Macdonald
Maritime History
Series

THE SHIPMASTER'S ASSISTANT AND COMMERCIAL DIGEST

BY

JOSEPH BLUNT

Macdonald and Jane's
London

Reprinted from a copy in the collections of the
G. W. BLUNT WHITE LIBRARY
MARINE HISTORICAL ASSOCIATION
MYSTIC SEAPORT, CONN.

Reprinted from the edition of 1837, New York
This edition first published 1970 in the United States of America
First published in Great Britain 1974

ISBN 0 356 04764 4

MACDONALD AND JANE'S
ST. GILES HOUSE, 49-50 POLAND STREET, LONDON W1A 2LG
Printed in the United States of America
Bound in Great Britain

THE

SHIPMASTER'S ASSISTANT,

AND

COMMERCIAL DIGEST:

CONTAINING INFORMATION USEFUL TO

MERCHANTS, OWNERS, AND MASTERS OF SHIPS;

IN WHICH THE FOLLOWING SUBJECTS ARE PARTICULARLY ELUCIDATED:

1. Ships.
2. Navigation Acts.
3. Custom-House Laws.
4. Fisheries.
5. Revenue Cutters.
6. Ship-Owners.
7. Ship-Masters.
8. Seamen.
9. Consuls.
10. Freight.
11. General Average.
12. Salvage.
13. Bottomry and Respondentia.
14. Marine Insurance.
15. Factors and Agents.
16. The Navy.
17. Pensions.
18. Crimes.
19. Slaves.
20. Wrecks.
21. Quarantine Laws.
22. Passengers.
23. Pilots.
24. Bills of Exchange.
25. Exchange.
26. Weights and Measures.
27. Harbour Regulations in the United States.
28. Commercial Regulations of Foreign Countries.

TOGETHER WITH THE TARIFF FOR 1832.

BY JOSEPH BLUNT,

COUNSELLOR AT LAW.

NEW-YORK:

PUBLISHED BY E. & G. W. BLUNT, 154 WATER-STREET,

CORNER OF MAIDEN-LANE.

1837.

may be committed at sea or in harbour, and within the jurisdiction of the United States' court.

As much of the common law relative to average, salvage, bills of exchange, factorage, marine loans and freight, as is necessary to guide a person in the ordinary course of business, is also presented. The law of insurance, and that prescribing the rights and duties of owners, masters and seamen, is inserted more at length, because of the difficulty of procuring advice on those subjects when it is most wanted.

In the chapter on bills of exchange, the various modes of estimating damages in the United States on returned bills, are given with references to the statutes establishing the rule.

The chapters on the different monies, and weights and measures of the world, have been prepared with much care; and as great modifications have been made, within 15 years, in the monies, weights and measures of several countries with which we have commercial intercourse, it is believed that they will be found to contain new and important information.

Such commercial regulations in those ports with which our trade is chiefly carried on, as were of general interest, have been arranged in alphabetical order in the last chapter. They have been mostly taken from a work compiled by order of Congress, and they will be found to contain much valuable information.

For the tariff the author is indebted to Selleck & Lyons, custom-house brokers, in this city; and the high character of those gentlemen for knowledge and experience, is a guaranty for the accuracy of the table here inserted.

CONTENTS.

CHAPTER I.

CHAPTER II.

CHAPTER III.

CHAPTER IV.

CHAPTER V.

CHAPTER VI.

CHAPTER VII.

CHAPTER VIII.

CHAPTER IX.

CHAPTER X.

CHAPTER XI.

CHAPTER XII.

CHAPTER XIII.

CHAPTER XIV.

CHAPTER XXIII.

CHAPTER XXIV.

CHAPTER XXV.

CHAPTER XXVI.

PREFACE.

The following work, although purporting to be a second edition, is, in reality, almost altogether new. The changes in the commercial laws of this country, since the publication of the former edition, have been such as to effect a revolution in its mercantile system. Great changes have also taken place in other countries.

The elementary principles of marine law, originally derived from the Rhodian law, the Consolato del Mare, the laws of Oleron and Wisby, and the marine ordinances of Louis XIV., which have been incorporated into the jurisprudence of most maritime powers, are indeed the same; but the modifications made by different governments to suit their respective interests, have produced a mass of discordant legislation, difficult, but at the same time necessary, for those engaged in navigation, to understand. Even in the United States, although the federal constitution has vested in Congress the power to regulate commerce with foreign nations, and between the states, no attempt has yet been made to establish a commercial code for the Union.

From some reason, (probably from a deficiency of mercantile information in that body,) this important subject has been neglected, and the regulation of many portions of this matter has been trusted to state legislation, always incompetent to establish a general rule, and liable to infringe the dormant powers of Congress, or to clash with laws already enacted. The pilot laws, those relating to wrecks, quarantine, passengers, and to the police of vessels in port, for instance, are entirely enacted by the states.

These laws, so far as they affect navigation, have been digested for this work. The utility of collecting these laws into one volume, will be manifest to every shipmaster. Every person of this class must often have experienced the difficulty of ascertaining the various legal provisions in those Atlantic states he has been compelled to visit, in the prosecution of his business. Without regarding the different legislative jurisdictions to which he is subjected at different times, a master naturally acts as if the same law was in force throughout the United States, and becomes liable to penalties, which a little acquaintance with their statutes would have enabled him to avoid. In enacting laws relating to commerce, the state legislatures have evidently seldom, if ever, consulted the provisions on the same subject in the sister states; and in this independent method of legislation, a system discordant in its provisions, overburdened with details, and incongruous in itself, has grown up with the increase of our trade, to the vexation and dismay of the owners and masters of ships. In this work they will find, under their proper heads, such laws as most immediately affect them; and if these are not in every state best calculated to promote the interests of commerce, still an acquaintance with their provisions will prevent them from incurring penalties, to which they often, from ignorance, render themselves liable.

Even in the revenue laws, passed by Congress, there is evinced a similar want of method and order.

The revenue law, enacted upon the organization of the government, was soon found to be defective, and in 1799, an attempt was made to establish a perfect system. Since that time, modifications have been made at almost every session, to correct either real or imaginary evils. Amendments have been heaped upon amendments, not repealing the original act, except by implication; new regulations have been engrafted upon the old, until the laws of the custom-house have become as mysterious and obscure as the ancient oracles, only to be comprehended and expounded by the initiated.

In the first chapters of this work, an attempt has been made to reduce this mass of legislation to a system. The laws relating to the revenue and to navigation are arranged in different chapters: not according to their dates, but according to the nature of the subject which they profess to regulate. For instance, the various provisions concerning drawbacks are placed in one chapter; the laws dividing and regulating the collection districts, are digested and condensed in a table, which, at one view, shows the extent of the district, its various ports of entry and delivery, and its local regulations and privileges; the regulations as to the entry of goods, form one head, and those as to their clearance, another. This same system of arrangement has been adopted with regard to all the acts of Congress relating to commerce.

A digest is also given of the laws of Congress, prescribing the duties of consuls, the regulations for marine hospitals, the United States navy, pensions, the fisheries, the registering and licensing of vessels, together with the navigation laws, and the acts defining crimes which

CHAPTER XXVII.

CHAPTER XXVIII.

APPENDIX.

CHAPTER I.

OF SHIPS.

Bill of Sale.—A bill of sale is the true and proper muniment of title to a ship, and to which all maritime courts look for proof of ownership. In England it is made necessary by statute, as between British subjects. The usual evidences, in the United States, of property are, the bill of sale and register. Other evidence, however, in the absence of those, may be admitted. Possession and acts of ownership are presumptive proofs, and may be sufficient to vest title; but they are liable to be rebutted by documentary evidence.

A title to a ship may, also, be given by sale under a decree in admiralty, as in case of capture or libel for wages, or on a bottomry bond. Sales of vessels, too, are frequently made abroad, by order of some admiralty court, as of vessels unfit for service.[a] As such sales are often collusive, and founded on the petition of the master for fraudulent ends, they are regarded with suspicion; and they must be founded upon the most obvious necessity, and conducted with the clearest good faith, in order to be held valid.

The power to condemn vessels as unseaworthy and unworthy of repairs, is in general exercised as an incident to the admiralty power. As congress has not established any rule on the subject, it may at present be exercised under the express provisions of state laws, or as a power incident to the surveying power.

When a ship is sold in port, delivery of possession is required to perfect the title; otherwise the vessel may be seized upon an execution in behalf of a judgment creditor of the seller.

Where a sale is by a part owner, delivery of the muniments of title only are necessary, unless the part owner himself be in actual possession.

When the ship is abroad, too, delivery of the muniments of title, and a bill of sale, is all that is necessary, but possession must be taken upon her arrival, and the buyer takes her subject to all prior incumbrances, and to all legal contracts made by the master respecting the employment or hypothecation of the ship, prior to notice of the transfer.[b]

Registry.—The registry is not a document required by the laws of nations to prove the national character of the vessel, nor is it a document conclusive as to the ownership. The registry acts are to be considered as municipal laws, enacted to promote purposes of public

---

[a] 10 Wheaton, 4. 11. [b] 3 Kent, 132.

policy; and they do not change the common law mode in which ships may be transferred.[a]

The registry, however, is evidence of national character, and in a time of general peace, is the only document that need be on board, to comply with the warranty of national character.[b]

If the bill of sale recite the register inaccurately, the vessel loses her American privileges, but the sale is not thereby avoided.[c]

A vessel may sail in a foreign trade with a sea letter, or certificate of ownership, and without a register; but she loses the privileges of an American vessel.

Every American vessel, whether registered or not, is entitled to a passport from the custom house.[d]

All commercial nations have, for the encouragement of the mercantile part of the community, to increase their tonnage, and secure employment to their seamen, conferred various privileges upon ships belonging to their own citizens.

The government of the United States was early impressed with the propriety of adopting this policy. In the first administration of Washington, in the second session of the second congress, 31st December, 1792, and 18th February, 1793, acts were passed prescribing regulations for vessels employed in the foreign trade, coasting trade, and fisheries of the United States, which have continued, with but few alterations, to the present time.

These acts relate to all ships employed at sea, which may be divided into five classes: 1. Ships of the United States employed in foreign trade, which are entitled to be *registered.* 2. Ships of the United States employed in the coasting trade or fisheries, which are entitled to be *enrolled and licensed.* 3. Ships built out of the United States, but owned by citizens, which are entitled to a *certificate of ownership.* 4. Ships built in the United States, but owned wholly or partly by foreigners, which are entitled to be *recorded.* 5. Ships built out of the United States, and owned by foreigners, which are considered alien vessels to all intents and purposes.

Vessels actually registered, and vessels duly qualified for carrying on the coasting trade and fisheries, or one of them, are alone denominated and deemed *ships* or *vessels of the United States,* entitled to the benefits and privileges appertaining to such vessels; and they continue to enjoy the same no longer than they continue to be wholly owned and commanded by a citizen or citizens of the United States.[e]

Vessels built within the United States, and vessels captured by citizens in war, and condemned as prizes, or seized and condemned for a breach of revenue laws, and wholly belonging to citizens, may be registered.[f]

No citizen who usually resides in a foreign country, can, during such residence, entitle himself to have registered a ship owned in whole or in part by him, unless he be a consul, or an agent or partner in

---

a 1 Mason, 306. b 1 Paine, 594. c 1 Wash. C. C. 226. d Act, 1st June, 1796.
e Act, 31st Dec. 1792, ch. 1. f Ibid. sec. 2.

some house of trade or partnership, consisting of citizens actually carrying on trade within the United States.[a]

An American vessel, transferred by parol while at sea to an American citizen, and resold to her original owners on her return to port, does not lose her privileges as an American vessel.[b]

If one of two partners obtain a registry of a vessel, by swearing that he and his partner, of the city of New-York, are the owners, when, in fact, his partner is domiciliated abroad, the vessel is liable to forfeiture.[c]

No ships can be registered, or, if registered, can be entitled to the benefit thereof, if owned, in whole or in part, by any naturalized citizen residing for more than one year in the country from which he originated, or for more than two years in any foreign country, unless he be a consul or public agent. But such ships may be registered anew on a *bona fide* sale to any citizen resident within the United States.[d]

No registered ship, which has been seized or captured, and condemned by a foreign power, can be registered anew, except regained by the original owner, at the time of capture or seizure, or by his executors or administrators ; but such ship is deemed a *foreign vessel*, though purchased or owned by any other citizen.[e]

Ships entitled to be *recorded*, and entitled to the benefits of *recorded ships* in the United States, are ships built in the United States, and belonging wholly or in part to foreigners.[f]

Vessels entitled to be *enrolled* are vessels of twenty tons or upwards, possessing the same qualifications and requisites as are made necessary for registering ships, i. e., they must be built within the United States, and be owned wholly by citizens. If under twenty tons, they are entitled to a *license*. No ships, unless enrolled and licensed, are deemed ships of the United States, entitled to the privileges of ships employed in the coasting trade or fisheries :[g] and if any not enrolled or licensed, be found engaged in the coasting trade or fisheries, having on board any foreign articles or distilled spirits, other than sea stores, they are subject to forfeiture, unless the vessel be at sea at the expiration of the time for which the license was granted ; in which case the forfeiture is not incurred, provided the master prove the fact, and deliver his license to the collector of the district in which he shall first arrive, within forty-eight hours after his arrival.

In the United States, no vessels are *required* to be registered. But to entitle them to the privileges of vessels of the United States, they must be registered ; otherwise, they are deemed alien ships. As is before stated, vessels engaged in the coasting trade or fisheries, are liable to forfeiture if they have foreign articles on board, unless they are *enrolled and licensed*.[h]

The place of registry is the *collector's district* where the vessel

---

[a] Act, 31st Dec. 1792, sec. 2. [b] 4 Cranch, 48. [c] 8 Cranch, 253.
[d] Act, 27th March, 1804, sec. 1.
[e] Acts, 27th June, 1797, sec. 1, and 27th March, 1804, sec. 2.
[f] Act, 31st Dec. 1792, sec. 20. [g] Act, 18th Feb. 1793, sec. 1, 2.
[h] Act, 18th Feb. 1793, sec. 12.

belongs at the time of her registry. This is deemed to be that at, or nearest to which, the owner, or, if more than one, the husband or acting owner of the vessel, usually resides, and the registry must be made by the collector of such dictrict.[a]

Where, however, a citizen of the United States purchases a vessel entitled to be registered, which *is in another district*, such vessel may be registered by the collector of the district where the vessel is at the time of the purchase, upon the purchaser's complying with the provisions of the law. And the usual oath or affirmation may be taken by the owner at his option, either before such collector, or the collector of his own district. But upon the vessel's arriving within the district to which she belongs, the certificate of registry granted to her must be delivered up to the collector thereof, who is to grant a new certificate in lieu of the first, upon compliance with the provisions of the law; and he is to transmit the certificate delivered up to the collector who granted it. If the certificate be not delivered up, it becomes void, and the purchaser and the master incur a penalty of $100; and the same penalties are inflicted for false swearing, as in the case of an oath made by an agent.[b]

If a vessel entitled to be registered is purchased by an agent or attorney, for or on account of a citizen of the United States, such vessel being in a district of the United States more than fifty miles distant, (taking the nearest usual route by land,) from that to which such vessel ought to be deemed to belong, the collector of the district where the vessel is, is to register the vessel, upon the application of the agent or attorney, and upon his complying with the requisites of the law. In the oath or affirmation he must state, that he is agent or attorney for the owner, and that he has purchased the vessel *bona fide* for the person whom he names as owner. If he swear falsely, there is a forfeiture of the vessel or her value, to be recovered of such agent or attorney.[c]

These clauses, declaring the vessel or her value to be forfeited for any false oath taken to procure a register, have been construed so that the absolute property of the ship does not, in fact or in law, vest in the United States upon the taking of the false oath, but remains in the owner, until the United States have manifested their intention to take the ship, and not the value.[d]

The ship may be recovered of the owners, but the value must be recovered of the person taking the false oath.[e]

Where a vessel, registered as American, belongs partly to a foreigner, and is sold to a purchaser ignorant of the fraud, she is not liable to forfeiture in the hands of such purchaser.[f]

Upon the vessel arriving in the district to which she belongs, the certificate must be delivered up, and a new one granted, in the same manner and under the same penalties as in the last preceding case.[g]

In order to obtain the registry of a vessel in the United States, it is necessary, according to the act of 31st December, 1792, that an oath

---

[a] Act, 31st Dec. 1792, sec. 3. [b] Ibid. sec. 11. [c] Act, 18th Feb. 1793, sec. 12.
[d] 3 Cranch, 338. [e] Ibid. [f] 2 Adm. Decisions, 452. [g] Act, 31st Dec. 1792, sec. 12.

or affirmation be taken and subscribed by the owner before the proper officer. This oath or affirmation, among other things, states, the place of residence and citizenship of the party applying; that he is sole owner, or if the fact be otherwise, the names of the other part owners, their residence and citizenship, and if such part owners be resident in a foreign country, that they are consuls or agents, or partners in a house consisting of citizens of the United States, and trading within the United States. It further states the name and burthen of the vessel, the place where, and the year when built. If a prize, it further states, that she was, after the 31st March, 1793, captured by citizens of the United States, and legally condemned. If forfeited for breach of the laws of the United States, it states that she has been so adjudged; and in both cases an authenticated copy of the condemnation must be produced. It further states, that the master is a citizen of the United States, and whether by birth, naturalization, or otherwise; and that no foreigner hath directly or indirectly any interest in the ship. In case the master be within the district at the time of the registry, he, and not the owner, makes oath to his citizenship. If the master swears falsely, he forfeits $1000.[a] This oath only respects the legal ownership, and does not require a disclosure of any equitable interests vested in citizens of the United States.[b]

By the act concerning the commerce of Florida, it is provided, that vessels having Spanish registers on the 10th July, 1821, and belonging to residents of Florida, may be registered, or enrolled and licensed as American vessels.[c]

In case a new ship is to be registered, it is necessary to produce a certificate under the hand of the master carpenter, by whom or under whose direction she was built, testifying that she was built by him or under his direction, and specifying the place where, and the time when, and the person for whom built, and describing her build, number of decks and masts, length, breadth, depth, tonnage, and such other circumstances as are usually descriptive of the indentity of a ship; and such a certificate authorizes the removal of a new ship in ballast from the district where built, to another district in the same, or an adjoining state, where the owner actually resides.[d]

The oath or affirmation is taken before the collector or other officer authorized to make the registry. If there be two or more owners, it is to be taken by at least one of them, and the other owners, who are resident within the United States, must transmit to the collector, who grants the certificate of registry, a like oath or affirmation within ninety days after the same is granted, and the same may be taken by them, either before the same or any other collector, or a judge of the supreme or district court of the United States, or of a superior court of original jurisdiction of some one of the states. If such oath or affirmation be not taken and transmitted within 90 days, the certificate of registry is forfeited and void.[e]

---

[a] Act, 31st Dec. 1792, sec. 4. [b] 1 Mason's Rep., 306. [c] Act, 30th March, 1822.
[d] Act, 31st Dec. 1792, sec. 8. [e] Ibid. sec. 4 and 5.

Before a ship can be registered in the United States, she must be measured by a surveyor, or a person appointed by him, or by the collector, or a person appointed by him, when there is no surveyor in the port where she is. The officer who measures the ship for the information of, and as a voucher to the person who makes the registry, must grant a certificate, specifying the build of the ship, her number of decks and masts, her length, breadth, depth, tonnage, and such other particulars as identify a ship, and that her name, and the place to which she belongs, are painted on her stern in the manner required by the act. This certificate is to be countersigned by the owner, or by some other person who may attend the admeasurement on behalf of the owner, in testimony of its truth; and without this, the certificate is invalid. This admeasurement need not be made upon any subsequent registry, unless the ship has undergone some alteration in burthen.[a]

When the terms of the act of the United States have been complied with, the collector is to make a record or registry of the ship, and grant an abstract, or certificate thereof, in the particular form prescribed by law.*

Where a new certificate is granted on a transfer, the words are so varied as to refer to the former certificate of registry for her admeasurement. So, where the master makes oath of his citizenship, the words are varied accordingly.[b]

Before granting a certificate of registry, the act of the United States requires that the husband, or acting or managing owner of the ship, should, with the master and a surety or sureties, give bond to the United States, if such vessel be of burthen not exceeding fifty tons, in the sum of $400; if of burthen above fifty tons, and not

---

[a] Act, 31st Dec. 1792, sec. 6. [b] Ibid. sec. 9.

* *Form of Certificate of Registry:*

"In pursuance of an act of the Congress of the United States of America, entitled, "An act concerning the registering and recording of ships or vessels," [inserting here the name, occupation, and place of abode, of the person by whom the oath or affirmation aforesaid shall have been made,] having taken or subscribed the oath (or affirmation) required by the said act, and having sworn (or affirmed) that he (or she, and if more than one owner, adding the words, 'together with,' and the name or names, occupation or occupations, place or places of abode, of the other owner or owners) is (or are) the only owner (or owners) of the ship or vessel, called the [inserting her name] of [inserting here the port to which she may belong] whereof [inserting here the name of the master] is at present master, and is a citizen of the United States, and that the said ship or vessel was [inserting here, when and where built] and [inserting here, the name and office, if any, of the person by whom she shall have been surveyed or admeasured] having certified that the said ship or vessel has [inserting here, the number of decks] and [inserting here, the number of masts] and that her length is [inserting here, the number of feet] her breadth [inserting here, the number of feet] her depth [inserting here, the number of feet] and that she measures [inserting here, her number of tons] that she is [describing here, the particular kind of vessel, whether ship, brigantine, snow, schooner, sloop, or whatever else, together with her built, and specifying whether she has any, or no gallery or head] and the said [naming the owner, or the master or other person, acting in behalf of the owner or owners, by whom the certificate of admeasurement shall have been countersigned as aforesaid] having agreed to the description and admeasurement, above specified, and sufficient security having been given, according to the said act, the said ship or vessel has been duly registered at the port of [naming the port where registered.] Given under my hand and seal, at [naming the said port] this [inserting the particular day] day of [naming the month] in the year [specifying the number of the year, in words at length."]

exceeding one hundred, in the sum of $800; if of burthen above one hundred tons, and not exceeding two hundred, in the sum of $1200; if of burthen above two hundred tons, and not exceeding three hundred, in the sum of $1600; and if of burthen exceeding three hundred tons, in the sum of $2,000, with condition that the certificate shall be solely used for the ship for which it is granted, and shall not be sold, lent, or otherwise disposed of to any person; and that in case the ship shall be lost, or taken by an enemy, burnt or broken up, or otherwise prevented from returning to the port to which she belongs, or in case she shall be sold when at sea or in a foreign port to a foreigner, or for his benefit, the certificate shall be delivered up within eight days after the arrival of the master within any district of the United States, to the collector of such district; and in case of a sale to any foreigner when the ship is within a district of the United States, that it shall be delivered up to the collector thereof within seven days; and every such certificate, so delivered up, must be forthwith transmitted to the register of the treasury, to be cancelled. If the same has been delivered up to a collector, other than of the district in which it was granted, the register of the treasury must notify the collector of that district of the delivery.[a]

If any certificate of registry be fraudulently or knowingly used for any ship not then actually entitled to the benefit of it, such ship is forfeited.[b] This section extends to vessels which have not, as well as to those which have, been previously registered.[c]

When the master of a registered ship is changed, the owner or the new master is to report such change to the collector of the port where such change happens, or where the ship shall first be after the change. He must, also, produce to him the certificate of registry, and make oath or affirmation that the new master is a citizen of the United States, and the manner in which he is so. The collector is thereupon to endorse upon the certificate a memorandum of the change, specifying the name of the new master, and transmits a copy of it to the collector of the district where the ship is registered, if it be not his district; and such collector must make a like memorandum of such change in his book of registers, and transmit a copy of it to the register of the treasury. If this change be not reported, the registry is void, and the master forfeits $100.[d]

So, if a registered ship be sold or transferred, in whole or in part, to a foreigner, by way of trust, confidence, or otherwise, the sale or transfer must be reported in the same manner, or the ship will be forfeited; but if the ship be owned in part only, the shares of the owners, conusant of the sale or transfer, are only forfeited.[e]

The name of every registered ship in the United States, and the port to which she belongs, must be painted on her stern, on a black ground, in white letters of not less than three inches in length, under the penalty of $50.[f]

If any registered ship in the United States be altered in form or

---

[a] Act, 31st Dec. 1792, sec. 7. [b] Ibid. sec. 27. [c] 3 Wheat. 101.]
[d] Act, 31st Dec. 1792, sec. 15. [e] Ibid. sec. 16. [f] Ibid. sec. 3.

burthen by being lengthened or built upon, or from one denomination to another by the mode of rigging or fitting, she must be registered anew by her former name, or she will cease to be deemed a ship of the United States. When the new registry is applied for, the former certificate is to be delivered to the collector to whom application is made. If not so delivered up, the owner forfeits $500, unless it is lost, destroyed, or unintentionally mislaid.[a]

The certificates granted to registered ships in the United States must be numbered progressively, beginning anew at the commencement of every year; and an exact copy of each certificate must be entered in a book kept for the purpose, and transmitted by the collector once in three months to the register of the treasury.[b]

Upon such entry, an oath or affirmation must be made, that it contains the names of all the owners of the ship, or if any part has been transferred since the granting the register, that such is the case; and that no foreigner has any share by way of trust, confidence, or otherwise, in the ship. This oath or affirmation is to be taken by the owner or part-owner, if the entry be at the port where they reside, otherwise by the master. If the owner or master refuse to take the oath or affirmation, the ship loses the privileges of an American ship.[c]

If the certificate be lost, destroyed, or mislaid, a new register may be granted by the collector of the port where the ship shall first be, after such loss, destruction or mislaying, upon oath or affirmation made by the master or other person having the command of the ship,* upon complying with the other requisites of the act in order to the registry of ships. The new register, if granted in any other district than that to which the ship belongs, is valid only for ten days after her first arrival within the district to which she belongs, and must then be given up, and a new one granted: otherwise a penalty of $100 is incurred.[d]

In cases where the master is required to deliver up the certificate to the *collector*, if he refuse, he incurs a penalty, and the ship loses her right to the privileges of an American ship.[e]

The act of 1792, requires that upon every transfer there shall be some instrument in writing, in the nature of a bill of sale, which recites at length the certificate of registry, otherwise the ship is incapable of being registered anew, and loses the privileges and benefits of a ship of the United States.[f] But the act

---

[a] Act, 31st Dec. 1792. sec. 14 and 6. [b] Ibid. sec. 19. [c] Ibid. sec. 17.
[d] Ibid. sec. 13. [e] Ibid. sec. 13 and 17. [f] Ibid.

* *Form of Oath:*

"I [inserting here the name of the person swearing or affirming] being master (or having the charge or command) of the ship or vessel, called the [inserting the name of the vessel] do swear (or affirm) that the said ship or vessel hath been, as I verily believe, registered according to law, by the name of [inserting again the name of the vessel] and that a certificate thereof was granted by the collector of the district of [naming the district where registered] which certificate has been lost, (or destroyed unintentionally, and by mere acccident mislaid, as the case may be,) and (except where the certificate is alleged to have been destroyed) that the same, if found again, and within my power, shall be delivered up to the collector of the district in which it was granted.

does not invalidate the contract as between the parties, but leaves it to the general operation of law. It only deprives the ship of her former character, and treats her as a *foreign* ship.

Whenever a registered ship of the United States is sold or transferred in whole or in part to a citizen of the United States, she must be registered anew by her former name, and the requisites of the law in common cases of registry must be complied with, otherwise she ceases to be a ship of the United States. And in this case her former registry must be given to the collector, to whom application is to be made for the new registry. In case of a transfer of a registered vessel while at sea, a new register is not necessary to protect the vessel from alien duties when she arrives, or the cargo which was actually imported while the old register was in force. If the alienation be to a foreigner, her privileges are *ipso facto* forfeited, but if to a citizen, they are not forfeited until after she should have been registered anew, and the oath which entitles her to enter does not require such new register.[a] If the certificate of registry is not delivered up, upon such sale or transfer, the owner forfeits $500, unless the same is lost, destroyed, or unintentionally mislaid, and oath or affirmation is made thereof.[b]

When the register of a ship is delivered up agreeably to law to the collector of the district in which it was granted, the *bond* given at the time of granting it, is to be *cancelled;* but if delivered up to any other collector, he is to give a receipt or acknowledgment of the delivery, and specify the time when; and upon this receipt being produced to the collector, who granted the register, he is to cancel the bond.[c]

In case of a sale and transfer by *process of law*, if the former owners do not surrender up the register, upon proof of the facts, to the secretary of the treasury, he may direct the collector of the district to which the ship belongs, to grant a new registry to the purchasers, upon their complying with the other conditions required in ordinary cases.[d]

Vessels captured and condemned by a foreign power are considered as foreign vessels, and are not entitled to be registered anew, unless the former owner regain his title.

In the act of 2d March, 1803, provision is made for cases of ships abroad at the time of sale. By this act, when a registered ship is sold or transferred, in whole or in part, to a citizen of the United States, while she is without the limits of the United States, she is to be entitled to all the privileges of registered ships, provided all requisites of law for the registry of ships are complied with, and a new certificate of registry obtained for such ship, within three days from the time at which the master or other person having command of the ship is required to make his final report, upon her first arrival afterwards in the United States, agreeably to the 30th section of the act of 2d March, 1799;

---

[a] 4 Cranch, 57. [b] Act, 31st December, 1792, sec. 14. [c] Ibid. sec. 18. [d] Act, 2d March, 1797.

and the tonnage duties of such ships are payable at any time within the three days.

There is no clause in the acts of congress, requiring the assent of the other owners to the transfer of a part of a registered ship to a foreigner. But every such transfer, whether by way of trust, confidence, or otherwise, must be made known, otherwise a forfeiture is incurred of the ship.[a] A sale, however, by a part owner, does not forfeit the shares of those owners who were ignorant of the transfer to a foreigner, but only of those who knew of such foreign ownership.

It has moreover been the policy of the legislature of the United States, for the purpose of encouraging ship-building among our citizens, to confer certain privileges on ships built within the United States, even when owned by *foreigners.* These privileges are not equal to the privileges enjoyed by citizens of the United States, but they are superior to those of foreign built ships. Such ships are entitled to be *recorded.*

Every such ship must be recorded in the office of the collector of the district in which she was built. In order to entitle her to be recorded, the carpenter who built her is to make *oath or affirmation* before the collector, that he built her, and to give a description of her, as below; which oath or affirmation, must be subscribed by the person making the same, and recorded by the said collector. She must also be countersigned, and a certificate of the *record* granted, as below.[b] * This certificate is recorded by the collector, and a copy transmitted to the register of the treasury.

Every change of the master must be endorsed on the certificate, and recorded and transmitted in the same manner, as in cases of registered ships.[c] On *entry,* the certificate of the record must be produced to the collector, where the ship is entered. Neglect or refusal in either case, occasions a forfeiture of the privileges of a recorded ship.

---

[a] Act, 31st Dec., 1792, sec. 16. [b] Ibid. sec. 20, 21, 22. [c] Ibid. sec. 23.

* "In pursuance of an act, entitled 'An act concerning the registering and recording of ships or vessels,' I [inserting here the name of the collector of the district,] of [inserting here the name of the district,] in the United States, do certify, that [inserting here the name of the builder,] of [inserting here the place of his residence, county, and state,] having sworn or affirmed, that the [describing the ship or vessel, as in the certificate or record,] named [inserting here her name,] whereof [inserting here the name of the master] is at present master, was built at [inserting here the name of the place, county, and state, where built] by him, or under his direction, in the year [inserting here the number of the year,] and [inserting here the name of the surveyor, or other person, by whom the same admeasurement shall have been made] having certified, that the said ship or vessel has [inserting here her number of decks,] is, in length [inserting here the number of feet,] in breadth [inserting here the number of feet,] in depth [inserting here the number of feet,] and measures [inserting here the number of tons.] And the said builder and [naming and describing the owner, or master, or agent for the owner or owners, as the case may be, by whom the said certificate shall have been countersigned] having agreed to the said description and admeasurement, the said ship or vessel has been recorded in the district of [inserting here the name of the district where recorded] in the United States. Witness my hand seal, this [inserting here the day of the month] day of [inserting here the name of the month,] in the year [inserting here the number of the year."]

On the great lakes upon the northern, northeastern, and northwestern frontiers of the United States, there is a large and increasing commerce, which is essentially a coasting trade. American vessels navigating these waters, are enrolled and licensed, and may be employed in the coasting or foreign trade. They, however, are in other respects subject to the regulations made to prevent any violation of the general revenue system of the United States.[a]

LICENSING AND ENROLLING VESSELS.

Vessels engaged in the coasting trade or fisheries, in order to be entitled to the privileges of ships of the United States, must be enrolled, possess the same qualifications, and the same requisites must be complied with, as are necessary for registering ships. And the same duties and authorities are given and imposed on all officers respectively in relation to such *enrolments*, and the same proceedings are to be had in similar cases, touching such enrolments; and the ships so enrolled, with the master or owner, are subject to the same requisites, as are in those respects provided for ships registered. A record of the enrolment is to be made, and a certificate or copy granted, in the form prescribed.[b] *

If a ship be under twenty tons, she need not be *enrolled*, but must be *licensed.* Ships enrolled, must moreover have a license for the coasting trade or fisheries, before they are entitled to the privileges of ships of the United States.[c] The husband, or managing owner, must give a bond with one or more sureties, in a sum varying according to the tonnage of the ship, from $100 to $1000, that the ship shall not,

---

[a] Act, 2d March, 1831. [b] Act, 18th Feb., 1793, sec. 1. [c] Ibid. sec. 2.

* "Enrolment, in conformity to an act of the congress of the United States of America, entitled 'An act for enrolling and licensing ships or vessels to be employed in the coasting trade and fisheries, and for regulating the same,' [inserting here the name of the person, with his occupation and place of abode, by whom the oath or affirmation is to be made,] having taken the oath (or affirmation) required by this act, and having sworn (or affirmed) that he [or she, and if more than one owner, adding the words 'together with,' and the name or names, occupation or occupations, place or places of abode, of the owner or owners] is (or are) a citizen (or citizens) of the United States, and sole owner (or owners) of the ship or vessel, called the [inserting here her name,] of [inserting here the name of the port to which she may belong,] whereof [inserting here the name of the master] is at present master, and is a citizen of the United States, and that the said ship or vessel was [inserting here when and where built,] and [inserting here the name and office, if any, of the person by whom she shall have been surveyed, or admeasured] having certified, that the said ship or vessel has [inserting here the number of decks,] and [inserting here the number of masts,] and that her length is [inserting here the number of feet,] her breadth [inserting here the number of feet,] her depth [inserting here the number of feet,] and that she measures [inserting here the number of tons,] that she is [describing here the particular kind of vessel, whether ship, brigantine, snow, schooner, sloop, or whatever else, together with her built, and specifying whether she has no gallery or head;] and the said [naming the owner or the master, or other person acting in behalf of the owner or owners, by whom the certificate of admeasurement shall have been countersigned] having agreed to the description or admeasurement above specified, and sufficient security having been given, according to the said act, the said ship or vessel has been duly enrolled at the port of [naming the port where enrolled.] Given under my hand and seal, at [naming the said port,] this [inserting the particular day] day of [naming the month,] in the year [specifying the number of the year, in words at length."]

during the existence of the license, be engaged in any trade whereby the revenue of the United States shall be defrauded. The master must swear or affirm, that he is a citizen of the United States, and that the license shall not be used for any other ship, or any other employment, than that for which it is specially granted, or in any trade or business, whereby the revenue of the United States may be defrauded. If the ship be of less burthen than twenty tons, the husband or managing owner must swear or affirm that she is wholly the property of citizens of the United States. The license is then to be granted in the form prescribed by law, and is in force generally for a year only, and while she continues to be owned by the same person, and to be of the same description, and employed in the same business, as are stated in the license.[a]*

Vessels engaged in the mackerel fishery are also entitled to be licensed, and are subject to all the regulations and provisions of the act of 18th February, 1793.[b]

Enrolments and licenses may be granted by any surveyor of a port, who has been authorized by the secretary of the treasury; and in that case he performs the same duties, and receives the same fees as collectors.[c]

Registered vessels may be enrolled upon giving up their register, and so, *vice versa*, vessels enrolled may be registered upon giving up their enrolment and license. When any vessel is in another district than that to which she belongs, the collector of such district, upon the application of the master or commander, and his taking an oath or affirmation that, according to his best knowledge and belief, the property remains as stated in the register or enrolment proposed to be given up, and upon his giving the bonds required for granted registers, must make the exchanges. The enrolment and license, or register so granted, must be delivered to the collector of the district where the vessel belongs, within ten days after her arrival therein,

---

[a] Act, 18th Feb., 1793, sec. 4. [b] Act, 24th May, 1828. [c] Act, 11th Feb., 1830.

* "License for carrying on the [here insert coasting trade, whale fishery, or cod fishery, as the case may be.]

In pursuance of an act of the congress of the United States of America, entitled 'An act for enrolling and licensing ships or vessels to be employed in the coasting trade and fisheries, and for regulating the same,' [inserting here the name of the husband or managing owner, with his occupation and place of abode, and the name of the master, with the place of his abode,] having given bond that the [insert here the description of the vessel, whether ship, brigantine, snow, schooner, sloop, or whatever else she may be,] called the [insert here the vessel's name,] whereof the said [naming the master] is master, burthen [insert here the number of tons, in words] tons, as appears by her enrolment, date [naming the district, day, month, and year, in words at length,] (but if she be less than twenty tons, insert, instead thereof,) proof being had of her admeasurement, shall not be employed in any trade while this license shall continue in force, whereby the revenue of the United States shall be defrauded; and having also sworn (or affirmed) that this license shall not be used for any other vessel, or for any other employment, than is herein specified, license is hereby granted for the said [inserting here the description of the vessel,] called the [inserting here the vessel's name,] to be employed in carrying on the [inserting here, coasting trade, whale fishery, or cod fishery, as the case may be] for one year from the date hereof, and no longer. Given under my hand and seal, at [naming the said district,] this [inserting the particular day] day of [naming the month,] in the year [specifying the number of the year in words at length."]

and be by him cancelled, under the penalty of $100, to be paid by the master.[a]

Vessels not enrolled and licensed, or under twenty tons burthen, not licensed, (other than *registered ships,*) found trading between district and district, or between different places in the same district, or carrying on the fisheries, pay the same fees and tonnage at every port they touch at as foreign ships; but if they have on board any articles of foreign growth or manufacture, or distilled spirits, other than sea stores, they are, with their lading, forfeited.[b] Vessels found with a false license, or making use of a license belonging to another ship, are, together with their cargo, forfeited.[c] Vessels *licensed,* if transferred to any person not a citizen of, and resident within the United States, or if employed in any other trade than that for which they are licensed, are, together with their cargo, forfeited.[d] Vessels enrolled and licensed, if proceeding on a foreign voyage without delivering up the enrolment and license, and being duly registered, are, together with the cargo imported, forfeited.[e] A coasting vessel is not forfeited for proceeding on a foreign voyage, if she has not broken ground with an intention to commence such voyage.[f] It is the actual proceeding, and not the intention, that is punishable.[g] Such a forfeiture can be enforced in prize courts.[h] If the port from which the ship is about to sail, be not within the district of her enrolment, the collector must give to the master a certificate, specifying that the enrolment and license have been received by him, and the time when they were received, which certificate must afterwards be delivered by the master to the collector who granted the enrolment and license. But vessels licensed for the fisheries, may obtain permission to touch and trade at foreign ports, and may thereupon take on board goods of foreign growth or manufacture: but if found with such goods on board within three leagues of the coast, without having such permission, they are, together with such goods imported therein, forfeited.[i] But these forfeitures do not apply to any part of the cargo which is owned by other persons than the master, owner or mariners of the ship.[j]

Steamboats owned wholly or in part by an alien residing within the United States, if employed only in a river or bay of the United States, may be enrolled and licensed; the oath as to ownership, of course, conforming to the fact. A bond with sufficient surety is to be given by the owner, in the penalty of $1000, that such steamboat shall not be used out of the rivers and bays of the United States.[k] Where a steamboat, or vessel employed in the whale fishery,[l] is owned by an incorporated company, the register, enrolment, and license, is to be issued in the name of the president or secretary, and is not vacated by a sale of shares among the stockholders. A new one is taken out upon a change in the officer taking out the old one.

The oath, in such case, as to ownership, states the boat to belong to the company, without designating the names of the stockholders;

---

[a] Act, 18th Feb., 1793, ch. 8. sec. 3. [b] Ibid. sec. 6. [c] Ibid. sec. 5. [d] Ibid. sec. 32.
[e] Ibid. sec. 8. [f] 1 Gallis. 43. [g] Ibid. 45. [h] 1 Mason, 24.
[i] Act, 18th Feb., 1793, ch. 8. sec. 21. [j] Ibid. sec. 33. [k] Act, 12th March, 1812.
[l] Act, 3d March, 1831.

and that no part of such boat has been, or is then, owned by any foreigner. It is made by the president or secretary.[a]

Registered ships are not interdicted from trading between district and district, but their privileges are not so great as those of licensed ships.[b] They are subject to the same regulations, penalties, and forfeitures, (except as to fees,) and the like duties are imposed on like officers, for licensed vessels.

This does not, however, extend to registered vessels having goods of foreign growth or manufacture, on which the duties have not been paid or secured. Foreign vessels are not permitted to carry on the coasting trade, but they may proceed coastwise, with a certified manifest to deliver their cargoes, brought from a foreign port, and consigned to different ports in the United States.[c]

The licenses granted must be numbered progressively, beginning *anew* every year. Ships licensed or enrolled, or registered *anew*, or exchanging the one for the other, are to hold their former names, and are to have their names, and the ports where they belong, painted on their sterns.[d] Every change of the masters of such ships is to be reported to the collector, and endorsed upon the license; and a neglect in this particular subjects the ship to pay the fees and tonnage of registered ships, and the new master to pay **$10.**[e]

The license must be given up to the collector of the district, who may have granted the same, within three days after the expiration of the time for which it was granted, in case such vessel be then within the district; or, if she be absent within three days from her first arrival within the district; or, if she be sold out of the district, within three days after the arrival of the master within any district, to the collector, taking his certificate therefor;[f] and if the master thereof neglect or refuse to deliver up the license, he forfeits $50; but if such license have been previously given up to the collector of any other district, and a certificate thereof be produced, or if such license be lost or destroyed, or unintentionally mislaid, so that it cannot be found, and the master make oath or affirmation thereof, and that the same, if found, shall be delivered up, then the penalty is not incurred. And if such license be lost, destroyed, or unintentionally mislaid, before the expiration of the time for which it was granted, upon the like oath or affirmation being made by the master, the said collector is authorized to license such vessel anew.

It is lawful for the owner or owners of any licensed vessel, to return such license to the collector who granted it, within the year for which it was granted, who thereupon licenses such vessel anew.[g]

Whenever a vessel is transferred by process of law, and the certificate of the enrolment, or license, is retained by her former owner, a new one may be obtained, without the return of the old one,[h] as in the case of registered vessels. (Vide p. 17.)

Any officer concerned in the collection of the revenue, may inspect the enrolment or license of any vessel; and if the master does

---

[a] Act, 3d March, 1825. [b] Act, 18th Feb., 1793, sec. 6. 20. 33.
[c] Act, 1st March, 1817, sec. 4. [d] Act, 18th Feb., 1793, sec. 7. 11. [e] Ibid. sec. 12.
[f] Ibid. sec. 9. [g] Ibid. sec. 10. [h] Act, 2d March, 1797.

not exhibit the same, when thereunto required by such officer, he forfeits $100.[a]

Before any vessel, of the burthen of five tons, and less than twenty tons, can be licensed, the same admeasurement must be made of such vessel, and the same provisions observed relative thereto, as in the case of admeasuring vessels to be registered or enrolled ; but where such vessel, or any other licensed vessel, has been once admeasured, it is not necessary to measure such ship or vessel anew, for the purpose of obtaining another enrolment or license, except such vessel have undergone some alteration as to her burthen, subsequent to her former license.[b]

Any officer of the revenue may board any vessel, within or without his district, and the same inspect, search and examine ; and if it appear that any breach of the laws of the United States has been committed, whereby such vessel, or the goods on board, or any part thereof, is liable to forfeiture, make seizure of the same.[c]

The license act does not extend to any boat or lighter, not being masted, or if masted, and not decked, employed in the harbour of any town or city.

For the more convenient regulation of the coasting trade, the seacoast and navigable rivers of the United States are divided into three great districts, which are subdivided into collection districts, for which see third chapter, on custom house regulations.

Every vessel, of the burthen of twenty tons or upwards, licensed to trade between the different districts of the United States, is authorized to trade between the districts included within the said great districts respectively, and between a state in one, and an adjoining state in another great district, subject only to the regulations that are by law required to be observed by such vessels, in trading from one district to another in the same state, or in the next adjoining state.[d]

Every vessel, of the burthen of twenty tons or upwards, licensed to trade as aforesaid, is required, in trading from one to another great district, other than between a state in one, and an adjoining state in another great district, to conform to the regulations that are required to be observed by such vessels, in trading from a district in one state to a district in any other than an adjoining state.[e]

Every American vessel, whether registered or not, upon clearing out to a foreign country, should be furnished with a passport.

In order to be entitled to passports, the masters of vessels become bound in the sum of $2000 not to misuse the same. In case of the loss or sale of the vessel, the passport must be delivered up to the collector from whom it was received; within three months, if the loss happened within the United States; within six months, if at any place nearer than the Cape of Good Hope ; and within 18 months, if at a more distant place.[f]

---

[a] Act, 18th Feb., 1793, sec. 13. [b] Ibid. sec. 26. [c] Ibid. sec. 27. [d] Act, 2d March, 1819. [e] Ibid. [f] Acts, 1st June, 1796,—March 2 1801, and Feb. 12, 1831.

No sea letters, or documents certifying a vessel to belong to citizens of the United States, can be issued, except to vessels duly registered, or enrolled and licensed, or owned wholly by citizens.[a]

Vessels of the United States, departing therefrom, bound to any foreign country, other than some place in America, without the passport, the master forfeits $200.

Persons making, uttering, or using, false sea letters, Mediterranean passports, or certificates of registry, &c. forfeit not exceeding $5000; and if an officer, he becomes incapable of holding an office.

The power vested in the secretary of the treasury to remove disabilities incurred under the act of 31st December, 1792, and that of the 18th of February, 1793, extends to the remission of any foreign duties incurred by reason of such disabilities.

A duty of fifty cents per ton, denominated "light money," is levied on all foreign vessels, not entitled to the privileges of American vessels, entering the ports of the United States.

Unregistered vessels, owned by citizens, in possession of a sea letter, proving the vessel to be American property, do not pay light money, provided, upon the entry of such vessels from a foreign port, oath is made that the sea letter, &c. contains the names of all the owners, &c. and that no foreign subject hath any share, &c. If the owner does not reside at the port of entry, the master is to make oath. If the owner or master refuses to swear, the vessel is not entitled to this privilege.[b]

By the law imposing tonnage duties on vessels, a distinction is made in favour of American vessels, except with regard to the vessels of those nations which place vessels of the United States on the same footing as their own ships.

American vessels, officered by Americans, and having three fourths of the crew Americans, and foreign vessels entitled to the privileges of American vessels, pay no tonnage duty.[c] All other vessels pay 50 cents per ton, and foreign vessels pay the "light money" in addition, making $1 per ton. Foreign vessels, upon arriving in the United States, must deposit their register, &c. with the foreign consul, within 48 hours after entry at the custom house; penalty for neglect is from $500 to $2000. Before entry it is produced to the collector. The consul must keep it and the other papers deposited, until the master produce a clearance in due form from the collector. If he deliver them without such clearance, he forfeits from $500 to $5000.

This extends only to vessels of nations where the papers of American vessels are deposited with the American consuls there.[d]

Similar privileges are granted by other laws of the United States, which will be found under their proper heads.

Where a ship was purchased by an American citizen in trust for an alien, it was held to be a fraud upon the registry acts, and that the ship could not enjoy the privileges of American ships.[e]

American citizens may employ foreign vessels in neutral trade, but they will be liable to the alien duties.

---

[a] Act, 26th March, 1810. [b] Act, 3d March, 1805.
[c] Acts, 13th July, 1832, and 31st May, 1830. [d] Act, 3d March, 1817. [e] 4 Dall. 314.

Liability of Vessels.—A vessel is liable, in admiralty, to respond to shippers for damages to the goods shipped on board: a lien existing on the ship for damage to the goods, in the same manner as goods are held for freight.[a]

Where repairs have been made, or necessaries furnished to a foreign vessel, in a port of a country to which she does not belong, the marine law gives a lien on the vessel to the party furnishing them, and he may sue in admiralty to enforce his right.[b]

For repairs and necessaries furnished at home, the question is governed by the local law of the state to which the vessel belongs.

According to the common law, there is no lien for repairs, or for stores and materials furnished for the vessel.[c] But by a statute of the State of New-York, there is such a lien in favour of shipwrights, and those who supply stores or materials. This lien ceases after security is given for the debt, or when the vessel leaves the state,[d] and twelve days after her departure to another port in the state.

Where the owners have contributed to give a vessel in the home port a foreign character, and to hold the captain as legally authorized to exercise the rights over his vessel, appertaining to a foreign vessel, she would be liable for repairs in favour of the party furnishing them.[e]

DOCUMENTS NECESSARY FOR AMERICAN VESSELS.

The Passport.—This is a permission from the government, for the vessel to proceed on the voyage proposed, and contains the name and residence of the master, the name and description of the vessel, number of crew, and guns mounted. This document is only necessary for vessels going to Europe.

The Sea Letter, specifies the nature and quantity of the cargo, and place of destination. It is in the French, Spanish, English, and Dutch languages, and is only necessary for vessels bound round Cape Horn and the Cape of Good Hope.*

---

[a] Crane vs. The Rebecca, District Court of Maine, 1631. [b] 4 Wheat. 438.
[c] Ibid. [d] 2 Rev. Stat., 493. 500. [e] 9 Wheat. 409.

* JAMES MONROE, President of the United States of America, to all who see these presents, greeting:

Be it known, that leave and permission are hereby given to master or commander of the called of the burthen of tons or thereabouts, lying at present in the port of bound for and laden with

to depart and proceed with his said on his said voyage, such having been visited, and the said having made oath before the proper officer, that the said belongs to one or more of the citizens of the United States of America, and to him or them only.

In witness whereof, I have subscribed my name to these presents, and affixed the seal of the United States of America thereto, and caused the same to be countersigned by
at the day of in the year of our Lord Christ

By the President.

Most Serene, Serene, most Puissant, Puissant, High, Illustrious, Noble, Honourable, Venerable, Wise and Prudent, Lords, Emperors, Kings, Republics, Princes, Dukes, Earls,

The Register, or Proof of Property, which shows the names and residences of the owners, where the vessel was built, and when, and a particular description of the vessel. This must be returned to the custom-house upon the return of the vessel.

In peace this is necessary, to show that the ship really belongs to a neutral state. If she appear to either belligerent to have been built in an enemy's country, proof is generally required, that she was purchased by the neutral before, or captured and legally condemned since the declaration of war; and in the latter case, the *bill of sale*, properly authenticated, ought to be produced. Even *Hubner* admits that these proofs are so essential to every neutral vessel, for the prevention of frauds, that those which sail without them will have no reason to complain if they are interrupted in their voyages, and their neutrality disputed.

The List of Crew contains the names, ages, quality, place of residence, place of birth, of every person of the ship's company, &c. This must be returned with the reporting officer's certificate of the number of men still on board.

The *French* call this *Role d'Equipage.* This document is of great use in ascertaining a ship's neutrality. It must naturally excite a violent suspicion, if the majority of the crew be found to consist of foreigners; still more, if natives of the enemy's country.

The Charter-party, when one is given. This instrument serves to authenticate many of the facts, on which the proofs of the ship's neutrality must rest.

The Bill of Lading, by which the captain acknowledges the receipt of the goods specified therein, and promises to deliver them to the consignee, or his order. Of this there are usually several duplicates: of which, one is delivered to the captain, one kept by the shipper of the goods, and one transmitted to the consignee. This instrument, being only the evidence of a private transaction between the owner of the goods and the captain, does not carry with it the same degree of authenticity as the charter-party.

The Invoices, which contain the particulars and prices of each parcel of goods, with the amount of the freight, duties, and other charges thereon, which are usually transmitted from the shippers to their factors or consignees. These invoices prove by whom the goods

---

Barons, Lords, Burgomasters, Schepens, Counsellors, as also Judges, Officers, Justiciaries, and Regents of all the good cities and places, whether Ecclesiastical or Secular, who shall see these presents, or hear them read. We
make known, that the master of appearing before us,
has declared upon oath, that the vessel, called the
of the burthen of about tons, which he at present navigates, is of the United States of America, and that no subjects of the present belligerant powers have any part or portion therein, directly nor indirectly, so may God Almighty help him. And as we wish to see the said master prosper in his lawful affairs, our prayer is, to all the before mentioned, and to each of them separately, where the said master shall arrive with his vessel and cargo, that they may please to receive the said master with goodness, and to treat him in a becoming manner, permitting him, upon the usual tolls and expenses, in passing and repassing, to pass, navigate, and frequent the ports, passes, and territories, to the end to transact his business, where and in what manner he shall judge proper: Whereof we shall be willingly indebted.

In witness and for cause whereof, we affix hereto the seal of were shipped, and to whom consigned. They carry with them, however, but little authenticity, being easily fabricated where fraud is intended.

The Log Book, or ship's journal, which contains an accurate account of the ship's course, with a short history of every occurrence during the voyage. If this be faithfully kept, it will throw great light on the question of neutrality. If it be in any respect fabricated, this may in general be easily detected.

The Bill of Health, which is a certificate properly authenticated, that the ship comes from a place where no contagious distemper prevails, and that none of the crew, at the time of her departure, were infected with any such distemper.

The General Clearance contains the name of the captain, vessel's name, number of men on board, number of guns, and description of cargo, with permission to proceed to port of destination.

The Clearing Manifest, containing the description of cargo and values, to be left in the custom-house; and if bound to France, Sweden, Brazil and Portugal, there must be a duplicate manifest, certified by the foreign consul, to be kept on board.

ON ENTERING.

Manifest, containing a statement of cargo, and description of packages and contents, names of shippers and consignees, residences of consignees, and ports of destination; and *list of passengers*, and *remaining sea stores.—List of seamen.*

List of Passengers,—showing names, occupations, sex, age, and whether citizens of the United States—sworn to by the captain—for the custom-house, and one for the mayor's office.

CHAPTER II.

NAVIGATION LAWS.

The nations of Europe have always been desirous of monopolizing the commerce of their different colonies. In order to effect that object, and also to secure to their merchants a disproportionate share of the carrying trade with other countries, navigation laws have been adopted by some of them, and England in particular has been noted for the exclusive character of her navigation system. For the purpose of meeting these restrictive measures, and to protect our own mercantile interest, various laws have been adopted by our government since the general pacification of Europe.

By the act concerning the navigation of the United States,[a] which may be regarded as the basis of the navigation laws of the United States, perfect reciprocity is tendered to all commercial nations, and, at the same time, restrictions on foreign vessels are imposed, of a retaliatory character. By this act, foreign vessels are prohibited from importing into the United States, under penalty of forfeiture of vessel and cargo, any merchandise, except of the growth, production, or manufacture of the country where such vessels belong. This law, however, extends only to vessels of foreign nations which have adopted a similar regulation. Merchandise usually shipped in the first instance from any particular country, are considered the productions of that country. By the same act, foreign vessels are prohibited from importing merchandise from one port of the United States to another port of the United States under penalty of forfeiting the goods. They are permitted, however, to carry from one port to another in the United States part or the whole of the original cargo imported in such vessels, provided it has not been unladen.[b]

By an act passed May 24th, 1828, the principle of reciprocity was still farther extended; and the president of the United States was authorized to issue his proclamation, doing away with all discriminating tonnage and impost duties upon vessels belonging to nations that had abolished discriminating duties upon American vessels in their ports.

He was also empowered to suspend their collection upon foreign vessels for a limited time, where the discriminating duties upon American vessels were only suspended for such period.[c]

In 1830, all tonnage duties on American vessels were abolished, and the same exemption was extended to vessels of other countries where no discriminating or countervailing duties were levied on American vessels.[d]

This principle of reciprocity, both as to tonnage and import duties, and as to the character of the cargoes, is carried out in various treaties between the United States and other nations. In those trea-

---

[a] Act, 1st March, 1817. [b] Ibid. sec. 4. [c] Act, 24th May, 1828. [d] Act, 31st May, 1830.

ties it is provided, that the citizens of both parties are placed in their respective ports upon the footing of the most favoured nation, without conditions, if the concession were made freely: otherwise upon similar conditions; that they shall have free access to all ports, places or rivers where foreigners are admitted; may have ware-houses for their business, and enjoy complete protection for their commerce; that the import, export and tonnage duties, bounties and drawbacks, shall be the same for both parties.

Treaties of this character have been concluded with Mexico, April 5th, 1830; Chili, May 16th, 1832; Russia, December 18th, 1832; Austria, August 27th, 1829; Prussia, May 1st, 1828; Brazil, December 12th, 1828; Hanseatic Republics of Lubec, Bremen and Hamburg, December 20th, 1827; Sweden and Norway, July 4th, 1827; Central America, December 5th, 1825; Denmark, April 26th, 1826; Columbia, October 3d, 1824; Tunis, February 24th, 1824; Algiers, June 30th, 1815; Great Britain, July 3d, 1815; United Netherlands, October 8th, 1782; Morocco, June 28th, 1786; Dukedom of Oldenburg, Proclamation, September 18th, 1830; Sardinia, Act of 7th January, 1824; Papal Dominions, Proclamation, June 7th, 1827; Hanover, Proclamation, July 1st, 1828.

The particular provisions of these treaties, sometimes establishing entire free trade between the contracting parties, will be found under the head of the respective countries in the chapter on commercial regulations. Foreign vessels paying the same tonnage duties as American, British,[a] Netherlands,[b] Prussian,[c] Columbian,[d] Swedish,[e] Danish,[f] Hanseatic,[g] Portuguese,[h] Chilian,[i] Mexican,[j] Russian,[k] Austrian,[l] Brazilian,[m] Central American,[n] Tunisian,[o] Algerine,[p] Hanoverian,[q] Papal Dominions,[r] Sardinia,[s] Oldenburg,[t] Moorish,[u] French vessels from French islands, and with the produce of those islands.[v] Spanish vessels from Spain pay the same tonnage duties that American vessels pay in Spain; from Spanish colonies the same tonnage duties that American vessels pay in the colonial port from which they last sailed,[w] and a further tonnage duty, equivalent to the discriminating duty levied in Havana, on exports from that port in American vessels.[x]

A similar tonnage duty is levied on Spanish vessels bound from the United States to Cuba or Porto Rico, with a cargo equal to the discriminating duty levied in Havana upon the same cargo, if imported in an American vessel; and if clearing out to another place, a bond with security is taken, that the cargo shall not be taken in either of those islands, or landed elsewhere with the intention of sending it there. This bond is cancelled, upon producing a certificate from an American consul, of its having been landed elsewhere.[x] This is

---

[a] Treaty, 3d July, 1816. [b] Act, 7th Jan., 1824. [c] 24th May, 1828. [d] 20th April, 1826. [e] Treaty, 4th July, 1827. [f] 26th April, 1826. [g] 20th December, 1827. [h] Act, 25th May, 1832. [i] Treaty, 16th May, 1832. [j] 5th April, 1830. [k] 18th Dec. 1832. [l] 27th Aug. 1829. [m] 12th Dec. 1828. [n] 5th Dec. 1825. [o] 24th Feb. 1824. [p] 30th June, 1815. [q] Proclamation, 1st July, 1828. [r] 7th June, 1827. [s] Act, 7th Jan. 1824. [t] Proclamation, 18th Sept. 1830. [u] Treaty, 28th June, 1786. [v] Acts, 3d March and 9th May, 1828, and 13th July, 1832. [w] Act, 13th July, 1832. [x] Act, 30th June, 1834.

in retaliation of the discriminating duties levied on American vessels in Cuba.

British vessels, rafts, &c. on the lakes, between the United States and Canada, pay in our ports the same tonnage duties, and custom-house charges, that are levied on the American vessels in the ports of Canada.[a] Laws, too, were passed by Congress, April 18th, 1818, May 15th, 1820, and March 1st, 1823, for the purpose of preventing British vessels engaged in the trade between the United States and the British West Indies, from enjoying greater privileges than American vessels enjoyed.

By the first of these acts, the ports of the United States were closed against British vessels coming from British ports usually closed to American vessels, and British vessels clearing out from the United States were compelled to give bond to land their cargoes in ports not usually closed to American vessels. The second act closed the ports of the United States against British vessels from Lower Canada or New-Brunswick; prohibited any importations from British colonies in the West Indies or America, except wholly of the growth or production of that colony; and compelled British vessels to give bond to land their outward cargoes elsewhere than in a British colony. These acts compelled the British government to forego the intercourse between the islands and the United States, or to open it to American vessels. This was proposed by the act of parliament of 1822, which opened certain colonial ports to foreign vessels, laden with certain enumerated articles. This was met, by the act of March 1st, 1823, opening the ports of the United States to British vessels direct from those enumerated ports, and permitting produce, &c. to be exported in such vessels, to any of those enumerated ports. It also proposed to put the tonnage and impost duties in that trade upon the same footing in American and British vessels. These laws all aimed at placing the trade upon the footing of exact reciprocity, or of compelling England to supply her islands through the Danish or Swedish islands, at great expense.

Finding this inconvenient, she concluded to modify her colonial system. An act was accordingly passed by parliament, July 5th, 1825, with the real object of making certain ports free ware-house depots for the South American trade, but professedly opening the colonial trade upon certain conditions.

As these conditions were not accepted by the American government, the trade between the United States and the islands was closed by an order of council, and by a proclamation of the president, March 17th, 1827, and so remained during Mr. Adams' term.

Upon the accession of his successor, the negotiation was resumed, and conducted with so little skill on the part of the American government, that it terminated in an arrangement, by which the retaliatory acts of congress of April 18th, 1818; May 15th, 1820; and March 1st, 1823, were repealed,[b] and the colonial trade placed almost wholly under the regulation of the British government. A law was accordingly at once passed by parliament, burdening the direct trade be-

---

[a] Act, 2d March, 1831. [b] Act, 29th May, 1830.—Proclamation, 5th Oct., 1830.

tween the United States and the British West Indies with heavy duties, (of which a schedule will be found under the proper head among commercial regulations.) The trade between the northern colonies, and the islands from which all foreign vessels were excluded, was then exempted from duties. In this manner a bounty was in effect given upon produce for the United States imported through the northern colonies, and so large a bounty as to compensate for the delay, and increased expense of the circuitous voyage.

Upon this footing the intercourse now stands: American and British vessels sailing upon equal terms in the direct voyage, which is so bounded with duties, that the trade is carried on chiefly through the northern colonies, and the longer voyage from those colonies to the West Indies is entirely in the hands of the British navigators.

The French government also imposed discriminating duties upon American vessels in French ports, and the government of the United States was compelled to adopt measures of retaliation against French commerce.

A law was accordingly passed, imposing a duty of $18 per ton upon French vessels arriving in the United States.[a]

This soon brought about a convention between the parties, concluded at Washington, June 24th, 1822, by which it was agreed, that a discriminating tonnage duty of 94 cents per ton should be levied on French vessels, and $3 75 per ton on French merchandise, imported in French vessels for two years; and provision was made for a yearly diminution of 25 per cent. of these duties on merchandise, after 1824, until the discriminating duty should be abolished. A law was then passed by congress abolishing the duty of $18 per ton, and carrying the treaty into effect, and French vessels from France, except the tonnage duty of ninety-four cents, are now on the same footing, in the ports of the United States, with American vessels, and American vessels, except a tonnage duty of five francs, enjoy the privileges of French vessels, in the ports of France.[b] The intercourse between the United States, Martinique and Guadaloupe, is also upon the footing of reciprocity, certain privileges having been extended, by an ordinance of February 5th, 1826, to American vessels in those islands; and all French vessels arriving in the United States from those islands in *ballast*,[c] or laden with productions thereof, which may be exported in American vessels, are admitted upon the same terms as American vessels therefrom.[d]

Where there is no treaty, and where a discriminating duty is imposed by any government upon American ships, a tonnage duty of $1 per ton is levied upon ships of that country in ports of the United States,[e] except French ships, which pay 94 cents per ton, and Spanish, from the West Indies, which pay $1 50, and from Spain, 5 cents. On all foreign vessels arriving in the United States, from ports with which American vessels are not usually permitted to trade, a tonnage duty of $2 per ton must be paid.[f]

---

[a] Act, 15th May, 1820.
[b] Act, 3d March, 1823.
[c] Act, 13th July, 1832.
[d] Act, 9th May, 1828.
[e] Acts, 20th July, 1790, and 27th March, 1804.
[f] Act, 3d March, 1817.

A duty of fifty cents per ton is levied upon every vessel of the United States, entered in a district in one state, from a district in another state, except from an adjoining state, or a coasting vessel between Long-Island and Rhode-Island, having on board merchandise, taken in one state to be delivered in another state. This is not paid on a fishing vessel, or on a vessel having a license to trade between the different districts of the United States, more than once a year.

A retaliatory law was also passed March 3d, 1817, prohibiting the importation of plaster of paris, the production of any country from which American vessels are not permitted to bring the same article. Upon this act being passed, the legislature of Nova Scotia repealed the obnoxious law, which produced the act of congress, and the president of the United States, by a proclamation, which he was authorized to issue, exempted that province from its operation.

Cargoes of merchandise of any description not prohibited, and the produce of any country, may be imported upon the same footing as in vessels of the United States, in the vessels of Denmark, Sweden and Norway, and the Swedish islands, Austria, the Hanseatic cities, Brazil, Colombia, Central America, and the Dukedom of Oldenburg.

In the vessels of the following nations, the cargoes to be placed upon the same footing, must consist of the produce or manufacture of the particular country, viz: Great Britain, Netherlands, Sardinia, Russia, France, Mexico, Portugal, Hanover and the Papal dominions; British vessels from the British West Indies or the North American colonies, laden with the productions of those colonies, or of Great Britain, and French vessels from the French West India islands.

CHAPTER III.

CUSTOM-HOUSE LAWS.

In this chapter the provisions and regulations prescribed for the collection of the revenue will be found under their respective heads.

The careless manner in which these laws have been enacted—blending so many different subjects in one act, and often, in one section, repealing parts of former laws by implication; enacting new regulations by way of proviso; and the general want of method and of knowledge which has been evinced by those who have had the management of the revenue system of the United States, have burdened the statute books with a mass of legislation, always intricate and burdensome to the merchant, and often contradictory and unintelligible to the public officers. An attempt is here made to reduce the various laws which have been enacted since the organization of the government, to something like a system.

The subject naturally divides itself into the following heads, and the references to the various laws will be found in the notes.

1st Part. Organization of the custom-house, and the duties of officers.
2d. Regulations for American vessels in the foreign trade.
3d. " for the importation of foreign goods.
4th. " for entering foreign goods.
5th. " concerning distilled spirits, wines, and teas.
6th. " for landing goods.
7th. " for goods remaining on board.
8th. " for appraising imported goods.
9th. " for foreign vessels.
10th. " for collecting duties.
11th. " drafts, tares, and allowances, for breakage, discount, &c.
12th. " for clearing vessels and exporting goods.
13th. " for coasting vessels.
14th. Collection districts and local regulations.
15th. Drawbacks.
16th. Fees.

1st. *Organization of custom-house, and duties of officers.*

The sea coast of the United States is divided into three great coasting districts, viz: The first, including all the sea coast and navigable rivers from the eastern boundary of the United States to the southern limits of Georgia. The second, from the river Perdido to the western limits of the United States. The third, from the southern limits of Georgia to the river Perdido.

These are again subdivided into smaller, or collection districts, in each of which a collector is appointed to enforce the execution of the revenue laws. In the larger districts a naval officer and surveyor are appointed to aid the collector in the execution of his duties; in some of them a surveyor only is appointed to co-operate with the collector. Inspectors are also appointed to superintend the loading and unloading of vessels, and to prevent any evasion of the revenue laws. Appraisers, weighers, measurers, and gaugers, are also appointed to perform the various functions prescribed by the laws; but they are all subordinate to the collector.

The act of March 2d, 1799, which is the basis of the revenue system of the United States, provides for the appointment of collectors, naval officers, and surveyors, in the various collection districts of the United States.[a] Other laws have been subsequently passed altering those districts; for which, see part 14th of this chapter.

Laws, too, have been enacted, creating appraisers[b] in Boston, New-York, Philadelphia, Baltimore, Charleston, Savannah, and New-Orleans.

All officers and persons appointed in the revenue service, before entering upon the duties of their offices, must take and subscribe an oath or affirmation, diligently and faithfully to execute the duties of their respective offices.[c]

For oath, vide note infra.*

The oath, or affirmation, if taken by a collector, may be taken before any magistrate authorized to administer oaths within the district; but if taken by another officer, must be taken before the collector of his district; and, being certified under the hand and seal of the person taking the same, must, within three months thereafter, be transmitted to the comptroller of the treasury. In default of taking the oath, or transmitting a certificate thereof, the party failing forfeits $200.[d]

Collector.—At the ports where there are a collector, naval officer, and surveyor, the collector receives all reports, manifests, and documents, to be made or exhibited on the entry of any vessel; records in books kept for that purpose, all manifests; receives the entries of all vessels, and of the merchandise imported in them, and,

---

[a] Sec. 1. to sec. 17. [b] Act, 1st March, 1823, sec. 16.
[c] Act, 2d March, 1799, sec. 20. [d] Ibid.

* *Form of Oath:*

"I, A. B., having been appointed collector (or other officer, as the case may be) of the district (or port of) do solemnly, sincerely, and truly swear, (or affirm,) that I will diligently and faithfully execute the duties of the said office of and will use the best of my endeavours to prevent and detect frauds in relation to the duties imposed by the laws of the United States. I further swear (or affirm) that I will support the constitution of the United States.

Sworn (or affirmed) and subscribed, this day of before me.

together with the naval officer, or alone where there is none, estimates the amount of the duties payable thereupon, endorsing the amount upon the respective entries; receives all moneys paid for duties, and takes all bonds for securing the payment thereof; grants all permits for the unlading and delivery of goods; with the approbation of the principal officer of the treasury department, employs proper persons as weighers, gaugers, measurers, and inspectors, at the several ports within his district; and also, with the like approbation, provides at the public expense, store-houses for the safe keeping of goods, and such scales, weights, and measures, as may be necessary.[a]

The inspectors hold their appointments only while the collector appointing them continues in office.[b]

The collector, every three months, must make returns to the treasury department, and also to the secretary of state. To the latter he transmits lists of seamen registered within his district, and also an account of any impressments made from American vessels which have been reported to him.[c]

To the register of the treasury he also makes quarterly returns of the state of the commerce between the United States and foreign countries,[d] of the tonnage in his district, and of the certificates granted by him under the acts for registering[e] and for enrolling vessels.[f]

The collector must cause one package in every invoice of woollen or cotton goods, except coming from beyond the Cape of Good Hope, and one package in every twenty packages of each invoice, and if necessary, a greater number, to be opened and examined. If upon examination any variation be found from the *original entry*,[g] either in quantity, quality, or price, the whole goods contained in that entry must be examined; and if any package be found not contained in the invoice, or if such package or invoice be made up with intent to defraud the revenue, the same are forfeited.

Goods liable to appraisement cannot be delivered until a report has been made to the collector, that they have been inspected, and found to be correctly and fairly invoiced and put up. The collector, however, may deliver them upon the owner's giving bond, with security, in double the estimated value of the goods, to deliver them to the order of the collector within ten days after the report made on the package sent to the public store. This bond is forfeited if the packages are opened in the meantime, or if they are not delivered to the collector's order. The collector or surveyor may also permit them to be opened, but the permit must be in writing, and an inspector must be present when they are opened.[h]

When goods are entered for re-exportation, with benefit of drawback, the collector must cause them to be inspected and compared with the original invoices before granting a permit for loading. If they do not agree with the entry, they are forfeited.[i]

---

[a] Act, 2d March, 1799, sec 21. [b] 2 Gallison, 361. [c] Act, 28th May, 1796, sec. 7.
[d] Act, 10th Feb., 1820. [e] Act, 31st Dec., 1792, sec. 19.
[f] Act, 18th Feb., 1793, sec. 7. [g] Act, 14th July, 1832, sec. 14.
[h] Act, 28th May, 1830, sec. 4. [i] Ibid. sec. 5.

The original invoice must be deposited with the collector; and the same in case of transporting goods, with right of drawback, from one district to another. An authenticated copy, signed by the merchant, with the oath made on the entry of the goods annexed, must be preserved in the custom-house.

By the tariff of 1832, it is made the duty of the collector to cause the actual value of goods on which an ad valorem duty is imposed, or where the duty is regulated according to the value of the square yard, or of any other quantity or parcel thereof, to be ascertained by appraisement; also the number of such yards, parcels or quantities. The value is calculated at the place of exportation, and the time of purchase.[a]

By the appraisement act, the secretary of the treasury is empowered to authorize the collector of any importing district to require importers to give an additional bond, equal to the value of the goods imported, that he will produce, within a reasonable time, such proof as may be in his power to obtain, to enable the collector to ascertain the class or description of manufacture, or rate of duty, to which they are liable.[b]

Naval Officer.—The naval officer receives copies of all manifests and entries, and together with the collector, estimates the duties on all merchandise subject to duty; (and no duties can be received without such estimate;) keeps a separate record thereof; countersigns all permits, clearances, certificates, debentures and other documents, to be granted by the collector; he also examines the collector's abstracts of duties, and other accounts of receipts, bonds, and expenditures, and if found right he certifies the same.[c]

Where the collector is directed to grant any enrolment, license, certificate, permit, or other document, the naval officer must sign the same.[d]

Surveyor.—The surveyor superintends and directs all inspectors, weighers, measurers, and gaugers, within his port, and once every week reports to the collector the names of such inspectors, weighers, gaugers, or measurers, as may be absent from, or neglect their duty; visits or inspects the vessels which arrive therein; and makes a return in writing every morning to the collector, if any, at the port where he resides, of all vessels which have arrived from foreign ports the preceding day, specifying the names and denominations of the vessels, the masters' names, from whence arrived, whether laden or in ballast, whether belonging to the United States, or to what other nation belonging; and if American vessels, whether the masters thereof have or have not complied with the law, in having the required number of manifests of the cargo on board, agreeing in substance with the provisions made necessary by law. He is also required to put on board each such vessel one or more inspectors, immediately after their arrival. The surveyor also ascertains the proof, quantities, and kinds of distilled spirits imported, rating such spirits according to their respective degrees of proof, as defined by the laws imposing duties on

---

[a] Act, 14th July, 1832, sec. 7. [b] Act, 28th May, 1830, sec. 8.
[c] Act, 2d March, 1799, sec. 21. [d] Ibid. sec. 25.

spirits; he must examine and ascertain the quality, kind, and quantity of all wines imported; also the quantity and kind of all teas and sugars imported; and grants certificates for the said spirits, and makes returns thereof. He also examines whether the goods imported in any vessel, and the deliveries thereof, agreeably to the inspector's returns thereof, correspond with the permits for landing the same; and if any error or disagreement appear, he reports the same to the collector, and to the naval officer, if any there be. The surveyor also superintends the lading, for exportation, of all goods entered for the benefit of any drawback, bounty, or allowance, and examines and reports whether the kind, quantity, and quality of the goods correspond with the entries and permits granted therefor. He also, from time to time, and particularly on the first Mondays in January and July, in each year, examines the weights, measures, and other instruments used in ascertaining the duties on imports, with standards provided at the public expense; and where disagreements or errors are discovered, he reports the same to the collector. The surveyor, in all cases, is subject to the direction of the collector.

At ports to which a collector and surveyor only are assigned, the collector executes the duties of the naval officer: he also does the same in case of the disability or death of the naval officer, until a successor is appointed, unless there is a deputy duly authorized under the hand and seal of the naval officer, who, in that case, continues to act until an appointment takes place. At the ports to which a collector only is assigned, such collector executes the duties of the naval officer, and, as far as may be, the duties prescribed to the surveyors. At the ports to which surveyors only are assigned, such surveyor performs all the duties enjoined upon surveyors, and also receives and records the copies of all manifests transmitted to him by the collector; all permits granted by such collector, distinguishing the gauge, weight, measure, and quality of the goods specified therein, and takes care that no goods be unladen or delivered from any vessel without a proper permit for the purpose.[a]

At such ports as may be designated by the secretary of the treasury, the surveyors may also perform the duties, and receive the fees of collectors, under the enrolment and license act.[b]

The surveyor must also make monthly returns to the collector of the district, of all the manifests certified or received, and of permits granted or received by him, under the enrolment and license act.[c]

At such ports of delivery only to which no surveyor is assigned, the collector of the district, from time to time, may employ a proper person to do the duties of a surveyor, who is entitled to the like compensation with inspectors.

The collectors, naval officers, and surveyors, must attend in person at their respective ports; keep fair and true accounts and records of all their transactions, as officers of the customs, in manner and form as directed by the proper department; and must at all times submit their books, papers, and accounts, to the inspection of persons appointed for that purpose. The collector must

---

[a] Act, 2d March, 1799, sec. 21. [b] Act, 11th Feb., 1830. [c] Act, 18th Feb., 1793, sec. 25.

pay to the order of the officer authorized to direct the payment thereof, the whole of the moneys received by virtue of the act of 2d March, 1799; and, once in every three months, or oftener if required, transmit their accounts for settlement to the officer whose duty it shall be to make such settlement. If any collector, naval officer, or surveyor, omit to keep fair and true accounts, or refuse to submit forthwith their books, papers, and accounts to such inspection; or if any collector omit to render his accounts for settlement, for a term exceeding three months after the same shall have been required by the proper officer, the delinquent officer forfeits, for the use of the United States, $1000, to be recovered, with costs of suit.[a]

Every collector, naval officer, and surveyor, in cases of occasional and necessary absence, or of sickness, may respectively perform their several duties by deputy, duly constituted under their hands and seals, for whom, in the execution of their trust, they are respectively answerable. In case of the disability or death of a collector, the duties and authorities vested in him devolve on his deputy, if any there be, for whose conduct the estate of such disabled or deceased collector is liable; in defect of a deputy, upon the naval officer of the same district; if there be no naval officer, upon the surveyor of the port, if any; and if none, upon the surveyor of the port nearest thereto within the district. In case of the disability or death of a surveyor, the collector may nominate some fit person to perform his duties, who acts until a successor be duly appointed, and ready to enter upon the execution of his office.[b]

The duties of surveyors and officers of inspection, concerning teas, distilled spirits, and wines, will be found in part 6th of this chapter.

Officers of the customs must seize and secure any vessel or merchandise liable to seizure, as well without as within their respective districts.[c]

Officers or other persons executing or aiding in the seizure of goods, who may be sued for any act committed in the performance of their duty, may plead the general issue, and give the special matter in evidence. If in such suit the plaintiff is nonsuited, or judgment pass against him, the defendant recovers double costs; and in suits, or informations where any seizure is made pursuant to the act of 1799, the *onus probandi* is upon such claimant. If any person forcibly resist, or impede any officers of the customs, or any person assisting them, in the execution of their duty, such person may, for every such offence, be fined, not exceeding $400. If any master of a vessel, coming into the United States, obstruct or hinder any officer of the revenue in going on board such vessel, for the purpose of carrying into effect the revenue laws, he forfeits a sum not exceeding $500, nor less than $50; but the *onus probandi* lies on the claimant only where probable cause is shown for such prosecution, to be judged of by the court.[d]

The public weighers, gaugers, and measurers, within three days

---

[a] Act, 18th Feb., 1793. sec. 22. [b] Ibid [c] Act, 2d March, 1799, sec. 70. [d] Ibid. sec. 71.

after any vessel is discharged, must make returns of the articles weighed, gauged or measured, out of such vessel.[a]*

[a] Act, 2d March, 1799, sec. 72.

* *Weigher's Return.*

Return of [here insert the number of packages and contents] weighed from on board the [here insert the denomination and name of the vessel] whereof [insert the name] is master, from [insert the port or place from which arrived.]

Date of vessel's entry.	To whom consigned as per permit.	Marks.	Numbers.	Packages.	Contents and quality.	Weight.	Tare as allowed by law.	Tare as marked on the packages.	Amount of drafts.

District of
Port of

A. B., Weigher.

Form of the Return to be made by the Gauger:

Return of [here insert the number of casks and packages] gauged from on board the [here insert the denomination and name of the vessel] whereof [insert the name] is master, from [insert the port or place from which arrived.]

Date of vessel's entry.	To whom consigned as per permit.	Marks.	Numbers.	Casks or Packages.	Contents and quality, as marked by the inspector of the revenue.	Gauge.	Wantage.	What casks empty or taken to fill up others.

District of
Port of

C. D., Gauger.

Form of the Return to be made by the Measurer:

Return of the [here insert salt or coal, as the case may be] measured from on board the [here insert the denomination and name of the vessel] whereof [insert the name] is master, from [insert the port or place from which arrived.]

Date of vessel's entry.	To whom consigned as per permit.	Number of bushels in words at length.	Quality, whether salt or coal.	Average weight of salt per bushel.

District of
Port of

E. F., Measurer.

The returns must be made by the weighers, gaugers, and measurers, in books to be prepared by them for that purpose, and kept in the custom-house.

The collector is authorized, upon a vessel's first coming within his district, to put and keep on board such vessel, whilst remaining within such district, or in going from one district to another, one or more inspectors, to examine the cargo, and to superintend the delivery thereof, and to perform such other duties, according to law, as they shall be directed. Collectors only have power to put on board vessels, inspectors to go from one district to another. Surveyors may put inspectors on board to remain while the vessel is within the district. The inspectors must make known to the person having the charge of such vessel, the duties they are to perform, and suffer no goods to be landed or removed from such vessel, without a permit in writing from the collector of the port, and naval officer, where any.

They must enter in a book, the names of persons in whose behalf such permits are granted, together with the particulars therein specified, and the marks, numbers, kinds, and description of the respective packages unladen pursuant thereto; and also keep a like account in said book of all merchandise sent to the public store, which book must be delivered to the surveyor in the month of January in every year for his inspection, and immediately after such inspection, be transmitted by the surveyor, with such observations as he may think necessary, to the collector, to be deposited in his office. Inspectors must attend to the delivery of the cargoes under their care, at all times when the unlading or delivery is lawful, particularly from the rising till the setting of the sun, Sundays and the 4th day of July excepted. For which purpose they must constantly attend and remain on board the vessels, the deliveries from which they are to superintend, or at any other stations where their inspection is necessary. They must not quit such stations or places without leave of the surveyor, who must appoint another inspector (if necessary) to supply his place during his absence. Any inspector, neglecting or violating his duty, for the first offence forfeits the sum of $50, and for the second offence, is displaced, and made incapable of holding any station under the revenue laws, for a term not exceeding seven years. No inspector can perform any other duty or service, on board any vessel, the superintendance of which is committed to him, for any person whatever, other than what is required by law, under the penalty of being disabled from acting as inspector. The wages or compensation of such inspector, as may proceed from one district to another, are defrayed by the master of the vessel committed to their care. Every officer of the revenue, while performing any duty on board any vessel, not in a port of the United States, discharging her cargo, is entitled to receive from the master such provisions and accommodations as are usually supplied to passengers, or as the state and condition of such vessel will admit, on receiving therefor 50 cents per diem; and any master, who refuses provisions and reasonable accommodations, forfeits $100.[a]

---

[a] Act, 2d March, 1799, sec. 53.

Collectors, naval officers, surveyors, inspectors, and the officers of revenue cutters, are authorized to board vessels in any port of the United States, or within four leagues of the coast, if bound to the United States, whether in or out of their districts, for the purposes of demanding manifests, and of examining and searching the said vessels. They may have free access to the cabin and every other part of the vessel; and if any box, trunk, chest, cask, or other package be found in the cabin, steerage, or forecastle, or in any other place separate from the residue of the cargo, the revenue officer must take a particular account thereof, and of the marks and numbers, and a description thereof, and if he judge proper, put a seal or seals thereon; and he must forward such an account and description, without delay, to the collector of the district to which such vessel is bound. If upon her arrival at the port of her entry, the boxes, trunks, chests, casks, or other packages so described, or any of them, be missing, or if the seals put thereon be broken, the master forfeits for every such box, trunk, chest, cask, or other package so missing, or of which the seals are broken, the sum of $200. Inspectors who may be put on board of any vessel, are required to secure, after sunset in each evening, or previous to their quitting the vessel, the hatches and other communications with the hold, or any other part they may judge necessary, with locks or other proper fastenings. If the said locks or other fastenings, or any of them, be broken or removed, during the night, or before the rising of the sun, or without the presence of the inspectors, or without license first had and obtained; or if any goods be clandestinely landed, notice thereof must be immediately given by the inspector, to the collector and naval officer; and the master, for each offence, forfeits the sum of $50.[a]

When the delivery of merchandise has been completed, copies of the accounts or entries made thereof, by the officers charged with the delivery, are returned to the collector of the district and naval officer, if any there be, within three days, if at the port where such officers reside; and if at any other port, as soon as the nature of the case will admit, not exceeding fifteen days. The accounts or entries must comprise all deliveries made pursuant to permits, and all merchandise sent to the public stores; also, each and every package remaining on board, for the purpose of being exported to a foreign port, or to some other district of the United States. The returns are according to the form below.*

[a] Act, 2d March, 1799, sec. 54.

* Return of merchandise unladen under my inspection, pursuant to permits for that purpose, from on board the [insert the names of the vessel and master,] from [insert the port from which the vessel arrived.]

When delivered or sent to store.	Dates of permits.	Marks.	Numbers.	Description of packages.	Contents.	To whom delivered, or whether sent to store, or remaining on board.	Remarks.

The returns must be signed by the inspectors; and after examination, and being found correct, countersigned or certified by the surveyor, if any there be, at the port where the deliveries have been made; they must be transmitted by him to the naval officer, if any there be, who compares the same with the manifests and entries in his possession; and if any difference appear, the particulars thereof must be noted by endorsement on the said returns, and if no difference appear, it is so noted by like endorsement. He transmits the same to the collector of the district, who compares them with the manifests and entries; if any difference appear, the same is noted by endorsement on such manifests, specifying the particulars thereof; and if no difference appear, it is noted by like endorsement. The endorsement, in each case, is subscribed by the officer by whom such comparison is made.[a]

Goods destined for the district of entry, remaining on board more than fifteen working days, must be taken possession of by the inspector.[b] Where the vessel is of more than 300 tons burthen, and is from a foreign port, twenty days are allowed.[c] Such goods, however, may be taken possession of by the inspector, with the consent of the owner or consignee, or with the consent of the owner or master of the vessel, at any time after five days notice to the collector.

These goods are then taken to the public store, and kept there, at the charge and risk of the owner, and if not claimed, are to be sold.

For mode of sale, &c. see part 7.

The wages of inspectors, beyond the time allowed by law, are paid by the master or owner of the vessel; but the inspectors, before the clearance of the vessel, must render an exact account to the collector, of all the compensation paid or to be paid by the master or owner.[d]

Every collector, naval officer, and surveyor, or other person specially appointed by either of them for that purpose, has authority to enter any vessel, in which they have reason to suspect any merchandise, subject to duty, is concealed, and to search for, seize, and secure any such merchandise; and if they have cause to suspect a concealment thereof in any particular dwelling-house, or other place, they are, upon proper application on oath to any justice of the peace, entitled to a warrant to enter such house, or other place, (in the day time only,) and there to search for such goods, and to seize and secure the same for trial. All such merchandise, on which the duties have not been paid, or secured, is forfeited.[e]

Any officer of the revenue is also authorized to go on board of, and search any vessels either within or without his district; and if it appear that any breach of the laws have been committed, subjecting either vessel or goods on board to forfeiture, to seize the same.[f]

All merchandise seized by virtue of the revenue acts, must remain in the custody of the collector, or such other person as he shall ap-

[a] Act, 2d March, 1799, sec. 55. [b] Ibid. sec. 56. [c] Act, 3d March, 1821, sec. 1.
[d] Act, 2d March, 1799, sec. 56.
[e] Act, 2d March, 1799, sec. 68. [f] Act, 18th Feb. 1793, sec. 27.

point for that purpose, until it is ascertained whether the same have been forfeited, or not. If it be adjudged that they are not forfeited, they must be forthwith restored to the owners, or claimants thereof. If any person conceal or buy any merchandise, knowing them to be liable to seizure, such person forfeits double the value thereof.[a]

No officer of the customs, or other person employed in the collection of the duties, and on the tonnage of ships or vessels, can own, either in whole or in part, any vessel; or act as agent, attorney, or consignee for the owner of any vessel, or of any cargo or lading on board the same; nor can any officer of the customs, or other person employed in the collection of the duties, import, or be concerned directly or indirectly in the importation of any merchandise, for sale into the United States, under penalty of $500.[b]

Each collector, naval officer, and surveyor, must account to the treasury for all his emoluments, and all the expenses incident to his office; such accounts must be rendered on oath or affirmation, in forms, and supported by proofs, prescribed by the secretary of the treasury. All such accounts are settled at the treasury like other public accounts.[c]

By the general appropriation bill of 1834, these officers are directed to render these accounts quarterly; and the clerks and weighers employed by them, are directed to render quarterly accounts to the collectors, to be forwarded to the treasury, of their fees and emoluments, and of all the expenses incident to their respective offices. These accounts must be rendered upon oath or affirmation, and supported by proofs prescribed by the secretary of the treasury.[d]

They must, together with the accounts of the expenses, render a list of the clerks employed, stating the rate of compensation allowed to each, and the duties which they severally perform; and, also, an account of the sums paid for stationery, official or contingent expenses, fuel, and office rent, stating the purposes for which the premises rented are applied.[e]

No account for compensation of any person employed in the collection of the revenue, can be allowed, until such person shall have certified, on oath or affirmation, that he has received the full sum therein charged, to his own use and benefit, and that he has not paid, deposited, or assigned, nor contracted to pay, deposit, or assign, any part of such compensation to the use of any other person, nor in any way, directly or indirectly, paid or given, nor contracted to pay or give, any reward or compensation for his office or employment, or the emoluments thereof.[f]

In the ports of Boston, New-York, Philadelphia, Baltimore, Charleston, Savannah, and New-Orleans, no person can be an inspector, who at the same time holds any other office in the customs.[g]

Any officer of the customs, directly or indirectly taking or receiving any bribe or recompense, for conniving at any false entry of a vessel, or merchandise, forfeits a sum not less than $200, nor more

---

[a] Act, 2d March, 1799, sec. 68. [b] Ibid. sec. 86. [c] Act, 7th May, 1822, sec. 12.
[d] Act, 27th June, 1834, sec. 2. [e] Act, 7th May, 1822, sec. 13. [f] Ibid. sec. 16.
[g] Ibid. sec. 14.

than $2000 for each offence; and any person giving or offering any bribe or reward for such deception, or fraud, incurs a like penalty for each offence.[a]

By the act of May 7th, 1822, persons employed in the custom-house, are prohibited from receiving any fee, or compensation, other than that allowed by law, for any service performed in making any entry, or clearance, or preparing any papers, to be used or kept in the custom-house, under pain of removal from office, and $500 fine.[b]

False swearing or affirming, under the revenue laws, is declared perjury, and made punishable as such.[c]

Bonds are given by the various collectors, surveyors, &c., for the faithful performance of their duties, in the following sums, viz.:

Collectors of New-York and Philadelphia,	$60,000
Do. of Boston and Charlestown,	40,000
Do. of Baltimore and Charleston,	30,000
Do. Norfolk and Portsmouth,	15,000
Do. Portsmouth in New-Hampshire, of Salem and Beverly, Wilmington, (in the state of Delaware,) Annapolis, Georgetown, (in Maryland,) Bermuda Hundred and City Point, Alexandria, Wilmington, Newbern and Edenton, (in the state of North Carolina,) Newport and Providence, (in the state of Rhode Island,) and Providence Plantations,	10,000
Collectors of Newburyport, Gloucester, Marblehead, Plymouth, Nantucket, Portland and Falmouth, New-London, New-Haven, Fairfield, Perth Amboy, Yorktown, Dumfries, Washington, Camden, Georgetown, (South Carolina,) Beaufort and Savannah,	5,000
Collectors of Hudson, Middletown and Waldoborough,	4,000
And all the other collectors,	2,000
Naval officers of Boston and Charlestown, New-York, Philadelphia, Baltimore and Charleston,	10,000
And all other naval officers,	2,000
Surveyors of Boston and Charlestown, New-York, Philadelphia, Baltimore and Charleston,	5,000
And all other surveyors,	1,000

These bonds are filed in the office of the comptroller of the treasury of the United States, and are severally put in suit for the benefit of the United States, upon any breach of the condition thereof.[d] *

[a] Act, 2d March, 1799, sec. 88. [b] Act, 7th May, 1822, sec. 17.
[c] Act, 2d March, 1799, sec. 17. [d] Ibid. sec. 88.

* *Form of Bond:*

Know all men by these presents, that we are held and firmly bound unto the United States of America, in the full and just sum of dollars, money of the said United States; to which payment, well and truly to be made, we bind ourselves, jointly and severally, our joint and several heirs, executors, and administrators, firmly by these presents. Sealed with our seals, and dated this day of one thousand

The condition of the foregoing obligation is such, that, whereas the President of the United States hath, pursuant to law, appointed the said to the office of in the state of

Now, therefore, if the said has truly and faithfully executed and discharged, and shall continue truly and faithfully to execute and discharge all the duties of the said office, according to law, then the above obligation to be void and of no effect, otherwise it shall abide and remain in full force and virtue.

Sealed and delivered in the presence of }

All matters directed by the act of March 2d, 1799, to be done to or by the collector of a district, or by the naval officer, may be done to and by the person who is authorized to act in his place.[a]

Persons conscientiously scrupulous, are permitted to affirm, in place of swearing.[b]

Where the forms of official documents are substantially complied with, according to the true meaning, no penalty or forfeiture is incurred by a deviation therefrom. The officers of the treasury may, from time to time, prescribe additions to the said forms, for the purpose of adapting the same to any alterations made to the rates of duties on the importation of goods, and on the tonnage of vessels, and for the better collection of duties.[c]

Whenever a collector dies or resigns, the commissions, to which he would be entitled on the receipt of all duties bonded by him, are equally divided between the collector resigning, or the legal representative of such deceased collector, and his successor in office, whose duty it is to collect the same; and for this purpose all the public or official books, papers, and accounts, of the collector resigning or deceased, must be delivered over to such successor.[d]

Each collector, naval officer, and surveyor, must keep in some conspicuous place of his office, a fair table of the rates of fees and duties demandable by law, and give a receipt for the fees he receives, specifying the particulars, whenever required; and in case of failure therein, he forfeits $100 to the use of the informer. If any officer of the customs demands or receives any greater, or other fee, compensation, or reward, for executing any duty or service required of him by law, he forfeits $200 for each offence, for the use of the party aggrieved. If any inspector, gauger, weigher, or measurer, receives any gratuity, fee, or reward, for any services performed by virtue of this act, other than is by law allowed, or if any gauger, weigher, or measurer, employed as such by the public, in the districts of Portsmouth, Salem and Beverly, Boston and Charlestown, Providence, New-York, Philadelphia, Baltimore, Norfolk and Portsmouth, or Charleston, gauges, weighs, or measures any article or articles other than shall be directed by the proper officer in order to ascertain the duties to be received, or the drawbacks to be allowed thereon, or makes a return of the weight, gauge, or measure of any merchandise, laden, or to be laden on board any vessel for the benefit of drawback, without having actually weighed, gauged, or measured the same, as the case may require, after such merchandise has been notified to the collector and entered for exportation, they for the first offence forfeit $50, and for the second offence $200, and are discharged from the public service. If any inspector or other officer of the customs certify the shipment of any merchandise entitled to drawback on exportation, without having duly inspected and examined the same, after he has received the permit for lading; or, if the amount of such drawback is estimated according to weight, gauge, or measure, until such merchandise has been first weighed, gauged, or measured, he is subject to the like forfeitures, and must be discharged from the public service.[e]

---

[a] Act, 2d March, 1799, sec. 95. [b] Ibid. sec. 96. [c] Ibid. sec. 111.
[d] Act, 7th May, 1822, sec. 4. [e] Act, 2d March, 1799, sec. 73.

It is the duty of collectors, and all other officers of the customs, in states where the importation or admission of persons of colour is prohibited by the laws of the state, to notice the provisions of those laws, and to carry into effect the laws of those states, by seizing the vessel in which such importations are made; and also prosecuting the master thereof for the penalty of $1000, for each person of colour imported. The vessel is forfeited.[a]

An act was passed March 3d, 1815, empowering collectors, naval officers, surveyors and inspectors, to search vessels, boats, and rafts, in their own or the adjoining districts; and if they found any goods subject to duty on which duties had not been paid nor secured, to seize the same.[b]

They were also empowered by the same act to stop, in their own and in the adjoining districts, any vehicle, beast of burden, or persons travelling on foot, and search for goods introduced into the United States, in violation of the revenue laws, and if such were found, to seize the same.

If they suspect such goods to be concealed in any dwelling-house, or other building, they are authorized, upon application on oath to any judge or justice of the peace, and a warrant being granted, to enter such house or building, in the day time only, and to search therefor. If any such goods are found, they are authorized to seize them.[c]

In making such seizure, these officers are empowered to command any person within ten miles of the place of search or seizure to aid and assist them; and any person refusing to aid, is liable to be fined from $50 to $200.

In case of resistance, the marshal may be called upon, with the posse, to enforce the seizure; and any citizen or inhabitant of the district refusing to aid, may be fined $300, and imprisoned three months.[d]

When any prosecution is commenced on account of the seizure of any vessel or merchandise, made by any officer under an act of congress, and judgment given for the claimants, if it shall appear to the court, that there was a reasonable cause of seizure, the court must cause a proper certificate to be made thereof; and in such case the claimant is not entitled to costs, nor is the person who made the seizure, or the prosecutor, liable to a suit, on account of such seizure and prosecution; but the vessel and merchandise must be, after judgment, forthwith returned to such claimants, or their agents.[e]

Every collector may, with the approbation of the secretary of the treasury, employ within his district such persons as deputy collectors, as he shall judge necessary; and the deputy collectors, before they enter on the duties of their offices, must take and subscribe, before the collectors appointing them, or before some magistrate within their respective districts, authorized by law to administer oaths.[f]

By an act passed February 10th, 1820, for the purpose of showing annually the actual state of the foreign commerce of the United States, it is made the duty of the register of the treasury, under direction of

---

[a] Act, 28th Feb., 1803. [b] Act, 3d March, 1815, sec. 1. [c] Ibid. sec. 2. [d] Ibid. sec. 4.
[e] Act, 24th Feb., 1807. [f] Acts, 3d March, 1817, and 6th May, 1822.

the secretary of the treasury, annually to prepare statistical accounts of the commerce of the United States with foreign countries, for each preceding year, to be laid before congress.[a]

Such accounts state all goods exported from the United States to other countries; all goods imported into the United States from other countries; and all navigation employed in foreign trade of the United States.[b]

The kinds, quantities, and values of all articles exported, and of all articles imported, must be distinctly stated in such accounts, except where it may appear to the secretary of the treasury that separate statements of the species, quantities, or values, of any particular articles, would swell the annual statements without utility; and, in such cases, the kinds and total values of such articles must be stated together, or in such classes as the secretary of the treasury may think fit.[c]

The exports must be so stated as to show the exports to each foreign country, and their values; and separately, the exports of articles of the production or manufacture of the United States, and their values; and those of the production or manufacture of foreign countries, and their values.[d]

The imports must be so stated, as to show the imports from each foreign country, and their values.[e]

The navigation employed in the foreign trade of the United States, is stated, so as to show the amount of the tonnage of all vessels departing from and arriving in the United States for or from foreign countries; separating the tonnage of vessels of the United States, and the tonnage of foreign vessels: and the amount of tonnage belonging to each foreign nation; also the amount of the tonnage of all vessels departing for or arriving from every particular foreign country, and, separately, the tonnage of vessels of the United States, and the tonnage of foreign vessels.[f]

The collectors must keep separate accounts of the kinds, quantities, and values, of those parts of the imports subject to duties ad valorem, directed by the secretary of the treasury.[g]

All articles exported must be valued at their actual cost, or the true values at the time of exportation, in the ports from which they are exported; and all articles imported must be valued at their actual cost, or the true values in the foreign ports from which they were last exported, at the time of such exportation.[h]

Every collector must keep an accurate account of the national characters and tonnage of all vessels departing from or arriving in his district for or from foreign countries, and of the places for which such vessels depart or arrive.[i]

The several collectors must make quarter yearly returns to the register of the treasury of these facts.[j]

The secretary of the treasury gives directions to the collectors, and prescribes rules and forms to be observed by them, proper for attaining the objects of this act.[k]

The forms of the annual statements are determined by the secretary of the treasury.[l]

---

[a] Act, 10th Feb., 1820, sec. 1. [b] Sec. 2. [c] Sec. 3. [d] Sec. 5. [e] Ibid. [f] Sec. 6. [g] Sec. 9. [h] Sec. 10. [i] Sec. 12. [j] Sec. 13. [k] Sec. 14. [l] Sec. 1.

Where any forfeiture accrues from a violation of the revenue laws, it is the duty of the collector, or other proper officer, to give notice in the newspaper of the seizure, specifying the name of the vessel, description of goods, and the names and places of residence of the owners or consignees of the vessel, or goods seized.[a]

At common law, any person may seize for a forfeiture to the government; and if the government adopt the seizure, and the property is condemned, he is justified.[b]

2d. *Regulations for American vessels in the foreign trade.*

American vessels from abroad, to become entitled to be placed on the most favourable footing, must have the captain and all the mates, Americans;[c] and also two thirds of all other persons making a part of their crew, Americans, "or persons not the subjects of any foreign prince or state."[d] In this latter item, are included the seamen, the cook, the apprentices, the boys, and all other persons (not including the captain and mates) doing duty on board. They must also have an American register.

Importation of Goods.—No merchandise can be imported in any vessel belonging in whole or in part to a citizen or inhabitant of the United States, unless the master have on board a manifest in writing, signed by such master or other person having the command, containing the name of the port where such merchandise was received, and the port where consigned or destined to, within the United States; particularly noting the merchandise destined for each port respectively, and the name, description, and built of the vessel, with the marks and numbers on each package, with the names of the owners and the master; and every package on board must be truly and particularly described, as well as all goods stowed loose—to whom consigned, according to the bills of lading; or if to order; with the names of all passengers, distinguishing whether cabin or steerage passengers, or both, with their baggage, and an account of all remaining sea-stores.*

---

[a] Act, 18th February, 1793, sec. 38. [b] 4 Wheat. 100.
[c] Act, 31st Dec., 1792, sec. 1. [d] Act, 1st March, 1817, sec. 6 and 7.

* *Form of Manifest:*

Report and manifest of the cargo laden on board of the whereof is master, which cargo was taken on board at burthen tons, built at in the state of and owned by merchants, at as per register granted at the and bound for

Marks.	*Numbers inclusive.*	*Packages and Contents.*	*By whom shipped.*	*To whom consigned, or if to order.*	*Place of Consignees' residence.*	*Ports of destination.*

Returned Cargo.—[If any articles of the outward cargo are brought back, they are to be detailed, specifying by whom shipped outward, and to whom consigned inward.]

Return of passengers, and packages belonging to them respectively.

Manifests.—In a circular of the treasury department, dated Sept. 27th, 1819, it is stated to be the duty of masters of American vessels, arriving in the United States from foreign ports, to have their ***manifests made out, at the time of their leaving such ports;*** and that the time of lading the vessel is the most proper for making out the manifests. It is also stated, that the penalty of the law will be incurred, if the master does not have his manifests ready to be exhibited to any officer of the customs, that may board him within four leagues of the coast. The privilege of making out the manifests, after the arrival of the vessel within four leagues of the coast, is stated to be totally inadmissible.

If merchandise imported is destined to be delivered in different districts or ports, the said merchandise must be inserted in successive order in the manifest; and all spirits, wines, and teas, being the whole or any part of the cargo, inserted in like order, distinguishing the port where destined, and the kind, qualities, and quantities thereof; and if merchandise be imported by citizens or inhabitants of the United States, in vessels other than of the United States, the manifest must be of the same form, and contain the same particulars, except that the vessel be described as in note.*

American vessels arriving from abroad, with goods consigned by their manifest to persons residing in different ports of the United States, are to land at the first port such part of the goods as are consigned to persons at the first port; and may, at their own pleasure, land either the whole, or part, or none of the rest, until they reach the other ports to which they are destined.[a] The manifest must specify the articles destined to each port.[b] For whatever portion of the goods they keep on board, they are to give a bond for the landing of the same in the United States, and securing the duties thereon.[c] Such vessels may take on board any other articles, to be landed in any other port in the United States; for which goods, they must have the manifest of a coaster, and clear out as such. They must, however, pay tonnage duties in each port.[c]

Before the departure of the vessel, provided it be not within forty-eight hours after her arrival, the master is furnished by the collector with a copy of his report, and a certificate, showing on what part of the cargo the duties have been paid or secured, and what part remains on board. He then gives bond for reporting such goods on which the duties have not been paid or secured. The copy of the report the master must produce to the collector of the district where bound, together with the certificates of the collectors of other districts where

---

[a] Act, 1st March, 1817, sec. 5. [b] Act, 2d March, 1799, sec. 23. [c] Ibid. sec. 33.

[Here insert the names of the passengers, and whether cabin or steerage passengers; with the description and number of packages containing their baggage, or the tools or implements of a mechanical trade.]

Vessel and Cabin Stores.

[Here detail what are remaining.]

* Report and manifest of the cargo laden on board the whereof is master, burthen [here insert the nation where built,] bound to which cargo was taken on board at

goods have been landed, within twenty-four hours after his arrival, (except in the state of Georgia, where forty-eight hours are allowed,) under penalty of $500. The bond is cancelled, by producing from the collector of such district a certificate, within six months, of the due entry and delivery of such merchandise in such district, or upon due proof that such entry and delivery were unavoidably prevented, and that if the goods have not been lost, they have been duly entered.[a] *

The master also must apply to the surveyor or inspector of the port, for a copy of the report, similar to the report of the collector, relating to distilled spirits, wines, or teas, when there are any on board, to be delivered in different districts; (the want of which subjects such articles to forfeiture, and $500 penalty on the master;) and each surveyor must certify what quantity has been delivered from his respective district.[b]

---

[a] Act, 2d March, 1799, sec. 34. [b] Ibid. sec. 35.

* *Form of the Certificate, showing what goods were landed:*

District of

Port of

These are to certify, that the within is a true copy of the report and manifest of the cargo of the [insert the denomination and name of the vessel,] whereof [insert the name] is master, from [insert the port where from,] entered at this port the [insert the day and month of entry,] as exhibited on oath (or affirmation) by the said master: That no part of the said cargo, as expressed in such manifest, hath been unladen or landed at this port, (or as the case may require:) That there hath been unladen and landed at this port, and the duties paid or secured to be paid on the following articles, (or) That all the said cargo as expressed in the said manifest, hath been duly entered and landed in this district according to law, except the following articles: [here enumerate the marks, numbers, packages, and contents, or if articles in bulk, the quantities, whether landed or remaining on board, as the case may require;] and that bond hath here been entered as the law directs, for the delivery of the [insert the whole or remaining part, as the case may require] of the said cargo, at the [insert the port and district of destination.]

Witness our hands and seals, this day of

A. B., Collector.
C. D., N. Officer.

Form of the Bond:

Know all men by these presents, that we, [here insert the name of the master of the vessel, and the name or names of the sureties,] are held and firmly bound unto the United States of America, in the sum of to be paid to the said United States; for which payment well and truly to be made, we bind ourselves, our heirs, executors, and administrators, jointly and severally, firmly by these presents. Sealed with our seals. Dated this day of in the year of the independence of the said United States, and in the year of our Lord one thousand

Whereas, the following goods, wares, and merchandise, [here insert the marks, numbers, denomination, and number of packages and contents, as far as may be, or if articles in bulk, the quantity and quality,] imported into the district of in the [insert the denomination and name of vessel,] whereof [insert name] is master, from [insert name of port, &c.] on the [insert date of vessel's entry,] as per report and manifest then delivered by the said master; are now intended to be exported and conveyed in the said [insert the denomination and name of the vessel] to the district of [insert the district or districts where intended to be sent;] and, whereas, the duties that would have become due on the said goods, wares, and merchandise, had the same been unladen, would have amounted to the aforesaid sum of

Now, therefore, the condition of this obligation is such, that if the above bounden shall and do, within six months from the date hereof, produce to the collector of this district the certificates required by law, that the said enumerated [packages of merchandise, or articles in bulk, as the case may be,] have been duly entered and delivered at the aforesaid district of or any other port or district of the United States, then the above obligation to be void, otherwise to be and remain in full force and virtue.

Sealed and delivered }
in the presence of }

Each and every surveyor, or officer acting as inspector of the revenue, for any port at which a vessel may arrive with a certificate as aforesaid, must certify in manner aforesaid all deliveries of spirits, wines, or teas, made at their respective ports; which certificates must be annexed to the certificate granted at the port of original importation.[a]

American vessels, arriving from abroad, may put on their manifest, either the whole or part of their cargo, as destined for a foreign port. Such part as is thus destined, they will not be obliged to land in the United States, nor to secure the duties thereon; but they will have to give bonds for the landing of them abroad, the same as the debenture goods.[b] They may do this, although they have also goods destined for various ports in the United States; but if they go coastwise, they must clear out with a certified manifest. They may also take on board any other articles, to be landed in any other port of the United States. For such goods they must clear out coastwise. At the port where these vessels ultimately clear out for a foreign port, they may take on board any goods for abroad.

On entering any vessel from abroad, during quarantine time, viz., from May to October, you are required to produce, at the custom-house, a certificate from the board of health.

Previous to entry at the custom-house, the captain of an American vessel is required to deposit his letters at the post office.

He is also compelled, under a penalty of $100, to declare, on oath, whether any seamen have been impressed in the course of the voyage, and what course he adopted thereupon.[c]

The number of seamen employed on board during the voyage must also be reported, before entry, and 20 cents per month for hospital money paid to the collector for each seaman's wages.[d]

In all cases where a vessel is prevented by ice from getting to the place at which her cargo is intended to be delivered, the collector of the district in which such vessel may be obstructed, may receive the report and entry, and, with the consent of the naval officer, (where there is one,) may grant a permit or permits for unlading the merchandise imported in such vessel, at any place within his district most convenient and proper; subject to the same rules, regulations, penalties, and provisions, as if the said vessel had arrived at the port of her destination, and had there proceeded to the delivery of her cargo.[e]

---

[a] Act, 2d March, 1799, sec. 35.
[b] Ibid. sec. 32, and Act, 22d Feb., 1805.
[c] Act, 28th May, 1796, sec. 6.
[d] Act, 16th July, 1798, sec. 1.
[e] Act, 2d March, 1799, sec. 85.

Form of the second Certificate:

District of

Port of

These are to certify, that there have been unladen and landed at this port, from on board the [insert the denomination and name of the vessel,] whereof [insert the name] is master, from [insert district and port where from,] the following packages of merchandise, [here detail the several packages with their respective denominations, their marks and numbers, and if any articles in bulk, the quantities delivered,] for which the duties have been (paid or secured) at the aforesaid port of [insert the port.] Witness our hands and seals, this day of

A. B., Collector.
C. D., N. Officer.

If a vessel from a foreign port, compelled by necessity, put into a port of the United States, not being destined for the same, the master, together with the mate, or person next in command, must, within twenty-four hours after her arrival, make protest in the usual form, upon oath or affirmation, before a notary public, or other person duly authorized, or before the collector of the district, setting forth the cause of such distress, or necessity; which protest, if not made before the collector, must be produced to him, and to the naval officer, (if any,) and a copy thereof lodged with him. The master, within forty-eight hours after arrival, must make report in writing to the collector, of the vessel and her cargo, as in other cases. If it appear to the collector, by the certificate of the wardens of the port, or other officers usually charged with, and accustomed to ascertain the condition of vessels arriving in distress, or by the certificate of any two reputable merchants, named for that purpose by the collector, if no such officers there be, that there is a necessity for unlading the vessel, the collector and naval officer (where any) must grant a permit for that purpose, and appoint an inspector to oversee such unlading, who keeps an account of the same, to be compared with the report made by the master. All merchandise so unladen is stored under the direction of the collector, who, upon request of the master or owner, together with the naval officer, when there is one, and alone, where there is none, grants permission to dispose of such part of the cargo as may be of any perishable nature, or as may be necessary to defray the expenses attending such vessel and her cargo: *Provided*, That entry is made, and the duties thereon first paid, or secured to be paid. In case the delivery of the cargo do not agree with the report thereof made by the master, and if the disagreement be not satisfactorily accounted for, the master is liable to penalties as in other like cases. Merchandise not disposed of, may afterwards be re-laden under the inspection of the officer superintending the landing, or other proper person, and the vessel may proceed with the same to the place of her destination, free from any other charge than for the storing and safe keeping of the said goods, and fees to the officers of the customs, as in other cases.[a]

For all goods not included in the manifest, or imported without a manifest, the master forfeits a sum equal to their value; and all merchandise not included in such manifest, belonging or consigned to the master, mate, officers, or crew, is forfeited, unless it is made to appear to the satisfaction of the collector, naval officer, and surveyor, or the major part of them, or to a court on trial, that no part was unshipped, except what was mentioned in the report of the master, or that the manifest has been lost or mislaid, without fraud, or defaced by accident, or incorrect by mistake.[b]

The master of any vessel belonging to a citizen or inhabitant of the United States, and laden with goods as aforesaid, on arrival within four leagues of the coast, or within any bays, harbours, ports, rivers, creeks, or inlets thereof, must have a manifest on board; and on demand made by any officer of the customs first coming on board, must produce such manifest, and deliver him a copy thereof, signed

---

[a] Act, 2d March, 1799, sec. 60.   [b] Ibid. sec. 24.

by the master or other person having charge of such vessel. The officer certifies on the original the day and year the same was produced; the copy is compared with the original, and there is certified by such officer on the back thereof, the day and year such copy was delivered to him. The officer then forwards the copy to the collector of the district to which the goods are destined. The original manifest is delivered afterwards by the master to the collector. He is also obliged to provide another copy for the officer of the customs who first comes on board after her arrival, who also certifies on the original, and forwards his copy to the collector. If a manifest be produced without a certificate, the master must swear, that no officer has applied for, and that no endorsement has been made on the manifest. It is sufficient to show the original with the endorsements, to other officers.[a] *

The penalty on masters, for not producing the manifest, and delivering a copy thereof to the proper officer on demand, or for not informing such officer of the *true destination* of such vessel, is $500 for each offence, and the like penalty is incurred by such officer who neglects or refuses to certify such manifest; and the officer is required to return, in writing, the name of the vessel and master offending in any particular, to the collector of the district where such vessel may be bound.[b]

Any vessel so laden, within four leagues of the coast, or within the limits of any district, unloading goods without authority from proper officers, the master and mate forfeit one thousand dollars for each offence, and the goods are forfeited, except in case of accident, necessity, or stress of weather: which must be made known, and proved, under oath, before the collector, by the master, mate, and one other officer or mariner.[c]

Masters of vessels receiving goods so unladen, and all others aiding and assisting therein, forfeit treble the value of such goods; and the vessel receiving them is forfeited.[d]

If any vessel, having arrived within any district from any foreign place, departs or attempts to depart from the same, (unless to some more interior port, or by stress of weather, or pursuit of enemies,) before report and entry with the collector, the master forfeits $400; and the collector, naval officer, surveyor, or revenue officer, may cause her to be brought back.[e] A vessel passing through a river or bay, forming a boundary of the United States, to the foreign territory of which it is the boundary, is not deemed to have arrived within the United States, under the revenue laws.[f]

---

[a] Act, 2d March, 1779, sec. 25. [b] Ibid. sec. 26. [c] Ibid. sec. 27. [d] Ibid. sec. 28. [e] Ibid. sec. 29. [f] 9 Wheaton, 362.

* I, (A. B.) certify, that the within manifest was this day produced to me as the original manifest of the cargo on board the [insert the denomination and name of the vessel,] whereof [insert the name] is master, from [insert the port last from.] In witness whereof, I have hereunto signed my name, this day of

The form of the Certificate to be endorsed on the copy of a manifest, is:

I, (A. B.) certify, that I have examined the within manifest produced to me this day as a copy of the original manifest of the cargo on board the [insert the denomination and name of the vessel,] whereof [insert the name] is master, from [insert the port last from,] with the original, and find the same to agree. In witness whereof, I have hereunto signed my name, this day of

The master of any vessel arriving from a foreign port, must report her arrival to the collector, within twenty-four hours, if the hours of business at the custom-house will permit; and within forty-eight hours thereafter, he must report the name, burthen, &c., in writing, agreeable to the directions of section 23, and must make oath or affirmation to the truth of the same,[a] as below.*

The master or other person having command, neglecting to make such reports, or either of them, except that to the surveyor, or the declaration aforesaid, or to take the said oath, or to comply with the true intent of this section, forfeits $1000.

Ships of war, or packets of any state, not permitted by such state to carry goods in way of trade, are not required to make reports.

Masters of vessels, after arrival and entry, may proceed to foreign ports from the district where they first arrived, with goods, noted on the manifest at the time of entry for such foreign port, provided such manifest be delivered within forty-eight hours after her arrival, without paying duties thereon, on giving bond with one or more sureties to the amount of the duties, that the said goods shall be actually re-exported in such vessel to a foreign port, unless due entry be made, and the duties paid thereon. Bonds are not required when vessels

---

[a] Act, 2d March, 1779, sec. 60.

* *Form of Oath:*

I, (A. B.) do solemnly, sincerely, and truly swear, (*or affirm,*) that the report and manifest subscribed with my name, and now delivered to me by the collector of the district of contains, to the best of my knowledge and belief, a just and true account of all the goods, wares, and merchandise, including packages of every kind and nature whatsoever, which were on board the at the time of her sailing from the port of or *which have been laden or taken on board* at any time since, and that the packages of the said goods are as particularly described, as in the bills of lading signed for the same by me, or with my knowledge; that I am at present, and have been during the voyage, master of the said vessel; (*or how long;*) that no package whatsoever, or any goods, wares, or merchandise, have been unladen, landed, taken out, or in any manner whatever removed from on board the said since her departure from the said port of except such as are now particularly specified and declared in the abstract or account herewith, and that the clearance and other papers now delivered by me to the collector, are all that I now have, or have had, that any way relates to the cargo of the said vessel.—And I do further swear, (*or affirm,*) that the several articles specified in the said manifest, as the sea-stores for the cabin and vessel, are truly such, and were *bona fide* put on board the said for the use of the officers, crew, and passengers thereof, and have none of them been brought, and are not intended by way of merchandise, or for sale, or for any other purpose than above mentioned, and are intended to remain on board for the consumption of the said officers and crew. I further swear, (*or affirm,*) that if I shall hereafter discover or know of any other or greater quantity of goods, wares, and merchandise, of any nature or kind whatever, than are contained in the report and manifest subscribed, and now delivered by me, I will immediately and without delay, make due report thereof to the collector of the port or district of And I do likewise swear, (*or affirm,*) that all matters whatsoever in the said report and manifest expressed, are, to the best of my knowledge and belief, just and true: [*The following addition to the oath or affirmation to be inserted in cases where the manifest shall not have been certified by some officer of the customs in manner provided.*] I further swear, (*or affirm,*) that no officer of the customs has applied for any inspection of the manifest of the cargo on board the said vessel, and that no certificate or endorsement has been delivered to me on any manifest of such cargo.

So help me God.

(Signed) A. B.

Sworn (*or affirmed*) before me, this } day of }

put in, in distress. These bonds will be sued, unless legally performed immediately upon the expiration of the time.[a]

The master must particularly specify in the report or manifest the sea-stores; and in the oath to be taken by such master, on making such report, he declares that the articles so specified as sea-stores, are truly such, and are not intended by way of merchandise, or for sale; whereupon the said articles shall be free from duty. If it appear to the collector, together with the naval officer, where there is one, or alone, where there is none, that the quantities of the said articles, or of any part thereof, so reported as sea-stores, are excessive, it is lawful for them to estimate the amount of the duty on such excess. If any other or greater quantity of articles are found on board as sea-stores than are specified in such entry, or if any of the said articles be landed without a permit first obtained, all such articles may be seized; and the master of such vessel moreover forfeits treble the value of the articles so omitted or landed.[b]

Except into the districts on the northern, northwestern, and western boundaries of the United States, adjoining to the dominions of Great Britain, in Upper and Lower Canada, and the districts on the rivers Ohio and Mississippi, no merchandise of foreign growth or manufacture, subject to the payment of duties, can be brought into the United States in any other manner than by sea, nor in any vessel of less than thirty tons burthen, nor be landed or unladen at any other port than those designated by law, under the penalty of forfeiture of all such vessels, and of the merchandise imported.[c]

Importers of any horses, or other useful beasts, imported into the United States for the purpose of breed, make entry, as in the case of other merchandise, and obtain a permit for landing the same, and likewise make oath or affirmation, that they are actually imported for the purpose above mentioned; and any horses, cattle, sheep, swine, or other beasts, landed without the provisions above mentioned being fully complied with, are subject to seizure and forfeiture.[d]

No beer, ale, or porter, can be brought into the United States by sea from any foreign port, except in casks or vessels, the capacity whereof is not less than forty gallons, beer measure, or in packages containing not less than six dozen bottles; nor can any refined lump or loaf sugar be imported, except in vessels of one hundred and twenty tons burthen and upwards, or in casks or packages containing each not less than six hundred pounds weight; nor any distilled spirits, (arrack and sweet cordials excepted,) except in casks or vessels of the capacity of ninety gallons wine measure and upwards; nor can spirits be imported in casks or vessels which have been marked pursuant to any law of the United States, on pain of forfeiture, together with the vessel. This does not extend to spirits, provided such spirits be for the use of the seamen on board, and do not exceed the quantity of four gallons for each seaman.[e]

No duty is levied on the importation of peltries, nor on the goods and effects of Indians passing or re-passing the boundary line, unless

---

[a] Acts, 2d March, 1799, sec. 32, and 22d Feb., 1805. [b] Ibid. sec. 45. [c] Ibid. sec. 92. [d] Ibid. sec. 94. [e] Ibid. sec. 103.

the same be goods in bales, or other large packages unusual among Indians, which are not considered as goods belonging bona fide to Indians, nor entitled to exemption from duty. No higher or other tolls or rates of ferriage, than what are payable by citizens of the United States, are demanded of British subjects; and no duties are payable on any goods merely carried over any of the portages or carrying places within the territories of the United States, for the purpose of being immediately re-embarked, and carried to some other place or places. Persons may import any goods, of which the importation is not entirely prohibited, into the districts established on the northern and northwestern boundaries of the United States, and on the rivers Ohio and Mississippi, in vessels or boats of any burthen, and in rafts or carriages of any kind or nature whatsoever.[a]

The master of any vessel, except registered vessels, and every person having charge of any boat, canoe, or raft, and of any carriage or sleigh, and every person coming from any foreign territory adjacent to the United States into the United States, with merchandise subject to duty, must deliver, immediately on his arrival within the United States, a sworn manifest of the loading of such vessel, boat, canoe, raft, carriage, or sleigh, or of the merchandise so brought from such foreign territory, at the office of the collector or deputy collector nearest to the boundary line, or nearest to the road or waters by which such merchandise is brought. The oath is taken before such collector or deputy collector; and states, that such manifest contains a full, just, and true account of the kinds, quantities, and values, of all the merchandise so brought from such foreign territory.[b] The penalty for neglect, is forfeiture of the goods, vessel, or vehicle and horses, and four times the value of the goods.[c]

These vessels, rafts, and carriages, upon their arrival, must be reported to the collector of the district; the goods must be accompanied by manifests, and they are to be entered, and the duties paid under the same regulations, and subject to the same rules, as goods imported by sea.[d]

When goods are brought into these collection districts, for the purpose of being carried over portages within the United States, and are reported as destined to be immediately re-embarked, the owner must enter them, as in the case of payment of duties, and specify in the entry the route of transportation—swear to the destination of the goods; and further, that if he should ever discover that they have been consumed in the United States, he will report the same.[e] The collector causes the same to be inspected, and being satisfied as to the regularity of the entry, he grants a protection for the goods, under which they are transported to the place of exportation.[f]

If any person having charge of such goods should, with intent to defraud the revenue, open, or sell any package, or any part thereof, or break or deface any seal put thereon, or deface, alter, or forge the protection, he is liable to pay $500, and to imprisonment of from one to six months.[g]

---

[a] Act, 2d March, 1799, sec. 105. [b] Act, 2d March, 1821, sec. 1.
[c] Act, 2d March, 1799, sec. 106. [d] Act, 3d March, 1823. [e] Act, 2d March, 1799, sec. 107.
[f] Ibid. sec. 108. [g] Ibid. sec. 109.

Any deputy collector, stationed in any district of the customs contiguous to a foreign territory, to whom the manifest of merchandise is delivered, is authorized to require of the importer payment of duties, or security, either by bond, or deposite of merchandise equal to double the amount of the duties.[a]

3d. *Regulations for the importation of foreign goods.*

Persons residing out of the United States, and making any shipment verified to the United States, of goods paying a duty ad valorem, must have their invoices verified, before a consul or vice consul of the United States, or some public officer authorized to administer oaths, in which latter case his certificate must be authenticated by a consul, &c. of the United States.

In case there is no American consul or commercial agent in the country of exportation, the authentication of the certificate must be made by a consul of some friendly nation; and if there be no consul then by two respectable merchants.

The oath verifying the invoice must be made by the owner, and must state that the goods were purchased on his account, or for account of himself and partners; that the invoice annexed contains a true account of the actual cost, and of all charges thereon; and that no discounts, bounties, or drawbacks, are contained therein, except what have been actually allowed.[b] *

If the goods have not been acquired in the ordinary way of bargain and sale, or if they belong to the manufacturer, the oath must state that the invoice contains a true account of the goods at their fair market value, at the time and place, when and where they were procured or manufactured, and of all charges and discounts, &c. as above.[c] †

---

[a] Act, 2d March, 1821, sec. 2. [b] Act, 1st March, 1823, sec. 7. [c] Ibid. sec. 8.

* *Form of Oath:*

I, do solemnly and truly (*swear or affirm,*) that the entry now delivered by me to the collector of , contains a just and true account of all the goods, wares, and merchandise, imported by, or consigned to me, in the whereof is master, from that the invoice which I now produce, contains a just and faithful account of the actual cost of the said goods, wares, and merchandise, of all charges thereon, including charges of purchasing, carriage, bleaching, dyeing, dressing, finishing, putting up, and packing, and no other discount, drawback, or bounty, but such as has been actually allowed on the same; that I do not know nor believe in the existence of any invoice or bill of lading other than those now produced by me, and that they are in the state in which I actually received them. And I do further solemnly and truly (*swear or affirm,*) that I have not, in the said entry or invoice, concealed or suppressed any thing whereby the United States may be defrauded of any part of the duty lawfully due on the said goods, wares, and merchandise; and that if, at any time hereafter, I discover any error in the said invoice, or in the account now produced, of the said goods, wares, and merchandise, or receive any other invoice of the same, I will immediately make the same known to the collector of this district.

† *Form of Oath:*

I, do solemnly and truly (*swear or affirm,*) that the entry now delivered by me to the collector of contains a just and true account of all the goods, wares,

The secretary of the treasury is empowered at his discretion to admit goods to entry, even if unaccompanied by an invoice duly authenticated, upon the importers giving bond, with sureties, to produce one if practicable within eight months, for places this side of Capes Horn or Good Hope, and 18 months for places beyond.[a]

If no invoice of goods subject to duty ad valorem be received, the collector, upon oath being made of that fact by the importer or agent, is authorized, if he deem it expedient, to admit the same to entry, upon an appraisement of their value. A bond, however, is required of the owner or agent, with sureties, to produce the invoice if practicable, as above, and to pay the difference of duty if any.[b]

A fee of two dollars is paid to the consul for his certificate to the invoice; but all articles shipped by one person may be included in one invoice.[c] Counterfeiting the certificate is punishable by a fine of $10,000, and imprisonment of three years.[d]

The same punishment is inflicted upon consuls for falsely certifying.[e]

Persons who make purchases abroad, must have their invoices authenticated as above, even when they have partners residing in the United States interested in these purchases.*

---

[a] Act, 1st March, 1823, sec. 10. [b] Ibid. sec. 2. [c] Ibid. sec. 22. [d] Ibid. sec. 24. [e] Act, 3d March, 1835.

and merchandise, imported by, or consigned to me, in the whereof is master, from that the said goods, wares, and merchandise, were not actually bought by me, or by my agent, in the ordinary mode of bargain and sale, but that, nevertheless, the invoice which I now produce, contains a just and faithful valuation of the same, at their fair market value, including charges of purchasing, carriages, bleaching, dyeing, dressing, finishing, putting up and packing, at the time or times, and place or places, when and where procured for my account; (or for account of myself and partners;) that the said invoice contains also a just and faithful account of all charges actually paid, and no other discount, drawback, or bounty, but such as has been actually allowed on the said goods, wares, and merchandise; that I do not know, nor believe in the existence of any invoice or bill of lading, other than those now produced by me, and that they are in the state in which I actually received them. And I do further solemnly and truly (*swear or affirm*,) that I have not, in the said entry or invoice, concealed or suppressed any thing whereby the United States may be defrauded of any part of the duty lawfully due on the said goods, wares, and merchandise; and that if, at any time hereafter, I discover any error in the said invoice, or in the account now produced, of the said goods, wares, and merchandise, or receive any other invoice of the same, I will immediately make the same known to the collector of this district.

* *Form of Oath:*

} to wit.

I, (A. B.,) of merchant, solemnly, sincerely, and truly swear, that I and my partners, doing business at under the firm of A. B. & Co., are the true and lawful owners of certain goods, wares, and merchandise, as specified in the invoice by us subscribed with the proper signature of the firm, and here produced to C. D., the consul of the United States of America, and intended to be shipped at by E. F., for the port of in the United States of America; that the sum of two thousand three hundred and ninety pounds fifteen shillings and four pence, British sterling, exhibited in the said invoice, is the true value of the said goods, wares, and merchandise, in their actual state of manufacture, at that we, the said owners, are not the manufacturers, in whole or in part, of such goods, wares, and merchandise, as aforesaid; and that

According to the construction given to the words "country, state or empire," in the law, "England" is called one country, "Ireland" another, and "Scotland" another; also, any island, which does not belong to a cluster of islands, depending from a single consulate, may be taken, by itself, as "a country;" and each cluster of islands, belonging to the same power, may be taken as a "country."

No duty can be demanded on the importation of old copper, or such copper manufactures as have been worn out, or otherwise so damaged as to be unfit for any other purpose than that of supplying a raw material, to be manufactured anew. Where any doubt arises whether imported copper comes within the intent and meaning of the act, the collector appoints one person, and the owner, importer, or consignee, appoints another, who ascertains whether the copper imported comes under the denomination of old copper; and the proceedings in this instance are conducted in like manner and form as the proceedings in cases of incomplete entry, or of damage sustained by merchandise during the voyage.[a]

To constitute an importation into the United States, there must be a voluntary arrival within some port or haven, with intent to land the cargo.[b]

The mere act of coming into port is prima facie evidence of importation.[c]

If a vessel put in to avoid capture, or in stress of weather, it is not an importation.[d]

Duties accrue upon the arrival in port with an intent to unlade, and not upon an entry at the custom-house.[e]

4th. *Regulations for entering foreign goods.*

Within fifteen days after the master has made his report, the owners or consignees of goods imported into the United States, or in case of their absence or sickness, their agents, must enter the same with the collector, specifying the names of the vessel and master, the port of

---

[a] Act, 4th March, 1828. [b] 1 Gallis. 206. 348.—1 Peters' C. C. 256. [c] 1 Gallis. 239. [d] 1 Gallis. 206. [e] Ibid. 365.—1 Mason, 482.

we are not directly or indirectly concerned in the profits of any art or trade, by which they have been brought to their present state of manufacture.

Sworn before me, at the
day of 1832.

[Seal.[

C. D.
the consul, &c.

A. B.
In presence of

N. B. This certificate is to be annexed to the invoice.

In case the owner, taking the oath, is a manufacturer, the following addition is to be made to his oath, viz :—

And that the prices charged in the aforesaid invoice are the current value of the same at the place of manufacture, and such as I or we would have received, if the same had there been sold in the usual course of trade.

exportation, the contents, marks, and net cost of each package,* and produce the original invoice, documents, and bills of lading, verified by oath.[a] † For vessels of more than three hundred tons, twenty

[a] Act, 2d March, 1799, sec. 36.

* [Entry, when imported in an American vessel.]

Entry of Merchandise, imported by in the master, from New-York.

Marks.	Numbers.	Packages and contents.	Quantity per invoice of articles subject to specific duties.	Value of articles subject to specific duties.	Value subject to 7½ per cent. ad valorem.	Value subject to 15 per cent.	Value subject to 20 per cent.	Value subject to 25 per cent.	Value subject to 30 per cent.	Amount of free goods.	Charges not subject to duty.	Total amount per invoice.

[Entry, when imported in a foreign vessel.]

Entry of Merchandise, imported by in the master, from New-York.

Marks.	Numbers.	Packages and Contents.	Quantity per invoice of articles subject to specific duties.	Value of articles subject to specific duties.	Value subject to 8¼ per cent. ad valorem.	Value subject to 16½ per cent.	Value subject to 22 per cent.	Value subject to 27½ per cent.	Value subject to 33 per cent.	Amount of free goods.	Charges not subject to duty.	Total amount per invoice.

† *Form of Oath of Importer, &c:*

District of New-York,
Port of New-York.

I, do solemnly, sincerely and truly swear, that the entry now subscribed with my name, and delivered by me to the collector of New-York, contains a just and true account of all the goods, wares, and merchandise imported for sale, or intended to be landed, in this district, for me, or on my account, or on account of any house of trade or partnership in which I am concerned in this district, or which actually came consigned to me, or to any house of trade or partnership in which I am concerned, and intended for sale, or to be landed in this district, in the whereof is master, from that the said entry contains a just and true account in of the cost thereof, including all charges; that the invoice and bill of lading now produced by me, are the true, genuine, and only invoice and bill of lading by me received of the said goods, wares, and merchandise, imported or consigned as aforesaid, and the only invoice by which I have been charged, or for which I am to account; and that the said invoice or bill of lading are in the actual state in which they were received by me; and I do not know of any other invoices or account of the said goods, wares, or merchandise, different from what is, or are here produced. I do further swear, that if I hereafter discover any other or greater quantity of goods, wares, or merchandise, than is contained in days are allowed. If there be any distilled spirits, wines, or teas on board, a separate entry is made by the master, for which vide part 5th.

No one is allowed to enter goods, or secure the duties on them, as principal in the bonds, unless he is the owner or consignee at the time the vessel enters the port to which she is bound; or unless he is the agent or factor of the owner or consignee, and lodge with the collector a power of attorney, from the owner or consignee, authorizing him to enter the goods, and to execute the bonds for the duties. A sub-purchaser, after importation, is not permitted to enter goods imported.[a] A transfer, made while the goods are at sea, will be admitted at the custom-house, to prove the change of property, but not if made after the vessel has entered the port of destination.

Attorneys, duly authorized by their powers, may take the oaths prescribed by law for their principals.

In case the owner or consignee is not at the port where the importation is made, he may make an entry in the common form, and swear to it before the collector at the port where he happens to be. In this entry he must state who is the owner of the goods.

---

[a] 1 Mason, 482.

the entry aforesaid, or shall receive any invoice of the whole, or any part thereof, other in quantity, quality and price, than has been now exhibited, I will immediately, and without delay, report the same to the collector of this district. I also swear that nothing has been concealed or suppressed in the entry aforesaid, whereby to avoid the just payment of the duties imposed by the laws of the United States, and that all matters are justly and truly expressed therein, according to my best knowledge and belief.

So help me God.

Sworn this 183 }
before me.

Consignee, Importer or Agent's oath:

I, do solemnly and truly swear, that the invoice and bill of lading now presented by me to the collector of New-York, are the true and only invoice and bill of lading by me received, of all the goods, wares and merchandise, imported in the whereof is master, from for account of any person whomsoever, for whom I am authorized to enter the same; and that the said invoice and bill of lading are in the state in which they were actually received by me, and that I do not know nor believe in the existence of any other invoice or bill of lading, of the said goods, wares, and merchandise; that the entry now delivered to the collector, contains a just and true account of the said goods, wares, and merchandise, according to said invoice and bill of lading; that nothing has been, on my part, nor, to my knowledge, on the part of any other person, concealed or suppressed, whereby the United States may be defrauded of any part of the duty lawfully due on the said goods, wares and merchandise; and that if at any time hereafter, I discover any error in the said invoice, or in the account now rendered of the said goods, wares, and merchandise, or receive any other invoice of the same, I will immediately make the same known to the collector of this district. And I do further solemnly and truly swear, that to the best of my knowledge and belief is the owner of the goods, wares and merchandise, mentioned in the annexed entry; that the invoice now produced by me, exhibits the actual cost or fair market value, at of the said goods, wares, and merchandise, all the charges thereon, and no other or different discount, bounty or drawback, but such as has been actually allowed on the same.

Sworn to, this 1836, }
before me,

Collector.

Naval Officer.

These remarks apply as well to goods paying a specific duty, as to those paying an ad valorem duty. As to goods paying a specific duty, the oath which declares their true value, such as is contained in the entry, will be sufficient.

It is not necessary to insert the numbers upon packages in entries of goods subject to specific duty, on importation nor upon exportation, nor in any coastwise or other certificate, except where a separate certificate is required for each package, where the numbers must be inserted.[a]

Where the goods imported are subject to a duty ad valorem, they will not be admitted to entry, (*unless taken from a wreck,*) without an invoice, verified and authenticated according to law, except by special permission of the secretary of the treasury.[b]

When all the owners reside in the United States, an entry made and sworn to by one of the owners, in the common form, before the collector of the port at which the importation is made, will answer both for the oath to the invoice and for the oath to the entry; and not only for goods paying a specific duty, but also for goods paying an ad valorem duty.*

---

[a] Act, 1st March, 1823, sec. 33. [b] Ibid. sec. 1.

* *Form of Owners' oath:*

I, do solemnly and truly swear, that the entry now delivered by me to the collector of New-York, contains a just and true account of all the goods, wares, and merchandise, imported by, or consigned to in the whereof is master, from that the invoice which I now produce, contains a just and faithful account of the actual cost of the said goods, wares, and merchandise, of all charges thereon, including charges of purchasing, carriage, bleaching, dyeing, dressing, finishing, putting up, and packing, and no other discount, drawback, or bounty, but such as has been actually allowed on the same; that I do not know nor believe in the existence of any invoice or bill of lading, other than those now produced by me, and that they are in the state in which I actually received them. And I do further solemnly and truly swear that I have not, in the said entry or invoice, concealed or suppressed any thing whereby the United States may be defrauded of any part of the duty lawfully due on the said goods, wares, and merchandise; and that if, at any time hereafter, I discover any error in the said invoice, or in the account now produced, to the said goods, wares, and merchandise, or receive any other invoice of the same, I will immediately make the same known to the collector of this district.

Sworn to, this day }
of 183 before me, }

Collector.

Naval Officer.

Manufacturer's or Owners' oath:

I, do solemnly and truly swear, that the entry now delivered by me to the collector of New-York, contains a just and true account of all the goods, wares, and merchandise, imported by, or consigned to in the whereof is master, from that the said goods, wares, and merchandise, were not actually bought by me or by my agent, in the ordinary mode of bargain and sale, but that, nevertheless, the invoice which I now produce contains a just and faithful valuation of the same, at their fair market value, including charges of purchasing, carriage, bleaching, dyeing, dressing, finishing, putting up, and packing, at the time or times, and place or places when and where procured for my account, (or for account of myself and partners;) that the said invoice contains also a just and faithful account of all charges actually paid, and no other discount, drawback, or bounty, but such as has been actually allowed on the said goods, wares, and merchandise; that I do not know, nor believe in the existence of any invoice or bill of lading, other than those now produced by

In case of goods paying an ad valorem duty, if the owner is in the United States, and not at the port of importation, the importer or agent must give a bond before the goods can be entered, that the invoice, duly verified by the oath of the owner, shall be produced to the collector within four months. This oath must be taken before a collector, and if none there be where the owner is, then before some public officer authorized to administer oaths.[a] The penalty of the bond is $1,000.

If the owner be dead, or insolvent, the executors, administrators, or assignees, are permitted to take the oath in place of the owner.[b]

An executor, as such, has a right to enter goods belonging to his testator; and bonds given by him in his representative character for duties, bind the estate.[c] If the executor has wasted the estate, the United States can resort to the bond given to the surrogate.[c]

Where part of the owners reside in the United States, and part reside abroad, the oath of one of the owners residing in the United States will be sufficient, except where the owners residing abroad are concerned in the manufacture, either in whole or in part, of the goods imported. The oath of the owner abroad, in such case, must be obtained to the invoice.

Wherever the invoice of goods subject to an ad valorem duty has not been duly authenticated, and the secretary of the treasury has refused to grant permission to enter, or wherever the collector has reason to suspect such goods to have been invoiced below their true value, the goods must be appraised, under the act of 1st March, 1823. If, upon appraisement, the value shall be found to exceed the invoice prices twenty-five per cent., fifty per cent. are added to the appraised value, and the duty is estimated upon the aggregate amount.[d]

This penalty is not incurred for a difference of fifty per cent. between the invoice value and the current value in the country of production. The value alluded to is that at the place of exportation or of purchase. If the appraised value exceed by less than twenty-five per cent. the invoice value, the appraised value is to be the amount on which duties are estimated; but the duties are never estimated on an amount less than the invoice value.[e]

When the particulars of such merchandise are not known, an entry thereof is made according to circumstances; declaring on oath or affirmation, all the particulars the party knows or believes concerning the same; and where an imperfect entry is made, either for want of invoices, bills of lading, &c., the collector takes such merchandise

---

[a] Act, 1st March, 1823, sec. 6. [b] Ibid. sec. 9. [c] 3 Mason, 126.
[d] Acts, 1st March, 1823, sec. 12 and 13, and 14th July, 1832, sec. 4. [e] Sec. 14.

me, and that they are in the state in which I actually received them. And I do further solemnly and truly swear, that I have not, in the said entry or invoice, concealed or suppressed any thing whereby the United States may be defrauded of any part of the duty lawfully due on the said goods, wares, and merchandise; and that if, at any time hereafter, I discover any error in the said invoice, or in the account now produced, of the said goods, wares, and merchandise, or receive any other invoice of the same, I will immediately make the same known to the collector of this district.

Sworn to, this day }
of 183 , before me, }
Collector. Naval officer.

into his custody, until the quantity, quality, or value, can be ascertained. If the goods are subject to an ad valorem duty, they are appraised in the manner set forth in part 8th of this chapter.

The oath of importer, where there is no invoice, is in the form in note.*

If no entry be made, the collector is directed to send such goods to the public store, where they are kept at the expense and risk of the owner, if not perishable, for nine months, or eighteen months if brought from beyond Capes Horn or Good Hope. They are then sold at public auction as unclaimed goods.[a]

The tonnage duties, where any are levied, must be paid at the time of making entry, and before any permit for unloading can be obtained.[b] The register, or other document in lieu thereof, and the clearance, and other papers granted at the departure of the vessel from the port whence she came, must, before entry, be delivered to the collector, who keeps them until she obtains a clearance, when they are given to the master or owner.[b]

Wearing apparel, and other personal baggage, and the tools or implements of a mechanical trade only, of persons who arrive in the United States, are exempt from duty. Due entry thereof, but separate and distinct from that of any other merchandise, must be made with the collector by the owner thereof, or his agent, expressing the persons by or for whom such entry is made, and particularizing the several packages and their contents, with their marks and numbers. The person making the entry, takes an oath or affirmation before the said collector, as in note.[c] †

---

[a] Act, 1st March, 1823, sec. 3. [b] Act, 2d March, 1799, sec 63. [c] Ibid. sec. 46.

* *Form of Owner or Consignee's oath, on entering merchandise without invoice:*

I, do solemnly, sincerely and truly that the entry now subscribed with my name, and delivered by me to the collector of New-York, contains a just and true account of all the goods, wares, and merchandise, imported for sale, or intended to be landed, in this district, for me, or on my account, or on account of any house of trade or partnership in which I am concerned in this district, or which actually came consigned to me, or to any house of trade or partnership in which I am concerned, and intended for sale, or to be landed in this district, in the whereof is master, from That the bill of lading now produced by me, is the true, genuine, and only bill of lading by me received of the said goods, wares, and merchandise, and that I have not received, and do not know of any invoice, or other account whatever, having been received of the said goods, wares, and merchandise. I do further that if I hereafter discover any other or greater quantity of goods, wares, or merchandise, than is contained in the entry aforesaid, or shall receive any invoice of the whole, or any part thereof, I will immediately, and without delay, report the same to the collector of this district. I also that nothing has been concealed or suppressed in the entry aforesaid, whereby to avoid the just payment of the duties imposed by the laws of the United States, and that all matters are justly and truly expressed therein, according to my best knowledge and belief.

to this 183 } So help me God.
before me, }

Collector. Naval Officer.

† District of }
Port of } *ss.*

I, [here insert the name of the person making the entry,] do solemnly, sincerely, and truly swear, (or affirm,) that the entry subscribed by me, and hereunto annexed, contains, to the best of my knowledge and belief, a just and true account of the contents of the several [here insert whether chests, cases, or packages] mentioned in the said entry, imported in the [here insert the name of the vessel, and master's name,] from [here insert the port

In case the party is not the owner of the said articles, he gives bond, with sureties, in a sum equal to the amount of duties, if imported subject to duty.*

On compliance with the conditions above mentioned, a permit is granted for landing the said articles. Whenever the collector and naval officer (if any) think proper, they may direct such baggage to be examined; and if any articles be contained therein, which in their opinion ought not to be exempted from duty, due entry must be made therefor, and the duties thereon paid or secured. And the goods are subject to forfeiture, in case articles subject to duty, and not entered, are found therein; and the person in whose baggage they are found, forfeits treble the value.[a]

On merchandise, of the growth or manufacture of the United States, which has been exported and brought back to the said states, and upon which no drawback, bounty, or allowance, has been paid, no duty is demanded.[b]

Report and entry of such merchandise must be made, as in other cases of merchandise imported; and proof, by oath or affirmation, of the person having knowledge of the facts, made to the satisfaction of the collector, jointly with the naval officer, if any, that the said articles were exported from the United States, as of their growth, produce, or manufacture, and of the time when, by whom, in what vessel, and for what place they were so exported.

---

[a] Act, 2d March, 1799, sec. 46. [b] Ibid. sec. 47.

from which arrived,] and that they contain no goods, wares or merchandise whatever, other than the wearing apparel and other personal baggage, (or if the case require,) and the tools of the trade of [here insert what mechanical trade,] all of which are the property of [here insert to whom belonging, and family, as the case may require,] who has or have arrived, (or as the case may require,) who is or are shortly expected to arrive in the United States; and are not directly or indirectly imported for any other person or persons, or intended for sale. So help me God.

* *Form of Bond:*

Know all men by these presents, that we, [here insert the names of the principal and sureties,] are held and firmly bound unto the United States of America, in the sum of $ to be paid to the said United States; for payment whereof, we bind ourselves, our heirs, executors, and administrators, jointly and severally, firmly by these presents. Sealed with our seals. Dated the day of in the year of the independence of the United States, and in the year of our Lord one thousand

Whereas the above named has this day, for and in behalf of exhibited an entry, subscribed with his name, of the following packages of wearing apparel and other articles, as being exempted from duty, [here insert the number and description of packages, together with their marks and numbers,] and has made oath before the collector of the district of that the said articles are the property of the said that they are truly and bona fide intended for the sole use of himself, (and family, as the case may require,) and are not directly or indirectly imported for any other person, or intended for sale.

Now, therefore, the condition of this obligation is such, that if the said shall, within one year from the date thereof, take and subscribe the oath prescribed by law in such case, before the said collector; or if the said oath, duly authenticated, shall be produced to the said collector agreeably to the true intent and meaning of the said law, then this obligation to be void, or else to remain in full force and virtue.

Sealed and delivered
in the presence of }

If the collector receiving the entry, be not the collector of the district from which the articles were exported, a certificate of the latter must be produced to the former, proving the exportation thereof.

A permit must be granted for landing the same, if the said certificate cannot be immediately produced; and if the proof otherwise required be made, a bond must be given with sureties, in a sum equal to what the duties would be on the said articles, if not of the growth, product, or manufacture of the United States.

Upon receiving this bond, the collector and naval officer, where any, grants a permit for the landing of said articles, as if the said certificate had been produced; and in default of such certificate being produced within the time limited in such bond, the collector is required to enforce the payment thereof.*

All oaths or affirmations taken under the act of 2d March, 1799, must be administered by the collector, or officer, to or with whom report or entry is made, and must be reduced to writing, and subscribed by the person swearing or affirming, and also by the person administering the same. The collector, jointly with the naval officer, or alone, where there is none, must, according to the best of his judgment or information, make a gross estimate of the amount of the duties on imported merchandise, which estimate must be endorsed upon such entry, and signed by the officers making the same. The amount of the estimated duties having been first paid, or secured, the collector, together with the naval officer, or alone, where there is none, grants a permit to land the merchandise, whereof entry has been made;

---

* *Form of Bond:*

Know all men by these presents, that we, [insert the name of the principal and sureties,] are held and firmly bound unto the United States of America, in the sum of to be paid to the said United States, for which payment well and truly to be made, we bind ourselves, our heirs, executors, and administrators, jointly and severally, firmly by these presents. Sealed with our seals, and dated this day of in the year of the independence of the United States, and in the year of our Lord one thousand seven hundred and ninety

Whereas has this day made entry at the custom-house of the port of of the following articles, viz. [here particularize the packages, marks, numbers, and contents,] as per entry by him subscribed, and hath likewise sworn (or affirmed) before the collector of the said port, that the said articles are of the growth, product or manufacture of the United States, and that they were exported from the district of in the whereof was master, on or about the and whereas the duties on the aforesaid articles, if of foreign growth or importation, would amount to the aforesaid sum of

The condition therefore of this obligation is such, that if the above bounden do, within six months from the date hereof, produce, or cause to be produced, to the collector of the district of a certificate under the hand and seal of the collector (and naval officer if any) of the aforesaid port of of the said articles having been actually exported from thence as herein set forth, subject to no drawback, bounty or allowance, then this obligation to be void and of no effect, otherwise it shall be and remain in full force and virtue.

Sealed and delivered
in the presence of }

and then, and not before, it is lawful to land the said goods. All permits must specify, as particularly as may be, the goods to be delivered, namely, the number and description of the packages, whether trunk, bale, chest, box, case, pipe, hogshead, barrel, keg, or any other packages whatever, with the mark and number of each package, and as far as circumstances will admit, the contents thereof, together with the names of the vessel and master, in which, and the place whence they were imported; and no merchandise can be delivered by any officer of the customs, that does not fully agree with the description thereof in such permit.[a]

If any package reported as aforesaid be not found on board, or if the merchandise on board such vessel do not agree with the report or manifest delivered by the master, in every such case the master forfeits five hundred dollars, unless it appear to the satisfaction of the collector, naval officer, and surveyor, or to the major part of them, where those officers are established at any port, or to the satisfaction of the collector alone, where neither of the others is established; or, in case of trial for the said penalty, to the satisfaction of the court, that no part of the merchandise of such vessel has been unshipped, landed, or unladen since it was taken on board, except as specified in the report or manifest, and pursuant to permits, or that the said disagreement is by accident or mistake; but in all such cases the master must make a post entry of any and all merchandise omitted to be reported in such manifest. No permit can be granted to unlade any such merchandise so omitted, before such post entry has been made.[b]

If any merchandise, of which entry has been made, be not invoiced according to the actual cost thereof, at the place of exportation, with design to evade the duties thereupon, or any part thereof, all such merchandise, or the value thereof, to be recovered of the person making entry, is forfeited.[c]

The invoices of all goods imported into the United States, and subject to a duty ad valorem, must be made out in the currency of the place from whence the importation is made, and contain a true statement of the actual cost of such goods, in such foreign currency or currencies, without any respect to the value of the coins of the United States, or foreign coins current within the United States, in such foreign country.[d]

Before merchandise, taken from a wreck, can be admitted to entry, it must be appraised. Also, where a reduction of duties is claimed, on account of damage sustained in the course of the voyage.[e]

When merchandise has been admitted to entry upon invoice, the collector certifies such invoice, under his official seal; and no other evidence of the value can be admitted on the part of the owners, in any court of the United States, except in corroboration of such invoice.[f]

In all cases of entry of merchandise for the benefit of drawback,

---

[a] Act, 2d March, 1799, sec. 49. [b] Ibid. sec. 57. [c] Ibid. sec. 66.
[d] Act, 3d March, 1801. [e] Act, 1st March, 1823, sec. 21. [f] Ibid. sec. 23.

the time of twenty days is allowed from the date of the clearance of the vessel in which the same are laden, for giving the exportation bonds for the same: provided, that the exporter, in every other particular, comply with the regulations and formalities established for entries of exportation for the benefit of drawback.

Under the act for ascertaining the annual state of the foreign commerce of the United States, it is provided, that

The kinds and quantities of all imported articles free from duty, must be ascertained by entry, made by oath or affirmation, by the owner, or by the consignee or agent of the importer, or by actual examination, where the collector thinks such examination necessary; and the value of all such articles is ascertained in the same manner in which the values of imports subject to duties ad valorem are ascertained.[a]

The values of all inported articles subject to specific duties, are ascertained in the same manner in which the values of imports subject to duties ad valorem are ascertained.[b]

5th. *Regulations concerning wines, distilled spirits and teas.*

Distilled spirits, except brandy, cannot be imported in casks or vessels of less capacity than 90 gallons wine measure, on pain of forfeiture.[c] Brandy may be imported in casks of not less than 15 gallons. Those casks containing brandy, of less than 90 gallons, must be deposited at the expense and risk of the importer, in a public store, and must be removed therefrom in the manner provided for wines and distilled spirits.[d]

The master, or other person having charge of any vessel having distilled spirits or wines on board, within 48 hours after arrival, must make a report in writing to the surveyor or inspector of the revenue of the port, under the penalty of $500, and the loss of the spirits so omitted. See form in note.[e] *

The importer of wines or distilled spirits has the option, when he

---

[a] Act, 10th Feb. 1820, sec. 7. [b] Ibid. sec. 8. [c] Act, 2d March, 1799, sec. 37. [d] Act, 27th Feb., 1830. [e] Act, 2d March, 1799, sec. 30.

* Report of distilled Spirits, imported in the built in burthen whereof is master, from bound to

Marks.	Number.	Description of casks and packages inclusive.	Kinds and qualities of spirits and wines.	Estimated gallons of spirits of each kind.	Estimated gallons of wines of each kind.	To whom consigned.	Where consigned.

Sea-stores, consisting of spirits and wines. [Here insert the quantities particularly.]

(Signed) A. B., master of

To

Inspector of the Revenue

for the port of

makes his entry, either to secure the duties in the ordinary mode, or to send them to the public store or other warehouse, to be selected, for 12 months.[a] In the latter case, he gives a bond for the duties, payable in one year; and the wines and spirits are kept under the joint locks of the inspector and importer, and cannot be delivered without a permit from the collector and naval officer.

In order to obtain a permit for their delivery, the duties must be paid or secured by bond with sureties.

The credit for duties is computed from the date of the permit, provided it is not beyond one year originally allowed.[b]

If the duties be not paid or secured at the end of one year, the collector causes so much of the wines and spirits as may be necessary to pay duties and charges, to be sold at public auction. The overplus is to be returned to the owner or his agent. The amount of the bond taken for duties on wines and spirits delivered after being deposited, is endorsed upon the bond given by the importer when the wines and spirits are deposited.[c]

Embezzlement, or fraudulently hiding or removing such wines or spirits from the store where they are deposited, is punishable by the same penalties, as if they were fraudulently landed without payment of duty, and also by forfeiture of the wines and spirits.[d]

Provision was also made by the 62d section of the act of 1799, for the deposit of teas, in the same manner, for two years; but by a subsequent act, teas were declared free of duty, and of course the 62d section is obsolete.

Wines and spirits not deposited in a public store, lose the benefit of drawback. They may however be shipped coastwise, for the purpose of being immediately put on board some vessel in another district without being deposited. The transportation of such wines and spirits must be made by order of the collector, under the superintendence of an inspector, and a careful examination must be had as to the identity, quantity and quality.[e]

When they are to be transported coastwise, the importer of distilled spirits or wines makes a separate entry thereof, specifying the name of the vessel and master, in which, and the place from whence, such spirits, wines, or teas, were imported, together with the quantity and quality thereof, and a particular detail of the chests, casks, or vessels containing the same, with their marks and numbers. This entry must be subscribed by the person making the same, for himself, or in behalf of the person for whom such entry is made; and must be certified by the collector before whom it is made, as a true copy, and conformable to the general entry, in respect to all distilled spirits and wines therein contained. This entry, thus certified, must be transmitted to the surveyor or inspector of revenue for the port where it is intended to commence the delivery of such spirits or wines. Every permit granted for the unlading thereof, must, previous to such unlading, be produced to the officer of inspection, who

---

[a] Act, 1st March, 1823. [b] Act, 27th Feb., 1830, sec. 2. [c] Ibid. sec. 3. [d] Ibid. sec. 5.
[e] Act, 24th April, 1818, sec. 1.

records the contents thereof, and endorses thereupon the word "*inspected*," the time when, and his own name; after which he returns the permit to the person by whom it was produced. If the said spirits, wines, or teas, be landed without such endorsement upon the permit, the master, for every such offence, forfeits $500, and the goods so landed are forfeited.[a]

All distilled spirits and wines must be landed under the inspection of the inspector of the revenue for the port, on pain of forfeiture thereof. For this purpose the said officer, or his deputies, must, at all reasonable times, attend.[b]

The officers of inspection, upon the landing of distilled spirits or wines, and as soon as the casks, vessels, and cases, containing the same, are inspected, gauged, or measured, must mark, in durable characters, upon the same, the number of casks, vessels, or whether of spirits or wines, marked by each officer respectively, in each year, in progressive numbers for each of the said articles; also, the port of importation, the name of the vessel, and the surname of the master; also, each kind of spirits or wines for which different rates of duties are imposed, the number of gallons in each cask or case; the rate of proof, if spirits; also, the name of the surveyor, or chief officer of inspection for the port, and the date of importation; of all which particulars the chief officers of inspection must keep fair and correct accounts.[c]

The surveyor, or chief officer of inspection within the district, gives to the importer, consignee, or his agent, a certificate* of the whole quantity of the spirits landed; which certificate, besides the quantity, specifies the name of such importer, consignee, or agent, and of the vessel from on board which they have been landed, and the marks of each cask, vessel or case, containing the same.[d]

The surveyor, or chief officer of inspection, in addition to the general certificate† aforesaid, gives to the importer, or his agent, a particular certificate, to accompany each cask, vessel or case, wherever the

---

[a] Act, 2d March, 1799, sec. 37. [b] Ibid. sec. 38. [c] Ibid. sec. 39. [d] Ibid. sec. 40.

* District of
Inspector's Office, No.
Port of

I certify, that [here insert the name of the proprietor, importer, or consignee] imported into this district on the [here insert the date of importation,] in the [here insert the name of the vessel, and whether of the United States or foreign, and the name of the master,] from [here insert the place from which imported, the number of, and whether casks, vessels, or cases,] of [here insert whether spirits, and the kind of each,] marked as per margin, (insert in the margin the marks and numbers, if any, at the time of importation,) which [here insert whether casks, vessels, or cases] have been marked as follows, [here insert the marks of the inspector of the port,] containing [here insert the quantity of spirits,] according to returns made to this office. A. B., Inspector.

† No. District of
Port of

I certify, that there was imported into this district on the [here insert the date of importation,] by [here insert the name of the proprietor, importer, or consignee,] in the [here insert the name of the vessel, the surname of the master, and whether a vessel of the United States or a foreign vessel,] from [here insert the place from which imported,] one [here insert whether cask, vessel, or case, by the proper name,] of [here insert whether spirits, wines, and the kind of each,] numbered and marked as per margin, (the marks of the inspector to be inserted in the margin,) containing [here insert the number of gallons and rate of proof, if spirits, or gallons, if wines.] A. B., Supervisor.
Countersigned by C. D., Inspector.

same may be sent, within the limits of the United States, as evidence that the same have been lawfully imported.[a] No such certificate is required for wines or teas, but only for spirits.[b]

The surveyors of the several districts have blank certificates, under checks and devices prescribed by the treasury, and must number, sign, and deliver the same to the inspectors of revenue for the several ports in their respective districts; which blank certificates must be filled up and countersigned by the inspectors, who are accountable therefor to the surveyors; and the same inspectors must make regular and exact entries of all certificates so granted.[c]

The proprietor, importer, or consignee, or his agent, who receives said certificates, upon the sale or delivery of the said spirits, delivers to the purchaser or purchasers thereof, the certificate or certificates which ought to accompany the same, on pain of forfeiting the sum of $50 for each cask, chest, vessel, or case, with which such certificate shall not be delivered. If any casks, vessels, or cases, containing distilled spirits, which, by the foregoing provisions ought to be marked and accompanied with certificates, are found in the possession of any person unaccompanied with such marks and certificates, it is presumptive evidence that the same are liable to forfeiture, and any officer of the customs may seize them; and if, upon the trial, the owner or claimant do not prove that the same were imported according to law, and the duties thereupon paid or secured, they will be adjudged to be forfeited.[d] It is not, however, cause of forfeiture, that these casks contain a mixture of other spirits, or that they have been adulterated or changed.[e] In order to incur a forfeiture, three circumstances must be united: the cask must contain distilled spirits, must have been one used for foreign spirits, and must be unaccompanied with the requisite certificates.[e]

On the sale of any cask, vessel, or case, which has been marked as containing distilled spirits or wines, and which has been emptied of its contents, and prior to the delivery thereof to the purchaser, or any removal thereof, the marks and numbers set thereon by any officer of inspection, must be obliterated in the presence of some officer of the customs, who, on due notice being given, must attend for that purpose; at which time the certificate which ought to accompany such cask, chest, vessel, or case, must be returned and cancelled. Every person who obliterates, counterfeits, alters, or defaces any mark or number placed by an officer of inspection upon any cask, vessel, or case, containing distilled spirits or wines, or any certificate thereof; or who sells, or in any way alienates or removes any cask, vessel, or case, which has been emptied of its contents, before the marks and nnmber have been defaced or obliterated; or who neglects or refuses to deliver the accompanying certificate, on being thereto required by an officer of the customs, for each and every such offence forfeits $100.[f]

---

[a] Act, 2d March, 1799, sec. 41. [b] Act, 4th July, 1836.
[c] Act, 2d March, 1799, sec. 42. [d] Ibid. sec. 43. [e] 10 Wheat. 421.
[f] Act, 2d March, 1799, sec. 44.

6th. *Regulations in landing goods.*

All duties on goods imported into the United States, must be paid or secured before a permit can be obtained for landing them.[a]

Merchandise brought in any vessel from any foreign place, cannot be unladen or delivered but between the rising and setting of the sun, except by special license from the collector and naval officer, where there is one, nor at any time without a permit from the collector and naval officer, if any, for such unlading or delivery. If any goods be unladen or delivered from any such vessel, contrary to this regulation, the master, and every other person knowingly concerned, or aiding therein, or in removing, storing, or otherwise securing the same, forfeit each the sum of $400 for each offence, and are disabled from holding any office of trust or profit under the United States, for a term not exceeding seven years. The collector must advertise the names of all such persons in a newspaper, printed in the state in which he resides, within twenty days after each respective conviction; and all merchandise, so unladen or delivered, is forfeited, and may be seized by any of the officers of the customs; and where the value thereof, according to the highest market price at the port where landed, amounts to $400, the vessel, tackle, apparel and furniture, is subject to forfeiture and seizure.[b]

Goods, requiring to be weighed, gauged, or measured, in order to ascertain the duties thereupon, cannot, without the consent of the proper officer, be removed from any place upon which the same may be landed, before the same have been weighed, gauged, or measured; and if spirits, wines, teas or sugars, before the proof or quality and quantity thereof have been ascertained and marked thereon, by or under the direction of the proper officer for that purpose, under the penalty of seizure and forfeiture.[c]

Of all goods paying an ad valorem duty, one package out of every invoice, and one out of every twenty in each invoice, must be sent to the custom-house appraisers' store for examination, whether received from abroad or imported coastwise, if in the original packages of importation. On sending such goods coastwise, whether for the benefit of drawback or not, the importer must make out a copy of the extract from the invoice, which extract contains so much of the invoice as relates to the goods shipped; and which, duly sworn to by the importer, before the collector, and duly certified by the collector, is to accompany the goods.[d]

7th. *Regulations for goods remaining in bond.*

At the expiration of fifteen working days, (or twenty days where the vessel is of more than three hundred tons burthen, and from a

---

[a] Act, 2d March, 1799, sec. 62. [b] Ibid. sec. 50. [c] Ibid. sec. 51.
[d] Acts, 18th April, 1818, and 1st March, 1823, sec. 38.

foreign port,)[a] after the report of the master to the collector, made upon his arrival, any goods on board other than those reported for some other district, or some foreign port, the inspectors must take possession of. With the consent of the owner or consignee of any merchandise, or with the consent of the owner or master of the vessel, the said merchandise may be taken possession of at any time after five days' notice to the collector of the district. All merchandise thus taken is delivered to the collector, for which a certificate or receipt is granted.

These goods must be kept at the charge and risk of the owners for the term of nine months: if within that time no claim be made for the same, an inventory and an appraisement thereof must be made, and verified on oath or affirmation by two or more reputable merchants, before the collector, and remain with him. The collector must afterwards cause the said goods to be sold at public auction, (previously causing the same to be advertised in one or more of the public newspapers, printed at or nearest to the place of sale, for the space of one month,) and, retaining the duties and all charges thereon, he must pay the overplus, if any, into the treasury of the United States, there to remain for the use of the owners, who, upon due proof of property, are entitled to receive the same. The collector must transmit, with the overplus, a copy of the inventory, appraisement, and account of sales, specifying the marks, numbers, and descriptions of the packages sold, their contents, the name of the vessel and master in which, and of the place whence they were imported; the time when, and the name of the persons to whom the said goods were consigned in the manifest. The receipt or certificate of the collector exonerates the master or person having the charge or command of any vessel in which such goods were imported, from all claims of the owners thereof. Such quantities of goods so stored, as may be necessary to discharge the duties thereon, may be sold, at the time or times when such duties become due and payable. Where any entry has been duly made of such goods, the same need not be appraised; and where such goods are perishable, they must be sold forthwith. The limitation of fifteen days does not extend to vessels laden with salt or coal; but if the master or owner of any vessel laden with salt or coal require a longer time to discharge her cargo, the wages of the inspector, for every day's attendance exceeding the said fifteen days, must be paid by the master or owner; and thereupon the collector is required to allow such longer time as in his judgment he may think necessary to discharge such cargo, not exceeding fifteen days. If, by reason of the delivery of the cargo in several districts, more than fifteen working days in the whole be spent therein, the wages of the inspectors who may be employed on board, must, for every day of such excess, be paid by the master or owner; and such inspectors, previously

---

[a] Act, 3d March, 1821.

to the clearance of such vessel, must render an exact account to the collector of all such compensations as have been paid, or may be due and payable by such master or owner.[a]

If any package reported in the manifest be not found on board, or if the goods on board do not correspond with the manifest, the master, or person in command of the vessel, forfeits $500, unless it be made to appear, to the satisfaction of the collector, naval officer, and surveyor, or a major part of them, or of the collector alone, where there is no naval officer or surveyor, or, in case of trial, to the satisfaction of the court, that no part of the cargo has been landed or unladen, except as specified in the manifest, or pursuant to permits, or that the disagreement is owing to accident or mistake.[b] A post entry must then be made of such goods omitted, &c. Goods found concealed on board after the master has declared that the whole cargo was discharged, are not protected by this proviso from forfeiture.[c]

Imported goods not provided for in the 56th section of the act of 1799, and which have not been entered pursuant to the revenue laws, must be sent to the public store, where they remain at the expense and risk of the owner, until the invoice, properly authenticated, be produced.

If not entered within nine months, (except as to goods from places beyond Cape Horn or the Cape of Good Hope, when eighteen months are allowed,) they must be appraised, and the duties estimated as upon appraised goods. Such portion of the goods as may be required to pay duties and necessary charges, may be sold, from time to time, as the duties become due; and if perishable, or liable to waste, they may be sold before by order of the collector, notice being given in one or more newspapers at or nearest the place of sale.

The articles are to be appraised previous to the sale, and the duties estimated.

The proceeds of the sale are to be distributed at the end of nine or eighteen months, as the case may be, pursuant to the 56th section of the act of 1799.[d]

Any vessel may proceed with any goods brought in her, and which, in the manifest delivered to the collector, are reported as destined for any foreign port, from the district within which such vessel first arrives, to such foreign port, without paying or securing duties upon such goods as shall be actually re-exported in the said vessel. But such manifest, so declaring the intention to re-export such goods, must be delivered to the collector within forty-eight hours after the arrival of such vessel. And the master or commander of such vessel must give bonds, with sureties, in an amount equal to the duties, that the goods shall not be landed within the United States, unless the duties are first paid or secured. These bonds are cancelled in the same manner as drawback bonds.[e]

---

[a] Act, 2d March, 1799, sec. 56. [b] Ibid. sec. 57. [c] 3 Hall's Law Journal, 176.
[d] Act, 1st March, 1823, sec. 3. [e] Act, 22d Feb., 1805.

8th. *Regulations for appraising imported goods.*

By the act of 2d March, 1799, provision is made for the appraisement of goods subject to duty ad valorem, where the entry is incomplete, or where there is no specification of particulars, or where the goods are damaged.

The goods must be, in such case, sent to the public store, in the parcels or packages containing the same, there to remain at the expense and risk of the owner or consignee, under the care of some proper officer, until the particulars, cost, or value, as the case may require, have been ascertained, either by the exhibition of the original invoice, or by appraisement, and until the duties thereon have been paid or secured, and a permit granted by the collector for the delivery thereof.[a]

In respect to articles that have been damaged during the voyage, whether subject to duty ad valorem, or chargeable with a specific duty, either by number, weight, or measure, the appraisers ascertain and certify to what per centage the said goods are damaged; and the per centage of damage, so certified, is deducted from the original amount, subject to a duty ad valorem, or from the actual or original number, weight, or measure, on which specific duties would have been computed. To obtain allowance for damage on merchandise entered, on which the duties have been paid or secured, and for which a permit has been granted, proof to ascertain such damage must be lodged in the custom-house within ten days thereafter. Every person appointed to ascertain the damage during the voyage, of any merchandise, must take and subscribe an oath or affirmation, as in note.*

Goods that have been taken from a wreck, must also be appraised in like manner.[b]

Goods belonging to persons not residing in the United States, and unaccompanied with regular invoices, must be appraised, unless otherwise ordered by the secretary of the treasury. If he refuses permission, they must be sent to the public store for appraisement, and are subject to the same regulations as in the case of suspected invoices.[c]

One package in every invoice, and one package out of twenty packages in each invoice, to be designated by the collector, must be sent to the public store for inspection.

Where the duty is regulated by the value of the square yard, or any other quantity, all the goods are sent.

---

[a] Act, 2d March, 1799, sec. 52. [b] Act, 1st March, 1823, sec. 21.
[c] Act, 28th May, 1820, sec. 12.

* *Form of Oath:*
District of
Port of
I appointed by
merchant, to ascertain and appraise the damage sustained on certain goods, wares, or merchandise, imported by, or consigned to the said in the master, from do solemnly, sincerely, and truly that I will diligently and faithfully inspect and examine the said goods, wares, or merchandise, and truly report, to the best of my knowledge and belief, the amount of damage received by the same, during the voyage of importation. And I do also that I have no direct or indirect interest in the said goods, wares, or merchandise.
before me.

If, upon inspection, the goods are found not to correspond with the invoice, or are falsely charged, the whole entry must be inspected; and if subject to an ad valorem duty, they must be appraised as in the case of suspected invoices. If a package be found to contain any article not described in the invoice, it is forfeited.[a]

For the appraisement of merchandise, there are appointed in New-York three persons; and in Boston, Philadelphia, Baltimore, Charleston, Savannah, and New-Orleans, two persons, on the part of the United States, who are sworn diligently and faithfully to inspect and examine such goods as the collector may direct, and truly to report, to the best of their knowledge and belief, the actual cost thereof, when purchased, at the time and place when and where the same were purchased, or the actual value, if the same were procured otherwise than by purchase.[b] Where the goods are subject to a duty ad valorem, or where it is estimated upon the value of the square yard, and they have been imported from a country where they were not manufactured or produced, the current value in the country of production or manufacture at the time of exportation, is to be estimated.[c]

To this value, all charges, except insurance, are to be added, and the duties are to be estimated on the aggregate amount.[d]

In all other ports besides those enumerated, appraisements are made by two respectable resident merchants, appointed by the collector, who are sworn in the same manner.

The secretary of the treasury, however, has the power to direct the public appraisers for one district to attend in another district, for the purpose of appraising goods imported in such district.[e]

There are, besides, four assistant appraisers in New-York, and two assistant appraisers in Boston and Philadelphia, each practically acquainted with the value of goods, who act under the direction of the appraisers, subject to their revision.[f]

If the importer be dissatisfied with the appraisement, he may, at his own expense, employ two respectable resident merchants, to appraise the goods again in connexion with the public appraisers. They are also sworn; and if they agree with the others, the value is to be reported to the collector; and, if not, the circumstances of disagreement.

If the importer be dissatisfied with the second appraisement, he may refer the matter to the secretary of the treasury, who is empowered to decide thereon, or to require further testimony in the case, and to order the goods to be entered accordingly.[g]

If the collector deem the appraisement too low, he may order a re-appraisement, either by the principal appraisers, or by three American merchants designated by him.[h]

Whenever goods, composed wholly or in part of wool or cotton, of similar kind, but different quality, are found in the same package, charged at an average price, the appraisers must adopt the value of the best article as the average value of the whole.[i]

---

[a] Act, 28th May, 1830, sec. 15. [b] Act, 1st March, 1823, sec. 5.
[c] Act, 14th July, 1832, sec. 7. [d] Acts, 1st March, 1823, sec. 5, and 14th July, 1832, sec. 14-15.
[e] Ibid. sec. 16. [f] Act, 28th May, 1830. [g] Ibid. sec. 18. [h] Act, 18th May, 1830, sec. 2.
[i] Act, 14th July, 1832, sec. 13.

If such goods are found to vary from the entry, or any package to contain any article not entered, or to be made up with intent to evade or defraud the revenue, the package is forfeited.[a]

The re-appraisement of cotton and woollen goods, can be obtained upon application to the collector by the importer, in writing, stating the reasons. He makes oath that the appraisement is higher than the actual cost and charges, and that he believes it to be higher than the actual value, with charges, at the port of exportation. Two skilful merchants are then chosen, one by the collector, and one by the importer, with power to appoint an umpire; and if their appraisement do not agree with the former one, the collector must decide between them.[b]

The appraisers are authorized to examine any person, under oath, touching the value of goods to be appraised, and to require any letters, accounts, and invoices, to be produced. Any person failing to attend, or refusing to answer, or to produce such papers, forfeits $50; and if he be the importer or agent, the appraisement is final.[c]

Where the duty is regulated by the value of the square yard, or any other quantity, or where the duty is ad valorem, the collector must cause the actual value of the goods, at the time of purchase and place of exportation, to be ascertained by appraisement, and the number of yards, &c., to be ascertained.[d]

The appraisers are bound to use all reasonable means to ascertain the true value, without regarding the invoice or affidavit of the value, and also the number of such yards or quantities.[d]

All manufactures of wool, or of which wool is a component part, which are imported in an unfinished condition, must be appraised at the same value as if entirely finished.[d]

The secretary of the treasury, too, is authorized, under the direction of the president, to modify and change the regulations for appraising goods, to secure a true and faithful appraisement, and just and proper entries of the actual value, and of the square yards, &c., and of their actual value.[e]

The changes and the reasons, however, must be reported to congress, at the next session.[e]

The secretary of the treasury may also authorize collectors to require importers of goods to give bonds in a sum equal to the value of the goods, to produce within a given time satisfactory proof to enable the collector to ascertain the class of manufacture, or rate of duty, to which such goods are liable.[f]

A fine of $50 is incurred by a merchant who refuses or neglects to act as appraiser, after being appointed either by the collector or importer.[g]

Whenever the collector suspects that goods, subject to an ad valorem duty, imported into his district, have been invoiced below the true value, in their actual state of manufacture, at the place from

---

[a] Act, 14th July, 1832, sec. 14. [b] Ac , 28th May, 1830, sec. 3.
[c] Ibid. sec. 8. [d] Act, 14th July, 1832, sec. 8. [e] Ibid. sec. 7.
[f] Act, 28th May, 1830, sec. 8. [g] Act, 1st March, 1823, sec. 19.

which they were imported, he must direct the same to be appraised; and if the value at which the same are appraised, exceed, by twenty-five per cent. the invoice prices thereof, then there must be added fifty per cent. on the appraised value; on which aggregate amount the duties on such merchandise is estimated.[a]

Where the appraised value exceeds by less than twenty-five per cent. the invoice value, such appraised value is considered the true value upon which the duty is to be estimated; but in all cases the duty must be charged as much as it would be on the invoice value.[b]

9th. *Regulations for foreign vessels.*

The basis of the commercial system of the United States is perfect reciprocity. The act of March 1st, 1817, tenders to the vessels of all foreign nations the same privileges in the ports of the United States that American vessels enjoy, and imposes restrictions of a retaliatory character upon the vessels of nations, which do not place American vessels in their ports upon the same footing with their own vessels.

Foreign vessels are not allowed to carry on the coasting trade;[c] but they may proceed from port to port with a certified manifest, for the purpose of delivering such parts of the cargo as were originally destined for those ports.[d] Before clearing out, the master must deliver to the collector duplicate manifests of the lading on board; and if there be none, he must so state; swear to the manifest, and obtain a permit from the collector to proceed to his port of destination. Upon his arrival in another district, and within forty-eight hours, he must deliver to the collector the manifest of the cargo on board; or if in ballast, he must so state; swear to the manifest, and also, that such manifest contains an account of all the goods which were on board his vessel when he sailed from her last port of departure, or which have been since on board. He must also deliver the permit received from the collector of the port of departure.[d]

Any neglect or refusal of the master on these points, subjects him to a penalty of $100.

In 1823, authority was given to the president of the United States to suspend or discontinue the discriminating duties of tonnage or impost, so far as they affect vessels of any nation which does not impose any discriminating duties upon vessels of the United States.[e]

Foreign vessels placed on the same footing as American vessels, are as follows:

Those of France, Holland, Belgium, Sweden, Norway, Russia, Austria, Denmark, Prussia, Hamburg, Bremen, and Lubec.

Those of Mexico, Colombia, Brazils, and Chili, pay the same tonnage duties as American vessels.

Goods imported in such vessels, direct from the European ports of their respective countries, and which are of the growth, produce, or manufacture of such countries, or which are usually first shipped from them, pay no higher duties than if imported in American vessels.

---

[a] Act, 1st March, 1823, sec. 13. [b] Ibid. sec. 14. [c] Act, 1st March, 1817, sec. 4.
[d] Act, 18th Feb., 1793, sec. 24. [e] Act, 24th May, 1828, sec. 1.

British vessels from British ports in Europe, pay no more tonnage duty than American vessels. Goods of the growth, produce, or manufacture, of British ports in Europe, pay the same duty, when imported in British vessels, from such ports, as when imported in American vessels.

The footing on which the trade between the United States and the British colonies is placed, will be found in chapter I.

Vessels of the United States enjoy, in the ports of the countries above mentioned, (except in the British colonies,) the same privileges that their vessels possess in the ports of the United States. The intercourse between the United States and the island of St. Barts is also upon the footing of reciprocity; but the Swedish vessels must be naturalized at St. Barts, and owned by Swedes inhabiting that island.

No discriminating duties are imposed on goods imported in Portuguese vessels from Portugal, Madeira, Porto Santo, and the Azores.[a]

Spanish vessels from Spain pay the same tonnage duties that American vessels pay in Spain: from Spanish colonies the same tonnage duties that American vessels pay in the colonial port from which the Spanish vessel last sailed;[b] and a further tonnage duty, equivalent to the discriminating duty levied on the same cargo in the Spanish colony, if exported to the United States in an American vessel.[c] A similar tonnage duty is laid on Spanish vessels clearing out from a Spanish island with a cargo, equal to the discriminating duty levied in Havana upon the same cargo, if imported in an American vessel; and if clearing out for another port, an export bond must be given, with security, double the value of vessel and cargo, that the cargo shall not be landed in Cuba or Porto Rico.[d] This bond is cancelled upon the production of a certificate of its having been landed elsewhere, from an American consul.

Foreign vessels, coming from a port where the flag of the United States is not usually admitted, are not allowed to come to an entry in the United States.

Importations by all foreign vessels, which are not placed on the same footing as American vessels, are subject to an additional duty of 10 per cent; for instance, if the duty by an American vessel is 15, the duty by such foreign vessel will be 16½. No drawback is allowed on this additional duty.

In carrying into effect the act of March 1st, 1817, the treasury department, by a circular dated September 29th, 1819, directed the collectors to regard the term country, in the first section, as embracing all the possessions of a foreign state, however widely separated, which are subject to the same supreme executive and legislative authority. The productions and manufactures of a foreign state, and of its colonies, may be imported into the United States in vessels owned by citizens or subjects of such state, without regard to their place of residence within its possessions. Gold and silver coin and

---

[a] Act, 4th July, 1836, sec. 1. [b] Act, 13th July, 1823, sec. 2. [c] Act, 30th June, 1834, sec. 1. [d] Ibid. sec. 3.

bullion are not considered goods, wares, or merchandise, within the meaning of the act, and may, therefore, be imported into the United States in foreign vessels, without regard to the place of production or coinage.

To insure uniformity in the execution of the 3d, 5th, and 6th sections of that act, it is directed, that in all cases where proof is exhibited, on oath, according to their provisions, the witnesses should be cross-examined by the collector, whose duty it is to decide, for the purpose of avoiding imposition and detecting evasion.[a]

Whenever a Spanish vessel arrives in distress in any port of the United States, having been damaged on the coast, or within the limits of the United States, and her cargo has been unladen in conformity with the 60th section of the act of 2d March, 1799, the cargo, or any part thereof, may, if the vessel be condemned as not seaworthy, or be deemed incapable of performing her original voyage, afterwards be reladen on board any other vessel, under the inspection of the officer who superintended the landing thereof. And no duties, charges, or fees, whatever, are paid on such part of the cargo as may be reladen and carried away, either in the vessel in which it was originally imported, or in any other.[b]

This provision was made in consequence of the stipulations contained in the 10th article of the treaty between the United States and Spain.

Under the act of 2d March, 1799, it was declared, that British subjects, and also the Indians dwelling on either side of the boundary line of the United States, might freely pass and repass, by land or inland navigation, into and from the territories of the United States, and navigate all the lakes, rivers, and waters thereof, and freely carry on trade and commerce with the citizens of the United States: Provided, that this should not be construed to justify the admission of British vessels from the sea into the rivers of the United States, beyond the highest ports of entry for foreign vessels.[c]

It was also provided in the same act, that all goods, of which the importation was not prohibited, might be imported from Canada by British subjects upon the same terms as by American citizens.[c]

No custom-house fees are paid by a British colonial vessel, boat, or raft, entering a port of the United States on the northern, north-eastern, or northwestern frontiers.[d]

The same tonnage duties, and the same discriminating duties, are paid by British vessels, and on goods imported in British vessels, into the American ports on that frontier, that are imposed in the British ports on American vessels, and on goods imported in American vessels into the colonies.[e]

10th. *Regulations for collecting duties.*

The regulations concerning the duties on wines and distilled spirits, and the manner of collecting them, will be found in part 6th of this chapter.

---

[a] Treasury Circular, 29th Sept., 1817. [b] Act, 14th Feb., 1805.
[c] Act, 3d March, 1799, sec. 104. [d] Act, 3d March, 1831, sec. 1. [e] Ibid. sec. 2.

All duties on merchandise imported, must be paid or secured before a permit is granted for landing the same: where the amount of such duty on goods imported on account of one person only, or of several persons jointly interested, does not exceed $200, the same must be immediately paid: if it exceed that sum, it may, at the option of the importer, be paid or secured to be paid by bond, the one half in three, and the other half in six calender months from the date of each respective importation. Upon all woollen goods the duties must be paid in cash, but the goods may be deposited. The collector, in lieu of sureties, may accept of a deposit of so much of the said goods as shall in his judgment be sufficient security for the duties for which the bond shall have been given, and the charge of safe keeping and sale of the goods so deposited. These goods are kept by the collector, at the expense and risk of the owners, until the sum specified in such bond becomes due; at which time, if not paid, so much of the deposited goods as may be necessary, are sold at public sale, and the proceeds, after deducting the charges of safe-keeping and sale, applied to the payment of such sum, rendering the overplus arising on such sale, and the residue of the goods so deposited, if any there be, to the persons by whom such deposit has been made, or to their agent or lawful representative.

All bonds for moneys or duties to be paid, or services to be performed for the United States, are taken in the name of the United States of America. No person whose bond has been received, either as principal or surety for the payment of duties, or for whom any bond has been given by any other person, which may be due and unsatisfied, is allowed a future credit for duties until such bond be fully discharged. To prevent frauds arising from collusive transfers, all merchandise imported into the United States is deemed the property of the persons to whom the same may be consigned; any sale, transfer, or assignment, prior to the entry and payment, or securing the payment of the duties, and the payment of all bonds then due and unsatisfied by the said consignee, to the contrary notwithstanding.[a]*

---

[a] Act, 2d March, 1799, sec. 62.

* *Form of the bond for duties:*

Know all men by these presents, that we, [here insert the name of the importer or consignee, or if by an agent, the name of such agent, and of the importers or consignees and the sureties, their place of abode and occupation,] are held and firmly bound unto the United States of America, in the sum of   to be paid to the said United States; for payment whereof, we bind ourselves, our heirs, executors, and administrators, jointly and severally, firmly by these presents. Sealed with our seals. Dated this   day of   in the   year of the independence of the said United States, and in the year of our Lord one thousand

The condition of this obligation is such, that if the above bounden [here insert the principal, or agent for such principal, and the sureties,] or either of them, or either of their heirs, executors and administrators, shall and do, on or before the   day of   next, well and truly pay, or cause to be paid, unto the collector of the customs for the district of   for the time being, the sum of   or the amount of the duties to be ascertained as due and arising on certain goods, wares, and merchandise, entered by the above bounden, [insert the name of the importer or consignee, or

Credit on Duties.—On all goods, except woollens, the credit, beginning at the time the vessel makes her entry at the custom-house, is as follows,—one half in three, and one half in six months.

The duties on goods, manufactured in whole or in part of wool, where not exceeding $200, must be paid in cash.[a] If above that sum, the duties must be paid, one half in three, and one half in six months.

The importer, however, may send them to the public store, under bond, at his risk and expense, and subject to the payment of interest at the rate of 6 per cent. on the amount of duties while so stored. One half the duties must in that case be paid in three and one half in six months from the date of importation; and in case of default, the collector may cause so much of the goods as will be sufficient to pay the duties due, with charges, to be sold at public auction.[b]

The importer can withdraw the goods from the public store at any time, upon paying duties and expenses.[b]

Bond for Duties.—Bonds to the United States for the payment of duties entered into by a partner in the name of the firm, bind the other partners.[c]

No clerk or hired person in the constant employment of another, is permitted to be a party in the same bond with his employer.[c]

In all bonds for duties, the principals must be residents, and the sureties citizens of the United States.[d]

If the importer, at the time of entry, offer to pay the duties in cash where he is entitled to credit, the collector must allow him a discount at the rate of 4 per cent. per annum.[e]

Where any bond for duties is not satisfied on the day it becomes due, the collector must, without delay, cause a prosecution to be commenced for the recovery of the money. In all cases of insolvency, or where any estate in the hands of the executors, administrators, or assignees, is insufficient to pay all the debts due from the deceased, the debt due to the United States on such bond must be first satisfied; and any executor, or other person, who pays any debt due by such person or estate previous to the debt due to the United States, become answerable in their own person and estate for the debt so due to the United States. If the surety pay the bond, he is entitled to the same preference over other creditors which the United States have.[f]

Where a consignee bonds goods, and afterwards, together with the owner, becomes insolvent, the surety paying the bond is not entitled to a preference against the bankrupt owner, but only against

---

[a] Act, 14th July, 1832, sec. 5. [b] Ibid. sec. 5. [c] Act, 1st March, 1823, sec. 25. [d] Ibid. sec. 26. [e] Ibid. sec. 27. [f] Act, 2d March, 1799, sec. 65, and 2 Wash. C. C. R. 196.

agent for such importer or consignee,] as imported in the master, from as per entry dated then the above obligation to be void, otherwise to remain in full force and virtue.

Sealed and delivered }
in the presence of }

the consignee.[a] Insolvency here means a voluntary assignment of a person unable to pay his debts, as well as a bankruptcy declared by law, or where the effects of an absent or absconding debtor have been attached.[b]

Where a suit has been instituted upon a bond for duties, the district court gives judgment, upon motion, at the return term, unless the defendant makes an affidavit in open court, the U. S. district attorney being present, that an error has been made in liquidating the duties, specifying the errors, and stating that the collector was notified thereof before the commencement of the return term.[b]

The court may then grant a continuance to the next term, but no longer.[b]

Six per cent. interest is allowed on all bonds after they become due.[b]

In 1830, the collection of duties was placed under the superintendence of a solicitor of the treasury, who has charge of all property assigned to the United States for the payment of debts, and of all trusts created for the same purpose, and power to release or convey to the original debtor, his heirs or devisees, real estate which has become the property of the United States, in payment of a debt, upon payment thereof.[c] All lists, returns, reports, and accounts with the treasury, must be transmitted to him at Washington.[d] Collectors must immediately report to him all bonds delivered to the district attorney for collection, and all suits commenced for fines or forfeitures, and all seizures made.

The district attorney is thereupon charged with the bonds delivered to him; and at the end of each term the district attorney must report the situation of the causes, accompanied with a certificate of the clerk of the court.

With the last quarterly return of the year, the collector must report, under oath, the bonds in suit, with the amounts paid on each.[e]

The solicitor of the treasury gives directions to the district attorneys, marshals and clerks, in the different districts, respecting all suits where the United States is a party.[f] Under the rules established at his office, collectors are directed to take triplicate receipts from the district attorneys; one of which must be forthwith transmitted by mail to the solicitor of the treasury, with the date and amount of the bond, and the names of the obligors; one is sent to the first auditor with the first quarterly returns, and the other is retained by the collector.

Any payment made on the bond must also be stated, with the date and the amount.

The collector must, on his part, give triplicate receipts to the district attorney or marshal, for any moneys collected by those officers, and paid over to him. Similar returns must be made by the district attorneys and marshals; but, as they are legal officers, they are presumed not to need information as to the law.

After June 30th, 1842, all duties must be paid in cash, (as provided

---

[a] 1 Wash. C. C. R. 494. [b] Act, 2d March, 1799, sec. 65. [c] Act, 29th May, 1830, sec. 1. [d] Ibid. sec. 2. [e] Ibid. sec. 3 and 4. [f] Ibid. sec. 5.

by Mr. Clay's compromise bill of 1832;) and these regulations, as to bonds, &c., may be unnecessary after that year.

The preference given to the United States by the 65th section of the act of 1799, and the law of March 3d, 1797, overreaches the lien which a creditor acquires by a judgment on the land of the debtor.[a] Though it does not extend to cases where the debtor has not made an assignment of his whole property, unless it should appear that a portion of it was left out for the purpose of evading the law.[b] Neither does it extend to cases where the debtor is merely unable to pay, but where there is a known and legal insolvency manifested by some notorious act of the debtor.[c]

Duties do not accrue until the vessel arrive at the port of entry. Therefore, if a duty be increased or diminished by law, even after the arrival of the vessel in the collection district, but before her arrival at the port of entry, the increased or diminished duty only is to be paid.[d]

Goods brought into the United States by superior force or inevitable accident, are not deemed to be imported so as to be liable to pay duties. But if they are afterwards sold or consumed in the country, they become retroactively liable; otherwise, if they are exported.[e]

The collector may refuse a credit for duties on goods imported, where the real owner, having a bond in the custom-house due and unpaid, has collusively transferred the property to a third person, in order to obtain a credit on the custom-house.[f]

An action of debt will lie for duties unpaid, where from mistake or fraud no bond was given when the goods were imported.[g] A bond given by one of a firm for the amount of duties, extinguishes the debt, and makes it the sole debt of the obligor.[h] There is, however, no lien on the goods, for the duties which can be enforced in admiralty.[i]

The United States have no lien on the estate of the debtor, until suit brought, or notorious insolvency has taken place, or an assignment of all his property, or the withdrawal of his person from legal process.[j] If the debtor make a bona fide assignment of his property, or it has been seized under an execution, the lien of the United States is divested.[k] The preference of the United States does not divest a prior legal lien.[l]

An assignment, to entitle the United States to a priority, must be of all the debtor's property, but it need not be for the benefit of all his creditors.[m]

By an act passed March 2d, 1833, it is declared, that the jurisdiction of the United States circuit courts extends to all cases in law and equity, arising under the revenue laws of the United States; and persons injured either in person or property for any act done under any revenue law of the United States, are enabled to sue for the injury in those courts. Property taken under the authority of the revenue laws is declared irrepleviable, and subject only to the orders of the United States courts. Any person attempting to dispossess or rescue

---

a 2 Wheat. 396. b 3 Cranch, 73. c 8 Ibid. 431. d 5 Ibid. 368. e 9 Ibid. 387.
f 3 Dall. 308. g 1 Mason, 482.—3 Ibid. 324. h 3 Wash. C. C. R. 508..
i 1 Paine's C. C. R. 499. j 3 Cranch, 73.—8 Ibid. 431. k 2 Wheat. 396.—1 Peters, 195.
l Bee, 196. m 1 Paine, 186.

such property is guilty of a misdemeanour, and liable to be imprisoned for twelve months, and fined $300.[a]

Where a suit is commenced in a state court against any person for any act done under the authority of the revenue laws, the defendant may remove the cause into the circuit court of the United States by petition;[b] and if the state court will not refuse the record and proceedings, nor suffer copies to be made, the record and other defects may be supplied by affidavit or otherwise.[c] The proceedings in the state courts are in such cases stayed, and all subsequent steps are declared void. If the defendant be in actual custody, the marshal is authorized to take him into custody, and hold him subject to the order of the court.[b]

All duties and fees are payable in money of the United States, or in foreign gold and silver coins, at the following rates, that is to say—the gold coins of Great Britain, Portugal and Brazil, not less than 22 carats fine, at the rate of 94 cents 8 mills per pennyweight: the gold coins of France, $9\frac{1}{10}$ fine, at the rate of 93 cents 1 mill per pennyweight: the gold coins of Spain, Mexico, and Colombia, 20 carats $3\frac{7}{16}$ grains fine, at the rate of 89 cents 9 mills per pennyweight:[d] the milled dollar of Spain, Mexico, Peru, Chili and Central America, and those re-stamped in Brazil, at the rate of 100 cents for each dollar weighing 415 grains, and of not less fineness than 10 oz. 15 pennyweights of pure silver in 12 troy oz. of standard silver, and in like proportion for the parts of a dollar: crowns of France at the rate of 110 cents for each crown, the actual weight whereof shall not be less than 18 pennyweights and 17 grains, and in like proportion for the parts of a crown; the 5 franc pieces of France, at 93 cents when weighing not less than 384 grains, and of not less fineness than 10 oz. 16 pennyweights of pure silver in 12 troy oz. of standard silver.[e] No foreign coins are receivable which are not by law a tender for the payment of all debts, except in consequence of a proclamation of the president authorizing such foreign coins to be received.

Foreign moneys are valued at the custom-house at the following rates:

THOSE MARKED THUS (*) ARE FIXED BY LAW.

		Am. Currency.
*Antwerp, Amsterdam, Rotterdam, and all the Netherlands,	F. or Guilder,	$0 40
Batavia,	Rix Dollar,	75
*Bengal,	Sicca Rupee,	50
Bombay,	do.	50
Bremen, Rix Dollar, according to the value of the rix dollar, as certified by the American consul at Bremen.		
*Calcutta,	Rupee,	50
*China,	Tale,	1 48

N. B. Invoices from China are invariably made in dollars and cents federal value.

[a] Act, 2d March, 1823, sec. 2. [b] Ibid. sec. 3. [c] Ibid. sec. 4.
[d] Act, 28th June, 1834. [e] Act, 25th June, 1834.

*Denmark,	Rix Dollar,	1 00
———, Blue Dollar, according to the value, at the moment, of Rix Dollars, compared to Blue Dollars. (Vide N. B.)		
*England and Ireland,	£ sterling,	4 80
France,	Franc,	18 708c.
*———,	Livre, (no longer in use)	$18\frac{1}{2}$
Halifax,	£	4 00
Hamburg,	Mark Banco,	$33\frac{1}{3}$
———,	Rix Dollar,	1 00
*Holland,	F. or Guilder,	40
*India,	Star Pagoda,	1 84
Italy,	Ounce,	2 40
Leghorn,	Pezzo,	90 76c.
———,	Livre,	$15\frac{3}{4}$
*Portugal,	Mil Reas,	1 24
Russia, Paper Rouble, according to the value at the time and place of shipment.. (Vide N. B.)		
———,	Silver Rouble,	75
Smyrna, Piastre, according to the value at Smyrna, at the time of shipment.		
*Spain,	Real of Plate,	10
*———,	Real of Veion,	5
———,	Another real of plate, or $\frac{1}{8}$ of a dollar,	$12\frac{1}{2}$ c.
Sweden,	Rix Dollar,	1 00
Trieste, Specie Florin, which is the specie Florin of Bohemia, and other parts of the Austrian dominions, (ascertained at the treasury department,)		48
Paper Florin of Trieste, and other parts of the Austrian dominions, according to its value, at the time, when compared with the Specie Florin.		

N. B. Wherever invoices are made out in a currency, the value of which is not fixed by a law of the United States, a certificate must be produced from the American consul, at the place of exportation, of the true value of such currency in Spanish dollars; and the duties are charged upon that value. The collector may require a bond to procure such certificate where practicable. In the absence of such evidence, prices current and other authentic sources of information are resorted to.[a]

11th. *Drafts, tares, and allowances, for breakage, discount, &c.*

TARES ALLOWED AT THE CUSTOM-HOUSE.

Alum, in casks, 12 per cent.
Almonds, in bags, 4 per cent., in bales, 8 lb. each.
in frails, 10 per cent., double bales, 16 lb. each.
in casks, 15 do.

---

[a] Treasury Order, 14th May, 1831.

Almonds, in cases, 8lb. each.
 in zeroons, 10 do.
Bristles, 12 per cent.
Candles, in boxes, 8 per cent. legal ton.
Cassia, Chinese, in boxes, 18 per cent.
 in mats, 6 do.
 do. real tare, usually passed as 8 per cent.
Cheese, in boxes, 20 per cent. legal tare.
 in casks, 15 do.
 in hampers, 10 per cent. legal tare.
Chocolate, in boxes, 10 do. do.
Cinnamon, in chests or boxes, 25 per cent. and in mats, real tare.
Cloves, in casks, 12 per cent.
 in bags, 4 do.
 in zeroons, 8 do.
Coffee, in bags, 2 per cent. legal tare.
 In double bags the importer must claim an additional tare from the collector, and he will then direct the additional bag to be reweighed, and allow an extra tare equal to its weight.
 in bales, 3 per cent. legal tare.
 in zeroons, 6 per cent. custom-house tare.
 in casks, 12 per cent. legal tare.
 in boxes, 15 per cent. legal tare.
 African, imported in the hull, has an extra tare allowed of 18 per cent. for the hull. The importer should claim it at the time of entry at the custom-house.
Cocoa, in bags, 1 per cent. legal tare.
 in casks, 10 do. do.
 N. B. The real tare on cocoa in bags and casks is more than this. The invoice tare will, of course, be claimed in making the entry at the custom-house.
 in zeroons, 11 per cent.
Copperas, 12 per cent.
Cotton, in bales, 2 per cent. legal tare.
 N. B. The tare on Indian cotton is, in fact, 4 per cent. The importer should, therefore, at the time of entry at the custom-house, claim invoice tare.
 in zeroons, 6 per cent. legal tare.
Currants, in casks, 12 per cent.
 in boxes, 12 do.
Figs, in boxes, 10 per cent.
 in casks, 12 do.
 in frails, 4 do.
 in drums, 3 do.
Fish, dry, in casks or boxes, 12 per cent.
Glue, in casks, 20 per cent.
 in boxes, 15 per cent.
Gunpowder, $\frac{1}{4}$ casks, 5 lb. each.
 half hundred, 900.
 whole, 2300.

Hemp, in bales, 5 per cent. No allowance is made for bands.
Indigo, in bags, 3 per cent. legal tare.
in barrels, 12 per cent. legal tare.
in cases, 15 per cent. custom-house tare.
in hogsheads or other casks, not bbls. 15 per cent. legal tare.
in zeroons, 10 per cent. legal tare.
Iron, sheet, in boxes, 8 lb. each.
Lead, white, ground in oil, 8 per cent.
dry, 6 per cent.
red, dry, 5 per cent.
Mace, in casks or boxes, 18 per cent.
Nails, in casks, 8 per cent. legal tare.
Nutmegs, in casks, 12 per cent.
in bags, 4 per cent.
Ochre, yellow, in oil, 12 per cent.
dry, 10 per cent.
Pimento, in bags, 3 per cent. legal tare.
in casks, 16 per cent. legal tare.
in mats, 5 per cent.
Pepper, in bags, 2 per cent. legal tare.
in bales, 5 per cent. legal tare.
in casks, 12 per cent. legal tare.
Plums and Prunes, in boxes, 8 per cent.
Powder, hair, in casks, 12 per cent.
in boxes, 15 per cent.
Quicksilver, in bbls. 7 per cent.
Raisins, in boxes, 15 per cent.
in jars, 18 lb. per jar.
in casks, 12 per cent.
in frails, 4 per cent.
in drums, 10 per cent.
Malaga, of the usual size, of about 112 lb. gross, are taken as 100 lb. net.
Shot, in casks, 3 per cent. legal tare.
in bags, ½ per cent.
Snuff, in casks, 12 per cent.
in boxes, 15 per cent.
Soap, in boxes, 10 per cent. legal tare. N. B. Invoice tare is generally claimed, because it is usually more than 10 per cent.
Spikes, 8 per cent.
Starch, in casks, 10 per cent.
Steel, in tubs, put up as usual, is taken at its real net weight of 112 lb.
in cases, 8 per cent.
in bundles, no allowance is made for bands.
Sugar, in bags or mats, 5 per cent. legal tare.
in boxes, whether Brazil, Havana, or any other, 15 per cent. legal tare.
in canisters, 40 lb. each.
in zeroons, 8 per cent.
in casks, 12 per cent. legal tare.

Sugar Candy, in tubs, 15 per cent.
in baskets, 5 per cent.
in boxes, 10 per cent. legal tare.

Tea, Bohea, in whole chests, 70 lbs. each, legal tare.
in half chests, 36 lb. each, legal tare.
in quarter chests, 20 lb. each, legal tare.

Hyson, Hyson Skin, and other green teas, in boxes of the usual size, of about 70 lb. gross, - - - - -
Young Hyson, in chests of common size, of about 80 lb. gross.
Imperial Gunpowder and Gomee, in chests, of the usual size, of above 110 *a* 115 lb. gross, - - - - - } 20 lb. each.

Hyson, Young Hyson, Imperial Gunpowder, and Gomee, in half chests, or in ten catty boxes. Real tare ascertained by starting.

Souchong, Compoy, and Congo, in boxes, weighing over 80 lbs. 22 lbs. each, legal tare.

Souchong, Compoy, and Congo, in boxes, weighing 80 lbs. and under.—20 lb. each, legal tare.

Tallow, in casks, 12 per cent.
in tubs, 15 per cent.
in zeroons, 18 per cent.

Tobacco, manufactured, real tare.

Twine, in bales, 3 per cent. legal tare.
in casks, 12 per cent. legal tare.
in boxes, 15 per cent.

Whiting, or Paris White, 12 per cent.

Wire, real tare.

ALLOWANCE FOR DRAFT.

Any quantity of 1 cwt. or 112 lbs.	1
above 1 cwt. and under 2 cwt.	2
2 cwt. and under 3 cwt.	3
3 cwt. and under 10 cwt.	4
10 cwt. and under 18 cwt.	7
18 cwt. and upwards,	9

ALLOWANCE FOR LEAKAGE AND BREAKAGE.

Importation in casks.—After gauging ale, beer, porter, brandy, gin, molasses, oil, rum, wine, and other liquors in casks, and taking off the real wants on landing, 2 per cent. more is deducted, before casting the duty. On this gauge, after deducting the wants on landing and the 2 per cent., the duty is paid, if there be entered afterwards for home consumption any wines or distilled spirits stored in the custom-house stores for the benefit of drawback.

Importation in bottles.—On ale, beer, and porter, in bottles, 10 per cent. is deducted for breakage, before casting the duty. On wine, and all liquors other than ale, beer, and porter, 5 per cent. is deducted, before casting the duty. The importer has a right to claim real breakage on ale, beer, porter, wine, and all other liquors, instead of the 10 or 5 per cent. above named; and if he thus claim it, from the collector, at the time he makes his entry at the custom-house, real breakage will be allowed. This is quite important for any article subject to fermentation.

Unless he make such a claim, he will be charged with duty as follows:

Per dozen of ale, beer, and porter, on $2\frac{2}{3}$ gallons, after having deducted either the 10 per cent. for breakage, or the real breakage—that is, on an invoice of 100 dozen, if he do not claim real breakage and real contents, he will be charged with a duty on 240 gallons.

Per dozen of wine, on $2\frac{1}{2}$ gallons, after having deducted either the 5 per cent. for breakage, or the real breakage.

On empty bottles imported in hampers, no breakage is allowed, unless claimed as damage at the time the importer makes his entry at the custom-house; and if thus claimed, the appraisers will be instructed to allow the real breakage.

Empty bottles imported in bulk are counted, and no duty is charged on the broken ones.

DISCOUNTS ON INVOICES.

In many places there are fixed prices for staple goods; and every year a certain discount is agreed upon as the standard discount. In such a case, the invoice must be made out at the short price.

The only discounts which are admitted to be entered, as discounts on the invoice, are such as the importer expressly states, on oath or affirmation, were actually and bona fide allowed to the owner or owners of the goods, in payment made for the same, before their shipment.

It is, therefore, necessary that the invoices should exhibit the true value without any discount, except such as may be actually and bona fide allowed, in payment made for the goods.

No discount is allowed at the custom-house on account of the bounty paid by the British government upon linens exported from that country, unless the cost of the said linens does not exceed eighteen pence sterling per yard.

12th. *Regulations for clearing vessels, and for the exportation of goods.*

The master of any vessel bound to a foreign port, must deliver to the collector a manifest of all the cargo on board, and the value thereof, by him subscribed, and swear or affirm to the truth thereof. Thereupon the collector grants a clearance for such vessel and her cargo, without specifying the particulars thereof in such clearance, unless required by the said master. If any vessel, bound to a foreign port, depart on her voyage without delivering such manifest, and obtaining a clearance, the master forfeits $500.[a]

---

[a] Act, 2d March, 1779, sec. 93.

The collector is not bound to grant a clearance, without a manifest, sworn to by the person in command of the vessel, be produced to him.[a]

In an action against the collector for refusing a clearance, the plaintiff may recover for loss of freight.[b]

Form of the report and manifest in note.*

The collectors, and other officers of the customs, must regard the inspection laws of the states in which they may respectively act, in such manner, that no vessel having on board goods liable to inspection can be cleared out, until the master or other proper person shall have produced a certificate that all such goods have been duly inspected as the laws of the respective states may require, to be produced to the

---

[a] 1 Peters' C. C. R. 406. [b] 3 Wash. C. C. R. 381.

* Report and manifest of the cargo, laden at the port of on board the master, bound for

Marks.	Numbers.	Packages or articles in bulk.	Contents or qualities.	Value at the port of exportation.

Oath to be taken by the Master:

District of

I, [insert the name,] master or commander of the [insert the denomination and name of the vessel,] bound from the port of [insert the name of the port or place sailing from,] to [insert the name of the place or port bound to,] do solemnly, sincerely, and truly swear, (or affirm, as the case may be,) that the manifest of the cargo on board the said [insert the denomination and name of the vessel,] now delivered by me to the collector of this district, and subscribed with my name, contains, according to the best of my knowledge and belief, a full, just, and true account of all the goods, wares, and merchandise now actually laden on board the said vessel, and of the value thereof: and if any other goods, wares, or merchandise, shall be laden or put on board the said [insert denomination and name of vessel,] previous to her sailing from this port, I will immediately report the same to the said collector. I do also swear, (or affirm,) that I verily believe the duties on all the foreign merchandise therein specified have been paid or secured, according to law, and that no part thereof is intended to be relanded within the United States; and that if, by distress or other unavoidable accident it shall become necessary to reland the same, I will forthwith make a just and true report thereof to the collector of the customs of the district wherein such distress or accident may happen. And I further swear, that the said merchandise is truly intended to be landed at

So help me God.

Form of a Clearance, to be granted to a vessel on her departure to a foreign port:

District of
Port of } *ss.*

These are to certify to all whom it doth concern, that master or commander of the burthen tons, or thereabouts, mounted with guns, navigated with men built, and bound for having on board hath here entered and cleared his said vessel according to law.

Given under our hands and seals, at the custom-house of this day of one thousand and in the year of the independence of the United States of America.

collectors, or other officers of the customs. Receipts for the payment of all legal fees which have accrued on any vessel, before any clearance is granted, must be produced to the collector or other officer.[a]

By the act to obtain accurate statements of the foreign commerce of the United States, passed February 10th, 1820, it is provided, that the owners or consignees of every armed vessel sailing out of the ports of the United States, belonging wholly or in part to citizens thereof, must enter into bond to the United States, with sufficient sureties, prior to clearing out, in double the amount of the value of the vessel and cargo, including her armament, that the said vessel shall not be employed by such owners to cruise or commit hostilities against the subjects, citizens, or property, of any foreign prince or state with whom the United States are at peace.[b]

The collectors of the customs are required to detain any vessel manifestly built for warlike purposes, and about to depart from the United States, of which the cargo principally consists of arms and munitions of war, when the number of men shipped on board, or other circumstances, render it probable that such vessel is intended to be employed by the owners to cruise or commit hostilities upon the subjects, citizens, or property, of any foreign prince or state with whom the United States are at peace, until the decision of the president be had thereon, or until the owners shall give such bond and security.[b]

Before a clearance can be granted for any vessel bound to a foreign place, the owners, shippers, or consigners of the cargo on board must deliver to the collector manifests of the cargo, or the parts thereof shipped by them respectively, and verify the same by oath or affirmation. Such manifests must specify the kinds and quantities of the articles shipped by them respectively, and the value of the total quantity of each kind of articles. The oath or affirmation states that such manifest contains a full, just, and true account of all articles laden on board of such vessel, by the owners, shippers, or consignors respectively, and that the values of such articles are truly stated, according to their actual cost, or the values which they truly bear at the port and time of exportation; and, before a clearance is granted for any such vessel, the master of every such vessel, and the owners, shippers, and consignors of the cargo must state, upon oath or affirmation, to the collector, the foreign place or country in which such cargo is truly intended to be landed.[c]

When foreign goods, entitled to drawback, are exported by the merchant who imported them, the amount of the drawback should be deducted from the cost, including freight, charges, duties, &c. The remainder being what the merchant actually pays for the goods, should be stated as the value of the foreign articles so exported.

When foreign goods, entitled to drawback, are exported by any other than the merchant who imported them, the price paid for them, unless by the amount of the debenture payable on their re-exportation, should be considered as the value.

---

[a] Act, 2d March, 1821, sec. 93. [b] Act, 3d March, 1825, sec. 10.
[c] Act, 11th Feb., 1820, sec. 11.

With respect to the amount of the value of foreign goods exported, and entitled to drawback, to be stated at the foot of the abstract, the same rule should govern,—for instance, if the value of an article, entitled to drawback, is, upon the above-mentioned principle, set down at $100, the same amount should be at the foot;—if articles of the same kind are re-exported, amounting to $100, and one half only are entitled to drawback, $50 should be stated as the amount so entitled, without any reference, in either instance, to the value set on the article when first imported for the purpose of securing the duties.

(EXAMPLE.)

	COTTON, PIECE GOODS.	
	Printed and coloured.	White.
Total amount exported,	Dollars. 35,329.	Dollars. 37,217
Exported, entitled to drawback, . . .	17,664 50	37,217
Exported, not entitled to drawback, . .	17,664 50	"

The table in note will enable every merchant to make out his outward entry and manifest conformably to the general plan of the treasury.

To each article exported is to be affixed the actual value of the quantity shipped, expressed in federal currency, at the time and place of exportation.

As to exports of foreign produce, the returns to the treasury are entirely conformable to the above plan, changing, of course, the words relative to imports into words for exports.

For domestic produce, the outward entry, as well as the outward manifest, is to be made to conform to the treasury form of quarterly returns.*

---

* *Owner, Shipper, or Consignee's Manifest:*

Manifest of the cargo, shipped by in the master, for 1822.

Marks.	Numbers.	Packages and kinds.	Quantities.	Value of articles at this port.

District of
Port of

I do solemnly to the best of my knowledge and belief, that the within manifest contains a full, just and true account of all articles laden on board the within named vessel, by and that the articles are truly stated according to their actual value, which they truly bear at this port, and time, and that the said articles are truly intended to be landed in the of

to, this 183 } before me, } So help me God.

Collector.

N. B.—Each shipper is to make out and sign such a manifest as this, to swear to it before the collector; and having duly sworn to it, take it to the clearance clerk.

13th. *Regulations for the coasting trade.*

American vessels engaged in the coasting trade, to become entitled to be placed on the most favourable footing, must be enrolled and licensed for the coasting trade.[a] The master, in all cases, must be an American citizen;[b] and if she is carrying on that trade from one state to another, provided it be not to an adjoining state on the sea coast, or in the same state, then at least three fourths of her crew must be American citizens, "or persons not the subjects of any foreign prince or state"—or she will be subject to a tonnage duty of fifty cents per ton, though this can be exacted but once a year.[c] The license may be surrendered at any time within the year, and a new one obtained by the owners, upon complying with the regulations of the licensing and enrolment act.[d]

When the master of a licensed vessel is changed, such change must be reported to the collector of the port where the change is made; and if there be none, then at the port where the vessel may next arrive. The collector, upon proof of the citizenship of the new master, and upon his taking an oath not to defraud the revenue, endorses the change upon the license.[e]

Any revenue officer may require the enrolment or license to be produced at any time; and the refusal to exhibit the same subjects the master to a fine of $100.[f]

Steamboats, intended to be employed in rivers or bays of the United States, may be enrolled or licensed, even if owned by aliens residing in the United States.[g]

A bond, with sureties in the sum of $1000, must, however, be given, that the steamboat shall not be employed in other waters than the rivers and bays of the United States.[h]

When the enrolment or license of a coasting vessel expires on a voyage to, or after her arrival at, another district, she is obliged to obtain a "temporary register," which is not surrendered until she arrives at the port to which she belongs. Hospital money is to be paid for all the time she was sailing under the "temporary register," as well as for the time she sailed under the enrolment or license.

By a law passed 2d March, 1819, vessels of twenty tons burthen, or upwards, licensed to trade between the different districts of the United States, are authorized to carry on the coasting trade between states in such districts, or adjoining states in different districts, or between the different districts, upon the same terms, and subject to the same regulations, as were then prescribed in trading between the districts then established.[i]

According to the above law, it is necessary for coasting vessels (except those from Georgia and Alabama) going from any port of the first or second district into the third, or vice versa, to enter and clear coastwise.

---

[a] Act, 1st March, 1817, sec. 4. [b] Act, 18th Feb., 1793, sec. 2. [c] Act, 1st March, 1817.
[d] Act, 18th Feb., 1793, sec. 8. [e] Ibid. sec. 12. [f] Ibid. sec. 13.
[g] Act, 3d March, 1817, sec. 1. [h] Ibid. sec. 2. [i] Act, 2d March, 1819, sec. 2.

It is always necessary for such vessels to clear and enter when going from the first to the second district.[a]

Licensed coasters of twenty tons burthen and upwards, may carry on such trade within the limits of either of the three great districts, without being obliged to clear or enter at the custom-houses, provided they have not on board either

Distilled spirits,	in casks,	exceeding	500 gallons.
Wine,	in do.	do.	250 do.
Do.	in bottles,	do.	100 dozen.
Sugar,	in casks or boxes,	do.	3,000 pounds.
Tea,	in chests or boxes,	do.	500 do.
Coffee,	in casks or bags,	do.	1,000 do.

Or foreign merchandise, in packages as imported, exceeding $400; or goods of foreign growth or manufacture, or of both, whose aggregate value exceeds $800.[b]

The masters of licensed vessels, having on board either of the above enumerated articles, except what may be necessary for sea stores; and masters of licensed vessels bound from a port in one of the great districts to a port in another great district, must, before sailing, make out and subscribe duplicate manifests of the whole of the cargo on board, stating the marks and numbers of every cask, bag, box, chest, or package containing the same, with the name and place of residence of the shippers and consignees, and the quantity shipped by and to each; which manifest must be delivered to the collector, if one resides within five miles, if not, to the surveyor, before whom he must swear that such goods were legally imported, and the duties paid or secured.

If there be no cargo on board, he must so state in the manifest. If there be distilled spirits on board, of foreign manufacture, the oath must state, that the duties thereon have been paid; and if more than sea stores, the numbers and marks must be specified in the manifest, as well as the names and residence of shippers and consignees.

The collector or surveyor then certifies, and returns one of the manifests to the master, with the permit, specifying the lading on board, and authorizing the vessel to proceed to her port of destination.[c] Within twenty-four hours after his arrival, he delivers his certified manifest to the collector or surveyor of the district, if within five miles, or within forty-eight hours if at a greater distance, and swears that there have been no other goods on board than those specified in the manifest since sailing from the district of departure.[d]

If there be no cargo on board, he produces a certificate of that fact from the collector or surveyor of the district whence she last sailed.[d]

If the certified manifest or permit be lost or mislaid, a bond must be given for the payment of duties on all foreign goods or distilled spirits on board, as if first imported, within six months.

---

[a] Act, March 2d, 1819. [b] Act, 18th Feb., 1793, sec. 15. [c] Ibid. sec. 16. [d] Ibid. sec. 17.

This bond is cancelled, upon producing a certificate from the collector of the port whence she sailed, that the goods were regularly imported.[a]

If any other goods have been taken on board or landed since her departure, the master must make known and particularize the same to the collector or surveyor; if not, he must so declare, upon his oath or affirmation;[b] whereupon a permit is granted for the landing of the cargo. If no collector or surveyor reside within five miles of the said port, the goods may be landed; but the master, upon arriving at the first port where a collector or surveyor resides, must, within twenty-four hours, deliver the said manifest, stating the times and places of the landing of the said goods, upon his oath or affirmation, under the penalty of $100.[c]

If he fails to clear, having distilled spirits or goods of foreign growth or manufacture on board, he is subject to a fine of $100; if the cargo be of goods of the growth or manufacture of the United States only, or if he have no cargo on board, he is subject to a fine of $50;[b] and if he does not enter, to a fine of $100; and the goods, wares, and merchandise, of foreign growth or manufacture, or distilled spirits found on board, or landed from such vessel, belonging to the master, owner, or mariners, are forfeited; and if the same amount, to the value of $800, such vessel, with her tackle, apparel, and furniture, is also forfeited. The collector or surveyor, upon his entrance, gives a permit for the landing of the cargo. If part of the goods enumerated above only be landed, an endorsement thereof is made by the collector on the manifest.[d]

The master of a coasting vessel is at all times bound to have a manifest of the cargo laden on board, whether it is of a nature to require him to enter and clear or not; and on failure thereof, if the lading of such vessel consists only of goods, the produce and manufacture of the United States, (distilled spirits excepted,) he is subject to a fine of $20.[e] If there be distilled spirits, or goods, wares, or merchandise, of foreign growth or manufacture on board, he is subject to a fine of $40;[f] if he refuses to inform any officer of the customs, from whence such vessel last sailed, and how long she has been in port, he is subject to a fine of $100; and if any of the goods laden on board such vessel, belonging to the master, owner, or mariners, be of foreign growth or manufacture, or spirits distilled within the United States, so much of the same as may be found on board not included in the manifest, are forfeited.[e]

If any goods of foreign growth or manufacture be found on board a coasting vessel, on which the duties have not been paid or secured, they are forfeited. Upon putting into a port other than the port of destination, the master must, within twenty-four hours after arrival, report to an officer of the customs, if any reside there, the arrival of the vessel, the names of the places he came from, and where bound, with an account of his cargo. Penalty for neglect, $20.

---

[a] Act, 18th Feb., 1793, sec. 23. [b] Ibid. sec. 16. [c] Ibid. sec. 15. [d] Ibid. sec. 17. [e] Ibid. sec. 18. [f] Ibid. sec. 22.

If vessels licensed for the fisheries are found within three leagues of the coast with foreign goods on board, exceeding $500 in value, without a permit, they are liable to seizure, with the foreign goods.[a]

Where licensed vessels, bound to a district in the same or an adjoining state, have on board only domestic produce or manufactures, or distilled spirits not more than five hundred gallons, wine in casks not more than two hundred and fifty gallons, or in bottles not more than one hundred dozen, sugar in casks or boxes not more than three thousand pounds, tea in chests or boxes not more than five hundred pounds, coffee in casks or bags not more than one thousand pounds, or foreign merchandise in packages, as imported, of not more value than $400, or goods, consisting of such enumerated or other articles of foreign growth or manufacture, or of both, whose aggregate value shall not be more than $800, the master need not deliver a manifest thereof, or obtain a permit, previous to her departure, or on her arrival make any report; but such master must be provided with a manifest, by him subscribed, of the lading which was on board at the time of his departure from the district from which she last sailed; and if the same or any part consists of distilled spirits, or goods of foreign growth or manufacture, with the marks and numbers of each cask, bag, box, chest or package containing the same, with the name of the shipper and consignee of each, such manifest must be by him exhibited, for the inspection of any officer of the revenue, when thereunto required. He must also inform such officer from whence such vessel last sailed, and how long she has been in port. If the master be not provided, on his arrival, with a manifest, and exhibit the same, as required, if the lading consist wholly of goods the produce or manufacture of the United States, (distilled spirits excepted,) he forfeits $20; or if there be distilled spirits, or goods of foreign growth or manufacture on board, excepting sea-stores, he forfeits $40; or if he refuse to answer the interrogatories truly, he forfeits $100. If any of the goods are of foreign growth or manufacture, or of spirits distilled within the United States, so much of the same as may be found on board such vessel not included in the manifest, are forfeited.[b]

The collector of the district of Pennsylvania may grant permits for the transportation of goods, of foreign growth or manufacture, across the state of New-Jersey to the district of New-York, or across the state of Delaware to any district in Maryland or Virginia; and the collector of the district of New-York may grant like permits for transportation across the state of New-Jersey; and the collector of any district of Maryland or Virginia, like permits for transportation across the state of Delaware. Such permit must express the name of the owner, or person sending such goods, and of the consignee, with the marks, numbers and description of the packages, and the kind of goods contained therein, and the date when granted; and the owner or person sending such goods must swear or affirm, that they were legally imported, and the duties thereupon paid or secured. The owner or consignee of such goods, within twenty-four hours after

---

[a] Act, 10th Feb., 1793, sec. 21. [b] Ibid. sec. 18.

their arrival, must report the same to the collector of the district where they arrive, and must deliver up the permit. If he neglect or refuse to make entry within the time and in the manner herein directed, all such goods are forfeited. If the permit be not given up within the time limited, the person to whom it was granted forfeits $50 for every twenty-four hours it shall be withheld. Where the goods are of less value than $800, the said oath and permit are not to be deemed necessary, nor is the owner or consignee obliged to report to the collector.[a]

Masters employed in the transportation of goods from district to district, that put into a port other than the one to which they are bound, must, within twenty-four hours, if there be an officer residing at such port, make report of their arrival to such officer, with the name of the place they came from, and to which they are bound, with an account of their lading, under the penalty of $20.[b]

If the master of any vessel have lost or mislaid the certified manifest, or the permit which was given therefor, the collector of the district where he arrives must take bond for payment of the duties on the goods of foreign growth or manufacture, or distilled spirits, within six months, in the same manner as though they were imported from a foreign country. Such bond is cancelled, if the said master cause to be delivered to the collector taking such bond, and within the term therein limited for payment, a certificate from the collector or surveyor of the district whence he sailed, that such goods were legally exported in such vessel, from such district.[c]

The master of every foreign vessel, bound from a district in the United States to any other district within the same, must, previous to her departure, deliver to the collector duplicate manifests of the lading on board, or if there be none, he must so declare; and to the truth of such manifests or declaration he must swear or affirm, and also obtain a permit from the said collector, authorizing him to proceed to the place of his destination. The master of every such vessel, on his arrival within any district from any other district, must, within forty-eight hours after his arrival, and previous to unlading any goods, deliver to the collector of the district a manifest of the goods on board, or if in ballast only he must so declare, and to the truth of which manifest or declaration he must swear or affirm; and also, that such manifest contains an account of all the goods which were on board such vessel at the time, or have been since her departure from the place whence she sailed. He must also deliver to such collector the permit which was given him from the collector of the district. If the master neglect so to do, he forfeits $100.

Goods subject to an ad valorem duty, shipped coastwise.—If in the original packages in which they were imported, they must be accompanied by an invoice, or a copy thereof, or an extract therefrom sworn to by the importer, as in the case of goods imported before the collector with whom they were entered, and certified by the same collector.

---

[a] Act, 18th Feb. 1793, sec. 19. [b] Ibid. sec. 22. [c] Ibid. sec. 23.

This invoice and certificate must be produced at the port to which they are transported; and the goods are subject to inspection and appraisement, as if they had been imported directly from abroad.

No appraisement, however, can be made, so as to change the amount of duties charged at the original port of entry, unless there were no government appraisers at such port.

If the invoice be not produced, the goods will be placed in the public store at the expense of the owner, until it be produced.[a]

This certificate must accompany all shipments of goods coastwise, although not shipped for the benefit of drawback.

If they are not in the original packages in which they were imported, they should be accompanied by the oath of the shipper taken before the collector, stating the fact, and that the duties thereon have been paid, or secured to be paid, according to law.

14th. *Collection districts, and local regulations.*

The Atlantic coast of the United States is divided into three great districts, which are again divided into smaller or collection districts. In the following table will be found a description of the different collection districts, with an account of the principal local regulations.

---

[a] Act, 20th April, 1818.

PORTS OF ENTRY AND DELIVERY.

COLLECTION DISTRICTS.—The following table shows the Collection Districts, as now established, with the various local regulations. As alterations have been made almost every session, the dates of the statutes making the alterations have not been inserted. A general reference will, perhaps, be deemed sufficient by the most curious reader, which will be found at the end of the table.

The following table shows the districts of each state; their names and extent; ports of entry and delivery, distinguishing those for foreign vessels, and those for such as arrive from the Cape of Good Hope, and beyond; residences of collectors, naval officers, and surveyors; with remarks, showing where first to come to, deposit manifests, enter, &c.

EXPLANATION OF THE TABLE.

The words printed in Roman capitals, thus, BOSTON, designate those places where a collector, naval officer and surveyor reside; those in Italic capitals, thus, *GLOUCESTER*, where a collector and surveyor reside; those in small capitals, thus, MARBLEHEAD, where a collector resides; those in Italics, thus, *Beverly*, the places of residence of surveyors. Ports of entry and delivery for foreign vessels are marked thus, †; ports of entry for vessels from the Cape of Good Hope, and beyond, thus, ‡. Foreign armed vessels are permitted to enter only such harbours as are marked thus, §, except when in distress, or pressed by an enemy.

N. B. The entry must always be made within the time limited by law; but may, in all cases, be with the collector of the district where the vessel is owned, or from which she may have sailed on the voyage from which she shall have returned. Foreign ships, however, can enter only in the district of delivery.

☞ All ports of entry are ports of delivery.

MAINE—12 Districts.

Names and extent of Districts.	*Ports of Entry.*	*Ports of Delivery.*	*Remarks and Directions.*
1st. Kennebunk: comprehending the towns of Wells and Arundell, and the shores and waters thereof.	‡ KENNEBUNK.	‡ KENNEBUNK, Wells, Cape Porpoise.	May proceed to her port of delivery, and enter at port of entry afterwards.
2d. York.	YORK.	YORK.	See the remarks under Portsmouth, New-Hampshire.
3d. Saco.	†‡ SACO, BIDDEFORD.	†‡ SACO, BIDDEFORD. Scarborough.	May proceed to her port of delivery, and enter at port of entry afterwards.
4th. Portland and Falmouth.	†‡§ *PORTLAND* and †‡ Falmouth.	†‡§ *PORTLAND*, †‡ Falmouth, North Yarmouth, Brunswick, Freeport, Harpswell.	If bound to a port of delivery only, in this district, except North Yarmouth, Freeport and Harpswell, must first come to at the port of entry, enter, report, &c. See Newburyport and law.
5th. Bath.	†‡ BATH.	†‡ BATH, Hallowell, Pittstown, Georgetown, Brunswick, Boudoinham.	If bound to a port of delivery only, in this district, except Georgetown and Brunswick, must first come to at the port of entry, enter, report, &c.
6th. Wiscasset.	† WISCASSET.	† WISCASSET, Booth-Bay.	Vessels belonging to the towns of Edgcomb and Newcastle, in the state of Maine, having entered at Wiscasset, and taken an officer on board, may unlade in the parts of those towns which adjoin Sheepscut river.

MAINE continued—12 Districts.

Names and extent of Districts.	*Ports of Entry.*	*Ports of Delivery.*	*Remarks and Directions.*
7th. Belfast, and all the waters and harbours on the W. shore of Penobscot bay, from Cambden to Bangor, both inclusive.	†BELFAST.	† BELFAST, *Bangor*. Prospect.	May proceed to her port of delivery, and enter at port of entry afterwards.
8th. Penobscot.	†‡ CASTINE, ‡ Penobscot.	†‡ CASTINE, Frankfort, Bluehill, Hampden, Deer Island.	Ditto.
9th. Frenchman's Bay.	† FRENCHMAN'S BAY.	† FRENCHMAN'S BAY, Union River.	Ditto. The custom-house in this district is at Ellsworth.
10th. Machias.	†MACHIAS.	† MACHIAS.	Ditto.
11th. Passamaquoddy.	PASSAMAQUODDY.	PASSAMAQUODDY, *Eastport*, Calais, Pembroke.	Ditto.
*12th Waldoborough: all the waters and shores from the middle of Damarascotty river, to the southerly side of the town of Northport.	WALDOBOROUGH.	WALDOBOROUGH, Bristol, Nobleborough, Warren, Thomaston, Cushing, Cambden, and that part of Ducktrap between Campden and Northport.	Ditto.

NEW-HAMPSHIRE—1 District.

District of Portsmouth: the whole state to the northern boundary line, and also the towns of Kittery and Berwick, in Maine. The district of White Mountains, created by a law of March, 1811, reannexed to this district, by a law passed May 7th, 1822.	†‡ PORTSMOUTH.	†‡ PORTSMOUTH, Newcastle, Dover, Exeter, Kittery, and Berwick.	Vessels bound to the district of Portsmouth may proceed to their port of delivery, and enter at a port of entry afterwards; if bound to Kittery or Berwick, may, at the option of the master, enter at York, in Maine, and take permits to land from him.

* Within Maine the collector of the several districts, whose limits are not marked out by the act, are from time to time to agree upon divisional lines, and transmit them to the comptroller of the treasury: such divisions, so agreed upon, include all the waters, shores and islands within the same, and all the lands adjoining the British colonies of New-Brunswick and Lower Canada, within the state of Maine; in case of disagreement, the President of the United States determines the divisions.

MASSACHUSETTS—13 Districts.

Names and extent of Districts.	*Ports of Entry.*	*Ports of Delivery.*	*Remarks and Directions.*
1st. Newburyport: from the State of New-Hampshire, to the north line of Ipswich.	†‡ NEWBURYPORT.	†‡ NEWBURYPORT, Almesbury, Salisbury, Haverhill, Newbury.	If bound to a port of delivery only, must first come to at the port of entry, report, enter in writing, and pay or secure all legal duties, port fees, charges, &c., before proceeding to the port of delivery.
2d. Ipswich.	IPSWICH.	IPSWICH.	May proceed to her port of delivery, and enter at port of entry afterwards.
3d. Gloucester: all the waters and shores in the towns of Gloucester and Manchester.	†‡ *GLOUCESTER.*	†‡ *GLOUCESTER* and Manchester.	Bound to the district of Gloucester, may proceed to the port of delivery, and report and enter at port of entry afterwards, within the time prescribed by the act of March 2d, 1799.
4th. Salem and Beverly: all the waters and shores within the towns of Beverly, Salem and Danvers.	†‡ SALEM, †‡ *Beverly.*	†‡ SALEM, †‡ *Beverly* and Danvers.	May proceed to her port of delivery, and enter at port of entry afterwards.
5th. Marblehead: the waters and shores within the town of Marblehead.	†‡ *MARBLEHEAD.*	†‡ *MARBLEHEAD.*	Ditto.
6th. Lynn.	† LYNN.	† LYNN.	
7th. Boston and Charlestown: all the waters and shores within the counties of Middlesex, Suffolk, and Norfolk.	†‡§ BOSTON, †‡ Charlestown.	†‡§ BOSTON, †‡ Charlestown, Medford, Cohasset, Hingham, Dorchester, Weymouth, Roxbury and Cambridge.	Ditto.
8th. Plymouth: all the waters and shores within the county of Rochester, excepting the towns of Wareham and Rochester.	†‡ PLYMOUTH.	†‡ PLYMOUTH, Scituate, Duxbury, Kingston, Marshfield.	Ditto.
9th. Barnstable: all the waters and shores within the county of Barnstable.	BARNSTABLE.	BARNSTABLE, Sandwich, Falmouth, Hardwick, Wellfleet, Provincetown, Chatham.	Ditto.
10th. Nantucket: the island of Nantucket.	†‡ PORT OF NANTUCKET.	†‡ PORT of NANTUCKET.	Ditto.
11th. Edgarton: all the waters and shores within the county of Dukes.	†‡ EDGARTON.	†‡ EDGARTON.	Ditto.
12th. New-Bedford: all the waters and shores within New-Bedford, Dartmouth, Westport, Rochester and Wareham, together with all the islands within the county of Bristol.	†‡ NEW-BEDFORD.	†‡ NEW-BEDFORD, Westport, Rochester, Wareham.	Ditto.
13th. Fall river: all the waters and shores on Taunton river, and in the town of Rehoboth.	† FALL RIVER, formerly Dighton.	† FALL RIVER, Swansey, Freetown, Berkely, Taunton.	Ditto.

PROVIDENCE and RHODE-ISLAND—4 Districts.

Names and extent of Districts.	*Ports of Entry.*	*Ports of Delivery.*	*Remarks and Directions.*
1st. Newport: all the waters, shores, bays, harbours, creeks and inlets from the west line of the state and along the sea coast, and northward up the Narraganset Bay, as far as the most southerly part of Warwick Neck, and from thence nearly a northward course, to the south end of Rumstick Point, at high water mark, and includes the several towns, harbours, and landing places of Westerley, Charleston, South Kingston, North Kingston, East Greenwich, and all that part of Warwick south of Warwick Neck; and also all the towns, harbours and landing places of Tiverton, Little Compton, and all other towns, landing places and harbours of the island of Rhode Island, Jamestown, Prudence, New-Shoreham, and every other place and island within the states southward of Warwick Neck and Rumstick Point.	†‡ NEWPORT.	†‡ NEWPORT, *North Kingston*, *East Greenwich*, *Pawcatuck* river in Westerley, *Tiverton.*	May proceed to her port of delivery, and enter at port of entry afterwards.
2d. Providence: all the waters, shores, bays, harbours, creeks and inlets, within the state of Rhode-Island, northward of a line running nearly north-east, from the south end of Warwick Neck to the south end of Rumstick Point, at high-water mark, including only the waters bounded by the east and west shores of said Rumstick Point and Warwick Neck, leading up the bay of the port of Providence.	†‡ PROVIDENCE.	†‡ PROVIDENCE, *Patuxet.*	Ditto.
3d. Bristol: that town, and all the shores and waters round the same, in the following limits, viz.—a line beginning at the middle of the bay between Mount Hope and Common-Sense Point, running south-westwardly through the middle of Bristol Ferry, and continuing such course until it strikes a point of equal distance between Rhode-Island and Prudence-Island, from thence northwardly on a straight line to the westernmost part of Nahant Point, except what is included within the district of Warren and Barrington.	†‡ *BRISTOL.*	†‡ *BRISTOL.*	Ditto.
4th. Warren and Barrington: towns of Warren and Barrington, and all the shores and waters round the same, in the following limits, i. e. a line drawn west from Bluff Point, on Pawpoose Square Point, to intersect the line dividing Bristol district from Providence district,	†‡ WARREN.	†‡ WARREN.	Ditto.

CONNECTICUT—5 Districts.

Names and extent of Districts.	*Ports of Entry.*	*Ports of Delivery.*	*Remarks and Directions.*
1st. New-London: from the east line of Connecticut to Lyme, including that place and the several towns or landing places of Stonington and Groton.	†‡§ *NEW-LONDON.*	†‡§ *NEW-LONDON*, *Stonington*, Lyme, Groton.	Must proceed to the port of entry, enter, report, &c. unless bound to the port of Stonington. The surveyor at Saybrook may inspect vessels bound to Lyme.
2d. Norwich: including that town, and all the territory between the south line thereof and the north limits of New-London district.	NORWICH.	NORWICH.	
3d. New-Haven: from the west line of the district of New-London westwardly to Oufatumnick river.	†‡ *NEW-HAVEN.*	†‡ *NEW-HAVEN*, Guilford, Branford, Milford, Derby.	May proceed to the port of delivery, and enter at port of entry afterwards.
4th. Fairfield: all places and ports in Connecticut west of the district of New-Haven.	†‡ FAIRFIELD.	†‡ FAIRFIELD, Norwalk, Stratford, Stamford, Greenwich.	Ditto.
5th. Middletown: the towns and landing places of Saybrook, Killingsworth, Haddam, East Haddam, Middletown, Chatham, Weathersfield, Glastonbury, Hartford, East Hartford, Windsor and East Windsor.	†‡ *MIDDLETOWN.*	†‡ *MIDDLETOWN*, *Saybrook*, Killingsworth, Haddam, East Haddam, Middletown, Chatham, Weathersfield, Glastonbury, *Hartford*, East-Hartford, Windsor, and East Windsor.	Must proceed to the port of entry, enter and report, except bound to Saybrook, Killingsworth, Haddam and East Haddam. ☞Observe—vessels from foreign ports, or having on board goods on which the duties have not been secured, bound to any port of Connecticut river, must take on board an inspector at Saybrook, and if bound to any district of this state, and coming through Sandy-Hook, must leave a manifest of her cargo on board, with the collector of New-York, under the penalty of $500.

NEW-YORK—8 Districts.

1st. Sag Harbour: all the bays, harbours, rivers and shores within the two points of Oyster Pond and Mantauck.	SAG HARBOUR.	SAG HARBOUR.	
2d. New-York: all parts of the coasts, rivers, bays and harbours of the state, which are not included in the other districts.	†‡§ NEW-YORK, Albany.	†‡§ NEW-YORK, New-Windsor, Newburgh, Poughkeepsie, Esopus, Kinderhook, *Albany*, Hudson, Troy, Rhinebeck.	May proceed to the port of delivery, and enter at port of entry afterwards. N. B. The President of the United States may appoint, if he deem it expedient, one other surveyor, to reside at such other place than Albany, as he may think fit.

NEW-YORK continued—8 Districts.

Names and extent of Districts.	*Ports of Entry.*	*Ports of Delivery.*	*Remarks and Directions.*
3d. Champlain: all such shores and waters of Lake Champlain, and the rivers connected therewith, as lie within the state of New-York, extending westwardly along the northern boundary line of the state, to the place where it is bounded by the River St. Lawrence.	Port and residence of a collector to be appointed by the President of the United States.	Ports and residences of two surveyors to be appointed by the President of the United States.	May proceed to port of delivery, and enter at port of entry afterwards. Masters of steam-boats on Lake Champlain, bound into Lower Canada, may deliver a manifest of the cargo on board, or take a clearance from the collector of the district through which she shall last pass when leaving the United States, without regard to the place of her commencing the voyage, or of landing. When the duties on goods imported shall have been secured, the goods may be landed in any part of the district, or in any other next the lake.
4th. St. Lawrence: all the shores and waters of the St. Lawrence in the state of New-York, east of the west boundary of the county of St. Lawrence, and west of the western boundary of Champlain district.	OGDENSBURGH.	OGDENSBURGH, Waddington.	
5th. Oswego: all the shores and waters of the River St. Lawrence, from the western boundary of St. Lawrence county, and all the shores and waters of Lake Ontario, and the rivers and waters connected therewith, within the state of New-York, to the west of Sodus bay.	OSWEGO, SACKETT'S HARBOUR, CAPE VINCENT.	OSWEGO, SACKETT'S HARBOUR, CAPE VINCENT.	May proceed to the port of delivery, and enter at port of entry afterwards. By the language of several statutes it would seem that Cape Vincent and Sackett's Harbour were separate districts, but as the statutes describing their boundaries cannot be found—they are included in the Oswego district.
6th. Rochester: all the shores and waters of Ontario, within the state of New-York, from the western extremity of Sodus bay to the eastern extremity of Oak Orchard Creek.	ROCHESTER.	ROCHESTER.	Ditto.
7th. Niagara: all the shores and waters of Lake Ontario, and the waters connected therewith, within the state of New-York, to the westward of the west bank of Genesee River.	LEWISTOWN.	LEWISTOWN.	Ditto.
8th. Buffalo: all the shores, rivers, and waters that empty into Lake Erie, or the River Niagara, within the state of New-York.	BUFFALO.	BUFFALO.	Ditto.

VERMONT—1 District.

Names and extent of Districts.	*Ports of Entry.*	*Ports of Delivery.*	*Remarks and Directions.*
The whole state, to include all such shores and waters of Lake Champlain, and the rivers connected therewith, as lie within the said state, and shall also extend along the northern boundary line of the state, adjoining to the British colony of Lower Canada.	Derby, Allburg.	Not to be more than two, and appointed by the President of the United States.	By the act of 2d March, 1799, the President was authorized, at his discretion, to divide this into 2 districts.

NEW-JERSEY—6 Districts.

1st. Newark: all that part of New-Jersey lying north and east of Elizabethtown and Staten Island, extending eastward as far as the mouth of the Kill Van Kull, where it empties into New-York Bay, together with the Passaic and Hackensack Rivers.	† NEWARK.	† NEWARK, Jersey City.	Jersey City is declared to be in Newark district by a treasury circular: by the law it is placed within the district of New-York.
2d. Perth-Amboy; all that part of New-Jersey, known by the name of East New-Jersey, (except what is within Newark and Little Egg Harbour district,) together with all the waters thereof, in the jurisdiction of that state.	†‡ PERTH-AMBOY.	†‡ PERTH-AMBOY, *New Brunswick*, Middletown-Point, Elizabethtown, and Newark.	May proceed to the port of delivery, and enter at port of entry afterwards.
3d. Burlington: that part called West New-Jersey, to the eastward and northward of the county of Gloucester, with all the waters thereof, formerly in the jurisdiction of the same state.	† BURLINGTON, LAMBERTON.	† BURLINGTON, LAMBERTON.	Must, before passing Philadelphia, deposit with the collector there a manifest of the cargo on board, and receive an inspector on board if ordered; may then proceed to the port of delivery, and enter afterwards at the port of entry, under penalty of $500.
4th. Bridgetown: the counties of Gloucester, Salem, Cumberland, and Cape May, (excepting the parts of Gloucester and Cape May within Great Egg Harbour district,) and all the waters thereof, heretofore within the jurisdiction of the said state.	BRIDGETOWN.	BRIDGETOWN, Salem, Port Elizabeth, on Maurice river, *Camden*.	May proceed to the port of delivery, and enter at port of entry afterwards. The surveyor of Camden is authorized to grant enrolments and licenses to all vessels owned north of Alloway's Creek.
5th. Great Egg Harbour: the river of Great Egg Harbour, with all the inlets, bays, sounds, rivers and creeks along the sea coast, from Brigantine Inlet to Cape May.	Somers' Point.	Somers' Point.	
6th. Little Egg Harbour: all the shores, waters, bays, rivers and creeks from Barnegat Inlet to Brigantine Inlet, both inclusively.	TUCKERTON.	TUCKERTON.	

PENNSYLVANIA—2 Districts.

Names and extent of Districts.	*Ports of Entry.*	*Ports of Delivery.*	*Remarks and Directions.*
1st. Philadelphia: all the shores and waters of the river Delaware, and the rivers and waters connected therewith, lying within the state of Pennsylvania.	†‡§ PHILADELPHIA.	†‡§ PHILADELPHIA, *Delaware City.*	The limits of the port of entry and delivery of Philadelphia are, the navy yard on the south, and on the north, Gunner's Run.
2d. Presque-Isle: all the shores and waters of Lake Erie, and the rivers and waters connected therewith, within the state of Pennsylvania.	PRESQUE-ISLE.	PRESQUE-ISLE.	

DELAWARE—1 District.

The whole state.	†‡ WILMINGTON.	†‡ WILMINGTON, † Newcastle, † Port Penn, *Delaware City.*	May proceed to port of delivery, and enter at port of entry afterwards.

MARYLAND—7 Districts.

1st. Baltimore: Patapsco River, Turkey Point, Spes Utiæ Island, all the waters and shores on the west side of Chesapeake Bay, from the mouth of Magetty River; Chester River, all the waters and shores on the east side of Chesapeake Bay, from the south side of Elk River, and Wye River inclusive.	†‡ BALTIMORE.	†‡ BALTIMORE, † CHESTER, Georgetown, on Sassafras River, HAVRE-DE-GRACE, Port Deposite.	Ditto.
2d. Oxford: all the waters and shores on the east side of Chesapeake Bay, from the north side of Wye River, and the eastern Bay, to the south side of Great Choptank River, inclusive.	† OXFORD.	† OXFORD, Cambridge, Easton.	Ditto.
3d. Vienna: all the waters and shores on the eastern side of Chesapeake Bay, from the south side of Great Choptank River, to the south side of Hooper's Point; Hayne's Point, Wycomico River inclusive.	† VIENNA.	† VIENNA, Salisbury.	Ditto.
4th. Snowhill: all the waters and shores on the sea coast, from the north line of Virginia to the south line of Delaware, together with all the waters and shores on the eastern side of Chesapeake Bay, from the south side of Pocomoke River inclusive, as far as the state of Maryland extends.	† SNOWHILL.	† SNOWHILL, Sinnipuxent, for the West India trade only.	Ditto.

MARYLAND continued—7 Districts.

Names and extent of Districts.	*Ports of Entry.*	*Ports of Delivery.*	*Remarks and Directions.*
5th. Annapolis: Magetty River, and all the waters and shores from thence to Drum Point, on Patuxent River, together with the said river, and all the navigable waters emptying into the same.	†‡ ANNAPOLIS.	†‡ ANNAPOLIS. †NOTTINGHAM. Benedick, Lower Marlborough, *Town Creek*, Sylvey's landing.	May proceed to port of delivery, and enter at port of entry afterwards. But must, before passing Town C eek, deposit a manifest of the cargo on board, and r ceive an inspector on board if ordered, with the surveyor there, under the penalty of $5 0.
6th. St. Mary's: all the waters of the Potowmack, within the jurisdiction of the state of Maryland, from Point Look-out to Pomonky Creek, inclusive.	† ST. MARY'S.	† ST. MARY'S, † *Nanjemoy*, Cedar Point, *Lewellensburgh.*	May proceed to port of delivery, and enter at port of entry afterwards.
7th. Georgetown: all the waters and creeks from Pomonky Creek, on the north side of the Potowmack, to the head of the navigable waters of the said river, within the jurisdiction of the state of Maryland.	†‡ GEORGETOWN.	†‡ GEORGETOWN, † Digge's Landing, † Carrolsburg.	Ditto. See Alexandria.

VIRGINIA—9 Districts.

1st. Norfolk and Portsmouth: all the waters, shores, bays and inlets, within the southern boundary of the state, to the mouth of James River; thence up the south side of James River to Hood's, inclusively, and up Elizabeth River to the highest tide water thereof; and all the waters, shores, bays, harbours, and inlets, between the south side of the mouth of York River, and along the west shore of Chesapeake Bay, thence up the northern side of Chicahominy River.	†‡§ NORFOLK, †‡ Portsmouth.	†‡§ NORFOLK, †‡ Portsmouth, *Suffolk*, *Smithfield.* † *Hampton*, South Quay.	Must first come to at the port of entry, report, enter, &c. When bound to South Quay, or to any port of the state to the south of Cape Henry, must deposit with the collector of Edenton, before passing that place, a manifest of the cargo on board.
2d. Petersburgh: Petersburgh itself, City Point, all the waters, shores, bays, harbours and inlets of James River, from Hood's, and the junction of the Chicahominy, to the junction of the James and Appamattox Rivers; from thence to the highest tide water of Appamattox, and also to the highest tide water mark of the Chicahoming. ☞ The preceding word is so spelt in the act.	From *PETERSBURGH* to † *City Point.*	The same as the port of entry.	A revenue cutter is stationed off Norfolk to board vessels bound up James River, and to endorse their manifests, and place a revenue officer on board. When not boarded by the revenue cutter, masters with a foreign cargo on board must deposite with the surveyor at Hampton a copy of the manifest, and an inspector is to be received on board if ordered. If the vessel has goods on board for this district, and that of Richmond also, the master must deliver duplicate manifests at the time of her entry, one to be forwarded to the collector of the other district, under the penalty of $500. The vessel in this case must be entered in the district where her owner, consignee, or acting manager resides.

VIRGINIA continued—9 Districts.

Names and extent of Districts.	*Ports of Entry.*	*Ports of Delivery.*	*Remarks and Directions.*
			The delivery of the goods is authorized by permits from the collector of the district in which the goods were entered. All entries made by agents for persons residing in other districts, must be made in the district where the vessel may discharge.
3d. Richmond: Richmond itself, Manchester, and Bermuda Hundred, and all the waters, shores, bays, harbours and inlets of James River, from Bermuda Hundred, including the harbour thereof, to the highest tide water of James River.	From *RICHMOND* and Manchester to † *Bermuda Hundred.*	The same as the port of entry.	The same regulations are to be adopted on going to any district up James River, above Sewall's Point. If the vessel has goods on board for this district and that of Petersburgh, she must deliver duplicate manifests at the time of entry, one to be forwarded to the collector of the other district. Vessels consigned to persons in Richmond, and loaded in whole or in part in the district of Petersburgh, may be cleared out at Richmond. N. B. By the old law at Bermuda Hundred, City Point, and Rocket's Landing, foreign vessels, not from the Cape of Good Hope and beyond, might enter, &c. and unlade; the act dividing that district, does not specify any alteration in this respect; it is presumed, therefore, that the law is as before.
4th. Yorktown: All the waters, shores, bays, harbours and inlets, between the point forming the south shore of the mouth of Rappahannock River, and the point forming the south shore of the mouth of York River, and thence up the said river to West Point, and thence up the Pamunkey and Mattapong Rivers to the highest navigable waters thereof.	† YORKTOWN.	† YORKTOWN, † *West Point*, Cumberland.	Must first come to at the port of entry, report, enter, &c.
5th. East River; all the waters, shores, &c. of the North and East Rivers, Mobjack Bay, and all other navigable waters, shores, &c. within the county of Matthews.	The President to appoint the port of entry and delivery.		
6th. Tappahannock: all the waters shores, harbours, bays and inlets, between Smith's Point, at the mouth of Potomack River, and the point forming the south shore of the Rappahannock River, up to its highest tide water; Yeocomico River and Kinsale, and from Smith's Point, on the south side of the Potomack, including all the waters, shores, bays, harbours, creeks and inlets along the south shore of Potomack River to Cockpit Point.	† TAPPAHANNOCK.	† TAPPAHANNOCK, † *Urbanna*, † *Port Royal*, † *Fredericksburgh*, including Falmouth, *mouth of Rappahannock River*, Yeocomico and † Kinsale, DUMFRIES, † Newport.	Must first come to at port of entry, report, enter, &c. unless bound to Urbanna or Edenton, but must always, before passing Urbanna, deposit a manifest of the cargo on board, and receive an inspector on board, if ordered, with the surveyor there, under penalty of $500.

VIRGINIA continued—9 Districts.

Names and extent of Districts.	*Ports of Entry.*	*Ports of Delivery.*	*Remarks and Directions.*
7th. Alexandria; all the waters, bays, shores, harbours, creeks and inlets, on the south side of the Potowmack, from Cockpit Point to the highest tide water.	†‡ *ALEXANDRIA.*	†‡ *ALEXANDRIA.*	Articles inspected in one part of the District of Columbia are not subject to a second inspection in any other port in that district.
8th. Folly landing; all the waters, shores, bays and harbours of the county of Accomack.	Folly Landing; collector to reside at Accomack court-house.	Folly Landing.	
9th. Cherrystone; all the waters, bays, shores, harbours and inlets, within Northampton county.	CHERRYSTONE.	CHERRYSTONE.	

NORTH-CAROLINA—8 Districts.

1st. Wilmington; all the waters, shores, bays, harbours, creeks and inlets, from Little River Inlet, inclusive, to New River Inlet inclusive.	†‡ WILMINGTON, Smithville.	†‡ WILMINGTON, Smithville.	
2d. Newbern; all the waters, shores, bays, harbours, creeks and inlets, from Dog Island, together with that part of Pampticoe sound, which lies southward and westward of the shoal projecting from the mouth of Pampticoe river towards Royal shoal, and southward of the same.	†‡ NEWBERN.	†‡ NEWBERN, *Swansborough.* The President of the United States may establish a port of delivery, either at Shellcastle or at Beacon island.	May proceed to the port of delivery, and enter at port of entry afterwards.
3d. Beaufort: all the water and shore north and east of the said town to Harbour Island, and south and west of the said town to Dog Island inclusive.	† BEAUFORT.	† BEAUFORT.	
4th. Washington: all that part of Pampticoe sound not included in Newbern district, as far north as the marshes.	†‡ WASHINGTON TOWN.	†‡ WASHINGTON TOWN.	
5th. Ocracocke, to include Ocracocke Inlet, Shell and Beacon Islands, and all the other shores, islands, bays, waters and shoals, within two miles of said inlet, on each side thereof.	The port of entry designated by the President. N. B. Vessels coming in at Ocracocke Inlet, and obliged to employ lighters before they pass the Royal shoal. They may enter at any port of entry connected with the waters where bound; and if coming in ballast, for the purpose of loading with-		No duties shall be paid, or secured to be paid, in this district, upon articles bound to another port connected with the waters of this inlet, unless upon goods cast away within the district. Vessels arriving must be reported to the collector, who shall superintend the unloading of all vessels from which goods must be discharged in lighters; all such goods shall be secured by fastenings under the seal of the collector, who gives permits, describing the goods, vessel, owners of the goods, and port of destination. The masters of the lighters give triplicate receipts, and if the goods should not be transported to the port of destination, unavoid-

NORTH-CAROLINA continued—8 Districts.

Names and extent of Districts.	*Ports of Entry.*	*Ports of Delivery.*	*Remarks and Directions.*
	out the shoals, at any port connected with the waters of the inlet.		able accidents excepted, or if the seals or fastenings should be broken, the master forfeits $500. These deliveries are endorsed by the collector on the original manifests of the vessels to be exhibited to the collector of the interior district.
6th. Edenton; all the waters, bays, harbours, creeks, and inlets, from the marshes, inclusive, northward and westward, except those included in the district of Cambden.	†‡ EDENTON.	†‡ EDENTON, *Hertford*, *Murfreesborough*, Princeton.	If intending to proceed to Plymouth, Windsor, Murfreesborough, or Princeton, must come to and enter at Edenton; if bound to Hertford, may proceed there, report, enter, &c. afterwards at port of entry.
7th. Plymouth; the rivers Roanoak and Cashie, and all the waters and harbours belonging thereto.	† *PLYMOUTH.*	† *PLYMOUTH, Windsor.*	
8th. Cambden; North River, Pasquotank and Little Rivers, all the waters, shores, bays, harbours, creeks and inlets, from the junction of Currituck and Albemarle sounds, to the north extremity of Black Bay.	† ELIZABETH CITY, on Pasquotank river.	† ELIZABETH CITY, on Pasquotank river, *Currituck.*	May proceed to her port of delivery, and enter at port of entry afterwards.

SOUTH-CAROLINA—3 Districts.

1st. Georgetown: all the shores, inlets and rivers, from the boundary of North-Carolina, to the point of Cape Romain.	†‡ GEORGETOWN.	†‡ GEORGETOWN.	May proceed to the port of delivery, and enter afterwards at port of entry.
2d. Charleston: all the shores, inlets and rivers, from Cape Romain to Combahee river, inclusive.	†‡§ CHARLESTON.	†‡§ CHARLESTON.	
3d. Beaufort: the shores, inlets and rivers, from Combahee River to Dick River, in Georgia.	†‡ BEAUFORT.	†‡ BEAUFORT.	

GEORGIA—5 Districts.

1st. Savannah; all the waters, shores, harbours, rivers, bays, creeks and inlets, from the said river to the north point of Ossabaw Island, and Great Ogeechee River, inclusive.	†‡ SAVANNAH.	†‡ SAVANNAH, and by permit from the collector, any other place within the district.	An inspector is to be taken on board, if a permit to land any where but at the port of delivery, be granted, and the collector think it necessary.
2d. Sunbury, and all the waters, shores, harbours' rivers, creeks, bays and inlets, south of the north point of Ossabaw Island and Great Ogeechee River, exclusive, and north of the south point of Sapelo Island, inclusive, except such part as is included in Hardwicke district.	†‡ SUNBURY.	†‡ SUNBURY, and by permit from the collector, any place within the district.	Ditto.

GEORGIA continued—5 Districts.

Names and extent of Districts.	*Ports of Entry.*	*Ports of Delivery.*	*Remarks and Directions.*
3d. Brunswick; all the waters, shores, harbours, creeks, bays and inlets, from the south point of Sapelo Island, exclusive, to the south point of Jekyl Island, inclusive.	† DARIEN.	† DARIEN, *Brunswick*, Frederica, and by permit, from the collector, any other place in the district.	May proceed to the port of delivery, and enter at the port of entry afterwards; if a permit be granted to land at any other place than the port of delivery, the collector may order an inspector on board.
4th. Hardwicke: all the waters, shores, bays, harbours, creeks and inlets, between the south point of Ossabaw Island and the south point of Warsaw Island.	HARDWICKE.	HARDWICKE.	
5th. St. Marys: all the waters, islands, shores, bays, harbours, creeks and inlets, from the south point of Jekyl Island, exclusive, to the river St. Mary.	† ST. MARYS.	† ST. MARYS, and by permit, any other place in the district.	If a permit be granted to land at any other place than the port of delivery, the collector may order an inspector on board.

FLORIDA—6 Districts.

1st. St. Johns: all the ports, harbours, shores and waters in Florida, and of the islands opposite thereto, from St. Marys to the south side of St. Johns.	ST. JOHN.	ST. JOHN.	
2d. St. Marks; all the ports, &c. from Ochlockney Bay to Charlotte Harbour.	MAGNOLIA.	MAGNOLIA.	
3d. St. Augustine: all the ports, harbours, shores and waters, of Florida and of the islands opposite and nearest thereto, from the river St. John to Cape Sable.	†‡ St. Augustine.	†‡ St. Augustine.	
4th. Key West: all the ports, &c. from Cape Sable to Tampa Bay.	‡ KEY WEST.	† Key West.	
5th. Apalachicola: all the ports, &c. from Tampa Bay to Cape St. Blas.	† APALACHICOLA.	† APALACHICOLA.	
6th. Pensacola; residue of the ports, &c. of Florida.	†‡ *PENSACOLA.*	†‡ *PENSACOLA.*	

ALABAMA—1 District.

Mobile: all the shores, inlets, and waters of Mobile bay, and of the rivers, &c. emptying into the Gulf of Mexico, east of Mobile River, and west thereof to the eastern boundary of Louisiana.	†‡ Mobile.	†‡ Mobile.	

LOUISIANA—2 Districts.

Names and extent of Districts.	*Ports of Entry.*	*Ports of Delivery.*	*Remarks and Directions.*
1st. Mississippi; all the waters, shores and inlets, of the river Ohio, with the rivers, shores, and waters connected therewith; all the waters, shores, and inlets of the river Mississippi, and all other navigable rivers and waters connected therewith, lying within the jurisdiction of the United States; and all the navigable waters, rivers, creeks, bays and inlets, within the United States, emptying into the Gulf of Mexico, lying west of the eastern boundary of the state of Louisiana, and east of the Atchafalaya, except those comprehended within the collection districts of Teche, Natchez and Pearl River.	†‡ NEW-ORLEANS.	†‡ NEW-ORLEANS, *Pittsburg*, *Louisville*, *Bayou St. John*, Charlestown, Marietta, Cincinnati, Limestone, Massac, Wheeling, Nashville, St. Louis, Port Ponchartrain, Vermilion.	The surveyor at Louisville gives a temporary register, which can be changed at New-Orleans, and a permanent register obtained, upon the usual conditions. Must come to at the port of entry, report, &c., take an inspector on board if ordered, under penalty of $500. Vessels trading at Bayou St. John, may clear out at New-Orleans and enter, the same as if they came by the way of the Mississippi. If bound to any other port in this district, must report, enter, and take an inspector on board at New-Orleans, before proceeding to her port of delivery, under penalty of $500. All vessels bound to Port Ponchartrain must report and enter at New-Orleans, and also clear out at New-Orleans. When foreign goods are to be imported into Pittsburg, Wheeling, Cincinnati, Louisville, St. Louis, Nashville, or Natchez, the importer should deposite in the hands of the surveyor at the place of destination a schedule of the goods, and their cost. Notice is then given by the surveyor to the collector at New-Orleans, with an estimate of the duties, and also that a bond is given therefore. The goods, upon their arrival at New-Orleans, are entered and left with the collector, until reshipped, with duplicate manifests, up the Mississippi; upon their arrival at the port of destination, the goods are inspected, and compared with the manifests.
2d. Teche: all the shores, bays, and rivers, within the United States, to the west of Atchafalaya, including the river Teche.	FRANKLIN.	FRANKLIN, *Vermilion.*	

MISSISSIPPI—2 Districts.

Names and extent of Districts.	*Ports of Entry.*	*Ports of Delivery.*	*Remarks and Directions.*
1st. Natchez: all the ports, shores, and waters of the Mississippi, within the state of Mississippi.	Natchez.	Natchez.	All vessels boun l to Natchez must be reported at New-Orleans, where a custom-house officer is put on board, whose expenses to Natchez, and returning to New-Orleans, are paid by the owner of the vessel.
2d. Pearl River: all the bays, waters, and shores on Lake Borgue and the Gulf of Mexico, and all the rivers empting therein within the limits of the state of Missisippi.	At such place at the mouth of Pearl River as the President shall designate.		

NORTH WESTERN STATES and TERRITORIES —9 Districts.

1st. Cleveland: all the waters, shores, and inlets of Lake Erie, within the jurisdiction of the United States, and the rivers and waters connected therewith, from the west line of the state of Pennsylvania to the west bank of Vermilion River.	Cuyahoga.	Cuyahoga, Fairport.	Goods not prohibited may be imported into these districts in vessels or boats of any burthen, and in rafts and carriages of any kind, which must, however, be reported to the custom-house officer of the district, accompanied with like manifests, and otherwise subject to the same regulations as if imported by sea. When the goods are imported for the purpose of being immediately exported to some place out of the United States, the owner in his entry must specify the route, portage, and carrying-place, over which it is intended to transport them. After due search and inspection, a certificate or protection for the goods is given by the collector, to remain in force for six months. Any person attempting to defraud the revenue, by breaking open or unpacking the goods on their passage, defacing the seal, &c. shall forfeit $500, and be imprisoned not more than six months.
2d. Sandusky: all the shores and rivers of Lake Erie, within the United Sates, from the western bank of Vermilion River to the western cape of Sandusky Bay.	Portland.	Portland.	
3d. Miami: all the shores and rivers of Lake Erie, within the United States, from the western cape of Sandusky to the north cape of Miami Bay.	President to designate ports of entry and delivery.		

NORTH WESTERN STATES and TERRITORIES continued—9 Districts.

Names and extent of Districts.	*Ports of Entry.*	*Ports of Delivery.*	*Remarks and Directions.*
4th. Detroit: all the shores and inlets of the Lakes Erie, St. Clair, and Huron, within the jurisdiction of the United States, and the rivers and waters connected therewith, and north and west of Miami Bay, as far as Presque Isle and Lake Huron.	DETROIT.	DETROIT.	The President of the United States may establish two others, with a surveyor for each.
5th. Michigan: all the territory between the south shore of Grand Traverse Bay, on lake Michigan, and the most northerly point of Indiana on Lake Michigan.	ST. JOSEPH.	ST. JOSEPH.	Two other places may be designated by the President as ports of delivery.
6th. Indiana; all the shores of Lake Michigan, between the south boundary of Michigan and the east boundary of Illinois, where it intersects the lake.	MICHIGAN CITY.	MICHIGAN CITY.	
7th. Illinois: all the territory in that state bordering on Lake Michigan.	CHICAGO.	CHICAGO.	Another port of delivery may be appointed by the President.
8th. Wisconsin: all the shores of Lake Michigan, north of Illinois and south of Menominee River.	MILWAUKEE.	MILWAUKEE.	Ditto.
9th. Michilimakinac; the island of that name, and the land adjoining, ceded by the treaty of Greenville; all the waters, shores, and inlets, to the westward and northward of the Lakes Michigan and Superior, and the rivers, waters, shores, and lakes connected therewith, lying within the jurisdiction of the United States, unto the northern and northwestern boundaries thereof, and also all the territory between the south shore of Grand Traverse Bay on Lake Michigan, and Presque Isle, Lake Huron.	To be established by the President of the United States, at or near Michilimakinac, and to be the residence of the collector.	Three, besides that of entry, with a surveyor at each, to be appointed by the President of the United States.	

☞ Vide law of March 2d, 1821, relative to the Northwestern District, in this chapter, part 4.

The statutes prescribing and altering the preceding districts are as follows:

March 2, 1799.
May 10, 1800.
Feb. 18, 1801.
Feb. 25, 1801.
March 2, 1801.
March 3, 1801.
March 16, 1802.
May 1, 1802.
May 3, 1802.
March 3, 1803.
Feb. 24, 1804.
March 27, 1804.
Jan. 11, 1805.
March 3, 1805.
Jan'y. 11, 1806.
Jan. 22, 1806.
March 8, 1806.
April 21, 1806.
Feb. 13, 1807.
Dec. 15, 1807.
April 25, 1808.
March 2, 1811.
March 2, 1811.
July 22, 1813.
April 9, 1814.
April 24, 1816.
April 26, 1816.
March 1, 1817.
March 3, 1817.
March 9, 1818.
April 11, 1818.
April 18, 1818.
April 20, 1818.
March 2, 1821.
March 3, 1821.
March 30, 1822.
April 17, 1822.—Two acts.
May 7, 1822.—Two acts.
May 26, 1824.
March 3, 1825.—Two acts.
Feb. 22, 1827.
March 2, 1828.
Jan. 21, 1829.
March 23, 1830.
March 31, 1830.—Two acts.
May 20, 1830.
May 28, 1830.
March 2, 1831.—Two acts.
July 13, 1832.—Two acts.
Feb. 5, 1833.
March 2, 1833.
June 30, 1834.

N. B. For Tariff of duties *vide* Appendix.

15th. *Drawbacks.*

Upon the exportation to a foreign country, not immediately adjoining the United States, of goods, by a vessel actually cleared out *within three years*[a] from the entry of the vessel in which they were imported, a drawback of the duties will be allowed, provided the exporter complies with the formalities required by law, and that the amount of duties on each exportation is not less than $50 of the same importation.[b]

Before the act of Jan. 6, 1836, the collector made a deduction of two and a half per cent. on the drawback before paying it to the exporter, but that act authorized the payment of the whole duty.

Goods exported for drawback must be exported in the original cask, chest, or package in which they were imported.[b]

To secure the drawback on wines and spirits, they must be kept while on shore under the keys of the custom-house.[c] They may, however, be sent coastwise, for the purpose of being immediately laden on board of a vessel for exportation, without being sent to the public store. The transferring from one vessel to another, however, must be by order of the collector, and under the superintendence of an inspector, who examines the same as to identity, quality, quantity and packages.[d]

No drawback is allowed on the following goods, viz: chain cables, butter, whale and fish oil, playing cards, salted provisions, foreign dried, pickled, or salted fish.[e] Nor is any drawback allowed on the ten per cent. additional duty imposed upon goods imported in certain foreign vessels.[e]

In order to entitle goods imported to the benefit of drawback, they must be landed.[f]

Goods may be transported coastwise into two other districts,[g] and still remain entitled to debenture.[h] By the original act allowing drawback, this privilege was limited to a transportation into one district besides the district of original importation; but by acts subsequently passed, it is extended to two districts.

To secure that privilege, a coastwise entry must be made before shipping the goods; the entry handed to the debenture clerk. The importer must swear to it before the collector; a permit, obtained for shipping, to accompany the entry, and handed to the surveyor, who will direct the permit to a shipping officer; and when the shipping officer has made his return, the coastwise certificate for debenture is given, which must be sent to the person to whom the goods are consigned.

For ad valorem goods, state in the outward coastwise entry; and cause to be stated in the coastwise certificate for debenture the value of each package separately.

Goods transported from one district to another, with benefit of drawback, must be accompanied with a copy of the invoice of the cost certified by the collector, which must be produced to the collector who clears out the goods for exportation.[i]

---

[a] Act, 6th Jan., 1829, sec. 1. [b] Act, 2d March, 1799, sec. 75.
[c] Act, 20th April, 1818, sec. 4. [d] Act, 1st March, 1823, sec. 34.
[e] Act, 27th April, 1816, sec. 4. [f] 1 Wash. C. C. R. 158. [g] Act, 1st March, 1823, sec. 28.
[h] Act, 12th Feb., 1831. [i] Act, 1st March, 1823, sec. 29.

The consignee, before the landing of the goods, must make an inward coastwise entry at the custom-house of the port of landing; swear to it before the collector; get a permit for the landing of the goods; call on the surveyor to direct this permit to the proper officer; and see that nothing be landed, except in presence of this officer.

Goods may be transported coastwise, by land, for the benefit of drawback, between Boston and Newport, via Taunton and Rhode-Island Bridge,[a] between Boston and Charlestown, Salem and Beverly, and Newburyport and Ipswich, and Marblehead, by the turnpike or other main road;[b] between Boston and Providence, by the post-road,[c] and between Boston and Bristol, (R. I.) by the way of Dighton and Taunton.[d]

Goods may be transported coastwise, for the benefit of drawback, partly by water and partly by land, from the port of Philadelphia or Delaware district, by the way of Burlington, Bordentown, Lamberton or New-Brunswick, and South Amboy, to New York; or from the port of New-York by the way of South Amboy, New-Brunswick or Lamberton, Bordentown or Burlington, to Philadelphia or Delaware district[c]; or from the port of Philadelphia or Delaware district, by way of Wilmington, Newport, Christiana Bridge, New-Castle, Port Penn, or Apoquinimink, and Sassafras river,[e] and Elkton, Frenchtown or Bohemia, to Baltimore; or from the port of Baltimore, by the way of Elkton, Bohemia, or Frenchtown, and Port Penn, Apoquinimink, and Sassafras river, New-Castle, Christiana Bridge, Newport or Wilmington, to Philadelphia or Delaware district.[b]

By an act passed Feb. 12, 1831, authority was given to transport goods with the benefit of drawback partly by land and partly by water, or wholly by land, from the district of importation into two other districts, from either of which the goods may be exported.[f]

The same regulations and formalities relating to the transportation from one district to another, must be complied with upon the transportation from the second to the third district. Those conditions are, upon loading and unloading the vehicle in which the goods are transported, the same as loading or unloading vessels where goods are transported coastwise for the benefit of drawback. Besides those, due entry must be made with the collector of the district, from which it is intended to transport any merchandise, and the collector causes the merchandise so entered to be inspected and marked in durable characters, by an officer of the customs, with the name of the officer, and the date of such inspection, and grants a permit for the transportation thereof; therein designating the route, and expressing the marks, numbers and contents of each chest, bale, box, or other package, and all other particulars, to be inserted in a certificate for the transportation coastwise, of goods entitled to drawback; and whenever he may deem the same necessary for the security of the revenue, he may cause each chest, bale, box, or other package, to be secured with proper fastenings, or under the seal of his office—and

---

[a] Act, 25th April, 1810. [b] Act, 3d March, 1804. [c] Act, 2d March, 1799, sec. 79.
[d] Act, 6th Feb., 1818. [e] Act, 27th Feb., 1801. [f] Act, 12th Feb., 1821.

within twenty-four hours after the arrival of the goods so transported, report and entry must be made to the collector of the district of destination, as in the case of goods transported coastwise. The permit is then surrendered, and the goods inspected and compared therewith. If any merchandise so permitted to be transported be transported by any other route than that expressed in the permit, or be not accompanied with the said permit, or if due entry be not made at the port of arrival, and if the permit be not surrendered, or if the said merchandise be unpacked, or the contents, or any part thereof, changed before entry and inspection at the port of arrival, or if any mark, fastening or seal, placed thereon by direction of any officer of the customs, be defaced or broken, in each and every such case the merchandise, in respect to which such omission or wrong doing shall happen, or the value thereof, is forfeited, and may be recovered of the person making default in either case.[a]

When goods subject to an ad valorem duty are transported coastwise by land, or partly by land and partly by water, for the benefit of drawback, it is necessary that each package should be marked with the date of shipment and the signature of the inspector. The numbers upon the packages of goods subject to specific duty need not be inserted in the coastwise or other certificates, unless a separate certificate be required for each package.[b]

When making an importation coastwise, the importer should preserve the custom-house certificate which was granted at the port of importation, after the collector has put upon it the date of the importation. It is necessary to produce this certificate, at the time of exportation for a foreign port, to get the drawback.

When goods, subject to an ad valorem duty, are transported coastwise, for the benefit of drawback, the safest plan is, to put, in the coastwise certificate, the value of each package separately.

On shipping goods to foreign ports, for the benefit of drawback, the exporter must go to the collector's room in the custom-house, with an "outward foreign entry, for the benefit of drawback;" get the importer to swear to it; then hand the entry to the debenture clerk; have a permit to accompany the entry; hand it to the surveyor, who will direct it to the shipping officer; see that no article be put on board except in the presence of the shipping officer; and furthermore, articles liable to a specific duty must not be shipped, until a weigher and gauger has certified, on the entry, the weight or gauge.

All goods entered for re-exportation with right of drawback, whether in the original district of importation or in another district, must be inspected and compared with the original invoices, and if found not to agree therewith, they are forfeited. The original invoice must be deposited with the collector when the goods are entered, and an authenticated copy signed by the person entering them, with his oath attached, preserved in the custom-house.[c]

After the vessel has cleared out, the exporter must go to the debenture clerk; receive the entry; swear to it, before the collector; sign

---

[a] Acts, 2d March, 1799, sec. 79, and 18th Feb., 1793, sec. 19.
[b] Act, 1st March, 1823, sec. 33. [c] Act, 28th May, 1830, sec. 5.

the debenture bond, and get some responsible person to sign this bond with him, and receive his debentures or his debenture certificate. All this must be done within twenty days from the date of the clearance of the vessel.

If either of these formalities be neglected, the exporter loses the debenture.

By the act of 1st March, 1823, persons who had reshipped goods entitled to debenture for transportation coastwise before the necessary certificates were issued by the collector, were allowed to enter them in the district to which they were transported, with benefit of drawback, provided they produced within two months thereafter, and before entry for exportation, a certificate from the collector of the port from which the goods came, that the coastwise certificates were not issued at the time when the vessel in which they were transported sailed.[a]

The exporter, too, in case he has neglected to complete his entry by taking the oath or giving the bond, may obtain permission to complete the same from the secretary of the treasury.

The application to the secretary must be sworn to, and must be accompanied by a statement from the collector of all the circumstances.[b]

The entries should state the marks, numbers, quantities and contents; the name of the vessel and of the captain in which the original importation was made; the date of importation, and the place where from; the name of the vessel and of the captain in which the exportation is made, and where bound, specifying some particular port or place; to whom the goods were sold and delivered, if they have been sold; and if imported coastwise, by what vessel or wagon, what captain or driver, and the date of the coastwise importation.

No drawback is allowed on sail duck, unless the quantity exported in one shipment amounts to fifty bolts;[c] nor on cordage, unless the quantity amounts to five tons.[d]

In entering outward wines and spirits for drawback, the importer, in addition to the date of the entry of the vessel, should state the dates and number of bonds given on receiving his various permits.

The debentures are paid by the collector, on the payment of the bonds for the duties on the same goods.

When the exportation is from the district in which the importation was made, debentures are issued. But when the goods have been transported coastwise, they issue a certificate of exportation; with which, at the port of importation, the debentures are obtained.

Both the debentures and the certificates are issued payable to the order of the exporter, and are transferred, by endorsement and delivery, the same as a note of hand, or bill of exchange.[e]

Goods shipped to any state or territory immediately adjoining that of the United States, except to ports situated to the westward or southward of Louisiana, are not entitled to drawback.[f]

---

[a] Act, 1st March, 1823, sec. 31. [b] Act, 3d March, 1825. [c] Act, 19th May, 1828, sec. 4.
[d] Act, 14th July, 1832, sec. 11. [e] Act, 2d March, 1799, sec. 80.
[f] Acts of 2d March, 1799, sec. 75, and 5th Jan. 1805.

Drawback, however, is allowed on goods shipped to the northwest coast of America.

No drawback is allowed on exportations made in vessels less than thirty tons burthen; and none unless the goods are exported by sea.[a]

No drawback is allowed on any article, unless the vessel in which the exportation is made, is actually cleared out within three years from the date of the entry of the vessel in which the importation was made.

Drawback is allowed on exportation only from the district of original importation; or from a district in which vessels can enter from the Cape of Good Hope, and places beyond the same.[b]

By the act of 7th May, 1822, Florida is placed on the same footing, as to the allowance of drawbacks, as the rest of the United States.[c]

A broken package, or a cask or case of which a part has been sold, is not entitled to drawback.

Exporters of any liquors in casks, or any unrefined sugars, may fill up the casks or packages out of other casks or packages included in the same original importation, or into new casks or packages corresponding therewith, to be marked and numbered as the original casks or packages, in case the original casks or packages, in the opinion of the officer appointed to examine the same, be so injured as to be rendered unfit for exportation, and in no other case. The filling up or change of package must be done under the inspection of a proper officer of the port from which such liquors, coffee, or unrefined sugars are intended to be exported; and the drawback on articles so filled up, or of which the packages have been changed, shall not be allowed without such inspection.[d]

Where articles are imported in bulk, they must be exported in the packages in which they were landed; for which purpose, the officer delivering the same returns the packages with their marks and numbers. They are not entitled to drawback, unless exported in such packages, nor unless they fully agree with the return made by the said officer; and in respect to distilled spirits, or wines, the certificates issued by the inspector of the revenue must be given up; and the drawback is not allowed on any spirits or wines that do not agree on examination with the certificates so given up.[d]

Any goods may be transferred into other packages from those in which they were imported, by permission of the collector.[e]

Notice having been given to the collector, of the necessity, he appoints an inspector to ascertain if such necessity exists; and if found necessary, the inspector superintends the transfer, and marks and numbers the new packages in the same manner as the old were marked.[e]

In order to entitle the exporter of any goods to the benefit of drawback, he must, previous to putting the same on board of any vessel for exportation, give twenty-four hours' notice to the collector

---

[a] Act, 2d March, 1799, sec. 92.
[b] Ibid. sec. 77.
[c] Act, 7th May, 1822, sec. 10.
[d] Act, 2d March, 1799, sec. 75.
[e] Act, 1st March, 1823, sec. 32.

of the district from which the same are about to be exported, of his intention to export the same, (unless in the case of distilled spirits, when six hours' notice is sufficient,) and make entry in writing of the particulars thereof, and of the casks and other packages or parcels containing the same, and of their respective marks, numbers, and contents; and if imported articles, the name of the vessel and master's name in which, the person for or by whom, and the places from which they were imported; also the district into which the said goods were imported, if other than the district from which they are intended to be exported.[a]*

Proof must be made to the satisfaction of the collector and naval officer, if any, by the oath of the persons (including exporters) through whose hands the goods have passed, according to the best of their knowledge and belief, respecting the due importation of the goods according to law, and in conformity to such notice of their identity, and of the payment, or securing the duties. In case of the actual sickness or absence of the importer or other person through whose hands the goods have passed, and not otherwise, the proof required of them may be accepted from their known agent, or the person who usually transacts their business. The collector directs the surveyor, where any, to inspect the goods.[a]†

In inspecting goods entered for exportation, with drawback, they

---

[a] Act, 2d March, 1799, sec. 76.

**Form of Entry:*

Entry of merchandise intended to be exported by [here insert the name or names,] on board of the [insert the denomination and name of the vessel,] whereof [insert the name of the master] is master, for [insert the port or place to which destined,] for the benefit of drawback, which were imported into the district of [insert the district of original importation,] on the [insert the date of importation,] by [insert the name of the importer,] in the [insert the denomination and name of the vessel,] from [insert the foreign port or place whence they were imported,] and brought into the district on the [insert the date of the vessel's entry,] in the [insert the denomination and name of the vessel and master,] from [insert the port from whence they arrived.]

Marks.	Numbers.	Packages and contents.	Net cost of ad valorem articles having paid duties.	Weight or gauge.	Tare and draft, or allowance for leakage.

†*Form of the direction to inspect the said goods; and permit for lading for exportation.*

District of
Port of

The surveyor will cause the articles specified in [insert the name of the person making entry] entry to be examined, and if found to agree exactly therewith, will have them (weighed, gauged, or measured, as the case may require,) and then permit the same to be laden on board the [insert the denomination and name of the vessel, and the master's name,] master, for [insert the port of destination,] for benefit of drawback.

A. B., Collector.
C. D., Naval Officer.

To the surveyor of the port of

must be compared with the original invoices.[a] If found to agree therewith, the collector, together with the naval officer, if any, grants a permit for lading the same on board of the vessel named in such notice and entry; which lading must be performed under the superintendence of the officer by whom the same have been inspected. The exporter likewise makes oath that the goods, previous to the clearance, or within ten days thereafter, are truly intended to be exported

---

[a] Act, 28th May, 1830, sec. 5.

Where the persons making entry, as aforesaid, are the persons by whom the merchandise were originally imported:

I, [insert the name,] do solemnly, sincerely and truly swear, (or affirm,) that the articles specified in the above or annexed entry, were imported by me, (or consigned to me, as the case may be,) in the [insert the denomination and name of the vessel,] whereof [insert the name] was master, from [insert the name of the port or place where from,] that they were duly entered by me, at the custom-house of this port, and the duties paid, (or secured to be paid thereon, as the case may be;) that they are the same in quantity, quality and package (and value, if articles paying an ad valorem duty) as at the time of importation, necessary or unavoidable wastage or damage only excepted, and are now actually laden on board the [insert the denomination and name of the vessel,] whereof [insert the name] is master; and that they are truly intended to be exported by me in the said vessel to the port of [insert the name of the port or place,] and are not intended to be relanded within the limits of the United States.

So help me God.

Oath to be taken by the importer, when goods are sold, to be exported by another person:

I, [insert the name,] do solemnly, sincerely and truly swear, (or affirm,) that the articles specified in the above or annexed entry, as imported by, (or consigned to me, as the case may be,) were truly imported by, or consigned to me, in the [insert the denomination or name of the vessel,] whereof [insert the name] is master, from [insert the port or place;] that they were duly entered by me at the custom-house of and the duties thereon paid, (or secured to be paid, as the case may be;) that they were the same in quantity, quality and package, necessary or unavoidable wastage or damage only excepted, (and value, if articles paying an ad valorem duty,) at the time of sale or delivery to [insert the name of the person or persons to whom sold or destined,] as at the time of importation.

So help me God.

Oath to be taken where goods are exported by a person other than the importer:

I, [insert the name,] do solemnly, sincerely and truly swear, (or affirm,) that the articles specified in the above or annexed entry, were purchased by me, of [insert the name of the person or persons from whom purchased,] that they are now actually laden on board of the [insert the denomination and name of the vessel,] whereof [insert the name] is master, and were at the time of such lading, and are now, the same in quantity, quality, and package, necessary or unavoidable wastage or damage only excepted, (and value if articles paying an ad valorem duty,) as at the time of purchase; that they are truly intended to be exported by me, in the said vessel, to the port of [insert the name of the port or place,] and are not intended to be relanded within the limits of the United States.

So help me God.

Oath to be taken by any other person than the importer or exporter of merchandise, who may have bought and sold the same, or in whose possession the same may have been:

I, [insert the name,] do solemnly, sincerely and truly swear, (or affirm,) that the articles of merchandise specified in this entry, were purchased by me from [insert the name of the person from whom purchased,] and were sold by me to [insert the name of the person to whom sold,] and that they were not, to the best of my knowledge or belief, altered, or in any respect changed, in quantity, quality, value, or package, necessary or unavoidable wastage or damage only excepted, while in my possession, or from the time of said purchase until the time of said sale.

So help me God.

to the place whereof notice has been given, and are not intended to be relanded within the United States.[a]

When goods are transported into another district, with benefit of drawback, they must be accompanied with a certificate from the collector of the district, and naval officer, if any, into which they were originally imported, specifying the marks, numbers, and descriptions of the casks or other packages, with the names of the master and vessel in which, the time when, and the place from whence they were imported; and where the articles are subject to duty, by weight, measure, or gauge, the quantity thereof; and where they are articles subject to duty ad valorem, the net amount of each package, on which duty has been paid or secured to be paid; and in all cases, the amount of the duties paid or secured, and by whom, and the names of the vessel and master in which they are shipped from such district, and by whom; and in order to entitle any person to such certificate, he must make out an entry of all such merchandise,* specifying the marks, numbers, and descriptions of the casks or packages and their contents, the names of the master and vessel in which, the time when, by whom, and the place from which they were imported; the names of the master and vessel in which they are intended to be laden, and district in the United States to which they are destined; and prove the truth of such entry, in like manner as is required for merchandise exported from a district of original importation; the collector and naval officer, if any, then grants such certificate. Such goods must be entered with the collector of the district into which they shall be brought from the port of original importation, by the persons so importing them, or to whom they may be consigned, specifying the names of the master and vessel in which, and the district from whence they are imported, together with the particulars of the packages, their marks, numbers, and their contents. A permit must be obtained for the same previous to the landing or unlading thereof; and any merchandise landed without such entry being made, and permit obtained, is not entitled to drawback.[b]

---

[a] Act, 2d March, 1799, sec. 76. [b] Ibid. sec. 77.

* *Form of an entry of goods to be transported coastwise, for the benefit of drawback.*

Entry of merchandise intended to be shipped by [insert the name or names,] on board the [insert the denomination and name of the vessel,] whereof [insert the name] is master, for [insert the port and district where bound,] to be exported from thence for the benefit of drawback, which were imported into this district on the [insert the date of the vessel's entry in which they were imported,] by [insert the name of the importer,] in the [insert the denomination and name of the vessel, and the master's name,] from [insert the name of the foreign port or place.]

Marks.	Numbers.	Packages and contents.	Cost of articles paying duty ad valorem.	Weight or gauge.	Tare and draft, or allowance for leakage.

When the entry is made, the exporter makes an oath that the duties have been paid or secured.[a] *

[a] Act, 2d March, 1779, sec. 77.

Form of a certificate for the transportation coastwise:

District of

Port of

We certify, that the merchandise hereinafter specified, which are now shipped by on board the of master, bound for the port of were duly imported into this district, on the day of by in the of master, from and the duties thereon paid, or secured to be paid, according to law.

Tare allowed.	Marks.	Numbers.	Packages, contents, value, and rates of duty collected or secured.	Amount of duties.
			Here insert each package in detail, the contents, quality and value, if articles subject to duty ad valorem, with the rates of duty collected or secured, as the case require.	

The amount of duties paid or secured being dollars.

A. B., Collector.
C. D., Naval Officer.

* *Form of an entry for goods arriving coastwise, accompanied with a certificate:*

Entry of merchandise transported coastwise, for [insert the name or names of the consignee,] in the [insert the denomination and name of the vessel,] whereof [insert the name] is master, from [insert the name of the port or district,] for the purpose of being exported from the district of, [insert the district in which they are to be unladen,] for the benefit of drawback; which were imported in the district of [insert the district of original importation,] on the [insert the date of importation,] by [insert the importer's name,] in the [insert the denomination and name of the vessel, and master's name,] from [insert the foreign port or place from whence imported.]

Marks.	Numbers.	Packages.	Contents.

Form of Oath:

I, [insert the name,] do solemnly, sincerely and truly swear, (or affirm,) according to the best of my knowledge and belief, that the entry by me subscribed is just and true; that the merchandise therein mentioned have been duly imported, and the duties thereupon paid, or secured to be paid, according to law.

Form of a permit for unlading goods transported coastwise, for the purpose of obtaining a drawback:

Port of

Permit [insert the name of the person making the entry,] to land, from on board the [insert the denomination and name of vessel, and name of master] master, from [insert the port and district from which arrived, and the number of packages and contents, with their marks and numbers, agreeably to the entry,] having been brought coastwise from thence, for the purpose of being exported from this district, for the benefit of drawback.

A. B., Collector,
C. D., Naval Officer.

To the Surveyor of the port of

When any merchandise, subject to drawback, is entered for exportation from any other district than the one into which they were originally imported, the person intending to export the same, besides producing the certificate before directed, must give the same notice, and make entry in like manner, and the merchandise must undergo the same examination, and be laden on board under the same regulations, as if exported from the place of original importation.[a]

For all merchandise entitled to drawback exported from the district into which they were originally imported, the exporters are entitled to receive from the collector debentures for the amount of the drawback, payable at the same times, respectively, on which the duties become due. And the collector must discharge such debentures out of the product of the duties arising on the importation of the goods exported.[b]

In respect to any merchandise on which the whole or part of the duties have been paid prior to an entry for exportation, the debenture for the amount of the drawback of such duties as shall have been paid, is made payable in 15 days from the time of signing the bond. All debentures are made payable to the original importer of the merchandise entered for exportation, whenever the same is requested, in writing, by the exporter, and not otherwise.

Where merchandise are exported from any other district than the one into which they were originally imported, the collector, together with the naval officer thereof, where there is one, must grant to the exporter a certificate* that such merchandise were exported from such district, with the marks, numbers, and descriptions of the packages, and their contents, the names of the master and vessel in which, and the port to which they were exported, and by whom, and the names of the vessel and master in which they were brought, and by whom shipped at the district from whence they came, and the amount of the drawback to which they are entitled. Such certificate entitles the possessor thereof to receive, from the collector of the district with whom the duties on the said goods were paid or secured, debentures

---

[a] Act, 2d March, 1779, sec. 78. [b] Ibid. sec. 80.

* *Form of a certificate to be granted on exportation from a district other than the district into which such goods were originally imported:*

District of

Port of

We hereby certify, that the merchandise hereinafter specified, which were imported into the district of on the of by in the of master, from and landed in this district in the month of out of the of master, from (having been previously entered at this office by) have been exported hence by in the belonging to master, bound for having been previously inspected and (weighed, gauged, or measured, as the case may require) and that the said with both of have entered into bond, in pursuance of the laws in that case made and provided.

for the amount of the drawback expressed in the said certificate, payable at the same time, and in like manner, as directed for debentures on merchandise exported from the port of original importation. The collector may refuse to grant such debentures, in case any error has arisen, or any fraud has been committed ; and in case of such refusal, if the debentures claimed exceed $100, the collector represents the case to the comptroller of the treasury, who determines whether such debentures shall be granted or not. In no case of exportation of goods is a drawback paid, until the duties on the importation thereof have been first received.[a]

The debentures are assignable by delivery and endorsement of the parties, who receive the same. In all cases where payment shall be refused by the collectors of the districts where the said debentures were granted, in consequence of the non-payment of the duties for a longer time than three days after the same have become due and payable, (such refusal to be proved in the same manner as in the case of non-payment of bills of exchange,) the possessor or assignee of such debenture may maintain, in the proper circuit or district

[a] Act, 2d March, 1819, sec. 80.

Marks.	Numbers.	Packages, contents, and rates of duties.	Amount of duties.
		Here insert in detail, the packages exported, their quality and contents, the value, if articles subject to duties ad valorem, the tare, if articles on which tare is allowed, and the rates of duties paid.	

Net amount of drawbacks payable, dollars and cents.

A. B., Collector.
C. D., Naval Officer.

Form of the debentures:

No. District of
Debenture for Port of

In pursuance of law, I hereby certify, that the sum of [here insert the amount,] will be due from the United States of America, payable at this office, to [here insert the name of the exporter, or his known agent or attorney,] or order, on the [here insert the time when payable,] for drawback of duties on merchandise imported by [here insert the name of the importer, and the denomination and name of the vessel in which they were imported,] and exported by the said [here insert the name of the exporter]—Provided the duties arising on the importation of the said merchandise shall have been discharged prior to the said time.

A. B., Collector.

Countersigned,
C. D., Naval officer.

court of the United States, a suit against the person to whom such debenture was originally granted, or against any endorser thereof to recover the amount of such debenture, with interest at the rate of six per centum per annum, from the time when the same became due and payable. In all suits for the recovery of money upon debentures, the court grants judgment at the return term, unless the defendants in open court exhibit some plea, on oath or affirmation, by which the court shall be satisfied that a continuance, until the next succeeding term, is necessary to the attainment of justice; in which case, and not otherwise, a continuance until the next term may be granted.[a]

Before the receipt of any debenture, in case of exportation from the district of original importation, and in case of exportation from any other district before the receipt of any certificate, the person applying therefor must, previous to such receipt, and before the clearance of the vessel in which the goods are laden for exportation, or within 20 days after such clearance, give bond, with one or more sureties, to the satisfaction of the collector, in a sum equal to double the amount of the sum for which such debenture or certificate is granted, that the said goods, or any part thereof, shall not be relanded within the limits of the United States, and that the said exporter or exporters will produce, within one year, if the exportation be made to any part of Europe or America, or two years if to any part of Asia or Africa, proofs and certificates of the delivery of the goods without the limits of the United States.[b] *

This bond may be discharged, and not otherwise, by producing, within one year from the date thereof, if the exportation be made to any part of Europe or America, or within two years, if made to any

---

[a] Act, 2d March, 1799, sec. 80. [b] Ibid. sec. 81.

* *Form of Bond*:

Know all men by these presents, That we of the of are held and firmly bound unto the United States of America, in the sum of for the payment of which, well and truly to be made, we bind ourselves, our heirs, executors and administrators, jointly and severally by these presents. Witness our hands and seals, this day of one thousand

Whereas, the following merchandise has been duly imported into the United States, to wit—[here particularize the person or persons by whom the several articles were imported, the denomination and name of vessel, master's name, from whence, into what district, and when imported, together with the marks, numbers, description of, and number of packages, with their contents,] which said merchandise hath been reshipped by the above bounden in order to export the same in the of master, now in the port of and bound for

The condition of this obligation, therefore, is such, that if the aforesaid recited merchandise, or any part thereof, be not relanded in any port or place within the limits of the United States, and if the certificates and other proofs required by law of the delivery of the same at the aforesaid port of or at any other port or place without the limits of the United States as aforesaid, shall be produced at this office, within from the date hereof, then this obligation shall be null and void, but otherwise to remain in full force and virtue.

Sealed and delivered in the presence of }

part of Asia or Africa, a certificate, under the hand of the consignee at the foreign port or place to whom the said merchandise shall have been addressed,* therein particularly describing the articles so exported, their marks, numbers, description of packages, the number thereof, and their actual contents, and declaring that the same have been received by them, specifying the names of the master and vessel from which they were so received; and where such merchandise are not consigned to any particular person, but where the master or other person on board may be the consignee, a certificate from the person to whom such merchandise may be sold or delivered by such master or other person, must be produced, to the same effect as that required if the persons receiving the same were originally intended to be the consignees thereof. In addition to the certificate aforesaid, it is necessary to produce a certificate under the hand and seal of the consul or agent of the United States, residing at the said place, declaring either that the facts stated in the certificate of such consignee, or other person aforesaid, are, to his knowledge, true, or that such certificate is deserving of full credit; which certificates must, in all cases, as respects the landing or delivery of the said merchandise, be confirmed by the oath or affirmation of the master and mate,† if living, or

---

* *Form of the certificate of a consignee, declaring the delivery of merchandise at a foreign port:*

I, (A. A., or we, B. B. and C. C.,) of the (city or town) of (merchant, or merchants and copartners in trade,) do hereby certify, that the goods or merchandise hereinafter described, have been landed in this (city, town or port,) between the and days of from on board the of whereof G. G. is at present master, viz. [here insert the particular articles delivered in manner following, as the case may require—namely,

A. B. No. 1. *a* 10. ten hogsheads, } containing fourteen thousand pounds weight of
C. D. No. 3. 6. 9. 15. four tierces, } coffee.
E. F. No. 14. 18. 22. 25. 27. 30. 33. 36. } Eight hogsheads, containing ten thousand pounds weight of brown sugar.
G. H. No. 21. *a* 30. Ten chests, containing seven hundred weight of hyson tea.
I. K. 7. 16. 19. Three bales, containing one hundred and fifty pieces of nankeen—

which, according to the bills of lading for the same, were shipped on board the at the port of in the United States of America, on or about the day of and consigned to (me or to us) by of aforesaid merchant, (or by the master of the said).

Given under (my or our) hands, at the (city of) this day of

† *Form of the oath of the principal officers of a vessel, confirming the landing of merchandise at a foreign port:*

Port of

We, G. G., master, and H. H., mate of the of lately arrived from the port of in the United States of America, do solemnly (swear or affirm) that the goods or merchandise enumerated and described in the preceding certificate, dated the day of and signed by A. A., of the city of merchant, were actually delivered at the said port, from on board the said within the time specified in the said certificate.

Sworn or affirmed, at the city of }
before me, this day of }

in case of their death, by the oath or affirmation of the two principal surviving officers of the vessel in which the exportation was made.* Where there is no consul or agent of the United States residing at the place of delivery, the certificate of the consignee, or other person hereinbefore required, must be confirmed by the certificate of two reputable American merchants residing at the said place, or if there are no such American merchants, then by the certificate of two reputable foreign merchants,† testifying that the several facts stated in such certificates are, to their knowledge, just and true, or that such certificate is, in their opinion, worthy of full faith and credit; which certificate must also be supported by the oath or affirmation of the master and mate, or other principal officers of the vessel, in manner as before prescribed. The oath or affirmation of the master and mate, or other principal officers, in all cases, when taken at a foreign place, must be taken and subscribed before the consul or agent of the United States residing at such foreign place.[a]

In cases of loss by sea, or by capture or other unavoidable accident, or when, from the nature of the trade, the proofs and certificates before required cannot be procured, the exporters are allowed to adduce to the collector of the port of exportation such other proofs as the nature of the case will admit; which proofs, with a statement of all the circumstances attending the transaction, within the knowledge of such collector, must be transmitted to the comptroller of the treasury, who has power to allow a further reasonable time for obtaining the proofs; or if he be satisfied with the truth and validity of the proofs adduced, to direct the bonds of such exporters to be cancelled. If the amount of such bond do not exceed the penal sum of $200, the collector, with the naval officer, and alone, where there is none, may, pursuant to certain rules prescribed by the comptroller of the treasury, admit such proofs as may be adduced; and if he deem the same satisfactory, cancel such bond accordingly.[a]

---

[a] Act, 2d March, 1799 sec. 81.

* *Form of a verification of the delivery to be executed by a consul or agent of the United States:*

I, M. M., consul (or agent) of the United States of America, at the city of do declare, that the facts set forth in the preceding certificate, subscribed by A. A., of the said city, merchant, and dated the day of are, to (my knowledge, just and true, or are, in my opinion, just and true,) and deserving full faith and credit.

In testimony whereof, I have hereunto subscribed my name, and affixed the seal of my office, at this day of

M. M., Consul.

† *Form of a verification to be executed by American or foreign merchants:*

We, residing in the city of do declare, that the facts stated in the preceding certificate, signed by of the said (city) merchant, on the day of are (to our knowledge, just and true, or are, in our opinion, just and true, and worthy of full faith and credit.) We also declare that there is (no consul or other public agent for the United States of America, or American merchants, as the case may require,) now residing at this place.

Dated at this city of this day of

R. S.
T. L.

The consuls or agents of the United States may demand 25 cents for administering each oath or affirmation, and one dollar for granting each certificate. If any consul or agent demand other or greater fees, his bond is forfeited.[a]

If any merchandise, entered for exportation to obtain any allowance given by law, on the exportation thereof be landed within the limits of the United States, it is subject to forfeiture, together with the vessel from which such merchandise shall be landed, and the vessels or boats used in landing the same; and all persons concerned therein shall, on indictment and conviction thereof, suffer imprisonment not exceeding six months. For discovery of frauds, and seizure of merchandise relanded contrary to law, the revenue officers have the same powers, and, in case of seizure, the same proceedings are had, as in the case of merchandise imported contrary to law.[b]

If any merchandise, entered for the benefit of drawback or bounty, upon exportation be entered by a false denomination, or erroneously as to the time when, and the vessel in which they were imported, or be found to disagree with the packages, quantities, or qualities, as they were at the time of original importation, except such disagreement as may have been occasioned by necessary or unavoidable wastage or damage only, except also in cases where permission has been obtained according to law, to alter or change the quantities or packages thereof; all such merchandise, or the value thereof, to be recovered of the owner or person making such entry, is forfeited. The forfeiture is not incurred, if it appear to the satisfaction of the collector and naval officer; and if no naval officer, to the satisfaction of the collector, or of the court in which a prosecution for the forfeiture be had, that such false denomination, error, or disagreement, happened by mistake or accident, and not from any intention to defraud the revenue.[c]

In addition to the forfeiture of the goods, the value thereof is also forfeited as a penalty, and in case the goods cannot be found, twice the value.[d]

Goods on which the duties were paid in the Baltimore district, are liable to forfeiture if transported across the state of Delaware to Philadelphia, without a permit from the collector of Baltimore: the same not belonging to the owner, master, or mariner, of the vessel in which they were imported, or in which they were transported from Baltimore to Philadelphia.[e] This decision is applicable to the transportation of goods from any one district to another.

Bounty.—There is also a species of drawback or bounty granted on the exportation of certain imported articles, which have been used in the domestic manufactures of the United States.

The articles entitled to bounty, under the existing laws, are, refined sugars, pickled fish, distilled spirits, printed and coloured silks.

On sugar, refined in the United States, there is a drawback of five

---

[a] Act, 2d March, 1799, sec. 81. [b] Ibid. sec. 82. [c] Ibid. sec. 84. [d] Act, 20th Feb., 1819. [e] 4 Dall. 28.

cents per lb., provided the bounty amount to $12 or upwards, in one exportation.[a]

This bounty ceases as soon as the exports of sugar equal the imports.[a] The exporter must, to be entitled thereto, swear that the sugar was refined from foreign sugar, and the collector may require the certificate of a sugar refiner to the same effect.[b]

The same regulations that are required in other cases of exportation for bounty, must be complied with.

The exporter must also give six hours' notice, before lading, of his intention to ship the sugars, to the inspector, stating the number of packages, the marks thereon, the places of deposit, the name of vessel, and of the place to which they are to be exported.[c] The sugars are then inspected, and laden in the presence of the inspector, and a return is made to the collector of the quantity and particulars.[c]

The exportation bond for landing abroad must be the full value of the sugars, and signed by the exporter and two sureties, of whom the master must be one.[d]

Upon a change of voyage, the collector will grant a permit to reland the sugars.[e]

If the sugar be unshipped without a permit, or, in case of necessity, within the United States, or within four leagues of the coast, it is forfeited, together with the vessel and tackle.[f] In case of distress, the unlading must be immediately reported to the principal officer of the customs in the nearest port.[f] The bond is discharged in the same manner that other debenture bonds are cancelled, except that the oath in confirmation of the certificate must state, in case the certificate be not signed by a consul or by American merchants, that there were not to be found, upon diligent inquiry, two merchants of the United States in the port where the sugars were landed.[g]

Where the proof of landing is not exactly regular, and other proof is offered, if the drawback amounts to $100, the dispensing with the strict proof must be referred to the comptroller of the treasury.[f]

Printed and coloured silks.—The same drawback is allowed on silks which have been stamped, coloured, printed, stained, dyed or painted, in the United States, as upon plain silk cloths. Such silks, however, must be entered at the custom-house at the time of importation, as intended for exportation, with privilege of drawback; and before they are delivered from the public store, they must be inspected, weighed, or measured, the quality ascertained, a sample of each piece preserved at the custom-house, and the original package marked with a custom-house mark, and a particular account thereof, and the samples must be presented at the custom-house to compare with the original package when entered for exportation. The silks, when entered for exportation, must be entered in the original package with the custom-house mark, and no drawback is allowed except on the contents of entire packages. The silks are then again inspected,

---

[a] Act, 21st Jan., 1829. [b] Act, 30th April, 1816, sec. 6. [c] Act, 24th July, 1813, sec. 9. [d] Ibid. sec. 10. [e] Ibid. sec. 11. [f] Ibid. sec. 12. [g] Ibid. sec. 13.

measured, or weighed, and compared with the original entry, registry and samples; and if the collector be satisfied that they are the identical goods, and not altered except by being coloured, stained, printed, dyed, or painted, the exporter is then permitted to take the oath, and give the exportation bond, as in other cases of exportation, for the benefit of drawback.[a]

If any silk goods are entered for exportation for drawback, when not entitled thereto, they are forfeited.[a]

Pickled fish.—Pickled fish, when exported, are entitled to a bounty of twenty cents per barrel, when the shipment amounts to fifty barrels.[b] They are entered for exportation with the collector and naval officer of the district.

The only pickled fish entitled to bounty, on exportation, are those which have been cured and packed solely with foreign salt; on which the duty has been paid, inspected,[c] and the casks branded, according to the laws of the state where exported; in addition to which, the words "for bounty," and the name of the place whence exported, branded thereon, are requisite.

On exportation of pickled fish of American fishery, for bounty, the exporter must make an outward entry, of which the blank form is in note.* He must fill up all but the oath; date the entry, and sign it;

---

[a] Act, 22d May, 1824, sec. 4. [b] Act, 29th July, 1813, sec. 2. [c] Ibid. sec. 3.

* Entry of pickled fish intended to be exported, for the benefit of bounty, by in the whereof is master, bound for

Marks, as branded on the casks.	Number of barrels.	Description or species of fish.	Quality, that is, No. 1, 2, or 3.

[To be signed here by the shipper before shipment.]

District of

I, do solemnly swear, that the pickled fish mentioned in the annexed entry, and now actually laden on board the whereof is master, and bound for are truly and bona fide of the fisheries of the United States; that the said fish are intended to be exported to as mentioned in said entry, and are not intended to be relanded within the limits of the United States. I do also verily believe, that the said fish was wholly cured with foreign salt, on which the duties have been secured or paid.

So help me God.

† *Form of Permit:*

District of

18

The surveyor will cause the barrels of pickled fish, specified in the within entry, to be examined, and if found to agree exactly therewith, and is fully satisfied that they are of the fisheries of the United States, will then permit the same to be laden on board the vessel within named, for benefit of drawback, and immediately make return to this office.

Collector.
Naval Officer.

To the surveyor and inspector of the

hand it to the collector, who signs the permit on the back of the entry; it is then handed to the surveyor, who directs it to the inspector to examine the same. If, upon inspection, the shipment be found to correspond with the entry, and the inspector is fully satisfied that they are of the fisheries of the United States, and cured with foreign salt, they are put on board under his superintendence. The inspector then makes a return of the shipment to the collector.[a]

In addition to the oath of the exporter, an oath must be made by the person who caught the fish, and by the inspector, that the fish were solely cured with foreign salt.

Within twenty days after the clearance of the vessel, the exporter must fill up his oath at the foot of his entry; swear to it before the collector; carry it to the accounting room; and give bonds in double the amount of the bounty, for the landing abroad of the pickled fish. These bonds will be cancelled, on the production of a certificate of the same kind as those produced for debenture goods; and the certificate of its being landed may be included in the same certificate as the debenture goods. These formalities must be punctually performed, otherwise the bounty will be lost.[a]

This bounty is payable at the time the certificate of landing is produced, but not, however, sooner than six months from the sale of the bond.[b]

Distilled spirits.—Rum, manufactured in the United States, from foreign molasses, is entitled, on exportation, to a bounty of four cents per gallon, provided it is at least first-proof, when exported to any foreign place, except immediately adjoining the United States.[c] The quantity so exported must amount to one hundred and fifty gallons, to entitle the exporter to drawback, and exported in vessels not less than thirty tons burthen.[d]

To entitle the exporter to the benefit of drawback, the vessels containing the same must be branded, or otherwise marked, in durable characters, with progressive numbers, with the name of the owner, the quantity, to be ascertained by actual gauging, and the proof. The exporter of such spirits, previous to putting the same on board of any vessel for exportation, must give six hours' notice to the collector of his intention to export the same; and make entry in writing, of the particulars thereof, and of the casks or vessels containing the same, their respective marks, numbers and contents, the places where deposited, the place to which, and the vessel in which they are to be exported.*[e]

---

[a] Acts, 2d March, 1799, sec 83, and 29th July, 1813. [b] Ibid. and 3d March, 1817.
[c] Act, 29th May, 1830. [d] Act, 30th April, 1816, sec. 1. [e] Ibid. sec. 2.

* *Form of Entry:*

Entry of domestic spirits intended to be exported by [here insert the name or names,] on board the [insert the denomination and name of the vessel,] whereof [insert the name of the master] is master, for [insert the port or place to which destined,] for the benefit of drawback:

Marks.	Numbers.	Casks and contents.	Gauge.

The collector, in writing, then directs the surveyor or inspecting officer to inspect the spirits so notified for exportation, and if found to correspond with the notice, and so it be certified by the inspecting officer, the collector, together with the naval officer, if any, grants a permit for lading the same, on board of the vessel named in the entry. This lading must be performed under the superintendence of the inspecting officer; and the exporter makes oath, previous to the clearance, or within twenty days thereafter, that the said spirits are truly intended to be exported to the place designated in the notice, and are not intended to be relanded within the United States.[a]

Where drawback is claimed on the exportation of spirits distilled from molasses, the oath of two persons, of whom one must not be the exporter, must be produced, that the molasses was of foreign production; and the collector may also require, in addition, the certificate of a distiller to the same effect.[b]

The exporter also takes an oath, and gives an exportation bond for landing abroad, as in other cases of exportation for benefit of drawback.[b]

These regulations having been complied with, the exporter is entitled to receive from the collector debentures for the amount of the drawback.[b]

The collector may refuse to grant such debentures, in casé it shall appear to him that any error has arisen, or any fraud been committed. In case of such refusal, if the debentures claimed exceed $100, the collector must represent the case to the comptroller of the treasury, who determines whether such debentures shall be granted or not.[c]

The bond is in the same form, and is discharged in the same manner, as exportation bonds in ordinary cases.[c] The bounty on spirits distilled from foreign molasses, and on refined sugars, are payable thirty days after the date of their issue, and are paid out of the duties upon imports and tonnage.[d]

Rail-road iron.—The secretary of the treasury is also authorized to allow a drawback of the duty upon all rail iron, which has been actually laid upon any rail-road or inclined plane, by a state or incorporated company.[e] If the rail iron imported for such object cannot be laid down before the bonds for duties become due, the secretary is authorized to extend the bonds for three years since 1836.[f]

For amendments, since 1836, vide Appendix.

16th. *Fees.*

TO THE COLLECTOR AND NAVAL OFFICER.

Entry of a vessel of 100 tons or upwards, - -	$2 50
Clearance do. do. do. to a foreign port, -	2 50
Entry of a vessel under 100 tons, - . - -	1 50

---

[a] Act, 30th April, 1816, sec. 2. [b] Ibid. sec. 5. [c] Ibid. sec. 3. [d] Ibid. sec. 4.
[e] Act, 3d March, 1821. [f] Act, 14th July, 1832, sec. 1.

Entry of American licensed coasters, of 50 tons and over,	$0 50
——————————————— if under do. - -	0 25
Clearance of a registered vessel coastwise under 100 tons,	1 50
——— of American licensed coasters of 50 tons, -	0 50
———————————————— if under do. -	0 25
Every post entry, - - - - - - -	2 00
Foreign vessels, on arriving coastwise, entry, - -	5 50
——————, clearing out coastwise, - - -	3 10
Light money, per ton, - - - - - - -	0 50
Permit to land goods, - - - - - - -	0 20
Every bond taken officially, - - - - -	0 40
—— Permit to load goods, for the exportation for drawback,	0 30
—— Debenture, or other official certificate, - -	0 20
—— Bill of health, - - - - - - -	0 20
—— List of crew, - - - - - - -	0 65
—— Sea letter, - - - - - - - -	0 20
—— Official document (registers excepted) required by any person, - - - - - - - - -	0 20

Foreign vessels pay no hospital money to the United States.

TO THE SURVEYOR.

Admeasuring and certifying the same, of every vessel of 100 tons and under, - - - - - - -	1 00
Admeasurement of every vessel above 100 tons, and not exceeding 160 tons, - - - - - - -	1 50
Above 160 tons, - - - - - - - -	2 00
For all other services on board any vessel of 100 tons and upwards, having on board goods subject to duty, -	3 00
For like services on board any vessel of less than 100 tons,	1 50
On all vessels not having on board goods subject to duty,	0 66½

TO EACH INSPECTOR.

For every day actually employed in aid of the customs, to be paid by the collector, unless the landing of the cargo require more than 15 days, when the wages for the extra days paid by the owner or master, is - - - - -	3 00

The fees to the inspectors, measurers, weighers and gaugers, with the above exception, are paid by the United States, out of the revenue.

FEES UNDER THE REGISTRY ACT.

Certificate of registry on record and bond, - - -	2 25
Endorsement on do. - - - - - - -	1 00
Every bond taken under the registry act, - - -	0 25
——————— for a Mediterranean passport, - - -	0 40
Seaman's protection, - - - - - - -	0 25

FEES UNDER THE COASTING ACT.

Admeasurement of a vessel, in order to the registry, enrolment, licensing or recording, if of 5, and less than 20 tons,	$0 50
——— if of 20, and not exceeding 70 tons	0 75
——— if of 70 do. 100 do.	1 00
——— if above 100, - - -	1 50
For every certificate of enrolment, - - - - -	0 50
Endorsement on do. - - - - - - - -	0 20
Every license, including the bond, if not above 20 tons, -	0 25
——— above 20, and not more than 100,	0 50
——— above 100, - - -	1 00
For recording certificate, manifest, and granting permit for a licensed vessel to proceed to another district, if less than 50 tons, - - - - - - - -	0 25
For do. if more than 50 tons, - - - - - -	0 50
For certifying manifest, and granting permit for registered vessels, - - - - - - - - -	1 50
For receiving manifest, and granting permit to vessels not belonging to American citizens, - - - - -	2 00
For receiving manifest, and granting permit to unload on arrival, - - - - - - - - -	1 50
Do. as to foreign vessels, - - - - - - -	2 00
Granting permit to carry on fishery in a foreign port,	0 25
For report and entry of foreign goods imported in such vessel,	0 25

By a subsequent section, their compensation is limited, so that it shall not exceed a certain sum.

The fees received by surveyors for certifying, or receiving certified manifests, or granting permits, are for their own use. All other fees are received and accounted for monthly by the collector.

If there is only a collector, he keeps the whole. If there be a surveyor, that officer is entitled to one third; and if there be a naval officer, they are equally divided.

Where there is more than one surveyor in the district, each surveyor receives one third of the fees collected in his own port.[a]

Penalties.—All penalties and forfeitures incurred under the revenue acts, are prosecuted in the courts of the United States.

If any officer, entitled to a share in the penalty or forfeiture, be necessary as a witness on the trial, he may be examined, but in such case his share of the same accrues to the United States.[b]

The proceeds of all penalties and forfeitures under the revenue acts, after deducting all proper costs, are divided as follows: one half to the United States, and where not otherwise specially appropriated the other half is equally distributed between the collector, naval officer of the district, and surveyor of the port. In districts where there is

---

[a] Act, 18th Feb., 1793, sec. 34.

[b] Act, 2d March, 1799, sec. 91.

only one such officer, he takes such moiety. Where the recovery is in consequence of any information given to the collector, the informer is entitled to one half of such moiety, and the other half is divided as above.[a]

Where the information is given by an officer of a revenue cutter, one fourth is reserved for the United States, one fourth to be divided as above, and one half is divided among the officers of the cutter in proportion to their pay.[a]

Where the amount of goods forfeited is less than $250, the part reserved to the United States is applied to pay the costs of the prosecution.[a]

One half of the excess of duty accruing in consequence of the fifty per cent. added to the value of goods, which have been sent to the public store for appraisement as suspected goods, is divided among the custom-house officers in the same manner as penalties, except that no appraiser is admitted to a share.[b]

The share in forfeitures and penalties belongs to the collector who made the seizure, or brought the suit, and not to his successor, when one is appointed before a judgment in the suit therefore.[c]

After a final decree of condemnation, and no appeal made, the right of the collector to the forfeiture is vested and absolute, and the secretary of the treasury has no right to remit the share belonging to the revenue officers.[d] Under the act of March 3d, 1797, however, he has power to remit until the money has been actually paid over to the collector for distribution.[e] In deciding a question of forfeiture, the court disregards the refusal of the secretary to remit the penalty.[f]

Forfeiture attaches in rem the moment an offence is committed, and the property is at once divested.[g]

Upon a piratical capture, the property of the original owners is not forfeited by the violation of the municipal laws of the country to which she is carried by the piratical captors.[h] Where the capture is by a lawful cruise, it is otherwise.[h] Property may be forfeited by an act committed without the knowledge or procurement of the owner.[i]

A change of property will not purge the forfeiture, where the circumstances are such as to put the purchaser on his guard.[j]

To entitle an informer to a share of the forfeiture, it is merely necessary that the information induced the prosecution and contributed to the recovery; it is not necessary that it should be as full as the evidence would warrant.[k]

Where there is any fact put in issue, the trial takes place in the judicial district where the penalty has accrued; and the collector of the district where the seizure was made, or where the forfeiture was incurred, must prosecute without delay; and he is authorized to re-

---

[a] Act, 2d March, 1799, sec. 91. [b] Act, 1st March, 1823, sec. 20.
[c] 1 Wheat. 462.—8 Ibid. 312.—4 Ibid. 74. [d] 2 Gallis. 515.—1 Mason, 431. [e] 1 Paine, 209.
[f] 1 Ibid. 23. [g] 3 Wheat, 246. [h] 5 Ibid. 338. [i] 1 Gallis. 26. [j] 1 Ibid. 41.
[k] 3 Wash. C. C. R. 464.

ceive the sums recovered from the court or the proper officer; and he must distribute the same upon the receipt thereof, and account quarterly with the treasury for all sums received for fines, penalties, and forfeitures. Fourteen days' notice is given in some newspaper published near the place of seizure, and also by posting the same in some public place near the court-house, of the seizure and prosecution of all vessels and merchandise libelled.[a]

Proclamation is also made for claimants of the property; and if no claimant appear and give bond to defend the suit, the court decides the cause according to law. If the claimant pray to have the property delivered to him, three appraisers are appointed by the court, to appraise, under oath, the value of the vessel or goods, at the expense of the claimant. Upon the return of the appraisement, bonds with proper sureties are given by the claimant, for the payment to the United States of a sum equal to the value as appraised, and a certificate of the duties having been paid or secured being produced, the property is delivered to the claimant.[a]

If judgment be given for the claimant, the bond is cancelled; but if against him, he must, within twenty days thereafter, pay into court the amount of the appraised value, with the costs, or judgment will be forthwith granted upon the bond, on motion in open court.[a]

The court may, if it think proper, where judgment is given in favour of the claimant, grant a certificate that there was a reasonable cause for seizure; and in such case the claimant is not entitled to costs, and the prosecutor, or person making the seizure, is not liable to an action for damages, provided the property be delivered forthwith after judgment to the claimant.[a]

All property not bonded, must be sold after condemnation, by the marshal, at public auction, giving fifteen days' notice of the time and place of sale, in one or more public newspapers in or near the place of sale.[b]

The proceeds of the sale, after deducting charges, are to be paid to the collector in ten days after the sale.[b]

Any person who has incurred any fine, penalty, forfeiture, or disability, or is interested in any vessel or merchandise subject to seizure, forfeiture, or disability, may prefer his petition to the judge of the district in which such fine, &c. accrued, setting forth the circumstances of his case, and praying that the same may be mitigated or remitted. The judge then inquires, in a summary manner, into the circumstances of the case, first causing reasonable notice to be given to the person claiming such fine, and to the attorney of the United States, to show cause against the mitigation or remission thereof; and causes the facts to be stated and annexed to the petition, and directs their transmission to the secretary of the treasury, who may mitigate or remit such fine, forfeiture, or penalty, or remove such disability, or any part thereof, if, in his opinion, the same was incurred without wilful negligence, or any intention of fraud, in the persons incurring

---

[a] Act, 2d March, 1799, sec. 89. [b] Ibid. sec. 90.

the same; and he may direct the prosecution to be discontinued, upon such terms as he may deem reasonable.[a]

This practice cannot, however, affect the right or claim of any person, to that part of any fine, penalty, or forfeiture, which such person may be entitled to, the amount of which right and claim must be assessed and valued by the proper judge, or court, in a summary manner.[b]

---

[a] Act, 3d March, 1797, sec. 1.

[b] Ibid. sec. 3.

CHAPTER IV.

FISHERIES.

VESSELS engaged in the fisheries, must be enrolled and licensed. The manner of enrolling and licensing fishing, as well as coasting vessels, is pointed out in chapter I. pages 19 and 20.

Laws have been passed by congress for the encouragement and regulation of fishing vessels belonging to the United States, of which the following are the principal provisions.

Before sailing on a fishing voyage, the master (if the vessel be above twenty tons) must make a written agreement with every fisherman on board, except apprentices or servants, stating the terms of shipment; whether the same is to continue for one voyage, or for the fishing season; and also, that the fish, or the proceeds of such fishing voyage or voyages, which may appertain to the fishermen, shall be divided among them in proportion to the quantities which they may respectively have caught. This agreement must be endorsed or countersigned by the owner, or his agent. If any fisherman, having engaged himself for a voyage, or for the fishing season, in any fishing vessel, and signed an agreement therefor, shall, during such agreement, desert or absent himself, without leave of the master or owner, or his agent, he is liable to the same penalties as deserting seamen in the merchant service, and may, in like manner, be apprehended and detained. If, during such fishing voyage, he refuse or neglect his duty, being thereto required by the master, or otherwise resist his just commands, to the detriment of such voyage, besides being answerable for all damages arising thereby, he forfeits, to the use of the owner, his share of any public allowance upon such voyage.[a]

Any fish caught on board such vessel, must be delivered to the owner, or his agent, for cure, and must be sold by said owner or agent. The vessel, for the term of six months after such sale, is answerable for the skipper's and every other fisherman's share of such fish, and may be proceeded against in admiralty therefor. Upon such process, the owner and agent are compelled to produce a just account of the sales and division of such fish, according to such agreement, otherwise the vessel is answerable for the highest value of the shares demanded. But the owner, or his agent, appearing to answer to such process, may offer his account of general supplies made for such fishing voyage, and of other supplies, to either of the demandants, and may produce evidence thereof in answer to their demands; and judgment is rendered for the respective balances. When process is issued, if the

---

[a] Act, 19th June, 1813, sec. 1.

owner or his agent give bond, with sufficient security, to the satisfaction of two justices of the peace, one named by such owner or agent, and the other by the complainants, to pay whatever sum shall be recovered on such process, there must be an immediate discharge of such vessel.[a]

On all pickled fish of the fisheries of the United States, exported therefrom, there is allowed a bounty of twenty cents a barrel, to be paid by the collector of the district from which the same is so exported. In order to entitle the exporter to the benefit of such bounty, he must make entry with the collector and naval officer of the district, and specify the names of the master and vessel in which, and the place where, such fish are intended to be exported, together with the particular quantity; and proof must be made, to the satisfaction of the collector and naval officer, that the same are of the fisheries of the United States.[b]—Vide chapter III. page 133.

Before entry for exportation, all pickled fish must be inspected and marked pursuant to the inspection laws of the respective states where inspection laws are in force, in regard to any pickled fish; and the casks containing such fish must be branded with the words "for bounty," with the name of the inspector or packer, the species and quality of the fish contained therein, and the name of the port of exportation. The collector of such district, together with the naval officer, where there is one, then grants an order for an inspector to examine the pickled fish as expressed in such entry; and if they correspond therewith, and the said officer is fully satisfied that they are of the fisheries of the United States, he grants a permit to lade the same, agreeably to such entry, on board the vessel therein expressed.[c]

The lading must be performed under the superintendence of the officer examining the same, who makes returns of the quantity and quality, to the officers granting the order. The exporter, when the lading is completed, and returns made, makes oath or affirmation, that the pickled fish expressed in such entry, and then actually laden on board the vessel as therein expressed, are truly and bona fide of the fisheries of the United States; that they are truly intended to be exported as therein specified, and are not intended to be relanded within the limits of the United States. He also gives bonds, in double the amount of the bounty, with one or more sureties, that the same shall be landed and left at some foreign port, which bonds are cancelled at the same periods, and in like manner, as provided in respect to bonds given on the exportation of goods entitled to drawback. The bounty is not paid until six months after exportation, to be computed from the date of the bond, and until the exporter produces to the collector with whom such outward entry is made, such certificates, or other satisfactory proof, of the landing of the same as aforesaid. The bounty is not paid, unless the same amount to $10 upon each entry.[d]

It must be proved, to the satisfaction of the collector, that the pickled fish for which the bounty shall be claimed, was wholly cured with foreign salt, on which a duty was secured or paid.[e]

---

[a] Act, 19th June, 1813, sec. 2. [b] Ibid. sec. 3.
[c] Acts, 2d March, 1799, sec. 83, and 29th July, 1813. [d] Ibid. sec. 2. [e] Ibid. sec. 3.

Fraudulent entries, with intent to obtain the bounty, when the fish are not entitled thereto, are punished by forfeiture of the fish, or the value thereof, to be recovered of the person making the entry.[a]

A bounty is paid on the last day of December, annually, to the owner of every vessel, or his agent, by the collector of the district where such vessel belongs, qualified, agreeably to law, for carrying on the bank and other cod fisheries, and which shall actually have been employed therein at sea for the term of four months of the fishing season next preceding, i. e. from the last day of February to the last day of November, in every year, for each and every ton of such vessel's burthen; if of more than five tons, and not exceeding thirty tons, $3 50; if above 30 tons, $4; and if above thirty tons, and having had a crew of not less than ten persons, and having been actually employed at sea for the term of three and a half months, but less than four months of the season, $3 50,[b] of which allowance three eighth parts belongs to the owner, and the other five eighths thereof divided by him among the several fishermen employed in such vessel during the season, in such proportions as the fish they respectively have taken may bear to the whole quantity of fish taken on board such vessel during such season.[c] The allowance on any one vessel, for one season, cannot exceed $360.[b]

Where a fishing vessel is prevented, by illegal capture, under authority from a foreign government, from being at sea for any part of the four months required, the time of detention is computed as part of the four months.[d] If the fishing vessel, having completed her lading, be wrecked on her return to port, the owner and crew, on satisfactory proof thereof to the comptroller of the treasury, are entitled to the same bounty as if she had arrived in the United States.[e]

Bounties are restricted, by an act of March 1st, 1817, to fishing vessels, whose officers, and at least three fourths of whose crews, are proved, to the satisfaction of the collectors of the district where they belong, to be citizens of the United States.

The original adjustment and settlement of the fares among the owners and fishermen, (together with a written account of the length, breadth, and depth, of said boat or vessel, when less than twenty tons, and the time she has actually been employed in the fishery in the preceding season,) must be produced, and sworn or affirmed to before the collector of the district, in order to entitle the owner to receive the allowance. If within one year after payment of such allowance, it appear that any fraud or deceit has been practised in obtaining the same, the boat or vessel, if found within the district, is forfeited; otherwise the owner, having practised such fraud or deceit, forfeits $100.[f]

The owner of every fishing vessel of twenty tons and upwards, must, previous to receiving the allowance, produce to the collector authorized to pay the same, the original agreement made with the fishermen, and also a certificate, by him subscribed, mentioning the

---

[a] Act, 29th July, 1813, sec. 4. [b] Act, 3d March, 1819. [c] Act, 29th July, 1813, sec. 5.
[d] Act, 4th April, 1818. [e] Act, 26th May, 1824, sec. 1. [f] Act, 29th June, 1813, sec. 6.

particular days on which such vessel sailed and returned on the several voyages made in the preceding fishing season, to the truth of which he must swear or affirm.[a]

No vessel of twenty tons or upwards, can be entitled to the allowance, unless the master, before he proceeds on any fishing voyage, makes an agreement in writing, or in print, with every fisherman employed therein, according to the provisions of the act of June 19th, 1813.[b]

False swearing, in procuring the bounty, under the fishery acts is punishable as perjury.[c]

Masters of fishing vessels that intend to touch at a foreign port during the cruise, should have a permit for that purpose from the collector of their district; as they are liable to forfeiture if they are found within three leagues of the coast, with any foreign merchandise of the value of $500 on board, unless they have the permit. The masters, upon their return, must also deliver manifests, and make entries within the same time, under the same penalty as is provided in the case of American vessels arriving from a foreign port.[d]

A vessel, licensed for the fisheries, is liable to forfeiture under the 32d section of the license act, 18th February, 1793, for sailing without a license therefor with a load of goods even of domestic growth, and not liable to duties, with intent to carry them to another place. The cargo is not liable to forfeiture under the next section of the same act, unless it belong to the master, or owner, or some mariner of the vessel.

---

[a] Act, 19th June, 1813, sec. 7. [b] Ibid. sec. 8. [c] Ibid. sec. 9.
[d] Act, 18th Feb., 1793, sec. 21.

CHAPTER V.

REVENUE CUTTERS.

THE president of the United States was authorized, by the act of March 2d, 1799, to cause ten revenue cutters to be built, to aid in the collection of the impost and tonnage duties.[a] He was also authorized to cause others to be built instead of those which became unfit for service; the expense of building and equipping the same to be paid out of the duties received. Those unfit for service are sold at auction, and the proceeds paid into the treasury.[b]

Each of the revenue cutters has one captain, and not more than three lieutenants or mates, first, second and third; and not more than seventy men, including non-commissioned officers, gunners and mariners. The revenue cutters, whenever the president of the United States directs, co-operate with the navy of the United States, during which time they are under the direction of the secretary of the navy, and the expenses thereof are defrayed by the agents of the navy department.[c]

The officers are appointed by the president of the United States, and are deemed officers of the customs, and subject to the direction of such collectors of the revenue, or other officers thereof, as, from time to time, are designated for that purpose. They have authority, and are required, to board all vessels which arrive within the United States, or within four leagues of the coast, if bound for the United States; and to search and examine the same, and every part thereof; and to demand, receive, and certify the manifests required to be on board; and to affix proper fastenings on the hatches and other communications with the hold; and to remain on board until they arrive at the port of destination. The master, or other person having at any time the command of any of the revenue cutters, must make a weekly return to the collector, or other officer of the district under whose direction they are placed, of the transactions of the cutter under their command; specifying therein the vessels that have been boarded, their names and descriptions; the names of the masters, and from what port they last sailed; whether laden or in ballast; whether vessels of the United States, or to what other nation belonging, and whether they have the necessary manifests; and generally, all such matters as it may be necessary for the collectors, or other officers of the customs, to be made acquainted with. The officers of the cutter must likewise execute such other duties, for the collection and security of the revenue, as, from time to time, may be directed by the secretary of the treasury, not contrary to law.[d]

---

[a] Act, 2d March, 1799, sec. 97. [b] Ibid. sec. 100. [c] Ibid. sec. 98. [d] Ibid. sec. 99.

The collectors of the respective districts may, with the approbation of the secretary of the treasury, employ open row and sail boats, in each district, for the use of the surveyors and inspectors in going on board of vessels, and otherwise for the better detection of frauds; the expense of which is defrayed out of the product of the duties.[a]

The cutters and boats, employed in the service of the revenue, must be distinguished from other vessels by an ensign and pennant, with marks thereon prescribed by the president of the United States; and, in case any vessel, liable to seizure or examination, does not bring to, on being required, or, being chased by any cutter or boat displaying the pennant and ensign prescribed for vessels in the revenue service, it is lawful for the captain or other person having command of such cutter or boat to fire at, or into, any vessel which does not bring to, after such pennant and ensign has been hoisted, and a gun fired by such cutter or boat as a signal; and such captain, or other person, and all persons acting by or under his direction, are indemnified from any penalties, or actions for damages, for so doing; and if any person shall be killed or wounded by such firing, and the captain, or other person aforesaid, shall be prosecuted, or arrested therefor, he is forthwith admitted to bail. If any vessel or boat, not employed in the service of the revenue, within the jurisdiction of the United States, carry or hoist any pennant or ensign prescribed for vessels in the revenue service, the master of the vessel so offending forfeits $100.[b]

The flag used by the revenue cutters and boats, is distinguished by the stripes being perpendicular, instead of horizontal.

---

[a] Act, 2d March, 1799, sec. 101. [b] Ibid. sec. 102.

CHAPTER VI.

OWNERS OF SHIPS.

Title to vessels.—Persons may become owners of ships in various ways; viz. by purchase, by building, by capture from an enemy, followed by a sentence of condemnation, or by inheritance or bequest.

To entitle vessels to the privileges of American ships, the owners must be natives or naturalized citizens, and the vessels must be registered or qualified to carry on the coasting trade. *Vide* chap. I., on Ships.

Those who intend to acquire the property of a ship by purchase, should previously ascertain that the person who proposes to sell is legally empowered to do so: for, although a sale of other goods, by the person who is in possession of them, may, in many cases, vest the property in the buyer, even when the seller himself has neither property in them or authority to dispose of them, it is not so with respect to ships; for the sale of which there is no open market. Written documents always determine this species of property; and the buyer has therefore the means of ascertaining the title of any one who offers to sell, and can seldom be deceived, unless by his own fault.

The requisite documents not only furnish the owner with proof of his property, but also enable him to dispose of it when the ship is at sea, or in a foreign port. When a ship is at home, and a delivery of actual possession is possible, such delivery is necessary to give a perfect title to the buyer, in case of the sale of a whole ship; for, although as between buyer and seller, it may be completed by payment of the price without delivery of possession; yet, if the buyer suffer the seller to remain in possession and act as owner, and an execution issue upon a judgment against the seller, the sale may, perhaps, be deemed fraudulent and void as against the party who has obtained the judgment.

In case of a sale, or an agreement for a sale *of a part only*, it has been thought sufficient, if the vendor, having delivered the muniments of his title, ceased from the time to act as a part owner, actual delivery of a part being considered impossible. This, however, is to be understood with some limitation: for, if a part owner has the *actual* possession of the ship, it is not impossible for him to deliver the possession: but, if he has *not* the actual possession, the possession of the other part owners may reasonably be considered to be the possession of the vendee after the sale.

In the case of an absolute sale it can rarely happen, in practice, that the seller should continue in possession; but the rule extends also to mortgages of ships, and with regard to them has often been regularly enforced. But, when a ship is abroad, a perfect transfer of the property may, at the common law, be made at home, by bill of sale and delivery of that and the other documents relating to the ship; as the delivery of the key of a warehouse to the buyer of goods contained therein is held to change the property of the goods, according to the rule of the civil law; such delivery, in each case, being not merely a symbol, but the mode of enabling the buyer to take actual possession, so soon as circumstances will permit.[a]

It has often occurred that a ship has been sold abroad by order of an admiralty court, as unfit for service. Such sales are not unfrequently collusive, and in such cases it is held that the title to the vessel is not transferred.[b] The practice, however, is very convenient, when the fact of necessity is obvious; and although in England it is supposed, that under the law of nations the admiralty courts have no such power, Lord Stowell said, that feeling the expediency of the power, the court would go far to sustain the title of the purchaser.[c] The validity of the title under such a sale, would in a great measure depend upon the necessity of a sale, and upon the fairness of the proceedings.

Liability of owners.—The owners of a vessel are of course liable for repairs made, and necessaries furnished, by order of the master. It is, however, frequently a question, who is to be regarded as the owner. This question is determined, not by the register, but by the fact to whom credit was given. The repairer may sue either master or owner; but if he undertake to repair on a special contract with either, the other is discharged.

If the master of a ship buy provisions for her, and have money of the owners to pay for the provisions, but sail without paying the money, the owners are liable to pay, in proportion to their respective shares in the ship; the master being but a servant to the owners.[d]

Whoever supplies a ship with necessaries, has a double security. 1. The person of the master. 2. The personal security of the owners, *whether they know of the supply or not.* The master is personally liable as making the contract. The owners are liable in consequence of the master's act, because they choose him as their agent in the management and conduct of the ship.[e]

Where a vessel has been sold, and the title remains in the vendor merely as security, he is not liable as owner on the contracts, nor for the conduct of the master.[f]

A mortgagee of a ship not in possession, is not liable for repairs and necessaries furnished to the ship.[g]

After an abandonment and acceptance, the insurers become the owners, and are liable for all repairs, &c. after the loss, in proportion to the amount of their subscriptions.

Charterers are considered as the owners of the ship, while on the voyage for which she is chartered; but if the owner retain the management, hire and pay the crew, and provide them with provisions, he is to be still deemed the owner, and the freighter is not liable for repairs,

---

[a] 1 Abbott, 11. [b] 3 Kent, 174. [c] 1 Edwards, Ad. Rep. 117.—5 Mason, 474. [d] 2 Vern. Rep. 643. [e] 3 Kent, 161. [f] Ibid. 134. [g] 7 Cowen, 697.

&c. If the freighter assume these duties, he becomes owner for the voyage, and he only is liable for repairs, &c.[a] In Massachusetts, this liability is extended to responsibility for embezzlement by the crew.[b] Where the owner retains the management, he is entitled to the freight, and may sue the consignee on the bill of lading, or enforce payment by detaining the goods.

If a ship be repaired, the ship itself is not liable at common law, but the owners. By a law of the state of New-York, vessels are liable for all debts contracted by the master, owner, or consignee, on account of any work done, supplies or materials furnished towards the building, repairing, or equipping such vessels. When the claim exceeds $100, the party applies to a court of record, and procures an attachment to seize the vessel. Upon the return thereof, he sets forth the particulars of his demand, and the court may refer the action to indifferent persons, whose report, when confirmed by the court, is conclusive. The vessel may be released from an attachment by giving satisfactory security to abide the judgment of the court.

The lien upon the vessel ceases after the vessel has left the state; and in no case does it continue more than twelve days after the vessel has left the port in which she has been arrested.[c] If a ship be repaired abroad, the ship is liable, and the master may hypothecate (or pawn) her for payment of the charges.[c]

If goods be spoiled by default of the master of a ship employed by the owners, the owners are liable; but the action must be brought against all the owners. So if the goods be lost or embezzled by the crew, or any other person.

In contracting for the transportation of goods, the master acts as agent for the owners, and his liability under the bill of lading is merely co-extensive with theirs.

Their liability under this head, will therefore be more properly found in the next chapter. The same remark is applicable to charterers, when they are regarded as owners.

In many parts of Europe, the responsibility of owners for the acts of masters, is limited to the value of vessel and cargo; and in Massachusetts, such a limitation is established by statute;[b] but, by the common law, the owners are bound for the whole amount of the injury done by the master and crew.[d]

The owners are liable for damage improperly done on the high seas, or in a harbour, to another vessel by collision.

Part owners.—The several part owners of a vessel are not partners, but tenants in common.[e] Where one of them is appointed to manage the concerns of the ship, he is termed the ship's husband, and the other owners are liable for his acts. His duty is to see to the proper outfit and equipment of the vessel. He has not, however, authority to insure for the other owners, nor to bind them for the expenses of law suits.[f]

---

[a] 8 Wheat. 605.—4 Cowen, 470. [b] Rev. Stat. Mass. part 1, chap. 32, sec. 1, 2, 3.
[c] 2 Rev. Stat. N. Y. 493. [d] 3 Kent, 217. [e] Ibid. 151. [f] 6 Daw. 134.

If several part owners wish to send the ship on a voyage, but two or three other part owners refuse their consent, the former may send her on the voyage, but they must enter into a recognizance for her safe return.

If complaint be not made in admiralty, or no dissent expressed to the other part owners before the sailing of the vessel, no redress can be had for her loss in the course of the voyage; inasmuch as a part owner cannot recover against another for sending the ship upon a voyage in which she was lost.

Where there is no agreement between the owners as to the employment of a vessel, the court of admiralty, in authorizing a majority of the owners to employ her, takes care to secure the interests of the minority, by taking a stipulation from the majority in a sum equal to the interest of the dissenting owners, to bring back and restore the ship, or to pay the minority the value of their shares.[a]

The voyage is then made at the risk and expense, and for the benefit of the majority; the minority not being entitled to any part of the freight.

This security is obtained upon application of the minority to the district court of the United States. If it be not obtained, and the ship be sent to sea and lost, the minority have no remedy, unless the majority have been guilty of some tort.

If the owners be equally divided as to the employment of the ship, either party may obtain security. If the minority have possession, and refuse to employ her, the majority may obtain possession, and send her to sea, upon giving security. In Davis & Brooks vs. Brig Seneca, where the owners were equally divided as to the employment of the vessel, and neither would recede, the circuit court ordered the vessel to be sold.[b] If a part owner sell his share, he can only sell his undivided right. His conveyance does not affect the property of the other owners.[b] When a vessel is owned by a firm, one partner can sell and convey the whole vessel.

A part owner is liable for repairs ordered by another owner, upon the ground that, one part owner on the spot has an implied authority from the one absent, to order what is necessary for the preservation of the vessel.

In settling accounts for supplies and repairs between part owners, who are not partners, the accounts are to be taken, and the assets distributed, as if each had a distinct and separate interest.

Where a vessel has been abandoned to separate insurers, they are not responsible as partners, but each is responsible for the expenses of the vessel, only to the extent of his interest as an insurer.

If part owners join in an adventure, a different rule prevails, and they are considered as partners in the adventure.[c]

---

[a] 3 Kent, 152. [b] Ibid. 155. [c] 20 Johns. 611.

CHAPTER VII.

MASTERS OF VESSELS.

NOTHING more materially concerns the master of a ship, than to know what degree of responsibility is attached to his situation, and what privileges it invests him with. The master and owner are, however, so intimately connected together, that many observations in the preceding chapter of owners, will be found to be necessary knowledge for the master of a ship. The doctrine of marine assurances, too, he should be well acquainted with, in order that he may not, by his conduct, inadvertently prejudice his owners' claim on the underwriters.

The master of a vessel is the legal agent or representative of his owners, and is subject to the same rules as to honesty and good faith, with other agents. In cases which are not included within his written orders, and which depend upon his judgment alone, he is to act as if the property intrusted to him were his own.

It is almost the invariable practice of owners to furnish their masters with written orders or instructions, embracing the principal part of their duty during their voyage. It is extremely hazardous for the master to depart from these instructions; as he will be responsible for the least damage which may accrue from a wanton and unnecessary deviation. He should consult them in every case of doubt or difficulty, and follow them with exact precision. Many permanent duties, however, are connected with the situation of a master, which he must always perform, but which are never specified in his orders. He is clothed with the power and discretion requisite to meet unforeseen emergencies during the voyage.

Authority of masters.—At sea, his authority is necessarily summary, and often absolute; but in proportion to his power is his legal accountability. It is essential that he should preserve perfect order and discipline on board, under the guidance of justice and moderation. For this purpose, he is armed with extensive power over the crew, and in case of necessity, over the passengers, who may, if turbulent and violent, be placed under restraint.[a]

The master has the power of appointing his officers and crew, and has the entire command over them during the voyage for which they are shipped. He may, and it is his duty, for the preservation of peace and order on board his vessel, to administer moderate chastisement: but this chastisement must not be a blow with the fist or a stick; the seamen ought to be flogged with a rope, before the crew, who at the same time should be apprized of the offence. In case of mutinous behaviour, or such gross mal-conduct of any seaman, as to endanger the safety of vessel and cargo, the master is justifiable in putting him

---

[a] 1 Camp. N. P. 58.

in irons. Repeated disobedience or neglect is a sufficient cause for the master to discharge a seaman; but this disobedience and neglect should be obstinate and continued, or often repeated, to justify such an exertion of authority in the master.

A seaman may likewise be discharged when infected with any contagious distemper—the master providing for his maintenance and medical attendance.

A seaman may also be discharged for habitual drunkenness, mutinous conduct, or theft; but the master is responsible, in all cases, if he discharges him without just cause.[a]

This power of discharge extends to the mate and other subordinate officers, it being a discretionary power vested in the master for the general welfare of the whole. The law, however, looks upon its exercise with a jealous eye, and holds the master to the strictest accountability. Besides his liability to damages, he is also liable to be fined to the extent of $500, and to be imprisoned not exceeding six months, if he discharge or leave behind, in a foreign port, any officer or seaman maliciously, and without justifiable cause.[b]

In case of the mate, who is selected by the owners to succeed the master in case of death, the disobedience, negligence, or want of skill, should be gross and palpable to justify the master in discharging him.

After a seaman has been discharged for neglect or disobedience, the marine law requires the master to receive him, in case he offer to return to his duty, or make satisfaction; and if he will not receive him, the seaman may follow the ship and recover his wages.[c]

He has authority, in virtue of his character as master, when abroad, to borrow money on the credit of his owners, for necessary expenses and repairs. If money be advanced to the master when abroad, the lender, in order to charge the owner, must prove the actual necessity of the repairs for which the money was advanced. If the money was fairly lent, its misapplication by the master will not discharge the owner. He may also borrow money to pay the export duty on the return cargo, provided he do it for the benefit of his owners. He may also sell a part, or hypothecate the whole of the cargo, to repair the ship when necessary on the voyage; but his authority to do this is at an end upon his arrival at the port of destination; neither can he sell or hypothecate the cargo after the ship is so disabled as to be unable to prosecute the voyage, and such sale will be considered as wrongfully made, though he obtain an order of a vice admiralty court for a sale.

In case of absolute necessity, where the voyage is wholly broken up, he may sell the ship and cargo for the benefit of all concerned.[d]

The absolute necessity, however, must be clear and palpable; and he does this as agent, ex necessitate, for all the parties—his character as master being at an end.

A master has authority to repair the ship, and to supply her with provisions, &c. when necessary; but he renders himself liable to those who furnish him with necessaries, unless he takes care, expressly to confine the credit to his owners.

---

[a] 1 Peters' Adm. R. 186.
[b] Act, 3d March, 1825, sec. 10.
[c] 3 Kent, 183.
[d] Ibid. 173

He is not, however, liable for stores ordered before, but delivered after his appointment.

When a vessel is driven, by stress of weather, into a port other than that to which she is bound, and the cargo, if of a perishing nature, be injured, the master, notwithstanding such injury, will be perfectly secure in proceeding on his voyage with the first opportunity. But the interests of his owners and shippers will, for the most part, in such cases, induce him immediately to sell such part of his cargo as is likely to perish. If, however, the master should risk this proceedure, he should obtain the most unequivocal proofs of the state of his cargo, either from the officers of the port, or from the most respectable commercial characters in the place, by their affidavits under oath; and he should likewise enter his protest before a notary, and see that his accounts are fair and regular, so as to manifest his own integrity; and even after doing all this, he should be reasonably sure of the acquiescence of the owners, shippers and freighters, before he runs the hazard of a sale.

If goods have been thrown overboard, or ransom paid during the voyage, upon arriving in port the master should enter his protest; and he, with some of his crew, must swear that some of the goods thrown overboard, money paid, or other loss sustained, were for the safety of the ship and goods, and for the preservation of the lives of those on board, and for no other purpose. The average, if not settled before, should then be adjusted and paid before the cargo is landed, or at least, before it is delivered; for the owner of the ship has a *lien* upon the goods on board, not only for freight, but also to answer all averages and contributions that may be due. Should this be neglected, the particular sufferer is not without his remedy; as it is the duty of the master to detain the goods until the contribution be made, or to take bonds for the same, to be paid when adjusted. An action would lie against him, or against the owners, for a neglect of this duty.

A protest should be made by the master in every case of accident either to vessel or cargo, at the first port he shall put into. Every occurrence during the voyage, which may operate to the detriment or disadvantage of any concerned in the voyage, should be protested against. This protest must be made within twenty-four hours after his arrival.

A master has no authority to sell the ship except in case of extreme necessity, and no person can safely purchase a ship of the master, in any case, which does not clearly fall within the principle. Although the master be himself a part owner of the ship, yet his sale thereof will not be good for more than his own part; for the interest of part owners is so far distinct, that one of them cannot dispose of the share of another.

If a ship has received an irreparable injury, the captain, acting bona fide, and for the benefit of the owners, may sell her;[a] he may hypothecate the ship, but this only when the voyage would be retarded if he should not take up the money; and not even then, if he have

---

[a] 5 Esp. Cas. 65.

goods of his owners sufficient to defray the necessary expenses, nor if the owners have agents or consignees in the place who have funds, or are bound to provide funds for this purpose. The loan, too, must not exceed the necessity, and must be made under circumstances to afford relief, and when he has no funds of his own.

It is doubtful if an hypothecation to the consignee could be sustained. It would, at all events, be subjected to severe scrutiny.

The master has also authority to make contracts which bind the owners, relative to the usual employment of the ship. He can also bind them in respect to the means of employing her. He may, in a foreign port, bind the ship and freight by a charter-party, and he may do the same at home, if the owners' assent can be presumed. Sir William Scott doubts whether a master has authority even in a foreign port, and in a case of extreme distress, to bind the owners beyond the value of the ship and freight.

It may, however, be considered the law, that the liability of the owner, in such case, is to the extent of the necessary advances.

In case of distress, and putting into port to repair, if there be no consignee or agent of the owner, the master may draw on his owner for the expense of the necessary repairs.

If money cannot be obtained on a bill, he may raise the funds by a bottomry bond on ship, freight and cargo;[a] and in case a bottomry loan cannot be effected, he may sell a portion of the cargo to defray the expense of the necessary repairs.[b] This is what is termed a forced loan, taken by the ship's owner from the cargo, and is payable when the ship arrives at the port of destination, according to the value at that port, of that part of the cargo taken, compared with that which is delivered.

A forced loan can only be made at an intermediate port, and among strangers.

Great judgment and caution are required in deciding in such cases between the different modes of raising funds for necessary repairs. In some instances, the sacrifice by sale of part of the cargo amounts to three fourths of its value; and a little address on the part of the master may enable him to avoid this loss, by including the cargo in the bottomry bond.

Responsibility of the master.—It has already been stated, that as his authority is great, on the other hand his responsibility is great.

He is responsible for the performance of those contracts he may make for the employment of the ship. He is also responsible to his owners, if he does not manifest reasonable care, prudence, and fidelity in the performance of his duty, and for any damage which may result from a neglect or breach of orders. He is liable for the mariners' wages, even though they were shipped by the owners.

He is also liable for goods lost or embezzled during the voyage, according to the net value at the port of delivery.

Also, for any damage committed by the ship, if it could have been avoided by proper care and diligence; but not if the pilot has command of the ship.

---

[a] 3 Rob. Adm. 240. [b] 3 Kent, 173.

If, through mere wantonness or negligence, he run foul of another vessel, an action will lie as well against him as the owners.

A vessel beating to windward upon the larboard tack, must luff or bear away if she meet another beating to windward upon the starboard tack, or her owner and master will be liable for all damage arising from their collision.

A vessel that has the wind free must get out of the way of one that is close hauled, or the master and owner become responsible for all damages.

So, too, where there is a neglect of due means to check the headway of a vessel entering a roadstead or harbour, where vessels are lying at anchor, the master and owner are responsible for all damages.

Where the collision is accidental, the loss must be borne where it falls.

Where the neglect is imputable to both parties, the loss is equally apportioned between the vessels; though their cargoes are not bound to contribute.

If the master has goods delivered to him on shore, he is answerable for them as much as if delivered on board the ship; so is he answerable by the common law, for the safety of goods from plunder or damage, while they are in his boats or barges to be put on board or landed, because those boats or barges are considered as attached to, and making a part of the ship.

The master is liable for all injuries to the goods, occasioned by bad stowage, or exposure to wet; for losses by theft or embezzlement; for the master, at his peril, must see all things forthcoming that are delivered to his charge, acts of God, national enemies, and perils of the sea only excepted: but for fire, thieves, and the like, he must answer as a common carrier.[a]

In stowing the cargo, the master should allow six inches for dunnage in the flat bottom, and nine in the bilges. Hogsheads should have three beds under each. Casks of liquor, molasses, &c. should be placed with their bungs up, well chocked, and not to exceed four heights of riders.

No liquor should be stowed over sugar, or any other goods liable to be damaged by its leakage; salt, from its tendency to moisture, should be separated by bulk heads from other goods; cargoes of grain stowed in bulk should be secured by planks, so as to prevent its shifting when the vessel lies over.

The master is bound, during the voyage, to take all possible care of the cargo; and although he is not responsible for injury done to it in consequence of a leak occasioned by a storm, tempest, or other inevitable accident, yet if a leak be occasioned by rats, and the goods be spoiled, the master has been held liable for the damage, because guilty of fault.[b]

If the cargo be injured from any defect in the vessel, whether latent or obvious, the master and owner are liable for the damage. If damage arise from worms perforating the bottom, they are liable,

---

[a] Marshall, 157. [b] Abbott, 221.

unless the holes were made during the voyage, and the shipper knew that the ship was not copper bottomed.

The master is bound at all times to provide ropes, &c. proper for the actual reception of the goods into the ship, and for the delivery of them on shore; for if a cask be accidentally staved in letting it down into the ship's hold, or in landing it, the master must answer for the loss.[a]

Goods lost in a lighter.—If goods are lost after the owner of them has taken them from the ship into a lighter, it is his own loss; but it is otherwise if the goods are sent from the ship by the ship's boat, which is considered as part of the ship and voyage. Yet, if the owner of any goods send his servant with them, the master, or lighterman, is not liable if they be lost.

When the charge of goods ceases, depends in some measure upon the custom of the place.

If the vessel can be moored alongside of a wharf or quay, there is no difficulty; as the goods are then delivered to the wharfinger. But when she is obliged to discharge in a river or open roadstead, and boats or other craft are employed in delivering the cargo, it is necessary to ascertain the custom. In discharging the cargo, the master should take a receipt upon the bill of lading for the goods delivered.

If the master take on board his ship any contraband or unlawful goods, whereby other parts of the cargo, or the ship, may be liable to forfeiture or detention, he is responsible; or if he takes on board any false or suspicious papers, which may subject the ship to capture or detention, he is also liable for the damages.[b]

The master of a ship is liable for goods of which the ship is robbed in the harbour, but he may reimburse himself out of the mariners' wages, for a loss happening by their neglect.

It should be recollected that the master, in his transactions with other persons, may incur a double responsibility; viz. to the persons with whom he contracts, and to his owners, if he should exceed his authority.

He may, however, by special contract with the parties dealing with him, expressly confining the credit to the owner, exempt himself from that responsibility.

Duty of the master.—The master should always preserve order and discipline on board of his ship. He is to take care that she be properly stowed, equipped and manned, and provided with the necessary documents to show her character. During the voyage, he must conduct her with skill and prudence by the most direct route to her destined port.

Passengers on board a vessel, are entitled to all the accommodations, conveniences, and attentions from the master, which the nature of the vessel and voyage, and the terms of their agreement, will admit; and the master is liable to an action, should the passengers be

---

[a] Goff v. Clinkard, cited 1 Wills. 282.

[b] Molloy, Book 2. ch. 2. sec. 7.—Abbott, 11.

deprived of them, or be not conveyed to the port of destination according to his contract.

Masters of vessels bound to the United States, must, on their arrival within four leagues of the coast, make out a true manifest of the cargo, and have two copies in readiness to be delivered to the proper officers, subscribed by themselves, one of which must be delivered to the revenue officer, when demanded within that distance, and the other to the officer of the customs in the district of delivery in which he shall first arrive, under penalty of $500.[a]

On entering ports, or navigating difficult passages, where the custom of the trade has stationed pilots, it is the duty of the master to take one on board, and by no means to proceed without; and not to discharge his pilot, except at the accustomed places. A neglect of this part of his duty destroys the policies on vessels and cargo, and renders both master and owners liable to the assured. A master should note on his log-book, the time and place of his taking the pilot on board.

When in the foreign trade, it is the duty of the master to put his ship under the charge of a pilot, both in the outward and homeward voyage, whenever within the usual limits of a pilot's employment.[b]

When driven by stress of weather, or chased by an enemy, he is justified in attempting to enter the port without a pilot.

So, too, where at a foreign port he has failed (after trying) to get a pilot, and attemps to enter in the exercise of a sound discretion.[c]

The pilot, when on board, is for the time considered as master, and has the exclusive control of the ship.

If any loss be sustained through his negligence, default or unskilfulness in navigating the vessel, the owner is responsible to the party injured, in the same manner as if she had been under the command of the master; and although Lord Mansfield expressed some doubt on the subject, the better opinion is, that for such loss, the master is not responsible.[d]

Port laws and regulations should be carefully observed. In almost every port there are certain laws for the government of the shipping, which cannot be transgressed with impunity. A master should, therefore, inform himself of this on his first arrival, and be scrupulous in conforming to them during his stay. All the damage which ensues in consequence of a breach of them, will eventually fall on him.

The master is bound to observe the health and revenue laws of whatever country he may be in; for, if by his negligence or misconduct he violates them, and the vessel be seized, or the cargo taken, he is answerable to the owners for the loss.

Port dues and charges are payable by the captain; and his vessel, cables, anchors, &c. may be distrained.

The laws of the different states respecting discharging ballast and anchorage in rivers, and those of the southern states respecting the coloured population, must also be observed.

---

[a] Vide chap. 3, p. 52. [b] 3 Kent, 175. [c] 2 Barn. & Ald. 380. [d] 3 Kent, 176.

He never should attempt a breach of embargoes, blockades, or other restraints, being, in most cases, personally responsible, if any damage should ensue.

Unnecessary deviations from the direct course of the voyage, ought never to be attempted.—Not only the policies on both vessel and cargo are by this means vacated, but the property subjected to other risks which often prove fatal.

The master should note in the log-book all the material occurrences which happen during the voyage. The log-books on board of merchant ships are in general badly kept, as to grammar, penmanship and cleanliness—being often defaced and torn, and in case of dispute, giving rise to suspicions of alterations.

In Norway the log-books are issued by the government, and stamped and numbered in the pages, so as to prevent any alteration.

Upon his arrival he must inform his consignee, and if subject to quarantine, report himself to the health officer of the port.

The regulations imposed by the revenue laws of the United States, will be found in the previous chapters.

Passengers dying on board.—If any passenger die on board, the master is obliged to inventory his effects; and if no claim be made to them within a year, the master becomes proprietor of the goods, but answerable for them to the deceased's legal representatives.

Captain dying.—If a captain die, leaving money on board, and the mate becoming captain, improve the money, he must, on allowance for his care, account both for interest and profits.

Whenever a vessel belonging to a citizen of the United States, is sold in a foreign country, and her company discharged; or when a citizen of the United States, with his own consent, is discharged in a foreign country, it is the duty of the master to produce to the consul, or commercial agent, the list of the ship's company, certified as aforesaid, and to pay to such consul, for every mariner so discharged, being a citizen of the United States, three months' pay over and above the wages due: two thirds thereof to be paid by such consul, or commercial agent, to each mariner so discharged, upon his engagement on board of any vessel to return to the United States, and the other remaining third to be retained for the purpose of creating a fund for the payment of the passages of American seamen, who may be desirous of returning to the United States, and for the maintenance of those who may be destitute, in such foreign port.

Masters of American vessels must make a protest when any of their seamen have been impressed, and transmit the same to the nearest consul, or the minister of the United States, and keep a duplicate for the secretary of state.

They must also declare on oath, before entry, whether any of their crew have been impressed, under penalty of $100.

Masters must take, under the penalty of $100 in case of refusal, all American seamen put on board by the consul or agent of the United States, in a foreign port, at a price not exceeding $10 for each person, provided that no more than two men for every hundred tons be put on board without his consent.

Where seamen have been transported from foreign ports in which there is no consul or agent of the United States, there is allowed to the master or owner such sum as may be deemed equitable by the comptroller of the treasury, in addition to the legal allowance.[a]

By an act of congress, passed February 28, 1803, before a clearance of any vessel bound on a foreign voyage, the master must deliver to the collector a list sworn to, containing the names, places of birth, and residence, and a description of the persons who compose his ship's company; and the collector delivers him a certified copy thereof; the master enters into bond with security, in the sum of $400, to exhibit the copy to the first boarding officer at the first port in the United States, at which he shall arrive on his return, who examines the men with such list, and reports the same to the collector; the collector transmits a copy of the list to the inspector of the port from which the vessel originally sailed. In case any of the persons not produced have been discharged in a foreign country with the consent of the consul, or commercial agent there residing, under his hand and official seal, or died, absconded, or have been forcibly impressed into other service, satisfactory proof thereof must be also exhibited to the collector.

Every master of a vessel, belonging to citizens of the United States, on his arrival at a foreign port, must deposite his register, sea-letter, and Mediterranean passport with the consul, vice-consul, or commercial agent, (at such port,) and in case of refusal or neglect, he forfeits $500. The consul, on such master producing to him a clearance from the proper officer, delivers to him all his said papers.

Rights of masters.—A master may detain the baggage or goods of passengers on board, until they have paid the passage money.

The master of a ship is not bound to deliver goods shipped on freight, when arrived at the port of destination, without a receipt from the consignee. An endorsement of the bill of lading is an *assignment* of the goods themselves; but it is not negotiable by the custom of merchants; nor is the master bound to deliver the goods, where there is no express stipulations, until his freight be paid; the goods, while in his hands, being bound for the payment of the freight, and if he part with them, he loses his *lien* on the goods for the payment of the freight.

If the consignee has failed, he should (where the consignee interposes his claim) deliver the goods to the agent of the consignor; but if the consignee have assigned the bill of lading, and no satisfactory indemnity be offered by either of the claimants, the master should deliver them into the hands of some responsible merchant, to abide the legal decision of the conflicting claims.

The master has no lien on the vessel for his wages, and in England he has no lien for monies advanced for stores and repairs.

In the United States, however, it has been held, that the master has a lien on the freight for all monies advanced abroad on account of the ship;[b] and in the case of the Grand Turk, the circuit court of the United States, in New-York, decided, that he had a lien on the ship

---

[a] Act, 28th Feb. 1811.

[b] 3 Mason, 255.

for advances made to pay sailor's wages.[a] As to his own wages, the law has always considered the captain as contracting personally with the owner, and the case of the captain has, in that respect, been distinguished from that of all other persons belonging to the ship. This rule of law has its foundation in policy, looking to the benefit of navigation; for, as ships may be making profit and earning every day, it might be attended with great inconvenience, if, on the change of a captain for misbehaviour, or any other reason, he should be entitled to keep the ship till he was paid.

---

[a] 1 Paine, 72.

CHAPTER VIII.

SEAMEN.

The rights and duties of seamen are well defined in the general maritime law of nations; and they are also made subject to special regulations prescribed by acts of congress.

These latter, of course, are paramount here, and supersede the maritime law as laid down by the old writers, and by judicial decisions. We shall, therefore, in the first place, set forth the statute provisions.

By the act of congress for the government and regulation of seamen in the merchant service, shipping articles are prescribed to be entered into before sailing, between the master and every mariner on board, (except apprentices or servants,) for every vessel bound to a foreign port, and for every vessel of more than fifty tons bound to any port except to one in an adjoining state. This contract must be in writing, and must declare the voyage or period for which the seamen shipped,[a] and the day and hour when they are to render themselves on board.[b]

If a seaman be shipped without signing such articles, he is not bound by the articles, or by the act, and the master forfeits $20 for every seaman not signing, and is also bound to pay the highest rate of wages paid at the shipping port for similar voyages for three months previous.[c] It has been decided, under this act, that articles stating a voyage from New-York to Curracoa and *elsewhere*, mean a voyage terminating at Curracoa.

This act, however, does not apply to voyages commencing from a foreign port to the United States, but merely to voyages commencing here.[d]

If any seaman, having signed the articles, neglect to render himself on board at the time mentioned, the master, or other officer, must at the time make an entry in the log-book, of the name of such mariner, and note the time that he so neglected to render himself, (after the time appointed;) and every such mariner forfeits for every hour one day's pay, to be deducted out of his wages. If he wholly neglect to render himself on board, or desert, so that the vessel proceeds to sea without him, he forfeits, to the master, owner, or consignee, double the sum advanced to him.[b]

If the mate, and a majority of the crew of a vessel bound to a foreign port, after the voyage is begun, (and before the vessel has left the land,) discover that she is too leaky, or otherwise unfit to proceed on the intended voyage, and require such unfitness to be inquired into,

---

[a] Act, 20th July, 1790, sec. 1. [b] Ibid. sec. 2. [c] 1 Hall's L. J. 209. [d] 3 Kent, 185.

the master must forthwith proceed to or stop at the nearest or most convenient place, where such inquiry can be made, and there apply to the judge of the district court, if he there reside, or if not, to some justice of the peace, taking with him two or more of the crew applying. Such judge or justice is then required to issue his precept directed to three of the neighbourhood, (the most skilful in maritime affairs,) requiring them to repair on board, and examine the same, and report to him, in writing, under their hands, or the hands of two of them, whether in any, or in what respect the said vessel is unfit to proceed on the intended voyage, and what addition of men, provisions, stores, or what repairs or alterations will be necessary. Upon such report being made he adjudges and endorses thereon his judgment, whether the said vessel is fit to proceed; and if not, whether such repairs can be made, or deficiencies supplied, where the vessel then lies, or whether it be necessary for her to return to the port whence she first sailed, to be there refitted; and the master and crew must conform to the judgment. The master must, in the first instance, pay all the costs to be taxed on a fair copy of the judgment, certified by the judge. But if the complaint of the crew appear to have been without foundation, then the master, or owner, deducts the amount thereof, and of reasonable damages for the detention, (to be ascertained by the judge or justice,) out of their wages. If, after such judgment, such vessel is fit to proceed on her intended voyage, or after procuring men, provisions, stores, repairs, or alterations, as directed, the mariners, or either of them, refuse to proceed, any justice of the peace may commit such mariner to the gaol until he pay double the sum advanced, together with costs allowed by the justice, and inserted in the warrant. The sureties of such mariner are also liable for such payment.[a]

If any person harbour or secrete any mariner belonging to any vessel, every such person, on conviction thereof, must pay $10 for every day which he harbours or secretes such mariner. No sum, exceeding one dollar, is recoverable from any mariner by any one person, for any debt contracted during the time such mariner actually belongs to any vessel, until the voyage for which he engaged is ended.[b]

If any mariner, subscribing such contract, absent himself from on board without leave of the master or officer commanding; and the officer having charge of the log-book, make an entry therein of his name at the time, such mariner forfeits three days' pay for every day's absence, to be deducted out of his wages; but if any mariner absent himself for more than forty-eight hours at one time, he forfeits all the wages due to him, and all his goods and chattels on board, or in any store where they may have been lodged at the time of his desertion, to the use of the owner, and moreover is liable to pay all damages sustained by reason of his desertion, with costs.[c]

This forfeiture is remitted, if the seaman return and is restored to his duty.

---

[a] Act, 20th July, 1790, sec. 3. [b] Ibid. sec. 4. [c] Ibid. sec. 5.

Mariners are entitled to receive one third part of the wages due to them at every port of delivery, unless the contrary be expressly stipulated in the contract. As soon as the voyage is ended, and the cargo and ballast is fully discharged at the last port of delivery, every mariner is entitled to the wages then due; and if such wages be not paid within ten days after such discharge, or if any dispute arise touching the wages, the judge of the district where the vessel is, or in case his residence be more than three miles from the place, or, of his absence, any judge or justice of the peace may summon the master, to show cause why process should not issue against such vessel, her tackle and apparel, according to the course of admiralty courts, for the said wages. If the master neglect to appear, or, appearing, do not show that the wages are paid, or otherwise satisfied, or forfeited, the judge or justice certifies to the clerk of the court of the district that there is sufficient cause of complaint, and thereupon the clerk issues process against the said vessel, and the suit is proceeded on, according to the course of admiralty courts. In such suit, all the mariners (having cause of complaint of the like kind) are joined as complainants; and the master must produce the contract and log-book, if required, to ascertain any matters in dispute; otherwise the complainants are permitted to state the contents thereof, and the proof of the contrary lies on the master. A mariner may also sue at common law for his wages, or he may obtain process in admiralty against the vessel, or in case she shall be about to proceed to sea before the end of ten days next after the delivery of her cargo or ballast.[a]

This is in conformity with the decisions in admiralty, and it is held that a seaman need not libel a vessel at the port of discharge, but may follow the ship, and pursue his lien for wages even against a bona fide purchase, and in preference to a bottomry bond.

In France, however, the mariner's lien is extinguished after a sale, and a voyage has been made in the name of the purchaser.

Fishermen engaged in the fisheries must also sign articles; and they are liable to the same penalties, entitled to the same remedies, and subject to similar regulations, as other sailors.[b]

If any mariner, who has signed a contract to perform a voyage, desert, or absent himself without leave, any justice of the peace (upon the complaint of the master) may issue his warrant to apprehend such deserter, and bring him before such justice. If it then appear that he has signed such contract, and that the voyage agreed for is not finished, altered, or the contract otherwise dissolved; and that such mariner has deserted, or absented himself without leave; the justice may commit him to the house of correction or common gaol, until the vessel is ready to proceed on her voyage, or until the master require his discharge. He is then to be delivered to the master, he paying all costs, and deducting the same out of his wages.[c]

Every vessel, belonging to a citizen of the United States, of the burthen of 150 tons or upwards, navigated by ten or more persons, and bound on a foreign voyage, must be provided with a chest of

---

[a] Act, 20th July, 1790, sec. 6. [b] 4 Pick. 298. [c] Act, 20th July, 1790, sec. 7.

medicine, put up by some apothecary of known reputation, and accompanied by directions for administering the same. The medicines must be examined by some apothecary, once at least in every year, and supplied with fresh medicines in the place of such as have been used or spoiled; and in default of having such medicine chest, the master must provide and pay for all such advice, medicine, or attendance of physicians, as any of the crew may stand in need of in case of sickness, without any deduction from the wages of such mariner.[a]

The provisions of this section were extended by a subsequent act to all vessels of more than seventy-five tons, and navigable by six or more persons bound to the West-Indies.[b]

It has been decided that a clause in the shipping article by which the seamen engaged to pay for all medicine and medical aid further than the medicine chest afforded, was void as inequitable and contrary to the policy of the act. The expense of curing a seaman taken sick during the voyage, is, by the general maritime law, a charge upon the ship.[c]

Every American vessel, bound on a voyage across the Atlantic, when she sails, must have on board, well secured under deck, at least sixty gallons of water, one hundred pounds of salted flesh meat, and one hundred pounds of wholesome ship bread, for every person on board, besides such other provisions, stores and live-stock, as may, by the master or passsengers, be put on board; and in like proportion for shorter or longer voyages. Otherwise, in case the crew be put upon short allowance during the voyage, the master or owner must pay to each of the crew one day's wages beyond the wages agreed on for every day of short allowance.[d]

During the late war with Great Britain, a law was passed, which was to operate only in reference to the subjects of any power which might adopt similar regulations respecting the employment in their vessels of native citizens of the United States before naturalization.[e] This law provides that no person, except a citizen of the United States, and no person of colour except a native of the United States, should be employed on board any American vessel.[f] It also provides that naturalized citizens in merchants' ships must produce their certificates of naturalization to the collector, and if in public armed vessels, to the commander.[g]

The collector must examine and certify the list of the crew, and no person can be employed on board unless his name be on the list. The names are also to be recorded in a book kept for the purpose by the collector.[h] Foreign seamen cannot even be received as passengers in a foreign port, without the written consent of the proper officer of the country to which they belong.[i] Any violation of this act subjects the commander of a public vessel to a fine of $1000, and the master and owner of a merchant vessel to a fine of $500, for every person employed or taken as a passenger.[j] As no other nation passed

---

[a] Act, 20th July, 1790, sec. 8. [b] Act, 2d March, 1805.
[c] 2 Mason, 541. [d] Act, 2d March, 1805, sec. 9. [e] Ibid. sec. 10.
[f] Act, 3d March, 1813, sec. 1. [g] Ibid. sec. 2. [h] Ibid. sec. 3. [i] Ibid. sec. 5. [j] Ibid. sec. 6.

any similar law respecting the employment of American seamen, this act became a dead letter, and so far as it respects the employment of foreign seamen, may be regarded as inoperative.

An act was passed in 1796, requiring the collectors in the different districts to keep books, in which American seamen, upon producing proof of their citizenship, may have their names entered, and obtain a protection or certificate of citizenship containing a description of their persons.[a]

If a seaman should be impressed, it is made the duty of the master to make a protest at the first port, stating the manner of the impressment, together with the name, place of residence and nation of the person impressed.[b] This protest must be sent to the American consul or minister resident in the country where the vessel is; and upon the arrival of the master in the United States, a duplicate must be sent to the secretary of state.[b]

The master, before his vessel is admitted to entry, must declare on oath, whether any of the crew have been impressed in the course of the voyage, and if so, what he did thereupon. By the neglect of this he incurs a penalty of $100.[c] Before clearance, he delivers the collector a list, sworn to, of his crew, describing their persons, &c. and takes a certified copy thereof, which, upon his return, he must exhibit to the first boarding officer, who compares it with the crew, to ascertain that none are missing.[d]

A report must also be made of the number of seamen employed on board during the voyage, and twenty cents per month must be paid to the collector by each seaman out of his wages for hospital money.[e] A like report must also be made before taking out a new enrolment in the coasting trade, and twenty cents per month paid for each seaman for the time he was actually employed.[f] The making a false return is punishable by a fine of $500.[f]

The collectors make quarterly returns of these monies to the treasury; and the money thus collected, as well as that collected from foreign seaman, is appropriated for the temporary relief and maintenance of sick and disabled American seamen when in port, and the surplus is invested under the direction of the president of the United States, for the purpose of erecting marine hospitals.[g]

The same sum is exacted from the raftmen and boatmen on the Mississippi, and they are entitled to the same privileges. Foreign seamen are to be admitted into the hospitals, when it can be done with convenience, who are to be charged 75 cents per day for each person, which charge must be paid before the vessel to which they belong can obtain her clearance. This money goes into the same fund.

Twenty cents per month is also deducted from the pay of the officers, seamen and mariners, in the navy of the United States, for the same purpose; and they are entitled to relief from the navy hospital fund, which is a different fund, under the direction of the secretary of the navy department.

---

[a] Act, 28th May, 1796, sec. 4. [b] Ibid. sec. 5. [c] Ibid. sec. 6. [d] Act, 28th Feb. 1803, sec. 1.
[e] Act, 16th July, 1798, sec. 1. [f] Ibid. sec. 2. [g] Ibid. sec. 5.

All fines imposed on navy officers, seamen and mariners, are appropriated to the navy hospital fund. When any of these persons are admitted into a navy hospital, the institution is allowed one ration per day by the United States; and, if he is entitled to a pension, such pension, during his stay, is paid to the commissioner, and deducted from his pension account.

In the state of New-York, steerage passengers, mates and seamen, are compelled to pay $1 for each foreign voyage, towards the state hospital fund; and the captains and cabin passengers $1,50; and the officers and mariners of coasting vessels pay 25 cents for the same purpose upon their arrival; provided that those from New-Jersey, Connecticut and Rhode Island, need not pay oftener than once a month. This hospital money must be paid at the office of the health commissioners, by the masters of coasters, within twenty-four hours after the arrival of their vessel, under the penalty of $100.

For the sums to be paid in other ports under statute laws, *vide* Quarantine Laws.

The hospital fund requires the attention of the government. It is not large enough to support an establishment commensurate with the wants of the seamen, and, at the same time, many are admitted to participate in its advantages who should, in equity, be debarred, but who are comprehended by the letter of the law. We mean those who do not go to sea more than a fourth part of their time, or who, perhaps, have never made more than one voyage.

An act has also been passed by congress, authorizing the apprehension of deserters while in port, from the vessel of any nation having a treaty with the United States for the restoration of deserters. Application must be made in writing, by the consul, to a magistrate, with proof that the deserter then belonged to the vessel, by the exhibition of the register and shipping list. The deserter is thereupon to be apprehended, and delivered to the consul. He cannot, however, be detained in prison longer than two months after his arrest, unless he shall have committed some crime, when his surrender is to be delayed until after trial and execution of the sentence.[a]

There are also laws in some of the states in relation to seamen, when in port, that are deserving of notice.

In Delaware, when engaged in a vessel, no mariner can be arrested for a debt contracted above ten shillings in amount.[a]

In Virginia, foreign seamen, parties to the shipping list, who absent themselves without leave from their vessel, (whether American or foreign,) may be carried before a justice of the peace by a warrant, and committed to gaol until the vessel is ready to sail, and then delivered to the master.

Apprentices, regularly bound to the master or owner for a term of years, may be dealt with in the same manner. If, however, the seaman or apprentice prove, before the justice, that he has been cruelly or improperly treated by the master, or that he has good reason to apprehend personal danger from the master should he be compelled to remain on board, the justice may discharge him from confinement.[b]

---

[a] Act, 2d March, 1829. [b] Act, 9th Jan., 1805.

If masters discharge or land any sick or disabled seamen without providing for their maintenance or cure, they forfeit $60; and if they land any passenger without the means of procuring their maintenance for one month, they forfeit $50.[a]

Tavern keepers, selling drink on credit to a sailor in actual employ of a vessel, lose the debt, and forfeit $2 to the master of the vessel. The same penalty is incurred by harbouring or entertaining a sailor in actual pay, without the consent of the master.[b]

In Georgia, persons giving credit to seamen for more than five shillings, lose the debt; and if a person, without leave of the master, harbours a sailor who has signed the shipping articles, he forfeits 40 shillings for every twenty-four hours he harbours him.

Persons selling a seaman spirituous liquor to the amount of more than one shilling and six pence per day, or suffering a sailor to drink in their houses after nine in the evening, forfeit $5.

In Alabama, persons secreting deserters from any merchant vessel are liable to a penalty of $10 for every day they continue so to harbour such seamen.[c] Masters employing seamen belonging to or pretending to be discharged from another vessel in that state, must obtain a certificate of their discharge, under penalty of $50.[c] A seaman absenting himself from his vessel without leave, is liable to be committed to the house of correction until the vessel sails.[c]

In Louisiana, captains of vessels arriving in New-Orleans are required to give to all sailors discharged from their vessels a certificate of discharge. If a sailor desert, the master must, within twelve hours, affix a notice in the mayor's office of the desertion, with the names of the vessel and deserter, and a description of the latter, signed by the master. Masters employing seamen without a certificate of discharge, are liable to a fine of $50; and if a sailor applies to enter without such certificate, the master must notify the other masters in port who have given such notice. If the master refuse to give such discharge, the sailor, if entitled to it, can compel him to do so before the parish court.

Any keeper of a public or boarding house harbouring or secreting a deserter from a merchant vessel, is liable to a fine of $100, and to imprisonment of thirty days, at the discretion of the court.[d]

The general rights and duties of seamen, however, depend upon the principles of the maritime law, which has been incorporated with, and forms part of the common law of the land.

Duty of seamen.—The mariners must obey all the commands of the master relating to the navigation of the ship, and the preservation of good order. In case of disobedience, he may correct them in a reasonable manner. Such an authority is necessary to the safety of the whole. But he should be very careful not to suffer his authority to degenerate into cruelty or oppression, as he may be called upon, by an action, to answer for the same upon his return to this country; and if he cannot show that there was a sufficient cause for chastisement, the seaman may recover damages proportionate to the injury.

---

[a] Act, 10th Feb., 1819. [b] Act, 22d Feb., 1819. [c] Act, 21st Dec., 1823. [d] Act, 11th Jan., 1822.

A mariner may be discharged in a foreign port by the master for misbehaviour; but slight and venial offences will not justify a discharge; and a master is responsible in damages if he discharge a sailor without just cause; and the sailor, in such case, is entitled to his wages for the voyage.[a] So, too, if he repent of his misconduct, and offer amends, and return to his duty, and the master refuse to receive him.[b]

The sailor, however, must follow the ship in her voyage. If the master, where a sailor might have been properly discharged for misbehaviour, instead of discharging him, send him to prison, and leave him in gaol abroad, the sailor will be entitled to his full wages until his return to the United States, after deducting the time he was imprisoned.[c]

A mariner cannot be discharged because of any disability from accident or sickness contracted in the voyage. On the contrary, the expense of medical aid, and of curing the sailor, is a charge upon the vessel, and is in the shape of additional wages during sickness. In case the sailor be left sick in a foreign port, he is entitled to his wages for the whole voyage.[d]

For the benefit of seamen, discharged in a foreign country without having given cause by misbehaviour, it has been enacted, that three months' pay, over and above the wages due to them, shall be paid to the American consul at that port, two thirds of it for their use when they take passage for the United States.[e]

If a sailor be discharged abroad, it is necessary to obtain the consent of the American consul or commercial agent at the port; and that consent, under his hand and seal of office, must be produced to the collector at the port of arrival in the United States, in order to discharge the bond given when the vessel clears out from the United States.[f]

The consul has the power of sending home American seamen in distress abroad, and may put them on board any American vessel to transport them to the United States, at the rate of $10 per head.

The seamen, if able, are bound to do duty on board, and the comptroller of the treasury may, at his discretion, where there was no consul at the port, make a further compensation.[g] Not more than two seamen to every 100 tons can be put on board without the consent of the master.[h]

Wages.—If a seaman die during the voyage, it was held by the district and circuit courts in Pennsylvania, that full wages for the voyage are due to his representatives;[i] but in the district courts in Massachusetts and South Carolina, it was decided that wages were due only up to the time of his death. As freight is the mother of wages, no wages are due to the mariners, unless freight be earned. If a ship be lost before she arrive at any port of delivery, the seamen lose all their wages. But if the ship be forfeited through the misconduct of the owners or master, the rule that the voyage should be performed does not deprive them of their wages, unless they had notice that

---

[a] 3 Rob. Ad. R. 92.—2 Pet. Ad. R. 420. [b] 1 Pet. Ad. R. 193. [c] 12 Serg. & R. 266
[d] 3 Kent, 184. [e] Act, 28th Feb., 1803, sec. 3. [f] Ibid. sec. 1.
[g] Act, 28th Feb., 1811. [h] Act, 28th Feb., 1803, sec. 4. [i] 3 Kent, 189.

the voyage was illegal. In such case they will be entitled to wages up to the time of the loss of the voyage, and such additional remuneration as shall be adjudged reasonable.

They cannot insure their wages, either directly, or through the owner ; therefore the owner is not liable for wages in case of the loss of the ship, if he receive freight from the insurers. But he is liable, if freight be paid by captors to a neutral.

A mariner cannot claim higher wages, in consequence of a promise made to him in time of distress, to animate him to greater exertions.

If the ship be lost after coming to a port of delivery, they only lose their wages from the last port of delivery ; and even where the officers and mariners gave bonds not to demand wages unless the ship returned to London, and she arrived at a delivering port, and afterwards was taken by an enemy, they had their wages to the delivering port. If they run away, though after coming to a port of delivery, they lose all their wages.

If a ship outward bound arrives at her destined port, unloads there, receives freight to return, and is taken by enemies on her return, the mariners shall have their wages to the time she arrived at the port she unloaded in, and for half the time she staid there to unload.[a]

So if she be shipwrecked on her return. By the maritime law, wages are due pro rata at each delivering port, even if the charter-party has made the freight to depend upon the safe accomplishment of the voyage out and home.

The wages pro rata are due upon the arrival out, even though she arrived in ballast, as it was the owners' fault that freight was not earned.[b] If part of the freight have been advanced, the seamen are entitled to a proportional part of their wages, even if the ship be lost on her outward voyage.[b]

Capture by an enemy puts an end to the contract for wages ; and Sir William Scott held that it was not revived by recapture—the sailor claiming, not then being on board. In the United States, however, it is held, that as the owner, in such event, recovers his freight, the seaman shall recover his wages, and such is now the law in England.[c]

It is the same when a foreign power seizes the ship and she is afterwards released, and the crew resume their duties and complete the voyage;—they are entitled to wages from the commencement of the voyage. If a neutral ship be captured, and even condemned, and the sentence be afterwards reversed, and freight allowed in damages, the seamen are entitled to wages ;[d] but wages are denied if the seamen refuse to re-enter the vessel when in their power.

When any part of the cargo is saved, or of the ship from shipwreck, the mariners are entitled to a proportion of their wages,[c] and the demand for wages takes precedence of a bottomry bond. In case of shipwreck, the claim on the vessel is rather a claim for salvage. Desertion from the ship without just cause, or a discharge by the master

---

[a] 1 Peters' C. C. R. 182. [b] 3 Kent, 191. [c] Ibid. 192. [d] 3 Mason, 161.

for bad conduct, will work a forfeiture of wages. The forfeiture is saved if the seaman repents, makes compensation or an offer of amends, and is restored to his duty. It is the duty of the seamen to stay by the vessel in distress as long as reasonable hope remains, and if they leave her in time of danger, when by their presence and exertions they might have prevented damage or saved the vessel, they forfeit their wages, and are answerable in damages.

A seaman is entitled to wages for the whole voyage, if compelled to leave the ship from cruelty, ill-treatment, or for personal safety, or from any wrongful discharge during the voyage.

In cases of embargo, or capture and recapture, if the ship afterwards perform the voyage and earn freight, the seamen are entitled to their wages for the whole time, provided they stay by the ship. In case of capture and recapture, however, their wages must contribute on account of salvage. If the voyage be broken up, extra wages are allowed according to the discretion of the court.

For an illegal voyage no wages can be recovered.

Where a vessel was captured, and the cargo and freight lost, but the master, to induce the sailors to stay by the ship pending the trial, agreed to allow them so much a month while they staid by her, it was held, that although freight is the mother of wages, still a special agreement was binding, and the seamen were entitled to their wages.

A mariner forfeits his wages by embezzlement of any part of the cargo.[a] If the embezzlement cannot be fixed on any particular person, the whole crew are bound to contribute out of their wages to make good the loss.[b]

The circumstances, however, must be such as to fix suspicion upon some of the crew; and when they are so situated as to be able to repel the presumption of guilt, they are exempted from contributing.[c]

Negligence of mariners.—Masters may reimburse themselves out of the wages of their mariners, for losses happening by their negligence.

Suing for wages in the district courts.—The convenience arising to mariners prosecuting for wages in the admiralty, or United States district courts is so great, that, out of regard to that useful body of men, it is permitted that they may sue for wages there by attaching the ship. But although this liberty is given to mates and mariners, it is denied to the master; for, the master contracts upon the credit of the owners, and the mariners upon the credit of the ship. The convenience and benefit accruing to the mariners from this practice, are, 1st. That they may *all join* in a suit there for wages, (thereby lessening the expense,) which could not be done in the courts of common law; and, 2d. In the district courts, the ship itself is answerable, and not the owners.

Even if a master of a ship design to go on a voyage, and hire and take on board seamen in order to accomplish it; but afterwards the owners cannot agree about sending the ship on the voyage, and the sea-

---

[a] 2 Cranch, 266. [b] 3 John. 17. [c] 3 Kent, 194.

men are thereupon discharged; the seamen have the same remedy in the district courts for their wages as if the ship had gone the voyage.

The claim of the sailors for wages takes precedence of every other lien on the vessel. It follows the vessel into the hands of a bona fide purchaser, and, also, the proceeds, whenever they can be found and identified.

CHAPTER IX.

CONSULS.

By the custom of all maritime nations, consuls or commercial agents are appointed, in the principal ports of civilized countries, to attend to the interests of the citizens of their respective countries, who may be obliged to have recourse to the public authorities of the foreign country. They are considered as representing the commercial interests of their governments, in the various places where they are stationed.

By the laws of the United States, consuls and vice consuls of the United States have the right, in the places to which they are severally appointed, of receiving the protests or declarations which such captains, masters, crews, passengers and merchants, as are citizens of the United States, and also such as any foreigner may choose to make before them, relative to the personal interest of any citizens of the United States; and the copies of the said acts, duly authorized by the said consuls or vice consuls, under the seal of their consulates, respectively, receive faith in law, equally as their originals would in all courts in the United States.[a] It is their duty, where the laws of the country permit, to take possession of the personal estate left by any citizen of the United States, other than seamen belonging to any vessel, who may die within their consulates, leaving there no legal representative, partner in trade, or trustee by him appointed, to take care of his effects They must inventory the same, with the assistance of two merchants of the United States, or for want of them, of any others, at their choice: collect the debts due to the deceased in the country where he died, and pay the debts due from his estate which he may have there contracted; sell at auction, after reasonable public notice, such part of the estate as is of a perishable nature, and such further part, if any, as may be necessary for the payment of his debts, and at the expiration of one year from his decease, the residue; and transmit the balance of the estate to the treasury of the United States, to be holden in trust for the legal claimants. But if, at any time before such transmission, the legal representative of the deceased appear and demand his effects in their hands, they must deliver them up, being paid their fees, and cease their proceedings. On information of the representative of the deceased, it is the duty of the consul or vice consul, immediately to notify his death in one of the gazettes published in the consulate; and also to the secretary of state, that the same may be notified in the state to which the deceased belongs; and as soon as may be, to transmit to the secretary of state an inventory of the effects of the deceased.[b]

---

[a] Act, 14th April, 1792, sec. 1. [b] Ibid. sec. 2.

Consuls and vice consuls, where vessels of the United States are stranded on the coasts of their consulates, as far as the laws of the country will permit, must take measures for saving the vessels, their cargoes and appurtenances; for securing the merchandise saved; and for taking an inventory thereof: and the merchandise and effects saved, with the inventory, after deducting the expense, must be delivered to the owners. But no consul or vice consul has authority to take possession of any property, when the master, owner, or consignee thereof is present, or capable of taking possession of the same.[a]

Every consul and vice consul of the United States may receive the following fees of office: for authenticating, under the consular seal, every protest, or other act, which captains, or others, citizens of the United States, may respectively choose to make, the sum of two dollars. For the taking into possession, inventorying, selling, and finally settling and paying, or transmitting, as aforesaid, the balance due on the personal estate left by any citizens of the United States who shall die within the limits of his consulate, five per centum on the gross amount of such estate. For taking into possession any such estate, which shall be delivered over to the legal representative before a final settlement of the same, two and an half per centum on such part delivered over as shall not be in money, and five per centum on the gross amount of the residue. It is the duty of the consuls and vice consuls of the United States, to give receipts for all fees, expressing the particular services for which they are paid.[b]

Consuls and vice consuls, before they enter on the execution of their trusts, must give bonds, with sureties, in a sum of not less than 2000 nor more than $10,000, conditioned for the true and faithful discharge of the duties of their office, according to law, and also for truly accounting for all money, goods and effects, which may come into their possession by virtue of their office; and the said bond must be lodged in the office of the secretary of the treasury.[c]

Consuls, also, may have other powers and duties besides these specified, either resulting from the nature of their appointments, or any treaty or convention under which they may act.[d]

No consul of the United States, residing on the Barbary coast, can own, in whole or in part, any vessel, to be concerned, directly or indirectly, in the exportation from, or importation to, any of the states on the coast of Barbary, of any merchandise, under penalty, for every offence, of a sum not exceeding $1000.

By an act passed April 20th, 1818, owners of goods subject to an ad valorem duty, living out of the United States, must declare on oath, before a consul of the United States, if one be in the country from which they are imported, that the prices charged in the invoice are the current prices at the place of manufacture, and also whether they are the manufacturer's in whole or in part; otherwise they cannot be entered at the custom-house. If there be no consul, the oath

---

[a] Act, 14th April, 1792, sec. 3. [b] Ibid. sec. 4. [c] Ibid. sec. 6. [d] Ibid. sec. 9.
[e] Act, 1st May, 1810.

must be made before a notary public, whose official character must be certified by a consul of some power in amity with the United States.

The fee of the consul for such certificate is $2.

When a seaman is discharged from an American vessel in a foreign port, it is necessary for the master to obtain the consent of the American consul in writing, signed and authenticated with his official seal.[a]

The ship register, sea letter, and Mediterranean passport, must be deposited with the American consul, upon an American vessel arriving in a foreign port, under the penalty of $500, to be recovered by the consul; and they are to be kept by the consul until the master produces a regular clearance, and until the provisions of the acts of April 14, 1792, and February 28, 1803, are fully complied with.[b]

Three months' pay must be paid to the consuls for each seaman discharged abroad: two thirds for the seamen, and one third towards a fund for the relief of American seamen in foreign ports. The consuls must account every six months for the same with the treasury department.[c]

It is the duty of the consuls, vice consuls, commercial agents, and vice commercial agents of the United States, to provide for the mariners of the United States found destitute within their districts, sufficient subsistence, and passages to the United States, at the public expense. All masters of vessels belonging to citizens of the United States, and bound home, are required to take such mariners on board, at the request of the consuls, and to transport them to the port in the United States to which such vessels may be bound, on such terms, not exceeding $10 for each person, as may be agreed between the master and consul. The mariners are bound to do duty on board according to their several abilities. No master of any vessel is obliged to take a greater number than two men to every one hundred tons burthen. If any master refuse, he forfeits the sum of $100 for each mariner so refused. The certificate of any such consul or commercial agent, given under his hand and official seal, is *prima facie* evidence of such refusal.[d]

The secretary of state is authorized to reimburse the consul, &c. for such reasonable sums as may be advanced for the relief of American seamen abroad.[e]

The consul, vice consul, commercial agent, or vice commercial agent of the United States, receives for every certificate of discharge of any mariner in a foreign port, fifty cents; and for a commission on paying and receiving the amount of wages payable on the discharge of seamen in foreign ports, two and a half per cent.[f]

If any consul, vice consul, commercial agent, or vice commercial agent, falsely and knowingly certify that property belonging to foreigners is property belonging to citizens of the United States, or to any invoice or other paper which he is authorized to sign,[g] he forfeits a sum not exceeding $10,000, and may be imprisoned not exceeding three years.[h]

---

[a] Act, 28th Feb., 1803, sec. 1. [b] Ibid. sec. 2. [c] Ibid. sec. 3. [d] Ibid. sec. 4. [e] Ibid. sec. 5—1 Paine, 336. [f] Ibid. sec. 6. [g] Act, 3d March, 1835. [h] Act, 28th Feb., 1803, sec. 7.

If any consul, vice consul, commercial agent, or vice commercial agent, grant a passport, or other paper, certifying that any alien, knowing him or her to be such, is a citizen of the United States, he forfeits a sum not exceeding $1000.[a]

The American consuls in Hamburg, Lubec and Bremen, have, by treaty, the right to arrest deserters from American vessels, in order to send them back to the United States. To do this they must apply in writing to the proper authorities, proving, by exhibiting the shipping list or other documents, that the persons demanded were part of the crew, and within two months they must send them back to the United States, or the deserters will be set at liberty.[b]

It should be remembered, that though an American consul is protected by his official character whilst he confines himself to his official duties, the English admiralty courts have refused to consider consuls in any other light than merchants, after they have engaged in commerce: that is, they will not permit them to take advantage, as merchants, of the privileges of their official characters. It is to be presumed and hoped, that the government of the United States will in this, as in all other cases, adopt the rule of reciprocity.

---

[a] Act, 28th Feb., 1803, sec. 9.

[b] Treaty, additional article, 4th June, 1828.

CHAPTER X.

FREIGHT.

Freight is the sum agreed on as the hire of a ship or carriage of goods, but it is sometimes improperly used to signify the cargo itself.

The taking of a ship to freight is the hiring her from her master or owners, either in part or in the whole, by the month, for an entire voyage, or by the ton. The contract, when reduced into writing, is called a *charter-party;* but it may be done by a *verbal agreement* only.

A charter-party is a contract of affreightment in writing, by which the owner lets the whole or part of his ship to a merchant, for the transportation of goods on a particular voyage, in consideration of the freight.

It settles the terms upon which the cargo is to be carried, as the bills of lading determine the contents of the cargo; the master or owners usually binding themselves, the ship, tackle, and furniture, that they shall be delivered (danger of the seas excepted) well-conditioned at the place of discharge agreed upon. They likewise generally covenant to provide a sufficiency of tackle and mariners, and to fit the ship in every respect for performing the voyage. This is the duty of the owner without a special contract. He is also bound to keep her properly equipped during the voyage, and to furnish her with proper documents, and to have the cargo safely and properly stowed. Unless with the consent of the shipper, or sanction of custom, the goods must be stowed under deck; otherwise they are at the risk of the master. The merchant or freighter, on his part, stipulates to comply with the payment promised for freight on delivery of his goods; to load and unload in a given time, and to allow so much for demurrage for detention beyond that time, and both parties oblige themselves in penalties for non-peformance.

A charter-party may be made by the master, for *himself and owners;* in which case, the master may release the freighter without advising with the owners. But, if the owners let out to freight the ship, *whereof* J. J. *is master*, then, though the master covenant in the same charter-party, and subscribe it, his release will not bind the owners; but the owners' release will include the master.

So likewise may a factor enter into a charter-party. If the ship be only freighted outwards, and loaded by the factor, the goods shipped are alone liable for the freight: and no demand can be made on the freighters by virtue of the charter-party: but the consignee of the goods is to pay the freight, according to the bills of lading.

Freight will also arise, not only by the terms of a charter-party or verbal agreement, but by *common usage;* for, when goods are sent on board generally, such freight becomes payable, as is customary for like goods in similar voyages.

Where goods of several merchants, unconnected with each other, are sent on board without any particular contract for the entire ship, she is called a *general* ship, because open to all. A merchant hiring a vessel, may either load it with his own goods, or wholly underlet it.

A trading voyage.—If a ship be freighted from one port to another, and thence to a third and fourth, and so home to the port whence she first sailed, (commonly called a trading voyage,) this is all but *one* voyage; but it must be performed conformably with the charter-party or agreement.

Freight by the ton or parcels.—If a ship be freighted by the ton, and she be full laden according to the charter-party, the freight is to be paid for her whole tonnage; otherwise, but for so many tons as the lading amounts to.

If the ship be named to be of a certain burthen, and she be found less, there is no more paid than only for the number of tons actually laden on board.

If the burthen be expressed to be two hundred tons or *thereabout*, the addition of *thereabout* is commonly understood to be within five tons more or less.

If a ship, freighted by the ton, or by parcels, be cast away, and part thereof be saved from the wreck, it has been doubted whether, *pro rata*, freight should not be paid.

Freight by the great.—If a ship be freighted by the great, and her burthen be not expressed, still the sum certain is to be paid.

If a burthen be expressed, and she be found not to amount to that burthen, still the sum certain is to be paid.

If a ship, freighted by the great, be cast away, the freight is lost.

Freight by the month.—In freighting a ship by the month, calender months are meant.

Where a ship is let by the month, the time does not begin to run until the ship breaks ground, unless otherwise agreed.

If either party be not ready at the time appointed for loading the ship, the other party, if the charterer, may seek another ship; or if the owner, another cargo; and the suffering party hath his remedy in an action for damages against the other. If the ship, when hired for the voyage, be loaded only in part, the charterer is entitled to the full enjoyment of the ship; for he is answerable for the freight not only for the cargo actually taken on board, but for what might have been taken, had a full cargo been furnished.

The master has no right to take goods of other persons on board without the consent of the charterer. But if the charterer did not agree to furnish a full cargo, and only to pay for the goods put on board, no freight is to be paid except for the goods shipped.

If the charterer agree to furnish a return cargo, and he lets the vessel return in ballast, he must pay the freight as if a return cargo were on board. This is called *dead* freight. If the master bring back the outward cargo, because it could not be disposed of, or landed, he is entitled to freight, though the charter-party has no stipulation as to a return cargo.[a]

---

[a] 2 Taunt. 286.

When the ship is hired, and the cargo put on board, the duties of the master and owner arise in relation to the commencement, progress and termination of the voyage.

The master is then bound to sail as soon as wind and tide will permit, unless prevented by well-founded apprehensions of danger from tempests or enemies.[a]

If, by the charter-party, the ship is to sail by a given day, the master must do it unless prevented by necessity; and in case sailing with convoy be stipulated, he is bound to go to the place of rendezvous, and place himself under the protection and control of the convoy, and so to continue as far as practicable during the voyage.[b]

If a master weigh anchor and sail after the time agreed for his departure, and any damage happen at sea after that time, he must make good all such misfortune. Yet, if a *charter-party* be made, that the master shall sail from New-York to Lisbon with the first fair wind and opportunity, &c. in consideration of which the merchant covenants to pay so much for freight, and the ship departs not with the first fair wind and opportunity, but afterwards *breaks ground*, and arrives at her port, the freight in this case becomes due; and there is nothing that can debar the ship of her freight but non-departure.

If the covenant is to go to a loading port, within a given time, the master must do it, or abide the forfeiture; and if forced out of his course by marine perils, he must regain it as soon as possible.[c]

Nothing but some just and necessary cause, such as apprehension of enemies, or tempests, to procure supplies or repairs, or to relieve a vessel in distress, will justify a deviation from the regular course of the voyage.

When a ship puts into any other port than the one she was bound to by agreement, the master must answer all damages that accrue thereby; unless she was forced in by a storm, enemies, or pirates, in which case he must afterwards proceed to that he was obliged to by contract.

If a ship on her voyage happen to be taken by an enemy, and afterwards retaken by another ship in amity, and restitution be made, and she proceeds on her voyage, the contract is not determined, though the taking by the enemy devested the property out of the owners; yet, by the laws of war, that possession was defeasible; and, being recovered afterwards, the owners became reinvested, and the entire freight becomes due.

If the ship in her voyage become unable, without the master's fault, or if the master or ship be arrested by any foreign prince or state in her voyage, the master may either mend his ship, or freight another.

If the freighter will not consent thereto, the master will be entitled to his full freight. If there be another vessel in the port where the disabled vessel is, or in one contiguous thereto, the master is bound to hire it, if he have the means, unless his own can be repaired within a reasonable time.

If the ship be capable of being repaired in a reasonable time, the owner ought to repair her, and continue his voyage, so as to claim

---

[a] Roccus. U. 56. [b] 3 Kent, 209. [c] 3 Burr, 1637.

his freight, which will be due if he offer to carry the goods on, though they are damaged, unless they are physically destroyed.[a]

If the charter-party contain a stipulation on the part of the owner to keep the ship in good order during the voyage, the entire expense of repairs in such case must be borne by him, and it does not become the subject of general average. If there should be a latent defect in the vessel unknown to the owner, he is still answerable for all damages occasioned by the defect.

In order to transport the cargo, the master has power to sell part, or hypothecate the whole. If the cargo be perishable, or so much damaged as not to be worth transporting, he may cause it to be sold.

A loss by fire proceeding from any other cause than lightning, has been held chargeable upon the owners.[b] Upon the arrival of the ship, the master must give notice to his consignee, and the goods are then to be delivered upon the wharf, to some person authorized to receive them. Such a delivery discharges the master. A delivery on the wharf, without notice to the consignee, will not discharge him.[c]

He is not bound, however, to deliver them until the freight be paid. Where the consignee will not either send for the goods or pay the freight, the master should send them to some storehouse, to be held subject to his order until the freight be paid. When the goods are transferred from a ship to a warehouse, the obligations of the master as a common carrier ceases, and losses by fire, &c. fall upon the owners of the goods.

A loss from striking on a sand bar or rock, which is generally known, and when the ship is not driven upon it by adverse winds or tempests, or in the night, is to be borne by the master.

When goods are to be delivered to the consignee upon payment of freight, he becomes responsible therefor by receiving the goods. The buyer of the goods from the consignee, however, is not liable, even if they be entered in the custom-house in his name. If part of the cargo be sold from necessity during the voyage, the owner of the ship pays its value at the port of delivery, deducting full freight.

In the course of the voyage, the master is bound to take all possible care of the cargo, and is responsible for every injury which might have been prevented by foresight, prudence and nautical skill.

Duties of the shipper.—He must, when chartering the ship, comply with his stipulations in the charter-party. He must use the ship in a lawful manner. If he put on board prohibited or contraband goods, whereby the ship is detained or forfeited, he is answerable to the owner for all damages, and he will have to pay the freight agreed for.[d] If the charterer detain the vessel beyond the stipulated time, or employ her in any service besides that agreed upon, he must answer for the damages.

If the detention be beyond the time stipulated for loading and unloading, the damages is usually settled at so much per day as demurrage.

---

[a] 3 Johns. 321. [b] 5 Term. R. 398. [c] 15 Johns. R. 39. [d] 3 Ibid. 105.

If part of the goods be on board, and some intervening misfortune prevent the master from taking in the remainder, the merchant may ship them on board another, discharge the first, and recover damages against the master and owners for the rest.

So, if some intervening misfortune prevent the merchant from shipping the whole in time, the master is at liberty to contract with another, and shall have freight, by way of damage, for the time that those goods were on board after the time limited. For, a failure as to a complete loading will end, and the contract, unless afterwards *affirmed by consent.*

If goods are fully laden on board, and the ship hath *broken ground,* and the merchant determines again to unload them, and not to prosecute the adventure, by the *marine law* the freight is due.

Where no freight was to be paid for the cargo *outwards*, but freight for the cargo *homewards*, and the freighter's factor abroad had no goods to load on board of her, payment of the freight was decreed.

If a ship be freighted out and home, and she delivers her cargo at the place agreed on: or if a ship be freighted to go to any place to load, and arrive there, and the freighter's factor cannot put any thing on board, the master must stay the days of demurrage agreed on by the charter-party, and make a regular protest for his freighter's non-compliance, who will, in this case, be obliged to pay him, empty or full: though, should the master not wait the time stipulated, or omit to make his protest, he will lose his freight. In case the master, on his finding no goods provided, should load some on his own account, this will not prevent his recovering the freight; but, if the master take in such goods on his own account, before the days of demurrage are expired; and still, by the contract with the freighter, he may claim freight, then the freighter is to have the benefit of the freight of those goods, in deduction of the said freight due from him.

If, in consequence of the ship's not being duly equipped, she be not used, the charterer is not bound to pay any freight; but if he actually employs her, he must pay the freight, and seek his remedy in an action for damages, under the charter-party.

It is requisite that the ship break ground in order to give a title to freight. If the ship be captured after loading, and before breaking ground, and be afterwards recaptured, and the voyage be broken up, the owners are not entitled to freight, though they were at the expense of loading her.

If, before the departure of the ship, there should happen an embargo, occasioned by war, reprisals, or otherwise, with the country to which the ship is bound, so that she cannot proceed on her voyage, the *charter-party* is dissolved without damages or charges to either party, and the merchant must pay the expenses of unloading.

If the ports be only shut, and the vessel stopped for a time, the *charter-party* is valid, and the master and merchant are reciprocally obliged to wait the opening of the ports, and the liberty of the ship, without any pretensions for damages on either side.

However, the merchant, at his own charges, may unlade his goods during the shutting up of the port, upon condition either to relade them, or to indemnify the master.

If the voyage become unlawful, or impossible to be performed, or broken up by war, or interdiction of commerce, or if the port be blockaded and the vessel returns to the port of destination, the contract of affreightment is at an end, and no freight is due.[a]

If the impediment be merely temporary in its nature, it is only a suspension of its performance. If the cargo be not perishable, and can endure the delay, an embargo or blockade is construed to be merely a temporary impediment, and the owner may retain the cargo until he can safely prosecute the voyage, or his full freight be paid to him.

In case a ship be freighted at the rate of $500 for every month that she shall be out, to be paid after the arrival at the port of New-York, and the ship be cast away coming up from the Hook, but the lading is all preserved, freight becomes due; for the money arises monthly by the contract, and the place mentioned is only to show where payment is to be made. The freight becomes due on the delivery or bringing up of the commodities, and not the ship, to the port of New-York.

If a ship be freighted out, and the master covenants that the ship should sail out of the port to Cadiz with the first fair wind and opportunity, and the freighter covenants, that, for the freight of all the premises, he would pay unto the master $2000; if the master do not show that the ship arrived at Cadiz, he cannot recover the freight. By the special terms of the contract, the master was in the nature of an insurer for the amount of the freight agreed on.

When a ship is freighted *out* and *home*, there is no freight due till the whole voyage is performed: so that, if she be cast away coming home, the freight *outwards* as well as *inwards* becomes lost.[b]

If freight be contracted for the transporting of women, and they happen in the voyage to be delivered of children, no freight becomes due for the infants.

A master of a ship is not bound to answer for freight to the owners for passengers, where they are not able to pay.

If freight be agreed on for a lading of certain cattle, from New-York to Barbadoes, and some of them happen to die before the ship's arrival, the whole freight becomes due, as well for the dead as the living. But, if the contract be to transport them at so much *per* head, freight will become due only for such as are living at the ship's port of discharge.

When cattle are sent on board, without any previous agreement about transporting them, freight is payable for the dead as well as the living.

Where goods have been carried to the port of destination, though spoiled so as to be of no value, the owner cannot abandon the goods for the freight, but must pay to the master his full freight.[c]

But where wine has leaked out of their hogsheads, or where sugar has been so wet, in consequence of tempestuous weather, as to leak

---

[a] 2 Johns. 336. [b] 2 Chitty's Rep. 666. [c] 3 Ibid. 321.

out, no freight can be recovered for the empty hogsheads, unless the leakage was caused by imperfection in the casks.[a]

An abandonment of the cargo is not a satisfaction for the freight, and the master may resort to the owner of the goods. Where part of the goods are lost or damaged, freight must be paid for the remainder, which have been delivered, and the freighter must look to the vessel, owner, or master, for damages, under the contract of affreightment. If part of the contents of casks leak out, freight is due, although the ship-owner may be in fault, and answerable in damages for his neglect.

Cargo answerable for the freight.—The lading of the ship is *tacitly* bound for the freight, which, in point of payment, is preferred before all other debts to which the goods so laden are liable, although such debts, as to the time, were *precedent* to the freight; for the goods remain, as it were, *bailed* or pledged to the master for the freight, nor can they be attached in his hands. But, as the goods are bound to the ship for hire, so is the ship to the owner of the goods, in case of damage or waste through the defect of the vessel or sailors.

The owner of the goods, or the consignee, is not personally liable for the freight until the goods are all delivered, or until after refusal of delivery.

If a vessel is compelled to put into port, short of the place of destination, and is unable to prosecute the voyage, and the goods are there received by the owner, he must pay freight according to the proportion of the voyage performed.[a]

But freight *pro rata* cannot be recovered, unless the goods be accepted at a place short of the destined port.

Where the master is consignee and joint owner of the cargo, his selling at a port of necessity will be deemed an acceptance by him as owner, so as to render *pro rata* freight due.[b]

The rule in apportioning freight is to calculate how much of the voyage had been performed when the goods arrived at the port of necessity.

Freight paid in advance can be recovered back where the voyage is not performed, unless the failure is owing to the shipper.

The owner's lien for freight is lost where the charterer is constituted owner for the voyage, or where the payment of freight is, by agreement, postponed beyond the time, or is inconsistent with the time and place for the delivery of the goods.

The intent, however, must be plain.

A bill of lading.—A bill of lading is a writing wherein masters of ships acknowledge the receipt of goods on board, and oblige themselves to deliver the same in good order and condition at the place whither they were consigned. There are always three made out, of which one should be remitted, by the first post, after signing, to the person the goods go to; another be sent him by the ship; and the third remain with the shipper: besides which, a fourth should be made out, to be given to the master for his government.

---

[a] 2 Johns. 327. [b] 2 Caines, 13.

The bill of lading contains the names of the ship and master, the shipper and consignee, the marks and quantities of the goods shipped, the places of departure and discharge, and the price of the freight.

It is the document and title of the goods shipped, and if it be to order or assigns, it transfers, by endorsement and delivery, the property in the goods, from the time of the delivery.

If the several bills be endorsed to different persons, the prior endorsement prevails, where the equities are equal.

The difference between a bill of lading and a charter-party is, that the first is required and given for a single article or more, laden on board a ship that has sundry merchandise shipped for sundry accounts: whereas, a charter-party is a contract for the whole ship. Bills of lading ought to be signed by the master within twenty-four hours after the delivery of the goods on board. But, upon delivery of the goods, the master, or other person officiating for the master in his absence, is to give a common receipt for them, which is to be delivered up, upon the master signing the bill of lading.

Upon delivering the goods at the port of destination to the shipper's factors or assigns, giving up the bill of lading sent to the factors or assigns is a sufficient discharge, but the master may insist on a receipt.

Demurrage.—Demurrage is an allowance made to the master of a ship by his freighters, for staying longer in a place than the time first appointed for his departure.

CHAPTER XI.

GENERAL AVERAGE.

General average is a contribution by all parties concerned, towards a loss sustained by some of the parties in interest, for the common benefit.

Whatever the master of a ship does in distress for the preservation of the whole, in cutting away masts or cables, or in throwing goods overboard to lighten his vessel, which is what is meant by jettison or jetson, is brought into a general average: in which all who are concerned in the ship, freight and cargo, are to bear an equal or proportionate part of the loss of what was so sacrificed for the common welfare; and it must be made good by the insurers in such proportions as they have underwritten.

In order to make the act of throwing the goods overboard legal, the ship must be in distress, and the sacrificing a part must be necessary to preserve the rest.

If practicable, the officers and the supercargo, when on board, should be consulted.

The sacrifice must be of something deliberately selected for that purpose; as, for instance, the cutting away of the mast for the purpose of righting the ship, when on her beam ends. If the sacrifice be only a necessary consequence, or continuation of some specific injury previously suffered, it is not the subject of general average; as, if the gale have dismasted the ship, and the wreck of the mast remains attached by the rigging, beating against her side, and endangering her safety. The cutting away of the rigging in order to relieve the vessel is not a deliberate sacrifice, but merely the continuation of the original injury; and the loss of the mast, &c. must be borne by the owner.

As soon as the interests are separated by the whole being in safety, specific charges again commence.

If a ship ride out the storm, and arrive in safety at the port of destination, the captain must make regular protests, and must swear, in which some of the crew must join, that the goods were cast overboard for no other cause but for the safety of the ship and the rest of the cargo.

There can be no contribution (which is another word used frequently for this species of *average*) without the ejection of some goods, and the saving of others; but it is not always necessary for the purpose of contribution, that the ship should arrive at the port of destination.

If the jettison does not save the ship, but she perish in the storm, there shall be no contribution of such goods as may happen to be saved; because the object for which the goods were thrown overboard was not attained. But if the ship, being once preserved by such means, and continuing her course, should afterwards be lost, the property saved from the second accident must contribute to the loss sustained by those whose goods were cast out upon the former occasion.

All losses sustained, and expenses incurred, voluntarily and deliberately, with the view to prevent a *total loss* of the ship and cargo, ought to be equally borne by the ship and her remaining lading. Such, for instance, is the damage sustained in defending the ship against an enemy or pirate; such is the expense of curing and attendance upon the officers or mariners wounded in such defence; and such also is the sum which the master may have promised to pay for the ransom of his ship to any privateer or pirate, when taken. A master who has cut his mast, parted with his cable, or abandoned any other part of the ship and cargo in a storm, in order to save the ship, is well entitled to this compensation; but if he should *lose* them by the storm, the loss falls only upon the ship and freight; because the tempest only was the occasion of this loss, without the deliberation of the master and crew; and it was not done with a view to save the ship and lading. Upon the same principle it is established, that, when a ship arrives at the mouth of a harbour, and the master, finding that his ship is too heavy laden to sail up, is obliged to put a part of the cargo into hoys and barges, the owners of the ship and of the goods that remained are obliged to contribute if the lighters perish. But if the ship should be lost, and the lighters saved, the owners of the goods so preserved are not to contribute to the proprietors of the ship and cargo lost.

The difference is this, the lightening of the ship is an act of deliberation for the general benefit; whereas, the circumstance of the lighters being saved, and the ship lost, is accidental, and no way proceeding from a regard for the whole.

It is not only the value of the goods thrown overboard that must be considered in a general average, but also the value of such as receive any damage by wet, &c., from the jettison of the rest.

If a ship be taken by force, carried into port, and the crew remain on board to take care of and reclaim her, not only the charges of reclaiming must be brought into a general average, but the wages and expense of the ship's company during her arrest, from the time of her capture, and being disturbed in her voyage.

But sailors' wages and victuals, when they are under the necessity of performing quarantine, do not come into general average; although charges occurring by an extraordinary quarantine are the subject of general average.

Warehouse rent for the cargo, when discharged, is a specific charge.

The expenses attending the detention of a vessel by an embargo, are the subject of particular average only.[a]

In Pennsylvania, however, it has been determined, that wages and provisions, in case of such detention, are the subject of general average.[b]

[a] 3 Caines, 155. [b] 2 Binney, 547.

The loss of a mast, through a press of sail, in escaping from an enemy, is not the subject of general average.[a] If the ship, in case of extremity, be voluntarily run on shore and lost, it was decided, in Sims v. Gurney, that it was a case of general average;[b] but in the New-York courts it was held, that the cargo, which in such case was saved, should not contribute for the loss.[c]

A jettison of goods on deck, although expressly mentioned in the policy, cannot be brought into general average; not so as to the ship's boat.[d]

The wages and provisions of the crew, during the detention of a captured vessel, may be brought into general average.[e]

So if compelled to put into a port to refit, by stress of weather, from the moment of bearing away, until the period of sailing again in prosecution of the voyage.[f]

The expenses of unloading, loading, storage and repairing, are also subjects of general average in the above case; and if there be a total loss after the expenses have been incurred, they must be paid by the insurer, in addition to the total loss.[g]

If a ship, in a case of extremity, should be voluntarily run ashore, and afterwards should be got off and perform the voyage, the damages caused by the stranding are subjects of general average; but if the ship be destroyed, and the cargo saved, the cargo is not bound to contribute.[h]

If a vessel have been injured on her voyage by tempests, but arrives and delivers her cargo, the expenses, during her detention at the port of delivery, for necessary repairs, viz: wages and provisions, are not to be brought into general average.[i]

But where a ship is obliged to go into port for the benefit of the whole concern, the charges of loading and unloading the cargo, and taking care of it, and the wages and provisions of the workmen hired for the repairs, become general average.

By the ancient laws of Rhodes, Oleron and Wisbuy, the ship and all the remaining goods must contribute to the loss sustained. The most valuable goods, though their weight should have been incapable of putting the ship in the least hazard, as diamonds or precious stones, must be valued at their just price in this contribution, because they could not have been saved to the owners but by the ejection of the other goods. Neither the persons of those in the ship, nor the ship's provisions, nor the respondentia bonds, are estimated, nor wearing apparel in chests and boxes, nor such jewels as belong to the person merely; but if the jewels are a part of the cargo, they must contribute.

The common rule is, that those articles which pay freight contribute, and none others; and they contribute according to their value, and not according to their weight.

The wages of sailors do not contribute. This is to reconcile them more easily to a jettison,—their wages being the same in either event.

---

[a] 5 Bos. and Pull. 378. [b] 4 Binney, 513—2 Serg. and Rawle, 237. [c] 9 Johns. 9. [d] 3 Ibid. 178. [e] 1 Caines, 573. [f] Ibid. 274. [g] 8 Johns. 307. [h] 9 Ibid. 9. [i] 11 Ibid. 315.

In case of ransom, however, they do contribute.

The rule of adjustment, in settling a general average, is to value the goods sacrificed, as well as the goods saved, at the net price, after deducting the freight they would have brought at the port of discharge.

The value of the vessel is to be taken at the end of the voyage, and the owners contribute according to that value, and also according to the net amount of freight and earnings. The value of the vessel, when lost, is estimated according to her value at the port of departure, making a reasonable deduction for wear and tear up to the time of the disaster; and where spars, masts, cables, sails, &c. have been destroyed, it is usual to deduct one third from the price of the new articles.

The contribution is in general not made till the ship arrive at the place of delivery; but accidents may happen, which may cause a contribution before she reach her destined port. Thus, when a vessel has been obliged to make a jettison, or by the damages suffered, soon after sailing, is obliged to return to her port of discharge, the necessary charges of her repairs, and replacing the goods thrown overboard, may then be settled by a general average.

The way of fixing a right sum, by which the average ought to be computed, can only be by examining what the whole ship, freight and cargo, if no jettison had been made, would have produced net, if they all had belonged to one person, and been sold for ready money. And this is the sum whereon the contribution should be made, all the particular goods bearing the net proportion.[a]

It is the duty of the master, in case of general average, to cause an adjustment to be made upon his arrival at his port of destination, as he has a lien upon the cargo for contribution.

When this adjustment has been fairly made in a foreign port, according to the usage there, it is held binding, though contrary to the usage at the home port.

If the case, however, is not a proper subject of general average, the foreign adjustment founded in mistake is not binding.

For payment of average, each person may sue for his share when adjusted; but it is usual, where the ship has many consignees, for the master to take a bond from each of the different merchants, to pay his proportion of the average when adjusted.

A bona fide owner of the cargo is liable for such proportion, whether he has signed a bond or not; but a consignee is not; and if he do not give a bond, the master would have to resort to the owner, or to coerce payment by retaining the goods.

It is necessary here to add, that, as all sums which are paid on account of general average may be recovered by action from the underwriters, so any person, whose goods have been thrown overboard, or who has expended money for the general preservation of ship and cargo, may obtain repayment by application to a court of equity for a general contribution.

---

[a] 1 Magens, 69.

The following examples of adjusted averages are here subjoined:

Average accruing to the ship Sea-horse, from Riga to New-York, for assistance in getting off the strand of Elsineur.

To sundry charges paid at the sound for lighters and assistance in getting the ship off - - -		$120 00
Protests and postages - - - - - - -		2 00
		$122 00
Should the ship arrive at New-York, she will make freight		$700 00
Wages for all the people, 1 month and 10 days,	$139 50	
Victuals for ditto - - - - - -	110 50—	250 00
Freight to contribute - - - - -		450 00
Ship Sea-horse valued at - - - - - -		4000 00
Freight valued at - - - - - - - -		450 00
F. J. for value of hemp, as *per* invoice - - -		6000 00
D. N. for value of flax - - - - - - -		1000 00
T. R. for value of iron - - - - - - -		350 00
		$11,800 00

If $11,800 loss give $122, what will $100 loss give?

Answer—\$1.03 $\frac{39}{100}$ or nearly $\frac{2}{5}$ *per cent.*

The ship must bear $4000 at \$1.03$\frac{2}{5}$, (which the insurers return,) - - - - - - - - -	$41 36
Freight $450, at \$1.03$\frac{2}{5}$ *per cent.* - - - - -	4 65
F. J. pays the captain for $6000 at the same rate -	62 03
D. N. pays the same for $1000 - - - - -	10 34
T. R. pays the same for $350 - - - - - -	3 62
	$122 00

The sloop Betsey, captain Watson, on her passage from St. Ubes to New-York, met with a very heavy gale of wind, the sea breaking over her, and the vessel making much water; the captain determined on *cutting away* the jib, as he could not take it in; but, before that could be done, a sea struck the vessel, and *broke the bowsprit.* The wreck of the bowsprit, jib, &c., broke the lashing of the larboard anchor, and carried it and the cable overboard. In order to preserve ship and cargo, he cut the whole of this wreck away. During the said gale of wind, the masts having lost great part of their support in the loss of the bowsprit, he prevailed on one of his men, for a gratuity of five guineas, to go aloft, and cut away the topsail, topgallant-sail, yards, mast and rigging; and, at last, the vessel reached her port of delivery.

Had the jib been *cut away,* it would have been general average; and it was only under the particular circumstances of being carried away, while that was in contemplation, it was allowed as a particular average on the ship, as was likewise the bowsprit. The entangling with the anchor and cable, though a consequence of the above, yet being *cut away*, came into general average, as did the topmast, &c. The gratuity to the seaman was not allowed, on the principle that a seaman is bound, by his duty and wages, to do *all* in his power for the good of the ship, and he can therefore earn no more.

General average.

Blocks for topmast rigging	$10 50
Running rigging	52 10
Topsail-yard	8 40
Topsail	40 00
Top-gallant-sail	20 00
Cable	49 00
	180 00
One third off for new	60 00
	120 00
Surveyors $15, protest $10	25 00
Anchor	35 00
Anchor-stock	10 70
Postages	4 30
	195 00

N. B. No deduction is made from the value of an anchor.

Ship	$2000
Cargo	1400
Net freight	500

$3900, at 5 *per cent.* is $195.

Particular average on the ship.

Blockmaker's bill	$26 50
Ropemaker's account for stays, &c.	25 20
Bowsprit, &c.	23 30
Jib	60 00
Carpenter's and smith's bill	25 00
	160 00
One third off	53 33
Ship $2000, at $5\frac{1}{2}$ *per cent.*, is	$106 67

N. B. The above average comes above 5 *per cent.*; had it been below, the underwriters would not have been liable to pay it.

CHAPTER XII.

SALVAGE.

Salvage is an allowance made for saving a ship or goods, or both, from the dangers of the seas, fire, pirates, or enemies.

This allowance is made whether the property is saved in whole or in part, and that whether saved from impending danger or rescued from actual loss. In the case of shipwreck or derelicts at sea, and rescue, and most other cases, the law has not fixed any certain rates of salvage, and it is left to the discretion of the court of admiralty under all the circumstances.

The amount to be allowed varies according to the labour and danger incurred by the salvors; the merit of their conduct; the value of the property saved; and the degree of damage to which it was exposed.

It fluctuates between one half and one fourth of the net proceeds of the property saved, and is distributed among the salvors according to their respective merits.

In general, a passenger, seaman, or pilot, is not entitled to any compensation by way of salvage, for ordinary assistance given to a vessel in distress, as it is no more than their duty. A passenger, however, for extraordinary exertions beyond the line of his duty, has been deemed entitled to such allowance; and extraordinary exertions and hazard in time of extreme peril, have been held sufficient to entitle the pilot to salvage.

If the ship have been abandoned, so as to discharge a seaman from his contract, he may become entitled to salvage, by subsequently contributing to save the vessel.[a]

So, if the ship have been captured, any exertion by a seaman in recapturing her, will entitle him to salvage.[b] In case of shipwreck, although the contract of the sailors is not at an end, and it is their duty to remain and labour to preserve the wreck and cargo, they are entitled by way of salvage to their wages, which form a lien on the property saved. Where the danger in rescuing property from a wreck is great, it may form a claim on the part of the sailors for compensation, even beyond their wages.[c]

The regulation of salvage by the act of congress, is confined to cases of recapture.[d]

By that act, it is provided, that all vessels other than vessels of war or privateers recaptured from an enemy, and not having been condemned as prizes by competent authority, shall be restored to the former owners, they paying in lieu of salvage, if retaken by a public vessel of

---

[a] 2 Cranch, 240. [b] 1 Rob. Adm. 271—3 Ibid. 292. [c] 2 Mason, 319.
[d] Act, 3d March, 1800.

the United States, one eighth part, and if retaken by a private vessel of the United States, one sixth part of the value, allowing and excepting all duties. If the vessel so retaken appear to have been armed as a vessel of war before such capture, or afterwards, and before the retaking, the former owners must pay, in lieu of salvage, one moiety of the value.

Any vessel or goods recaptured, which before belonged to the United States, and not having been condemned as prizes by competent authority before the recapture thereof, the same must be restored to the United States. And in lieu of salvage, there is paid from the treasury of the United States, pursuant to the final decree in such case, by any court of the United States having jurisdiction, for the recapture of an unarmed vessel, or any goods therein, one sixth part of the value, when made by a private vessel of the United States; and one twelfth part when made by a public armed vessel of the United States; and for the recapture of a public armed vessel, or any goods therein, one moiety of the value, when made by a private vessel of the United States, and one fourth part when made by a public armed vessel of the United States.[a]

Vessels or goods appearing to have before belonged to foreign states in amity with the United States, are restored to the former owners, they paying, in lieu of salvage, such proportion of the value, as, by the law or usage of such state within whose territory such owners shall be resident, is required, on the restoration of any vessel or goods of a citizen of the United States, under like circumstances of recapture; and where no such law or usage shall be known, the same salvage is allowed, as is provided for property of American citizens. But such vessel or goods are not restored, where the same haveb een, before recapture, condemned as prize by competent authority, nor in any case where, by the law or usage of the state within whose territory such former owners are resident, the vessel or goods of a citizen of the United States, under like circumstances of recapture, would not be restored to such citizen of the United States.[b]

All sums of money which may be paid for salvage, when accruing to any public armed vessel, are divided among the commanders, officers and crew thereof, as provided by law; and when accruing to any private armed vessel, among the owners and company concerned in such recapture, according to their agreements; and in case there be no agreement, then in such proportions as the court having jurisdiction thereof shall appoint.[c]

It has been decided, that a neutral captured by a belligerent was entitled to be discharged without paying salvage—as the neutral, acting properly, would be discharged by the courts of the captors. When belligerent captors and courts were notorious for their rapacity, as were those of England and France, during the wars growing out of the French revolution, an exception was made to the rule, and one sixth of the net value was decreed for salvage, in case of recapture of a neutral; thus, for the time, classing the vessels of war and courts

[a] Act, 3d March, 1800, sec. 2. [b] Ibid. sec. 3. [c] Ibid. sec. 4.

of these enlightened nations in the same rank, but differing in degree, with the cruisers and self-constitued courts of piratical communities.

The wearing apparel of the master and seamen are always excepted from the allowance of salvage.[a]

The valuation of a ship, in order to ascertain the rate of salvage, may be determined by the policy of insurance, if there be no reason to suspect she is undervalued; and the same rule may be observed as to goods, where there are policies upon them; if that, however, should not be the case, the salvors may insist upon the proof of the *real* value, which may be obtained from the merchant's invoices, and they must be paid for accordingly.[a]

The insured may recover from the insurer the expenses of salvage; yet he cannot receive a double satisfaction for the same loss. Thus, if the insurer should have paid to the insured the expenses arising from salvage, and afterwards, on account of some particular circumstance, the loss should be repaired by some unexpected means, the insurer shall stand in the place of the insured, and receive the sum thus paid, to atone for the loss.[b]

Cases frequently arise in which the salvage is so high, the other expenses so great, and the object of the voyage so far defeated, that the insurer is allowed to *abandon* his interest in the property saved to the insurer, and to call upon him to contribute, as if a total loss had actually happened.

The right to share in salvage is forfeited by embezzlement of any part of the cargo saved.[c]

If a vessel be abandoned at sea, in distress, by all except one, who is left either by accident or design, he is entitled to claim salvage if he assist in saving the ship.[c]

Any irregular proceedings on the part of the salvors serves to diminish their salvage.

No salvage is allowed for recapturing a vessel which has been taken by a friendly power.[d]

---

[a] Lex Mercatoria, 147. [b] Randall v. Cochrane, 1 Ves. 98. [c] 2 Cranch, 240.
[d] 1 Johns. 165.

CHAPTER XIII.

BOTTOMRY AND RESPONDENTIA.

Bottomry is in the nature of a mortgage of a ship, when the owner or master borrows money to enable him to carry on the voyage, and pledges the keel, or *bottom* of the ship, as a security for the repayment: and it is understood that, if the ship be lost, the lender also loses his whole money; but, if it return in safety, then he shall receive back his principal, and the premium or interest stipulated to be paid, although it may exceed the usual or legal rate of interest. When the ship and tackle are brought home, they are liable, as well as the person of the borrower, for the money lent. When the loan is not made upon the vessel, but upon the goods and merchandise laden thereon, which, from their nature, must be sold or exchanged in the course of the voyage, then the borrower only is *personally* bound to answer the contract, who, therefore, in that case, is said to take up money at *respondentia.* In this consists the difference between *bottomry* and *respondentia;* that the one is a loan upon the ship, the other upon the goods. In the former, the ship and tackle are liable; in the latter, for the most part, recourse must be had to the *person* of the borrower. Another observation is, that, in a loan upon bottomry, the lender runs no risk, except upon the ship; and upon respondentia, the lender must be paid his principal and interest, though the *ship* perish, provided the goods are saved. If the borrower have not goods on board to the value of the sum borrowed, the contract, in case of loss, is reduced proportionably, and the borrower is bound to return, in all events, the surplus sum borrowed, with legal interest. In all other respects, the contract of bottomry and that of respondentia are upon the same footing.

These terms are also applied to another species of contract, which does not exactly fall within the description of either; namely, to a contract for the repayment of money, not upon the ship and goods only, but upon the mere hazard of the voyage itself; as if a man lend $1000 to a merchant to be employed in a beneficial trade, with a condition to be repaid with extraordinary interest, in case a specific voyage named in the condition shall be safely performed. This species of contract has been prohibited in France, and in England it is restrained by statute as to East India voyages. The weight of authority, however, at common law, is in favour of their validity.

The contract of bottomry and respondentia seems to deduce its origin from the custom of permitting the master of a ship, when in a foreign country, to hypothecate the ship, in order to raise money to refit. Such a permission is absolutely necessary, and is impliedly given him in the act of constituting him master, by the marine law, which in this respect is reasonable; for, if a ship happen to be at sea, and spring a leak, or the voyage is likely to be defeated from want of necessaries, it is better that the master should have it in his power to pledge the ship and goods, or either of them, than that the ship should be lost, or the voyage defeated. But he cannot do either for any debt of his own, but merely in case of *necessity*, and for *completing the voyage*. Although the master of the vessel has this power while abroad, because it is absolutely necessary for the purposes of commerce and navigation, yet the very same authority which gave that power in those cases, has denied it when he happens to be in the same place where the owners reside. All the cases which have been determined upon the subject, seem to require, that the ship should be *abroad*, as well as in a *state of necessity*, to justify the captain or master in taking money on bottomry. Molloy, in express terms, declares, that a master has no power to take up money on bottomry in places where his owners dwell.

To authorize the master to hypothecate the vessel, it must be necessary to borrow money to enable the vessel to proceed on her voyage; it must be made after the voyage has commenced in a port where the owners do not reside, and it must be proved to be necessary. It is not essential that the port should be in a foreign country. It may be in a distant port in the same country, in a case of extreme necessity, where it is difficult to communicate with the owners. The master may hypothecate at the port of destination, as well as at any foreign port.[a] And if the owners disagree as to sending the ship to sea, the majority shall carry it, and the master may then take up money on bottomry for their proportion who refuse, although they reside on the spot, and it will bind the vessel.

In other cases, however, bottomry loans cannot be made by the master, where either he or the owners have goods sufficient to repair the ship. No other means of procuring funds at that place should exist, and the sum loaned must be advanced solely on the faith of the vessel.[b] The master cannot hypothecate for a pre-existing debt; but when the loan has been properly made, its misapplication by the master, without the knowledge or assent of the lender, will not affect its validity. The consignee, or agent of the owner, under special circumstances, may take a bottomry bond to secure advances.[c]

It is the essence of a contract of bottomry, that the lender run the risk of the voyage, and that both principal and interest be at hazard; for, if the risk go only to the interest of premium, and not to the principal also, though a real and substantial risk be inserted, it is a contract against the statute of usury, and therefore void.

The risk also must be actually run, to entitle the lender to the extraordinary interest. If the voyage be broken up, therefore, the extra interest is not earned. But after the voyage has commenced, and the loan has been for a moment put at hazard, though the vessel be forced back by the perils of the sea to the port of departure, and the voyage broken up, the lender is entitled to his principal and marine interest.

If money be taken up on bottomry, and the ship is to sail on a specified voyage, but in fact performs a different voyage, the vessel is

---

[a] 3 Johns. 352. [b] 2 Peters' Ad. 301. [c] 1 Dodson, 278.

liable on the bottomry bond, the borrower having no right to risk the security of the lender on a different voyage.[a]

It remains to be shown what these risks are to which the lender undertakes to expose himself. They are, for the most part, mentioned in the condition of the bond, and are nearly the same, against which the underwriter, in a policy of insurance, undertakes to indemnify. These accidents are, tempests, pirates, fire, capture, and every other misfortune, except such as arise from the defects of the vessel, or from the misconduct of the borrower. There is great similarity between contracts of bottomry and insurance, and they are frequently governed by the same principles.

A bottomry bond of later date, fairly given in the course of the voyage, is entitled to priority of payment over one given at the commencement of the voyage—it being given to furnish the means of preserving the ship and the former loan. It also supersedes a previous mortgage of the ship, and must be paid before prior insurance.

Capture, in a bottomry bond, does not mean a mere temporary taking, but it must be such a capture as to occasion a total loss. And, therefore, if a ship be taken, and detained for a short time, and yet arrive at the port of destination within the time limited, (if time be mentioned in the condition,) the bond is not forfeited, and the obligee may recover.

A lender on bottomry, or at respondentia, is neither entitled to the benefit of salvage, nor liable to contribute in case of a general average.

In Pennsylvania the lender on respondentia is entitled to the benefits of salvage, and is liable to particular and general average. The principle that the lender on *respondentia* or *bottomry*, is not bound to contribute in case of general average, which was laid down by Lord Mansfield, has been justly questioned. It is contrary to the maritime law of the rest of Europe, and to equity and justice.

If the ship and cargo be lost, not by the perils of the sea, but by the fault of the borrower or master, the bond is forfeited, and must be paid. The doctrines of sea-worthiness, deviation, diligence and correct conduct, on the part of the borrower, are equally applicable to this contract, as to that of insurance.

The loan may be made after the departure of the vessel, and it is not necessary that the money should be used in the outfit.[b]

After the arrival of the vessel, the marine interest ceases, and legal interest is substituted. The admiralty courts exercise an equity jurisdiction over these contracts; and if an undue advantage has been taken of the master's necessities, they may moderate it or refuse to carry it into effect.

Nothing but the actual destruction of the subject hypothecated will discharge the borrower; but the property saved continues subject to hypothecation. If that be not equal to the loan, the lender must bear the loss of the residue.

---

[a] 2 Peters' Ad. 295. [b] 1 Peters' U. S. R. 386.

If the vessel or cargo be lost, not by marine perils, but by the default of the borrower, the hypothecation bond is forfeited, and must be paid. So, too, if the ship be lost, and the cargo forwarded by another ship, the borrower must pay the debt.

The lender does not assume the risk of barratry or loss by the fraud or misconduct of the borrower, or his agent.

The French code prohibits all marine loans upon sailors' wages, and the prohibition is founded in good policy.

CHAPTER XIV.

MARINE INSURANCE.

INSURANCE is a contract by which the insurer undertakes, in consideration of a premium equivalent to the hazard run, to indemnify the person insured against certain perils and losses, or against some particular event. Marine insurance is a contract of *indemnity* against those perils to which ships and goods are exposed, in the course of their voyages from one place to another.

The *origin of insurance* has occasioned much doubt among the writers upon mercantile law. Indeed, it is involved in so much obscurity, that, after all the researches which have been made, no very satisfactory solution of this doubt can be promised. It however is clear, that wherever commerce extended its influence, insurance must have soon followed as a necessary attendant. Some writers have ascribed the origin of this contract to Claudius Cæsar, the fifth Roman Emperor. Other respectable authorities have given the honour of it to the Rhodians; thus laying a foundation for the idea that the law of insurance obtained a place in most of the ancient codes of jurisprudence. It was introduced into England by the active and industrious Lombards, who went thither in the thirteenth century; and about the end of the fifteenth century, many considerable regulations were made at Barcelona, in Spain, respecting marine insurances. The progress which this branch of law had made in England previously to the time of Lord Mansfield, was very low; but, during the long period that venerable judge presided in the court of King's Bench, its progress towards perfection was equally rapid.

A complete system cannot be suddenly erected; but it is the boast of this age, that in it the great foundations of marine jurisprudence have been laid, by clearly developing the principles on which policies of insurance are founded, and by applying those principles to particular cases. In the following treatise we shall endeavour to render the law of it clear to the merchant, owner, freighter and man of business. To effect this, we have divided the subject, and it will be discussed in the following order:

I. The policy.
II. The construction of the policy.
III. Perils of the sea.
IV. Capture and detention of princes.
V. Barratry of the master or mariners.
VI. Partial losses, and of adjustments.
VII. Abandonment.
VIII. Fraud in policies.
IX. Sea-worthiness.
X. Illegal voyages.

XI. Warranty.
XII. Deviation.
XIII. Changing the ship.
XIV. Reinsurance and double insurance.
XV. Return of premium.

I. *The policy.*

The policy is the instrument by which the contract of indemnity is effected between the insurer and insured; and it is signed only by the insurer, who is called the underwriter. Of policies there are two kinds, *valued* and *open;* and the only difference between them is this, that, in the former, goods or property insured are valued at prime cost, at the time of effecting the policy; in the latter, the value is not mentioned, but, in case of loss, must be proved.

Policies of insurance, when once they are underwritten, can, generally speaking, never be altered by any authority whatever; because it would be an opening to fraud, and would introduce uncertainty into a species of contract, of which certainty and precision are the most essential requisites. It may be observed, however, that cases frequently exist, in which a policy, *upon proper evidence*, may be altered; and, after signing, policies are frequently altered by *consent* of the parties.

A policy of insurance is the property of the insured; and, if it be *wrongfully* withheld, either by his broker or any other person, he may recover it by an action of trover.

Policies of insurance are generally printed, leaving blanks for the insertion of names and all other requisites. It is, therefore, frequently necessary to insert written clauses, which are to be considered as part of the contract; and the court will look to them to find out the intention of the parties, and will suffer them to control the printed words.

We will now proceed to consider, first, what persons may be the insurers; secondly, what things may be insured; thirdly, what the requisites of a policy are.

1st. All persons, whether aliens or citizens, may insure each other against marine losses.

This rule, however, does not extend to alien enemies. Such a contract is deemed contrary to public policy, and has been adjudged illegal by the courts. Insurance in the United States is generally carried on by incorporated companies.

2dly. The most frequent subjects of marine insurance, are *ships*, *goods*, *merchandise*, and the *freight* or *hire* of ships. But, although insurances upon such property must frequently occur, yet there are cases which can hardly fall within any of those descriptions.

The *bottomry* and *respondentia* are a particular species of property, which may be the subject of insurance; but then it must be particularly expressed in the policy to be *respondentia* interest; for, under a general insurance on *goods*, the party insured cannot recover money lent on *bottomry*. It, however, has since been ruled, that money expended by the captain, for the use of the ship, and for which *respon-*

dentia interest was charged, may be recovered under an insurance on *goods, specie and effects,* provided *the express usage of the trade,* which in matters of insurance is always of great weight, sanction it.

Contraband of war may be insured, although the British lawyers are inclined to make such contracts illegal.

In France and Spain, freight not earned cannot be insured, but it is otherwise in the United States and England.

Profits are also proper subjects of insurance in the United States and England, but not in France.

Commissions are also insurable.

Captors of ships secured as prizes may insure their interest therein before condemnation; nor are they entitled to a return of premium, if the capture be ultimately adjudged no prize, and restitution be awarded to the owners, by the court of admiralty.

Insurances upon the wages of seamen are forbidden; a regulation founded in wisdom and sound policy. This regulation, however, does not mean to prevent mariners from insuring those wages which they are entitled to receive abroad, or goods which they have purchased with those wages in order to bring them home; but, in such a case, they are to be considered in the same light with other men.

It has, however, been determined, that, where the mate of a ship, or a sailor, is to receive something at the end of the voyage, in lieu of wages, he cannot insure it, any more than he could insure wages payable in money.[a]

A wager policy was valid at common law, in New-York; but to entitle the plaintiff to recover, the loss must be total and final.[b] Such a policy is now prohibited by statute.

Wager policies are not valid in Massachusetts, Pennsylvania, or France. In England, however, any interest, even a reasonable expectation of profits, is insurable. It is not necessary in a policy to state the particular interest.[c]

The words "policy to be proof of interest," are not evidence of a wager policy.

The owner of a vessel hypothecated, has an insurable interest in her, and may insure generally;[d] but the owner of a vessel under a bottomry, for more than her value, cannot insure her.[e]

Profit, freight and bottomry interest, must be described by name in the policy.

Goods may be insured, though purchased with the proceeds of a former illegal cargo.

3dly. The essentials in a policy of insurance are, first, the name of the person for whom the insurance is made; secondly, the names of the subscribers or underwriters, and the sums insured; thirdly, the names of the ship and master; fourthly, whether they are ships, goods, or merchandise, upon which the insurance is made; fifthly, the name of the place where the goods are laden, and whither they are bound; sixthly, the time when the risk begins, and when it ends;

---

[a] Webster v. De Tastet, 7 Term Rep. 157. [b] 3 Caines, 141. [c] 1 Ibid. 276. [d] 1 Johns. Rep. 385. [e] 2 Caines, 110.

seventhly, all the various perils and risks which the insurer takes upon himself; eighthly, the consideration, or premium, paid for the risk or hazard run ; ninthly, the month, day and year, on which the policy is executed.

1st. *Of the names of the persons insured.*

Where the policy states the insurance to be for account of A., it is equivalent to a representation that A. is owner.[a]

A policy in the name of one joint owner, "as property may appear," without stating the insurance to be for the benefit of all concerned, does not cover the interest of another joint owner.[b]

An insurance will be valid if made "for account of A., or of whom it may concern."

If a partner insure in his own name only, the policy will cover only his undivided interest in the partnership. But if the policy has the words, "and whomsoever it may concern," it will cover the whole partnership interest, and any person having even a special interest, as by lien, &c.[c]

If the insurer knows that a policy in the name of the broker is in fact effected on account of another, a debt due from the broker cannot be set off against the loss.

2d. *The names of the subscribers or underwriters.*

This was always requisite; as, without it, there would be no insurer.

3d. *Of the names of the ship and master.*

It is customary to insert the names of the ship and master, in order to ascertain the bottom upon which the adventure is to be made, and the captain by whose direction the ship is to be navigated. Sometimes, however, there are insurances generally "upon any ship or ships" expected from a particular place; and although it is more accurate to insert the name of the captain, the insurance would not be void, if a different captain from that mentioned in the policy came into the ship; as the policy always contains the words—"or whosoever else shall go for master in said ship."

With respect to insurances *upon any ship or ships*, it has been recently determined that they are not only legal and valid, but that the insured has a right to cover, by such policy, whatever ship he thought proper that fell within the terms of it.

4th. *Whether they are ships, goods, or merchandise, upon which the insurance is made.*

It is absolutely necessary that there should be a specification, upon *which* of these the underwriter insures. But it is another question,

---

[a] 3 Johns. Cas. 130. [b] 2 Cranch, 431. [c] 1 Wendell, 561.

whether, in policies upon goods, it be necessary to declare the *particulars.* The practice is very unsettled. But when goods are coming from abroad, it is better to insure under general expressions, on account of the various casualties which may happen to obstruct the purchase of the particular commodities intended to be sent.

There are certain kinds of merchandise which are of a perishable nature, on account of which, there is inserted a memorandum at the foot of the policy, by which it is declared, that, in insurances upon bar and sheet iron, iron wire, tin plates, salt, grain of all kinds, tobacco, indian meal, fruits, (preserved or otherwise.) cheese, dry fish, vegetables and roots, hempen yarn, cotton bagging, pleasure carriages, household furniture, skins and hides, musical instruments, looking-glasses, and other articles that are perishable in their own nature, the underwriter will not be answerable for any partial loss, but only for general average; that, in insurances on hemp, they consider themselves free from partial losses not amounting to thirty per cent.; on sugar, flax, flaxseed, and bread, on losses not amounting to seven per cent.; and on coffee and pepper in bags or bulk, on losses not amounting to ten per cent., unless it arise from a general average; and that no loss or particular average shall be paid, unless amounting to five per cent.

A memorandum that corn, &c., shall be free from average, unless general, protects the insurer from every claim for a total loss, unless there has been an actual physical destruction of the subject insured.[a]

There are some kinds of property which do not fall under the general denomination of *goods* in a policy, and for the loss of which the underwriters are not answerable, unless they are specifically named; such as *goods lashed on deck, the captain's clothes, and the ship's provisions.* A policy on *goods*, means only such goods as are merchantable, and a part of the cargo; and, therefore, when goods like those are meant to be insured, they are always insured by name, and the premium is greater.

It has been questioned whether a cargo of dollars, or other coin, jewels, &c., if lost, be recoverable under a policy upon *goods and merchandise* generally; but Magens states explicitly, that gold and silver, coined and uncoined, pearls and other jewels, may be insured at London and Hamburg, and several other places, under the general expression of *merchandise.*

5th. *The name of the place at which the goods are laden, and to which they are bound.*

This has been always held to be necessary in policies, and must be so, on account of the evident uncertainty which would follow from a contrary practice, as the insurer would never know what the risk was which he had undertaken to insure; and, therefore, if a ship be insured from New-York to   , a blank being left by the lader of the goods, to prevent a surprise by an enemy, and if in her voyage she happen to be cast away, though there be private instructions for her port, yet the insured must sit down with his loss, by reason of the uncertainty.

---

[a] 1 Johns. Cas. 226.—1 Caines' R. 196.—3 Ibid. 108.

26

Where the insurance was to Barbadoes and a market, it was decided by the supreme court of New-York, that the vessel might go *bona fide* from island to island, for the purpose of selling her cargo, and that the risk was not determined until the whole was disposed of.[a]

If the insurance be to several ports, and the insured intend to go but to one, he can go to either ; but if to more than one, he must follow the order in which they are described in the policy.[b]

It is also customary to state in the policy, at what port or place the ship may touch and stay during the voyage, so that it shall not be considered as a *deviation* to go to any of those places.

The term *port* must be taken in reference to the subject-matter to which it is applied. It generally means a harbour ; but where there are no harbours, it may mean a road or anchoring place for the purpose of loading and unloading.[c]

6th. *The time when the risk commences, and when it ends.*

Policies expressly declare, that " the adventure shall begin upon the said goods and merchandise, *from the loading thereof on board the said ship*, and so shall continue, until the said ship, goods and merchandise shall have arrived at L. ; and upon the said ship till she has been moored at anchor twenty-four hours in good safety ; and *upon the goods, till the same be there safely discharged and landed.*" From these words, it is obvious that the insurers are not answerable for any accident which may happen to the goods, in lighters or boats going aboard, *previous* to the voyage ; yet, as the policy says the risk shall continue *till the goods are safely landed*, it seems the insurer continues responsible for the risk to be run in carrying the goods in boats to the shore. If there be a loss, however, in these cases, the accident must have happened while the goods were in the boats or lighters belonging to the ship ; and in a case where the owner of the goods brings down his own lighter, receives the goods out of the ship, and, before they reach land, an accident happens, whereby the goods are damaged, the insurer is discharged, although the insurance be upon goods to New-York, *and till the same be safely landed there.*

In a case so early as in the time of James II., a policy of insurance was construed to run until the ship had ended, and was discharged of her voyage : for arrival at the port to which she was bound was not a discharge, *till she was unloaded.*

But, although this construction be right where the policy is general from A. to B., yet if it contain the words usually inserted—" *and till the ship shall have moored at anchor twenty-four hours in good safety,*" the underwriter is not liable for any loss arising from seizure after she has been twenty-four hours in port, even if such seizure was in consequence of an act of barratry (such as *smuggling*) of the master *during the voyage.*

It has, however, been decided, that an arrival in port, where the vessel is at once ordered back to perform quarantine, is not an arrival which will discharge the insurer from a loss at quarantine, as the

---

[a] 1 Johns. Rep. 333. [b] 2 Ibid. 264. [c] 10 Ibid. 126.

arrival and mooring in good safety must be construed to mean an opportunity of loading and unloading.

So, too, where a vessel arrived at a port where an embargo had been previously laid on vessels of the same nation, and which vessels were afterwards declared prizes of war, the underwriters were held liable.

But where a ship had arrived at the wharf on the 12th of January, and was laid on the outside of the tier, there being no room to lay her on the inside; where the sails were unbent, topmasts struck; three anchors out; and she was also lashed to another ship, and so continued till the 19th, when several ships and a quantity of ice forced her adrift, and she was wholly lost: Lord Kenyon was of opinion she was completely moored on the 19th; and, as the accident did not happen till above twenty-four hours after that time, the underwriters were not liable.

Where the vessel is obliged, by the municipal regulations of the country, to stop without the harbour to be examined, the risk continues until she has been moored in safety within the harbour for twenty-four hours.[a]

In an insurance upon *freight*, if an accident happens to the ship *before any goods* are put on board, which prevents her from sailing, the insured upon the policy cannot recover the freight which she would have earned if she had sailed.

In insurance upon freight, the risk begins from the time the goods are sent on board; but if a ship, sailing under a contract, be lost on her way to the port of lading, or at the port of lading, before taking in her cargo, the insurer is liable—the right to freight having commenced.

But if the policy be a *valued* policy, and *part* of the cargo be on board when such accident happens, the rest being ready to be shipped, the insured may recover the whole amount of the freight.

So, likewise, in an *open* policy on freight, *at and from London and Teneriffe to any of the West India Islands*, (*Jamaica excepted.*) The ship was under a charter-party to depart out of the river Thames, and proceed to Teneriffe, there to receive on board 500 pipes of wine, to be delivered in the West Indies, for the freight of which the freighters covenanted to pay 35*s.* per pipe. She sailed from London in ballast, and was captured before her arrival at Teneriffe. The court held, that the instant the ship departed from the Thames, the contract for freight had its *commencement*, and the plaintiff was entitled to recover.

If the cargo be temporarily landed, from necessity, during the voyage, it is still protected by the policy.

When a ship is insured *at and from a place*, and it arrives at that place, as long as the ship is preparing for the voyage upon which it is insured, the insurer is liable; but, if all thoughts of the voyage be laid aside, and the ship lie there five, six, or seven years, with the owner's privity, the insurer is not liable.

Where a vessel is bound to a West India Island, as Jamaica, and insured from the port of departure to Jamaica generally, it is laid down, that the outward risk upon the ship ended twenty-four hours

---

[a] 11 Johns. Rep. 358.

after her arrival in the first port in the island to which she was destined; but that the outward policy *upon goods* continues till they were landed.

In insurance upon East India voyages, the insurers in England have been held liable, not only for events which may possibly happen from the port of discharge to that of delivery, but also *for all intermediate or country voyages.* And this construction of East India policies prevails, whether the words of them be large and comprehensive, such as, with liberty to touch, stay and trade, at any port or place whatsoever; or restrained and limited, such as, to touch and stay at any port or place in this voyage. At the same time, though the general rule be so, yet the parties contracting may, by their own agreement, prevent such a latitude of construction. In order to do this, it is not necessary that the express words of exclusion should be inserted in the policy; but if, from the terms used, the court can collect that such was the intention of the parties, that construction, which is most agreeable to their intention, will prevail.

In the unloading of goods there should be no unreasonable delay, but this must always depend upon circumstances.

The risk on the body of the ship is generally to commence "from her beginning to load at   and so shall continue and endure until the said ship shall arrive at   and hath there been moored at anchor twenty-four hours in good safety." This mode of stating the commencement of the risk must commonly be applied to insurances on ships outward bound; for, when insurance is made on the homeward risk, the beginning of the adventure is sometimes stated to be "immediately from and after her arrival at the port abroad;" at other times, "from the departure;" and, in short, it is very variable, depending upon the inclination of the insurer.

The construction of policies, as to loading and unloading, is according to the usage of trade at the place, and this is liberally construed.

Where the policy authorized the unloading of the goods at Gibraltar, and their reshipment in British vessels for England or Holland, and the goods were unloaded and put into a store-ship, (there being British ships in port,) a loss from the wrecking of the store-ship, which was there always regarded as a storehouse, was held to be within the policy.

So, too, in a loss by fire, in a warehouse at Canton, where the rigging was stored, the insurers were held liable—it being the universal and well known usage for European vessels (except the Dutch, who are denied the privilege) to deposit their rigging, &c., in such warehouses, upon their arrival at Canton.

7th. *Of the various perils and risks against which the underwriter insures.*

The words now used, expressive of the insurer's risk, are very extensive, including "perils of the seas, men of war, fire, enemies, pirates, rovers, *thieves*, jettisons, letters of mart and countermart, surprisals, takings at sea, arrests, restraints, and detainments of all kings, princes and people, of what nation, condition, or quality soever; barratry of the master or mariners; and all other perils, losses and misfortunes, that have or shall come to the hurt, detriment, or damage of the said goods and merchandises, and ship, or any part thereof."

The policy is so general in its terms, as to embrace every species of risk to which ships and goods are exposed, from the perils of the sea, and all other causes incident to maritime adventures. The perils, however, may be enlarged or abridged, at the pleasure of the parties.

Where there is no representation of neutrality, the insurer takes upon himself war risks.[a]

Damage in consequence of detention from pestilence in the port, is a loss within the policy.[b]

The interdiction of commerce with the destined port is a peril within the policy, and the vessel is not bound to proceed to the nearest port, neither is the affreighter bound to receive his goods there.[c]

The danger, however, must be so great, as to amount almost to a certainty of capture. An interdiction of commerce with the destined port, or a denial of entrance at the port by blockade, or by the government, is not deemed, in England or in Massachusetts, a loss within the policy.

It is doubtful whether a loss by fire, proceeding from negligence, is covered by a policy against fire. An insurance against *all* risks does not comprehend any arising from the fraud of the insured.

The law is totally silent as to the description of *thieves* meant by the policy; whether the insurer undertakes as well against thefts committed by the master or mariners, as against thefts committed from without. That he is liable in the latter case, cannot be doubted.

In addition to these, it is frequently the practice to insure her, *lost or not lost;* in which, if the ship should be lost at the time of the insurance, still the underwriter, provided there be no fraud, is liable. The practice is peculiar to American and English policies, not being adopted by other nations.

8th. *The consideration or premium for the risk or hazard run.*

This is expressed to have been received at the time of underwriting: "We, the insurers, confessing ourselves paid the consideration due unto us for this insurance by the insured." This being subscribed by the underwriter, it is proper to inquire whether, if the premium were not actually paid at the time, he could afterwards maintain an action for it against the *insured*, who might then produce his subscription as evidence against himself. Questions upon policies of insurance stand most broadly upon the usage of the place where the policy is effected; and this question would, no doubt, be determined by usage.

The premium of consideration paid, given, or contracted for, *must*, like the risk, be inserted.

9th. *The day, month, and year, on which the policy is executed.*

This insertion seems very necessary, because, by computing the date of the policy with the date of facts which happened afterwards, or are material to be proved, it will frequently appear whether there

---

[a] 1 Caines, 217. [b] 2 Ibid. 1. [c] 1 Johns. 249.

is any reason to suspect fraud or improper conduct on the part of the insured.

II. *The construction of the policy.*

In the construction of policies, two rules chiefly prevail, namely, to give effect to the *intentions* of the parties, and to the *usage of trade*, with respect to the particular voyages or risks to which the policy relates.

If any of the terms used in the policy have, by the usage of the trade, or in the common understanding between insurers and insured, acquired a peculiar sense, they are to be construed accordingly.[a]

Except for the purpose of explaining the usage of trade, parol evidence is inadmissible to vary or contradict a policy.[b]

When an insurance is made on one species of property, the damage sustained by loss of property, different from that named in the policy, cannot be recovered. Thus, a man who has insured a cargo of *goods*, cannot recover the *freight* which he has paid for the carriage of that cargo; nor can an owner, who insures the *ship merely*, demand satisfaction for the loss of *merchandise* laden thereon; or ask from the insurers *extraordinary wages paid to the seamen, or the value of provisions consumed*, by reason of the detention of the *ship* at any port longer than was expected.

On a policy on a *ship*, sailors' wages or provisions are not allowed in England in settling the damages; and if a ship be detained in consequence of any injury received in a storm, the underwriter must make good that damage; but he is not held bound to pay for the wages and provisions of the crew during the necessary detention of the vessel for repairs. In the United States the law is otherwise, and he must pay for them as comprehended within the perils of the sea. In a fishing vessel, the loss of lines and tackle employed in fishing, was held, in England, not to be within a policy on the vessel, tackle, &c.

It is necessary that the cargo laden on board should be of the same form and species with that insured. A policy on a cargo of wheat will not, for instance, cover a cargo of flour.[c] A policy of cargo, or goods generally, will not cover goods stowed on deck, nor live stock. Local usage, however, may give such an extension to the terms.[c] Bills of exchange may be insured.

The policy generally contains the words "lost or not lost;" but the better opinion is, that these words are not necessary.

It is a settled rule of construction, that the peril upon which the policy attaches, must be the immediate, and not the remote cause of the loss; and where a partial is followed by a total loss, the former is merged in the latter.

III. *Perils of the sea.*

It may, in general, be said, that every thing happening to a ship, in the course of her voyage, by the intermediate act of God, without

---

[a] 7 Johns. Rep. 385. [b] 3 Ibid. 1. [c] 3 Kent, 259.

the intervention of human agency, is a peril of the sea. Thus, every accident happening by the violence of wind and waves; by thunder or lightning; by driving against rocks; by the stranding of the ship; or by any other violence which human prudence could not foresee, nor human strength resist, may be considered as a loss within the meaning of such a policy; and the insurer must answer for all damages sustained in consequence of such accident. But, if a ship be driven by stress of weather on an enemy's coast, and be there captured, it is a loss by capture, and not by perils of the sea.

In order to charge the underwriter for a loss by perils of the sea, the ship must be equipped with every thing necessary for the voyage; she must be seaworthy, and have a sufficient crew, and a captain and pilot of competent skill.

The ignorance and incompetency of the master and mariners, is not a peril of the sea against which the underwriter undertook to insure.

It is, however, difficult oftentimes to discriminate between damage occasioned by the ordinary wear and tear of the voyage, which falls upon the owner, and by a peril of the sea.

The loss of an anchor by friction of the rocks, the destruction of the ship by worms, the ordinary leakage of fluids in casks, the spontaneous combustion of hemp, are all instances of losses not within the policy. Even damage done to the ship by rats, has been questioned, as a loss for which the insurer is not answerable.

If a ship has been missing, and no intelligence received of her within a reasonable time after she sailed, it will be presumed that she foundered at sea.

There is no precise time, after which, a vessel that has not been heard of, is to be presumed to be lost; but the presumption must depend upon the circumstances of the case.[a]

The usual, and not the utmost length of the voyage, is the basis of the calculation.[b] In France, it is one year in ordinary voyages, and two years in long ones. In Spain, one year and a half.

If the vessel be obliged to put in for repairs, and be afterwards lost on the voyage, the insurer is entitled to recover the partial loss from the previous damage and general average thereon, in addition to the total loss.[c]

Where the insurers took no risk in port but sea-risk, it was held, that a loss occasioned by the vessel's being driven on shore, so that she could not be got off unless at an expense exceeding half her value, and where afterwards she was burnt by an armed force, was a loss by the perils of the sea, and not by burning.[d]

In an action on a policy, in which there was a warranty against captures and seizures, (the ship never having been heard of after sailing,) it was insisted for the defendant, that as captures and seizures were excepted, it lay upon the plaintiff to prove that the loss happened in the particular manner stated. Lord Chief Justice Lee said, it would be unreasonable to expect certain evidence of such a loss, where every body

---

[a] 2 Johns. Rep. 150 [b] 1 Caines, 525. [c] 10 Johns. Rep. 487. [d] 11 Ibid. 9.

on board is presumed to be drowned ; and all that can be required is, the best proof the nature of the case admits of, which the plaintiff has given. The jury found a verdict for the plaintiff.

The enumerated perils of the sea, pirates, rovers and thieves, include the violent acts of individuals, whether felons or as a mob, or plunderers from the wreck and also the plundering or injury committed by a mutinous crew.

IV. *Capture and detention by princes, or foreign powers.*

A ship is to be considered as lost, by *capture*, when taken, though she be never condemned at all, nor carried into any port or fleet of the enemy, and the insurer must pay the value. If, after condemnation, the owner recover or retake her, the insurer can be in no other condition, than if she had been retaken or recovered before condemnation. The insurer runs the risk of the insured, and undertakes to indemnify ; he must therefore bear the *loss actually* sustained. So that if, after condemnation, the owner recover the ship in her complete condition, but has paid for salvage, or been at any expense in getting her back, the insurer must pay the loss actually sustained. No capture by the enemy can be so total a loss as to leave no possibility of recovery. The chance does not, however, suspend the demand for a total loss upon the insurer ; but, in case of a recapture, justice is done by putting him in the place of the insured.

Where a capture has been made, whether it be legal or not, the insurers are liable for the charges of a *compromise* made, *bona fide*, to prevent the ship from being condemned as a prize, or to avoid the greater expense of prosecuting an appeal.

A vessel was captured and deprived of her papers ; upon recapture and restoration, on payment of salvage, it was held that the insured was justified in breaking up the voyage, and that there was a total loss by capture, the ship not being able to proceed without her papers.[a]

After capture and recapture, the insurer is liable only for the salvage and for losses within the policy, but not for the expenses of an auction sale by the direction of the consignee of the insured.[b]

He is liable for the expenses of prosecuting an appeal against captors, where he does not dissent after notice of the proceedings, though they surpass the amount of his subscription.[c]

The jury, however, must decide as to the propriety of those expenses and the insurers' proportion.[c]

Insurers are bound to pay any necessary and reasonable expenses occasioned by capture.

If an insurer underwrite property belonging to another country, between which and our own hostilities break out subsequent to the policy being effected, which said property is captured, lost, or destroyed during the war, the underwriter is not liable.[d]

The underwriter is answerable for all loss or damage arising to the insured, "*by the arrests, restraints, and detainments of all kings, princes and people, of what nation, condition, or quality soever.*"

---

[a] 10 Johns. 79. [b] 1 Caines, 49. [c] Ibid. 276. [d] 3 Kent, 254.

The only question then is, what shall be considered as such detention? Lord Mansfield said, that the insured may abandon in case merely of an arrest or embargo by a prince, not an enemy; and, consequently such an arrest is also within the meaning of the word *detention.*[a]

Detention in port on suspicion of a breach of neutrality, is a loss within the policy.[b]

Where a vessel, chartered by the month, is detained by an embargo, the charterer cannot recover, upon an insurance of the cargo, the hire of the vessel while detained.[c]

Although the words of this part of the policy are, "*arrests, restraints, and detainments, of all kings, princes, or people, of what nation, condition, or quality soever;* yet the word *people* must be understood as applying to *those people who are the ruling power of the country,* and not to any assemblage or people who arrest the ship in a violent and riotous manner.

In case of a detention by a foreign power, which in time of war seizes a neutral vessel at sea, and sends her into port to be searched for enemy's property, all the charges consequent thereon must be borne by the underwriters; and whatever costs may arise from an improper detention, must always fall upon them.

In the following case, the plaintiff obtained a verdict on the principle "that the condemnation of any vessel by a foreign court of admiralty is conclusive here only as to the *express ground* of the sentence." The policy of the American ship Mercury was subscribed by the defendant as an underwriter for £200. On her passage from Virginia to Bremen, she was captured by a French privateer, and carried into Nantes, where she was condemned by a French court of admiralty, "as belonging to the enemies of the French republic." But as the ship was provided with all the proper and usual documents, it was held that the underwriters were responsible.

But, though an underwriter is liable for all damages arising to the owner of the ship or goods from the restraint or detention of princes, yet that rule is not extended to cases where the insured navigates against the laws of those countries, in the ports of which he may chance to be detained, or to cases where there is a seizure for non-payment of customs.

If, indeed, any of those acts were committed by the master of the ship, without the knowledge of the insured, the underwriter would be liable, not for losses by *detention,* but for a loss by the barratry of the master.

V. *Barratry of the master or mariners.*

Barratry is committed, when the master of the ship or the mariners cheat the owners or insurers, whether it be by running away with the ship, sinking her, deserting her, embezzling the cargo, or by carrying a ship, a different course from their orders. It includes

---

[a] 2 Burr, 696. [b] 2 Caines' Cas. 158. [c] 3 Ibid. 155.

every breach of trust with dishonest views. These definitions are so very comprehensive, that they seem to take in every case of barratry. From a review of the decisions on this subject, it appears, that any act of the master, or of the mariners, which is of a criminal nature, or which is grossly negligent, tending to their own benefit, to the prejudice of the owners of the ship, *without their consent or privity*, is barratry.

It is not necessary, in order to entitle the insured to recover for barratry, that the loss should happen *in the act of barratry*. It is immaterial whether it take place *during* the *fraudulent* voyage, or *after* the ship has returned to the regular course; for the moment the ship is carried from its right track, with an evil intent, barratry is committed.

But the loss, in consequence of the act of barratry, must happen *during the voyage insured*, and within the time limited by the policy; for, if the captain be guilty of barratry by smuggling, and the ship afterwards arrive at the port of destination, and *be there moored at anchor twenty-four hours in good safety;* the underwriters are not liable, if, after this, she should be seized for that act of smuggling.

The sailing out of port, without paying duties, whereby the ship is subjected to forfeiture, is barratrous.

To constitute barratry, it must be *without the knowledge or consent of the owners*.

It need not be made to appear affirmatively that the master was benefited by the fraudulent act, the law will intend that it was done to the injury of the owner.[a]

Trading with an enemy, without the leave of the owner; and for a neutral to resist search, are acts of barratry.

Breach of an embargo is an act of barratry in the master.

Barratry implies something contrary to the duty of masters and mariners *in the relation in which they stand to the owners of the ship*. They may make themselves liable to the owners of *goods* for misconduct, but not for *barratry*, which can by committed against the owners of the ship, and them only.

If the owner be also the master of the ship, any act, which, in another master, would be construed barratry, cannot be so in him; but where the person, who acts as master, is proved to have carried her out of her course for fraudulent purposes of his own, this is *prima facie* evidence of barratry; and it is incumbent on the underwriter, if he can, to prove that such person was owner as well as master.

If the owner of a vessel let her on charter, retaining the management, and hiring and paying the master and crew, and furnishing them with provisions, the hirer is not considered the owner, *pro hac vice*, but the original ownership continues; and if the captain at the request of the hirer, go out of his course, it is barratry.[b]

But if it be let to the master for a certain time, and he covenant to victual and man her at his expense, he is to be deemed the owner, and no act of his will amount to barratry;[c] and the insurer will not be liable to an innocent owner of goods on board.

---

[a] 2 Caines, 57. [b] 1 Johns. 229 [c] 8 Ibid. 272.

If the parties insert in the policy that the insurance shall be upon the ship, *in any lawful trade,* and the captain commit barratry by smuggling, the underwriters are answerable. For, otherwise, the word *barratry* would be struck out of the policy; and most clearly the stipulation in the policy, respecting the employment of the ship *in a lawful trade,* must mean, as was said by Lord Kenyon, in delivering the unanimous opinion of the court, *the trade on which she is sent by the owners.*

A master endowed with a discretionary power, of making the best purchases with despatch, will not be warranted in trading with an enemy's settlement, (although with their permission,) unauthorized by his owners, in consequence of which the ship was seized and confiscated. Nor does it make any difference that the benefit of his owners was intended; as the act is barratry.

So, also, if the master of a ship, *contrary to the instructions of his owner,* cruise for and take a prize, and the vessel is afterwards lost, he is guilty of *barratry,* even though he prosecute the prize in the court of admiralty in the name of himself and his owner, and though the owner had procured a letter of marque solely with a view to encourage seamen to enter, and without any intention of using it for the purposes of cruising; for, whatever is done by the captain to defeat or delay the performance of the voyage, is barratry in him, it being to the prejudice of the owners; and, though the captain might *conceive* what he did was for their benefit, yet, if he acted contrary to his duty to them, it is barratry.[a]

It has been contended, that, if a vessel deviated from the voyage insured, *through the ignorance of the captain,* it amounted to barratry. But the court of King's Bench, after considerable argument, were unanimously of opinion, that there must be *fraud* to constitute barratry.

VI. *Partial loss and adjustment.*

Partial loss implies a damage, which the ship may have sustained, in the course of her voyage, from any of the perils mentioned in the policy. When applied to the cargo, it means the damage which goods may have received, without any fault of the master, by storm, capture, stranding, or shipwreck; although the whole, or the greater part thereof, may arrive in port. These partial losses fall upon the owners of the property so damaged, who must be indemnified by the underwriter. But the underwriters of New-York expressly declare, as appears from a memorandum at the foot of the policy, that they will not answer for partial losses, not amounting to 5 *per cent.* This clause was intended to prevent the underwriters from being continually harassed by trifling demands. But, at the same time that they provide against trifling claims for *partial* losses, they undertake to indemnify against losses, however inconsiderable, that arise from a *general* average.

If, in adjusting the losses under this memorandum, the partial loss be found on survey and sale to have been 5 per cent., the insurer

---

[a] Moss. v. Byrom, 6 Term Rep. 379.

pays the damages and expenses; if less than 5 per cent., the insurer pays nothing. The expenses are not to be estimated in calculating the loss.

When we speak of the underwriters being liable to pay, whether for total or partial losses, it must always be understood, that they are liable only in proportion to the sums which they have underwritten. Thus, if a man underwrites $100 upon property valued at $500, and a total loss happen, he is answerable for $100, and no more; that being the amount of his subscription: if only a partial loss amounting to 60 or 70 per cent. upon the whole value, he pays $60 or $70, that being his proportion of the loss.

There are two kinds of indemnity which may be obtained under a contract of insurance: to pay what the goods would have brought if they had reached the place of destination; the other, to pay only the first cost of the goods, and the expenses incurred.

An adjustment of general average at a foreign port is conclusive, both between the parties to the policy and the parties in interest in the adventure.

The adjustment of partial loss is different from that of general average, in being only *prima facie* evidence of the claim, and the party will not be concluded without a full disclosure of all the circumstances. It also differs in the rule of estimating the value of the goods. In the former, it is according to the value at the time and place of departure of the vessel; in the latter, according to the value at the foreign port.

If extra freight and extraordinary expense be incurred in transporting the cargo in another vessel, it is charged upon the insurer.

He is, also, liable for all the labour and expense attendant upon an accident which forces the vessel into port.

In adjusting partial loss, the insurer has nothing to do with the state of the markets or with the loss on landing expenses; freight and duty accruing in consequence of the deterioration. The loss is to be adjusted only upon a comparison of the gross proceeds of the sound and damaged goods.[a]

Where goods are damaged in the course of the voyage, the way to ascertain the damage is to compare the market price at which the same goods would have sold, if sound. The freight is not to be estimated in an open policy. The market value of the property insured is to be estimated at the time of the commencement of the risk, that being the object for which an indemnity was stipulated.

When there is no special stipulation, the insurer is not liable for loss occasioned by *ordinary* leakage. When the leakage is caused by an extraordinary accident, the difference is to be estimated between that and ordinary leakage, and an allowance made for the latter.

When the quantity of damage sustained in the course of the voyage is known, and the amount which each underwriter of the policy is liable to pay is settled, it is usual for the underwriter to endorse on the policy, "*adjusted this loss at so much per cent.*," or some words to the same effect.—This is called an adjustment.

---

[a] 3 Kent, 337.

After an adjustment is signed by the underwriter, if he refuse to pay, the owner has no occasion to go into a proof of his loss, or any of the circumstances respecting it, unless fraud were used in obtaining the adjustment; or unless there had been some misconception of the law or fact upon which it was made.

If an nisurer pay money for a total loss, and in fact it be so at the time of adjustment, and it afterwards turn out to be only a partial loss, he shall not recover back the money so paid to the insured; for substantial justice is done by putting him in the place of the insured, and giving him all the advantages that arise from the salvage.[a]

An adjustment made by the agent of the insurer does not bind him so far but that he may show it to be erroneous.[b]

If the goods be valued in the policy at so much per lb., their weight must be estimated according to the standard of the place where the contract was made.[c]

The premium may be resorted to as a guide to discover the amount intended to be insured.[d]

In an open policy on cargo, the invoice price of goods is the value which the insured can recover upon a total loss, and that without any deduction for the drawback on exportation.

By the invoice price of goods, is meant the prime cost. The insured, in an open policy, cannot charge commissions on the purchase of goods by himself, though he may add the premium of insurance.[e]

A total loss and an average loss cannot be recovered under the same policy.[f]

The jury may allow interest on the amount of a partial loss.[g]

In estimating the loss in case of repairs, the insurer is entitled to a deduction of $\frac{1}{3}$ new for old, whether the vessel be old or new.[h]

It is the duty of the master to cause an adjustment upon his arrival at the destined port, and he has a lien upon the cargo for the amount of the contribution.[i]

VII. *Abandonment.*

The insured, before he can demand a recompense from the underwriter for a total loss, must cede or abandon to him, his right to all the property that may be recovered from shipwreck, capture, or any other peril stated in the policy.

A total loss does not always mean that the property insured is irrecoverably lost or gone, but that, by some of the perils mentioned in the policy, it is in such a condition as to be of little use or value to the insured, and so much injured as to justify him in abandoning it to the insurer, and in calling upon him to pay the whole amount of his insurance, as if a total loss had actually happened. Here it is sufficient to remark, that, in case of a total loss, literally so called, the *prime cost* of the property insured, or the value mentioned in the policy, must be paid by the underwriter, at least as far as his proportion of the insurance extends. The insurer has nothing to do with the market; he has no concern in any profit or loss which may arise to

---

[a] 4 Burr, 1766. [b] 1 Caines, 444. 2 Ibid. 30. [d] 10 Johns. 79. [e] Ibid. 273. [f] 1 Ibid. 249. [g] Ibid. 315. [h] 11 Ibid. 315. [i] Ibid. 323.

the merchant from the sale of the goods. If they be totally lost, he must pay the value of the thing he insured at the *outset;* he has no concern in any subsequent value. The right of abandonment does not depend upon the certainty, but upon the probability of a total loss.

It is unnecessary, where the object is entirely destroyed, but only where the loss is constructively total.

Where a vessel is hopelessly stranded, it is unnecessary to abandon freight.[a]

The right to abandon must arise upon the object of the insured being so far defeated that it is not worth his while to pursue it; such a loss is equally inconvenient to him as if it had been total. For instance, if the voyage had been absolutely lost, or not worth pursuing; if the salvage be very high—suppose a half; if further expense be necessary; if the insurer will not engage at all events to bear that expense, though it should exceed the value, or fail of success: under these and many other like circumstances, the insured may disentangle himself, and abandon, notwithstanding there has been a recapture.

There may be circumstances in which it would be unjust to suffer the insured to abandon; for, a ship might be taken, and escape immediately, which would be no hindrance at all to the voyage; or she might be taken and instantly ransomed, which would amount only to a partial loss; in which cases, the insured shall not be allowed to demand a recompense for a total loss.

The right to abandon must depend upon the nature of the case at the time of the action brought, or at the time of the offer to abandon.

The owner, therefore, cannot abandon, unless at some period or other of the voyage there has been a total loss; and, therefore, if neither the thing insured, nor the voyage be lost, the owner is not allowed to abandon.

In case of stranding, the goods must be deteriorated to half their value, to justify an abandonment.[b]

If certain articles be mentioned in the policy, and a moiety of them be lost, the insured may abandon as for a total loss, though the loss be not equal to a moiety of the cargo.[c]

So, if part be lost by jettison, and a part damaged, so as to reduce the residue of the goods to less than a moiety, notwithstanding the damaged goods sold (at a port into which the vessel is obliged to enter for repairs) for a sum, which, deducted from the cost of the damaged and lost part, would reduce it to less than a moiety of the the cost of the whole.[d]

If the vessel should be so much injured as not to be worth repairing, it is a total loss.[e]

A damage exceeding the moiety of value of the subject insured, is sufficient to authorize an abandonment. At least, this has been adopted as the rule in the most respectable states in the union, though it has never been understood as extending to a cargo consisting of memorandum articles.[f]

---

[a] 8 Taunt. 755. [b] 1 Johns. 435. [c] Ibid. 406. [d] 6 Ibid. 129
[e] 1 Johns. Cas. 34. [f] 8 Cranch, 47.

A total loss may either be technical or real. The latter is always a question of fact, but the former often depends upon the construction of the law.[a]

An embargo by a foreign friendly power constitutes a total loss, and authorizes an immediate abandonment.

The insured has a right to call upon the underwriters for a total loss, and of course to abandon, as soon as he hears of such a calamity having happened ; his claim to an indemnity not being at all suspended by the chance of a future recovery of part of the property lost ; because by the abandonment, that chance devolves upon the underwriter, by which means the intention of the contracting parties is fully answered, and complete justice is done.

In a modern decision, it was held by the court of King's Bench, that as soon as the insured receive account of such loss as entitles them to abandon, they must, in the first instance, make their election, whether they will abandon or not : and, if they abandon, they must give the underwriter notice in a reasonable time, otherwise they waive their right to abandon, and can never afterwards recover for a total loss.[b]

It is a question for a jury to decide, what time is reasonable.[c] Five days delay has been held too late. If the insurer reject the abandonment, he must also do it in a reasonable time.

A technical total loss must continue to the time of the abandonment.

If the same conveyance brings the account of the vessel's detention, &c., and of her release from restraint, the insured cannot abandon, but the expenses must be paid by the insurers.

An agent, who insures, has authority to abandon for his principal.[d]

The effect of an abandonment, if legal, is to put the insurers into the place of the insured, and to make the agents of the latter their agents.

It has a retrospective effect, and without any deed of cession, it transfers to the insurer the right of property to the extent of his insurance.

After the insured knows that the voyage is completed, he cannot abandon.[e]

The insured may abandon immediately upon being advised of the capture of his vessel.[f]

A capture by a friend, is a good cause to abandon.[g]

An abandonment should describe the causes of abandonment with certainty, and it should be explicit and unconditional.[h]

After a waiver of an abandonment, the insured can recover only an average loss.[i]

After an abandonment of the vessel, and acceptance, the insurer is entitled to the freight which may be earned subsequently, and he is chargeable with the subsequent wages of the crew, as owner.[j] Such

---

[a] 4 Cranch, 42. [b] 1 Term Rep. 608. [c] 6 Cranch, 338. [d] Ibid. 272.
[e] 3 Johns. Cas. 156. [f] 7 Johns. R. 514. [g] 2 Johns. Cas. 263. [h] 1 Johns. R. 181.
[i] 3 Johns. Cas. 39. [j] 7 Johns. R. 431.

an abandonment is binding and conclusive between the parties, and the rights flowing from it become vested, and are not to be divested by subsequent events.

But, if the insured, hearing that his ship is much disabled, and has put into port to repair, express his desire to the underwriters to abandon, and he be dissuaded from it by them, and they order the repairs to be made, they are liable to the owner for all the subsequent damage occasioned by that refusal, though it should amount to the whole sum insured.[a]

When a case proper for abandonment has occurred, and it be duly made, the insurer cannot destroy its effect by an offer to pay for the repairs.

Upon a valid abandonment, the master and the consignee become the agents of the insurer, and the insured is not bound by the subsequent acts, unless he adopt them. When the ship is abandoned, the freight earned previous to the disaster, according to the law of the state of New-York, belongs to the owner, the residue to the insurer. In England, the same rule applies.

According to the law of Pennsylvania, the entire freight goes to the insurer.

The same rule is adopted in France.

The insurer is not bound, after abandonment and acceptance, to go on and complete the voyage, although he is entitled to the freight if he does.

VIII. *Fraud.*

The contract of insurance is regarded as founded in good faith; and both parties, but especially the insured, are bound to communicate all the facts within their knowledge which affect the risk.

It is necessary to consider this in three divisions: 1st. The allegation of any circumstances, as facts, to the underwriter, which the person insured knows to be false; 2dly. The suppression of any circumstances which the insured knows to exist, and which, if known to the underwriter, might prevent him from undertaking the risk at all; or, if he did, might entitle him to demand a larger premium; and 3dly. A misrepresentation.

In a case before Lord Chief Justice Holt, in the reign of William and Mary, that learned judge held, that if the goods were insured as the goods of a Hamburgher, who was an ally, and the goods were, in fact, the goods of a Frenchman, who was an enemy, it was a fraud, and that the insurance was not good.

A *false assertion* in a policy will vitiate the contract, even though the loss happen in a mode *not* affected by that falsity.

If the misrepresentation was by fraudulent design, it avoids the policy, whether material or not; but, if unintentional, it does not affect the policy, unless material and untrue.

If the information be stated on belief only, or as mere opinion, and be made in good faith, it does not affect the policy.

---

[a] Da Costan v. Newham.

A representation to one underwriter, is not evidence of a representation to a subsequent underwriter on a different policy, though upon the same vessel, and against the same risks.[a]

To constitute a representation, language equivalent to the assertions of a particular fact must be used.[b]

A misrepresentation to avoid a policy, must be of some fact, which, if untrue, would materially alter the risks of the voyage [c]

The second species of fraud, which affects insurances, is, *the concealment of circumstances known only to one of the parties entering into the contract.* The facts, upon which the risk is to be computed, lie, for the most part, within the knowledge of the insured only. The underwriter must, therefore, rely upon him for all necessary information; and must trust to him, that he will conceal nothing, so as to make him form a wrong estimate. If a mistake happen, without any fraudulent intention, still the contract is annulled, because the risk is not the same which the underwriter intended.

Every fact known to the insured, which would, if disclosed, enhance the premium, should be communicated to the underwriters.[d]

The insured need not disclose that the vessel has papers on board which are necessary to the prosecution of the voyage, according to the usage of the trade; though the possession of such papers increase the risk of capture.[e]

One having a doubtful account of his ship that was at sea, namely, that a ship, described like his, was taken, insured her, without giving any notice to the insurers of what he had heard, either as to the hazard or the circumstances, which might induce him to believe that his ship was in great danger, if not actually lost, and the policy was declared void.

The case of *Grieve* v. *Young*, decided by the court of sessions in Scotland, in 1782, is correspondent in principle. A letter was sent by the owner of a ship to his correspondent in Edinburgh, to make an insurance on her. After the letter was put into the post, but before the post departed, the ship was lost, and was known to be so by the said owner. He did not write to countermand the insurance, as he might have done by the *same post*, in which case the insurance could not have been effected. The court were of opinion, that it was not incumbent on the owner to countermand it by *an express*, but being satisfied that there was time for so doing by the *ordinary course* of the post, which it was his duty to do, gave judgment for the underwriters.

But although the rule is laid down thus generally, that one of the contracting parties is bound to conceal nothing from the other, yet it is by no means so general as not to admit of an exception. There are many matters as to which the insured may be innocently silent.

The insured need not mention what the underwriter ought to know; what he takes upon himself the knowledge of; or what he waives being informed of. The underwriter need not be told what lessens the risk agreed, and understood to be run by the express terms

---

[a] 2 Johns. 157. [b] 7 Cranch, 506. [c] 5 Ibid. 100. [d] 1 Johns. Cas. 1. [e] 6 Cranch, 278.

of the policy. He needs not be told general topics of speculation; as, for instance, the underwriter is bound to know every cause which may occasion natural perils; as the difficulty of the voyage, the kind of season, the probability of lightning, hurricanes, and earthquakes. He is bound to know every cause which may occasion political perils, from the rupture of states, from war, and the various operations of war. He is bound to know the probability of safety, from the continuance and return of peace; from the imbecility of the enemy, through the weakness of their councils or their want of strength. If an underwriter insures private ships of war, by sea and in harbour, from port to port, and from places to places, any where, he need not be told the secret enterprises upon which they are destined; because he knows some expedition must be in view; and, from the nature of his contract, he waives the information, without being told. If he insure for three years, he need not be told any circumstance to show that it might be over in two; or, if he insure a voyage with liberty of deviation, he need not be told what tends to show there will be no deviation.

The insured is not bound to disclose all by-gone calamities: he need only disclose the material facts known to him by the latest intelligence. The insurer is bound to know the nature and general course of the trade and the voyage. If, after having given instruction for insuring, the party receive any intelligence affecting the risk, he must forthwith communicate it to the underwriter.

The policy will not be affected by the master's fraudulently withholding information of the loss, provided the insured act in good faith.

If the insured is bound to disclose fairly all circumstances that may affect the risk, still more strongly is he called upon not to change the condition of his ship against the consent of the underwriter. Thus, in an insurance upon a ship and cargo, from Liverpool to Oporto, the ship sailed, but was driven back by contrary winds: and, before she could sail again, an embargo was laid; the insured applied to the underwriters for leave to put guns on board, and to take out a letter of marque. The underwriters consented to the guns for her defence, but refused the letter of marque. Notwithstanding which, a general letter of marque was obtained, and was put on board; the ship sailed, and was taken on her voyage out. The jury thought that the letter of marque was intended to be used only in the voyage home. The court, however, determined that this vacated the policy.

We now come to the third division, namely, to cases in which policies are void by *misrepresentation*. Before we proceed to state the cases under this head, it will be proper to distinguish between a *warranty* and a *representation*. A warranty or condition is that which makes a part of the written policy, and must be literally and strictly performed; and, being a part of the agreement, nothing *tantamount* will do or answer the purpose. A representation is a statement in the case, not a part of the written instrument, but collateral to it, and entirely independent of it; and it is sufficient that a representation be *substantially* performed. Warranties will be further noticed hereafter. If there be a misrepresentation, it will avoid the policy, as a fraud, but not as a part of the agreement. Even written instructions, if they are not inserted in the policy, are only to be considered as representations;

and, in order to make them valid and binding, as a warranty, it is absolutely necessary to make them a part of the instrument, by which the contract of indemnity is effected. If a representation be false in any material point, it will avoid the policy; and, if the point be not material, the representation can hardly ever be fraudulent. The materiality of the information withheld, is a question of fact for the jury.

If the broker, at the time when the policy is effected, in representing to the underwriters the state of the ship, and the last intelligence concerning her, does not disclose the whole, and what he *conceals* shall appear *material* to the jury, they ought to find for the underwriter, the contract in such case being void, although the concealment should have been *innocent:* the facts not mentioned having appeared *immaterial* to the broker, and having not been communicated merely on that account.

In order to vitiate the contract, the thing concealed must be *material*—it must be *some fact,* and not merely a supposition or speculation of the insured; and the underwriter must take advantage of any misrepresentation the first opportunity, otherwise he will not be allowed to claim any benefit from it at a future period. If, therefore, the insured merely represent that he *expects* a thing to be done, the contract will not be void, although the event should turn out very different from his expectation.

Wherever there has been an allegation of a falsehood, a concealment of circumstances, or a misrepresentation, it is immaterial whether such allegation or concealment be the act of the person himself who is interested, or of his agent; or whether it arise from inattention or negligence; for, in either case, the contract is founded in deception, and the policy is consequently void.

Actual fraud, such as wilfully burning or wrecking the ship, not only avoids the policy, but subjects those concerned therein to criminal punishment. Vide chapter XVII.

If the insured be supposed to be guilty of fraud, the proof of it falls upon the underwriter; direct and positive proof is not necessary; but, circumstantial evidence is all that can be expected, and, indeed, all that is necessary to substantiate such a charge.

It remains to be considered, how far the insurer may retain the premium, or is bound to return it, in cases where the policy is void, on account of the frauds which have been treated of in this division. This question was decided in the case of *Chapman and others* v. *Fraser*, where it was expressly determined, that, in cases of *actual* fraud on the part of the insured, or his agent, the underwriter might retain the premium. Hence, too, it would seem that the underwriter is bound to return the premium, where *fraud* is rather by the construction of the law, than by the actual conduct of the insured.

So, if an underwriter be guilty of concealment, he is liable to return the premium.

The insurers and insured are equally bound to disclose circumstances that are within their knowledge; and, therefore, if the insurer, at the time he underwrites, can be proved to have known that the ship had safely arrived, the contract will be equally void as if the insured had concealed from him some accident which had befallen the ship.

IX. *Sea-worthiness.*

Every ship insured must, at the time of the insurance, be able to perform the voyage, unless some external accident should happen: and, if she have a latent defect, though wholly *unknown* to the parties, it will vacate the contract, and the insurers are discharged. This doctrine is founded upon that general principle of insurance law, that the insurers shall not be responsible for any loss arising from the insufficient or defective quality or condition of the thing insured.

But, although the insured ought to know whether the ship was seaworthy or not, at the time she set out upon her voyage, yet he may not be able to know the condition she may be in after she is out a twelvemonth; and, therefore, whenever it can be made to appear that the decay, to which the loss is attributable, did not commence till a period subsequent to the insurance, as she was seaworthy at the time, the underwriter would be liable. It is sufficient if she be so at the time of her sailing. She may cease to be so in twenty-four hours after departure, and yet the underwriter will continue liable.[a] Every case of this kind, it is true, must depend upon its own circumstances; but, when they are once ascertained, the rule of law is clear and decisive.

A vessel, seaworthy at the time of leaving port, foundered the day after her departure from a leak, without any apparent cause: the court held it to be a loss by the perils of the sea, on a demurrer to the evidence;[b] though it was afterwards decided that those facts formed a legal presumption that the vessel was not seaworthy.[c]

Whether a vessel is seaworthy or not, is a question for the jury.

Masters and owners of vessels should recollect that the policies used in this port and in the southern ports contain a clause, usually called the rotten clause, in the following words, viz., that if the vessel, after a regular survey, shall be condemned for being unsound or rotten, the underwriters shall not be bound to pay the subscription on the policy. The effect of this is, to have the interest of the insured tried in foreign ports, where he may have no proper agent. Captains should be very careful not to permit a condemnation to be made on the above ground, unless it should be evident that the vessel was unseaworthy at the commencement of the voyage.

From carelessness in this respect, the liability of the insurer is often unjustly destroyed. The policies in the eastern ports have not this clause; and other things being equal, the underwriters, who do not insert it, offer better terms than those who retain it in their policies.

Where it becomes necessary to have a condemnation in foreign ports, masters should direct the attention of the surveyors to that subject, if the vessel belongs to any of the southern ports.

If the survey and condemnation do not proceed upon the above ground alone, and unconnected with other circumstances, they are not conclusive.[d]

---

[a] 1 Doug. 708. [b] 1 Johns. 241. [c] 2 Ibid. 124. [d] 8 Ibid. 163.

So if the report does not refer to the rottenness existing at the commencement of the voyage.[a]

It is not only necessary that the ship itself should be sufficient for the voyage, but it is also an implied condition, that she should be furnished with every thing necessary for the purpose of safe and careful navigation. Not only must the ship herself be seaworthy, but she must have a sufficient crew, sufficient equipments, means to sustain the crew, a captain of competent skill, and *a pilot on board,* wherever a pilot is customarily employed.

There must also be a competent mate, who, in case of any accident befalling the master, is capable of taking his place and conducting the voyage. Mere practical seamanship is not all that is wanted in a master or mate. They ought both to have knowledge of mercantile business, judgment and forethought, to meet the many emergencies of the voyage.

X. *Illegal voyages.*

Whenever an insurance is made upon a voyage expressly prohibited by the law of the country where the policy is made, the policy is of no effect, being void from the beginning.

Even if it be told to the underwriter, that the voyage is illicit, he is not bound, because the contract is null and void.

A vessel was insured from Norfolk to Lisbon, and the insured warranted that a British license should be obtained; a loss having happened, the insurers set up for defence the illegality of the voyage. The court decided that it was illegal for an American vessel to sail with a British license, in time of war between the United States and Great Britain, and that the insured could not recover.[b]

If a ship, though neutral, be insured on a voyage prohibited by an embargo, laid *in time of war*, by the prince of the country in whose ports the ship happens to be, such an insurance is also void.

Though a ship may have committed some act in a former voyage, for which she is liable to seizure, yet an insurance on her for a particular voyage is legal; as if it were otherwise, the consequence might be extended *ad infinitum.*

If a ship be insured at and from A. to B., and there be any illegality in her traffic during her stay at A., the insured cannot recover on a policy for a loss happening between A. to B.

In time of war, to bring, even in a neutral ship, goods purchased by an agent in the enemy's country, after the eruption of hostilities, even though they were not purchased of the enemy, is illegal; and the benefit of an insurance, effected for the commission of these acts, is forfeited.

We may conclude with this principle: that all insurances upon a voyage generally prohibited, such as to an enemy's garrison, or upon a voyage directly contrary to an express act of congress, are absolutely null and void.

---

[a] 3 Cranch, 187. [b] 15 Johns. 352.

All goods, the traffic in which is not prohibited by the law of this country, are lawful goods, within the meaning of the policy, although they may be contraband of war,[a] or owned by the subject of a belligerent.[b]

It is not, however, deemed unlawful to insure voyages, where the insured aims to violate the revenue laws of a foreign country; and where the insurer has been informed of the object of the voyage, he is held liable on the policy, although the loss was seizure and condemnation for smuggling.

Where the insurer is ignorant of the illegality of the voyage, he is not liable.

A warranty against illicit trade was introduced into some of the American policies in 1788.

This does not, however, extend to seizures for offences committed against the law of nations, nor to arbitrary seizures, under the pretence of illicit trade. It only applies to illicit trade, actually attempted to be carried on.

XI. *Warranty.*

A warranty, in a policy of insurance, is a condition that a certain thing shall be done, or happen; and, unless that is performed, there is no valid contract. It is perfectly immaterial for what view the warranty is introduced; but being once inserted, it becomes a binding condition on the insured; and unless he can show that he has *literally* fulfilled it, or that it was *literally* performed, the contract is the same as if it had never existed.

But, as a warranty must be *strictly* complied with in favour of the underwriter, and against the insured, equal justice demands, that, if a strict and literal compliance with the warranty will support the demand of the insured, the decision ought to be in his favour; especially when, by such a decision, *all* the words in the policy will have their full operation.

If a ship be warranted to sail on or before the 1st of August, and she be prevented by any accident from sailing till the 2d of August, as, by the sudden want of any necessary repair, or by the appearance of an enemy at the mouth of the port, the captain would do right not to sail; but there would be an end of the policy.

In order to make written instructions valid and binding as a warranty, they must appear on the face of the policy itself: even though a written paper be *wrapt up in the policy*, when it is brought to the underwriter to subscribe, and shown to them at that time: or even though it be *wafered to the policy*, at the time of subscription; still it is not in either case a *warranty*, or to be considered as part of the policy itself, but only as a *representation.*

But, if a policy of insurance *refer* to certain printed proposals, the proposals will be considered as part of the policy.

---

[a] 1 Johns. Cas. 1. [b] 2 Ibid. 77.

Every warranty is part of the contract, and differs from a representation in this, that it is a condition precedent, and must be strictly performed. It is either express, when it must appear on the face of the contract; or implied—as, that the vessel is seaworthy; and whether the thing warranted be material or not. And whether the loss happened by reason of a breach of the warranty, is of no consequence; a breach of warranty avoids the contract.

It has likewise been determined that a warranty, written in the margin of the policy, was to be considered equally binding, and subject to the same strict rule of construction, as if inserted in the body of the policy itself.

The warranties which most frequently occur, and upon which the greatest questions have arisen, may be reduced to three classes: warranty as to the time of sailing, warranty against illicit trade, and warranty as to neutrality.

1st. *As to the time of sailing.*—It has been held, that when a ship has been warranted to sail on a particular day, though the ship be delayed for the best and wisest reasons, or even though she be detained by force, the warranty has not been complied with, and the insurer is discharged from his contract.

If the warranty be to sail *after* a specific day, and the ship sail before, the policy is equally avoided, as in the former case; because the terms of the warranty are as much departed from in one case as in the other.

But, when a ship is warranted to sail on or before a particular day, if she sail from her port of loading, with all her cargo and clearances on board, to the usual place of rendezvous at another part of the same island, merely for the sake of joining convoy, it is a compliance with the warranty, though she be afterwards detained there by an embargo beyond the day. The ground is, that when the ship leaves her port of loading, when she has a full and complete cargo on board, and has no other object in view, but the safest mode of sailing to her port of delivery, her voyage must be said to commence from her departure from that port. If, indeed, her cargo was not complete, it would not have been a commencement of the voyage.

The second species of warranty, which most frequently occurs in insurance, is that against illicit and contraband trade. To constitute a breach of this warranty, it is not sufficient that there has been a condemnation under pretence of such a trade—there must be an illicit or prohibited trade, in fact, existing.[a]

And if the insurer know, at the time of insuring, that there are other goods which are contraband shipped on board of the same vessel, he will not be protected by the warranty.[b]

The underwriter is liable for a loss happening from illicit trade barratrously carried on by the master, notwithstanding the warranty.[c]

A warranty against prohibited trade, protects the insurer from loss, in consequence of the vessel's being denied an entry at her port of destination.[d]

---

[a] 2 Johns. Cas. 481. [b] 1 Caines, 489. [c] 2 Ibid. 222. [d] 1 Johns. 181.

This warranty extends only to partial losses, occasioned by temporary detention, not followed by condemnation.[a]

The third species of warranty is that of *neutrality;* or, that the ship or goods insured are neutral property. If the ship and property be neutral at the time when the risk commences, this is a sufficient compliance with a warranty of neutral property: because it is impossible for the insured to be answerable for the consequence of war breaking out during the voyage.

A warranty of neutrality is not complied with merely by the ship and cargo being neutral. They must have all the insignia of neutrality. The ship must be documented as a neutral; and the ship and cargo must not be accompanied by any documents falsifying the warranty. She must also be conducted throughout the voyage with a strict regard to treaties, and the general rules prescribed for the conduct of neutrals.

If a warranty of property belonging to any neutral power be rendered void by any act of the master of a ship, (except barratry,) after the commencement of the voyage, and the ship be, in consequence, condemned by a belligerent power, the insured cannot recover.

Where a policy contains no warranty of neutrality, the insurers take upon themselves all risks, belligerent as well as neutral.[b]

The sentence of a foreign court of admiralty, is not conclusive as to the breach of the warranty of neutrality in New-York.[c]

A transfer by the insured of the thing insured, after it has been captured to a belligerents' subject, is a breach of the warranty of neutrality.[d]

The character of the property is to be determined by the domicil of the owner.[e]

If the neutral enter after receiving notice of a blockade, there being none in fact, it is not a breach of the warranty of neutrality.[f]

Concealment of papers amount to a breach of neutrality,[g] except when the underwriters know that it is customary to take such papers on board. A warranty of neutrality is broken by an entrance of a blockaded port.[h]

XII. *Deviation.*

Deviation means a *voluntary departure,* without necessity, or any reasonable cause, from the regular and usual course of the specific voyage insured. Whenever a deviation of this kind takes place, the voyage is determined, and the underwriters are discharged from any responsibility. It is necessary to insert, in every policy of insurance, the place of the ship's departure, and also of her destination. Hence it is a condition, on the part of the insured, that the ship shall pursue the most direct course, of which the nature of things will admit, to arrive at the destined port. If this be not done, and if there be no special agreement to allow the ship to go to certain places out of the usual track, or if there be no just cause assigned for such a deviation

---

[a] 2 Johns. Cas. 481. [b] Ibid. 157. [c] Ibid. 451. [d] 2 Caines, 73. [e] 1 Johns. Cas. 363
[f] 2 Caines, 1. [g] 7 Cranch, 506. [h] 4 Ibid. 434.

the underwriter is no longer bound by his contract. Nor is it at all material, whether the loss be or be not in actual consequence of the deviation; for, the insurers are in no case answerable for a subsequent loss, in whatever place it happens, or to whatever cause it may be attributed. Neither does it make any difference, whether the insured was or was not consenting to the deviation.

The shortness of the time, or the distance of the deviation, makes no difference as to its effect upon the contract.

A vessel having liberty to touch at Leith, on her voyage down the Frith of Forth touched at another port equally in her way, and it was held a deviation.

If the master of a vessel put into a port not usual, or stay an unusual time, it is a deviation, and discharges the insurer.

It has been held, that, even where there is a permission given *to touch and stay* at a place, it confers no privilege on the insured to break bulk, or to unload any part of the cargo.

Unless there be some usage proved, or some special facts, to vary the general rule, the party insured must go to the several places mentioned in the policy, *in the order in which they are named;* and that, to depart from that course is a deviation. If they are not specifically named, then the insured must touch at them in their geographical order.

So, where a ship was insured, "at and from Lisbon to a port in England, with the liberty to call at any one port in Portugal for any purpose whatever," Lord Kenyon was of opinion that the liberty given must be restrained to mean some port lying in the fair course of the voyage.

These principles being once established, it follows as a necessary consequence, that, however short the time of deviation may be, if only for a single night, or even for an hour, the underwriter is equally discharged as if there had been a deviation for weeks or months; for, the condition being once broken, no subsequent act can ever make it good.

If a merchant ship carry letters of marque, she may *chase* an enemy, though she may not *cruise*, without being deemed guilty of a deviation.

A voluntary deviation from the voyage insured, vitiates a policy upon *freight*, as well as upon ship and goods.

A vessel, which is permitted by her policy to chase, capture, and man prizes, is not warranted in *shortening sail* and *lying to*, in order to let the prize keep up with her for the purpose of being protected or convoyed into port, although such port be within the limits of the voyage insured.

But, whenever the deviation arises from *necessity* and a *just cause*, the underwriter still remains liable, although the course of the voyage is altered.

The first ground of necessity, which justifies a deviation, is that of *going into port to repair*. If a ship be decayed, or receives material and imminent danger in her voyage, which cannot be repaired at sea, and goes to the *nearest place* to refit, it is no deviation, because it is for the general interest of all concerned, that the ship should be put in a proper condition to perform the voyage.

The next excuse for leaving the direct course is *stress of weather.* Upon this point the rule is this: that, whenever a ship, in order to escape a storm, goes out of the direct course, or when, in the due course of the voyage, she is driven out of it by stress of weather, it is no deviation. It has also been held, that, if a storm drive a ship out of the course of her voyage, and she do the best she can to get to her port of destination, she is not obliged to return to the point from which she was driven.

If a ship be driven out of her port of loading by stress of weather into another, and then does the best she can to get to her port of destination, it is not deemed a deviation, though she do not return to the port whence she was driven.

A deviation may also be justified, if done to avoid an enemy, or to seek for convoy; because it is in truth no deviation to go out of the course of a voyage, in order to avoid danger, or to obtain protection against it.

If a vessel, on being pursued by a cruiser or pirate, put into a port to avoid capture, it is not a deviation.[a]

So, to avoid a probable danger of capture, when obliged to wait for wind.[b]

Stopping or going out of the way to relieve a vessel in distress in order to save life, was held by Judge Washington not to be a deviation; and Chief Justice Marshall, in Mason v. ship Blairean, observed, that the court had great doubts whether stopping to relieve a vessel in distress could be considered a deviation.[c]

If, by the usage of any particular trade, it is customary to stop at certain places lying out of the direct course from A. to B., it is not a deviation to stop there, because it is a part of the voyage; but, in order to justify the captain of a ship in quitting the straight and direct line from the port of loading to that of delivery, there must be a precise, clear, and established usage upon the subject, not depending merely upon one or two loose and vague instances.

So, also, if a ship be insured upon a trading voyage, it is incumbent on the parties insured to carry on that trade with the usual and reasonable expedition: otherwise their conduct will amount to a deviation, and discharge the policy.

But though an actual deviation from the voyage insured is fatal to the contract of insurance; yet a deviation merely *intended*, but never carried into effect, is considered as no deviation; and the insurer continues liable for a loss happening before the vessel arrives at the dividing point.[c]

If a vessel be captured and taken out of her course by reason of her having contradictory papers on board, it is a deviation.[d]

If a vessel remain in a port of necessity longer than is necessary to complete the repairs, or avoid the danger, it is a deviation.[e]

---

[a] 10 Johns. 179. [b] 2 Ibid. 138. [c] 2 Cranch, 257.
[d] 1 Johns. Cas. 341. [e] 7 Cranch, 487.

An alteration of the voyage must be after the commencement of the risk to constitute a deviation.[a]

If, however, it can be made to appear, by evidence, that it never was intended or came within the contemplation of the parties to sail upon the voyage insured; if all the ship's papers and documents be made out for a different place from that described in the policy, the insurer is discharged from all degree of responsibility, even though the loss should happen before the dividing point of the two voyages, and the premium is to be returned. This, however, is not a deviation.

If a ship be insured from a day certain, from A. to B., and before the day she sail on a different voyage from that insured, the insured cannot recover; even though the ship afterwards fall into the course of the voyage insured, and be lost after the day on which the policy was to have attached.

In cases of deviation, the premium is not to be returned; because, the risk having commenced, the underwriter is entitled to retain it.

XIII. *Changing the ship.*

Changing the ship, or, as it is commonly called, changing the bottom, will operate as a bar to the insured's recovering upon a policy of insurance against the underwriter. Except in some special cases of insurance upon *ship or ships*, it is essential, to render a policy of insurance effectual, that the name of the ship on which the risk is to be run should be inserted. This being done, it follows that, the insured shall neither substitute another ship for that mentioned in the policy, before the voyage commences, nor, during the course of the voyage, remove the property insured to another ship, without the consent of the underwriter, or without being compelled by a case of *unavoidable necessity.*

And this doctrine, relative to the changing the bottom of the ship, was alluded to by Lord Mansfield, when delivering the opinion of the court in the case of Pelly against the Royal Exchange Assurance Company. "One objection," said his lordship, "was formed, by comparing the case to that of changing the ship's bottom, on board of which goods are insured; *which the insured have no right to do.*"

This is to be taken as a rule, subject to the exceptions of inevitable or urgent necessity: for it has been held, that the owners of goods insured, by the act of shifting the goods from one ship to another, do not preclude themselves from recovering an average loss, arising from the capture of the second ship, if they act from necessity, and for the benefit of all concerned.

XIV. *Reinsurance and double insurance.*

Reinsurance may be defined to be a contract, which the first insurer enters into, in order to relieve himself from those risks which he has incautiously undertaken, by throwing them upon other underwriters, who are called reinsurers.

---

[a] 11 Johns. 241.

The reinsurer is wholly unconnected with the original owner of the property insured; and as there was no obligation between them originally, so none is raised by the subsequent act of the first underwriter. The risk of the insurer forms the object of the reinsurance, which is a new independent contract, not at all concerning the insured; who consequently can assume no power or authority with respect to it.

The insurer is not bound to abandon or give notice to the reinsurer when the first insured abandons to him; but the reinsurer may avail himself of any defence which the first insurer might have urged against the insured.[a]

A *double insurance* is where the *same* man is to receive *two* sums instead of one, or the same sum twice over, for the same loss, by reason of his having made two insurances upon the *same* goods or the *same* ship. The distinction between these two contracts is, that a reinsurance is a contract made by the first underwriter, his executor, or assigns, to secure himself or his estate; a double insurance is entered into by the insured. Where a man has made a double insurance, he may recover his loss against which of the underwriters he pleases, but he can recover no more than the amount of his loss. It being thus settled, that the insured shall recover but one satisfaction, and that, in case of double insurance, he may fix upon which of the underwriters he will for the payment of his loss; it is a principle of natural justice, that the several insurers should all of them contribute in their several proportions, to satisfy that loss, against which they have all insured.

Where the vessel was valued on one policy at $2000, and there was a prior insurance for $3000, the insured was allowed to prove the vessel to be worth enough to cover both policies.[b]

In the year 1763, it was ruled by Lord Mansfield, and agreed to by the course of practice, that upon a double insurance, though the insured is not entitled to two satisfactions, yet, upon the first action, he may recover the whole sum insured, and may leave the defendant therein to recover a ratable satisfaction from the other insurers.

Although a man, by making a double insurance, should not be allowed to recover a double satisfaction for the same loss, yet various persons may insure various interests on the same thing, and each to the whole value, (as the master for wages, the owner for freight, one person for goods, another person for bottomry,) and such a contract does not fall within the idea of a double insurance.

Policies sometimes have a clause inserted to avoid the rule of contributions, and to make the insurers responsible according to the date of their policies.

XV. *Return of premium.*

The next object of inquiry is, in what cases, and under what circumstances, there shall be *a return of premium.*

---

[a] 3 Caines, 190. [b] 1 Johns. 385.

The principle, upon which the whole of this doctrine depends, is simple and plain. The risk of peril is the consideration for which the premium is to be paid. If the risk be not run, the consideration for the premium fails; and equity implies a condition, that the insurer shall not receive the price for running a risk, if, in fact, he runs none.

So, if the insurance be made for a greater amount of property than the insured has on board, there is to be a ratable return of premium.

If the risk has not been run, no matter from what cause, the premium is to be returned.

Whether the cause of the risk not being run is attributable to the *fault, will, or pleasure,* of the insured, still the premium is to be returned.

If the policy should become void by a failure of the warranty, there being no fraud, the insured is entitled to a return of the premium.[a]

If the property be insured to a larger amount than the real value, the overplus premium is recoverable by the insured.[b]

After the risk has attached, though but for a moment, there can be no return of premium.[c]

Where the insured supposed at the time of insuring that he has an interest in the subject matter, in which he is mistaken, he is entitled to a return of the premium; though if he had been interested, the risk would have attached.[d]

There is often, in policies, an agreement inserted, that if the voyage shall have been begun and terminated at the time of insuring, there shall be no return of the premium.

The famous ordinances of Louis XIV., declare that, if the voyage be entirely broken up before the departure of the ship, *even by the act of the insured,* the insurance shall be void, and the underwriter shall return the premium, reserving one half *per cent.* for his trouble. Accordingly, it has always been the custom, when the policy is cancelled, to return the premium, deducting one half *per cent.*

This deduction of one half per cent. is always made when the premium is returned.

In the common law there are two general rules established, which govern almost all cases. The first is, that where the risk has not been run, whether that circumstance was owing to the fault, the pleasure, or will of the insured, or to any other cause, the premium shall be returned. Another rule is, that if the risk has *once* commenced, there shall be *no* apportionment or return of premium afterwards. Hence, in cases of deviation, though the underwriter is discharged from his engagement, yet, the risk being once commenced, he is entitled to retain the premium.

When, however, from the nature of the agreement between the parties, or the nature of the voyage, the contract becomes divisable, "a part of the premium shall be retained for the risk run, and part shall be returned, as the risk has never commenced."

In an insurance for twelve months, at £9 *per cent.*, the ship was captured within two months after the contract was made, and a return of premium was demanded. But the contract in this case was entire;

---

[a] 3 Johns. 307. [b] 2 Johns. Cas. 329. [c] 8 Johns. 1. [d] 3 Johns. Cas. 269.

the premium was a gross sum stipulated, and paid for twelve months; and the parties, when they made the contract, had no intention nor thought of a subsequent division or apportionment, and therefore there could be no return of premium.

When the contract is entire, whether it be for a *specified time or for a voyage*, there shall be no apportionment or return, if the risk has *once commenced.* And, therefore, when the premium is entire in a policy, on a voyage where there is no contingency at any period, out or home, upon the happening or not happening of which the risk is to end, nor any usage established upon such voyages, although there be several distinct ports at which the ship is to stop, yet the voyage is one, and no part of the premium shall be recoverable.

Where there is any fraud on the part of the insured, or of his agent, the premium is not returned.

So, if the voyage be illegal, there is no return of premium.

CHAPTER XV.

OF FACTORS AND AGENTS.

FACTOR, broker, and agent, are terms nearly synonymous; yet custom has created distinctions in applying these different names to particular descriptions of agency. Hence, *factor* appears to be exclusively applied to agents employed in the purchase or sale of goods. *Brokers* are generally factors, and employed, also, in the shipping and money transactions of merchants and masters of ships. *Agents* have other distinctions, as those to the army and navy, who receive and advance pay or proceeds, on account of officers and others. The latter term, however, as it implies a person duly authorized to act for another, comprehends all the rest, and may therefore be indiscriminately applied to the whole.

Commercial agents are persons frequently appointed to settle accounts, and dispose of the effects of merchants and other persons dying or failing, in foreign countries, or at home. Their commission terminates with the particular business for which they were engaged, and they generally give security for the trust reposed in them.

Supercargoes are persons employed by commercial companies, or private merchants, to take charge of the cargoes they export to foreign countries, to sell them there to the best advantage, and to purchase returning cargoes of the most advantageous kind. The supercargoes generally go out and return with the ships, on board of which they were embarked, and therein differ from factors, who reside abroad at the settlements of the companies for which they act.

Ships' husbands.—The chief employment of this class of agents is in the principal sea-ports, where they purchase the ship's stores for her voyage; procure cargoes on freight; settle the terms, and obtain policies of insurance; receive the amount of freight; pay the captain, or master, his salary and disbursements, and, finally, make out an account of all these transactions for their employers, the owners of ships, to whom they may be considered as stewards on land, as the officer bearing that name is on board the ship, when at sea. The ship's husband is often part owner himself.

A factor is one who acts for another, and who buys, sells, or negotiates, conformably with the orders of his employer, under various circumstances of limitation.

The factor generally receives, from the merchant or person by whom he is employed, a commission of factorage, according to the usage of the place where he resides, and the business he transacts. It is requisite that he keep strictly to the tenor of his orders, as a division from them, even in the most minute particular, exposes him to make ample satisfaction for any loss that may accrue from his non-observance.

The usual compensation to a factor is made by a commission of so much per cent. on the goods sold; but sometimes he acts under a *del credere* commission; or, for an additional premium beyond the usual commission, he undertakes for the credit of the persons to whom he sells the goods to him consigned. In the latter case, the undertaking, though verbal, is not affected by the statute against frauds, which, in general, invalidates any verbal undertaking to be responsible for the debt of a third person; and the factor is usually sued as if he himself was the purchaser.

Del credere is an Italian mercantile phrase, which has the same signification as the English word *guaranty*, and the Scotch word *warrandice*.

A factor, authorized to sell goods in his own name, generally debits the buyer to himself; though, if money be not paid, he is not liable to his principal for it; (unless under a commission del credere;) yet he has a right to receive it, and his receipt is the proper discharge. The factor may bring his action, and the buyer cannot at law set off a former sum due to him from his principal.

An agent who is intrusted with general powers, must exercise a sound discretion. If his powers be special and limited, he must strictly conform to them. If a special agent exceed his powers, his principal is not bound; but a general agent binds his principal so long as he keeps within the general scope of his authority, although he exceeds his private instructions.[a]

A factor selling goods as his own, by endorsement of the bill of lading, though no delivery is made, the goods being at sea—the buyer shall keep possession, unless collusion appears between them.

A factor, empowered by general orders to dispose of goods to the best advantage, is bound to exercise that degree of diligence which a prudent man exercises in his own affairs. If it appear that he has done so, and sold the goods to persons in reputed good circumstances, and to whom he would have given credit on his sole account, he will not be liable, although some of these should fail. A factor is liable only for fraud or gross neglect; and while acting with good faith he is only bound to exercise ordinary diligence and attention.[b] But by neglecting to comply with the directions of his principal, he renders himself liable.[c]

Though if he be sued by his principal for a breach of trust, or orders, whereby he has put himself in the place of the vendee, he may use any defence of which the vendee could have availed himself, had the suit been brought against him.[c]

A consignee to whom the disposal of goods on particular terms is intrusted, may, bona fide, dispose of them in another manner, provided a compliance with these terms should be found impracticable.[d]

He may sell goods sent to him as a commission merchant, and take a note according to the custom of the market; and if the vendee, before the time of payment of the note, should become insolvent, the factor will not be liable.

---

[a] Sumner's Rep. C. C. U. S. 537.—15 Johns. R. 44. [b] 1 Johns. Cas. 175. [c] Ibid. 437. [d] 2 Caines, 310. [e] 3 Johns. R. 319.

A generally empowered factor is paid by a commission of so much per cent. upon the goods sold, and is sure of his commission, whether the event be favourable or otherwise. Hence, to preclude risk to the merchant, the agreement called *del credere* was invented, by which the factor, for an additional premium beyond the usual commission, when he sells the goods on credit, becomes bound to warrant the solvency to the purchaser. A commission *del credere* is an absolute engagement to the principal from the broker, (or factor,) and makes him liable in the first insurance. Thus, when a factor, under a commission *del credere*, sold goods, and took accepted bills from the purchasers, which he endorsed to a banker at the place of sale, and, having received the banker's bill, (payable to the factor's own order,) on a house in London, endorsed and transmitted it to his employer, who got it accepted: it was holden that, on the failure of the acceptor and drawer of this bill, the factor was answerable for the amount.

A sale by a factor creates a contract between the owner and buyer, although unknown to each other; and this rule holds even in cases where the factor acts upon a *del credere* commission. Hence, if a factor sell goods, and the owner gave notice to the buyer to pay the price to him and not to the factor, the buyer will not be justified in afterwards paying the factor, and the owner will be entitled to recover the price in an action against the buyer, unless the factor has a lien on such price.

If goods be bought by a person as a broker, though without disclosing the name of the purchaser till he has become insolvent, the purchaser, thus knowing that the party acted as an agent, cannot set off the price of the goods against a debt due to him from the broker, but is still liable to the vendor. But, when a factor, acting under a *del credere* commission, sells goods as his own, and the buyer does not know of any principal, the buyer may, in an action brought against him by the principal, set off a debt due to him from the factor.

The agent is personally responsible only where the principal is not known, or when he exceeds his power, or when he contracts, to be personally liable. The party dealing with the agent, too, is bound to the principal, and not to the agent. If the agent buy in his own name, and the goods come to the use of the principal, the latter is liable.[a]

The circumstance of persons selling goods being described in the catalogue of sale as sworn brokers, is not sufficient notice to the purchaser that they are only agents in that transaction, to prevent him from dealing with them as principals; and, when goods are sold by a broker without disclosing his principal, the purchaser is justified in paying him in the same or in a different manner from that stipulated for by the terms of the contract; though it would be otherwise when the principal is disclosed at the time of sale. When, however, a factor sells goods as a principal, and before they are all delivered, or any part of them paid for, the purchaser is informed that they belong to a third person: in an action by the latter for the price of them, the purchaser cannot set off a debt due to him from the factor.

---

[a] 2 Kent, 631.

If a broker be authorized by one man to sell goods, and to buy such goods for another, an entry in his books of sale of these goods, from the one to the other, signed by him, is in general a binding contract between the parties. The bought and sold note, which is a copy of this entry, is not sent to the parties for their approbation, but to inform them of the terms of the contract. The authority, however, of the broker, may be countermanded at any time before a memorandum of the contract of sale is written and signed by him, pursuant to the statute against frauds, although he has previously entered into a verbal agreement to sell the goods.

Should unlimited orders be given to a factor, he is left to buy or sell on the best conditions he can.

The factor, being merely a trustee for his principal, if the latter, having goods in the other's hands, owe him money by simple contract, and then dies indebted by specialty more than his assets are worth, the factor cannot retain the goods.

So, if he sell the goods, and take a negotiable note payable to himself, it is held in trust for his principal, and subject to his order; and if it be endorsed by the factor, and the maker fail to pay it, the factor is not liable on the note to the principal.[a] A payment to the factor, after notice from the principal, would not discharge the party from the note or debt.

If a factor receive a commission merely to sell and dispose of goods, this did not formerly enable him to trust; yet it is now held that he may sell on credit, unless the usage of the trade be to the contrary.

A factor, as such, has not any authority at common law to *pledge*, but only to sell, the goods of his principal. Hence, if the factor pledge the goods, the owner may recover the value of them in an action of trover against him with whom they are pawned. If the factor pledge the goods as his own, the pawnee cannot claim to retain them against the principal for the amount of the factor's general lien at the time of the pledge; but the factor may deliver them as security, with notice of his lien to a third person to keep possession as his agent, in order to preserve that lien.[b]

The same rule holds with respect to a bill of lading which has been endorsed to a factor by his principal; for the bill of lading, which is the *symbol of the delivery of possession*, cannot give the factor a greater authority than the actual possession of the goods themselves. Hence, as a factor cannot pledge the goods, so neither can he pledge the bill of lading; for though the endorsement of a bill of lading gives the endorsee, or person to whom endorsed, an *irrevocable right to receive* the goods, yet it will not have that operation where it is intended as an assignment of the property in the goods, or where it is intended as a deposite only, by a person not authorized to make such deposite.

There is an exception to this rule in the case of negotiable paper, which may be pledged by the factor for his own debt, so as to bind the principal, where there is no notice to the bailee of the fraud.[c]

---

[a] 7 Mass. R. 36. [b] 4 Johns. 103. [c] 1 Bos. and Pull. 648.

This rule of the common law was so often productive of hardship to persons making advances on goods, that in 1825, an act was passed by the British parliament, declaring that the person in whose name the goods were shipped should be deemed the owner, so as to entitle the consignee to a lien for all moneys due to him from the consignor, unless he knew that the consignor was not the real owner. Every factor, too, who is intrusted with the possession of goods for sale, or as security for advances, or with the bill of lading, or custom-house permit, or warehouse keeper's receipt, is to be deemed the owner, so far as to render valid any contract for the sale or disposition thereof, for moneys advanced, or responsibility assumed, upon the faith thereof.

The real owner may have his goods, however, upon repayment of the moneys advanced, and on satisfying the lien of the factor.

In 1830, the legislature of New-York, and in 1831, that of Rhode Island, adopted the same law.[a]

The maxim that the principal is civilly responsible for the acts of his agent, prevails universally in courts of law and equity; and, upon this principle it was held, by Chief Justice Holt, that a merchant was answerable for the deceit of his factor, who had sold some silk to the plaintiff as silk of a superior, knowing it to be of an inferior, quality.

If the principal direct his factor to load a vessel with certain goods, and he should load her with goods of a different description, the former is not bound to accept them, nor is he liable for any of the charges upon them.[b]

The several merchants who employ the same factor must run the joint risk of his actions, although they are strangers to each other; thus, if five merchants remit to him five distinct bales of goods, and the factor makes a joint sale of them to one man, who is to pay one moiety down, and the other at six months' end: if the buyer fail before the second payment, each merchant must bear a proportional share of the loss, and be content to accept of his dividend of the money advanced.

But if the factor draw a bill of exchange upon all those five merchants, and one of them accepts the same, the others shall not be obliged to make good the payment.

The authority and trust reposed in factors being very great, they ought to be very prudent in their actions for the benefit of their principals. If a factor gave time to a man for payment of moneys contracted on sales of his employer's goods, and after the time is elapsed, sell goods of his own to the same persons for ready cash, leaving the other unpaid, and such man become insolvent, the factor ought to make good the loss, although he cannot be compelled by the law.

If goods be remitted to a factor, and he make a false entry of them at the custom-house, or land them without entry, whereby they incur seizure or forfeiture, he must make good the damage to his principal; but, if he make his entry according to invoice, or his letters of advice, and these prove erroneous, the goods are lost, and he is discharged.

---

[a] 2 Kent. 629. [b] 4 Johns. 103.

The same probity exacted from the factor is, by the law, exacted from his employer, judging that the act of the one is that of the other; therefore, if a merchant consign counterfeit jewels to his factor, who sells or disposes of them as if genuine, and incurs a loss or damage thereby, the merchant shall not only make it good, but render such other satisfaction as may be adjudged. It is established that a principal shall answer for his factor in all cases; and, in contracts, if a factor buy goods on account of his principal, especially if accustomed to do so, the contract of the factor will compel the principal to a performance of the bargain.

The proceeds of goods sold by a factor must be carefully disposed of. If applied without the limits of his commission, or order, he becomes responsible. Conforming to this, if he be robbed, the theft discharges him; and if he buy goods which afterwards suffer injury, the loss becomes that of the merchant. If the factor take money that is false, he must make good the loss; but, if the money which he receives be afterwards lessened in value by edict or proclamation, the loss is that of the merchant.

The caution of the factor is particularly required to letters of credit; as to whether for a time limited, or to what value, &c.

It is now held, that, if a merchant remit goods to his factor, and shortly after draw a bill on him, which is accepted, and he then break, the factor has a general lien upon all goods in his hands for the value of his acceptance, and whatever may be due to him.

Bills remitted to a factor are, while unpaid, considered as goods unsold; and if the factor become bankrupt, must be returned to the principal, subject to the lien of the factor. A factor has a lien on consigned goods for incidental charges, and also as an item of general account for balance due to him, so long as he keeps possession of them; if he part with them, he parts with his lien.

A general lien is for a general balance of accounts, and is construed strictly; but a particular lien, which is for special advances, or expenditures on account of the goods in question, is construed favourably. Possession, and that rightfully obtained, is necessary to create a lien.[a] A lien is destroyed by an express stipulation to pay over the proceeds.[b]

If a factor, who enters into a charter-party with a master for freightment, personally covenant for the performance of it, he is obliged by the contract; but, if he load abroad generally, the goods, the principals, and the lading, are made liable, and not the factor.

If a factor, possessing money belonging to his principal, receive orders from him to make insurance on ships and goods so soon as he has loaded, and he neglect to do so, he shall make good the damage that may accrue from such neglect. In case of loss, he ought not to make a composition without orders from his principal.

Joint factors are answerable for each other, and one may account without his companion.

A factor should be extremely punctual in the advices of his transactions, in sales, purchases, affreightments, and especially in drafts by

---

[a] 2 Term. R. 585. [b] 6 Ibid. 258.

exchange. If he sell on trust, without giving advice thereof, and the buyer break, he is liable for his neglect; and, if he draw without advising that he has so done, he may expect to have his bill returned protested. If he deviate from the orders he receives for purchasing goods, in any respect; or if, after they are bought, he send them to a different place from that directed to, they must remain for his own account, unless the merchant, on advice, admits them. If he sell a commodity under the price ordered, he may be compelled to make good the difference; and, if on purchasing goods for another, at a price limited, the price rise, and he take them for his own account, and send them to another part, he will be obliged to satisfy his principal for damages.

Again, if a factor, in conformity with a merchant's orders, buy with his money or credit that which he shall be directed to purchase, and, without giving advice, sell it again to profit, appropriating the advantage to himself, the merchant may recover it from him, and amerce him for the fraud.

If a merchant order his factor to ship him a sum of money, in the current coin of a kingdom, when its exportation is prohibited, and the money be seized, the loss is the merchant's, and not the factor's.

If a factor pay the money of a merchant, without his orders, it is at his own risk; so, also, if he lend his cash without leave, although he proposes that the interest shall be for the merchant.

If, at the expiration of the credit on which goods are sold, the factor take a note payable to himself at a future day, he makes the debt his own.[a]

The authority of an agent is terminated, first, by the death of the agent or of the principal, or either, if there be two; by the express revocation of his powers; by a change in the condition of the principal, such as his bankruptcy, his lunacy, or by marriage, if the principal be a female; and by the execution of the business which he was constituted to perform.

---

[a] 1 Martin's Louis. R. 368.

CHAPTER XVI.

NAVY.

National ships are not required to conform, like merchant vessels, to the ordinary revenue regulations of the countries which they visit. Bearing the national flag, and representing, as it were, the country to which they belong, it is presumed that nothing will be done to contravene municipal laws. Their commanders must, however, make known the character of their vessels, and they must conform to the quarantine and port regulations, and to the law of nations.

The discipline on board is of course conformable to martial law, and to the following rules and regulations prescribed by congress for the government of the navy of the United States.

Art. 1. The commanders of all ships and vessels of war, belonging to the navy, are strictly enjoined and required to show, in themselves, a good example of virtue, honour, patriotism, and subordination; and be vigilant in inspecting the conduct of all such as are placed under their command; and to guard against, and suppress, all dissolute and immoral practices, and to correct all such as are guilty of them, according to the usage of the sea service.

2. The commanders of all ships and vessels in the navy, having chaplains on board, shall take care that divine service be performed in a solemn, orderly, and reverent manner, twice a day, and a sermon preached on Sunday, unless bad weather, or other extraordinary accidents prevent it; and that they cause all, or as many, of the ship's company as can be spared from duty, to attend at every performance of the worship of Almighty God.

3. Any officer, or other person, in the navy, who shall be guilty of oppression, cruelty, fraud, profane swearing, drunkenness, or any other scandalous conduct, tending to the destruction of good morals, shall, if an officer, be cashiered, or suffer such other punishment as a court martial shall adjudge: if a private, shall be put in irons, or flogged, at the discretion of the captain, not exceeding twelve lashes; but if the offence require severer punishment, he shall be tried by a court martial, and suffer such punishment as said court shall indict.

4. Every commander, or other officer, who shall, upon signal for battle, or on the probability of an engagement, neglect to clear his ship for action, or shall not use his utmost exertions to bring his ship to battle, or shall fail to encourage, in his own person, his inferior officers and men to fight courageously, such offender shall suffer death, or such other punishment as a court martial shall adjudge; or any offi-

---

[a] Act, 23d April, 1800.

cer neglecting, on sight of any vessel or vessels of an enemy, to clear his ship for action, shall suffer such punishment as a court martial shall adjudge; and if any person in the navy shall treacherously yield, or pusillanimously cry for quarters, he shall suffer death, on conviction thereof by a general court martial.

5. Every officer or private, who shall not properly observe the orders of his commanding officer, or shall not use his utmost exertions to carry them into execution, when ordered to prepare for, join in, or when actually engaged in battle: or shall, at such time, basely desert his duty or station, either then or while in sight of an enemy, or shall induce others to do so—every person so offending shall, on conviction thereof, by a general court martial, suffer death, or such other punishment as the said court shall adjudge.

6. Every officer or private who shall, through cowardice, negligence, or disaffection, in time of action, withdraw from, or keep out of battle, or shall not do his utmost to take or destroy every vessel which it is his duty to encounter, or shall not do his utmost endeavour to afford relief to ships belonging to the United States: every such offender shall, on conviction thereof by a general court martial, suffer death, or such other punishment as the said court shall adjudge.

7. The commanding officer of every ship or vessel in the navy, who shall capture, or seize upon, any vessel as a prize, shall carefully preserve all the papers and writings found on board, and transmit the whole of the originals, unmutilated, to the judge of the district to which such prize is ordered to proceed; and shall transmit to the navy department, and to the agent appointed to pay the prize money, complete lists of the officers and men entitled to a share of the capture: inserting therein the quality of every person rating, on pain of forfeiting his whole share of the prize money resulting from such capture, and suffering such further punishment as a court martial shall adjudge.

8. No person in the navy shall take out of a prize, or vessel seized as a prize, any money, plate, goods, or any part of her rigging, unless it be for the better preservation thereof, or absolutely necessary for the use of any of the vessels of the United States, before the same shall be adjudged lawful prizes by a competent court; but the whole, without fraud, concealment, or embezzlement, shall be brought in, and judgment passed thereon, upon pain that every person offending herein shall forfeit his share of the capture, and suffer such further punishment as a court martial, or the court of admiralty in which the prize is adjudged, shall impose.

9. No person in the navy shall strip off their clothes, or pillage, or in any manner maltreat, persons taken on board a prize, on pain of such punishment as a court martial shall adjudge.

10. No person in the navy shall give, hold, or entertain, any intercourse or intelligence to or with any enemy or rebel, without leave from the president of the United States, the secretary of the navy, the commander in chief of the fleet, or the commander of the squadron, or, in case of a vesssel acting singly, from his commanding officer, on pain of death, or such other punishment as a court martial shall adjudge.

11. If any letter or message, from an enemy or rebel, be conveyed to any officer or private of the navy, and he shall not, within twelve hours, make the same known, having opportunity so to do, to his superior or commanding officer; or if any officer commanding a ship or vessel, being acquainted therewith, shall not, with all convenient speed, reveal the same to the commander in chief of the fleet, commander of a squadron, or other proper officer whose duty it may be to take cognizance thereof: every such offender shall suffer death, or such other punishment as a court martial shall adjudge.

12. Spies, and all persons who shall come or be found in the capacity of spies, or who shall bring or deliver any seducing letter or message from an enemy or rebel, or endeavour to corrupt any person in the navy to betray his trust, shall suffer death, or such other punishment as a court martial shall adjudge.

13. If any person in the navy shall make, or attempt to make, any mutinous assembly, he shall, on conviction thereof by a court martial, suffer death; and if any person as aforesaid shall utter any seditious or mutinous words, or shall conceal or connive at any mutinous or seditious practices, or shall treat with contempt his superior, being in the execution of his office; or, being witness to any mutiny or sedition, shall not do his utmost to suppress it, he shall be punished at the discretion of a court martial.

14. No officer or private in the navy shall disobey the lawful orders of his superior officer, or strike him, or draw, or offer to draw, or raise any weapon against him while in the execution of the duties of his office, on pain of death, or such other punishment as a court martial shall inflict.

15. No person in the navy shall quarrel with any other person in the navy, nor use provoking or reproachful words, gestures, or menaces, on pain of such punishment as a court martial shall adjudge.

16. If any person in the navy shall desert to an enemy, or rebel, he shall suffer death.

17. If any person in the navy shall desert, or shall entice others to desert, he shall suffer death, or such other punishment as a court martial shall adjudge; and if any officer, or other person belonging to the navy, shall receive or entertain any deserter from any other vessel of the navy, knowing him to be such, and shall not, with all convenient speed, give notice of such deserter to the commander of the vessel to which he belongs, or to the commander in chief, or to the commander of the squadron, he shall, on conviction thereof, be cashiered, or be punished at the discretion of a court martial. All offences committed by persons belonging to the navy, while on shore, shall be punished in the same manner as if they had been committed at sea.

18. If any person in the navy shall knowingly make or sign, or shall aid, abet, direct, or procure the making or signing, of any false muster, or shall execute, or attempt, or countenance any fraud against the United States, he shall, on conviction, be cashiered, and rendered for ever incapable of any future employment in the service of the United States, and shall forfeit all the pay and subsistence due him, and suffer such other punishment as a court martial shall inflict.

19. If any officer or other person in the navy, through inattention, negligence, or any other fault, suffer any vessel of the navy to be stranded, or run upon rocks or shoals, or hazarded, he shall suffer such punishment as a court martial shall adjudge.

20. If any person in the navy sleep upon his watch, or negligently perform the duty assigned him, or leave his station before regularly relieved, he shall suffer death, or such punishment as a court martial shall adjudge; or, if the offender be a private, he may, at the discretion of the captain, be put in irons, or flogged, not exceeding twelve lashes.

21. The crime of murder, when committed by any officer, seaman, or marine, belonging to any public ship or vessel of the United States, without the territorial jurisdiction of the same, may be punished with death, by the sentence of a court martial.

22. The officers and privates of every ship or vessel, appointed as convoy to merchant or other vessels, shall diligently and faithfully discharge the duties of their appointment; nor shall they demand or exact any compensation for their services, nor maltreat any of the officers or crews of such merchant or other vessels, on pain of making such reparation as a court of admiralty may award, and of suffering such further punishment as a court martial may adjudge.

23. If any commander, or other officer, receive, or permit to be received on board his vessel, any goods or merchandise other than for the sole use of his vessel, except gold, silver, or jewels, and except the goods or merchandise of vessels which may be in distress, or shipwrecked, or in imminent danger of being shipwrecked, in order to preserve them for their owner, without orders from the president of the United States or the navy department, he shall, on conviction thereof, be cashiered, and be incapacitated, for ever afterwards, for any place or office in the navy.

24. If any person in the navy waste, embezzle, or fraudulently buy, sell, or receive any ammunitions, provisions, or other public stores; or if any officer or other person knowingly permit. through design, negligence, or inattention, any such waste, embezzlement sale, or receipt, every such person shall forfeit all the pay and subsistence then due him, and suffer such further punishment as a court martial shall direct.

25. If any person in the navy unlawfully set fire to, or burn any kind of public property, not then in the possession of an enemy, pirate, or rebel, he shall suffer death. And if any person in any other manner destroy such property, or shall not use his best exertions to prevent the destruction thereof by others, he shall be punished at the discretion of a court martial.

26. Any theft, not exceeding twenty dollars, may be punished at the discretion of the captain, and above that sum, as a court martial shall direct.

27. If any person in the navy, when on shore, plunder, abuse, or maltreat any inhabitant, or injure his property in any way, he shall suffer such punishment as a court martial shall adjudge.

28. Every person in the navy shall use his utmost exertions to detect, apprehend, and bring to punishment, all offenders, and shall, at all times, aid and assist all persons appointed for this purpose, on pain of such punishment as a court martial shall adjudge.

29. Each commanding officer shall, whenever a seaman enters on board, cause an accurate entry to be made in the ship's books of his name, time, and term of his service; and, before sailing, transmit to the secretary of the navy a complete list or muster roll of the officers and men under his command, with the date of their entering, time and terms of their service, annexed; and shall cause similar lists to be made out on the first day of every second month, to be transmitted to the secretary of the navy, as opportunities shall occur: accounting, in such lists or muster rolls, for any casualties which may have taken place since the last list or muster roll. He shall cause to be accurately minuted on the ship's books the names of, and times at which any death or desertion may occur; and in case of death, shall take care that the purser secure all the property of the deceased for the benefit of his legal representative or representatives. He shall cause frequent inspections to be made into the condition of the provisions, and use every precaution for its preservation. He shall, whenever he orders officers and men to take charge of a prize, and proceed to the United States, and whenever officers or men are sent from his ship, for whatever cause, take care that each man be furnished with a complete statement of his account, specifying the date of his enlistment, and the period and terms of his service; which account shall be signed by the commanding officer and purser. He shall cause the rules for the government of the navy to be hung up in some public part of the ship, and read once a month to his ship's company. He shall cause a convenient place to be set apart for sick or disabled men, to which he shall have them removed, with their hammocks and bedding, when the surgeon shall so advise, and shall direct that some of the crew attend them and keep the place clean; and, if necessary, shall direct that cradles, and buckets with covers, be made for their use. And when his crew is finally paid off, he shall attend in person, or appoint a proper officer, to see that justice be done to the men, and to the United States, in the settlement of the accounts. Any commanding officer offending herein, shall be punished at the discretion of a court martial.

30. No commanding officer shall, of his own authority, discharge a commissioned or warrant officer, nor strike, nor punish him, otherwise than by suspension or confinement; nor shall he, of his own authority, inflict a punishment on any private beyond twelve lashes with a cat of nine tails; nor shall he suffer any wired, or other than a plain cat of nine tails, to be used on board his ship; nor shall any officer who command by accident, or in the absence of the commanding officer, (except such commander be absent for a time by leave,) order or inflict any other punishment than confinement, for which he shall account on the return of such absent commanding officer. Nor shall any commanding officer receive on board any petty officers or men turned over from any other vessel to him, unless each of such officers and men produce to him an account, signed by the captain

and purser of the vessel from which they came, specifying the date of such officer's or man's entry, the period and terms of service, the sums paid, and the balance due him, and the quality in which he was rated on board such ship. Nor shall any commanding officer, having received any petty officer or man as aforesaid, rate him in a lower or worse station than that in which he formerly served. Any commanding officer offending herein, shall be punished at the discretion of a court martial.

31. Any master at arms, or other person of whom the duty of master at arms is required, who shall refuse to receive such prisoners as shall be committed to his charge, or, having received them, shall suffer them to escape, or dismiss them without orders from proper authority, shall suffer in such prisoners' stead, or be punished otherwise at the discretion of a court martial.

32. All crimes committed by persons belonging to the navy, which are not specified in the foregoing articles, shall be punished according to the laws and customs in such cases at sea.

33. All officers, not holding commissions or warrants, or who are not entitled to them, except such as are temporarily appointed to the duties of a commissioned or warrant officer, are deemed petty officers.

34. Any person entitled to wages or prize money, may have the same paid to his assignee, provided the assignment be attested by the captain and purser; and in case of the assignment of wages, the power shall specify the precise time they commence. But the commander of every vessel is required to discourage his crew from selling any part of their wages or prize money, and never to attest any power of attorney until he is satisfied the same is not granted in consideration of money given for the purchase of wages or prize money.

35. General courts martial may be convened as often as the president of the United States, the secretary of the navy, or the commander in chief of the fleet, or commander of a squadron, while acting out of the United States, shall deem it necessary; but no general court martial shall consist of more than thirteen, nor less than five members; and as many officers shall be summoned on every such court as can be convened without injury to the service, so as not to exceed thirteen, and the senior officer shall always preside, the others ranking agreeably to the date of their commissions; and in no case, where it can be avoided, without injury to the service, shall more than one half the members, exclusive of the president, be junior to the officer to be tried.

36. Each member of the court, before proceeding to trial, shall take the following oath or affirmation, which the judge advocate, or person officiating as such, is hereby authorized to administer:

"I, A. B., do swear (or affirm) that I will truly try, without prejudice or partiality, the case now depending, according to the evidence which shall come before the court, the rules for the government of the navy, and my own conscience; and that I will not by any means divulge or disclose the sentence of the court, until it shall have been approved by the proper authority; nor will I, at any time, divulge or disclose the vote or opinion of any particular member of the court, unless required so to do before a court of justice in due course of law."

This oath or affirmation being duly administered, the president is authorized and required to administer the following oath or affirmation to the judge advocate, or person officiating as such:

"I, A. B., do swear (or affirm) that I will keep a true record of the evidence given to, and the proceedings of, this court; nor will I divulge or by any means d sclose the sentence of the court, until it shall have been approved by the proper authority; nor will I, at any time, divulge or disclose the vote or opinion of any particular member of the court, unless required so to do before a court of justice in due course of law."

37. All testimony given to a general court martial shall be on oath or affirmation, which the president of the court is hereby authorized to administer; and if any person shall refuse to give his evidence as aforesaid, or shall prevaricate, or shall behave with contempt to the court, it shall and may be lawful for the court to imprison such offender at their discretion; but the imprisonment in no case shall exceed two months. And every person who shall commit wilful perjury, on examination on oath or affimation before such court, or who shall corruptly procure, or suborn any person to commit such wilful perjury, shall and may be prosecuted by indictment or information in any court of justice of the United States, and shall suffer such penalties as are authorized by the laws of the United States in cases of perjury, or the subornation thereof. And in every prosecution for perjury, or the subornation thereof, under this act, it shall be sufficient to set forth the offence charged on the defendant, without setting forth the authority by which the court was held, or the particular matters brought, or intended to be brought before the said court.

38. All charges, on which an application for a general court martial is founded, shall be exhibited in writing to the proper officer; and the person demanding the court shall take care that the person accused be furnished with a true copy of the charges, with the specifications, at the time he is put under arrest. Nor shall any other charge or charges, than those so exhibited, be urged against the person to be tried before the court, unless it appear to the court that intelligence of such charge had not reached the person demanding the court, when the person so to be tried was put under arrest, or that some witness, material to the support of such charge, who was at that time absent, can be produced; in which case, reasonable time shall be given to the person to be tried to make his defence against such new charge. Every officer so arrested is to deliver up his sword to his commanding officer, and to confine himself to the limits assigned him, under pain of dismission from service.

39. When the proceedings of any general court matial shall have commenced, they shall not be suspended or delayed on account of the absence of any of the members, provided five or more be assembled; but the court is enjoined to sit from day to day, Sunday excepted, until sentence be given. And no member of said court shall, after the proceedings are begun, absent himself therefrom, unless in case of sickness, or orders to go on duty from a superior, on pain of being cashiered.

40. Whenever a court martial shall sentence any officer to be suspended, the court shall have power to suspend his pay and emoluments for the whole, or any part of the time of his suspension.

41. All sentences of courts martial, which shall extend to the loss of life, shall require the concurrence of two thirds of the members present; and no such sentence shall be carried into execution, until confirmed by the president of the United States; or if the trial take place out of the United States, until it be confirmed by the commander of the fleet or squadron. All other sentences may be determined by a majority of votes, and carried into execution on confirmation of the commander of the fleet, or officer ordering the court, except such as go to the dismission of a commissioned or warrant officer, which are first to be approved by the president of the United States.

A court martial shall not, for any one offence not capital, inflict a punishment beyond one hundred lashes.

42. The president of the United States, or, when the trial takes place out of the United States, the commander of the fleet or squadron shall possess full power to pardon any offence committed against these articles, after conviction, or to mitigate the punishment decreed by a court martial.

45. Courts of inquiry may be ordered by the president of the United States, the secretary of the navy, or the commander of a fleet or squadron. But such courts cannot consist of more than three members, who shall be commissioned officers, and a judge advocate, or person to do duty as such; and such courts have power to summon witnesses, administer oaths, and punish contempt, in the same manner as courts martial. But such court shall merely state facts, and not give their opinion, unless expressly required so to do in the order for convening; and the party, whose conduct shall be the subject of inquiry, shall have permission to cross-examine all the witnesses.

The proceedings of courts of inquiry must be authenticated by the signature of the president of the court and judge advocate, and shall, in all cases not capital, or extending to the dismission of a commissioned or warrant officer, be evidence before a court martial, provided oral testimony cannot be obtained.

The judge advocate, or person officiating as such, must administer to the members the following oath or affirmation:

"You do swear (or, affirm) well and truly to examine and inquire, according to the evidence, into the matter now before you, without partiality or prejudice."

After which, the president shall administer to the judge advocate, or person officiating as such, the following oath or affirmation:

"You do swear (or affirm) truly to record the proceedings of this court, and the evidence to be given in the case in hearing."

46. In cases where the crews of the ships or vessels of the United States shall be separated from their vessels, by the latter being wrecked, lost, or destroyed, all the command, power, and authority, given to the officers of such ships or vessels, shall remain, and be in full force, as effectually as if such ship or vessel were not so wrecked,

lost, or destroyed, until such ship's company be regularly discharged from, or ordered again into, the service, or until a court martial shall be held to inquire into the loss of such ship or vessel; and if, by the sentence of such court, or other satisfactory evidence, it shall appear that all, or any, of the officers and men of such ship's company did their utmost to preserve her, and, after the loss thereof, behaved themselves agreeably to the discipline of the navy, then the pay and emoluments of such officers and men, or such of them as shall have done their duty as aforesaid, shall go on until their discharge or death; and every officer or private who shall, after the loss of such vessel, act contrary to the discipline of the navy, shall be punished, at the discretion of a court martial, in the same manner as if such vessel had not been so lost.

47. All the pay and emoluments of such officers and men, of any of the ships or vessels of the United States taken by an enemy, who appear by the sentence of a court martial, or otherwise, to have done their utmost to preserve and defend their ship or vessel, and after the taking thereof, have behaved themselves obediently to their superiors, agreeably to the discipline of the navy, shall go on and be paid them until their death, exchange, or discharge.

48. The proceeds of all ships and vessels, and the goods taken on board of them, which shall be adjudged good prizes, shall, when of equal or superior force to the vessel or vessels making the capture, be the sole property of the captors; and when of inferior force, shall be divided, equally, between the United States and the officers and men making the capture.

49. Prize money, belonging to the officers and men, is distributed in the following manner.

1. To the commanding officers of fleets, squadrons, or single ships, three twentieths, of which the commanding officer of the fleet or squadron has one twentieth, if the prize be taken by a ship or vessel acting under his command, and the commander of single ships two twentieths; but where the prize is taken by a ship acting independently of such superior officer, the three twentieths belong to her commander.

2. To sea lieutenants, captains or marines, and sailing masters, two twentieths; but where there is a captain, without a lieutenant of marines, these officers are entitled to two twentieths and one third of a twentieth, which third, in such case, is deducted from the share of the officers mentioned in article No. 3 of this section.

3. To chaplains, lieutenants of marines, surgeons, pursers, boatswains, gunners, carpenters, and master's mate, two twentieths.

4. To midshipmen, surgeon's mates, captain's clerks, schoolmasters, boatswain's mates, gunner's mates, carpenter's mates, ship's stewards, sailmakers, masters at arms, armorers, cockswains, and coopers, three twentieths and a half.

5. To gunner's yeomen, boatswain's yeomen, quartermasters, quartergunners, sailmaker's mates, sergeants and corporals of marines, drummers, fifers, and extra petty officers, two twentieths and a half.

6. To seamen, ordinary seamen, marines, and all other persons doing duty on board, seven twentieths.

7. Whenever one or more public ships or vessels are in sight at the time any one or more ships are taking a prize or prizes, they all share equally in the prize or prizes, according to the number of men and guns on board each ship in sight.

No commander of a fleet or squadron is entitled to receive any share of prizes taken by vessels not under his immediate command; nor of such prizes as may have been taken by ships or vessels intended to be placed under his command, before they have acted under his immediate orders; nor can a commander of a fleet or squadron, leaving the station where he had the command, have any share in the prizes taken by ships left on such station, after he has gone out of the limits of his said command.

50. A bounty is paid by the United States, of twenty dollars, for each person on board any ship of an enemy at the commencement of an engagement, which is sunk or destroyed by any ship or vessel belonging to the United States, of equal or inferior force: the same to be divided among the officers and crew in the same manner as prize money.

The navy ration is, on Sunday, fourteen ounces of bread, one and a quarter pounds of beef, half a pound of flour, one quarter of a pound of suet, one half pint of distilled spirits. Monday, fourteen ounces of bread, one pound of pork, half pint of peas, one half pint of distilled spirits. Tuesday, fourteen ounces of bread, one pound of beef, two ounces of cheese, one half pint of distilled spirits. Wednesday, fourteen ounces of bread, one pound of pork, half pint of rice, one half pint of distilled spirits. Thursday, fourteen ounces of bread, one and a quarter pounds of beef, half pound of flour, quarter pound of suet, one half pint of distilled spirits. Friday, fourteen ounces of bread, four ounces of cheese, two ounces of butter, half pint of rice, half pint of molasses, one half pint of distilled spirits. Saturday, fourteen ounces of bread, one pound of pork, half pint of peas, half pint of vinegar, one half pint of distilled spirits.[a]

All the vessels in the service of the United States, mounting twenty guns and upwards, must be commanded by captains; those not exceeding eighteen guns (except galleys) by masters or lieutenants, according to the size of the vessel, to be regulated by the president of the United States.[b]

The annual pay of the officers of the navy of the United States is as follows:—

Senior captain.—At all times when in service, $4,500: when on leave of absence, or waiting orders, $3,500.

Other captains.—When in command of squadrons on foreign stations, $4,000: when on other duty, $3,500: when off duty, $2,500.

*Commanders.**—When attached to vessels for sea service, $2,500: when attached to navy yards, or on other duty, $2,100: when on leave of absence, or waiting orders, $1,800.

Lieutenants.—Commanding, $1,800: on other duty, $1,500: waiting orders, $1,200.

---

[a] Act, 3d March, 1801. [b] Act, 25th February, 1799.

* These officers were known until the Act of 3d March, 1837, as masters commandant.

Assistant surgeons.—Waiting orders, $650: at sea, $950: after passing, and found qualified for promotion to surgeon, $850: at sea, $1,200: when stationed at navy yards, hospitals, rendezvous, and receiving ships, $950: after being passed and stationed as above, $1,150.

Surgeons.—For the first five years after the date of commission, $1,000: for the second five years, $1,200: for the third five years: $1,400: for the fourth five years, $1,600: after he shall have been commissioned as a surgeon twenty years and upwards, $1,800.

All surgeons of the navy, under orders for duty at navy yards, receiving vessels, rendezvous, or naval hospitals, shall have an increase of one fourth of the foregoing amount of their respective annual pay, from the date of their acceptance of such orders.

All surgeons of the navy ordered to any of the ships or vessels of the United States, commissioned for sea service, shall have an increase of one third of the foregoing amount of their respective annual pay, from the date of their acceptance of such orders.

All surgeons of the navy, ordered as fleet surgeons, shall have an increase of one half of their respective annual pay, from the date of their acceptance of such orders.

Chaplains.—When attached to vessels for sea service, or at navy yards, $1,200: when on leave of absence, or waiting orders, $800.

Professor of mathematics.—When attached to vessels for sea service, or in a yard, $1,200.

Secretaries.—To commanders of squadrons, when commanding in chief, $1,000: to commanders of squadrons, when not commanding in chief, $900.

*Masters.**—Of a ship of the line, for sea service, $1,100: when on other duty, $1,000: when on leave of absence, or waiting orders, $750.

Second masters.—When attached to vessels for sea service, $750: when on other duty, $500: when on leave of absence, or waiting orders, $400.

Passed midshipmen.—On duty, $750: waiting orders, $600.

Warranted masters' mates.—When attached to vessels for sea service, or at navy yards, $450: when on leave of absence, or waiting orders, $300.

Midshipmen.—When attached to vessels for sea service, $400: when on other duty, $350: when on leave of absence, or waiting orders, $300.

Clerks.—Of a yard, $900: first clerk to a commandant of a navy yard, $900: second clerk to a commandant of a navy yard, $750: to commanders of squadrons, captains of fleets, and commanders of vessels, $500.

Boatswains, gunners, sailmakers, carpenters.—Of a ship of the line, for sea service, $750: of a frigate for sea service, $600: when

* These officers were known until the Act of 3d March, 1837, as sailing masters.

on other duty, $500: when on leave of absence, or waiting orders, $360.

Officers temporarily performing the duties belonging to those of a higher grade, receive the compensation allowed to such higher grade, while actually so employed.

No officer is put on furlough but at his own request; and all officers so furloughed, receive one half only of the pay to which they would have been entitled if on leave of absence.

If any assistant surgeon have been absent from the United States, on duty, at the time others of his date were examined, he is, if not rejected at a subsequent examination, entitled to the same rank with them; and if from any cause his relative rank cannot be assigned to him, he retains his original position on the register.

One ration per day only is allowed to all officers when attached to vessels for sea service.

No allowance is made to any officer in the naval service of the United States, for drawing bills, for receiving or disbursing money, or transacting any business for the government of the United States; nor is he allowed servants, or pay for servants, or clothing or rations for them, or pay for the same, nor for rent of quarters, or to pay rent for furniture, or for lights or fuel, or transporting baggage. The yearly allowance is all the pay, compensation and allowance that can be received under any circumstances whatever, by any such officer or person, except for travelling expenses, when under orders, for which ten cents per mile are allowed.[a]

The pursers in the navy of the United States are appointed by the president of the United States, by and with the advice and consent of the senate. No person can act in the character of purser, who shall not thus have been nominated and appointed. And every purser, before entering upon the duties of his office, must give bonds, with two or more sufficient sureties, in a penalty of twenty-five thousand dollars, conditioned faithfully to perform all the duties of purser in the navy of the United States.[b]

According to a resolution of congress, ships of the first class are to be called after the states of the Union; those of the second class after the rivers; and those of the third class after the principal cities and towns, taking care not to call two vessels after the same name.[c]

The flag of the United States consists of *thirteen* horizontal stripes, alternate red and white, and the Union is twenty-four white stars, in a blue field. On the admission of every new state into the Union, a star is added to the union of the flag on the next 4th of July to such admission. It now has twenty-six stars, just double the number of the revolutionary thirteen.

---

[a] Act, 3d March, 1835. [b] Act, 30th March, 1812. [c] Act, 3d March, 1819.

CHAPTER XVII.

PENSIONS.

The people of the United States have not been unmindful of their duty to those seamen who have been wounded or disabled in the public service. In pursuance of that liberal policy which characterizes a wise government, and which in the end amply rewards those who pursue it, they have, by various acts, made suitable provision for wounded and disabled seamen. To constitute a fund for payment of pensions, it has been enacted,[a] that all the money accruing to the United States, from the capture of prizes authorized by law, must be paid to the treasurer of the United States.

It is the duty of the treasurer of the United States to receive all the money so accruing, and to disburse the same, pursuant to warrants from the secretary of the navy, countersigned by the accountant of the navy; and to render a distinct quarterly account of the moneys thus received and disbursed to the accounting officers of the treasury.

The commissioner of the navy pension fund is the secretary of the navy.

The commissioner of the navy pension fund is authorized to make regulations for the admission of persons on the roll of navy pensioners, and for the payment of the pensions.

It is also his duty to receive applications for pensions, to grant the same according to the provisions of the pension acts, and to direct and control the expenditures out of the navy hospital fund.[b]

If any officer, non-commissioned officer, marine, or seaman, belonging to the navy of the United States, be wounded or disabled while in the line of his duty, he is placed on the list of invalids, at such rate of pay, and under such regulations, as the president shall think proper; and inferior disabilities entitle the person so disabled to receive a proportionate pension. Officers, seamen, or marines, are entitled to receive for life, or during the disability, a pension according to the nature of his disability, not however exceeding half the monthly pay of the pensioner. The commissioners of the navy pension fund, if they deem that allowance insufficient on account of the peculiar disability or situation of the pensioner, are authorized to increase it to the full amount of his monthly pay.

The money accruing from the sale of prizes is appropriated as a fund for the payment of pensions and half pay, and if insufficient, the public faith is pledged to make up the deficiency; and if more than sufficient, the surplus is to be applied to make further provision for the comfort of disabled seamen, and of those who may merit, by long and faithful services, the gratitude of their country.

---

[a] Act, 26th March, 1804.   [b] Act, 10th July, 1832, sec. 1.

Applications for payment of pensions must be accompanied by the affidavits of two surgeons, (whose credibility must be certified by the magistrate,) stating the continuance of the disability, and its rate at the time—unless the disability be for a total disability, in consequence of a cause which cannot be removed.

If any officer of the navy or marines were killed, or died by reason of a wound received in the line of his duty, leaving a widow, or, if no widow, a child or children under sixteen years of age, such widow, or, if no widow, such child or children are entitled to receive half the monthly pay to which the deceased was entitled at the time of his death, which allowance was to continue for the term of five years. In case of the death or intermarriage of such widow before the expiration of five years, the half pay for the remainder went to the child or children of the said deceased officer; and such half pay ceased on the death of such child or children.[a]

The same rate of pensions, and upon the same terms, was allowed for ten years to the widow or children of a seaman or marine killed, or dying from any casualty happening, or disease contracted in the service; but by an act passed 3d March, 1837, the pension is to be allowed to the widow or children of any officer, seaman or marine, dying in the service from any cause; the allowance to be half of the pay allowed by the act of 3d March, 1835, and to be paid to the children upon the death or intermarriage of the widow. Upon the arrival of the children to 21 years of age, the pension ceases, unless the widow be living; and the pension is to be paid to her for life if she remain a widow.

The secretary of the navy is authorized to place on the pension list any officer, seaman, or marine, who, on board of any private armed vessel bearing a commission of letter of marque, was wounded or otherwise disabled, in any engagement with the enemy: allowing to the captain, a sum not exceeding $20 per month; to lieutenants and sailing master, a sum not exceeding $12, each, per month; to marine officer, boatswain, gunner, carpenter, master's mate, and prize masters, a sum not exceeding $10, each, per month; to all other officers, a sum not exceeding $8, each, per month, for the highest rate of disability, and so in proportion; and to a seaman, or acting as a marine, the sum of $6 per month, for the highest rate of disability, and so in proportion.

The commanding officer of every vessel having a commission of letters of marque and reprisal, must enter in his journal the name and rank of any officer, and the name of any seaman, who, during his cruise, has been wounded or disabled, describing the manner and extent, as far as practicable, of such wound or disability.[b]

The officers and seamen of the revenue cutters, who may be wounded or disabled in the discharge of their duty, whilst co-operating with the navy by order of the president of the United States, are entitled to be placed on the navy pension list, at the same rate of pension, and under the same regulations and restrictions, as officers and seamen of the navy.

---

[a] Act, 20th Jan., 1813 [b] Act, 18th Feb., 1813.

CHAPTER XVIII.

CRIMES.

The courts of the United States have jurisdiction over offences committed on the ocean by any citizen of the United States; and various statutes have been passed, declaring the crimes and the punishments of the offenders. By an act passed upon the organization of the government, it is declared, that if any person, owing allegiance to the United States of America, levy war against them, or adhere to their enemies, giving them aid and comfort within the United States, or elsewhere, and shall be thereof convicted, on confession in open court, or on the testimony of two witnesses, to the same overt act of the treason whereof he stands indicted, such person shall be adjudged guilty of treason against the United States, and suffer death.[a]

If any person, having the knowledge of the commission of treason, conceal, and do not, as soon as may be, disclose the same to the president of the United States, or some one of the judges thereof, or to the president or governor of a particular state, such person, on conviction, shall be adjudged guilty of misprison or treason, and be imprisoned not exceeding seven years, and fined not exceeding $1,000.[b]

If any person, within any fort, arsenal, dockyard, magazine, or in any other place under the sole and exclusive jurisdiction of the United States, commit the crime of wilful murder, such person, on being thereof convicted, shall suffer death.[c]

Murder or rape committed upon the high seas, or in any arm of the sea, or in any river, haven, creek, basin or bay within the admiralty jurisdiction of the United States, and without the jurisdiction of a state, or wounding, striking, or poisoning a person, so that he afterwards die upon shore, is punishable by death.[d]

The same punishment is inflicted upon persons wilfully burning any dwelling-house, or any out house parcel of any dwelling-house, within any place under the jurisdiction of the United States; and also upon their abettors.[e]

For setting fire maliciously to any arsenal, armory, magazine, rope-walk, ship-house, block-house or barrack, or any out house not parcel of a dwelling-house, or any light-house or beacon, or any vessel built or building, or any materials for building or repairing vessels, or any munitions of war, or any arms or victuals, in any place under the jurisdiction of the United States, the person offending is liable to be fined not exceeding $5,000, and to be imprisoned not exceeding ten years.[f]

---

[a] Act, 30th April, 1790, sec. 1. [b] Ibid. sec. 2. [c] Ibid. sec. 3. [d] Act, 3d March, 1825, sec. 4. [e] Ibid. sec. 1. [f] Ibid. sec. 2.

The burning or destroying a public armed vessel of the United States on the high seas, or in any waters within admiralty jurisdiction, and out of the state jurisdiction, and the aiding or abetting therein, is punishable with death.[a]

If any person, having knowledge of the actual commission of wilful murder, or other felony, upon the high seas, or within any place under the sole and exclusive jurisdiction of the United States, conceal, and do not, as soon as may be, disclose the same to some one of the judges or other persons in civil or military authority under the United States, on conviction thereof such person shall be adjudged guilty of misprison of felony, and shall be imprisoned not exceeding three years, and fined not exceeding $500.[b]

If any person, within any place under the sole and exclusive jurisdiction of the United States, commit the crime of manslaughter, and be thereof convicted, such person shall be imprisoned not exceeding three years, and fined not exceeding $1,000.[c]

If any person commit upon the high seas, or in any river, haven, basin or bay, out of the jurisdiction of any particular state, murder or robbery, or any other offence which, if committed within the body of a county, would, by the laws of the United States, be punishable with death: or if any captain or mariner of any vessel piratically run away with such vessel, or any goods or merchandise to the value of fifty dollars, or yield up such vessel voluntarily to any pirate: or if any seaman lay violent hands upon his commander, thereby to hinder his fighting in defence of the ship or goods committed to his trust, every such offender shall be adjudged to be a pirate and a felon, and being thereof convicted, shall suffer death. The trial of crimes committed on the high seas, or in any place out of the jurisdiction of any particular state, must be in the district where the offender is apprehended, or into which he may first be brought.[d]

A vessel lying in an open roadstead in a foreign country, is "upon the high seas," within the meaning of this section.[e]

This section applies only to offences committed in some river, &c. not within the jurisdiction of a particular state.[f]

A robbery committed on the high seas, is piracy under this section, though such robbery, if committed on land, would not be punishable with death; and the courts of the United States have jurisdiction in this case.[g]

This act extends to all persons on board all vessels who commit piracy on other vessels.[h]

A commission, issued by an officer of a nation whose existence is not acknowledged by the United States, *de facto* or *de jure*, will not authorize captures at sea; but the person will not be deemed guilty of piracy, unless it appears that the capture was made with intent to steal, and not by the right of war.[h]

If any citizen commit any piracy or robbery aforesaid, or any act of hostility against the United States, or any citizen thereof, upon the high seas, under colour of any commission from any foreign prince

---

[a] Act, 3d March, 1825, sec. 11. [b] Act, 30th April, 1790, sec. 6. [c] Ibid. sec. 7.
[d] Ibid. sec. 8. [e] 5 Wheat. 200. [f] 4 Cranch, 135. [g] 3 Wheat. 310. [h] 5 Ibid. 144.

or state, or on pretence of authority from any person, such offender shall, notwithstanding the pretence of any such authority, be adjudged to be a pirate, felon and robber, and on being thereof convicted, shall suffer death.[a]

Every person who, either upon the land or the seas, knowingly and wittingly aids, procures, commands, or advises any person to commit any murder or robbery, or other piracy aforesaid, upon the seas, which affects the life of such person, and such person thereupon commits such piracy or robbery, such person so aiding, procuring, commanding, or advising the same, shall be adjudged to be accessory to such piracies before the fact, and being thereof convicted, shall suffer death.[b]

After such offence has been committed, every person who, knowing that such pirate has committed such piracy or robbery, receives, entertains, or conceals such pirate, or receives into his custody any vessel, goods or chattels, which have been by such pirate piratically or feloniously taken, shall be adjudged to be accessory after the fact; and on conviction thereof, shall be imprisoned not exceeding three years, and fined not exceeding $500.[c]

If any seaman or other person commit manslaughter on the high seas, or confederate, or endeavour to corrupt any master, officer or mariner to yield up or to run away with any vessel or with any goods, or to turn pirate, or to go over to or confederate with pirates, or in any wise trade with any pirate, knowing him to be such, or furnish such pirate with any ammunition, stores or provisions, or fit out any vessel with a design to trade with, or supply or correspond with any pirate or robber upon the seas: or if any person consult, combine, confederate or correspond with any pirate or robber on the seas, knowing him to be guilty of any piracy or robbery: or if any seaman confine the master of any vessel, or endeavour to make a revolt in such ship, such person, being thereof convicted, shall be imprisoned not exceeding three years, and fined not exceeding $1000.[d]

If one or more of the crew unlawfully, or by force or threats, usurp the command of any American vessel upon the high seas, or in any waters within admiralty jurisdiction, or if they obstruct the commander in the exercise of his authority, the offenders are liable to a fine of $2000 and an imprisonment of ten years.[e]

Combining or attempting to make a mutiny, or unlawfully confining the master, is punishable by fine to the extent of $1000, and imprisonment not exceeding five years.[f]

If the master or officer of an American vessel, without justifiable cause, maltreat any of the crew, or maliciously withhold from them suitable food and nourishment, or inflict any cruel or unusual punishment, the offender is liable to a fine of $1000, and to be imprisoned five years.[g]

If any person, within any of the places upon the land, under the sole and exclusive jurisdiction of the United States, or upon the high seas, in any vessel belonging to the United States, or to any citizen

---

[a] Act, 30th April, 1790, sec. 9. [b] Ibid. sec. 10. [c] Ibid. 11. [d] Ibid. sec. 12.
[e] Act, March, 1835. sec 1. [f] Ibid. sec. 2. [g] Ibid. sec. 3.

thereof, of malice aforethought, unlawfully cut off the ear or ears, or cut out or disable the tongue, put out an eye, slit the nose, cut off the nose or a lip, or cut off or disable any limb or member of any person, with intention to maim or disfigure such person, the person so offending, their counsellors, aiders and abettors, shall be imprisoned not exceeding seven years, and fined not exceeding $1000.[a]

If any person, within any of the places under the sole and exclusive jurisdiction of the United States, or upon the high seas, take and carry away, with an intent to steal or purloin, the personal goods of another; or if any person having the charge or custody of any arms, ordnance, munition, shot, powder, or habiliments of war, belonging to the United States, or of any victuals provided for the victualling of any soldiers, gunners, marines, or pioneers, embezzle, purloin, or convey away the same, the person so offending, his counsellors, aiders and abettors, shall be fined not exceeding the fourfold value of the property so stolen, embezzled, or purloined: the one moiety to be paid to the owner of the goods, or the United States, as the case may be, and the other moiety to the informer and prosecutor, and be publicly whipped, not exceeding thirty-nine stripes.[b]

If any person, within any part of the (sole and exclusive) jurisdiction of the United States, receive or buy any goods, knowing the same to be stolen, or receive, harbour, or conceal, any felons or thieves, knowing them to be so, he shall be liable to the like punishments as in the case of larceny.[c]

If any person receive or buy stolen goods, or bank notes, or money, (knowing them to be stolen,) on the high seas, or in any waters within admiralty jurisdiction, and out of the jurisdiction of a state, it is punishable by a fine of not more than $1000, and imprisonment of not more than three years.[d]

If a master of an American vessel maliciously leave an officer or seaman of his vessel in a foreign country, without good cause, he is liable to a fine of $500, and six months' imprisonment.[e]

Offences committed on board of an American vessel while lying in a foreign port, by one of the ship's company, or a passenger, upon any person belonging to the vessel, or upon a passenger, is punishable in the same manner as if committed upon the high seas. If tried abroad, however, the offender is not again tried in the United States.[f]

If any offence be committed in a dockyard, or in any place within the exclusive jurisdiction of the United States, for which no punishment is specially provided by the United States, they are to be adjudged to the same punishment provided by the laws of the state in which such place is situated, had such offence been committed in the body of the country.[g]

If any person commit perjury, or procure any person to commit corrupt and wilful perjury, in any suit, controversy, matter, or cause depending in any of the courts of the United States, or in any deposition taken pursuant to the laws of the United States, every person so offending shall be imprisoned not exceeding three years, and fined

---

[a] Act, 30th April, 1790, sec. 13. [b] Ibid. sec. 16. [c] Ibid. sec. 17.
[d] Act, 3d March, 1825, sec. 8. [e] Ibid. sec. 10. [f] Ibid. sec. 5. [g] Ibid. sec. 3.

not exceeding $800, and stand in the pillory for one hour, and be thereafter rendered incapable of giving testimony in any of the courts of the United States.[a]

If any person, knowingly and wilfully, obstruct, resist, or oppose any officer of the United States, in serving or attempting to serve or execute any mesne process, or warrant, or any rule or order of any of the courts of the United States, or any other legal or judicial writ or process whatsoever, or assault, beat, or wound any person duly authorized in serving or executing any writ, rule, order, process, or warrant aforesaid, every person so offending shall be imprisoned not exceeding twelve months, and fined not exceeding $300.[b]

Any person, not being an owner, who, on the high seas, wilfully and corruptly cast away, burn, or otherwise destroy any vessel unto which he belongs, being the property of any citizen of the United States, or procure the same to be done, shall suffer death.[c]

If any person on the high seas wilfully and corruptly cast away, burn, or otherwise destroy any vessel of which he is owner, in part or in whole, or in any wise direct or procure the same to be done, with intent or design to prejudice any underwriter, or of any merchant that shall load goods thereon, or of any other owner of such vessel, the person so offending shall suffer death.[c]

The combining and conspiring with any other person to burn or destroy a vessel, with such intent, or to defraud a lender on bottomry or respondentia, and the building or fitting out a vessel for such an object, is punishable by fine not exceeding $10,000, and an imprisonment of ten years.[d]

Any person guilty of any crime arising under the revenue laws of the United States, or incurring any fine or forfeiture by breaches of the said laws, may be prosecuted, tried, and punished, provided the indictment or information be found within five years after committing the offence, or incurring the fine or forfeiture.

If any person import, or bring from any foreign place into the United States, any false, forged, or counterfeit gold or silver coins, which are by law made current, or are in actual use and circulation as money within the United States, with the intent to utter, or make payment with the same, knowing the same to be falsely made, forged, or counterfeited; or utter, as true, any such false, forged, or counterfeited coins of gold or silver, for the payment of money, with intention to defraud any person, the person so offending shall be sentenced to imprisonment for not more than ten years, and fined not exceeding $5000.[e]

Importing copper coin of the United States, counterfeit, is punishable by a fine of $1000, and imprisonment of three years.[f]

If any persons commit the crime of piracy, and be brought into the United States, they shall suffer death.

Persons committing robbery upon any ship, or any of the ship's company upon the high seas, or in any open roadstead, or in any haven, basin, bay, or river, where the sea ebbs and flows, are to be considered pirates, and to suffer accordingly.

---

[a] Act, 30th April, 1790, sec. 18. [b] Ibid. sec. 22. [c] Act, 26th March, 1804.
[d] Act, 3d March, 1825, sec. 23. [e] Acts, 21st April, 1806, and 3d March, 1825, sec. 20.
[f] Act, 3d March, 1825, sec. 21.

If any person engaged in a piratical cruise or enterprise, land from the piratical ship, and commit robbery on shore, he shall be adjudged a pirate, and suffer death.[a]

If any person upon the high seas, or in any arm of the sea, or in any river, haven, creek, basin, or bay, within the admiralty jurisdiction, and out of the jurisdiction of the United States, maliciously attack a vessel, with intent to plunder her, he is punishable by a fine of $5000, and an imprisonment of not more than ten years.[b] The entering a vessel upon the high seas, or in such a place, with a felonious intent, or maliciously cutting or injuring her cordage, fasts, cables, buoys, or buoy rope, is punishable by a fine of not more than $1000, and an imprisonment of not more than five years.[c]

The assaulting a person on board of an American vessel on the high seas, or in one of the places above named, with a dangerous weapon, or with a felonious intent, is punishable by a fine not exceeding $3000, and an imprisonment not exceeding three years.[d]

The plundering or destroying any property belonging to a vessel wrecked or in distress, or obstructing the escape of any person from a wreck; and the holding out any false light, or extinguishing any true light, with intent to bring a vessel in danger, is punishable by a fine of $5000, and an imprisonment of ten years.[e]

American citizens engaged in the slave trade, either in foreign vessels, or in those belonging to citizens of the United States, are considered as pirates, and shall suffer death.[f]

They are guilty of the same crime, and liable to the same punishment, if they land on any foreign shore, or seize or decoy any negro or mulatto not held to service by the laws of the United States, on board of any ship, with intent to make him a slave; or if they in any way be aiding or abetting in forcibly detaining such negro or mulatto with that intent; or if they on board of a slave ship, or on the high seas, or any where on tide water, offer to sell him as a slave, or land him with that intent.[f]

There are other regulations by the United States, and by several of the states, against this abominable traffic, which will be mentioned more at large in the next chapter.

To prevent any interference on the part of American citizens in the quarrels between other nations, it has been enacted, that

If any citizen of the United States, within the territory or jurisdiction thereof, accept and exercise a commission to serve a foreign prince, or people, in war, against any prince, or people, with whom the United States are at peace, the person so offending may be fined not more than $2000, and imprisoned not exceeding three years.[g]

If any person, within the said territory or jurisdiction, enlist, or hire or retain another person to enlist or to go beyond the limits or jurisdiction of the United States, with intent to be enlisted in the service of any foreign prince, or people, as a soldier, or on board of any vessel of war, every person so offending shall be fined not exceeding $1,000, and imprisoned not exceeding three years. This act is not

---

[a] Act, 15th May, 1820, sec. 3. [b] Act, 3d March, 1825, sec. 6. [c] Ibid sec. 7. [d] Ibid, sec. 22. [e] Ibid. sec. 9. [f] Act, 15th May, 1820, sec. 4. [g] Act, 5th June, 1794, sec. 1.

to be construed to extend to any subject or citizen of any foreign prince, or people, transiently within the United States, who shall, on board of any vessel of war, letter of marque, or privateer, which, at the time of its arrival within the United States, was fitted and equipped as such, enlist, or hire or retain another subject or citizen of the same foreign prince or people, who is transiently within the United States, to enlist on board such vessel of war, if the United States then be at peace with such foreign prince or people.[a]

If any persons, within the limits of the United States, fit out and arm, or are knowingly concerned in the fitting out, or arming, of any vessel, with intent that such vessel be employed in the service of any foreign prince or state, to cruise or commit hostilities against the subjects, citizens, or property of any foreign prince or state with whom the United States are at peace; or issue or deliver a commission within the territory or jurisdiction of the United States, for any vessel, to the intent that she may be employed as aforesaid, every person so offending shall be fined not more than $10,000, and imprisoned not more than three years; and every such vessel, with her tackle, apparel, and furniture, together with all materials, arms, ammunition, and stores, which may have been procured for the building and equipment thereof, shall be forfeited, one half to the use of the informer, and the other half to the use of the United States.[b]

If any citizen of the United States, without the limits thereof, fit out and arm, or knowingly aid or be concerned in the fitting out, or arming, any private vessel of war, with intent that such vessel shall be employed to cruise or commit hostilities, upon the citizens of the United States or their property; or enter on board of such vessel for the intent aforesaid, or purchase any interest, with a view to share in the profits thereof, such person so offending shall be fined not more than $10,000, and imprisoned not more than ten years.[c]

If any person, within the territory or jurisdiction of the United States, increase or augment, or knowingly be concerned in increasing or augmenting, the force of any ship of war, which, at the time of her arrival, was a ship of war in the service of any prince or state, or belonging to the citizens of such prince or state, the same being at war with any foreign prince or state with whom the United States are at peace, by adding to the number of the guns of such vessel, or by changing those on board of her for guns of a larger calibre, or by the addition thereto of any equipment solely applicable to war, every person so offending shall be fined not more than $1000, and imprisoned not more than one year.[d]

If any person, within the territory or jurisdiction of the United States, begin or set on foot, or provide or prepare the means for, any military expedition or enterprise, to be carried on from thence against the territory or dominions of any foreign prince or state with whom the United States are at peace, every person so offending shall be fined not exceeding $3,000, and imprisoned not more than three years.[e]

---

[a] Act, 5th June, 1794, sec. 2. [b] Ibid. sec. 3. [c] Act, 14th June, 1797.
[d] Act, 5th June, 1794, sec. 4. [e] Ibid. sec. 5.

The district courts take cognizance of complaints, by whomsoever instituted, in cases of captures made within the waters of the United States, or within a marine league of the coasts or shores thereof.[a]

In every case in which a vessel is fitted out and armed, or in which the force of any vessel of war, cruiser, or other armed vessel, is increased or augmented, or in which any military expedition or enterprise may be begun or set on foot contrary to law; and in every case of the capture of a vessel within the jurisdiction or protection of the United States, and in which any process issuing out of any court of the United States is disobeyed or resisted by any person or persons having the custody of any vessel of war, or any other armed vessel of any foreign prince or state, or of any subjects or citizens of any foreign prince or state, it shall be lawful for the president of the United States, or such other person as he shall have empowered for that purpose, to employ the land or naval forces of the United States, or of the militia thereof, for the purpose of taking possession of, and detaining any such vessel, with her prizes, and also for the purpose of preventing the carrying on of any such expedition or enterprise.[b]

The president of the United States, or such person as he may empower for that purpose, may employ the land or naval forces of the United States, or of the militia thereof, to compel any foreign vessel to depart from the United States; in all cases in which, by the laws of the nations or the treaties of the United States, they ought not to remain within the United States.[c]

The crime of perjury, the punishment of which is declared by the act of April 30, 1790, is committed by swearing falsely in the courts of justice of the United States. It is also defined to be the crime of perjury to swear falsely in the custom-house, &c., or to any of the matters required by the registry acts, or under any laws of the United States; and it is punishable by a fine not exceeding $2,000, and an imprisonment not exceeding five years. Subornation of perjury is punishable in like manner.[d]

If any person forge, erase, alter, or falsify any document mentioned or required by the registry acts, or any other custom-house document, or aid or abet therein, he is punishable by a fine of $1,000, and an imprisonment of three years.[e]

If any person assault, resist, obstruct, or hinder any officer in the execution of the revenue act, or of any act mentioned therein, he shall forfeit $500.[f]

If any collector or other officer be concerned in making or granting any false register or record, enrolment or license, or grant any document contrary to the true intent of the registry acts, or take any greater fees than are allowed by law, or receive any reward or gratuity for any service performed pursuant thereto; or if a surveyor or other person appointed to measure any vessel, wilfully deliver to the

---

[a] Act, 5th June, 1794, sec. 6. [b] Ibid. sec. 7. [c] Ibid. sec. 8.
[d] Act, 3d March 1825, sec. 13. [e] Ibid. sec. 19. [f] Act, 2d March, 1799.

collector or naval officer a false description of any vessel to be enrolled, licensed, registered or recorded, they forfeit, if the offence relates to a vessel to be registered or recorded, $1000, but otherwise, $500, and in either case are incapacitated from serving in any office of trust or profit in the United States; and if any person neglect or refuse to perform the duties of his office, they forfeit, for the first offence, $500, the like sum for the second, and are incapacitated as above.[a]

If any officer of the United States be guilty of extortion by colour of his office, he is liable to a fine of $500, and an imprisonment of one year.[b]

The wilful destruction of a vessel at sea, or the conspiring to do it, either on shore or at sea, with the view of defrauding the underwriters, is also punishable by some of the state laws, so far as it falls without the jurisdiction of congress.

In Maine, the casting away or destroying a vessel within the state, with intent to defraud the underwriters, or aiding or abetting therein, is punished by imprisonment for life, or not less than five years, at the discretion of the court.

The fitting out of a vessel, or making out a false invoice of goods, or swearing to a false affidavit or protest, or procuring a false affidavit or protest for such a purpose, is punishable by a fine of $5000, or imprisonment not exceeding five years.[c]

In Massachusetts, the wilful destruction of a vessel within the state, with intent to defraud any person, is punishable by imprisonment for life, or a term of years.[d]

The equipment or fitting out a vessel with intent that she shall be cast away or destroyed, to defraud any owner or insurer, or aiding therein, is punishable by a fine of $5,000, and imprisonment from three to twenty years.[d]

The making out false invoices or other papers, with intent to defraud the underwriters, or the making out a false protest with such intent, is punishable by imprisonment of ten years, or by a fine of $5,000, and an imprisonment of two years.[d]

In Connecticut, any owner, officer, or mariner of a vessel, casting away or destroying her with intent to defraud the underwriters, or persons having goods on board, is punishable by imprisonment from seven to ten years.[e] Burning a vessel belonging to another is punishable in the same manner.[f]

In New-York, the wilful burning of vessels or goods, for the purpose of defrauding the owners or insurers, is punished with imprisonment in the state prison from seven to ten years.[g]

For wilfully burning a vessel in the day time, the imprisonment is from one to seven years.[g]

From some omission on the part of the legislature, the offence of conspiring, within the state, to cast away vessels for the purpose of defrauding underwriters, is punishable only as a misdemeanor.

In Delaware, the forcible or secret removal of a vessel from any of the waters of the state, is punishable by a fine of £500, and the offender is also responsible to the owner for damages.[h]

---

[a] Act, 31st Dec. 1792. [b] Act, 3d March, 1825, sec. 12. [c] Act, 27th Feb., 1821.
[d] Revised Statutes, 725. [e] Rev. Laws, 1825, tit. 21, sec. 24. [f] Ibid. sec. 32.
[g] 2 Rev. Stat. 667. [h] Act, 1782.

In Maryland, persons wilfully burning or stealing a vessel, are punishable by imprisonment of from two to twelve years.[a]

Conspiring or attempting to burn a public armed vessel, is punishable by death.[a]

In Georgia, if any person wilfully set fire to any vessel above the value of $200, alongside of any wharf, or at anchor in any river, or within any of its waters, or assist therein, he is fined not exceeding $1000, and imprisoned for a term not exceeding ten years.[b]

---

[a] Act, Nov. 1809. [b] Penal Code, 1817, sec. 209.

CHAPTER XIX.

SLAVE TRADE.

As this inhuman traffic has ceased to be a legal trade, it remains only to point out the penalties and punishments to which any American, who should so far forget his duty to his country and his God, as to engage in any manner in this commerce, will subject himself. To say nothing of the prohibitory acts of the provincial and state legislatures before the adoption of the constitution, so long since as 1794, citizens were prohibited, by congress, from fitting out vessels to carry on the slave trade under the penalty of $2,000; and owners of foreign vessels suspected of an intention of going to Africa to carry on the slave trade, were required, before clearance, to give sufficient security that no slaves should be taken on board of said vessels within nine months thereafter. In 1800, citizens and residents were prohibited from holding any right in vessels employed in this trade, on pain of forfeiting their right and double its value, and double the value of the slaves. The vessels, with their tackle and furniture, were made liable to forfeiture.

By the statute passed the 28th February, 1803, masters were prohibited from bringing into any state, whose laws forbid the importation thereof, any negro or mulatto, not a native, citizen, or registered seaman, under the penalty of $1,000; and the vessel cannot be admitted to entry. If any negro, &c. be landed, the vessel is forfeited, and a moiety is given to the informer.

Citizens of the United States, or foreigners residing within the United States, are prohibited from owning any part of a vessel engaged in the slave trade, under the penalty of forfeiture of the vessel and double the value thereof, and double the value of any slaves transported therein.[a]

Citizens of the United States, voluntarily serving on board of a foreign or American vessel engaged in the slave trade, were formerly subject to fine and imprisonment,[b] but now they are regarded as pirates, and suffer death.[c]

Of late years much attention has been attracted to this subject. By a statute of April 20, 1818, it is made unlawful to import or bring in any manner whatsoever into the United States, from any foreign country, any negro, mulatto, or person of colour, as a slave, or to be held to any service or labour, under penalty of forfeiture of the vessel.[d]

The second section of this act subjects to forfeiture any vessel, her tackle, apparel, furniture and lading, that is built, fitted, or loaded within the United States, or that sails from the United States for the

---

[a] Act, 10th May, 1800, sec. 1. [b] Ibid. sec. 2, 3. [c] Act, 15th May, 1820, sec. 4. [d] Ibid. sec. 1.

pose of procuring any negro, mulatto, or person of colour from any foreign country, to be transported to any port or place, to be held, sold, or otherwise disposed of as slaves.[a]

Persons building, fitting out, equipping, loading, or otherwise preparing or sending away, and causing it to be done, with intent to employ such ship or vessel in such trade or business, or any way concerned in aiding or abetting therein, severally forfeit a sum not ex-exceeding $5,000, and moreover may be imprisoned for a term not more than seven, nor less than three years.[b]

If anv citizen of the United States, or other person resident within the United States, take on board, or transport from any foreign country, or from sea, any negro, not being an inhabitant, nor held to service by the laws of either of the states or United States for the purposes aforesaid, he forfeits a sum not exceeding $5,000, nor less than $1,000, and moreover suffers a like imprisonment. Every vessel on board of which such negro, &c. may have been taken, forfeits her tackle, and the goods and effects found on board, or which have been imported therein, and every such vessel shall be condemned.[c]

It has been held, that this act prohibits the carrying of slaves on freight, even if the property of foreigners, and carrying them from one port in a foreign country to another.[d]

Sec. 5th prohibits any person from holding any right in such negro under any importer, or those claiming under him.

Sec. 6th subjects any person who shall sell such prohibited negro, &c. to a penalty of $10,000, and seven years' imprisonment.

If any person purchase or dispose of any negro, &c. for a slave, or to be held to service or labour, who shall have been imported or brought in any way from any foreign country, he shall forfeit and pay $1,000. This forfeiture does not extend to the seller or purchaser of any negro, &c. who may be sold by virtue of any regulations made by any legislature of any state.[e]

Sec. 8th lays the burden of proof upon the defendant, so that when he has been proved to be in possession of any person of colour, he must prove that he has not violated this act.

Sec. 9th provides that the offender may be prosecuted within five years after the offence.

These provisions were substituted in place of the six first sections of the act passed March 2d, 1807. The remaining sections of the latter act provides, that

Vessels found in any river, port, or bay, within the jurisdictional limits of the United States, or hovering on the coast, having on board any negro, &c. for the purpose of selling them as slaves, are to be forfeited, together with their tackle and goods on board.[f]

The president may employ armed vessels to cruise on any part of the coast, and instruct commanders of armed vessels to seize and bring in vessels found on the high seas contravening the provisions of this law. Masters of vessels seized are liable to prosecution, and to a

---

[a] Act, 15th May, 1820, sec. 2. [b] Ibid. sec. 3. [c] Ibid. sec. 4. [d] 9 Cranch, 403.
[e] Act, 15th May, 1820, sec. 7. [f] Act, 2d March, 1807, sec. 7.

fine not exceeding $10,000, and to imprisonment from two to four years. The proceeds of vessels, &c. seized, prosecuted, and condemned, are to be divided equally between the United States and the officers and men, and distributed as in the case of prizes. The officers and men thus entitled, are to keep safe every negro, mulatto, &c. and deliver them to persons appointed to receive them.[a]

Masters of vessels of less than forty tons burthen, shall not take on board, nor transport any negro, &c. to any port or place whatever, for the purpose of disposing of him as a slave, under the penalty of $800. But nothing in this section is to prohibit the transporting, on any river or inland bay of the sea within the jurisdiction of the United States, any negro, &c. not imported contrary to the provisions of this act.[a]

Masters of vessels, of the burthen of forty tons or more, sailing coastwise, and having on board any negro, &c. to be transported and sold as slaves, must make out and subscribe duplicate manifests of every negro, describing name, sex, age, and stature of each person of colour, whether negro or mulatto, and the names and residences of the owners, and deliver the manifests to the collector or surveyor. The master and owner must swear that the persons were not imported after the 1st of January, 1808, &c. and that under the laws of the state they are held to service or labour. The collector or surveyor is then to certify, grant a permit to proceed, &c.[b]

Vessels departing without the master's having made out and subscribed duplicate manifests of every negro, &c. on board, or taking on board any other negro than those specified in the manifests, may be forfeited, together with their tackle and apparel.[b]

The master forfeits $1,000 for every negro, &c. transported contrary to this act. A moiety of the forfeiture goes to the person prosecuting.[b]

The master of every vessel, of forty tons or more, sailing coastwise, and having on board any negro, &c. to sell or to be held to service or labour, arriving in any one port of the United States from another, must, before suffering any of the said negroes to go on shore, deliver the certified manifest, and swear to the truth of it. If the collector be satisfied, he is to grant a permit for the landing of the negro, &c.[c]

Masters neglecting or refusing to deliver the manifests, or landing any negro, &c. before delivering the manifests, forfeits $10,000.[c]

By the act of congress of March 3d, 1819, the president is authorized to employ the armed vessels of the United States on the coasts of the United States and of Africa, &c. to enforce the acts of congress prohibiting the importation of slaves.[d]

Vessels unlawfully engaged in the transportation of negroes, &c. may be seized and brought into port, and condemned.[d]

The proceeds of offending vessels are to be divided between the United States and the captors, whether armed vessels or revenue cutters.[d]

---

[a] Act, 2d March, 1807, sec. 8. [b] Ibid. sec. 9. [c] Ibid. sec. 10. [d] Act, 3d March, 1809, sec. 1.

Proviso: that the officers and men shall safely keep the negroes, &c. and deliver them to the marshal of the district.[a]

The officers and crews of offending vessels are to be taken into custody, and delivered to the civil authority.[a]

The president is authorized to make regulations for safe keeping, support, and removal out of the United States, of the negroes, &c. and may appoint agents on the coast of Africa to receive them [b]

A bounty of $25 for every negro delivered to the marshal, is to be paid to the captors by the secretary of the treasury.[c]

The district attorney is to prosecute by information, in the case of persons holding negroes unlawfully imported.[d]

Upon the verdict of a jury, the court is to direct the marshal to take the negroes into custody, subject to the orders of the president.[d]

Informers are entitled to a bounty of $50 for every negro so taken, besides the portion of penalties accruing to him.[d]

Vessels captured under the provisions of this act are to be sent into a port of the state or territory where they belong, if that can be ascertained, if not, then into any port.[e]

By a subsequent statute of May 15, 1820, it is declared piracy in American citizens to be in any way concerned in the slave trade.

Congress, too, since 1828, has been in the habit of making annual appropriations for the suppression of the slave trade.

American citizens engaged in the slave trade, either in foreign vessels, or in those belonging to citizens of the United States, are considered as pirates, and shall suffer death.[f]

They are guilty of the same crime, and liable to the same punishment, if they land on any foreign shore, and seize or decoy any negro or mulatto, not held to service by the laws of the United States, on board of any ship with intent to make him a slave; or if they in any way be aiding or abetting in forcibly detaining such negro or mulatto with that intent; or if they, on board of a slave ship, or on the high seas, or any where on tide water, offer to sell him as a slave, or land him with that intent.[g]

Regulations have also been made in the several states to prevent and punish the kidnapping of negroes and mulattoes.

By a statute of the legislature of the state of New-York, any person sending, or attempting to carry out of the state, any slave or servant, or aiding or abetting therein, (before proving, to the satisfaction of the mayor, recorder, or judge of the common pleas, that such slave was his property during the ten years preceding, and obtaining a license for that purpose,) is fined not more than $2,000, or he is imprisoned at hard labour in the states' prison from two to four years, or both, at the discretion of the court. Masters of vessels taking said slaves or servants to sea, without the license having been first proved, forfeit $500. If any person kidnap a negro, mulatto, or person of colour, with intent to carry him out of the state, or be aiding or abetting therein; or if a master of a vessel sell or dispose of

---

[a] Act, 2d March, 1807, sec. 1. [b] Ibid. sec. 2. [c] Ibid. sec. 3. [d] Ibid. sec. 4. [e] Ibid. sec. 5. [f] Act, 15th May, 1820, sec. 4. [g] Ibid. sec. 5.

such person, in any foreign place, he is fined as above, or imprisoned for not more than fourteen years.[a]

All slaves imported into the state become free; but if a slave secrete himself on board of a vessel while lying in the harbours of other states, the master, or his agent, may take him before the police magistrate in the city of New-York, and upon proof being made that such person of colour did secrete himself on board of said vessel, without the knowledge or consent of the master, they give him a a warrant to send or carry the slave back to the same port. This is to prevent the masters from becoming subject, when innocent, to the penalties of the laws of other states, prohibiting the exportation or kidnapping of persons of colour.[b]

Laws for the same purpose have been made in the other states with similar penalties: as kidnapping or the carrying away of negroes is punished in all the states with more or less severity.

In Connecticut, persons engaged in any manner in the slave trade, forfeit $170 for every slave, and $1,700 for every vessel in which they are concerned; and all insurance on such a trade is void.[c]

Any person importing a slave into a state, to be left therein, forfeits $350 for every one imported.[d]

In the states where slavery exists, there are also laws respecting the introduction of people of colour, whether free or slaves, which masters should become acquainted with, as heavy penalties are inflicted for their infraction.

In Delaware, the exporting or transporting, or decoying a slave from the state, with intent to sell him, or abetting therein, is punishable by a fine of $500, and the slave is declared free. A person, however, may remove from the state, and take his slave with him.

The importing a slave into the state, except where a person removes with his slaves into the state, is punishable by a fine of $100. The master of a vessel prepared for the exportation of slaves, and stationed in any waters within the state for such purpose, is liable to a fine of $1000.[e]

Masters of vessels exporting a slave, are liable to a fine of $500, and imprisonment from one to three years.[f]

In Maryland, masters of vessels suffering a slave to frequent or remain on board, forfeit 20s. for every hour such slave is on board.

They may, however, hire slaves to work on board from their owners.[g]

Persons importing, or transporting out of the state a free negro or mulatto, with the intent to sell him, forfeit $800, and in default of payment, are compelled to work on the roads five years.[h]

Masters importing any felon, convict, or slave, from a foreign country, knowing him to be such, or importing a negro or mulatto from a foreign country, with the intent to sell him as a slave, are liable to imprisonment from one to five years.[i]

In Virginia, masters of vessels carrying a slave out of the state,

---

[a] 1 Rev. Stat. 658. [b] Ibid. 659. [c] Rev. Laws, tit. 96, sec. 7. [d] Ibid. sec. 5.
[e] Act, 7th Feb., 1827, sec. 9. [f] Act, 19th Jan., 1826, sec. 4. [g] Act, October, 1753.
[h] Act, Nov., 1796. [i] Act, Nov., 1809, sec. 7.

without the consent of the owner, are punishable by a fine of from $100 to $500, and imprisonment of from two to four years, and are also liable to pay double the value of the slave; and they are deemed to be guilty, if such slave be carried away on board of their vessels.[a] A penalty of $500 is also incurred by transporting a negro or mulatto out of the state, without a magistrate's certificate. This is obtained by producing the negro or mulatto before the magistrate in a county adjoining the river where the vessel lies, and by depositing with the magistrate a description of his person, age, name, place of birth, and destination of the vessel, and also producing the certificate of his freedom, or the consent of his owner.[b]

Without doing this, the master of the vessel is liable to an action by the owner, in addition to the above penalty. Masters even permitting a slave to come on board of their vessels, without the written consent of the owner or overseer, or buying or receiving any thing from a slave, without such consent, forfeit $220. These penalties are recoverable by an attachment of the vessel, or any property of the master.[c] Bonds must be given where the vessel is attached, to pay any damages sustained by the owner, in case the plaintiff fail in suit.[d]

In Virginia, trading with slaves, without the consent of the owner or overseer, is punished by a fine of $20, or 39 lashes, and $10 in addition, if on Sunday.[e] Masters, importing a free negro or mulatto, forfeit $333 33. This does not extend to those employed on board.[f]

Free negroes.—In Virginia, masters bringing any free negro or mulatto into the state, are liable to be fined from $500 to $1000, and imprisoned from six to twelve months. This law does not extend to negroes, &c., employed on board; but such negro or mulatto is liable to arrest, and to 39 lashes, if found on shore without a pass. Masters receiving and harbouring a slave on board, or advising a slave to abscond, are liable to be imprisoned from two to five years. If a slave be found on board after the vessel has left her port, the master is presumed to be guilty. Justices of the peace are authorized to issue warrants to search the vessel for slaves. Double the value of the slave may be recovered against any person who aids in their escape.[g]

In North Carolina, masters of vessels carrying a slave out of the state, without the written consent of the owner, or permitting the same to be done on board their vessels, or concealing a runaway slave on board with intent to carry him off, are liable to capital punishment.[h]

Masters permitting a slave to be on board, between sunset and sunrise, or on Sunday, without a pass from his owner, or a justice of the peace, expressing the time and business for which he goes on board, are liable to a fine of £5 for the first, and £10 for the second offence.[i]

Masters, or any person belonging to a vessel, are liable to a penalty of £30, for trading with a slave without the permission of his owner.[j] If in the night time, the penalty is £50.[k]

---

[a] Rev. Laws, 1819, vol. 1, p. 428. [b] Ibid. 432. [c] Ibid. 443, 444. [d] Act, 24th Feb., 1827. [e] Rev. Stat. 426. [f] Ibid. 438. [g] Act, 11th March, 1834. [h] Act, 1779, c. 142. [i] Act, 1791, c. 335. [j] Act, 1788, c. 285, or Act, 1805, c. 690. [k] Act, Nov. 1819, c. 1001.

The transportation of slaves from the state of North Carolina, with the intention of enabling such slaves to effect their escape from their masters, is punishable with death.[a]

Five hundred dollars penalty is incurred by having a slave on board after the vessel has weighed anchor.[b]

Masters bringing free negroes, or persons of colour, into the state, must keep them on board, and take them away when they sail, under the penalty of $500.[c]

The delivery of any fire-arms, powder, or lead, to a slave, is punishable by fine and imprisonment.[d]

Trading in any manner with a slave, without the permit of the master, is punishable by a fine of $100.[e]

South Carolina—Slaves.—Any person trading or dealing with a slave, without a permit from his owner or overseer, is punishable by a fine of $1000, and twelve months' imprisonment, and he must keep the permit when he buys.[f]

Free negroes.—Free negroes are prohibited from coming into the state. Masters having free negroes or persons of colour on board, are required to give bonds in the sum of $1000, with sureties, to carry them away upon their departure; and on their refusal so to do, they are compelled to anchor one hundred yards from the shore, and to remain there until their departure, under a penalty of $1000, and six months' imprisonment. The negro or person of colour also is liable to be closely confined in gaol until the vessel sails, and is to be warned never to enter the state again.[g]

The master is bound to pay $2 to the justice who performs these services.[g]

A penalty of $100, too, is incurred by every master, by having such free negro or person of colour on board; and for the second offence, the penalty of $1000, and an imprisonment of six months.[g]

This act does not extend to public armed vessels of any nation; nor to free Moors, Lascars, or natives of countries beyond the Cape of Good Hope.[g]

In Georgia, the importing of slaves into the state is punishable by a fine of $500.

The carrying a slave out of the state without the consent of the owner, or the concealing or harbouring a slave, is punishable by fine and imprisonment. Also, the trading with a slave without the like consent.[h]

Passengers.—Within twenty-four hours after arrival, the master must report all persons of colour on board to the mayor, or other chief magistrate of the town, under penalty of $ 00. He must also give bonds to keep him on board after dark, and to carry him away with him.[i]

Louisiana—Slaves.—If a slave be transported out of this state without the owner's consent, his full value can be recovered of the owners of the vessel in which such slave is carried away; and the owner of the slave has a lien upon the vessel for the same, with damages. The suit, however, must be commenced within five years.[j]

---

[a] Act, 1832, chap. 9. [b] Sess. 1825, c. 1289. [c] Sess. 1830, c. 30. [d] Sess. 1828, c. 32. [e] Sess. 1826, c. 13. [f] Act, 18th Dec., 1817. [g] Act, 19th Dec. 1835. [h] Act, 23d Dec., 1833. [i] Act, 26th Dec., 1827. [j] Act, 26th March, 1835.

CHAPTER XX.

WRECKS.

Maine.—Commissioners of wrecks are appointed by the governor in the several counties, who give bonds, with securities, for the faithful performance of their duties.

Upon being informed that any wrecked property, to the amount of $100, is found, the commissioner must, forthwith, repair to it, and if no lawful claimant be present, must take charge of the same; and he may command any person to assist him. Penalty for refusing is $10. An inventory must then be taken of the property, and it is to be kept for the owner for one year, unless perishable, when it may be sold, after advertisement, in sixty days. Enough, too, may be sold at public auction to discharge the duties in thirty days. At the end of a year the remaining portion is sold, and the proceeds, after allowing a reasonable salvage, are to be paid into the state treasury.

In case the owner claim the goods before sale, he must allow salvage to the commissioner and those who assisted, and the amount, if they cannot agree, is to be settled by referees, mutually chosen, from whose decision an appeal may be made to the supreme court.

The commissioner may allow salvage to the amount of $50 to any person who saved goods previous to his arrival. Any person intermeddling with, or secreting wrecked property, except under the directions of the commissioner after his arrival, forfeits $1000.

The commissioner must, after the wreck, publish an account thereof, and of the goods found, in a newspaper, or forfeit $50.[a]

Massachusetts.—Sworn commissioners, who give bonds for the faithful discharge of their duty, are appointed by the governor in the several counties on the sea-board, whose duty it is to repair to the place where any wreck or shipwrecked property is, immediately upon receiving information thereof, and to take charge of the same; to make an inventory; and to deliver the property to the owner, or his authorized agent. For doing this, he is to be paid by the owner. If they cannot agree, the compensation is to be fixed by arbitration. If any person, unauthorized by the owner or commissioner, meddle with the property after the arrival of the commissioner, he forfeits $1,000.

The commissioners may call on all persons to assist them, and any person refusing forfeits $10.

Advertisement of the particulars of the shipwreck and of the goods, must be inserted in the nearest newspaper, under the penalty of $50. Within thirty days so much of the goods shall be sold as will pay

---

[a] Act, 27th Feb., 1821.

the duties; the remainder shall be kept one year, unless it be perishable, when it shall be sold, after sixty days' advertisement of the sale.

If no owner appear within one year, the inventory, or if sold, the account of sales, are to be handed to the state treasurer, and the proceeds paid over to him. The commissioner may be compelled to do this by action.[a]

Connecticut.—The selectmen of the town, and justices of the peace, are ex-officio wreck-masters, and it is their duty to aid in securing any property wrecked. Whenever any wrecked property is discovered on the coast, upon application being made to a justice of the peace, he must issue a warrant, calling forth the assistance required to secure the same. Notice is then given to a judge of the county court, who directs the sheriff to take and keep the property until the further order of the court. If no claimant appear, it is ordered to be sold after a year and a day, and if perishable, it may be sold sooner. The proceeds, after deducting all charges and salvage to be allowed by the court, are paid into the state treasury.

Enough may be sold to pay charges and salvage, if no claimant appear at any time after one month.[b]

New-York.—The sheriff, coroner, and the wreck-masters, in the maritime counties, are enjoined to aid and assist in saving and securing the cargoes of any vessel cast ashore, for which they shall have a reasonable salvage. If any person secrete any shipwrecked goods, or do not deliver them to the wreck-master within forty-eight hours, they forfeit treble the amount to the owner, and will be further punished by fine or imprisonment for the misdemeanor. The goods saved are to be kept by the sheriff, coroner, or wreck-master, for a year and a day, to be restored to the owner if he should call within that time, he paying expenses, &c. At the end of that time they are sold at public vendue, and the proceeds paid into the public treasury.

If property be perishable, the first judge of the county, upon a sworn petition proving the fact, may order it to be sold sooner. It may also be sold at the end of three months after a claimant appears, unless the salvage and expenses be paid. If the parties cannot agree as to salvage, the amount is to be ascertained by three disinterested freeholders, who are appointed by the county court. The salvage cannot exceed half of the property saved, and the fees of the appraisers, two dollars per day, form a charge upon the property. Notice of the sale must be published for two weeks in one or more of the newspapers in the city of New-York, and a description of all wrecked property in the hands of the wreck-master, with marks, brands, letters and figures, and the names of the vessel and master, must be published by the wreck-master in the same newspaper for four weeks. Any officer violating the wreck laws forfeits treble damages to the party, and is also guilty of a misdemeanor. Any person obliterating or defacing marks on wrecked property, or in any manner disguising its appearance, or destroying or suppressing any invoice or other document of the ownership of wrecked property, is

---

[a] Rev. Stat. 1834, chap. 57, tit. 14, pt. 1. [b] Rev. Laws, 1835, tit. 117.

guilty of a misdemeanor, and punishable by a fine of $2,000, and an imprisonment of three years.[a]

New Jersey.—Commissioners for each district on the seaboard are appointed by the courts of common pleas in the counties on the sea-coast, who give bonds, with two sureties, in a sum from $5,000 to $20,000, and are sworn to the faithful performance of their duty. Their duty is, upon application to them by the owner, or any other person having charge of a vessel or cargo cast on shore, or in danger thereof, to employ as many men as shall be agreed upon between him and the owner, or other person, to assist in the preservation of the vessel or cargo; which men are to be under the direction of the owner or person having charge of the said vessel or cargo.

The compensation of the commissioners, and persons employed by them, is to be settled by two freeholders, one chosen by the owner, the other by the commissioner, with power in them, in case of disagreement, to choose a third person, whose decision may be appealed from within fifteen days by the owner or person having charge of the vessel; and the court shall, at the next term, hear and decide thereon in a summary way.

Until this compensation is paid, or security given therefor, the property must remain in the possession of the commissioner. In case of appeal, the vessel and cargo may be released upon payment of the sum awarded to the commissioner, who must restore whatever may be taken therefrom, by the judgment of the court of common pleas. If the compensation be increased, judgment is given against the owner for the increase and execution issued.

The commissioners cannot dispose of any part of the cargo or vessel when there is any owner or insurer, supercargo, master, or agent present. They must make and subscribe an inventory of the property saved before it is removed, describing the numbers and marks on the packages and casks, and the kind of goods or liquors therein contained, if it can be done without injury to the goods, or unnecessarily breaking the packages, and the quantity thereof. This inventory is to be transcribed into a book, subject to be inspected by any person interested, and to be called for by the court of common pleas.

If any person, unauthorized by the commissioner, attempt to board any vessel in distress, without leave of the person having charge of her, or molest any person in saving the same, or wilfully deface any mark on any part of the cargo, before the above inventory shall be made, he forfeits $100 to the use of the owner; and if he do not pay the same within twenty days, he may be imprisoned for any time not exceeding six months.

If any goods, stolen or unlawfully taken from a wreck, be found in possession of any person, they shall be restored to the owner or his agent upon demand, and the person in whose possession they shall be found, shall be liable to pay double the value thereof.

Should no person be present to claim the property for the owner or insurer, the commissioner must take possession thereof, and make an inventory as above; which, together with a description of the ves-

---

[a] 1 Rev. Stat. 699.

sel, must be advertised for four weeks, in one or more newspapers in New-Jersey; and if the value of the goods exceed $500, in one newspaper in New York, and in another in Philadelphia, for the same time.

If no person claim them within a year, the same must be advertised at two or more places within the county, not less than ten nor more than twenty days; and afterwards sold at public auction. The proceeds, after deducting expenses and compensation, to be settled by a judge of the common pleas, are paid into the public treasury, to be kept for the owner for two years from the date of the first advertisement, deducting one per cent; after that time to go to the state. If the goods are perishable, they may be sold after being advertised at two places within the county, not less than five days.

If stranded goods are found, above the value of twenty dollars, information must be given to the commissioner of the district, for which the finder is allowed his reasonable expenses. If he conceal or convert the stranded goods to his own use, or does not give information as above within four days, he must pay to the commissioner double the value of the goods,—out of which the owner is entitled to be compensated for all the damage he may have suffered by reason of the conversion or failure to give information, in case he claim his property within a year from the judgment against the offender.

Persons stealing or embezzling stranded goods, forfeit double the value of the property stolen or embezzled, and are liable to be punished as in other cases of theft or receiving stolen goods.

If the commissioner be guilty of fraud, connivance, or wilful neglect, he must pay to the aggrieved party double the damage sustained, and be incapacitated from office.

If any person refuse to give assistance when required by the commissioner, he forfeits $5.

If any lights be put up for the purpose of decoying vessels into danger, the person so doing is fined not exceeding $1,000, or imprisoned not more than three years, or both.

No person related within the third degree to the person claiming compensation, and no person who has received compensation for saving any vessel or cargo within three years, is eligible to adjust the compensation as aforesaid.[a]

Persons assisting in preserving a vessel or cargo in distress, are entitled to salvage, which, when it has been ascertained by the arbitrators before mentioned, must be paid in cash, and not in a portion of the cargo. No commissioners can be interested directly or indirectly in such salvage, or in the purchase of any stranded or wrecked vessel or goods. The goods must be sold in such parcels as are likely to bring the best price; and any moneys unclaimed after the time prescribed by the act of March 3, 1820, must be paid over to the trustees of the school fund.[b]

Delaware.—Sheriffs, justices of the peace, and the custom-house officers, are all authorized to act as wreck-masters; with authority, when applied to in behalf of a vessel in distress, to summon men to

[a] Act, 3d March, 1820. [b] Act, 9th March, 1836.

aid her, and if any person refuse, he is liable to a penalty of £5. Masters of vessels riding at anchor near the vessel in distress, may be required by them to render assistance with all their spare hands and boats, under a penalty of £100, to be paid to the master or owner of the vessel in distress. All persons so assembled must obey the orders of the master of the vessel in distress, and in case of his absence, the sheriff—in his absence, the justice of the peace, and lastly, the custom-house officers.

Any person going on board without their orders, or hindering or molesting any one employed in the preservation of the vessel, or defacing the marks of goods saved, must within thirty days make double satisfaction to the party aggrieved, or be imprisoned at hard labour twelve months.

Persons pressing on board without leave, may be repelled by force. If no person appear to claim the goods saved from a wreck, an inventory must be made of them by the person finding them, and the goods and inventory delivered to a justice of the peace. If they are not claimed within one year, they are sold at public auction; and, if perishable, they are, after being advertised, sold forthwith. The proceeds, after deducting all charges, are paid into the state treasury, to be accounted for to the legal owner, who must obtain an order, after proving property, from the judges of the supreme court.

Persons plundering goods, &c. from a wrecked vessel, or assaulting, or hindering the escape of any person from a wreck, or showing false lights, or otherwise contriving to bring a vessel into danger, are punished as felons convicted of grand larceny. A justice of the peace is authorized, upon application being made to him, and upon affidavit, to grant a search warrant for wrecked goods, to take possession of the same wherever found, and to commit the offender to gaol for trial. Salvage is due to the wreck-masters, and other persons aiding in the preservation of wrecked goods; and in case of disagreement as to the amount, three freeholders are to be chosen by the owners and salvors to adjust it. Their award is binding, and the goods are liable for the salvage.

A wreck-master, or person acting under him, is liable in treble damages for an abuse of his trust.[a]

Maryland.—A wreck-master is appointed by the governor, who gives a bond and security to the amount of £1000, for the faithful performance of his duty on the sea-board.

His duty is, upon application made to him by any person in behalf of any vessel in distress, to proceed to her assistance with as many men as may be necessary; and if a vessel belonging to a citizen of Maryland be near, he may take such boats and men as can be spared from her, for the assistance of the vessel in distress, under a penalty, in case of refusal, of £100, to be paid by the master.

If no person claim the goods, the wreck-master must take possession of them, and make an inventory thereof, with a true description of the marks, numbers, and kinds of goods, which must be inserted for four

---

[a] Act, 2d Feb., 1786.

weeks in the Easton, Baltimore, and Philadelphia papers. If they are not claimed within three months, they are sold at public auction, (but, if perishable, they may be sold forthwith,) and the proceeds, after deducting expenses, &c. paid to the state treasurer for the benefit of the owners.

The compensation of the wreck-master is determined by the county court, or orphan's court, but is not to exceed twenty per cent. of the property saved.

The amount of salvage to be paid to those employed by him, is determined by an associate justice of the county in a summary way, upon the master's request, the parties having five days' notice of the time and place of trial. An appeal lies to the chief justice, if made within ten days, by whom it must be determined in thirty days. If the amount be not paid within thirty days after the decision, the wreck-master may sell as much of the cargo for that purpose as may be necessary.

If any person besides those authorized attempt to enter a vessel in distress, without leave of the master, or if any person molest and endeavour to hinder those employed in assisting her, or deface the marks of the goods before the wreck-master shall have made his inventory, he forfeits £50 to the owner; and in case of non-payment, is to receive thirty-nine lashes.

The commander or master may repel any such person by force. Persons in whose possession goods stolen or embezzled from a wreck shall be found, must deliver them to the owner, wreck-master, or the agent of one of them, upon demand, or pay four times the value.

If the wreck-master be guilty of fraud or negligence, he shall forfeit four times the damages to the party aggrieved, and be incapacitated.

If any person refuse or neglect to assist upon being summoned, he shall forfeit £10, and be liable to the same damages.

If any person make a hole in a vessel, steal a pump or goods from a vessel in distress, or wilfully do any thing tending to her immediate destruction, he shall suffer death.

The goods remain in the possession of the wreck-master until the expenses and salvage are paid or secured.[a]

The wreck-master is also authorized to hire labourers to aid him, and is entitled to salvage not exceeding 20 per cent., to be allowed by the county court, or orphan's court.[b]

Persons finding a boat or vessel adrift, must give notice to a justice of the peace, and advertise the same, under penalty of £2 10s.[c]

Virginia.—Two commissioners are appointed by the governor in each county on the sea-board, who each give bonds and security in the sum of £1000, Virginia currency, for the faithful performance of their duty. Their duty is, upon hearing of any vessel being stranded, or in danger thereof, to summon as many men as may be necessary, and to repair to the assistance of the said vessel. If any person besides those employed by the commissioners attempt to enter the vessel, he may be repelled by force, and he is liable to a penalty of

---

[a] Act, Nov., 1799. [b] Act, 3d Jan., 1807. [c] Act, Oct., 1753.

£10, or to be whipped. Any person molesting those employed in saving goods from the wreck, or any person defacing the marks upon the goods before an inventory is made, forfeits £10. In case any goods stolen or embezzled are found in the possession of any person, he forfeits treble the value thereof. Persons refusing to assist, when summoned by the commissioner, forfeit 25 shillings, and are liable also for treble damages to the owner. The goods saved are retained by the commissioner until the expenses and salvage are paid. If the owner and commissioner disagree as to the amount of compensation, the dispute must be submitted to the decision of two indifferent persons, chosen by the parties, whose decision shall be final.

If no person claim the goods, the commissioners take possession of them; make an inventory, with a true description of the marks, numbers, and kinds of goods, which shall be published four weeks in the state paper, or as it is called in the statute, the Virginia gazette. If the goods be not claimed within three months, they are sold at public auction, (if the goods be perishable, they may be sold immediately,) and the proceeds, after deducting charges, &c. paid into the public treasury for the use of the owner.

If any person wilfully contribute to the destruction of a vessel, or steal from a vessel in distress, he shall suffer death.

If commissioners be guilty of fraud, or wilful neglect, they shall pay treble damages, and be incapacitated from being a commissioner.[a]

If a vessel or boat be found adrift the finder must apply to a justice of the peace to have the same valued and advertised. At the end of a year and a day, if no claimant appear, it becomes the property of the finder.[b]

The penalty for taking away a boat or vessel without leave is $10, over and above all damages. The penalty is incurred by each person.[c]

North Carolina.—This state is divided into the following wreck districts, viz. Currituck county, 8 districts—1st, from the Virginia line to Judy's Cove; 2d, from do. to Caffey's inlet; 3d, from do. to Killyhank bay; 4th, from do. to New inlet; 5th, from do. to Ira Midgetts, and 6th, from Ira Midgetts to the Bald Beach, south of Chickamicomico; 7th, from do. to Cape Creek, near the light-house; 8th, thence to Carteret county line. Carteret county, 3 districts—1st, from the county line to Cedar inlet; 2d, thence to the old Topsail inlet; 3d, thence to Bogue inlet. Onslow county, 2 districts—1st, thence to New River inlet; 2d, thence to the New Hanover line. New Hanover county, 2 districts—1st, from the new Topsail inlet to Masenborough inlet; 2d, thence to New Brunswick county line. New Brunswick county, 2 districts—1st, from New inlet to Lockwood's Folly; 2d, thence to South Carolina line.

In each of these districts a wreck commissioner is appointed by the governor, who is sworn, gives a bond, &c. with two sufficient sureties, in the amount of $15,000, for the faithful performance of his duty. This commissioner must not be an officer of the United States.

---

[a] Act, 20th June, 1782. [b] Rev. Stat. 445. [c] Act, 7th Feb., 1819.

It is the duty of the commissioner, upon application made to him by any person on behalf of any vessel in danger of being stranded, to command a sheriff or constable to summon as many men as may be necessary for her assistance, who must obey the summons under the penalty of 40 shillings, and who are to be under the direction of the master or owner. Where there is an owner, consignee, supercargo, or captain present, the commissioner is to assist him as he may direct, for which he is to be paid over and above his salvage, and must not undertake to sell the property. For the services of the commissioner and men employed, they are paid within forty days, and in default thereof, the property saved remains in the custody of the commissioner. If the parties disagree as to the amount of the reward, it is determined by two indifferent persons, one to be chosen by each party.

If any person attempt to enter a vessel in distress, without being authorized by the commissioner, or by leave of the master or owner; or if any person molest them in saving the vessel or goods, or deface the marks or the goods before an inventory be taken, they shall forfeit £100 to the owner.

If any goods, stolen or carried from a wreck, be found upon any person, he must deliver them upon demand to the owner or commissioner, or the agent of one of them, or forfeit treble their value.

If no person be present to claim the property wrecked, the commissioner must take possession thereof, and make an inventory, with a true description of the marks, numbers, and kinds of goods, which shall be published in a public gazette eight weeks; and if the goods be not claimed within twelve months, they shall be sold. If perishable, they may be sold after advertisement in two places within the county, not less than ten nor more than twenty days. If the value thereof exceed $1000, the advertisement must be published in some newspaper and one other public place, except of such part as requires immediate sale. The proceeds, after deducting reasonable charges, must be paid to the clerk of the county for the owner. If the amount exceed the amount of the clerk's bond, then it must be paid to the clerk of the district where the vessel was stranded.

If the proceeds be not claimed within a year and one day, they shall be paid, after deducting one per cent., to the treasurer, for the use of the state.

If any person find stranded property, he must immediately give information thereof to the nearest commissioner, and deliver it to him, for which he receives reasonable salvage, to be ascertained as above. If he convert the same to his use, or fail to give information thereof within ten days to the nearest commissioner, he shall forfeit double its value.

If any person embezzle or steal any stranded property, or conceal it, knowing it to have been stolen, he shall forfeit double its value, and be liable to a prosecution as in cases of theft.

The commissioner is entitled to five per cent., in full, for all services in cases of wrecked or stranded property, where no owner appears.

If any commissioner be guilty of fraud, or wilful neglect, he shall pay treble damages to the party aggrieved, and be incapacitated.

The commissioner must advertise and sell the property at public auction, unless the captain, owner, supercago, or consignee, shall choose to superintend the sale himself, or to remove it without selling. The commissioner must record all sales, and deliver to the party concerned a true account thereof. He is entitled for the sale, &c. two and a half per cent. on the amount.[a]

Persons displaying false lights or beacons on the sea-coast, with intent to mislead vessels, are punishable by fine and imprisonment.[b]

South Carolina.—Any justice of the peace or militia officer is a wreck-master; and it is his duty, when a vessel is ashore, to notify another justice or officer, and call together a party of the militia, and to employ proper persons to aid in saving the property, and also to examine, upon oath, persons concerning the same. For this each wreck-master is allowed three dollars per day.

Where goods stranded have been concealed, the justice may issue a search warrant, and if the person having them refuse to deliver them on demand, he forfeits to the owner treble their value. Persons carrying away goods saved forfeit the same. Persons informing where such goods are concealed, so that they are recovered, are entitled to a salvage, not exceeding 25 per cent., to be adjusted by the next justice.

If any wrecked goods, unlawfully taken, be exposed for sale, the person to whom they are offered, or any justice or militia officer, may seize and hold them for ten days; if within that time proof be not furnished by the person offering them, of his rightful possession, they are, by order of the justice, delivered to the owner: five per cent. is to be paid to the person seizing them; and the person offering them for sale forfeits twice their value to the owner.

Persons not empowered attempting to come on board a vessel on shore, or interfering in her preservation, may be repelled by force; and any person assaulting or interrupting persons employed in saving effects from a wreck, are punished by fine and imprisonment, at the discretion of the court. Where goods of small value are stolen without violence, the offender forfeits treble the value to the owner, to be ascertained by a justice; but where persons plunder or destroy goods from a wreck, or where they do any act wilfully tending to the destruction of a vessel, they are liable to capital punishment.

Persons saving a vessel or goods, in the absence of the master, owner or mariners, and giving noticet hereof to a custom-house officer, or justice of the peace, or militia officer, are entitled to salvage; and in case of disagreement, the amount is to be settled by one or more justices, not exceeding three.

If no person appear to claim a vessel or goods cast on shore, the wreck-masters take possession thereof, and deliver the same to the

---

[a] Hayward, 668. [b] Act, 1831.

collector of the district, keeping a schedule thereof. The collector publishes the same in the newspapers for eight months, and if no claim be made within a year, they are sold at auction, (if perishable forthwith,) and the proceeds, after deducting charges, are paid into the state treasury, subject to the claim of the owner.[a]

Georgia.—Plundering from a wreck or vessel in distress, is punished by confinement at hard labour, for a term not less than one nor more than five years.

---

[a] Act, 1783.

CHAPTER XXI.

QUARANTINE LAWS.

By an act of congress, passed February 25, 1799, respecting quarantine and health laws, it is provided, that the quarantines and other restraints which shall be required and established by the health laws of any state, or pursuant thereto, respecting any vessels arriving in, or bound to, any port or district thereof, whether from a foreign port or place, or from another district of the United States, shall be duly observed by the collectors, and all other officers of the revenue of the United States, appointed and employed for the several collection districts of such states respectively, and by the masters and crews of the several revenue cutters, and by the military officers who command in any fort or station upon the sea-coast; and all such officers of the United States are authorized and required, faithfully to aid in the execution of such quarantines and health laws, according to their respective powers and precincts, and as they shall be directed from time to time by the secretary af the treasury. The secretary is authorized, when a conformity to such quarantines and health laws require it, and in respect to vessels subject thereto, to prolong the terms limited for the entry of the same, and the report or entry of their cargoes, and to vary or dispense with any other regulations applicable to such reports or entries: provided, that no state is thus enabled to collect a duty of tonnage or impost without the consent of congress thereto; and provided, that no part of the cargo be taken out, or unladen therefrom, otherwise than as by law is allowed, or according to the regulations hereinafter established. When, by the health laws of any state, or by the regulations made pursuant thereto, any vessel arriving within a collection district of such state, is prohibited from coming to the port of entry or delivery, by law established for such district, and it is required or permitted by such health laws, that the cargo of such vessel may be unladen at some other place within, or near to, such district, the collector authorized therein, after due report to him of the whole of such cargo, may grant his special warrant or permit for the unlading and discharge thereof, under the care of the surveyor, or one or more inspectors, at some other place where such health laws permit, and upon the conditions and restrictions which shall be directed by the secretary of the treasury, or which such collector may, for the time, reasonably judge expedient for the security of the public revenue: provided that, in every such case, all the articles of the cargo, so to be unladen, shall be deposited at the risk of the parties concerned therein, in such public or other warehouses or inclosures as the collector shall designate, there to remain under the joint custody of such collector, and of the owner or owners, or master, or other person having charge of such vessel, until the same be entirely unladen or discharged, and until the goods so deposited may be safely removed, without contravening such health laws; and when such removal may be allowed, the collector having charge of such goods may grant permits to the respective owners or consignees, their factors or agents, to receive all goods which shall be entered, and whereof the duties accruing shall be paid or secured, upon the payment by them of a reasonable rate of storage, which shall be fixed by the secretary of the treasury for all public warehouses and enclosures.

Suitable warehouses, with wharves and enclosures, are provided, where goods may be unladen and deposited for any vessel subject to a quarantine, pursuant to the health laws of any state as aforesaid, at such convenient place or places therein, as the safety of the public revenue, and the observance of such health laws may require.

When, by the prevalence of any contagious or epidemical disease in or near the place by law established as the port of entry for any collection or district, it shall become dangerous or inconvenient for the collector and the other officers of the revenue employed therein to continue the discharge of their respective offices at such port, the secretary, or in his absence, the comptroller of the treasury of the United States, may direct and authorize the removal of the collector and the other officers employed in his department, from such port to any other more convenient place within, or as near as may be, to such collection district, where such collector and officers may exercise the same authorities, and are liable to the same duties, according to existing circumstances, as in such lawful port or district: and of such removal, public notice must be given as soon as may be.

The above law refers to the several health laws of the different states, and, as far as they could be obtained, abstracts of their respective provisions are herein given.

In Maine, the health officers are appointed by each town. Masters having on board any person sick with a contagious disorder, must obtain permission in writing from the selectmen before they can bring their vessels up to a town, or before they suffer any person or thing to be landed, under the penalty of $200. The selectmen of each town are authorized, at their discretion, to establish quarantine regulations, which the pilots must make known to masters when they come on board. Persons violating these regulations forfeit $500, and may be imprisoned six months. The same punishment may be awarded to masters coming up to town, in violation of a quarantine, or for making false declarations as to the port or place from which they came. By refusing to answer questions touching the health of his crew, or the place from whence he came, $200 fine is incurred by the master.

A red flag must be hoisted at the main-mast head during the quarantine.[a]

In New-Hampshire, vessels arriving at Portsmouth with any person on board sick with any contagious or infectious disorder, or who has been so sick during the voyage, or having any goods on board which may be reasonably supposed to be infected, must notify the

---

[a] Act, 10th March, 1821.

selectmen, and go into such quarantine as they may direct. If the master permit any person or thing to be landed without a permit from the selectmen, he forfeits $400; and the person coming on shore is liable to be imprisoned thirty days. The goods so landed may be seized by the selectmen, and cleansed, at the expense of the owner.

Vessels arriving between the 15th of May and the 1st of November, from any place subject to the yellow fever, or any malignant contagious disorder, must be visited by the health officers; and if they, or any two of them, determine that the vessel, being at or near the town, would be injurious to the health of its inhabitants, she must go into quarantine for not exceeding thirty days.

Refusal to go into quarantine, or a violation of its regulations, subjects the owner and master to a penalty of $2,000, and the vessel may be taken to the quarantine ground by the health officers, at the expense of the owners.[a]

By a subsequent act, the health officers of Portsmouth were authorized to make quarantine regulations for that port, which being approved of by two justices of the peace, became law; and any violation thereof is punishable by a fine of $500, and an imprisonment of three months.

Any pilot taking a vessel up to town in violation of the quarantine regulations, forfeits his branch, and incurs a penalty of $100.

Any master attempting to evade the quarantine by false declarations as to his port of departure, or suffering any person or thing to be landed from his vessel without permission from the health officers, forfeits $500, and is liable to be imprisoned three months. A similar penalty is incurred by neglecting to comply with the directions of the health officers, as to purifying the vessel.

Any diseased mariner or other person, sent on shore at the place appointed by the said health officer for the reception and cleansing of the sick, is to be there kept, maintained, provided for, and cleansed, at his own expense, or that of his parents or masters, if able, otherwise at the charge of the town to which he belongs. In case such person have no legal settlement within this state, then at the charge of the state.

Every person who comes on shore from any vessel infected, or justly suspected to be so, or subject to, or ordered for quarantine, or performing it, or who leaves the place appointed for the sick, or for purification, not having obtained permission from the health officers, forfeits $100, or suffers three months' imprisonment, at the discretion of the court.

Vessels in quarantine must hoist a red flag of six feet in length at the head of the main-mast, in the day time, during the whole term of the quarantine, until said vessels be entirely cleansed.

If any person, without leave of the health officers, go on board any vessel performing quarantine, or go within the limits appointed by said officers, circumscribing infected persons and substances on shore,

---

[a] Act, 3d Feb., 1789.

he is considered as contaminated with infection, and held to undergo purification in the same manner as performing quarantine.

If any vessel attempt to pass the forts at New-Castle, after having been hailed and forbidden to pass, the commander is authorized to fire a shot ahead of the vessel; if she do not then come to, to fire another astern; and if she still persist in her attempt, to fire into her, until she bring to; and the master must pay to the commanding officer $5 for every shot so fired, before the vessel can leave the quarantine ground.

Massachusetts.—Any town may establish a quarantine ground, and the board of health in each seaport may make such quarantine regulations as they deem proper.

The board of health is chosen at an annual town meeting, and in case none be elected, the selectmen act as a board of health. In Boston, the common council forms the board of health.

The quarantine regulations extend to all persons and goods arriving in vessels subject to quarantine, and to all persons going on board; and any person violating them forfeits from $5 to $500.

Vessels suspected to be foul or infected, may be ordered by the board of health into quarantine, to be cleansed; and all persons on board handling the cargo, may be ordered to the hospital. All the expenses of the quarantine must be paid by the owner of the goods or vessel, or by the person on whose account they were respectively incurred.

Any master or person belonging to the vessel, refusing to answer, on oath, the questions of the health officer, relative to the health of the vessel, crew, or the port of departure, forfeits $200, and in default of payment is imprisoned six months.[a]

Rhode-Island.—The several town councils are *ex officio* boards of health, and are empowered to make all quarantine regulations. They may also appoint a sentinel to hail vessels, and to direct them to anchor within the quarantine limits, until visited by the health officer. By refusal so to do, a penalty of $20 is incurred, and the vessel may be ordered back to quarantine ground. Masters having, or who have had on board during the passage, any person sick with a contagious disorder, or who have come from a place where any contagious disorder prevailed, must not approach within one mile of any port or any public landing place, or suffer any person to come on board or to be landed without the license of the town council, under the penalty of $400 His colours, too, must be hoisted in his shrouds upon his first arrival.

Persons landing without a permit forfeit $40, and may be sent back to the vessel.

All persons sick with a contagious disorder are to be sent to the hospital, and all other persons to a suitable place to undergo quarantine.

Persons are put on board to take care of the vessel, and to cleanse and air such goods as require purification. These expenses constitute a lien on the goods.

---

[a] Rev. Stat. 1834, part I, tit. 9, c. 21.

Goods not requiring airing, are to be landed without delay.

Goods, landed without permission of the health officer and a certificate of health, are forfeited.

The town council allows the accounts of the quarantine officers, and the seamens' wages may be stopped to pay the charges of the town for any expense incurred in medical aid to them.[a]

Quarantine regulations for the town of Providence.

All vessels which arrive in the harbour of Providence on and after the first day of June, from any place, except from ports north of the forty-eighth degree of north latitude, and all vessels from any port in the United States, south of Chesapeake Bay, and including the port of Norfolk, notwithstanding they may have touched at any intermediate port during their homeward passage, having on board their original cargoes, or any part thereof: likewise, all vessels, with their officers, crew and passengers, that have touched or landed at the port of Norfolk, are not to pass the quarantine ground, which comprises that part of the harbour lying westward of the main channel of the river, and extending northward from Sassafras Point to the distance of one fourth of a mile from said point. The health officer may, on inspection and examination of such vessel, permit her to proceed up to the town.

No vessel coming from any port or place within the south of Europe, or within the Straits of Gibraltar, or from any port or place on the American continent situated between the tropics, including all the West India islands, and places in the Bay of Mexico, or from any other port where it is ascertained that contagious sickness hath recently prevailed, is permitted to unload at any of the wharves in this town. Such vessels, with their officers, crew and passengers, after having been subjected to all the regulations of quarantine to the satisfaction of the health officer, may, on a certificate obtained of him to that effect, be permitted to discharge their cargoes into scows or lighters, any where southward of the creek and west of the channel, and such craft may bring the same up to the town. Vessels laden with salt are not included in this decree, but may, on a certificate of the health officer to that effect, be permitted to unlade at the wharves in the town.

All vessels arriving at this port, after having discharged their cargoes in any other port of the United States, agreeably to the quarantine regulations of such port, must anchor at the quarantine ground, and be visited and examined by the health officer, and be subject to the provisions of the quarantine regulations.

All vessels, subject on their arrival at this port to be visited and examined by the health officer, which pass Fields' Point after 9 o'clock, P. M., must anchor on the quarantine ground, notwithstanding they may not have been hailed by the sentinel.

If any officer of the customs, or any other person, go on board of

---

[a] 1 Rev. Laws of 1822, p. 261, 264.

any inward bound vessel, or put any person or persons on board of any vessel that is subject to quarantine, such officer, person or persons, so going or put on board, shall not be permitted to land in the town until the time of the quarantine of such vessel shall have expired.

No untanned hides, skins, horns, or any other article whatsoever, that may be thought by the health officer capable of generating disease, can be landed from any vessel whatever within the limits of the town, during the existence of the quarantine, without a permit therefor first had and obtained of the board; nor can any vessel having sickness on board, or having had any person sick of a malignant or contagious disease during the voyage, be permitted to come to any wharf in the town within twenty-five days after being unladen and properly cleansed, which time is considered to commence from the date of a certificate to that effect from the health officer: nor then during the existence of the quarantine, except to the wharves at Fox Point, or India Point, under special permission from the board.

If the captain or commanding officer on board of any vessel arriving at the port of Providence, and subject to quarantine, refuse to answer any or all interrogatories or inquiries put to him by the health officer, or evade such inquiries, or in any way or manner make, or cause to be made to the said health officer, a false or equivocal statement or report relative to the officers, crew and passengers on board thereof, or of the state of the health of all or any of the officers, crew and passengers, or neglect to report to the said health officer any death that may have occurred on board during the said voyage, or refuse to sign the written examination of such captain or commander, taken at the time by said health officer, after being requested so to do, such captain or commander, so offending, forfeits not exceeding $300, nor less than $100.

If any person ordered to the hospital from on board of any vessel arriving at the port, or from any part of the town, refuse to go thither, or being there, depart from or leave the limits of said hospital without permission first obtained from the board, or from the health officer, in writing, such person, for each offence, forfeits not exceeding $100, nor less than $20.

The following rules and regulations must be observed on board of all vessels while at quarantine:

1st. All vessels must, during their quarantine, wear colours in their shrouds.

2d. No provisions, spiritous liquors, or other articles, can be admitted on board of such vessels without permission from the health officer.

3d. The health officer, on all occasions, must direct what goods shall be delivered from on board such vessels, the places where, and the manner in which they shall be landed.

4th. No boat, except the health officer's, can be permitted to go alongside of any such vessel, nor to lie at anchor, or to remain in any other manner within one hundred yards of them.

5th. Such vessels must be removed and stationed at such places as the health officer may, from time to time, under the direction of this board, direct and appoint.

6th. The bilge water must be pumped from such vessel at least twice a day, until the water, so pumped, shall be free from offensive smell.

7th. The direction of the health officer for cleansing the vessel, clothing and other things on board, must be strictly complied with by the officers and crew.

8th. The commanders of such vessels are answerable for all irregularities and breaches of these regulations by the people on board.

9th. All permissions and directions of the health officer, as aforesaid, must be in writing.

If any person be guilty of a breach of the foregoing orders and regulations, such person incurs a penalty not exceeding the sum of $200, nor less than $10, at the discretion of the court.

Connecticut.—The civil authority and selectmen of the several towns have authority to constitute a board of health in their respective towns, who may examine into nuisances on board of vessels or in other places, and cause the same to be removed, and make orders to prevent the same. The violation of their orders is punished by a fine of not less than $15, nor more than $100.

Between 1st June and 1st November, the board of health of any town may compel vessels from any foreign port, or any port south of the capes of the Delaware, to perform quarantine, unless they have a clean bill of health from a port north of Delaware. Masters, in such case, upon coming near the place assigned for quarantine, must make a signal for a health officer, by hoisting a flag in the shrouds, or, if necessary, may send a person on shore to notify the health officer of his arrival. This person, however, must return forthwith on board, under a penalty of $50.

The health officer must forthwith examine the vessel, and if necessary, he orders it into quarantine; and any violation or neglect of the quarantine is punished by a penalty of not more than $500, and imprisonment of not more than six months.

False declarations, with a view of avoiding quarantine, are punished in like manner.

The health officer may direct the vessel to be cleansed and purified, and the passengers to be secluded on shore for four days, and persons sick of a contagious disorder to be removed to the hospital.

Vessels from ports north of Delaware Capes may also be subjected to quarantine, after three days' printed notice of such regulation.

Fees of health officers for visiting vessels cannot exceed $5.

Other vessels may be ordered into quarantine at the discretion of the board of health.

Persons violating or attempting to elude quarantine, and masters anchoring elsewhere than at the quarantine ground, or making false declarations as to the port of departure, or permitting any person or thing to be landed, or any person to enter their vessel before examination, are punishable by a fine of from $100 to $500, and imprisonment of six months.

Persons breaking quarantine forfeit $100.[a]

---

[a] Rev. Laws, tit. 94.

Whenever any certificate of health has been given for any cargo, vessel or person, if the board of health, on examination, find that the same was obtained by fraud, or any false or unfounded representation, or be of opinion that such vessel, person or cargo should perform further quarantine, on notice thereof being given to such person, or to the owner, master, supercargo or consignee of such vessel or cargo, as the case may be, the same is liable to be proceeded with in the same manner as if no certificate of health had been given.

Quarantine laws of the state of New-York.

The board of health in the city of New-York, of which the mayor is president, is appointed by the common council.

The health officer, president, physician, and health commissioner of the city, are the commissioners of health.

The health officer may appoint an assistant, who may perform all the duties required of the health officer.

The health officer is entitled to the following fees for visiting and examining vessels.

For each vessel from a foreign port, $6 50.

For each vessel from a place in the United States south of Cape Henlopen, if above 160 tons, $3; if not exceeding 160, and above 100 tons, $2; if below 100 tons, $1.

All such fees must be paid by the masters of vessels.

The board of health must appoint an inspector of vessels, who is entitled to the following fees:

For each cargo inspected by him under the direction of the board of health, $3.

For each vessel cleansed and purified by him under the like direction, $5.

Which fees must be paid by the owner or consignee of the cargo inspected or vessel purified.

The anchorage place for vessels at quarantine must be as near as may be to the marine hospital on Staten Island, and is designated by buoys, to be fixed under the direction of the health officer; and every vessel subject to quarantine must anchor within them.

Every vessel subject to quarantine, must, immediately on her arrival, proceed to, and anchor at, the place assigned for quarantine; and remain there with her officers, passengers and crew, during her quarantine, subject to the regulations of quarantine.

Vessels arriving in the port of New-York are subject to quarantine, as follows:

1. All vessels from a foreign port, having forty or more passengers, or on board of which, during the voyage, or whilst at the port of departure, any person shall have been sick, arriving between the first day of April and the first day of November, in any year.

2. All vessels arriving between the thirty-first day of May and the sixteenth day of October, from any place, in the ordinary passage from which they must pass to the south of Cape Henlopen.

3. All vessels from any place (including islands) in Asia, Africa, or the Mediterranean, or from either of the West Indies, Bahama, Bermuda, or Western Islands, or from any place in America, in the ordinary passage from which they must pass south of Georgia, arriving between the first day of April and the first day of November, in any year.

4. All vessels from any place, where yellow, billious malignant, or other pestilential or infectious fever existed at the time of their departure, or on board of which, during the voyage, any case of such fever shall have occurred, arriving between the first day of April and the first day of November, in any year.

5. All vessels, which, if they had arrived direct from their foreign port of departure, would have been included in the fourth class, that arrive at any place in the United States or British North America, and proceed thence to the port of New-York, between the first day of June and the first day of October, in any year. Penalty for violation, $2,000, or twelve months' imprisonment.

Every vessel included in the first two classes, are subject to such length of quarantine, and other regulations, as the health officer may designate and enjoin.

Every vessel included in the third class, which may arrive between the thirty-first day of May and the first day of October, in any year, must remain at quarantine for two days, and for such further period as the health officer shall deem expedient; but vessels from Canton and Calcutta are excepted, unless they have been at some place in the West Indies, or in America, south of St. Mary's, in Georgia, and north of the equator, or on the continent or islands near the continent of Africa, after the fifteenth day of May, in the year of their arrival. Penalty for neglect, $2,000, or twelve months' imprisonment.

Every vessel in the fourth class, which may arrive within the days mentioned, and every vessel in the fifth class, must remain at quarantine for at least thirty days after her arrival, and in all cases, at least twenty days after her whole cargo has been landed, and perform such further quarantine as the health officers shall prescribe.

All vessels subject to a regular quarantine, if navigated by steam, are subject only to such length of quarantine, and other regulations, as the health officer shall enjoin. Penalty for neglect $2,000, or twelve months' imprisonment.

The quarantine of vessels subject thereto, where no period of regular quarantine is prescribed, is limited by the direction of the health officer: but, unless under special circumstances, and with the sanction of the board or commissioners of health, it cannot exceed the time requisite for a due examination of the vessel and cargo.

Every vessel arriving in the port of New-York coastwise, after the first day of June, which has been to the West Indies, or America, south of Georgia, is subject to the same regulations as are imposed on such vessels under similar circumstances that have arrived direct at the port of New-York. Penalty for neglect, the same.

The mayor of the city of New-York, or the board or commissioners of health, whenever in their judgment the public health may require it, may order any vessel at the wharves of the city, or in its vicinity, to the quarantine ground, or other place of safety, and may require all persons, articles or things, landed or introduced into the city from such vessel, to be seized and returned on board, or removed to the quarantine ground. In case the master, owner or consignee of the vessel cannot be found, or shall refuse or neglect to obey the order of removal, the mayor, or the board of health, has power so to remove the vessel, at the expense of such master, owner or consignee. Penalty for neglect, $2,000, or twelve months' imprisonment.

No vessel nor person so ordered out can return to the city, without the written permit of the board of health, the mayor, or the commissioners of health, under the like penalty.

If any vessel arriving at the quarantine ground, be bound to some port eastward of the city of New-York, and beyond this state, the health officer, after having duly visited and examined her, may permit her to pass on her voyage through the sound; but no such vessel can, in that case, be brought to anchor off the city, nor can any of her crew or passengers land in, or hold any intercourse or communication with the city, or with any person therefrom.

It is the duty of each pilot belonging to the port to use his utmost endeavours to hail every vessel entering the port, and to demand of the master whether any person has died or been sick on board during the passage, and whether any pestilential fever existed, at the time of her sailing, at the port whence she sailed.

If any of the above questions be answered in the affirmative, the pilot must immediately give notice to the master, that he, his vessel, crew, passengers and cargo, are subject to the examination of the health officer; and must direct him to proceed and anchor his vessel at the quarantine anchorage, to await the further directions of the health officer.

It is the duty of every pilot who conducts into port a vessel subject to quarantine—

1st. To bring such vessel to anchor within the buoys marking the quarantine anchorage.

2d. To prevent any vessel or boat from coming alongside of the vessel under his charge, and to prevent any thing on board from being thrown into any other vessel or boat.

3d. To present to the master of the vessel a printed copy of the quarantine laws.

4th. To take care that no violations thereof be committed by any person on board, and to report such as may be committed, as soon as may be, to the health officer.

The health officer must board every vessel subject to quarantine immediately on her arrival, and make strict search and inquiry into the health of the officers, crew and passengers, and into the state and condition of the vessel and cargo.

In the discharge of this duty, he may put all such questions to the persons on board as he shall judge necessary and proper to enable him to ascertain the condition of the vessel, and the length of quarantine to which she ought to be subjected; and the persons to whom such questions may be put, must, if required, answer the same under oath, which the health officer is authorized to administer.

Every vessel subject to a regular quarantine of two days, must, during its quarantine, be thoroughly ventilated and cleansed, and the clothing and bedding of the crew and passengers well washed and aired. Penalty for neglect $2000, or twelve months' imprisonment.

Captains and passengers arriving from healthy ports and in healthy vessels, subject to a quarantine of two days, may, on their arrival, be permitted to come into the city, without any baggage.

The master, owner or consignee of every vessel subject to a regular quarantine of thirty days, must, forthwith, upon the requisition, and under the direction of the health officer, cause such vessel to be unladen, cleansed and purified. Penalty for neglect $2000, or twelve months' imprisonment.

Every vessel last mentioned, must, during her quarantine, be at least three times thoroughly whitewashed in every part of the inside, except such parts as have been painted or varnished, which must be purified as the health officer shall direct; and such vessel must be fumigated with mineral acid gas, when required by the health officer. There must be an interval of at least four days between each whitewashing, and when the weather permits, wind-sails must be kept in each hatchway of the vessel. Penalty for neglect $2000, or twelve months' imprisonment.

When the regular period of quarantine has expired, if the health officer judge the vessel clean and free from infection, the board of health may release the vessel from quarantine.

It is the duty of the health officer to cause the cargo of every such vessel to be landed at the quarantine ground, or at some other suitable place out of the city, and there to be properly ventilated and cleansed, for at least twenty days. Penalty for refusing to obey $2000, or twelve months' imprisonment.

From such ventilation and cleansing, alum, chalk, coals, distilled, expressed and fermented liquors, drugs and medicines, dye-woods, glass, stone and earthenware, fruit in a sound state, honey, ivory, lignumvitæ, mahogany, metallic substances, marble, oils, paints, resin, salts, spices, syrups, tar, turpentine, turtle-shell, wax, and such other articles of the cargo as may be sufficiently purified by washing with water, or are not liable to retain infection, are excepted.

No other articles can be conveyed to the city without the permit of the board of health, which cannot be given, until the health officer or some special agent shall have reported that such cargo is free from infection. Penalty for violation $2000, or twelve months' imprisonment.

None of the officers, passengers or crew, can proceed to the city, until fifteen days after the sailing of the vessel from her foreign port of departure, nor until fifteen days after the last case of infectious fever that shall have occurred on board, nor until ten days after landing at quarantine. Penalty for violation $2000, or twelve months' imprisonment.

The health officer, if he judge it necessary, may cause any bedding or clothing on board a vessel subject to quarantine, or any portion of her cargo that he may deem infected, to be destroyed.

If there be any West India merchandise, other than articles enumerated, on board of any coasting vessel subject to quarantine, the health officer, except in cases hereafter mentioned, must order it to be landed for purification, at the quarantine ground, subject to his orders, or if not landed at the quarantine ground, to those of the mayor and commissioners of health. Penalty for neglect of this provision $500, or six months' imprisonment.

The landing of such merchandise from such vessel is not required, if the master exhibit satisfactory proof that it is free from damage, and has been landed in the United States or some British port of North America more than twenty days; or that the port in the West Indies where it was shipped was healthy at the time of such shipment, and that the vessel in which it was imported was also healthy from the time of her departure from the United States or British port of North America until her return. Penalty for neglect of this section $500, or six months' imprisonment.

All rags, hides and skins, arriving in vessels subject to the examination of the health officer, between the 31st day of May and the 1st day of October in any year, must be discharged at the quarantine ground: and if the health officer, on examination, find the articles so discharged to be sound, he may grant a permit for their removal to those parts of the city where their entry is permitted, unless they arrived under the circumstances next mentioned; but he may retain such articles until they have been cleansed or purified, or until, in his judgment, they may be removed with safety.

All cotton, all the articles enumerated in the last preceding section, and all other articles likely to imbibe and retain infection, must be detained at the quarantine ground or at some other suitable place without the limits of the city, until the first day of November, if they arrive be-between the 31st day of May and 1st day November, in any vessel on board of which any person has been sick of any infectious fever during the time the cargo was on board, or which shall have brought such articles from a port where such fever existed at the time of, or shortly previous to their shipment.

The health officer, the board of health, or the mayor and commissioners of health, may permit such articles to be shipped for exportation by sea, or transportation up the North or East rivers, in any vessel, which shall not approach whilst loading, or when loaded, nearer than three hundred yards to the wharves of the city.[a]

All articles arriving in vessels subject to quarantine, whose exportation by sea, or transportation up the North or East rivers, and which may, without danger to the public health, be shipped from the wharves of the city of New-York, may, by permission of the board of health, or the mayor and commissioners of health, be brought to the city of New-York for the above object.[b]

---

[a] Rev. Stat. part 1, chap. 14. [b] Act, 2d May, 1836.

If any vessel subject to quarantine of less than thirty days, and laden in whole or in part with cotton of the United States, have on board any sick person, the character of whose disease cannot be immediately ascertained, the health officer may detain such vessel and cargo at quarantine for a term not exceeding ten days; and if in his opinion the disease of such sick person be not of a malignant nature, he may either release the vessel and cargo from quarantine, or detaining the vessel, may permit the cotton to be sent directly to the city of New-York, or to be put on board of any vessel at the wharves of the city for exportation.

Every vessel subject to quarantine must be designated by colours, to be fixed in a conspicuous part of the main shrouds of the vessel until the expiration of her quarantine, under the penalty of $50, and $3 per hour.

No boat from any outward or inward bound vessel can land at the quarantine ground after sunset; nor can boats of any description, at any time, pass through the range of vessels lying at quarantine, without the permission of the health officer, under the penalty of $50.

No lighters can be employed to load or unload vessels at quarantine but by the permission of the health officer, and subject to such restrictions as he shall impose.

No vessel subject to quarantine can approach the city of New-York beyond the place assigned for quarantine, without a written permit from the health officer.

The health officer, whenever he shall deem it expedient, may require any person placed under quarantine to execute a bond, with such sureties as he may approve, to the commissioners of health and their successors in office, in the penalty of not less than $500, nor more than $2000, that the person executing it shall not, during his period of quarantine, approach nearer the city-hall in the city of New-York than the distance of three miles, except in passing the city by water, and that he shall not go into any city or town of the United States, in violation of the quarantine laws thereof.

All passengers placed under quarantine, who are unable to maintain themselves, must be provided for by the master of the vessel in which they arrived.

If the master omit so to provide for them, they must be maintained on shore, and the expense of their maintenance charged to their vessel.

The health officer, upon the application of the master of any vessel under quarantine, may direct to be confined, in some suitable place on shore, any mate or mariner on board, who shall have committed an offence punishable by the laws of this state or of the United States, and who cannot be properly secured for punishment on board of his vessel. Such confinement shall continue during the residue of the quarantine of the offender, or until he shall be proceeded against in due course of law; and the expenses of maintaining the offender shall be charged and paid in the same manner as the expenses of maintaining poor passengers.

All vessels and persons remaining at quarantine on the first day of October, are subject only to such quarantine and restrictions as vessels and persons arriving on or after that day.

The master of every vessel released from quarantine, and arriving at the city of New-York, must, within twenty-four hours after such arrival, deliver the permit of the health officer at the office of the mayor and commissioners of health, or to such person as they shall direct.

No vessel subject to a regular quarantine of two days, unless she sailed from some port in the West Indies, or in America south of Louisiana, and north of the equator, or from some port in the United States south of Georgia, before the first day June in the year of her arrival, can, when released from quarantine, approach within three hundred yards of that part of the island of New-York which lies southward of Bank-street on the North river, and of Eighth-street on the East river, until after the first day of October in the year of her arrival, unless by virtue of a special permission to be granted by the board of health, or the mayor and commissioners of health; which permission shall not extend to embrace any time between the first day of June and first day of September in the year of her arrival, unless under the circumstances following:

If such vessel came from any place in the Mediterranean, in Asia, in America south of the equator, or from the Madeira, Canary, Cape de Verd, Western Bermuda, or Bahama islands, the mayor and commissioners of health may, by a special permission in writing, direct her to be hauled to a wharf south of the bounds so prescribed; and in their discretion may first order her cargo, or any portion thereof, to be unloaded, subject to their orders and regulations. Penalty for violating these provisions $2,000, or twelve months' imprisonment.[a]

If any coasting vessel, subject to a regular quarantine of two days, be wholly laden with lumber or timber, the mayor and commissioners of health may permit her cargo to be discharged at any wharf they shall designate. The vessel is to be properly cleansed after discharging, and a report thereof made to the mayor and commissioners, who order her to a wharf specified, and to remain there until October, or the offender incurs a penalty of $2,000, or twelve months' imprisonment.

All vessels wholly loaded with salt, being healthy and from healthy ports, may be permitted to unload in the same manner.[a]

Any vessel regularly employed in trading to one port or island in the West Indies, or America south of Georgia and north of the equator, for the period of twelve months' immediately preceding her arrival at the port of New-York, and the port or island being free from any infectious fever, as well as the crew and passengers, and having performed her regular quarantine of two days, and been properly ventilated, and permitted by the health officer to proceed to the stream three hundred yards from the city, may be permitted by the mayor and commissioners of health to come to the wharf with her cargo on board, on and after the first day of October.

Any new vessel, or any other vessel not employed before in the West India or southern trade, south of Georgia, is subject to the same

---

[a] Act, 2d May, 1836, and Rev. Stat. part 1, chap. 14.

regulations, if employed in such regular trade, although for less than one year, provided she is in all other respects similarly circumstanced, and the same penalties are incurred.

All vessels from the West India islands, and America south of Georgia and north of the equator, being healthy and from healthy ports, after performing two days' quarantine, and being properly ventilated, and being permitted by the health officer to come to the stream three hundred yards from the city, may, after their cargoes have been discharged, and the vessel cleansed and purified, be permitted by the mayor and commissioners of health to come to such wharf as they may designate, to receive their outward cargoes, at any time after the first of October.

If any vessel subject to a regular quarantine of two days, arrived from any place in the West Indies, or in America south of Georgia and north of the equator, or from any place on the continent or the islands near the continent of Africa; or have been at any of these places after the fifteenth day of May, in the year of her arrival, no portion of her cargo can be brought into the city before the first day of October, until it has been inspected, unless by a special permission, in writing, of the mayor and commissioners of health. Penalty for violation $2,000, or twelve months' imprisonment.

When such inspector has made his report to the mayor and commissioners of health, they may direct such cargo, or any part thereof, to be brought into the city, subject to such regulations as they may prescribe, or may order it to be landed at some suitable place out of the city, there to be detained at least twenty days and properly ventilated, and then to be brought into the city, subject to their regulations. Penalty for neglect $2,000, or twelve months' imprisonment.

No vessel subject to a regular quarantine of thirty days, when permitted to proceed, can approach within three hundred yards of the city of New-York, between the first day of June and the first day of October in the year of her arrival, unless permitted by the board of health, or the mayor and health commissioners, in the manner prescribed for vessels subject to two days' quarantine. Penalty for violation $2,000, or twelve months' imprisonment.[a]

No cargo or part of the cargo of any vessel, on board of which, during her voyage, a case of any pestilential fever has occurred, can be brought into the city of New-York between the first day of June and the first day of November, except by the permission, in writing, of the board of health, under a penalty of $2,000, or twelve months' imprisonment.

No vessel arriving from any place in the United States north of Cape Henlopen, or in British North America, between the thirty-first day of May and the first day of October in any year, having on board West India produce or merchandise, can approach within three hundred yards of the island of New-York, southward of the bounds before, in this article, prescribed, until permitted by the mayor and commissioners of health, and health officers. Penalty for neglect of this section $500, or six months' imprisonment.

---

[a] Act, 2d May, 1836.

If the master of any such vessel exhibit, to the mayor and commissioners of health, such satisfactory proof that the vessel and port of departure are healthy, they may permit the vessel to be hauled to any wharf of the city, and such produce or merchandise may be there landed; otherwise it must be sent to some suitable place out of the city for purification, subject to their regulations. Penalty for neglect $500, or six months' imprisonment.

No person who shall have been one of the crew, or a passenger, in any vessel, at whatever place arriving, on board of which any person shall have been sick of any pestilential fever, can enter the city of New-York, until fifteen days after the last case of such fever that occurred on board such vessel, under the penalty of $50.

No person can bring into the city of New-York any clothing, bedding, or merchandise, that shall have been on board of any such vessel, until such article shall have been cleansed and purified; and all such articles brought into the city, contrary to this section, may be seized and sold by the commissioners of health, for the use of the marine hospital, and a penalty of $50 is incurred.

The mayor of the city of New-York, or the president, at the time, of the board of health, may issue his proclamation, declaring any place where there shall be reason to believe a pestilential or infectious fever actually exists, to be an infected place, within the meaning of the health laws of this state.

Such proclamation must fix the period when it shall cease to have effect; but such period, if they shall judge the public health to require it, may from time to time be extended by the board of health, and notice of such extension must be published in one or more of the newspapers of the city.

After such proclamation has been issued, all vessels arriving in the port of New-York from such infected place, are subject to a quarantine of at least thirty days, and, together with their officers, crews, passengers and cargoes, to all the provisions, regulations and penalties, in relation to vessels subject to a similar quarantine.

The board of health may, in their discretion, prohibit or regulate the internal intercourse by land or water, between the city of New-York and such infected place; and may direct, that all persons who shall come into the city of New-York, contrary to their prohibitions or regulations, shall be apprehended and conveyed to the vessel or place from whence they last came; or, if sick, that they be conveyed to the marine hospital, or such other place as the board of health shall direct.

Every master of a vessel subject to quarantine, arriving in the port of New-York, who refuses or neglects—

1. To proceed with and anchor his vessel at the place assigned for quarantine, at the time of his arrival.

2. To submit his vessel, cargo and passengers, to the examination of the health officer, and to furnish all necessary information to enable that officer to determine to what length of quarantine and other regulations they ought respectively to be subject.

3. To remain with his vessel at quarantine during the period assigned for her quarantine; and whilst there, to comply with the directions and regulations of this chapter, and with such as any of

the officers of health, by virtue of the authority given to them in this chapter, shall prescribe in relation to his vessel, his cargo, himself, or his crew; or who proceeds to the city with his vessel without permission, or who neglects to deliver his permit to proceed to the mayor for twenty-four hours:

Shall be considered guilty of a misdemeanor, and punished by fine or imprisonment; the fine for each offence not to exceed $2,000, nor the imprisonment twelve months.

Every master of a vessel hailed by a pilot, who shall either—

1. Give false information to such pilot relative to the condition of his vessel, crew, passengers, or cargo, or the health of the place or places whence he came, or refuse to give such information as shall be lawfully required.

2. Or land any person from his vessel, or unlade or transship any portion of his cargo before his vessel shall have been visited and examined by the health officer.

3. Or shall approach with his vessel nearer the city of New-York than the place of quarantine to which he shall be directed:

Shall be considered guilty of the like offence, and for each offence shall be fined in a sum not exceeding $500. And every person who shall land from any such vessel, or unlade or transship any portion of her cargo, under the like circumstances, shall be considered guilty of the like offence, and be subject to the like penalty.

Every person who shall oppose or obstruct the health officer in performing the duties required of him in this title, shall be considered guilty of a misdemeanor; the fine for each offence not to exceed $500, nor the imprisonment three months.

Every person who, without the authority of the health officer or board of health, shall go within the enclosure of the quarantine ground, shall be considered guilty of the like offence; the fine for each offence not to exceed $100, nor the imprisonment thirty days.

Every person who shall go on board of, or have any communication, intercourse or dealing with, any vessel at quarantine, without the permission of the health officer, shall be considered guilty of a misdemeanor, and punished by fine or imprisonment.

Such offender shall also be detained at quarantine so long as the board of health shall direct, not to exceed twenty days, unless he shall be taken sick of some pestilential or infectious disease.

It shall be the duty of the health officer to give immediate information to the board of health, of every such transgression, the circumstances attending it, and the condition of the vessel with which a communication shall have been had, that the board may determine how long the offender ought to be detained at quarantine.

Every person under quarantine is subject to a penalty of $50, who elopes from, or goes beyond the bounds assigned to him for his quarantine; and it shall be the duty of every justice of the peace, or other magistrate before whom any such offender shall be brought, to order him by warrant to be reconveyed to the quarantine ground, there to remain for the residue of his term of quarantine.

Every pilot who refuses or neglects to perform the duties enjoined on him, shall be considered guilty of a misdemeanor, and shall be fined for each offence in a sum not exceeding $200.

Whenever the commissioners of health, or either of them, shall charge in writing any pilot with any violation or neglect of duty, the warden of the port shall suspend such pilot from his office, until he shall have entered into a recognizance before some magistrate in the city of New-York, in the sum of $200, and with sufficient sureties, to appear and answer to the offence charged at the next court of general sessions for the city and county of New-York.

Every person who refuses or neglects to obey or comply with any order, prohibition or regulation made by the board of health in the exercise of their powers, shall be considered guilty of a misdemeanor, and punished by fine or imprisonment, in the discretion of the court by which the offender shall be tried.

The board of health, or the mayor and commissioners of health, when they shall judge it necessary, may cause any cargo, or part of a cargo, or any matter or thing, within the city, that may be putrid or otherwise dangerous to the public health, to be destoyed or removed; such removal, when ordered, shall be to the quarantine ground, or such other place as the board of health shall direct.

The board of health, the mayor, or either of the commissioners of health, may send to the marine hospital, or such other place as the board of health shall direct, all persons in the city, not residents thereof, who shall be sick of any malignant or contagious fever.

Every master, owner or consignee of a vessel lying at a wharf, or in the harbour of the city of New-York, between the 31st May and the 1st November, must report within twelve hours the name of every sick person on board such vessel: and no such person shall be removed therefrom without a written permit for that purpose from the mayor, the board, or one of the commissioners of health. Penalty for neglect $250, or six months' imprisonment.

No salted provisions can be packed or repacked at any season of the year, in that part of the city of New-York lying south of a line drawn from the Hudson river, through the centre of Canal-street to Sullivan-street, through Sullivan-street to Grand-street, through Grand-street to Walnut-street, and through Walnut-street to the East river.

From the first day of May to the first day of October in any year, no salted or pickled beef, pork or fish, except smoked beef and fish, shall be deposited in the city south of the line above described

This is not to be construed to prevent retail grocers or other small dealers from keeping on hand, for the use of their customers, small quantities, not exceeding five barrels of each kind of the provisions therein mentioned, if the provisions so kept be sound and in good order.

All salted or pickled provisions, and all hides, skins and cotton, that remain deposited in the city, south of the line described in the tenth section of this title, on the first day of June in any year, shall be reported by the owner or person having charge thereof to the mayor, the board, or one of the commissioners of health, that the same may be examined, and if necessary, destroyed or removed.

If such articles, when ordered to be removed by the board of health, shall not be forthwith removed by the owner or person having charge thereof, the board of health shall cause them to be removed to some safe place, there to remain at the risk of the owner.

The expense of the removal and subsequent storage of such articles must be borne by the owner or person having charge thereof when removed, and if paid in the first instance by the board of health, may be recovered by them in an action against such owner or bailee; or if payment of such expenses be refused by the owner or bailee, the board may cause such articles to be sold, and account for the proceeds, deducting such expenses and the costs of sale.

This does not extend to provisions exposed to sale by butchers in the public markets, or kept by the heads of families for family use.

Every person who shall refuse or neglect to obey these directions, shall be fined for each offence in a sum not exceeding $500, or be imprisoned for a term not exceeding six months.

No rags, hides or skins, arriving in the port of New-York, between the 31st day of May and the 1st day of October in any year, shall be taken to any place in the city, south of a line beginning at Spring-street on the North river; thence along that street to the Bowery; thence down the Bowery to Grand street; thence through Grand-street to Walnut-street, and thence through Walnut-street to the East river; and all such articles brought into the city contrary to the above provision, may be seized and sold by the commissioners of health for the use of the marine hospital.

The board of health, or the mayor and commissioners of health, may, however, permit sound hides and skins to be brought into the city, south of the line last described, in small quantities, and for the purpose of immediate manufacture, but not otherwise.

It is the duty of the master and owner of every vessel that may have brought cotton into the city, between the first day of May and the first day of November in any year, and of the owner and consignee of such cotton, if, upon examination, it shall appear damaged or otherwise unsound, to make an immediate report thereof to the mayor or commissioners of health.

Every master, owner, or consignee, refusing or neglecting to perform the duties so enjoined, for each offence forfeits to the commissioners of health the sum of $500.

All persons sent to the marine hospital, or any other hospital provided by the board of health, other than those who shall have paid hospital money, and such poor persons as the board of health shall exempt, shall pay a reasonable sum for their board, medicine and attendance; and for the recovery of such sum, the commissioners of health may sue in their name of office.

The health commissioner is entitled to receive the following sums from the master of every vessel that arrives in the port of New-York, namely:

1. From the master of every vessel from a foreign port, for himself, and each cabin passenger, $1 50; for each steerage passenger, mate, sailor, or mariner, $1.

2. From the master of each coasting vessel, for each person on board 25 cents; but no coasting vessel from the states of New-Jersey,

Connecticut and Rhode-Island, shall pay for more than one voyage in each month, computing from the first voyage in each year.

The moneys so received shall be denominated "hospital moneys," and shall be appropriated to the use of the marine hospital, deducting a commission to the health commissioner of two and one half per cent for collection.

Each master paying hospital moneys, shall be entitled to demand and recover, from each person for whom they shall be paid, the sum paid on his account.

Every master of a coasting vessel shall pay to the health commissioner, at his office, in the city of New-York, within twenty-four hours after the arrival of his vessel in the port, such hospital moneys as shall then be demandable from him, under the provisions of this title; and every master, for each omission of such duty, shall forfeit the sum of $100.

No vessel having on board any person infected with any pestilential or infectious disease, or coming from a place so infected, can enter any other of the ports or harbours of this state, until such quarantine as the mayor, or, in his absence, the recorder, of Albany, Troy and Hudson, may direct.

Every person so subject to quarantine, who shall violate any of the regulations prescribed, shall be fined in a sum not exceeding $500.

The health officer in each of the cities of Albany and Hudson, must assist in carrying into effect these provisions; and from the master of each vessel from a foreign port that he shall visit and examine, shall be entitled to receive the sum of $7 50.

The board of trustees of the city of Brooklyn, constitute a board of health for that city, and annually appoint a physician, then being an inhabitant, to be the health physician.

The health physician is to visit and inspect all vessels coming to the wharves, landing places, or shores, in the city of Brooklyn, and suspected to have on board any pestilential disease, and all stores or warehouses suspected to contain putrid or unsound provisions, and damaged hides, cotton, or other articles; and to make a report of their condition to the president of the board of health.

No vessel subject to quarantine in the port of New-York, can proceed beyond the place of quarantine on Staten Island, to the city of Brooklyn, without a permit from the health officer of the city of New-York.

The master of every such vessel arriving in the city of Brooklyn, must, within six hours after such arrival, deliver the permit of the health officer to the president of the board of health, or he is for each offence deemed punishable by fine or imprisonment, or both: the fine not to exceed $250, nor the imprisonment six months.

The board of health of the city, whenever the public health requires it, may order any vessel at any wharf, landing place, or shore of that city, to be removed at least five hundred yards from the shores of the city, within six hours of the service of such order.

Every such order must be in writing, and be signed by the president of the board, or by a majority of the members of the board; and may be served by a delivery thereof to the person having at the time the care or command of the vessel to be removed, or to the master, owner, or consignee thereof.

Every person upon whom such order shall have been duly served, who omits to comply with its requisitions, shall be punished by fine or imprisonment, or both; the imprisonment not to exceed six months, nor the fine for each day the vessel remains in violation of the order, more than $250.

Every practising physician in the city of Brooklyn, must forthwith make a report in writing, to the board of health, of every patient he shall have labouring under any pestilential or infectious disease, or forfeit $50.

Every keeper of a boarding or lodging-house in the city of Brooklyn, between the first day of June and the fifteenth day of November in each year, must report in writing to the board of health every seafaring man or traveller sick in his house, within six hours after each case of sickness shall have occurred, under the penalty of $100, or six months' imprisonment.

No sick person, between the days last mentioned, can be removed from any vessel lying near the shores of the city of Brooklyn, or from any other place, into the city, until a written permit for such removal has been granted by the board, under the penalty of $100, or six months' imprisonment.

The board of health of the city of Brooklyn has power,

1. To issue their proclamation, prohibiting or regulating the internal intercourse by land or water, between that city and any other place where they shall have reason to believe that a pestilential or infectious disease then prevails.

2. In case of the prevalence of any such disease in any part of the city, to enclose and shut up such infected part, so as to prevent all intercourse therewith.

3. To remove to the public hospital of the city, or such other place as they may deem fit, all persons within the city, not being residents thereof, who shall be sick of any pestilential or infectious disease, and all articles and things affected by, or tainted with pestilential disease; and,

4. To cause any bedding or clothing, or any unsound or putrid articles found within the city, to be destroyed, whenever in their judgment such destruction shall be necessary to prevent infection; and every person violating such regulation, is punishable by fine or imprisonment, or both.

Any two justices of the peace, in any town of this state, may cause all persons sick of any infectious or pestilential disease, and not being residents of such town, by an order in writing, to be removed to such place of safety within the town as they shall deem necessary for the preservation of the public health.

New-Jersey.—Quarantine vessels arriving at Perth Amboy, between 31st May and 1st October, from any place south of Georgia, the West Indies, or the Bahama or Bermuda islands, or from any place where an infectious disorder prevails, or on board of which any person has died, while at a foreign port or on the return passage, must anchor south of a line drawn from the south ferry wharf in

Perth Amboy, and Caleb Ward's house, Staten Island, to be examined. The health officer, if he deem proper, may order the vessel to be unloaded and purified, and to be quarantined for twenty days. All intercourse with Amboy may be prohibited, and the crew and passengers prohibited from landing at Amboy ; and any violation of the law may be punished by a fine of $100, or an imprisonment of two months. The health officer is entitled to a fee of $5 for his first visit, and $2 for every subsequent visit, made upon the request of the master or the health committee.[a]

The governor, too, may issue his proclamation in aid of the quarantine laws of New-York or Pennsylvania, forbidding all persons from entering on board, or landing any thing from any vessel performing quarantine in the Delaware or the bay of New-York, under a penalty of $300.[b]

Pennsylvania.—A board of health is established, which is a body corporate, consisting of eleven members, chosen annually, six members to be elected by the corporation of Philadelphia, two by the commissioners of the incorporated part of the Northern Liberties, one by the commissioners of Penn township, one by the commissioners of Southwark, and one by the commissioners of Moyamensing.

The board sit upon their own adjournment as they find necessary, but meet at least once in every day between the 1st of June and 1st of October in every year. The board has full authority to make general regulations, for the government of the lazaretto, and the vessels, cargoes, and persons there detained, or under quarantine, and of the health office and quarantine regulations in general.

The governor appoints the lazaretto physician, and one physician in the city of Philadelphia, denominated the port physician, one health officer, and one quarantine master, who all are under the direction and control of the board of health, and must be removed from office by the governor, at the request of the majority of the board of health.

The following fees are paid to the health officer on the arrival of vessels. All American vessels sailing under coasting licenses, (except vessels engaged in the Pennsylvania coal trade, which pay no fees,[c]) arriving at the port of Philadelphia, from any port in the United States between the river St. Croix and the river St. Mary's, (except ports or places between Sandy Hook and Cape Charles,) pay $2 50 for each arrival, during quarantine months ; and the said vessels during that time (if having goods capable of containing contagion, persons, baggage, or clothing, from any foreign port or place, or any diseased person) stop at the lazaretto, and are there examined by the lazaretto physician and quarantine master. All American vessels from any port in the United States where they may have touched, or traded from a foreign port, pay the same sum as if from such port. All American vessels with coasting documents, arriving from any port between Sandy Hook and Cape Charles, including the bay and river Delaware, during quarantine months, having on board merchandise of foreign growth or manufacture, or persons, baggage, or cloth-

---

[a] Act, 3d Feb., 1812. [b] Act, 19th Nov., 1799. [c] Act, 12th June, 1832.

ing, from any foreign port, or from any place to the northward or eastward of Sandy Hook, or westward of Cape Charles, must stop at the lazaretto for examination, and pay for each arrival, during quarantine months, $2 50. All American vessels arriving from any place in New-Brunswick, Nova Scotia, Canada, or the islands or ports adjacent to the river St. Mary's, the coast of Florida, bay of Mexico, including New-Orleans and parts adjacent, and from thence along the bay of Honduras and coast of Terra Firma, as far as the river Amazon, including all the islands generally denominated West India, Bahamas or Bermudas, pay on arrival $5. All American vessels arriving from any place in Europe, in the Western Madeira, Canary or Cape de Verd islands, the west coast of Africa, as far as latitude 34 degrees south, and from any place in the Mediterranean or straits thereof, or from any place from the river Amazon inclusive, and round the coast of Brazils as far as latitude 34 degrees south, pay $10 each. All American vessels arriving from any place beyond latitude 34 degrees south, or round Cape Horn or the Cape of Good Hope, pay $20 each. All foreign vessels arriving as aforesaid, (except prizes to American vessels,) pay 25 per cent. each, additional, unless otherwise regulated by treaty. Prize vessels, taken by foreign armed vessels, pay 25 per cent. each more than American vessels. Prize vessels, taken by American vessels, pay on arrival $10 each. Public armed vessels and privateers, pay $6 each. Any vessel of the burthen of 150 tons and upwards, arriving at the lazaretto from any foreign port, or coastwise, may come to in the outer channel, as near to the west end of the island of Little Tinicum, opposite the lazaretto, as her draught of water, wind and weather will permit, for the purpose of receiving the visit from the lazaretto physician and quarantine master; and if the said vessel do not receive her visit in the inner channel, she must pay an additional sum of $5, of which $2 are paid to the lazaretto physician, and $1 to the quarantine master, as a compensation for their extraordinary services, and $2 into the treasury of the board.

Every vessel coming from any foreign port, or any port south of Cape Fear, and every vessel from any port which has discharged, within thirty days previous, goods or baggage brought in such vessel from a foreign port,[a] if arriving between the first of June and the first of October, must come to anchor in the river Delaware, as near the lazaretto as the draught of water and the weather will allow, before any part of the cargo or baggage be landed, or any person who came in such vessel leaves her, or any person be permitted to go on board, and must submit to an examination. If any master or pilot leave his station before the said lazaretto, or if any master permit any part of the cargo or baggage, or any person arriving in such vessel from any port beyond the limits of the United States, to be landed, or suffer any person, except the pilot, to come on board before such examination, and a certificate obtained, the person so permitting, and the person so landed or going on board, (unless imminent danger of the loss

[a] Act, 2d April, 1821.

of the vessel or lives of the crew shall render assistance necessary,) must pay a fine not exceeding $500; and it is the duty of the lazaretto physician and quarantine master, so soon as any vessel shall be anchored near the lazaretto, between sunrise and sunset, immediately, wind and weather permitting, to go on board, and there thoroughly examine the vessel, crew, passengers, cargo and baggage on board, and to demand answers under oath or affirmation, to be administered by either the said physician or quarantine master, to all such questions touching the health of the crew and passengers during the voyage, and the nature and state of the cargo, as the board of health may direct to be asked. If upon such examination it appear to the physican and quarantine master, that the said vessel came from a place at which no contagious disease prevailed at the time of her departure, that the persons on board are free from every contagious disease, (the measles excepted,[a]) and that the said vessel has had no malignant disease on board, either during the homeward bound voyage or during her continuance in a foreign port, and they see no cause to suspect that the cargo or any part thereof is infected, they must forthwith deliver to the master a certificate of the facts, and he may thereupon proceed to his destination, and must present such certificate at the health office in Philadelphia within twenty-four hours after his arrival and safely mooring there; but if it appears upon such examination that the vessel came from a place at which a contagious disease prevailed, such vessel shall be detained at the lazaretto not exceeding twenty days; and the letter-bag of the vessel, when purified, and such letters as the master or passengers think proper to write to their owners, consignees, or friends, must be transmitted to the health office in Philadelphia, which shall safely deposit the same in the post office. And thereupon the board of health must direct measures to be pursued to cleanse the vessel and cargo, purify the clothing and baggage, and restore the health of diseased persons on board, which direction is carried into execution under the inspection of the lazaretto physician and quarantine master, at the expense of the master, owners, or consignees of the vessel and goods respectively. Wine, rum, salt, sugar, spirits, molasses, mahogany, manufactured tobacco, dye woods, preserved fruits, and such other articles as the board of health, by their general regulations, permit, may be conveyed immediately to the city in lighters, at the expiration of the said time. If it appear to the said physician and quarantine master that no person has been sick with a contagious disease (the measles excepted[a]) on board, either during the voyage homeward, or during her continuance in a foreign port, nor any person from on board such vessel during the performance of quarantine, and the said physician and quarantine master certify the said facts to the board of health; and that in their opinion the vessel, crew, cargo and passengers, may be safely suffered to proceed to the city, the master may proceed with the same according to his destination, unless the board of health deem it necessary to cause a further detention of the said vessel or cargo, or of the crew or passengers,

[a] The small-pox was also excepted until the Act of 29th March, 1824.

or of any baggage on board said vessel, in which case the same shall be detained until the board of health authorize the same to proceed and enter the city. Upon the arrival of the said master at Philadelphia, he must present the said certificate at the health office within twenty-four hours after his arrival. If upon examination of any vessel, or during the performance of quarantine by any vessel, it appear to the said physician and quarantine master that there has been any person sick on board with any contagious disease, either during the voyage homeward, or during the continuance of the vessel in a foreign port, or during the performance of quarantine at the lazaretto, (or that any person on board has been affected with such disease,) then in such case the vessel is detained such further time as the board of health may deem necessary, and the cargo and baggage, (except such part thereof as in the opinion of the board of health may be supposed incapable of retaining infection, which said part may be transported to the city in lighters,) unless otherwise ordered and directed by the board of health, unladen and thoroughly cleansed and purified, and the crew and passengers, and the cargo and baggage, except as before excepted, cannot enter the city before the first day of October thence next ensuing, without permission of the board of health. Such vessel, after she has been purified, if no malignant disease appear on board, may be allowed to take in freight at the lazaretto by means of lighters, and proceed to sea. If any master, or other person on board, do not true answers make to all such questions as the lazaretto physician, quarantine master, health officer, or port physician may ask, or knowingly deceive, or attempt to deceive the officers aforesaid, in his answers to their official inquiries, such person, for each offence, forfeits not exceeding $500, and moreover, imprisonment at hard labour for not less than one year, and not exceeding five years. If any master neglect to present his certificate at the health office within twenty-four hours, he forfeits $300. If any master, or any other person on board, neglect to comply with the directions of the lazaretto physician or quarantine master, made agreeably to law, with respect to the detention of any vessel, or the landing of any person, or of any goods, bedding, baggage, or clothing, or refuse to carry the same into effect, such person, for each offence, forfeits not exceeding $500, nor less than $200.

Any vessel coming from any place within the United States, at which she had only touched upon her arrival from a foreign port, is subject to all the rules, regulations and restrictions preceding, and examined and treated, as well the vessel itself as the cargo, crew, passengers and baggage on board, in the same manner as if she had directly arrived at the lazaretto from a foreign port. All vessels, as well vessels of war as merchant vessels, coming from any place within the United States, and bound to the port of Philadelphia, between the first day of June and the first day of October, and having on board any goods, the growth or produce of any foreign country, or any person, or bedding or clothing, from any foreign port, must come to an anchor opposite the lazaretto, and be examined by the said lazaretto physician and quarantine master. If the master produce such satisfactory proof as the board of health may, in that case, direct, that the said goods have been landed in the United States more than twenty days, and are free from damage, and that the said vessel, bedding, clothing and persons, are free from infection, (the measles excepted,) then the said physician and quarantine master must give to the captain a certificate of the facts, permitting such vessel to proceed to the city, which certificate the said captain must present at the health office in Philadelphia, within twenty-four hours after his arrival and safely mooring there. If he neglect so to do, he is sentenced to a fine of $200. If the said captain fail to produce such satisfactory proof as aforesaid, the said vessel, goods, merchandise, bedding, clothing and persons, must be detained at the lazaretto, and proceeded with in the same manner as in the case of vessels coming directly from a foreign port. If the master of such vessel, having on board any goods or merchandise, bedding, clothing, or persons, as aforesaid, refuse or neglect to come to an anchor opposite the lazaretto, and pass the same with intent to proceed to the city, without examination and certificate obtained as aforesaid, he forfeits $500, and the said vessel, goods, merchandise, bedding, clothing and persons, must be sent back to the lazaretto.

Every vessel coming from the Mediterranean is subject to a strict examination; and if it appear that the said vessel came from any place where the plague existed at the time of her departure, or has spoken with any vessel on board of which any person was affected with the plague: or if any person be affected with the said disease on his arrival at the lazaretto, or have been affected during the voyage, the said vessel cannot be suffered to proceed to the city, and the cargo and baggage must be unloaded, and thoroughly cleansed and purified, and no part suffered to enter the city without the permission of the board of health; and the crew and passengers perform a quarantine of not less than twenty days, nor more than forty. Such vessel, after she has been thoroughly purified, may be allowed to take in freight at the lazaretto by means of lighters, and proceed to sea.

Any person, and all goods, bedding and clothing, arriving at any port within the United States, from any foreign port, at which any contagious disease, (the measles excepted,) prevailed at the time of their departure, or in any vessel in which any such disease existed while they were on board the same, are prohibited from entering the city or county of Philadelphia, or the county of Delaware, (except the township of Tinicum,) at any time between the first day of June and the first day of October, either by land or water, without permission of the board of health, under the penalty of $500 for each offence, and the forfeiture of all such goods, bedding or clothing; all goods, bedding, clothing and merchandise, seamen or passengers, landed from on board any vessel belonging to the port of Philadelphia at any other port of the United States, are subject to perform twenty days' quarantine, previously to entering the city or county of Philadelphia, under the same penalty, without permission first obtained from the board of health.

No person, goods, bedding or clothing, from any place at which any contagious disease (the measles excepted) prevailed at the time of their departure, or from on board any vessel in which any such disease existed while they were on board, can enter the city or county of Philadelphia at any time between the first day of June and the first day of October, by land or water, without the permission of the board of health, under the penalty of $500 for each offence, and the forfeiture of all such goods, bedding and clothing.

Whenever the board of health receive information that any contagious disease (the measles excepted) prevails in any place within the United States, or on the continent of America, all communication with such infected place, is subject to such regulations as the board of health may think proper to direct and publish in one or more newspapers published in the city of Philadelphia. All vessels from such place, bound to the port of Philadelphia, must stop at the lazaretto, and be proceeded with in the same manner as in cases of vessels coming from foreign ports; and every person having entered the city or county of Philadelphia, from such place, may also be conveyed to such place for purification as the board may appoint for that purpose, and be there detained not exceeding twenty days, at the expense of such person.

The lazaretto physician, immediately on the arrival of any vessel liable to be detained for purification, must cause the sick on board to be removed to the building appointed for their reception, and diligently and impartially, with his best skill, attend upon and administer medical assistance to each and every sick person therein lodged.

The quarantine master, immediately after the arrival and examination of any vessel liable to be detained for purification, must cause such vessel to be properly moored near the lazaretto, at such distance from any vessel under quarantine as may prevent the communication of any infectious disease to or from the same; and the cargo, bedding and clothing must be landed, cleansed and purified, under the direction of the lazaretto physician; and it is the particular duty of the quarantine master to prevent any personal intercourse between the persons on board the different vessels under quarantine, and for that purpose, to take possession and secure the boats of such vessels from sunset to sunrise of the succeeding day, until their respective terms of quarantine shall be completed.

By an act passed 30th January, 1827, free communication is permitted between the officers and crews of national vessels detained at quarantine, and the naval asylum on the Schuylkill.

The port physician, upon receiving information that any person on board of any vessel in the port of Philadelphia, is suspected to be afflicted with any contagious disease, or that there is just cause to suspect that the cargo, or any part thereof, is infected with such disease, must visit and carefully examine such vessel, and if he discover any sick person on board, he may thereupon direct such sick person to be removed to the lazaretto, or to some other safe place specified by the board of health. The said physician must, without delay, report the state of said vessel, cargo and crew, to the board of health, who shall direct and determine how the crew, passengers, vessel and cargo shall be disposed of, for the restoration of their health and purification. On the arrival of any vessel from any foreign port, from the first day of October to the first day of June in the next succeeding year, the said physician, provided such vessel has not been previously visited and examined by the physician resident at the lazaretto and quarantine master, and before any of the passengers, crew, cargo or baggage are landed, must visit and carefully examine such vessel in manner and form as the said lazaretto physician and quarantine master are bound to do, and demand answers, under oath or affirmation, to be administered by the said port physician. If the crew, passengers, vessel and cargo, be in a healthy state, and if there be no ground to suspect that any of the crew or passengers have died on the voyage of any dangerous contagious disease, (the measles excepted,) or that the cargo, bedding or clothing is infected, then, and in such case, the said physician must give to the master a certificate of the facts, which the said master must present at the health office within twenty-four hours after such examination, or forfeit $200. If on examination any suspicion arise touching the health of the crew or passengers, or the infectious state of the vessel, cargo, bedding or clothing on board, no part thereof can be landed, but the said physician must immediately report the same to the board of health, who shall direct what measures shall be pursued relative thereto. Every vessel arriving at the port of Philadelphia must be visited by the port physician previously to her being hauled to any wharf within the city or Wind Mill Island; and every person so hauling such vessel to any wharf as aforesaid, shall pay the sum of $200, unless it be made to appear that there was, at the time, imminent danger of the loss of such vessel, or of the passengers or crew thereof.

The health officer must keep a public office in the city of Philadelphia, where all masters must deliver the certificates of bills of health granted by the lazaretto physician and quarantine master, or port physician.

The letter mail, during the quarantine season, leaves the lazaretto and fort Mifflin for the health office, in the city of Philadelphia, and returns once or twice in each juridical day,[a] at such hours as the board of health may determine, and is free for the transmission of letters to and from persons within the bounds of the lazaretto, or on board of vessels detained there. The health officer, immediately after the arrival of the lazaretto mail, must deposit in the post office the letters received, excepting those addressed to the board of health.

Every diseased person sent to the lazaretto, by either of the aforesaid physicians, quarantine master, or health officer, must be there kept and maintained until the lazaretto physician grant a discharge in writing; and if before obtaining a discharge, such person absent himself from the lazaretto, the health officer, or any constable or other person whom he shall call to his assistance, may pursue and apprehend him, and again deliver him, to be detained until duly discharged; and, moreover, the person so absenting himself shall, for each offence, suffer such temporary confinement in the lazaretto, not exceeding three months, as the board of health shall ordain. If any master knowingly receive or employ on board of his vessel, or if any inhabitant of this commonwealth knowingly receive, or in any way

[a] Act, 12th June, 1832.

entertain any person so absenting from the lazaretto, each master and inhabitant so offending shall forfeit $200. If any person arriving in any vessel detained at the lazaretto, absent himself without having first obtained a discharge, signed by the lazaretto physician and quarantine master; or if any person other than those detained at the lazaretto, go on board or alongside of any vessel whilst under quarantine; or if any person not authorized by the board of health go within the limits of the lazaretto, such person must perform such quarantine as the board of health may direct, and forfeit $200. If any diseased or other person sent to the lazaretto, or any person arriving in any vessel detained at the lazaretto, refuse or neglect to obey the directions of the lazaretto physician or quarantine master, the person so refusing or neglecting, for each offence forfeits $200. The expense and charge of boarding, lodging, nursing, medicine, maintenance, and other necessaries provided for the diseased persons sent to the lazaretto, and also of burying them in case of their death, must be paid by the importer, master, owner, or consignee of the vessels in which such diseased persons were respectively imported. When the diseased persons are passengers, and not servants, the said charges must be repaid by them, their executors or administrators, to the master, owner, or consignee, who pays the same.

When any vessel comes up to the city of Philadelphia, or the shores of Southwark, or the Northern Liberties, with a certificate of health from the lazaretto physician and quarantine master, or the port physician, if the said vessel appear to the board of health to be infected with any contagious disorder dangerous to the community, the said board may order the said vessel to the lazaretto, to undergo purification; and the said board are authorized to remove any vessel from any part of the city or shore aforesaid as shall be infected with such disorders as aforesaid, to such convenient distance as they may deem proper, although such vessel may not be infected.

Pilots in good health may bring vessels to the lazaretto without performing quarantine, and they take a certificate from the lazaretto authorizing them to proceed to the capes; but they are not permitted to come to the city. If infected, pilots perform quarantine as part of the crew.

Whenever the said board of health receives information that any contagious disease rages in any place within the United States, or on the continent of America, the said board may prohibit all communication by land and water with such infected places, by stopping all vessels coming into the port of Philadelphia, at the lazaretto, in the same manner, and under the same penalties and forfeitures, as in cases of vessels coming from foreign ports.

No master of a vessel or other person can remove any sick person lying in the river Delaware, before the city of Philadelphia, the district of Southwark, or the township of the Northern Liberties, before such sick person has been visited by the port physician, and a written permit granted by him for such removal, under the penalty of $50, or an imprisonment of three months.

If any person wilfully and knowingly obstruct or resist the board of health, or any of the members thereof, or any persons by them appointed, in the performance of duties enjoined on them, such person forfeits $500. If, after the expiration of the quarantine, any mariner or other person commit any violence on the person of a member of the board of health, or any of the officers attached to the same, for any thing done in the execution of his duty, such person shall be subject to a fine of $200, and to imprisonment at hard labour not exceeding three years.

The quarantine master must accompany the lazaretto physician, on the arrival of vessels at the lazaretto, and have them moored, and, when necessary, well cleansed and white-washed, for which he must be paid by the master, owner, or consignee. He is allowed to charge, for lime and brushes, the usual prices at which such articles are retailed in the city of Philadelphia; (he is also authorized to receive all letters and papers to be forwarded to Philadelphia by the lazaretto mail, and by any other conveyance he may think proper;) and no person can be permitted to go on board any vessel under quarantine, except the lazaretto physician and quarantine master, unless at the request of either of them, to perform some necessary service.

All prosecutions against any master, owner, or consignee of any vessel, or other person, must be brought within twelve months next after the commission of the offence.

The vessel is liable for the payment of the penalties incurred for a breach of quarantine regulations.[a]

Between the first day of June and the first day of October, no vessel laden with, or having on board any vegetables, fish, or hides, can be unladen at the port of Philadelphia, until a permit is obtained from the board of health. If any master, or other persons, presume to unlade any vegetables, fish, or hides, without first having obtained a permit from the board of health, every such master, or other person so offending, must pay a fine not exceeding $500.

Between the first day of June and the first day of October, within forty-eight hours after the discharge of the cargo of every vessel at the port of Philadelphia, it is the duty of the master or consignees, and other persons having the direction of the discharge of the same, under the penalty of $100, to give to the board of health notice that the same cargo is discharged, and to permit the board of health to examine the condition of the hold, ballast and limbers of such vessel. If the board of health deem it for the safety and health of the city of Philadelphia, they may designate a proper place to which the said vessel shall be taken, and that her hold, ballast and limbers shall there be cleansed and purified, or at the expense of such master, owners, consignees, or other person having the direction of the discharge of the cargo, may send such vessel to a proper place, and have her hold, ballast and limbers cleansed and purified.[b]

Delaware.—Masters having on board more than forty persons, or any persons sick with an infectious disorder, or coming from any sickly place, are liable to a penalty of $1000 for approaching their

---

[a] Act, 29th January, 1818. [b] Act, 2d April, 1821.

place of landing, nearer than one mile, or for landing any person or thing from their vessels without a permit from the health officer. There are health officers at Newcastle, Wilmington, Lewes, one near Nanticoke river in Sussex county, and one in Kent county. It is their duty to visit any vessel after being notified by the master, and to inquire into her state of health. Any concealment by the master as to the condition of the vessel or persons on board, from her departure from port until her arrival, is punishable by a fine of $100. The health officer's fee is $10.

In case the health officer refuses to grant such permit, application may be made to two justices of the peace, or to a trustee of the poor and the nearest justice, and they may grant a permit.

Persons visiting, without permission, a vessel having an infectious disorder on board, before a permit is granted, forfeit $10.[a]

The local authorities of Wilmington and Newcastle, and also of the other towns, have the power, whenever the occasion exists, to subject vessels, from any port where a contagious disorder prevails, to quarantine regulations, and a violation of those regulations is punishable by a fine of $500.[b]

Maryland.—The constitution confers upon the governor the power to make quarantine regulations where he thinks necessary.

Any violation of quarantine is punishable by a penalty of £100 sterling.[c]

In Baltimore, health officers and assistants are appointed to visit vessels, and if they deem it necessary, they may order them to perform a quarantine of not less than ten nor more than twenty days; at the end of that time a second visit is paid, and, if necessary, an additional quarantine of ten days may be ordered. Vessels not having a clean bill of health, or having more than thirty persons on board, or a contagious disorder on board, must not approach nearer Baltimore than Hawkins' Point, without permission of the health officer, under the penalty of $1000.

The same penalty is incurred by landing any infected person or goods without such permission. A penalty of $300 is incurred by concealing, or not truly stating the state of health of persons on board during the voyage, or not answering the inquiries of the health officer or his assistant.[d]

The mayor of Baltimore is authorized to prohibit persons from sickly places from entering the city, for fifteen days after leaving such place, under the penalty of $300.

The mayor, health officer and health commissioners, are authorized to prohibit the landing of damaged or infected articles, under the penalty of $300. And whenever they deem it necessary, may order such articles to be removed, under a penalty of $100, and $20 per hour for neglecting such order.

The health officer and his assistant during quarantine months, i. e. from the first of April to the first of November, give attendance at fort M'Henry from eight in the morning until six in the evening.

---

[a] Act, 24th Jan., 1797. [b] Act, 1799 and 1800. [c] Act, Nov., 1766. [d] Ibid. 1793.

A book is kept there of all marine intelligence collected, and of the masters arriving; and all letters on board are delivered to the health officer, to be transmitted to the post-office. Vessels from the East or West Indies, from Africa or South America, from the Mediterranean, and the west coast of Spain, as far as Cape Vincent, from the first of May to the first of November, are detained one day, during which they are twice visited by the health officer. If he deem it necessary, he orders them to go into quarantine not exceeding ten days, and he gives a written order specifying the number of days. Before the end of that time he visits again, and he may extend the quarantine five days. Vessels leaving the quarantine ground before the expiration of the quarantine, forfeit $500, to be paid by the person having charge of her.

Masters having on board any person sick with a contagious disorder, or coming from a sickly place, without a clean bill of health, incur a penalty of $300 by passing the quarantine ground, or by landing such infected person, or any goods, without permission of the health officer.

Pilots must bring vessels in their charge, from foreign ports and other suspected ports, during quarantine months, to the quarantine ground, and if the vessel approach nearer to Baltimore, a penalty is incurred of $100; and if he know that there exists any contagious disorder on board, $500.

If any person go on board, or have communication, except by speaking, he incurs a penalty of $300, and may be compelled to go into quarantine.

Persons leaving the vessel without the health officer's permission, forfeit $300. Pilots forfeit the same by coming into the city within fifteen days after leaving the vessel, except by like permission.

Vessels in the months of June, July, August, September and October, coming from any places above mentioned, loaded with articles liable to putrefaction, must land their cargoes, or discharge them into other vessels, within and near to Love Point, unless specially permitted to come into port by two commissioners of health and the mayor. If the health officer deem it necessary, he may order such cargo to be stored for purification at the lazaretto, and to remain there until properly aired. He may also order all vessels with such cargoes, and the bedding and clothing of the crews, to be cleansed and aired; and any violation of such orders is punished by a fine of $500.

If the master of any vessel discharged from quarantine discover any part of the cargo to be damaged, he must stop discharging, and notify the health officer thereof, or he incurs a penalty of $300.

The health officer, if he deem it necessary, may cause the vessel to be removed to the quarantine ground, and to discharge the cargo there, or he may have it put into lighters to be transported there.

By landing goods contrary to the direction of the health officer, a penalty of $100 is incurred.

All sick persons must be sent to the lazaretto; and if they leave there, without permission from the attending physician, to come to Baltimore, they forfeit $50.[a]

---

[a] Ordnance, 1807.

No sick person can be removed from a vessel lying in the harbour without a written permit from the consulting physician and mayor, or some member of the board of health: penalty $20.[a]

No ballast can be landed between May and October, without permission from the board of health.[b]

Virginia.—The governor is authorized to establish quarantine for such times, and in such manner as he shall think fit, by proclamation.

Masters having persons on board sick with a contagious disorder, must make it known to the health officer of the port, and the vessel must remain in some open road, without communicating with the shore, until the order of the governor be received, or they incur a penalty of $1500.

Vessels from places where a contagious disorder prevails, must wait until visited by the health officer, to whom is communicated the name of the vessel, where laden, and what places she touched at; whether any contagious disorder prevailed at any of those places; how long the vessel has been on her passage; the number of persons on board; whether any and who have died, and of what disorder; whether any are sick on board, and generally every thing touching the health of the vessel.

Any concealment or falsehood on these points, subjects the master to $1500 fine. A similar fine is inflicted by refusing to deliver to the health officer the bill of health, manifests, log-book and journal, by refusing to go into quarantine when required, or by violating quarantine.

Persons attempting to escape from quarantine, may be compelled to return; and any person going on board a vessel when quarantined, may be compelled to remain.

The health officer guilty of neglect or breach of duty, forfeits $3000, and is liable to the party aggrieved in treble damages, for embezzlement, or wilful damage of any goods performing quarantine.[c]

North Carolina.—The commissioners of navigation and justices of the peace act as health commissioners, and appoint places for quarantine grounds, in their respective ports and inlets. Masters arriving from sickly ports, or having a contagious disorder on board, must come to an anchor at such places, and notify the commissioner, or the nearest justice, or they will incur £500 penalty, and may be imprisoned one year. The pilot, also, is liable.

A physician is then sent on board to examine the vessel and crew; and, upon his report, the board of health, consisting of three justices or commissioners, may order such vessel into quarantine. If any person violate the regulations of the board as to quarantine, or leave the vessel and land without permission of the board, he incurs a penalty of £100; and if the master consent, he also is liable. For a violation by the master, the vessel is liable. Persons visiting the vessel without permission, forfeit £50, and may be compelled to perform quarantine; and if the master do not inform such persons that the vessel is in quarantine, he forfeits £100, and £200 for permitting them to leave

---

[a] Ordnance, 1827. [b] Ibid. 1821. [c] Act, 26th Dec., 1792.

without the order of the board of health. The sheriff may be called upon to enforce the quarantine laws. Persons landing any thing from vessels in quarantine, and putting any thing in another vessel, without the leave of the board, forfeit £100.

Masters may be compelled to declare on oath, the state of health of the crew and passengers, and of the place whence they came; and by a false declaration, they incur a penalty of £1000.

Fresh provisions are furnished to the vessel during the quarantine by the commissioners, and the master, vessel and cargo, are liable therefor.

Port physicians are appointed, and their fees prescribed by the respective boards of health, to examine vessels, and certify as to their state of health; and by giving a false certificate, they incur a penalty of £1000.[a]

South Carolina.—Vessels arriving in any port in this state, must come to and wait to be examined by a health officer before suffering any person to land. Pilots and other persons taking any vessel past the quarantine ground, without examination, forfeit £100 sterling.

Masters must declare the state of health of the vessel and crew, and of the place of departure; and if the health officer deem it proper, the vessel is ordered into quarantine. Persons violating quarantine regulations, whether as to intercourse with the inhabitants, or the shore, or the cleansing the vessel, forfeit from $100 to $1000. Persons visiting vessels in quarantine, forfeit £500, and may be ordered to remain. When pilots are compelled to perform quarantine, they are entitled to $4 per day, and to be found, unless such pilot was then in quarantine, or omitted to inquire as to the health of the vessel and crew.

Vessels from the Mediterranean, or any sickly port, must produce a clean bill of health, sworn to by the master, or they will be ordered into quarantine; and the vessel and cargo are to be purified. Masters producing a false bill of health, or health officers giving a false certificate, forfeit £1000. The authority of regulating vessels in quarantine, is vested in the intendant and wardens of Charleston, and in Beaufort and Georgetown in the commissioners of streets.[b]

All two decked vessels in Charleston harbour, between the first of June and the first of November, must have a wind-sail extending to the lower hold, and twice a week they must admit a quantity of water into the hold, to be pumped out again, or a penalty of $10 is incurred, and the harbour master, or his deputy, may order it to be done at the expense of the master. If a vessel be deemed foul, the health commissioners may order her to be removed for fumigation, and to be cleansed; and if the owner or consignee do not remove her within twenty-four hours, he incurs a penalty of $100, and all expenses of cleansing.

The harbour master, or his deputy, also have a right to examine vessels; and if they deem the further landing of the cargo to be dangerous to the health of the city, they may order the hatches to be

---

[a] Acts, 1794, 1802, and 1817. [b] Brevard's Dig. tit. 50.

closed, and every violation of that order is punished by a penalty of $20.[a]

A hospital tax of 10 cents per ton, is imposed on all American vessels arriving at Charleston.[b]

Georgia.—Vessels from sickly ports are subjected to quarantine when arriving in any port in this state; and no person or goods can be landed or put on board another vessel during such quarantine.

Masters and persons having charge of such vessel are prohibited from landing any persons or goods, or permitting the same to be done. If persons go on board a vessel performing quarantine, they are subject to quarantine themselves, and persons landing may be compelled to return to quarantine.[c]

Persons violating quarantine regulations are liable to a fine of $50, and if not paid, to be imprisoned for one month.[d]

The goods on board must be aired, and after having performed quarantine, the master obtains a certificate of health from the health officer or justice. The health officer at Savannah receives $2 for each square rigged vessel, and $1 for each schooner, sloop, &c., except coasters, within the state.

Pilots on boarding must inquire of the masters as to the health of their vessels, and masters are compelled to answer truly to all the inquiries of the pilots. If any contagious disorder exist on board, the pilots are prohibited from boarding the vessel.[e]

The jurisdiction of the corporation of Savannah, in cases of quarantine, extend from Ossabaw Sound to Tybee, and all rivers, &c., within those limits.[f]

The corporation are also authorized to compel, by resolution, any vessel from a suspected port to perform quarantine, at such place as it shall appoint.[g]

Alabama.—The mayor and corporation of Mobile are authorized to make quarantine regulations.[h]

Louisiana.—Authority is given to the common council of New-Orleans to establish quarantine regulations, with this limitation, that no vessel shall be prohibited from entering the port of New-Orleans, nor any passengers, unless such vessel has on board some person sick with a contagious disorder, or the vessel has a damaged cargo.[i]

---

[a] Act, 21st July, 1800. [b] Act, 29th April, 1816, Congress. [c] Act, 14th Dec., 1793. [d] Act, 10th Dec., 1803. [e] Act, 14th Dec., 1793. [f] Act, 10th Dec., 1803. [g] Act, 2d Dec., 1805. [h] Act, 21st Dec., 1823. [i] Act, 19th Feb., 1825.

CHAPTER XXII.

PASSENGERS.

With the view of preventing too many passengers from being crowded into one ship through the cupidity of the owner or master, it was enacted by congress, March 2, 1819, that if the master or other person on board of any vessel, take on board at any foreign port, or convey into the United States from any foreign port, or transport from the United States to any foreign port, a greater number of passengers than two for every five tons of such vessel, every such person so offending, and the owner of such vessel, severally forfeit $150 for each passenger so taken on board.

If the number of passengers exceed the said proportion by the number of twenty passengers in the whole, every such vessel is forfeited to the United States.

Every vessel bound on a voyage from the United States to any port on the continent of Europe, at the time of leaving the last port whence such vessel shall sail, must have on board, well secured under deck, at least sixty gallons of water, one hundred pounds of salted provisions, one gallon of vinegar, and one hundred pounds of wholesome ship bread, for each passenger on board, over and above such other provisions, stores and live stock, as may be put on board by such master or passenger for their use, or that of the crew, and in like proportion for a shorter or longer voyage; and if the passengers on board such vessel, in which such proportion of provisions have not been provided, at any time be put on short allowance, the master and owner of such vessel shall severally pay to each passenger put on short allowance, the sum of $3 for each day they may have been on such short allowance.

The master of any vessel arriving in the United States from any foreign place, at the same time that he delivers a manifest of the cargo, and, if there be no cargo, then at the time of making a report of the vessel, must also deliver to the collector a list of all the passengers on board, in which list the master must designate, particularly, the age, sex and occupation of the said passengers, the country to which they severally belong, and that of which it is their intention to become inhabitants; and further set forth whether any, and what number, have died on the voyage. This report is sworn to by the master; and the refusal or neglect of the master to comply with this, incurs the same penalties, disabilities and forfeitures, as is provided for a refusal or neglect to report and deliver a manifest of the cargo.

Every collector must, quarter yearly return copies thereof to the secretary of state, by whom statements of the same are laid before congress at each session.

There are also laws passed by the states generally, respecting alien passengers, requiring reports to be made by masters of vessels to the municipal authorities of the port, and also requiring security that the passengers shall not become a public charge. Doubts have been raised as to the constitutionality of these state laws, on the ground that the power to regulate commerce is exclusively vested in congress by the constitution. These doubts were, however, settled by the decision of the supreme court of the United States in 1837, in the case of the corporation of New-York v. Miln, where it was decided, that these passenger laws were constitutional, being merely regulations of police. These laws are briefly as follows:

Maine.—In Maine, masters having passengers on board, who are not inhabitants of the state, must, within forty-eight hours after arriving, deliver a list of their names and places of residence to the mayor, selectmen, or overseers of the poor of the town, and obtain a permit to land them, or give bonds in the sum of not more than $500 for each passenger, to indemnify the town and state from all expenses for three years. By landing, or permitting passengers to land, without such permission or bonds, a penalty is incurred of $200 for each person landed, for which the vessel may be attached.[a] They must also give notice to the town clerk of any birth or death happening on board. Penalty $1.

The carrying a person out of the state without his consent, is punished by a fine of $2000, or an imprisonment not exceeding five years, or both.[b]

The transporting any minor or apprentice beyond the sea, without the consent of his parent, master, or guardian, subjects the master to $200 penalty, besides damages.[b]

Masters landing foreign convicts, or any person of notoriously dissolute and abandoned character in the state, forfeit $400.[b]

New-Hampshire.—In New-Hampshire, masters having passengers on board, who have no legal settlement in the state, are required, before permitting them to land, to report their names and places of residence to the overseers of the poor, or selectmen of the town; and if notified, within two days thereafter to give bonds with sureties in the sum of $500 for each passenger, to indemnify the town and state from all charges for three years. If they land such passengers without giving bonds, they forfeit $200 for each passenger.[c]

Persons bringing any indigent person into the state, who has no legal settlement there, forfeit from $50 to $300.[d]

Massachusetts.—In Massachusetts, masters, upon arriving in any port, before permitting any alien passenger to leave the vessel, must report to the mayor of a city, or the selectmen of a town, the names of the passengers, and their places of embarkation. The master must then give a bond in the sum of $200 for every alien passenger, with sureties, to hold the town and state harmless for their maintenance and support for three years. The municipal magistrates may, if they think fit, dispense with such bond, or they may commute upon receiving $5 for each alien passenger.

---

[a] Act, 28th Feb., 1835. [b] Act, 24th Feb., 1821. [c] Act, 14th June, 1820. [d] Act, 18th June, 1807.

The landing a passenger in violation of those regulations, is punished by a penalty of $200 for every alien so landed.

The landing an alien passenger at any port besides that to which the vessel is destined, with the view of avoiding giving bonds, is punished by a fine of $100 for every person so landed.[a]

Any person bringing and leaving any poor or indigent person in a town in which he is not entitled to a settlement, forfeits $100.

Masters landing any person convicted of an infamous crime, or any person of notoriously dissolute and abandoned life and character, forfeits $500 for each offence.[a]

Rhode Island.—Masters must report all passengers on board within twenty-four hours after arrival, to the overseers of the poor of the town, stating names, ages, nation, character and condition, under the penalty of $100 for each offence.[b]

By bringing into the state or landing therein any convict or person of notoriously dissolute and abandoned character, knowing him to be such, they forfeit $400 for every such offence.[b]

The transporting out of the state, without his consent, any free citizen, is punished by a fine not exceeding $2,000, and an imprisonment not exceeding two years.[c]

Connecticut.—If any person bring into the state any poor and indigent person, and leave him in a town where such poor person is not an inhabitant, he forfeits $67 for every person so brought and left.[d]

New-York.—Masters of vessels from any port out of the state must, within twenty-four hours after arriving at the port of New-York, report in writing, under oath, to the mayor, or in case of his absence, to the recorder, the name, age, occupation, place of birth, and last legal settlement of all passengers on board, or such as have been landed, or put on board another vessel during the return voyage, either from a foreign country to the United States, or from any other state to the city of New-York, or they incur a penalty of $75 for every passenger not reported or falsely reported.

Upon such report, the mayor or recorder may require the master to give bonds, with two sureties, in a sum not exceeding $300 for each passenger, to indemnify the city for their maintenance for two years thereafter; and if such bonds be not given within three days after arriving, the master, owner and consignees incur a penalty of $500 for each alien passenger for whom such bonds may be required.

These bonds are usually commuted by a payment of $1 for each passenger: but this is discretionary with the mayor or recorder. If those officers think that any of such passengers, being citizens, are likely to become paupers, they may order them to be removed forthwith to their last place of settlement, and if not removed by the master and owner, they are severally liable for the expense of their maintenance and removal.

Aliens entering the city with the intention of residing, must, within twenty-four hours, report themselves to the mayor or recorder, sta-

---

[a] Rev. Stat., 1834, chap. 46. [b] Rev. Laws., 1822, p. 178–9. [c] Ibid. 353.
[d] Rev. Laws, 1835, tit. 53, sec. 10.

ting name, age, occupation, the time and place where landed, and the name of the vessel and master, or they incur a penalty of $100. The vessel is liable to be attached for any such penalties incurred by the master or owner, and will be released only upon sufficient bonds given to pay the same.[a]

New-Jersey.—Masters having passengers on board from any foreign port, may be compelled by the overseers of the poor of the town in which they arrive, to give bonds in the sum of $200 each, for the maintenance and support of any sick, infirm, or poor passengers; and if they land such passengers without license from the overseers of the poor before giving such bonds, they incur a penalty of $100 for each passenger.[b]

For importing and landing a convict, a penalty of $200 is incurred, and security must also be given to transport such convicts without the United States.[c]

By an agreement made between this state and New-York, the passengers' laws of New-York are to govern the bay of New-York, even as to vessels lying at Jersey City; and in the Kill-van-Kull, as far as the western end of Shooter's Island. They also govern as to all vessels bound to New-York, in all the waters of the sound, from Shooter's Island to Woodbridge creek.

Vessels moored at the wharves or shore of Staten Island are also subject to the passenger laws of New-Jersey.[d]

Pennsylvania.—Masters were prohibited, by an act of January 29, 1818, from bringing more than one passenger to two tons, but as that subject is regulated by an act of congress, passed 2d March, 1819, that part of the state law is not in force. They were also required to provide necessary provisions and vinegar, and to attend to the cleanliness of the passengers.

Masters must pay to the health officer of Philadelphia $1 for every alien passenger: two children between five and twelve years of age being counted as one passenger.

If a master or other person trust a passenger for more than $4, duing the voyage, he is not allowed to recover the debt.

Redemptioners—On the arrival of a vessel with German passengers, she is visited by a German interpreter, who is entitled to $2 for the first, and $1 for every subsequent visit, to be paid by the master or owner.[e]

The master must give a bill of lading to each passenger, for all goods belonging to him, to which they do not require access during the voyage. Penalty for neglecting or refusing, $100.

Passengers are entitled to be put on shore immediately after paying or tendering to the master the passage money, and the $1 due to the health officer; and any master refusing to land such passenger with his goods, forfeits $50, besides being liable for damages; but the captain may detain passengers on board opposite Philadelphia for thirty

---

[a] Act, 11th Feb., 1824. [b] Act, 10th Feb., 1819. [c] Act, 28th Jan., 1797.
[d] U. S. Laws, 28th June, 1834. [e] Act, 29th June, 1818.

days, unless their passage is paid for, and at the end of that time may bind them out to service for a term of years, before the mayor or register of German passengers. The captain must provide all necessaries for passengers during the time they are detained, charging them therefor. Sick passengers are removed to the hospital.

Vessels arriving after the first of December must provide a house on shore for the passengers during the thirty days detention, and they are to be provided for there in the same manner.

Husband and wife must be bound out to the same master, unless with their consent; and the consent of the passengers is necessary when bound to any person residing out of Pennsylvania.

Masters bringing German passengers must, within fifteen days after arriving at Philadelphia, report to the register of German passengers the names and ages of those who have died on board, or they incur a penalty of $300.

The goods of the passengers are pledged for their passage, and the master or owner may at any time after thirty days apply to an alderman or justice of the peace for an execution against the goods; and if, after five days' notice, the passenger do not show cause why an execution should not issue, judgment is given for the passage money due, and an execution issued against the goods.

Masters permitting German passengers to land, and retaining their goods on board as security, must give a certificate to each of them, specifying the goods belonging to him, the sum due, and the time and terms of redemption. No storage can be charged for the goods retained.

All bonds and contracts given by one passenger while on shipboard for the passage of another, are void; but after paying his own passage a passenger may become security for another.

German passengers are entitled to ask for special courts for the trial of any cause between them and the master, or owner, or crew of the vessel, in relation to the voyage, and they may sue separately or jointly.

Where passengers dying on board leave effects, the master must, within ten days after arriving at Philadelphia, file with the register of wills an inventory thereof, or he incurs a penalty of $500.

Minors cannot bind themselves for their passage beyond the age of twenty-four years.[a]

All actions for penalties must be commenced within two months after the arrival of the vessel at Philadelphia, or after the offence, and the proceeds go to the support of the poor.

The register of German passengers mentioned here, is a public officer, understanding both German and English, who superintends the importation of German passengers, and ascertains whether they are likely to become chargeable; and all indentures of the passengers must be made before, and certified by him. In the indentures of minors he must insert a clause, requiring the master to give six weeks' schooling each year.[a]

Masters or other persons importing any convicts into Pennsylvania,

---

[a] Act, 7th Feb., 1818.

incur a penalty of £50; and if they offer a convict for sale, they are liable to three months' imprisonment. They must also give security to transport such person out of the United States, or in default thereof, they are committed to gaol until such security be given.

Every master of any vessel arriving at the port of Philadelphia, from any country out of the United Sates, or from any other of the United States than this state, within twenty-four hours after arrival, must report, in writing, on oath or affirmation, to the mayor, or in case of his sickness or absence, to the recorder, or to any alderman or justice of the peace, the name, place of birth and last legal settlement, (if known,) age and occupation, of every person brought as passengers in such vessel, on her last voyage, from any country out of the United States, into the port of Philadelphia; and of all passengers who have been landed at any place during such voyage, or have been put on board any other vessel, with the intention of proceeding to said port; and of the names of the owners and consignees of such vessel, under the penalty, on such master, and the owners or consignees, severally, of $75 for every person not reported, or whose name, place of birth, and last legal settlement, age and occupation, or names of the owners or consignees shall be falsely reported. The mayor, recorder, alderman or justice, may require, by a short endorsement on the report, every such master to pay to the guardians of the poor the sum of $2 50 for each passenger, not being a citizen of the United States, or at the option of the said guardians of the poor, to be bound with two sufficient sureties, for $150 for each passenger not being a citizen of the United States, to indemnify the said city, districts and townships, from all expenses which may be incurred for the maintenance of such persons, or of the child or children of such persons, for the term of two years. The master pays $2 for preparing said bond. If such master neglect to pay $2 50 for each passenger, or to give such bond within five days after such vessel arrived at Philadelphia, such master, and the owners or consignees, severally, are subject to a penalty of $500 for each person not being a citizen of the United States, for whom the mayor or recorder may determine that bond should be given.

Every vessel, on board of which any person not being a citizen of the United States may have been a passenger, is liable for the said penalties. The attachment can be dissolved by the master, owner or consignee of the vessel, by giving bonds with sufficient security to the sheriff for the payment of the penalties, or for paying the value of such vessel, towards the satisfaction of said penalties, and for the appearance of the master, owner, or consignee to answer to the suit.

Delaware.—A penalty of $600 is incurred by bringing a greater number of passengers into this state than are provided with provisions and other necessaries, particularly vinegar.

The berths for all passengers over fourteen years of age must be six feet by eighteen inches wide, for each, and the same for every two persons under that age.

The height of each forward berth must be three feet nine inches, and in the steerage and cabin, two feet nine inches.

No more than two adults and four children can be put in one division or bedstead.[a]

How much of this law is in force since the passage of the act of congress of 2d March, 1819, may well be questioned.

Masters and owners of vessels, having foreign emigrants on board, forfeit $500 for every emigrant landed without a license from the trustees of the poor and a justice of the peace. This license is obtained upon application, by paying $1 for each passenger landed.[b]

Masters or others bringing convicts into the state, forfeit $5 for each convict, and must also give security in the sum of $50 for each convict for his good behaviour for one year; £20 penalty for every convict landed is incurred by landing them without giving such security.

Maryland.—Masters arriving at Baltimore must, within twenty-four hours after entering at the custom-house, report to the mayor or recorder the names, ages and occupations of all alien passengers on board during the voyage, or they incur a penalty of $20 for each passenger not reported.

Within forty-eight hours the master must pay $1 50 for each passger[c] above five years of age; and if any such passenger be landed before making such payment, the master incurs a penalty of $100 for each person landed. The same penalty is incurred by landing an alien passenger within fifty miles of the city, unless payment be made for such person within forty-eight hours, or a bond be given to prevent his becoming a public charge.

The same report must be made to the municipal authorities upon arriving at any other port in the state, but the master has the option of paying $1 50 for each passenger, or of giving a bond for $150 for each person, to indemnify the country from all charges incurred for two years. A penalty of $100 for each passenger landed is incurred by landing aliens in any port before complying with these requisitions.[d]

There is also a register of German and Swiss emigrants at Baltimore, whose duty it is to regulate the apprenticeship of such passengers, who pay their passage by temporary service. All indentures of that character must be drawn up by him, or they are void. He must keep an account of the ages, names, sexes, term of service, country, and to whom bound, of all such emigrants. Minors can be bound only by their next of kin, or in default thereof, by the orphan's court, and their indentures must contain a stipulation to give them two months' schooling annually.

Emigrants cannot be bound to more than four years' service, except males under seventeen, or females under fourteen, who may be bound, the former to twenty-one, and the latter to eighteen years of age. German and Swiss emigrants cannot be detained on board for their passage money longer than thirty days after arriving, and the master is bound to furnish them, during that time, with provisions free of charge.

---

[a] Act, 24th Jan., 1797, sec. 5. [b] Act, 12th Feb., 1829, sec. 15. [c] Act, 17th Feb., 1835. [d] Act, 22d March, 1833.

At the end of that time they may apply to the register, whose duty it is to cause them to be brought on shore, where they may be further detained for thirty days in addition, at the expense of the master, and at the end of that time, if not indented, the claim for passage money becomes an ordinary debt, and the emigrants are discharged.

No child can be made responsible for the passage of his parents, nor can parents or husband or wife be made responsible for the passage of any person deceased, notwithstanding any contract.

Masters must, within ten days after arriving, deliver to the register aforesaid, an inventory, under oath, of all property on board belonging to any deceased passenger, or they incur a penalty of $200.

This property is appraised by the register, and may be sold at public auction, or be taken by the master or owner in payment or part payment of his claim for passage money; but if the passenger died before half of the passage was performed, no passage money is due.[a]

Masters knowingly bringing any convict into the state, or importing any free person of colour, with intent to sell him, are liable to be imprisoned from one to five years.[b]

Virginia.—Masters of vessels bringing convicts into the state, forfeit £50 for each convict landed, and are also liable to three months' imprisonment.[c]

Masters bringing any free person of colour into the state, are liable to a fine of from $500 to $1,000, and to be imprisoned from six to twelve months.

This law does not extend to persons belonging to the vessel, but all such, if found on shore without a pass, are liable to punishment.[d]

For this, and laws as to slaves found on board vessels, vide chapter X, page 267.

There was also a law passed 26th Dec., 1792, making masters of vessels liable for all debts of passengers transported by them out of the state, unless such passenger gave six weeks' notice of his intended departure in the newspaper; but we presume this relic of antiquity has become obsolete, as unsuited to the age, or that it has been repealed.

North Carolina.—Masters of vessels transporting slaves out of the state, without the consent of their masters, or for the purpose of enabling them to escape, are liable to capital punishment.[e]

Persons bringing slaves into the state from states where laws exist for the liberation of slaves, may be compelled to give bonds in the sum of £50 for each slave, to remove them from the state within three months.[f]

Masters bringing free persons of colour into the state, must keep them on board and take them away with them, or they incur a penalty of $500.[g]

A similar penalty is incurred if a slave be found concealed on board after the anchor is weighed, when departing.[h]

---

[a] Act, 1817. [b] Act, Nov., 1809. [c] Act, 13th Nov., 1788. [d] Act, 11th March, 1834.
[e] Acts, 1792 and 1832. [f] Act, 1783. [g] Act, 1830. [h] Act, 1825.

South Carolina.—Masters having free persons of colour on board, except Moors, Lascars, or natives of countries beyond the Cape of Good Hope, must give bonds in the sum of $1,000, with sureties, to carry them away with them, and the negro, &c., is liable to be imprisoned until the departure of the vessel. If the master refuse to give bonds, the vessel is quarantined at anchor, one hundred yards from the shore, until she is ready to sail.[a]

The carrying away a slave without the consent of the owner, is felony, and punished by death.[b]

Masters having redemption passengers on board, must deliver a list to the collector, and must make affidavit that none of them are convicts; and masters landing convicts forfeit £500, and in default of payment, may be imprisoned twelve months.[c]

The vessel having convicts on board is compelled to leave the state in ten days, and is not permitted to take in any cargo.[c]

Masters having passengers on board who are likely to become chargeable, are compelled to give security to carry them out of the state within three months, or to indemnify the town for their support.[d]

Georgia.—Any master of any vessel arriving between the first of July and last day of October, inclusive, at Savannah, must, within twenty-four hours after entry, make a report, in writing, on oath, to the mayor, of the age, name and occupation of every passenger in such vessel on her last voyage, upon pain of forfeiting $75 for every alien neglected to be reported.

Masters must give bonds, with two sureties, in a sum not exceeding $300 for each passenger, to indemnify the city against any expense that may be incurred, for the maintenance and support of any such person so introduced, and for the maintenance and support of the child or children of any of such persons which may be born after such importation, in case such person or such child at any time within six months after the said importation, become chargeable to the said city.

Masters of vessels who permit any passengers, not citizens of the United States, to land in the city, before such bonds shall be given, and without a written permission from the mayor, are subject to a penalty of $300 for each person so landed. The like penalty is provided in case any passenger, not a citizen of the United States, be permitted to land within fifty miles of the city, with intent to proceed to the city, and the vessel may be attached therefor.[e]

Masters having persons of colour on board, must, within twenty-four hours after arrival at any port, report them to the mayor or chief magistrate, or they incur a penalty of $100. They must also give bonds with security to keep them on board from 6 P. M. to 5 A. M., and to carry them away with them.[f]

The importing a slave illegally, and the carrying one out of the state without the consent of the owner, is punishable by imprisonment not exceeding seven years.[g]

---

[a] Act, 19th Dec., 1835. [b] Act, 1754. [c] Act, Nov. 1788. [d] Act, 1758.
[e] Act, 22d Dec. 1819. [f] Acts, 20th Dec., 1826, and 26th Dec., 1827.
[g] Penal Code, 1817, sec. 235.

Masters carrying out of the state any person of colour, without a certificate of freedom from the county clerk, are liable to be fined $500, if prosecuted within five years.[a]

A late law subjects all vessels having a coloured person on board, (except Lascars, free Moors, American Indians, or natives of countries beyond the Cape of Good Hope,) to a quarantine of forty days, and prohibits all coloured persons from going on board.[b]

Louisiana.—Masters must, within twenty-four hours after entry at the custom-house, deliver to the mayor or the recorder of New-Orleans, a statement under oath, of the names, ages, professions and means of subsistence of his passengers, under the penalty of $100 for every foreigner, and $50 for every other passenger omitted in the return.

A bond must also be given, with two sureties, that such passengers shall not become a public charge within two years, either from want or crime; and if any passenger be landed without such a bond, a penalty of $250 is incurred.

If a certificate legalized by the American consul be produced, that any passenger is of good character and of a useful profession, the mayor may dispense with the bond.[c]

By transporting a slave out of the state without the owners consent, the owners of the vessel become liable to pay his full value.[d]

---

[a] Act, 20th Dec., 1826. [b] Act, 22d Dec., 1829. [c] Act, 16th March, 1818. [d] Act, 26th March, 1835.

CHAPTER XXIII.

OF PILOTS AND PILOTAGE.

The business of a pilot is to conduct any ship or vessel into a road or harbour, over bars or sand, or through intricate and dangerous channels, being occasionally called in to the master's assistance when sailing in such places, or by unknown shores, and diffident of his own skill and judgment. Where the approach or entrance to harbours, &c., is hazardous and difficult, the taking a pilot is obligatory on the master; otherwise, in case of a loss, he must make it good. The pilot is responsible for any accidents which may happen through his ignorance or negligence. After a pilot is taken on board, the master has no longer any command of the ship till she is safe in the harbour; but then the master resumes the government of the same, and is to see to her bed and lying, the pilot being no longer liable, though for his own convenience he may still be on board. While the pilot is on board and acting as pilot, he has the exclusive direction of the ship, and is considered as master, *pro hac vice*, and the master is not liable for any damage committed by the ship through the negligence or unskilfulness of the pilot.[a] If the owner be on board in such case, an action will lie against him.[b] The same rule holds good if a pilot go on board only to conduct a ship through some dangerous place: after passing it, the master must resume the command, and the pilot is no longer responsible. If the pilot continue on board for the remainder of the voyage, he is only to be considered as a common passenger, after he has conducted the ship through the hazardous passage, for which purpose he came on board: neither can he charge any wages, salary, or fee, though he should keep the helm during the whole voyage, except for the duty done in passing the passage, unless by contract.

If a master of a ship find himself, in tempestuous weather, in any reputed dangerous place, usually denominated *pilot's* water, and a pilot offer to come on board, which offer he refuses to accept, the master in such case is liable to his owners, freighters, or insurers, for the damage or loss of ship and cargo, if either happen in his attempting a passage without a pilot.

If the master at a foreign port attempt to obtain a pilot, and fail, and then in the exercise of his best discretion, endeavour to enter the port, and ground, the insurer is not discharged.[c]

If the master approach a port in the night, he must make signals for a pilot, and wait a reasonable time for one, and if he attempt to enter the port without one, except in case of extreme necessity, the insurers are discharged.[d]

---

[a] 1 Johns. Rep. 305. [b] 5 Boss. & Pull. 446. [c] 2 Barn. & Adolph. 380. [d] 3 Kent, 176.

The business of regulating pilots and pilotage properly belongs to congress; but that body, at the formation of the government, found itself unacquainted with the local details necessary for forming a general pilot law.

A law was therefore passed, declaring that all pilots in the bays, inlets, rivers, harbours and ports of the United States, shall continue to be regulated in conformity with the existing laws of the states respectively where such pilots may be, or with such laws as they may hereafter enact for the purpose, until further legislative provision shall be made by congress.[a]

The state pilot laws then existing, were of course rendered valid: and presuming that the provision relating to future laws was also valid, (of which there is good reason to doubt,) the states have gone on to pass pilot laws, as if the power had belonged solely to them. In general no inconvenience resulted from this course, as the state legislatures were sufficiently well inclined to facilitate the entrance of vessels into their harbours.

The legislature of New-York, under the influence of party feelings, however, determined to limit the number of pilots of that important port to sixty, and thus by monopolizing the business in the hands of a few, to reward their political favourites.

The natural consequence followed: pilots neglected their calling, and the loss of life resulting from their negligence, roused the public indignation; and the legislature of New-York still refusing to throw open the business of piloting vessels, the legislature of New-Jersey enacted a law for the establishment of branch pilots for Sandy Hook bay and the Hudson river, and congress, by a law passed 2d March, 1837, declared, " that it shall and may be lawful for the master or commander of any vessel coming into or going out of any port situate upon waters which are the boundary between two states, to employ any pilot duly authorized by the laws of either of the states bounded on the said waters, to pilot the said vessel to or from said port; any law, usage, or custom, to the contrary notwithstanding."

This law entirely breaks up, not only the monopoly of the New-York pilots, but it places the pilots of Delaware bay, whether licensed by the governors of Pennsylvania, Delaware or New-Jersey, on an equal footing: also the pilots of Chesapeake bay, whether licensed by the governors of Maryland or Virginia. Full and free competition is thus effectually secured. The state pilot laws passed since 1789, and before 1837, are also recognised, at least so far as to licensing pilots and establishing rates of pilotage.

The laws by the states, contain the following regulations:

Maine.—Pilots are appointed by the governor and council, upon the recommendation of a majority of the ship-owners and masters in the port for which they are appointed.

The pilots are sworn and give bonds in the sum of $5000 for the faithful discharge of their duties; and if any vessel or cargo be lost or

---

[a] Act, 7th August, 1789.

run aground through the unskilfulness or neglect of the pilot, he is liable for all damages.

The governor and council are empowered to hear complaints against pilots, and to remove or suspend them.

They also fix and determine the rates of pilotage for each port, and a schedule thereof must be hung up in the collector's office.

Any master may pilot his own vessel without paying pilotage.[a]

Pilots forfeit $50 by piloting vessels with any person on board sick with a pestilential disorder up to a town, before permission be given by the selectmen, and $100 for piloting a vessel up in violation of a quarantine.[b]

New-Hampshire.—Pilots for Piscataqua river are appointed by the governor and council. They have power to appoint substitutes, and also deputies, who must be approved of by the governor. The pilots and their deputies give bonds in the sum of $1,000, and also take an oath for the faithful performance of their duties. Pilots must take charge of vessels drawing nine feet or more, except coasting and fishing vessels, and show to the masters their warrants and list of fees.

The cruising ground of pilots is from the Ragged Neck, in Rye, to the southwest of Portsmouth harbour; thence easterly to the middle ground, between the islands of the shoals, and the harbour's mouth, and as far as the easternmost of the Sisters; and the branch pilots and each of the deputies must always keep a suitable boat in good repair.

Masters bound out of the port may take their vessels to sea without a pilot, and pay no pilotage; but vessels inward bound must pay half pilotage if they refuse to take a pilot, unless the vessel be within the light-house before a pilot offers, in which case no pilotage is due, if the pilot be not employed. The governor and council fix the fees of pilots and hear complaints against them, and suspend or remove them for misconduct. Pilots are liable for all damages sustained through their neglect or want of skill.[c]

Massachusetts.—The governor, with the advice of the council, appoints pilots for the several harbours, except for Boston, where two commissioners of pilots are appointed, and New-Bedford, where five commissioners are chosen. These commissioners appoint the pilots for Boston, and for New-Bedford and Fairhaven. The pilots give bonds in the sum of $2,000 for the faithful performance of their duties, except for Newburyport and New-Bedford, where the penalties are $500 and $1000. For Boston, Salem and Newburyport, pilots are appointed only upon the recommendation of the marine societies respectively of those towns. The appointing power may revoke the appointments, and may suspend at their discretion.

The pilots for Boston must render quarterly an account of the fees received by them, and must pay to the commissioners five per cent. of the amount received. The five per cent. they are authorized to add to the pilotage established by law. The fees of the pilots in Mas-

---

[a] Act, 24th Feb., 1821. [b] Act, 10th March, 1821, sec. 9 and 12.
[c] Acts, 18th June, 1805, and 22d June, 1785.

sachusetts are set forth in their respective warrants, and all vessels, except fishing vessels, coasting vessels of less than 200 tons, and vessels trading between ports within the state, are bound to employ pilots or pay full pilotage, unless no pilot offers before vessels have arrived within the following limits, i. e. within the chops of the harbour of Salem, Marblehead or Gloucester; within the gurnet of Plymouth harbour, or within any bar of a barred harbour; or within the entrance of Boston harbour, being a line drawn from Harding rocks to the Outer Graves, and thence to Nahant head. In such case the master may refuse to employ a pilot, and the vessel pays no pilotage.

The penalty for piloting a vessel in or out of Boston harbour without being licensed, is $50 for each offence.

The pilots are assigned as follows: the pilots for Salem and Marblehead cruise from Nahant rock to Norman's Woe; the Gloucester pilots, from Norman's Woe round the Cape to Chebacco bar; the Newburyport pilots, from Chebacco bar to the Isle of Shoals; the Plymouth pilots, from the highlands of Marshfield to Cape Cod; the Nantucket pilots take charge of any vessels bound over the shoals. Each of the pilots is bound to keep a one decked boat in good order, and a sufficient number of row boats. One of the decked boats for the port of Plymouth must be stationed in that harbour, two in Salem harbour, two in Marblehead, one in Gloucester, one in Sandy bay, four at Gay Head, four at Holmes' Hole, and two at Edgartown; and they are bound to cruise on their respective pilot grounds at all times when the weather permits. If a vessel sustain any damage through the negligence or unskilfulness of the pilot, he is liable for all damages, and also to be removed.

For vessels drawing more than nine feet of water, bound in or out of New-Bedford harbour, the pilotage is $2 per foot for all vessels inward bound, and $1 per foot for vessels outward bound. When a vessel, bound into New-Bedford or Fairhaven, has a pilot on board not commissioned for that port, and a commissioned pilot comes on board, the non-commissioned pilot must surrender the vessel, and receives for pilotage as follows: if the vessels have arrived in the upper harbour of New-Bedford, he receives full pilotage; if into Tarpaulin Cove at anchor, one half; if through Quick's Hole into Buzzard's bay, two thirds; if within a line drawn from the south part of Noman's land to Seconnet point, one-fourth; if within a line drawn from the Hen and Chickens to the light-house to Cuttyhunk, three fourths; if within a line drawn due east and west across the north part of Great Ledge, seven eighths; and these amounts are to be deducted from the sums that would otherwise be due to the warrant pilots. If a vessel, bound into New-Bedford harbour, decline to receive a warrant pilot, she is liable to pay half pilotage. Any person piloting vessels through Vineyard Sound, over Nantucket Shoals, to her port of destination in Boston bay or eastward thereof, is entitled, from the first of November to the thirty-first of March, for vessels of less than eleven feet water, $3 50 per foot; between eleven and fourteen feet, $4 per foot; more than fourteen, $4 50 per foot; and from the first of April to the thirty-first of October, on each of the above classes, $1 per foot less. If the person acting as pilot, be landed between Cape Ann and Portsmouth, he is entitltd to $5 more, and if to the eastward of Portsmouth, $10. This, however, does not apply to cases where there is a special contract. Fishing and coasting vessels are not liable to pay pilotage to the New-Bedford pilots.[a]

For the pilot laws of New-York, vide Appendix.

New-Jersey.—The act to establish and regulate pilots for the ports of Jersey City, Newark and Perth Amboy, by the way of Sandy Hook, provides for the appointment, by the governor and council, of seven commissioners from the counties of Bergen, Essex, Middlesex and Monmouth; one, at least, from each of the counties, who have full power to appoint pilots, and give them certificates of appointment.

Persons receiving certificates as pilots or deputy pilots present them to the governor, who, after administering an oath to each that he will diligently and truly perform the duty of pilot or deputy, and obey the instructions of the commissioners, and not be in partnership with more than nine others—directs the treasurer to take a bond in the sum of $500 from the party, with two sureties, for the faithful discharge of their duty—which done, the governor must deliver to him a license, signed by himself, authorizing him to act as pilot or deputy, as the case may be.

A preliminary examination must be had by the commissioners before granting any certificate, into the competency, skill and experience of the parties applying, and in particular touching his knowledge of the tides, soundings, bearings and distances of the several shoals, rocks, bars and points of land, in that navigation for which he seeks to be licensed. This examination is to be had in the presence of one or more of the branch pilots.

Commissioners may require pilots or deputies to renew their licenses and bonds whenever it is deemed necessary, and they may take away the license of any pilot or deputy for wilful infringement or violation of their duty, or of the order of the commissioners, or for negligently losing any vessel, or mental derangement, or habitual intemperance, provided due notice be given to such pilot, and an opportunity be afforded him of being heard in his own defence.

If a pilot do not give up his license, a notification of its revocation is to be published in a Jersey City or Newark paper.

Commissioners may make all needful rules and regulations for the government of the pilots, and establish penalties for the breach thereof. Fines for misbehaviour of pilots while on duty, $25, or suspension.

A fine of $100, one half to the informer, the other to the master of the vessel, is imposed on any pilot or deputy who refuses or neglects, when practicable, to go to any vessel on the coast having a signal flying for a pilot, or which he shall hear firing guns.

When cruising off, or standing out to sea, pilots must go to the vessel nearest shore, or in most distress, under a penalty of $50; and for refusing to go on board a vessel when required, a penalty of $100 is

---

[a] Rev. Stat. part 1, tit. 12, chap. 32.

imposed, and in either case, upon complaint and conviction, the pilot may be suspended.

Pilots offering their services must show their licenses, or they incur a penalty of $10.

For carelessly or negligently losing a vessel, a pilot is broke, on conviction, and rendered incapable ever after of acting as pilot, and is liable moreover for damages, at common law. If a vessel be run ashore by a pilot, no pilotage can be charged; and if negligently done, the pilot is liable for all damages sustained.

No more than nine pilots can be in partnership, nor in any manner concerned in business together, under a penalty of $200 on each pilot so concerned, one half to the informer, the other half to the state.

No commissioner can have any interest in the pilotage business.

Any vessel carrying off a pilot, must pay $75 per month to the commissioners, for the use of said pilot, until he return, over and above the usual pilotage.

Rates of pilotage "to or from the eastward or southward of the white buoy, on the east edge of the outer middle," to or from Newark, Jersey City or Perth Amboy, for vessels of the United States, or, by treaty, on a footing with those of the United States—

For vessels under 14 feet,	$1 50	per foot,
" over 14 feet, and under 18,	1 75	"
" over 18 feet,	2 25	"

and for all other vessels, an addition of one fourth to these rates; the full pilotage to be paid, even though the vessel be moored, at the master's request, at any place within Sandy Hook, other than the ports of Amboy, Newark or Jersey City, and then the pilot must be discharged within twenty-four hours. Half pilotage is only chargeable if the pilot board to the westward of the white buoy, and none, if offering to take charge above or to the northward of the upper middle, unless such vessel be above 100 tons, and make signal for a pilot, when half pilotage may be charged.

And further, from the first of November to the first of April, $4 additional is to be charged for every vessel drawing ten feet and upwards, and $2 for below ten feet; and one fourth addition to the whole rates, for a pilot boarding a vessel so distant, that Sandy Hook light could not, in fair weather and in day light, be seen from the deck.

Three dollars a day are allowed for pilots tending, when requested, on vessels bound out or in, over and above the usual detentions of getting vessels from the wharf to sea, and from sea to the wharf.

Extraordinary services or exertions by pilots are to be paid as may be agreed on; or according to the award of the commissioners, in case of non-agreement.

The following section was enacted with the view of testing the right of the legislature of New-York, to exact half pilotage from vessels in charge of New-Jersey pilots; but as congress has allowed the pilots of either state equal privileges, it is inoperative.

If the master of any vessel, (except schooners and sloops employed in the coasting trade, licensed for that purpose, and not making the usual signal for a pilot,) coming into the ports of Jersey City, Newark or Perth Amboy, or into any of the waters of New-Jersey, refuse to receive on board and employ a pilot who shall have offered to go on board and to take charge of the pilotage of such vessel, the master, owner or consignee of such vessel shall pay to the pilot half pilotage, from the place at which such pilot shall have offered himself, to the port of destination; but no half pilotage shall be collected from any vessel in charge of a New-York pilot, provided vessels in charge of a New-Jersey pilot be permitted to enter and traverse the waters of New-York, without being compelled to pay half pilotage.

Each pilot must have at least two apprentices, who must be duly instructed by the pilots to whom they are indented in piloting and working ships and square rigged vessels; these apprentices have the preference for appointments as deputies, &c., and the piloting business is confined to branch pilots, deputy pilots, apprentices indented, and boat-keepers to be selected from apprentices.

The commissioners are required, in the month of May, annually, to examine the apprentices, touching their qualifications as pilots.

The pilot in charge of a vessel, inward or outward bound, must have the lead regularly hove, and see that the line is properly marked, under the penalty of forfeiture of pilotage.

In case of disagreement about amount of pilotage, commissioners tax and certify the pilot's charge.

Penalty for intoxication while in charge—for the first offence, forfeiture of pilotage, six months' suspension, and $50 fine; for the second offence, to be broke, and rendered incapable for the future of piloting.

All forfeitures, fines, penalties, &c., are paid over to the pilot's charitable fund.

Pilots make monthly returns to the commissioners of the fees received, from which said commissioners receive a commission of five cent. per for their services.[a]

Pennsylvania.—Pilots for Philadelphia are appointed by a board of wardens after examination by wardens and two pilots; and there are three classes of pilots—the first for vessels of any description, the second for vessels drawing twelve feet of water and less, the third for vessels drawing nine feet of water and less. The licenses are only in force one year, but are renewable by the pilots, unless good reason exist for refusing.

Thirty dollars penalty is incurred, by any person not licensed, piloting a vessel to or from Philadelphia. The New-Jersey and Delaware pilots have, of course, under the above act of congress, a right to pilot vessels, without being subject to this penalty.

Before they can obtain a license, the first class of pilots must serve an apprenticeship of six years; the second class five years; and the third class four years; and must have conducted a square rigged vessel twice up and twice down the river, under the inspection of the master. They must also give a bond, with security, in the sum of $500, for the faithful performance of their duties. Pilots neglecting or re-

---

[a] Act, Feb., 1837.

fusing for two weeks to act, forfeit their warrants; also, if they combine to prevent other persons from performing their duty as pilots.

If the number of pilots necessary for the port be reduced by disease or otherwise, so as to occasion much inconvenience to the trade of the state, the wardens, or any three of them, may grant certificates to such persons as they may find qualified to act as pilots, for six months, renewable, if occasion require it; subject to the like rules as other pilots.

The apprentices on board of pilot boats must be taken up and down the Delaware four times in each of the four last years of his apprenticeship, in a square rigged vessel, by his master, in order to teach him his business as pilot.[a]

The pilot who first offers himself to any inward bound vessel, is entitled to take charge thereof, if his license authorize him to pilot a vessel of such draught of water, and if required, he exhibits his license to the master. And if the draught of water be greater than he is licensed to carry, he may, nevertheless, with the consent of the master, take charge of such vessel, until a pilot, duly qualified, offer; but if such qualified pilot offer before such vessel shall have passed Reedy Island, he must be received, and the former pilot is entitled to pilotage, according to the distance he may have conducted such vessel, and the latter to the residue, which is ascertained by the master warden. And the master of such vessel must display a signal for a pilot, until a pilot duly qualified, offer; and on refusal or neglect so to do, or to receive a pilot duly qualified, the master, owner or consignee, pays the wardens half pilotage, to the use of the society for the relief of distressed and decayed pilots.

In all cases, when extraordinary services have been rendered by any pilot, the board of wardens, if the parties cannot agree, determine the compensation for such services.

The pilot must inform the master of every vessel he conducts to the port of Philadelphia, of the rules and regulations necessary in reporting at the warden's office.

The master of any outward bound vessel must remain twenty-four hours after his arrival at the capes, to give the pilot an opportunity to be taken out, and on refusal, if it can be done without endangering the vessel, the master must pay to such pilot, his executors, &c., a sum not exceeding $800.

If any first rate-pilot, having a boat attending him, be carried to sea in any ship contrary to his inclination, by stress of weather, or other unavoidable accident, the master, owner or consignee, must pay him the wages the master receives, until his return to the capes, or in case of his death while absent, to his executors, &c., to the time of his death; a second rate pilot, the same wages as the first mate receives; and a third rate pilot, the same wages as the seamen receive; but if not having a boat attending them, half the said wages.

If any inward bound vessel, having a pilot on board, be prevented by ice, or other cause, from proceeding to the port of Philadelphia, and be compelled to proceed to any other place, not in the river De-

---

[a] Order of Wardens, 22d Nov., 1824.

laware, or bay, he receives full pilotage as if he had conducted the vessel to the port of Philadelphia, and eight cents for each mile he travels to the place of his abode.

Two dollars a day are allowed to the pilot of each ship compelled to perform quarantine; and the pilot cannot be discharged in less than six days without his consent.

The license of each pilot is 50 cents, for the support of the warden's office, and $1 to pilots attending examination.

The compensation to pilots for conducting vessels from Philadelphia to the capes of Delaware, or from the capes to Philadelphia, is for every half foot of water which any inward bound vessel draws under and up to twelve feet, $1 50; outward bound, $1 12½; for every half foot of water which such vessel draws more than twelve feet, and less than fifteen feet, $2 08⅛; outward bound, $1 66⅝; for every half foot over fifteen feet, inward bound, $2 22; outward bound, $1 78;[a] and he also receives over and above the said sums, for every vessel not being registered or owned[b] in the United States, the sum of $2 67; and for conducting all ships or vessels to or from Philadelphia, between the 20th day of November and the 10th day of March inclusive, the additional sum of $10. No pilot can receive any reward for any supernumerary inches under six. If any pilot be detained by any master, owner or consignee, over twenty-four hours, or by the ice, he is entitled to $2 per day.

Pilots' compensation for conducting dismasted or crippled vessels, in any wise injured, so as to occasion extraordinary care or trouble, is double what they would otherwise be entitled to, of which the board of wardens judge. Pilots demanding or receiving more than legal fees, may be suspended one year.[c]

Every vessel arriving from, or bound to, any foreign port or place, and every vessel of the burthen of seventy-five tons or more, sailing from or bound to any port or place not within the river Delaware, is obliged to receive a pilot. The master, within thirty-six hours after arrival, must report her name, draught of water, and the name of the pilot, also as to the sobriety and competency of the pilot;[d] when outward bound, the same, under $10 penalty for neglect. The master must pay half pilotage on refusal or neglect to take a pilot, unless no pilot offered before she reached Reedy Island; or in case of an outward bound vessel, no pilot could be obtained for twenty-four hours after being ready for sea.[c]

American vessels engaged in the Pennsylvania coal trade, pay no half pilotage.[e]

When any inward bound vessel, having a pilot on board, is detained by ice, and is conducted by him to a place of safety, the master of such vessel, after being detained forty-eight hours, may discharge his pilot, and the pilot receives full pilotage, as if he had conducted the ship to the port of Philadelphia; and if detained more than forty-eight hours, he receives $2 a day for every day he is so detained.[c]

---

[a] Act, 1837. [b] Act, 2d April, 1804. [c] Act, 29th March, 1803.
[d] Act, 25th March, 1816. [e] Act, 12th June, 1832.

Misbehaviour may be punished by the wardens, after a hearing, either by fine or suspension, and the owner also has a right of action for damages.

Pilots must report, within forty-eight hours after arrival, to the wardens, the name of any vessel piloted by them to Philadelphia, and the number of persons on board, under the penalty of $12.

If any pilot, endeavouring to assist or relieve any vessel in distress, suffer loss or damage in his boats, sails, tackle, rigging, or appurtenances, the master, owner or consignee of such vessel, must pay the value of such loss or damage, to be ascertained by the board of wardens.

The board of wardens are entitled to 6 cents per ton on every vessel clearing out at the port of Philadelphia, which may be recovered of the owner or consignee.[a] This duty is applied first to pay the salaries of the wardens, and the residue to improve the navigation of the Delaware.

It is the duty of the pilots, between the 1st of March and the 20th of December, to cruise six miles east of the five fathom bank, twenty miles south of Cape Henlopen, and twenty miles north of Cape May.[b]

Delaware.—Vessels of seventy-five tons and upwards, bound into or from any port in this state, unless owned by citizens of Delaware, are obliged to take a pilot, or pay half pilotage from the capes to Philadelphia to the Philadelphia society for the relief of distressed and decayed pilots. If no pilot can be obtained for an outward ship within twenty-four hours after she be ready for sea, or in case of an inward bound vessel, before she reach Reedy Island, half pilotage is not due.

Within thirty-six hours after arrival, the master must report to the collector of Wilmington the name of the vessel, her draught of water, and the name of her pilot, under penalty of $60. In case of an outward bound vessel, a similar report is required.[c]

Maryland.—A board is constituted for examining and appointing pilots for Chesapeake bay, whose warrants, which are under the seal of the board, are for one year only. The pilots give bonds, with sureties, in $500, for the faithful discharge of their duty, and are divided into three classes—the first class for vessels of any draught of water; the second class for vessels not exceeding twelve feet; the third class for vessels not exceeding nine feet. Every pilot, or his company, must keep a decked pilot boat of twenty-six feet keel, under the penalty of $150 for every vessel piloted, and the name of the boat must be painted in large letters on her stern, mainsail and foresail.

Any person acting as a pilot, without a warrant, forfeits $150, and is liable for all damages. Any person, however, may aid or conduct a vessel in distress, but he must surrender his charge to the first pilot coming on board, and he is then entitled to half pilotage.

---

[a] Acts, 2d April, 1804, and 20th March, 1811. [b] Order of Wardens, 26th Dec., 1825.
[c] Act, 5th Feb., 1819, and 31st Jan., 1825.

No more than six pilots can be partners, under the penalty of $200 each.

The board of examiners make rules for the government of pilots, and may break or suspend them; and a pilot acting as pilot while broke or suspended, forfeits $100.

Masters of vessels over one hundred tons burthen, and drawing nine feet or more of water, inward bound, must receive the first pilot offering below the Horse Shoe, and must keep him unto the first port of discharge, or pay half pilotage.[a] When outward bound, they must take that pilot or one of his company, if they apply, as pilot to the capes, or pay half pilotage;[b] but coasting vessels of less than one hundred and thirty tons, outward bound from Baltimore to the capes, are not obliged to employ a pilot.[c] Masters incur a penalty of $30 by refusing to show a pilot the register or license, and the pilot incurs a penalty of $50 by taking other than legal pilotage.[b] Disputes relative to the pilotage of coasters, are to be settled before a justice of the peace.[c]

Vessels following a vessel having a pilot on board, pay half pilotage.

A pilot cruising or standing out to sea, must offer his services first to the vessel nearest the land or in most distress. If a pilot refuse to go on board a vessel when required as a pilot, he forfeits $100, and is liable to suspension. Pilots must show their warrants to masters when offering their services, or forfeit $10, and also a copy of the act when receiving their pilotage, under a penalty of $20, and if required, $60.

A pilot losing a vessel through negligence, is liable for damages, and is incapacitated from again acting as pilot. If he run a vessel ashore, he loses his pilotage, and is also liable for damages if done through carelessness.

Pilotage from sea to Baltimore,	.	$3 50 per foot,
" " Baltimore to sea,	.	2 50 "

but no supernumerary inches less than six can be charged for.[d]

From the mouth of the Potomac to Georgetown, and vice versa, 20 per cent. in addition, and so in proportion for any less distance, which is to be fixed by the board of examiners. During December, January and February, American vessels sailing to or from Baltimore, pay 75 cents per foot in addition to the above rates; foreign vessels from prohibited ports pay one third more.[a] If the vessel touch at Hampton Roads, except forced in by distress of weather, the pilot is entitled to $12 for piloting in, and $10 for piloting her out of the roads. If she touch at Annapolis, except from the same cause, the pilot is entitled to $3 for each day he is detained. If detained at quarantine, $2 per day. If the master require his attendance at a particular time and place, the pilot is entitled to $4 for each day he is detained by the master's not being ready, and if attending upon request of the master with his boat, he is entitled to $8 per day.

Foreign vessels must take a pilot if one offers, or pay full pilotage, and they pay one third more than American vessels. Pilots receiving

---

[a] Act, 1818. [b] Act, 11th Feb., 1830. [c] Act, 27th Feb., 1833. [d] Act, 24th Feb., 1824.

or demanding more than lawful pilotage, forfeit $50. If a pilot be carried to sea against his inclination, he is entitled to receive as follows: 1st class, if his boat be in attendance, $30 per month; otherwise, ... $20 per month,
2d class, $24 per month, or . . . 16 " "
3d class, 20 per month, or . . . 12 " "
until his return or death; and if his boat be ready to take him off, and the same can be safely done, the master must pay him in addition $300.

A pilot refusing to aid a vessel in distress in the bay, or within eighteen miles of either cape, is rendered incapable of again acting as pilot.

A pilot is entitled to a reasonable reward for aiding a vessel in distress, but all contracts between masters of vessels in distress and pilots are void.

Every pilot must have one white apprentice on board; and no person can obtain a warrant until after having served three years in the business of pilot in Chesapeake bay.

No pilot can undertake to pilot a vessel into a port in Virginia unless such vessel be below the Horse Shoe, and no Virginia pilot offer to pilot her. The Maryland pilot must also give up the vessel in such case, without any charge, to the Virginia pilot, who offers to take charge of her. This provision, however, is operative only in case the Virginia legislature makes a similar regulation as to vessels bound to the ports of Maryland.[a]

Persons employing their vessels as pilot boats, without being licensed, incur a penalty of $50 for each offence.[b]

These acts of Maryland are, of course, modified by the act of congress of 1837, and all Virginia pilots are placed upon the same footing as those of Maryland.

Virginia.—Five examiners are appointed to grant branch warrants for pilots, who must be white men. The examiners are appointed by the county court or the municipal magistrates of the town where a vacancy occurs, and they are sworn to execute their duties impartially.

The pilots give bonds, with security, in the sum of $500, for the faithful performance of their duty; and they are divided into three classes—the pilots of the first class having the power to pilot vessels of every description; those of the second, only vessels drawing twelve feet of water or less; and those of the third, vessels drawing not more than nine feet.

Non-residents are not allowed to act as pilots, unless they are Maryland pilots.

Branch pilots must keep at least one sufficient boat of not less than eighteen feet keel, under the penalty of $150; and the name of the boat and port must be marked ten feet below the head of her foresail in letters nine inches long.

No more than four pilots can be in partnership, under the penalty of $100 each.

---

[a] Act, Nov., 1803. [b] Act, 1818.

No person can officiate as a pilot, without a branch, under the penalty of $30, unless assisting a vessel in distress. In that case, he delivers the vessel up to the first pilot coming on board, and receives half pilotage.

Apprentices properly qualified may act with a copy of their master's branch, in the same capacity as their master.

Any pilot first boarding a vessel, may conduct her into Hampton Roads, York River, or Mobjack Bay; there pilots qualified for the different ports where she is bound, take her in charge.[a]

Masters are obliged to take the first pilot offering below a line where Cape Henry bears west of south, or to pay full pilotage to the first port of discharge. Coasting vessels of less than seventy-five tons burthen are not compelled to take a pilot, nor are other vessels, unless a pilot offers, before they arrive within the line above described.[b]

Pilots, cruising or standing out to sea, must offer their services first to the vessel nearest to land, or in most distress.

Vessels having no pilot, and following one having a pilot, pay half pilotage.

If a pilot or his apprentice lose a vessel by negligence or misconduct, the pilot may be suspended six months, besides being liable for all damages. A pilot, upon meeting a vessel, must inquire into the health of her crew, and if he find her liable to perform quarantine, he must direct her to follow his pilot-boat to the nearest quarantine ground, and there inform the superintendent of her arrival, under the penalty of being suspended two months. For this he receives an extra fee of $7, to be paid by the master, and if he be decoyed on board, and be obliged to perform quarantine, he is allowed $3 per day.[a]

Masters must receive pilots when offering to take their vessel to sea. Coasting vessels, that come in without a pilot, are not compelled to take a pilot when outward bound;[b] but pilots that brought a vessel in, when tendering their services, have a legal preference, if they are in readiness.[c]

Pilots refusing, when requested to go on board a vessel to pilot her, may be suspended by the board of examiners, besides being liable to all damages.

Consignees and supercargoes are liable for pilotage; and the pilot may make out a bill of his fees, and obtain it through the collector, who is authorized to demand the same before clearing the vessel, and to retain two and a half per cent. commission.[d]

PILOTAGE RATES.

	American vessels in foreign trade. *per foot.*	*Coasters.*
From sea to Hampton Roads,	$1 25	$10 or $5 for refusing.[b]
Hampton Roads to sea,	1 00	5 00
Hampton Roads or Sewell's Point to—		*per foot.*
Norfolk or Portsmouth,	50	50

[a] Act, 10th Feb., 1819. [b] Act, 26th Feb., 1821. [c] Act, 27th Jan., 1825. [d] Act, 15th Feb., 1820.

	American vessels in foreign trade. *per foot.*	*Coasters.* *per foot.*
Sleepy Hole or Look Out,	$ 75	$ 61
Pagan Creek,	60	50
Jamestown,	1 00	1 00
Martins Brandon,	} 2 00	1 33
Flower de Hundred, or	} 2 00	1 42
City Point or Bermuda Hundred,	} 2 00	1 83
Four Mile Creek or Turkey Island,	2 12	2 12
Osborne's or Warwick,	2 80	2 50
Richmond,	3 00	3 00

On York River—	*F. T.*	*Coasters.*
From sea to Yorktown,	12 00	10 00
Back River or Egg Island to— Yorktown,	6 00	5 00
Yorktown to sea,	7 50	6 67

	F. T.	*Coasters.*
Westpoint,	1 33	81
Cumberland,	1 63	1 00
Highest landing on Pamunkey river,	2 07	1 25
Shepherd's,	1 47	92
Meredith's, Moor's, or the highest landing on Mattapony,	1 97	1 19

	F. T.	*Coasters.*
Cape Henry to any river on Mobjack Bay,	12 00	10 00
Mobjack Bay to sea,	7 50	
From the capes to Urbanna,	15 00	13 33
From Urbanna to— Sea,	12 00	10 00

	F. T.	*Coasters.*
Tappahannock,	1 40	83
Naylor's Hole,	1 38	81
Leed's or Micou's,	2 13	1 29
Port Royal,	2 97	1 83
Fredericksburg,	2 70	2 29

	F. T.	*Coasters.*
From sea to Piankebank,	15 00	13 33
Piankebank to sea,	12 00	
From Cape Henry to Smith's Point in South Potomac,	25 00	20 00
And going out between the same places,	20 83	16 67

From Smith's Point to—	*F. T.*	*Coasters.*
Coan or Yeocomico,	74	50
Machodack,	84	58
Upper Machodack,	1 12	81
Nangomy,	1 37	1 00
Body's Hole,	1 47	1 08
Qaunfico,	1 58	1 21
Occoquan,	1 78	1 29

American vessels in foreign trade.		*Coasters.*
Piscataway,	2 10	1 58 *per foot.*
Alexandria,	2 48	1 89
Eastern Branch,	2 62	2 00

And the same fees by the foot on their return.

Foreign vessels pay one fourth more, unless placed on the same footing as American vessels.

Vessels of war pay the same pilotage as merchant vessels, unless drawing over eighteen feet of water, when they pay fifty cents per foot in addition.

From Cape Henry to Yorktown, vessels of fifty guns and upwards pay $24; between fifty and twenty guns, $18:

From Cape Henry to Mobjack, $20:

From the cape to Smith's Point, $45: and the same prices back.

Pilots waiting in attendance after the time appointed for their attendance, receive $1 75 per day, and the same when outward bound, and detained in Hampton Roads after a fair wind for going to sea. Masters not intending to go to sea may, however, discharge their pilots in Hampton Roads.

When attending with their boats upon a vessel at the request of the master or owner, pilots are entitled to $7 per day. When carried to sea, pilots are entitled to the same wages as the mate of the vessel. If a vessel be first boarded within the capes, the pilots are only entitled to half pilotage to Hampton Roads.

Pilots must carry a copy of the pilot laws, and must produce the same when required by masters. If they exact more than their legal fees, they forfeit double the sum received.[a]

By a law of 26th February, 1821, vessels in distress were allowed to employ a Maryland pilot when no Virginia pilot was in sight, but now, by the law of congress, they are authorized to employ either for any port in either state.

Pilots guilty of a misdemeanor or neglect of duty, or of intoxication when in charge of a vessel, may be suspended by the commissioners of pilotage for Norfolk and Hampton. These commissioners also determine all disputes respecting pilotage, and their judgment is final.[b]

North Carolina.—Pilots are appointed by the commissioners of the respective ports, who grant them for those ports branches which contain the pilotage fees. They also have power to fine pilots £100. Any person undertaking to act as a pilot without a branch forfeits £100;[c] for Cape Fear river, £20; but any person may pilot a vessel, in danger or leaky, into Brunswick. The pilots give bonds, with two sureties, in the sum of £250, for the faithful performance of their duties.[c]

Pilots seeing a vessel on the coast with a signal for a pilot, or firing guns for assistance, must go on board. By neglect or refusal, a penalty of £20 is incurred;[d] and they may also be removed by the commissioners.[e]

By refusing to attend on board a vessel in port, after notice from the master or consignee, a penalty of £5 is incurred for each and every day's delay of the vessel.[c]

---

[a] Act, 10th Feb., 1819. [b] Acts, 5th March, 1824, and 27th Jan., 1825.
[c] Act, 1784. [d] Act, 1783. [e] Act, 1790.

Masters refusing a pilot, either in Cape Fear river, or in or out of its inlets, except when merely making a harbour,[a] or when bound into Ocracock inlet, with vessels exceeding forty tons,[b] must pay full pilotage to the pilot refused.[c]

The bar pilots for Cape Fear river must keep a good spy-glass in the pilot boat.[d]

The bar pilots take vessels over the bar to and from fort Johnson, and the river pilots take vessels to Wilmington and back again to the fort.[c]

The pilots for the bar and river inlet must keep as many good decked boats, sufficient for tempestuous weather, as may be ordered by the commissioners.[d]

Each pilot must keep one and may keep two apprentices, who may be authorized by the commissioners to pilot vessels for their master.[e]

No more than three of the pilots can be in partnership, and the river pilots cannot be in partnership.[e]

A Cape Fear river pilot forfeits his branch by bringing a vessel past the quarantine ground without the certificate of the health officer.[f]

Also, if he permit ballast to be discharged in the river, without informing the commissioners within ten days.[g]

If a slave be permitted to board a vessel, for the purpose of piloting her over any bar in or out of an inlet, unaccompanied by a pilot, his owner forfeits the value of the slave.[h]

The commissioners of pilotage for Cape Fear river have authority in all matters concerning the navigation of that river from Negro Island downward, and out of all the inlets, and the commissioners at Wilmington decide all disputes about mooring of vessels, &c.[e]

Masters give bonds not to transfer debtors or slaves out of the state, and also to pay their pilotage.[g]

Pilots who bring vessels into port over the main bar or new inlet bar of Cape Fear river, are entitled to carry them out, provided they attend when the vessel is ready to go out. If not, any other branch pilot for the bar over which she departs may be employed.[f]

Pilots attending to carry a vessel from her station to any other place in the river, are entitled to 10s. per day while detained, if the wind and weather permit her removal; and pilots boarding a vessel which is blown off, are entitled to 10s. per day while at sea.[g]

Pilotage for vessels over forty tons, not belonging to North Carolina, from sea to Beacon Island road, or Wallace's channel, if of less than eight feet water, $7; if between eight and ten feet, $1 per foot; more than ten feet, $1 50 per foot.

For taking each vessel over either of the Swashes, $2.

From the Swash Straddle to Newbern or Washington, $1 50 per foot; to Edenton, $15; to Camden, $12 50. The same fees down and out.[i]

The commissioners have authority to make a distinction between

---

[a] Act, 1823. [b] Act, 1783. [c] Act, 1831. [d] Act, 1790. [e] Act, 1786. [f] Act, 1797.
[g] Act, 1784. [h] Act, 1812. [i] Act, 1805.

bar pilots who use deck boats and those who do not, by allowing the former more.[a]

South Carolina.—The city council of Charleston elect annually seven commissioners of pilots, who examine and certify as to the qualifications of pilots. The city intendant then gives a license, after administering an oath that the applicant will faithfully perform his duty, and use his best endeavours to board all vessels bound to Charleston, and that he will not be in partnership with more than one pilot. He also gives a bond, with two sureties, in the sum of $500, if of the second class, and $1000, if of the first class, for the faithful discharge of his duty.

The commissioners have power to make the pilots renew their licenses, and to suspend or revoke them in case of misbehaviour. No pilot can absent himself from the port, or hire out his boat without leave, and the commissioners cannot grant leave if there be less than three pilot boats in port. No pilot can employ another whose branch has been taken away. Penalty $100, and he may also be broke as a pilot.

Pilots standing out to sea, or cruising, must offer their services to the vessel nearest the bar, or in most distress, under the penalty of $50, and he may also be broke.

Vessels subject to perform quarantine, the pilot must conduct to the quarantine ground, and must remain on board, unless released by the port physician. The pilot is entitled to his provisions, and $4 per day while detained, and he is liable to a fine of $50, and to be suspended twelve months, if he disobey the law.

The pilot who brought the vessel in, has the exclusive right to pilot her out, unless he misbehaves himself when coming in.

He must, however, attend on board, or substitute a pilot of the same class, within twenty-four hours after notice in writing has been left at his place of abode by the master or harbour master, requiring him to attend. At the expiration of that time, the master may employ another pilot of the same class. Pilots bearing down to vessels to the leeward of the bar, and boarding vessels ten leagues from land, are entitled to $4 per day until they arrive in port, over and above their pilotage.

Pilots directed by the master to anchor in the roads when inward bound, and afterwards to bring the vessel up to the city, are entitled to $4 extra.

Pilots have a right to their pilotage before they pilot a vessel out; and a pilot who has notice that the inward pilotage is unpaid, is liable therefor, if he carry her out, until all pilot charges are paid.

Any white person or free person of colour is entitled to $5, if he give instructions to a vessel outside of the bar, when requested to repair on board for the purpose, and to $2 per day if he be requested to remain on board to bring the vessel to the bar. He cannot, however, pilot her over the bar except in case of distress, without a license, under a penalty of $100.

---

[a] Act, 1796.

Pilots of the second class incur the same penalty for bringing in a vessel drawing more than twelve feet. The master and crew may bring the vessel in without incurring such penalty; but the master is liable to pay full pilotage to the first pilot who offered his services outside of the bar, and showed his license, unless the pilot be of the second class, and his vessel draws more than twelve feet water.

Outward bound vessels must, when ready for sailing, hoist a pilot signal, i. e. a jack at the foretopmast head.

Pilots, when detained after the time appointed, except by wind and weather, are entitled to $4 per day.

When carried to sea, they are entitled to their provisions and other necessaries, and to $2 per day until their return, unless no pilot boat appear to take off the pilot, and the vessel lie to sixteen hours off the bar to discharge him.

The harbour master must keep in his office a list of the pilots of both classes, and also the pilot law, for the inspection of masters.[a]

Pilotage to or from Charleston—

For 6	feet water or under,			- - - -	$8
7	do.	do.	do.	- - - -	9
8	do.	do.	do.	- - - -	10
9	do.	do.	do.	- - - -	11
10	do.	do.	do.	- - - -	14
11	do.	do.	do.	- - - -	16
12	do.	do.	do.	- - - -	19
12½	do.	do.	do.	- - - -	20
13	do.	do.	do.	- - - -	21
13½	do.	do.	do.	- - - -	23
14	do.	do.	do.	- - - -	25
14½	do.	do.	do.	- - - -	29
15	do.	do.	do.	- - - -	31
15½	do.	do.	do.	- - - -	35
16	do.	do.	do.	- - - -	42
16½	do.	do.	do.	- - - -	50
17	do.	do.	do.	- - - -	60[b]

The pilots at Beaufort and at Georgetown, are appointed by commissioners for those places, and they are authorized to make all necessary rules and regulations for their government, and to suspend or discharge any pilot violating them.[c]

Georgia.—Pilots are regulated by commissioners, who have authority to determine all disputes between them and masters in relation to pilotage; and the party refusing to abide by their decision, incurs a penalty of $100. Any damage or injury sustained through the neglect or default of a pilot exceeding $100, the pilot is liable for.

Any person acting as a pilot, without authority, is liable to a fine of $100, and ten days' imprisonment.

A master refusing a pilot, is bound to pay full pilotage to the first

---

[a] Act, 17th Aug., 1807. [b] Act 31st July, 1815. [c] Act, 1784.

pilot offering. Coasting vessels, to and from Charleston, however, only pay half pilotage for refusing a pilot outside of the bar; and vessels coasting between ports of the state, pay no pilotage unless they employ a pilot.

The pilotage is established for the several ports by the commissioners of pilotage; and if a warrant pilot ask more than his established fees, he forfeits double the amount.

Masters incur a penalty of $100 by employing any pilot, when outward bound, except the one who brought them in, unless they have good cause.

The pilot incurs the same penalty by neglecting to attend when notified after the vessel is ready for sea.

Pilots bringing vessels in must see them safely moored, and also give directions for their safe riding.

Pilots belonging to one port, when required at sea, are compelled to take charge of any vessel bound into a Georgia port, and are entitled to $2 per day while on board, besides their usual pilotage.

Masters must give security, if required, to pay the pilot fees.

Pilots must be citizens of the United States, and must give bonds, with sureties, in the sum of $2000, for the faithful performance of their duties.

Ten commissioners of pilotage for Savannah are elected by the mayor and aldermen.

The commissioners may fine the pilots, or suspend and revoke their licenses, subject to an appeal to the superior county court.

No person can obtain a certificate until after two years' service in a decked boat, and until he has given proof of his qualifications. He then serves eighteen months as a certificate pilot before he obtains a full branch.[a]

Pilots, when carried away without fault on their part, are entitled to $1 per day, besides their expenses, until their return.[b]

Alabama.—Pilots for Mobile are licensed by the harbour master and board of wardens, consisting of five, who are appointed by the legislature, and have power to sue for fines, &c.

The harbour master has discretionary powers to regulate and station, and to remove from time to time the vessels in the port, and a fine of $50 is inflicted for disobedience to his directions.

A similar fine is inflicted on a pilot for refusing to obey his order to return to his station on Mobile point.

The harbour master may appoint a deputy, and he is entitled to three cents per ton for the registered tonnage of every vessel loading, unloading, or making fast to any of the wharves in the city.

The harbour master also receives the pilotage for piloting a vessel to sea, or from sea to within the bars. A pilot is entitled to $2 per day while waiting for a wind. Where a vessel does not employ a pilot, half pilotage is paid. Pilots are entitled to an extra allowance for exerting themselves for the preservation of a vessel in distress,

---

[a] Act, 23d Dec., 1830. [b] Ibid. 1835.

to be determined upon by the board of wardens. Persons acting as pilots, except where vessels are in distress, forfeit $25.

The pilots are furnished with printed instructions, to be shown to masters as soon as they take charge of vessels.[a]

Pilotage over the outer bar of Mobile, for vessels under fourteen feet water, $2 per foot; exceeding fourteen, $2 50 per foot; do. over Dog river bar in Mobile bay, $1 per foot.[b]

The harbour master and wardens have power to appoint the pilots at Mobile, and when called upon to survey a vessel, and certify as to the manner in which the hatches were secured, they are entitled to $3, and for surveying damaged goods, $5 per day.

They also have power to fix the time of sale of damaged goods after two days' advertising, and are entitled to a per centage for attending and certifying to the sale, i. e. 5 per cent for $200; over 200 and to 500, $2\frac{1}{2}$ per cent; over $500 and to 1000, $1\frac{1}{2}$ per cent; $5000, $\frac{1}{2}$ per cent; over $5000, $\frac{1}{4}$ per cent.[c]

Louisiana.—The harbour master and wardens of the port of New-Orleans are authorized to make regulations for the government of pilots, and to impose fines to the extent of $1000, for their contravention.

Every branch pilot must keep a decked pilot boat, of not less than thirty feet keel, exclusively employed as a pilot boat, and he cannot employ any person to pilot a vessel, unless such person has been in his constant employ for six months previous. Deputy pilots cannot obtain employment with a branch pilot, unless they produce a certificate of good conduct from their last employer.

Penalty for neglect of these provisions, $50.

A similar penalty is inflicted on any person who pilots a vessel in or out of the Mississippi, when a branch or deputy pilot offers to do so. No public house can be kept at or within three miles of the Balize or other pilot station, without a license, and no license can be obtained without a recommendation from a majority of the pilots.

No branch pilot can leave his station for more than three consecutive days, without the written permission of the master and wardens, under the penalty of $50, and no permission can be granted to two branch pilots at the same time.

Pilots must register their names with the harbour master, and he may order them to return to the Balize, and a refusal to return there, subjects the pilots to a fine of $50. Master pilots give bonds, in the sum of $1000, with two sureties, for the faithful performance of their duties.

Pilotage from sea to the block-house at the Balize, or from within the river to the eastward and southward of the bars, a distance of about three miles, is $2 per foot for the vessel's draught of water. At the block-house the pilots live and leave the vessel; and there outward bound vessels take pilots, and pay the same pilotage as inward. No pilots are appointed for the river, and no regular pilotage is established. Few vessels except foreigners take any. It is better

---

[a] Act. 23d Dec., 1822. [b] Act, 13th Jan., 1831. [c] Ibid. 1828.

to be without them. The Balize pilots take vessels up the river if desired, and have what they can agree for with the masters.

Besides the pilotage per foot, a pilot is entitled to $2 per day for every day that he may be detained on board any vessel by the master, waiting for a fair wind or otherwise. Any master of a vessel who refuses to take a pilot when one offers, pays half pilotage; provided, that nothing is payable by any vessel employed between New-Orleans and any other port in Louisiana, for refusing to take a pilot. If any person not duly appointed, pilot a vessel in or out of the Mississippi, when a branch or deputy pilot offers, he is fineable $20. Any pilot who is taken off to sea through the default of the master of the vessel, is entitled to mate's wages until his return to New-Orleans.

Pilots are entitled for extra services to vessels in distress, to such allowance as shall be made by the harbour master and wardens.[a]

No harbour master nor warden can be interested in a pilot boat, and they have power to make regulations for their government. These regulations are furnished to the pilots in French and English, and must be communicated by the pilot upon boarding to the master of the vessel.[b]

Master pilots are empowered to appoint deputy pilots, and are answerable for their negligence or misconduct.[c]

---

[a] Act, 1st March, 1826. [b] Act, 31st March, 1805. [c] Act, 7th June, 1806.

CHAPTER XXIV.

BILLS OF EXCHANGE.

A BILL of exchange is a written order or request, by one person to another, in favour of a third, for the payment of a certain sum of money at an appointed time. It is a security originally invented to enable merchants of different countries to remit money from one to another in a safe and easy manner, and it has since been extended to other purposes of commerce. It is negotiable, contrary to the usual policy of the common law, which prohibits the transfer of other simple contract debts.

There are three persons generally concerned in this contract, but every endorsement creates a new party.

The custom prescribes the form of a bill, and raises a contract.

It is not requisite to observe the same nicety in a bill of exchange as in deeds and wills.

A bill, payable out of a particular fund, is no bill of exchange.

A bill, payable out of the fifth payment, as it shall become due, is not good: but

Pay J. S., or order, at my quarterly half-pay per advance, is a negotiable bill.

A bill, payable to me, or my order, is a good bill.

The *drawer* is the person who draws the bill of exchange.

The *drawee* is the person upon whom it is drawn; and he is so called before he accepts the same: but after he has accepted, he is then called the *acceptor*.

Every person, before he can pay away or pass a bill of exchange, must, if it be made payable to his order, write his name on the back of the bill; and he is therefore called an *endorser*, and becomes security for its payment.

An *endorsee* is any person who is in possession of a bill of exchange, in consequence of its having been endorsed to him.

The *payee* is the person in whose favour the bill is drawn; as, if A draw upon B., directing him "*to pay to* C, *or order*," C is called the payee; and, before C can pass away the same, he must *endorse* it.

If the bill have not the words payable "to order, or bearer, or assigns," it is not transferable, so as to enable the assignee to sue in his own name.

The payee may be the buyer or remitter, and so may be the endorser.

Where the payee is the owner of the bill, there are but three parties; but if it be remitted to a fourth party, the payee endorses it, and becomes the endorser, and this, either specially or in full.

Where a bill of exchange is drawn upon a person residing in another country, it is called a foreign bill; but when upon a person in the same country, it is called an inland or domestic bill.

44

A bill drawn by a person in one of the United States, upon a person residing in another of the states, is called a foreign bill;[a] except in the state of New-York, where it is called an inland bill.[b]

The terms of a bill vary according to agreement or custom.

Some are drawn at sight, or at a certain number of days or months after sight, or after date, or at *usance*, which means the customary term between two places.

Days of grace are a certain number of days granted to the acceptor after the time of the bill has expired.

In reckoning, the day of date or of presentment is not included; and where months are mentioned, calendar months are meant.

In all bills dated the 28th, 29th, 30th or 31st of January, and payable one month after date, the term expires on the last day of February, and they are payable the 3d of March.

In drawing bills, the law of the country where the bill is drawn prevails as to the validity and meaning of the contract.

When a bill is presented it is frequently left until the next day for acceptance; but this is only from courtesy, and the holder may require an answer without leaving it.

An acceptance, at common law, may be verbal, but it is usual for the drawee to write his name on the face of the bill, with the word "accepted."

An act of parliament, passed 1819, has made it necessary, in order to charge the acceptor, that the acceptance should be written on the bill.

In New-York, by the revised statutes, it is made necessary that the acceptance should be in writing, and signed by the acceptor or his lawful agent.

If the acceptance be written on another paper, it only binds the acceptor in favour of a person who has seen the acceptance, and received the bill for a valuable consideration on the faith thereof.

An unconditional acceptance in writing, to accept a bill before it is drawn, binds the acceptor only to the same extent.

A holder may require an acceptance to be written on the bill, and on refusal to do so, may protest for non-acceptance.

If a payee destroy a bill left with him for acceptance, or refuse to return the same to the holder, he becomes liable for the amount of the bill.[c]

Damages may be recovered of a person who refuses to accept a bill after promising to do so, by the drawer or negotiator thereof, on the faith of such promise.

In the other states of the Union, except Louisiana, it is presumed the common law doctrine obtains; but in France, Germany, Netherlands, Belgium and Spain, a written acceptance is necessary.

According to the common law, any act giving credit to a bill amounts to an acceptance.

A very small matter will amount to an acceptance; and any words

---

[a] 2 Peters' U. S. R. 586. [b] 5 Johns. Rep. 375. [c] 1 Rev. Stat. 768.

will be sufficient for that purpose, which show the party's assent or agreement to the bill.

Verbal acceptance is sufficient; and an action lies against the acceptor thereon. But there must be a witness. These words, "the two bills of exchange which you sent me, I will pay, in case the owners of the Queen Ann do not," are a sufficient acceptance.

Acceptance, to pay when the goods are sold, is a good acceptance.

Acceptance, to pay half in money and half in bills, is good.

Acceptance, to pay according to the tenor of the bill, after the day of payment is past, is good.

A bill may be accepted for part, and the sum accepted for is good against the acceptor.

Acceptance of a bill, drawn upon two partners, by one of them, binds both, if it concern the joint trade.

Acceptance of a servant, usually transacting business for his master, is good; yet the servant should express such acceptance to be for his master, or he is liable himself.

Where an acceptance has once been made it cannot be revoked.

Acceptance may be made after the time appointed for payment, and in such case it is to pay on demand.

Protest and notice.

If the drawee refuse to accept or pay the bill, the payee must cause it to be protested.

A protest signifies to the drawer that the party upon whom he drew his bill was unwilling, not to be found, or insolvent; and is to let him (the drawer) have timely notice thereof; and also to enable the party to recover against the drawer.

A foreign bill must be protested on the last day of the three days of grace allowed, (after the time expressed upon the bill,) and if not paid upon the last of the three days, the party ought immediately to protest the bill and return it; but, if the last of the three days be a great holiday or Sunday, the day before is the day of payment.*

Bills of exchange must be sued for within six years after their becoming due, or they are barred by the statute.

---

* *Number of days grace allowed in the United States and chief cities of Europe.*

Amsterdam	6	Madrid	14
Antwerp	6	Milan	0
Bremen	8	Naples	3
Cadiz	6	Paris	10
Cologne	6	Petersburg	10
Copenhagen	8	Rome	0
Dantzick	10	Rotterdam	6
England	3	Scotland	3
Geneva	5	Sicily	0
Genoa	30	Stockholm	6
Gibraltar	14	Trieste	3
Hamburg	12	Turin	5
I land	3	United States	3
Leghorn	0	Venice	6
Leipsic	0	Vienna	3
Lisbon	6		

If two or three bills be drawn for the same sum, they carry a condition with them that only one should be paid.

If, before a bill be accepted, and even before it be due, it be endorsed to any person, the said endorsee may, immediately after the drawee has refused to accept it, bring an action against the endorser.

A protest is absolutely necessary on a foreign bill, where it is refused acceptance or payment, in order to charge the drawer.

The payee must demand acceptance from the drawee before protest.

If a payee die before presentation, there can be no protest before probate or administration.

If a bill, left for acceptance, be lost, the drawee must give a note for the payment thereof; otherwise it may be protested.

If a bill be lost, and no new one can be had, and the drawee does not insist on having the original, but refuses payment on another account, a protest made on a copy is sufficient.

A protest on a foreign bill is necessary to recover, against the drawer, not only interest and costs, but also principal; and such protest must be made in due time, and timely notice given to the drawer. What is a *timely* notice must be determined by the customs of the merchants. Convenient notice must be given to the drawer of an inland bill; which notice, as to time, must also rest upon the custom and verdict of a jury.

But, in case of non-acceptance or non-payment of either foreign or inland bills, the safest way is to give as early notice to the person of whom it was received, as possible—that is, by the first post or conveyance; otherwise you may lose the security of the drawer.

In the state of New-York no protest is necessary on inland bills, except to enable the holder to recover damages. In the other states, where inland bills mean only those drawn by and on persons residing in the same state, bills drawn by a person in one state upon a person in another state are governed by the same rule as foreign bills.

Where the drawer of the bills has no funds in the hands of the drawee, notice of non-acceptance or non-payment is not necessary.

Where the drawer of a bill has become bankrupt, and assignees have been appointed, notice should be given to the assignees.

A third person, after protest for non-acceptance, may intervene and accept for the honour of the drawer or any particular endorser. His acceptance is termed acceptance supra protest, and he subjects himself to the same obligations as if the bill had been directed to him. He can recover against the person for whom he accepts, and against all who stand prior to him on the bill.

There is no precise time in which bills payable at sight, or so many days after sight, must be presented for acceptance; only there must be no unreasonable delay, and this would depend upon the circumstances of the case.

The French code requires that bills drawn in Europe upon any part of France must be presented within six months from date, and in default, the drawer is discharged.[a]

---

[a] L. 1, T. 8, sec. 11.

A bill payable at a given time after date, need not be presented before the day of payment.

If the drawee cannot be found, due diligence must be used to find him, before protest for non-acceptance.[a] If he has absconded, no demand, in general, need be made.[b] If he has removed to another town, the holder must make the demand there, but if he has left the state, a demand at his former residence is sufficient.[c]

If there be no evidence or knowledge of his residence except the date of the bill, demand and inquiry must be made there.[d]

Notice of non-acceptance or non-payment must be given by the first direct and regular conveyance. When by mail, it must be by the first mail after the day next to the last day of grace; and each party into whose hands a dishonoured bill passes, is allowed one entire day to give notice.[e]

The notice may be sent by private conveyance, and it will be sufficient, even if it arrive a little behind the mail.[e]

Where the drawer lives in the same city, and within the district of the letter carrier, the notice may be sent through the post-office. If there be no penny-post, the notice must be personal, or sent to the house or place of business of the drawer.

The notice must state that the bill is dishonoured, and it is usual to state that the holder looks to the drawer for payment. The same in the case of an endorser. In the state of New-York it is provided by statute, that in case of a contagious disease prevailing in the city of New-York, presentation of bills may be made to the county clerk against all houses that do not register with the clerk some place out of the infected district, where all bills upon them may be presented, and notice may be given through the post-office to all houses usually doing business in such district.[f]

If the drawee refuse to accept because he has no effects of the drawer, notice is not necessary,[g] unless drawn upon the ground of some fair mercantile agreement.[h] The party receiving notice, is bound to give notice to those who stand prior to him on the bill, or he loses their security.

Of endorsements.

Every man who writes his name upon the back of a bill, becomes bound to the next holder for the amount thereof. It matters not whether he has received any value for the bill. The endorsement of his name implies that he receives the value of the bill, and the law will compel him to be answerable for the same to the holder thereof.

An endorsement may be blank or special. When blank, the bill is transferable by simple delivery; but when special, it orders the bill to be paid to some particular person or his order, or it transfers the bill without recourse to the endorser.

An endorsement cannot be made of less than the full amount re-

---

[a] 8 Barn. & Cress. 387. [b] 4 Mass. Rep. 45. [c] 14 Johns. Rep. 114. [d] 4 Serg. & Rawle, 480. [e] 3 Kent, 106. [f] 1 Rev. Stat. 769. [g] 1 Term. Rep. 405. [h] 3 Kent, 110.

maining due of the bill. If the holder die or become bankrupt, his personal representatives or assignees become the owners of the bill. If the executors or administrators endorse it, they bind themselves only, and not the estate. Where a bill is payable to a firm, any of the partners may transfer it by endorsement.

Possession is prima facia evidence of property in a bill of exchange payable to bearer, or endorsed in blank; and where it is payable to a fictitious person, an innocent holder may sue on it as payable to bearer. An innocent holder may recover, even where the bill is founded in usury, or has been stolen; but, in the latter case, he is liable to be defeated if he took the bill under circumstances which should have awakened suspicion as to the manner in which the bill was obtained.

A bill negotiated after it has become due, is open to all defences existing when it was negotiated.

When a bill is payable on demand, it is not subject to the operation of that rule, unless negotiated in an unreasonable time after the date. Two and a half months have been held an unreasonable time.

Liability.

Every drawer, endorser, and acceptor of a bill of exchange, is separately liable to the payment thereof.

On non-payment, the payee (the person to whom it is to be paid) may sue the acceptor and drawer; but he can have but one satisfaction: that is, he can only recover from them jointly the amount of the bill in his hands.

He who accepts for the honour of the drawer, is liable to the payment, although he may have no effects. The acceptance is an undertaking for the payment.

If a bill be endorsed to the drawer of it, he may maintain an action, as the endorsee, against the drawee, if the latter had effects of the drawer at the time of drawing the bill; otherwise not.

The last endorser of the bill of exchange may maintain an action against any of the former endorsers, and so any endorser may against all that precede him.

An endorser of a bill, who has paid it, must prove payment in an action against the acceptor.

The endorser of a foreign bill of exchange may be charged, without first resorting to the drawer. The acceptor, as well as the endorser, is liable, though the maker's name be forged.[a] This is, however, only to an innocent holder.

Of waiving security of drawer and endorser.

Giving time to the acceptor by an agreement, or for a consideration, will discharge the previous parties; but taking collateral security from the acceptor, or forbearing to sue, will not discharge them: nor will mere indulgence, without a consideration.[b] Accepting a com-

---

[a] 3 Kent, 114. [b] Ibid. 111.

position in discharge of the acceptor, will discharge the previous parties; but receiving part payment of the bill will not. Discharging any of the endorsers, or making any composition with them, discharges all subsequent parties, but not those before the party discharged.

It is not necessary to prove the hand of the drawer in an action against the acceptor, nor can the acceptor set up the forgery of the bill.

If a bill be assigned for a just debt, equity will not relieve, though the bill was at first given without consideration.

If A. sell goods to B., and B. is to give a bill in satisfaction, B. is so far discharged that he cannot be sued for the goods, though the bill be never paid, for the bill is payment; but he is liable to be sued for the bill.

A note or bill is no absolute payment, though agreed to be such, if the giver of it know the persons upon whom it is drawn to be in a failing condition.

Damages.

If the bill be returned dishonoured, the drawer or the endorser is liable to the holder for damages, besides the amount of the bill.

In Europe, those damages are what will enable the holder to purchase a new bill at the current rate of exchange, together with interest and all charges, such as protest, postages and commissions. In the United States a different practice has obtained, and a certain per centage is allowed on the amount by way of damages.

The damages in most of the United States are regulated at present by statutes passed by the different states; but it is to be hoped that congress will soon pass a general law, establishing some uniformity of usage on this subject.

By the revised statutes of the state of New-York, if a bill be drawn upon any person in the states of Maine, New-Hampshire, Vermont, Massachusetts, Rhode-Island, Connecticut, New-Jersey, Pennsylvania, Delaware, Maryland, Virginia, or the District of Columbia, three per cent. damages are given; if in the states of North or South Carolina, Georgia, Kentucky or Tennessee, five per cent; and if in any other place upon or adjacent to this continent, north of the equator, comprehending all the islands in the West Indies and Atlantic Ocean, or Europe, ten per cent. The damages, by custom, upon other places, are twenty per cent. In New-York, the amount due, and the damages, are calculated after the rate of the exchange when the bill is returned, and not upon the face of the bill.*

---

* *Examples of estimating damages at New-York on a foreign bill returned from London.*

£100	444 44
9 per cent. premium at the time when bill is returned	39 99
Damages 10 per cent. calculated on the nominal par,	44 44
The amount to be paid to holder,	$528 87

Bill returned from Paris.

100 francs at 5. 15,	$194 14
Damages 10 per cent. on nominal par, or 5 33⅓ francs for $1,	18 75
The amount to be paid to holder,	$212 89

If the contents of the bill be expressed in federal money, the amount due and damages are ascertained without reference to the rate of exchange.

The damages are in lieu of interest and of all charges previous to notice of non-payment, but seven per cent. interest is allowed on principal and damages from the demand thereof.

The damages in the state of Maine on foreign bills, consist of the amount of the bill at par, the charges of protest, with six per cent. interest on those sums from the time when the bill became due, and ten per cent. damages on the face of the bill, with interest thereon, from the demand upon the drawer.

In Maryland and Indiana, the damages on foreign bills are fifteen per cent., calculated at the rate of exchange, and charges of protest and interest from the time of protest.

In South Carolina, the damages on foreign bills, except payable in North America and the West Indies, are fifteen per cent., and calculated as in Maryland; on those payable in the West Indies and North America, out of the United States, twelve and a half per cent.; on those within the United States, ten per cent.; charges and interest are allowed, and damages are calculated at the rate of exchange. In Connecticut, Delaware, Illinois, Missouri, Alabama and Louisiana, the damages on foreign bills are twenty per cent. In Ohio, twelve per cent.; but if drawn on a drawer in any of the other states of the Union, six per cent.[a] In Pennsylvania, the damages are twenty per cent. on bills drawn on Europe or European islands; but if drawn on Mexico, the Spanish Main, Madeira, the Canary, Western, or Cape de Verd Islands, the damages in that state are fifteen per cent.; if drawn on Louisiana, or any other places in North America out of the United States, (except Mexico, or any of the Bahamas or West Indies, or the North-West Coast,) ten per cent; if drawn upon any of the United States, except Louisiana, five per cent.; and if drawn upon any foreign place, except those above described, twenty-five per cent.[b]

The damages and amount of bill are calculated after the rate of exchange, and charges and interest from the time of notice are allowed. In Virginia, Georgia,[c] Mississippi, and Rhode-Island, the damages on foreign bills are ten per cent., calculated at the current rate of exchange, and charges and interest from date of protest are also allowed.

In Kentucky, ten per cent. interest is allowed on foreign bills protested from date until paid, in lieu of damages; but they mustbe demanded of drawer within eighteen months from date of bill.

In Massachusetts, the damages on bills drawn on places beyond the Cape of Good Hope, or in Asia, Africa, or the islands thereof, amount to twenty per cent. on the par value of the bill; if on any other foreign place, the value of the bill, at the current rate of exchange at the time of demanding payment, is five per cent. and damages thereon, and interest from the date of the protest. If on New-York, Vermont, Connecticut, Rhode-Island, New-Hampshire or Maine, three per cent.;

---

[a] Act, 1831. [b] Act, 1821. [c] Act, 1827.

if on New-Jersey, Pennsylvania, Delaware, Maryland, Virginia, or the District of Columbia, five per cent.; if on North Carolina, South Carolina or Georgia, six per cent.; and if on any other of the United States, nine per cent. One per cent. is allowed on returned bills, if drawn on places in Massachusetts more than seventy-five miles distant from the place where the bill was negotiated.[a]

In North Carolina, the damages on bills drawn upon any state of the Union, except Louisiana, are six per cent.; upon any other part of North America, except the West Indies, ten per cent.; upon Europe, South America, or the African islands, fifteen per cent.; and elsewhere, twenty per cent.[b]

In Tennessee, the damages on bills drawn upon any of the other states, are three per cent.; upon any place in North America bordering upon the Gulf of Mexico, or the West Indies, fifteen per cent.; and upon any other place, twenty per cent.[c]

In Connecticut, the damages on bills drawn upon the city of New-York, are two per cent.; upon any other part of the middle states, New-England or Virginia, three per cent.; upon North or South Carolina, Georgia or Ohio, five per cent.; any other part of the United States, eight per cent., and lawful interest on amount and damages from time of notice.

The damages allowed in the other states on bills drawn on places out of the state where the bill is negotiated, and within the United States, are as follows: i. e., in Rhode-Island, five per cent., and charges and interest from date of protest; in Maryland, eight per cent., and charges and interest; in Virginia, one per cent.; in North Carolina, ten per cent. and charges; in Missouri, Alabama, Louisiana, Ohio, Indiana and Illinois, ten per cent.

This want of uniformity in calculating damages, is productive of much inconvenience; and it is to be regretted that congress has not established some uniform rule for awarding damages on protested bills, both domestic and foreign, under its power of regulating commerce.

The drawer of bills

Should be well satisfied that they will be accepted and duly honoured before he draws; to this end, it is requisite that he be assured of having effects in the hands of the person drawn upon; and also that he be a man of integrity and punctuality, who will not dishonour his paper, but pay it regularly as it becomes due: otherwise he may be subject to heavy damages.

The acceptor

Should be careful to accept no bill but what he has effects in his hands to answer; to insist upon his correspondent advising of each bill so soon as drawn, specifying the number, date, sum, time, and to

---

[a] Rev. Stat. 1834. [b] Act, 1828. [c] Act, 1830.

whom payable: for, if he should accept or pay a forged draft, the loss will fall on himself; to adjust and balance all accounts of this nature at least once in three months, and oftener if the drafts are large and continual.

The bill holder

Should exchange no draft for a stranger, when he is not convinced of the validity thereof from the *writing* of the drawer or acceptor. If he be not satisfied on this head, he may offer to send the bill to one of the parties, and, when in cash, that he will account with him for the value.

He should see that the bill be drawn properly, and make the person paying the bill endorse his name on the back; also take a regular copy of the particulars of the bill in a book.

If the bill be not already accepted, he should present it for acceptance. If the person it is drawn upon will not accept, and also adds he will not pay it when due, he should return it to the endorser or drawer immediately, taking a good bill or cash for the same.

But, if the drawee says he may pay it when due, he should wait till that day, present it for payment, and if then refused, have it protested, and for the amount call upon the endorser. But as the holder has at present the endorser and drawer as security, he should be cautious how he gives up the bill to either for their single security, if doubtful.

When remitting a bill, endorse on the back thereof, "Pay the contents to A. B. of C. or order. D. E." This will prevent the bill's being negotiated, should it fall into bad hands.

If the bill be payable to bearer, write, upon the face thereof, "Sent by post, December, 1821, to A. B. of C. D. E.," in red ink. Endorse no bill until you pay it away.

Promissory note.

A promissory note is a written instrument by which a person promises to pay to another person, or order, or bearer, a certain sum of money at the expiration of a fixed term. They are in general considered in the same light as inland bills of exchange: the maker corresponding to the acceptor, and the first endorser to the drawer of a bill of exchange.

Checks.

A check is negotiable like an inland bill of exchange, and governed by the same rules.[a]

Form of a letter of credit.

Letters of credit are granted by merchants or others, in favour of persons travelling into foreign countries. They are commonly open

---

[a] 3 Kent, 77.

or unsealed, and contain an order from the writer or grantor to his factor or correspondent to furnish such a man, the bearer, with a certain sum, at one or several times, and to place it to the account of him who grants the letter. It is ordinary and necessary for the grantor of a letter of credit to give his correspondent a letter of advice, by post or otherwise, in which he describes the person to be honoured with credit, from his stature, complexion, garb, or any mark on his body, or by some token, as he who can relate such a circumstance, &c. The design of which is to prevent fraud: for, the bearer of the letter may lose it, or he may be robbed, and the finder or rogue go and present it. Letters of credit may be of various forms, and yet valid.

A guaranty is a promise to answer for the payment of some debt, or the fulfilment of some engagement by another person, who is first liable. It must be in writing, and must express on its face the consideration that induced the person signing it to assume the responsibility.

This is in consequence of the construction of the statute of frauds; and in Virginia, where *legal* construction is not so strict, the *promise* only need be in writing.

CHAPTER XXV.

EXCHANGE.

Exchange may be compared with barter; as it is the paying or receiving of money in one country for its equivalent in the money of another, by means of bills of exchange. Or it has been more fully defined, as the reduction of different coins, or any denominations of money, from one to another; or, as the method of finding how many of one species or denomination are equal to a given number of another; in order to which, it is necessary to know the value of the coins of different countries, and the proportion to each other, according to the settled rate of exchange. The several operations, in this case, are only different applications of the rule of three.

The *par of exchange* is the real or intrinsic value of the different species of foreign money, equalized to those of the United States, and *vice versa.*

The *course of exchange* is the current price of a sum of money between two places. This price is constantly fluctuating, according to the circumstances of trade, or as cash or bills are more or less plentiful; and fluctuating thus, it is seldom at par, but generally either above or below it.

Usance is the usual term of bills between certain places: as, one, two, or three months after date; and double usance, treble, or half, means double, treble, or half the usual time. When necessary to divide a month upon half usance, the division contains fifteen days.

Days of grace are a certain number of days exceeding the term expressed, which is generally granted before the bill is paid. The number of these days varies according to the custom of different countries.

Course of exchange at New-York.

New-York gives $4 80 for £1 sterling, at sixty days, on London.

The conventional par of exchange is $4.44.4, to which a premium of eight per cent. must be added to make it equal to the real par, which is the relative price of gold in the two countries, less expenses. The best mode of calculating exchange would be to call £100 for so many dollars and cents, without alluding to the premium: but the practice is to estimate $4.44.4 for £1.

New-York does this in exchange on Paris, giving $1 for 5.33⅓ francs, at sixty days.

New-York gives in exchange on Amsterdam, forty cents for one guilder, at sixty days.

New-York gives in exchange on Hamburg, thirty-five cents for one mark banco, at sixty days.

All payments and bills from the United States on other places are made through the above places, or regulated by the exchange on London at the time and place of payment.

Example of the London course of exchange.

Uncertain prices.					*Certain prices.*
Rotterdam	*gives*	12	Florins current	*for*	1 Pound sterling.
Madrid	*receives*	39	Pence sterling	"	1 Dollar of Exchange.
Lisbon	"	66	Pence sterling	"	1 Milrea.
Leghorn	"	50¼	Pence sterling	"	1 Pezza of 8 reals.
Genoa	"	49	Pence sterling	"	1 Pezza fuori di Banco.
Naples	"	39	Pence sterling	"	1 Ducat di Regno.
Venice	"	57	Lire Piccole	"	1 Pound sterling.

Paris, three months date, gives	25 francs 82½ c.	for	£1 sterling	
Amsterdam, " "	12 guilders 4¾ stivers	for £1	do	
Hamburg, " "	13 ma. ba. 11¾ schillings	for £1	do	

	Private Bills.	*E. I. Comp.'s Bills.*
Calcutta, for 1 Company's rupee, *receives*	22¾d	23d
Bombay, " " " " "	23¼d	23½d
Madras, " " " " "	–	23½d

Course of exchange at Paris.

		30 *Days.*	3 *Months.*	
London	*receives*	25.32½fr.	25.12½fr.	for 1 Liv. sterling.
Amsterdam	"	57 1/16	57 5/16	den. de gros for 3 Francs.
Hamburg	"	187	185¼	for 100 Marcs.
Madrid	"	15.17½	15.12½	for 1 Pistole.
Lisbon	"		525	Re. for 3 Francs.
Livourne	"	511½	508¾	for 1 Piastre.
Naples	"	432½	429½	for 1 Ducat.
Trieste	"	251½	249	for 100 Florins.
Vienna	"	251½	449¾	do.
Milan	"	84⅛	83½	for 100 Liv. Austrich.
Auguste	"	253¼	250½	for 100 Florins.
Petersburg	"		110½	for 100 Roubles.

Course of exchange at Amsterdam.

London	*receives*	guilders	12.07½ short,		per Pound sterling.
"	"	"	11.97½ 2 m.		
Paris	"	"	56 11/16		per 120 Francs.
Hamburg	"	"	35⅜		per 40 Marks B°.
Lisbon	"	"	44⅝	3 m.	40 Crusados.
Cadiz	"	"	103¼		40 Ducats.

In this chapter, the principal countries with which the United States have commercial intercourse are arranged alphabetically, and the chief towns and seaports are placed under the head of the country to which they belong.

Money is either *real* or *imaginary*. Real money includes all coins, whether of gold, silver, copper, or the like; such as eagles, dollars, cents, guineas, pistoles, or ducats, &c., &c. Imaginary money, or money of account, is that which never existed, or at least which does not exist in real specie; but it is a denomination invented or retained to facilitate the stating of accounts, by keeping them on a permanent basis; not to be changed like currency, which the authority of the government sometimes raises or depresses according to the exigencies of the state. Of this kind are dollars, cents, pounds, livres, marks, &c.

With regard to the imaginary or *nominal* moneys hereafter quoted, their *actual* value in *British sterling* is placed opposite to them, except as to a few, uninfluenced by the fluctuations, which are the result of a favourable or unfavourable state of commercial exchange between one country and another; and it is therefore to be remembered, in perusing the following pages, that, in bill transactions, where, for example, a sum of money is to be remitted to, or received from, a foreign country, the said sum must not be calculated according to the actual value of the currency, but by the course of exchange of the day.

The value in federal money can be easily ascertained by the common rule of three; and to assist in this operation, the value of British sterling is given in federal currency in the tables.

UNITED STATES OF AMERICA.

The legal currency, which is chiefly used by correct merchants, is composed of eagles, dollars, dimes, cents and mills; each denomination being a decimal part of the preceding.

There are besides, four different currencies, or rates, at which any one species of coin, of the same value, is reckoned in the denominations of account, which have, perhaps, from the first settlement of America, been, and still continue to be, used in differents parts of the Union. In the New-England states, viz. New-Hampshire, Massachusetts, Maine, Rhode Island, Connecticut, Vermont, and in Virginia, and Kentucky, the dollar is received at six shillings; in New-York and North Carolina, at eight shillings; in New Jersey, Pennsylvania, Delaware, and Maryland, at seven shillings and six-pence; and in South Carolina and Georgia, at four shillings and eight-pence.

In the trade and intercourse with the different parts of the United States, brief rules, for reducing the currency of one state to that of another, are particularly useful; and for this purpose those which follow have been composed.

Rules for reducing the colonial currencies of the different states to a par with each other: as also for reducing the money of account of the United States to those currencies, and, vice versa, *by decimals.*

1. To reduce New-England, &c. to New-York and North Carolina currency, to any given sum add its third part; and, *vice versa*, subtract a fourth part.

2. To reduce New-England, &c. to New-Jersey, &c. currency, add to any given sum its fourth part; and, *vice versa*, subtract a fifth part.

3. To reduce New-England, &c. to South Carolina and Georgia currency, as 8 to 7; and, *vice versa*, as 7 to 8; so is the one currency to the other.

4. To reduce New-York and North Carolina to New-Jersey, &c. currency; as 16 to 15; and, *vice versa*, as 15 to 16; so is the one to the other.

5. To reduce New-York and North Carolina to South Carolina and Georgia currency, as 12 to 7; and *vice versa*, as 7 to 12; so is the one to the other.

6. To reduce New-Jersey, &c. to South Carolina and Georgia currency; as 45 to 28; and *vice versa*, as 28 to 45; so is the one to the other.

7. To reduce any of the above currencies to the money of account of the United States, let the inferior denominations, if any, in the given sum, be annexed to the pounds in decimals, and divide, if the rate of the dollar be six shillings, by 3; if eight shillings, by 4; if seven shillings and six-pence, by 375; if four shillings and eight-pence, by 23; and pointing off the decimal according to rule, the figures on the left will be dollars, those to the right decimals of a dollar, or dimes, cents and mills. To reduce the money of account of the United States to either of the aforesaid currencies, multiply respectively by the decimals, by which, in the former case, it was directed to divide, and the product will be pounds and decimals of a pound.

The coins of the United States, as established by law, are as follows:—

Eagles coined before 1834, contain 247.5 grains of fine gold in 270 grains of standard gold, or 11 parts pure to 1 of alloy,[a] and are valued at $10 66$\frac{1}{2}$.

Half and quarter eagles, coined before that year, are valued in proportion, and are receivable in all payments at the rate of 94 cents 8 mills per pennyweight.[b]

Eagles coined since July 31, 1834, contain 232 grains pure gold in 258 grains standard gold, and are valued at $10.

Half eagles coined since July 31, 1834, contain 116 grains pure gold in 129 grains standard gold, and are valued at $5.

Quarter eagles coined since July 31, 1834, contain 58 grains pure gold in 64$\frac{1}{2}$ grains standard gold, and are valued at $2 50.

Silver coins.

	containing	Grains of pure silver.	coined before 1837,	Grains of standard do.	coined since 1837	Grains of standard do.
Dollars		371 4-16		416		$412\frac{1}{2}$
Half dollars		185 10-16		208		$206\frac{1}{4}$
Quarter dollars		92 13-16		104		$103\frac{1}{8}$
Dimes		37 2-16		41 3-5		$41\frac{1}{4}$
Half dimes		18 9-16		20 4-5		$20\frac{5}{8}$

[a] Act, 2d April, 1792. [b] Act, 28th June, 1834.

The standard weight of the silver coins was diminished by the act of 3d March, 1837, but as the proportion of fine silver was increased, the same amount of pure silver was retained.

In the coins minted previous to that act, the standard for silver coins was 1485 parts of pure silver to 177 parts of alloy: the alloy being pure copper.[a] The act of 1837 directed the standard of gold and silver to be 9 parts of pure metal to 1 of alloy.

Previous to that act, there was a female head surrounded with 13 stars, and the date, on one side of all the coins; and a spread eagle with a shield, a designation of its value, and the inscription, United States of America, on the other.

That act directed that there should be upon the coins struck at the mint the following devices and legends: upon one side an impression emblematic of liberty, with an inscription of the word LIBERTY, and the year of the coinage; and upon the reverse the figure or representation of an eagle, with the inscription, United States of America, and a designation of the value of the coin; but on the reverse of the dime and half dime, cent and half cent, the figures of the eagle are omitted.

Copper coins.

Cents, value each 1-100 doll.	containing	166	grains.
Half cent, - - 1-200 doll.	containing	183	grains.

Mills.	*Cents.*	*Dimes.*	*Doll.*	*Eagle.*
10 equal - -	1			
100 equal - -	10 equal - -	1		
1000 equal -	100 equal - -	10 equal - -	1	
10000 equal -	1000 equal -	100 equal - -	10 - -	1

Mint regulations.

The principal mint of the United States is at Philadelphia.[a] There are also three branches; one at New-Orleans for the coinage of gold and silver, one at Charlotte, North Carolina, and one at Dahlohnega, Georgia, for the coinage of gold only.[b]

The officers of the mint are a director, treasurer, assayer, melter and refiner, chief coiner and engraver, appointed by the president and senate.[c] The director has the control and superintendence of the mint, and the general regulation and supervision of the branches, and reports annually to the president their operations. The treasurer receives and keeps all the bullion and coin, and on the warrant of the director delivers the same to the persons entitled to receive the same.[c]

The standard of gold and silver is now nine hundred parts pure metal, and one hundred parts of alloy. The alloy of silver is copper, and the alloy of gold is copper and silver; but the silver must not be in greater proportion to the copper than one half.[c] The proportion of gold to silver in foreign coins established by act of 2d April, 1792, was one to fifteen of silver; it now varies. The proportion of gold

[a] Act, 2d April, 1792, 3d March, 1801, and 19th May, 1818.
[b] Act, 3d March, 1835. [c] Act, 3d March, 1837.

to silver in the American coins, is 1 lb. of pure gold = 16 lbs. $12\frac{4}{10}$ grains of pure silver. Gold and silver may be deposited by any person to be coined, provided the metal exceed $200 in amount, and be not too much debased.[a]

The bullion is weighed in the presence of the depositors when practicable, and a receipt is given stating the description and weight. If the bullion require to be melted before ascertaining its value, the weight after melting is the weight specified. When gold and silver are combined, and either metal is in such small proportions that it cannot be advantageously separated, no allowance is made for such metal.

From every parcel a sufficient portion is reserved to be assayed, but what remains after assaying is returned to the treasurer.

Charges by the mint.

For refining when bullion is below standard; for toughening when metals are contained in it which render it unfit for coinage; for copper used for alloy when the bullion is above standard; for silver introduced into the alloy of gold; and for separating the gold and silver when these metals exist together in the bullion; and the rate of these charges are fixed, from time to time, by the director, with the concurrence of the secretary of the treasury, so as not to exceed, in their judgment, the actual expense to the mint of the materials and labour employed.[a]

Where the gold or silver is of standard fineness, one half per cent. is the charge for coining, and the coin is payable in five days. If not required to be delivered for forty days after being deposited, no charge is made for coining.[b]

Mode of accounting.

From the report of the assayer, and the weight of the bullion, the treasurer estimates the whole value of each deposite, and also the amount of the charges or deductions, if any, and gives a detailed memorandum to the depositor; he also gives a certificate of the net amount of the deposite, to be paid in coins of the same species of bullion as that deposited.

The bullion is transferred, from time to time, in parcels, to the refiner, recording the weight and character, and it is then formed into ingots of legal standard, and suitable for coinage. These ingots are then assayed, and if they do not differ from the legal standard for gold more than two thousandths, and for silver more than three thousandths, they are delivered to the chief coiner to be made into coin.

In adjusting the weights of the coins, the following deviations from the standard weight must not be exceeded in any of the single pieces: in the dollar and half dollar, $1\frac{1}{2}$ grains; in the quarter dollar, 1 grain; in the dime and half dime, $\frac{1}{2}$ grain; in the gold coins, $\frac{1}{4}$ grain; in the

---

[a] Act, 3d March, 1837. [b] Act, 28th June, 1834, chap. 95.

copper coins, 1 grain in the pennyweight; in weighing a large number of pieces together, when delivered from the chief coiner to the treasurer, and from the treasurer to the depositors, the deviations from the standard weight must not exceed the following limits: 4 pennyweights in 1000 dollars; 3 pennyweights in 1000 quarter dollars; 1 pennyweight in 1000 dimes; 1 pennyweight in 1000 half dimes; 2 pennyweights in 1000 eagles; 1½ pennyweights in 1000 half eagles; 1 pennyweight in 1000 quarter eagles.[a]

An account is kept by the treasurer of the ingots delivered to the melter; and this account is settled annually, crediting him with an allowance for waste not exceeding two thousandths of the whole amount.[a]

An account is also kept with the chief coiner, of the standard weight of metal delivered to him, crediting him with a similar allowance for silver, and one thousandth for gold, for waste, and with all coins of legal standard received from him, and also with the weight of the clippings. This account is also to be settled annually.

The coins not of legal standard are returned to the melter to be recoined.

At every delivery of coins made by the chief coiner to the treasurer, it shall be the duty of the treasurer, in the presence of the assayer, to take indiscriminately a certain number of pieces of each variety for the annual trial of coins, (the number being prescribed by the director,) which must be carefully labelled, and deposited in a chest appropriated for that purpose, kept under the joint care of the treasurer and assayer, and so secured that neither can have access to its contents without the presence of the other.

When the coins which are the equivalent to any deposite of bullion are ready for delivery, they are paid over to the depositor, or his order, by the treasurer, on a warrant from the director; and the payment must be made, if demanded, in the order in which the bullion was brought to the mint, giving priority according to priority of deposite only. In the denominations of coin delivered, the treasurer must comply with the wishes of the depositor, unless when impracticable or inconvenient to do so; in which case, the denominations of coin are designated by the director.

One million of dollars are kept at the mint, in order to facilitate the delivery of coin to depositors.

An annual trial, on the 2d Monday of February, is made before commissioners designated by the president, of the coins reserved; and if a greater than the legal difference be found to exist, either in fineness or weight, it is reported to the president.

Copper bullion is purchased from time to time, in planchets, to be coined, and no allowance is made for waste. Copper coins may always be obtained at the mint for other coins, and the money received therefor is used as a fund to buy copper planchets.[a]

Some foreign coins also pass in the United States at values established by law. They consist of the gold coins of Great Britain,

---

[a] Act, 13th March, 1837.

Portugal, France, Spain, Mexico, Columbia and Brazil, the milled dollar of Spain, Mexico, Peru, Chili, Central America and Brazil, and five franc pieces of France.

A material change has been made in the legal value of foreign coins, by the acts of June 25th and 28th, 1834.

Previous to that period, foreign coins, except crowns, dollars and five franc pieces, passed by weight, as bullion, and of varying value.

In 1821, a report was made by the secretary of the treasury of the result of the assays made at the mint upon various coins.

It was there stated, that

The gold coins of Great Britain and Portugal are constantly found to be of the same quality with those of the United States, (those of Portugal, however, being rather bare,) weight 270 grs. The value of these coins is $1 for 27 grs. of 88.82 (say 88.89) cents per dwt.

The gold coins of France average 21 carats $2\frac{5}{12}$ grs. fine, in 24 carats. Their value is $1 for 27.49 grs., or 87.29 cents per dwt.

The gold coins of Spain average 20 carats, $3\frac{1}{4}$ grs. fine, in 24 carats. Their value is $1 for 28.54 grs., or 84.09 cents per dwt.

The standard quality of the silver coins of the United States was then 10 oz. 14 dwts. $4\frac{5}{13}$ grs. fine, in 12 oz., and the weight of the dollar 17 dwts. 8 grs. Their value per oz. was $115\frac{5}{13}$ cents.

The average quality of silver French crowns is 10 oz. 18 dwts. 13 grs. fine, in 12 oz. Their value is 117.73 cents per oz.

The average quality of silver five franc pieces of France is 10 oz. 16 dwts. fine, in 12 oz. Their value is 116.36 cents per oz.

The average quality of Spanish dollars is 10 oz. 15 dwts. 18 grs. fine, in 12 oz. Their value is 116.23 cents per oz.

The above average values of foreign coins differed at that time but little from those established by acts of congress then existing.

Table, showing the value, by weight, of those coins according to those averages; according to the acts of congress then existing, and under the acts of 25th and 28th June, 1834:

	By the above averages.	*By acts before* 1834.	*Acts of* 1834.
British and Portuguese gold coins, at	88.89 cts. per dwt.	88.89 per dwt.	94.8 per dwt.
French do. - - - - -	87.29 do.	87.27 " "	93.1 " "
Spanish do. - - - - -	84.9 do.	84.21 " "	89.9 " "
Silver French crowns - -	117.73 per oz.	117.6 per oz.	117.62 per oz.
Silver five franc pieces - -	117.36 " "	116 " "	116.25 " "
Spanish dollars - - -	116.23 " "	115.66 " "	115.76 " "

The rate at which foreign coins are received in payment, according to the existing law, is

			cts.	m.	
Gold coins of	Great Britain, Portugal and Brazil, 22 carats fine . .		94	8	per dwt.
" "	France . . .	9 1-10 fine . . .	93	1	" "
" "	Spain, Mexico and Colombia . . .	20 carats, 3 7-16 grains .	89	9	" "

Silver coins.—Milled dollar of Spain, Mexico, Peru, Chili and Central America, and those restamped in Brazil, ... } weighing 415 grains and 10 oz. 15 dwts. of pure silver in 12 oz. of standard silver, } $1

Halves, quarters, &c. in proportion.

Five franc pieces, weighing 384 grains, and having 10 oz. 16 dwts. of pure silver in 12 oz. of standard silver, ... 93 cts.

Assays are made annually of these silver coins at the mint, and the results must be reported to congress.[a]

In order to secure the standard of gold coins of the United States, three from each parcel are set aside for assay, and if upon the annual assay a greater difference than 1 part in 384 in fineness, or 1 part in 500 in weight, be found to exist, it is certified to the president, and the officer in fault is disqualified.[b]

AMERICA.

British colonies.

Accounts are kept in Canada, New-Brunswick and Nova Scotia, in pounds of 20 shillings or 240 pence each. This currency is 10 per cent. worse than sterling or £100 currency = £90 sterling or $432.

In some parts of Lower Canada accounts are kept in livres of 20 sous or 240 deniers each, according to the old French system. The proportion between the shilling and livre is as 5 to 6, or 5 shillings = 6 livres.

ARABIA.

At Mocha accounts are kept in piastres of 80 caveers current. This piastre is an imaginary coin: payments being generally made in Spanish dollars, which pass for 1 piastre, $\frac{215}{1000}$.

Foreign gold coins pass by weight, except the Venetian sequin, which passes for 2 piastres 25 cancers.

Gold and silver are weighed by the Vakia, = 10 coffalas or 100 carats, being nearly the same as one ounce Troy.

AUSTRIA.

At Vienna and in Austria proper, accounts are kept in guldens or florins, each of 60 creutzers, each creutzer = 4 phenings or hellers. The florin is also divided into 20 groschen of 3 creutzers each, and also into 80 groschels of 6 hellers each.

The rix dollar specie is worth 2 florins. The rix dollar currente is worth $1\frac{1}{2}$ florins. The specie guilder is worth $2\frac{1}{2}$ paper guilders or government paper.

The principal gold coins are double souverains of $26\frac{2}{3}$ florins, worth $3 37 7, and single and half souverains in proportion; imperial ducats, of $4\frac{1}{2}$ florins, worth $2 29 9, with double and quadruple ducats in proportion; Hungarian or Kremnitz ducats, of 4 florins 32 creutzers, worth $2 29 6.

The silver coins are specie rix dollars, of 2 florins; florins, worth 48 cents 6 mills, and half florins; copstucks = 20 creutzers, and half and quarter copstucks; Brabant and crown dollars = $2\frac{1}{2}$ florins.

The copper coins are creutzers, half creutzers, groschels, phenings and hellers. Usance is fourteen days after acceptance. Days of grace, three.

At Prague, and in all Bohemia, accounts are kept in guldens or florins of 60 creutzers, each creutzer = 4 phenings.

---

[a] Act, 25th June, 1834. [b] Act, 28th June, 1834, chap. 95.

The florin also is divided into 20 Bohmens or Kayser groschen = 80 groschel or 180 white phenings. The 20 florin rate (in which the Cologne mark of fine silver is coined into 20 florins) prevails in Austria and Bohemia.

At Trieste, accounts are kept as at Vienna. Also, in lire of 20 soldi or 240 denari, Trieste currency, 100 lire de Trieste = $9 18; also, in lire or florin di piazzi, of 20 soldi or 240 denari, 100 lire di piazza = $8 98; also, in lire Austrian of 100 centesimi, 100 lire Austrian = $16 20 2 mills.

The florin Austrian = $5\frac{5}{17}$ lire de Trieste, or $5\frac{7}{17}$ lire di piazza.

The Austrian coins pass at the rate of 90 lire de Trieste for 17 Austrian florins, or 30 soldi for 17 creutzers, except the Terentzer piece, which passes for 12 soldi.

The imperial ducat is reckoned at $4\frac{1}{2}$ florins, or $22\frac{1}{2}$ lire de Trieste, or 23 lire di piazza.

At Venice, accounts are now kept in livre Austrian of 100 centesimi, 1000 millesimi or 10,000 dix millesimi. There were formerly three other kinds of money in use, which are still occasionally referred to, viz.: moneta piccola, valuta currente, and banco, or that in which the bank of Venice kept accounts. Banco is 20 per cent. better than valuta currente, and $54\frac{5}{6}$ better than moneta piccola.

Accounts were formerly kept in livres of 20 soldi, or marchetti of 12 denari each, moneta piccola.

The ducato currente = 24 grossi, of which each grosso = 12 grossetti or denari di ducato.

The ducat banco = 24 grossi, each of 12 denari.

$6\frac{1}{5}$ livre piccola = a ducat currente, and $9\frac{3}{5}$ livre = a ducat banco.

The gold coins are the sequin of 22 livre, pistoles of 38 livre, and ducats of 14 livre.

The silver are the della croce of 12 livre 8 soldi, the ducatone of 11 livre, the ducato effetivo of 8 livre, the lirazzo of 30 soldi, the tallaco of 10 livre, the ozella of 3 livre 18 soldi.

There are also subdivisions of these pieces into halves and quarters.

The copper coins are soldi and half soldi, or begattini.

The new Austrian coins consist of $1\frac{1}{2}$, 1, and $\frac{1}{2}$ livre, or 18, 12, and 6 creutzers, and copper pieces of 10, 5, 1, and 1 soldi.

100 livre picole = 59 livre Austrian, $11\frac{2}{5}$ centesimi = $9 57 8 mills.

In Austria, the fineness of gold is expressed in carats and grains: the mark or absolute weight being divided into 24 carats of 12 grains each = 4333 English grains Troy. The fineness of silver is expressed in loths and grains: the mark being divided into 16 loths of 18 grains each. Wrought silver is 14 loths or $\frac{7}{8}$ fine. A mark of gold 23 carats 8 grains fine, is minted into $80\frac{2}{5}$ ducats; and as 5 marks of Vienna equal 6 of Cologne, 67 ducats must weigh a Cologne mark.

A Vienna mark of silver, $13\frac{1}{3}$ loths fine, is coined into 10 rix dollars or 20 florins. A mark $9\frac{1}{3}$ fine, is coined into 42 pieces of 20 creutzers, or into 35 copstucks.

A mark $8\frac{2}{3}$ fine, into 46 pieces of 17 creutzers.

A mark 8 fine, into 72 pieces of 10 creutzers.

A mark $6\frac{13}{18}$ fine, into $86\frac{1}{2}$ pieces of 7 creutzers. This is the conventional rate of coinage established in 1753, and adopted in the greater part of Germany.

In the Austrian dominions, with the exception of the Italian territories, where the metrical system prevails, gold and silver are weighed by the Vienna mark, being divided into 8 oz., 16 loths, 64 quintins, 256 phenings, 65,536 richtphenings = 4333 English grains Troy.

The weight of the ducat is divided into 60 parts, called mandel weights.

Diamonds and precious stones are weighed by the carat = 48$\frac{1}{8}$ Richtphenings, or 3.18 English grains Troy.

BARBARY STATES.

In Algiers, accounts were formerly kept in saimes or doubles of 50 aspers, and in patakas-chicas of 8 tomins, or 232 aspers. A piastre = 3 patakas-chicas, and a tomin = 29 aspers. A sultanin passed for 8$\frac{1}{2}$ patakas-chicas; a sequin for 10, and a Spanish dollar for 4$\frac{3}{4}$. Since Algiers has become a French possession, the French coins have been introduced. In Fez, Salle, Mogadore, and in all western Barbary, accounts are kept in mitkuls of 10 ounces, each ounce being 4 blankeels of 24 fluce each.

The principal coins are Spanish doubloons and dollars, with their divisions, and a gold coin worth $10, coined at Madrid for the Barbary trade.

The gold mitkul, or miscal, or ducat of 10 ounces, and the bendiky of 27 ounces.

The silver ounce or dirhem of 4 blankeel.

In copper, 6 and 4 fluce pieces.

A bendiky is worth $2. A mitkul, $74.07.

At Tripoli, accounts are kept in piastres of 13 grimellini, or 52 aspers.

The grimellini is valued at 8 sous, the piastre at 75 cents, or 3s. 3d. sterling.

The coins are sultanais, $\frac{1}{3}$ heavier than Egyptian; the ghersch, called quarter dollar, worth 18 cents 5 mills, or 9$\frac{1}{4}$d. sterling, half and quarter ghersch in proportion.

Spanish dollars and Venitian sequins also pass, but their value is not fixed.

At Tunis, accounts are kept in piastres of 16 carobas, or 52 aspers. The asper is divided into 2 bourbes. The only gold Tunisian coin is the mahbub or sultanin, valued at 4$\frac{1}{2}$ piastres, with halves and quarters in proportion. The silver coins are the piastre, with halves and quarters and doubles, valued at 24 aspers. The value of foreign coins is uncertain.

BELGIUM.

At Antwerp and throughout Belgium accounts were kept as at Amsterdam, in guilders or florins of 20 stivers or sols, each stiver being 12 deniers or 16 pfennings. In 1816 the decimal system was introduced into Holland, and of course was extended to Belgium. The florin now is divided into 100 centimes, and is worth 40 cents United States currency.

Accounts are also kept in pounds, shillings and pence, Flemish. The pound Flemish = $2\frac{1}{2}$ daalder, or rix dollar = 6 guilders = 20 shillings = 120 stivers = 240 groats = 480 liards = 1440 deniers = 1920 Brabant pfennings = 5760 mitres, and is worth $2 37 7 mills United States currency. Six florins of exchange = 7 florins current.

Usances as at Amsterdam. Days of grace, five.

The weight of gold and silver is the same as in the Netherlands, viz. the Troy mark of 8 oz. of 20 engels each. The engel is divided into 32 aas or azen. The mark = 3798 grains Troy weight.

BRAZIL.

Accounts are kept as in Portugal in rees, reas or reis; 1000 reas make a milrea; 100,000 reas = 100 milreas, and 1,000,000 reas = 1000 milreas, commonly called a conto of reas: 100 milreas are worth $104 $16\frac{2}{3}$.

The gold coins are pieces of 1,000 reas, 2,000 reas, and 4,000 reas, also the Portuguese coin.

The silver coins are pieces of 640, 600, 480, 320, 300, 240, 160, 150, 120, 80, 75 and 60 reas; also the Spanish dollar, which now passes for 960 reas: formerly it passed for 800 reas.

The pataca = 320 reas, and the crusado novo 180 reas.

The paper currency consists in bills of the junta of Rio de Janeiro, but it has no value abroad.

The copper coins are pieces of 1 and 2 vintems, or 20 and 40 reas.

BUENOS AYRES.

Accounts are kept in pesos or dollars of 8 reals each: being the same as in Mexico and New Grenada. The coins are the same also.

The paper money is at a great depreciation, being in 1836 nearly eight pesos for one of specie.

CENTRAL AMERICA.

Accounts are kept as in Mexico in pesos of 8 reals each. Coins the same as in Mexico, being the doubloon and dollar, halves and quarters, &c.

CHILI.

Accounts are kept as in Mexico. Coins the same also.

CHINA.

Accounts are kept in China in tales, mace, candarimes or scandarimes, and cash; the tale = 10 mace = 100 candarimes = 1000 cash. Cash is the only money coined in China. It is six parts copper and four lead, round, with a square hole in the centre, through which a string is passed.

Foreign coins circulate freely, especially dollars. For change they cut them in parts and the fragments are weighed. The tale is worth $1 48, but the East India Company value it at 6*s.* 8*d.* The fineness of gold and silver is expressed by dividing the weight into 100 parts, of which each is called touch. Thus, 93 touch would contain 7 alloy and 93 fine gold or silver.

DENMARK.

At Copenhagen, in Denmark, the accounts were formerly kept in rix-dollars, Danish currency; but, since the establishment of the rix-bank, in the year 1813, they have been kept in rix-dollars, of 6 marks or 96 skillings. By the regulation then issued, all payments are required to be made in rix-bank money, either in silver coin or notes, so soon as a sufficient sum may be issued to pay off the old coin or notes. Until then, specie money is to pass at the rate of one specie dollar silver coin, for two rix-bank dollars silver coin; or one specie dollar in notes, for two rix-bank dollars, one half in silver coin, and the other half in notes, at the exchange between silver coin and notes, which is to be fixed and published by the bank twice a year, viz. the first of February and the first of August. Danish bank notes *currency* are to pass at the rate of six dollars currency for one *rix-bank* dollar.

The Cologne mark of fine silver, which is equal to 3608 English grains, is coined into $18\frac{1}{2}$ rix-bank dollars; consequently, 2 rix-bank dollars are of the same value as one old specie dollar, $9\frac{1}{4}$ of which were coined from a mark of fine silver; and one new rix-bank dollar is equal to $27\frac{1}{4}$ pence sterling, and to $\frac{5}{8}$ of the old current dollar.

The sound duties are charged in specie, which nominally bears a fixed agio of $19\frac{1}{2}$ per cent. on specie rix dollars, reduced to crowns, by 6 stivers to every specie rix dollar, and 3 stivers for every crown dollar.

The accounts are kept in rix dollars and stivers. Such articles as do not appear in the tariff, pay in privileged ships (or those of nations having a treaty of commerce with Denmark) one per cent. on the value of the cocket, or other custom-house document, or original invoice; and, in unprivileged ships, one and a quarter per cent. When no authenticated value appears, the custom-house officers fix it according to their own judgment; and it is extremely difficult to obtain any deduction from their charges.

The Swedish specie is about $2\frac{5}{6}$ per cent. worse than specie, which means the account money of the Altona bank. Crown money is $15\frac{35}{51}$ per cent. worse.

Money of account $6\frac{1}{4}$ per cent. worse.

Holstein money 25 per cent. worse.

In specie, the old rix dollar is reckoned at 6 marks Danish, and equals $1\frac{1}{2}$ sletdaler = 4 orts = 6 marks = 96 schillings = 192 fyrkes = 288 witlen = 1152 pfenings Danish, and half those denominations in Hamburg money.

Danish standard gold is 18 carats fine, or 3 pure to 1 alloy.

Danish standard silver is 13 lods 6 grains, or 240 grains fine, or 5 pure to 1 alloy.

The fineness of gold is expressed in carats and grains, the mark being 24 carats of 12 grains each. The fineness of silver, in lods and grains, the mark being 16 lods of 18 grains each.

The lb. used in weighing gold and silver consists of 2 marks, 32 lods, 128 quintines, or 512 orts = 7266 English grains Troy. At the mint the Cologne mark is used in coining.

The new Holstein currency, coined since 1788, consists of the specie rix dollar = 48 specie skillings or 60 Holstein skillings, and 32, 16, 8, 4 and 2 specie skilling pieces, or 40, 20, 10, 5 and 2½ skillings Holstein currency.

At Altona accounts are kept in marks of 16 skilling lubs—each skilling being 12 pence lubs, as at Hamburg.

The ducats coined by the king of Denmark or duke of Holstein, are of the same weight and fineness as those of the German empire, 67 weighing a Cologne mark and 23⅔ carats fine.

No usance is established at Copenhagen. Days of grace eight.

At Altona the usances and days of grace are as at Hamburg.

EAST INDIES.

Coins, moneys and weights.

Before the colonies were established, particularly while the Mogul's power prevailed in Hindostan, the monetary system was very simple. There was current, throughout those dominions, one principal coin of silver, called the *sicca rupee*. It was of a certain weight called the sicca; which served also as a standard for weighing other articles.

There were, however, gold coins minted; but their price was not fixed, silver being the only standard of value. The principal piece of gold was the *mohur:* it was of the same weight as the sicca rupee, and both are supposed to have been originally coined without any alloy.

These denominations of money are still current in India; but they differ from each other, and all have departed from their original purity. The British East India Company, however, have kept as near to it as the necessary firmness of coins seems to require.

The moneys of some of the native princes are still in a high degree of firmness, but they are subject to frequent alterations; and hence the necessity of *shroffs*, who are a kind of money-brokers or assayers, appointed to set a value upon the different coins that may require examination.

The principal money of account in India is the current rupee. It is an imaginary money to which real coins are generally reduced before they are entered into books of account. This reduction is performed by allowing a certain per centage called the *batta*, which varies according to circumstances.

BRITISH POSSESSIONS.

Moneys and weights.

The monetary system of the British possessions in India have undergone various alterations from time to time; but the principal object in this place is to show the present state of their money and mint regulations. It should be observed, that there are mints established in each of the presidencies, where assay-masters are engaged that have been instructed by the king's assay-master at the London mint. These establishments are open to the public as well as to the company.

CALCUTTA.

Coins and moneys.

Accounts are commonly kept here in current rupees, the rupee being divided into 16 annas, and each anna into 12 pice. The East India Company, however, keep their accounts in sicca rupees, similarly divided, which bear a *batta* of 16 per cent. against current rupees; and in their financial statements, which are submitted to parliament, each sum of sicca rupees is reduced to current rupees by adding to this batta, and the current rupee is then reckoned at 2 shillings sterling, (46 cents 2.7 mills, United States currency.)

Thus, a sicca rupee of account is worth 2 shillings $3\frac{7}{8}$ pence sterling; (53 cents 7.7 mills, United States currency;) but it is commonly reckoned at 2 shillings and 6 pence, or 57 cents 8.7 mills, United States currency. The value in the United States is 50 cents.

A lac of rupees is 100,000, and a crore 100 lacs, or 10,000,000 of rupees.

In the inferior departments of business accounts are kept in cowries, a species of small sea-shells, which, as long as they remain unbroken, are used as money in small payments. 2560 cowries are generally reckoned for a current rupee; but they have intermediate divisions, viz.: 4 cowries make 2 gunda; 20 gundas 1 punn; 4 punns 1 anna; 4 annas 1 cahaun; and 4 cahauns 1 current rupee; but the last proportion is variable.

Coins.

There are under the presidency of Bengal three mints, the principal of which is at Calcutta, and the subordinate one at Benares, and the other at Furruckabad.

At the mint of Calcutta there are coined gold mohurs, and silver sicca rupees; one of the former is by authority to pass for 16 of the latter.

The fineness of both metals is $\frac{11}{12}$, like English standard gold. The following is a statement of the weight, fineness and value.

Name.	Pure grains.	Alloy grains.	Gross w. grains.	Sterling value.	Value in U. S. curr'cy.
Gold mohur,	187.651	17.059	204.710	33s. 2.52d.	7 doll. 67 cts. 7 mills.
Sicca rupee,	175.923	15.993	191.916	2s. 0.56d.	0 48 " 0 "

It should be observed, that the sicca rupee was formerly of the sicca weight, viz. $179\frac{2}{3}$ English grains, with $\frac{1}{48}$ part only of alloy, making the pure quantity as above; but in 1819 the alloy was increased to $\frac{1}{12}$, the same as the gold.

The charge for coining at the Calcutta mint is 2 per cent. if the bullion be of the standard fineness; but when it differs, there is a proportional charge made for refining, which varies from $\frac{1}{4}$ to $2\frac{1}{2}$ per cent.

At the subordinate mints silver only is coined, as follows:

Name.	Pure grains.	Alloy grains.	Gross w. grains.	Sterling value.	Value in U. S. currency.
Benares rupee,	168.875	6.125	175	23.58 pence.	45 cents 4.9 mills.
Furrackabad rupee,	165.220	7.780	173	23.07 "	44 " 5 "

Gold and silver are weighed by the dhan or grain of 4 punkhos. 25 grains make 1 anna; and 32 grains 1 massa. 10 massa equal 1 sicca weight, which is $179\frac{2}{3}$ grains Troy, or 6.57066 drachms Avoirdupois. Thus, $12\frac{1}{2}$ massa, 16 annas, or 1 tolah, are equal to 224.588 English grains.

MADRAS, OR FORT ST. GEORGE.

Coins and moneys.

There are different monetary systems in Madras, which may be distinguished under the head of the old system and the new.

According to the old system, accounts are kept in star pagodas, fanams and cash; 80 cash equal 1 fanam, and 42 fanams 1 pagoda. The East India Company and other European merchants keep their accounts at 12 fanams the rupee, and 42 fanams or $3\frac{1}{2}$ rupees the star pagoda; but the natives reckon the rupee at 12 fanams 60 cash, and the star pagoda at 44 fanams 50 cash. The bazar exchange fluctuates from 35 to 45 fanams.

The gold coins are, star or current pagodas; and the silver coins, arcot rupees. Double and single fanams and copper pieces of 20 cash, called pice, are current here; also, pieces of 10 and 5 cash, called doodee and half doodee, and single cash pieces. These copper coins are struck in England, and the value is marked upon each.

The star pagoda weighs 52.56 English grains, and the gold is $19\frac{1}{5}$ carats fine; it contains, therefore, 42.048 grains of fine gold, and is worth 7 shillings $5\frac{1}{4}$ pence sterling, or $1.72 cents $1\frac{1}{2}$ mills United States currency; but is commonly valued at 8 shillings sterling, or $1.85 cents 1.76 mills United States currency.

The Arcot rupee, which is also coined at the fort St. George mint, weighs 176.4 grains, and contains 166.477 grains of fine silver; its value, therefore, is $23\frac{1}{4}$ pence sterling, or about 44 cents 8.5 mills United States currency. It is divided into 16 annas, or 192 pices, like the other rupees.

Many other coins circulate on the Coromandel coast, of which the following are the most generally current:

The old pagoda, with three swamy or figures, coined at Madras and Negapatam, which is about $20\frac{2}{3}$ carats fine, and which generally bears a batta of 10 per cent. against the new coins of the same places:

The new pagoda of Negapatam and Tutocoryn, which is $18\frac{1}{4}$ carats fine, and is reckoned about 4 per cent. worse than the star pagoda:

The Porto Novo pagoda, which is $17\frac{3}{4}$ carats fine, and is about 20 per cent. worse than the star pagoda:

The Pondicherry pagoda, which was originally equal in value to the star pagoda; but its standard has been lowered to 17 carats, and even less. All these different pagodas are nearly of the same weight.

In 1811 a coinage from Spanish dollars took place, consisting of double rupees, single rupees, halves and quarters, and pieces of 1, 2, 3 and 5 fanams. One rupee weighs 186.70 grains Troy, and contains 166.477 grains of pure silver, which is the same quantity as is contained in the Arcot rupee. It is therefore worth 23.247 pence sterling, or about 44 cents 8.5 mills United States currency.

A silver coinage of half and quarter pagodas, of dollar-silver fineness, also took place then. The silver half pagoda weighs 326.73 grains Troy, and is equal to $1\frac{3}{4}$ Arcot rupee, or about 78 cents 4.87 mills United States currency.

New system, (since 1818.)

By a proclamation, dated January 7th, 1818, the silver rupee is in future to constitute the standard coin of the presidency. The public accounts are, in consequence, converted from the star pagoda into the Madras rupee, at the exchange of 350 rupees for 100 pagodas; and all the engagements of the government are also transacted in the same rupees.

The new coinage of silver consists of rupees weighing $7\frac{1}{2}$ dwts. and $\frac{11}{12}$ fine. Thus the rupee contains 165 grains of pure silver, and 15 grains of alloy, making together 180 grains, with half rupees, quarters, eighths and sixteenths in proportion. The sixteenth is the anna, and the eighth the double anna.

The new coinage of gold consists of rupees, halves and quarters, of the same weight and fineness as the silver rupee. Thus the former contains 165 grains of pure gold and 15 grains of alloy.

The new gold rupee, valued at the mint price of gold in England, is worth £1 9 shillings 2.42 pence sterling, or $6 75 9.3 mills United States currency.

The new silver rupee valued at the old mint price of silver in England, is 1 shilling 11.04 pence sterling, or about 44 cents 4 mills United States currency; but as the 15th part of the gold rupee, it is worth 1 shilling 11.36 pence, or 45 cents 0.6 mills United States currency. The coinage of the pagoda has been discontinued.

The charge for coining at the Madras mint is 3 per cent. for gold, and 4 per cent. for silver, including the charge for refining.

Gold and silver are sometimes weighed by the star pagoda weight, which is 52.56 English grains, as above stated.

BOMBAY.

Coins and moneys.

Accounts are kept in rupees; each rupee being divided into four quarters, and each quarter into 100 reas. The rupee is also divided into 16 annas or 50 pice. An urdee is 2 reas; a dorea 6 reas; a dooganey or single pice 4 reas; a fuddea or double pice 8 reas. A punchea is 5 rupees, and a gold mohur 15 rupees. Of these, the annas and reas only are imaginary coins.

The coins of Bombay are the mohur or gold rupee, the silver rupee, and their divisions; also the double and single pice, the urdee and dorea, which are copper coins, with a mixture of tin or lead.

The old Bombay rupee was the same as that formerly coined at Surat under the Mogul; it weighed 178.314 English grains, and contained 124 per cent. of alloy.

By an agreement of the English government with the Nabob of Surat, the rupees coined by both were to circulate at an equal value, and they mutually pledged themselves to keep up the coin to its exact standard of weight and fineness. The Nabob rupees, however, were soon afterwards found to contain 10, 12, and even 15 per cent. of alloy; in consequence of which most of the Bombay rupees were melted down and recoined at Surat. The coinage of silver in the Bombay mint was suspended for 20 years, and the Surat rupees were the only ones seen in circulation. At length, (in 1800,) the company ordered the Surat rupee to be struck at Bombay, and since that period the rupees of both places have been kept at an equal value, weighing 179 English grains, and valued at 23 pence sterling, or 44 cents 3.65 mills United States currency.

In the company's financial accounts, which are submitted to parliament, the Bombay rupee is reckoned at 2 shillings and 3 pence, and then it bears a batter of 16 per cent. against current rupees.

In 1774 the gold mohur was ordered to be made of the same weight as the silver rupee, and to be equal in fineness to a Venitian sequin: by this the proportion of gold to silver in the Bombay coins was nearly as 15 to 1. When the Surat rupees, however, were introduced into circulation, this proportion ceased; and gold coined according to the regulation of 1774, was exchanged for only 13 times its weight of silver.

In order to remedy this, it was settled in 1800, that the mohur should be of the same weight and fineness as the silver rupee, and that it should pass for 15 such rupees.

The following is the new system.

Name.	Pure grains.	Alloy grains.	Gross w. grains.	Sterling value.	Val. in U. S. currency.
Gold rupee,	164.74	14.26	179	29 shill. 1 78d.	$6.74 cents 6 96 mills.
Silver rupee,	164 74	14.26	179	1 " 11d.	44 cents 3.65 mills.

The charge for coinage in the Bombay mint is $2\frac{1}{2}$ per cent. for gold, and 3 per cent. for silver, including the charge for refining.

Gold and silver are weighed by the tola of 40 valls, 100 gonze or Bombay grains, or 600 chows. 24 tolas make 1 seer; and 32 tolas 13 valls, equal £1 Troy.

BATAVIA.—(In the Island of Java.)

Coins and moneys.—Old system.

Accounts are kept in rix dollars, an imaginary money of 48 stivers, valued at $1 15 cents 7.35 mills United States currency, or 5 shillings sterling.

The principal currency is composed of rupees of 4 shillings, 12 dubbeltjees, 15 cash, 30 stivers, or 120 doits. This rupee is valued at 72 cents 3.34 mills; (3 shillings 1½ pence sterling;) the cash at 4 cents 8.22 mills; (2½ pence sterling;) the stiver at 2 cents 4.11 mills; (1¼ pence sterling;) and the others in proportion. There are also sooka of 2 satalies, 6 cash, or 12 stivers. Certain Chinese denominations are likewise used, especially in the bazar.

10 condorines make 1 cash; 4 cash 1 mace; and 10 mace 1 tale.

The principal coins of the islands are patacks and cash. The patack is worth 6 mace or 24 cash. There are, besides the above, pieces called pities, composed of 4 parts of lead and 1 of tin, 50 of which make 1 stiver.

Foreign coins pass here at a certain number of stivers each; but these rates are subject to variation; and coins, both of gold and silver, are mostly valued according to their weight and fineness.

New monetary system.

A new system of moneys has been recently established here by the king of the Netherlands; it somewhat differs from that which has been introduced into Holland, (for which see *Amsterdam*.)

The monetary unit is the new guilder or florin of the Netherlands; but instead of decimal divisions it is here divided into 4 shillings, 12 dubbels, 24 Dutch stivers, 30 Indian stivers, or 120 doits.

A paper currency has also been established, consisting of bills of 1000, 600, 300, 100, 50, 25, 10, 5 and 1 guilders, (gulden,) which are converted into specie on demand. For this purpose exchange offices have been established at Batavia, Samarang, and Sourabaya. The two latter places, however, issue no paper of greater value than 100 guilders.

The following coins are current, and are received at the government treasury at the annexed rates of exchange:

Rupee of Java, Surat and Arcotat - -	120
Sicca rupee - - - - -	126
American dollar - - - - -	240
Spanish dollar - - - - -	264
Old ducaton - - - - -	312
Milled ducaton - - - - -	320
Gold ducat of the Netherlands - - -	528
Gold rupees - - - - -	1926

Gold and silver are weighed by the Dutch mark Troy, which is divided into 9 reals, each weighing 422 English grains.

COCHIN.—(*Malabar coast.*)

Accounts are kept here in rupees of 16 annas, which are reckoned equal to the Surat rupees. Accounts are also kept in fanams, 20 of which equal the rupee. A schilling is 4 fanams.

Venitian sequins are worth 72 fanams; Dutch ducatons, 50; Spanish dollars, 40; Dutch rix dollars, 32; and Negapatam pagodas, 64 fanams.

Gold and silver are weighed by the sicca weight, for which see *Calcutta.*

GOA.—(Malabar coast.)

Accounts are kept here in pardos, tangas, vintins and budgerooks; but there are good and bad tangas, &c. A pardo is worth 4 good tangas or 5 bad ones, 16 good ventins or 20 bad; 300 good budgerooks or 360 bad. The pardo is also divided into 240 good or 300 bad reas.

The coins are, the St. Thomas, a gold piece of nearly the weight of a ducat, which passes for 11 good tangas, more or less. The silver coins are the pardo xeraphin of 5 good tangas, and the common pardo of 4 good tangas. The copper and tin coins are good and bad budgerooks.

MALACCA.—(On the Malay peninsula.)

Accounts are kept in rix dollars of 8 shillings, or 48 stivers; the stiver being again divided into 4 doits. The rix dollar is an imaginary money, in which all contracts for goods are made; but the principal current coins are rupees, Dutch shillings, dubbletjees, 2 stiver pieces, and doits.

The Spanish dollar is from 25 to 40 per cent. better than the rix dollar of account; hence, at a medium, this rix dollar is worth 77 cents 1.56 mills, or about 3 shillings 4 pence sterling. A Dutch ducaton passes for 13 shillings; an English crown for 10 shillings; a Bombay or Surat rupee for 5 shillings; a Madras or Arcot rupee for 4 shillings, more or less. A stamped Japan copang passes for 10 rix dollars.

MANILLA.—(In Luconia, one of the Philippine Islands.)

Accounts are kept in dollars or pesos of 8 reals; the real being divided into 34 maravedis.

The course of exchange between Bengal and Manilla is generally from 38 to 45 Spanish dollars per 100 current rupees.

MAURITIUS, OR THE ISLE OF FRANCE.—(In the Indian ocean.)

Coins and moneys.

Accounts are kept here in two different ways, namely, in dollars of 100 cents, which is the mode generally adopted in public or government accounts; or in dollars of 10 livres or 200 sols, which mode is mostly used by merchants. These are called colonial livres, 2 of which equal 1 French franc.

The principal French coin in common currency, is the sol marqué, which is of copper, and worth 3 colonial sols.

Hence $66\frac{2}{3}$ marqué equal 1 dollar.

Thus, 2 sols equal 1 cent; 1 marqué $1\frac{1}{2}$ cent, and 1 livre 10 cents.

The ten livre pieces struck in the colony under the French government, the 5 franc pieces of France, and the German crown pieces, have the same value in exchange as the Spanish dollar.

PEGU.—(On the further Peninsula.)

The trade is here mostly carried on by barter; gold and silver are not coined in the country, but exchanged as merchandise. The tical, a certain weight of silver, which is sometimes used as a money of account, is divided into 16 toques or touch.

There is, however, a small coin, called ganza, which is a mixture of copper, lead, and tin, and worth about 2 cents 4 mills, or $1\frac{1}{4}$ pence sterling; but the price varies according to the demand and supply. Gold, silver, pearls, spices, and other valuable articles, are generally paid for in this money.

Gold and silver are weighed by the tical, and their fineness is expressed by dividing the weight into 16 parts called touch, answering to 100 touch in China, or 10 touch on the Malabar coast.

PONDICHERRY.—(Coromandel coast.)

Accounts are kept in pagodas of 24 fanams; and the fanam is subdivided into 60 cash.

The coins are gold pagodas, and silver rupees and fanams, which have been mentioned under the article Madras; also copper cash and dudus, a copper coin, 20 of which are reckoned to a fanam.

Gold and silver are weighed by the seer, pagoda, rupee, and fanam. A seer weighs $24\frac{3}{8}$ rupees, $81\frac{1}{4}$ pagodas, or $731\frac{1}{4}$ fanams; a rupee weight equals 30 fanams, or 480 nellos; a pagoda weighs 9 fanams or 144 nellos. Thus, 3 rupees are equal in weight to 10 pagodas. The seer equals 4293 English grains.

PRINCE OF WALES'S ISLAND.—(Off the western coast of Malay.)

Accounts are kept in Spanish dollars, copangs, and pice; 10 pice making 1 copang, and 10 copangs 1 Spanish dollar.

The current pice are coined in the island; they are pieces of tin, 16 of which weigh 1 catty or $1\frac{1}{3}$ English pound. On the exchange of dollars into pice there is a loss of 2 per cent.; on dollars without the king's head, 10 per cent.; and from 5 to 10 per cent. on all dollars defaced.

Gold and silver are weighed by the buncal, which is divided into 16 miams, and is of the weight of 2 Spanish dollars nearly, or 1 ounce, 9 pennyweights, $10\frac{7}{12}$ grains Troy. 20 buncals make 1 catty, which equals 29 ounces, 15 pennyweights, $11\frac{2}{3}$ grains Troy.

EGYPT.

At Alexandria, accounts are kept in piastres current of 40 medini, each medini = 8 borbi = 6 fiorli = 3 aspers.

A ducatello	= 10 medini.	A sequin	= 146 medini.
A griscio	= 30 do.	A zumabob	= 120 do.
A zenzeri	= 107 do.		

At Cairo, accounts are kept in piastres of 33 medini or 80 aspers.

The mahbub sequin = 120 medini.

The funducli do. = 146 do.

The pataccas formerly passed for 85 medini, but they vary in value.

The coins of Turkey are all current in Egypt.

ENGLAND AND IRELAND.

Accounts are kept in pounds sterling of 12 shillings, and 240 pence = 960 farthings. The pound being worth \$4 80 federal currency, legal value; the gold sovereign, however, is worth \$4 84.

REAL MONEY.

Gold.

Guinea	\$5 07
Half guinea	2 53.5
Sovereign	4 84

Half, double and five sovereign pieces in proportion.

Seven shilling piece	1 68

Since 1816, gold coins alone are a legal tender for a debt over 40 shillings.

Silver.

Crown	\$1 20
Bank token	72
Half crown	60
Shilling	24
Sixpence	12

Copper.

	Cents.	Mills.
Penny	2	
Half-penny	1	
Farthing		5

A pound, Scotch, old currency = 1s. 8d.
A shilling " " " = 1d.
A penny " " " = $\frac{1}{12}$d.
A pound sterling = £1 1s. 8d. Irish currency.
A shilling " = 1s. 1d. "
A penny " = 1d. $\frac{1}{3}$ farthing Irish.

The currency is now, however, in Scotland and Ireland, the same as in England.

The fineness of gold in England is expressed in carats and grains. The pound or absolute weight being 24 carats of 4 grains each.

The carat pound = 10 dwts. Troy, and the carat grain = 60 grains Troy.

The fineness of silver is expressed in ounces and pennyweights, the pound being 12 oz. of 20 dwts. each.

The standard fineness of gold is 22 carats, and is expressed in fractions $\frac{22}{24}$, or decimally 0.917.

Wrought gold has two legal standards; one of 22 carats, (like the coin.) the other 18 carats, for jewellery. A lb. of standard gold is coined into 44$\frac{1}{2}$ guineas, 46$\frac{29}{40}$ sovereigns, or 133$\frac{1}{2}$ 7 shilling pieces.

The standard fineness of silver before 1817, was 11 oz. 2 dwts. fine, by which 62 shillings were coined from a lb. of standard silver, or 5s. 2d. per oz., and this is still the mint price in comparing foreign coins.

In 1817, the lb. of standard silver was directed to be coined into 66s., or 5s. 6d. per oz. The standard fineness is still 11 oz. 2 dwts. of pure silver with 18 dwts. of alloy, and it is expressed in fractions $\frac{37}{40}$, or decimally 0.925. Wrought silver has also two legal standards; one the same as the old silver coin, the other 11 oz. 10 dwts. fine, or new, sterling.

FRANCE.

In France, accounts are now kept in francs, decimes and centimes; or in livres, sous and deniers.

1 franc = 10 decimes = 100 centimes.

1 livre = 20 sous = 240 deniers.

1 ecu of exchange = 3 francs.

In the old system of coinage, the fineness of gold was reckoned at 24 carats, each 32 parts, and of silver at 12 deniers, each 24 grains; but in the new the fineness of both metals is decimally expressed.

Accounts were formerly kept in livres tournois, which was formerly of the same value as the franc; but now francs are 1$\frac{1}{4}$ per cent. better.

The livre tournois was divided into 20 sols, or 240 deniers.

The old coins were as follows:

Gold.—Old Louis d'Or, from 1640 to 1709, weighing 103$\frac{3}{35}$ Troy grains, and 21$\frac{3}{4}$ carats fine.

Sun Louis d'Or, from 1709 to 1716, weighing 125$\frac{1}{2}$ grains, and 21$\frac{1}{2}$ carats fine.

Noailles, from 1716 to 1718, weighing 188$\frac{2}{3}$ grains, and 21$\frac{2}{3}$ carats fine.

Chevalier, or L. L. Louis d'Or, from 1718 to 1723, weighing $149\frac{7}{10}$ grains, and $21\frac{1}{2}$ carats fine.

Mirlitons, from 1723 to 1726, weighing $102\frac{1}{5}$ grains, and $21\frac{7}{12}$ carats fine.

Old shield Louis d'Or, from 1726, weighing $125\frac{1}{2}$ grains, and $21\frac{2}{3}$ carats fine.

Double and single Louis d'Ors, of 48 and 24 livres respectively. The single Louis d'Or weighed $117\frac{2}{3}$ grains, and was 21 carats fine.

Silver.—Ecu or Louis blanc, from 1640 to 1709, weighing $400\frac{9}{10}$ grains.

Crowns, from 1709 to 1718, weighing $199\frac{3}{4}$ grains.

Navarre dollars, from 1718 to 1724, weighing $375\frac{8}{1}$ grains.

Bidet neuf, from 1724 to 1726, weighing $360\frac{8}{10}$ grains.

Ecus or crowns, coined since 1726, of 6 livres, and halves, fifths, tenths and twentieths, in proportion.

Also, 2, $1\frac{1}{2}$ sols, and 6 liard pieces.

Copper.—Sols, half sols, and liards.

In the old system of coinage, the absolute fineness of gold was reckoned at 24 carats, each 32 parts; of silver at 12 deniers, each 24 grains.

In the new system, the fineness of both metals is decimally expressed.

There are three legal degrees of fineness for wrought gold, to wit: 1st, $\frac{920}{1000}$, or $22\frac{8}{100}$ carats; 2d, $\frac{840}{1000}$, or $20\frac{16}{100}$ carats; 3d, $\frac{750}{1000}$, or 18 carats.

For wrought silver there are two: 1st, $\frac{950}{1000}$, or $11\frac{2}{5}$ deniers; 2d, $\frac{800}{1000}$, or $9\frac{3}{5}$ deniers.

The new moneys of France.

The franc may be considered as the unity of the new French coins. It is nearly the same with the livre tournois, and worth about 10 pence English, or 18 cents 7 mills. Francs and livres were formerly similar; but, in one coinage, the 5 livre pieces were, by accident, made too heavy, being worth $101\frac{1}{4}$ sols, instead of 100. The new franc has been therefore adopted in conformity with this value, and the franc or new livre is equal to 213 deniers, being $1\frac{1}{4}$ per cent. better than the old livre tournois = 210 deniers.

By a decree which passed the French legislative body on the 30th of March, 1803, for a new coinage, the silver pieces were appointed to be $\frac{1}{4}$ francs, $\frac{1}{2}$ francs, $\frac{3}{4}$ francs, 2 franc pieces, and 5 franc pieces; and 200 francs are to be coined from a killogram (or 2 lbs. 8 oz. 3 dwts. 2 grains Troy) of silver $\frac{9}{10}$ fine. The gold coinage to be 20 and 40 franc pieces; and 150 pieces of 20 francs are to be coined from a killogram of gold $\frac{9}{10}$ fine. The copper pieces to be those of $\frac{2}{100}$, $\frac{3}{100}$, and $\frac{5}{100}$ of a franc. Pieces of billon of 10 centimes are also minted $\frac{200}{1000}$ fine. The gold and silver coins are of $\frac{9}{10}$ pure and $\frac{1}{10}$ alloy; or as assayed at the mint of the United States, the gold coins are 21 carats $2\frac{5}{12}$ grains fine, and the silver 10 oz. 16 dwts. in 12 oz.

Gold coins.

40 francs	\$7 70.2
20 francs	3 85.1

Silver.

5 francs	93$\frac{1}{2}$cents.
2 francs	39.4
1 franc	18.708
$\frac{3}{4}$ of a franc	14.031
$\frac{1}{2}$ of a franc	9.354
$\frac{1}{4}$ of a franc	4.577

Copper.

2 decimes, $\frac{1}{5}$th of a franc	3$\frac{3}{4}$ cents.
A decime, $\frac{1}{10}$th of a franc	1.708 Mill.
A sol, or 5 centimes	$\frac{15}{16}$ or 9.35
3 centimes	.4$\frac{1}{6}$
2 centimes, $\frac{1}{50}$th of a franc	.3.41
A centime, $\frac{1}{100}$th of a franc	.1.7

Paper.

The bank of France has a capital of 90,000,000 of francs, and its notes are payable in specie on demand. None are issued for less than 500 francs. It receives money and articles of value on deposit, discounts commercial paper, and advances money on pledges, and public or other securities.

GERMANY.

Germany being divided into a number of separate states, the particulars of each will be found under its proper head. But as there are certain regulations and usages which are common to most parts of that country, the following general view of them may be useful as well as satisfactory.

The most common way of keeping accounts, is in rix dollars of 90 creutzers, or in guldens or florins of 60 creutzers; the rix dollar of account, or (as it is generally called) rix dollar current, is reckoned at 1$\frac{1}{2}$ florins, and the rix dollar specie, or rix dollar effective, at 2 florins convention money, or 2 florins 24 creutzers Muntze. The rix dollar current is in some places divided into thirds and fourths, the first called kaysergroschen, of 30 creutzers, and the second called batzer, of 22$\frac{1}{2}$ creutzers. The above way of keeping accounts prevails in a considerable part of Germany, including Austria and its dependencies, Bohemia, Bavaria, Suabia and Franconia. In Prussia, Saxony, Hanover, Brunswick and Lunenburgh, accounts are kept in rix dollars of 24 good groschen, each good groschen being divided into 12 pfenings, or in rix dollars of 36 marien good groschen, each marien groschen being divided into 8 pfenings. Hamburgh, Altona, Lubeck, Holstein, and Mecklenburgh, keep accounts in marks of 16 skilling lubs, each skilling being divided into 12 pfenings, and the rix dollar is reckoned at 3 marks. The other countries bordering on the Baltic and North sea, and the countries on the left bank of the Rhine, have various ways of keeping accounts.

Every independent state or city of Germany has its own coins; most of which, however, may be referred to or compared with the following: namely, in gold, the ducat, the pistole, and the gold florin, or gulden; and in silver, the rix dollar specie and its sub-divisions.

The rate of coinage of ducats is the same all over Germany. 67 ducats are to weigh a Cologne mark, and the gold must be $23\frac{2}{3}$ carats fine. Ducats, however, in most places, are allowed to circulate, provided the deficiency in weight or fineness does not amount, in all, to more than the sixth part of a carat, and they are then called passier ducats.

The fineness of gold is valued throughout Germany in carats and grains—the mark being 24 carats of 12 grains each. The fineness of silver in loths and grains—the mark being 16 loths of 18 grains each.

Under the name of pistoles are comprehended the Saxon Augustan d'Ors, the Prussian Frederick d'Ors, the Carl d'Ors of Brunswick, the George d'Ors of Honover, the Christian d'Ors of Danish Holstein, and the pistoles of Hesse Palatinate, Hildesheim and Mecklenburgh, all reckoned at 5 rix dollars convention money, and 35 pieces weighing a Cologne mark of gold $31\frac{3}{4}$ carats fine.

According to the convention rate of silver coinage established in 1753 by Austria and Bavaria, and adopted by Saxony in 1763, one Cologne mark of silver, 13 loths 6 grains fine, is to be coined into $8\frac{1}{3}$ specie rix dollars, $16\frac{2}{3}$ convention florins, or $33\frac{1}{3}$ half florins; this makes the Cologne mark of fine silver 20 florins.

The same weight, 9 loths 4 grains fine, is coined into 35 kopfstucks, or pieces of 20 creutzers: the same weight, 8 loths fine, into 70 pieces of 10 creutzers: the same weight, 6 loths fine, into 105 pieces of 5 creutzers.

The creutzer pieces are $12\frac{73}{100}$ per cent. worse than larger pieces.

The common standard for silver coins throughout Germany, except Prussia, Hanover, Liege, Swedish Pomerania, Hamburg, Lubec and Holstein, is the convention or 20 florins rate of coinage.

In this rate the Cologne mark of fine silver is coined into or valued at 20 florins = 10 rix dollars effective, or $13\frac{1}{3}$ rix dollars of account. The cologne mark, every where, is the standard weight for coins, and is divided into 8 ounces = 16 loths = 256 pfenings = 512 hellers = 4352 eschen = 65536 richtphenings.

The weight for gold and silver in bullion is not the same in all parts of Germany. The fineness of gold is expressed in carats: the mark being 24 carats of 12 grains each. That of silver in loths: the mark being 16 loths of 18 grains.

At Cassel accounts are kept in rix dollars of 32 albuses, each albus being 9 pfenings or 12 hellers current. The rix dollar = $1\frac{1}{2}$ reichsflorin = 24 good groschen = 36 marien groschen = 90 creutzers. The coins are coined after the convention rate.

At Cologne accounts are kept in rix dollars specie of 80 albuses, or rix dollars current of 78 albuses, each albuse being 12 hellers.

The rix dollar specie is divided into $1\frac{1}{39}$ florins current = $1\frac{1}{4}$ rader florin = $1\frac{1}{2}$ florins specie = 2 herren florins = $3\frac{1}{2}$ Cologne florins = 4 orts = 8 skillings = 20 blafferts = 30 groschen = 60 stivers = 80 Cologne albuses = 90 creutzers = 100 light albuses = 120 fettmangens = 960 hellers, being worth 2s. $7\frac{1}{2}$d. sterling, or 60 cents $5\frac{1}{3}$ mills.

The rix dollar current is worth 2s. $6\frac{3}{4}$d. sterling, or 59 cts. $\frac{1}{3}$ mills.

At Frankfort and Hanan accounts are kept in rix dollars of 90 creutzers, or in guilders of 60 creutzers—each creutzer being 4 pfenings. The rix dollar of account is divided into $1\frac{1}{2}$ florins = $22\frac{1}{2}$ batzens = 30 kaisergroschen = 45 albuses = 90 creutzers. The rix dollar specie = $1\frac{1}{3}$ rix dollar of account.

The guilder = 40.5 cents United States currency.

At Leipsic, Dresden, and throughout Saxony, accounts are kept in specie rix dollars of 24 good groschen, each groschen being 12 pfenings.

The convention or specie dollar = $1\frac{1}{3}$ rix dollar, or 32 good groschen, and is worth 97 cents 2 mills. The rix guilder = 16 good groschen = 48 cents 6 mills. The Meissen guilder = 21 good groschen, 63 cents 8 mills. An old schock = 20 do. A new schock = 60 do.

At Augsburg and Munich, and throughout Bavaria, accounts are kept in guldens or florins of 60 creutzers current, of 4 denari each. The florin also contains 15 batzen = 20 kaisergroschen = 24 land muntze = 30 albuses. A current rix dollar is worth $1\frac{1}{2}$ florins, or 2s. $7\frac{1}{2}$d. sterling. A batzen = 4 creutzers. A guilder = 40 cents 5 mills. In smaller payments in Bavaria, the Cologne mark of fine silver is reckoned at 24 florins, or 16 rix dollars of account.

In the kingdom of Hanover, the grand duchies of Mecklenburg and Saxe Weimar, and the duchy of Saxe Gotha, accounts are kept in rix dollars of 24 good groschen, of 12 pfenings each, convention rate. The specie rix dollar = $1\frac{1}{3}$ rix dollar current. In Mecklenburg, the rix dollar = 2 Mecklenburg guilders = 3 marks = 192 wittens. In the duchies of Nassau, Anhalt, Koethen, Coburg, and Saxe Meinungen, accounts are kept in guilders of 60 creutzers, each creutzer being 4 pfenings or hellers, convention rate. In Coburg they also use the rix dollar of 90 creutzers.

In the duchy of Oldenburg, accounts are kept in rix dollars of 72 groots, each groot being 5 schwar; also, in rix dollars of 48 shillings or 54 stivers, each stiver being 4 orts.

In Stutgard and the kingdom of Wirtemburg, accounts are kept as in the duchy of Coburg. The 24 florin rate is also used here in small payments as in Saxony.

In Brunswick, accounts are kept in rix dollars of 36 marien groschen of 8 pfenings each. The rix dollar being worth about 68 cents 9 mills.

HANSEATIC CITIES.

Bremen.—Accounts are here kept in rix dollars of 72 grotes, a grote equal to 5 schwaren.

Coins of Bremen.—In gold, ducats at $2\frac{3}{4}$ rix dollars.

In silver, 1, $\frac{1}{2}$, and $\frac{1}{4}$ specie dollars, kopfstuck of 12 grotes, 6, 3, 2, 1, and $\frac{1}{2}$ grote pieces.

In copper, $2\frac{1}{2}$ and single schwaren pieces.

Foreign coins.—In gold, ducats at $2\frac{3}{4}$ rix dollars, and Louis d'Ors, &c., at 5 rix dollars.

In silver, $\frac{2}{3}$ pieces at 48 grotes, with about 10 per cent. gain against currency.

The thaler or rix dollar = 68 cents 9 mills.

Usance from Germany, 14 days after sight; England and France, 1 month after date. Days of grace, 8.

At Hamburg, in Germany, accounts are kept in marks of 16 schillings; a schilling is equal to 12 pfening lubs; and also in £ s. d. Flemish.

Payments are made in four different ways, viz.:

1st. In specie dollars of 3 marks, for which the bank allows on receiving 1 per mille; but, on re-paying the same, is charged $1\frac{5}{8}$ per mille, viz. for 1000 dollars, on paying into the bank, the owner's account is credited 3003 marks, and on his withdrawing a like sum, debited 3004 marks and 14 schillings.

2d. In banco valuta, in which the bank books are kept.

3d. In currency, which is generally about 23 per cent. less than banco.

4th. In light money, consisting of Louis d'Ors of 5 dollars, or 15 marks; ducats of $2\frac{3}{4}$ dollars, or $8\frac{1}{4}$ marks; and specie dollars of $1\frac{1}{3}$ dollar, or 4 marks; which money is afterwards compared with a certain loss against banco, or currency.

Moneys of exchange.

1 rix dollar = 3 marks, or 48 schillings.
A mark banco = $2\frac{2}{3}$ schillings, or 32 groats Flemish.
3 marks banco = 8 schillings, or 96 groats Flemish.
1 pound Flemish = 20 schillings Flemish = $2\frac{1}{2}$ rix dollars.
1 schilling do. = 12 groats Flemish, or 6 schillings of Lubeck.
1 do. Lubeck = 2 groats Flemish, 4 dreylings, or 12 pfenings of Lubeck.

The exchange dollar, by which bills between Hamburg and Amsterdam are negotiated, is 2 marks, or 32 schillings of Lubeck, or 64 groats Flemish.

The value of the mark banco at par was fixed at $33\frac{1}{3}$ by an act of congress now repealed. Hamburg gives at par 3 marks banco for a dollar.

Hamburg coins.

In gold, double and single ducats.

In silver, 1, $\frac{1}{2}$, and $\frac{1}{4}$ specie dollars, of 3, $1\frac{1}{2}$, and $\frac{3}{4}$ marks; 2 and 1 mark pieces, 8, 4, and 2 schilling pieces, and schillings, sechilings, and dreylings of 12, 6, and 3 pfenings.

Foreign coins.

In gold, pistolen, or Louis d'Ors, at 10 marks $13\frac{3}{4}$ schillings banco, or $13\frac{7}{16}$ marks currency, more or less. Dutch and German ducats at

6 marks fixed, with $4\frac{1}{2}$ per cent. loss against banco, or at 7 marks 12 schillings currency.

In silver, old specie rix dollars at 3 marks, with about 1 per cent. gain against banco, or at about $3\frac{3}{4}$ marks currency. Several kinds of new $\frac{2}{3}$ and $\frac{1}{3}$ pieces, at 2 and 1 marks light money, with 33 per cent. loss against banco.

Usance for German, English and French bills as at Bremen. Holland bills also have 1 month after date, and Spanish, Portuguese, and Italian bills 2 months. Days of grace, 12.

At Lubeck, accounts are kept as at Hamburg.

1 rix dollar is equal to 3 marks 48 schillings, or 576 pfenings.

The other moneys, and the course of exchange in general, are the same as at Hamburg. The agio varies from 20 to 24 per cent. between banco and current.

The merchants constantly draw on Hamburg at 3 days date in banco money, receiving from $\frac{1}{8}$ to $\frac{1}{4}$ agio; and they draw on other places in the same manner, at 2 months.

Usance as at Hamburg, and 10 days' grace allowed.

ITALY.

Ecclesiastical states.

At Ancona accounts are kept in scudo of 20 soldi, subdivided into 12 denari.

The scudo is also divided into 12 paoli, or 100 bajochi, or 80 bolognini.

At Bologna Ferrara accounts are kept in lire, of 20 soldi of 12 denari each; also in scudi of 5 lire or 100 soldi.

The scudo is also divided into 10 paoli, 100 soldi, 500 quatrini, or 1200 denari.

At Rome accounts are kept in crowns, or scudo of 10 paoli, and each paoli in 10 bajochi. The scudo is also divided into $3\frac{1}{3}$ testoni = 500 quatrim = 1000 mezzi quatrini.

The silver crown or scudo in the ecclesiastical states is worth \$1 $\frac{2}{3}$ mills, and weighs $408\frac{15}{100}$ grains Troy, and is $10\frac{23}{24}$ fine. The gold sequin weighs $52\frac{9}{10}$ grains Troy, and is $23\frac{5}{8}$ carats fine, and is worth \$2. The Roman lb. for gold and silver is divided into 12 ounces, 288 denari, or 6912 grains = 5234 grains Troy.

Tuscany.—At Leghorn accounts are kept in pezza da otto reali of 20 soldi, or 240 denari di pezza each, or in lire of 20 soldi = 240 denari di lire. The same divisions exist in scudo d'Ors = $7\frac{1}{2}$ lires, and the scudo corrente or ducatone = 7 lire. The testone = 2 lire.

In Moneta Buona or money of Florence, $5\frac{3}{4}$ lire = 6 lire in Moneta lunga, or money of Leghorn. The lire is worth 15 cents 6.6 mills; the ducat current, \$1 9 6.

At Florence books are kept in lire of 20 soldi or 240 denari, or in ducati of 20 soldi or 240 denari di ducato. The coins and values are as at Leghorn. The fineness of gold is expressed in carats and ottavi

—the pound being 24 carats of 8 parts each: that of silver in oncie and denari—the pound being 12 oncie of 24 denari each. The pound = 5240 grains Troy.

In the duchies of Parma, Modena, and Lucca, accounts are kept in lire of similar subdivisions.

At Lucca they are also kept in scudo di cambio of 20 soldi or 240 denari di cambio. The lire is worth 24 cents 3 mills—the scudo di cambio = $1 7. The scudo d'ors of Florence = 8¼ lire of Lucca, and the lire of Florence = 22 soldi.

At Modena and Parma accounts are now kept in lire Italiani of 100 centesimi = 18 cents 7.1 mills. The lire di Modena = 7 cents 1.76 mills. The lire di Reggio = 7 cents 7.8 mills. The lire di Parma = 4 cents 5⅓ mills.

PIEDMONT AND SARDINIA.

At Turin accounts are kept in lire of 20 soldi, or 240 denari Piedmontesi = 2 cents 1¾ mills. The scudo contains 6 lire.

The nuove lire coined since 1821 = the French franc = 18 cents 7.01 mills. 5 lire of Sardinia = 8 lire of Turin. The lire of Sardinia = 35 cents 1.28 mills; the lire of Turin = 21 cents 7.59 mills.

At Genoa accounts are kept in lires of 20 soldi, or 240 denari di lire.

Banco voluta was 25 per cent. better than moneta buona or fuori banco.

The scudo d'oro = 10 lire 16⅕ soldi moneta buona = $1 66 6⅓.

The scudo d'oro marche = 9½ lire moneta buona = $1 64 9.

The scudo d'argento = 8 lire 14 soldi moneta buona = $1 34 7¼.

The scudo di cambio = 4 lire 12 soldi moneta buona = 71 cents 8⅔ mills.

The piastre = 5¾ lire moneta buona = 88 cents 5.77 mills.

The fineness of gold is expressed in carats and grains—the absolute weight being 24 carats of 24 grains each; that of silver in denari and grains, i. e., 12 denari of 24 grains. In weighing gold or silver, the ounce is divided into 24 denari of 24 grains. The gold coins are 21¾ carats fine, and the silver 10⅞ denari fine without remedy.

LOMBARDY.

At Bergamo, Mantua, Milan, Padua, Verona, as well as at Venice, accounts are kept in lire of 20 soldi or 240 denari. Also in lire Italiani, introduced under the French government, of 100 centesimi. Also in lire di Austria of 100 centesimi = 1000 millesimi = 10,000 dix millesimi.

1 lire Italiani	= 18	cents	7.1	mills.	United States.
1 " d'Austria	= 16	"	2.02	"	
1 " correnti at Milan	= 14	"	3.7	"	
1 " of Mantua	= 5	"	7.85	"	
1 " of Bergamo	= 9	"	8.3	"	
1 " of Verona	= 9	"	7.21	"	
1 " picola of Venice	= 9		7.81	"	

NAPLES AND SICILY.

At Naples accounts are kept in ducati del regno of 10 carlini, or 100 grani.

The new system of coinage of 1818 has for its unit the silver ducat, weighing 515 Neapolitan grains, or 354 Troy grains, and being $5\frac{1}{6}$ pure, divided as above. It is worth 80 cents 6.45 mills.

Spanish dollars pass for 1 ducat 24 grani, or 124 grani. The gold coins are 996 pure in 1000, with a remedy of $\frac{1}{1000}$ in the fineness. Formerly the fineness of gold was expressed by 24 carats of 8 parts each, and that of silver by 12 ounces of 12 sterlini each. Gold and silver are weighed by the libbra of 12 ounces or 360 trapezi = 4950 grains Troy.

Coins.

In gold: Doppien of 46 carlini; Sicilian oncies at 30 carlini.

In silver: Ducat del regno of 10 and 5 carlini, Sicilian scudi at 12 and 6 carlini, tari pieces of 2 carlini, and pieces of 26 and 13 grani, 24 and 12 do.

At Palermo, in Sicily, accounts are kept in oncies of 30 tari, or 60 carlini.

One oncia = $2\frac{1}{2}$ scudi = 5 fiorini, or 30 tari = $2 46.

One taro = 15 ponti, or 20 grani (grains) = 120 picioli.

The scudo = 12 tari: the florin 6 tari: the ducat = 10 tari. The scudo = 94 cents 6.8 mills. The Sicilian coins have but half the value of those of the same denomination in Naples. The Sicilian ounce at Naples = 15 tari.

JAPAN.

Accounts are kept in Japan in tales or tayels of 10 mas or 100 condorines. The tale = $1 40 7.4.

Payments are generally made in silver ingots, value depending on weight.

The Spanish dollar is valued at from 7 mas to 74 condorines.

Gold coins.

Itchebo	= 15 mas	=	$2 14 $\frac{1}{2}$.
Old copang	= "	=	$10 31 9.7.
Oban	= "	=	$30 95 9.1.

At Madras the old copang is worth $9 68 3; the new copang, $4 91 9.

Silver coins.

The Schnit weighing 4 oz. 18 dwts. 16 grs. = £1 5s. 3d. sterling, or $6 6.

The Kodama, varying in size and value.

Copper or iron coins.

Cash, of which 600 = 1 tale.

MEXICO.

Accounts are kept in pesos or dollars of 8 reals. The real is divided into halves and quarters, and into 24 parts called grains.

The gold coins are doubloons of 8 escudos d'oro, or 16 pesos. There are halves, quarters, &c.

The silver coins are pesos, halves, quarters, eighths or reals, and sixteenths.

The fineness of gold is expressed in quilates, 24 being the number into which the castellano or other weight is divided. A quilate contains 4 grains, and the grain is divided into 8 parts.

The doubloon contains 374 grains of pure gold, having 3 parts alloy to 21 parts of pure gold.

The fineness of silver is expressed in dineros, the mark being divided into 12 dineros, and the dinero into 24 grains. The peso contains 374 grains Troy of pure silver, being $1\frac{1}{4}$ parts alloy to $10\frac{3}{4}$ parts of pure silver, or 5 parts alloy to 43 parts of pure silver.

NEW GRANADA.

Accounts are kept in pesos or dollars of 8 reals, 16 medias, or 32 cuartillas.

The peso is also divided into halves and quarters. The real $= 12\frac{1}{2}$ cents, the media $= 6\frac{1}{4}$, and the cuartilla $= 3\frac{1}{8}$ cents.

The gold and silver coins are the same as in Mexico.

NETHERLANDS.

At Amsterdam and in the Netherlands, accounts are kept in florins or guilders, or gulden. Previous to 1816, the florin was divided into 20 stivers of 16 pfennings each; but it is now decimally divided, each florin being = 100 centimes, or 40 cents United States, and weighing 166.17 grains, or 7 esterlings.

The gold coins are the 10 florin piece, halves and quarters; the ruyder = 14 florins, and halves and quarters; the ducat = 5 florins 5 stivers.

The silver coins are the ducatoon = 63 stivers.

Rix dollar	= 50	do.
Albert's dollar	= 50	do.
Lowen dollar	= 42	do.
Crown	= 40	do.
Escaling	= 6	do.
Sesthalfs	= $5\frac{1}{2}$	do.
Doubleties	= 2	do.
Stiver.		
3, 2, 1, $\frac{1}{2}$, and $\frac{1}{4}$ florin pieces.		

The copper are the duyt or grote, equal to $\frac{1}{8}$ stiver.

Payments are made either in banco or currency; the former is from 3 to 5 per cent. generally better than the latter, which difference is called banco agio.

1 pound Flemish is equal to 20 schillings Flemish, or 6 Dutch florins; 1 florin is equal to 40 grotes Flemish, 12 grotes to 1 schilling Flem-

ish, 1 stiver to 2 grotes Flemish, and 1 rix dollar to $8\frac{1}{3}$ schillings Flemish.

A gold florin, used in the sale of grain, is equal to 28 stivers. 5 gold florins = 7 florins; 3 florins = 10 schillings Flemish; 25 schillings Flemish = 3 rix dollars; 2 rix dollars = 5 florins.

The fineness of gold was reckoned in carats and grains, the absolute weight being 24 carats of 12 grains each.

The fineness of silver is reckoned in pennyweights, deniers and grains; the pennyweight being 12 deniers of 4 grains each. Gold and silver are weighed by the mark of 8 oz. or 3798 Troy grains. The ounce is divided into 20 engels or esterlings of 32 aas each. The fineness of gold and silver is now reckoned decimally.

PERSIA.

Accounts are kept in Persia in tomans of 50 abassis = 100 mamoodis = 200 shafrees or chayés = 1000 dinars-bisti = 2000 kasbequis = 10,000 dinars.

The toman and dinar are imaginary.

The gold coins are the cherassi, which vary in value—thus, the iman riza is worth 4s. 2d., the aboul-faiz, 12s. 3d., and the koulikhan, 30s. 6d.

The silver coins are haser-denaries of 10 mamoodis, daezajies of 5, larins of $2\frac{1}{2}$, abassis of 2, and single and half mamoodis.

The copper kasbequis = 5 dinars.

In large payments the coins are weighed. The toman is worth $5 54 $7\frac{1}{2}$.

PERU.

Accounts are kept as in Mexico, in pesos of 8 reals. The coins the same also. Vide page 387.

POLAND.

Accounts are kept in guldens or florins of 30 groschen, or grosz of 18 pfennings each.

Florins are also called zloti.

Also in guilders of 30 groschen of 10 deniers each.

The florin contains $2\frac{1}{2}$ shostacks = 90 shillings.

The rix dollar is worth 6 florins in Great Poland, and 3 florins in Little Poland.

The gold coins are double ducats of 50 florins, ducats of 25 do., and ducats of 18 florins.

The silver are specie rix dollars = 8 florins Polish, or 4 florins Prussian; thalers or crowns; 5, 2, and 1 florin pieces, and halves and quarters.

The copper coins, 3, 1 and half groschen pieces, and 1 shilling Polish.

The Polish florin, calculated at $6\frac{2}{3}$ florins for the Russian silver ruble, is worth 11 cents $2\frac{1}{3}$ mills United States currency.

PORTUGAL.

In Lisbon and throughout Portugal, accounts are kept in rées, reis or reas, of which 1000 make a milreis.

The milreis, in accounts, is separated from the reis by a crossed cypher, called cifrao, and the million from the milreis by a colon : thus —rs. 2 : 700 ⊕ 500, being 2,700 milreis and 500 reis.

The old crusado = 400 reis ; the new crusado = 480 ; the testoon = 100, and the vinten = 20 reis.

The coins before 1722 are worth 20 per cent. more than those of later date.

The gold coins are the debraon - - = 12.800 reis.
Half debraon or ionese - - - = 6.400 "
Quarter do. - - - - - = 3.200 "
Escudo = 1,600, half do. and quarter do., or crusada-velbo.

The silver coins are the new crusado = 480 reis, halves, quarters and eighths ; the 6, 5, 3 and $2\frac{1}{2}$ vinten pieces, being 120, 100, 60 and 50 reis.

The Brazilian pataco or dollar passes for 240 reis.

The Spanish dollar - - - = 810 reis.

Payments in Portugal have of late been made in what is called currency—being one half specie and one half government paper. Legal currency is therefore $13\frac{1}{2}$ per cent. worse than specie, and may be even worse than that.

Usance for Spanish bills 15 days after sight.
English " 30 " " "
French " 60 days after date.
German and Dutch 2 months after date.
Italian and Irish, 3 " " "

Six days of grace are allowed on foreign bills accepted.

The fineness of gold is expressed in quilates or carats and grains—the mark being 24 carats of 4 grains each. The standard for coins is 22 carats fine; for wrought gold $20\frac{1}{2}$ carats, and gold dust $21\frac{3}{4}$ to 22 carats. The fineness of silver is expressed in dinheiros and grains —the mark being 12 dinheiros of 24 grains each. The standard for coins is 10 dinheiros 19 grains fine: for wrought silver $10\frac{1}{4}$ dinheiros.

Gold and silver are weighed by the marco divided into 8 oncas, 640 tharas, 192 escropulos, or 4,608 graõs = $3,541\frac{1}{2}$ grains Troy.

The carats for precious stones is heavier, being 151 carats to 1 English ounce Troy weight.

PRUSSIA.

At Berlin, Magdeburg, Stetin, and throughout the electorate of Brandenburg, accounts are kept in thalers or rix dollars of 24 good groschen, each groschen being 12 pfenings current. Bank books are kept in thalers banco.

The gold coins are ducats, reckoned at $2\frac{3}{4}$ rix dollars ; and then they pass at 20 per cent. premium on currency, or 3 thalers 8 groschen, worth $2 19 3.4 mills United States.

Double, single, and half Fredericks = 10, 5, and $2\frac{1}{2}$ rix dollars, or 8, 4, and 2 thalers banco.

The silver coins are rix dollars, worth 69 cents 4.43, halves, thirds, quarters, sixths and twelfths, being $31\frac{1}{4}$ per cent. worse than banco.

There are also base silver pieces of 6, 4, and 3 pfenings; and copper pieces of 3 and 1 pfening.

The Cologne mark of gold, $21\frac{3}{4}$ carats fine, is coined into 35 Fredericks; the Cologne mark of fine silver is coined into 14 rix dollars. The fineness of silver and gold is expressed in grains, the mark being 288 grains. The proportion of gold to silver is $14\frac{14}{29}$ to 1. Gold and silver in bars are weighed by the mark of 8 oz. or 16 loths = 3608 grains Troy.

At Konigsberg, in Prussia, accounts are kept in florins, (gulden or guilders,) of 30 groschen, and a groschen is equivalent to 18 pfenings.

3 florins	=	1 dollar of 90 groschen.
1 florin	=	8 gute groschen.
4 gute groschen	=	15 groschen.

The usance on London is 3 months date. Days of grace, 3.

Foreign coins (variable.)—In gold, new Dutch ducats at 9 florins and 21 groschen; Louis d'Ors at 16 florins and 10 to 20 groschen.

In silver, albertus dollars at 4 florins and 15 groschen; silver rubles, old, at 3 florins and 18 to 24 groschen; new, at 3 florins and 8 groschen.

At Dantzic, accounts were formerly kept as at Konigsberg; but they are now kept as at Berlin, Prussian currency.

1 Dantzic dollar is equal to 3 florins, 90 groschen, or 270 schillings.

1 Prussian dollar is 4 florins, 120 grosh, or 360 schillings of Dantzic.

Payments are made, 1st, in exchange money, in which the Dutch ducat is fixed at 12 florins Dantzic currency; 2d, in Dantzic currency, which is $33\frac{1}{8}$ per cent. less than Prussian currency, viz. 100 florins Prussian = $133\frac{1}{3}$ florins Dantzic.

Dantzic coins.—In gold, ducats at 12 florins and 17 groschen m. o. l.

In silver, florins of 30 groschen, tympff of 18 gr. Sixers of 6 groschen, and duitgens of 3 groschen.

In copper, schillings of 6 pfenings.

Foreign coins (variable.)—In gold, English guineas at 25 florins and 13 groschen; Frederick d'Ors at 21 florins and 20 groschen; and Dutch ducats at 12 florins and 14 groschen.

In silver, old specie or banco dollars at 6 florins, albertus dollars at 5 florins and 24 groschen, and Russian rubles at 4 florins and 25 groschen.

Usance at Dantzic is 14 days after acceptance; Berlin and Konigsberg the same. At Stetin, it is on French and English bills 1 month from date. Hamburg 4 weeks, and Amsterdam 6 weeks.

Days of grace 3, except at Dantzic, where 10 are allowed. Bills drawn at longer than 14 days, have only 3 days' grace.

RUSSIA.

In Petersburg and throughout Russia, accounts are kept in paper rubles of 100 copecks, the value of which in specie is fixed from time to time by imperial decrees. The ruble also is divided into 10 grievens, $33\frac{1}{2}$ altins, or 50 groschen, and the copeck is divided into 2 denushkas or 4 polushkas.

At Riga, in Russia, accounts are also kept in rix dollars of 90 groschen, and in florins of 30 groschen. Payments are made in albertus dollars and the currency of Riga, or ferdings money. The latter is legally $33\frac{1}{3}$ per cent. less than albertus; but, in commercial transactions, the difference frequently amounts to 42 per cent.

The gold coins are the imperial and half imperial of 10 and 5 rubles, with ducats, double and single; the double ducat being worth 5 rubles 60 copecks, and the single ducat 2 rubles 80 copecks.

In silver, rubles of 100 copecks, half rubles of 50, and quarter rubles of 25 copecks, and 20, 15, and 10 copeck pieces.

In copper, 10, 5, 2, 1, $\frac{1}{2}$ and $\frac{1}{4}$ copeck pieces.

1 ruble in silver is worth 74 cents 9.1 United States currency.

The value of the paper ruble is fluctuating; but its average value in silver as quoted for the last 10 years, has been 3 rubles 74 copecks in bank notes for 1 silver ruble, and the exchange on London 1 bank ruble for $10\frac{1}{2}$d. sterling. At this rate, the bank ruble is worth 20 cents 3 mills United States currency.

The paper currency consists in bank bills on white paper of 100, 50, and 25 rubles each; on red paper, of 10 rubles, and on blue paper, of 5 rubles. This is the currency of the country, and forms the medium of foreign exchange. The only gold coin now struck is the half imperial or 5 ruble piece, worth $3 62 $6\frac{1}{3}$ mills United States.

The fineness of gold and silver is expressed in solotnicks, 96 being the unit, and the solotnick being divided into 96 parts called dolis.

The present standard of gold is $\frac{88}{96}$, being $\frac{1}{8}$ grain better than the English standard.

The standard of silver is $83\frac{1}{3}$.

The introduction of foreign small coins was expressly prohibited on the 1st of January, 1812, and their prohibition has since been renewed in 1828.

Mint regulations.—It is declared by an ukase of 1810, that all expenses incident to the coinage of silver shall be borne by the crown, except a small deduction for refining, where the fineness of such shall be found below the proof of $\frac{64}{86}$ or $\frac{2}{3}$.

						Worth
Silver ruble of		Peter the Great	- 312.1	grain of fine	silver,	84 cts. 0.7
"	"	Catharine I.	- 309.9	"	"	83.4.7
"	"	Peter II.	- 310	"	"	83.5
"	"	Anne	- 317.2	"	"	85.4.4
"	"	Elizabeth	- 321.8	"	"	86.6.8
"	"	Peter III.	- 277.5	"	"	74.7.5
"	"	Catharine II.	- 275.9	"	"	74.3.2
"	"	Paul	- 280.8	"	"	75.6.4
"	"	Alexander	- 278.1	"	"	74.9.1

No usance in Russia. No days of grace are allowed on bills payable at so many days after sight. Days of grace on bills at sight 3, on all others 10.

SPAIN.

In Spain there are different modes of keeping accounts in the different provinces; but the most general mode is in reals of 34 maravedis.

The mode at Barcelona is in libras of 20 sueldos, each sueldo being 12 dineros, and each dinero 2 mallas; 37½ sueldos = 1 hard dollar; and the libra = 54 cents United States currency.

At Bilboa, Madrid and Malaga, accounts are kept in reals vellon, or copper reals of 34 maravedis.

At Cadiz in reals de plata antiquas, (or reals of old plate,) of 16 quartos, or 34 maravedis each.

In Navarre in reals of old plate of 36 maravedis each: also in libras of 20 sueldos.

At Valencia in libras of 20 sueldos, each sueldo being 12 dineros. Sometimes in reals of new plate of 24 dineros each.

In Spain the reals have 9 varieties, 4 being general and 5 local.

The four principal moneys of Spain are vellon, new plate, old plate, and Mexican plate; and in order to obtain a distinct view of them, it may be proper to make the real vellon the basis of all the rest. It is the twentieth part of the hard dollar, (peso duro,) universally known by the name of the Spanish dollar. The real vellon is also the twentieth part of the gold dollar, (coronilla,) and its value in this metal is 2½ pence sterling, or 5 cents.

The real vellon or billon is divided into 8½ quartos, 17 ochavos, or 34 maravedis vellon; 68 blancas = 136 comadas = 340 dineros.

The real of new plate is double the real vellon, and is divided into 34 maravedis of new plate, or 68 of vellon, with quartos and ochavos in proportion. It is a coin, but not a money of account in any general way, and is worth 10 cents.

The real of old plate is better than the real vellon in the proportion of 32 to 17. Thus, 17 maravedis of old plate equal 32 of vellon. This real is also divided into 16 quartos or 32 ochavos, and is worth 9 cents 5 mills.

The real of old plate is not a coin, but a money of account in particular provinces, and is the most general money of exchange; 8 of these reals make the peso de plate or piastre, which is also called the dollar of exchange, and when plate only is mentioned, old plate is understood.

The real of Mexican plate is divided into halves and quarters, called medio and quartillo. It is the eighth part of the hard dollar, and is therefore worth 2½ reals vellon, 1¼ real of new plate, or $1\frac{21}{64}$ real of old plate.

The real of Mexican plate is the chief money of account in Spanish America, where it is divided into 16 parts; but in Spain it is sometimes divided into 21 parts, and is worth 12 cents 4.71 mills United States currency.

It may be noticed that vellon is the root of several other moneys employed in domestic and inland trade. Thus, 60 reals vellon equal the doubloon de plata sencillo; 15 = the peso sencillo, and 11 = the ducado de vellon.

Besides the abov there are five reals which are only of local use. They are not coins, but moneys of account, and sometimes moneys of exchange. Thus,

The real of Alicant	$13\frac{9}{32}$	of which equal the hard dollar.
" of Catalonia	$12\frac{19}{48}$	" "
" ardite of Catalonia	$18\frac{19}{32}$	" "
" current of Gibraltar	12	" "
" of Valencia	$17\frac{17}{24}$	" "

The peso de plata or piastre is also equal to 15 reals 2 maravedis vellon, and 4 piastres make the doubloon de plata or pistole of exchange. The hard dollar = $10\frac{5}{8}$ reals. The ducado de plata or ducat of exchange = 11 reals 1 maravedi of plate.

The ducat of freight (in which freight is often contracted to be paid) is 12 reals of plate.

The escudo at Bilboa is counted 10 reals vellon.

Gold coins.

Doubloon or quadrupel of 4 pistoles, at	320	reals de vellon	=	$15 53.5
Double pistoles - -	160	"	=	7 76.8
Single pistoles - - -	80	"	=	3 88.4
Escudo or half pistoles - -	40	"	=	1 94.2
Coronilla, or medio escude d'oro	20	"	=	93.3

Silver coins.

Dollar or peso duro - - -	20	reals	=	$1 00
Half dollar or escudo vellon -	10	"	=	0 50
Quarter do. or peseto Mexicana -	5	"	=	0 25
Real of Mexican plate - - -	$2\frac{1}{2}$	"	=	0 $12\frac{1}{2}$
In base silver.				
Peseto provincial - - -	4	"	=	0 20
Real of provincial plate - -	2	"	=	0 10
Real vellon - - - - -	1	"	=	0 5

Copper coins.

Double quartos or ochavos of 8 maravedis de vellon, and quartos of 4, and ochavos of 2 maravedis de vellon.

The paper currency consists of royal bonds called vales reales, first issued in 1800, bearing an interest of 4 per cent., and transferable by endorsement. The value varies, and they are quoted at so many per cent. loss. Thus, 75 per cent. means that they are worth 25 per cent. of their face.

Days of grace, except at Cadiz, 14. At Cadiz, 6.

Gold and silver are weighed by the Castilian mark, which is divided, for gold, into 50 Castellanos, 400 tomines, or 4800 grains, and for silver, into 8 ounces, 64 ochavos, 128 adarmes, 384 tomines, or 4608 grains, and equals $3550\frac{1}{2}$ grains Troy.

Diamonds, &c., are weighed by the ounce of 140 carats, or 560 Castilian grains = 431.48 Troy grains.

The fineness of gold is expressed in quilates or carats and grains. The mark or absolute weight being divided into 24 carats of 4 grains each, and the grain having 8 parts.

The fineness of silver is expressed in dineros and grains—the mark being 12 dineros of 24 grains each.

Before 1786 back to 1772, the standard of gold was $21\frac{1}{2}$ carats fine, and before 1772 back to 1730, the standard of gold was 22 carats, and that of silver, 11 dineros fine; since 1772 the stand of silver has been $10\frac{3}{4}$ dineros, except for pesotas and reals, which is $9\frac{3}{4}$ dineros; and since 1786 the standard of gold has been 21 carats fine, except for the coronilla, which is $20\frac{3}{8}$ carats.

SWEDEN.

Accounts are kept in Sweden in riksdalers of 48 skillings, each skilling being 12 rundstycken or öre.

This riksdaler is the Swedish specie dollar, which, by a decree of 1777, is made the money of account. Before that, accounts were kept in dahlers of 4 marks or 32 öre, either silver or copper coin. The former being 3 times the value of the latter.

One riksdaler is worth $1 6 9.

The gold coins are ducats of 94 skillings specie, and double and half ducats.

The silver specie riksdaler, and $\frac{2}{3}$, $\frac{1}{3}$, $\frac{1}{6}$, $\frac{1}{12}$, and $\frac{1}{24}$, in proportion.

The copper single and double slants of 1 and 2 öre silver.

Rundstycken of 1 öre copper and half do.

The paper currency is of two sorts, banco and riksgold. The former issued by the national bank, and the latter by the riksgold bank.

Banco is 50 per cent. better than riksgold, and 2 dahlers banco = 3 dahlers riksgold.

Banco is a legal tender; and the bank is under the control of the Diet composed of the deputies of the four orders of the community.

The riksgold bank is under the direction of the government.

The fineness of gold is expressed in carats and grains—the mark being 24 carats, and the carat 12 grains: of silver, is expressed in lods and grains—the mark being 16 lods, and the lod 18 grains.

The standard gold for coinage is 23 carats 5 grains fine, and it is sold by ducats—$60\frac{1}{2}$ ducats weighing 1 mark. Wrought gold is of three sorts: 1st. ducat gold, 23 carats 5 grains fine; 2d. pistolet gold, 20 carats 4 grains fine, with an allowance of 2 grains in the mark for remedy; and, 3d. crown gold, 18 carats 4 grains fine, with the same allowance.

Standard silver for the specie riksdaler is $396\frac{4}{5}$ grains English, or 535 aas Swedish, of pure silver, in $451\frac{2}{3}$ grains English, or 609 aas Swedish, of standard silver. Wrought silver is $13\frac{1}{4}$ lods fine.

At Bergen, in Norway, accounts are kept in rix dollars of 6 marks—the mark being 16 skillings Danish.

At Christiana and other places in Norway, they reckon in rix dollars of 4 orts, each rix dollar being 24 skillings Danish.

SWITZERLAND.

No general mode of keeping accounts prevails through Switzerland, each canton having its own customs. During the existence of the Helvetic republic a uniform mode was introduced, consisting of francs or livres of 10 batzen, each batzen being 10 rappen; but in 1803 Switzerland again became a federative republic, and each canton assumed the right of coinage. This France called the Swiss livre, and was worth $1\frac{1}{2}$ francs French, or 28 cents.

In July, 1814, the cantons agreed to bring the Swiss rate of coinage to the value of the old livre tournois, and they also agreed to relinquish the right of coining all coins under 1 franc, for 25 years; and in 1825 the cantons of Bern, Basil, Luzern, Friburg, Aargan and Pay de Vaud, agreed to a uniform rate of coinage upon that basis.

At Basil accounts are kept in the Swiss livre of 10 batzen or 100 rappen. The livre is also divided into 20 sols de Suisse of 12 deniers each. Accounts are also kept in pounds of 20 shillings, each shilling being 12 pfennings; also in guilders of 15 batzen, each batzen being 10 rappen; also in guilders of 60 creutzers or 480 hellers.

Gold coins.

New Louis d'Or=16 francs	=	$4 49.6.
Pistole	=	4 30.5.
Ducat	=	1 97.

In Bern accounts are kept in the Swiss franc or livre of 10 batzen; also in guilders of 15 batzen or 60 creutzers.

A Bern guilder=42 cents United States currency.

The batzen= 2.8 mills United States currency.

Gold coins: new Louis d'Or of 16 francs, and the ducat of $7\frac{1}{2}$ livres =$2 $10.7\frac{1}{2}$ mills. Silver newthaler of 4 francs=$1 12.4 mills United States currency, with halves and quarters; 10 sol pieces=14 cents, batzen and creutzers.

At Geneva accounts are kept in two different ways, viz: in livres of 20 sols or 240 deniers, which is used by bankers, and is called current money; and in florins or guilders, consisting of 12 sous, 48 quartz, or 144 deniers, which mode is adopted by retail dealers. The sous and deniers of the latter are called sous or deniers of the florin petite monnaie, to distinguish them from the sous and deniers of the livres, which are called current.

One livre is equal to $3\frac{1}{2}$ florins, and therefore 1 florin is $\frac{2}{7}$ of 1 livre, or $5\frac{5}{7}$ sous current; also 10 sous current are equal to 21 sous of a florin.

The ecu or patagon in which accounts are sometimes kept, is a real coin, worth 3 livres, $10\frac{1}{2}$ guilders, 60 sous, 126 sous of a florin, 504 quartz, 720 deniers current, or 1512 deniers of a florin.

Coins of the canton, in gold—old pistoles of 10 livres currency, or 35 guilders petite monnaie; also new ones, since 1752, of $10\frac{1}{2}$ livres, or $40\frac{1}{4}$ guilders.

In silver—new dollars, and half ones of the same value and fineness as the French, viz: of $12\frac{3}{4}$ guilders, and $6\frac{3}{8}$ guilders or florins respectively.

Old patagons of 3 livres current, or $10\frac{1}{2}$ guilders petite monnaie, half and quarter livres of 15 sous current or $2\frac{5}{8}$ guilders, and 5 sous current or $\frac{7}{8}$ guilders.

At Lausanne accounts are kept in livres of 20 sous, of 12 deniers de Suisse each, and also in livres of 10 batzen or 1000 rappen.

Six livres tournois are reckoned at 4 livres de Suisse, and 40 francs for 27 livres de Suisse.

At Neufchatel accounts are kept in livres tournois de Neufchatel divided into 20 sols, each sol being subdivided into 12 deniers; and also in franken or francs of 10 batzen, each batzen being divided into 10 rappen.

The old system of keeping accounts which is still partially retained in local business, consists in livres foibles, of 12 gros or 144 deniers each.

At St. Gall accounts are kept in florins of 60 creutzers or 480 hellers. The florin or guilder is also divided into 10 shillings, 15 batzen, 60 creutzers, 240 pfennings, or 480 hellings.

The Swiss franke, which is a new money of account, contains 10 batzen or 100 rappen.

Accounts are kept either in specie, which is the money of exchange, or in currency.

1190 florins specie are equal to 1383 florins current, which makes the difference between specie and currency $16\frac{26}{119}$ per cent.

In Zurich accounts are kept in guilders of 60 creutzers of 8 hellers each. The guilder is also divided into 40 shillings of 12 hellers each, or into 16 batzen of 10 augsters each.

1 florin of Geneva	= 8	cents	$8\frac{3}{4}$	mills.
1 livre of Geneva	=31	"	$1\frac{1}{10}$	"
1 livre tournois of Neufchatel	=26	"	$2\frac{4}{5}$	"
1 livre foible of Neufchatel	=10	"	$5\frac{}{10}$	"
1 florin of St. Gall, specie	=52	"	$9\frac{1}{4}$	"
1 florin or guilder of St. Gall, currency	=43	"	$9\frac{1}{3}$	"
1 guilder of Zurich	=45	"	$3\frac{1}{3}$	"
1 guilder of Bern	=42	"		
1 livre de Suisse	=28	"	1	"

TURKEY.

At Constantinople accounts are kept in piastres or grouch of 40 paras of 3 aspers each. There is also the imaginary piastre which is divided into 80 parts, and also into 100 parts, called aspers or minas.

The common bag, called chise, contains 500 piastres; a bag of gold, called kitze, 30,000 piastres, or 15,000 sequins; and by *juck* is understood the sum of 100,000 aspers.

The gold coins are the fonducli or sequin of 5 piastres, with halves and quarters; the altunen of $3\frac{1}{2}$ piastres; the zerimabub or zindsjerli of $1\frac{3}{4}$ piastres.

The silver coins are the piastres of different dates, which vary in value from 46 cents 3 mills to 17 cents 3 mills, the present value, and the beslick and 10 para piece.

There are no days of grace or usance.

In Smyrna accounts are kept in piastres or gooroosh called dollars. The piastre is divided into 12 tomens, and into 40 paras or medini.

The English and Swedes divide the piastre into 80 aspers, the Dutch, French and Venitians into 100 aspers, and the Turks, Greeks, Persians and Armenians into 120 aspers.

The value of the piastre has diminished within 30 years from 36 cents to 5 cents, its present value.

The coins are chiefly Turkish.

VENEZUELA.

Accounts are kept as in New Granada, in pesos of 8 reals, or $12\frac{1}{2}$ cents; medias of $6\frac{1}{4}$ cents, and cuartilles of $3\frac{1}{8}$ cents. The peso or dollar is also divided into halves and quarters.

The Spanish dollar, and that of the United States and the Spanish American republics, are also current at par; also, the gold ounce of Spain and of the Spanish republics, and their fractional parts. The French franc passes for 20 cents, and the 5 franc piece for $1; the English shilling at 25 cents, and the Portuguese and Brazilian piastre at $1.

The gold ounce passes for $16, and the peso for 10 common reals.

WEST INDIES.

British West Indies.

The currency of these islands consists of Spanish, Portuguese and English coins.

In the Bermudas and at Jamaica, accounts are kept in pounds of 20 shillings, or 240 pence currency. The exchange with England is fixed at 40 per cent., and, according to this, £5 sterling are equal to £7 Jamaica currency; but the English guinea passes here for £1 12s. 6d., at which rate £100 sterling are equivalent to £154 15s. $2\frac{6}{7}$d. of the above currency, being £14 15s. $2\frac{6}{7}$d. above the rate fixed by government. This regulation is not, however, strictly observed, as the exchange is generally from 12 to 18 per cent. above the legal par, viz. £152 to £158 Jamaica currency being paid for £100 sterling.

The following are the gold coins which circulate at Jamaica, with their legal weight and value.

		Dwts.	Grs.	Currency.		
Portuguese	joannes, or joe	18	12	£5	10	0
	Half joannes, or joe	9	6	2	15	0
	Quarter do.	4	15	1	7	6
	Moidore	6	22	2	0	0
	Half do.	3	11	1	0	0
Spanish . .	Doubloons	17	18	5	0	0
	Double pistole	8	16	2	10	0
	Pistole	4	8	1	5	0
	Half do.	2	4	0	12	6
English . .	Guineas	5	8	1	12	6
	Half do.	2	16	0	16	3
	7 shilling piece	1	19	0	10	10
	Sovereign			1	14	00

If gold coin be lighter than the weight expressed above, 3 pence are deducted for every grain deficient.

Silver dollar = 6s. 8d.
Bit = 7½d.
Pistareen = 1s. 3d.

The doubloon weighs 17 dwts. 8 grains, and passes for $16.

At Barbadoes, accounts are kept as at Jamaica; but the currency is different. An English guinea passes here legally for £1 10s. 0d., the Portuguese joannes for £5, the doubloon for $16, or £4 10s. 0d., and the moidore for £1 17s. 6d., and all these coins must have the same weight as at Jamaica. The Spanish dollar is current at 6s. 3d. Mutilated coins are out of circulation in the British islands, except at Grenada, where half joannes plugged up to 7½ dwts. pass for $7 33.

In the Bahamas, accounts are kept in pounds, shillings, and pence. The English guinea, weight 5 dwts. and 4 grains, passes for £1 18s. The French, weight 5 dwts. and 2 grains, for £1 16s. The joannes, weight 18 dwts., for £6 8s. The moidore, weight 6 dwts. and 16 grains, for £2 8s. The doubloon, weight 17 dwts. and 8 grains, for £6 8s. For every grain short of the above weight, a deduction of 3½d. is made. The English shilling passes for 1s. 9d., and the pistareen for 1s. 6d.

The dollar = 8s. currency; the sovereign = £1 14s. 3½d.

BRITISH WINDWARD ISLANDS, *improperly called* LEEWARD ISLANDS, viz. *Barbuda, St. Christopher's, or St. Kitts, Nevis, Antigua, Montserrat, Dominica, St. Lucia, St. Vincent, Grenada, Tobago, and Trinidad.*

Accounts are here kept in pounds, shillings and pence. The English guinea passes for 45s. the par; therefore, between the currency of these islands and sterling, is 114$\frac{2}{7}$ per cent., or £100 sterling are equal to £214 5s. 8$\frac{4}{7}$d. currency.

The Portuguese half joannes, or half joe, passes here for £3 6s., the Spanish doubloon for £7 4s., and the Spanish dollar for 9s. currency. All gold passes for 9s. per dwt. At Grenada the doubloon passes for $16, frequently at a premium of 10 per cent.

The general price of gold is $1 per pennyweight.

Silver.

Round dollar = 9s.
Cut dollar = 8s. 3d. currency.
Bit = 9d. Moco, or the piece cut from the dollar, has different values.

Copper.

Dog = 1½d.
Stampe = 2¼d.
In Grenada the moco = 6d.

In the French islands, viz. Martinique, Guadaloupe, Deseada, and Mariegalante, accounts are kept in livres of 20 sols, each sol equal to

12 deniers. The colonial livre is one third less than the livre tournois of France. The currency of the Windward islands is also adopted.

Gold coins.

Doubloon	=	144 livres.
Napoleon	=	66 livres, 13 sols, 4 deniers.
Louis d'Or	=	40 " 10 "
Guinea	=	45 "
Sovereign	=	4 "

Silver.	Dollar	=	9 livres.
	Moco	=	2 " 5 sols.
	Pistareen	=	1 " 10 "
	Trois petites pieces	=	1 " 2 " 6 deniers.
	Bit	=	15 "
Copper.	Tempé	=	3s. 9d.
	Dog	=	2s. 6d.

At St. Domingo, in general, accounts are kept in dollars of 10 dimes or 100 centimes, and the dollar is here valued at 4s. 6d. sterling.

Spanish doubloons pass for $16; half joannes or joes for $8; French crowns for a dollar and 9 centimes.

5 franc pieces = 9 escalins = 81 cents.

A dollar = 11 escalins = 99 cents.

SPANISH ISLANDS.

At Cuba and Porto Rico, accounts are kept in pesos or dollars of 8 reals. The real is divided into halves and quarters, and also into 34 maravedis.

The gold coins are doubloons = $16, and halves and quarters. The doubloon occasionally passes for $17.

VIRGIN ISLANDS.

In the Danish islands of St. Thomas, St. John, and St. Croix, or Santa Cruz, accounts are kept in rix dollars (also called piastres or pieces of eight) of 8 shillings or bits, or 48 stivers; likewise in dollars of 10 dimes or 100 centimes; but in negotiating bills with England, the Windward island currency is adopted.

Gold is valued at $1 per dwt.

The rix dollar current is reckoned 20 per cent. worse than Danish currency; but the Danish coins are valued at 25 per cent. more.

Thus, the 2 rix dollar ducat passes for $2\frac{1}{2}$ rix dollars, or 20 bits.

The silver coins are quadrupe, double and single bits, and 1 and 3 stiver pieces.

The Spanish dollar passes for $12\frac{1}{2}$ bits, and each bit for $6\frac{1}{4}$ stivers.

In the Dutch islands, viz. St. Martin's, St. Eustatia, and Saba, accounts are kept in pieces of 8, i. e. piastres of 8 reals, each real being divided into 6 stivers.

The Spanish dollar passes for 11 reals, the joe for 11 piastres, and the Spanish single pistole for $4\frac{1}{2}$ piastres.

At the Dutch settlements of Surinam, Berbice, Demarara, and Essequebo, accounts are kept in guilders or florins of 20 stivers, or 240 pfennings. $17\frac{1}{2}$ florins are estimated as equal to £1 sterling.

The stiver is also divided into 8 dwts.

The Dutch coins pass here at about 20 per cent. premium.

Spanish dollar = 3 guilders; the bit = 5 stivers; doubloon = 42 to 44 guilders; the joe = 22 guilders.

TABLE

Showing the value of dollars, from 1 to 10,000, in the colonial currencies of the different states of the United States of America.

Dollars.	New-England, Vermont, Virginia & Kentucky.		New-York and North Carolina.		N. Jersey, Pennsylvania, Delaware & Maryland.			South Carolina and Georgia.		
$	£	s.	£	s.	£	s.	d.	£	s.	d.
1	0	6	0	8	0	7	6	0	4	8
2	0	12	0	16	0	15	0	0	9	4
3	0	18	1	4	1	2	6	0	14	0
4	1	4	1	12	1	10	0	0	18	8
5	1	10	2	0	1	17	6	1	3	4
6	1	16	2	8	2	5	0	1	8	0
7	2	2	2	16	2	12	6	1	12	8
8	2	8	3	4	3	0	0	1	17	4
9	2	14	3	12	3	7	6	2	2	0
10	3	0	4	0	3	15	0	2	6	8
20	6	0	8	0	7	10	0	4	13	4
30	9	0	12	0	11	5	0	7	0	0
40	12	0	16	0	15	0	0	9	6	8
50	15	0	20	0	18	15	0	11	13	4
60	18	0	24	0	22	10	0	14	0	0
70	21	0	28	0	26	5	0	16	6	8
80	24	0	32	0	30	0	0	18	13	4
90	27	0	36	0	33	15	0	21	0	0
100	30	0	40	0	37	10	0	23	6	8
200	60	0	80	0	75	0	0	46	13	4
300	90	0	120	0	112	0	0	70	0	0
400	120	0	160	0	150	0	0	93	6	8
500	150	0	200	0	187	10	0	116	13	4
900	270	0	360	0	337	10	0	210	0	0
1,000	300	0	400	0	375	0	0	233	6	8
2,000	600	0	800	0	750	0	0	466	13	4
3,000	900	0	1,200	0	1,125	0	0	700	0	0
4,000	1,200	0	1,600	0	1,500	0	0	933	6	8
5,000	1,500	0	2,000	0	1,875	0	0	1,166	13	4
9,000	2,700	0	3,600	0	2,375	0	0	2,100	0	0
10,000	3,000	0	4,000	0	3,750	0	0	2,338	6	8

TABLE

Showing the number of cents and decimals in any number of shillings and pence, less than a dollar, in the same currencies.

Shillings and pence currency.		New-England, Vermont, Virginia & Kentucky.	New-York and North Carolina.	N. Jersey, Pennsylvania, Delaware & Maryland.	South Carolina and Georgia.
s.	d.	Cents.	Cents.	Cents.	Cents.
0	1	1.38	1.04	1.11	1.78
0	2	2.77	2.08	2.22	3.57
0	3	4.16	3.12	3.33	5.35
0	4	5.55	4.16	4.44	7.14
0	5	6.74	5.20	5.55	8 92
0	6	8.53	6.24	6.66	10.71
0	7	9.72	7.28	7.77	12.50
0	8	11.11	8.32	8.88	14.28
0	9	12.50	9.37	10.00	16 07
0	10	13.88	10.41	11.11	17.85
0	11	15.27	11.45	12.22	19.64
1	0	16.66	12.50	13.33	21.42
2	0	33.33	25.00	26.66	42.85
3	0	50.00	37.50	40.00	64.28
4	0	66.66	50.00	53.33	85.71
4	8	77.77	58.32	62.22	100.00
5	0	83.33	62.50	66.66	
6	0	100.00	75.00	80.00	
7	0	. . .	87.50	93.33	
7	6	. . .	93.75	100.00	
8	0	. . .	100.00		

TABLE OF MONIES OF ACCOUNT.

Containing the Value of the Monies of Account of different Places, (expressed in Pence Sterling and Decimals of Pence,) according to the Mint Price, both of Gold and Silver, in England; that is, £3 17s. 10½d. per Oz. Standard for Gold, and 5s. 2d. per Oz. Standard for Silver, and also in Federal Currency.

		Value in Silver.	In Gold.	In Fed.
		d.	, .	$ c. m.
Aix La Chapelle..	Rixdollar current..................	31, 40	31, 43	62 9
licant..........	Libra or Peso.......................	39, 40	37, 38	75 2
msterdam.......	Rixdollar............................	52, 54	variable*	1 09 0
	Florin (Old)........................	21,	ditto	40 0
	Florin (New)........................	20, 72	ditto	40 0
	Pound Flemish......................	124, 32	ditto	2 40 0
Antwerp..........	Pound Flemish (money of exchange)..	123, 25	123, 87	2 37 7
	Florin (money of exchange)..........	20, 54	20, 64	39 6
	Pound Flemish current.............	105, 65	106, 18	2 03 5
	Florin current.......................	205,	205,	40 0
Arragon..........	Libra Jaquesa........................	49, 25	46, 75	94 0
Augsburg.........	Florin Giro, or money of exchange....	32,	31, 83	61 7
	Florin current.......................	25, 20	25, 07	48 6
Barcelona.........	Libra Catalan........................	28, 14	26, 70	53 4
Basil.............	Rixdollar, or Ecu of exchange........	47, 27	47,	94
	Rixdollar current....................	42, 45	42, 20	84 4
Bergamo........	Scudo of 7 Lire.......................	35, 67	36, 50	68 7
Berlin............	Pound Banco........................	47, 25	variable	94 5
	Rixdollar current....................	36,	ditto	69 5
	Rixdollar in Fredericks...............	——†	39, 68	72 4
Bern.............	Ecu of 3 Livres.......................	42, 64	42, 90	84 0
	Crown of 25 Batzen..................	35, 53	35, 75	70 0
Bologna..........	Lira corrente.........................	10, 86	10, 62	20 9
	Lira, money of exchange..............	11, 12	10, 89	21 2
Bolsano..........	Florin Giro, or money of exchange...	33, 26	33, 08	66 0
	Florin moneta lunga, or currency.....	25, 20	25, 06	48 6
Bremen...........	Rixdollar current....................	37, 80	variable	68 9
	Rixdollar in Carl d'ors...............	——	39, 38	71 4
Canary Islands....	Real current.........................	3, 95	3, 66	7 3
Cassel............	Rixdollar current....................	37, 80	variable	75 6
Cologne..........	Rixdollar specie of 80 Albuses.......	31, 38	ditto	60 5
	Rixdollar current of 78 Albuses......	30, 60	ditto	59 0
Constantinople....	Piastre, or Dollar, 1819...............	9, 45	uncertain	18 9
Dantzic...........	Gulden or Florin......................	9,	9,	17 4
Denmark.........	Rixdollar specie......................	54, 72	——	1 5 6
	Rixdollar Sundish specie.............	53, 21	——	1 2 6
	Rixdollar Crown money..............	48, 37	——	93 3
	Rixdollar Danish currency...........	44, 27	44, 88	85 4
	Rixdollar Holstein currency..........	43, 78	44, 16	84 5
England..........	Pound Sterling......................	240,	240,	4 80
	Shilling...............................	12,	12,	24
	Penny................................	1,	1,	2
	Farthing..............................	25	25	5
Florence.........	Lira...................................	8, 12	8, 53	15 7
	Ducat, or Crown current.............	56, 84	59, 71	1 09 6
	Scudo d'oro, or Gold Crown.........	——	63, 97	1 17 9
France...........	Livre Tournois.......................	9, 58	9, 40	13 0
	Franc (new system)..................	9, 70	9, 52	18 7
Frankfort.........	Rixdollar, Convention money.........	37, 80	37, 65	73 0
	Rixdollar Muntze, or in small coins...	31, 50	——	60
Geneva...........	Livre current.........................	16, 13	16, 93	31 1
	Florin.................................	4, 60	4, 84	8 7
Genoa...........	Lira fuori Banco.....................	7, 99	7, 83	15 4
	Pezza, or Dollar of exchange........	45, 92	45, 50	88 5
	Scudo di cambio, or Crown of exchange	36, 75	36, 02	71 9
	Scudo d'oro..........................	85, 49	83, 77	1 66 6
Germany.........	Rixdollar current....................	37, 80	variable	75 6
	Rixdollar specie......................	50, 40	ditto	97 2
	Florin of the Empire.................	25, 20	ditto	48 6
	Rixdollar Muntze.....................	31, 50	ditto	63
	Florin Muntze........................	21,	ditto	42
Hamburg.........	Mark Banco (at a medium)...........	18, 22	variable	35 0
	Pound Flemish Banco................	136, 65	ditto	2 63 6

* In the places marked *variable*, the price of the coins is not fixed; and, therefore, the intrinsic value in gold of the monies of account cannot be ascertained for any length of time.

† Where the columns are marked with a dash, it is to be understood that there is no coin in the metal of that column, by which the monies of account can be computed.

		Value in Silver. d.	In Gold. d.	In Fed. $ c. m.
Hamburg	Mark current	14, 82	ditto	28 6
	Pound Flemish current	111, 15	ditto	2 14 4
Hanover	Rixdollar, in cash	42,	42, 26	80 7
	Rixdollar, Gold value	39,	39, 24	75 2
Ireland	Pound Irish old	221, 54	221, 54	4 43 1
Konigsberg	Gulden or Florin	12,	variable	23 1
Leghorn	Pezza of 8 Reals	46, 25	49, 16	89 2
	Lira moneta buona	8, 13	8, 55	15 7
	Lira moneta lunga	7, 79	8, 19	15
Leipsic	Rixdollar Convention money	37, 80	variable	75 6
	Rixdollar in Louis d'ors or Frederick's.	———	29, 68	56 3
Lucca	Lira		———	24 3
	Scudo d'oro	55, 50	58, 27	1 12 7
	Scudo corrente	51, 80	54, 39	1 00
Malta	Scudo, or Crown	21, 32	23, 34	41 1
Milan	Lira Imperiale	10, 41	10, 53	20
	Lira corrente	7, 45	7, 30	14 4
	Scudo Imperiale	60, 90	61, 60	1 20 2
	Scudo corrente	42, 32	42, 78	85 5
Modena	Lira	3, 72	33, 15	66 3
Munich	Gulden or Florin	21,	21, 28	42 6
Nancy	Livre (money of Lorraine)	7, 38	7, 26	14 5
Naples	Ducato di regno	41, 20	uncertain	80 6
Navarre	Real	4, 90	4, 67	9 3
	Libra	8, 20	7, 79	15 6
Neufchatel	Livre Tournois	13, 63	13, 40	26 3
	Livre foible	5, 45	5, 36	10 5
Novi	Scudo d'oro marche	35, 49	83, 77	1 64 9
Parma	Lira	2, 35	2, 30	4 5
Persia	Toman of 100 Mamoodis	287, 60	———	5 55
Poland	Gulden or Florin	6, 03	6, 27	11 2
Portugal	Milree	uncertain	67, 34	1 34 7
	Old Crusado	uncertain	26, 94	55 9
Prague	*(See Vienna)*			
Riga	Rixdollar Alberts	52, 54	variable	1 0 1
	Rixdollar currency, (agio at 40 per cent.)	37, 53	ditto	72 4
Rome	Scudo or Crown	52, 05	51, 63	1 0
	Scudo di Stampa d'oro	79, 37	78, 73	1 53 1
Russia	Ruble	variable		
St. Gall	Florin, money of exchange	27, 44	variable	52 9
	Florin current	22, 76	ditto	43 9
St. Remo	Lira	8, 46	8, 90	17 8
Sardinia	Lira	18, 21	18, 82	35 1
Sicily	Ounce	123, 54	124, 80	2 38 3
	Scudo, or Crown	49, 02	49, 92	96 7
Spain	Real of old plate	4, 88	4, 57	9 4
	Real of new plate	5, 18	4, 86	10
	Real of Mexican plate	6, 48	6, 07	12 5
	Real vellon	2, 59	2, 43	5
	Dollar of old plate or of exchange	39,	37, 30	75 2
Stralsund	Rixdollar of account	28, 35	variable	54 7
	Pomeranian Gulden	14, 18	ditto	27 3
Strasburg	Livre and Franc *(see France)*			
	Florin	19, 08	18, 76	36 9
Sweden	Rixdollar	55, 41	56, 43	1 06 9
Switzerland	Franc (new system)	15, 14	———	28 1
Trieste	Florin, Austrian currency, Convention	25, 20	25, 05	48 6
	Lira, Trieste currency	4, 76	4, 73	9 2
	Lira di Piazza	4, 65	4, 63	9
Turin	Lira	11, 28	11, 23	21 8
United States	Dollar	50, 9	50,	1
	Cent	5	5	1
Valencia	Libra	39, 45	36, 59	75 2
Venice	Lira piccola (in the old coins)	5, 07	variable	9 6
	Lira Austriache	8,	ditto	16 2
Vienna	Florin	25, 20	25, 05	48 6
Zante	Lira	4, 06	variable	8 1
Zurich	Florin, money of exchange	25, 85	ditto	45 3
	Florin current	23, 50	ditto	42

The foregoing Table has been computed from the proportion which the monies of account bear to the coins of each place respectively, valued according to the British Mint Regulations. Thus, the intrinsic par of exchange may be calculated both in gold and silver, where the moneys of exchange are the same as those of account; but dealers in bills, coin, and bullion, generally prefer computations from actual assays.

NEW TABLE OF GOLD COINS.

Containing the Assays, Weights, and Values of the principal Gold Coins of all Countries, computed according to the Mint Price of Gold in England, and from Assays made both at London and Paris; also, the value in Federal Currency, at the rate established by the Act of 31*st July*, 1834.

		Standard Weight. dwt.	gr.	mi.	Con. in pure go. grains.	Value in Sterling. s.	d.	Value in Federal. $	c.	m.
Austria........	Souverain	3	13	15	78, 6	13	10,92	3	37	8
	Double Ducat	4	20	5	106, 4	18	9,97	4	58	9
	Ducat	2	10	2	53, 2	9	4,98	2	29	6
	Ducat Kremnitz, or Hungarian	2	10	3	53, 3	9	5,91	2	27	9
Belgium........	Gold Lion, or 14 Florin Piece	5	7	16	117, 1	20	8,65	5	04	6
	Ten Florin Piece (1820)	4	5	15	93, 2	16	5,93	4	01	9
Denmark........	Ducat current	1	21	19	42, 2	7	5,62	1	81	2
	Ducat specie	2	9	8	52, 6	9	3,70	2	26	4
	Christian d'or	4	5	16	93, 3	16	6,14	4	02	1
England........	Guinea	5	9	10	118, 7	21	0	5	7	5
	Half Guinea	2	16	15	59, 3	10	6	2	54	
	Seven Shilling Piece	1	19	0	39, 6	7	0	1	69	8
	Sovereign	5	3	5	113, 1	20	0	4	84	6
France........	Double Louis (coined before 1786.)	10	5	6	224, 9	39	9,64	9	60	7
	Louis	5	2	12	112, 4	19	10,71	4	84	6
	Demi Louis	2	13	6	56, 2	9	11,38	2	42	3
	Double Louis (coined since 1786.)	9	15	19	212, 6	37	7,53	9	15	2
	Louis	4	19	19	106, 3	18	9,75	4	57	5
	Double Napoleon, or Piece of 40 Francs	8	3	0	179,	31	8,36	7	70	2
	Napoleon, or Piece of 20 Francs	4	1	10	89, 7	15	10,5	3	85	1
	New Louis (Double, &c.) the same as the Napoleon.									
Germany...	Augsburg Ducat	2	8	8	52, 1	9	2,64	2	21	3
	Baden Ducat	2	3	2	46, 9	8	3,60	2	02	2
	Bavaria Carolin	5	5	10	115,	20	4,23	4	95	7
	Max d'or, or Maximilian	3	14	0	77,	13	7,44	3	31	8
	Ducat	2	19	11	52, 8	9	4,12	2	27	5
	Brunswick Pistole	4	19	5	105, 7	18	8,48	4	54	9
	Double in proportion.									
	Carl d'or, before 1802	4	4	15	92, 5	16	4,44	3	93	
	Double in proportion.									
	Carl d'or, since 1802	4	3	11	92,	16	3,38	3	91	
	Double in proportion.									
	Ducat	2	8	9	51, 8	9	2,	2	23	
	Cologne Ducat	2	9	8	52, 6	9	3,70	2	26	4
	Frankfort Ducat	2	9	14	52, 9	9	4,34	2	27	7
	Hamburg Ducat	2	9	14	52, 9	9	4,35	2	27	7
	Double in proportion.									
	Hanover George d'or	4	5	3	92, 6	16	4 66	3	93	9
	Ducat	2	10	3	53, 3	9	5,19	2	29	6
	Gold Florin	1	18	6	39,	6	10,83	1	67	
	Double in proportion.									
	Hesse Cassel Pistole	4	4	8	92,	16	3,39	3	77	
	William d'or of 1815	4	4	9	92, 1	16	3,6	3	77	2
	Hesse Darmstadt Carolin	2	15	0	58,	10	3,18	2	46	4
	Ducat	2	8	16	52, 3	9	3,07	2	25	1
	Liege Ducat	2	10	0	53, 2	9	4,98	2	28	9
	Lorraine Leopold	7	3	15	157, 4	27	10,28	6	68	6
	Francis	4	6	1	93, 6	16	6,78	3	97	6
	Manheim Carolin	5	4	10	114, 4	20	2,96	4	85	9
	½ and ¼ in proportion.									
	Pistole	4	4	16	92, 3	16	4,02	3	92	
	Ducat	2	9	10	52 8	9	4,13	2	27	
	Mentz Ducat	2	9	12	52, 9	9	4,34	2	27	7
	Nuremberg Ducat	2	9	8	52, 6	9	3,71	2	26	4
	Double, &c. in proportion.									
	Ratisbon Four Ducat Piece	9	11	0	77, 2	36	10,81	8	85	6
	Treves Ducat	2	9	8	52, 6	9	3,71	2	26	4
	Wirtemberg Carolin	5	4	0	113, 7	20	1,47	4	82	9
	Ducat	2	8	12	51, 9	9	2,22	2	23	2

		Standard Weight.			Con. in pure go.	Value in Sterling.		Value in Federal.		
		dwt.	gr.	mi.	grains.	s.	d.	$	c.	m.
Germany....	Wirtzburg Ducat	2	9	8	52, 6	9	3,71	2	26	4
Holland, now Netherlands.	Double Ryder	12	21	0	283, 2	50	1,46	12	20	8
	Ryder	6	9	0	140, 2	24	9,75	6	04	3
	Half Ryder	3	4	10	70, 1	12	4,87	3	02	1
	Ducat	2	9	12	52, 8	9	4,13	2	27	5
Italy......	Genoa Doppia, or Pistole	4	5	14	93, 4	16	6,36	4	02	7
	Pieces of 2, 4, &c. in proportion.									
	Sequin	2	10	6	53, 4	9	5,41	2	30	2
	Genovina of 100 Lire	17	22	0	394, 2	69	9,20	15	41	3
	½, &c. in proportion.									
	New Genovina, of 96 Lire or 4 Pistole Piece of the Ligurian Republic	16	1	15	357, 7	63	3,6	14	79	7
	Ditto of 48 Lire	8	0	18	178, 9	31	7,9	7	39	8
	Pieces of 24 and 12 in proportion.									
	Lucca Pistole	3	13	0	77, 9	13	9,44	3	34	8
	Milan Sequin	2	10	0	53, 2	9	4,98	2	29	
	Doppia, or Pistole	4	0	8	88, 4	15	7,74	3	80	7
	40 Lire Piece of 1808	8	4	0	179, 7	31	9,64	7	74	2
	Naples Six Ducat Piece of 1752	5	9	8	118, 7	21	0,09	5	12	
	Six Ducat Piece of 1767 and 1772	5	7	14	116, 8	20	8,06	5	4	
	Six Ducat Piece of 1783	5	12	18	121, 9	21	6,89	5	24	9
	Four Ducat Piece, or Pistole of 1752	3	14	6	79, 2	14	0,20	3	48	
	Four Ducat Piece of 1767 and 1770	3	11	6	76, 8	13	7,10	3	37	5
	Two Ducat Piece, or Sequin of 1762	1	16	6	37, 4	6	7,42	1	59	1
	Three Ducat Piece, or Oncetta of 1818	2	15	1	58, 1	10	3,40	2	49	
	Piedmont Pistole or Doppia, 1741 to 1785	6	2	8	134, 2	23	9,01	5	79	
	Pistole, coined since 1785	5	17	0	125, 6	22	2,75	5	41	1
	½, &c. in proportion.									
	Sequin	2	9	12	52, 9	9	4,34	2	28	
	½ in proportion.									
	Carlino, coined before 1785	30	11	14	670, 8	118	8,64	27	34	
	Carlino, coined since 1785	28	20	0	634, 4	112	3,33	25	80	
	½, &c. in proportion.									
	Piece of 20 Francs, called *Marengo*	3	18	4	82, 7	14	7,63	3	56	4
	Rome Doppia or Pistole, of Pius VI	3	12	5	77, 2	13	7,59	3	31	
	Ditto of Pius VII. 1802	3	11	12	76, 6	13	6,68	3	30	
	½, &c. in proportion.									
	Zecchino, or Sequin, coined before 1760	2	8	0	51, 4	9	1,16	2	22	
	Sequin, coined since 1760	2	9	0	52, 2	9	2,86	2	25	1
	Scudo of the Republic	16	16	6	367,	64	11,43	15	81	1
	Sicilian* Ounce of 1734	2	18	14	61, 2	10	9,97	2	62	5
	Ounce of 1741	2	18	4	60, 7	10	8,91	2	60	5
	Ounce of 1751	2	15	8	58, 2	10	3,60	2	50	4
	Double Ounce of 1758	5	7	14	117,	20	8,48	5	04	4
	Tuscany Ruspone	7	7	8	160, 8	28	5,50	6	93	
	Zecchino, or Sequin	2	10	14	53, 6	9	5,83	2	31	8
	Ruspone of the Kingdom of Etruria	7	7	13	161,	28	5,93	6	93	8
Malta..........	Double Louis	9	18	18	215, 3	38	1,25	9	36	
	Louis	4	21	16	108,	19	1,37	4	68	
	Demi Louis	2	11	3	54, 5	9	7,75	2	34	
Parma.........	Quadruple Pistole	17	12	18	386,	68	3,78	16	62	8
	Double, &c. in proportion.									
	Pistole or Doppia of 1787	4	10	4	97, 4	17	2,85	4	19	4
	Ditto of 1796	4	8	14	95, 9	16	11,67	4	13	5
	Maria Theresa (1818)	4	1	10	89, 7	15	10,5	3	86	1
Poland........	Ducat	2	9	12	52, 9	9	4,34	2	27	5
Portugal......	Dobraon of 24,000 Rees	34	12	0	759,	134	3,96	32	70	6
	Meio Dobraon of 12,000 Rees	17	6	0	379, 5	67	1,98	16	35	3
	Dobra of 12,800 Rees	18	6	0	401, 5	71	0,70	17	30	1
	Joannese of 6,400 Rees	9	5	16	203, 4	35	11,98	8	65	
	Half Joannese of 3,200 Rees	4	14	12	101, 5	17	11,56	4	32	5
	Moidore or Lisbonnine	6	22	0	152, 2	26	11,24	6	55	7
	½, &c. in proportion.									
	Piece of 16 Testoons, or 1600 Rees	2	5	14	49, 3	8	8,70	2	12	1
	Piece of 12 Testoons, or 1200 Rees	1	16	0	36, 7	6	5,94	1	57	
	Piece of 8 Testoons	1	4	6	26,	4	7,21	1	12	6
	Old Crusado of 400 Rees	0	14	18	13, 6	2	4,88		58	8
	New Crusado of 480 Rees	0	16	2	14, 8	2	7,43		63	5

* Much variation is found in the fineness of the Sicilian gold coins.

		Standard Weight. dwt.	gr.	mi.	Con. in pure go. grains.	Value in Sterling. s.	d.	Value in Federal. $	c.	m.
Portugal	Milree (coined for the African Colonies) 1755	0	19	15	18, 1	3	2,44		73	
Prussia	Ducat of 1748	2	9	14	52, 9	9	4,34	2	27	9
	Ducat of 1787	2	9	6	52, 6	9	3,71	2	28	7
	Frederick (Double) of 1769	8	9	18	185,	32	8,90	7	97	5
	Frederick (Single) of 1778	4	5	4	92, 8	16	5,08	3	99	7
	Frederick (Double) of 1800	8	9	6	184, 5	32	7,84	7	95	1
	Frederick (Single) of 1800	4	4	13	92, 2	16	3.42	3	97	5
Russia	Ducat of 1751	2	8	4	51, 5	9	1,37	2	22	5
	Double Ducat of St. Andrew of 1756	4	17	16	104, 4	18	5,72	4	50	
	Ducat of 1796	2	10	0	53, 2	9	4,98	2	29	7
	Ducat of 1763	2	9	8	52, 6	9	3,71	2	26	7
	Half Ducat of 1785	1	14	6	35, 1	6	2,54	1	51	
	Gold Ruble of 1756	1	0	10	22, 5	3	11,78		96	7
	Ditto of 1799	0	18	14	17, 1	3	0,31		73	7
	Gold Poltin of 1777	0	9	0	8, 2	1	5,41		35	5
	Imperial (coined before 1763)	10	16	0	234, 7	41	6,45	10	04	
	Imperial of 1763	8	9	10	184, 7	32	8,06	7	94	
	Imperial of 1772	8	10	8	185, 5	32	9,96	7	97	5
	Half Imperial of 1780	4	2	4	90,	15	11,14	3	87	
	Imperial of 1801	8	6	8	181, 9	32	2,31	7	82	9
	Half Imperial of 1801	4	3	4	90, 9	16	1,05	3	91	8
	Ditto of 1818	4	3	12	91, 3	16	1,98	3	93	3
Saltzburg	Ducat	2	9	8	52, 6	9	3,71	2	26	7
Sardinia	Carlino	9	23	16	219, 8	38	10,	9	47	2
	½ in proportion.									
	Doppietta	1	23	13	43, 7	7	8,81	1	88	
Saxony	Ducat of 1784	2	9	8	52, 6	9	3,71	2	26	7
	Ducat of 1797	2	9	14	52, 9	9	4,34	2	27	9
	Augustus of 1754	4	3	8	91, 2	16	1,69	3	92	5
	Augustus of 1784	4	4	12	92, 2	16	3,81	3	97	6
Spain	Quadruple Pistole, or Doubloon, (coined before 1772.)	17	1	8	375, 3	66	5,06	16	02	8
	Double Pistole, (before 1772)	8	12	14	187, 7	33	2,63	8	1	4
	Single and half in proportion.									
	Quarter Pistole, or Gold Dollar (before 1772)	1	2	8	24, 2	4	3,39	1	0	5
	Doubloon of 1772	16	21	16	372,	65	10,05	15	53	5
	Double and Single in proportion.									
	Half Pistole, of 1772	2	2	10	46, 3	8	2,33	1	99	
	Quarter Pistole, of 1772	1	2	2	23, 9	4	2,75	1	1	
	Quadruple Pistole, of 1801	16	9	6	360, 5	63	9,62	15	53	
	Double Pistole of 1801	8	4	13	180, 3	31	10,92	7	76	8
	Pistole of 1801	4	2	6	90, 1	15	11,35	3	88	4
	Coronilla, Gold Doll. or Vintem of 1801	1	0	18	22, 8	4	0,42		98	3
Sweden	Ducat	2	8	12	51, 9	9	2,22	2	28	5
Switzerland	Ducat of Lucerne	2	9	8	52, 6	9	3,71	2	26	7
	Double Ducat of Lucerne	4	6	12	94, 1	16	7,94	4	06	
	Piece of Five Ducats of Lucerne	10	23	18	241, 9	42	9,74	10	42	
	Ducat of Schwitz	2	6	4	49, 7	8	9,55	2	14	
	Ducat of St. Gall	2	7	12	51,	9	0,31	2	20	
	Ducat of Uri	2	8	0	51, 4	9	1,16	2	22	
	Pistole of Lucerne	4	19	9	105, 9	18	8,91	4	56	
	Pistole of Soleure	4	19	12	106,	18	9,12	4	57	
	Pistole of the Helvetic Republic of 1800	4	19	9	105, 9	18	8,91	4	56	
	Basil Ducat	2	4	10	48, 1	8	6.14	2	07	
	Pistole	4	18	13	105, 1	18	7,20	4	51	5
	Bern Ducat	2	2	1	45, 9	8	1,48	1	98	6
	Double, &c. in proportion.									
	Pistole	4	19	0	105, 5	18	7,86	4	54	2
	Geneva Pistolè, Old	4	4	18	92, 5	16	4,45	3	98	5
	Pistole, New	3	15	4	80,	14	1,9	3	44	4
	Zurich Ducat	2	9	8	52, 6	9	3,71	2	26	7
	Double and ½ Ducat in proportion.									
Turkey	Sequin Fonducli of Constantinople of 1773	1	23	6	43, 3	7	7,94	1	86	6
	Sequin Fonducli of 1789	1	22	16	42, 9	7	7,11	1	84	8
	Double Sequin, Mahbub of 1773	3	7	14	73, 1	12	11,26	3	15	
	Sequin Mahbub, of 1789	1	7	10	28, 9	5	1,37	1	25	
	Sequin of Cairo of 1773	1	9	16	31,	5	5.83	1	33	5
	Sequin of Cairo of 1789	1	5	6	26, 9	4	9,13	1	14	
	Half Misseir (1818)	0	13	5	12,16	2	1,82	1	83	
	Sequin Fonducli	1	22	7	42, 5	7	6,26	1	85	

		Standard Weight. dwt	gr.	mi	Con. in pure go. grains.	Value in Sterling s	d.	Value in Federal. $	c	m.
Turkey.........	Rubieh..............................	0	10	18	9, 9	1	9,		42	
	Yermeebeshlek........................	13	4	13	70, 3	12	5,30	3	02	8
United States...	Eagle, coined before 1834.............	11	6		247,10	44	8,	10	66	5
	½ and ¼ in proportion.									
	Eagles coined since 31st July, 1834.....	10	18		232,	41	3,	10		
	½ and ¼ in proportion.									
Venice..........	Zecchino, or Sequin...................	2	10	10	53, 6	9	5,83	2	31	
	½ and ¼ in proportion.									
	Doppia, or Pistole....................	4	7	0	94, 4	16	8,48	4	6	5
	Scudo d'oro, or Gold Crown...........	29	6	2	643, 6	113	10,87	26	18	
	Ducato d'oro, or Gold Ducat...........	1	12	6	33, 3	5	10,72	1	43	
	Osella d'oro.........................	9	17	18	214, 5	37	11,55	9	33	
	EAST INDIES.									
East India......	Mohur of Shah Allum (1770)...........	8	11	15	186, 8	33	0,72	7	97	5
	Mohur of the same....................	8	13	13	188, 5	33	4,33	8	12	
	Mohur, Half, (1787)...................	4	6	10	94,	16	7,64	4	06	
	¼ in proportion.									
	Mohur Sicca, of Bengal, dated 19th Sun.	8	15	0	189, 8	33	7,09	8	17	5
	Mohur of Bombay, old, still in circulation..............................	7	17	8	170,	30	1,04	7	33	
	Mohur of the Dutch East India Company (1783).........................	8	8	0	183, 4	32	5,50	7	89	
	Mohur of ditto, (1797)................	7	22	8	174, 5	30	10,60	7	51	
	Mohur, Half ditto, (1801).............	4	18	18	96, 2	17	0,30	4	15	
	Rupee, Tippoo's......................	8	6	0	181, 5	32	1,46	7	81	
	*Rupee, Zodiac......................	7	14	16	167, 6	29	7,9	7	23	
	Rupee, Bombay, (1818)................	7	11	13	164, 7	29	1,78	7	09	6
	Rupee of Madras, (1818)...............	1	12	0	165,	29	2,42	7	11	
	Pagoda, Star.........................	1	21	11	41, 8	7	4,77	1	79	8
	Pagoda, with a crescent and 3 figures..	2	0	18	44, 8	7	11,14	1	93	
	Pagoda, with a crescent and one figure.	1	22	5	42, 4	7	6,04	1	84	7
	Pagoda, Arcot, old....................	1	20	4	40, 5	7	2,01	1	75	
	Pagoda, Arcot, new...................	1	11	4	32, 4	7	8,59	1	89	
	Pagoda, Onore.......................	2	0	4	44, 2	7	9,87	1	91	5
	Pagoda, Mangalore....................	2	0	12	44. 6	7	10,72	1	93	4
	Pagoda, Pondicherry..................	1	16	6	37, 2	6	7,	1	60	
	Pagoda, Hyderee Hoon.................	1	23	4	43, 8	7	7,96	1	86	6
	Pagoda, Sultanee Hoon................	2	2	16	46, 6	8	2,97	2		
	Saik Sai, a Mahratta coin.............	6	7	16	139, 2	24	7,63	6		
	Tippoo's Faruki......................	2	0	18	44, 8	7	11,14	1	93	
	Japan Copang, old....................	0	14	8	233, 2	41	3,27	9	98	
	Japan Copang, new...................	6	2	14	134, 5	23	9,65	5	80	

* These Rupees are stamped with the Signs of the Zodiac: they are now very scarce, being only preserved as objects of curiosity.

TABLE OF SILVER COINS.

---

*Containing the Assays, Weights, and Values of the Principal Silver Coins of all Countries, computed at the rate of 5s. 2d. per Ounce Standard, from Assays made both at the London and Paris Mints; and the value in Federal Currency, calculated at $4 80 the Pound Sterling, except those marked with a *, which indicates the value at the Custom-House; and those marked with a †, which indicates the real value in the United States.*

		Standard Weight.			Conts. in pure Sil.	Value in Sterling.		Value in Federal.		
		dwt	gr.	mi	grains.	s.	d.	$	c.	m.
Austria........	Rixdollar, *Constitution*, before 1753....	17	13	10	390,	4	6,45	1	08	9
	Rixdollar, *Convention*, coined since 1753	15	22	4	353, 7	4	1,39		98	8
	Rixdollar Ditto, of Francis II. 1800.....	16	0	4	355, 5	4	1,64		99	3
	Rixdollar of the Kingdom of Hungary..	16	6	1	360, 9	4	2,39	1	00	8
	Half Rixdollar, or Florin, *Convention*..	8	2	1	179, 6	2	1,07		50	1
	Copfstuck, or 20 Creutzer Piece.	2	16	3	59, 4	0	8,29		16	6
	17 Creutzer Piece	2	9	18	53, 5	0	7,47		14	9
	Halbe Copf, or 10 Creutzer Piece......	1	7	1	28, 8	0	4,01		8	
Denmark........	Ryksdaler, old, of 6 Marks Danish.....	15	12	5	344, 4	4	0,92		97	8
	Crone, or old piece of 4 Marks..........	10	4	7	226,	2	7,55		63	1
	Crone, or Crown, of 1747..	10	10	16	232, 9	2	8,52		(5	
	Ryksdaler, specie, of 1798..........	17	11	17	388, 4	4	6,23	1	05	5
	New Piece of 4 Marks..................	11	16	14	259, 8	3	0 27		72	5
	Half Ryksdaler..........	8	17	8	194, 2	2	3,11		54	3
	Mark, specie, or 1-6 Ryksdaler.......	2	21	12	64, 4	0	7,59		15	2
	Rixdollar, specie of Sleswig and Holstein	17	12	6	389, 4	4	6,37	*1	00	
	Pieces of $\frac{2}{3}$ and $\frac{1}{3}$ in proportion									
	Piece of 24 Skillings....................	3	2	10	68, 9	0	9,62	19	24	
England........	Crown, old..............................	19	8	10	429, 7	5	0	†1	10	
	Half crown..............................	9	16	5	214, 8	2	6		†55	
	Shilling.	3	21	0	85, 9	1	0		24	
	Sixpence...............................	1	22	10	42, 9	0	6		12	
	Crown, new.............................	18	4	7	403, 6	4	8,36	†1	10	
	Half crown..............................	9	2	4	201, 8	2	4,18		†55	
	Shilling................................	3	15	6	80, 7	0	11,27		24	
	Sixpence	1	19	14	40, 3	0	5,63		12	
France..........	Ecu of 6 Livres.........................	18	7	16	403, 1	4	8,28	†1	10	
	Demi Ecu	9	1	18	201, 5	2	4,13		†55	
	Piece of 24 Sous........................	3	16	19	83, 4	0	11,64		23	8
	Divisions in proportion.									
	Piece of 30 Sous........................	4	12	4	100, 2	1	1,99		26	
	$\frac{1}{2}$ in proportion.									
	Piece of 5 Francs of the Convention....	15	5	14	338, 3	3	11,24		†93	
	Piece of 5 Francs (Napoleon) of 1808...	15	12	4	344, 9	4	0.16		†93	7
	Piece of 2 Francs of 1808..............	6	6	2	138, 8	1	7,38		†37	5
	Franc of 1809..........................	3	3	1	69, 4	0	9,69		†18	7
	Demi Franc...........	4	13	6	34, 7	0	4,84		†9	3
	Franc (Louis) of 1818, same as Franc of 1809.									
Germany...	Aix la Chapelle Rathsproesentger..........	2	13	9	56, 9	0	7,94		15	8
	Double ditto............................	5	5	16	116, 3	1	4,24		32	5
	Baden Rixdollar	16	3	1	358, 1	4	2	1		
	Bavaria Rixdollar, Convention of 1780.....	15	22	4	358, 7	4	1,39		97	2
	Rixdollar of 1800.......................	15	13	13	345, 6	4	0,25		95	5
	$\frac{1}{2}$ in proportion.									
	Copstuck	2	16	3	59, 4	0	8,29		16	6
	Bremen Piece of 48 Grotes................	8	22	1	198,	2	3,64		55	3
	Brunswick Rixdollar, Convention..........	16	4	4	359, 2	4	2,15		97	2
	Half Rixdollar.......................	8	2	2	179, 6	2	1,07		50	
	Gulden, or Piece of $\frac{2}{3}$, fine, of 1764......	9	1	1	200, 8	2	4,03		56	
	Gulden, common, of 1764............	8	2	10	180,	2	1,13		50	2
	Gulden, ditto of 1795...............	8	23	7	199, 1	2	3,80		55	6
	Half Gulden, or Piece of $\frac{1}{3}$, of 1764.....	4	1	5	90,	1	0,56		25	1
	Cologne Rixdollar, old....................	16	18	15	372, 5	4	4,01	1	04	
	Rixdollar, Constitution..................	18	4	14	404,	4	8,41	1	12	8
	Rixdollar, Convention.................	15	22	4	353, 7	4	1,39		97	2
	Frankfort Rixdollar, Convention of 1772.....	16	8	16	363, 5	4	2,75		99	8
	Rixdollar, ditto, of 1796................	16	6	0	360, 8	4	2,38		99	

		Standard Weight. dwt.	gr.	mi.	Conts. in pure Sil. grains.	Value in Sterling. s.	d.	Value in Federal. $	c.	m.
Germany....	Hamburg Rixdollar, specie	17	21	12	397, 5	4	,4	1	11	
	Double Mark, or 32 Schillings Piece	9	11	8	210, 3	2	,30		†70	
	Single in proportion.									
	Piece of 8 Schillings	2	6	4	50, 1	0	,09		13	9
	Piece of 4 Schillings	1	6	12	28, 3	0	3,35		7	0
	Hanover Rixdollar, Constitution	18	0	14	400, 3	4	7,89	1	11	
	Florin, or Piece of ⅔, fine	9	0	10	200, 3	2	3,86		55	9
	Half Florin, or Piece of ⅓, ditto	4	11	4	99, 2	1	1,85		27	7
	Quarter, or Piece of 6 good Groschen, do.	2	4	10	48, 6	0	6,73		13	6
	Florin, or Piece of ⅔, base	8	23	15	199, 6	2	3,87		55	7
	Hesse Cassel Rixdollar, Convention	15	22	6	353,	4	1,39		97	2
	Florin, or Piece of ⅔	7	23	3	176, 8	2	0,68		49	4
	½ in proportion.									
	Thaler, or Rixdollar of account of 1778.	12	4	3	270, 3	3	1,74		75	5
	Thaler of 1789	11	17	5	259, 7	3	0,26		72	5
	Ecu, Convention, (1815)	15	21	2	349, 3	4	0,77		96	5
	Six Bon Gros	2	23	0	65, 1	0	9,80		19	6
	Bon Gros	0	11	5	10, 3	0	1,43		2	9
	Liege Ducatoon of 1671	20	22	18	465, 3	5	4,97	1	29	9
	Patagon, old	16	17	14	371, 6	4	3,89	1	3	7
	Patagon of 1792	16	6	11	361, 3	4	2,45	1		
	Escalin of 1771	2	1	6	45, 6	0	6,36		12	7
	Escalin of 1792	1	22	0	42, 6	0	5,94		11	9
	Lorraine Ecu, called Leopold, (1704)	17	5	6	382, 3	4	5,38	1	6	6
	Ecu, (1710)	19	5	10	426, 9	4	11,61	1	19	2
	Lubec Rixdollar, specie	17	15	12	391, 9	4	6,72	1		
	Double Mark	9	11	8	210, 3	2	5,36		58	7
	Mark	4	17	14	105, 1	1	2,67		30	
	Manheim Rixdollar, fine	17	20	6	396, 7	4	7,39	1	10	7
	Florin, or Piece of ⅔, fine	8	22	8	198, 3	2	3,69		55	3
	Rixdollar, Convention	16	4	3	359, 0	4	2,13		97	2
	Mecklenburg Florin, or Piece of ⅔	8	23	5	199, 1	2	3,80		55	
	Mentz Rixdollar	16	6	0	360, 8	4	2,38		98	
	Copstuck	2	16	13	59, 8	0	8,35		16	7
	Nuremberg Rixdollar, Constitution	18	2	15	402, 2	4	8,16	1	12	3
	Rixdollar, Convention	16	4	2	359, 0	4	2,13		97	3
	Copstuck	2	16	13	59, 8	0	8,35		16	7
	Ratisbon Rixdollar, specie	16	4	2	359, 2	4	1,58		97	4
	½, &c. in proportion.									
	Saltzburg Rixdollar, Convention	16	6	0	360, 8	4	2,38		97	2
	24 Creutzer Piece	2	16	4	59, 4	0	8,29		16	3
	Saxony Rixdollar, Convention	16	3	4	358, 2	4	2,01		97	2
	½ and ¼ in proportion.									
	Old Rixdollar of Dresden	17	23	14	399, 3	4	7,75	1	11	5
	Ditto of Leipsic	15	9	16	342,	3	11,75		93	5
	Piece of 16 Groschen of Leipsic	7	14	16	169, 1	1	11,61		47	2
	Piece of 8 Groschen	3	20	8	85, 6	0	11,95		47	9
	Rixdollar current of Saxe Gotha	11	4	2	248. 1	2	10,64		69	3
	1-6 Thaler of 1804	2	0	19	45, 3	0	6,32		12	5
	Ditto of 1808	1	21	8	42, 1	0	5,87		11	7
	Ditto of Jerome Buonaparte of 1809	1	23	6	43, 7	0	6,10		12	2
	Treves Rixdollar, specie	16	4	2	359,	4	2,13		97	2
	Wirtemberg Rixdollar, specie	16	14	2	359, 1	4	2,14		97	2
	Copstuck	2	16	12	59, 8	0	8,35		17	7
	Wurtzburg Rixdollar, specie	16	4	16	359, 7	4	2,22		97	3
	Copstuck	2	16	6	59, 3	0	8,28		16	6
***Holland**, now called Netherlands..*	Ducatoon	21	4	15	471, 6	5	5,85	1	30	7
	Piece of 3 Florins	20	2	12	446, 4	5	2,33	1	24	7
	Piece of 3 Florins of Batavia	19	15	0	435, 7	5	0,84	1	21	7
	Rixdollar (the Assay varies)	16	20	8	375, 9	4	4,99	1	6	
	Daalder, or 30 Stiver Piece	9	18	18	217, 3	2	6,34		60	7
	Half Rixdollar	8	8	8	185, 4	2	1,89		51	7
	Florin, or Guilder	6	14	14	146, 8	1	8,49		*40	
	½ in proportion.									
	12 Stiver Piece	4	3	18	92, 4	1	0,90		25	8
	Sesthalf, or 5½ Stiver Piece	1	17	4	38, 1	0	5,32		10	6
	8 Stiver Piece	2	18	8	61, 5	0	8,58		17	2
	Florin of Batavia	6	9	2	141, 6	1	7,77		*40	
	Rixdollar, or 50 Stiver Piece of the Kingdom of Holland	16	13	18	367, 9	4	3,37	1	2	7
***Italy**.......*	Genoa Scudo della croce	25	11	8	565, 5	6	6,96	1	57	9
	Scudo di S. Giambatista of 5 Lire	13	5	12	293, 8	3	5,02		82	

		Standard Weight. dwt.	gr.	mi.	Conts. in pure Sil. grains.	Value in Sterling. s.	d.	Value in Federal. $	c.	m.
Italy..........	Double Madonnina..................	[illegible]	[illegible]	12	116, 2	1	4,22		32	4
	Single and half in proportion.									
	Scudo of 8 Lire, of 1796	20	14	10	457, 4	5	3,87	1	27	7
	½, ¼, &c. in proportion.									
	Scudo of the Ligurian Republic	20	11	2	454, 3	5	3,43	1	26	9
	Lucca Scudo..........................	16	18	10	372, 3	4	3,98	1	02	7
	Mezzo, or ½ Scudo	8	0	7	177, 9	2	0,84		51	3
	Terzo, or ⅓ Scudo..................	5	17	2	126, 8	1	5,70		34	4
	Quinto, or 1-5 Scudo...............	3	3	19	70, 3	0	9,81		20	6
	Barbone............................	1	7		29, 3	0	4,09		8	2
	Milan Scudo of 6 Lire................	14	9		319, 6	3	8,62		89	2
	½ in proportion.									
	Lira, new..........................	2	9	0	52, 8	0	7,37		14	7
	Lira, old..........................	2	9	4	52, 9	0	7,38		14	8
	Piece of 30 Soldi, Francis II..........	3	11	8	77, 2	0	10,78		21	5
	Scudo of the Cisalpine Republic.......	14	10	4	320, 2	3	8,71		89	4
	Piece of 30 Soldi of ditto............	3	11	8	77, 2	0	10,78		21	5
	Modena Scudo of 15 Lire, of 1739..........	17	8	9	385, 2	4	5,78	1	7	5
	Double, &c. in proportion.									
	Scudo of 5 Lire, of 1782	5	17	2	126, 8	1	5,70		35	
	Scudo of 1796..........................	12	22	12	287, 4	3	4,13		80	3
	Naples Ducat, old......................	13	17	18	305, 2	3	6,61		85	2
	½ in proportion.									
	Piece of 12 Carlini (before 1784)........	15	18	12	350, 3	4	0,91		97	8
	Ducat, new..........................	13	7	8	295, 4	3	5,24		82	5
	½ in proportion.									
	Piece of 12 Carlini of 1792............	16	0	18	356,	4	1,71		99	4
	Ditto of 1796..........................	15	22	12	353, 9	4	1,41		98	8
	Ditto of the Neapolitan Republic (1799).	15	22	12	353, 9	4	1,41		98	8
	Ditto of 1805	15	23	18	355, 2	4	1,60		99	2
	½ in proportion.									
	Ditto of 10 Carlini (1818)..............	13	7	0	295, 1	3	5,20		82	4
	Parma Ducat, of 1784..................	15	18	18	350, 6	4	0,95		97	9
	Ducat of 1796........................	16	2	18	357, 9	4	1,97		99	9
	½ in proportion.									
	Piece of 3 Lire........................	4	2	2	90, 7	1	0,66		25	3
	Piedmont Scudo (1690)	17	3	12	380, 7	4	5,16	1	06	3
	Scudo (1733)	18	20	16	418, 8	4	10,48	1	16	9
	Scudo (1755)..........................	22	0	16	488, 9	5	8,26	1	36	5
	½, &c. in proportion.									
	Scudo (1770)..........................	22	1	16	490, 0	5	8,42	1	36	8
	½ and ¼ in proportion.									
	Piece of 2 Lire (1714)................	7	16	13	170, 8	1	11,85		47	7
	5 Franc Piece (1801)	15	11	12	343, 7	3	11,99		95	9
	Ragusa Tallaro, or Ragusina (1759)...	11	13	2	256, 4	2	11,80		71	6
	Ditto (1774)........................	11	9	16	253, 3	2	11,37		70	7
	Ditto (1794)........................	12	1	6	267, 7	3	1,38		74	7
	Ducat (1797)........................	4	8	16	97,	1	1,54		27	1
	Rome Scudo, or Crown (before 1753).......	20	2	2	446,	5	2,27	1	24	5
	Testone, old.	5	18	2	127, 8	1	5,84		35	7
	Paolo, old.	1	21	16	42, 4	0	5,92		11	8
	Scudo, or Crown (coined since 1753)...	16	17	13	371, 5	4	3,87	1	3	7
	Mezzo Scudo, or half Crown..........	8	8	16	185, 7	2	1,93		51	8
	Testone (1770)	5	0	0	111, 1	1	3,51		31	
	Ditto (1785)	4	23	4	110, 3	1	3,40		30	8
	Paolo (1785)	1	16	4	37, 2	0	5,19		10	2
	Grosso, or Half Paolo, (1785)...........	0	20	0	18, 5	0	2,58		5	1
	Papetto (1775)........................	3	6	12	72, 7	0	10,15		20	3
	Scudo of the Roman Republic (1799)...	16	13	18	368, 1	4	3,40	1	2	8
	Scudo of Bologna (Pius VI.)..........	16	19	8	373, 2	4	4,11	1	4	2
	Testone ditto........................	5	0	6	111, 5	1	3,56		31	1
	Scudo of the City of Bologna..........	17	6	18	383, 9	4	5,60	1	7	2
	Ditto of Pius VII (1800)..............	16	21	4	371, 5	4	3,78	1	5	5
	Sicilian Scudo..........................	15	16	6	348, 2	4	0,62		97	2
	½ in proportion.									
	Piece of 40 Grains..................	5	7	2	117, 5	1	4,40		32	8
	Ditto of 20 Grains..................	2	15	18	59, 1	0	8,25		16	5
	Tuscany Ducatone (1676)................	20	17	4	460,	5	4,23	1	28	5
	Livornina (1723)....................	17	4	13	381, 7	4	5,30	1	6	6
	Pezza della rosa (1726)...............	16	14	2	368, 2	4	3,41	1	2	8
	Francescone (1738)..................	17	9	14	386, 4	4	5,95	1	7	9
	½ in proportion.									

		Standard Weight. dwt. gr. mi.	Conts. in pure Sil. grains.	Value in Sterling. s. d	Value in Federal. $ c. m.
Italy	Leopoldone (1790)	17 7 8	384, 3	4 5,66	1 7 3
	Piece of 10 Paoli of the Kingdom of Etruria (1801)	17 5 18	382, 9	4 5,46	1 6 9
	Scudo Pisa of ditto (1803)	17 8 4	385, 0	4 5,76	1 7 5
	Piece of 10 Lire ditto (1803)	26 1 12	578, 7	6 8,80	1 61 6
	Ditto of 5 Lire ditto (1803)	13 0 18	289, 4	3 4,41	80 8
	Lira (1803)	2 9 16	53, 4	0 7,45	14 9
	Venitian Scudo della Croce	20 15 8	458, 2	5 3,98	1 27 9
	Giustina, or Ducatone	17 22 8	398, 1	4 6,47	1 8 9
	Ducato*	12 15 8	280, 8	3 3,21	78 4
	Lirazza, or Piece of 30 Soldi	2 0 10	44, 9	0 6,26	12 5
	Tallaro	16 12 16	367, 1	4 3,26	1 2 5
	½, &c. in proportion.				
	Osella	6 9 16	142, 3	1 7,87	39 7
	Scudo of 10 Lire (1797)	16 10 16	365, 2	4 2,99	1 1 9
	Piece of 2 Lire, or 24 Creutzers (1800)	1 12 2	33, 4	0 4,66	9 3
	Ditto of 1 Lira	0 18 7	16, 9	0 2,35	4 7
	Ditto of 2 Lire, called Moneta Provinciale (1808)	1 11 8	32, 8	0 4,58	9 2
	Ditto of 1 Lira	0 18 8	17, 5	0 2,44	4 9
	Ditto of 2 Lire (1802)	1 8 19	30, 5	0 4,25	8 5
	½ and ¼ in proportion.				
Malta	Ounce of 30 Tari of Emmanuel Pinto	15 4 14	337, 4	3 11,11	94 2
	Ounce of Emmanuel de Rohan	17 2 2	379, 3	4 4,96	1 3 9
	½ in proportion.				
	Scudo of the same	6 5 0	137, 9	1 7,25	38 5
	Double in proportion.				
	Ounce of Ferdinand Hompesch	17 4 3	381, 3	4 5,24	1 6 5
	2 Tari Piece	0 19 2	17, 7	0 2,47	4 9
Netherlands, now called Belgium	Ducatoon, old	21 9 0	474, 6	5 6,27	1 32 5
	Ducatoon of Maria Theresa	20 1 12	445, 5	5 2,20	1 24 4
	Crown	17 19 4	395, 2	4 7,18	1 10 3
	½, &c. in proportion.				
	Escalin	1 23 8	43, 8	0 6,11	12 2
	Double in proportion.				
	Plaquette	0 21 12	20,	0 2,79	5 6
	5 Stiver Piece	1 9 18	31, 3	0 4,37	8 7
	Silver Lion of 1790	19 21 6	441, 5	5 1,65	1 23 3
	Florin of 1790	5 14 9	124, 3	1 5,35	34 7
	Piece of 10 Stivers of 1790	2 18 6	61, 8	0 8,62	17 2
	Florin of 1816	6 16 6	148, 4	1 8,72	17 4
	Half Florin	3 9 2	75,	0 10,46	20 9
	Divisions in proportion.				
Poland	Rixdollar, old	16 6 0	360, 8	4 2,38	1 0 8
	Rixdollar, new (1794)	11 11 6	254, 3	2 11,51	71
	Florin, or Gulden	3 18 16	84,	0 11,72	23 4
Portugal	New Crusado (1690)	10 19 0	239, 2	2 9,40	66 8
	Ditto (1718)	9 1 0	200, 2	2 3,95	55 9
	Ditto (1795)	9 1 18	201, 6	2 4,15	56 3
	Doze Vintems, or Piece of 240 Rees (1799)	4 12 10	100, 4	1 2,01	28
	Testoon (1799)	1 22 18	43, 4	0 6,06	12 1
	New Crusado (1802)	8 23 16	199, 7	2 3,88	55 7
	Ditto (1809)	8 23 0	198, 2	2 4,67	57 3
	Seis Vintems, or Piece of 120 Rees (1802)	2 2 8	46, 6	0 6,50	13
	Testoon (1802)	1 22 0	42, 5	0 5,93	11 9
	Tres Vintems, or Piece of 60 Rees (1802)	1 1 4	23, 3	0 3,25	6 5
	Half Testoon (1802)	0 22 0	20, 4	0 2,84	5 7
Portuguese Col. or Brazil	Pataca of Brazil, old, of 640 Rees	12 2 2	268, 3	3 1,46	74 9
	Ditto of 600 Rees (1755)	11 2 12	246, 6	2 10,43	68 9
	Ditto of 640 Rees (1768)	11 8 14	252, 3	2 11,23	70 5
	Ditto of 640 Rees (1801)	11 19 10	262, 2	3 0,61	73 2
	½ and ¼ in proportion.				
	Piece of 12 Macutas, of Portuguese Africa	10 22 18	243, 2	2 9,96	67 9
	Ditto of 8 ditto	7 4 14	159, 8	1 10,31	44 6
	Ditto of 6 ditto	5 7 12	118,	1 4,47	32 9

* The Venitian Silver Ducats vary in weight from 13 dwts. 18 grs. to 14 dwts. 19 grs.; some (of 1763) weighing only 13 dwts. 10 grs. The fineness also varies from W. 1 oz. 6 dwts. to W. 1 oz. 3¾ dwts.

		Standard Weight. dwt	gr.	mi.	Conts. in pure Sil. grains.	Value in Sterling. s.	d.	Value in Federal. $	c.	m.
Portuguese Colonies, or Brazil	Ditto of 4 ditto	3	12	8	78, 1	0	10,90		21	8
Prussia	Florin, old, of the Elector of Brandenburg	9	5	11	204, 9	2	4,61		57	2
	*Rixdollar, Prussian currency	11	9	0	252, 6	2	11,27		70	5
	½ in proportion.									
	Rixdollar, Convention	16	4	2	359,	4	2,13		97	2
	Florin, or Piece of ⅔	8	22	8	198, 4	2	3,70		55	4
	Florin of Silesia	7	16	0	170, 3	1	11,78		47	5
	Drittel, or Piece of 8 good Groschen	3	20	4	85, 3	0	11,91		47	8
	Piece of 4 Groschen	1	20	10	41, 2	0	5,75		11	5
	Piece of 6 Groschen	2	19	6	62, 3	0	8,69		17	3
	Rixdollar, old, of Bareuth	10	1	6	223, 3	2	7,18		62	3
	Piece of ⅔ ditto	6	2	18	135, 9	1	6,97		37	9
	Piece of 30 Creutzers ditto	3	7	16	73, 8	0	10,30		20	6
	Rixdollar, old, of Anspach	11	6	18	250, 6	2	10,99		69	9
	Piece of ⅔ ditto	7	2	14	158,	1	10,06		44	1
	Rixdollar of Anspach and Bareuth Convention	16	4	2	359,	4	2,22		97	2
Russia	Ruble of Peter the Great	14	1	8	312, 1	3	7,58		84	
	Ditto of Catherine I. (1725)	13	23	0	309, 9	3	7,27		83	5
	Ditto of Peter II. (1727)	13	23	4	310,	3	7,28		83	5
	Ditto of Anne (1734)	14	6	16	317, 2	3	8,29		85	4
	Ditto of Elizabeth (1750)	14	11	16	321, 8	3	8,93		87	7
	Ditto of Peter III. (1762,	12	12	0	277, 5	3	2,75		74	7
	Ditto of Catherine II. (1780)	12	10	6	275, 9	3	2,52		74	3
	Ditto of Paul (1799)	12	15	10	280. 8	3	3 21		75	6
	Ditto of Alexander (1802)	17	7	2	273,	3	2,12		74	
	Ditto of ditto (1805)	12	12	12	278, 1	3	2,83		74	9
	Poltin, or ½ Ruble of Anne	6	19	8	151, 2	1	9,11		42	7
	Ditto of Elizabeth	7	1	10	156, 8	1	9,89		43	8
	Ditto of Catharine II	6	5	2	137, 9	1	7,25		37	1
	Ditto of Paul	6	7	2	139, 7	1	7,50		37	8
	Ditto of Alexander (1804)	6	3	10	136, 5	1	7 06		37	
	Polpoltin, or ¼ Ruble, old	3	4	18	71, 1	0	9.92		19	
	Ditto of Paul	3	0	8	67,	0	9,35		18	
	Ditto of Alexander (1802)	3	4	10	70, 8	0	9,88		19	
	20 Copeck Piece (1767)	2	19	0	62. 6	0	8 74		17	
	Ditto (1784)	2	12	18	56, 2	0	7,84		15	6
	15 Copeck Piece (1778)	1	19	18	40, 5	0	5 65		11	3
	10 Copeck Piece	1	14	16	35, 9	0	5,11		11	2
	Ditto (1798)	1	6	16	28, 5	0	3 97		7	
	Ditto (1802)	1	6	11	28. 3	0	3 95		7	
	5 Copeck Piece (1801)	0	15	10	15, 3	0	2,13		4	2
Sardinia	Scudo, or Crown	14	15	0	324, 7	3	9,34		90	7
	½ and ¼ in proportion.									
Sierra Leone Company	Piece of 10 Macutas	14	21	12	330, 8	3	10.19		92	4
	Ditto of 5 Macutas	7	12	18	167, 4	1	11.37		46	7
	Ditto of 2 Macutas	2	22	6	65,	0	9 07		18	1
	Ditto of 1 Macuta	1	11	8	32, 5	0	4,53		9	1
Spain	Dollar, old Mexican square (1747)	16	22	10	376, 1	4	4.51	†1		
	Half ditto	8	11	5	188,	2	2,25		†50	
	Dollar, old, called Sevillan (1731)	16	22	10	376, 1	4	4.51	†1		
	Old Mexican Peceta of 2 Mexican Reals (1736)	4	5	2	93. 6	1	1.07		†25	
	Real of Mexican Plate (1746)	2	2	11	46. 8	0	6,53		†12	5
	Dollar, Mexican, with globes and pillars (1765)	17	0	0	377, 4	4	4 79	†1		
	Peceta of two Reals of Plate (1721)	3	5	14	71, 9	0	10,04		†16	
	Real of Plate (1721)	1	14	19	35, 9	0	5 01		†8	
	Dollar,‡ of late coinage	16	17	0	370, 9	4	3,79	†1		
	Half Dollar, ditto	8	8	10	185, 4	2	1,88		†50	
	Mexican Peceta (1774)	4	3	16	92. 3	1	0,88		†25	
	Real of Mexican Plate (1775)	2	1	20	46, 1	0	6 43		†12	5
	Peceta Provincial of 2 Reals of new plate (1775)	3	6	0	72, 2	0	10.08		†16	
	Real of new plate (1795)	1	15	0	36, 1	0	5,04		†8	
Sweden	Rixdollar (1762)	17	19	10	395. 5	4	7 22	1	10	4
	Rixdollar of late coinage	17	12	0	388, 5	4	6,22	1	8	5

* The Prussian Coins having been debased at different periods vary in their reports.

‡ This is the coin which is universally circulated under the name of the Spanish Dollar.

		Standard Weight.			Conts. in pure Sil.	Value in Sterling.		Value in Federal.		
		dwt.	gr.	mi.	grains.	s.	d.	$	c.	m.
Sweden........	Double Plott, or Piece of ⅔...........	11	16	12	259, 6	3	0,25		72	5
	Single Plott, or Piece of ⅓.............	5	20	6	129, 8	1	6,12		36	2
	Piece of 8 Skillings....................	2	21	2	63, 8	0	8,90		17	8
	Ditto of 4 Skillings.....................	1	14	0	31, 5	0	4,95		9	9
Switzerland.....	Ecu, or Rixdollar of Lucerne (1715)...	16	5	8	360, 1	4	2,28	1	0	5
	½, &c. in proportion.									
	Old Gulden, or Florin of Lucerne (1714)	7	2	8	157, 5	1	9,99		43	9
	Ecu of 40 Batzen of Lucerne (1796).....	18	13	14	412, 3	4	9,57	1	15	1
	Half Ditto..............................	8	20	12	196, 7	2	3,46		54	9
	Florin, or Piece of 40 Skillings of Lucerne (1793)....................	4	8	14	96, 8	1	1,51		27	
	Half Florin of Lucerne..............	2	3	0	47, 3	0	6,60		13	2
	Piece of 10 Batzen (1782)............	4	3	14	92, 2	1	0,68		25	3
	Quarter Rixdollar of Friburg..........	5	0	18	111, 9	1	3,62		31	2
	Piece of ⅛ Rixdollar of Ditto...........	2	10	0	53, 6	0	7,48		14	9
	Piece of 20 Batzen of Soleure.........	8	20	12	196, 7	2	3,46		54	9
	Ditto of 10 Batzen of Ditto............	4	13	0	101, 5	1	2,17		28	3
	Ecu of 40 Batzen of the Helvetic Republic (1798)..................	18	10	14	409, 5	4	9,18	1	14	3
	½ in proportion.									
	Piece of 10 Batzen....................	4	13	17	100, 5	1	2,03		28	1
	Ditto of 5 Batzen......................	2	5	8	49, 3	0	6,88		13	7
	Ecu of 4 Franken (1801)..............	18	8	12	407, 6	4	9,18	1	10	3
	Basil Patagon, or Ecu, old................	17	0	10	377, 9	4	4,76	1	5	5
	Thaler, or Rixdollar, of 1763..........	13	10	10	298, 4	3	5,66		83	3
	Patagon, or Ecu, of 1795...............	15	1	5	334, 3	3	10,68		93	4
	Double, &c. in proportion.									
	Piece of 10 Batzen....................	4	12	4	100, 1	1	1,97		27	9
	Bern Patagon, or Crown....................	8	7	14	406, 7	4	8,79	1	13	5
	¼ in proportion.									
	Piece of 10 Batzen....................	4	14	17	102, 5	1	2,31		28	6
	Piece of 5 Batzen......................	2	3	2	47, 2	0	6,59		13	2
	Geneva Patagon............................	15	19	8	351,	4	1,03		98	1
	Piece of 21 Sous........................	2	11	5	54, 8	0	7,65		15	3
	Piece of 12 Florins 9 Sous, called Genevoise, or Gros Ecu, (1794)..........	18	4	16	404,	4	8,41	1	12	8
	Ditto of 1796............................	18	9	6	408, 2	4	9	1	14	
	½ in proportion.									
	Piece of 15 Sous of 1794.............	1	15	1	36, 1	0	5,04		10	
	Neufchatel Piece of 21 Batzen.............	8	11	0	187, 8	2	2,22		52	4
	Piece of 10½ Batzen...................	4	5	10	93, 9	1	1,11		26	2
	St. Gall Rixdollar..........................	16	2	4	357, 3	4	1,98	1		
	½ in proportion.									
	24 Creutzer Piece......................	2	17	2	60, 2	0	8,40		16	8
	Zurich Rixdollar, or Ecu (1753)...........	16	21	8	375,	4	4,36	1	4	7
	Half Rixdollar (1753)..................	8	4	12	181, 8	2	1,28		50	7
	Ecu (1761)................................	15	22	14	354,	4	1,43		98	9
	Half Ecu (1761).........................	7	21	4	175,	2	0,43		48	9
	Ecu (1773)................................	15	14	18	346, 8	4	0,42		96	8
	Half Ecu (1773).........................	7	19	9	173, 4	2	0.21		48	4
	Ecu (1794)................................	14	19	18	329, 3	3	9,98		91	9
	Half Ecu (1786).........................	7	10	10	165, 2	1	11,06		46	1
	Piece of 20 Schillings (1798)..........	2	14	6	57, 6	0	8,04		16	1
Turkey.........	Altmichlic of 60 Paras (1757)..........	11	16	0	259,	3	0,16		72	3
	Piastre of Mustapha III. (1775)........	7	6	0	161,	1	10,48		44	9
	Altmichlic of 1773......................	10	6	12	228, 1	2	7,85		63	7
	Piastre of Abdul-hamed, 1773.........	6	15	8	147, 5	1	8 59		41	2
	Another of the same period...........	7	4	10	159, 6	1	10.28		44	6
	Piece of 100 Paras of Selim (1789)......	10	8	4	229, 7	2	8 07		40	1
	Double Piastre of ditto	8	9	10	186, 4	2	2.03		28	
	Piastre of Selim of 1801..............	4	7	8	95, 7	1	1,36		26	7
	Half Piastre............................	1	14	16	35, 9	0	5,01		10	
	Piastre of Crim Tartary, 1778	4	2	4	90, 9	1	0.69		24	3
	Piastre of Tunis, 1787.................	4	8	6	96, 5	1	1,47		26	9
	Piastre, 1818............................	3	1	4	67, 7	0	9,45		18	9
	Beshlie....................................	12	10	8	276,	3	2,54		77	
	Piece of Ten Paras.....................	8	14	0	7, 5	0	1,04		24	1
United States...	Dollar, 1795..............................	16	19	16	373, 5	4	4,15	†1		
	½, &c. in proportion.									

		Standard Weight. dwt. gr. mi.	Conts. in pure Sil. grains.	Value in Sterling s. d.	Value in Federal. $ c. m.
United States ..	Dollar, 1798	16 21 6	374, 9	4 4,35	†1
	Dollar, 1802	16 14 0	368, 3	4 3,42	†1
	Dollar, an average of 8 years	17 8 0	371, 2	4 3,68	†1
	Half & quarter in proportion.				
	Dollar of 1837 and subsequent	17 4 10	371, 2	4 3,	1
	Half & quarter in proportion.				
	Dime, or 1-10 Dollar, 1796	1 18 14	37, 5	0 5,71	†10
	Half Dime, 1796	0 21 0	18, 5	0 2,72	†5
	Dime of 1837	1 17 5	37, 2	5, 5	†10
	EAST INDIES.				
East India	Rupee of Mohammed Shah	7 14 9	168, 7	1 11,55	47 1
	.... of Ahmed Shah	7 18 16	172, 8	2 0,12	48 2
	.... of Ahmed Ghir, 1759	7 22 0	175, 8	2 0,54	49
	.... of Shah Allum, 1772	7 21 4	175,	2 0,43	48 9
	.... of the same, Benares, 1774	7 13 0	167, 5	1 11,38	46 8
	.... of the same, 1779	7 23 8	176, 8	2 0,68	49 3
	.... Benares, 1818	7 14 5	168, 9	1 11,58	47 2
	.... Sicca, coined by the East India Company at Calcutta	7 22 0	175, 8	2 0,54	*50
	.... Calcutta, 1818	8 0 0	175, 9	2 0 56	*50
	.... Arcot, 1759	7 14 16	169, 1	1 11,61	47 2
	.... Ditto, 1782	7 12 4	166, 8	1 11,29	46 6
	.... Ditto, 1788	7 15 12	169, 8	1 11,71	47 4
	.... Ditto, of the latest coinages	7 12 2	166, 5	1 11,25	46 5
	.... Bombay, old	7 21 4	174, 9	2 0,42	48 8
	.... Bombay, new, or Surat, 1818	7 10 4	164, 7	1 11,01	46
	.... Lucknow	7 12 2	166, 5	1 11,25	46 5
	.... Sultanny	7 12 0	166, 3	1 11,22	46 4
	.... Madepoor, or Nowsee	7 1 16	157, 1	1 9 93	43 9
	.... Madras Rajapoor	7 10 4	164, 8	1 11,01	46
	.... Jeypoor	7 16 8	170, 6	1 11,82	47 6
	.... Furruckabad, 1818	7 10 14	165, 3	1 11,07	46 1
	.... Chanderry	7 4 8	159, 5	1 10,27	44 5
	.... Oukery	6 14 0	146, 9	1 8,51	41
	.... Shree Sicca of Poona	7 3 6	158, 5	1 10,13	44 3
	.... Halee Sicca	7 17 2	171, 2	1 11,90	47 8
	.... Ougein	7 10 4	164, 8	1 11,01	46
	.... Maisore, or new Holkar	7 10 8	165, 1	1 11,05	46 1
	.... Indore Holkar	7 8 6	163, 1	1 10,77	45 5
	.... Chinsouree	7 6 6	161, 2	1 10,50	45
	.... Broach, old	7 0 10	164, 3	1 10,94	45 9
	.... Broach, new	7 1 18	157, 2	1 9 95	43 9
	.... Brodera, old	7 6 17	161, 8	1 10,59	45 2
	.... Brodera, new	7 2 2	157, 3	1 9,96	43 9
	.... Ana Sai, coined at Cairo	6 23 14	155, 1	1 9,65	43 3
	.... Ana Sai, coined at Pitlad	6 19 4	151,	1 9 08	42
	.... Amedabad Sicca	7 3 18	159, 1	1 10,21	44 5
	.... Mungull Sai	7 2 4	157, 4	1 9,97	43 9
	.... Mumo Sai	7 2 14	157, 9	1 10,04	44 1
	.... Seea Sai, coined in Futty Sing's time	7 0 4	155, 6	1 9,72	43 4
	.... Cambay	6 19 2	150, 9	1 9 07	42 1
	.... Persian, 1745	7 19 10	173, 5	2 0,22	48 4
	.... Dittto 1789	7 20 0	173, 9	2 0,28	48 6
	.... Madras, 1818	7 12 0	165,	1 11,04	46 1
	Fanam, Cananore	1 11 10	32, 9	0 4,5	9
	.... Bombay, old	1 13 16	35,	0 4,88	9 7
	.... Pondicherry	1 1 2	22, 8	0 3,18	6 4
	.... Ditto, double	1 18 2	39,	0 5,44	10 9
	Larin	3 6 0	72, 1	0 10,06	20 1
	Bussora Crux	5 7 14	118, 1	1 4,49	32 9
	Gulden of the Dutch East India Company, 1820	6 16 6	148, 4	1 8,72	41 4

CHAPTER XXVI.

WEIGHTS AND MEASURES.

UNITED STATES.

THE authority to establish a uniform system of weights and measures was conferred upon congress, at the organization of the federal government. But no laws have as yet been passed by that body for that purpose. Some steps have been taken to obtain information, and elaborate reports have been made by Mr. Jefferson, Mr. Adams, and Mr. Hassler, upon this important subject. Standard weights and measures, similar to those in use in England before 1825, have been prepared by Mr. Hassler, for the use of the custom-house, and a complete set furnished to the governor of each of the states.[a]

No reform in the system of weights and measures, however, has been made, and the old English system, with such modifications as provincial customs or state laws have engrafted upon it, may be regarded as that adopted in the United States.

The weights are Troy and avoirdupois.

The measures of capacity are wine or beer for fluids, and dry or coal measures for other substances.

There is also long and square measure for cloth and land, and cubic measure for solid substances or for wood.

Weights.—The weights are those denominated the Troy and avoirdupois weights. The Troy and avoirdupois weights are nearly in the proportions to each other of the specific gravity of wheat and spring water, viz. as 5760 to 7000. An avoirdupois pound = 7000 grains Troy. Troy weight is divided as follows:

24 grains are equal	to a pennyweight.
20 pennyweights	to an ounce, and
12 ounces	to a pound = 5760 grains.

Troy weights are used for gold, silver, medicine, &c.

8 lbs. Troy are considered as equal to a gallon; 16 lbs. equal to a peck; and 64 lbs. to a bushel, where weight and measure are reduced into each other.

In the avoirdupois weight are reckoned 16 drachms, or drams, equal to 1 ounce; 16 ounces equal to 1 pound; 28 pounds equal to 1 quarter of a hundred weight, or of 112 pounds; and 20 hundred weight equal to 1 ton in weight.

This weight is used for all gross goods, as butter, cheese, sugar, hemp, flax, &c., and is the pound of commerce. That used at the custom-house is derived from the Troy pound in the mint according to the above proportion.

Diamonds and other precious stones are weighed by carats, the

---

[a] Resolution, 14th June, 1836.

carat being divided into 4 grains, and the grain into 16 parts. The diamond carat weighs $3\frac{1}{5}$ grains Troy.

Liquid measures.—Liquid measure is derived from the pound Troy, as well as the measure of grain; 12 ounces or a pound being considered as equal to a pint, and 8 pints equal to a gallon (containing 231 cubic inches) of wine, brandy, cider, &c., of which the standard is preserved in the state department at Washington.

The English wine measures are smaller than those of beer, and are proportioned as four to five; hence, 4 gallons beer measure are nearly equal to 5 gallons wine measure; of which latter a gallon is 231 cubic inches, and weighs 8 pounds, 5 ounces, and $6\frac{1}{4}$ drams, avoirdupois, of rain-water. A beer gallon contains 282 cubic inches, and weighs 10lb. 2oz. $11\frac{1}{2}$dr.

* *Wine measure.*	*London beer measure.*
2 pints are one quart.	8 pints are one gallon.
4 quarts are one gallon.	9 gallons, one firkin.
42 gallons, one tierce.	18 gallons, one kilderkin.
63 gallons, one hogshead.	36 gallons, one barrel.
84 gallons, one puncheon.	54 gallons, one hogshead.
2 hogsheads, one pipe or butt.	27 gallons, one half hogshead.
2 pipes or butts, one tun, or 252 gallons.	The tun of beer = 2 butts, or 4 hogsheads, or 6 barrels.

In a tun of wine are	*In a barrel of beer are*
2 pipes or butts.	2 kilderkins.
3 puncheons.	4 firkins.
4 hogsheads.	36 gallons.
6 tierces.	72 pottles.
252 gallons.	144 quarts.
504 pottles.	256 pints.
1008 quarts.	
2016 pints, and it weighs	
2016 pounds Troy.	

Vinegar is measured as wine; but the measures for brandy vary. From France, Spain and Portugal, brandy is usually shipped in large casks, called pipes, butts and pieces, according to the places whence they are exported; and differing in their contents, not only from one another, but very often among those embarked at the same place.

Olive oil is also shipped in casks of various sizes, according to the custom of the places where it is embarked, and for the conveniency of stowage. Gallipoli, Leghorn, France, Majorca, and several parts of Spain and Portugal, supply the northern parts of Europe with this commodity, as well for eating as for cleansing woollens, and for making soap. In England it is sold by the tun of 236 gallons, and at Amsterdam by the tun of 717 mingles, or 1434 pints; the casks in

* The wine and ale gallon bear the same proportion to each other as the Troy and avoirdupois.

which it is imported contain from 20 to 70 steckans, at 16 mingles a steckan, the mingle weighing 2 lbs. and from 2 to 4 ounces, according to the place of the oil's growth.

The hogshead of molasses should contain 100 gallons wine measure.

Dry measure.

4 gills are - - - -	1 pint	2 bushels are - -	1 strike.
2 pints - - - - - -	1 quart.	4 bushels - - -	1 coom.
2 quarts - - - -	1 pottle.	2 coom or 8 bush.	1 quarter.
2 pottles - - - - -	1 gallon.	4 quarter - - -	1 chaldron.
2 gallons - - - -	1 peck.	5 quarters - - -	1 wey or load.
4 pecks - - - - - -	1 bushel.	2 weys - - -	1 last.

The Winchester bushel, which is the measure for corn and seeds, should be $18\frac{1}{2}$ inches wide, and 8 inches deep. Its contents are, therefore, 2150.42 cubic inches. Corn and seeds are measured by striking the bushel from the brim, with a round piece of light wood, about two inches in diameter, and of equal thickness from one end to the other. All other dry goods are heaped.

Coal measure.

4 pecks are equal to - - - - -	1 bushel.
12 bushels - - - - - - -	1 sack.
3 sacks - - - - - - -	1 vat.
4 vats, or 12 sacks, or 36 bushels - -	1 chaldron.
21 chaldrons - - - - - -	1 score.

The coal bushel holds one Winchester quart more than the Winchester bushel; it therefore contains 2217.62 cubic inches. This bushel must be $19\frac{1}{2}$ inches wide from outside to outside, and 8 inches deep. In measuring coal, it is to be heaped up in the form of a cone, at the heighth of at least 6 inches above the brim. The outside of the bushel must be the extremity of the cone, and thus the bushel should contain at least 2814.9 cubic inches. Hence, the chaldron should measure 58.64 cubic feet.

Long measure.—3 barleycorns = 1 inch; 12 inches = 1 foot; 3 feet = 1 yard; 2 yards = 1 fathom; $5\frac{1}{2}$ yards, or $16\frac{1}{2}$ feet = 1 pole or perch; 40 poles = 1 furlong; 8 furlongs = 1 mile or 1760 yards; $69\frac{1}{10}$ miles = 60 geographical or sea miles, or 1 degree of latitude; 3 miles = 1 league.

An ell English is $1\frac{1}{4}$ yards; an ell Flemish $\frac{3}{4}$ yard; an ell French $1\frac{1}{2}$ yards.

Square or land measure.—144 square inches = 1 foot; 9 feet = 1 yard; $30\frac{1}{4}$ yards = 1 perch; 40 perches = 1 rood; 4 roods = 1 acre, or 43.560 square feet; 640 acres = 1 square mile.

Land is usually measured by a chain of 4 poles, or 100 links. The pole = 22 yards or 792 inches.

Cubic measure.—Wood is measured in the United States by the cord of 8 feet in length, 4 feet high, and 4 feet wide.

In measuring timber, 48 cubic feet make 1 ton of shipping; 40 feet of rough timber, or 50 feet of hewn timber, make a load.

In enumerating articles in England, the following denominations are used; most of them are also used in the United States:

A quire of paper is 24 sheets.
A ream of paper 20 quires.
A ream of paper, perfect, is 21½ quires.
A bale of paper 10 reams.
A roll of parchment or vellum, 5 dozen, or 60 skins.
A dicker of hides, 10 skins.
A dicker of gloves, 10 dozen pair.
A last of hides, 20 dickers.
A load of timber, unhewn, 40 feet.
A load of square timber, 50 feet.
A load of 1 inch plank, 600 square feet.
A load of 1½ inch plank, 400 square feet.
A load of 2 inch plank, 300 square feet.
A load of 2½ inch plank, 240 square feet.
A load of 3 inch plank, 200 square feet.
A load of 3½ inch plank, 170 square feet.
A load of 4 inch plank, 150 square feet.
A hundred of deals, 120.
A chaldron of coals, 36 bushels.
A hogshead of wine, 63 gallons.
A hogshead of beer, 54 gallons.
A barrel of beer, 34 gallons; but, within the bills of mortality, 36 gallons.
A barrel of ale, 32 gallons.
A gross, 144, or 12 dozen.
A wey of cheese, 236 pounds.
Eight gallons, a bushel of corn.
Eight bushels of corn, a quarter.
A last of corn or rape seed, 10 quarters, or 80 bushels.
A last of pot-ash, cod-fish, white herrings, meal, pitch and tar, 12 barrels—of salt, 18 barrels.
A last of flax and feathers, 17 cwt.—of gunpowder, 24 barrels, or 2400 lbs.—of wool, 4361 lbs.
A faggot of steel, 120 lbs.
A burden of gad steel, 180 lbs.
A seam of glass, 24 stone of 5 lbs. each, or 120 lbs.
A puncheon of prunes, 10 to 12 cwt.
A gallon of train oil, 7½ lbs.
A tun of wine, 252 gallons.
An anker of wine, 9 gallons.
A rundlet of wine, 18 gallons.
Oil of Greenland, ditto.
A tun of olive or sweet oil, 236 gallons.
A tod of wool, 28 lbs.
A pack of ditto, 364 lbs.
One hand in length, is 4 inches.
A firkin of butter, 56 lbs.
A firkin of soap or herrings is equal to a firkin of ale, two making a barrel.
A pipe, or butt, is 120 gallons.
A quintal, or kintal, 1 cwt.
A load of brick, 500; and plain tiles, 1000.
A stone of fish in London, 8 lbs., but in the country, commonly 14 lbs.—a stone of wool, 14 lbs.—the same for horseman's weight, hay, iron, shot, &c.
A stone of glass, 5 lbs. and a seam of ditto, 24 stone.
A cade of red herrings, 500.
A cade of sprats, 1000.
4 or 5 gallons of sturgeon, 1 keg.
1728 solid inches, a cubic foot.
27 solid feet, a cubic yard.
48 solid feet of timber, a ton.
A long dozen is 13.
A long score, 21.
A long hundred, 120.

Barrels of sundry commodities.

Anchovies, 30 lbs.
A double barrel, 60 lbs.
Nuts and apples, 3 bushels.
Pearl and pot-ash, or barilla, 200 lbs.
Oil, 31¼ gallons.
Candles, 10 dozen pounds.
Raisins, 1 cwt.
Spanish tobacco, 2 to 3 cwt.
Gunpowder, 1 cwt., and 24 barrels equal to 1 last.
Soap, 256 lbs.
Herrings, 32 gallons.
Salmon and eels, 42 gallons.
Figs, 3 qrs. 14 lbs. to 2¼ cwt.

Articles in wholesale trade, bought and sold by the thousand.

Cuttle bones.
Oranges and lemons.
Chair-nails.
Tacks and tender-hooks.
Pomegranates and tazels.
Goose-quills, rough, and thimbles.
Bricks.
Clinckers, or Flanders tiles.
Billets and leaves of horn.
Barrel hoops.
Squirrel-skins.
Slate and hilling stones.

Pins and small needles by the 1000 dozen.

Articles bought and sold at six score to the hundred.

Banks and barlings.
Barrel and pipe-boards.
Boom-spars and bow-staves.
Canspars and caprevans.
Herrings and deal boards.
Nails, eggs, and cod-fish, cole, ling, and Newfoundland fish, and stock-fish of all sorts.
Ells of canvass, and most foreign linens.
Hogshead-staves.

There are some modifications and alterations of the weights, measures, and assizes of casks, in a few of the states, which, as far as they could be obtained, are as follows:

Maine.—The dry measure is the Winchester bushel of $18\frac{1}{2}$ inches diameter, measured inside. The ale quart, wine quart, and wine gallon, and the avoirdupois and Troy weights are established.[a]

New-Hampshire.—Diameter of bushel $18\frac{1}{2}$ inches, for things sold by heaped measure.[b]

Measure for charcoal, basket of 2 bushels, or 18 gallons level measure.[c]

Massachusetts.—Beef and pork barrels must be 28 inches long, and 17 for beef, and $17\frac{1}{2}$ inches for pork, between the chimes, to contain 200 lbs. of meat. Pork barrels must contain 31 to $33\frac{1}{2}$ gallons. Fish barrels must contain 200 lbs. of fish, and from 28 to 29 gallons.

The other New-England states have adopted the inspection laws of Massachusetts.

The bushel is to contain 32 Winchester quarts, and to be $18\frac{1}{2}$ inches diameter. The cwt. is to be 100 lbs. avoirdupois. The bushel of wheat weighs 60 lbs., of rye or Indian corn 56 lbs., of barley or buckwheat 46 lbs., of oats 30 lbs., and of salt 70 lbs.

The weights and measures established in this state by the revised statutes of 1834, are those of England previous to 1824, except the beer measure, which is not used.

Connecticut.—In this state the half bushel, corn measure, contains 1099 cubic inches, the bushel being nearly 48.58 cubic inches larger than the Winchester bushel. This is the old standard half bushel under the law of 1800. The charcoal half bushel contains 1282 inches.—100 lbs. make a cwt., and 2000 lbs. a ton.[d] The beer gallon contains 282 cubic inches. The wine gallon 231 cubic inches. The quart, corn measure, contains 68.67 cubic inches. The pint, 34.38 inches. The standard weight of wheat is 60 lbs. to the bushel.

New-York.—The standard measure of length in this state is the yard of 3 feet, which is in the proportion of 1,000,000 to 1,086,141 to a pendulum, vibrating seconds in a vacuum, at the temperature of melting ice at Columbia College in the city of New-York.

---

[a] Act, 5th Feb., 1821. [b] Act, 15th Dec., 1797. [c] Act, 29th Dec., 1828. [d] Rev. Stat., 1835.

The standard lb. is the weight of $\frac{2}{125}$ part of a cubic foot of distilled water at its greatest density, weighed in a vacuum with brass weights, i. e. $62\frac{1}{2}$ lbs. = a cubic foot of such water, which is also equal to 1000 oz.

The standard gallon is to contain 10 lbs. of distilled water at its greatest density, at the mean pressure of the atmosphere at the level of the sea.

The gallon is the measure from which all others are derived as parts or multiples, 2 being the divisor or multiplier.

The bushel is to contain 80 lbs. of such water as aforesaid, and is to be made round, with a plain and even bottom, being $19\frac{1}{2}$ inches from outside to outside. The half bushel $15\frac{1}{2}$, and the peck $12\frac{1}{3}$ inches.

In measuring articles sold by heaped measure, the cone must extend to the outer edge of the measure, and must be as high as possible.

The bushel weighs 60 lbs. of wheat, and 56 lbs. of rye or Indian corn.

The cwt. consists of 100 lbs., and 20 cwt. make 1 ton.

Beef and pork for the navy of the United States must be packed in white oak barrels, 28 inches long from one end of the stave to the other, and from the outside of each head 26 inches. From 17 to 16 inches between the chimes. To contain from $28\frac{1}{2}$ to 30 gallons, and 200 lbs. weight of meat. The beef to be cut into pieces of 10 lbs. each, the pork into pieces of 8 lbs.

Beef and pork barrels, for exportation, 28 inches long, and $17\frac{1}{2}$ inches between the chimes. Flour barrels 22 inches long, and 14 inches diameter at the head, or 27 inches long, and 12 inches diameter at the head, to contain 98 lbs.—or the larger size of stands 27 inches long, and $16\frac{1}{2}$ inches diameter, to contain 196 lbs. Fish barrels are 28 inches long; distance between the chimes 26 inches; diameter of the head $16\frac{1}{2}$ inches. Half barrels 24 inches long, 13 inches head. Pot and pearl ashes, barrels 30 to 31 inches long, 20 to 19 inches in diameter at the head for pot, and 23 to 21 inches for pearl.

New-Jersey.—Here the wine barrel contains $31\frac{1}{2}$ gallons, the half barrel 16 gallons.

Pennsylvania.—In Pennsylvania, 16 gallons, wine measure, make a half barrel, $31\frac{1}{2}$ one barrel, 64 one double barrel, 42 one tierce, 84 one puncheon; 2 hogsheads make 1 pipe or butt, and 2 pipes make 1 tun, or 256 gallons. Beer, ale, cider, pork, beef, and oil, are sold by the above measure. The width of the stave is fixed at 3 inches. Tobacco hogsheads must be 4 feet long, 32 inches in the head, and 4 hogsheads to the tun, equal to the gauge of Maryland. The flour barrel is double the gauge for wine measure, as in New-York, and 63 gallons, wine measure.

Delaware.—Weights and measures the same as in Pennsylvania. Beer is sold by beer measure.

Maryland.—English weights and measures are used, except the beer gallon.

Tobacco hogsheads must be 4 feet long, and 70 inches in the whole diameter within the staves at the croze and bulge. Flour casks must contain $31\frac{1}{2}$ gallons, wine measure.

Pork and beef barrels, 220 lbs. net of meat. The staves must be 29 inches long, and 18 inches diameter at the head.

Fish barrels to contain not less than 29, nor more than 31 gallons. Tierces to hold 45, and halt barrels not less than 15 gallons.

Virginia and Kentucky.—English weights and measures, except the beer gallon, are used. The tobacco hogshead shall contain 1250 lbs. net of tobacco, being 54 inches long, and 34 inches at the head within the croze.

Pork and beef barrels to contain 204 lbs. net of meat, and from 29 to 30 gallons. Fish barrels from 30 to 32 gallons. Flour barrels 27 inches long, and $17\frac{1}{2}$ inches diameter at the head, and to contain 196 lbs. The tar and pitch barrels must contain $31\frac{1}{2}$ wine gallons. The barrel of salt to contain 5 bushels. The bushel contains $2150\frac{2}{3}$ cubic inches.

District of Columbia.—In Alexandria, District of Columbia, the weights and measures are the same as in Virginia; in Georgetown and Washington, the same as in Maryland.

North Carolina.—The standard weights and measures of this state are derived from English standards, according to a statute passed while a province. The beer gallon is not among them; of course the measure for liquids is the wine gallon only.

South Carolina.—English weights and measures are used.

Georgia.—English weights and measures, except the beer measure, are used.

Mississippi and Alabama.—English weights and measures are used. Flour barrels contain 196 lbs. Pork and beef barrels 200 lbs. net of meat.

Louisiana.—Weights and measures are according to those established by the revenue laws of the United States. A dry measure is ordained by the name of a barrel, to contain $3\frac{1}{2}$ bushels, equal to 6988.86 cubic inches.

It corresponds nearly with the assize of the flour barrel of the different states, and with the ancient Bourdeaux half hogshead.

Before its cession to the United States, the weights and measures in use in Louisiana were of French origin, and the lineal and superficial measures now used by the French and Spanish inhabitants are still of that character. The English weights and measures of capacity were more readily adopted.

Louis, the old French measure of length, was the king's foot of 12 inches, of 12 lines each; the toise of 6 king's feet; the perch of 3 fathom or 18 feet; the linear arpent of 10 perches; the league of 84 arpens; the ell of Paris of 3 feet, 7 inches, $10\frac{5}{6}$ lines.

The king's foot bears to the English foot the proportion of 16 to 15.

Old French superficial measure.

The	square foot of	144	square	inches.
The	" fathom of	36	"	feet.
The	" perch of	9	"	fathoms.
The	" arpent of	100	"	perches.
The	" league of	7056	"	arpens.

Wood measure.—The cord of 4 feet height, 8 feet length, and the billets of wood 4 feet long.

They, however, also occasionally use the American foot both for wood and land.

The surveyor's chain of 22 yards contains 10 fathoms, 1 foot, $10\frac{9}{10}$ inches.

Tennessee.—There is no standard other than the English for weights and measures in this state.

Ohio.—The English weights and measures are used, but the half bushel is by statute to contain $1075\frac{1}{5}$ cubic inches, and is to be the standard for dry measure.

Indiana.—The English weights and measures, except the beer measure, are used in this state, and the half bushel is as in Ohio.

The assize of hogsheads of tobacco, and of casks or barrels of flour, beef and pork, is the same as in Virginia.[a]

Illinois.—The English measures, except the beer measure, are established by law of 2d March, 1819. The half bushel is to contain $1075\frac{59}{100}$ cubic inches, or 18 quarts, 1 pint, 1 gill wine measure. The lb. avoirdupois is to contain 7020 grains Troy and the usual divisions.

Missouri.—The English weights and measures, except the beer measure, are used. The half bushel is to contain $1075\frac{1}{5}$ cubic inches: the quart $57\frac{3}{4}$ cubic inches.[b]

AMERICA.

British colonies in North America.—In Canada, New-Brunswick and Nova Scotia, the weights and measure of Great Britain were established by act of parliament in 1808. In the corn trade in Lower Canada the old French minot is still retained, it being about $\frac{1}{10}$ more than the English or Winchester bushel—90 minots being 100 bushels.

---

[a] Act, 21st Jan., 1818. [b] Act, 8th Dec., 1834.

ARABIA.

At Mocha the weight of commerce is the bahar of 15 farzils or 150 maunds each.

The maund contains 40 vakias, each vakia being about 1 oz. Troy weight.

A rattle is 15 vakias: but in weighing coffee, 14½ vakias are reckoned to a rattle, 2 rattles to a maund, and 10 maunds or 290 vakias to a farzil. The rattle is the weight used in the bazar.

The bahar of Mocha = 18 mounds of Mocha, or 450 lbs. avoirdupois.

Dry measure is the teman of 40 mecmedas or kellas. The teman weighs, filled with rice, 168 lbs. avoirdupois.

Liquids are sold by the cuda or gudda, of 8 nusfies or messeahs, or 128 vakias each. It is nearly equal to 2 gallons English.

Long measure is the guz of 25 inches English, the cobido or hand covid of 19 inches, and the long covid of 27 inches English.

At Hodeida the weights are of the same denomination, but 30 vakias = 1 maund; 10 maunds = 1 farzil, and 40 farzils = 1 bahar of 813 lbs. avoirdupois.

AUSTRIA.

At Vienna the weight of commerce is the pound or pfund of 4 quarters, 16 ounces, 32 loths or 128 quintelins, and equal to 8643 English grains.

The centner of 100 lbs. = 123½ lbs. avoirdupois.

Dry measure.—The muth contains 30 metzen, 128 viertels or 240 achtels, and equals 1,745 bushels English.

Wine measure.—The fuder of wine contains 32 eimers, 128 viertels, 1,280 maasses or 5.120 seidels, and equals 14.94 gallons English.

The dreiling is an old measure of 30 eimers, now no longer in use.

Long measure.—The foot of Vienna measures 12.45 English inches.

The fathom or klafter is 6 feet Vienna measure.

The ell of Vienna and of all Lower Austria is 30.66 English inches, but the ell of Lintz or Upper Austria is 31.5 inches English. Hence

100 ells of Vienna = 85.167 }
100 " Lintz = 87.5 } yards English.

At *Prague* the lb. of commerce consisted of 32 loths, and weighs 7940 grains English, and the centner contained 6 stone of 20 lbs. each.

The dry measure was the strick of 4 viertels, 16 massels or 192 seidels, and contained 3.03 English bushels.

The wine measure was the fas of 4 eimers, 128 pints, 512 seidels, and contained 67.8 English gallons.

The long measure, the ell, measuring 32.2 inches English.

But they have fallen into disuse since the Austrian weights and measures have been introduced.

At *Venice* the commercial weights are the peso grosso, divided into 12 oncie, 72 sazzi, 2304 carati or 9216 grani, or 7363 grains Troy or heavy weight, and the peso sottile or light weight, of which the pound contains 4650 English grains.

The following is the comparison of the two weights—

$104\frac{3}{5}$ lbs. peso grosso are equal to $165\frac{1}{4}$ lbs. peso sottile.

1 migliajo is equal to 40 miri of 25 liri each, or 1,000 lbs. peso grosso.

1 carrico is equal to 4 quintals of 100 lbs. each, or 400 lbs. peso sottile.

$106\frac{1}{2}$ lbs. peso grosso, or 168 lbs. peso sottile, are equal to 112 lbs. English.

The French kilogramme is also used in the custom-house, called libbra Italiana.

Dry measures.—A sacco of corn is divided into 1 stari, 26 quarti, or 64 quartucci. The staro contains 4941 English cubic inches; and 39 stari equal $11\frac{1}{5}$ quarters English.

The Moggio contains 4 staja or stari, 16 quarte, or 64 quartucci or quartaroli, and is equal to 2.27 English bushels.

Liquid measures.—An amphora of wine is divided into 4 bigoncie, 8 mastalli, 16 quarti, 48 sacchi, and contains 137 English gallons. The botte contains 5 bigonzi.

Oil is sold both by measure and weight. A migliajo of oil is divided into 40 mini, and contains 38526 English cubic inches. It weighs 1210 lbs. peso grosso, or 1200 lbs. of Hamburg weight.

Cloth measures.—100 bracci of silk equal $68\frac{2}{3}$ English yards; and 100 bracci of woollen equal 73 English yards.

The Venitian foot equals 13.68 inches English.

At Trieste there are two kinds of weight, of which one is called the Vienna weight, and by this goods coming from the interior of Germany are weighed; the other, called the Venice weight, is used for goods imported from other parts.

The comparison of the two weights stand as follows:

17 lbs. Vienna weight equal 20 lbs. Venice grosso weight.
7 lbs. - - " 13 lbs. Venice sottile weight.
91 lbs. of Vienna weight, 107 lbs. Venice grosso weight, and
168 lbs. of Venice sottile weight, each equal 112 lbs. English.
100 lbs. of Venice weight equal $115\frac{3}{4}$ lbs. Hamburg.

BARBARY.

Morocco.—At Morocco, Mogadore, Salee, Fez, &c. the libra or pound of Castile is generally used for weighing goods. This is divided into 2 marcs, 16 ounces, or 9216 grains.

The measures of Spain are also used, as the cahiz, or corn measure, containing 12 fanegas, 48 quartillas, or 144 celemines. The almude or wheat measure of Salee is 40 celemines of Castile = $5\frac{1}{3}$ bushels.

Cloths are measured by the cana of 12 covados of Morocco = 21 inches.

In some parts of Barbary the pic is used = 26 inches.

Algiers.—Here the common cantaar or quintal consists of 200 rotolos; but that for weighing figs, raisins, butter, honey, dates, oil, and soap, of only 166 rotolos; that for iron, lead, thread and wool of 150; that for almonds, cheese and cotton, 110; and, lastly, that for bronze, copper, wax and drugs, of 100 rotolos.

The rotolo is divided into 16 ounces = 1.19 lbs. avoirdupois.

The mitigal, for weighing diamonds, pearls, gold and silver, is equal to about 73 grains of Troy weight.

The measure for corn and dry goods is called tarrie = $2\frac{1}{4}$ pecks English; 16 tarries make a caffise.

The measure for oil is called metalli = 37 lbs. 6 oz. avoirdupois.

Of cloth measure, the pik, or Turkish pike, is divided into 8 robi. The pik Moorish is used for measuring linen. 100 of the latter equal 75 of the former.

1 pic Moorish = $18\frac{2}{5}$ inches.

Tunis.—Here the cantaar, or quintal, consists of 100 rotolos, or 1600 ounces.

A caffise of corn contains 16 tumulos, and a tumulo of good wheat weighs about 50 lbs. of Tunis.

A mataro of oil contains 2 mataros of wine; it weighs 32 rotolos, and is equal to $5\frac{1}{8}$ English gallons, and weighs 34 lbs. avoirdupois.

The wine measure is the millerolle of Marseilles = 16.99 gallons English.

Of cloth measure, several pikes are used; and 45 pikes cloth measure make 48 pikes of that for silk stuffs, or 64 pikes linen measure.

The cloth pik = $26\frac{1}{2}$ inches.
The silk pik = 24.8 "
The linen pik = 18.6 "

Precious metals and jewels are weighed by the ounce, consisting of 8 termines, and equivalent to 485.8 grains Troy.

Tripoli.—At Tripoli the cantaar or quintal consists of 100 rotolos, the rotolo of 16 ounces, and the ounce of 8 termines = 112 pounds.

The caffise, corn measure, is equal to 20 tiberi = 1.154 bushels English.

A mataro of oil weighs 42 rotolos.

Cloth is measured by the pike, which is equal to $2\frac{1}{5}$ palmi of Genoa.

Gold and silver, either in bars or coins, are weighed by the metacolo, 50 of which are equal to the Venitian marc, and it is equal to 73.66 grains Troy weight.

BELGIUM.

The weights formerly and which are still occasionally used, are the charge of 400 lbs., the ship pound of 300 lbs., the centner of 100 lbs., the chariot or cart load of 165 lbs., and the stone of 8 lbs. The pound was 2 marks of 8 oz. each, and the ounce = 4 loots of 10 engels each.

1 lb. Brabant = $1\frac{335}{1000}$ lbs. avoirdupois, or 7235.5 grains English.

In 1820 it was determined to adopt the French system of weights and measures into the Netherlands, of which Belgium then was a part; but to retain the ancient denominations.

For this system, vide the Netherlands.

Wine is still sold by the old aam or ahm, which contains 50 stoops, or $36\frac{1}{2}$ gallons English. It is also sold by the velt = 5 gallons. A tun of beer contains 54 stoops. 2 ells are used, i. e. that for silk = 27.32 inches English, and that for woollens = 26.966 inches.

BUENOS AYRES.

The weights and measures are the same as in Central America, which see. There are, however, some variations; as, for instance, the fanega, which is estimated at $3\frac{7}{8}$ Winchester bushels; and it is not allowed to use at the custom-house the Spanish terms mayo and alquiers. The term cascos is avoided, and barrels or pipes substituted.

The libra = 1 lb. 4 drs. avoirdupois.
The arroba = $25\frac{2}{5}$ lbs. "
The quintal = 101 lbs. 7 oz. "
The vara = $33\frac{1}{3}$ niches.
The contaro = $4\frac{1}{5}$ gallons.

CENTRAL AMERICA.

The weights and measures in this, as in all the former possessions of Spain, are founded on the Spanish system.

The commercial weight is the quintal = 4 arrobas, or 100 lbs.
The lb. = 16 onzas = 1 lb. 4 drs. avoirdupois.
The oz. = 8 drams, or 16 adarmes.
The adarme = 36 grains.

Long measure.

1 vara = 4 palmos, or 33.384 inches.
1 palmo = 9 pulgados, or $8\frac{1}{3}$ inches.
1 pie or foot = 12 pulgados, or 11.128 inches

Dry measure.

1 cahiz = 12 fanegas, or 144 celomines.
1 fanega = 1.599 bushels. The celomine is divided into halves, quarters, &c.

Liquid measure.

1 botta = 30 arrobas.
1 moyo = 16 "
1 arroba = 8 azumbras, or 32 quartillos.
The arroba of wine = 4.245 gallons English.
The arroba of oil = $3\frac{1}{3}$ gallons.

CHILI.

The same as in Central America.

CHINA.

The principal commercial weights are the pecul, the catty, and the tale. The pecul is divided into 100 catties, and each catty is again divided into 16 tales. The comparative value of these weights is as follows:

		Avoirdupois.		
	lbs.	oz.	drams.	
1 tale =	0	1	5.333 or	$1\frac{1}{3}$ oz.
16 tales, or 1 catty =	1	5	5.333 or	$1\frac{1}{3}$ lbs.
100 catties, or 1 pecul =	133	5	5.333 or	$133\frac{1}{3}$ "

The pecul weighs 162 lbs. 8 dwts. 13 grains Troy.

The weights are sometimes denominated differently, viz.. the catty is called gin; the tale is called liang; the mace, tchen; the candarine, fwen; and the cash, lis.

No commercial measures are used in China, dry goods and liquors being sold by the weight. In delivering cargoes, English weights are used, and afterwards turned into China peculs and catties.

Long measure.—The long measure is the covid or cobre; it is divided into 10 punts, and equals 14.625 inches.

100 covids are equal to 40.625 yards.

There are 4 different measures answering to the foot, viz.:

	English inches.
The foot of the mathematical tribunal - - -	13.125
The builders' foot, called kong pa - - - -	12.7
The tailors' and tradesmen's foot - - - -	13.33
The foot used by engineers - - - - - -	12.65

The li contains 180 fathoms. and each fathom contains 10 engineers' feet. The li, therefore, equals $1897\frac{1}{2}$ English feet; and $192\frac{1}{2}$ lis are equal to a mean degree of the meridian only.

DENMARK.

Commercial weights.

1 last	= 5200 lbs.
1 shippond	= 320 "
1 bismerpond	= 12 "
1 lispond	= 16 "
1 vog	= 36 "
1 centner or quintal	= 100 "
1 pound	= 2 marks, 32 lods.

128 quintins, or 512 orts = 7720 grains avoirdupois.

Dry measure.—1 toende or barrel = 8 skieps or skeppels, 32 viertels, or 144 pots, and contains 8,488 cubic inches.

A last of corn is divided into 12 toendes, 96 skeppels, or 384 foertels.

21 toendes (or barrels) equal $10\frac{1}{4}$ English quarters; and 100 equal $4\frac{2}{5}$ Hamburg lasts.

Coals are sold by the barrel of 176 pots. 18 barrels are a last. A keel of Newcastle coals makes about 130 barrels or toendes.

The last of oil, butter, herring, and other fat substances, is 12 toendes, and should weigh 224 lbs. net.

Liquid measure.—Wine and other liquors are measured by the hogshead of 30 viertels.

1 viertel = 4 kans, 8 pots, or 32 poegels, and contains $2\frac{41}{100}$ gallons.

There is also the fuder of 6 ahms, or 4 oxhofts. An ahm is divided into 4 ankers, 40 stuebgens, $77\frac{1}{2}$ kans, or 155 pots, equal to 9,128 English cubic inches, or nearly 40 gallons.

59 ankers are equal to 61 ankers of Hamburg.

The strick contains $7\frac{1}{2}$ ahms.

Cloth measure.—100 ells equal $68\frac{2}{3}$ English yards, and 21 equal 23 Hamburg ells; 105 feet equal 108 English feet.

The favne, or fathom, contains 6 Danish feet. The miil, or mile, is equal to 4 geographic or nautic miles.

Of long measure, the ell of 2 feet is about three quarters of an inch more than 2 English feet; and by this ell, with its fractions, all piece goods are measured. The Danish foot is longer than that of England, the proportion being nearly as 14 to 15.

The ell = 2 feet. The ruth = 10 feet.

EAST INDIES.

BENGAL.—*Great weights.*

16 chittauks	= 1 seer	= 1 lb.	13 oz	13 drms.	33 decim.
40 seers	= 1 factor maund	= 74 "	10 "	10 "	66 "

Bazar weight is 10 per cent. more than factory weight.

1 bazar maund	= 82 "	2 "	2 "	133 "

MADRAS.

Table of great weights.

10 pagodas	weight make	1 pollam.
40 pollams	"	1 vis.
8 vis	"	1 maund.—wt. 25 lbs. avoir.
20 maunds	"	1 candy.—wt. 500 lbs. "

BOMBAY.

Table of great weight.

30 pice	= 1 seer.	
40 seers	= 1 maund	= 38 lbs. avoirdupois.
20 maunds	= 1 cady	= 76 lbs. "

BATAVIA.

Great weights.

1 catty		= 1 lb. 4 oz. avoir.
100 catties	= 1 pecul	= 125 lbs. "
3 peculs	= 1 bahar	= 357 lbs. "

Equal to 16 Madras maunds, 1 vis, and 24 pollams.

EGYPT.

The commercial weight is the cantaro of 100 rottoli = 95 pounds avoirdupois.

A rottoli = 144 drams. The occa = 400 drams.

The cantaro varies for different kinds of goods.

The cantaro of iron	= 233⅓	rottolis	= 921⅔	lbs.
" lead	= 140	"	= 133	"
" red lead	= 130	"	= 123⅓	"
" black lead	= 150	"	= 142½	"
" gum arabic and balm	= 133	"	= 126⅓	"
" arsenic and other drugs	= 125	"	= 118¾	"
" dye woods	= 120	"	= 114	"
" almonds and fruits	= 115	"	= 109¼	"
" cloves, nutmegs, sarsaparilla and elephant's teeth	= 110	"	= 104½	"
" coffee and wire	= 105	"	= 99⅔	"
" quicksilver, pewter, tin in bars, vermillion and sugar	= 102	"	= 97	"

Silk is weighed by the occa of 400 drams; but the silk of Cyprus, Brusa and Sagoro, by the occa of 404 drams.

Long measure is the pic = 26.8 inches.

ENGLAND, SCOTLAND AND IRELAND.

Troy weight, or the weight for gold and silver, is the same as in the United States, and the pound denominated the imperial Troy pound is declared by statute to be the standard brass pound, made in 1758, and in the custody of the clerk of the house of commons.

The commercial weight (called avoirdupois) is also the same as in the United States, and the pound weighs 7000 grains Troy, being to the Troy pound as 7000 to 5760.

If the standard Troy pound be lost, it is to be restored by comparison with a cubic inch of distilled water, weighed by brass weights, at the temperature of 62° Fahrenheit, and the barometer at 30 inches. Such cubic inch is to weigh 252.458 grains, and the pound Troy 5760 grains.

Long measure is the same as in the United States. The standard yard is declared to be the distance between the centres of the two points on the gold studs in the straight brass rod, now in the custody of the clerk of the house of commons, made in 1760—the brass being at the temperature of 62°, and it is denominated the imperial standard yard.

The dimensions for measuring land are the same as in the United States; the acre containing 4840 square yards.

If the standard yard be lost, it is to be restored by comparing it with the pendulum vibrating seconds of mean time, in the latitude of London, in a vacuum on the level of the sea. The yard being in the proportion of 36 parts to 39.1393 of the pendulum.

Dry and liquid measures.—These were formerly the same as used in the United States, and of course were of different characters like them. The gallon being the same, but the divisions and subdivisions being different for dry and liquid measurement. By the act of 17th June, 1824, the standard measure of capacity for liquids, as well as for dry goods, not measured by heaped measure, is declared to be the gallon containing 10 pounds avoirdupois, of distilled water, weighed in air at the temperature of 62°, and the barometer at 30 inches; and all measures are to be taken in parts and multiples. The gallon contains 277.274 cubic inches. The gallon used at the custom-house is 7 inches in diameter and 6 deep.

The standard measure for coals and other things sold by heaped measure, is declared to be the imperial bushel, containing 80 pounds avoirdupois of water, as aforesaid—the same being round, with a plain and even bottom, and 19½ inches from outside to outside.

Goods sold by heaped measure must be heaped up in the bushel in the form of a cone, 6 inches high—the outside of the bushel being the extremity of the base. 3 bushels = 1 sack, and 12 sacks = 1 chaldron.

For articles not sold by heaped measure such as grain, &c., the same is stricken off with a round straight stick of equal diameter throughout.

The law of imperial measure does not extend to Ireland, for any articles usually sold by weight.

This law altered the old measures of England, Scotland and Ireland; but the old measures were permitted to be used, provided their contents in imperial or the new measurement be marked on them.

	Cubic inches.	Weight, Avoirdupois.
The imperial gallon contains	277.274	10 lbs.
" old corn gallon	268.8	9 lbs. 10 oz. 1¾ dr.
" old wine gallon	231.	8 lbs. 5 oz. 6¼ dr.
" old ale gallon	282.	10 lbs. 2 oz. 11½ dr.

Wine gallons multiplied by 5 and divided by 6 gives imperial. Corn gallons multipled by 31 and divided by 32 gives imperial. Ale gallons multiplied by 59 and divided by 60 gives imperial. The coal measure is scarcely changed by the statute from the old measure.

These new measures are now of course the legal measures of Great Britain and Ireland.

There are, however, used, other divisions, and of different denominations from those used in the United States for weighing particular articles, in various parts of the kingdom.

Thus, there are three quintals: First, of 100 pounds, by which sugars, &c., are bought and sold in the British West Indies, &c. Secondly, of 112 pounds, by which all gross goods are weighed throughout England. Thirdly, of 120 pounds, called the stannary hundred, by which tin, &c., is weighed to the king's farmers.

Of *Wool*, if commonly bought by the tod, 7 lbs. avoirdupois are equal to 1 clove; 14 lbs. equal to a stone; 28 lbs. equal to a tod; 182 lbs. equal to a wey; 364 lbs. equal to a sack; 4368 lbs. equal to a last. Or, otherwise, 2 cloves are equal to 1 stone; 2 stones equal to 1 tod; 6½ tods equal to 1 wey; 2 weys to 1 sack; and 12 sacks equal to 1 last. But, when it is stapled, or sorted, it is sold by the pack, containing 6 score, or 120 lbs.

Lead is sold by the fodder, and a load is equal to 3 cwt.

A fodder at Leith	is equal to	20	cwt.	of 112 lbs. to the cwt.
at London	" "	19½	cwt.	
at Newcastle	" "	21	cwt.	
at Stockton	" "	22	cwt.	
at Hull	" "	19½	cwt.—of 120 lbs. to the cwt.	
at Chester	" "	20	cwt.—of 120 lbs.	

Gunpowder: 100 lbs. avoirdupois to a barrel; 24 barrels equal to a last.

From the pound avoirdupois are formed other weights; as a *stone* of 7 lbs., 8 lbs., 14 lbs., 16 lbs., and 20 lbs.; and, in some parts, a *clove* of 7 lbs., 8 lbs. and 10 lbs.; and sometimes a *tod* of 20 lbs., 32 lbs., &c.

The stone is generally 14 lbs. avoirdupois.

For butcher's meat or fish it is 8 lbs.

A stone of glass=5 lbs. A seam of glass=120 lbs. A quarter is 8 bushels. A wey 10, and a last 20 bushels.

Hay and straw are sold by the load of 26 trusses. The truss of new hay is 60 lbs., but after the 1st of September the truss is 56 lbs. The truss of straw is 36 lbs. For other enumerations of articles vide United States of America, page 415.

Of *Wood-fuel.*—Wood-fuel is assized into shids, billets, faggots, fall-wood, and cord-wood. A shid is to be 4 feet long, and, according as they are marked and notched, their proportion must be in the girth, viz.—If they have but one notch, they must be sixteen inches in the girth; if 2 notches, 23 inches; if 3 notches, 28 inches; if 4 notches, 33 inches; and if 5 notches, 28 inches about. Billets are to be 3 feet long, of which there should be 3 sorts, viz. a single cask, and a cask of two; the first is 7 inches, the second 10 inches, and the 3d 14 inches about: they are sold by the hundred of 5 score. Faggots are to be 3 feet long, and at the band 24 inches about; besides the knot of such faggots, 50 go to the load. Bavins and spray wood are sold by the hundred, which are accounted a load. Cord-wood is the bigger sort of fire-wood, and it is measured by a cord or line, whereof there are two measures; that of 14 feet in length, 3 feet in breadth, and 3 feet in heighth. The other is 8 feet in length, 4 feet in heighth, and 4 feet in breadth.

Measures of wood.

1000 Billets of wood are equal to			1 Cord.
10 cwt. of do.	"	-	1 Cord.
1 Cord of wood	"	-	½ Chaldron of coals.
100 lbs. of wood	"	-	1 Quintal of wood.

At Newcastle the chaldron of coal is not a measure but a weight of 53 cwt. avoirdupois.

Eight Newcastle chaldrons=1 keel or 15⅓ London chaldrons,

The London chaldron of coal=4 vats, 12 sacks, 36 bushels, or 144 pecks. The coal bushel holds 1 Winchester quart more than the Winchester bushel, and contains 2,217.62 cubic inches.

Newcastle Grindstone measure.

1 Grindstone,	8 Feet,	1 Chaldron.	9 Grindstone,	4 Feet,	1 Chaldron.
3 "	7 "	2 "	18 "	3 "	1 "
3 "	6 "	1 "	27 "	2 "	1 "
5 "	5 "	1 "	36 "	1 "	1 "

*** 8 inches are 1 foot; measure across the stone and one edge.

Scotish weights and measures.—At the time of the Union, in 1707, it was enacted, that the same weights and measures should be used throughout the United Kingdom as were established in England, and this is also the law by the new act of 1824; nevertheless, in a great part of Scotland, the use of the Scotish weights and measures is still retained. The weights, indeed, are now used only for the sale of certain commodities; for other articles the English avoirdupois weight being substituted; but the measure for corn are almost uniformly Scotish, and they are different, in almost every county, from the Scotish standard measure.

General weights.—The English Troy weight and apothecary's weight are used throughout Scotland, in the same manner as in England, with the exception, that the Scotish jewellers divide the Troy ounce into 16 drops, each drop being 30 Troy grains; whereas the English divide it into 20 pennyweights, and a pennyweight into 24 grains.

The English avoirdupois weight is used for the sale of leather, soap, sugar, tea, flour, candles, and other groceries; also, for selling resin, wax, pitch, wrought metals, some Baltic goods, and all goods brought from England.

Scotish Troy weight, also called Dutch and French weight, is used for weighing iron, hemp, flax, Baltic and Dutch goods, meal, butcher meat, unwrought pewter and lead, &c. The pound, 16 of which compose a stone, contains 7600 Troy grains. It is consequently nearly 9 per cent. heavier than avoirdupois, or 35 lbs. are equal to 38 lbs. avoirdupois.

Trone weight.—This weight was abolished by act, in 1618; its name is, however, still retained for selling butter, cheese, tallow, wool, lint, hemp, hay, and some other home commodities, but the Trone stone and pound are generally denominated by avoirdupois pounds and ounces. The Trone pound contains 16 ounces avoirdupois as the stone contains 16 pounds. The weight of the Trone pound, however, varies in different places from 20 to 28 Dutch ounces.

Liquid measures.

4 Gills are equal to - -	1 Mutchkin.
2 Mutchkins " - - -	1 Chopin.
2 Chopins " - - -	1 Standard Pint.
2 Pints " - - -	1 Quart.
4 Quarts " - - -	1 Gallon.
8 Gallons " - - -	1 Barrel.

The Stirling pint jug is the unit of both the liquid and dry measures of Scotland. It contains 103.404 English cubic inches. Wine and spirituous liquors are now in general bought and sold in Scotland by English wine measure.

Dry measures.

4 Lippies are equal to		1 Peck.
4 Pecks	" - -	1 Firlot.
4 Firlots	" - -	1 Boll.
16 Bolls	" - -	1 Chalder.

The standard firlot for measuring wheat, peas, beans, rye and white salt, contains 2197.335 English cubic inches, and the boll for the same purpose contains, therefore, 8,789.34 cubic inches, or 100 bolls are equal to about 51 quarters 1 bushel Winchester measure.

The standard firlot for measuring barley, oats and malt, contains 3,205.524 English cubic inches, and the boll contains 12,822 cubic inches, or 100 bolls are equal to about 74 quarters 4 bushels Winchester measure.

Long measures.

3 Feet	$=1$ Ell $=37\frac{1}{5}$ English inches.
6 Ells	$=1$ Fall or Rood.
24 Ells	$=1$ Chain.
10 Chains	$=1$ Furlong.
8 Furlongs	$=1$ Mile $=5,952$ English feet.

But, by act of 44 James VII., (I. of England,) the Scotch mile is ordained to be like the English, viz. 5,280 feet.

Square measures.

6 Square Feet, Scots,	= 1 Square Ell.
36 Square Ells	= 1 Square Fall.
40 Square Falls	= 1 Square Rood.
4 Roods	= 1 Acre.

The Scotish acre contains 1 acre, 1 rood, $3\frac{1}{3}$ perches English; and, therefore, 48 Scotish acres equal 61 English acres nearly.

Irish weights and measures.—The weights of Ireland are the same as those of England; the measures are also the same, with some exceptions and customary regulations. Corn meal and flour are sold in sacks by weight, chiefly by the stone of 14 lbs. avoirdupois, and the common appellation of quantity is the barrel, which weighs as follows: 20 stone of wheat, peas, beans, and rye; 16 stone of barley, bere, and rapeseed; 14 stone of oats, (and in some places 12,) and 12 stone of malt.

Dry measure.—Coals and lime are sold by the bushel, by which also the duty on malt is levied. The coal bushel is 20 inches in diameter at the bottom, 21 at the top, and must contain 10 gallons Winchester measure.

The duties on coals imported are levied by a measure containing a tun weight.

The lime bushel was formerly 8 Winchester gallons; but by a late act the half barrel has been adopted, which is to be 21 inches diameter at the bottom in the clear, 22 at the top, and 12 deep, containing 20 Irish gallons, or 4,352 cubic inches.

The malt bushel measures 2,178 cubic inches. It is generally called the Winchester bushel, though it contains 27.58 cubic inches more, or about $1\frac{1}{4}$ per cent.

Liquid measure.—The Irish gallon measures 217.6 cubic inches; and as that of England is 231 cubic inches, 100 gallons of the latter equal $106\frac{1}{8}$ of the former. Dealers generally allow 6 per cent. for the difference.

Long measure.—The inch, foot, and yard, are the same here as in England; but the Irish perch or pole is 7 yards, and that of England only $5\frac{1}{2}$. Hence 11 Irish miles are equal to 14 English miles.

Land measure.—The proportion between the land measures of England and Ireland is deduced from the square perch of each country. Thus, $30\frac{1}{4}$ Irish acres = 49 English acres. The former is called plantation measure, the latter statute measure.

1 Irish acre = 1 acre, 2 roods, $19\frac{21}{121}$ perches English; and 1 acre of the latter = 2 roods, $18\frac{38}{49}$ perches of the former.

FRANCE.

Before the revolution, a variety of weights and measures prevailed in France.

The old French weights and measures.

Long measure.—The toise or fathom of France equals 6 feet, (pied de roi;) the foot 12 inches, (pouce;) and the inch 12 lines, each subdivided into 12 points. 76 French feet are nearly equal to 81 English feet; or, more accurately, 40,000 French feet, inches, or lines, equal 42,638 English feet, inches, or lines. Thus, 1 French foot equals 1.06597 English, or 12.78934 English inches; and hence 1 English foot equals 11.26 French inches. The Paris aune was $46\frac{17}{20}$ English inches.

Old French road measure.—The lieue or league is 2 French miles, each mile 1000 toises; hence the French league equals 2 English miles, 3 furlongs, and 15 poles.

The French league, however, in different parts of France, has been applied to different distances. The marine league (20 to a degree) equals 2,853 toises, or 6,081 English yards; and the astronomical league (25 to a degree) equals $2,282\frac{2}{7}$ French toises, or 1,865 English yards.

The arpent, or acre of land, contained in general 100 square perches; but the perch was various in different provinces.

The old French weight for gold and silver, (called poids de marc,) makes the pound or livre contain 2 marcs, 16 ounces, 128 gros, 384 deniers, or 9,216 grains.

The French marc = 3,780 grains Troy weight.

For *commercial weight*, the poids de marc was likewise used; and the quintal of 100 livres = 108 lbs. avoirdupois, very nearly.

Commercial weight, however, as well as measures of capacity, varied considerably in the different provinces.

Corn measure was the muid of 12 setiers, 24 mines, 48 minots, 144 bushels, or 2,304 litrons = $53\frac{1}{8}$ bushels English.

Wine measure was the muid of 36 setiers, 144 quarters, or 288 pintes = 70.8 gallons English.

This system, which varied in the different provinces, produced great inconvenience. To obviate this, the French government attempted to settle a weight and measure taken from nature, regulating each other and themselves. For this purpose they chose the distance from the equator to the pole, the quadrant or fourth part of the circle of the meridian, (or rather of the polar circumference of the earth,) and divided this estimated space into ten millions of parts, each of which is termed a *metre*. This space was ascertained by the determinations of different degrees of the meridian, which were made at various times by men of the first class in science and talent; including particularly the accurate admeasurements made between the Mediterranean and the North Sea, viz. from Barcelona to Dunkirk, which were completed in 1799. The result is, that the *metre* is fixed at 36 French inches, and 11.296 lines, equal to 39 English inches, and .371 decimal parts. Hence,

1. *New measures of length, with their corresponding value in English measures.*

				English inches.
Millimetre, 1000th part of the metre				.03937
Centimetre, 100th of the metre				.39371
Decimetre, 1-10th of a metre				3.93710
METRE, the principal unity of the French measure				39.37100
Decametre	=	10	metres	393.71000
Hecatometre	=	100	"	3937 10000
Chiliometre	=	1000	" (8 *are nearly* 6 *E. M.*)	39371.00000
Myriometre	=	10000	"	393710.00000
Grade, or decimal degree of the meridian, (100,000 metres, or 1-100th of the quadrant)				3937100.00000

2. *Measures of capacity.*—The LITRE is the unity for dry and liquid measures; it is equal in its contents to a cubic decimetre, or a cube of $\frac{1}{10}$th part of the METRE. The litre in liquids is used instead of the *pinte*, of which it is $1\frac{1}{20}$th part; and in dry measure it supersedes the *litron*, of which it makes $\frac{1}{4}$. Hence,

		Cubic inches English.	
A Millimetre	1-1000th of a litre	.06103	
Centilitre	1-100th of a litre	.61028	
Decilitre	1-10th of a litre	6.10280	
LITRE, a cubic decimetre		61.02800	= nearly 2 1-8 wine pints.
Decalitre	10 litres	610.28000	= 14 = nearly 3 wine pints.
Hecatolitre	100 "	6102.80000	
Chiliolitre, or kiliotre	1000 "	61028.00000	= 1 tun 12.75 wine gallons.
Myriolitre	10000 "	610280.00000	

3. *Weights.*—A gramme is the unity of gravity; it is the exact

weight of a column of pure water, equal to a cubic centimetre, or the cube of the $\frac{1}{100}$th part of the metre, when the water is at its greatest density, or of the temperature of thawing ice. It has been found equal to 18.827 French grains, or 15.434 grains Troy; and 489.5058 grammes make a pound of the standard of the mint at Paris.

		Cubic inches English.	
Milligramme......	1-1000th of a gramme......	.0154	
Centigramme.....	1-100th of a gramme......	.1544	
Decigramme......	1-10th of a gramme......	1.5444	
GRAMME...........	a cubic centimetre.......	15.4440	
Decagramme.....	10 grammes.............	154.4402	= { 6 dwts. 10.44 gr. Troy, or 5.56 dr. avoirdupois.
Hecatogramme..	100 "	1544.4023	= 3 oz. 8.5 dr. "
Chiliogramme....	1000 "	15444.0234	= 3 lbs 3 oz. 5 dr. "
Myriogramme....	10000 "	154440.2344	= 22 lbs. 1.15 oz. "

100 myriogramme = 1 tun, wanting 32.8 lbs.

4. *Agrarian, or land measures, &c.*—The ARE, or square decametre, is the unity of agrarian or land measures. It is equal to 3.95 perches. The deciare is $\frac{1}{10}$th part of the are; the centiare is $\frac{1}{100}$th part, and is equal to a square metre. The hecatare is equal to 100 ares, or 2 acres, 1 rood, 35.4 perches. The myriare is equal to 10,000 acres.

For fire-wood, &c.—The STERE is the unity of measure for fire-wood, &c. It is a cubic metre, equal to 35.3171 cubic feet English. The decistere is $\frac{1}{10}$th of the stere, and equal to 3.5317 feet English.

This is called the metrical or decimal system, and has a new nomenclature.

The introduction of this new system of weights and measures experienced general opposition, which was probably much increased from the adoption of the new Greek denominations. The imperial government, therefore, about the year 1812, with a view to connect the respect due to ancient habits with the preservation of the new system, allowed for a limited time that, instead of decimal fractions of the new weights and measures, others, called *usuelle* should be formed, bringing them as nearly as possible to the value of those formerly in use. In consequence, the *half kilogramme* forms, at present, a new measure called the LIVRE USUELLE; it is not exactly the old livre, *poids de marc*, but nearly 3 gros more. It was permitted to divide this half kilogramme, not by decimals, but, like the old livre or pound, into 16 ounces, and the other divisions as in the poids de marc. Similar concessions were made with respect to the divisions of measures of extent and capacity; and these changes are acceptable, because they accord with old habits.

The system of 1812, called the "system usuelle," is metrical; but with binary divisions and the old denominations.

Extract of the resolution passed by the Minister of the Interior, 28th March, 1812, *for the execution of the foregoing decree.*

ART. I. It is permitted to employ, for the use of commerce—

1. A measure of length equal to 2 *metres,* called *toise,* and divided into 6 feet.

2. A measure equal to $\frac{1}{3}$d of the metre, or $\frac{1}{6}$th of the toise, called foot, (*pied.*) divided into 12 inches, (*pouce,*) and the inch into 12 lines.

II. Each of these measures bear on one side the corresponding divisions of the metre, that is, the toise, 2 metres divided into decimetres, and the first decimetre into millimetres; and the foot, $3\frac{1}{3}$ decimetres, divided into centimetres and millimetres; in all $333\frac{1}{3}$ millimetres.

III. The measurement of linens and stuffs may be made with a measure equal to 12 decimetres, and called *aune.* This measure is divided into halves, quarters, eighths and sixteenths, as well as into thirds, sixths and twelfths. It bears on one side the corresponding divisions of the metre in centimetres only, viz. 120 centimetres numbered in tens.

IV. Corn and other dry goods may be measured retail with a measure equal to $\frac{1}{8}$ of the hectolitre, called *boisseau*, and its double, halves and quarters.

V. Each of these measures is marked with its name, and also the indication of its proportion with the hectolitre.

VI. For the retail sale of corn, small shot, meal, dry or green vegetables, the litre may be divided into halves, quarters and eighths.

VII. For the retail sale of wine, brandy, and other liquors, measures of the quarter, eighth and sixteenth of a litre may be employed. Each of the said measures is marked with its name, indicative of its proportion with the litre.

VIII. For the retail sale of all substances whose price and quantity are regulated by weight, the merchants may employ the following *poids usuels*, viz.

The *livre*, equal to the half kilogramme or 500 grammes, which shall be divided into 16 onces.

The *once*, the 16th of the livre, which shall be divided into 8 gros.

The *gros*, the 8th of the once, which shall be divided into 72 grains.

Each of these weights is likewise divided into halves, quarters and eighths. They bear, besides their own name, the indication of their value is grammes.

The divisions ordained in the foregoing decree are stated in the following table, with their proportions to the metre, and also to English weights and measures.

Comparison of weights.

Pois usuels.	Grammes.	Troy weight, grains.
Livres usuelle.	500	7717

With halves, quarters, &c., in proportion.

Comparison of linear measures.

Measures usuelle.	Metres.	English measure. Feet.	Inches.	Parts.
Toise usuelle	2	6	6	9
Pied, or foot	$0\frac{1}{3}$	1	1	$1\frac{1}{2}$
Inch	$0\frac{1}{42}$	0	1	$1\frac{1}{8}$
Aune	$1\frac{1}{5}$	3	11	3

With halves, quarters, &c., in proportion.

Dry measures.—The boisseau usuel = 12.41 litres = 0.35474 English bushels, with halves, quarters, &c. in proportion.

Liquid measures.—The litron usuel = $2\frac{1}{9}$ English pints.

GERMANY.

The weights used in Germany are very various; but those that usually occur in chymical books are the apothecaries' weights, commonly known by the name of the Nuremburg medicinal weights. They are divided precisely as our English apothecaries' weight, or as follows:

24 grains make - - - -	1 scruple.
3 scruples - - - - -	1 dram.
8 drams - - - - -	1 ounce.
12 ounces - - - - -	1 pound.

According to Gren, 1 Nuremburg pound = 0.959266 of a Troy pound. The same ratio exists between the respective ounces, drams, scruples and grains. Hence, to reduce Nuremburg weights to their respective English, we have only to multiply by 0.959266.

There is another weight in common use in Germany, namely, the Cologne marc, or marc of Charlemagne. It is employed in weighing gold and silver, and therefore often occurs in chymical books. It is thus subdivided:

256 standard parts (Richtpfennings) make	1 pfenning
4 pfennings (pennyweights or deniers)	1 quintin.
4 quintins (drams) - - - -	1 loth.
2 loths - - - - - -	1 ounce.
8 ounces - - - - - -	1 mark.

It appears from Gren that 1 Cologne ounce is equal to 0.939018 of a Troy ounce, and the Cologne marc is equal to 3608 Troy grains. From these data it is easy to reduce the Cologne weights to the English standard.

The common measure of length in Germany is the Rhinland foot, which, like our own, is divided into 12 inches.

1 Rhinland foot = 12.36 English inches.
1 Rhinland inch = 1.02842 "

At Emden, 1 ship-pound equals 3 centners, or 300 pounds. The pound is divided into 32 loths.

100 pounds of Emden equal 102 pounds Hamburg, or $109\frac{1}{8}$ pounds English.

Of the measures, one last of corn is divided into 15 tons, 60 verps, or 120 scheffels, or 144 kruesen.

One last, or 15 tons, equal $10\frac{3}{4}$ quarters English. $16\frac{1}{2}$ tons = 1 last of Hamburg. 47 ells = 55 Hamburg ells. 100 ells = $73\frac{1}{3}$ English yards. 100 feet = $97\frac{1}{4}$ English feet.

Rostock, in Mecklenburg.—The commercial weights of this place are, 1 ship-pound equal to 20 lispounds of 16 pounds each, or 320 pounds. 1 pound is equal to 32 loths: and 100 pounds equal to 112 pounds English. A ship-pound of iron and lead is only 280 pounds.

The weight of Lubeck is also used in Mecklenburg, which is about 5 per cent. lighter than the above.

Dry measures.—A last of corn is divided into 8 droemts, or 96 scheffels, equal to 384 fossers, or 1456 spints = 105.952 bushels English.

The *liquid measures* are the same as those of Hamburg.

SAXONY.

At Dresden the commercial pound is divided into 2 marks, 16 oz. 32 loths, 123 quintelins, 512 pfennings or 7680 grains, and equal 7266 grains Troy.

Dry measures.—The scheffel is divided into 4 quarts, 16 masschens = 3 bushels English. The wispel contains 2 malters, 24 scheffels.

Liquid measures.—The fuder contains $2\frac{2}{5}$ fasses, 12 eimers, or 756 hannen. The eimer = 17.87 gallons English.

The fuder is also divided into 4 oxhofts, 6 ahms, or 24 ankers. The anker being 32 quarts or 64 nossels.

Long measures.—The Saxon ell measures 22.22 inches English, The Saxon foot 11.11 inches English, and the mile = 5.628 miles English.

At Leipsic the weights and long measures are the same; also the legal dry measure. The old Leipsic scheffel, however, is larger, measuring 8481 cubic inches English, or 2025 inches more than the Dresden scheffel.

The Leipsic liquid measures have the same divisions, but they are larger than those of Dresden.

The Leipsic eimer contains $20\frac{1}{10}$ English gallons.

COLOGNE.

At Cologne the mark, which is the standard weight throughout Germany, for the precious metals, is divided into 8 ounces, 16 loths, 64 quintlins, 256 pfennings or deniers, 4352 eschen, or 65.536 Richtpfennings = 3608 grains Troy, or 233.769 grammes.

The pound of commerce contains 2 marks. The centner = 106 Cologne pounds, or $109\frac{1}{4}$ pounds avoirdupois.

Dry measures.—The last of corn contains 20 malters, or 480 fasses = 91.995 bushels English.

Wine measures.—The ahm = 26 veirtels; 104 masses, or 416 pintgers = 41.129 gallons English. The tun = 160 masses.

Long measures.—The Cologne foot = 10.83 inches English. The long ell = 27.347 inches English. The short ell = 22.625 inches English.

HANSE TOWNS.

At Bremen, the commercial weights are, the pound, equal to 2 marks, 16 ounces, 32 loths, 128 quinters, 512 orts = 7690 English grains; the centner of 116 pounds; the ship-pound of $2\frac{1}{2}$ centners or

20 pounds; the psundschwer of 300 pounds, or for cartage 308 pounds.

100 pounds are equal to 110 pounds English; 97 pounds = 100 of Hamburg; 102 pounds = 103 of Amsterdam.

One stone of flax = 20 lbs.; 1 stone of wool and feathers = 10 lbs.; 1 waage of iron = 120 lbs.

A lispound 14 lbs. A tun of butter, great measure = 300 lbs., of small measure = 220 lbs.

Dry measures of Bremen.—A last of corn is divided into 4 quarts, 40 scheffels, 160 viertels, or 640 squints.

10 lasts of Bremen = 9 lasts of Hamburg. 1 last = $9\frac{7}{8}$ quarters English: or 41 scheffels = 1 last English.

A keel of Newcastle coal is equal to $10\frac{3}{4}$ lasts, or 127 tonnes or barrels.

Liquid measures of Bremen.—A fuder of wine contains 6 ahms, 120 viertels, 270 stuebgens, 1080 quarts, or 4320 mingels.

7 stuebgens = 8 stuebgens at Hamburg; 75 stuebgens = 63 gallons English. A tonne of beer contains 48 stuebgens. A tonne or barrel of whale oil contains 6 steckanns of 16 mingels each.

Cloth measures of Bremen.—100 ells = 107 Hamburg ells, or $63\frac{1}{3}$ English yards. 35 feet = 36 Hamburg feet. 20 feet = 19 English feet.

The ell = 2 feet, or 24 inches of 10 parts each. A clafte = 6 feet. A ruth = 16 feet.

HAMBURG.

At Hamburg the commercial weights and measures are as follows:

Weights.—1 ship-pound is equal to 20 lispounds of 14 lbs., or 280 lbs.; 1 centner is equal to 8 lispounds, or 112 lbs.; and 1 lb. is equal to 32 loths, or 7476 English grains.

100 pounds of Hamburg are equal to $103\frac{3}{8}$ lbs. of Berlin, or $106\frac{2}{3}$ lbs. English.

One stone of flax is equal to 20 lbs.; 1 stone of wool or feathers is equal to 10 lbs. A pipe of oil is 820 lbs. net weight.

Dry measures.—A last of corn is divided into 3 wispel, 30 scheffel, 60 fass, 120 himten, or 480 spints = 89.6 bushels English.

A fass contains 3215 cubic inches. A last of Hamburg is $11\frac{1}{2}$ quarters English.

Coals are sold by the barrel, (tonne,) and a keel of Newcastle coals will deliver about 114 barrels.

Liquid measures.—A fuder of wine is divided into 6 ahms, 24 ankers, 30 eimers, 120 viertels, 240 stuebgens, 480 kanns, or 960 quarts. A stuebgen contains 220.72 English cubic inches; and 45 stuebgens is equal to 49 English gallons.

Whale oil is sold by steckhanns, 6 of which make a Hamburg barrel; and 49 steckhanns are equal to 252 gallons, or an English tun. The ahm = $38\frac{1}{4}$ gallons English.

Cloth measures.—The Hamburg ell contains 22.5783 English inches. 100 ells equal $62\frac{2}{3}$ English yards.

The Hamburg foot contains 3 palms. The Rhinland foot used by surveyors contains 12 inches of 10 lines each, and equals 12.36 inches English.

The Hamburg ell = 2 feet Hamburg. The fathom 6 feet. The ruth 14 feet, and also 16 feet.

The Rhinland ruth = 12 Rhinland feet, or $13\frac{1}{7}$ feet Hamburg.

The Brabant ell = 27.585 inches English.

A Hamburg mile contains 2000 Rhinland ruthes, or 8244 yards English = 4.684 miles.

The morgen or acre of land contains 600 square ruthes, each ruthe 256 square feet Hamburg, and equals 2 acres $6\frac{1}{2}$ perches English.

LUBECK.

At Lubeck the centner of 112 lbs. is equal to 114 lbs. English. The ship-pound contains $2\frac{1}{2}$ centners, equal to 20 lispounds, or 280 lbs.

A lispound is either of 16 or 14 lbs. 1 stone of flax is equal to 20 lbs.: 1 stone of wool or feathers is equal to 10 lbs. 1 lb. is equal to 2 marks, 16 ounces, 32 loths, 64 drams, 256 pennyweights, or 128 quintlins, or 512 pfennings = $7479\frac{1}{2}$ grains English.

104 pounds of Lubeck are equal to 112 lbs. English.

Three English yards are equal to 4 Brabant yards, and 5 Brabant yards are equal to 6 Lubeck ells; 1 ell = 2 feet Lubeck, or 22.692 inches English.

14 Lubeck ells are equal to 9 yards of English.

141 do. = 142 ells of Hamburg.

Flax, Codilla hemp, tallow, iron and hops, are sold by the ship-pound of 280 lbs. Linseed, tar and whale oil, by the barrel. Mats by the 100 pieces. Raven ducks and flems by the piece.

Coffee, sugar, cocoa, cotton, indigo, pepper, ginger, pimento, wax, bristles and tin, by the pound weight; and rice, logwood, vitriol and starch, by the 100 lbs.

Dry measures.—The last of corn = 8 dromts, 24 tonnes or barrels, 96 scheffels, 384 fasser.

The scheffel contains 2041 cubic inches English, or $\frac{949}{1000}$ of a bushel. The oat scheffel = 2395 cubic inches English.

Liquid measures the same as at Hamburg.

ITALY.

At Rome the lb. is divided into 12 once, 288 denari, or 6,912 grani = 5,234 grains English.

There are 3 quintals, viz. of 100 lbs., 160 lbs., and 250 lbs.; also, the migliajo of 1000 lbs.

Dry measure.—The rubbio contains 4 quarte, 22 scorzi, or 88 quartucci; also, 12 stari and 16 stari = 8.356 bushels English.

In measuring salt, the rubbio is divided into 2 quarte, 12 scorzi, or 48 quartucci.

Liquid measure.—The barile of wine contains 32 boccali, or 128 fogliette = 15.409 gallons English.

Long measure.—The Roman foot = 11.72 inches English. The canna mercantile = $78\frac{1}{3}$ inches English, and is divided into 3 palmi or 24 parti. 40 Roman miles = 37 miles English.

TUSCANY.

At Florence and at Leghorn, heavy goods are weighed by the migliajo of 1000 lbs., or centinajo of 100 lbs. Sugar by the cantaro of 151 lbs. Flour by the cantaro of 150 lbs. Codfish, &c., by the cantaro of 160 lbs. All fine goods are sold by the pound.

The pound, for weighing precious metals, &c., consists of 12 oncie, or ounces, 96 drams, 288 denari, equal to 52 English grains. $132\frac{1}{2}$ lbs. equal 100 lbs. English, and 41 equal 29 lbs. of Hamburg. The pound, commercial weight, is 1 per cent. heavier than the pound used for weighing precious metals.

Dry measure.—The maggio is composed of 2 rubbi, $7\frac{1}{2}$ sacci, $22\frac{1}{2}$ staji, or 2880 busoli. The sacco contains 4498 English cubic inches.

The principal corn measure is the stajo of 2 mine, 4 quarti = 32 mezzette or 64 quartucci = 0.6913 bushels.

The rubbo is 1440 busoli, the sacco 384, and the stajo, 128.

Liquid measure.—A barile or barrila of wine contains 20 fiaschi, 40 boccali, 80 mezzetti, or 160 quartucci. It is equal to 2564 English cubic inches, or 12.842 English gallons.

A barrila of oil contains 16 fiaschi, 32 boccali, 64 mezzetti, or 128 quartucci; equal to 1940 English cubic inches, or $8\frac{1}{2}$ English gallons, or 60 lbs. of Hamburg.

Cloth measure.—A canna is composed of 4 bracci, or 8 palmi. The braccie for woollen contains 23.255, and that for silks 22.913 English cubic inches.

100 bracci of woollens equal $101\frac{9}{10}$ bracci of silks. 31 equal 20 English yards.

SARDINIA.

The commercial lb. contains 12 once = 6125 grains Troy.

In Turin the lb. = 5692 grains Troy. The rubbo = 25 lbs.

Dry measure.—In Sardinia the restiere of corn contains 3 starelli or 48 imbuti. The starello = 1.389 bushels English.

In Turin the sacco = 3 staje, 6 mine, 12 quartieri, or 48 copelli = 3.26 Winchester bushels.

Liquid measure.—In Turin the wine measure is the brenta = 6 rubbi, 36 pinte, or 72 boccali. The rubbo = 2.48 gallons English.

In Sardinia the long measure is the palmo = 9.78 inches English, and the raso or ell = $21\frac{5}{8}$ inches English.

In Turin the foot = 12.72 inches English, and the reso or ell = 23.3 inches English.

At Genoa the cantaro of peso grosso is equal to 6 rubbi, 100 rottoli, or 150 lbs. of 12 oz. each.

Peso grosso (great weight) is 10 per cent. heavier than peso sottile. 100 lbs. peso sottile equal 69.89 lbs. English; 1 lb. peso sottile = $4891\frac{1}{2}$ grains Troy.

Dry measure.—The mina of corn is divided into 8 quarti, or 96 gambette, and contains 7116 English cubic inches, or 3.426 bushels.

Of salt, a monda is 8 mine.

Liquid measure.—A mezzarola of wine contains 2 barrili, or 100 pintes. The pinte contains 91.5 English cubic inches; a mezzarola, therefore, is equal to $39\frac{1}{4}$ English gallons.

A barrila of oil is divided into 2 mezzi barrili, 4 quarti, or 128 quarteroni, and weighs $7\frac{1}{3}$ rubbi, of 25 lbs. each, or $183\frac{1}{3}$ peso sottile, which renders 122 lbs. at Hamburg equal to $17\frac{1}{2}$ English gallons.

Cloth measure.—A canna grossa is 12 palmi, a canna picoli 9 palmi, a canna linen measure 10 palmi, a braccio is $2\frac{1}{3}$ palmi, and a palmo is equal to 9.715 English inches.

In a ship's cargo, a last is computed as equal to 20 boxes of lemons, 26 barrili of oil, and 44 barrili of wine.

NAPLES.

At Naples the commercial weights are that called grosso or great weight, and piccola or lesser weight.

The cantaro grosso equals 100 rotoli of $33\frac{1}{3}$ oncies or ounces each.

1 rotolo is equal to $31\frac{3}{7}$ oz. avoirdupois.

100 rotoli equal $196\frac{1}{2}$ lbs. avoirdupois.

A cantara piccola is equal to 150 libri, or 106 lbs. avoirdupois.

1 libra or pound is equal to 12 ounces, or 4966 grains Troy.

Dry measure.—The carro of corn is composed of 36 tomoli, or 864 mezarrette; and a tomolo of wheat weighs from 45 to 48 rotoli. The carro contains 112276 English cubic inches, and is equal to $6\frac{1}{2}$ quarters. The tomolo = $1\frac{1}{2}$ Winchester bushels.

Liquid measure.—A carro of wine contains 2 botti, 24 barrili, or 1440 carrafi. A pipe is composed of 14 barrili. A barrilo contains 2600 English cubic inches.

12 barrili or 1 botto are equal to 140 wine gallons; and 1 barrilo = 11 gallons wine measure.

A salma of oil is composed of 10 staje, of 32 pignatti each, and contains $42\frac{3}{4}$ wine gallons; 11 salme are computed as a ship's last.

Cloth measure.—A canna is composed of 8 palmi, or 96 oncc, equal to 83.05 English inches.

10 canne equal 23 English yards; 100 feet equal $86\frac{3}{5}$ English feet.

At Palermo and Messina the commercial weights are of 3 denominations: 1st, the rotolo grosso of $2\frac{3}{4}$ lbs. or 33 ounces; 2d, the rotolo sottile of $2\frac{1}{2}$ lbs. or 30 ounces; 3d, the pound (libre) of 12 ounces (oncies) = 4900 grains Troy.

Hence 10 rotoli grossi equal 11 rotoli sottili.

1 contaro grosso equals 100 rotoli grossi.

100 rotoli grossi	= 193	lbs. English.
100 rotoli sottili	= 175	" "
100 libri or pounds	= 70	" "

Dry measure.—The salma grosso is composed of 16 tomoli, 64 quarti, or 64 modelli, and is equal to $9\frac{3}{4}$ Winchester bushels. The salma generali (used chiefly for corn) is also composed of 16 tomoli; but it is about 20 per cent. less than the salma grosso, or 7.85 Winchester bushels.

Liquid measure.—Of wine, the tonna contains 12 salme, and a salma is composed of 8 quartari, or 96 quartucci, equal to 5340 English cubic inches, or 23 gallons.

The salma of Syracuse is $\frac{1}{8}$ part less than that of Palermo and Messina.

At Palermo oil is sold by the cantaro peso grosso, equal to 24 English gallons. At Messina it is sold by the caffisso, equal to $12\frac{1}{2}$ rotoli grossi of 33 ounces each, and equal to nearly 3 gallons English.

Cloth measure.—A canna is divided into 8 palmi, equal to 76.24 English inches.

60 canne, or 480 palmi, equal 127 English yards.
100 palmi equal $79\frac{1}{4}$ English feet.

JAPAN.

The picul = 100 catti, or 1,600 tales, or 16,000 mas, and weighs 130 lbs. avoirdupois.

Dry measure.—Rice is measured by the managoga = 10,000 ickmagogs, 1 ickmagog = 1000 ickogas, or 100,000 gantas.

Long measure is the inc or tattamy = $6\frac{1}{4}$ feet English.

MEXICO.

Weights and measures the same as in Central America, page 425.

NEW GRANADA.

Weights and measures the same as in Central America.

NAPLES.—(Vide page 442.)

NETHERLANDS.

At Amsterdam the ship-pound was formerly = to 20 lispounds = 3 centners = $37\frac{1}{2}$ stone, or 300 lbs.

One pound was 16 ounces, or 32 loths = 7625 English grains. 100 lbs. = $108\frac{3}{4}$ lbs. English, or 102 lbs. of Hamburg.

Dry measure.—The last of corn was divided into $21\frac{3}{5}$ tons, 27 mudden, 36 sacks, and a sack into 3 schepels, 12 vierdevats, or 96 koops.

One last was $10\frac{1}{2}$ English quarters.

Coals are sold by the hoed of 33 maaten.

Salt is sold by the hundert of 4004 maaten, equal to $8\frac{1}{5}$ English lasts.

Liquid measure.—An aam of wine contains 4 ankers, 8 steckanns, 21 viertels, 64 stoopen, or 128 mingels: equal to 9318 English cubic inches, or $40\frac{1}{3}$ gallons.

Whale oil is sold per 12 steckanns, in quarteels, containing from 18 to 21 steckanns.

12 steckanns = $62\frac{1}{2}$ English gallons.

Cloth measure.—100 ells = $75\frac{1}{2}$ English yards; and 14 feet = 13 English feet. The Rhenish foot = $12\frac{9}{25}$ inches English was also used.

Of a ship's cargo, the last is 8 hogsheads of wine, 14 barrels of herrings, 12 barrels of pitch, 13 barrels of tar, 7 quarteels of whale oil, 4000 lbs. of iron, copper, &c., 2000 lbs. of wool and feathers. The last of wheat is 10 per cent. more than the last of rye, and the latter 20 per cent. more than the last of oats. The last of 400 lbs. is equal to 2 English tons, and freight is still adjusted by the last.

In 1820, however, it was determined to introduce a more simple system of weights and measures, retaining the ancient denominations. The French metrical system was therefore adopted, and at present the weights and measures, both in the Netherlands and in Belgium, are as follows:

Weights.

Korrel, equal to	1 Decigramme.
Wigtje, "	1 Gramme.
Lood, "	1 Decagramme.
Ons, "	1 Hectogramme.
Pond, "	1 Kilogramme.

Liquid measures.

Vingerhoed, equal to	Centilitre.
Maatje, "	Decilitre.
Kan, "	Litre.
Mingel, "	1.2 Litres.
Stoop, "	2.4 "
Anker, "	38.4 "
Vat, "	1 Hectolitre.

Dry measure.

Maatje, equal to	1 Decilitre.
Kop, "	1 Litre.
Schepel, "	1 Decalitre.
Mudde "	1 Hectolitre.
Last, "	3 Kilolitres, or 30 mudden.
Ton, "	2 Hectolitres, or 2 mudden.
Seaton, "	10 Hectolitres, or 10 "

Long measure.

Streep, equal to	1 Millimetre.
Duim, "	1 Centimetre.
alm, "	1 Decimetre.
El "	1 Metre.
Roede, "	1 Decametre.
Myl, "	1 Kilometre.

PERSIA.

There are two sorts of weights, i. e. the batman of Chevray, and the batman of Tauris; the former being double the latter. The batman = 6 rattels, or 300 derhams, or 600 miscals. The batman of Tauris = 6.34 lbs. avoirdupois.

Dry measure.—The artaba = 25 capichas = 50 chenicas = 200 sextarios = 1.86 Winchester bushels.

Long measure is of two sorts, the royal guerze, or monkelser = 37½ inches, and the common guerze = 25 inches. The arish = 38¼ inches.

PERU.

The weights and measures the same as in Central America. Vide page 425.

POLAND.

In 1819, weights and measures founded upon the metrical system of France were introduced into Poland. The weight of commerce is the kilogramme, which is divided into 16 oz. 32 loths, or 128 drams. The dram is 3 scruples of 24 grains each. 100 kilogrammes = 1 centner, or 220½ lbs. avoirdupois.

Formerly the lb. of Cracow = 6250 grains, and the lb. of Warsaw = 5832 grains Troy.

Dry and Liquid measure is the French litre, called kwarty.

128 litres = 1 korgez ; 30 korgez = 1 last.

The korgez is divided into 4 quarters, or 8 garcy, and contains 3.6325 Winchester bushels.

Long measure is the ell of 2 feet = 24.3 inches English. The Cracow foot = 14.03 inches English.

PORTUGAL.

At Lisbon and Oporto the commercial weights are,

The quintal, equal to 4 arrobas; and 1 arroba is equal to 32 libri or pounds.

1 libra is equal to 16 oncas or ounces = 7084 English grains.

The libra is divided into 2 marcos, 4 quartas, 16 ounces, 120 ottavas, or 9216 graös.

Dry measure.—A mojo, or moys, of corn and salt, is divided into 15 fanegas, 60 alquieres, 120 mejos, 240 quartos, 480 octavos, or 1920 selemines, and contains 23.03 Winchester bushels.

Liquid measure.—A tonnelada of wine is divided into 2 pipes or botas, 52 almudas, 104 alquieres or potas, 624 cannadas, or 2496 quartillos. The almuda of Lisbon contains 1040 English cubic inches, equal to 4⅓ gallons. 31 almudas are at London reckoned to a pipe of Lisbon wine, equal to 140 gallons.

The pipe of wine at Oporto contains 21 almudas; and, as the almuda contains 1530 English cubic inches, the pipe is equal to nearly 139½ gallons, though generally reckoned at only 138 gallons.

Cloth measure.—This is of 2 kinds: the one called the vara, and the other covado. A vara is divided into 5, and the covado into 3 palmes.

21 varas equal 34 covados; 147 covados of Lisbon equal 150 covados of Oporto; 27 covados of Lisbon equal 20 English yards, and 11 equal 13 ells of Hamburg. 5 varas equal 6 English yards; 23 = 44 ells of Hamburg. 9 feet equal 10 English feet.

In a ship's cargo, 4 chests of sugar, 4 pipes of oil, and 4000 lbs. of tobacco, are computed to the last for freightage.

The *long measure* is divided as follows: 1 covado or cubit = 2 pes, 3 palmas, 24 inches or pallegadas = 36 dedos or 144 graös.

The milha or mile = 9389.3 palmos, or $1\frac{1}{4}$ miles English.

The pe or foot = 12.944 inches English. Land is surveyed mostly by the vara. 4840 varas = 1 acre, or 1 acre, 1 rood, $30\frac{2}{5}$ perches English.

PRUSSIA.

In 1820 a new system of weights and measures was introduced into Prussia, the standard of which is the Rhinland foot of 12 inches, connected with the Cologne mark.

The pound = 2 Cologne marks, or 7218 grains Troy. It weighs the sixty-sixth part of a cubic foot, Rhinland, of pure water weighed in air at 15° Reaumur.

4 quentins	equal to	1 loth.
2 loths	"	1 ounce.
16 ounces	"	1 pound.
110 pounds	"	1 centner or quintal.
4000 pounds	"	1 ship last.

Besides these may be added the following, often used, viz.:

14 pounds	equal to	1 lispfund.
20 lispfunds	"	1 shipfund.
22 pounds	"	1 stein or stone.
100 pounds	"	103.11 lbs. avoirdupois.

The Cologne mark is equal to 3609 grains Troy weight.

Long measure.

12 inches	equal to	1 foot, Rhinland.
$25\frac{1}{2}$ inches	"	1 ell.
6 feet	"	1 fathom.
2 fathoms	"	1 ruthe.

The Rhinland foot is equal to $12\frac{356}{1000}$ English inches.

Liquid measure.

5 oessels	equal to	1 quart.
30 quarts	"	1 anker.
2 anchors	"	1 eimer.
2 eimers	"	1 ahm.
$1\frac{1}{2}$ ahms	"	1 oxhoft.
4 oxhofts	"	1 fuder.

The tun, beer measure, contains 100 quarts.

The eimer is the principal wine measure, and contains 3840 Prussian, and 4192 English cubic inches, and 18.14 English gallons.

Dry measure.—The principal corn measure is the scheffel, which is divided into 16 metzen, or 48 quarts, and measures 3072 Prussian, or 3353.6 English cubic inches; it is equal to 1.5594 English bushels.

At Dantzick the corn measure is divided thus, viz.:

4 metzens equal	- - - - -	1 viertel.
4 viertels "	- - - - -	1 scheffel.
16 scheffels "	- - - - -	1 malter.
2 malters "	- - - - -	1 wispel.
3 wispels "	- - - - -	1 last of wheat or rye.
2 wispels "	- - - - -	1 last of oats or barley.

Lumber is sold by the shock of 60 pieces. A ship last for reckoning the burthen of vessels, is equal to 4000 pounds, or 2 tuns, nearly.

At Stetin 1 small stone (kliener) = 10 lbs. A stone of wood is 21 lbs.

1 last of corn is divided into 3 wispel, 6 droemts, 72 scheffels or 1152 metzen.

Coals are sold by the barrel of 8 scheffels. 18 barrels are equal to 1 Newcastle chaldron.

Liquid measure.—The loth of wine is divided into 1⅓ pipes, 2 oxhofts, 3 ahms, 12 ankers, 60 viertels, or 360 stofs. A stof contains 89 English cubic inches.

The beer measure is the last of 6 fass, 12 barrels, or 1152 stofs. A stof is divided into 2 halves or 4 quarts, and contains 116 English cubic inches.

Cloth measure.—100 ells equal 73 English yards; 100 feet = 100½ English feet.

Of a ship's cargo.—Ships are commonly freighted by the Dutch last, of which 5 are equal to 1 Stetin last. To the Dutch last are reckoned 4000 lbs. of iron and other heavy goods; 2000 lbs. of hemp, tow, and other light articles; 56½ scheffels of grain; 5 schock of pipe staves; 7 schock of hogshead staves, or 12 schock of hogshead headings; 9 schock of barrel staves, or 14 schock of barrel headings; 65 cubic feet of oak timber, or 70 cubic feet of fir timber.

Ships are also freighted by the mille; and in 1 mille are reckoned 20 schock or 1200 pipe staves; 30 schock or 1800 hogshead staves; 40 schock or 2400 barrel staves; 60 schock or 3600 headings; 260 cubic feet of oak timber, and 280 feet of fir.

At Dantzig, or Dantzick, the commercial weights are,

The ship-pound, equal to 20 lispounds of 16½ lbs. each, or 330 lbs.

1 centner equal to 110 lbs.

1 grosser or large stone = 33 lbs.

1 kliener or small stone is equal to 20 lbs.

1 pound is equal to 16 ounces or 32 loths = 7238 English grains.

Dry measure.—The last of corn is divided into 24 tons, 56½ scheffels, 240 viertels, or 960 metzen. The scheffel contains 3172.72 English cubic inches.

Liquid measure.—The last of wine contains 2 fuders, 8 oxhofs, 12 ahms, 48 ankers, 240 viertels, or 1320 stofs. A stof contains 105 cubic inches. 1 oxhoft, or 165 stofs, is equal to 75 English gallons.

The last of beer is divided into 6 fass, 12 barrels, 1080 stofs, or 4320 quarts. The beer stof contains 141 English cubic inches. A barrel, or 90 stofs = 45 English beer gallons.

Cloth measure.—100 ells = 73 English yards, and 100 feet equal 100½ English feet, as at Stetin.

17 Dantzick feet are equal to 16 English feet.

The pipe staves of Dantzick are of 3 different sorts: crown, brack, and bracks brack. The gauge for crown staves is $4\frac{1}{2}$ inches broad, $1\frac{3}{4}$ inches thick, and 64 inches in length, which they must be at the least; but they are expected greater in every respect.

Pipe staves are from 64 to 68 inches long; 6, 5, and $4\frac{1}{2}$ at least broad; and $1\frac{1}{2}$ to 3 thick.

Brandy staves, at least 54 to 58 inches long, as thick and broad as pipe staves.

Hogshead staves, 42 to 45 inches long; breadth and length as pipe staves, all English measure.

The different sorts are distinguished by proper marks. *Crown pipe staves* are stamped at the end with K. Brack, in the middle, I. Bracks brack, II. *Hogshead crown*, at the end, OK. Brack, in the middle, I. Bracks brack, II. *Brandy hogshead crown*, at the end, BK. Brack, in the middle, ⋈. Bracks brack, ⋈ ⋈. *Oak plank* is assorted in the same manner. *Crown plank*, in the middle, is marked C. Brack, in the end and middle, B; and bracks brack, BB.

To distinguish $1\frac{1}{2}$ from 2, and $2\frac{1}{2}$ from 3 inches, the $1\frac{1}{2}$ is marked with I, and $2\frac{1}{2}$ with ⋈.

At the end, in rough strokes with coloured paint, brack is yellow, I. Bracks brack, white, II. Crown, red, III.

In a SHIP'S CARGO, pearl ashes are sold by the ship-pound; and 11 ship-pounds, net weight, are reckoned for a last. The tare is fixed at 7 per cent.; but it is sometimes 8 or 10 per cent., according to the size of the casks, which weigh from 5 to 10 ship-pounds. A barrel of weed ashes weighs about a ship-pound, and 12 barrels make a last.

Sowing linseed is packed in barrels, of which 24 make a last of $56\frac{1}{2}$ scheffels.

60 grosser or large stones, or 1980 lbs. make a last of flax.

40 of the same, or 320 lbs. make a last of feathers.

At MEMEL, the corn measure is the last of $56\frac{1}{2}$ scheffels, as at Dantzick, which is from $10\frac{1}{2}$ to $10\frac{3}{4}$ quarters, Winchester measure. Timber, masts, and yards, are sold by the British running foot. Linen cloth is measured by the Berlin ell, of which $137\frac{1}{5}$ make 100 yards English. Flax and hemp are sold by the stone of 23 lbs. Linseed by the barrel of $2\frac{1}{4}$ scheffels. Salt by the last of 6000 lbs.

RUSSIA.

The Russian pound contains 32 loths, 96 solotnicks = 6318 grains Troy.

Petersburg.—At Petersburg the commercial weights are as follows:

One berkowtz, equal to 10 poods or $360\frac{4}{5}$ English pounds; one pood being equal to 40 lbs. or $36\frac{1}{12}$ English.

100 lbs. Russian = $90\frac{1}{6}$ English.

Dry measures.—The chertwert of corn is divided into 2 osmins, 4 pajocks, 8 chertwericks, or 64 garnetz, and contains 12447 English cubic inches, or 5.952 Winchester bushels. 16 chertwerts make a Russian last, equal to $11\frac{1}{2}$ English quarters.

Coals are sold by measure, and by weight. In measure, a keel of Newcastle coals should make 157 chertwerts; and in weight, 1316 poods.

Liquid measures.—A pipe of wine—divided into 40 vedras, 320 krushkas, or 3520 charkas. The vedra contains 751.82 English cubic inches, or 3.246 wine gallons: and the pipe, therefore, should contain 130 gallons.

The oxhoft = 6 ankers = 12 stekars = 18 vedras, or 240 bottles.

Cloth and Linear measures.—The arsheen of Russia contains 28.0114 English inches.

The English and Rhenish foot are both used in Russia.

97 Rhenish feet equal 100 English feet.

One sashe equal 7 English or $6\frac{4}{5}$ Rhenish feet.

The werst, or mile of Russia, contains 500 sashes or sashen, 1500 arsheen, 3500 English feet, or 3400 Rhenish feet.

The arsheen is divided into 16 vershocks.

Land measures.—The dessetina contains 2400 Russian square fathoms, or 21.600 arsheens, and equals 2 acres, 2 roods, 32 perches English.

In a ship's cargo the following quantities are reckoned equal to a gross or great last:

Of potatoes, bristles, hemp, tallow, linseed oil, caviar and iron, 120 poods.

Of soap and wax, 100 poods.

Of aniseed, carraway seed and cable yarn, 80 poods.

Of flax, hemp, Russian yarn and isinglass, 60 poods.

Of corn or linseed, 16 chertwerts.

Of small mats, 600; of buckskins or large mats, 400.

To the preceding information may be added, that—

10 Poods are a berquet: 6 berquets 1 last.

63	"	of hemp, iron and flax - -	=	a ton English.
$62\frac{1}{2}$	"	of tallow - - - - -	=	do.
44	"	of isinglass, hides, bristles or horse-hairs, and caviar - -	=	do.
60	Pieces	of sail-cloth - - - - -	=	do.
80	"	of flems or sheeting - -	=	do.
90	"	of raven ducks - - -	=	do.
120	"	of drillings - - - -	=	do.
3500	Hare-skins	- - - - - -	=	do.
6000	Arsheens	broad diapers and linens -	=	do.
8000	"	huckaback and narrow " -	=	do.
6000	"	crash - - - - - -	=	do.

$5\frac{1}{2}$ Winchester bushels make a chertwert, by which grains, &c. is sold.

3 Russian krushkas are equal to a gallon of beer in London.

Libau.—At Libau the commercial weights are,

One ship-pound, equal to 20 lispounds of 20 lbs. each, or 400 lbs.

One pound is equal to 32 loths, or 6373 English grains.

$109\frac{1}{2}$ lbs. are equal to 100 lbs. English.

57

At Libau the weight of Lubeck and Hamburg is also used, which is 17 per cent. heavier than the Libau weight.

The *Dry measures* of Libau are the last of wheat, rye, barley and peas, which is of 48 loofs. A last of oats and malt is of 60 loofs.

The last of wheat, rye, &c., equal $11\frac{1}{2}$ English quarters; and that of oats, &c., $14\frac{1}{3}$ English quarters.

Salt is sold by the last. $12\frac{1}{2}$ lasts of Liverpool salt are equal to 9 lasts of Libau. A keel of coals is estimated at $9\frac{1}{6}$ lasts or 440 loofs.

Riga.—At Riga the commercial weights are,

The last of 12 ship-pounds.

The ship-pound, equal to 4 loofs, 20 lispounds, or 400 lbs.

One lispound is equal to 20 lbs.: one pound is equal to 6454 English grains.

45 lbs. at Riga is equal to 46 lbs. Russian standard: 38 = 35 lbs. English.

Dry measures.—The last of wheat and barley contains 24 tons, (barrels,) or 48 loofs; a last of oats, 30 tons, or 60 loofs; and a last of rye, $22\frac{1}{2}$ tons, or 45 loofs.

48 loofs equal $11\frac{1}{2}$ English quarters, or a chertwert of Russia.

Salt and linseed are measured by the ton, or barrel. Salt is 18, and linseed 12, barrels to a last. Of Liverpool white salt about $2\frac{1}{2}$ tons make a last at Riga.

Liquid measures.—A fuder of wine is divided into 6 ahms, 24 ankers, 120 viertels, or 720 stofs.

One ahm, or 120 stofs, equal $38\frac{1}{4}$ English gallons.

Cloth measures.—Five ells equal 3 English yards. Ten feet of Riga equal 9 of England.

SPAIN.

At Cadiz the commercial weights are,

The quintal, equal to 4 arrobas; and 1 arroba equal to 25 libri.

One libra or pound equal to 2 Castilian marks, or 16 onces = 7101 grains Troy.

The ounce is divided into 16 darmes.

100 libri or pounds equal 102 lbs. English.

The apothecaries weight is also the Castilian mark, but it is divided into 8 drams, 24 escrupulos, 48 obolos, 144 carracters, or 576 grains.

Dry measures.—The last of corn and salt is divided into 4 cahiz, 48 fanegas, 144 celomines, or 576 quartillos. The fanega contains 3439 English cubic inches, and is equal to 1.599 Winchester bushels.

100 lasts of salt are equal to 81 lasts English or 77 lasts of Dantzick.

Liquid measures.—A majo of wine contains 16 cantaros, or arrobas majores; a pipe 27, and a botta 30 cantaros. This arroba = 4.245 gallons English.

The pipe of oil contains 34 arrobas menores, which are equal to $110\frac{1}{3}$ gallons English.

The capacity of the arroba menora is 771 English cubic inches, equal to $3\frac{}{3}$ English wine gallons.

Cloth measures.—100 varas are equal to $91\frac{1}{2}$ English yards; and 100 feet to $92\frac{1}{3}$ English feet.

The Burgos foot is used in commerce, being equal 0.91428 of the English foot. It is divided into 12 inches, 144 lines. 3 of these feet make one vara, which is divided into quarts, sixths, eighths, and sixteenths.

At Malaga, the commercial weights and cloth measures are the same as at Cadiz.

Dry measures.—A fanega of corn is divided into 12 almudas, or 48 quartillos, and contains 3696 English cubic inches.

Liquid measures.—An arroba of wine is divided into 8 azumbres or 32 quartillos, equal to 960 English cubic inches, or $4\frac{1}{6}$ gallons.

A pipe of wine contains 30 arrobas, or 125 English gallons.

A pipe of oil is estimated at about 116 gallons English.

At Majorca the commercial weights are,

The quintal, equal to 4 arrobas, or 100 lbs.

One libra, or pound, equal to 12 ounces=6487 English grains.

100 libri, or pounds, are equal to $92\frac{1}{2}$ lbs. English.

Dry measure.—A quartera of corn is divided into 6 barsellas, or 36 almudas, and contains 4097 English cubic inches.

Liquid measures.—A pelexo of wine contains 12 cortanes.

A pipe of oil contains 107 cortanes, equal to 116 gallons English.

Cloth measures.—A canna, equal to $1\frac{7}{8}$ English yards; and 8 canna equal to 15 ditto.

At Alicante the commercial weights are as follows:

One carga is equal to $2\frac{1}{2}$ quintals, or 10 arrobas.

One quintal is equal to 4 arrobas=96 lbs. mayor, (great,) or 144 lbs. menor (small) weight.

One libra or pound mayor equals 18 oz., and also 8004 English grains.

One libra or pound menor equals 12 oz., and also 5336 English grains.

Dry measures.—A caffise of corn, divided into 12 barsellas, contains 15019 English cubic inches.

Liquid measures.—A tonnelada of wine contains two pipes: the pipe is divided into 40 arrobas or 50 cantaros. A cantaro contains 655 English cubic inches; 50 cantaros or a pipe are, consequently, equal to $141\frac{2}{3}$ gallons.

Cloth measures.—A vara is divided into 4 palmes. 100 varas equal 83 English yards.

At Barcelona the commercial weights are,

The quintal equal to 4 arrobas or 104 lbs.

One libra or pound equals 12 ounces=6313 English grains.

100 lbs. equal 90 lbs. English.

Dry measures.—A salma of corn is divided into $1\frac{3}{5}$ cargas, 4 quarteras, or 48 cortanes, and estimated to be equal to one English quarter.

Liquid measures.—A cargo of wine is divided into 16 cortanes, 32 quarteras, or 128 quartas, and contains 6660 English cubic inches; equal to 29 gallons. A cargo of oil is divided into 11 arrobas, 30 cortanes, or 120 quartas.

A pipe of oil from Majorca contains 107 cortanes, equal to about 116 gallons.

Cloth measures.—A canna is divided into 2 varas or 8 palmes. 100 canne are equal to 173 English yards.

In Spanish America the weights and measures are the same as at Cadiz: and generally through Spain, except as above, where custom has established some variation, the Castilian weights and measures are used, as at Cadiz. The standard of long measure is preserved at Burgos; of dry measure at Aula; of liquid measure at Toledo; and of weight at Madrid.

SWEDEN AND NORWAY.

At Stockholm the weights are of four distinct denominations, viz., 1st. the miner's pound, called the mark, of 5801 Troy grains, and of which 100 are equal to 83 lbs. English; 2d. the inland pound, or mark, of 5526 Troy grains, and of which 100 = 78 lbs. English; 3d. the iron or export weight, called, also, light weight, of 5250 grains Troy; 4th. the victualie or skaal weight, which is the standard weight, or that by which almost all goods are weighed.

One ship-pound of iron is divided into 20 markpounds of 20 marks each, or 40 marks. A mark contains 5250 Troy grains.

One ship-pound of victualie weight is divided into 20 lispounds, of 20 lbs. each, or 400 lbs.

One quintal is equal to 120 lbs. 1 vog = 165 lbs. 1 stone = 32 lbs. 1 lispound = 20 lbs.

One pound victualie weight = 32 loths = 6563 English grains. 100 lbs. victualie = 125 lbs. iron weight, or $93\frac{3}{4}$ lbs. English.

100 lbs. iron weight = 75 lbs. English.

One last of iron = 15 ship-pounds: one last of victualie = 12 ship-pounds.

Dry measures.—A last of corn contains 24 tons or barrels. A barrel is divided into 2 spanns, 4 half spanns, 8 quarts, 32 kopper, or 56 kanns, and measures 8940 English cubic inches, equal to about $4\frac{1}{6}$ bushels, or the last, of 24 barrels, to $12\frac{1}{2}$ quarters.

Coals are sold by the barrel; 155 to 160 barrels are equal to a Newcastle keel.

Liquid measures.—A fuder of wine is divided into 2 pipes, 4 oxhofts, 6 ahms, 12 eimer, 24 ankers, 360 kanner, 720 stoops, or 2880 quarts. A kanner contains 160 English cubic inches; and 1 oxhoft, or 90 kanner, equals $62\frac{1}{3}$ English gallons.

Cloth measure.—100 ells equal 65 English yards; 38 feet Swedish = 37 feet English.

NORWAY.

At Bergen the commercial weights are,

One ship-pound, equal to 20 lispounds, of 16 lbs. each, or 320 lbs.

One centner, equal to $6\frac{1}{4}$ lispounds, or 100 lbs.

One vog, equal to 3 bismer pounds, or 36 common pounds.

One bismer pound is equal to 12 lbs.

One pound is equal to 32 loths, or 7703 English grains.

100 lbs. equal to $110\frac{1}{4}$ lbs. English.

Dry measure.—A last of corn measures 12 toender or barrels. One barrel of corn contains 144 pots, or 8489 English cubic inches.

21 barrels equal $10\frac{1}{4}$ quarters English. 1 barrel of tar equals 320 pots.

Liquid measures.—A fuder of wine is divided into 6 ahms, 24 ankers, 240 stuebgens, 465 kanns, or 930 pots. The ahm contains 9128 English cubic inches, equal to nearly 40 English gallons.

Cloth measures.—21 Norway ells equal to 23 Hamburg ells. 100 = $68\frac{2}{3}$ yards English. 34 feet equal 35 English.

In a ship's cargo the last of Spanish and French salt, and the last of coal, contains 18 toender or barrels, and the barrel of 176 pots. 7 vog of stockfish are reckoned as a last, and 120 barrels of tar to the keel.

SWITZERLAND.

At Geneva the commercial weight is of two sorts, viz., the poid fort and the poid foible.

The lb. of the pound fort contains 18 oz., and the lb. of the pound foible only 15 oz. The oz. of both weights is divided into 24 deniers, or 576 grains.

100 lb. fort = 121.4 lbs. avoirdupois. 100 lb. foible = 101.2 lbs. avoirdupois.

Dry measure is the coupe or sack = 2.203 Winchester bushels, and containing 110 lbs. of wheat.

Wine measure is the char divided into 12 setiers, 288 quarterons, or 576 pots.

The setier = 11.9 wine gallons.

Long measure is the foot = 19.2 inches English.

The Geneva ell = 45 inches English.

At Neufchatel the commercial weight is of two sorts, viz., the old poids de marc of France and the poids de fer.

100 lbs. poids de fer = 114.7 lbs. avoirdupois.

Wine measure is the muid of 5 gerle: 12 setiers, or 192 pots = 18.548 wine gallons.

Long measure is the foot = 11.81 inches English, and the ell = 43.8 do.

Dry measure here and at Bern is the mutt of 12 maas, 48 immi, 96 echterli, 192 sechzehnerli = 4.771 Winchester bushels.

The commercial weight at Bern is the centner of 100 lbs. The pound = 16 oz. 32 loths or 128 quintleins, and weighs 8060 grains Troy.

The *Wine measure* is the landfass of 6 saums, 24 brenten, or 600 maas. The common fass is $\frac{2}{3}$ of a landfass. The maas is divided into halves, quarters, &c., and contains 3.532 pints English.

Long measure at Bern is the ell of 82 inches of 12 lines each, and = 11.545 inches English.

At Zurich the commercial weight is of two sorts, the light lb. of 16 oz., for weighing silks, being 2 marks, or 32 loths, and the heavy lb. of 18 oz., or 36 loths.

The light lb. = 1.033 lbs. avoirdupois.

The heavy lb. = 1.162 lbs. avoirdupois.

Dry measure is the mutt of 4 viertels; 16 viertels or 64 masslings = $2\frac{1}{3}$ Winchester bushels.

Liquid measure is the kopk of 2 maas, which is of 2 sorts, i. e. the land maas = 0.48 wine gallons, and the city maas = 0.43 wine gallons.

Long measure is the foot of 12 inches = 11.81 inches English, and the ell of 2 feet, or 23.62 inches English.

TURKEY.

At Constantinople and Smyrna, the commercial weights are, the cantaar or quintal, of $7\frac{1}{3}$ great, or $29\frac{1}{3}$ small, batmans, 44 okas, 100 rotolos, 176 yusdromes, or chequees. The chequee is divided into $66\frac{2}{3}$ miscals, or 100 drachmas.

One great batman is equal to 4 toppie or 8 okas.

One small batman is equal to 1 toppie or 2 okas.

One oka is equal to 2 rotolos or rottels.

The cantaar or quintal is equal to 124 lbs., 9 oz., 12 drams, avoirdupois.

A toppo of cotton weighs about $4\frac{3}{5}$ lbs. avoirdupois.

Dry measure.—The fortin of corn, containing 4 kisloz. 99 kisloz are equal to $11\frac{1}{5}$ quarters English, or one last of Hamburg. The kilò or kisloz of rice weighs about 10 okas.

Liquid measure.—The principal liquid measure is called the almud, equal to 1 gallon, 3 pints.

The almud of oil should weigh $22\frac{5}{8}$ lbs. avoirdupois.

Cloth measure.—The standards are called pikes, and are two lengths, the great, called halibi or archim, and small, called endaseè. 31 great pikes equal 32 smaller. 50 great pikes equal 36ı English yards.

At Smyrna, the cantaar or quintal consists of $7\frac{1}{2}$ batman, $22\frac{1}{2}$ chequees, 45 okas, 100 rotolos, or 18,000 drams.

A cantaar of cotton-wool and of tin is only 44 okas.

The rotolo is 180 drams, and the oka, which is 400 drams, equals $2\frac{3}{4}$ lbs. avoirdupois.

A chequee of 800 drams of goats' wool generally renders at London $5\frac{1}{6}$ lbs. avoirdupois; a teffee of Brussa silk, of 610 drams, $2\frac{3}{4}$ lbs.; a chequee of opium, of 250 drams, $1\frac{5}{8}$ lbs.; a quintal of fruit of 100 rotolos, one hundred weight; and a quintal of cotton-wool, of 100 rotolos, 106 lbs.

Gold and silver lace is sold by the metical of $1\frac{1}{2}$ drams.

The pike is 27 inches English.

Dry measure is the killow=1.456 Winchester bushels, or $13\frac{1}{2}$ wine gallons.

WEST INDIES.

In the West Indies the weights and measures vary in the colonies of the different nations. In the British islands they are the same as in England; observing only that, at Trinidad, the quintal contains but 100 lbs.

At Cuba, and the other Spanish settlements, the Spanish weights and measures are used.

At St. Domingo, in the Haytien or western part, the weights and measures of France are still used; but, in Hispaniola, or the eastern part, those of Spain.

At St. Thomas's, St. John's, and St. Croix, the usual weights and measures are those of Denmark.

In Brazil the weights and measures are the same as those of Portugal.

A GENERAL TABLE

OF THE

AGREEMENT WHICH THE WEIGHTS OF THE PRINCIPAL PLACES IN EUROPE HAVE WITH EACH OTHER.

Note.—As the weights of Amsterdam with the OLD WEIGHTS of Paris, Bordeaux, Strasbourgh, Besançon, and several other places, have but the minutest difference, they are all comprehended under the head of Amsterdam, as those of Nuremburg are under Frankfort, and others in the same manner.

By means of this Table, the agreement which the weights of one place have with those of another, may easily be discovered. For example: Suppose it is wanted to be known how many pounds 100 English make at Amsterdam, look for England in the first column, and thence along the line to the column under Amsterdam, and it will there be found, that 91 lbs. 18 oz. Dutch, correspond with 100 lbs. English; and so with any other weight sought for, and *vice versa*. The calculations are in pounds of 16 ounces each.

100 lbs. weight of … are equal to	Of U. S. of A. and of England		Of Amsterdam, Paris, &c.		Of Antwerp or Brabant.		Of Rouen the viscounty-weight.		Of Lyon, the city weight.		Of Rochelle.		Of Toulouse and Upper Languedoc.		Marseilles or Provence.	
	lb.	*oz.*	*lb.*	*oz.*	*lb.*	*oz.*	*lb.*	*oz.*	*lb.*	*oz.*	*lb.*	*oz.*	*lb.*	*oz.*	*lb.*	*oz.*
U. S. of A. and of England	100	0	91	8	96	8	88	0	106	0	93	9	107	11	113	0
Amsterdam, Paris, &c.	109	8	100	0	105	8	96	4	116	0	99	0	118	0	123	8
Antwerp	103	12	94	12	100	0	91	4	110	0	93	13	111	12	117	0
Rouen	113	14	104	0	109	12	100	0	120	8	102	15	122	11	128	8
Lyon	94	3	86	0	90	12	82	12	100	0	85	2	101	8	106	4
Rochelle	110	9	101	0	106	8	97	3	117	0	100	0	119	3	124	12
Toulouse, &c.	92	5	84	12	89	6	81	8	98	5	83	15	100	0	105	4
Marseilles	88	11	81	0	85	8	78	0	94	0	80	3	95	9	100	0
Geneva	123	0	112	6	118	8	108	0	103	5	111	6	102	9	128	4
Hamburg	107	5	98	0	103	6	94	4	113	10	97	0	115	10	121	0
Frankfort, &c.	111	11	102	0	107	8	98	3	118	5	101	0	120	6	126	0
Leipsic	104	5	95	4	100	0	91	12	110	8	94	4	112	6	117	12
Genoa	73	0	66	2-3	70	5	64	0	77	5	66	0	78	10	82	5
Leghorn	75	8	69	0	72	12	66	6	80	0	68	5	81	6	85	4
Milan	65	3	59	8	62	12	57	4	69	0	58	14	70	3	73	8
Venice	65	11	60	0	63	6	57	12	69	10	59	6	70	13	74	2
Naples	64	10	59	0	62	4	57	0	68	7	58	6	69	10	72	14
Seville, Cadiz, &c.	103	7	94	8	99	12	91	0	169	10	93	9	111	8	116	11
Portugal	95	4	87	8	92	0	84	4	101	8	86	0	103	4	108	0
Liege	104	0	95	0	100	3	91	7	110	3	94	0	112	0	117	5
Russia, or Muscovy	88	12	81	4	85	2-3	78	0	94	1-12	80	6	95	9	100	5
Sweden	93	7	85	8	90	2	82	3	99	0	84	9	100	9	105	9
Denmark	111	12	102	4	107	13	98	5	118	7	115	15	125	5	126	4

100 lbs. weight of … are equal to	Of Geneva.		Of Hamburg		Of Frankfort, &c.		Of Leipsic, &c.		Of Genoa.		Of Leghorn.		Of Milan.		Of Venice.	
	lb.	*oz.*	*lb.*	*oz.*	*lb.*	*oz.*	*lb.*	*oz.*	*lb.*	*oz.*	*lb.*	*oz.*	*lb.*	*oz*	*lb.*	*oz.*
U. S. of A. and of England	81	7	93	5	89	7	96	1	137	4	132	11	153	11	152	0
Amsterdam, Paris, &c.	89	0	102	0	98	0	105	0	150	0	45	0	168	0	166	0
Antwerp	84	5	96	10	92	13	99	8	142	2	137	6	159	3	157	1-3
Rouen	92	9	106	0	102	0	109	4	156	0	150	13	147	11	172	2-3
Lyon	76	8	87	12	84	4	90	5	129	0	124	11	144	8	142	3-4
Rochelle	89	14	103	0	99	0	106	0	151	8	146	7	169	11	167	10
Toulouse, &c.	75	7	86	7	83	0	89	8	127	2	122	14	142	6	140	0
Marseilles	72	0	82	10	79	6	85	8	121	8	117	7	136	1	134	8
Geneva	100	0	114	10	110	2	118	0	168	9	163	0	188	13	186	8
Hamburg	87	4	100	0	89	11	102	15	147	0	142	2	164	10	162	11
Frankfort, &c.	90	12	104	0	100	0	107	1	153	0	147	14	171	6	169	5
Leipsic	84	12	92	2	93	5	100	0	142	13	138	1	160	0	158	2
Genoa	59	5	68	0	65	5	70	0	100	0	96	11	112	0	110	11
Leghorn	61	6	70	6	67	10	72	8	103	8	100	0	116	0	114	8
Milan	53	0	60	1	58	5	62	8	89	4	86	4	100	0	98	12
Venice	53	6	61	3	58	13	63	0	90	0	87	0	100	13	100	0
Naples	52	8	60	2	57	13	62	0	88	8	85	8	99	2	98	0
Seville, Cadiz, &c.	84	2	96	6	93	10	99	4	141	12	137	0	158	12	156	14
Portugal	77	14	89	4	85	12	91	13	131	4	126	13	147	0	145	14
Liege	84	8	96	14	93	0	99	12	142	8	137	12	159	9	157	11
Russia, or Muscovy	72	4	82	13	79	6	85	4	121	13	117	13	136	7	134	15
Sweden	76	1	87	2	83	9	89	12	128	3	124	0	143	9	142	0
Denmark	91	0	104	4	99	14	107	5	153	5	148	4	171	11	169	13

100 lbs. weight of … are equal to	Of Naples.		Of Seville Cadiz, &c.		Of Portugal.		Of Liege.		Of Russia.		Of Sweden.		Of Denmark.	
	lb.	*oz.*	*lb.*	*oz.*	*lb.*	*oz.*	*lb.*	*oz.*	*lb.*	*oz.*	*lb.*	*oz.*	*lb.*	*oz.*
U. S. of A. and of England	154	10	97	0	104	13	96	5	112	2-3	107	1-24	89	1-2
Amsterdam, Paris, &c.	169	0	106	0	114	8	105	4	123	1-12	117	0	97	13
Antwerp	160	2	108	0	108	8	99	11	116	2-3	110	11-12	92	3-4
Rouen	175	12	110	4	119	0	109	7	128	0	121	15-24	101	5-8
Lyon	145	6	91	3	98	8	90	8	106	1-4	101	0	84	0
Rochelle	170	11	107	0	115	10	106	5	124	1-3	117	11-12	98	13
Toulouse, &c.	143	4	89	13	97	0	89	3	104	9-16	99	5-12	83	1-8
Marseilles	136	14	85	13	92	12	85	4	99	2-3	94	3-4	79	3-16
Geneva	189	14	119	2	128	8	118	4	138	1-4	131	7-16	109	7-8
Hamburg	165	10	103	13	112	4	103	2	120	11-16	114	17-24	95	7-8
Frankfort, &c.	172	6	108	2	116	13	107	6	125	7-8	119	2-3	100	1-16
Leipsic	161	0	101	0	109	0	100	4	117	1-4	111	5-12	93	1-8
Genoa	112	11	70	11	76	5	70	6	83	7-8	79	3-4	66	5-8
Leghorn	116	9	73	0	79	0	72	10	84	7-8	80	2-3	67	7-16
Milan	100	8	63	0	68	2	62	10	73	1-4	69	2-3	58	1-4
Venice	101	6	63	9	68	11	63	2	74	0	70	5-8	58	11-16
Naples	100	0	62	8	67	9	62	0	72	13-16	69	5-8	57	7-8
Seville, Cadiz, &c.	159	12	100	0	108	3	99	14	116	0	110	1-3	92	5-16
Portugal	148	0	92	12	100	0	92	0	107	13-16	102	1-8	85	3-8
Liege	160	10	100	9	108	12	100	0	116	15-16	111	1-8	92	15-16
Russia, or Muscovy	137	4	86	3	93	1	85	8	100	0	95	0	79	7-16
Sweden	144	7	90	9	97	15	90	0	105	1-4	100	0	83	1-4
Denmark	172	12	109	1	117	1	107	10	125	5-6	119	7-12	100	0

A TABLE

Representing the conformity which the Long Measures of the principal trading cities of Europe have with each other.

The Ells of Amsterdam, Haarlem, Leyden, the Hague, Rotterdam, and other cities of Holland, as well as the Ell of Nuremburg, are equal among themselves, and are comprehended under the Ell of Amsterdam, and the Ell of Bern and Basle under that of Hamburg, Frankfort, and Leipsic.

MEASURES.		Yards of United States and Great Britain.	Ells of Holland and Amsterdam.	Ells of Antwerp and Brussels.	Ells of Hamburgh, Frankfort, Leipsic and Cologne.	Ells of Bergen and Drontheim.	Ells of Sweden and Stockholm.	Canes of Marseilles and Montpelier.	Canes of Toulon, Albi, and Castres	Canes of Genoa, of 9 palmes.	Vares of Castile & Biscay.	Vares of Cadiz & Andalusia.	Vares of Portugal or Lisbon.	Covedoes of Portugal or Lisbon.	Brasses of Florence, Leghorn & Lucca.
100 yards of the U. S. and G. Britain	make	100	133$\frac{1}{3}$	131$\frac{2}{3}$	160	146$\frac{2}{5}$	154	46$\frac{2}{3}$	50	40$\frac{2}{3}$	107	109$\frac{1}{5}$	81$\frac{1}{3}$	133$\frac{1}{3}$	154$\frac{3}{4}$
100 ells of Holland and Amsterdam . . .	make	75	100	98$\frac{3}{4}$	120	110	114$\frac{1}{2}$	35	37$\frac{1}{2}$	30$\frac{1}{2}$	80	81$\frac{4}{5}$	61	100	116$\frac{1}{2}$
100 ells of Antwerp and Brussels, ...	make	76	101$\frac{1}{4}$	100	121$\frac{1}{2}$	111$\frac{4}{5}$	116	35$\frac{4}{5}$	38	30$\frac{1}{5}$	81	84	61$\frac{3}{5}$	101$\frac{1}{4}$	118
100 ells of Hamburg, Frankfort, &c. . .	make	62$\frac{1}{2}$	83$\frac{1}{8}$	82$\frac{1}{3}$	100	91$\frac{3}{4}$	95$\frac{1}{2}$	29$\frac{4}{5}$	31$\frac{1}{4}$	25$\frac{4}{5}$	65$\frac{4}{5}$	68$\frac{1}{5}$	50$\frac{4}{5}$	83$\frac{1}{3}$	97
100 ells of Bergen and Drontheim	make	67$\frac{1}{2}$	90	89	108	100	103	31$\frac{1}{2}$	33$\frac{3}{4}$	27$\frac{4}{5}$	72	74$\frac{3}{4}$	55	90	105
100 ells of Sweden and Stockholm	make	65$\frac{3}{4}$	87$\frac{1}{2}$	86$\frac{1}{2}$	105	96$\frac{1}{4}$	100	30$\frac{1}{2}$	32$\frac{3}{4}$	26$\frac{3}{4}$	70	71$\frac{1}{2}$	53$\frac{1}{2}$	87$\frac{1}{2}$	102
100 canes of Marseilles and Montpelier	make	214$\frac{1}{2}$	286	282$\frac{4}{5}$	343$\frac{1}{5}$	314$\frac{3}{5}$	327$\frac{1}{2}$	100	107$\frac{1}{4}$	87$\frac{1}{4}$	228$\frac{4}{5}$	234	174$\frac{3}{4}$	286	333$\frac{1}{5}$
100 canes of Toul. & Upper Languedoc	make	199$\frac{3}{4}$	266$\frac{2}{3}$	263$\frac{1}{3}$	320	193$\frac{1}{3}$	304	93$\frac{1}{3}$	100	81$\frac{1}{4}$	213$\frac{1}{3}$	213	162$\frac{3}{4}$	266$\frac{2}{3}$	309$\frac{1}{8}$
100 canes of Genoa, of 9 palmes	make	245$\frac{1}{4}$	327	323	392$\frac{4}{5}$	359$\frac{3}{4}$	374$\frac{1}{2}$	114$\frac{1}{2}$	122$\frac{3}{5}$	100	261$\frac{3}{4}$	268$\frac{1}{5}$	199$\frac{1}{2}$	327	381
100 vares of Castile and Biscay	make	93$\frac{3}{4}$	125	123$\frac{3}{5}$	150	137$\frac{1}{2}$	143$\frac{1}{4}$	43$\frac{3}{4}$	46$\frac{4}{5}$	38$\frac{1}{5}$	100	102$\frac{1}{3}$	76$\frac{1}{4}$	125	145$\frac{3}{5}$
100 vares of Cadiz and Andalusia	make	91$\frac{3}{4}$	122$\frac{1}{4}$	119	146$\frac{3}{5}$	134$\frac{1}{2}$	139$\frac{4}{5}$	32$\frac{2}{3}$	45	37$\frac{1}{4}$	97$\frac{2}{3}$	100	74$\frac{2}{3}$	122$\frac{1}{4}$	142
100 vares of Portugal or Lisbon	make	123	164	162	196$\frac{4}{5}$	180$\frac{4}{5}$	187$\frac{3}{4}$	57$\frac{1}{5}$	61$\frac{1}{2}$	50	131$\frac{1}{5}$	134	100	164	191
100 covedoes of Portugal or Lisbon. . .	make	74	100	98$\frac{3}{4}$	120	110	114$\frac{1}{2}$	35	37$\frac{1}{2}$	30$\frac{1}{2}$	80	81$\frac{4}{5}$	61	100	116$\frac{1}{2}$
100 brasses of Florence, Leghorn, &c. .	make	65$\frac{1}{5}$	85$\frac{1}{2}$	84$\frac{4}{5}$	102$\frac{3}{6}$	94	98	30	32	26$\frac{1}{5}$	68$\frac{4}{5}$	70$\frac{1}{3}$	32$\frac{1}{5}$	95$\frac{1}{2}$	100

N. B. By means of this Table, the reader may please to observe, that 100 yards of England make 133$\frac{1}{3}$ ells of Holland; and in like manner he will find how the measures of other places in the table correspond with each other. By the common rule of three, or proportion, he will easily make his computations for any quantity required.

General table of the agreement which the corn measures in the principal places of Europe have with those of England and Amsterdam.

10¼ quarters English, or 82 Winchester bushels, (or a last at Amsterdam, Dantzic, Elbing, and Konigsburg,) make, at

Aiguillon, 41 sacks.
Albi, 25 setiers.
Alicante, 12 cahizes.
Alkmaar, 36 sacks.
Amesfort, 16 muddes.
Amsterdam, 1 last.
Antwerp, 32½ viertels.
Arles, 49 setiers.
Bayonne, 36 sacks.
Beaucaire, 28 setiers.
Beaumont, 38 sacks.
Bergen-op-Zoom, 63 setiers.
Bois-le-Duc, 20½ mouwers.
Bommel, 18 muddes.
Bordeaux, 38 boisseaux.
Breda, 33½ viertels.
Bruges, 17½ hoedts.
Brussels, 25 sacks.
Bueren, 21 muddes.
Cadillac, 33⅓ sacks.
Cadiz, hanegas.
Cahors, 100 cartes.
Campen, 24½ muddes.
Carcassone, 35 setiers.
Clairac, 34½ sacs.
Cleves, 16¼ mouwers.
Condom, 41 sacs.
Copenhagen, 42 tons.
Dantzic, 1 last.
Delft, 29 sacks.
Deventer, 36 muddes.
Doesbourg, 22 mouwers.
Dort, or Dordrecht, 24 sacks.
Dunkirk, 18 razieres.
Edam, 27 muddes.
Elbing, 1 last.
Emben, 15¼ tuns.
Erfelsteyn, 21 muddes.
Frankfort, 27 malders.
Gand or Ghent, 56 halsters.
Genoa, 25 mines.
Gimond, 20 sacks.
Gravelines, 22 razieres.
Haarlem, 38 sacks.
Hamburg, $\frac{}{13}$ of a last.
Heusben, 17¼ muddes.
Hoorne, 44 sacks.
Konigsburg, 1 last.
Brille, 40 sacks.
La Reole, 30 sacks.
Lavaur, 21 setiers
Leyden, 44 sacks.
Libourne, 35 sacks.
Liege, 96 setiers.
Lisle, in Flanders, 38 razieres.
Lisbon, 216 alquieres.
Leghorn, 40 sacks.
Louvain, 27 muddes.
Lubeck, 95 scheffels.
Middlebourg, 41½ sacks.
Montfort, 21 muddes.
Muyden, 44 sacks.
Naerden, 44 sacks.
Nerack, 33¼ sacks.
Nieuport, 17½ razieres.
Oudewater, 21 muddes.
Paris, 19 setiers.
Porto Port, 180 alquieres.
Pumerens, 27 muddes.
Rabastens, 17 setiers.
Rhenen, 20 muddes.
Ruremond, 68 schepels.
Riga, 46 loopens.
Rotterdam, 29 sacks.
St. Gilles, 40 charges.
St. Omer, 22½ razieres.
St. Valery, 19 setiers.
Saumer, 19 setiers.
Steenbergen, 25 viertels.
Stockholm, 23 tuns.
Terveer, 39 sacks.
Thiel, 21 muddes.
Toulouse, 26 setiers.
Tongres, 15 muddes.
Tonningen, 24 tuns.
Venloo, 21¾ mouwers.
Vianen, 20 muddes.
Utrecht, 25 muddes.
Zurick Zee, 40 sacks.

The weight of each piece or bolt of British sail cloth, as required by law; the length being 38 yards, and breadth 24 inches.

Double threads.			*Single threads.*		
No. 1	to weigh	44 lbs.	No. 7	to weigh	24 lbs.
2	"	41 "	8	"	21 "
3	"	38 "	9	"	18 "
4	"	35 "	10	"	15 "
5	"	32 "			
6	"	29 "			

CHAPTER XXVII.

HARBOUR REGULATIONS IN THE UNITED STATES.

THE chief commercial regulations in the United States have been so fully considered in the foregoing chapters, that there is nothing to mention here but the harbour regulations established in some of the principal ports.

Maine—Harbour regulations.—Masters incur a penalty not exceeding $10 by anchoring on the herring grounds near the Manannas and Mohegan islands, unless compelled by stress of weather or any disaster.[a]

A penalty of $60 is incurred by discharging ballast in any road, port, or harbour within the state.[b]

A penalty of $7 is incurred by taking any stone or ballast from any shore, without the consent of the owner.[b]

Vessels.—Fishing boats under 2 tons are not liable to attachment when owned in the state.[c]

Vessels are liable here to all material men and mechanics employed to do any work upon them, and they have precedence to other attachments where there is no lien.[d]

New-Hampshire—Harbour regulations.—Persons discharging ballast or any rubbish into the river Piscataqua or Portsmouth harbour, are liable to be fined from 20s. to 40s. A harbour-master is chosen annually at the town meeting.[e] Masters must, within 48 hours after arriving, deposit all the gunpowder on board in the public magazine, or they forfeit £30.[f]

Boston, the capital and largest seaport in Massachusetts, is seated on a peninsula at the bottom of Massachusetts' bay, and has an excellent harbour, easy to be defended, and with water deep enough for the largest ships, though the channel is narrow. Lat. 42° 23′ N., long. 71° 4′ W.

Gunpowder must be in casks of 25, 50, or 100 lbs., and marked on the head "gunpowder," and the year, &c.

Vessels with gunpowder on board cannot lie within 200 yards of any wharf in Boston; or, if with more than 25 lbs. on board, not within 200 yards of any wharf in Charlestown or Roxbury. Gunpowder, when landed in Boston, must be carried to Tileston's wharf, and then to the public powder-house on Pine Island, in boats or carts, which shall have been approved of by the fire wards, and marked by them. It is to be sent on board in a similar manner. If more than 5 lbs. be kept on board any vessel, or on any wharf, it is forfeited.

---

[a] Act, 30th March, 1831. [b] Act, 2d March, 1821. [c] Act, 19th March, 1835.
[d] Act, 12th Feb., 1828. [e] Act, 16th June, 1792. [f] Act, 18th Feb., 1794

Lime cannot be shipped unless contained in casks of 100 gallons, or of 50 gallons, made of well seasoned heads and staves, with 10 hoops on each cask, and branded by the inspector, under the penalty of $1 50 for each cask.

A penalty of not more than $10 for every 100 lbs. is exacted of masters receiving pickled fish on board which have not been inspected. The fish also are forfeited.

A similar forfeiture, and a penalty of $8 per barrel, are incurred for beef and pork, which have not been inspected, received on board, $20 per cask for pot or pearl ashes, and $1 50 for butter or lard

Rubbish and ballast must not be thrown into the harbour, under the penalty of £20.

Rhode Island—Harbour regulations.—The harbour-master of Providence is appointed by the town council, which also establishes the harbour regulations, and the fees of the harbour-master.[a]

Connecticut—Harbour regulations.—Persons casting ballast or any rubbish that may obstruct navigation, into any channel, harbour, or river, forfeit $17.[b]

If in Connecticut river, the fine may be increased to $500.[c]

New-York, the chief seaport in the state of New-York, is situated on the island of Manhattan, at the junction of the Hudson and East rivers. It has an excellent harbour, and may be called the commercial metropolis of the United States. Its imports and exports—the productions of all parts of the world. Lat. 40° 42′ N., long. 74° W.

Masters having more than 28 lbs. of gunpowder on board, must not approach within 300 yards of any wharf south of 14th-street, (near the penitentiary,) before discharging their powder, under the penalty of forfeiting the same.

The powder must be sent to the magazine within 48 hours after arrival, or it is forfeited; but it may be forthwith put on board another vessel for immediate exportation without being landed.

Vessels of war are excepted.

Harbour-masters' regulations.

Article I. No vessel shall be moored in the stream in the East river, nearer than three hundred yards from the docks of the city of New-York, from the first day of May to the first of October. All vessels having on board gunpowder, shall moor or anchor near Buttermilk Channel, and shall hoist, and keep a red flag hoisted, at the foretop-gallant-mast head, during the time they are discharging or receiving. [This regulation is considered very important to guard steamboats from a too near approach to vessels discharging or receiving.] Nor shall any vessel lie at single anchor within that distance, more than twenty-four hours. No vessel shall be moored in the North river nearer than three hundred yards from the wharf; nor any vessel lie at single anchor, within that distance, more than twenty-four hours.

Article II. Agreeably to a statute of the state of New-York, all

[a] Act, 25th June, 1830. [b] Rev. Laws. tit. 73, sec. 5. [c] Ibid. sec. 6.

vessels lying in the North or East rivers, are requested to hoist a lantern with a light in the rigging, in some conspicuous place, under the penalty of said statute, which makes all vessels liable for damages by a non-compliance.

"Whenever any vessel navigating that part of the Hudson river which is north of the Battery, at the southern extremity of New-York, or navigating Lake Champlain, shall be at anchor in the night-time, the master of such vessel shall cause her peak to be lowered, and shall cause a good and sufficient *light* to be shown in some part of her rigging at least twenty feet above her deck, and from her taffril, under the penalty of fifty dollars. And in case such penalty cannot be collected from the master, the owners of such vessel shall be liable therefor, 'jointly and severally, in the same manner as if they were sureties of such master.'"

By the law of April 29th, 1829, "the provisions of the above section are extended to the harbour of New-York, embracing the bay, as far as the village of Castleton, on Staten Island; and thence up the East river, as far as the south point of Blackwell's Island."

Article III. Vessels lying at the wharves or piers, or in basins or slips, shall, unless otherwise directed, lie with their heads up to the docks; those on the east side of the docks, to have their yards topped by their larboard lifts: and those on the west side, topped by their starboard lifts. To be regulated agreeably to the cut in the margin, and not to be changed without the special permission of the harbour-master or harbour-masters, except to paint or bend sails. The moveable fore and aft spars and spritsail yards rigged in; stern davits, quarter davits, bumpkins, and martingales, unshipped. Those on the east side of the docks, shall have the crown of their starboard anchor taken in on the forecastle, and their larboard cable bent and clear. Those on the west side of the docks to have the palms of their larboard anchor taken in on the forecastle, and to have the starboard cable bent and clear.

Those in the North river, lying on the south side of the docks, to have their yards topped by their larboard lifts; and those lying on the south side to have the palm of the starboard anchor taken in on the forecastle, and the larboard cable bent and clear; those on the north, to have their larboard anchor taken in on the forecastle, and the starboard cable bent and clear. Any vessel wanting a berth will apply at the office, or sub-office, or to the harbour-master of the district in which he may wish a berth, stating where the vessel lies; nor shall any vessel exchange, or bargain berths, except by permission of the harbour-master or harbour-masters.

Article IV. All vessels at the end of the wharves or piers, shall haul either way, to accommodate vessels going in or coming out.

Article V. All vessels not discharging or receiving cargoes, shall make room for vessels needing immediate accommodation: vessels wishing to discharge to have the preference of berth to those loading. Vessels returning, or putting into port in distress, always to be first accommodated. As to the fact of vessels being *bona fide* employed in these particulars, the harbour-master is the sole judge.

Article VI. All vessels have on board a ship-keeper, or person to take care of them; and, if any vessel shall be required to remove, and no person be found on board for that purpose, the harbour-master will cause the same to be removed, at the expense of the master, owner, or consignee, who shall also be liable for all damage occasioned by such vessel.

Article VII. No vessel shall be moored or fastened in such place or manner as shall, in anywise, obstruct or interfere with the steam or team ferry-boats at any ferry of this city.

Article VIII. No ballast shall be thrown overboard, on this side of Sandy-Hook, below low-water mark; and in the harbour, all ballast must be landed above high-water mark—to have a tarpaulin between the vessel and the dock, to prevent ballast falling in the water.

Article IX. No person shall encumber any of the wharves, piers, or docks, with spars, boats, goods, or other things.

Article X. No pitch, tar, or other combustibles, shall be heated on board of any vessel at any of the wharves, piers, slips, or basins, of this city; but all such business shall be done on floating stages or boats, or on the wharves, at least six feet from the edge of the wharf, and with a bucket of water always ready.

Article XI. No vessel shall be permitted to hoist a stern-boat, quarter-boat, or boat under the bowsprit.

All persons failing to comply with the foregoing regulations, are liable to a penalty of fifty dollars for each offence, and for all damages, with costs of suit.

There are three harbour-masters, who have, for the better accommodation of the public, divided the city into three districts; and for the convenience of the public their general office is kept at Messrs. E. & G. W. Blunt's Nautical store, 154 Water-street, corner of Maiden-lane.

Harbour-masters' fees. On all vessels of the United States, and on all foreign vessels permitted by law to enter on the same terms as vessels of the United States, which shall enter, and load or unload, or make fast to any wharf, one cent and a half per ton, according to the tonnage in the vessel's register or papers. On all other vessels double that rate. The fees are payable in forty-eight hours after the vessel's arrival, (at the custom-house,) under the penalty of paying double the amount, and costs of suit.

All sloops or schooners in the coasting trade, on application to the harbour-master or harbour-masters, for a berth, shall pay two dollars; and for adjusting any difference respecting the situation or position of any sloop or schooner engaged in the coasting trade, on the application of the person having charge of such vessel, *two dollars* to be paid by the party in fault.

The harbour-masters have authority to regulate and station all vessels in the stream of the East and North rivers, within the limits of the city of New-York, and the wharves thereof, and to remove, from time to time, such ships or vessels as are not employed in receiving and discharging their cargoes; to make room for such others as require to be more immediately accommodated for the purpose of receiving or discharging theirs; and as to the fact of their being fairly and *bona fide* employed in receiving and discharging their cargoes, the said harbour-masters, or either of them, are hereby constituted the sole judges; and have authority to determine how far and in what instances it is the duty of the masters and others having charge of vessels, to accommodate each other in their respective situations. If any person having charge of any vessel refuse or neglect to obey the directions of the said harbour-masters, or either of them, in matters within their authority to direct; or if any person resist or oppose the said harbour-masters, or either of them, in the execution of the duties of their office, such person, for every such offence, forfeits $50.

It shall be the duty of the harbour-masters to superintend and enforce the execution of all laws of this state, and by-laws of the corporation of the city of New-York, for cleaning the docks and wharves, and for preventing and removing all nuisances in or upon them, or either of them; and if the person whose duty it shall be to remove such nuisance, refuse or neglect to remove the same within 48 hours after notice from the harbour-masters requiring such person to remove the same, the said harbour-masters may thereupon demand and receive from such person $2 50.

Masters should be careful not to go into any of the docks belonging to the corporation, as they are liable to pay for so doing $10 each day they shall be there, a penalty which is rigorously exacted. They are also liable to a similar penalty if they should anchor their vessels so as to incommode the ferry-boats from New-York to Brooklyn.

A like penalty is imposed if they cast an anchor in or near any of the wharves or docks, or place a cable or line across the entrance of any slip, or lie at the end of the pier with the jib-boom rigged out, or take any stones, earth, timber or ballast from, or throw them into any dock, or bring any masts or other timber, or stages or platforms, for working on, within any of the docks or wharves.

There is a marine court in this city for the decision of all disputes between mariners and the master or owner.

Rates of wharfage.—Owners of wharves in the city of New-York, may ask and receive the following rates of wharfage for all vessels using their wharves, that is to say:

For every vessel under the burthen of 50 tons, at the rate of 50 cents per day.

For every vessel of 50 tons, and under 100 tons, $62\frac{1}{2}$ cents per day; and $12\frac{1}{2}$ cents per day for every 50 tons above 100 tons, in addition to the rate last mentioned.

Whenever any vessel shall be brought to any dock or wharf to repair or careen, and it is found necessary to sling or erect any stage or stages on her sides, for the more convenient caulking or repairing the same, or that any boats, scows, or floating stages, are brought alongside said vessel, for the purpose of caulking, repairing, or careening, as aforesaid, it shall be lawful for the owner of said wharf to demand and receive $33\frac{1}{3}$ per cent. in addition to her wharfage.

Every vessel which makes fast to any other vessel fastened to any wharf, and being so fastened, loads, unloads, or careens, pays half wharfage.

The master or owner of any vessel discharging ballast upon any wharf, or into a dock, without the consent of the owner, incurs a penalty of $250, and is also liable for wharfage so long as the ballast remains upon the wharf.

A penalty of $5 is incurred by throwing any thing into a dock which may obstruct it.

Disputes as to wharfage are to be settled by one of the port-wardens, whose decision is final. The expenses of the decision must not exceed $1 25, and are borne by the losing party. The master and owner are both liable for wharfage; but a consignee or agent is not, unless an account thereof be presented or left, and payment demanded, before the vessel sails.

Rates of craneage.

	Sloops of 80 tons, and less.	More than 80 tons.
For taking out and putting in a mast - - -	$6 25	$10 00
	Schrs. of 200 tons, and less.	More than 200 tons.
Do. do. do. - - -	$5 00	$6 25
	Square rigged vessels of 200 tons, and less.	More than 200 tons.
Do. do. do. - - -	$6 25	$7 50

Coasting vessels owned in the states of New-York, New-Jersey, or Connecticut, may lie at the public docks by the year, upon the following conditions, viz.:

If they first arrive between the 1st of May and 31st of July.............50 cents per ton.
if between the 1st of August and 31st of October.....40 "
if between the 1st of Nov. and 31st of January.......25 "
if between the 1st of Feb. and 30th of April..........12½ "

and all vessels, of not more than 5 tons burthen, pay $2 on their first coming to at a public dock, which gives them the right of wharfage there until the 1st of May then next ensuing.

A law of the corporation requires vessels which lie at the public docks, by the year, to move their situation once in 21 days, except between the 20th December and March, in each year, or to pay, in addition to the above rates, for every day beyond that term,

if under 20 tons - - - - - 5 cents.
if 20 tons, and under 40 tons - - - 10 "
if 40 tons, and under 60 tons - - - 15 "
if 60 tons, and under 100 tons - - - 20 "

Other coasting vessels pay to the lessee of the public docks the same wharfage as to owners of other wharves above mentioned.

A penalty of $10 is exacted for careening a vessel in any of the corporation docks, and $10 per day while careening.

Vessels with lime on board are not permitted to lie at the public docks, except while discharging, or whilst the same is bona fide for sale.

Vessels with charcoal on board cannot unload or expose it for sale at any slips in front of the markets, under the penalty of $10.

To bring a wreck into any of the public docks, subjects the person to a penalty of $25, and $10 per day whilst lying there; and to throw any dirt into the same, to a penalty of $5.

To kindle a fire on the wharf, except for the purpose of boiling tar, $10.

RATES OF COMMISSIONS,

Allowed by the New-York Chamber of Commerce, when no agreement subsists to the contrary.

ON FOREIGN BUSINESS.

	Per cent.
On the sale of merchandise	5
or purchase of stocks	1
specie	$1\frac{1}{2}$
On the purchase and shipment of merchandise, with funds in hand—on the aggregate amount of costs and charges	$2\frac{1}{2}$
On drawing or endorsing bills in all cases	$2\frac{1}{2}$
On vessels, selling or purchasing	$2\frac{1}{2}$
procuring freight	5
collecting freight on general average	$2\frac{1}{2}$
outfits or disbursements, with funds in hand	$2\frac{1}{2}$
On effecting marine insurance, in all cases:	
When the premium does not exceed 10 per cent. on the amount insured	$\frac{1}{2}$
When the premium exceeds 10 per cent. on the amount of premium	5
On collecting dividends on stock	$\frac{1}{2}$
delayed or litigated accounts	5
On adjusting and collecting insurance losses	$2\frac{1}{2}$
On receiving and paying moneys, from which no other commission is derived	1
On remittances in bills, in all cases	$\frac{1}{2}$
On landing and reshipping goods, from vessels in distress—on the value	$2\frac{1}{2}$
On receiving and forwarding goods, entered at the custom-house—on the value	1
And $2\frac{1}{2}$ per cent. on responsibilities incurred.	

ON INLAND BUSINESS.

	Per cent.
On the sale of merchandise	$2\frac{1}{2}$
On the purchase and shipment of merchandise, or accepting for purchases, without funds or property in hand	2
On the sale or purchase of stocks	1
specie	$\frac{1}{2}$
On the sale of bills of exchange with endorsement	$\frac{1}{2}$
On the sale of bank notes or drafts not current	$\frac{1}{2}$
On selling or endorsing bills of exchange	$2\frac{1}{2}$
On vessels, selling or purchasing	$2\frac{1}{2}$
On do.—chartering to proceed to other ports to load	$2\frac{1}{2}$
On do.—procuring or collecting freight	$2\frac{1}{2}$
On do.—outfits or disbursements	$2\frac{1}{2}$
On do.—collecting general average	$2\frac{1}{2}$
On effecting marine insurance, in all cases:	
When the premium does not exceed 10 per cent. on the amount insured	$\frac{1}{2}$
When the premium exceeds 10 per cent. on the amount of premium	5
On adjusting and collecting insurance losses	$2\frac{1}{2}$
On collecting dividends on stocks	$\frac{1}{2}$
On collecting bills, and paying over the amount, or receiving and paying moneys from which no other commission is derived	1
On receiving and forwarding goods—on the value	$\frac{1}{2}$
On the same when entered for duty on debenture	1
On remittances in bills, in all cases	$\frac{1}{2}$

The above commissions to be exclusive of the guaranty of debts for sales on credit, storage, brokerage, and every other charge actually incurred. The risk of loss by fire, unless insurance be ordered, and of robbery, theft, and other unavoidable occurrences, if the usual care be taken to secure the property, is in all cases to be borne by the proprietor of the goods. When bills are remitted for collection, and are returned under protest, for non-acceptance or non-payment, the same commission to be charged as though they were duly honoured. On consignments of merchandise, withdrawn or reshipped, full commission to be charged to the extent of advances or responsibilities incurred, and half commission on the residue of the value.

RATES OF STORAGE,

Chargeable per month, as established by the Chamber of Commerce.

	Cents.
Almonds, in frails or other pack., cwt...	6
Alum, in casks or bags, per ton.........	40
Ashes, pot and pearl, bbl..................	8
Beef, bbl...................................	6
Bottles, quart, in mats, cr. or hamp. gr.	8
Bark, quercitron, in casks, ton.........	60
Bagging, cotton, loose or in bales, pc...	3
Butter, in firkins of 60 lbs., per firkin..	2
Brandy, see liquors.	
Candles, in boxes of 50 or 60 lbs., box..	2
Chocolate, in boxes of 50 lbs., box......	2
Cocoa, in bags, per cwt....................	2½
——— in casks, "	3
Coffee, in casks, "	2½
——— in bags, "	2
Copperas, in casks, per ton...............	40
Copper, in pigs, "	20
——— in sheets or bolts, ton............	30
——— braziers' bottoms, "	75
Cordage, per ton............................	50
Cassia, in mats or boxes, per cwt.......	10
Cotton, Amer., in sq. bales, 300 lbs....	12½
——— do. in round bales, "	16
——— W. Ind., in proportion to round.	
——— E. India, in bales, per 300 lbs..	9
Cheese, casks, boxes, or loose, cwt.....	3
Duck, heavy, per bolt......................	1½
—— Ravens or Russia sheeting, pc....	¾
Dry goods, in boxes or bales, 40 cu. ft...	40
Earthenware, in crates of 25 to 30 ft...	15
———— in hhds. of 40 to 50 ft...	30
Fish, pickled, per bbl........................	6
—— dry, in casks or boxes, cwt........	4
——— in bulk, per cwt.................	2½
Figs, in frails, boxes, or drums, cwt....	2½
Flax, per ton................................	60
Flaxseed, or other dry articles, in tierces of 7 bushels, per tierce...................	10
Flour, or other dry articles, in bbls.......	4
Grain, in bulk, per bushel.................	1
Gin, see liquors.	
Ginger, in bags, per cwt....................	2
Glass, window, in boxes of 50 ft........	1½
Hardware, in casks of 40 cubic ft.......	40
Hemp, per ton..............................	75
Hides, dried or salted, per hide..........	1½
Indigo, in ceroons or boxes, per cwt...	4
Iron, in bars or bolts, per ton............	20
—— in hoops, sheets, or nail rods, ton..	30
Lard, in firkins of 60 lbs..................	2

	Cents.
Leather, per side............................	1
Lead, pig or sheet, per ton...............	20
—— dry or ground in oil, per ton......	40
Liquors, in puns. of 120 gals., per pun..	30
——— in quarter casks.................	6¼
——— in pipes or other cks. 120 g....	30
——— bottled, in cks. or bxs. dz. b....	1½
Molasses, per hhd. of 110 gals., (other casks in proportion,)......................	30
Nails, in casks, per cwt....................	2
Oil, in hhds. or other casks, 110 gals...	30
—— in chests of 30 flasks, per chest....	4
—— bottled in boxes or baskets, doz.....	1½
Paints, in casks or kegs, ton.............	40
Pepper, in bags, per cwt..................	2½
Pimento, in casks or bags, cwt..........	2½
Pork, per bbl................................	6
Porter, see liquors.	
Rags, in bales, per cwt....................	6
Raisins, Malaga, in casks..................	3
——— " in boxes.................	1
——— in other packages, per cwt....	2
Rice, in tierces, per tierce................	12
—— in half do. per half do...............	8
Rum, see liquors.	
Saltpetre, in bags, per cwt................	2
——— in casks, per cwt................	2½
Salt, in bags or bulk, per bushel.........	1½
Shot, in casks, per ton......................	37
Soap, in boxes of 50 to 60 lbs............	2
Steel, in bars or bundles, per ton........	30
—— in boxes or tubs, per ton...........	40
Sugar, raw, in bags or boxes, per cwt...	2
——— do. in casks, per cwt............	2½
——— refined, in casks or other pack..	3
Tallow, in casks or seroons, cwt........	2
Tea, bohea, in whole chests...............	15
—— do. in half chests.....................	8
—— green or black, in qr. chests........	4½
—— in boxes, in proportion to qr. chests.	
Tin, block, per ton.........................	20
—— in boxes of the usual size, per box..	1½
Tobacco, in hhds., per hhd................	37½
——— in bales or seroons, per cwt.	4
——— manufac. in kegs of 100 lbs.	2
Wines, see liquors.	
Woods, for dying, under cover, ton.....	50
——— " in yards...............	25
Whiting, in hhds., per ton.................	37½

On articles on which the rate is fixed by weight, it is understood to be on the gross weight; and on liquors, oils, &c., on which the rate refers to gallons, it is understood to be on the whole capacity of the casks, whether full or not. The proprietor of goods is to be at the expense of putting them in store, stowing away, and turning out of store. All goods taken on storage to be subject to one month's storage; if taken out within 15 days after the expiration of the month, to pay half a month's storage; if after 15 days, a whole month's storage.

Fees for measuring timber.

For short ship timber - -	25 cents	per ton of 40 cubic feet.
For square timber, - -	14 "	per ton, cubic measure.
For boards, plank, or scantling -	37½ "	per 1000 superficial feet.

City measurers.

Salt or grain - - - -	75 cents	per 100 bushels.
Lime - - - - -	12½ "	per load of 16 bushels.
Charcoal - - - - -	1 "	per bushel.
Sea coal - - - - -	25 "	per chaldron.

Weighmasters' fees.

Hemp, flax, and hides - - - -	3	cents	per cwt.
Brazilletto wood - - - - -	4	"	"
Anchors, above 800 wt. - - - -	5	"	"
Do. under 800 wt. - - - -	2	"	"
Cables, above 800 wt. - - - -	5	"	"
Do. under 800 wt. - - - -	2	"	"

All other articles 2 cents per cwt.; but if the amount does not exceed $10, then 3 cents per cwt.

The weighmaster must make a return of the articles weighed, and mark the weight on each article in legible and durable figures. Penalty for neglect or extortion, $50. Each weighmaster may demand the expense of removing his scales and weights, provided the same does not exceed $1.

Gaugers' fees.

For gauging and ullaging each standing cask,	50	cents.
" ullaging " "	12½	"
" gauging each lying cask	12½	"
" " each quarter cask	8	"
" " barrel or half barrel . .	8	"
" " ullaging do.	4	"

Gaugers' and weighers' fees are paid one half by the buyer and one half by the seller.

Philadelphia, the capital and only seaport of Pennsylvania, is situated on the west bank of the Delaware, between that river and the Schuylkill, 120 miles from the sea, and is accessible by vessels of 500 tons. Lat. 39° 57′ N. Long. 75° 09′ W.

Port regulations.—Vessels may occupy a vacant place at any wharf after applying to the owner or agent for permission, and may continue there so long as may be necessary for the despatch of her business, subject to the directions of the port-warden.

Persons finding an anchor or cable in the Delaware, must file a written notice at the warden's office, and publish the same in a Philadelphia newspaper twice a week for two months, under a penalty of $50. Upon proof of property the same is delivered to the owner or his agent, he paying to the finder one half its value, if found below the north point of Reedy island, and one third if found above;

the valuation to be determined by two appraisers chosen by the parties. If not claimed within two months it becomes the property of the finder.

The harbour-master of Philadelphia is appointed by the governor, and gives bond, with two sureties, in the sum of $4,000, for the faithful performance of his duties.

His duties are to enforce the laws and regulations for cleaning the docks and wharves of the port of Philadelphia; for preventing all nuisances at the wharves and in the docks aforesaid, by burning or breaming any ships or vessels, or otherwise howsoever; for regulating and stationing all ships or vessels in the stream of the river Delaware, or at the wharves within the boundaries of the city of Philadelphia; for removing, from time to time, ships and vessels in order to accommodate and make room for others, or for admitting the river craft to pass in and out of the docks, and for compelling the masters and captains of vessels to accommodate each other, so that vessels arriving from sea shall, for a reasonable time, not exceeding six days, be entitled to berths next to the wharves, until they have landed their cargoes, and for that purpose such vessels lading, may be removed, and take in their cargoes across the decks of the vessels lying nearest to the wharves; for directing the paying of vessels when applied to for that purpose, between the north boundary of the city and Peg's run in the Northern Liberties, and the south boundary of the city and Catharine-street in the district of Southwark; and if any master of any vessel refuse or neglect to comply with the directions of said harbour-master, in matters within the jurisdiction of his office, or if any person whomsoever shall obstruct or prevent the harbour-master in the execution of his duties, such master, or other person, forfeits $100.[a]

The harbour-master is entitled to a fee of $1 on every vessel arriving at Philadelphia, except coasting vessels under 75 tons,[b] and steamboats.[c]

A tonnage duty of four cents per ton must be paid to the port-wardens before sailing, upon every vessel cleared for a foreign port, for the purpose of improving the navigation of the Delaware.

No vessel, having more than five kegs of gunpowder on board, can anchor north of the pier next above the Point house on the Delaware; and all gunpowder must be landed at that pier, and no greater quantity than three kegs, of 25 pounds each, can be landed or shipped on board of any vessel lying between that pier and the wharf of Conroe & Co.

All gunpowder, over 30 pounds, must be delivered at the magazine, within 48 hours after arrival, and before coming to any wharf, of any vesssel importing the same, under the penalty of £20 for every cask not delivered.

Gunpowder, to be exported, must be delivered from the magazine into some boat, and from thence carried immediately to the vessel, under the penalty of £20 if the boat be not ready to receive it, and £15 for every hour such boat remains at the wharf after receiving it.

---

[a] Act, 29th March, 1803. [b] Act, 2d April, 1804. [c] Act, 25th March, 1814.

No fire shall be kept on board any vessel after 8 P. M., under the penalty of 10 shillings, except by special license from the mayor.

Vessels are liable in the state of Pennsylvania for repairs and materials, upon attachment, from the time of repairing until the vessel has proceeded to sea, and then the lien ceases. The tradesmen may all join in the libel. Upon security being given to answer the demands then filed, the vessel is released from the arrest.

The burning or breaming a vessel at any wharf between South and Vine streets is punishable by a penalty of $150.

Rules and regulations of the wardens.—Every vessel that shall come to anchor in the Delaware, any where between Almond and Vine streets, having previously caused her gunpowder, if any she had on board, to be landed as the law directs, may remain in that situation twenty-four hours, and no longer, taking care to lay as near to the island or sand bar as may be consistent with their safety. But if, from the circumstance of a vessel having servants on board, or from any other cause, it may be thought necessary or convenient to lay a longer time in the stream, then the owner, master, pilot, or other person having the charge or direction of such vessel, shall remove her from opposite the city, and shall moor her (or cause her to be moored to the northward of Vine-street) with one anchor and cable up, and one anchor and cable down the stream, and in both the above mentioned situations, the regulations contained in the next succeeding article to be duly attended to. Vessels in the Schuylkill cannot remain at anchor in the stream longer than 12 hours.

When any vessel shall be hauled into any wharf or dock, or alongside of another vessel that may be lying at such wharf or dock, the owner, master, pilot, or whoever may have the command, care or direction of her, shall have her securely made fast; and if outside of another vessel, shall get one good fast from each end of the vessel to the shore, with sufficient fenders between them and the inside vessel, and shall cause the flews of their anchors to be taken on board; and if in the Delaware, must, within twenty-four hours thereafter, cause her jib-boom, spritsail yard, main boom, spanker, and ringtail booms, if any they have, to be rigged in, and their lower yards topped up, in such a manner as least to interfere with vessels passing.

If any vessel properly moored in the stream shall have her anchor or cable overlaid by another vessel, in anchoring or mooring, the master, or person having the care or direction of such last mentioned vessel, shall immediately, or as soon as may be, after application made to him by the party aggrieved, cause the said anchor or cable, so overlaying, to be taken up and cleared.

If the fasts of vessels, when moored at a wharf, shall extend across a dock, so as to obstruct the passing or re-passing of shallops, lighters, or other craft or vessel, the master, or other person having the command of such ship or vessel, shall, upon the first application, immediately cause such fast or fasts to be cast off, or slacked down.

No outward bound vessel, putting off from a wharf, shall lay longer in the stream between Vine and Almond streets, in the district above mentioned, than twenty-four hours, nor in the Schuylkill longer than six hours; and if vessels lying at the end of wharves, so much interlock with each other as to prevent vessels hauling in and out of dock, the master, owner, or pilot, or other person having charge of the same, shall immediately, on application from any person so wanting to haul his vessel in or out of the dock aforesaid, have the vessels so interfering moved in such manner as to accommodate the one applied for; in which case, the vessel making room for another to haul in or out, shall have liberty to make her warps fast to the most convenient place adjacent, for a reasonable time; and that all sea vessels, when transporting or wanting to haul into a wharf or dock, or to make sail in order to proceed to sea, shall have the same privilege.

When any vessel may be lying alongside any wharf, and not taking in or discharging, she shall make way for, and permit any vessel that wants to unload or load, to come inside next the wharf, until she discharges or loads her cargo: and the said vessel, when so discharged or loaded, shall haul outside and give way to the vessel that first occupied the wharf; provided, that from the 10th day of December to the first day of March, no vessel shall be compelled to move, except those lying at Gloster Point pier, from her berth, excepting to let vessels in and out of docks.

No vessel loading or discharging hemp at any wharf, or within any dock, shall be allowed to have any fire on board; neither shall any vessel lying outside or near her, be permitted to have fire on board, while it may be considered dangerous. And no tar, turpentine, rosin, or pitch, shall be heated on the wharf or on board any vessel lying at any wharf within the limits of the city.

All vessels and boats are prohibited from discharging or taking in their cargoes, or any part thereof, or discharging any ballast in the stream of the river Schuylkill; and from throwing any oyster shells, clam shells, or other heavy articles from off any wharf, or from on board of any vessel or boat into the said river below low-water mark, from the permanent bridge to its junction with the river Delaware, under the penalty of twenty dollars.

Baltimore, the chief seaport in Maryland, is situated near the head of the Chesapeake Bay, on the river Patapsco. Ships of burthen come to at Felt's Point, but coasters go up to the town. Lat. 39° 23′ N. Long. 76° 39′ W.

By an ordinance of the mayor and city council of Baltimore, passed in July, 1818, "to provide for the preservation of the navigation of the port of Baltimore," it is ordained, that "no person shall, without permission of the wardens of the port, throw or deposit dirt, mud, gravel, stones, or other materials, in or on the shores or banks of the basin, Jones' Falls, Gwinn's Falls, Patapsco river, or of any other streams of water within the limits of the city, or four miles thereof, under a penalty, for each offence, of 50 dollars, to be recovered, one half to the informer, the other half to the use of the corporation."

The fourth section of an ordinance of 1820 prohibits the throwing any "animal, or fruit, or vegetable matter into the basin or docks, or into Jones' Falls, between the first day of June and the first day of November," under the penalty of ten dollars.

No spars, arks, logs, or lumber, with the bark or sap on, and also square timber, shall remain in the water of the harbour of Baltimore, or in any situation where a common tide can reach the same, within

200 yards of any dwelling or wharf, without a written permission from the board of health, between the first day of June and first day of November, in every year; and the owners of such spars, &c., are required to keep the same more than 200 yards from any dwelling or wharf, (unless they have such permission,) or have them deposited on dry land. For a violation of this ordinance, a forfeiture is prescribed not exceeding $20, and the further sum of $10 for every 24 hours they neglect to comply with it.

The harbour-master at Baltimore is entitled to $5 on every foreign vessel, in addition to his ordinary fee.[a]

By throwing oyster shells in any river, a penalty of $5 is incurred.[b]

Maryland rivers.—No vessel is permitted to anchor, unless compelled by unavoidable necessity, in any fishery on the Susquehanna, or at the head of the Chesapeake, between the 1st of April and the 20th of May, after being ordered to depart, under the penalty of $20, and $5 for every hour she remains.

A penalty of $20 is also incurred by wantonly sailing through a seine extended in any of those fisheries.[c]

The casting ballast into any river or bay below high-water mark, or into the Chesapeake above Cedar Point, subjects the master to £50 penalty.[d]

Virginia—Trading.—Masters of vessels trading and retailing goods on the waters in this state, must obtain a license as pedlars.[e]

Harbour-masters.—Harbour-masters are appointed by the county and corporation courts, and have authority to regulate where vessels shall lie, and to dispose of their spars, &c., so as not to obstruct the navigation, &c.

Disobedience to such regulations, is punishable by a fine of $50. Harbour-masters, on their part, are liable to a fine of $50 if they neglect to direct where vessels shall be moored longer than 24 hours after their arrival; and also liable for all damages sustained. They must also attend to the unmooring and to the remooring of vessels driven from their stations, and are allowed half fees for such services. The fees for square rigged vessels are $2, schooners and sloops, $1.[f]

All vessels merely putting into Norfolk on their homeward passage, are exempt from harbour-masters' fees;[g] and so are all coasting vessels of less than 75 tons, and all vessels in Dismal Swamp canal trade,[h] and all steamboats and passenger packets.

Ballast-masters.—Ballast-masters are appointed by the county courts adjacent to the Chesapeake bay, whose duty it is to superintend the discharging of ballast, and receive 83 cents per day while so employed. If they neglect to attend to their duty, they forfeit $60; and if masters land or cast overboard their ballast without giving notice in writing to the ballast-master, or contrary to his directions, they forfeit $150. Where there is no ballast-master, the captain must apply to a freeholder to act as one. Failure to produce the certifi-

---

[a] Act, 25th Jan., 1806. [b] Act, 13th March, 1834. [c] Act, Nov., 1807.
[d] Act, 1774. [e] Act, 23d Feb., 1820. [f] Act, 16th Feb., 1819. [g] Act, 3d March, 1821
[h] Act, 17th Jan., 1829.

cate of a ballast-master, incurs $30 fine. Masters must bury all persons dying on board of their vessels while within the state, at least 4 feet above high-water mark, under the penalty of $150.[a]

North-Carolina—Harbours and rivers.—Masters throwing ballast or oyster shells overboard in any river or channel in this state, are liable to a penalty of £100; and by pulling down any beacon or other mark, they incur a penalty of £50.[b]

Charleston is the principal seaport in South Carolina. It stands on a peninsula, formed by the rivers of Ashley and Cooper, the former of which is navigable for ships of burthen 20 miles above the city. Lat. 32° 46′ N. Long. 79° 48′ W.

Passengers.—Every master, upon his arrival, must give to the harbour-master a list of his passengers, and their servants, describing their places of residence, their occupations, christian and surnames, and stating whether he considers any, and which, as likely to become burdensome, under the penalty of $10 for each passenger. If any passenger likely to become a public charge, cannot procure sufficient security, the master must take him away within three months, or must become his security himself.

Port regulations.—No vessel shall remain unmoored more than one tide after her arrival, and one tide on her departure.

All vessels arriving must anchor 50 fathoms from the nearest wharf; and bound out, 100 fathoms from the nearest wharf.

No vessel shall, under any pretence whatever, be hauled to any wharf or into any dock, until her yards are topped, her jib and spanker booms rigged in, her spritsail yards put fore and aft, and such of her anchors as are not in use have on the forecastle deck, or other suitable part of the vessel, so as not to obstruct the passage of other vessels by her sides.

No vessel shall be placed so as to prevent others from hauling in and out of the docks.

No fasts shall be run athwart any of the docks.

Every vessel lying at the head of a wharf shall lay out a bower anchor, E. by N., and a stream or bower anchor E. by S.; the cables to be laid under the inner counter, and from the inner bow.

All vessels lying at the head of Chisholm's south wharf, and Blake's wharf, and from Prioleau's to Gadsden's wharf, shall lay their heads to the northward. All vessels at the other wharfs shall lay their heads to the southward, except when the harbour-master directs otherwise.

Every vessel lying fore and aft in a dock, shall have a bower out abaft, and the cable laid under her inner counter, and the anchor laid E. by N. or E. by S., or as the harbour-master shall direct.

No vessel shall take or keep a berth at any wharf, contrary to the harbour-master's directions. He is to fix the berths of all vessels.

All vessels in ballast, light, or taking in a cargo, or retailing a cargo, at any wharf, shall give an inside berth to a loaded vessel that wants to discharge.

---

[a] Act, 7th April, 1831. [b] Rev. Laws, chap. 194, sec. 8.

No vessel shall be allowed more than 15 days to discharge her cargo; 10 days if under 200 tons, and 5 days if under 100 tons.

No naval stores shall be landed at any wharf except Gadsden's or Blake's wharf, South bay. Not more than two bundles of hay or blades, or more than one dray load, shall be landed at one time. [By applying to the harbour-master, and getting his special permit, hay and blades, also naval stores, may be landed as he shall direct, on any wharf: provided, no hay, blades, or naval stores are left on the wharf after sunset.]

No pitch, tar, or turpentine, shall be boiled on any wharf, or on board any vessel; but, for such boiling, a tub of sand shall be put into a boat, and moored to a buoy in the stream.

No ballast, dirt, or rubbish, shall be hove into the docks or stream.

No vessel shall be left entirely vacant, but must have a white ship-keeper on board, capable of taking care of her.

No gunpowder shall be landed in the city from any vessel; no vessel shall be hauled into any dock or wharf, having gunpowder on board, until the same is discharged, under the penalty of one hundred dollars, with costs, for each offence.

All masters of vessels, as soon as they have made their entry at the custom-house, shall deliver to the harbour-master a complete list of all his passengers, servants, and others, signed with his own hand; their christian and surnames, place of nativity, residence, professions, and circumstances; and if there is any pauper or paupers, give bonds for them to the intendant, as the law directs; penalty for neglect 100 dollars.

All vessels in ballast or light, shall give their inside berth to a vessel that wants to take on board her cargo immediately.

No vessel in ballast or light shall be allowed to take an inside berth, until her cargo is ready to be taken on board.

No vessel shall be allowed to hold an inside berth, to take her cargo on board, more than one week, if under 100 tons; 11 days, from 1 to 200 tons; 15 days, from 2 to 300 tons, and 20 days, if over 300 tons. No vessel shall retain her berth more than 24 hours, after her hold is stowed. No vessel is allowed to clean their bottoms in any of the docks where vessels load and discharge, but go to the ship-yards, or on the hard to clean or repair. The harbour-master shall order any empty vessel or vessels, that encumber the docks, into the stream, and be moored 100 fathoms from the nearest wharf; and have power to cut the fast of any empty vessel that refuses to move, when he directs her to be removed: if he is obliged to have her removed, he shall charge the expense to the owner or captain, who is by law obliged to pay the same.

Every captain, commander, or owner of a vessel, refusing or neglecting to comply with any of the foregoing regulations, shall forfeit and pay, for the use of the city, the sum of 20 dollars, with costs, for the first day, and 50 dollars, with costs, for every subsequent day which he so refuses or neglects to comply with any such regulation.

No master of a vessel can employ any slave to work on board his vessel, except such slave hath a city badge to work out.

And it is the bounden duty of the harbour-master, and he is vested with full power and authority, not only to take care, and use his best exertions, that the foregoing regulations be in every respect promptly and punctually observed, maintained, enforced, and executed; but to take legal measures against any persons that may violate or transgress any of the said regulations, and to prosecute without delay every such offender before a court of justice, having competent jurisdiction to try and punish every such offence; and the harbour-master shall also have full power and authority to cut the fast or fasts of any vessel, within half an hour after notice is given, when the captain or commander thereof refuses or neglects, within that time, to slack the same, or to moor such vessel according to law; he hath power, also, to remove any vessel, by the aid of such hands as shall be furnished by the wharf-owner, or master of a vessel applying for a berth, provided they are competent for the purpose. And if any person or persons whatsoever, shall molest or obstruct the harbour-master in the performance of his duties, or in the exercise of any of his powers, as aforesaid, they shall, for every such offence, forfeit and pay to the use of the city, the sum of 50 dollars, with costs.

A negro working on board a vessel, if he hath a badge, is entitled to receive 87½ cents per day; half a day's labour 43¾; for one hour 12½ cents. If found with 3 meals on board, the captain may deduct 18¾ cents, or 6¼ cents for each meal.

No negro or person of colour shall be guilty of whooping or hallooing, or of making any clamorous noise, or singing aloud any indecent song on board any vessel; the negro offending, to be whipped at the work-house; the captain to forfeit and pay 20 dollars for suffering such offence to be committed on board his vessel.

No master of a vessel shall suffer a dog or dogs to go ashore on any wharf, or into any part of the city, except the persons accompanying said dog shall have sufficient rope or chain fastened to the dog's neck, and one end of the rope or chain held by the person so accompanying said dog, to prevent his biting any person—penalty from 10 to 20 dollars for violating the law, and cost of prosecution, and the dog liable to be killed by any one.

Port-wardens are appointed by the city corporation to inspect any vessels arriving in distress, and to report the state of the vessel and cargo, and to survey damaged goods, and to report whether damaged or not, and the degree of damage. The expenses of the survey must be paid by the owner, master, or consignee. They take an oath faithfully to perform the duties of their office, and are allowed the following fees:—

For survey of a vessel - - - - - - -	5 dollars.
" " a vessel and cargo - - - - -	6
" " cargo - - - - - - -	5
" " stowage of the hold of any vessel - -	5
" " goods after landed - - - - -	5
For warrant and record thereof - - - - -	2
For a copy of the survey - - - - - -	2

Foreign vessels pay an advance of 50 per cent. on the above rates.

Savannah.—The chief seaport of Georgia, is situated on the south bank of Savannah river, 17 miles from its mouth. Lat. 5° 02′ N. Long. 81° 03′ W.

Port regulations.—The commissioners have power to place anchors, buoys and chains in the port of Savannah, and to Five-fathom Hole, for the use of which they may demand,

From all vessels under 200 tons	- . - -	5 dollars.
" " above 200, and less than 300	-	10
" " above 300	- - - - - -	12

To displace or cut the same, subjects the offender to a penalty of $300.

The same are placed in Darien river, for the use of which, vessels, except coasters, shall pay 3 cents per ton.

No master shall throw out any rubbish or ballast in the rivers or ports in this state, except above high-water mark, under a penalty not exceeding 300 pounds sterling.

If any vessel or boat be intentionally suffered to sink in Savannah river, between Ray's Hole and the sea, the owner or captain shall be fined not more than 500 dollars.

Wharfage.	*s.*	*d.*
For every ship, snow or brig loading at a wharf, per day -	1	4
For such vessel lying and not loading at a wharf, per day -	2	8
For every sloop or schooner loading, per day - -	0	10
For do. lying and not loading, per day - - - - -	1	8

Besides these there are fees for goods laden from one vessel to another.

Tonnage.—A duty of 3 pence per ton is imposed by a law of Georgia, to which congress has assented, on all vessels entering this port, to be applied to improving the navigation of the river. This is in addition to the tonnage duty of the United States, and of the state duty of 4 cents per ton for the health fund.

Gunpowder.—Where a package, &c., of gunpowder, brought into the state of Georgia, exceeds 5 lbs., it must be marked as such in large letter, or it is liable to forfeiture.[a]

Mobile.—The port wardens at Mobile are chosen annually by the mayor and aldermen, and they are entitled to 3 cents per ton for all vessels entering at the custom-house, and loading or discharging, (steamboats, river craft, and the Pensacola and New-Orleans packets only excepted.[b])

By an act for the improvement of the navigation of the port of Mobile, the collector is required to levy a tonnage duty of 5 cents per ton on every vessel drawing more than 7 feet, arriving at or departing from that port, and the masters of such vessels are required to declare the tonnage under oath, under the penalty of $100 for refusal.[c]

Louisiana—Harbour regulations.—The harbour-master of New-Orleans and three wardens are appointed by the governor, with the consent of the senate, and he gives a bond for the faithful discharge of

---

[a] Act, 26th Dec., 1831. [b] Act, 21st Jan., 1832. [c] Act, 20th Dec., 1825.

his duty, in the sum of $2500. He has the power of regulating the stations of vessels upon the river, within the limits of the city, and any resistance to his authority is punished by a fine of $50.

The harbour-master and wardens also examine vessels when required, for which they are allowed $2 50 per day, and $2 for a certificate, and $1 for a duplicate.

They also examine damaged goods, which are sold under their direction, after advertising in two newspapers.

The fees are $2 50 per day, and $2 for a certificate.

Where, upon an examination by the wardens, separate certificates are required by the different consignees, the wardens are entitled to charge fees in each case.[a]

Anchors and cables found in the Mississippi, must be deposited at some place designated by the master and wardens, and if not claimed within three months, and salvage paid for their recovery, they become the property of the persons finding them.

Fines and penalties are applied to the use of the Charity Hospital. The master and wardens are entitled to receive $5 for every vessel arriving in port.

---

[a] Act, 17th Feb. 1821.

CHAPTER XXVIII.

COMMERCIAL REGULATIONS OF FOREIGN COUNTRIES.

The limits of this work will not permit the insertion of all the information collected on this subject. Such matter, accordingly, has been selected, as has been deemed must useful, and concerning those ports with which our trade is chiefly carried on.

ALEXANDRIA AND ROSETTA,

The chief ports of Egypt. These places are distant from each other about 50 miles, and from Cairc about 400 miles, and it is at the one or the other that the ships discharge their goods destined for Cairo, and take in their return cargoes. Of these two harbours, Rosetta is by far the most considerable. The exports from Egypt are many kinds of drugs, Mocha coffee, wax, wool, mother-of-pearl, white and coloured linens, sugars, spices, elephant's teeth, hides, &c. The imports are arsenic, black lead, antimony, quicksilver, vitriol, brass wire, tin, Venitian steel, lead, paper, satins of Florence, cloths of all sorts, dye-woods, hardware, and glass beads. Lat. of Alexandria, 31° 13′ N. Long. 30° 16′ E. Lat. of Rosetta, 31° 24′, Long. 30° 58′.

ALGIERS,

A seaport on the south shore of the Mediterranean, on the coast of Barbary. Latitude 36° 49′ N. Long. 20° 13′ E. It is likely, at no very distant period, to rise into some importance as a commercial port, from the more than ordinary fertility of the soil, and their favourable situation for commerce. At present the exports are wheat and barley, olive oil, fruits, wax, honey, hides and skins, wool, ostrich feathers, and some live cattle. The imports are spices of all sorts, rum, superfine cloths of the most gaudy colours, fine muslins, gold and silver embroideries, damasks, calicoes, and linen of fine quality, lead, tin, pewter, and dye-woods, but these in small quantities.

Algiers is now a French port, and on the 17th September, 1830, the following order was issued:—

The duty on anchorage, fixed heretofore at 100 francs for French and foreign vessels entering the port or harbour of Algiers, shall, from the date of this order, be reduced to 50 francs for vessels of 50 tons and under; to 75 francs for vessels of 50 tons to 100 tons; vessels above 100 tons, and none other, are to pay the duty of 100 francs.

No duty is exacted on vessels of less than five tons.

Vessels equipped for the fisheries are also exempt from duty.

All vessels, French, Algerine and foreign, entering the port, or anchoring in the harbour, are requested to send their manifests to the custom-house, with a detail of their cargoes, within 24 hours.

Nothing is allowed to be discharged or taken on board without written permission of the custom-house, under the penalty of fine and confiscation.

This fine is fixed at 200 francs.

If goods are discharged which are not in the manifest, or if goods are discharged without permission, the captain of the vessel will be compelled to pay a sum equal to the value of the goods, and to a fine of 200 francs.

The infractions above mentioned inflicting fine and confiscation, shall be decided by *proces verbeaux*, signed by at least two officers of the customs, and referred, in cases of appeal, to the tribunal, which shall decide definitely.

The custom-house duties are fixed as follows, viz.:

On imports by French or Algerine vessels, 4 per cent.; and by other vessels, 6 per cent., on the value of the merchandise.

On exports by French or Algerine vessels, 1 per cent.; and by other vessels, 2½ per cent. ad valorem.

Gold and silver, in coin or ingots, (French coin excepted,) shall pay a duty of 3 francs per kilogramme for gold, and 20 centimes per kilogramme for silver, provided the quantity exceeds five kilogrammes of gold, and twenty-five of silver.

In lieu of the duties of Otroi, there shall, on importation, be levied one tenth of the import duties as fixed above on the following articles: coal, garlic and onions, oranges and lemons, straw, butter, soap, bougies, melons and olives.

AMSTERDAM,

The largest seaport in the Netherlands, is situated at the mouth of the Amstel. The city is built upon piles, and has a good harbour. Lat. 52° 22′ N. Long. 4° 51′ E.

The chief articles of natural produce and manufacture, and therefore primary articles of export, from Amsterdam and the kingdom of the Netherlands, are wheat, beans, peas, oats, barley, of corn; clover, rape, hemp, and line, of seeds; butter, cheese, linen, sail-cloth, woollen and cotten stuffs of different qualities; oils of rape, hemp and whale; and the spirit called Geneva, of manufactures. Besides these, which may be denominated staple commodities, madder, oak bark, tallow, white lead, &c., may be added. Amsterdam imports most kinds of West India and American goods, especially coffee, sugar, tobacco, cocoa, cotton and dye-woods; from the East Indies, spices, raw silk and cotton, and goods manufactured of both these articles; from Spain, wool, indigo, cochineal and Peruvian bark; from France, wine and brandies; and from Great Britain, all kinds of colonial produce, hardware, rock salt, tin plates, and printed calicoes.

Regulations as to tare and leakage.—All weight is regulated according to the Amsterdam weight, and long measure by the Hague ell.

All entries of goods, in the southern provinces of the kingdom, permitted to be made according to the metrical system, are rendered by the administration of the customs into Dutch weight and measure.

The tare on goods, rated by weight where there is no fixed tare, is, for wooden casks 15 per cent. on the gross weight; for packages in leather, linen, canisters, &c., 8 per cent.

Merchants, dissatisfied with the rated allowance of tare, may apply to the director of the customs in their district, or where there is no director, to the receiver, to regulate the same by the actual packages.

An allowance for leakage shall be made to the merchant upon all liquids, including molasses and honey, in the following proportions, viz:—

Coming from England and the northern ports of Europe, also from France by inland navigation, six per cent.

Coming from France by sea, and from other countries by the rivers Rhine and Waal, twelve per cent.

Coming from any other port or place, 14 per cent.

Finally, from whatever place the same may come, upon train oil, twelve per cent.; blubber, six per cent.

In case the importer is dissatisfied with the allowance for leakage, he shall be permitted to pay the duty upon the actual quantity, to be ascertained by sworn gaugers at the importer's expense.

Transit.—All merchandise, not specially prohibited, may pass freely through the kingdom of the Netherlands, from and to any other country, either by land or by water, upon the payment of the transit duty.

The goods intended for transit must be so declared at the first office of customs, or before unlading at the place of discharge, and they must be transported without delay, unless permitted to remain by the chief officer of the customs. This delay in the warehouse cannot exceed six months.

The carriages and horses of any travellers coming into, or proceeding out of the kingdom of the Netherlands, shall be free of duty.

All the formalities prescribed for the declarations on importations must be observed for the transit; the person making the declaration must also give security for what the goods would pay more, if declared for home consumption, or, if the importation is prohibited, for double the value these securities are discharged on presenting, within six weeks after the term granted on the passport for re-exportation—a certificate to that effect, at the back of the passport, signed by two officers. With respect to goods which are not prohibited, the person declaring them has a right, during the whole time granted for the passage in transit, to withdraw his declarations, and make a new one for home consumption.

Law on the tea trade.—The general law of 30th October, 1816, respecting the import and export duties, is declared applicable to tea; and, therefore, every body is allowed to import it into the kingdom, and to dispose of it immediately after payment of the import duties below specified.

For Bohea and ordinary Congo - -	8 florins per 100 lbs.
For all other sorts - - -	16 do. do.

But teas coming directly, without breaking bulk, from China or the East Indies, on account of the inhabitants of the Netherlands, and in ships built in the kingdom, pay only an import duty.

Bohea and ordinary Congo - -	2 florins 50 cents per 100 lbs.
All other sorts - - -	5 do.

Only such tea to be considered as Bohea and ordinary Congo, as is imported unmixed in whole chests, without any smaller chests being packed among them.

Tea which, though imported in whole chests, is worth a florin and above per pound, according to the current price, at the time of the declaration, is not considered as ordinary Congo.

On teas to be exported only the scale duty is paid, according to the general dispositions of the tariff of the 3d October, 1816.

The transit is prohibited without exception. In calculating the duties on teas when they are in the usual chests, there is a deduction from the gross weight for tare as follows—

From chests of 110 pounds and upwards - - -	18 per cent.
From chests under 110 pounds - - - - - - -	25 do.

Unfree territory.—The law establishes two lines on the frontier: one on the frontier line, the other at the distance of a league, more or less, in the interior, called the line of the interior for the seacoast. This line is fixed at the distance of 1700 Rhinland ells from the coasts, including the isles of Rosenburg, Texel and others, situated to the north. The district between these lines is called the unfree territory. It is forbidden to have magazines or depots of goods in this territory, in places or communes where the aggregate population is only 2,000 souls, under the penalty of confiscation and a fine of 100 florins. This regulation does not extend to the production of the soil, or of the manufactories, in respect to the depot in these establishments; nor does it concern retail dealers, provided the quantity of goods in their ware-houses or shops does not exceed what may reasonably be supposed necessary for their trade. Goods transported within the unfree territory must be accompanied with passports, which are given gratis, for goods of which the exportation is prohibited, on giving security in their value; for those which pay export duty, in the amount of the duty; and for those which are free, without security.

Declarations.—The declaration of goods imported must be made at the frontier bureau, and of goods exported, at the interior bureau of the unfree territory, within twenty-four hours after arrival, signed by the master and mate, and the vessel's papers exhibited. The declaration must contain,

1. The name of the vessel, and of the master; if by land, that of the driver.
2. The name of the place or country whence the goods come; on exportation, their destination.
3. An exact specification of the goods, with their precise names.
4. The marks and numbers of all the pieces, bales, parcels, baskets, or chests.
5. The quantity or number of the pieces, specifying whether they are halves, quarters, or other divisions, the weight and the measure, according to the kind of each, or by bales, pieces, barrels, &c.
6. The value, calculated according to the price current at the moment of making the declaration; the whole without figures, and in words at length.

The goods and merchandise exempt from duty, either on importation or exportation, must, however, be equally expressed in this declaration, unless they are specially denominated in the law; those which enjoy this faculty, and of which it is not necessary to make a declaration, are precious stones, gold and silver, coined, and in bars or ingots, herrings, whale blubber and oil, fish, fresh, salted, or in pickle, from the national fisheries. All these articles require no permit. If the captain, master, or driver, is not able to make this declaration as prescribed, the goods must be deposited in the public warehouses, whence they are sent to the chief bureau, after having been sealed *plombees*. The persons interested may also affix their seal to them, and the whole is at their expense. Within the year, the goods may be withdrawn on making the declaration prescribed. In every case it may be required that an inventory shall be made, at the moment of importation, by the receiver, at the expense of the persons interested. In this case, the inventory shall be made out and signed in duplicate; the person making the declaration has the right to change or correct it, as long as it has not been given to the examining clerks, or that a seizure has not been made.

As for goods coming by sea, the merchants or consignees, if they are ignorant of the exact quantity, &c., have a right to have the goods which they receive numbered, measured, gauged and weighed, under the direction of the custom-house officers, and in a place pointed out by them, before they make their declaration, but at their own expense; the persons interested are not obliged to calculate the duties to be paid according to the declaration; they may have it done by the receivers, who are responsible to the treasury for the errors which they may commit in their calculations. The declaration being made and duly signed, the receiver gives a passport either to pass the line of the unfree territory into the interior, where the circulation requires no permit; or in case that the duties are not paid on entrance, to the unloading places where the duties are to be paid. It is essential to observe, that those goods which are exempt from import duties, but are subjected to scale duty, excise, &c., are to be declared at their entrance to the receivers of those duties, if there are any in the frontier places where the importation takes place.

Goods not declared, or declared under a false denomination, or falsely declared in respect to the quantity; those unloaded without previous permission, as well as the excess above the weight declared, are liable to confiscation; but this confiscation does not include those articles which are duly declared: that is to say, *not* the whole of the goods declared, but the pieces, packages, bales, &c., in particular, the declaration of which is false. However, if the excess of weight or measure is above a twelfth of the whole quantity, the confiscation extends to the whole.

The master or driver who has made his declaration at the frontier bureau, is obliged to produce, at the place of unloading, all the articles so declared, under the penalty of 100 florins for every barrel, chest, bale, or piece missing, unless he can prove that the deficiency has arisen from theft, or from some extraordinary cause.

The passports which are granted by the officers of the customs, must mention a proper space of time, after which they are to be null and void. But the chief officer in the place has the power of prolonging them during the time that the passports are valid; the merchant may demand the repayment of the export duties paid, on proving that the goods upon which they have been paid, have not been exported.

The merchant may obtain an abatement of the import duties, in case that by an error, goods damaged or spoiled on the voyage have been declared as good merchandise; but this claim must be made before the goods are put into his warehouses or those of the custom-house. This abatement is regulated, first, if the merchandise is sound and good, and in case it is sold publicly, upon the sum by which the proceeds of the sale are less than their value; or, if it is damaged, according to an estimate made by two sworn brokers—one named by the custom-house officers, one by the merchant, and a third, if necessary, by the municipality; the whole at the expense, and at the option of the merchant.

Merchandise paying duty ad valorem, may be taken by the custom-house officers, if they deem the goods are undervalued in the declaration, upon adding 10 per cent. to the valuation; with the exception of goods the value of which is fixed by government. This pre-emption must be declared by the officer immediately after his summary visit, and for the whole quantity, and payment must be made before the officer takes even a sample of the goods. If payment be not made within 24 hours, 11 per cent., and at the end of 48 hours, 12 per cent. are added; and at the end of 72 hours, the right of pre-emption is lost, and the officer must pay 3 per cent. damages to the owner.

Salvage.—The salvage of goods thrown into the sea, and of stranded ships, is not considered as an importation; goods so circumstanced may therefore be taken on shore at all times, and in all places, without any formality in respect to the board of convoys and licenses. Such goods and merchandise as may be saved, if they were loaded, and destined for foreign countries, are exempt from all duties; if they are re-exported goods that have been loaded in a port of the kingdom, destined for abroad, without having been landed in any foreign country, and these again re-embarked, are exempt from import duty.

All pieces of wreck, masts, sails, anchors, cordage, and other appurtenances of shipwrecked vessels, are exempt from all import duty.

Importation by sea.—The officers of the customs take care that the captains, &c., may be informed at the first bureau of the orders and formalities prescribed by the law.

The captains are bound to make, within 24 hours, and before they proceed to their destination, a declaration of their cargoes in writing, and in duplicate, signed by the captain and mate, or pilot.

The officers must deliver one of these declarations, compared and signed by them, to the captains, and inform them that the declaration must be sworn to at the places of their destination.

If the captain is impelled by necessity to pass beyond the first bureau, he must make his declaration at the first port where he shall stop. Should the captain delay to make his declaration above 24 hours, or pass the first bureau without necessity; or, should he suppress in his declaration any part of the goods or merchandise, he incurs a fine of 500 florins; and, if the master of a vessel, 300 florins.

If the captains are not acquainted with the quantities, qualities, &c.,

they may make their declaration under the general term of "merchandise;" but in this case the bills of lading must be exhibited with the declaration, and the custom-house puts a guard on board at the captain's expense. The goods declared are placed under the guard of the custom-house till the declaration is made conformable to the law; the whole at the expense of those interested.

In case the captains make any difficulty in signing without reserve to the formula of the declaration, they may refer to the manifests and other papers that show the contents of the cargo, of which the captains are there bound to exhibit the duplicates which are annexed to the declaration; but this is not to hinder them from declaring upon oath, or by a solemn affirmation, that they have not loaded or unloaded any other merchandise in this kingdom.

The duties are paid indifferently upon the whole cargo, at the place of destination of the vessel, though a part of the cargo may have another destination, and be conveyed thither by lighters.

Ships touching at a port, either to wait for orders, or obliged by some accident at sea, are not subject to any duty relative to the convoys and licenses; but they are placed under the *surveillance* of the custom-house officers, and must make a declaration. If there be prohibited goods in the ship, a guard is put on board, at the expense of the captain, unless he prefers depositing the goods in a warehouse belonging to the customs. The unloading and reloading can in no case take place without a permit; in respect to merchandise landed to remain in the country, they are subject to all the usual formalities; and in case of the sale or unloading of any goods, the vessel is liable to the tonnage duty.

Exportation by sea.—The declaration must be made on paying the duties at the place of embarkation: that is to say, at the place where the goods are embarked, whether in vessels destined to a foreign country, or in lighters or other vessels, or boats, to be conveyed on board the ships—the passport must mention the name of the captain or boatman charged with the conveyances. It is forbidden to take on board any goods or merchandise not accompanied with a passport; and if the vessel has already passed the last bureau, the passport must have a declaration on the back, that the goods have been examined by the officers of the last bureau. If, after the examination has taken place, and before passing the last bureau, the captain receive more goods, he must make a signal to the officers to come on board, that they may make a new examination, under a penalty of 300 florins. The captains or masters of vessels must sign a declaration, stating that they have not any merchandise besides those mentioned in the passports, and are to exhibit at the last bureau their reckoning, with the receipt of the officer to whom they have paid the duties on the last articles taken on board, and then they receive an act of clearance.

All these formalities must take place on board. The officers are forbidden to take away the passports. However, in case there is a presumption of fraud, they may retain them; but they must declare their intention in this respect within 2 hours, if the delay could interrupt the voyage.

The pilots are forbidden, under a penalty of 300 florins, to permit merchandise to be taken on board or landed without regular passports, or to take a ship to sea, which is not furnished with an act of clearance.

Entrepôt.—All goods, whether for transit, or simply imported, may be placed in entrepôt bonded; but the declaration to that effect must be made on the importation. They pay warehouse rent according to a value settled between the municipal administration and the board of convoys and licenses.

The right of making use of the entrepôt is fixed for 2 years; but the board of convoys and licenses may prolong it. In the latter case the proprietor or consignee renounces the favour of transit. The duties are paid on taking the goods out of the entrepôt, at the expiration of the term.

No change of packages, casks, or marks, can be made in the entrepôt, unless necessary for the preservation of the goods. All damage while in entrepôt, unless owing to the negligence of the public officers, is borne by the owner; and no allowance is made in calculating duties for waste or loss, except from fire, inundation, or other extraordinary events. Goods in entrepôt may be transferred from the owner to other persons, and no charge is made for the care of the goods. There are three kinds of entrepôts: public, established, (or designated by a merchant, and approved by the customs,) and private, (or in the custody of the merchant.)

Tonnage duty.—Vessels serving exclusively to convey mails and passengers, may make an arrangement with the board concerning this duty.

The tonnage duty is regulated as follows:

Foreign vessels - - - -	1 franc 5 stivers per ton.
Dutch and American - - -	45 centimes " "

Foreign vessels belonging to any nation where the vessels of the Netherlands are treated on the same footing as the ships of that nation, enjoy the same favour, with respect to the tonnage duty, as the vessels of the Netherlands. Ministers to and from foreign courts exempt from duty.

Pilotage from Amsterdam to the Texel.

A vessel drawing	9 feet per last of 2 tons -	14 francs	15 stivers.
Do.	10 feet -	15 "	10 "
Do.	11 feet -	17 "	10 "
Do.	12 feet -	22 "	10 "
Do.	13 feet -	32 "	10 "

Light duties from America, $13\frac{1}{3}$ stivers per last; East Indies, $21\frac{1}{3}$ stivers.

Export and import duties the same on American as on Dutch vessels.

Foreign vessels from the Dutch East India colonies pay no import duties, on producing evidence of having paid the export duties in the colonies.

Americans are entitled by treaty to all the privileges, rights and immunities, and exemptions in commerce of the citizens of the most favoured nations in the ports of Holland. Neither are they obliged to pay any other duties or imposts. They may transact their own business, or employ such agents, &c., as they please. Citizens of each party may dispose of their effects by will or otherwise. Between the Netherlands and the United States, free ships make free goods, except they are in the actual service of a belligerent; but vessels are required both at sea and in port to exhibit to cruizers their sea-letters and other documents, and if they have no contraband on board they are allowed to pass. If they have contraband on board, the vessel must be sent in without breaking the hatches or opening packages, and only the contraband goods are to be condemned. If no contraband be found on board, the captor must pay costs and damages. American property rescued from pirates, shall be restored, and shipwrecked property, if claimed within a year and a day, paying reasonable salvage, &c. In case of war, 9 months shall be allowed them to retire with their property.

No citizen of either party is to be allowed to enter the service of a country at war with the other party.

Armed vessels of either party visiting and examining the merchantmen of the other party, must remain out of cannon shot, and send a boat to examine their papers.

A vessel entering the ports of Holland, and not willing to break bulk or take in any cargo, shall not be obliged to pay any duties in or out, or to render any account of their cargo, unless suspected of carrying contraband to an enemy. Masters of vessels may ship American seamen in Amsterdam, &c., without being subjected to any penalty, except they belong to a Dutch ship.

In time of war, American vessels should be furnished with sea-letters, and the other documents prescribed by treaty. In case of vessels recaptured by privateers, one third salvage shall be paid if they have not been 24 hours in the possession of the enemy; if more than that time, the whole shall belong to the recaptor. If recaptured by a public vessel, one thirtieth and one tenth shall be paid under like circumstances.

ANTWERP

Stands on the Sheldts, which is 400 yards wide. It is the principal commercial place of the new kingdom of Belgium. It is 65 miles south of Amsterdam, lat. 51° 13′ N., long. 4° 23′ E. Having been part of the same kingdom, much that has been said of one applies to the other. The imports here are pretty much the same as at Amsterdam; and its advantages from ships of the largest burthen being able to come up to the town, and the extraordinary facility with which goods destined for the interior are circulated again by canals, gives it a great preponderance of advantage. Nearly all the trade of the Belgic provinces passes through the hands of the Antwerp merchants, the articles of import being landed there, and those of export being sent thither to be shipped. The exports, beside what these southern provinces have in common with the northern ones, viz., corn, seeds, and linens, are chiefly lace, carpets, hair cloth, and tapestry, from the capital, Brussels; flax of fine quality, and hops of superior flavour; tallow and hides.

All vessels arriving with a cargo at Flushing, are accompanied up the river by two custom-house officers; their fees are 1½g. each for every day they remain on board, coming up the river, and 4½g. for their expenses back to Flushing.

The pilotage from sea to Flushing, up and down the river, and back again to sea, is paid according to the draft of water and the tariff.

No vessel is allowed to go in or out of the dock, or move in the river, without having a pilot on board, who receives 1g. for every tide, whether large or small vessels.

The charges for clearing in and out of Flushing are more or less, according to the size of the vessel and the quantity of goods on board; they seldom overrun 20 to 25g., but if liable to quarantine they are much higher; the doctor's fees alone are from 10 to 35g., according to circumstances and the number of men on board, besides other expenses.

These four articles not being regular port charges, are only filled in, in case the master thinks it necessary to make a protest; then they come to about 36g. together.

The expenses for sealing the hatches and ship's provisions depend upon the time the vessel is discharging, and the quantity of provision on board; they may amount from 4 to 12g., but seldom overrun that sum.

This charge is indiscriminately paid by every vessel, whether large or small.

The tonnage duty on all vessels assimilated to the Dutch, is 90 centimes, with 13 of additional duty on every ton measured at Antwerp, and is only paid *once* within the year, commencing the 1st of January, and finishing the 31st of December; whether they make 1 or 10 voyages during that time, to any port or ports of the Netherlands, they only pay the in and outward tonnage duty once, at their first entry.

Every vessel must have a clearance passport from the custom-house; the cost is from 3 to 15g., according to the place they come from.

The dock duty is paid according to the size of the vessel, and the following tariff:

50 to	100 tons, at	12 cents per ton		For 3 months.
101	150 "	16 "	"	
251	200 "	20 "	"	
201	250 "	26 "	"	
251	and above	36 "	"	

After the expiration of which time they pay one fortieth part of the whole amount for every week they remain longer.

The cooking-house dues are also calculated after the size of the vessel; they are as follows:

Under 36 tons . .	g.0 47 cents		Per week.
From 36 to 100 . .	0 94¼	"	
101 200 . .	1 41	"	
201 300 . .	1 89	"	
300 and upwards	2 36	"	

Which they are obliged to pay, whether they make use of them or not.

Sand ballast brought alongside the vessel, is 1g. per last, about 1½ tons in weight.

All vessels leaving Antwerp must be provided with a surveyor's certificate that they are sea-worthy; without this document they cannot obtain a pilot. When in ballast, it costs from 3g. to 6.75g.; and when loaded, from 5g. to 15g., according to the size of the vessel, besides 5.70g. for the tribunal certificate.

The consul's fees are charged according to their respective tariffs.

All vessels arriving at Antwerp are visited by the water bailiff; his fees are from 5g. to 25g., according to the size, and the number of sailors on board.

For charter-parties and stamps, when required, the charge is 4g.

The brokerage for clearing a vessel in and out, is fixed by law at 75 centimes per last.

Brokerage on a general cargo outward is 5 0-0; on a charter-party outwards, 3 0-0, according to law.

These expenses depend on the quantity of provisions on board; and the petty charges the captain may be at, never overrun 10g. to 15g.

Pilotage from Antwerp to Flushing, being stipulated in palms, 3 of which are a little better than a foot, in order to ascertain the exact draught of water, all the vessels are hooked by the pilotage officer, who charges 1g. to 1½.

The difference in the port charges between a vessel going away with a cargo, or in ballast, only exists in the pilotage, the brokerage, and some trifling charges as stated above, but then she saves the ballast. All the other charges remain the same.

The tare on goods rated by weight, and for which there is no established tare in the tariff, is regulated as follows:

For all wooden casks, without distinction, 15 lbs. per 100 lbs., gross weight.

For all packages in leather, mats, baskets, canisters, linen, and the like, 8 lbs. per 100 lbs., gross weight.

Liquid merchandise is entitled to the following allowance for leakage:

On those from England, Embden, Bremen, Hamburg, and other neighbouring places known by the name of Rhine Coast, and those from France by the rivers, 6 per cent. On those coming from France, by sea, or from other countries, by the Rhine and Waal, 12 per cent. On those from other more distant countries, 14 per cent.

Lastly, 12 per cent. for whale oil, and 6 per cent. for whale blubber, without regard to their origin.

In case the declarant should consider the deduction allowed insufficient, he shall have the privilege of paying the duty on the actual quantity.

Similar privileges are secured to Americans in Belgium to those secured to them in the Netherlands. Vide page 484.

AUSTRALASIA,

Comprehending New South Wales, Norfolk Island, Van Dieman's Land, and other settlements in the vicinity of this continent.

The exports are already hemp, flax, and wool; the imports, every thing of which it may reasonably be supposed an infant colony, the population of which, in 1818, was near eighty thousand persons, and has been rapidly increasing, must stand in need. Ready made clothes of all kinds and quantities, cheese, hams, wine, hops, beer, porter, cutlery, glass, earthenware, and hardware, linen, calico, scythes, sickles, saddles and bridles, knives and forks, spoons, &c., are among the number of articles in general request. The jurisdiction of the governor of New South Wales extends from 10° 37′ to to 43° 49′ S. lat., and from the seacoast westward, to 135° E. long., and thence proceeding in an easterly direction, including all the islands in the Pacific Ocean within the before mentioned latitude. All the functions of government (except arbitrary taxation by 59 George III. c. 144) are vested solely in the governor, who is responsible to the government of the mother country alone for the exercise of his discretionary power. Some few of the regulations which attach upon vessels arriving in the harbour of these regions, it is proper to notice. The first is by statute of 59 Geo. III. f. 3. 122, by which every British vessel owned and navigated according to law, may trade between any place in the United Kingdom, and the said colony and its dependencies, and pass to the eastward of the Cape of Good Hope, though such vessel be of less than 350 tons, notwithstanding any former prohibitions.

At Port Jackson, which was the first, and still remains the chief harbour in this government, the following, among other regulations, have been promulgated by the colonial government.

No person but the pilot or other person specially authorized, is to board any vessel arriving, until a union or ensign is hoisted at the mast-head. The commander of every vessel is to report himself and ship at the naval officer's offices, and enter the ship agreeably to form, and produce a manifest of his cargo; to give a bond in £200 not to open the vessel's hatches for the sale of any article, till he receive a general permit for the purpose, and not to send any spirits, wine, beer, or other strong drink, even after such general permit, without a special permit in writing, properly signed and countersigned, specifying the quantities and qualities, with the name of each purchaser, nor to sell or send from the vessel any arms or ammunition to any person without special permit.

Liquors only to be landed at particular places, and not to be removed until security given for payment of the assessments. Forfeitures to be determined according to the British laws respecting manifests and smuggling.

No trade permitted with the inhabitants till the securities required be received, and no convict to be received on board any vessel without a proper pass from the governor, or other officiating magistrate; no boats to go on shore after dark; no seaman to go into the country without a pass; no clothing or bedding to be purchased from convicts, under specific penalties annexed to these different offences. Persons dying on board any vessel in the harbour, to be buried on shore, and no stone ballast or iron hoops to be thrown overboard below high-water mark, under the penalty of £5, two thirds to the informer. No merchant vessel to leave the harbour without a naval officer's certificate, countersigned by the governor, in compliance with the preceding regulations, on pain of being fired at and detained. The natives of the whole region before described, with all the neighbouring islands, being under the protection of Great Britain, all violations of their persons and property to be punished according to the laws adopted or made by the colonial government.

Purchases are generally made by barter. Dollars, however, valued at five shillings, are the chief money current in the colony; and a bank has been recently established, which issues small notes.

BORDEAUX,

A seaport of France, on the left bank of the Garonne, 13 leagues from the sea. It is built in the form of a bow, and its harbour is spacious, with a large and extensive quay. Its exports are wine, brandy, vinegar, olive oil, fruits, and the productions of the soil, mines, fisheries, and manufactories of France. Its imports are naval stores, pot and pearl ashes, codfish, cochineal, cocoa, coffee, sugars, gums, oil, pimento, rice, teas, hides, indigo, nankins, tobacco, and colonial produce; fustic, logwood, and other dye-woods; raw materials for manufactures; staves for wine casks, &c.

Bordeaux has an internal communication with the Mediterranean. Lat. 44° 50′ N. Long. 0° 34′ W.

By the late commercial treaty between the United States and France, articles of the produce or manufacture of the United States, when imported in American vessels, shall be liable to pay an additional duty of not more than 20 francs per ton over and above the duties paid on like articles imported in French vessels, and then only upon the excess of value of the imports over the exports.

No discriminating duty shall be imposed on such articles imported in vessels of the United States for transit or re-exportation.

The duties of tonnage, light money, pilotage, port charges, brokerage, and all other duties upon foreign shipping, shall not, upon vessels of the United States, exceed 5 francs per ton, the duties levied upon French vessels.

The consuls may cause deserters from American vessels to be arrested, in order to send them home, proving before the proper tribunals that the men belong to their respective vessels by their registers or ship's roll. If not sent back within 3 months, they shall be discharged.

It was also agreed by the treaty of July 4, 1831, that the duties on French wines imported into the United States should, for 10 years, be as follows,

On red wines in casks, per gallon - - - - -	6 cts.
On white wines in casks " - - - - - -	10 "
On all wines in bottles " - - - - - -	22 "

And, in case of a reduction of the then duties on other wines, a proportional reduction must be made on French wines.

It was also agreed that the duty on long staple cotton imported into France, in American or French vessels, should be the same as on short staple.

Custom-house regulations.—Vessels must be reported within 24 hours after arrival. Great care should be taken to make out the manifests correctly, as post entries are not allowed; and if there are more goods on board than are specified in the manifest, the excess is forfeited, and a penalty is incurred; if less, the duties must be paid on the whole quantity specified, and a penalty is also incurred. It may, however, be mentioned in the manifest, that the quantity is unknown.

A severe penalty is exacted if tobacco be found secreted on board by any person belonging to the ship. All custom-house business is done through the medium of brokers. Cotton and ashes are generally sold at 4 months' credit.

By the treaty of 1831, the following quantities are considered as forming the ton of merchandise for each of the articles hereinafter specified:—

Wines—four 61 gallon hogsheads, or 244 gallons of 231 cubic inches, American measure.

Brandies and all other liquids—244 gallons.

Silks and all other dry goods, and all other articles usually subject to measurement—forty-two cubic feet French, in France, and fifty cubic feet American measure, in the United States.

Cotton—804 pounds avoirdupois, or 365 kilog.

Tobacco—1600 pounds avoirdupois, or 725 kilog.

Ashes—pot and pearl, 2240 pounds avoirdupois, or 1016 kilog.

Rice—1600 pounds avoirdupois, or 725 kilog.

And for all weighable articles not specified, 2240 pounds avoirdupois, or 1016 kilogrammes.

The ad valorem duty is estimated on a declaration of the value of the goods on their arrival and before the receipt of the duties, and justified by an invoice from the place of exportation. The custom-house officers may keep the articles upon paying the estimated value and a tenth more. Duties are payable on the gross weight of the articles and their coverings, &c., except when the duty amounts to more than 40 francs per 100 kilogrammes, when they are estimated on the net weight. The tare may be real or legal, at the option of the importer.

Legal tare on sugar, raw or clayed, in bales or bags,	2	per cent.
raw, in boxes or hogsheads	15	"
clayed, in do.	12	"
coffee, cocoa and pepper, in boxes or hogsheads,	12	"
in bales, bags or packs,	3	"
indigo, in boxes or pipes	21	"
in seroons	9	"
cotton, from Turkey	10	"
of any kind in packages of less than 50 kilog. .	8	"
of 50 and more,	6	"
Potash, weedash, raw, tare, &c., in pipes . .	12	"
All other articles paying duty on net weight, if in boxes or casks .	12	"
if in bales, packs, baskets or hampers,	2	"

The net weight of liquids is ascertained by establishing the tare of the articles.

French manufactures returned, except laces and silks, after having been shipped, pay a duty of 51 centimes per 100 kilogrammes, or 15 centimes per 1000 francs value, at the option of the payer.

The same duty is exacted on goods allowed to cross the French territory, viz. raw materials and colonial produce. All imported goods are entitled to a right of entrepôt for 12 months, with the privilege of renewal. The duties are, on taking the goods from the warehouse, in cash, or at four months credit, with security.

There is no tonnage duty on French vessels from the United States.

One franc ten centimes are paid for every permit taken out by shippers.

Pilotage at Bordeaux is paid per station. From April till October inclusive, vessels entering pay for three stations—the rest of the year for three and a half. Vessels sailing pay for $3\frac{1}{3}$ stations. The rate per station for French vessels is 3 francs 50 centimes per foot when drawing upwards of 12 feet, and 3 francs 75 centimes per foot when drawing 12 feet or under, and never charged for less than 10 feet.

Port charges.

Duties of entry and clearance for

French vessels, above 300 tons	15 francs per ship.
from 150 to 300 tons	6 do.
below 150 to 30 tons	2 do.
Foreign vessels of 200 tons and less	18 do.
of more than 200 tons	36 do.
Discharges, permits and certificates, relative to cargo, for each	50 c. for French ships.
	100 c. for foreign do.
Passports for foreign ships	1 franc.
Health visit at quarantine	12 do.
Mooring to a berth	30 do.
Reporting at the navy office and court of commerce,	36 do.
Gauging	12 do.
Visiting officers	12 do.
Harbour-master	14 do.
Passport and clearance	36 do.

If they sail in ballast, they pay a navigation duty of 6 f. per ship not above 200 tons, and 7 f. when above.

Tonnage duties.

French vessels above 30 tons, from foreign countries, per ton,	45 centimes.
Foreign vessels	3 f. 75 "
American and Mexican vessels, per ton	5 f.

The vessels of the United States and Mexico, however, do not pay any discriminating duties for pilots, docks, or brokerage, to which other foreign vessels are subject.

The duties are payable according to the net or gross weight of the merchandise, as a general rule.

The general rule is, that the duties are payable on the united weight of the goods, the cases, casks, &c., containing them, and the oil cloths, cords, &c., which cover the whole.

Exceptions become necessary for goods, the packages of which are out of proportion to the bulk, and where the duties are heavy. These exceptions are established by law, such as cotton, indigo, sugar, &c., and include all goods taxed on the importation or exportation at more than 40 francs per 100 kilogrammes, which pay on the net weight.

Vessels of the United States and of Mexico, pay tonnage duty, a fixed sum of five francs per ton, instead of 4.12½, which are at this day for all foreign vessels, the stipulation of previous laws. In consequence of this fixed sum, vessels of the United States and of Mexico are to be treated as French vessels, as to the application of all the taxes which have a discriminating tariff for foreigners; this is immediately applicable to the duty of pilotage, of brokerage, and of all those that custom-house officers receive, to wit: The dock duty at Havre and Rochelle, and the duty of sauvetage at Quillebeuf.

To foreign vessels which, bound from a foreign to a foreign port, are forced by stress of weather, or otherwise, to enter a French port, without transacting any commercial operations: such vessels will only be subject to 50 centimes per ton, if laden wholly or in part, or 25 centimes per ton, if in ballast.

Storage duty.—Storage, by the custom-house, can only be charged when goods are forcibly detained for alleged breaches of the law, in any of the following cases:

1st. When goods are abandoned or proprietors unknown; when the charge for storage is ¼ centime daily for 50 kilogrammes gross.

2d. When it is necessary to discharge a vessel arriving in distress, and storage is furnished by the custom-house. The charge then is ½ per cent. on the value.

3d. When declaration of entry, in detail, is not made within three days. This being considered as want of attention, the charge is 1 per cent. on the value.

Diplomatic agents, being entitled to receive, free of duty, all articles for their own use, coming from their respective countries, in the first year of their mission; those articles are exempt also from custom-house charge for storage.

Quarantine.—A royal ordinance of 4th April, 1835, directs:

1st. Vessels coming from the United States of America, with clean bills of health, shall not in future be subject to any quarantine of observation.

2d. Bales of cotton coming from the United States of America, shall not in future be opened or sent to the lazaretto, when the vessels which bring them have foul bills of health.

Tobacco cannot be sold in France except to the administration of tobacco. It may, however, be stored for 12 months, and re-exported at a trifling expense of entrepôt.

BRAZIL.

This great and wealthy country extends from the Amazon to the Rio Grande. It is now independent of Portugal, though its government is in an unsettled state. Its chief ports are Maranham, San

Salvador, Rio Janeiro, and Pernambuco. Its imports are European manufactures, flour, salt, furniture, and naval stores. Its exports are sugar, cotton, coffee, cocoa, indigo, drugs, Brazil wood, from the northern parts; hides and tallow, from the southern; and the precious metals and stones, from the middle.

Franquia.—Vessels proceeding to Brazil, when intending to dispose of their cargoes at different ports, must clear out for "Brazil and other ports," or for "Pernambuco, Bahia, Ric de Janeiro, and other ports." They are then entitled to the privilege of franquia, and may land a part of their cargoes at one port, paying duties only on the goods so landed, and proceed with the remainder to other ports. But if they clear out but for one port, they are compelled to make a complete entry, and discharge the whole of the cargo.

In proceeding from one Brazilian port to another, it is necessary that a bill of health should be taken from the local authorities of each port; and where any part of the cargo is landed, the same must be noted on the original manifest by the customs officer of the port.

Anchorage.—Foreign vessels pay, in all the ports of the empire, 10 reis per ton per day, from the 5th day after their entry.

Light-house.—The light-house duty is 100 reis per ton, for all vessels over 40 tons, departing from ports where there is a light-house. Vessels under 40 tons are exempted from this duty.

Port duty.—On all vessels not crossing the bar at the harbour of Rio de Janeiro, the following charges are levied: of three masts, 12,800 reis; of two masts, 9,600 reis; and of one mast, 6,400 reis.

Seal.—The duty is 40 reis for every written half sheet.

Health.—Visit of the physician is fixed at 8,200 reis; but in case the vessel is made to perform quarantine, then another sum of 8,200 reis is payable on the admission of the vessels to free pratique.

Hospitals.—A vessel of three masts pays 6,000 reis; brigs, corvettes and yachts, 4,000; pinnaces, 2,560; barks, 1,280.

Each one of the ship's company of vessels sailing for a foreign port, pays 400 reis.

Provisions.—The secretary of the bureau of commerce receives 400 reis, where the ship's company is less than eight men; where it is more than eight men, 3,000 reis. The registering clerk receives, for vessels destined for Europe, Asia or Africa, 300 reis; and for each individual enrolled, 40 reis.

Provisions for the vessel pay no export duty; their quantity is, however, strictly calculated according to the estimated consumption of the crew.

No vessel can begin to take in her lading until her previous cargo is entirely discharged, nor until she has been visited by an officer of the customs, and taken her designated place of anchorage.

Goods charged with duties that are seized, either for non-compliance with the required formalities, or for attempts to defraud the customs, belong one half to the informer or person making the seizure.

Entrance to Rio de Janeiro.—On entering this port it is not necessary for vessels to heave to or hail on passing Fort Santa Cruz in the day-time; they must, however, come to anchor before they pass a line between Villaganhen, (on an island opposite the lower part of the city,) and the church of Boa Viagem, on a high rock on the eastern side of the bay, where they must remain, nor send a boat on shore till visited by the several government boats, when the captain will be informed by the last that he may land, accompanied by a soldier, who will conduct him to the house of his consignee. The vessel's manifest will be required by the custom-house boat. Should the vessel not come to anchor as above mentioned, she will be fired at from the fort, and made to pay a fine. Vessels entering the port at night will be hailed from Fort Santa Cruz: it is not necessary, however, to understand what is said, but merely to reply where from, the name of the vessel and nation, without heaving to, but proceeding to the anchorage. A gun will likewise be fired, and strong lights exhibited, which are not to be regarded on board, as they are only signals to the fort conveying intelligence of the arrival.

The custom-houses established are as follows:

Para, Maranhao, Parnahyba, Piauhy, Fortaleza, Aracaty, Rio Grande de Norte, Pernambuco, Alagoas, Maceyo, Sergype, Bahia, Porto Alegre, Espirito Santo, Parahibo, Rio Janeiro, Santos, Paranagua, San Catharina Rio Grande do sul, on which St. Jose do Norte is dependant.

All the fees heretofore paid in the custom-houses are abolished, and in lieu thereof a payment into the national treasury of half per cent. on the value of merchandise entered for consumption; together with one per cent. for charges on landing, denominated *do expediente.*

The commissioners and comptrollers of the custom-house are to count and classify the merchandise, identify them, calculate their weights, measures and tares, estimate any damage, and cause the packages to be opened for entry, after comparing the marks and numbers, and fix the value of those not included in the tariff, or custom-house valuation, when they are not specified in the invoice.

They are to examine the vessel's clearance, and see whether it agrees with the entry, and whether it is duly authenticated by the necessary certificates.

The duties of masters of vessels.—The master of a merchant vessel entering a port of the Brazilian empire where there is a custom-house, besides the special obligations required in the respective ports, will be obliged to comply with the following regulations.

To go directly with his vessel, from the entrance of the harbour to the anchorage ground in franquia, and if, on account of the tide, contrary wind, or any other just motive, he should be compelled to come to anchor, and remain anchored for 12 hours after said hindrances are removed, (except in case of being quarantined,) he shall pay a fine of 100||000 reis, and shall be compelled (by the fort, or by a government vessel of war, whichever may be nearest) to proceed immediately to the franquia anchoring ground.

He shall not suffer any kind of vessel to board him, nor any person to come on board, or to leave his vessel, before he has been visited from the custom-house, excepting only the pilot, health-officer, the head officer at the entrance, when there is one, and in case of shipwreck, or for saving of lives.

Even after the custom-house visit on arrival, and until the vessel is discharged, he shall allow no person to come on board without a written permission from the inspector of the customs, and this permission shall only be given in the following cases, viz.:

1. To allow the buyers of goods to go on board to examine the cargo they wish to purchase, when sufficient specimens cannot be seen ashore.

2. To workmen or labourers necessary to put the cargo in order, taking care to have them examined when they go on board or return. In case of the infraction of the above regulations, a fine shall be imposed on him from 100||000 to 200||000 reis for every vessel he allows to board him, and of 50||000 for each person who shall enter or leave his vessel without license, unless he is a passenger, or belonging to the crew; and every other person who goes on board or leaves the vessel shall pay 100||000 fine, and be kept in custody until payment is made. The one third part of these fines shall be divided among the watchmen or military who shall have taken up the offender.

He shall deliver to the Guarda-mor, when he makes his visit on arrival, his passport and cargo book.

He shall deliver to the commander of the guard boat, without the port, if he is there, or at the franquia, if he is there, the manifest, as described below.

He shall enter at the custom-house, within 24 hours after the Guarda-mor has been on board, not counting the days in which the custom-house is shut, and present himself to the inspector, and swear or affirm that he has not on board of his vessel any merchandise other than what is described in the manifest he has delivered, and that he has no further declaration to make; and if he does not enter within the 24 hours, he shall pay 100||000 reis for each day's delay additional.

If he shall detain his vessel at either of the anchorages more than 24 hours, when he shall be directed by the Guarda-mor or his representative to remove thence, he shall pay 100||000 reis for every day he delays.

He shall discharge no part of his cargo but by an order in writing from the inspector; and if he lands any without such order, he shall pay 100||000 reis for each package so landed.

He shall give notice to the officer attending to the discharge of the vessel, as soon as his cargo is discharged, that he has nothing remaining on board. If he omits to do this, on the same day, so that the vessel may be immediately examined, he shall be fined 100||000 reis.

The master of every vessel going with a cargo to any port of the empire, must have two manifests of the cargo, exact copies of each other, which shall exhibit the name, class, and tonnage of the vessel, the name of the captain, whose signature must follow the date; the name of the port where the articles stated in the manifest were taken on board; the name of the port or ports for which the vessel is destined; the marks or countermarks, and numbers of the packages, and their description, as, bales, cases, pipes, half pipes, barrels, &c.; a declaration of the quantity and quality of the merchandise of each package, or several similar ones of the same mark, and also of what is on board in bulk; the names of the consignees, or to order; all to be written at length, except the numbers of the packages.

When the vessel has taken in her cargo at more than one port, there must be two manifests from each port.

At the end of the manifest the captain shall declare the number of passengers, whether cabin or steerage, and the baggage for the use of each, and in addition, any declaration necessary for his security; and in good faith, he shall declare whether he has any package to add to the manifest, or whether any are deficient, with the cause of it, as no after declaration will relieve him from responsibility, for he will not be exempted upon the vague declarations frequently made, which do not account for deficiencies or differences.

The captain of any vessel bound to Brazil, when he has completed his cargo in the port or ports from which he is to sail, and made the manifests required, shall present his documents to the Brazilian consul residing in the port, who shall examine them, and if agreeable to these regulations, certify them.

In those ports where there is no Brazilian consul or substitute, the manifests shall be certified by two Brazilian resident merchants, or if there are none, by two merchants of the place; in either case, the signatures to be authenticated by legal authority.

Should any greater quantity of goods be found on board than are stated in the manifest or the declaration of the captain, the overplus shall be seized and divided among those who seize them, after paying the duties; and the captain shall pay a fine of half the value of the goods.

If there are any goods missing of those stated in the manifest or declaration of the captain, they shall be reputed to be concealed or smuggled, and he shall pay the value thereof to those who have discovered the deficiency, and half the value to the national treasury. These condemnations shall take place on the simple fact of there being an overplus or deficiency of goods, without further proof being required.

For each difference in the quality or mark of the package, the captains shall pay 2||000 reis, although in every other respect the goods discharged may agree with the manifest.

The captain whose manifests are not conformable to these regulations, shall be fined from 100||000 reis to one conto de reis, at the will of the collector, according to the degree of culpability that shall appear, and he cannot discharge until the fine is paid.

In case the captain brings no manifest, he may still be allowed to discharge by paying 5 per cent. on the value of the cargo, in addition to the usual duties.

The vessel shall be held liable for the fines incurred by the captain.

Goods entered for consumption.—If dry goods, may remain 3 years in the custom-house.

If wet goods, or perishable, they cannot remain more than 6 months.

When the time expires, public notice shall be given, and if not removed in 20 days, they shall be sold, and the proceeds, after deducting duties and charges, reserved for the owner on proof of property.

No vessel can have a permit of re-exportation to take on board at the anchorage ground of loading and unloading, other than pipes, half pipes, crates of earthenware, iron in bars, and other articles of great bulk. All other loading must be taken on board at the franquia anchorage.

When a guard will be placed on board at the vessel's expense, 2||000 reis per day—vessel to sail as soon as loaded.

Foreign vessels are permitted to tranship and re-export foreign merchandise from one port of the Brazilian empire to another.

The charges on reshipment are not to be deducted from the duties to which goods are liable in every port of the empire.

If a vessel is entered in franquia, the captains, owners, or consignees of goods, may discharge for consumption *part* of their goods, on paying 5 per cent. additional duty.

A foreign vessel in franquia may take the products of the country on board at that anchorage to take them to *foreign* countries. In which case, the inspector is authorized to allow the time of remaining at the anchorage which may be absolutely necessary.

Articles free of duty on entry for consumption.—1. Foreign coin, of silver or gold, or gold and silver in bars or pigs; 2. Printed books; 3. Articles for the use of foreign ministers, where reciprocity exists; 4. Wearing apparel of persons coming into the country; 5. Raw materials for national manufactures; 6. Machines, if not already in use in the provinces for which they are intended.

The articles Nos. 1, 3 and 4, are not subject to pay the expedients or storage, and may be immediately taken away by the owners. Nos. 5 and 6 will pay $\frac{1}{2}$ per cent., when by their nature they are obliged to be stored.

The machines are to be free of duty if they facilitate, shorten, and render the work more perfect, and reduce the expense of any species of manufacture or labour.

Machines also are free which cannot be made in the country, until otherwise ordered.

To be entitled to freedom from duty, the importer must leave with the custom-house an exact description and drawing of the machine, with its uses and mode of application.

Tares and allowances for breakage, &c.—On liquids in glass, in packages, 5 per cent. allowed on the value: in earthenware, 3 per cent.

3 per cent. also on glass and earthenware, in whatever packages they come.

On other articles subject to diminution, such as salt, the commissioners of the custom-house shall make reasonable allowance, and 2 per cent. on wine, oil, and other liquids, in casks or wooden vessels.

The abatements to be made when not allowed for in the pauta.

To any merchant a credit of 3 and 6 months is allowed for duties, on signing a bond with two good securities.

Vessels with foreign goods cannot enter for consumption at ports where there are no custom-houses, unless the duties have been paid at some custom-house of the empire; but in the province of S. Pedro the entry may be made at Rio Grande, or S. Jose de Norte, when they may unload, or go elsewhere in the province.

If any foreign goods are landed without the entry specified, the vessel and goods to be seized and sent to Rio Janeiro, Pernambuco, Maranhao, Para, and Rio Grande do sul, whichever is nearest, and sold at public sale.

Proceeds, after paying duties and charges, to belong to those who seize and send them on.

All goods landed where there are no custom-houses without the duty paid, to be seized wherever found, and proceeded against as smuggled, (extraviados.)

The goods to be sent, if possible, in the vessel that landed them, if it can be seized; if not, to be sent by the first safe conveyance to the nearest custom-house, with an exact account.

A vessel having goods on board, which have not paid the duties on entry for consumption, being compelled by distress to enter a port where there is no custom-house, shall justify the necessity to the competent authority of the place, and if his situation makes his departure impossible without absolutely necessary supplies, he may buy them when licensed by that authority, and embark them, after paying the duties and charges to the collector of the public revenue.

If the vessel is obliged necessarily to unload part or the whole of her cargo, it may be done by adopting the same proceedings as used in cases of similar necessity in ports where there are custom-houses, with this exception, that none of the cargo can be sold, and that the goods shall be deposited by order of the principal authority of the place, and an inventory made, which shall be compared with the manifest or cargo book, and the greatest care taken to preserve the goods in safety.

BUENOS AYRES.

This extensive country is known by the name of the United Provinces of South America. They extend from the Rio Grande to the Rio Negro. The city is situated on a peninsula, on the south bank of the river La Plata, 200 miles from the ocean. Lat. 34° 37′ S. Long. 58° 24′ W. The river in that part is 21 miles in breadth. It has no port, and vessels are obliged to anchor at 9 miles distance, and discharge their cargoes by means of lighters, which can reach the town only at high water, through a creek. It is well fortified, and is the depot of a great part of the treasures and merchandise of Potosi, Peru and Chili. Since its emancipation from colonial thraldom its trade has been considerable. Its exports are wheat and jerked beef to the West Indies and Brazil; gold, silver, copper, hides, tallow, oil, sugar, Vigonia wool, tobacco, cotton, Paraguay tea, beeswax, dye-woods and drugs, to the United States and Europe. Its imports are naval stores, furniture, lumber, salt, fish, boots, &c. Its inland trade with the western coast of the continent can be carried on only in the summer, on account of the impracticability of passing the Andes at any other season. The commercial regulations of this place, which we have been able to obtain, are as follows:—

Importation—Entry of vessels.—As soon as a foreign vessel comes to anchor, the inspector at the mole, or in case of hindrance to him, the officer of the bay, must board her with a guard appointed by the iuspector of service.

After announcing himself to the captain, the inspector will read to him the articles of "*regulations of active service*," dated 18th July, 1832, which prescribe specifically the formalities of entry. These articles, eleven in number, are printed in five columns, Spanish, English, French, Italian and German. A copy is, for his government, delivered to the captain, who must give a receipt for it.

The inspector will demand of the captain where from, what route he has pursued, in what ports he has taken in cargo, and to whom his vessel is consigned.

Manifest.—It is the duty of the captain immediately to deliver a general and exact manifest of all that he has on board; he must insert therein a list of his remaining stores and provisions. This manifest must be signed by the captain himself, or in his absence, by the supercargo.

The manifest must declare, in great detail, all the packages, their marks and numbers; and designating to whom the packages are consigned, all in conformity with the bills of lading, (*sobordo.*) The number of packages must be given in letters, and then in figures on the margin. Every article not in the manifest is irrevocably seized.

The manifest must contain the packages or private adventures of the crew: and, in a special paragraph, the packages imported under the title of *regalo*, (presents.) For this purpose the captain must exact from his crew and passengers the most exact account of every article they have on board.

No captain must come on shore before having delivered his manifest to one of the above named officers, who will note thereon the day and hour of its delivery.

The captain who shall not have delivered his manifest on coming to anchor, must deliver it to the inspection placed at the mole; which, as soon as received, will be transmitted to the inspectors of service, to be by them placed before the receiver, who will send it to the bureau of the *registros.*

Every captain whose manifest is not conformable to his deliveries, or his bills of lading, is punished by a fine of $1,000 in specie, which must be deposited by the consignee, reserving his right to charge them to the captain.

The captain must also present a certificate of his entire lading from the consul of the republic, residing at the port beyond sea where the vessel has laden, or if there be no consul, from the custom-house of the place.

The captain must also deliver the *sobordo*, or bills of lading, to be contrasted or compared with the general manifest.

The captain, after presentation of his manifest in the form prescribed, may make any additions and corrections he pleases, only he must make them at the bureau of the *registros*, within twenty-four hours after its delivery on board, or to the inspection *franche* at the mole. In case there are no additions to be made, the captain must, nevertheless, appear at the above bureau, to make and to sign such corrections as may be necessary.

If the manifest designates the quantity of articles by the words *moyes alquirs*, and other measures unknown in the country, the captain, in this case, in presenting himself to the bureau, will convert these measures into fanegas. Without such conversion, he cannot receive his permit to discharge.

Every captain must, also, in preparing his manifest, avoid using the word *caschs*, (casks,) it being forbidden by express law. The words *pipas*, (pipes,) *medias pipas*, (half pipes,) *tercitoras*, (tierces,) *cuarturolas*, (quarter casks,) *bariles*, (barrels,) must alone be applied to those packages of every description in their cargoes.

The manifest, if in a foreign language, must be literally translated into Spanish. The translation may be made on free paper. It must be signed by the translator.

The captain must sign, at the foot of his manifest, a note, acknowledging that he has been made acquainted with all the penalties to which he would be subjected in contravening the prescribed regulations.

If he refuse to sign such note, either because he does not understand the Spanish language, or, which seldom occurs, that he has no person on board who understands either of the four languages hereinbefore mentioned, this circumstance shall be certified by the inspector at the foot of the manifest, and be signed by the accompanying guard. A copy of the eleven articles mentioned shall always, with the customary formalities, be delivered to the captain.

Discharging.—When the captain shall have complied with all the indicated formalities, the agent of the house to which the vessel is consigned, in proceeding to the register of discharge or permit to unload, must address himself to the *commandancia* of the rolls, or the captaincy of the port, and present to the receiver a demand exactly conformable to the manifest delivered by the captain to the inspector *franche*, to pass the customary visit.

If the vessel belong to a nation having a consul at Buenos Ayres, the agent must, at the same time, deliver a certificate of all the papers deposited with the consul.

The bureau of the port will deliver an acquittal of the duties, and a certificate acknowledging either the delivery of the ship's papers, as above, to the consul, or their deposite in said bureau.

The port duties on entry are:

			Pesos.	Reals
Tonnage duties.	Foreign vessels,	English, per ton *		6
		Other, per ton	1	0
	National vessels, per ton - -			6
Health visit.	English, per ton - -		6	0
	Other, per ton - -		12	0
	National vessels, per ton - -		6	0
Duty for police regulations of the port, per ton - -			1	0

This latter regulation is the one which makes known to the cap-

* By treaty, being on an equality with vessels of the Republic.

tains and agents of commercial houses the duties they have to pay, and the time allowed for payment.

The agent must, afterwards, deliver at the custom-house, to the *writer*, the receipt for port duty entry, on a sheet of stamped paper, for fifteen dollars, for permission to unload.

To expedite the delivery of this permission, the agent of the consignee ought to obtain, from each of those interested in the cargo, a copy of their respective invoices; and, after having arranged the whole, he will present the exhibit to the bureau of the *writer*, to obtain his expedition. This copy cannot, in any manner, be regarded as a justificatory proof of the exactitude of the general manifest to be produced by the captain.

As soon as the receiver has authorized, upon the legalized copy of the general manifest, the delivery of the permit to discharge, this document is sent to the inspector of service, to be copied and inscribed in the register of the bureau of active service.

The permit to discharge, expedited in the form usual with compared invoices, is, after the above enregistering, immediately clothed with the *visa* of *active service*, and sent to the captain of the vessel, for the purpose of proceeding to discharge.

On the margin of the permit, the custom-house names the officer who is to remain on board, to attend the unlading until the vessel is entirely discharged.

The captain, if he remain on board, or the officer by whom he is represented, must carefully watch that nothing is unladen or received on board without a permit in writing from the receiver, under penalty for the captain of a fine of $1000 in specie, which must be deposited by the consignee of the vessel, and are integrally abandoned as being confiscated to the use of the informer.

All goods transported from the river to the shore, without a permit from the receiver, are seized and sent to the custom-house stores.

All vessels are required to discharge at the interior balizes, if there be not a lawful cause to prevent it.

Every vessel, which, because of its draught of water, cannot safely pass the interior balizes to unload, must apply to the receiver for authority to discharge at the exterior balizes.

The front of the principal bureau of *active service* is exclusively and rigorously appropriated to unlading.

This disposition does not apply to woods, coal, lime, salt in bulk, and other articles, on which, by decision of the receiver, it is easy to establish the identity, and which, may then be landed upon the mole or under tents, after previous information given to said receiver, in order that he may take measures to prevent that, in lieu of such articles, other merchandise is not landed.

The yard and the stores of the custom-house are open for the reception of goods from one hour after sunrise until 3 o'clock, P. M.

The agreement of the kinds of merchandise, and of the packages discharged, with the permit granted, must be carefully ascertained, in order that, if there be a material disagreement, application may be made of the regulation which prescribes the seizure and sending of the articles to the custom-house stores.

Special manifests.—As the articles specified in the manifest of every vessel cannot all be expedited from the custom-house, even after presentation of copies of the invoices, it is indispensable for every vessel to present two special manifests, of which the first must, independently of the signature of the introducer, have that of a surety inscribed on the register of the custom-house. Care must be taken that all merchants, indiscriminately, do not enjoy this prerogative.

The two special manifests must be immediately presented to the bureau of the *registros*, that he may note the same, and to the receiver, who inscribes on one the order to expedite, and affixes to the other a simple *paraphe*, (mark.) These formalities being fulfilled, the two manifests will be delivered to the visiter, who, after having confronted them with the manifest of expedition, will mark one of the two pieces, with which the person interested will present himself to the storekeeper of the customs, to ascertain at what hour delivery can be made of the goods specified in the manifest: those goods being previously submitted to a counter verification by the visiters or comptrollers, for their classification and valuation.

In the manifests, general and special, in all the permits destined to appear at the custom-house, all details must be given in letters, and the quantities inserted on the margin in figures.

Casks and cases must be well described, in such manner that there can be no doubt of their number or their nature.

Independently of port and custom-house duty, properly so called, all cargoes pay a duty of four per 1,000 on their estimated value, denominated *contribution direct.*

The rate of storage is fixed as follows:

For every pipe - - - - - -	3 pesos.
For every quarter cask or barrel, duty in proportion.	
For every *bulto* (package) of every kind - -	4 reals.
For every seven arrobas of merchandise by weight -	4 "

The following articles pay as follows:

Woods.—Planks, (tablazon,) per dozen - - -	4 reals.
Grains.—Wheat and corn, per fanega - - -	4 "

The following are free from charge for storage:

Wood.—Fire, in stocks, boards, beams, joists for masts, spars; bricks, tiles, coal, salt in bulk, salt in casks or bags, pays as pipes and their divisions. There is, in addition, a duty of amortigacion.

Duties, where the amount does not exceed $500, are paid in cash.

If, within eight days after coming to anchor, the person interested does not wish to unload, the vessel must proceed to sea, after being subject to the customary visit, and after advice has been given of this intention to depart to the receiver, by the inspector *franche.*

Transhipment.—The importer retains the privilege to tranship the whole or a part of the cargo declared in his manifest.

But the law limits this to twenty-five days from the vessel's anchorage. The delay having expired, the transhipment is not permitted.

Vessels arriving from sea, may tranship to another vessel bound to a foreign port. This latter vessel must measure at least 120 tons. The tonnage is ascertained by the inspector *franche.*

Transhipments, destined for a port of the rivers of the interior, situated out of the territory of the province, whether such port be national or foreign, are subject to the general regulations applicable to them always in reference to their origin. They will be, generally, the regulations prescribed for Montevideo, Brazil, and countries beyond sea.

Liquids, and all products of the soil, are allowed to be transhipped.

Products of industry, and all articles which ought to be submitted to the effective inspection of the visiters, are not entitled to the privilege of transhipment.

The permit to tranship is delivered in duplicate. It must be presented to the bureau of the *registros*, that he may take note thereof; to the visiter, for the valuation of merchandise inscribed therein; to the bureau of the customs, to receive his *visa;* to the guard of the vessel from which are extracted the merchandise transhipped, that he may ascertain the transhipment; to the inspection *franche*, at the mole, that it likewise may ascertain the embarking of the merchandise on board the vessel destined to receive them; to the bureau of liquidations, for the application of the duties according to the valuation made by the visiter on entry; to the bureau of control, for counter verification; to the cashier, for the payment of what is due; finally it is returned to the bureau of the *registros*, to be annexed to the ship's papers of the exporting vessel.

The transhipment permit must be signed by the same individual who has made the declaration of entry, under penalty, without this indispensable condition, of not being permitted to be expedited.

The duty on articles transhipped is the 175th of the duty of entry.

Permission is given to tranship on board a vessel bound to a foreign port without being subject to the required verification, but subject, to duties of export, hides coming from places situated out of the territory of the province.

CADIZ,

The first commercial city in Spain, with the finest port in Europe. It is situated on the western extremity of an isthmus, on an island belonging to the province of Andalusia, the northern part of which is called Cadiz, and the southern Leon, and which is connected with the main land by the bridge of Suaza, fortified at both ends. Lat. 36° 32′ N. Long. 6° 16′ W.

A consul resides at Cadiz from every commercial nation in the world; and partly from its local advantages, already enumerated, and partly from its deficiency of inland water communication with the capital and other large cities in Spain, it engrosses, either directly or indirectly, almost the whole trade of the kingdom, as well European as colonial.

Imports.—Linens, woollens, hardware, grain, mats, tar, pitch, tallow, fish, oil, &c.

Exports.—Cochineal, indigo, dye-woods, marilla, Peruvian bark, and other colonial produce; of home productions, wool, wines, in great variety; barilla, salt, iron, olive oil, fruits of various kinds; sherry wines and inferior brandies, distilled in a slovenly manner from the refuse of their fruit, but sold in large quantities for mixing with weak wines.

Tonnage duty.—One real per ton on all vessels. No drawback is allowed on goods exported in foreign vessels. Raw cotton of the United States is prohibited. Brazil and Levant cotton is admitted under a duty of 7 cents. The duty on flour is $2 50 per barrel, and charges 70 cents; on wheat, sufficient to make a barrel of flour, 60 cents. Papers required of foreign vessels, are the passport from the government, proof of property, contract for freight, log-book, and list of crew.

One uniform duty shall be paid on the importation or exportation of goods in foreign commerce, excepting the discrimination between those in national or foreign vessels.

In cases where importation or exportation is permitted under a foreign flag, the same import and export duties shall be paid, with the addition of one third more; but in cases where certain goods are exempt from duty, they shall be equally so whether belonging to foreigners or Spaniards.

Goods once subject to duty, whether of importation, exportation, consumption, or foreign circulation, shall pay the same, without any allowance of drawback from re-importation, re-exportation, or on any other account, excepting for the rectification of error in the amount of the duty.

Neither shall any premium, bounty, or reduction of duty be granted, with a view of encouraging the importation or exportation of any species of goods, from motives of utility, security, or any other.

The circulation of all kinds of merchandise from one port to another of the Spanish dominions, is only permitted to vessels under the national flag; subject to the regulations contained in the two following articles, which apply to all countries under the dominion of Spain.

National goods, circulated or exported coastwise, shall be subject, at the place of exportation, to a duty of 2 per cent. for the charges of administration; and they shall be free of duty at the places of importation, except such goods as are liable to the duty of consumption.

Foreign goods, having paid the import duties at any one port of the peninsula, may be exported, either coastwise or to any foreign port, on paying the 2 per cent. duty of administration; but if exported to any ultra-marine port of the Spanish monarchy, they will be subject to the second import duty to which foreign merchandise is liable; and the same rule applies to foreign merchandise exported from one Spanish colonial port to another, or to any port of the peninsula.

National vessels engaged in transporting foreign imported merchandise, or national produce, from one Spanish port to another, if they have been detained, and paid any charges in a foreign port, (although no mention is made of such detention in the bill of health, or muster of the crew,) shall pay, in the port of their destination or discharge, all the duties of importation and consumption on the goods set forth in the bills of lading, even though the permits and registers may state that the duties have already been paid. They shall be subject, also, to the penalties for infraction of the quarantine, maritime, and revenue laws.

Foreign vessels shall be admitted into all the ports of the Spanish monarchy, on the same footing as Spanish vessels are admitted into the foreign ports of the nations to which such vessels belong.

A foreign vessel entering into a Spanish port without intention to unload, but merely to avoid or repair damages, or to procure necessary supplies, shall be allowed to remain as long as may be necessary for these purposes; and if it be a merchant vessel, it shall be treated in the same manner as a Spanish vessel in like circumstances would be treated in the nation to which it belongs, paying or not paying, in perfect reciprocity, the duties of tonnage, anchorage, and the other charges of transit, demurrage, free intercourse, and quarantine.

Foreign vessels of more than 80 tons burthen may export from ports of deposit of the first class, foreign goods of lawful commerce, and of the produce of the country to which such vessels belong, subject to the regulations concerning deposited goods. And no other duty than the 2 per cent. of deposit shall be paid on goods so warehoused and re-exported, in ports so privileged, except the period allowed for warehousing be exceeded, and they be considered as imported, in which case they must pay the import duties.

In like manner, foreign vessels above 80 tons burthen, may export, from ports specially licensed for this purpose, both foreign and national goods, upon complying with the rules established in the general tariff.

Also, foreign vessels of the same burthen may import provisions and raw materials (in the same manner as the importation of them is permitted by license) into the ports of Spain from foreign countries, and all other goods which are not subject to any other duty than that of administration: it being required that the said goods shall be the produce of the nation to which the vessel belongs, and shall pay the duties without the benefit of deposit, and shall carry the goods to the appointed deposits.

Places of deposit for maritime commerce shall be established at such ports as the government may propose, and the cortes approve of. They shall be of two classes: the first class shall be for the deposit of national goods, subject to the duty of consumption, and also of foreign goods. The second class shall be for the deposit of national goods only, which are subject to the duty of consumption. The places selected for this purpose must be secure and well fortified, capable of defending shipping, possessing custom-houses, warehouses, and a junta of commerce, composed of three individuals chosen by the merchants of the place. Respect must also be had to the facilities for the greatest exportation of domestic produce.

Ships, both national and foreign, shall be considered as articles of commerce, and the sale or purchase of them shall be permitted, prohibited, or regulated by the general tariff of each year; and all those which belong to Spanish subjects shall become naturalized.

In determining the amount of duty for solids and liquids, the weights and measures of Castile shall alone be employed; and as it respects money, the effective reals de vellon, and not the nominal or imaginary reals, shall be used.

The productions of the dissident or American provinces, situated north of the equator, which come directly to the ports of entry of the peninsula in foreign vessels, shall pay, over and above the duty fixed for foreign flags by the tariff of February 21, 1828, one third more, as well as the duty established by the royal order of June 7, 1830.

The same productions of the dissident provinces, situated south of the equator, coming directly to the ports of entry of the peninsula in foreign vessels, shall pay four fifths of the duty to which the tariff of February 21, 1828, subjects foreign flags, as also the duty imposed by the royal order of June 7, 1830.

Productions coming from foreign ports of America and the West Indies, under a foreign flag, to the ports of entry of the peninsula, shall pay the duties prescribed by the tariff of imports.

The productions of the dissident provinces, situated either north or south of the equator, and those of the colonies and foreign countries which arrive in the ports of entry of the peninsula, coming from the warehouses of Havana or Porto Rico, under register from the same, shall pay, over and above the duties fixed by the tariff of February 21, 1828, one fifth more, and the additional duty imposed by the royal order of June 7, 1830, provided they have not touched at any foreign port during their passage. If they shall have touched at any foreign port during their passage, unless from stress of weather or damage, they shall pay the duties prescribed by the tariff of imports.

If the same productions be brought from the said warehouses, under the Spanish flag, without touching at any foreign port on the passage, they shall simply pay the duties of the tariff of February 21, 1828, and the additional duty imposed by the royal order of June 7, 1830. Should they, however, have touched at any port on the passage, except from damage or stress of weather, they shall be considered as coming from that port.

Productions of the dissident provinces, colonial productions, and those of foreign countries, coming directly from foreign ports in Europe, either under the Spanish or foreign flag, shall pay the duties established by the tariff of imports, and one third more, as also the duty imposed by the royal order of June 7, 1830.

The freedom granted to the port of Cadiz is confined, as respects prohibited goods, to a spot outside of the city, where the free and real deposit of such goods will be allowed; and as respects goods not prohibited, to the stores and houses of the merchants, where a *factitious* deposit of the same will be permitted.

The space of ground between Cadiz and the *Cortadura*, known by the name of Puntales, will be that in which the deposit of prohibited goods will be allowed, for an indefinite period, with the exception of those monopolized by the crown, and of articles contraband of war.

The deposit of said goods will be made in the private stores existing at Puntales, and in those that may be erected there henceforward; and for the purpose of defraying the expense of employées, a charge will be made of $\frac{1}{2}$ per cent. on their entrance only.

Within this enclosure, the sale, barter, or consumption of said goods will be permitted without restriction, but not their removal for importation into any part of the peninsula.

Their removal for exportation to foreign ports will be allowed, as also for the Spanish dominions in America and Asia; but in this latter case they are to be provided with a certificate from the custom-house.

All prohibited goods existing in the city and port of Cadiz, are to be conveyed to the spot above designated as soon as this decree shall be put into execution, and duplicate lists of the same are to be presented to the custom-house.

Business may be transacted at Puntales every working day, from morning to evening, and the owners of the goods will be permitted to inspect their property, to sell or barter it, or to perform any other operation of the kind they may think proper; and the officers appointed to superintend the stores, will not only not embarrass merchants by any unnecessary interference, but will afford them every facility compatible with this decree.

The factitious deposit of goods, not prohibited, will be allowed not only in the houses and stores of the merchants, but in the magazines of the custom-house.

The expedition of this kind of goods to any habitated part of the peninsula, with a certificate from the custom-house, may be effected without payment of any export duties.

Neither will any duties be charged on goods under factitious deposit, that may be sold, exchanged, or transferred from one store to another, with the intervention of the government officers.

Custom-house and gate duties will be charged on goods in factitious deposit, conveyed to Cadiz for their consumption there.

When said goods leave the depot direct for towns in the interior, custom-house duties only will be charged, and there, on their being sold, the provincial duties will be exacted.

Goods under factitious deposit will be allowed the term of 12 months for the payment of duties, which term may be lengthened, if a just motive be alleged.

In the factitious deposit of goods not prohibited, it shall be obligatory on the owners to observe the rule established in regard to manifests, licenses and other documents; and they are to give security for the fulfilment of the conditions contained in the preceding articles.

CAPE OF GOOD HOPE

Comprehends three bays or harbours, viz., on the east side, Saldanha and Table bays—on the west, False bay. Lat. 34° 24′ S. Long. 18° 28′ E.

The imports are principally beer of different kinds, blacking, books, boots, shoes and brushes; brass, iron, and tin ware; clothes of woollen, linen, and cotton; cutlery, glass, groceries, haberdashery, hats, hosiery, lead and lead shot, medicines, paint brushes and oil; perfumery, plate, spirits, stationary, saddlery; wines from France, Portugal, Spain, &c.

The exports are almost exclusively wines made in the country, which are rapidly improving; aloes, and a few animals, both wild and tame.

The most important local regulations are the following:—No boat can ship, tranship, or bring on shore any goods without a permit from the custom-house, with the nature and number of packages, &c. &c.; nor can they be landed any where but at the public wharf, without permission, and must be removed at the expiration of 24 hours, under pain of seizure.

No person to be received on board without a certificate from the proper officer, nor any person to be left behind without permission from the secretary's office.

No specie to be shipped without a special permit, under pain of 12 months' imprisonment, forfeiture of treble the amount, and confiscation of the craft conveying it to the ship.

Deserters and runaway slaves being harboured, subject to a penalty of 500 rix dollars; and notice of departure to be given 2 days previous to sailing, that search may be made after deserters, &c.

Charges at the custom-house.

	Rix dolls.		Rix dolls.
Entrance of ship . .	4	Manifest	1
Landing or shipping a cargo	10	Clearance	4
Landing and shipping a cargo	2	Pass for vessel trading on the coast . . .	2
Permit to import or export	1		
Permit for stores, &c. .	4		

Cape Town, Simonstown, and Port Elizabeth, are free ports; and the two first free warehousing ports.

American vessels are not permitted to land at the Cape of Good Hope any other than *American produce.* The ship and cargo is liable to be confiscated by breach of these regulations.

Barrels and casks, and hoops, staves and headings, imported into the Cape of Good Hope, may be sold there, free of duty.

CANTON,

A seaport of China, where Americans and Europeans are permitted to trade, situated on the river Pe Kiang, usually called the Tigris, which falls into a large bay at Bocca Tigris. Foreign vessels anchor at Whampoa, where one or more Chinese custom-house boats are stationed to each ship to prevent smuggling.

The exports are teas, silks, nankins, paper, chinaware, cottons, sugars, candy, matting and furniture, to India, and zinc.

The black teas begin to come down at the beginning of October, and by the beginning of November are plenty in market. The green teas begin to come down about the 15th of October, and are plenty about the 10th of November. Black teas do not lose much by being a year old, except their freshness of smell. The crispness which is produced by artificial heat, is lost by age; and old teas are often fired a second time to give them the crispness of new teas, and, in some degree, restore the flavour; for which they are often sold when mixed with new teas.

The imports are woollens, lead, tin, copper, dyes, quicksilver, furs, specie, ginseng, brandy, opium, (prohibited—still 3000 boxes are imported annually, being often taken on shore by the custom-house boats at the rate of $14 per box,) wine, pepper, beetle nut, cotton, pearl, bird's nests, and shark's fins.

Lat. 23° 7′ N. Long. 113° 14′ E.

Pilotage.

For a vessel of about 300 tons, from Macoa to Whampoa, inward $60
Outward the same.

Ships generally have a comprador, who supplies the ship with provisions, a linguist, an agent or Hong merchant, &c.

The ship's comprador will expect a cumshaw or present of ($200 or $300, according to the number of the crew;) and if you employ the hoppo man, or custom-house officer, in his stead, the linguist will expect a cumshaw of $200 in lieu of the above.

The linguist's own fee is $216, besides boat hire.

The water mandarin's, $19.

The cumshaw to the emperor, for every vessel, is 1950 tale, about $2778; besides which a tonnage duty is paid from 500 to 800 tale, according to the tonnage of the vessel.

A tale is worth $1 39 nearly. In purchase of teas, sugars, &c., 72 candarins (or candareens) are $1; chinaware and payments to comprador, &c., 75 candarins.

Chopped dollars are received by weight at 71.5 or 71.7 candarins, as you can agree; the dollar receive at the latter and pay at the former.

Bills on London, at 9 and 12 months' sight, vary every year in price, from 5s. to 6s. per dollar.

All goods are put on board by the seller free of duties and all other charges.

Goods are imported free of charge, except boat hire, if sold to a Hong merchant; the duty usually being included in the price.

All contracts with Chinese should be written in the English and Chinese languages, and read to them.

If the outside men, whose characters are not well established, buy of you, earnest money should be taken, as a penalty in case of non-fulfilment of the contract.

In the contract made with the Hong merchant, the prices and quantity of your outward and present cargoes should be mentioned.

Factories are generally hired here by the masters or supercargoes of ships, and it is usual for two ships' families to live in one factory. The house comprador, who generally charges from $80 to $100, furnishes it with furniture, provisions, &c., for which he is separately paid.

The impositions to which all foreigners are subjected in trading with the Chinese, are well known; and the greatest circumspection and prudence should be observed in all intercourse with them. Boats should never be permitted to come alongside in the night.

At Macoa masters must go on shore and report the vessel and cargo in general terms to the Chinese custom-house officers, and they must report a cargo in order to be admitted without delay. The pilot cannot be obtained under 24 hours. He is accompanied by a mandarin, who should be watched. He furnishes the first boat from Whampoa to Canton with a permit, for which he receives $2.

The fishermen at Macoa will offer to pilot the ship up for $50, but will take much less.

Tariff.—The custom-house of Canton is governed by a species of code, which dates its origin from the commencement of the last century, but which, since that period, has undergone numerous modifications and additions. The high superintendence of the custom-house, and of the collection of duties, is confided to the *Foo-yuen*, or governor of the province of Canton.

The duties are received by the hoppo. The application of the code, and the functions of the hoppo, are not restricted to the port of Canton; they extend throughout the province.

Printed copies of the custom-house code are very rare, perhaps even they do not exist; those printed regulations, published by the custom-house, are alone considered official. The code is only known by the manuscript copies, which serve as guides to the Chinese merchants.

Duties on foreign commerce.—All foreign vessels must, on their arrival at Canton, have their tonnage ascertained, which is done by multiplying the length by the breadth, and by dividing the product by 10.

Vessels are afterwards classed as is directed in the first part of the tariff.

The tariff of duties for tonnage is, for vessels of eastern ocean the same as for vessels of western ocean—except only an allowance to vessels of eastern ocean of two tenths.

The duty is, for every tael of measurement, 1 mace 2 cand.

A discount is allowed of 10 per cent., and the money is weighed with the scales of the treasury. There is also levied a duty of *port entry*, fixed as follows, on all vessels, without distinction of tonnage:

Inwards, primitive duty	.	1125 taels	0 m.	actual,	810 t.	6 m.	9 c.	1 cash.
Outwards, "	.	533 "	8	"	480	4	2	0 "

Duties are payable in money, (*sycee*,) and is weighed in the treasury scales.

	t.	m.	c.
All vessels arriving from foreign ports pay, for the first month after entry into port	2	6	0
For each month after the first	1	3	0
All foreign vessels pay besides, from the day of entering into port until their departure, per day . . .		6	0
Daily during their unlading	3	4	8
Those who apply for carpenters or painters at Whampoa, per man		1	0
Those who ask permission to transport sundries (chow chow)		1	0
For every lighter (chop) employed in loading or unloading merchandise		2	4
For every boat accompanying a lighter		1	2

All goods imported or exported are subject to the duties specified in the first part of the tariff.

An extra tax of 10 per cent. is added for insurance against loss by fire.

	t.	m.	c.	cash.
Every bale of merchandise, barrel, or case, on being landed from a foreign vessel, pays immediately .	2	0	0	0
All manufactures, called piece goods, pay per piece			1	1
This last duty is payable in *sycee* money, with 8 per cent. discount, and is weighed in the treasury scales.				
There is another duty of *pecalage* per 100 catties (1 pecul of merchandise)			3	8
And to every tael of duty is added			1	6
All foreign goods, which, after having been weighed, and after acquittal of duty, are sent into the interior to be there disposed of, pay per 100 catties .			1	0

The duties on merchandise exported by foreign vessels, collected conformably to the regulations in force, according to the rates fixed by the emperor Kien Long, in 1735, are payable in *sycee* money, with 8 per cent. discount, and weighed in the scales of the treasury. They pay besides, for every tael of value, 4 c. 9 cash. Discount and weighing as above.

At Lintin, dependent upon the province of Canton, the collection of duties is said to be somewhat more regular, and less prejudicial to foreign commerce.

Within a few years, a tariff, carefully revised and modified by the mandarins of the port, serves as the basis for the payment of duties; but here, as well as at Canton, the amount of receipts progressively diminishes in its progress from the receiver of customs to the hoppo and other high officers, through whose hands it passes to reach the imperial chest.

The charges on vessels are exorbitant and capricious; thus, pilotage in and out, $120; to the interpreter, (linguist,) $173; *comprador*, broker, $50; *cumshaw*, or present to the mandarin at Whampoa, $2,223; amount paid by each foreign vessel, $2,566—and without regard to her size or her cargo, unless it be of rice, when she is free from the cumshaw, and all port duties.

American vessels frequently avail themselves of this privilege by putting their opium, &c., on board of a hulk without making an entry, and then proceed to Manilla, where they take in a cargo of rice, with which they return, make their regular entry, and are exempted from the heavy charges of *cumshaw*, &c.

CENTRAL AMERICA.

The commercial intercourse between the United States and the republic of Central America, is placed, by the treaty of 1825, on the basis of perfect reciprocity and liberty of trade. Each of the contracting parties has the privilege of importing, at the domestic rate of duties, into the ports of the other, merchandise of whatever origin;

and in respect to tonnage or other charges, the vessels of the one pay in the ports of the other the same dues, in every case, that are exacted from national vessels.

This new state possesses many advantages in respect to maritime commerce, from its extensive coasts on the Atlantic and Pacific oceans. Its interior communication is also capable of being rendered very perfect, by means of numerous navigable streams and lakes. The soil of several of the provinces is of great fertility, and is susceptible of yielding grain, flax, hemp, cotton, and sugar, in abundance. It possesses, also, some valuable silver mines. The principal exports, however, are indigo, cochineal, and dye woods. The imports comprise every variety of manufactured articles, tea, coffee, spices, wines, oil, spirits, &c.

The ports of the north and of the south of the republic, recognized (*habilitados*) by the laws, shall be open to vessels of every nation at peace with the republic, and which does not manifest any opposition to its independence.

The law will protect all merchandise imported and exported through those ports, provided that the regulations of the present tariff are complied with, and that the duties which it imposes are paid.

Commerce of importation.—The following articles are duty free: 1. Books, printed or in manuscript, bound or stitched. 2. Instruments adapted to science. 3. Music, printed or in manuscript. 4. Instruments and implements for agriculture, mines, arts, and trades. 5. The seed of plants not cultivated in the republic. 6. Gold and silver, whether as bullion or coin.

The merchant who imports merchandise and coin in the same vessel, shall be allowed a deduction of 2 per cent. upon an amount of the merchandise equal to the amount of coin.

Every foreign vessel anchoring in a recognised port of the republic, shall pay a tonnage duty of 3 reals per ton; which, for the present, shall include anchorage and light money. National vessels shall pay one third less.

Twelve hours after vessels come to anchor, the commanders will present to the administrator of the customs, duplicate manifests, affirmed and signed, giving, 1. The name of the captain and of the vessel, the tonnage, a list of the crew, and from whence arriving. 2. The number of bales, packets, cases, barrels, jars, and the other packages, with their marks, numbers, consignees, and the kinds of merchandise; as tissues of flax and hemp, of wool, of silk, hardware, &c., and with a declaration at foot, that there are no other goods on board than those specified in the manifest.

The manifest will not only indicate the articles destined for the port where the vessel has anchored, but also those for transit or transhipment, and which are destined for other ports.

The manifest and other documents will be revised in the Spanish language, and with the greatest perspicuity.

The manifest, presented with the prescribed formalities, will be received by the administrator, who, after having examined it, will pass it to the bureau of control, where the copies will be compared with the original; and the comptroller, after a careful examination of the whole, will transmit one copy of the manifest to the chief wharfinger, and the other to the *alcayde* of the custom-house, for his government in opening all packages landed and placed in store.

The administrator, after having received the manifest, will designate the number of persons necessary to be placed on board the vessel, who shall be furnished with the permit to discharge, and who shall be present whilst she is discharging.

The captain will annex to the manifest the official and private correspondence with which he may be charged.

Before commencing to discharge, the captain and supercargo of merchant vessels must be informed of the formalities to be observed for the landing of the goods and payment of the duties.

The inspectors of customs will keep a register, prepared by the administrator, divided into three parts. The first will contain a literal copy of the manifest; the second will mention the entry of packages into store, with their marks and numbers, and with the names of the owners and consignees, referring to the permit; the third will present the details of the delivery from the store of the same goods, mentioning the certificates of delivery.

The discharging of vessels will commence immediately on receiving the permits, and must be completed with the least possible delay. It must not exceed 12 working days, except in cases of necessity, when the time may be prolonged by the administrator in concert with the comptroller.

Vessels of more than 300 tons will alone be allowed the privilege of correcting their manifests within 8 days immediately following the commencing to discharge. This privilege, however, is not extended to nations who do not grant similar advantages to the vessels of Central America.

As soon as a vessel is discharged, the administrator, the commandant of active service, and their respective subordinates, will make their visit on board. The administrator will satisfy himself that the merchandise declared for transit or transhipment remains on board; and if goods are discovered which are not in the manifest, they will be subjected to the consequences prescribed by the laws in cases of seizure.

Vessels, the agents of which will not submit to the regulations of this tariff, must depart within the prescribed delay of 6 days.

Foreign vessels putting into ports of the republic by stress of weather, or for supplies of water or provisions, cannot be permitted to remain longer than the time strictly necessary for repairs or taking in supplies. If they are merchant vessels, they must exhibit their manifests, and must submit to the visits and formalities that the commandant general of the place, and the administrator, may, under the circumstances, deem necessary.

Exportation.—The exportation of live cochineal, and of the seed of *xiquilite*, is alone prohibited. Infractions and contraventions will be punished according to law.

All produce of the soil, and all manufactures of the republic, are free of duty on exportation.

Also free of duty on exportation, all produce and foreign merchandise, provided they have paid the duty of importation; but if the goods have been reimported from some other port of the republic, they will pay full import duties.

Entrepots.—At present, and until otherwise ordered, the ports of entrepot are *Omoa* on the north coast, and *Union* on the south.

All produce and goods of every nation at peace with the republic, shall be admitted into those entrepots.

Foreign property deposited in the ports of entrepot, are placed under the guaranty of the laws, and cannot be violated either by reprisals or in any other manner.

Goods may remain in these entrepots as long as may be the wish of the proprietors, not exceeding one year. If, after this term, they are not withdrawn in the space of a month, they will owe the total duties of importation. They will equally be subject to those duties, if, in the course of the year, they are withdrawn from the entrepot to be sent into the interior.

Goods will pay, on their entry into entrepot, a duty of 1 per cent. on their valuation as fixed by the tariff, and a like duty when withdrawn.

Masters of merchant vessels having articles destined to be placed in entrepot, must present, within 12 hours after arrival, the manifest of such articles, designating their marks, numbers, and consignees.

The manifest being examined by the administrator, they will proceed immediately to unloading, in the manner and within the periods prescribed by preceding articles.

On being placed in entrepot, goods shall be weighed, and the weight marked thereon. The same shall be done when removed.

General regulations.—The merchants who export in produce and merchandise of the republic, other than gold and silver, a value equal to the value of their importations, shall be allowed a deduction of 2 per cent. of the duties paid on such imports.

All articles imported or exported, or attempted to be imported or exported, in contravention of the tariff, either by the ports, roadsteads, or frontiers not legalized for commerce, will be irrevocably confiscated.

CHILI.

The intercourse between the United States and the republic of Chili is now under the protection of a treaty, which places it on the basis of the most favoured nation, and stipulates that no favour shall be granted by one party to the commerce or navigation of other nations, that shall not, at once, become common to the other party. There is, however, an important exception to this stipulation, and reserved by Chili in consequence of "the intimate connection and identity of feelings and interests," which subsist among the new American states. It provides that the relations and conventions which now exist, or may hereafter exist, between the republic of Chili, and all the new nations within the ancient territory of Spanish America, whatever alterations may take place in their names, or organization, are not to be considered as included in the prohibition of granting specific favours to other nations.

Besides the direct trade carried on from the United States to Chili, there is a circuitous commerce in American vessels, between China and that republic. Teas, silks, nankeens, and drugs, are exchanged for gold and silver, and the results of the traffic have proved so beneficial, as to have had the effect of inducing the Chinese to improve their manufactures of silk, and adapt them to the Chilian taste. The consequence has been to throw an important branch of trade into American hands, and, at the same time, its tendency has been to exclude, to a considerable extent, French silks from the Chilian market. Our vessels engaged in this circuitous intercourse, when on their return from China, proceed sometimes to Europe, where they dispose of such articles as may not have been exchanged in the ports of Chili, or of such as were there shipped, and they may ultimately reach the United States with a cargo consisting wholly of European productions. A voyage of this kind is not officially known to the custom-houses of the United States, and, of course, does not enter into the treasury statements of the trade between them and Chili, in the annual reports of commerce and navigation made to Congress. It is in the harbours, also, of Chili, that American whaling vessels are often in the habit of entering, for the purpose of making repairs, or of taking in fresh stores, for their return homeward.

Valparaiso has, from its proximity to St. Jago, the capital of the republic, become the chief port of Chili for foreign commerce; under the ancient government nearly the whole of this commerce for all the possessions of Spain bordering on the Pacific Ocean was engrossed by Callao, the seaport of Lima. But so uninterrupted have been the civil commotions of Peru, and such has been the comparative tranquillity of Chili, for a series of years, that Valparaiso, from having been a mere dependency of Callao, is now in possession of nearly the whole foreign trade of the two republics, and is rapidly obtaining that ascendancy which its rival formerly enjoyed.

Entrepot and transit by sea.—Goods which are not placed in the custom-house stores will be exempt from duty of storage, but will pay two per cent. of transit on their exportation to foreign ports.

The duty of entrepot is fixed at three per cent. for the first year; two per cent. for the second; one per cent. for the third.

Warehouses of entrepot.—Valparaiso is the only port of the republic open to the entrepot of merchandise for transit.

The entrepot will comprise all descriptions of foreign merchandise, whatever may be their nature, or whence proceeding.

Merchandise in general, for which no exception is made by the present regulation, will be deposited in the public stores.

Articles of monopoly will be transported to the stores of the principal factory, (*factoria principal.*)

Gold and silver (*sellados*) coined, may also be deposited in private stores, whether wrought or in ingots, and silver plate, goldsmith's wares, and jewellery (*alhajas*) of all sorts, on paying the duty prescribed by this regulation.

Also will be entitled to the same favour, articles of supply intended for revictualing vessels of war, belonging to allies or neutral powers.

This extension, and the other exemptions granted to articles of supply for vessels of war, are applicable only in those cases where the articles arrive in our ports by vessels belonging to governments which have expedited or freighted them.

Gunpowder shall be stored in the public places destined to its reception.

There will be a warehouse denominated *maritime*, to receive the cargoes of vessels arriving in distress.

In the maritime warehouse, goods shall be considered as remaining on board.

The entrepot in this warehouse shall not exceed one year.

There shall be paid for maritime storage, for the four first months of entrepot, $\frac{1}{2}$ real per month per quintal of weight, and double for each of the remaining eight months.

The duties of entrepot, of transit, of storage, and of police. will be collected exclusively by the custom-house.

The duty of entrepot will be collected on all merchandise which will owe it, counting from the date of the manifest in detail.

When the consignees wish to renew the entrepot, they must make their demand with a new manifest in detail, and pay the accrued warehousing duties.

These formalities being complied with, the merchandise may remain in entrepot another term of three years.

The treasury shall be responsible for all damage which may happen to merchandise deposited in the public stores, or in those of the factory of tobacco.

This responsibility does not extend to unavoidable accidents, such as conflagration, earthquake, inundations, and other unforeseen events which may happen.

The accountability will only attach to injury resulting from abandonment, or culpable negligence of persons employed as guards and superintendents of the said warehouses.

When it shall be authentically and legally proven, that goods have sustained deterioration in consequence of neglect, or have been stolen from the stores without scaling or breaking of the walls or doors, the custom-house will reimburse their value to the persons interested.

This reimbursement must be preceded by the decision of a competent judge, and by the valuation or appreciation of the visiting judges.

No package placed in entrepot can be opened, except in presence of a warehouse keeper, of a visiter, and of the proprietor.

Commerce of transit.—The maritime commerce of transit is confined to the port of Valparaiso.

By this maritime commerce of transit is to be understood the movement of foreign merchandise, introduced by sea, into the warehouses of entrepot, and thence re-embarked for foreign ports.

All foreign merchandise deposited in the public warehouses, will be considered as on transit, until a destination is given to it.

Manifests.—The commander of every vessel, national or foreign, arriving from foreign ports into the principal ports of the republic, must present, four hours after anchoring, a manifest, exhibiting the entire cargo on board.

At present, the ports recognised as principal ports, are San Carlos, Constitution, Valdivia, Valparaiso, Talcahuano, Coquimbo.

Foreign vessels of war are not required to present manifests.

All vessels bringing supplies for the squadrons of foreign friendly powers, are considered as vessels of war.

But when such vessels, besides the supplies belonging to their respective governments, have articles on board for individual account, a manifest of the entire cargo must be presented.

Unforeseen causes rendering it impossible for the captain to prepare his manifest within the time prescribed, he may, in lieu thereof, present his original bills of lading.

The bills of lading thus presented, must be accompanied by a certificate (pliego) in which the captain shall declare, under his signature, the entire cargo on board, and that the merchandise inserted in the bills of lading by him presented, composes the entire lading of the vessel.

As soon as a vessel arrives from a foreign port, one of the officers on duty will repair on board, and deliver to the captain a copy of the articles mentioned in the preceding article.

To insure attention to the strict interdict under which the vessel is placed until a delivery of the general manifest, the said officer of the customs shall leave a guard on board, with orders to remain until delivery and reception of the manifest.

If, after the expiration of the time allowed for delivery of the manifest, this delivery shall not have taken place, the vessel of which the captain shall have omitted this formality, shall immediately depart.

Great vigilance shall be used, to prevent all communication with the vessel in the bay, before and after her departure.

Every captain, who, before the presentation of his manifest, shall permit persons to come on board, or to leave his vessel, or shall hold any correspondence, will be fined one hundred dollars for every contravention, whether with or without his knowledge.

The only exception to this rule, is for public correspondence, which may be forwarded through the captaincy of the port, even before presentation of the manifest.

All boats which shall come alongside a vessel having a guard on board, shall be confiscated, and no excuse admitted.

The general manifest shall be received in all languages. It must specify the quantity of packages, their denominations, that is to say, bales, pipes, barrels, cabas, (javas,) half cabas, &c. It shall also contain samples of valuable articles, and a statement of the provisions on board.

It is not required that articles in use shall be reported.

Household furniture, even if it has been used, or tissues of any kind in entire pieces, will not be reputed articles in use.

At the end of every manifest, the captain will annex, with his signature, the following note: " This manifest contains —— packages, which form the entire cargo, according to the bills of lading, and the provisions on board. Given on board said ship, in the port of Valparaiso, this —— day of ——." He will give the hour and date, and will fill the blank for packages in letters, not in figures.

When one or more packages shall have been omitted in the manifest, they will be confiscated; and in case of omission of the marks and numbers indicated in the bills of lading, the captain shall be fined $50 for every package on which these requisites shall be omitted.

Captain responsible for the fines.

The manifest being completed, the captain of the vessel will deliver it to the guard, and with his register will return to him the printed document, announcing his duties.

The officer on duty will be very particular in sending, 4 hours after a vessel has anchored, the custom-house boat, with an officer to require the manifest, and retire the guard.

If the manifest be not ready when the officer of active service presents himself on board, he will compel the captain to make sail immediately and depart.

If a captain, instead of a general manifest, present his original bills of lading, the officer or guard shall give him a receipt, specifying the number of bills of lading received.

When a vessel, driven into port by stress of weather, shall require assistance promptly and efficaciously, the officer who first visits her shall remain on board with the guard and give advice.

Of samples.—After delivery of the general manifest, the samples of goods composing the cargo may be landed, subject to the regulations which follow.

Of discharging.—Vessels will discharge every day, except days of civic fetes or of rigorous observance.

From the 1st October to 31st March, discharging will commence at 7 in the morning; from the 1st April to 30th September, at 8 in the morning. It will cease in both periods at 1 o'clock, afternoon.

Of visits to vessels.—The discharging being finished, the captain or consignee of the vessel will present a demand in duplicate, for proceeding to visit the ship.

Re-exportation.—Before commencing to load a vessel, the captain or consignee will, to obtain authority, make application in writing to the governor of the place.

Transhipment.—Transhipment may take place in all the great ports of the republic, when the vessel on which it is made sails directly for foreign countries.

The duty of transhipment shall be 1 per cent. for foreign goods on their valuation.

Importation.—When, for national consumption, a part of the goods in entrepot are demanded, the duty of importation may be settled at the custom-house of Valparaiso, or at any other of the principal custom-houses of the republic.

The principal custom-houses of the republic are those of Santiago, Chiloé, Valdivia, Conception, Constitution, and Serena.

For the payment of duties there shall be presented three bills of lading, specifying the destination of the goods.

Foreign letters and newspapers.—All letters, or sealed parcels of correspondence, periodicals or newspapers, are to be delivered by the captain, immediately on his arrival, to the resguardo (collector) or his deputy.

Letters, &c., for other ports at which the vessel is subsequently to touch, and those directed to the consignees, provided these last do not exceed 8 ounces in weight, are to remain in the custody of the captain or supercargo.

Not only the captain, but all other persons having letters in charge must make delivery of them to the resguardo. The penalty of the first offence will be a fine of ten times the amount of the postage and $10; for the second, double those sums; for the third, forty times the postage and $140, or fifteen days' imprisonment; doubling the penalty thus at each repetition of the offence.

Wheat and flour, and in general all goods on which there are fixed duties, and which come by sea to Chili, can only be imported at the said port of Valparaiso.

Foreign merchandise may remain in deposit in the custom-house warehouses in Valparaiso, for the space of three years, but only for four months in any of the other principal custom-houses of the republic.

The duties are payable at this place previous to the consignees removing the goods, and it shall be done under the formalities established by the regulations for the deposit warehouses, it being well understood that the clearing permission of the goods at the termination of the deposit spoken of in any of those articles, can only take place at the port of Valparaiso.

Gunpowder shall be considered as an exception from the two preceding articles; and in whatever port to which it is carried, will have to remain deposited in the public store destined for that object, until the owners request it for consumption, in which case they shall pay the storage as regulated in the following article.

During the first six months of the deposit, there will be charged for storage one quarter per cent. monthly on the valuation of the goods, and for any further time which they remain in deposit one eighth per cent. also monthly.

All merchandise which enters the warehouses will be liable to pay storage, even those which enjoy the privilege of being free from import duties.

To calculate the storage, reference will be had to the date of the manifest of the goods when stored, and they shall pay the whole month's storage for any one they have commenced.

The port charges shall be established under the following denominations, viz.: anchorage, tonnage, and roll duty.

These charges shall be as follows: anchorage, $2 each vessel: tonnage duty, 2 reals per ton measurement, and roll duty $2 for every vessel.

The charge for anchorage will be exacted, for the mere act of casting anchor in any of the ports of the republic.

And it will be recovered every time that a vessel comes to an anchor.

Vessels of war are exempted from the charge of anchorage.

Vessels which not having touched at any port, are obliged by bad weather, damage, or enemies, to return to the port from which they sailed, are likewise exempted from the anchorage charge.

All foreign merchant vessels which, coming from a foreign country, should anchor in any of the ports of the republic, will be liable to the payment of tonnage duty.

From this charge are exempt: vessels of war, national vessels, whalers of any flag, foreign merchant vessels which merely touch at our ports, foreign merchant vessels which arrive in ballast, vessels which put in to repair damages, and vessels which are obliged by pirates or enemies to seek a shelter in our territories.

When whaling vessels should land and dispose in our ports of articles of the fishery only, they will not be subjected to tonnage duty—but should they land any other description of merchandise, they will be obliged to pay it.

Foreign merchant vessels coming into a port of Chili in distress, will be allowed to deposit their cargoes in the custom-house stores, and even to reship them to foreign countries, without paying tonnage duty—but should part or whole of such cargoes be introduced for the consumption of Chili, then such exemption will not be made.

Vessels declared free from the payment of tonnage duty, will not lose this exemption even if they take on board foreign or country produce.

Neither will they lose this exemption by having on board or landing precious metals, coined or uncoined, because such articles of themselves will not cause any liability to the vessels exempted from the charge.

Tonnage duty once paid in any port in Chili, will not be exacted again from the same vessel, when proceeding direct to any other port of the republic, unless she remains longer than 30 days at sea, in which case it will again be exacted.

If any vessel, after having paid tonnage duty, should proceed to a foreign port, she becomes liable to the same charge on her return.

The roll duty will be exacted by the captain of the port from national and foreign merchant vessels, as sole compensation for the certified roll to be given them, and for the assistance which when asked he will be obliged to render, for the apprehension of runaway sailors.

Anchorage and tonnage duty will be recovered at the custom-house.

The stamped paper duty for sailing licenses, the register duty, the hospital duty, doctor's fees, and any others which, under the denomination of port charges, have heretofore been exacted from national and foreign vessels, are abolished.

CONSTANTINOPLE,

The capital of the Turkish empire, is situated on the strait dividing Europe from Asia. Lat. 41° 01′ N. Long. 28° 55′ E.

It cannot be strictly called a commercial city: but yet, standing in need of many European commodities, no inconsiderable trade is carried on by different nations, especially the French, English, and Netherlanders.

The great import article is woollen cloth of the finest quality, the smoothest surface, and the gaudiest colours. The best colours are violet, purple, green, crimson, scarlet, sky blue, flesh and cinnamon colours. Great quantities of silken stuffs are imported from France and Italy. Paper is one of the best articles carried to Constantinople, and generally one of the most profitable; most of it comes from France and Venice. The other imports are tin, brass, &c., from Hamburg and the north of Europe; from England, sugar, spices, camphor, lead, quicksilver, cochineal, dyewoods, &c.

The exports are very few in comparison with the imports, consisting in wool, buffalo, ox and cow hides, pot ashes, yellow wax, and some goat's hair.

The duties, both import and export, are generally 3 per cent. ad valorem.

The European merchants generally direct their correspondents at Smyrna to draw on Constantinople, or order remittances to be made to them from the capital in specie, in order to purchase the return cargoes at Smyrna.

By the treaty concluded between the United States and Turkey, the trade of the parties is placed on the footing of the most favoured nations. Antecedent to this, the American commerce was subject to an additional duty of 15 per cent. on the whole amount of the impost levied under the tariff. This surcharge is now abolished, and our trade is entitled to, and receives, all the favour so long extended to that of England, France, and Russia. The Porte seems now to be well disposed to cultivate the most friendly commercial and political relations with the United States. These propitious circumstances, although not at this moment likely to give much enlargement to our foreign trade, yet, in the event of an European war, they will be made greatly available. As neutrals, the whole commerce of the Black Sea, increasing daily in magnitude, will be opened to our enterprise.

American merchants established in the well defended states of the Sublime Porte, for the purposes of commerce, shall have liberty to employ *semsars* (brokers) of any nation or religion, in like manner as merchants of other friendly powers; and they shall not be disturbed in their affairs, nor shall they be treated in any way contrary to established usages. American vessels arriving at, or departing from, the ports of the Ottoman empire, shall not be subjected to greater visits by the officers of the custom-house, and the chancery of the port, than vessels of the most favoured nations.

If litigations and disputes should arise between the subjects of the Sublime Porte and citizens of the United States, the parties shall not be heard, nor shall judgment be pronounced, unless the American drogoman be present. Causes in which the sum may exceed 500 piastres, shall be submitted to the Sublime Porte, to be decided according to the laws of equity and justice. Citizens of the United States of America, quietly pursuing their commerce, and not being charged or convicted of any crime or offence, shall not be molested; and even when they may have committed some offence, they shall not be arrested and put in prison by the local authorities, but they shall be tried by their minister or consul, and punished according to their offence, following, in this respect, the usage observed towards other Franks.

American merchant vessels that trade to the dominions of the Sublime Porte, may go and come in perfect safety with their own flag; but they shall not take the flag of any other power, nor shall they grant their flag to the vessels of other nations and powers, nor to the vessels of rayahs. The minister, consuls, and vice consuls of the United States, shall not protect, secretly or publicly, the rayahs of the Sublime Porte, and they shall never suffer a departure from the principles here laid down and agreed to by mutual consent.

Merchant vessels of the United States, in like manner as vessels of the most favoured nations, shall have liberty to pass the canal of the imperial residence, and go and come in the Black Sea, either laden or in ballast; and they may be laden with the produce, manufactures and effects of the Ottoman empire, excepting such as are prohibited, as well as of their own country.

Merchant vessels of the two contracting parties shall not be forcibly taken for the shipment of troops, munitions, and other objects of war, if the captains or proprietors of the vessels shall be unwilling to freight them.

If any merchant vessel of either of the contracting parties should be wrecked, assistance and protection shall be afforded to those of the crew that may be saved; and the merchandise and effects which it may be possible to save and recover, shall be conveyed to the consul nearest to the place of the wreck, to be by him delivered to the proprietors.

COPENHAGEN

Is as well the capital as the seat of nearly the whole commerce of the kingdom of Denmark. It possesses one of the finest harbours in the Baltic, into which vessels of almost any burthen can enter. Lat. 55° 41′ N. Long. 12° 34′ E.

The imports are few, as the Danish West India islands are sufficient for the supply of colonial produce; and the duties are so high that, except tobacco, wines, and brandies, and some few articles of American produce, the Danes obtain but little, except from their own dependencies, and through the medium of their own factories and companies.

Their exports are, however, numerous—hides and skins in great quantities, horses, cattle, and oats, with some useful minerals of inferior value.

The greatest part of the trade of the Baltic passes and repasses and becomes tributary here, and the whole of it is so to the Danish dominions; for most of the merchandise which does not pass by Elsineur, goes through the canal of Holstein; and what does not pass through either of these two channels, which is but trifling, goes by way of Lubeck, yet still pays a toll, if sent by land carriage, in passing the skirts of Holstein to Hamburg or other places; so that the whole of the Baltic trade is tributary to Denmark.

Houses in the Baltic charge the Sound duties in the invoices, and have their own agents at Elsineur to clear all the merchandise shipped by them. If this be not the case, the merchants at Elsineur then draw upon the owners or agents where the goods are directed or addressed.

Masters must report within twenty-four hours after arrival, under penalty of two rix dollars per day, and produce authentic bills of lading. If they do not report all their cargo, they must pay 20 per cent. on that part omitted, except they swear it was unintentional. If it belongs to the master or mate it is liable to confiscation or double duty.

Masters must not sail without their told-zedel or passport, containing a list of the cargo, and certifying that the duties, &c., are paid, under penalty, if the cargo has not been duly entered, of confinement for life and treble duty on goods. If she be in ballast, the penalty is 10 rix dollars. The production of false passports incurs a forfeiture of ship and goods.

Copenhagen is the only Danish port where brandy, salt, tobacco and wine may be imported.

Duties are payable at the Sound on almost all merchandise. Masters are allowed 4 per cent. out of the duties paid.

Sound dues.—In making out invoices for goods which are to pass the Sound, care should be taken to set forth the quantity, exclusive of packages, and the value, as nearly as possible. Overcharges are thus avoided. This caution is particularly necessary in regard to articles which pay duty according to their value. If the shipper, however, does not wish to value his merchandise with so much accuracy on the invoice, he ought to address a letter either to his correspondent at Elsineur, (and it is desirable for merchants trading to the Baltic to have one there,) or to his captain, stating the value as nearly as possible.

The custom-house is open every day at Elsineur, including Sundays and holidays.

The best anchorage is near to the guard-ship. It is not necessary for captains to go on board this vessel; but as soon as they have come to anchor, they ought immediately to go on shore. They must take with them all their papers, as invoices, manifest, roll of equipage, &c. It is necessary that they land at the port, or otherwise they incur a fine. As soon as permission is received from the quarantine guard, to which they and their passengers, if any, must present themselves, they proceed to the custom-house and deliver their papers. If the wind will not permit them to double Cronberg Point, they may anchor between the fort and Cape Kullen, and may thence go on shore with their papers, always taking care to land at the port.

The fees, payable in rix dollars and stivers, are:

	IN BALLAST.		LADEN.	
	Rix dol.	Stiv.	Rix dol.	Stiv.
Light money	2	24	4	24
Passport	2	00	2	00
Interpreter	0	12	0	32*
Guard-ship	0	6	0	6
Under clerks, called *lopere*	0	12	0	12

* Of from one to three bills of lading, and for each one exceeding three, there is a charge of eight stivers.

There is also a tax payable to the inspector of the harbour of one dollar and six stivers. But this is not strictly due from privileged vessels, unless they are unprovided with a manifest from the custom-house of their port of departure.

The poor tax of one dollar is exacted when the vessel is despatched on a Sunday, holiday, or during hours allotted for repast.

Quarantine money for each person from beyond Cape Finisterre	2	rix bank thalers.
From between Cape Finisterre and Lanskrona	1	"
Vessels actually put under quarantine pay, instead of the above duties, for the first visit of the physician	5	"
To the inspector, while on board, per day	1	"
For the quarantine pass	2	"

These fees are paid in silver money.

By a treaty between the United States and Denmark, the commerce between the two countries is placed upon the footing of the most favoured nation, and of entire reciprocity.

DANTZIC

Is one of the first commercial cities in the north of Europe, and is situated on the west branch of the Vistula, near its entrance into the Baltic. Lat. 54° 22′ N. Long. 18° 37′ E.

The imports are chiefly coffee, sugar, rum, dye-woods, indigo, all kinds of spices, tobacco, nankins, printed calicoes, hardware, grindstones and coals. Earthenware is prohibited. Salt may be imported, but must be sold to government at a stated price, or exported again.

The exports are exceedingly numerous: grains of most kinds, but especially wheat and rye; timber, both oak and firs, especially in staves of different lengths; seeds of flax, hemp and rape; ashes, both pot and weed, of superior quality; feathers, bristles and horse hair; yarns and linen; wax and tallow; spruce beer, and a liquor called, emphatically, Dantzic.

DUBLIN,

The metropolis of Ireland, is situated on the river Liffey, seven miles from the sea, at the bottom of a beautiful bay. Lat. 53° 22′ N. Long. 6° 17′ W.

Three miles below the city is a commodious dock for packets and merchant vessels.

The exports are linens, beef, pork, butter, tallow, whiskey, &c.

The imports are American and West India produce.

The custom-house regulations in Dublin are similar to those at Liverpool. Irish produce and manufactures, (except linen, grain, cottons, refined sugar, molasses, and some few unimportant articles, which are free,) are subjected to an export duty of one pound per 100 pounds value, except exported to some place in Europe or the Mediterranean, when the duty is reduced to ten shillings. Besides this, specific export duties are imposed upon certain articles, too numerous to be mentioned.

EAST INDIES.

Under this title we include the British, Portuguese and Dutch possessions beyond the Cape of Good Hope, and also Mocha.

British possessions.

The greater part of the peninsula of India, containing nearly 200,000 square miles, is under the control of Great Britain. These territories are under three governments, viz., the port of Calcutta, of Madras and of Bombay. Besides this country, several islands are subject to the authority of that kingdom, viz., Prince of Wales, Ceylon, the Moluccas, Bencoolen and Mauritius.

By the act "for effecting an arrangement with the East India Company," the British territories in India are to remain under its government until 30th April, 1854. All the real and personal property of the company is to be held in trust by it for the crown for the service of India, discharged of all claim of the company to any profit or advantage, except an annual dividend of £10 10s. per centum per annum on the existing amount of the capital stock of the company.

The company ceases to trade, is to close all its commercial business, and to sell all its merchandise, stores, warehouses, vessels, lands, and other commercial assets, except such as may be retained for the purposes of the government of the country.

This ancient mercantile body is thus entirely deprived of all its commercial character and privileges. But it retains its political power; and from having united the functions of merchants and sovereigns in its shareholders, these are now sovereigns alone. Or, the new organization may, with more propriety, be viewed as a branch of the government of the British empire; endowed, it is true, with great prerogatives, but still limited and under the restraint of parliament.

The company collects the revenue from its possessions, appoints all officers, and directs the administration of affairs throughout its extensive territories.

The trade is opened from April, 1834, to all British subjects, to ports where there are custom-houses. They may, also, reside at such places, as also at any other place, without license, in such of the territories as were under the government of the company in the year 1800, or in those ceded by the Nabob of the Carnatic, in the province of Cuttack, and in the settlements of Malacca and Singapore. None but servants of the company can, without license, enter, proceed to, or reside in any other of the territories than those mentioned. The governor general in council can, with the consent of the court of directors, open other places.

Persons authorized to reside in any of the Indian domains, may also acquire and hold lands or lease-holds therein.

Offices are open to all natives or natural born resident British subjects, without regard to religion, place of birth, descent, or colour.

American vessels, by the treaty of 3d July, 1815, are received in some ports, and may trade with Bombay, Calcutta, Madras, Singapore and Prince of Wales island on the same footing with those of the most favoured European nations. They pay no higher duties on imports or exports; but all goods exported must be unladen in the United States, and they cannot carry on the coasting trade of the British settlements. They may touch for refreshment at the Cape of Good Hope, St. Helena, and all other places in the African or Indian seas.

The imports at these places, are spirituous liquors, wines, iron, fish, naval stores, spars and specie.

The exports are cotton, silks, sugar, saltpetre, indigo, cocoa, betel nuts and specie.

Dutch possessions

Are Java, Banca, Celeberian isles, and the Spice islands.

American vessels may trade with these settlements, and it is believed are on the same footing with Dutch vessels. At Batavia, the following duties are imposed:

The original invoice of imported goods must be produced, and 30 per cent. added to the amount. Dutch and American vessels pay six per cent. on the sum total; foreign ships from Holland pay nine per cent., and from other ports, twelve per cent.

It exports coffee, sugar, camphire, spices, of a good quality, but dear.

Regulations.—Duties for export, on all vessels, two per cent. on the value.

Duties for entrepôt, on all vessels, one fourth of the import duty.

The duties are in dollars and stivers, sixty-six of the latter to the Spanish dollar.

For regulating the trade with Batavia and other ports of Java, it is provided:

That the master of a vessel on his arrival is not to land himself, nor to suffer any of the crew or other persons on board to land, until the vessel be visited by an officer from the guard-ship.

On landing he is to report himself immediately to the master attendant, and then to the police office.

A manifest of the whole cargo must be delivered at the custom-house within four and twenty hours after the arrival of the vessel in the roads.

The captain must leave the ship's papers with the master attendant, when he first reports himself. These are returned to him when he receives his clearance.

It is not permitted to land any merchandise after sun-set, under a penalty of 500 florins. Nor is it allowed to ship any goods on Sunday without special permission.

Muskets and ammunition are prohibited to be imported, but fowling pieces, exceeding 100 florins in value, are admitted.

Export duties.—Coffee, exported in a foreign vessel, to a foreign country, pays a duty of five florins and a quarter per pecul, but if carried to a port in the Netherlands, without breaking bulk, one florin of the duty is returned. In a vessel of the Netherlands, to a port of that country, the duty is two florins.

Sugar, exported in a Netherland vessel, pays a duty of one florin per pecul; in a foreign vessel, two florins.

Rice, however exported, is charged with a duty of three florins per coyang of 27 peculs.

The export duty on other articles is as follows:

		Netherland vessels.	Foreign vessels.
		Florins.	Florins.
Nutmegs,	per pecul	9½	19
Cloves,	"	9½	19
Mace,	"	10	20
Bird's nests, first sort,	"	475	950
second sort,	"	316	632
third sort,	"	237	474
Arrack,	per leagre (*)	10	10
Tin, Banca,	per pecul	2	4
Camphor,	"	3½	7
Copper, Japan,	"	3⅛	7
Tortoise shell,	"	2	2
Rattans,	"	2	2
Hides,	per 100	2 p. ct.	2 p. ct.

Goods are received in entrepôt on paying a duty of one per cent. on the invoice valuation.

The money of account is in florins and centimes, as in the Netherlands.

By a resolution of the Netherlands East India government, of 18th February, 1833, the ports of Pentaniah and Sambos, on the western coast of Borneo, are declared free from all duties of import and export until the 1st of January, 1834 ; and from thenceforward no foreign vessel will be permitted to trade to any port of the said coast belonging to the Netherlands.

By a resolution of the 21st of the same month, the duty on coffee exported from Java in a foreign vessel, to a foreign country, is reduced to five florins per pecul. In other respects the export duty on coffee remains unchanged.

The king has modified the ordinance of 3d May, 1833, which fixed the duties on the importation of wines and spirituous liquors into the East India possessions of the Netherlands, as follows: on arrack, in bottles; brandy; *aguadiente*, foreign, in bottles; *bradewigin* of all sorts, in casks or bottles; foreign gin, in casks; rum, in bottles; sirups, in large or small bottles; and on wines, ordinary, red and white, in casks. The duties are made double of those imposed in 1833, on importations from foreign ports, in vessels of all nations, without distinction of flag.

On all goods in entrepôt, on which full duties are afterwards paid, the amount of entrepôt duty will be allowed.

Goods in entrepôt cannot be cleared out in less than fourteen days after entry.

Opium cannot be imported or exported in entrepôt, in less quantity than two peculs.

Tobacco, wine, or spirits, cannot be allowed in entrepôt, unless the

* The leagre is about 500 gallons.

value is equal to 4,000 rupees, nor cleared out in less quantity, except gin, which may be in not less than 100 cases.

Gin imported in foreign vessels, coming from foreign ports, shall pay duties as such, but when shipped from the Netherlands, proof must be given of its being shipped there, to secure the difference of duty.

Artificial vinegar, foreign gin, rum, arrack, or other spirits, will not be allowed in entrepôt.

MOZAMBIQUE.

Mozambique is the capital of the Portuguese settlements on the east coast of Africa. It has a good port. The cargoes must be reported and landed in the custom-house immediately on the arrival of the vessel, under penalty of forfeiture.

The imports are Malabar goods, glass beads, mock coral, cornelians, garnets, yellow nankins, blue cotton goods, tea, soap, sweet oil, palm oil, iron, hardware, gunpowder, for the government, or by license for individuals, muskets, drugs, spices, preserves, butter, wine in casks, olives, hams, cheese, sugar, woollen goods, hats, brandy and rum, cordials and dried fruit.

The import duty is five per cent. in Portuguese vessels; in foreign vessels it is twenty-four per cent. The former are allowed to tranship or unload, and re-export, on payment of but two per cent.

All articles intended for any fabric or manufactory established at Mozambique, are free of duty, as are also Portuguese manufactures. Naval supplies or stores pay half duties. Goods which have paid the duties of export and import at Goa, pay also but half duties.

The exports are slaves, amber, ivory in large quantities, ambergris, colombo root, cowries, elephant's hair, teeth of the sea horse, tortoise shells, coire and cables of coire.

GOA,

The capital of the Portuguese East India possessions, has dwindled away to but little commercial consequence. It was, at one period, a place of immense trade, but has been compelled to yield to bad government, and to more fortunate rivals. By the treaty of 1810, it is made a free port, for the reception of British produce.

Goa is made a warehousing port by the edict of 4th February, 1811.

Vessels touching at any of the Portuguese establishments beyond the Cape of Good Hope, coming from Europe or America, are permitted to sell any part of their cargoes on paying the duties for consumption or re-exportation; those re-exported pay but two per cent.

MOCHA,

A seaport of Arabia, on the Red Sea, famous for the excellence of its coffee. That which is raised at Udden has the preference. The coffee is brought to Mocha, in April, May and June, in a state unfit for the American market. It must be first cleansed, assorted and packed. This is generally done after a cargo has been ordered by the master, who buys it in the rough state, either at Mocha or Beetlefakee, about 115 miles distant. The refuse, which is called coke, will sell at half price, for consumption in Arabia. Salt is also made here; and it would be well for ships coming directly home, to ballast themselves with this article.

The other exports are myrrh, frankincense, cocoa, aloes, senna, ivory, gold and gums. To procure a full cargo of gums, a long stay at Mocha would be requisite, or it would be better at once to go to Muscat, a port on the other side of the peninsula, at the mouth of the Persian Gulf.

Anchorage duty, $400. If vessels land no merchandise, this duty is not exacted.

This duty of $400 is to be paid at Beetlefakee, if you purchase your cargo there, though it is not a seaport.

Gum also requires picking, &c., and there is a loss of from 10 to 15 per cent. in so doing. The senna is also very dirty, and requires much cleansing. The duties on imports and exports are 3 per cent; brokerage on sales, 1½ per cent.; commissions, 2¼ per cent.

The imports are glass, crockery, hardware, nails, common muskets, shot, knives, sabres, lead, tin and false pearls. Forage should be taken out from the United States for the subsistence of such live stock as may be taken on board at Mocha.

GIBRALTAR

Is situated on a peninsula commanding the entrance into the Mediterranean. Lat. 36° 06′ N. Long. 5° 20′ W.

This is a great commercial station, being a depôt for foreign produce, with which it supplies the adjacent provinces of Spain, and trades largely with the Moors of the opposite coast of Barbary.

Vessels lie within three moles: the old mole at the upper end of the town for merchant vessels, the sloop's mole, and the new mole for ships of war.

Gibraltar is a free port, subject to no duties, and to few restrictions. Spirits cannot be landed, unless accompanied by a cocket from England. All kinds of British manufactured goods are to be found here. The charges amount to about five per cent. on purchases, 7½ to 8 per cent. on sales, except on bulky articles of little value, such as earthenware, porter, &c., which are subject to much higher expenses, according to the time they remain unsold, in consequence of the extremely high rent of storehouses.

GREECE.

Peloponnesus is a peninsula joined to the rest of Greece by an isthmus, called the isthmus of Corinth, and surrounded by islands called the islands of the Archipelago.

Corfu is the principal depôt and mart of the islands, as well as of some places situate in the neighbouring peninsula.

In all parts of the peninsula, provisions are plentiful and cheap, and money of more value than in any other part of the Mediterranean: in consequence of which, there is no good market for any considerable quantity of manufactured goods. Lead and tin are always in demand, but only in small quantities at any one port. Ships that take cargoes of fish to Venice or Trieste, where there is always a great consumption, may take in ballast and run down the Gulf of Venice, and load immediately in the Morea, instead of waiting in those ports for a cargo. It would be a difficult task to attempt giving a particular description of the various articles, the produce of the Morea, they being so very numerous; currants, fustic, cotton, valonia for tanning, and olive oil, are among the principal; beside these, are to be reckoned some sorts of fruits, gums, drugs, madder, &c.

Currants, it has been observed, are a considerable article of export from the Morea. Petrasso is one of the best ports to ship them from; the fruit is rather larger, and more free from sand or gravel, than that of either Zante or Corfu. They are shipped in various sized casks, from twenty hundred weight to fifty pounds. The quantity shipped must weigh above five hundred weight net, otherwise they are liable to seizure. The casks are always included in the weight of the fruit, and paid for as such; the Morea currants have the preference in most countries, except in England, where the Zante currants are more merchantable.

Fustic also is chiefly shipped from Petrasso, as more of it grows in the Morea than in any other part; it is very convenient to stow amongst a dry cask cargo, where it is stowed to great advantage for the ship, and it may be cut up into convenient lengths without injuring the wood.

Valonia is a kind of acorn, of a bright stone colour, which it always preserves while it is kept dry; any kind of dampness injures it, as it then turns black, and loses both its strength and value. It is chiefly used by tanners. The first cost is usually from three pounds ten shillings to five pounds sterling per ton; though it is a very bulky article it is always bought and sold by weight; a ship can only take a small proportion of her registered tonnage, in consequence, the freight of valonia per ton is always very high.

The exports from Salonica are grain, (wheat, barley and Indian corn,) cotton, wool, tobacco and timber. The average exportation of wheat per annum, is 1,000,000 kilos, the kilo being about 55 pounds; of cotton, about 110,000 bales; of tobacco, about 30,000 bales, each bale containing about 275 pounds; of wool, about 1,000,000 pounds. Timber is exported to Malta and other parts of the Mediterranean.

The ordinary imports are sugar, coffee, dye-woods, indigo, cochineal, muslins, printed calicoes, iron, lead, tin, watches, &c.

Those from the gulf of Corinth are principally grain: as wheat, barley, oats, peas and maize; some cotton, wool, honey and cheese. Of wheat alone, which is indeed the principal article of export, about 250,000 kilos.

Tariff.—All merchandise or goods, of whatever nature, may be imported into or exported from Greece.

All merchandise or goods once paying duty, shall thereafter be considered free.

All merchandise or goods imported into Greece, are subject to a duty of ten per cent. ad valorem, with the exception of such as are separately mentioned in the tariff.

All goods or merchandise imported for the purpose of re-exportation shall pay one per cent. ad valorem.

All masters of vessels arriving in privileged ports shall, before the expiration of twenty-four hours, present their manifest at the custom-house; any goods landed and not noted in such manifest, will be considered as contraband.

All merchandise deposited in the transit stores, is understood to to be limited to one term of three months; previous to the expiration of which, the owners of such goods may apply for extension of the permit for a second term, liable to the same charge, and subsequently for a third term, if required. At the expiration of three terms, or nine months, goods deposited in transit must be exported or withdrawn into consumption at the duties contained in the tariff.

The owner of goods deposited in transit may, at any time, introduce the whole, or any part, into consumption, or export the same as other countries.

The owner of goods deposited in transit may, at any time, sell or make over the whole or any part of such property, but in all such cases he is bound to communicate the same to the director of the transit.

Any person wishing to export merchandise deposited in the transit stores, must apply to the director for permission, who is bound to give the necessary assistance in all cases where the owner of such goods will give security that a legal bill of lading shall be produced within the specified period.

The port of Syria shall be considered the only one affording the facilities of transit until such time as efficient stores can be constructed in some of the other ports of Greece.

Tonnage duties.—The merchant vessels of foreign nations shall be subjected to no higher duties than Greek vessels, so long as the latter are received in the ports of such foreign nations on a footing of complete reciprocity. But if, in the ports of another nation, there shall be levied on the merchant vessels of Greece, duties higher than those levied on them in the ports of Greece, then an increase of duty equal to such excess shall be levied on the vessels of such nation.

Every master of a vessel must, before his departure, pay at the custom-house of the port the duties set forth in the tariff. The certificate of payment is signed by the minister of finance.

The custom-house, after receiving the duties, will furnish a receipt, which must be presented to the officers of the port, who will deliver the permit for departure.

The master of a vessel who attempts to depart without a permit is subjected to a penalty of twenty times the amount of the duties owing by him; and a vessel which has no port duties to pay, that attempts to depart without a permit, is subjected to a fine of from one to ten drachms.

Observations on the tonnage duty.—Vessels arriving from abroad loaded, and which discharge their cargoes and depart loaded, pay the whole duty.

Vessels arriving from abroad loaded, and which depart in ballast, pay two thirds of the duty, which is also exacted if they arrive in ballast and depart loaded.

Vessels arriving from abroad in ballast, and departing without lading, or arriving and departing with cargo, and not discharging any of it, pay one third of the duty.

Vessels arriving from and going to another port of the kingdom, pay but one half the duty.

A vessel is considered as loaded whether she be so fully or partially.

Exceptions.—Every vessel forced to enter a port, either by a storm, or in consequence of damage, is exempted from all charges during eight days.

Every vessel entering a port, from whatever cause, and destined to another port, and the master of which shall immediately make a declaration to the captain of the port that he has no intention either of loading or discharging his goods, may remain five days without paying any duty except the light-house duty. He is permitted, also, to receive or deliver letters or money, unless otherwise provided for by special ordinances.

HANSE TOWNS.

These are Bremen, Hamburg and Lubeck; and a treaty exists between them and the United States, by which the commercial intercourse between them is put upon terms of perfect reciprocity, and the principles of free trade established. Citizens of either party are at liberty to dispose of their personal property within the jurisdiction of the other by will or otherwise.[a] The American consuls are empowered to arrest deserters from American vessels.

BREMEN

Is situated on the river Weser, and 45 miles from the sea. Its harbour is nine miles below the town. It has not, indeed, so much facility of internal communication with Germany by its particular river, as its great rival, Hamburg, has by the Elbe; but, as a balance to those natural advantages, the charges of receiving, forwarding and selling, as well as purchasing and shipping goods, are so moderate at Bremen, as to give it no inconsiderable advantage over other places in many instances. Wheat is considered not so good here as that from the Baltic. The imports are principally all sorts of manufactured goods, for the use of the interior of Germany; all kinds of West India and American produce, teas, tobacco, rums and brandies, tin plates, tallow, tar, oil, and tropical fruits. The exports are chiefly bark, bristles, glass, grain, hams, hides, rags, smalts, wines, and yarn and linens of all kinds, descriptions and qualities; table linen, shirting, gingham, bedticking, raven duck, sail cloth, flaxen osnaburgh, and hempen techlenburghs.

---

[a] Treaty, 4th June, 1828.

The customary tares are, 110 pounds per hogshead on Virginia and Kentucky tobacco and stems; 90 pounds on Maryland, or the real tare, if the casks weigh 120 and 100 pounds, respectively, and upwards; on sugar in casks, 17 per cent.; 70 pounds on Havana, and 20 per cent. on Brazil sugar, in boxes; 10 per cent. on East India sugars; on cotton, 4 to 6 per cent.; on black teas, 22 to 24 pounds, and on green, 20 to 22 pounds per chest; on ashes, 10 per cent.; on rice, coffee, and most other articles, the real tare.

Specification of the rates of exchange for regulating the payment of freight, &c.

For the payment of freight, that rate of exchange is fixed, which is quoted on the first mail-day after the expiration of the eighth day, subsequent to the arrival of the vessel in the Weser, and being moored at the wharf, and according to the intermediate price; or in case the rate shall not have been quoted upon that particular mail-day, then the rate current on the following mail-day is to be taken, with the addition of 2 rix dollars per £100 sterling, in bills on England at two months.

In case the rate of freight is not filled up in Louis d'ors, the foreign money is reduced to Louis d'ors, according to the rate of exchange on bills at sight, and the captain is obliged to receive the payment of his freight in the latter.

But in the case of vessels coming from America or the West Indies, where the freight is stipulated to be paid in dollars, the Spanish dollar is estimated at 1 rix dollar and 24 grotes.

Freights stipulated in guineas shall be reduced to pounds sterling, at 21 shillings per guinea, and thence to Louis d'ors, at the current rate of exchange.

The captain is entitled to demand his freight on the first "pay day" after the correct and faithful delivery of the cargo, when the merchant is obliged to pay the freight immediately in gold.

By port charges is understood the customary pilotage, and all disbursements which the captain is obliged to pay, according to law, not including, however, extra pilotage.

The time for discharging is fixed according to the following:

Large vessels arriving from sea and going up to the city, and loaded with grain or rape seed, are allowed 14 days; smaller ones 8 days, unless an extension of the time has been granted. By large vessels are understood all over 20 lasts.

Vessels laden with piece goods, or other merchandise, must be unloaded as soon as they arrive in the docks, or at the warehouses.

Any delay not occasioned by the fault of the captain, gives him the right to protest, and to have refunded to him, by the consignee, such additional wharfage as he may have paid, and the cost of the protest.

Every bill of lading which is made out for Bremen, obliges the captain to deliver the merchandise from his vessel, at the city, in case there is sufficient depth of water to accomplish that purpose.

If the captains are not bound by the bills of lading thus to act, and yet deliver the cargo from their vessels at the city, they are entitled to the customary lighterage.*

Vessels arriving from ports on the Elbe, or coasts of Holland or Germany, and East Friesland, are obliged to sail up to the city without additional compensation, if the state of the river will permit, and providing their bills of lading do not call for a different place of discharge.

Duty on merchandise sent here to be transported elsewhere.

All merchandise imported into this place, merely for the purpose of being forwarded, which comprehends such as is sent here by land or water for foreign account, with the express intention that it shall not remain for sale, but only to be forwarded by a resident to its place of destination, may be entered for transportation, and forwarded accordly, on payment of the customary duty; but if it should be retained for this market, it must be entered and assessed as are regular importations.

Merchandise brought here to the annual fair, and which remains unsold, is placed on the footing of transportation goods, if re-exported.

A formal declaration must be made within twenty-four hours after the arrival of such merchandise as is intended for transportation, on pain of a forfeiture of the privilege, containing a description of the articles, weight, mark and number of the bale, cask, &c., as also the place whence it came, and that of its destination. The declaration must also embrace an obligation to pay the duty within the time limited for the departure of the goods.

Merchandise to be forwarded is allowed to remain here but three months; but an extension may be granted for a similar period of three months, on payment of 25 per cent. on the original transportation duty. "Transportation goods" which shall not have been forwarded within the time allowed, forfeit the privilege, and are to be considered as subject to the rates imposed on importations and exportations, unless it be proven that they have been detained by causes beyond the control of the parties, such as attachments, severity of the winter, &c.

Transportation goods must be forwarded in the same bags, packages, barrels, &c., in which they were imported, unless it be necessary to unpack the same, for which purpose permission must first be obtained from the custom-house. If any repairs shall have been made, or marks altered, without the knowledge of the custom-house, the forwarding merchant shall be fined in double the transportation duty, and be obliged to enter the goods upon forwarding the same for exportation, as if they had been originally intended to be exported.

Importation and exportation duty.

All merchandise, imported by land or water, shall be subject to the importation duty, except such as is declared for transportation, or

* That is, besides the freight, they are allowed the sum which the employment of lighters would have cost, had the vessels not discharged their cargoes at the city.

such belonging to resident citizens, which had been sent to foreign fairs, but not being sold, has been returned. Merchandise coming by sea, and not landed within the city, but in the suburbs, is subject to the import duty, except goods that may be stored at Vegesack for re-exportation.

The value of importations is calculated according to the invoice price, adding thereto the freight and the rate of insurance current here; upon exportations it is adjusted upon the invoice price alone. Should there be no invoice of importation, it shall be the duty of the importer to make a correct estimate of the value upon his oath as a citizen; but the custom-house is vested with power to institute a closer examination if the estimate appears to be made too low.

The payment of the importation and exportation duties must be made without reserve, prior to the goods entering into, or passing out of the city.

It is requisite for the adjustment of the duty that the merchant who imports or exports merchandise, should specify to the custom-house, in a formal declaration, the manner in which the goods are packed, their contents, measure, number, weight and value; stating also the particular kind which is entered, especially of articles which have a general name, but are composed of a great variety of different sorts and value; for example, "manufactures," "tobacco," "drugs," &c.

Should the merchant be unable to give a conscientious statement of the value and measure of his importation, he is required to deposit the amount of the duty as he may estimate the same, and receive a certificate *ad interim*, but continuing bound to furnish a correct statement within four weeks, and to pay any deficiency; in default of which the deposited sum is forfeited to the treasury as a fine, and legal steps taken to enforce the liquidation of the duty.

Harbour of Bremen haven.—All vessels entering the harbour are subject to the superintendence of the harbour masters, whose directions are to be obeyed by the captains and crews.

No ballast or rubbish is to be thrown overboard, under a penalty of ten rix dollars for the first offence, which is increased in case of repetition; the offender, too, is obliged to remove the articles he may have so cast into the harbour.

It is not permitted to keep gunpowder on board, and any which may be in the vessel must be delivered up within two hours after she has reached her berth. Non-compliance with this subjects the party to a fine of from ten to fifty rix dollars. Nor is it permitted to discharge any firearms in port.

The use of all fire on board, from sunset to sunrise, is prohibited. The captain, however, may have a light in a closed lantern in his cabin.

The crews are not allowed to carry on shore any firearms, dirks, or other weapons.

Export duty $\frac{1}{3}$ per cent. ad valorem.

Import duty $\frac{3}{4}$ per cent. do.

HAMBURG

Is seated on the rivers Elbe and Alster, about 18 leagues from the sea. Lat. 53° 33′ N. Long. 9° 56′ E. It is the most considerable free Hanseatic city, and the place of greatest commercial importance in Germany.

The situation of Hamburg, on the river Elbe, is more advantageous for extensive internal communication than that of Bremen, on the river Weser.

Vessels of much greater burthen can come up to Hamburg than to Bremen.

Besides the Elbe, which enters the German ocean here, they have an immediate water communication with Lubeck and the Baltic. It is furnished by different rivers, which communicate with the Elbe; with the manufactories of Austria, Bohemia and Saxony; with the productions of Silesia, Moravia and Poland, even to the confines of Hungary; so that it has more articles of commerce for exportation than most cities in the world. The articles of export are linens, grain, wax, leather, flax, glass, iron, copper, smalts, rags, staves and various wooden articles. The linens go chiefly to America and the West Indies; platillas Britannia, uccome from Silesia; the striped and checked creas from Lusatia, where they are generally bought up by the Hamburg merchants. It is well therefore to give an order some months beforehand.

Wheat can frequently be shipped here at as low prices as in the Prussian and Mecklenburg ports. In fact, most Baltic articles, such as flax, iron, wax, &c., can generally be obtained as low from Hamburg, on account of the difference in the freight, as from the ports in the Baltic, whence they originally came. The export of Saxon smalts is very considerable; the quantities are F. F. G., H. M. C. and O. C.; rags, for the use of paper manufactories; quills, hides and drugs are also frequently shipped. The imports are coffee, chiefly from Martinique, St. Domingo and Surinam; Havana, Brazils and Martinique clayed sugars; also some foreign Muscovado rum, cocoa, dye-woods, cotton, rice, tobacco, indigo, spices, tea, wines, twist, &c. All merchandise imported or exported by sea, except such as are mentioned hereafter, pay a duty of 1½ per cent. currency ad valorem, calculated in banco, which must be paid before the landing of the same. Flour pays, in addition, an excise duty of one marc, eight shillings currency per 100 lbs. when imported; but no other article is subject to it, except what is paid by the consumer himself. If goods arrive here for immediate re-exportation, they may be bonded on arrival and pay no duty. Free of all import duty are corn, books, linen, yarns, tin, copper, coined silver and gold. Free of duty on exportation, are all Hamburg manufactured goods. The state duty levied by the Hanoverian government on merchandise coming or going by sea, is, for most articles, ½ per cent.—for some, more. The stamp duty on bills and policies is very inconsiderable. Brokerage on all articles, with few exceptions, is only paid by the seller, and varies, but most generally it is ⅚ per cent. currency on the value in currency. At auction sales the selling broker receives 1½ per cent.; the purchasing broker, 2 per cent. All other charges, as lighterage, landing, housing, weighing, delivering, warehouse rent, insurance against fire, &c., are very moderate.

All merchandise is either sold on two or three months credit, or with a discount of one to one and a half per cent. for ready money; even then no calculation can be made on receiving the money before eight or fourteen days after the delivery. The commission charged on purchase or sale, is two and a half per cent.; for guaranty of debt, one and a half per cent. if sold at two or three months credit, and half per cent. if sold for ready money, unless the consignee wishes to take the risk upon himself.

Conditions of sale—Imports.—Coffee is sold per pound in schill. banco, discount one per cent.; good weight is half per cent. Tare is as follows, viz.: on casks, real weight; on bags of 130 lbs. or less, two lbs.; above 130 lbs. and not above 180 lbs., 3 lbs.; above 180 lbs. and not exceeding 200 lbs., 4 lbs. On Mocha bales of about 300 lbs., 14 lbs.; if 600 lbs., 30 lbs.; on Bourbon, single bales, 2 lbs.; on double, 4 lbs.

Cocoa is sold per lb. in schill. currency, uncertain agio; discount, 1 per cent.; good weight and tare as coffee.

Cotton is sold per lb. in groats Flemish, with a rebate of $8\frac{2}{3}$ per cent.; discount, 1 per cent.; good weight, 1 per cent.; tare on bales, West Indian and North American, 4 per cent.; on square bales, 6 per cent.; on Bombay and Surah bales, 8 per cent.; on Bourbon bales, and Manilla seroons, 6 per cent.; on Caraccas and Guinea small seroons, 10 per cent. For the regulation of the state duty, all packages should be called bags or bales in the bill of lading.

East India piece goods are sold per piece in marcs banco; discount 1 per cent. For saving in the state duty, if more than 30 pieces are in a bale, the number of pieces should not be mentioned in the bill of lading, but only the number of bales.

Flour is sold per 100 lbs. in marcs currency, uncertain agio; discount, 1 per cent.; good weight, 1 per cent.; tare, 20 lbs. per barrel.

Fustic is sold per 100 lbs. in marcs currency; agio, 20 per cent.; discount, 1 per cent.; good weight, 1 per cent.; and frequently an allowance in weight is made, if the wood is not very solid.

Ginger is sold per lb. in groats, Flemish, with a rebate of $8\frac{2}{3}$ per cent.; discount, 1 per cent.; good weight, 1 per cent.; tare, like coffee.

Indigo is sold per lb. in schill. Flemish, with a rebate of $8\frac{2}{3}$ per cent.; discount, 1 per cent.; good weight, half per cent.; tare, if in seroons upwards of 120 lbs., 22 lbs.; in half seroons less than 120 lbs., 20 lbs.; in chests, real tare.

Logwood is sold like fustic.

Nankeens are sold per piece, in schill. banco; discount, 1 per cent. For saving in the state duty, if a bale contains more than 60 pieces, no number of pieces, but merely of bales, should be mentioned in the bill of lading.

Nicaragua wood is sold per 100 lbs. in marks currency, with uncertain agio; discount, 1 per cent.; good weight, &c., like fustic.

Pepper is sold per lb. in groats Flemish; discount, 1 per cent.; good weight, half per cent.; tare, if in single bales of 300 lbs., 3 lbs.; in double bales, 6 lbs.

Pimento is sold per lb. in schill. currency; agio, 20 per cent.; discount, 1 per cent.; good weight, 1 per cent.; tares, if in casks, real weight; if in bags of 120 lbs., 2 lbs.; in bags of 250 lbs., 3 lbs.

Quercitron bark is sold per 100 lbs. in marcs currency; agio, 20 per cent.; discount, 2 per cent.; good weight, 1 per cent. To determine the tare, the American tare is reduced to Hamburg weight.

Rice is sold per 100 lbs. in marcs currency; agio, 20 per cent.; rebate, $8\frac{2}{3}$ per cent.; discount, 1 per cent.; good weight, 1 per cent.; tare, real, and super tare for tierces, 4 lbs.; for half tierces, 2 lbs. Rum is sold per 30 quarts, in rix dollar currency, agio uncertain. Sugar, raw and clayed, is sold per lb. in Flemish groats, with a rebate of $8\frac{2}{3}$ per cent.; discount, 1 per cent., and sometimes $1\frac{1}{2}$ per cent.; Brazil or Havana chests, good weight, $\frac{3}{4}$ per cent., real tare; super tare, 10 lbs. for Brazil, and 5 lbs. for Havana sugar, per chest; Muscovadoes in casks, good weight, 1 per cent.; tare, if the casks weigh upwards of 1000 lbs., 18 per cent.; if less, 20 per cent.; clayed sugars, good weight, 1 per cent.; tare, 16 per cent.; East India sugars, in bags, good weight, $\frac{3}{4}$ per cent.; tare for white, 4 to 5 lbs.; for brown, 6 to 7 lbs.

Tea, per lb. in schill. currency, agio uncertain; discount, 1 per cent.; good weight, $\frac{1}{2}$ per cent. Tare of bohea, in chests of 400 lbs., 70 lbs.; of 150 to 180 lbs., 45 lbs. All black tea, 28 lbs. tare; green, 24 lbs. For the regulations of the state duty, the net weight should likewise be mentioned in the bill of lading. Tobacco leaf is sold per lb. in schillings currency, agio uncertain; discount, $1\frac{1}{2}$ per cent.; good weight, 1 per cent.; tare, per cask, 80 lbs. Brazil leaf, in seroons, tare, 5 per cent.; in rolls—canisters in baskets of about 100 lbs., good weight, 1 lb. per basket; tare, 14 lbs., if the basket is packed up in linen, and 12 lbs. if without linen. Porto Rico rolls, good weight, 1 per cent.; no tare, as the rolls are weighed by themselves; Brazil rolls, in seroons of 4 to 600 lbs., are sold per lb. in schillings banco; good weight, $\frac{3}{4}$ per cent.; tare, 8 lbs. per seroon. Tobacco stems, per 100 lbs. in marcs currency; agio uncertain; discount, $1\frac{1}{2}$ per cent.; good weight, 1 per cent.; tare, if in casks, real weight; if packed up with cords, 2 to 4 per cent., according to the thickness of the rope. As there is a great difference in the state duty for the different sorts of tobacco, it is necessary that, on shipping leaf tobacco, there should be inserted in the bill of lading, leaf tobacco, and the net weight. With tobacco in rolls, only the number of packages containing roll tobacco and the net weight, without mentioning the number of rolls, should appear in the bill of lading.

Exports.—Glass (window) is sold per chest, in marcs currency; agio uncertain; other glassware, per piece, dozen, or hundred, in schillings or marcs currency, with uncertain agio; discount, 1 per cent.

Hare skins (German, gray) are sold per 100 pieces, in rix dollar banco; Russian, gray, per 104 pieces, in rix dollar banco; white, in marcs currency; agio uncertain; discount, 1 per cent.

Iron is sold per ship-pound of 280 lbs. in marcs currency; agio uncertain; discount, 1 per cent.

Copper is sold per ship-pound of 280 lbs. in rix dollars banco; discount, 1 per cent.

Linen estopilles are sold per piece, in marcs banco, with a rebate of $8\frac{2}{3}$ per cent. Sail cloth, ravens' duck, and flems, per piece, in marcs currency; agio uncertain. Osnaburgs and Tecklenburgs, per 100 double ells, in rix dollars banco. All other linen per piece, in rix dollars banco; discount, 1 per cent.

The exchange business done at Hamburg is very great; for besides the business of the place, most of the merchants in the inland towns have their bills negotiated here.

When goods are sold with deduction (rabatt) of $8\frac{2}{3}$, or $4\frac{2}{3}$ per cent., it means a deduction of $8\frac{2}{3}$ for $108\frac{2}{3}$, or $4\frac{2}{3}$ for $104\frac{2}{3}$. The agio on many goods sold in currency is a fixed one, and either 20 or 25 per cent.; with others it is uncertain, and according to the agio existing at the moment.

The government of the Netherlands has laid such heavy duties on the transit of English manufactured goods, that a large portion of this trade is now attracted to Hamburg.

LUBECK

Stands at the head of the Hanseatic league, but it has lost its importance as a place of trade.

Merchandise charged with duty according to weight, shall be regulated by the gross weight of the city.

The *ad valorem* duties shall be levied on the value of the merchandise at the port of departure.

Weights, measures, and moneys of foreign nations, shall be calculated according to the table marked B.

Declaration—Payment of duty.—The payment of the import duty is based on the declaration, under oath, of all the merchandise presented for admission.

The persons who have the exclusive right of making such declarations under oath, are

The members of the colleges of burgesses, inasmuch as they have always possessed the right.

In case of their illness or absence, then their specially authorized agent may act for them, but always on their absolute responsibility.

Other burgesses or inhabitants, when the articles are imported from abroad by their order.

The declaration must indicate the contents, marks and numbers of the packages, as also the measure, number, or gross weight; and for goods, *ad valorem*, the prime cost, with the valuation in money, and the gross weight of Lubeck must be added.

This declaration must be signed by the declarant himself, with attestation, under oath, to the truth, expressed in these words, "true, so help me God."

The declaration is according to a model given, and must be on a stamped paper, (costing 1 mark 6 schillings.)

A similar declaration must be made for goods free of duty, except money to the amount of 1000 rix dollars per package.

If the consignee cannot make the declaration, he must, before the receipt of the merchandise, make the same known to the proper officer, who will, at the option of the consignee, either place the goods in the public warehouse, where they will remain for account of the consignee until the declaration is produced, or he will fix the duties, in which case he may, if necessary, open the packages.

The responsibility of declarants for the truth of their declaration is unlimited as to time.

The correction of a declaration is permitted when voluntary, and not forced by the proper authority, and when the declarant admits the error before the receipt of the merchandise, and before the verification has been begun.

The declaration of merchandise arriving by sea or by the river, should be made on the same day that the vessel or bark passes the first bar, or the first after the passage, under a penalty of 10 per cent. of the duties on the merchandise.

The payment of the duties must be made immediately after the transmission of the declaration to the chief bureau.

General rules.—Merchandise charged with duty according to weight, and entered in one and the same declaration, shall be free, when the weight does not exceed 50 pounds.

The duty for any weight of merchandise above 50 and under 100 pounds, shall be paid as for 50 pounds.

Goods brought by one and the same conveyance, and destined to one person, shall be free from duty, when the value does not exceed 50 marks.

Those articles of consumption which are subjected to an excise, by ordinances actually in force, and for which the excise is paid at the time of their entry into the city, are free of duty.

Goods which have once paid duty, and have been exported, and again imported, shall be free of duty, when their identity shall be attested in the declaration under oath.

HAVRE DE GRACE,

A seaport of France, situated on the right bank of the Seine, 1 league from Cape de la Heve. Most of the American trade is carried on through this port. Its harbour dries at low-water; but the tide does not begin to fall until 3 hours after high-water, which phenomenon is probably caused by the current of the Seine crossing the mouth of the harbour with great force at the beginning of the ebb. Lat. 49° 29′ N. Long. 0° 6′ E.

Its exports are woollens, linens, cottons, silks, perfumery, toys, watches, paper, hardware, and generally the manufactures of France.

Its imports, raw cotton, iron, naval stores, dye-woods, pot and pearl ashes, green hides, tallow, feathers, furs, colonial produce, &c.

For the privileges of American vessels and custom-house regulations, vide Bordeaux, page 489.

Port regulations.—There are 3 basins at Havre: the outer basin, the basin de la barre, and the basin of commerce. Ships may all lie afloat, except when the red flag is hoisted on the bridges, which is the signal of their letting the water out to clean the basins. The depth of the water on the entrance depends upon the winds: at neap tides you cannot come out of the basins with vessels drawing more than 14½ feet water; at spring tides there are 17½ to 18 feet. On entering the harbour, all fires and lights must be extinguished, under a penalty. No smoking of tobacco allowed on ships' decks, under a penalty. Lower yards must be topped, and fore-and-aft spars taken in.

All foreign sailors are taken up after the retreat drum is beat, unless they have a consul's pass.

Pilotage.

For the first 100 tons,	22 f.	For the fourth	12 f.
second	18	Each 100 beyond 4	22
third	15		

On foreign vessels, 50 per cent. more.

IONIAN ISLANDS.

These islands have for many years been severed from the Ottoman empire, and have, at different periods, been subject to the Venitians, to France, and to Russia. They now form a separate state, under the denomination of the United States of the Ionian Islands, and are placed under the immediate and exclusive protection of the king of Great Britain. This arrangement was made by the treaty of Paris, 5th November, 1815, between England and Russia. It was agreed in the same instrument, that the Ionian islands should regulate their internal organization, with the approbation of the protecting power, which, for this purpose, should appoint a lord high commissioner to reside there; the fortresses and forces to be under the authority of Great Britain; and the expenses thereof to be settled between the latter and the islands. The trading flag of the new states to be acknowledged as that of a free and independent state; and that the commerce between the United Ionian States and the dominions of the emperor of Austria shall enjoy the same advantages and facilities as that of Great Britain with the said United States. None but consuls and commercial agents, charged solely with the carrying on commercial relations, are to be accredited to the islands. All the allied powers then negociating at Paris acceded to the treaty, as also the grand sultan and the king of the Two Sicilies.

The exports from these islands are, raisins and other dried fruits, olives, olive oil, soap, silk, wine, &c., besides such merchandise as is imported from abroad and placed in entrepôt.

The imports are coffee, sugar, wines, brandy, grain, cured fish, manufactures of wool, cotton and silk, iron, &c.

Manifest.—On arrival at a port of the Ionian islands, the master of a vessel is required, immediately after having complied with the regulations of the health office, to deliver a manifest of all that is on board the vessel, indicating precisely—1st. Articles destined for the port at which his vessel has arrived; 2d. Articles which have another destination; 3d. Articles to be retained for the ship's use. The omission of these formalities is punished by a fine of from two to twenty pounds sterling, according to the magnitude of the offence.

The manifest may be revised by the captain, but the custom-house may require the production of the original, and the bills of lading.

Errors of the manifest may be corrected within twenty-four hours after the delivery. All goods not inserted therein originally, or on being corrected, are confiscated.

Visit.—Inspectors of the customs are authorized to remain on board till the vessel is discharging, and vigilantly to exercise their duties.

Nothing must be unladen until the formalities of entry shall have been complied with, under penalty of confiscation.

Whenever a captain, after having made his entry, shall express a desire to proceed to a different port, he shall be permitted to do so.

Declaration of the destination of merchandise.—The destination of goods, whether for consumption or for transit, must be declared within twenty-four hours after landing, in default of which they will be considered as placed in entrepôt, and liable to duty accordingly.

Liquidation of duties.—For duties ad valorem, the original invoice must be produced; in default of which the duties will be levied according to the prices current of the place.

The falsification or alteration of originals, or copies of documents, subjects to confiscation the articles contained in such document.

No articles, except such as are subject to quarantine, are allowed to be deposited within the lazarettos. Goods subject to quarantine are, when freed therefrom, to be removed to the custom-house.

Goods which have not paid the duties.—Every deposit beyond the limits of the custom-house bureaus, of merchandise suspected of not having paid the duties, is seized and confiscated, unless payment of the duty is proved, with a fine upon the offenders, for the first offence, equal to the value of the goods seized.

Coasting trade.—The transportation from island to island of the produce of Ionian soil and industry, in Ionian vessels, is free of duty, except the article of brandy, which pays an import duty of $2\frac{3}{4}$ deniers per gallon, and of wine and vinegar, which pay $1\frac{1}{2}$ deniers.

The transportation as above, by foreign vessels, is subject to the duties of importation or exportation.

All articles of foreign origin, which have paid duty in one of the islands, may be shipped to any of the others, free of duty, if in Ionian vessels. If in foreign vessels they pay two thirds of the duty on specified articles, and five per cent. of the duty ad valorem.

Free port.—Extracts from the act of August 1825, creating Corfu a free port:

All kinds of merchandise may be stored in the designated warehouses, free of all duties or charges, except rent, and *facchinaccio*, porterage, which are fixed in special rates. Prohibited articles, and those reserved to the government, as salt and gunpowder, are admitted to the warehouses.

Bond is given, that after one year the goods warehoused shall be exported to the places mentioned in the bond.

And should goods not be exported within thirty days after notice given by the authorities, they will be confiscated.

Merchandise drawn from the warehouses of the free port, for exportation or sale, is subject to a duty of one per cent. on the value, whatever time it may have been in entrepôt.

No sale or transfer of goods in depôt, of less than a whole package or bale, can be made, nor of articles not in packages or bales, of less than the value of one hundred dollars.

Sales or transfers are subject to a charge of 2*s.* 6*d.*

For damages, an allowance is made, on withdrawal from the warehouse, of five per cent. on pepper, coffee, and other similar articles; on spirituous liquors five per cent., and on wine four per cent.

No bale can be opened but in the presence of the owner.

General regulations.—Vessels coming to anchor in Ionian roads or ports, and not discharging or taking in cargo, are exempt from all duties; the purchase of provisions and taking in water for the crew, are not deemed taking in lading.

Captains or owners of vessels are answerable for all the port and quarantine duties, except the lazaretto and purgation charges.

Goods cannot be received into the lazarettos, nor taken from them, without an order in writing of the collector.

The duties of purgation and quarantine of goods must be paid before they are taken from the lazarettos.

LEGHORN

Is a fine town, with a capacious but shallow harbour; and on account of the comparative advantages and freedom which foreign nations enjoy here in all respects, its commerce is very extensive; and by the decay of that of Venice, Genoa and other Italian seaports, on the increase. Even Florence, the capital of Tuscany, within the territory of which Leghorn is situated, is dependent on the latter for its commerce, for it supplies the whole of the interior with the produce of the Levant, of Europe, and of the East and West Indies, and is the medium of all commerce with the coast of Barbary. Lat. 43° 33′ N. Long. 10° 22′ E.

The only obstruction to the trade of this port grows out of the rigor of the quarantine precautions. In compliance with these, vessels, when approaching the roads of Leghorn, are visited by a boat from the health office, which leaves on board two guards, one of whom always acts as pilot, and for which six crowns are allowed.

Generally, after the vessel is brought to a safe anchorage, one of the guards accompanies the captain in his boat to the health office, where his bill of health is demanded, and inquiry is made what vessels have been communicated with during the voyage, at what ports the vessel may have touched, and also as to what general incidents may have occurred.

Except the bill of health, no other papers are demanded of the captain, his flag alone being considered a sufficient voucher of his national character.

Should there be no bills of health, or a foul one, or if coming from a suspected port, and all vessels from the Levant and coast of Barbary are considered such, the quarantine is fixed from 18 to 40 days; all the goods on board subject to purification, which includes all articles of cotton, wool, silk, hemp, flax, hides, leather, feathers or paper, or articles of which the packing is formed of any of those articles, are transported to the lazaretto, where every package is open ed and undergoes a thorough purification of from twenty to forty days from the opening of the package, the quarantine counted from this period, and not from the day that the goods may have been discharged at the lazaretto. The expense of repacking the goods to be transported to the warehouses in the city, is a charge upon the goods, separate from the lazaretto duties. Vessels remain in the roads until at least one half of their cargoes is discharged, when they are allowed to enter the mole.

The quarantine on vessels having clean bills of health, and not coming from suspected places, is generally limited to from fifteen to twenty days, but the goods that are liable to contagion must be transported to the lazaretto.

The expense consequent upon this very rigorous adhesion to the regulations of quarantine, are serious drawbacks on the trade of Leghorn, as the lighterage and packing charges alone of a cargo of 250 tons, would amount to upwards of $500.

The allowance to the guards during the quarantine of the vessel is five pauls each per diem, together with their provisions, which is always a charge on the vessel, and not on the cargo.

Henceforth the lazaretto of St. Leopold shall be reserved to receive vessels infected or suspected of contagion, merchandise or persons from the two other lazarettos, in case of accident during quarantine, and in aid thereof when full. All vessels, with foul bills of health, will perform their quarantine in the lazaretto of St. James, which is more convenient and less expensive for captains and merchants; and to establish a more equitable proportion in the current value of goods and the tariff of quarantine duties, there shall immediately be prepared a tariff to take effect the first of September next, and which shall be annually renewed.

	MONTHS.		
	WINTER. 1st Dec. to Feb. inclusive.	SUMMER. 1st. March to Nov. inclusive.	Vessels of war.
YELLOW FEVER.			
Days of quarantine, according to causes of suspicion for arrivals from America.			
Clean bills of health.—Days of observation.			
First division, from the equator to the tropic of cancer.	7	10	To days less than merchant vessels.
Second division, from the tropic of cancer to Charleston inclusively, and from the equator to all South America	5	7	
Third divison, from the United States between Charleston and Canada			
Doubtful bill of health.—Days of quarantine.			
Lazaretto of St. Roch, all destinations and all seasons...	18	18	10
Without susceptible commodities, rigid	14	18	10
Foul bills of health.—Days of quarantine.			
Lazaretto of St. Roch, all seasons, and wherever from...	25	25	10
Without susceptible commodities	18	25	10
Susceptible commodities, rigid	...	...	13

The above regulations, where there are clean bills of health, are applied to vessels from America, which shall, at the same time, produce a declaration of the Tuscan consul, or at least of some other European consul, that the place enjoys good health, and that the adjacent country is free from yellow fever, or other contagious disease.

In cases where captains have not provided themselves with this consular declaration, the board of health will hold a special deliberation, to decide on the manner in which they shall be subjected to quarantine.

Articles subject to purification, in cases of doubtful bills of health respecting yellow fever, are indistinctly verified and purified on board in such manner as shall be effectual, and shall accomplish the disinfection of the vessel.

Articles subject to infection, in cases of foul bills of health, must be purified within the lazaretto.

Vessels subjected to treatment as having foul bills of health for yellow fever, as also those with foul bills of health, the "*plague bubonniene*," cannot be admitted to free pratique, until their interior shall have been disinfected with the perfumes of *guitton-morveau*, and with washings of chlorine of lime, according to the nature of their ladings; particular attention to be given to the parts of the vessel most frequented.

Regulations for cruisers and vessels in general, which have communicated at sea with other vessels.

	Vessels and persons.	May be increased to	
Cruisers, in time of general good health—days of quarantine	15	20	At the lazaretto of San Rocca.
Cruisers, in time of contagion	20	30	
Vessels in general, in time of good health	10 of observation.		
Vessels in general, in time of contagion	20	30	

If the vessel which shall have communicated at sea, can present circumstances or observations worthy of particular attention, the health office will decide as to the term of quarantine.

When it is discovered that the vessel has had communication at sea with another proceeding from a contaminated place, the vessel is subject to the same treatment as one arriving with a foul bill of health.

Regulations for vessels arriving, the health documents of which are irregular.

	Days of quarantine.	
Not having a bill of health, in which is noted the number of persons, or the name of the captain, a master not being properly identified	5	of observation.
Having on board an excess of persons	3	"
Having less persons on board than expressed	5	"
Wanting confidence in the goods subject to quarantine	5	"

If there should arise any suspicion that the merchandise is the product of the Ottoman Levant, or of any other places subject to a rigorous quarantine, and that it has not undergone any purgation, and that the captain or master of the vessel has not official or governmental documents to prove the place of their embarkation to be one of free pratique; the board of health office must deliberate on the proper measures to be pursued, as in the case in which the diminution of the persons on board shall not be properly accounted for.

The exports from all the Italian ports are much the same; silk, raw or manufactured, making one of the principal differences; fruit, oil, parmesan cheese, marble, hair powder, drugs, &c.

The imports are almost every thing which the world produces, excepting the commodities which have been enumerated, and the few others which Italy can boast, particularly hides, codfish, salmon, coffee, sugars dyes, spices, &c. Small fish are preferred to large, and white sugar to brown.

Goods in general are bought and sold for silver money; between which, and the money in which bills of exchange are bought, there is a difference of seven per cent. (agio) against silver—that is, $107 in silver are equal to $100 in gold On goods bought and sold, (unless it be in effective money, where there is no discount,) there is, generally speaking, a discount of three per cent.; on all cotton manufactures, four per cent. Charges on sales, including commissions, are generally from six to eight per cent.; on fish, eight to ten per cent.

LISBON,

The capital of Portugal, is situated on the river Tagus, and has one of the finest harbours in the world. Lat. 38° 42′ N. Long. 9° 9′ W.

Wine is the most considerable article of exportation, and the quantity shipped, both from Lisbon and Oporto, is very great. Salt is also an article of commerce, and the Portuguese salt has the quality of preserving provisions better than that of any other country. The country yields excellent white honey; fruits, such as lemons and oranges, which are, however, very inferior to the Spanish; almonds, with which the pigs are fed, and to which the Portuguese hams owe their celebrity; and figs are produced in Algarve, which are chiefly consumed in the country. The Portuguese wool is coarse and much inferior to the Spanish.

The imports are flax, iron, wheat, salted fish, copper, lead, provisions, grain, flour and West India produce.

To the north of Europe, the exports are wines, salt, fruits, and some colonial produce; and the returns consist in hemp, flax, iron, timber and deals, stock fish, pitch, tar, Russian and German linens, and particularly grain. A great smuggling trade is carried on with Spain, in sugar, tobacco, spices, &c.

The corn laws, which had their origin in 1815, have been subsequently amended and made still more rigorous. It is a policy but ill adapted either to the soil, climate, or habits of the people of Portugal. It is true, that in her early history, she produced more corn and less wine than in more modern times. But after its introduction the culture of the vine advanced so rapidly, as soon to nearly supplant that of grain. It is at this day, too, the favoured culture, and that kingdom is rich in the variety and flavour of its wines. By our laws, all the red wines of Portugal pay the same rate of duty as port, which is of superior quality and of higher price than the other wines of that country. Their white as well as red wines pay a higher duty than the wines of Austria, Germany, France and Spain. If their high and low priced wines were admitted into the United States at the same duties as are charged on the wines of other countries, and the flour and grain of America were as freely received in Portugal, a most beneficial interchange would ensue.

Duties.—The import duties are termed *dizima* and *siza*, amounting together to 20 per cent.; *donativo*, four per cent.; *consulado*, three per cent.; *fragata, comboy*, or war duty, three per cent.; making 30 per cent. They are levied on the value specified in the tariffs, or where omitted, on the invoice price or a valuation.

The *dizima* and *siza* are the old constitutional duties, and are considered as a portion of the royal patrimony; each of them are 10 per cent.

Donativo was an aid which the nation presented to the King in 1756, for the purpose of restoring the public edifices destroyed by the earthquake of 1755. It was continued for governmental expenses generally, by a decree of May, 1762. It is levied on all imports, by land or sea, from foreign countries or Portuguese colonies. It does not apply to goods imported for exportation.

Consulado is a duty imposed on all goods exported or imported, by a law of September, 1641, immediately after the separation from Spain.

Fragata, comboy, or war duty, was established in 1761, for the purpose of protecting the coasts; it was then extended to the protection of the colonial trade, and lately to other purposes.

Portagem is a small toll duty paid per bale, package, chest, barrel, &c., on the exportation of some few articles, such as figs, brought into Lisbon from Algarve, which pay 15 reis per arroba; almonds, 10 per bale; fruit in boxes, 20.

Baldeacao is a duty payable on a cargo transhipped from one vessel to another for re-exportation, or upon goods re-exported from the custom-house, for a foreign country. It is now fixed by royal decrees at two per cent.

By edicts of 1815, 1822, 1823 and 1824, the importation of foreign wheat is only permitted when the inspector general of the corn market, in conformity with the regulations established by this market, and when the price of native wheat is at 840 reis per alquiere, that of foreign hard wheat at 800, and of foreign soft wheat at 700, declares what quantity is required for the consumption of the country.

A royal order is then published, prescribing the quantity, quality and time of importations from foreign countries.

These importations can only be made into the port of Lisbon, unless specially permitted to others.

Rye, barley and oats, are admitted at any time for consumption or re-exportation. Flour is absolutely prohibited, unless admitted by a special edict.

By a decree of 13th August, 1831, rice, of the growth of the United States, imported direct from thence into the ports of Lisbon and Oporto, in Portuguese or American vessels, with a certificate of origin from a Portuguese consul, was admitted for consumption, on paying a duty of 23 per cent. on the current price. It can only be imported from the United States, Brazil, or the Portuguese colonies in

Asia and Africa, by special license. It is not allowed to be imported from other places, either for consumption, or warehousing for exportation.

An arrangement was made in January, 1833, with the king of Portugal, by which American rice is admitted into Portugal at the same rate of duty that is paid on rice from Brazil; and if the duty on the latter shall hereafter be reduced, that on the American article shall in like manner be reduced. As the duty on Brazil rice is, with other productions of that country, established at 15 per cent. by the treaty of 1825, the rice of the United States will now be charged at the same rate, being a reduction of eight per centum from the former duty.

When a cargo of goods which are allowed to be warehoused for re-exportation, is entered at the custom-house, the importer must make a declaration and entry for warehousing; otherwise they will be charged with the full duty of consumption. A similar declaration must be made if the cargo is intended for *baldeacao* or transhipment.

Materials for the construction of vessels pay one half of the import duties.

The coasting trade is only allowed to Portuguese vessels.

Merchandise liable to quarantine is entitled to a deduction of one fifth of the *siza* and *dizima*, on account of the expenses to which it is subject by quarantine charges.

Port charges.—There is no tonnage duty in Portugal, nor is there any countervailing or discriminating duty between Portuguese and American vessels. Both pay uniformly the same rates.

Pilotage is paid according to the customs of the different ports, and without difference between Portuguese and foreign vessels.

The following charges are paid at Lisbon:

	Reis.
Health officer at Belem	7,060
Custom-house at Belem	240
Measurement	240
Marco or wharfage; vessels coming into Lisbon with a cargo, and sailing thence, loaded with the produce of the country, pay per ton	105
And, likewise, if they depart in ballast, but with some deductions.	
Vessels entering and departing in ballast, or with their original cargoes, pay no marco dues.	
Vessels sailing from Portuguese ports in ballast, pay full light money, per ton	200
If with a cargo of the produce of Portugal, or of her colonies, per ton,	50
If loaded with one half of such a cargo	100
With a fourth of such a cargo	150
To the guarda-mor of the ballast office	1,000
To the officers of the college of commerce	1,500
To the officers of the light money,	480
Anchorage	500
Passport	10,720

	Reis.
Port captain	800
Bill of health	120
Castle of Belem	4,080
Custom-house of Lisbon	480
do.	160
do. visit	240

The port of Lisbon is free to the merchant ships of every country not at war with Portugal. Goods and merchandise, of whatever nature and kind, and under whatsoever flag imported, will be admitted to deposit therein.

Even in the event of war the merchandise deposited will not suffer embargo or confiscation; on the contrary, all private property which may be lying in the said port, or afterwards enter under a friendly or neutral flag, will be held sacred.

The merchandise so admitted to deposit may be freely re-exported, on payment of the duty of one per cent. only, with the expenses of labourers and of guards, to the time of its leaving the port.

In cases wherein such merchandise shall not enter into deposit, and it shall be transhipped on board of other vessels, it shall be subject to pay the duty of two per cent., and the other expenses of guards at reasonable rates.

The duty of *baldeacao* and that of re-exportation shall be computed on the price established in the custom-house tariff, or on the invoice value, where the article is not expressed in the tariff, and in default of both it shall be computed ad valorem.

No merchandise shall pay warehouse rent during the first year; but after that, it shall be subject to a monthly rent for all the time it shall remain in the warehouses beyond that period.

All merchandise which from its nature is very combustible, is excepted from the preceding rule, and cannot be deposited in the custom-house, but may be deposited in private warehouses, at the cost of its owners.

Port regulations.—All goods and merchandise, whatever may be their nature and origin, or the flag under which they shall be imported, are admitted to entry in the custom-houses of Lisbon and Oporto for home consumption, except live pigs, powder, olive and turnip-seed oil.

Tobacco, soap and orchilla, continue to be subject to the laws and conditions of the state contracts.

Vinegar, wines, brandies, and other spirituous liquors, of whatever quality, are admitted only in bottles or jars of half a canada, Lisbon measure, and in cases or packages of two dozen each. Rum is admitted in casks of any size.

LIVERPOOL,

A seaport in Lancashire, England, and the second town in the kingdom for commerce, is situated on the right bank of the Mersey, three miles from its mouth, where it is 1,500 yards wide. It has an excellent harbour, formed with great labour and expense; and docks for the reception of ships having been built, capable of containing more than 300,000 tons of shipping. Lat. 53° 22′ N. Long. 2° 52′ W.

The principal manufactures in this place are fine porcelain, earthenware, watches, stockings, glass, iron, salt, copperas, cordage and malt liquor, though coal and large assortments of all English manufactures, for the American market, may always be procured here, being situated near to the large manufacturing towns.

By treaty, American vessels are put on the same footing in British ports with British vessels, and are liable to no other duties. American produce is liable to the same duties, and entitled to the same drawback upon exportation, whether imported in American or British vessels; and British produce is subject to the same rule, whether exported in American or British vessels.

For custom-house regulations, vide London.

Tonnage.

The inward tonnage duty on any American vessel, from any part of Europe, except Ireland or the Isle of Man, the Mediterranean, the United States, or any part of America, except Newfoundland, or Labrador, or Africa	per ton	£0 1 0
Outward duty the same		0 1 0
To the trustees of the docks		0 2 0

This duty must be paid before passing through the custom-house.

A book containing the port regulations, is given to every foreign vessel.

Light-house duties, 2d. per ton; floating do. 1d.

Quarantine duty.

On vessels from the United States, performing quarantine, with a clean bill of health . .	per ton	£0 3 0
without do. do. . . .		0 10 0

Pilotage.

Inwards	9s. per foot.	Outwards .	5s per foot.

Terms of sale.—Cotton is sold upon a credit of ten days and three months, by drafts payable in London. That is, ten days after sale the purchaser gives bills, made equal to cash in three months and ten days from the day of sale.

Tobacco and ashes are sold on a credit of two and two months, by bills payable in London. That is, two months after the date of sale the purchaser gives a bill made equal to cash in four months from the day of sale.

Bark, flour, rice, staves and flaxseed, are sold on a credit of one and three months.

Naval stores are, generally, sold upon a credit of two and two months, the same as tobacco, but frequently these articles are sold for an acceptance at four months.

LONDON,

The metropolis of Great Britain, and the greatest commercial place in the world, is situated on the river Thames, nearly at the head of tide water. The port extends along its banks from Deptford to the bridge, about four miles in length. The wharves having been found inadequate to its increasing commerce, superb docks have been excavated to receive vessels from various parts of the world. West India dock, for outward bound vessels, is 2600 feet long, and 400 broad; that for inward bound vessels, 2600 feet long and 500 broad, and capable of receiving 300 vessels of 300 tons burthen.

London dock . . .	1260	feet long.
	690	broad.
East India discharging dock . .	1410	feet long.
	560	broad.
East India loading dock . . .	780	feet long.
	520	broad.

Lat. 51° 31′ N. Long. 0° 06′ W.

To this port are confined some branches of foreign commerce, viz., the company trade to the East Indies, Turkey and Hudson's bay. All English manufactures, and the productions of all other parts of the world, are to be found here. The most important of its peculiar manufactures are silk weaving, the making of optical and mathematical instruments, porter, &c.

The port regulations are too numerous to be here inserted. They are furnished to all vessels upon their arrival.

An additional shilling per ton is exacted here for quarantine duties, besides the quarantine duties paid in other ports.

Masters, upon their arrival off Dungeness, must display a signal for a pilot, and keep it flying until they have passed the buoy of the brake; and if a pilot comes within half a mile, with the pilot's signal flying, must take him on board, if possible, under penalty of £5 for every 50 tons, and double pilotage.

Ships coming to this port are not obliged by law to make a signal for, or receive a pilot on board, beyond the following limits or pilot water, viz.:

Five miles from or outside of Bembridge ledge.

Three miles from or outside Dunnose or St. Catharine, or three miles from the Needle's Point, coming in at that passage.

Pilots taken on board by the captain outside or beyond these limits, to receive the following pay according to law:

6 leagues distant	4	4	0
10 " "	6	6	6

and proportionably for any intermediate distance; and for every ten leagues beyond the meridian of Peverell Point, for ships not exceeding fourteen feet water, three guineas; and for ships of more than fourteen feet water, four guineas; and proportionably for intermediate distances. The pilotage into Cowes Roads is,

For ships drawing as far as	17 feet . .	5	shillings	per foot.
	17 to 20 . .	6	"	"
	above 20 feet draft	7	"	"

and the same rates outwards.

It would be advisable, to prevent disputes, that the captains should have an understanding with the pilot before giving him charge of the ship, that the question of distance and distance money might be settled beforehand.

Custom-house regulations.—No goods can be unladen, nor bulk broken, within four leagues of the British coasts, until report of the vessel and entry of the goods are made, and warrant granted; and the goods must be unladen at the times and places, and in the manner and by the persons appointed by the officers of the customs. If the goods are not reported or entered, or are unladen contrary to these provisions, they are forfeited. If bulk be illegally broken, the master is liable to a penalty of £100. Any alteration of the stowage of the cargo, or if any part be staved, destroyed, or thrown overboard, or any package be broken, it is deemed breaking bulk. The following articles, however, may be landed without report, entry, or warrant, viz.: diamonds and bullion; fresh fish, British taken, and imported in British ships; turbots and lobsters, fresh, however taken or imported.

Vessels must be reported within 24 hours after arrival, under penalty of £200.

The master of the vessel must, within 24 hours after his arrival, and before breaking bulk, make due report of the vessel, upon oath, setting forth an account of the particular marks, numbers and contents of all the parcels of goods on board,—of such as are stowed loose,—of the places where shipped,—the burthen of the vessel,—where built,—the country to which she belongs,—the name and country of the master and crew: it must also be stated whether bulk was broke in the course of the voyage, " and what part of the cargo, if any, be intended for importation at such port, and what part, if any, be intended for importation at another port in the United Kingdom,"—what part, if any, is prohibited, except to be warehoused for exportation only,—and what part, if any, is intended for exportation in such vessel to foreign places; also, the surplus stores which remain. If a British vessel, the report must contain a statement of the foreign made sails or cordage, not being standing or running rigging, on board. The master failing to make such report, or making a false one, forfeits £100. Yet he may amend his report, where no fraud seems to have been intended.

All British vessels, and all other vessels, loaded with tobacco, must have manifests, containing nearly similar particulars to those required in the report mentioned above, except that the tobacco must have a separate manifest, which must, " without fail, contain the particular weight of tobacco in each hogshead, cask, chest or case, with the tare of the same; and if such tobacco be the produce of the dominions of the Grand Seignor, then the number of the parcels or bundles within any such hogshead, cask, case or chest, must be stated in such manifest."

The tobacco manifest must have on it a certificate of the British consul or other chief British officer residing at the port from which the vessel departed, stating the date of the production of the manifest to him.

All letters must be delivered before the vessel will be permitted to enter; for each of which the master will receive, from the postmaster, two pence.

Manifests of the goods on board are to be made out and produced upon being demanded by the custom-house officers. Master and mate will forfeit £100 if they suffer bulk to be broke until properly authorized, or if the marks and seals are altered. If the report, manifest and cargo disagree, the master is subjected to a forfeit of £100, unless it appear that no fraud was intended.

Goods must not be thrown overboard in port, or within four leagues of the coast, except in distress.

Goods must be entered within fourteen days after report, or they will be sent to the public stores.

If any part of the cargo of a vessel for which a manifest is required, be reported for importation at some other port in the United Kingdom, or at some other port in the Isle of Man, the collector and comptroller of the port at which some part of the cargo has been delivered, shall notify such delivery on the manifest, and return the same to the master.

Vessels are required to come as quickly up to the proper place of mooring or unlading as practicable, without touching at any other place, and to bring to, at the stations appointed for the visits of the boarding officers.

Boarding officers* have free access to all parts of the vessel; may fasten hatchways, seal and secure goods, or may open locks, if keys be refused. If any goods be found concealed they are forfeited. The breaking any lock, mark or seal, placed by a customs officer, or secretly conveying away the goods, subjects the master to a penalty of £100.

Master and mate must give bonds in the penalty of £200 before clearance, not to land goods illegally.

Masters must bring to at the usual place of stationing revenue officers, under penalty of £100. Revenue officers are to have free access to the cabin or any part of the ship.

Goods cannot be shipped for exportation until a copy of the coquet or entry (with the endorsement) thereof be delivered to the searcher.

If imported goods be opened and carried away, or put into any other package after arrival, or if goods to be exported shall be concealed, the master or other offender shall forfeit £100.

Goods must be landed and shipped in presence of an officer, under severe penalties.

Passengers' baggage (except watches and fowling pieces) is not liable to duty. If the officers refuse to pass it under pretence that the articles are not of that description, they may be placed in the king's warehouse, free of duty, for six months.

Where goods are lost or accidentally destroyed, before landing, the duties will be returned. If goods which have not been reported should be found after clearing the vessel, they will be forfeited.

Bills of entry must be signed by the merchant importing or ex-

---

* They must be provided with sufficient room under deck for their bed or hammock.

porting goods, or by his agent. Entry must specify marks and contents of each package, and weight of each parcel rated by weight, and state whether goods be on British or alien account; and no entry can be made in the name of the children of aliens under 21 years of age.

Any produce of any of the United States, except specially prohibited, may be imported in American vessels; but if manufactured in any degree in foreign parts, they are prohibited.

When the duties, either import or export, are to be taken by the value, they are first deducted from the real value at the port of exportation. Goods undervalued may be detained by the officer, the importer receiving the value as declared and the duties which he paid. The commissioners may permit an amendment of the entry. The value declared on the prime entry governs the post-entry.

Returned goods are to pay the same duties as they would have been liable to on a regular importation.

If a bounty was received thereon at exportation, it must be returned on reimportation.

Goods by tale or measure are not allowed to have a post-entry; but by an article in the landing waiter's instruction, a post-entry may be allowed for linen if less than one ell per piece.

More goods are not to be left on board any vessel at clearing inwards, than such as the duties thereon would not amount to more than 40 shillings.

But vessels importing tobacco are not to be forfeited on account of having on board any quantity loose, for the use of the seamen or passengers, not exceeding 5 lbs. for each person.

Printed patterns of calico or linen may be admitted free of duty, provided they are intended to be used merely as patterns, and afterwards re-exported.

Exports.—No goods can be shipped, or water-borne to be shipped, for exportation, before due entry outwards of vessel and merchandise be made, and cocket granted. No stores for any such vessel, nor any goods, are deemed to be stores, unless the same be entered on the victualling bill. Any goods or stores shipped, or water-borne to be shipped contrary to these provisions, are forfeited.

The master of the vessel must make application to the proper officer for a victualling bill of such stores as he may require, and as shall be allowed by the collector and comptroller for the use of such vessel, according to the voyage upon which she is bound.

Before any goods can be taken on board, the master of the vessel must deliver the certificate from the proper officer of the clearance inwards, or coastwise, of such vessel of her last voyage, and at the same time make entry outwards, and give the name, country, tonnage, &c., of the vessel.

The searcher may open any package of goods shipped, and if found to correspond with the cocket and clearance, he must repack them at his own cost.

Officers may board any vessel after clearance, and if there be any goods or stores not entered on the cockets or victualling bills, the same are forfeited; and if any goods entered on the cockets be not on board, the master forfeits £20 for every parcel of goods omitted.

All vessels departing, are to bring to at such stations as are appointed within the port for the landing of customs officers, or for further examination, previous to such departure.

The exporter must deliver to the custom-house a shipping bill, with an endorsement, specifying the value, &c., of the goods.

If the true value of goods to be exported cannot be ascertained, they may be shipped on the merchant's giving a bond that he will produce a shipping bill and declaration of the real value, and pay the duty within 3 months. If a false declaration is then knowingly made, the value thereof is forfeited.

If the bill of goods be not produced, the importer shall forfeit £20.

If goods on which the export duties have been paid are lost at sea, a like quantity may be exported free, upon proof being made of their loss to the baron of the exchequer.

If goods to be exported be undervalued, they may be taken by the custom-house officer.

The export duty on British produce or manufactures (except linen, cotton, grain, molasses, refined sugar, and some few other goods which it is not necessary to enumerate, all which are free) is 10 shillings for every £100 value.

There is an additional duty on coals of 17 shillings per Newcastle chaldron; if sold by weight, 5s. 9d. per ton.

On culm, per chaldron, 4s. 6d.

Salt intended for exportation pays 1d. per bushel excise duty at the pit. When exported, the home consumption duty of excise paid at the entry thereof for exportation, is deducted from its value, and the balance is deemed to be the real value at the port of exportation; and a bond is required from the captain and two sureties that it shall not be relanded.

On the exportation of sugars, tobacco, cotton, indigo, ginger, fustic, or any dyewood, the produce of any English colony, or of any goods liable to excise, a bond must be given to land them in the United States, which bond shall be annulled by a certificate from the British consul, or, if none in the port of arrival, by a magistrate of the United States.

Debentures.—No entry can pass, or debenture be made out on exportation of goods entitled to drawback or bounty, but in the name of the real owner, if a resident in Britain, who is to make oath that he is the real owner; and if he has not obtained a right to the drawback or bounty, he must, at the time of entering the goods, declare upon the entry the name of the person who is entitled to such drawback, and that person is to sign the receipt to the debenture.

But persons residing upwards of 20 miles from the place of exportation, may export goods by and in the name of an agent; as also may any person, exporting from a place where he does not reside, goods of British manufacture, his property: such agent making oath, on the back of the debenture, to the name and place of abode of the real proprietor of the goods.

Drawback is not allowed, except the goods are shipped within three years from the importation, and if warehoused on importation within one year after the duty being paid, and claimed in two years after being shipped.

Warehouse system.—When goods are warehoused, the importer is at the expense of the rent; and if destroyed by fire, no duty is to be paid. When taken out, they are to be re-examined. When delivered for exportation, a bond is to be given in treble the amount by the exporter, the master, and a surety, for the due landing them, and the production of a certificate if in the United States, within 18 months.

No goods are to be delivered from the warehouse, except in the original package, or one equal thereto. If not taken out in two years, (except tobacco, which may remain three years,) they are to be sold; but if they will not sell for as much as the duties, they are to be destroyed. If delivered for home consumption, they are liable to such duties as are due at the time of taking them out, according to the account taken at the first examination; if for exportation, duties must be paid upon all deficiencies.

Goods may be removed from one warehouse port to another, upon giving bonds to deliver the same to the collector of the intended port without diminution. If, upon their arrival, there should be any deficiency, full duties shall be paid for such deficiency.

Tobacco can be warehoused free of charge for 18 months, and after that period it pays 1½d. per hogshead per week.

Goods sent to the king's stores, and remaining there three months, may be sold for the duty and charges of warehousing, &c., the overplus, if any, to be paid to the proprietor.

MARSEILLES,

A seaport of France in the Mediterranean, at the end of a gulf studded with islands. Lat. 43° 18′ N. Long. 5° 22′ E.

The imports are cotton, rice, indigo, and American and West India produce generally.

Cocoa—the consumption of this article is not extensive.

Tobacco—the annual quantity consumed in this port is 1200 hhds., which must be sold to government; but speculators sometimes purchase in entrepôt, for exportation, and not unfrequently sell to government.

Hides, Buenos Ayres—the autumn and the winter are the seasons when they are in the greatest demand, and find a ready sale.

Nankins, short, are in demand in February and March, when they are most saleable. From 50 to 75,000 pieces are required for the supply of the market, and that early in the season.

Cochineal is in constant demand here, as well for the manufactories in this vicinity, as for various parts of the Levant.

Coffee—the tare on coffee in casks is neat; in linen bags, 1 per cent.; in grass bags, neat, or as may be agreed on at the sale. The supplies for the south of France, Switzerland, and Piedmont, are principally drawn from this port, and small parcels are constantly shipped from this port by vessels going to the Levant.

Its exports are fruit, oil, perfumes, wines, drugs, and the manufactures of France.

For commercial regulations, &c., vide Bordeaux, page 489.

A very rigorous quarantine is kept up here, to prevent the introduction of the plague.

MEXICO.

This country comprehends all that part of North America lying south of the United States and Texas, and north of the 16th degree of N. latitude. Its products are universal, its soil being rich; and from the peculiar and elevated face of the country, it is enabled to bring forth the productions of various climates under the same degree of latitude. Its manufactures of wool, cotton, leather, segars, gunpowder, soap, and soda, are large and numerous, and the trade with this great empire will afford a large field to American enterprise. Its commerce with the United States, West Indies, and Europe, is chiefly carried on through the port of Vera Cruz, in lat. 19° 11′ N., long. 96° 4′ W. From this port Spain has received her chief supply of the precious metals, amounting in peace to about $17,000,000 per annum; cochineal, $2,400,000; sugar, $1,300,000, &c. The imports are bale goods, $9,000,000; paper, $1,000,000; quicksilver, $650,000; cocoa, $1,000,000.

The principal port of Mexico on the western side of the continent is Acapulco, once celebrated as the annual resort of galleons. Its harbour is a beautiful basin, ten miles long and three broad, and surrounded by volcanic mountains. This country having been declared independent, it is to be presumed that its resources hereafter will be more fully developed, and that its government will not delay to facilitate its commercial intercourse with other nations.

A treaty was formed on the 5th of April, 1832, between the United States and Mexico, by which the principle of reciprocity in trade was fully recognised, and both parties were put upon the footing of the most favoured nation; and providing that, to avoid all kinds of vexation and abuse in the examination of papers relating to the ownership of vessels belonging to the citizens of the two contracting parties, they have agreed, and do agree, that in case one of them should be engaged in war, the vessels belonging to the citizens of the other must be furnished with sea-letters or passports, expressing the name, property, and bulk of the vessel, and also the name and place of habitation of the master or commander of said vessel, in order that it may thereby appear that the said vessel really and truly belongs to the citizens of one of the contracting parties. They have likewise agreed that such vessels being laden, besides the sea-letters or passports, shall also be provided with certificates containing the several particulars of the cargo, and the place whence the vessel sailed, so that it may be known whether any forbidden or contraband goods be on board the same; which certificate shall be made out by the officers of the place whence the vessel sailed, in the accustomed form; without which requisites the said vessel may be detained, to be adjudged by the competent tribunal, and may be declared legal prize, unless the said defect shall be satisfied or supplied by testimony entirely equivalent to the satisfaction of the competent tribunal.

Contraband or prohibited goods.—First, cannons, mortars, howitzers, swivels, blunderbusses, muskets, fusees, rifles, carbines, pistols, pikes, swords, sabres, lances, spears, halberts, and granades; bombs, powder, matches, balls, and all other things belonging to the use of these arms; secondly, bucklers, helmets, breastplates, coats of mail, infantry belts, and clothes made up in a military form, and for military use; thirdly, cavalry belts, and horses with their furniture; fourthly, and generally, all kinds of arms, and instruments of iron, steel, brass, and copper, or of any other materials manufactured, prepared and formed expressly to make war by sea or land.

The citizens of the two countries respectively shall have liberty, freely and securely to come with their vessels and cargoes to all such places, ports, and rivers of the United States of America and of the United Mexican States, to which other foreigners are permitted to come; to enter into the same, and to remain and reside in any part of the said territories respectively; also, to hire and occupy houses and warehouses for the purposes of their commerce, and to trade therein, in all sorts of produce, manufactures, and merchandise; and, generally, the merchants and traders of each nation shall enjoy the most complete protection and security for their commerce.

And they shall not pay higher or other duties, imposts, or fees whatsoever, than those which the most favoured nations are or may be obliged to pay; and shall enjoy all the rights, privileges, and exemptions, with respect to navigation and commerce, which the citizens of the most favoured nation do or may enjoy; but subject always to the laws, usages, and statutes of the two countries respectively.

The liberty to enter and discharge the vessels of both nations of which this article treats, shall not be understood to authorize the coasting trade, which is permitted to coasting vessels only.

No higher or other duties shall be imposed on the importation into the United Mexican States of any article, the produce, growth, or manufacture of the United States of America, than those which the same or like articles, the produce, growth, or manufacture of any other foreign country do now or may hereafter pay; nor shall articles, the produce, growth, or manufacture of the United Mexican States, be subject, on their introduction into the United States of America, to higher or other duties than those which the same or like articles of any other foreign country do now or may hereafter pay.

Higher duties shall not be imposed in the respective states on the exportation of any article to the states of the other contracting party, than those which are now or may hereafter be paid on the exportation of the like articles to any other foreign country; nor shall any prohibition be established on the exportation or importation of any article, the produce, growth, or manufacture of the United States of America, or of the United Mexican States respectively, in either of them, which shall not in like manner be established with respect to other foreign countries.

No higher or other duties and charges on account of tonnage, light or harbour dues, pilotage, salvage in case of damage or shipwreck, or any other local charges, shall be imposed, in any of the ports of Mexico, on vessels of the United States of America, than those payable in the same ports by Mexican vessels; nor in the ports of the United States of America, on Mexican vessels, than shall be payable in the same ports on vessels of the United States of America.

The same duties shall be paid on the importation into the United Mexican States, of any article, the growth, produce, or manufacture of the United States of America, whether such importation shall be in Mexican vessels or in vessels of the United States of America; and the same duties shall be paid on the importation into the United States of America, of any article, the growth, produce, or manufacture of Mexico, whether such importation shall be in vessels of the United States of America or in Mexican vessels. The same duties shall be paid, and the same bounties and drawbacks allowed, on the exportation to Mexico of any articles, the growth, produce, or manufacture of the United States of America, whether such exportation shall be in Mexican vessels or in vessels of the United States of America; and the same duties shall be paid, and the same bounties and drawbacks allowed, on the exportation of any articles, the growth, produce, or manufacture of Mexico, to the United States of America, whether such exportation shall be in vessels of the United States of America or in Mexican vessels.

All merchants, captains, or commanders of vessels, and other citizens of the United States of America, shall have full liberty, in the United Mexican States, to direct or manage themselves their own affairs, or to commit them to the management of whomsoever they may think proper, either as broker, factor, agent, or interpreter; nor shall they be obliged to employ for the aforesaid purposes any other persons than those employed by Mexicans, nor to pay them higher salaries or remuneration than such as are in like cases paid by Mexicans: and absolute freedom shall be allowed in all cases to the buyer and seller to bargain and fix the prices of any goods, wares, or merchandise imported into, or exported from, the United Mexican States, as they may think proper; observing the laws, usages, and customs of the country. The citizens of Mexico shall enjoy the same privileges in the states and territories of the United States of America, being subject to the same conditions.

The citizens of neither of the contracting parties shall be liable to any embargo, nor shall their vessels, cargoes, merchandise, or effects, be detained for any military expedition, nor for any public or private purpose whatsoever, without a corresponding compensation.

The citizens of both countries, respectively, shall be exempt from compulsory service in the army or navy; nor shall they be subjected to any other charges, or contributions, or taxes, than such as are paid by the citizens of the states in which they reside.

Whenever the citizens of either of the contracting parties shall be forced to seek refuge or asylum in the rivers, bays, ports, or dominions of the other with their vessels, whether merchant or of war, public or private, through stress of weather, pursuit of pirates or enemies, they shall be received and treated with humanity, with the precautions which may be deemed expedient on the part of the respective governments in order to avoid fraud, giving to them all favour and protection for repairing their vessels, procuring provisions, and placing themselves in a situation to continue their voyage without obstacle or hindrance of any kind.

All vessels, merchandise, or effects, belonging to the citizens of one of the contracting parties, which may be captured by pirates, whether within the limits of its jurisdiction or on the high seas, and may be carried into or found in the rivers, bays, port , or dominions of the other, shall be delivered up to the owners, they proving, in due and proper form, their rights before the competent tribunal; it being well understood that the claim shall be made within one year, counting from the capture of said vessels or merchandise, by the parties themselves, or their attorneys, or by the agents of the respective governments.

When any vessel belonging to the citizens of either of the contracting parties shall be wrecked, foundered, or shall suffer any damage on the coasts or within the dominions of the other, there shall be given to it all the assistance and protection in the same manner which is usual and customary with the vessels of the nation where the damage happens; permitting them to unload the said vessel, if necessary, of its merchandise effects, with the precautions which may be deemed expedient on the part of the respective governments, in order to avoid fraud, without exacting for it any duty, impost, or contribution whatever, until they be exported.

In whatever relates to the succession of [personal] estates, either by will or *ab intestato* [and the right of] disposal of such property, of whatever sort or denomination it may be, by sale, donation, exchange, or testament, or in any other manner whatsoever, the citizens of the two contracting parties shall enjoy, in their respective states and territories, the same privileges, exemptions, liberties and rights as native citizens; and shall not be charged, in any of these respects, with other or higher duties or imposts, than those which are now or may hereafter be paid by the citizens of the power in whose territories they may reside.

It shall be lawful for the citizens of the United States of America, and of the United Mexican States respectively, to sail with their vessels with all manner of security and liberty, no distinction being made who are the owners of the merchandise laden thereon, from any port to the places of those who now are or may hereafter be at enmity with the United States of America or with the United Mexican States. It shall likewise be lawful for the aforesaid citizens respectively to sail with their vessels and merchandise, before mentioned, and to trade with the same liberty and security from the places, ports, and havens of those who are enemies of both or either party, without any opposition or disturbance whatsoever, not only directly from the places of the enemy, before mentioned, to neutral places, but also from one place belonging to an enemy to another place belonging to an enemy, whether they be under the jurisdiction of the same government or under several. And it is hereby stipulated that free ships shall also give freedom to goods, and that every thing shall be deemed free and exempt which shall be found on board the vessels belonging to the citizens of either of the contracting parties, although the whole lading or any part thereof should appertain to the enemies of either, contraband goods being always excepted. It is also agreed that the same liberty be extended to persons who are on board a free vessel, so that, although they be enemies to either party, they shall not be made prisoners, or taken out of that free vessel, unless they are soldiers, and in the actual service of the enemy. By the stipulation that the flag shall cover the property, the two contracting parties agree that this shall be so understood with respect to those powers who recognise this principle; but if either of the two contracting parties shall be at war with a third party, and the other neutral, the flag of the neutral shall cover the property of enemies whose governments acknowledge this principle, and not of others.

It is likewise agreed that in the case where the neutral flag of one of the contracting parties shall protect the property of the enemies of the other, by virtue of the above stipulation, it shall always be understood that the neutral property found on board such enemies' vessels shall be held and considered as enemies' property, and as such shall be liable to detention and confiscation, except such property as was put on board such vessel before the declaration of war, or even afterwards, if it were done without the knowledge of it: but the contracting parties agree that four months having elapsed after the declaration, their citizens shall not plead ignorance thereof; on the contrary, if the flag of the neutral does not protect the enemies' property, in that case the goods and merchandise embarked in such enemy's vessel shall be free.

All other merchandise and things not comprehended in the articles of contraband expressly enumerated and classified as above, shall be held and considered as free, and subjects of free and lawful commerce, so that they may be carried and transported in the freest manner by both the contracting parties, even to places belonging to an enemy, excepting only those places which are at that time besieged or blockaded; and to avoid all doubt in that particular, it is declared that those places only are besieged or blockaded, which are actually besieged or blockaded by a belligerant force capable of preventing the entry of the neutral.

The articles of contraband before enumerated and classified, which may be found in a vessel bound for the enemy's port, shall be subject to detention and confiscation, leaving free the rest of the cargo and the vessel, that the owners may dispose of them as they see proper. No vessels of either of the two nations shall be detained on the high seas on account of having on board articles of contraband, whenever the master, captain, or supercargo of said vessel will deliver up the articles of contraband to the captor, unless the quantity of such articles be so great and of so large a bulk, that they cannot be received on board the capturing vessel without great inconvenience; but in this, and in all other cases of just detention, the vessel detained shall be sent to the nearest convenient and safe port for trial and judgment, according to law.

For the greater security of the intercourse between the citizens of the United States of America and of the United Mexican States, it is agreed now for then, that if there should be at any time hereafter an interruption of the friendly relations which now exist, or a war unhappily break out between the two contracting parties, there shall be allowed the term of six months to the merchants residing on the coast, and one year to those residing in the interior of the states and territories of each other respectively, to arrange their business, dispose of their effects, or transport them wheresoever they may please, giving them a safe conduct to protect them to the port they may designate. Those citizens who may be established in the states and territories aforesaid, exercising any other occupation or trade, shall be permitted to remain in the uninterrupted enjoyment of their liberty and property, so long as they conduct themselves peaceably, and do not commit any offence against the laws; and their goods and effects, of whatever class and condition they may be, shall not be subject to any embargo or sequestration whatever, nor to any charge nor tax other than may be established upon similar goods and effects belonging to the citizens of the state in which they reside respectively; nor shall the debts between individuals, nor moneys in the public funds, or in public or private banks, nor shares in companies, be confiscated, embargoed, or detained.

The said consuls shall have power to require the assistance of the authorities of the country, for the arrest, detention, and custody of deserters from the public and private vessels of their country; and for that purpose, they shall address themselves to the courts, judges, and officers competent, and shall demand the said deserters in writing, proving, by an exhibition of the register of the vessel, or ship's roll, or other public documents, that the man or men demanded were part of said crews; and on this demand so proved, (saving always where the contrary is proved,) the delivery shall not be refused. Such deserters, when arrested, shall be placed at the disposal of the said consuls, and may be put in the public prisons at the request and expense of those who reclaim them, to be sent to the vessels to which they belonged, or to others of the same nation. But, if they be not sent back within two months, to be counted from the day of their arrest, they shall be set at liberty, and shall not be again arrested for the same cause.

Commercial regulations—Aliens.—The master of any vessel coming from a foreign port, shall immediately on his arrival in any of the ports of the republic, declare in writing to the chief of the maritime custom-house, the number of passengers he has on board, the country to which they belong, their trade or occupation, and the place where they embarked. The penalty for neglect to comply with this regulation, or the making a false statement, is $100, and an additional fine of $20 for each passenger omitted in the report. The vessel may be detained until the penalty be paid. Seamen whose names are entered on the roll are not considered as passengers.

Every foreigner shall, before he disembarks, declare his name, age, stature, place of birth, from whence he came, his destination, the object of his voyage, and his profession, which, when executed by the head of a family, will be sufficient for the women and children thereof.

The declaration mentioned above must be in writing, and signed by the person making the same.

This formality being complied with, the collector shall give to the foreigner a permit to disembark, subject, however, to the following rules:

1. That no Spaniard or subject of the Spanish government shall enter the republic.

2. That any foreigner provided with a passport from the general government may disembark.

3. That the citizens of the new states of America, and the subjects of nations who may have agents officially accredited to the republic, may also land, having passports granted or examined by any Mexican agent at the place of embarkation, or on security of their consul in the port where they may arrive, or on that of any Mexican citizen.

The subjects of nations who are not comprehended in the foregoing paragraph, shall only be permitted to land with a passport of the general government, or with one granted or examined by any Mexican agent residing in a foreign country.

The foreigner to whom such permit is granted, must, within 24 hours after having landed, present himself to the civil authority of the port.

Any foreigner permitted to introduce himself into the republic as aforesaid, shall, within one month thereafter, solicit of the supreme government, a *carta de seguridad,* (card of safety,) to remain in, and pass through the same for the period of one year; in order to obtain which, a certificate will be required from the officially accredited agent of the applicant, stating that he is a subject or citizen of the nation he represents, as also his occupation or profession.

Every foreigner, whatever his passport may be, must present himself to the civil authority of the place where he may have resided more than eight days; and, also, whenever he may change his place of residence. Non-compliance with that provision subjects the party to a fine of $20.

Foreigners introduced and established agreeably to the regulations herein prescribed, shall be under the protection of the laws, and enjoy the same civil rights that are conceded by said laws to Mexican citizens, with the exception of acquiring real estates, which can only be held by citizens.*

Any foreigner who shall disembark and introduce himself into the territory of the republic contrary to the provisions of this decree, shall be expelled therefrom. As also any foreigner who shall be adjudged guilty of having used, for the purpose of his disembarkation, any document belonging to another, or for having suppressed or falsified any of the statements required, or for having counterfeited or altered any passport or *carta de seguridad.*

Every foreigner wishing to leave the republic, must make application for the proper passport, either to the general government or the civil authority of the state in which he may be.

The supreme government, as well as its agents abroad, shall demand $2 for a passport, either to enter or depart from the republic; and $1 for the granting or renewal of each *carta de seguridad,* and $4 for each certificate of signature.

---

* This exception does not extend to lands belonging to mining establishments in which aliens may hold shares. Aliens may purchase and hold lands by permission of the general government for federal territory; or of the state governments for state territory. By the colonization law, aliens may also hold land, but one fourth part of the colonists must be Mexicans.

All foreigners, being the subjects or citizens of nations having accredited agents in the republic, must apply through their medium, for the *carta de seguridad*, or for a passport to leave the country.

Cartas de seguridad must be renewed annually, in the month of January; applications for which renewals must pass through the accredited agent of the applicant.

It has been frequently and earnestly recommended by the accredited agents of the United States residing in Mexico, that the passports of all Americans going to that country, should invariably be certified by the Mexican minister in the United States, or by the consul of the port of departure. The observance of this form will preserve the party from infinite vexation and hardship.

And it is well to add that owners of vessels should, on no occasion, fail to have their ship's papers verified by the signature of the resident Mexican consul.

Measurement of vessels.—Every master of a vessel must obtain from the captain of the port a certificate of her tonnage, which must be presented at the custom-house, when paying the duty.

The tonnage duty on all foreign vessels is 17 reals per ton.

The anchorage duty is abolished.

Regulations.—No foreign vessel is permitted to carry on the coasting trade.

Any merchant vessel arriving in the ports of the republic, merely to procure supplies for her crew, or to avoid average, and not embark or disembark articles of merchandise, is allowed to be admitted for the time which may be absolutely necessary to supply her wants, and is subject to no other charges than the customary port dues payable by national vessels. She is to receive an inspector on board during her stay.

Every vessel anchoring in a port of the republic, shall deliver to the custom-house three copies of her manifest, to be signed by the interventors;* one of said copies is to be delivered to the commissary general, to be transmitted to the secretary of the treasury; one remains in the possession of the treasurer of the customs, and the third in that of the appraisers.

The manifests of every cargo shall specify the marks, numbers, and contents of each package, the bales, cases, barrels, or other parcels; expressing, in general, their contents, and writing the numbers in letters and figures, with their corresponding marks and numbers.

If the manifest be not presented whilst the vessel is in the act of anchoring, the vessel, with all her appurtenances, shall be confiscated, always excepting her cargo.

The omission in the manifest, of a bale, barrel, case, or any other package of the cargo, shall be punished with a fine equal to the value of the parcel omitted; and if the person responsible for the manifest

* The interventors are officers appointed by the state in which the custom-house is located. They watch over the execution of the commercial regulations; prosecute breaches of the law, and report to their respective states; the authorities of which make to the general governments such communications on the proceedings of these officers as they deem proper.

does not pay the same, execution shall be levied on his effects, or the equipments of the vessel, or upon the vessel itself. If the omission shall consist of more than six bales, cases, or other parcels, the vessel shall be subject to confiscation.

Besides the general manifest, another manifest, in triplicate, shall be presented, of each importation, signed by the exporter, minutely expressing the contents of each case, bale, barrel, or other parcel, according to their several marks, to be delivered to the officers at the time of the anchoring of the vessel. These particular manifests must be certified by the consular agent of the republic nearest to the port from whence the cargo is despatched.

Every article which is not entered in the prescribed manner, or which does not conform to the foregoing provisions, in quality or quantity, is liable to confiscation.

A failure to present any of the manifests, as directed, or to comply with any other of the requisitions relating to them, is punished by a fine of from $1 to $25, where no other penalty is imposed, for which the vessel, or the owners of the goods are, according to the circumstances, responsible.

All expenses of landing and conveyance of merchandise to the public stores, must be paid by the respective consignees.

Heavy or bulky packages of goods may be despatched on the custom-house wharf, the interventors and custom-house officers being present; but this privilege is in no case to be extended, for any large amount, to linens, cottons, silks, woollens, small wares, &c. And if those officers suspect fraud, they can immediately order such packages to the custom-house.

The duty of average, and all others, under whatever denomination, except such as are mentioned in this act, payable to the general government, are suppressed.

Importers are responsible for the whole amount of the duties on merchandise imported by them, which shall be divided into two equal instalments; the first payable in 40 days after the landing, and the second at the end of 40 days after the first becomes due.

The collector will deliver no merchandise until the duties are paid, or a satisfactory bond given for them.

No return or reduction on duties actually paid into the custom-house shall be made, except in cases of error of account or payment.

The reshipment of merchandise imported shall not exempt it from the payment of the duties imposed in the tariff, or that may hereafter be imposed by law.

The collectors and receivers of the maritime custom-houses shall select from each class of merchandise imported, such packages as they may deem proper, for examination; and in case they do not agree with the specifications of the manifest, the examination shall be continued by pieces.

The duties on damaged merchandise shall be deducted in proportion to the injury sustained, being first examined by the inspectors in the presence of the collector.

The provisions of the tariff are not to affect special treaties of commerce entered into with foreign nations.

When seizures shall be made on the coasts, rivers, lakes, or harbours, of goods that are prohibited or fraudulently entered, or for other sufficient cause, the vessel, boat, or other craft, with their appurtenances, shall also be seized, and with the goods, be confiscated, whether they come from a part of the republic or from beyond seas.

Such seizures are regularly adjudicated, and the vessels and goods sold at auction. The proceeds, after the payment of the duties, are distributed among the captors, officers, and the government, the latter receiving one half.

In addition to the other penalties, the introducers of prohibited goods, or of such in which the government has the monopoly, shall pay a fine on the first conviction equal to one fifth of the value thereof. This fine is doubled on the second conviction, and trebled on the third.

Exemptions.—Foreign merchandise entered at the custom-house of Yucatan, or in the territories of California, pays but three fifth parts of the duties specified in the tariff; but if it be transported from thence to any other ports or frontier custom-houses of the republic, the remaining two fifths are then exacted. The same provisions apply to goods entered at the frontier custom-houses in the state of Chiapas.

The section of the law which exempted from one sixth of the duties goods imported direct from the place of origin in national vessels, is repealed by an act of 27th May, 1831.

National produce is exempt from duties in the maritime custom-houses.

Exportation of gold and silver bullion.—In future no person will be refused the necessary permission for the exportation of these metals through any of the ports of the republic.

The states from which these articles are exported are allowed to impose certain duties.

Gold and silver bullion in bars, double bars, &c., when transported from the interior to the ports of the republic, must be numbered and impressed with a mark designating its weight and purity, and accompanied with certificates of the payment of the above mentioned duties, and those of the mine.

Officers designated by the respective states and the general government shall give the certificates referred to.

Gold and silver bullion, which may be found in any port, unaccompanied with the requisites specified in the two preceding paragraphs, or the weight and purity of which is not conformable to the said documents, shall be confiscated, unless where the non-conformity arises from the fault of the proper officers.

The only duty on gold and silver bullion payable in the maritime or frontier custom-houses, through which the exportation may be made, shall be 7 per centum, *ad valorem.*

Clearance.—By a notification of the secretary of state, of the 11th August, 1830, foreign consuls are requested to retain in their possession the customary papers appertaining to the vessels of their respective nations, until a certificate of clearance from the custom-house be produced to them by the master or consignee.

The following ports of Mexico, and the departments appertaining thereto, have been closed to foreign commerce, by a decree of the Mexican government, dated 2d March, 1837:

On the Gulf of Mexico—Bacalar, Goatzacoalco, Alvarado. Matagorda, and Galveston.

On the Pacific—Huatulco, Manzanilla, Natividad, Mazatlan, La Paz, Loreto, San Diego, and San Francisco.

NAPLES,

Situated on the bay of that name, is well placed for commerce, and has all the luxuries of life in great profusion. Lat. 40° 51′ N. Long. 14° 11′ E.

The chief articles of manufacture are silk stockings, soap, boxes, and other ornamental articles made from lava, marble, minerals, and fossils of most kinds. The other productions are brimstone, fruits, wines, and above all Gallipoli oil.

The imports are colonial produce, linens, and salt fish of every sort, kind, and quality.

Articles of export are purchased for ready money. On imported articles, 2 to 4 months credit is generally given; and on British manufactured goods, even longer.

The charges on sales, including commissions, are generally from six to eight per cent.

Besides the duties specified in the tariff, an additional duty is levied at the custom-house at Naples on each package,

Amounting from 6 to 25 ducats	- -	11 grains.
" " 26 to 50 "	- -	22 "
" " 51 to 100 "	- -	33 "
" " 101 and upwards,	- -	44 "

And a duty of seal on each package exported, containing a duty of more than 10 carlines.

Goods deposited in the public warehouse pay for 1 month, per cantajo, 11 grains.

For 2 months,	- - - - - -	17 grains.
" 3 "	- - - - - -	23 "
" 4 "	- - - - - -	28 "
And for every subsequent month,	- -	11 "
On re-exportation, each bale pays	- -	22 "

If the goods are re-opened, the duty, per cantajo, will be 10 grains. The importation of fire and side arms, &c., is prohibited.

Extract from the Laws of Navigation and Commerce of the kingdom of the Two Sicilies, established by a decree dated February 28th, 1826.

The masters of all foreign vessels arriving in our ports, after having obtained the quarantine permit, must deposit their register at the custom-house, for which a receipt will be given. For duty of deposit, receipt, and certificate, fifty-five grains will be charged.

If there be a consul of the nation to which the vessel belongs, residing in the port, the custom-house officers, after having verified the register, and the duty being paid thereon, shall return the same to the captain, to be deposited with his consul; and should there be no consul or vice-consul of his nation residing in the port, the register shall remain in the custom-house, and not be restored to the captain until twenty-four hours preceding the departure of the vessel.

On all vessels, national or foreign, that shall anchor in the ports or roadsteads of the kingdom of the Two Sicilies, a tonnage duty shall be exacted, with the reservation of the exceptions which shall be hereafter noticed. This duty of tonnage is exacted from the vessel, and not from the cargo.

Vessels which are forced to enter our ports by stress of weather, or to procure clean bills of health, or other imperious circumstances, shall be exempt from tonnage duty, provided they make no operation of commerce. The embarking or disembarking of articles necessary for the maintenance of the crew, or service of the vessel, shall not be considered operations of commerce.

Vessels entering our ports by distress of weather, or damage suffered at sea, shall not be exempt from tonnage duty, whether they shall have discharged the cargo, or part thereof, unless the same shall be declared by experts officially appointed, as perishable, by being reshipped.

Vessels arriving from suspected places, and not permitted by the health officer to enter for trade, shall also be exempt from duty of tonnage.

All vessels stranded or abandoned by their captains, are likewise exempt from the duty of tonnage, notwithstanding their cargoes should be saved.

Flags of truce, cartels, or such other vessels as bring despatches for the government, shall also be exempt from the tonnage duty; provided, however, they have not any portion of merchandise on board.

Private armed vessels, or their prizes, having merchandise on board, belonging to the prize, are also exempt from tonnage duty. Vessels taken by armed cruisers, and declared unlawful prizes, are likewise exempt from the tonnage duty, provided no sale of the cargo, or any part thereof, is made in the kingdom: nevertheless, vessels taken by armed vessels, declared lawful prizes, shall not be exempt from the duty of tonnage.

Foreign vessels that shall enter any of the ports of the kingdom of the Two Sicilies, although they shall remain less than twenty-four hours, must pay the duty of tonnage at the rate of forty grains per ton.

Foreign vessels of war shall be exempt from the duties of tonnage, provided they are engaged in no trade or commerce; in such case, the tonnage duty, and every other duty of navigation, will be exacted. The aforesaid vessels arriving in our ports to take on board munitions or provisions, for fleets or squadrons stationed elsewhere, and having our sanction therefor, shall not be considered as trading.

Foreign vessels, empty or laden, having paid the tonnage duty in one port, shall pay the half of the same duty in every other port of our kingdom at which they may arrive, unless having taken in a cargo of indigenous merchandise, when, this circumstance being verified, no additional tonnage duties shall be exacted at any other ports to which they may proceed.

All foreign vessels that shall be hauled on shore in any ports of the kingdom of the Two Sicilies, for the purpose of repairing, shall pay a duty of six carlins per ton.

A bill of clearance shall be given to every national or foreign vessel that shall depart from any port of our two kingdoms.

Every foreign vessel that shall depart from any port of our kingdom, shall be provided with a passport; the same shall be granted by the officers of the customs, for which one ducat will be exacted.

Foreign vessels which shall enter into the port of Messina, shall be there considered, as to the rights of navigation, as vessels bearing our national flag; consequently, foreign vessels shall be subjected to the payment of the navigation duties which are imposed on vessels of the kingdom; and in cases in which the latter are exempt from duty, foreign vessels shall be equally exempt.

All captains of vessels, either national or foreign, that shall enter into any of our ports or roads, shall be obliged, within twenty-four hours after the arrival, to make their declaration to the officers of the health, customs, marine and police, under a penalty of not less than 200 ducats. In the said declaration, mention shall be made of the port from whence the vessel proceeded, the nature of the cargo, the particular incidents that may have occurred during the voyage; and the captains must, also, answer to all the questions made to them according to the form annexed to the present decree.

Captains of our national vessels, when arriving in foreign ports, in which our consuls may reside, shall present themselves to the same, and exhibit to them the register and roll of equipage; and, at the same time, make a declaration of the incidents that may have occurred during the voyage.

Exclusive of the papers demanded by the present decree, every captain departing from any one of the ports of the kingdom to another, or to a foreign port, shall be provided with a roll of equipage.

No vessel, national or foreign, shall depart before the captain shall have exhibited at the health office his bill of clearance.

Coasting trade.—The coasting trade is restricted to vessels bearing the royal flag. Foreign vessels, however, discharging their cargoes, or portions thereof in one port, or taking in cargo, or part thereof, being the productions of the kingdom, and proceeding to another port or ports of the same, are not considered as subject to the coasting restriction.

From the 1st of January, 1825, the circulation of articles, indigenous and foreign, shall be free, both by sea and land, throughout our two dominions, in the same manner as is now in practice in the kingdom of Naples; consequently, merchandise of all kinds may be taken coastwise from one place to another in Sicily, without payment of duty of import or export.

The custom-houses of Naples and Palermo being depôts of foreign merchandise, merchandise of this sort, coming to either, from other ports of the kingdoms, shall be subject to the duties of import, except such, however, as is provided with the *bollo* (seal) of the frontier custom-houses.

It is forbidden to send coastwise to Sicily from the ports of the kingdom of Naples, those productions thereof that are subject to the duties of export, when in Sicily they are exempt or subject to greater duties. It is likewise forbidden to export coastwise from Sicily to the kingdom of Naples, those articles which are there subject to a greater duty of export.

Prohibitions.—It is forbidden to introduce in the states, within or without the Phare, after a delay of six months from the publication of this decree, any description of foreign manufactures, enclosed or packed in cases of tin, or of other metal, or of earth.

Consequently, merchandise of this description, found in such packages, after the expiration of the above delay, will be considered as contraband, and will be confiscated.

Are not comprised, as among the packages designated above, cases of wood lined with tin, usually employed for the transportation of velvets and tissues of great value, and also tubes of tin in which are contained tulles of cotton and laces.

Quarantine.—The health office of Naples, for the purpose of facilitating the trade of American vessels arriving in that port, has determined that such of them as come furnished with certificates from Neapolitan consuls, showing the healthy condition of the place of departure and its environs, shall observe the following rules:

If the vessels are empty, they will be merely subject to observation for some days.

If laden with goods not capable of conveying contagion, they will be subjected to a few days observation, and allowed to discharge their goods in the mean time, before obtaining *pratique.*

If laden with goods capable of conveying contagion, they shall be subject to fourteen days' quarantine.

If they bring no certificates from Neapolitan consuls, the regulations will be enforced towards them, and they will be subjected to a quarantine of from twenty-one to twenty-eight days.

NEW GRANADA.

This country was formerly part of the republic of Colombia.

All vessels, whether national or foreign, must, before they can trade on any part of the Atlantic coast of New Granada, first enter some port near the part of the coast on which they wish to trade, and obtain a license to that effect; for which they must pay at the rate of one dollar and a half per ton. The license will be accompanied by receipt for said payment, without which papers, any vessel found trading on the coast will be confiscated with her whole cargo.

All vessels will be confiscated, with their whole cargoes, which are found trading with the Indians on said coast, in any of the articles known as contraband of war, such as arms, ammunition, war equipments, &c.—even though they should have obtained the above license and receipt.

The coasting trade can only be carried on in vessels of New Granada.

The coast referred to, extends from the confines of Venezuela, near Cape De Vela, to the Caman, near Cape Gracias a Dios, and comprehends what are known as the Goarjira, the Darien, and part of the Mosquito coasts.

The citizens of the United States have a right by treaty to frequent all the coasts and countries of the republic of Colombia, and reside and trade there in all sorts of produce, manufactures and merchandise, and shall pay no other or greater duties, charges or fees, whatsoever, than the most favoured nation is, or shall be obliged to pay ; and they shall enjoy all the rights, privileges and exemptions in navigation and commerce, which the most favoured nation does or shall enjoy, submitting themselves, nevertheless, to the laws, decrees and usages there established, and to which are submitted the subjects and citizens of the most favoured nations.

Merchants, commanders of vessels, and other citizens of both countries, to manage themselves their own business, and to be treated as citizens of the country in which they reside, or at least to be placed on a footing with those of the most favoured nation.

The citizens of neither of the parties to be liable to any embargo, nor to detention of vessels, cargoes or effects, for any military expedition, nor for any public or private purpose, without a sufficient indemnification.

If the citizens of either party seek refuge in the domains of the other, from stress of weather, pirates, or enemies, they and their vessels are to be received as friends, allowed to make repairs, procure provisions, and continue their voyage.

It shall be lawful for the citizens of the parties to sail with their vessels, with all manner of liberty and security, no distinction being made as to who are the owners of the goods laden thereon, from any port to the places of those who now are, or hereafter may be, at enmity with either of the contracting parties ; and that free ships shall also give freedom to goods, although the whole or a part of the lading may belong to the enemies of either ; contraband of war always excepted. It is provided, however, that this stipulation shall be understood as applying to those powers only who recognise this principle.

Where the neutral flag of one of the parties shall protect the property of the enemies of the other, by virtue of the above stipulation, it shall always be understood that the neutral property found on board such enemy's vessel, shall be deemed to be enemy's property, unless it were shipped before the declaration of war, or without the knowledge of its existence. After the expiration, however, of two months from the declaration of war, such ignorance will not avail. If the flag of the neutral does not protect the enemy's property, then the goods of the neutral embarked in such enemies' vessels shall be free.

All other merchandise not included in the list of contraband articles, shall be considered as free, and may be carried to the places of an enemy not blockaded. It is declared that those places only are besieged or blockaded, which are actually attacked by a belligerent force capable of preventing the entry of the neutral.

Articles of contraband which may be found in a vessel bound for an enemy's port, are subject to detention and confiscation, leaving free the rest of the cargo and the vessel, to the disposition of the owner. In cases of detention, the vessel shall be sent to the nearest safe port for trial.

Vessels sailing for an enemy's port, not knowing that it is blockaded, may be turned away, but shall not be detained; nor shall vessels that entered the port prior to the blockade, be restrained from quitting it with their cargoes; nor if found there after the surrender of the place, shall they be confiscated, but are to be restored to their owners.

Regulations.—Duties on goods paying an ad valorem duty, are calculated in the following manner, viz.: to the first cost of the goods in the foreign port whence the exportation is made, shall be added 20 per cent., and the duties shall be calculated and collected on that amount.

The invoices of all goods paying an ad valorem duty, must bear at the foot thereof, the oath of the owner of the goods, if he resides in the port or place where they were purchased; and if not, then of his agent, who purchased them, affirming that the value in the invoice is the true cost thereof in said port or place; which oath must be certified by the consul, vice consul or commercial agent of the government; or if no such officer resides at the port, then by the consul, vice consul or commercial agent of some friendly power, having a treaty of commerce with the republic; and if there be none such, then it must be certified by three merchants of the port whence the shipment is made.

Whenever any goods are imported not accompanied by the invoice, or the invoice shall not have the requisites prescribed above, the goods shall be valued at the current price in the port to which they are brought, and on that valuation the duties shall be calculated and collected. From this provision are excepted goods saved from shipwreck.

The owner, agent, or consignee, who shall receive goods from a foreign port, shall, immediately on the arrival of the vessel making the importation, present the invoice and bill of lading, and make oath before the proper officer of the customs, that the invoice and bill of lading which he delivers, are the originals which he has received.

If the administrator of the customs shall suspect that the goods have been put down in the invoice at less than the true value in the port whence they were exported, he shall cause them to be valued at the prices which they would bear at the place whence they came, at the time of exportation; and if the value thus assessed should exceed the value in the invoice by 20 per cent., then 50 per cent. shall be put upon the estimated value, and the duties shall be calculated and collected thereon: provided, however, when the estimated value as above shall not exceed the invoice value by 20 per cent., then the estimated value shall be considered the true value.

Two persons are named by the president to act as valuers in each port, who shall not be merchants. Whenever the owner or consignee is dissatisfied with the estimate fixed by the valuers, he may select two merchants of the place, who shall proceed, with the two first, again to examine and value the goods, and shall make a report of their proceedings to the collector; and if the owner or consignee be still dissatisfied, he may appeal to the governor of the province, whose determination shall be final.

Goods saved from shipwreck shall be valued at the current price at the port of exportation; and the same rule shall be observed whenever any deduction of duties is claimed on account of injury to the goods during the voyage.

The following rules are to be observed in the payment of duties, and on the arrival of the cargo, whether the goods pay a specific or ad valorem duty: The duties on importations shall be paid by halves, in two instalments; the first at the expiration of three months; the second at the expiration of six months; to be counted from the day of entry.

The owner or consignee of the goods must give bond for the duties, with two securities, residents of the place, to be approved of by the administrator of the customs.

If the payment of the duty is not punctually made, the administrator is to proceed immediately against the debtors, who, besides the costs, shall also pay an interest of one per centum a month upon the amount of the duty, from the day on which it was due, until paid. If the duty is paid in advance, a discount is made of one half of one per centum a month.

Masters of all vessels must, at the moment of entering the port, deliver to the officer who shall go on board a signed manifest of the number of packages belonging to himself, or to merchants, or passengers, with their marks, and also declare, under oath, that the manifest contains all those which he received on board.

The collector is to point out one from each ten in the invoice, which he shall cause to be opened and examined, and the goods valued, and 50 per cent. is to be added to the valuation, upon which the duties are then to be calculated. If any goods are found which are not mentioned at all in the invoice, the whole package in which they are, is forfeited.

It is provided in the laws, that when a general description of goods would embrace them at a certain rule of duty, and under a particular description, they are charged at a different rate; that rate under the last description is the true one.

All vessels arriving in the ports of the republic, must have the names of all persons on board on the roll, and they must also have passports, signed by the consul at the place of departure; every case of neglect in this particular, subjects the vessel to a penalty of $100.

By a decree of 14th January, 1833, it is ordered that vessels wishing to trade with the coast which extends to the Escudo de Veragua and Culebras river, including those of Darien, from San Blas to Caman, and that of Goarjira, except that part of the Mosquito coast which belongs to the republic of Central America, whether said vessels be national or foreign, must enter one of the ports nearest the said coasts, which has been declared open to foreign trade, to ask for a passport, pay the duty of 12 reals per ton, and obtain the documents which prove the entrance and payment; without which papers, any vessel found trading on the coast, is subject to forfeiture.

No vessel, whether foreign or national, must trade with the natives on the aforesaid coasts of Goarjira, Darien and Mosquito, in articles contraband of war; and those which may be found so doing, will be confiscated, with their whole cargoes, notwithstanding they should have complied with all the other requisites, and have obtained the papers to prove it.

The above regulations do not include the coasting trade, which can only be carried on in national vessels.

Export duties.—The exportation of the following articles is prohibited, viz.: platina, gold in dust or bars, and silver in bullion.

From this prohibition is excepted gold and silver which may be extracted from the mines in the "department of the isthmus," or which may be brought there from any foreign country. Such gold or silver may be exported by paying a duty of three per cent. on the gold which has previously paid the extraction duty, and six per cent. on that which has not paid that duty; and by paying 50 cents a mark* on the silver. This department embraces the provinces on the isthmus of Panama, including Forto Bello and Chagres, on the Atlantic, and Panama on the Pacific ocean.

Tobacco cannot be purchased for exportation from the growers; it is a monopoly in the hands of the government, and can be purchased only from its agents. This is the only monopoly retained by the government.

No bounty is allowed on the exportation of any article.

There is no drawback, properly so called, allowed upon the re-exportation of any imported article. A system of warehousing which does not require that the duties should be paid, or bonds given for them, has been partially introduced.

When the goods are taken out of the warehouse for sale in the country, the import duties are to be paid on the same terms, and at the same periods which are fixed by the general law. The time is to be calculated from the day on which the goods are withdrawn from deposit.

If the goods are taken out for re-exportation, there is no import duty to be paid; but on all goods deposited in warehouses, there is due a deposit duty, at the rate of 4 per cent. per annum on the amounts of the invoices, to be calculated from the day on which they were warehoused, to the day on which they are withdrawn for sale or re-exportation. This duty is to be paid at the time of taking the goods out.

When the goods are withdrawn from deposit for the purpose of re-exportation to any other port of the republic, the officer of the customs is to deliver to the owner or consignee a copy of the invoice,

* The mark is eight ounces.

expressing on it that the goods mentioned therein have not paid the import duties.

There is to be paid on all goods passing over the isthmus of Panama, from the one ocean to the other, a transit duty of two per cent., to be calculated on the value of the invoice, which is to be delivered, certified, and sworn to, agreeably to the provisions of the importation law.

The coasting trade from one port to another of the republic, is prohibited to all foreign vessels.

Tonnage duties.—The following rates are established in the payment of tonnage duties:

A national vessel, $12\frac{1}{2}$ cents per ton.

A foreign vessel, 50 cents per ton.

A national vessel of 20 tons and under, free.

National vessels, proceeding from one port of the republic to another, for each ton over 20 tons, $6\frac{1}{4}$ cents.

On the entry of the vessels into port, the proper officer shall receive from the master or supercargo the register; and on the sailing of the vessel, is to redeliver it to him, if the tonnage duty has been paid. Whenever a consul or commercial agent of the nation to which the vessel belongs, resides in the port, then the officer, after having received the register, and after having ascertained the tonnage of the vessel, shall pass over the register to the consul or commercial agent, upon his receipt, and undertaking that the duty shall be paid within ten days after the entry of the vessel.

The prohibition of aniseed and its essences, of sugar, molasses, cocoa and coffee, does not extend to the ports of the isthmus, where they may be introduced for the consumption of that portion of the inhabitants of the republic, or for transit from the Atlantic or from the Pacific oceans: paying, in those cases, corresponding duties, either of consumption or transit.

Foreign goods or merchandise crossing the isthmus from the Atlantic to the Pacific, or *vice versa*, shall pay two per cent. transit duty on the amount of the invoice, which is to be presented, sworn to and certified, in conformity with the existing laws.

The executive power will prescribe the rules which shall regulate the manner of admitting cargoes imported at the isthmus for transit to the Pacific, and will direct such precautionary measures as shall prevent such goods as are imported for transit, from being consumed in the country without paying the consumption duties.

Packages shall not be liable to confiscation in which may be discovered any goods not expressed in the manifest, and when it shall be found that the errors or omissions in some packages are made good in the totality of the cargo, so that the manifest agrees with the whole, nor when the difference, either more or less, which results from said packages, shall not exceed the value of $50 for each $1000 of the amount of the invoice, but in all cases the corresponding duties shall be paid.

The masters of vessels shall alone be held responsible for the errors or negligences which shall happen in their ships, after the merchants have entered their cargoes according to all the prescribed forms, and have exhibited at the port of entry the certified and sworn invoice.

Decree.—From the day on which this law shall come into operation, four reals per ton shall be paid by national vessels, and eight reals by foreign vessels, which shall enter the ports of New Granada coming from foreign ports.

Vessels, as well national as foreign, coming from foreign ports, which may have entered any of the ports of New Granada, for the purpose of leaving the whole or part of their cargo, and shall afterwards proceed to another qualified port of New Granada, either with part of their cargoes, or in ballast, or with export goods, shall only pay the tonnage dues in the port where they shall have first entered, and shall not pay them in the ports where they may afterwards enter.

National vessels, not exceeding twenty tons, and coming from foreign ports, shall pay no tonnage dues.

National and foreign vessels shall pay the tonnage dues above stated, whenever they do not exceed one hundred tons. Those which exceed this tonnage up to three hundred tons, shall pay for all beyond the first hundred; the former at the rate of two reals, the latter at the rate of four reals per ton. Beyond three hundred tons, the excess shall be paid at the rate of one real per ton for national vessels, and two reals for foreign.

National vessels alone can engage in the coasting trade; and the said vessels, when occupied in this trade, shall pay no dues of tonnage, anchorage, visit, or any other recognised port dues, which specifically affect the vessel, and not the merchandise, with the exception of *pratique*, where they require it.

Whaling vessels, which come to Panama, to refresh and take in provisions, shall pay no anchorage or tonnage dues.

In the absence of merchants at the custom-house at Matuntubo, the officers of that establishment may be named as valuers, and as third persons in case of disagreement between the valuers.

There shall be no difference made as to the payment of import duties on account of the place of departure of vessels, whether they come from Europe, Asia, the United States, or the European colonies in America.

The inspection and classification of the goods shall be made immediately that the discharge of the vessel is completed, or that the cargo shall have arrived at the custom-house, in the order of precedence in which the invoices shall have been presented to the chief of the customs, so that he who shall have first presented them may demand to be first despatched. This does not exclude giving precedence of inspection and classification to articles which are wasting, or which, as in the case of combustibles, cannot be admitted into the custom-house.

When the merchant does not assent to the classification made by the customs, it shall be proceeded in by competent persons named by the chiefs of the customs and by the party interested. If the chiefs of the customs do not agree as to the classification they should make, they shall name a third, who shall make the classification, and this shall be deemed to have been made by the customs. If the chiefs do not agree as to the individual to act as third, in case of difference, they shall name another to make the election, and the nomination of the third shall be deemed to be complete, when it is certified by him who was appointed for this purpose.

With respect to the custom-house of Matuntubo, the officers of the same may be named as the competent persons mentioned in this article.

Within three days after the completion of the inspection and classification of the goods, the account or liquidation of the duties incurred shall be delivered to the party interested. In this account shall be expressed the value of the goods according to the tariff, and according to the separation of classes established by this law, and the duty corresponding to each class, with the sum total of them, as well as that of *alcabala* and commerce. The *alcabala* shall be received upon the value of the goods, according to the estimation of the tariff, with an addition of 15 per cent.

The account of the duties being delivered to the merchant, he shall have the space of three days to revise it, and make such observations upon it as he shall consider just, which he shall present to the administrator; if the chiefs of the customs deem them well founded, they will make the consequent alterations.

If at the conclusion of the three days after the delivery of the account and liquidation of the duties to the importer, he and the chiefs of the customs shall not have agreed upon one or more observations made upon the account, the importer shall, nevertheless, authenticate the documents and drafts hereafter mentioned for the amount of the account delivered by the administrator, expressing in the draft that he reserves his right to claim those portions which he considers to be not conformable with law, which right shall be duly acknowledged.

The claim mentioned in the preceding article shall be made before the governor of the province in which the custom-house is situated, within the strict period allowed to the importer to make the last payment of the duties incurred. The governor shall require from the customs the necessary information, and shall transmit this, with the application to the executive, in order that it may decide upon the case, which decision shall be strictly enforced.

The term having expired which is allowed to the importer to examine the liquidation delivered to him by the customs, he shall, forthwith, give drafts in favour of the customs for the amount of the duties, and at the dates indicated by this law, which said drafts shall be signed by the party interested, and, as guarantees, by two merchants established and of long standing in the place, or by two persons of property, in either case to the satisfaction of the customs.

With respect to the custom-house at Matuntubo, the guaranty mentioned in this article may be effectuated in the capital of the province, and with the approval of the board of revenue.

The two signatures which are required of long-established merchants, or persons of property, constitute those who execute them securities for the drawer, in the same manner as if they were the principal payers: each of them, of the whole sum, and as if they were bound by public deed of warranty.

The importers of goods which give rise to duties of imports shall execute at least as many drafts as there are dates allowed them for making their payments, and each of these drafts shall be satisfied on arriving at maturity; but, if the customs require it, the amounts which are payable at the respective dates shall be divided into several sums, and drafts shall be signed for each of them at the dates corresponding with the divided amount.

Importers of goods may pay the eighth part of the import duties which arise from them, in certificates of the floating debt charged upon the customs, and payable in conformity with article 4 of the law of the 4th of January, 1832; and this eighth part shall be included in the total amount of duties, which determines the dates which are to be allowed.

When the importer, who has reserved his right to claim one or more portions against the customs' account of liquidation, shall obtain a decision in his favour, the same customs, at sight of this definitive decision, shall immediately make him the corresponding abatement or return, as the case may be.

When the importer is a Granadine, there shall be admitted, as his sureties, merchants or persons of property in his place of residence, who may previously have bound themselves to answer for a larger amount than that of the duties incurred; but in this case, the sureties must have been previously accredited by the board of revenue of the province in which the importer resides, binding themselves to place to his account, cost, and risk, at the custom-house where the importation was made, the amounts in which he may be indebted at the maturity of the respective dates, and to pay an interest of two per cent. for every month of delay or neglect.

The dates allowed for the payment of duties, which are to run from the day on which the account and liquidation of the duties are delivered to the party interested, are the following: three days, if the duties do not exceed 50 dollars; if the duties exceed 50 dollars, and up to 500, thirty days; if they exceed 500 dollars, and up to 1,000, fifty days; from 1,000 to 2,000 dollars, half at fifty days, and the other half at one hundred days; from 2,000 to 4,000 dollars, half at seventy-five days, and the other half at one hundred and fifty days; and from 4,000 dollars upwards, a third part at seventy-five days, another third at one hundred and fifty days, and the remaining third at two hundred and twenty-five days.

All goods which are not prohibited may be imported through the qualified ports of the isthmus of Panama, without paying any duties of import, transit, &c., whenever the said goods are intended to pass, and in fact do pass, from the Atlantic to the Pacific, or from the Pacific to the Atlantic; but if the said goods are destined for the consumption of the inhabitants of the isthmus, then they shall pay the import duties.

There may be brought into the port of Panama, without paying any import duties whatever, foreign goods or merchandise, for the purpose of being exported to other parts of the globe; and the said goods and merchandise shall remain deposited in the custom-house until the day on which the exportation shall take place; and the importers shall pay for deposit duty the first year three per cent., the second year two per cent., and afterwards one per cent., remaining in other respects subject to the dispositions of the law of the 4th of April, 1826, which are extended to the port of Panama, in the same terms as has been provided with respect to the port of Carthagena, by the law of 21st March, 1832.

The invoices are to be presented within 24 hours after the captain shall have declared his intention of discharging; but, up to the moment of receiving the goods, the owners or consignees shall not be obliged to indicate the merchandise or effects which they desire to leave in the store for the purpose of being placed in deposit.

The clearances issued by the customs for goods which pass from one place to another, shall be signed by the administrator and accountant. The omission of either of these signatures shall be imputible solely to the office where it takes place, and shall in no way prejudice the owners of the goods; and the government shall exact the responsibility from the respective officers.

All goods or assets which become confiscated shall be sold by public auction, and the proceeds divided into three equal parts: one for the person making the seizure, another for the informer, and the third part for the national treasury, by way of duties.

The packages of a cargo which appear to be broken, shall be examined, and if a deficiency should be the result, the duty shall, however, be paid upon the articles which are missing.

There shall be no ground for confiscation of a package in which shall be found some articles more or less than is stated in the manifests, when in the whole of the cargo it shall be found that the deficiencies of some are made good in others, or that the excess in one is deficient in others: provided always, that the cargo in its totality is conformable with the manifests. When it is ascertained that the excess or the deficiency in the packages of a cargo does not exceed the value of fifty dollars for every thousand of the total value of the goods manifested, according to the estimate of the tariff, in this case, also, there shall be no confiscation; but in every case, the duties corresponding with that which is in excess or deficiency, shall be paid in conformity with the law.

The captains of vessels are alone responsible for the omissions and errors which may be discovered in the cargo-books, when the merchants shall have delivered their cargoes with all the prescribed formalities, and shall have exhibited at the port of entry the corresponding sworn invoices.

When, from the cargo-books which the captain shall exhibit at the time of visiting the vessel, and from the investigation of the whole cargo, there shall appear to be an excess of one or more packages, they shall be confiscated whenever the said packages shall not have been included in the invoices or manifests delivered by the respective owners or consignees of the said goods; and if a deficiency be discovered, the captain shall pay the duties corresponding to the goods so deficient.

Prohibition.—No captain of a national or foreign ship is allowed to receive on board gold in ingots or in dust, either in small or large quantities; and the captain found guilty of admitting the same on board, will subject himself to the punishment which the laws have established against defrauders.

Whenever it can be found that any vessel has conveyed gold in dust or ingots, with the knowledge of the captain, the ship shall not be again admitted into any of the harbours of the state; and the captain, at whatever time he may be seized, shall be punished as a defrauder.

It is the precise duty of the consuls and commercial agent's of New Granada, in foreign countries, to examine and search all vessels proceeding from our ports, for the purpose of ascertaining whether gold has been received on board in dust or ingots; and if it should prove to be the fact, to make a report of the same to their government, accompanied by such proof and information as they may have collected.

New ports.—In the law of 25th May, 1835, it is enacted:

There shall be established, on the Atlantic, in the province of Veragua, a port of importation and exportation at the mouth of the river Conception.

The declared ports of exportation only, on the Pacific Ocean in the same province, are the ports of Montijo, in the canton of Santiago, and of Bocachica, in that of Alanje: provided, that exportations from these ports shall take place only in vessels which have received the necessary authority from the governor of Veragua.

The provisions of the law in regard to Sabanilla, and as far as the same extend to exportations alone, are applied to these ports.

A decree of 5th June, 1835, orders the erection of a custom-house at Conception. And by another decree of the 9th of same month, the following regulations for Montijo and Bocachica.

The productions of New Granada may be exported from these ports; but no foreign merchandise can be imported into them. Agreeably to the provisions of the law of April, 1833, the exportation by the said ports, of gold in dust or bars, or of silver in bars, and *pina*, produced from the mines of the ancient department of the isthmus, or imported there from abroad, or of platina, can take place but by the permission of the governor of Veragua.

A decree of 29th May, 1835, authorizes the exportation of mother of pearl, in foreign and national vessels, from the islands in the Pacific Ocean of the two provinces of the isthmus. To enjoy the privilege, vessels must be in ballast, and receive a permit, except whaling vessels, which may have on board the produce of their fishing, and such tobacco and brandy as may be required for their crews, viz.: seventy-five quintals of the former, and fifty arrobas of spirituous liquors.

NICE,

A free port in Piedmont, Sardinia. It is well situated for commerce with the interior of that kingdom, Switzerland, Savoy, and Tuscany. Lat. 43° 42′ N. Long. 7° 17′ E.

It imports coffee, sugar, pepper, nankins, fish, and manufactured and other goods.

Its exports are all silks, fruit, fish, rice, hemp, anchovies, and cordials.

Nice has the following advantages, viz.:

1st. That the articles suitable for the consumption of the place and the interior, sell for better prices than at any of the neighbouring ports.

2d. That all kinds of manufactured goods, as well as raw materials and productions, may be imported, exported, and transhipped, at very trifling expenses.

3d. That the custom-house regulations grant every facility to all commercial operations, both afloat and on shore.

4th. That it has a constant intercourse with Genoa, Marseilles, and Leghorn; and that whenever it may be found advantageous to send any goods to France, they can be transhipped by French vessels, by which means the difference, or savings in the import duty, will more than defray the expenses, freight and insurance included.

5th. That the charges on business, vessels' repairs and disbursements, are less here than at any other port in the vicinity.

6th. That sales are made without any extra tares, weights, or allowances, which are usually given at Genoa and Leghorn.

7th. That the quarantine regulations are the same as at Marseilles.

8th. All goods introduced via Nice, for the consumption of Piedmont and Savoy, pay one third less duties than those via Genoa, although in the same kingdom, which gives a decided preference to the port of Nice over that of Genoa.

Vessels drawing more than 12 feet of water should go first into Villa Franca, (or Ville-Franche,) 1½ miles east of this place. The entrance into Villa Franca is spacious, and clear of rocks and shoals, and has a light-house on the starboard hand; and the anchorage at the bottom of the bay is very good.

Captains and supercargoes should have ample and fair samples of their cargoes ready to be shown, on arrival, to the buyers, and to be sent to the interior and neighbouring ports.

American vessels may go from hence in ballast to Marseilles, where they can be loaded, repaired, &c., &c., without being subject to pay any tonnage duty whatever.

NOVA SCOTIA AND NEW BRUNSWICK.

Fishing vessels of the United States must not take, cure, or dry fish within three marine miles of any coast, bay, creek, or harbour, in the British settlements, except on that part of Newfoundland from Cape Ray to the Rameau islands, on the western and northern coasts of Newfoundland, from Cape Ray to the Quirpon islands, on the shores of the Magdalen islands, on the south coast of Labrador, from Mount Joly to the Straits of Belle Isle, and thence northwardly indefinitely, so long as the same remains unsettled.

They may, however, enter any of the ports in these provinces to repair damage, for shelter, wood, or water, subject to the above restrictions.

Plaster may be brought from the North American British settlements direct.

PERU.

This country, the government of which has not yet become settled, is bounded on the south by Chili, and on the north by the river Guayaquil. It has not a single harbour in the strict sense of the word, the anchorage being in bays or roads more or less open and insecure. Callao, the port of Lima, affords good anchorage in the road before the town, and is the great emporium of the trade of Peru.

Lat. 12° 2′ S. Long. 77° 4′ W.

Flour has been lately shipped in considerable quantities to Valparaiso, in Chili, and has brought good prices. Tobacco, particularly Kentucky, is a good article of import. In the trade with this country, while the government is in its present state, foreigners must expect to meet with much imposition and injustice from the public authorities as well as from individuals.

Importation.—Vessels of friendly or neutral nations, from whatsoever part they may arrive, shall have free entrance into the chief ports of Peru, which are for the present Callao, Islay, Arica, Huanchaco, and Payta.

The government protects the vessels and merchandise which may arrive in the ports of Peru, and their owners are required to observe the laws of the country in all that concerns them.

Captains or supercargoes, within 24 hours after the anchoring of their vessels, must deliver to the administrator of the custom-house duplicate copies, sworn to and signed, of the manifest, in gross, of all the cargo on board, stating, 1st, the name of the captain or supercargo, that of the vessel, the port of clearance, and the tonnage; 2dly, the packages, with their marks, numbers, and the kind of merchandise which they contain; 3dly, in the same form, those which come *in transitu*, with their places of destination. The whole manifest must be written out clearly, with figures in the margin only.

If the manifest should not be exhibited within the prescribed time, the captain of the vessel will be compelled to make sail for some other port, notwithstanding any excuse which may be offered.

In the discharging and other operations of vessels, their captains or supercargoes will be required to admit the persons employed in the preventive service, and allow the visits on anchoring, the inspections, and the other formalities prescribed by the laws.

The owner or consignee, within 48 hours after the anchoring of the vessel, shall present duplicate copies, without abbreviations, and with figures in the margin only, of the manifest, in detail, of all the cargo, stating, in letters, the form and nature of the packages and their contents; or, if fruits, their weight or measure, exact or approximate.

If circumstances should render it impracticable for the owner or consignee to specify the contents of any packages, they will state so in the manifest, in which case the packages will be brought on shore, in order that they may be examined and classified by the inspectors, in the presence of the administrator of the custom-house, or his deputy, and two of the principal officers of the preventive service; and a note of the whole being made in the manifest, the packages will be carried on board again, or deposited in warehouses.

Until the manifest in detail is exhibited, no permit will be granted for loading, discharging, or transhipping.

No one whose time for the payment of duties, whether for himself or as security, has expired, will be permitted to clear a vessel until he has satisfied them.

All the business with the custom-house must be transacted by the consignee or owner of the cargo, they being responsible for the payment of the duties.

Duties on foreign importations.—All merchandise imported in vessels under foreign or national flags, shall pay 30 per cent. as the only duty.

In order to the exaction of the prescribed duties, two merchants of known probity and intelligence, and two officers of the custom-house, to be named by the minister of finance, shall draw up, every six months, in the presence of the latter, a price current, adjusted by the actual market prices. This document, subscribed by them, and approved by the government, will be the invariable standard by which the valuations of the invoices exhibited in all the custom-houses of the republic shall be regulated.

If the quantity of any article, at the time of its examination in the custom-house, prove to be greater than that stated in the manifest or invoice, the surplus, if its value do not exceed three per centum, compared with the whole, shall pay double duties; but if it exceed this, the surplus will be confiscated, even though the article be of a kind not liable to duty.

If, at the time of examining and comparing the manifest or invoices with the goods, any deficiencies are observed in the latter, the duties will be exacted for the deficient goods in the same manner as if they had actually come and were present.

If, at the time of the examination of the goods by the inspectors, it be found that they are different, in quality or kind, from those specified in the manifest or invoice, they shall be confiscated, a minute inspection being previously made of them.

The payment of the import duties will be made in the following manner: As soon as the merchant proceeds to take the cargo from the custom-house to his warehouses, he shall give three notes of equal amount, the sum total of which shall be equal to the amount of import duties owing by him. The first note shall be payable in 40 days, the second in 120, and the third in 180 days. The government will receive and pass these notes at their intrinsic value, and will lend all the support of the laws to the last holder of them.

In case the merchandise should have suffered any detriment, testimony to that effect will be given by the officers of the preventive service on sea and land, so that it may duly appear, and the fact shall be stated in the permits of transportation from the port to the custom-house, in order that such detriment, or any other damage which may be observed in the goods, when they are examined by the inspectors for the purpose of being delivered to the parties interested, may be seen and duly appreciated.

The goods deposited in the warehouses of the custom-house shall be exempt from storage charges during the first three months; during the second three months, one real per month will be exacted for each package; but for every month after this term, the charges will be increased to four reals per package, until they are all withdrawn.

Goods entered, which are destined for other places, will remain deposited in separate warehouses, subject to the conditions expressed in the foregoing article.

The administrator of the custom-house is competent to grant by his own authority, permits for clearances and transhipments.

He is likewise competent to decide, by his own authority, all disputes, when the sum involved does not exceed $100.

Iron, and other bulky articles which it has not been usual to deposit in the custom-house, will be cleared as formerly.

Every foreign vessel which may enter the port with a cargo, or receive one afterwards for any place, shall pay four reals per ton for anchorage duties, and national vessels shall pay for the same two reals.

Whaling vessels, or any other vessels which may anchor in port for the purpose of taking in water or provisions, or repairing damages, will pay only the anchorage duty.

In order to contribute to the good and welfare of shop-keepers and retailers, it is henceforward prohibited to keepers of warehouses to make any petty sale whatever, under penalty of $500, to be paid to the informers.

Reshipments and transhipments.—Any owner or consignee who may desire to export the goods which he may have imported, can reship them again upon paying the transit duty of two per cent. ad valorem, if the goods be in the warehouses of the custom-house; but if they be in possession of the parties interested, the established duties will be exacted without any remission.

Transhipments are henceforward prohibited: only in the chief ports will they be permitted in unavoidable cases, and then the cargo must be brought to the wharf, and after it is examined by the administrator or his deputy, and by the proper officers of the preventive service, it may be transhipped, the subscriber of the policy paying the transit duty of one per cent. in cash. If, after the transhipment of any merchandise, it should be desired to enter it, the tariff duties will be exacted, without any reduction of what was paid for the transhipment.

Exports.—Stamped silver exported in any vessel will pay, as the only duty, five per cent.

Stamped gold exported in any vessel will pay, as the only duty, two per cent.

The exportation of silver bullion in lumps and bars, and that of gold bullion in plates and dust, is absolutely prohibited, under the penalty of confiscation.

Wrought gold and silver are excepted, the permit stating the number and weight of the pieces, and that 13 per cent. was paid upon the silver, the mark being valued at six dollars; and four per cent. upon the gold, the *castellano* being valued at two dollars.

No person will be allowed to export any sum of money exceeding $25, without having paid the duties on it, and taken out the requisite permit, under the penalty of confiscation.

The other natural products or manufactures of Peru, which may be exported in vessels under a foreign flag, will pay four per cent. upon the valuation by the current market prices.

The same articles, if exported in vessels under the flag of Peru, are free of all duty.

The export duties mentioned in the foregoing articles, must be paid at the time of shipping the commodities.

Coasting trade.—The coasting trade cannot be carried on except in vessels under the flag of Peru. If there should be no national vessels, foreign vessels may be employed; a special license therefor being previously granted by the government, upon consultation with the general commandancy of marine, the custom-house and consulate.

Those who violate any of the provisions of the foregoing articles, will incur the penalty of the confiscation of their merchandise; and captains of vessels, that of losing their vessels.

Any merchant whose goods may be confiscated, if he be a native of the country, shall also suffer the punishment of being banished, from six months to two years, according to the degree and nature of his offence; and if he be a foreigner, he shall be forever expelled the country.

Notices.—Vessels clearing from the chief or minor ports of Peru, must indispensably take out the requisite legal papers, and satisfy all fees.

PETERSBURG

Is built on both banks of the Neva, and is the centre and emporium of the commercial concerns of Russia, through however many channels conveyed, and these are necessarily numerous in this vast and diversified empire. There are no less than 12 principal ports, besides inferior ones, which contribute to the commerce of this capital, viz.: Abo, Archangel, Arensburg, Cronstadt, Liebau, Odessa, (a free port,) Pernau, Revel, Riga, Taganrog, Theodosia, and Wyburg.

The exports from Russia are hemp, flax, tallow, furs, iron, linseed, oil, leather, cordage, feathers, &c. For hemp, Riga is the best place in the Baltic, and Petersburg the next; that which is exported from the other ports is inferior in quality, and proportionably dearer. For pass hemp and tow, Liebau is a good place. Riga is also the chief port for ashes and flax, the sorting of the latter being very strictly attended to there; the quality from Pernau is equally good, and the sorting even better, but the quality exported bears no comparison to that from Riga. Tallow is regularly cheaper at Petersburg than in the other ports of the Baltic; it is also the best port in Russia for iron. For linseed, Riga and Pernau are the best places: timber is mostly exported from Archangel, Riga, Pernau, and Wyburg; oak timber, from Riga only. Archangel is the best place for tar; it was formerly the principal port in the Russian dominions, and it still exports in prodigious quantities, tar, deals, pitch, hemp, tallow, iron, and mats, with a less considerable quantity of linseed and leather.

In ordering goods from Archangel, it is usual to remit the amount to a house at Petersburg, which sends the money in specie to Archangel by post. Of late, a bank has been established at Petersburg under imperial authority, which promises to confer great facilities on commercial negotiations and transmissions of payment, being both a discount and deposit establishment.

The principal imports are coffee, sugar, and other colonial produce, indigo, dyewoods, spices, cotton, twist, salt, &c.

Entry of vessels.—The entry of vessels coming from foreign countries, and the importation of merchandise by sea, are only permitted in ports designated.

Merchandise saved from vessels shipwrecked excepted.

Captains and masters of merchant vessels of every nation, with or without cargo, when they approach a Russian port, must always, except in case of a tempest, come to anchor near the first revenue tender, and if even driven beyond this, must cast anchor without entering the port, as soon as the storm will permit.

If a captain or master of a vessel contravene this preceding article, the revenue boat will fire upon him, and he shall pay a fine of five silver roubles to the crown.

During the months when the navigation is open, there must always be an officer of the customs on board the revenue boat. He is always to accompany the commander of the boat, whenever the latter boards vessels newly arrived, to examine his passports and certificates of quarantine, if coming from places whence such certificates are necessary. It is the duty of the officer of the customs to demand of the captain his bills of lading, seal them up and return them. He will then enter in his book the name of the vessel, that of the captain, of what nation, from whence coming, and whether with or without a cargo.

So long as vessels just arrived are within view of the cutter, the custom-house officer must vigilantly watch that they neither load nor unload any articles of merchandise; and if detected therein, the offender must be seized and conducted to the custom-house.

The officer is required, as soon as possible, to report to the custom-house all vessels boarded from the cutter, as well as those which may have passed without being boarded.

In those ports where there are inspectors of the customs, they shall, as a vessel enters, proceed on board, seal up the hatches and all other openings, rendering it impossible to discharge any thing. It is prescribed to those inspectors, as also those of the maritime frontiers, carefully to prevent vessels, when proceeding from the cutter to the port, from receiving or discharging any articles. The offender and the articles to be seized and sent to the custom-house.

As soon as a vessel shall have entered the port, an officer will proceed on board and compare the number of seals with those reported by the inspector. He will leave on board an officer, to whom he will give a list, indicating the number and places of the seals. He will then enter in his book the arrival of the vessel, will receive from the captain the envelope containing his bills of lading, and will, without delay, despatch him to the custom-house with his report, in which he will indicate, 1st. The names of the vessel and captain. 2d. Of what nation. 3d. Whence from, and length of passage. 4th. Whether laden or not. 5th. Whether the hatches and other openings have been duly sealed by the inspector. 6th. What objects are in the cabin and other places not susceptible of being sealed. 7th. What places have been sealed, their number, and the name of the officer left in charge of the vessel.

In maritime ports where there are neither cutters nor inspectors, it is the duty of the superintendent of vessels to receive from the captain his bills of lading, to seal the hatches and other openings, and immediately afterwards to present the bills of lading to the custom-house with his report.

Every bill of lading presented to the custom-house with the report of the superintendent of vessels, will be signed by the director general, and with the seal of the customs affixed.

If a captain resists the placing of the seals, the inspector or the superintendent of vessels shall give notice to the custom-house, which shall take immediate and rigorous measures to affix the seals, and to reinforce the guard. If, on examination, the captain be found guilty, a fine of 500 silver roubles shall be levied on him for the benefit of the crown.

An inspector of the customs, or a superintendent of vessels, who shall permit a vessel to enter the port without having affixed the requisite seals, and who does not offer justifiable reasons for the omission, shall be dismissed.

Places of anchoring, and permissions to change those places, depend on the maritime administration of the port.

In ports where there is no maritime administration, the designation will be made by the superintendents of vessels.

Presentation of manifests.—Every captain of a vessel is obliged, within 24 hours, unless prevented by the weather, to present himself at the custom-house. His bills of lading will be returned to him, and he is to deliver a manifest of his cargo, or a declaration of his arrival in ballast, written in the language with which he is most familiar.

Any captain who does not present himself at the custom-house within 24 hours, and does not deliver his manifest within 48 hours, shall pay a fine to the crown of 10 roubles.

The manifest of the captain must exhibit,

1st. The name of vessel and captain, and to what nation belonging. 2. Whence from, length of passage, and name of consignee. 3d. The tonnage and draft of water. 4th. The articles comprising the cargo, with the marks and numbers, and the numbers to be in letters, not in figures, of all the packages, &c.; the names of the persons to whom the goods are to be delivered, or to specify if they are consigned to order. 5th. The number of passengers, and the effects belonging to each. 6th. The objects which belong to the captain and to the sailors, including therein their clothes and provisions, and rigging of the vessel, designating their quantity and quality. 7th. The names of the sailors, and the nation of each individual. 8th. The number of bills of lading for the entire cargo.

In fine, if the captain, by stress of weather, has been obliged to throw any part of his cargo overboard for preservation of his vessel and cargo, or if from any cause whatever he has discharged any part of his cargo in another port, he will declare this by protest, and will state it in his manifest.

The captain's manifest must conform to his bills of lading and the notes of lading, which, with his signature affixed, must be presented to the bureau of the customs, together with his passport and certificate of quarantine, if he have one.

Bills of lading must accompany all merchandise imported into Russia. This document is exacted in the ports of the White Sea, of the Baltic, of the Black Sea, and of the Sea of Azof, with the exception only of merchandise coming from the Ottoman provinces, and laden in Russian or Turkish vessels.

The bills of lading must specify,

1st. The name of the shipper. 2d. The place of shipment, and the destination. 3d. The kind of goods contained in each package expressed in general terms: thus, merchandise of cotton, wool, silk, steel, earthenware, china, glassware, sugar, coffee, &c. 4th. The quantity of each kind indicated in net or gross weight, separately for each package, or for all together: for example, 100 hhds. of sugar refined or not refined, weighing together so many pounds net or gross; 10 cases of prunes, weighing together so many pounds net or gross weight; 200 cases earthenware, weighing together so many pounds net or gross; 200 bales of cloth, weighing together so many pounds net or gross, &c. When articles of different kinds, such for example as tools, implements of iron, steel, or other metal, &c., the net or gross weight of each package must be separately designated under the appellation of "*hardware.*" 5th. The name of the captain and of the vessel. And, 6th. The net rate of freight. The bills of lading must be signed by the captain; and if any be presented which are not signed, the officers of the customs will cause them to be immediately signed.

The import duty on liquids being payable by measure, the bills of lading must specify the quantity contained in each vessel, or the contents of the whole.

Liquids contained in bottles or flasks, packed in cases or other packages, must, in the bills of lading, have the number of packages, and the contents of each designated.

Articles paying duty by the package according to the tariff, such as tar and pitch, are not subject to a specification of weight or measure in the bills of lading.

Nor will such specification be required for rude articles of the mineral kingdom used for ballast, such as salt, plaster, alabaster, marble, &c., when not in packages.

If goods are imported by sea without bills of lading, or if the bills of lading have interlineations or erasures, or if they are not according to prescribed formalities, or if, on visiting the vessel, they are found to differ from the real state of the cargo, in all such or other cases of informality, the goods will be subject, besides the regular duties, to an addition of 10 per cent. upon the same.

Goods free of duty will be admitted without bills of lading, and in case of irregularity, are exempt from fine.

Bills of lading are not required for goods belonging to the captain, to the passengers or sailors, except supercargoes, who are not exempt from presenting their bills of lading and their invoices.

If bills of lading giving the weights, do not express whether it is gross or net, reference will be made to the declaration of the merchant. But the goods will pay the additional duty of 10 per cent.

Goods to order may henceforth be imported. For payment of the duties, if not prohibited by the tariff, they are to be proceeded with according to the rules relative to imports.

The tonnage, lasts, or number of sea tons of every vessel, must be designated exactly in the captain's manifest, according to the certificates of the place where the vessel was built, or of that where she was measured, or according to the acquittance of tonnage dues in some port. If measured in a Russian port, the tonnage will be expressed according to the certificate of such port. A captain convicted of having diminished the measurement more than 10 lasts, shall pay two silver roubles for every last thus diminished.

If a captain pretends that he has no bills of lading or other documents relative to his cargo, he shall not on that account, or any other, be relieved from the necessity of producing his manifest, and of being responsible for its correctness.

If, after having presented his manifest, the captain discovers that he has through error specified too much or too little therein, and, if within 24 hours, he gives information thereof, he is to be permitted to make the necessary correction. Beyond this term, he cannot, under any pretext, make the slightest change in his manifest.

The director, or other officer of the customs, is required to receive the manifest of every captain, to note the day on which it is presented, to attach to it the bills of lading, and to affix the seal of the customs. He will cause it to be translated; the original will be enregistered and numbered, and an exact copy taken, according to which the cargo is to be discharged.

These formalities being complied with, an officer of the customs, accompanied by the superintendent of vessels, will, without delay, visit the vessel, whether laden or in ballast. He will remove the seals, affix others, note on the manifest whether it is found to be correct, or wherein erroneous. He will state the number of seals affixed by him, and the name of the inspector who is left with the vessel. He will then sign his name to the whole. During this visit, the captain is required to show all belonging as well to him as to his crew, and all places destined to contain cargo, under the penalty to the crown of 100 silver roubles.

Until the manifest is presented and the visit completed, no person is permitted to board or to leave the vessel. All the passengers and crew must consequently be examined when leaving the vessel, in order to ascertain that nothing is landed. If articles are discovered, other than goods free of duty, they shall be confiscated, and the party sentenced to fine as follows: for merchandise liable to duty, five times the amount of duty; for prohibited goods, double the value thereof.

In ports where there are two custom-houses, that is, one at the sea-shore, and one " principal" in the town, the first will immediately forward to the second the original declaration of the captain, sealed, with the documents of his cargo, and will send separately the translation of his manifest, &c. If the ship cannot get up to the principal customs with all her cargo, the custom-house, in advance, will deliver to the superintendent of vessels a legalized copy of the manifest.

No captain is to proceed to the principal custom-house, nor quit the station allotted to him, before having presented his manifest at the advanced customs.

Goods cannot be transported from one vessel to another, until permission is obtained from the customs. In contravention of this, whoever may be the proprietor, if even the imperial court itself, or whether imported by a vessel of war, or of commerce, the goods shall be condemned as if they were contraband, unless they be such as are duty free.

The captain is responsible for the observance, by his crew, of all the regulations of the customs.

The captain, no matter to what nation he belongs, is obliged, in Russian ports, to conform strictly to all the regulations of the customs.

Foreign ships of war, arriving for matters of commerce, will be considered as merchant vessels, and held to the same obligations and responsibilities.

Discharging cargoes.—Vessels in ballast at an advanced custom-house, and those which can proceed to the principal customs without discharging any part of their cargo, may do so, as soon as their manifest has been delivered, the vessel visited, and the seals affixed.

If vessels cannot proceed to the customs with their entire cargo, it is permitted to lighten them by transports.

Those lighters are neither to be laden nor discharged, except in presence of the captain of the ship, or his substitute, and in presence of the person commanding the lighter.

The hatches of the lighter are to be sealed as soon as she is laden, and an exact report made to the customs.

The officer of the customs, as soon as this report is received, will take bills of lading from the master of the lighter, and will send him with a passport containing all the requisite formalities, to the principal custom-house.

If desired by the captain of the vessel, or owner of the goods, they may, on their account, place a person on board the lighter to superintend their property.

The advanced custom-house makes report daily to the principal customs, of all arrivals and departures of vessels.

A lighter departing from the vessel before the requisite seals are affixed, shall subject the master thereof to a fine of fifty silver roubles to the crown.

No officer left in charge of a vessel or of a lighter, shall, on any pretext, absent himself.

Perishable articles are excepted from the general law in reference to transport by lighters. They may be hurried forward, under orders of the proper authority.

Vessels may discharge from sunrise to sunset, except on holidays. In the ports of the White Sea, where the navigation is so soon closed, vessels are to discharge during holidays.

Vessels must not discharge in the night, except in extraordinary cases, necessary to save some vessel or cargo.

A commander discharging at prohibited hours, shall pay a fine of 50 silver roubles, and the inspector in charge shall be dismissed.

No goods must be unladen except at permitted places, under penalty of 100 silver roubles to the crown.

The port-holes of vessels must be closed whilst discharging, except when opened by order of the officer, under the penalty of 25 silver roubles to the crown.

If a vessel or lighter gets aground, the inspector who has been placed on board must immediately inform the custom-house, who, conjointly with the proprietor, will take the necessary measures for the preservation of goods, vessel, and lighter.

Vessels or lighters proceeding from an advanced to a principal custom-house, are under the inspection of the superintendents of vessels attached to the latter.

If a vessel or lighter arrive without having the seals affixed, or if they are damaged, they shall be immediately affixed, and a report made to the principal customs.

As soon as a vessel has anchored, the custom-house will deliver a copy of the captain's manifest to the first superintendent of vessels, and to the inspector of custom-house stores, that the cargo may be discharged and received therein. In ports where there are no public stores, the goods may be deposited in private warehouses, under authority of the customs.

The first superintendent of vessels, as soon as he has received the manifest, must, with a deputy, examine the seals, and place inspectors to superintend the unlading.

In ports where there are no public lighters, flat bottomed boats may be employed, under the inspection and responsibility of the superintendents of vessels.

All goods discharged must be accompanied by an officer to the public store, where they will be received by the storekeeper.

The public storekeeper must note on the manifest what packages he has received. When heavy goods, difficult to be transported, are placed on the shore, they are under the care of the officers, who will give receipts for them to the storekeeper.

When a vessel is discharged, the superintendent and inspector are to make report thereof to the customs.

Damaged packages, and such as exceed the number contained in the manifest, shall be immediately opened in presence of an officer, the captain, owner, or his clerk.

The unlading of a vessel or lighter being completed, the officers of the customs will carefully search every part, to ascertain if any thing be concealed.

Discharged vessels and lighters which have been thus visited, are permitted to haul off as designated by the officer of the customs.

Vessels reported to be in ballast, must nevertheless be visited as ordered by the foregoing articles.

As soon as a vessel is discharged, the measurer of vessels shall measure her according to the prescribed rules, to ascertain her measurement in lasts.

It is strictly forbidden to all Russian and foreign vessels to take on board goods of any kind, in ports or places not designated, under penalty of 100 silver roubles, and under pain of confiscation and other payments.

It is also strictly forbidden to captains, merchants, and owners, to open any package on board the vessel. If they do, and if even no injury be done, a fine shall be paid of 100 silver roubles.

Prohibition is equally made to all boatmen and others, to take to, or receive any thing from vessels, without permission of the customs, and under penalty of confiscation.

Packages not in the manifest.—If, in unlading, more goods or packages are found than are expressed in the manifest, but are contained in the bills of lading, presented at the same time, this may be deemed an error, and may be corrected without penalty.

If, in unlading a vessel, more packages are found than are entered either in the manifest or bills of lading, and that before the time fixed for settling the duties, the owner of such goods proves by an invoice or bill of lading that they were shipped for his account, then they shall be delivered to him on payment of the duties, and an addition of 10 per cent. for having imported goods without bills of lading. The captain shall pay a fine equal to the amount of duties on said goods.

If the captain omits to insert in his manifest any packages belonging to a passenger, and the latter applies to claim his property at the customs, the captain shall be asked if the goods belong to such passenger. If the captain answers affirmatively, the goods shall be delivered accordingly, and the captain shall pay for each package thus omitted a fine to the crown of 10 silver roubles.

If the goods not inserted in the manifest belong to the captain himself, they shall be forfeited, unless the articles are free of duty, and then the penaly must be, for merchandise liable to duty, five times the amount of duty; for prohibited goods, double the value thereof.

Packages or articles neither marked in the manifest or bill of lading, if not claimed before the duties are payable, will be considered as belonging to the captain, and will be proceeded with as in the preceding paragraph.

If packages called for by manifests and bills of lading are not to be found when discharging, the captain shall be obliged to pay duty thereon at the rate of similar articles of first quality, and the captain shall be held accountable to the proprietor for the goods missing.

Goods in the manifest not found on board, and for which the captain presents either no bill of lading or an informal one, shall be reported to the customs, and the invoice demanded of the owner, which shall be presented within 24 hours, and agreeably to which the captain shall pay duty. If such invoice be not produced, the captain shall pay for each missing package a fine of 200 silver roubles.

If a package delivered to a lighter be lost, then all the responsibility and consequences mentioned above fall upon the commander of the lighter.

Of ship's provisions, and of permission given to captains for the sale of their goods by retail.

Captains of vessels arriving in Russian ports from places beyond the Sound, may have for the supply of their crew, free of duty, the following articles: for each individual, captain included, two anchors of rum, or other strong liquor; three anchors of beer and porter, one anchor of wine, ten pounds of coffee, one pound of sugar, and one pound of tea. Vessels from ports within the Sound can only thus appropriate one half the above quantity—the surplus must pay duty.

Vessels coming from foreign ports to complete their lading.

Vessels coming from foreign ports to a port in Russia, for completing their cargoes with Russian goods, must make known their object, and must prove by their bills of lading that the merchandise on board is not destined for a Russian port. He will then be permitted to complete his lading with Russian products, and will only pay duty thereon. The officers of the customs will, in this case, prevent the landing of any article clandestinely, and will place an inspector on board till the vessel's departure. The captain who may desire to sell a part, no matter how small, of his cargo not prohibited, will make his report to the customs, and pay the import duties.

If it shall be discovered that the captain has double bills of lading indicating the destination for another Russian port, all articles except such as are not liable to duty, shall be confiscated.

Cronstadt.—Every vessel must stop at the guardship on arrival, or if forced to pass her from distress or stormy weather, must anchor off the harbour, and not enter it till visited. For passing the guardship without stopping, the penalty is five silver roubles for every shot fired by the guardship.

At the guardship the Sound pass and the Elsineur bill of health must be produced, and if with cargo, bills of lading in duplicate. After the former are signed, and the latter sealed under cover, they will be returned to the master. The penalty for not giving up these documents is 100 silver roubles.

All masters are requested to read the admiralty instructions handed to them by the officer on board the guardship with particular care, and to attend to the same.

Every ship must have a pilot from the guardship.

Every vessel must have a buoy at her anchor when she brings up;

and if a vessel gives another a foul berth, she answers for all consequences should any damage ensue.

No person is allowed to board a vessel, or leave her from the period of quitting the guardship till entering the harbour, and until the harbour-masters have been on board to seal the hatches. The master is bound to inform them of every secret passage to the hold. The penalty for not allowing the hatches to be sealed, is 100 roubles silver.

On entering the harbour, the master must produce at the guardship at the Mole Head, the Sound pass, bill of health, passengers' passes, and make a true report of his crew. To the harbour-master's office he must deliver the sealed cover with his sealed bills of lading.

No vessel can be moored or moved in the harbour without leave asked, and never without the attendance of a pilot. The penalty for shifting the vessel's berth without leave, is 50 roubles silver.

All letters must be given up on arrival. A premium of 20 copecks is allowed for each letter so delivered. On departure, every letter must bear the post-office stamp. The penalty for concealing letters on arrival, as also for taking any on board when departing, without the post-office stamp, is 25 roubles for each letter.*

On being cleared at both places at the Mole Head, the master will go to the consular office, open from 7 A. M. to 9 P. M.

Every master, till his vessel is searched, must take silver in preference to bank notes for his current expenses.

No master can scrape or repair his vessel without leave.

Every master must appear in the custom-house within 24 hours after arrival, make his declaration within 48 hours, and is allowed 24 hours more for final correction of errors, unless at his request the vessel is already searched. The declaration must contain,

The cargo, as per bills of lading.

If in ballast, the quantity, and of what sort.

Goods without bills of lading, belonging to the master and crew.

Passengers' names, and their baggage.

Stores, provisions, clothing of master and crew, and small articles for their use.

Names of the crew, and of what nation.

The Sound pass, bill of health, and register, must also be brought to the custom-house with the declaration.

Every master is enjoined to attend most particularly to the writing out of his declaration. No alterations are admitted.

It is highly necessary for every master with an inward cargo to make a protest on arrival; the time limited by law is 24 hours after arrival.

The tonnage of the vessel must be correctly entered.

The vessels arriving from beyond the Sound are allowed to bring, duty free, for provisions for every man on board, two ankers of spirits, one anker of wine, three ankers malt liquor, ten pounds coffee, one pound tea, and one pood sugar.

Ships coming from within the Sound are allowed half the quantity.

Bills of health required.

---

* This includes unsealed letters, even of recommendation or introduction.

Flags to be hoisted after search.

Master required not to leave the ship after finishing his duties on shore till it is searched; or, if forced to go on shore, he must leave his keys with a confidential person, that every place may be searched.

No master is permitted to go up to St. Petersburg till such time as his declaration is made out, and his ship searched.

No master is permitted to begin to discharge any goods whatever before the searchers have been on board his ship.

Goods must not be moved from one ship to another without leave.

Heavy penalty for discharging goods in an illegal place.

Heavy penalty for putting goods into concealed places.

Penalty for opening a package on board, 100 roubles silver.

Goods not in bill of lading or declaration must be claimed within the time stipulated by law.

Goods in bills of lading and declaration not found on board, a sum equivalent to the highest duties must be paid.

If, for goods entered in the declaration, there are no bills of lading, and which are not found on board, the penalty is 200 roubles silver per each parcel wanting.

For each parcel of baggage not entered, penalty 10 roubles silver.

Prohibited goods brought to order, provided the master cannot discover the owner, the penalty is two roubles silver per lb., gross weight.

Whilst discharging, the ship's port-holes must be shut. For keeping them open without leave, a penalty of 25 roubles silver is to be levied.

Masters must inspect the condition of lighters.

Vessels may discharge every day excepting Sundays and holidays, and load every day, including Sundays and holidays.

Working hours are from sunrise to sunset.

It is particularly recommended to all masters of vessels to settle for their ballast before they are loaded.

Every master must apply for ballast prahms to the captain of the inner guardship.

After the vessel is discharged of her cargo or ballast, the master must give information thereof to the harbour-masters and ship-measurers.

No person must break bulk of a craft without the presence of the custom-house officer attached to his ship.

Every master is requested not to begin upon a craft on its arrival from St. Petersburg, till he has a regular note from the officer.

All fresh provisions actually necessary for the voyage, as well as for daily consumption, can be taken on board without entry.

Every master is particularly requested to give immediate information, should any part of his cargo be out of order.

Every master must give notice of his progress in loading.

Every master, when about to clear out, must produce his bills of lading, as the vessel cannot be cleared without them.

Admiralty passes being abolished, masters are requested to come to the office to settle accounts and receive the ship's pass.

Every master is requested to watch strictly the daily labourers he may engage, to prevent pilfering and fraud.

The smoking of segars and pipes on board of vessels, or on the deal yards and in the streets, is strictly forbidden.

Cook boats may be hired at five roubles b. n. per month.

The cook-house is under the immediate superintendence of the police.

Masters of vessels are most seriously requested to attend to the admiralty instructions about the discharging of ballast and throwing dirt overboard, as the law will be rigidly enforced. All dirt and scrapings from the ships must be taken on shore in boats to a place appointed by the captain of the inner guardship.

No captain must turn a seaman on shore, nor send him away, without a written discharge.

Every master is responsible for his crew, and for their adherence to custom-house regulations.

Boats of merchant vessels must land at the regular landing places appointed for them.

Provision yerricks must not be lent by one master of a vessel to another.

The penalty for leaving the port without the regular passes, is confiscation of the ship.

For obstructing custom-house officers in the execution of their duty, 500 roubles silver is to be levied.

Fires are not allowed in the mole, under any pretext whatever, nor lights in any part of the vessel, except in the cabin, and there in a candlestick with water.

Vessels laden with cotton, bound for the Russian ports in the Baltic, passing through the Sound, the Great or the Little Belt, or the Holstein canal, and coming from a place not known to be entirely healthy, are required to present, before entering into the Baltic, a certificate, in due form, delivered by the Danish quarantine establishment, declaring them to have been purified, or to be in a satisfactory state of health.

Every vessel arriving laden with cotton at a Russian port in the Baltic, from a place known to be entirely healthy, must exhibit, on its passage through the Danish seas, specific proofs of the satisfactory condition of the cotton.

Satisfactory proofs of the condition of the cotton, are—

1st. The passports delivered by the custom-house in ports which are not suspected, indicating also the quantity and the origin of the cotton laden at such ports.

2d. Certificates to the same effect delivered by our consuls, or by the consuls of the powers to which these vessels belong, if such documents have been delivered in the ports where the cotton was laden.

On exhibition of these certificates by the vessel, the Danish custom-house will attest upon the receipt which it gives for the payment of the Sound duties, that the proofs required with regard to the satisfactory condition of the cotton have been furnished.

When the vessels are provided with neither a custom-house passport, nor a consular certificate stating the quantity of the cotton, and that it comes from a place not suspected, or that it has been purified by a quarantine, and when these vessels have not even a quarantine certificate, they shall be obliged (if they come with cotton from a place entirely healthy, and are bound for a Russian port) to perform a quarantine in Denmark, and to provide themselves there with requisite certificates in due form, without which they will not be allowed to continue their voyage, as they will not be received in Russian ports.

No vessel laden with cotton shall be admitted into Russian ports, except those which exhibit a certificate from one of the Danish quarantine establishments, or a receipt from the Danish custom-house for Sound duties, with the endorsement of the custom-house declaring that the satisfactory proofs as to the condition of the cotton have been furnished.

Simple receipts for the payment of the Sound duties without the above mentioned endorsement, will not be considered sufficient, when exhibited by vessels laden with cotton; and these vessels shall be treated like all those which are not provided with sufficient certificates as to their healthy condition—that is to say, they shall be sent back to Elsinore.

A bill of health from the resident consul is also necessary.

Import and export duties are rated in silver, but paid in bank assignats at a certain agio, fixed in the beginning of every year, by which the whole payments of that year are regulated.

If the price of the goods in the declaration is suspected to be less than their current value, the goods may be taken by the custom-house officers, they paying to the owner the estimated price, and ten per cent. in addition.

Merchants may demand the real tare on imported dry goods only; on the others, the legal tare is conclusive.

Cotton, linen, wool and silk goods, are weighed in their envelopes, and no tare is allowed for the same.

Tare on imports.—Moist goods.

Anchovies, capers, salted or preserved fruits and olives, in glass or earthen vessels	40	per cent.
The same articles, except olives, in wooden vessels	30	"
Olives in wooden vessels	20	"
Mushrooms in brine, oil or vinegar	40	"
Colours		"
Nitric acid, or spirits of nitre, in wooden or earthen vessels	40	"
Sulphuric acid, in flasks or earthen vessels	40	"
Olive oil, in casks	17	"
——— of Italy or Provence, in flasks	20	"
——— other kinds, in flasks or earthen vessels	40	"
Oil for painters, in barrels	13	"
Oil of turpentine, in casks or wooden vessels	17	"
Liquorice, in casks	13	"
Fish, salted, in flasks or wooden vessels	30	"
Gums, liquid, and other liquid medicines, in casks or chests	12	"
All other liquids, in casks or wooden vessels	17	"
——— in earthenware and glass vessels	20	"

Tare on dry goods imported.

Cotton, spun, in bales	6	per cent.
——— in casks or chests	15	"
Rosin, in chests	17	"
Camel's hair, spun, not twisted, in chests	10	"
——— twisted, in do	25	"
Alum, Swedish or English, in do	8	"
Colours, white lead, (dry) minum	8	"
——— cochineal, for each sack weighing from 4 to 7 pounds	2	livres.
——— from 2 to $3\frac{1}{2}$ do	1	"
Indigo, in seroons of leather, weighing from $5\frac{1}{2}$ to 7 pounds	34	"
——— in half seroons, weighing from $2\frac{1}{2}$ to 4 do	20	"
——— of Guatimala, in casks without envelopes, or in chests lined and hooped	20	per cent.
Iron wire, in barrels	8	"
Marcassite and bismuth	6	"
Pewter, in rods or barrels	6	"
Mercury, in leather bottles	9	"
Zinc, in barrels	6	"
Table utensils of delf ware, in casks	20	"
——— in baskets	12	"
Pot and pearl ashes, in barrels	12	"
Gum lacquer	15	"
——— in chests	25	"
Wool, in bales	3	"
Upon other goods in casks, chests, or other wooden vessels	10	"
——— in earthen or glass vessels	20	"
——— in single sacks	2	"
——— in double sacks	4	"
——— in sacks of bark or matting	3	"
——— in sacks and mats together	5	"
——— in baskets	5	"

Tare of export goods.—Dry goods.

In barrels or chests	10	per cent.
In sacks	2	"
In mats, or sacks made of mats	3	"
Except Muscovy leather, on which are allowed	5	"

Moist goods.

Pressed caviac	15	per cent.
Soap	3	"
Meat and salt fish	10	"
Tallow	10	"
Honey	17	"
Treacle	10	"
All other moist goods	17	"

By the convention concluded between the United States and Russia, in April, 1824, regulating the commerce and navigation of the two nations on the northwest coast of America, it was stipulated that the ships of both nations might, during a term of ten years, frequent, without hindrance, the interior seas, gulfs, harbours and creeks of each nation on that coast, for the purpose of fishing and trading with natives of the country. The ten years expired in April, 1834; and formal notice has been given by the governor of the Russian colonies, to the masters of the American ships then trading there, that they could no longer claim, under the convention, the right of landing at all the landing places, without distinction, belonging to Russia on that coast. Those interested in the trade will not fail to observe that, under the second article of the convention, it is necessary for all American vessels resorting to any point on that coast, where there is a Russian establishment, to obtain the permission of the governor or commander.

Port charges paid by vessels in the port of Odessa.

Tonnage duty.—Every vessel pays, for the benefit of the crown, a tonnage duty of 50 copecks per ton, on entering, and the same on leaving the port.

Every foreign vessel arriving laden from a foreign port, pays, moreover, for the benefit of the city, 50 copecks on each last, or 120 poods weight of her cargo.

Anchorage money.—Foreign vessels pay 50 copecks per ton; Russian vessels, 25 copecks per ton, for the benefit of the city.

Light money.—Every vessel pays 25 roubles for the support of the light-house.

Quarantine.—Every vessel, coming from a foreign port, is furnished by the quarantine office with a quarantine flag, for which five roubles must be paid; and a set of printed regulations, the price of which is one rouble.

ROTTERDAM,

A seaport of Holland, situated at the junction of the Rotte and the Merme. Lat. 51° 54′ N. Long. 4° 28′ E.

The trade of Rotterdam is very similar to that of Amsterdam, but not so extensive. Rotterdam is, however, a much better place for most kinds of grain, and the white Zealand wheat, shipped from this place, is of a particularly fine quality. It is also the best market for madder and geneva; the latter of which is sold by the rume, but for the convenience of English smugglers, it is also sold in ankers and half ankers.

The commercial regulations are the same as at Amsterdam.

SIAM.

Siam proper extends from about the latitude of 23° north to the gulf of that name, and is bounded west by the Burman empire, and east by the Lai (Lau) mountains. This is the valley of Menam, the "Mother of Waters," the country of the true Siamese. This river, after watering and manuring the low, flat land, by its annual deposits, empties itself by three channels into the gulf of Siam. The boundaries of the Siamese dominions on the bay of Bengal, extend from the Burman, (or more correctly speaking in the present day,) the English Burmese dominions, as far south as the boundary line between the petty states of Perak and Quedah, in the straits of Malacca, in about the latitude of 5° north; in which is included the valuable island of Junk, Ceylon or Salung, containing a vast body of tin ore. It then extends nearly east across the Malay peninsula, in about the same latitude, between the provinces of Fringano and Pakang, whose shores are bathed by the China Sea; it then extends north to the head of the gulf of Siam. The Siamese government, during the year 1832, brought under their immediate subjection nearly the whole of the tributary states in the Malay peninsula. They possess, also, a large part of the late kingdom of Lao, including the former capital of the empire, called Lauchang, situated on the great river Camboja, in about the 16th degree of north lat., and which is represented to be very populous. They hold, also, (with the exception of a small portion of the southern part,) the province of Batabaug, in Camboja. The eastern boundary line is in about the longitude of 105°, and extends north to the latitude of 15°, being the dividing line between Lao and Camboja: and extending south to the Siamese gulf, the boundary being the island of Kong, alias Ko Kong, situate in north lat. 10° 43′, and long. 103° 17′ east. Extending north on the east coast of the gulf, lies Chautabun, once a part of the ancient kingdom of Camboja; it is well known as a rich and valuable possession of Siam.

The imports consist of British piece goods, white and printed, with some woollens; India goods of all descriptions, the coarse from Bengal, and the finer and more expensive from Surat; from China, silks and teas, porcelain, quicksilver, and almost every other article exported from that country. From other sources, powder, arms and cannon, glassware and crockery, cutlery, some drugs, arrack, wine, &c. Opium is strictly prohibited; but the Chinese and others introduce, clandestinely, large quantities for sale. There is an immense trade carried on at the capital, called Si-a-Yuthia, (pronounced See-ah-you-te-ah,) and on the opposite or right bank of the river at Bankok. The inland trade is a very important branch, especially with Lau and the Chinese province of Yunan, &c. This domestic traffic is carried on, on the Menam, in flat boats and on bamboo rafts. Boats leave Lau in August and September, when the river is swollen by the periodical rains, and arrive at Bankok in November and December. They bring stick, lac, benzon, raw silks, ivory, beeswax, horns, hides, timber, &c. The articles of merchandise exported into China through Lau, consist of coarse woollens, broadcloths, cutlery, gold, copper, lead, &c. The Chinese are the principal foreign traders. The Siamese prosecute a large foreign and coasting trade to China, Camboja, Cochin China, the Malay peninsula, to Singapore, to the eastern coast of Sumatra, to the bay of Bengal, &c. The traffic between the countries lying on the shores of the straits of Malacca and the bay of Bengal, is generally conducted by three different routes across the Malay peninsula, and then reshipped in boats on the gulf of Siam to the capital; the imports being British and Indian goods, opium, esculent swallow's nests, &c.

Abstract of a treaty with Siam.—The citizens of the United States are permitted to enter and depart from any port of the kingdom with cargoes of whatever description, and to buy, sell and exchange, without qualification or restriction, except that they are not to sell munitions of war to any other person than the king, or to import opium, or to export rice. The only charge to be exacted from American vessels, is a measurement duty of 1700 ticals or bats for every fathom of 78 American inches in breadth, upon ships selling merchandise, and of 1500 ticals or bats per fathom on those purchasing cargoes with specie; the measurement to be made in the middle of the vessel's length, upon the single deck, or if there be more than one deck, then upon the lower one; but no charge is to be made upon a vessel entering merely to refit, or for refreshment, or to inquire the state of the market. In case of a reduction of the duties upon the vessels of any foreign nation, the same reduction is to be made in favour of those of the United States.

American debtors who shall have honestly brought forward and sold all their property for the payment of their debts, are not to be proceeded against for the balance remaining due after the application of the proceeds of such sale. Merchants trading to Siam shall obey the laws and customs of the country; and if they wish to rent houses, they shall rent the king's factories, and pay the customary rent therefor. The king's officers may take account of goods brought on shore, but no duty shall be levied thereon.

In case of shipwreck of an American vessel on the Siamese coast, the persons escaping shall be hospitably entertained, and the property saved shall be restored to the owners; and if a vessel of the United States shall be captured by pirates, and brought into a Siamese port, the persons on board shall be set at liberty, and the property restored to the rightful proprietors.

If the privilege shall hereafter be granted to any foreign nation, other than the Portuguese, to have consuls resident in the kingdom, the same privilege shall be extended to the United States.

The treaty has removed all obstacles to a lucrative and important branch of our commerce, and but a single charge is now exacted, whether on imports or exports, &c.; the merchant being left free to sell or purchase where and of whom he pleases. Prior to this period, the American merchant was not allowed to sell to any individual the cargo he imported, nor purchase a return cargo; the king had the exclusive right of purchase and sale in both cases. He also fixed the prices of the articles wanted for return cargoes.

The duties on imports were not permanent; they varied from 8 to 15 per centum.

The export duty on sugar of the first quality was $1 50 (Spanish) per pecul, which was not less than from 25 to 30 per cent. upon the first cost; and other articles were charged in the same proportion.

Port charges and other exactions were not defined and fixed, but they generally amounted to not less than $3 50 (Spanish) per ton.

SICILY.

Palermo, (Lat. 38° 07′ N. Long. 13° 20′ E.) is the capital of Sicily, and has a good harbour; but Messina, (Lat. 38° 14′ N. Long. 15° 49′ E.) is better situated for the trade with Italy, being only at a short distance from the Italian coast. Its harbour is very commodious, but by no means safe.

The principal exports of Sicily are grain to Genoa, Leghorn, France and Spain; silk (the chief staple article) to Genoa, Leghorn

Marseilles, the United States and England; salt, shumac, almonds, tallow, olive oil, olives, cheese, nuts, barilla, wines, anchovies and sardines; kid, lamb, fox, hare and rabbit skins.

The imports are, from Leghorn, raw wool and woollen stuffs, raw and spun cotton, linens, calicoes, iron, copper, gunpowder, indigo, cochineal, pepper and other spices, dye-woods, flax, hemp and hides; from Genoa, velvets, paper, German linens, embroidered silks, &c.; from France, linens, cotton stuffs, hats, paper, lace, jewellery, camlets, serges and other stuffs; from Venice, quicksilver, turpentine, druggeries, cloth of Padua, wax, glass, &c.; from Naples, English and French merchandise, Calabrian pitch, timber, earthenware, &c.; from Trieste, German articles; from Spain and Portugal, sugar, tobacco, dye-woods, and other colonial produce; from Holland, linens and West India produce; from England, East and West India produce, watches, hardware, cutlery, toys, jewellery, copper, pewter, iron, lead, hides, &c.

For commercial regulations vide Naples.

SMYRNA,

The principal port in the Levant, has a very large and commodious harbour, and carries on a great trade with the interior of the Asiatic nations. The Armenians carry on the greatest trade with Smyrna; about 15,000 are established in this city, and the caravans from Persia are chiefly composed of them. These caravans arrive and depart at fixed periods, by which the Europeans regulate their shipping, in order that the Asiatics may carry with them the western merchandise, and the Europeans reload with that of Asia. Of the European nations, the English send the greatest number of ships to Smyrna. Lat. 38° 23′ N. Long. 27° 20′ E.

The imports are piastres, cloth, silken stuffs, paper, cochineal, argil, indigo, sugar, spices, dye-woods, East India goods, &c.

The exports are coffee, cotton, wool, camel's and goat's hair, currants, raisins, figs, wax, soap, pearls, precious stones, opium, rhubarb and other drugs, box-wood, Turkey carpets, silks, iron, &c.

The French trade to Smyrna is chiefly carried on from Marseilles, and that of the Italians, from Leghorn.

The principal imports into Smyrna, in vessels of the United States, are coffee, sugar, spices, dyestuffs, rum, coarse cottons and furniture; and they take away return cargoes of wool, opium, old copper, drugs, fruit, wine, oil of roses, and some few other articles.

The duties are so light, and so little attention do the Turkish authorities give to commerce, that Smyrna may, in fact, be called a free port. The duties are, however, rigidly exacted, and the lighters which transport merchandise to and from the shipping, stop at the custom-house, which is on the harbour, where the goods are examined by the proper officers. Efficient measures are taken, at the same time, to prevent smuggling, but the agents of government do not go on board the vessels, or examine their documents.

In coming to anchor, each vessel is bound not to interfere in any way with any other that may have already obtained its position; and if interference does take place, so as to cause damage, the offender must pay the award given by the consuls of their respective nations.

There are no light-house or harbour dues. The only charges to which vessels are subjected are those paid to the consuls, and are:

Deposit of papers, $2; clearance, $2; anchorage, $1; bill of health, $2; teskeret from the Turkish authorities, $1: total $8.

There are no established pilots, but there are persons who are sufficiently acquainted with the navigation, to act as such. It is not usual for vessels entering the port to take a pilot, but it is sometimes done when departing. The masters of vessels make their own bargains with the pilots before they sail. The usual charge for piloting a vessel out is from $3 to $5. American vessels, proceeding from Smyrna to Constantinople, generally take pilots, who are paid about $25, for which sum they navigate the vessel to Constantinople, remain on board whilst there, act as the captains interpreter, and bring her back to Smyrna.

The annual importation of coffee from the United States is about 2,000,000 pounds, and the annual consumption is near 6,000,000 pounds. The importations of sugar, (refined or Havana,) amount to about 1,500,000 pounds, of which a very large proportion is taken by vessels of the United States.

Cotton manufactures, termed bleached sheetings, of the American looms, were, from their superior texture, in great demand, and met with a ready sale throughout the Turkish possessions. But their reputation was soon destroyed by the introduction from England of immense quantities of an imitation of this article, of a quality, however, so inferior, as to exclude fair competition, and to efface the distinctive character of the American fabric. Smyrna requires, annually, some 400,000 pieces of cotton goods, and something over 100,000 pounds of twist.

This market receives an annual supply of 100 chests of indigo, 10,000 pounds of cochineal, 300 puncheons of rum, besides iron, tin, lead, brandy, &c.

The export of opium, chiefly by Americans, varies from 300,000 pounds to 400,000 pounds. It is greatly superior to the opium of Hindostan, and always commands a readier sale in China. The other exports are, 500,000 pounds of silk, 60,000 kintals of raw cotton, 100,000 pics of carpets, 70,000 pounds of old copper, 400,000 horse hides, 1,500,000 pounds madder roots, 25,000 kintals wool, besides goats wool and skins, valonia, olive oil, drugs, sponges, figs and raisins, in large quantities, &c.

The wool exported to the United States amounts annually to about 4,000 square bales, weighing from 300 to 600 pounds; the figs to 130,000 drums, and the raisins to 200 tons.

On an average of the exports and imports, the charges on sales amount to about 12 per cent., and on purchases to about 8 per cent.

STOCKHOLM.

Stockholm, the capital of Sweden, is built on several islands in the Molar sea, near its junction with the Baltic. The harbour is commodious and safe; but the entrance is rather dangerous, on account of the many rocks and small islands. The vessels employed in the trade of Stockholm are mostly Swedish, because all goods imported under other flags pay a heavy duty. Lat. 59° 21′ N. Long. 18° 04′ E.

The few articles that Sweden produces are much sought after by other nations, viz.: iron, steel, copper, tar, pitch and timber. Iron, however, is the chief article of Swedish commerce, if we except the deals of Norway, (which latter country is now part of the kingdom of Sweden,) and which are from Christiana, the best in the world. The greatest export of iron is to England, where it is in great request. The produce of the mines is frequently contracted for beforehand.

The imports of Sweden are chiefly salt and colonial produce. Not every port in Sweden has the privilege of shipping goods in its own ships; those places that have this privilege, are called staple towns; the principal of them are Stockholm and Gottenburgh.

The principal articles of export, are iron, steel, pitch, tar and timber; of iron, the annual export is about 400,000 ship-pounds.

The imports are salt and colonial produce; refined sugars are prohibited, as is also hardware. As the import trade is not very considerable, ship owners, generally, send a cargo of iron, tar, pitch, &c., to England, and let the ship take there a charter to the Mediterranean or America, which not unfrequently pays in one voyage for the loss of the vessel.

Foreign vessels may bring the produce of other countries, besides their own, upon paying 40 per cent. additional duty.

There is in Sweden a company who have the monopoly of wrecks. The rate of salvage on Swedish property, if goods are not landed, is six per cent.; if landed, eight per cent. on the whole, lost as well as saved. On foreign property, 10 per cent.; on articles raised from a sunken ship, 20 per cent. if Swedish, 25 per cent. if foreign. On heavy articles, 15 per cent., after payment of expenses by the owner.

By the treaty of September 4, 1816, the produce of the United States and West Indies, may be imported into Sweden in American vessels, on as favourable terms as in Swedish vessels, except an addition of 10 per cent. on the duties, imports and charges on West India produce.

The manufactures and produce of the United States, are admitted upon the same terms as the same articles the production of any other country. The certificate of the American collector proves the goods to be of American produce or manufacture. American vessels, not intending to break bulk, may depart without any charges, except pilotage, wharfage or light money, where the same would be payable by Swedish vessels. If they discharge part only of the cargo, duties are payable only on that part; but the charges, &c., of the vessel itself, are payable at the port where she first breaks bulk, and only there. Americans enjoy all the rights of entrepôt enjoyed by the subjects of the most favoured nation. American vessels in ballast, or importing produce of the United States, or exporting Swedish produce, are on the same footing as Swedish vessels. Shipwrecked goods may be claimed in a year and a day. American vessels, from ports of the United States to ports in Sweden or Norway, or vice versa, shall not be subject to any quarantine, except that necessary for the visit of the health officer, provided they have a clean bill of health from the health officer of the port of departure; unless some person be found on board afflicted with a malignant disease, or general quarantine regulations have been promulgated as to all vessels from that port.

Masters of vessels, loading merchandise for Sweden, at a port where there is a consul, must present to him the manifest and original bills of lading, when, on comparing them, and finding them to be correct, he notes the same and returns them. The master who omits to comply with this regulation is subject to a penalty of 200 riksdalers; or if the documents contain false statements of the number or quality of the goods, the fine is 300 riksdalers.

The tonnage duty on Swedish vessels, whether entering or departing, is twelve skillings banco, per last, and on foreign vessels, except such as are privileged by treaty, 36 skillings per last.* But any Swedish or privileged foreign vessel, performing in the course of one calender year, more than one voyage to and from the same revenue district, shall pay the inward tonnage duty only, on any succeeding voyage made within that period.

On goods imported, which, according to the tariff, pay duty at a certain per centage on their value, or pay dissimilar duties on different valuations, the owners or importers must declare their wholesale price at the place of unlading, including insurance, freight, and other charges, except duties and other charges made at the port; and on goods exported, their wholesale price at the port of shipment, exclusive of the duty and shipping charges. To the declaration of the owner or shipper, must be annexed the invoice, policy of insurance, and bill of lading; he being bound, if required, to confirm the same by his oath. But in case of non-compliance on the part of the owner or importer, then any custom-house officer, as well as the commissioned deputies of the respective manufacturing and mechanic societies, are authorized to redeem the same *in toto*, provided it all be of the same quality, adding ten per centum thereto, and upon which amount, thus raised in value, the duty must be paid agreeably to the tariff.

Goods, the quantity of which, by Swedish weight or measure, cannot be ascertained on ship board, must be conveyed either to the public stores, or to the city scales, or gauger's office, in order to be weighed and measured. After making entry at the custom-house, the owner or importer of the goods will receive a bill of the amount of duties payable on the same, after payment of which he shall be at liberty to dispose of them, or if he prefer it, he may store the same on credit (*credit uplag*) for the duty.

In order to facilitate commercial transactions, the warehousing on credit, (*credit uplag*,) or the privilege of postponing payment of the duties on goods designated in the tariff, by the minimum quantities therein specified, shall be permitted until otherwise ordered, in the ports of Stockholm, Gottenburg, Gefle, Carlscrona, Carlshamn, Mal-

* Vessels of the United States are privileged by the treaty.

mo, Norcoping, Calmar, Wisby, Helsinburg, Westerwick, Ystad and Uddewalla, on the following conditions, viz.:

That the goods must be stored under the joint lock and key of the custom-house and of the owner.

That the owner of such goods, on paying the whole import duty, if to be sold within the country, and on paying the transit duty, when intended for re-exportation, and actually exported, shall be permitted to withdraw from the credit warehouse larger or smaller quantities, but never less than one half the minimum quantity allowed to be stored.

That the warehousing credit is not to extend beyond one year from the time when the goods were imported; within, or at the expiration of which period, they must be either re-exported, or the whole duty paid at such rates as existed when they were stored; otherwise they will be sold at public auction for account of the owner, who shall receive the balance of such sale, the import duty and charges being first deducted.

That previous to the admission of goods to the warehousing credit, the value thereof must be definitively appraised, and the accruing duty rated accordingly, which is to be paid when they are withdrawn, without regard to such variations in price as similar goods may have experienced during the interval.

That goods may be transferred from the credit warehouse of one city to that of another; always, however, dating the credit from the time of the first storage.

That upon application to the superior board of customs, goods may be transferred from credit warehousing to bond warehousing, (entrepôt,) on payment of the transit duty, and a small retribution, termed *recognitions afgift.*

Shipmasters, native or foreign, who, for pressing reasons, or to receive orders as to future destination, enter a Swedish port where there is a custom-house, may take in there, without payment of tonnage duty, refreshments, or make necessary repairs; and under the due observance of the navigation laws, and after giving in a written declaration as to the quality and quantity of the goods obtained for other ports of the country, or for foreign ports, may discharge greater or less quantity of the cargo of such goods as are allowed for importation; and take in provisions and complete her cargo of such goods as are allowed for exportation, without paying duty or other charges for more than is unladen or taken in; but the tonnage duties must be paid in full, as soon as loading or unloading, whether much or little has taken place. A vessel, either Swedish or foreign, having taken a part of her cargo at a Swedish port, is allowed to complete the same in any other Swedish port where there is a custom-house, of such goods as are free for exportation; the customs duties being paid at each separate port, on what may be there taken on board, but the tonnage dues must be paid in full at the first place of loading, and a receipt thereof entered on the passport.

Masters of merchant vessels are required to state exactly, in their manifest, their stock of provisions; and such thereof as is necessary for the support of the crew whilst on board, along with the following quantities of wine, brandy, coffee and rice, shall be free from duty or other charges at the port of delivery ; but this, however, only once a year, or when the crew is discharged for the last time, viz.:

From the Baltic.—A captain whose crew is six men and under, is allowed an anker of wine and a half anker of brandy.

If from seven to ten men, two ankers of wine and of one of brandy.

If from eleven men and above, three ankers of wine and two of brandy.

The captain is allowed one lispund of coffee and two of rice.

In this classification are included captains arriving from Holland, England and France, at the custom-houses, in the districts of Holland, Gottenburg and Bohus.

From the Western Ocean.—A crew of ten men and under, is allowed three ankers of wine and two of brandy.

If from eleven to fifteen men, four ankers of wine and three of brandy.

If from sixteen men and above, a hogshead of wine and four ankers of brandy.

The captain is allowed two lispunds of coffee and four of rice.

Wine and brandy must not be exchanged, the one against the other.

The necessary supplies of provisions for ships' crews, shall be furnished free of duty, whether the vessel enter the port, or they be taken to her in her boats, except such provisions be taken from goods in bond, or from the credit depot, when the duty must be paid.

From the Mediterranean and Levant.—On goods which, during conveyance to their place of destination, have accidentally received damage, no reduction of it to be allowed, if the owner wishes to have the disposal thereof. But should he consider the damaged goods not of sufficient value to pay the duty thereon, he must adduce legal proof thereof to the custom-officers, who shall proceed to sell them at auction, in which case the duty chargeable on goods of fixed value will be regulated on the proportion between that value and the price obtained, and on goods paying an ad valorem duty, the per centage will be charged on the price paid at the auction. The difference between the produce of the sale and the amount of duty, to go to the owner.

Vessels of all nations may, from stress of weather, for want of provisions, or to make repairs, enter Slito, or other ports of the coast of Gothland, where there are custom-houses, without paying any other charge than that of pilotage and the ordinary fees to the customs officers.

Extracts from Navigation Act of 20th October, 1835.

Every master of a vessel, whether Swedish or foreign, who takes in goods destined for Sweden, at a port in which a Swedish consul resides, must, before his departure from that port, appear before the said consul, and deliver to him a duplicate copy of the manifest of his cargo, signed by the master of the vessel, together with all the original bills of lading of the goods. The consul will compare the bills of lading with the manifest, and if he finds them to agree, he will certify the fact on the manifest, and return it, together with the bills of lading attached under the seal of his consulate, to the master. When the cargo is shipped at a European port, the numbers, marks, gross weight and cubic contents of every package, (except the goods be in bulk,) must be specified on the bills of lading, according to the mode of estimating them at the port where they are taken in.

Every master of a vessel, whether Swedish or foreign, arriving in Sweden with a cargo from a foreign port in which a Swedish consul resides, must, on delivery of his manifest and bills of lading, produce a duplicate copy of the manifest, certified as prescribed above.

A master of a vessel, whether Swedish or foreign, bound to a Swedish port which does not possess general bonding or warehousing privileges, shall not bring for re-exportation any goods, the importation of which into Sweden is forbidden, unless he proves, by producing his manifest and bills of lading, that it is his intention to prosecute the same voyage to a specified foreign port; when this cannot be satisfactorily proved the goods will be confiscated.

TUNIS.

The commerce carried on at present between the Christian states on the northern shores of the Mediterranean and the country of Tunis, is very extensive, and the exports are chiefly the produce of the country, which may be always shipped by getting a permit from the Bey, for those articles that pay a duty. Tunis is the most considerable state in Barbary for commerce. Lat. 36° 32′ N. Long. 10° 34′ E.

The principal articles of export are wheat, barley, beans, olive oil, hides, skins of wild beasts, wool, wax, honey, madder, roots, ivory, gold dust, scarlet caps, jerbi shawls, senna, soap, sponge, cotton, ostrich feathers, orchilla weed, and live cattle; but the trade with Tunis has not been cultivated in proportion to the advantages of which it is susceptible.

The principal port for shipping corn from the country of Tunis, is Biserta, about 50 miles west from Tunis, but no corn can be shipped without first obtaining a tiskery from the Bey, for which must be paid as follows:

For wheat, 22 $1\frac{1}{2}$ piastres per caffisi.
barley, $11\frac{1}{4}$ " "

The caffisi of corn is divided into 18 weales; 100 caffisi are $127\frac{1}{2}$ Winchester quarters.

The price of corn is extremely fluctuating; it is generally cheapest at the end of harvest, in August and September.

Wheat fluctuates from 30 to 70 piastres per caffisi; barley fluctuates from 12 to 35 piastres per caffisi. There is always a great demand for grain to export to Minorca, Majorca, the east of Spain, the south of France, and the greatest part of Italy and Malta.

Olive oil is chiefly shipped from Tunis, Soliman and Susa; but the last is by far the best place to load at, especially in point of expedition. Before any shipment takes place, a tiskery must be obtained from the Bey, paying two and a half piastres per metal, Tunis measure, which will weigh about 40 pounds English. The French, from Marseilles, take large quantities of oil. Some of the Tunis oil finds its way to England under the name of Gallipoli, especially for the use of the clothiers, it being a stronger bodied oil than the Italian.

The Susa oil is in higher estimation than the Soliman, and the latter is reckoned better than the Tunis oil.

Sponge is gathered on the sea shore near Sphax and Jerbi; it is inferior to that found on the shores of the Black Sea, yet it will always meet with a ready sale, especially in Malta, Sicily, Italy and Spain.

Soap is made in the kingdom of Tunis, and is exported in great quantities; it is usually shipped from the ports of Tunis and Susa. It is generally much cheaper and of a better quality at Susa.

Immense quantities of wool are annually exported from Tunis; the quality entirely depends upon the part of the country that produces it. At Tunis, and in the western part of the country, the quality of the wool is very indifferent; at Susa it is much better; at Jerbi, Sphax, and the eastern part, it is very fine, being equal to the Spanish wool: but having a much longer staple, it is better adapted for the manufacture of shawls.

Ivory and gold dust are articles of export from Tunis, but not the produce of the country. They are brought by the caravans from the interior of Africa, the trade carried on by these caravans being chiefly in slaves, ivory and gold dust. The traders from the interior generally arrive at Tunis in the month of June, and disposing of their merchandise, make purchases of goods to take back with them; the goods they take in return, consist chiefly in long ells, coarse woollens, fire-arms, gunpowder, watches and hardware. The caravans again set out from Tunis in October for Tombuctoo and the coast of Guinea.

Ostrich feathers are sold by weight, and divided into classes according to the quality; the Moors use many artifices to increase the weight.

The imports into the kingdom of Tunis form no inconsiderable part of the commerce of the Mediterranean; they are chiefly—from Syria, India muslins by the caravans, via Bussora, cottons, carpetings, silks, raw and manufactured, opium, copper and tobacco; from the Morea, dried fruit and figs to make brandy; from Tripoli, madder, roots and senna; from Trieste, glassware of various kinds, wood in beams and plank, iron, fine linens and woollens, chiefly low priced; from Spain, wine, brandy, wool and naval stores of all kinds; from France, hardwares of all sorts, watches, trinkets, fine linens, woollen cloth of all kinds, sugars and coffee; from Leghorn, Swedish iron, narrow and flat bars, tin in bars and sheets, lead in pigs, and shot, quicksilver, aquafortis, spices of all sorts, black and red stick, lack gum, benjamin alum, copperas, sugars of all sorts, coffee, cloths of various kinds, cochineal, logwood, nails, white and black ginger, fine linens and sheet iron.

The Tunisians receive most of the British manufactures, &c., via Leghorn; but, nevertheless, they consume a considerable quantity of English manufactures, particularly coarse woollens; great quantities of long ells, made in the neighbourhood of Exeter, being sent out for this particular market. The bales for the Tunis market should be assorted as follows:

10 pieces light blues,	long ells.	10 pieces coffee coloured,	long ells.
9 pieces Turkey blues,	"	2 pieces yellow,	"
9 pieces Mazarine blues,	"	1 piece green,	"
9 pieces red	"	50 pieces in each bale.	

Arch imperials.

10 pieces blue,	long ells.	5 pieces assorted colours, (no green,)	long ells.
15 pieces red,	"	30 pieces in each bale.	

Scarlet, long ells, should always be sent in separate bales; two or three bales of scarlet are sufficient at one time, and for the other bales, assorted as stated. There is always a demand at Tunis for any quantity, as the caravans take immense quantities into the interior of Africa.

The fine cloth which the Tunisians chiefly use, has been generally of French manufacture only, because they esteem the colour rather than the quality of the cloth. Bales should be assorted thus:

1 piece scarlet,	long ells.	1 piece purple,	long ells.
1 piece crimson,	"	2 pieces mazarine blue,	"
1 piece light wine,	"	2 pieces light blue,	"
1 piece deep wine,	"	1 piece green,	"
2 pieces deroy,	"	12 pieces in each bale.	

The pieces should be from 18 to 20 yards each, seven fourths wide; the cloth should not be shorn bare, but have a tolerable dress upon it.

The best season for a ship to go to Tunis with a cargo of merchandise is in the months of September and October, particularly for woollens; the weather then becomes rather temperate, and the Moors never think of purchasing an article for their own wear until the moment it is wanted, though they often pay double for it. Spices of all sorts are always paid for in ready cash; lead and all sorts of naval and military stores, pay no duty whatever; all other articles imported in British ships are, by treaty, to pay three per cent. ad valorem, but the tariff does not amount to more than two per cent.

The French pay the same tariff as the English; American vessels pay six per cent. ad valorem, if loaded by foreigners; but if loaded with American produce the duty is the same as Tunisians would pay in the United States: and the Jewish merchants, who enjoy the whole of the trade between Tunis and Leghorn, pay ten per cent. tariff upon all their imports.

Anchorage duty.—If in ballast, nothing. If they bring or carry away a cargo, 17½ piastres.

VENEZUELA.

No treaty has been made between the United States and Venezuela, since its separation from the government of Colombia. The treaty, however, which was contracted with that confederation in 1825, is still in operation as well as regards New Granada, as Venezuela and Equador. In conformity with its provisions and the decree of the government, issued in 1826, the commercial relations of the two countries stand on the footing that goods of the growth, produce, or manufacture of either party, on board its vessels, are admitted into the ports of the other, on the same terms as if imported in national vessels.

Custom-house regulations.—Numerous changes have been made by the congress of Venezuela in the custom-house regulations of this part of ancient Colombia. Five laws, all dated 12th may, 1834, and which were to go into operation the first October following, have designated, 1st. The ports which shall be open, as well to the importation of foreign merchandise, as to the exportation of national products. 2d. The regulations to be observed in custom-house transactions. 3d. The duties on imports. 4th. The proceedings to be had, and the penalties to be inflicted in cases of seizure.

The following ports are declared open (*habilitados*) for importation and exportation:

Angostura, in the province of Guyana; Carupano and Cumana, in that of Cumana; Barcalona, in that of Barcelona; La Guayra, in that of Caracas; Puerto Cabello, in that of Carabobo; La Vela, in that of Coro; Maracaibo, in that of Maricaibo.

In the province of Margarita, the ports of Pampatar and Juan Griégo are open for exportation and importation, for the consumption of the island.

The shores of the river Oronoco, are, in like manner, open for the exportation of cattle and mules, in the space comprised between Angostura and the post of Yaya.

The ports of Guiria, in the province of Cumana, and Caranero, in that of Caracas, are, in like manner, declared to be open for the exportation of their products.

Visit to vessels—manifest.—All vessels arriving from foreign ports in ports open to external commerce, shall, at the moment of coming to anchor, be visited by the administrator, or by the persons authorized by him, and by the commandant (*commandante*) of active service, (*resguardo,*) where there is one, with a chief (*cabo*) and a superintendent, (*celador;*) they will require from the captain his vessel's papers, (*patents de navigacion,*) and the manifest (*sobordo*) of his cargo, which shall express the class and name of the vessel; the nation to which she belongs; her tonnage; the name of the commander; that of the port or place of exportation; the number and description of packages (*bultos*) composing the cargo, with a description of their marks and numbers, the names of consignees according to bills of lading, (*consirmientos;*) the port of destination, and the list (*nota*) of provisions for the consumption of the crew.

There will be left on board one or more inspectors, (*celadores,*) if the vessel arrives with cargo. If in ballast, a manifest (*sobordo*) will not be required; but the other pieces (*documentos*) or papers (*noticias*) designated will be carefully examined, to ascertain if the vessel be really in ballast.

Within 24 hours after the arrival of the vessel, the captain will present himself at the bureau of the administrator, and will make declaration that he has no other articles on board than those specified in the manifest, (*sobordo*,) and agreeing with the bills of lading signed by him; he will sign this declaration, but reserving the privilege to correct his manifest for articles omitted.

The captain who does not present his manifest, (*sobordo*,) will incur a penalty of $200, and will be compelled to present it in 24 hours, collated with the bills of lading, which shall be returned to him after this verification; the unlading cannot be previously commenced.

Vessels bound to Angostura and Maracaibo will be in charge of one or more inspectors from Yaya and the fort of St. Carlos, to prevent the unlading of any articles before the vessels shall have been regularly visited.

Discharging.—Within three days after the vessel shall have come to anchor, the consignee or proprietor of the cargo shall make known at the custom-house whether or not it is his intention to discharge. If the unlading is to take place, in whole or in part, the necessary permit (*permiso*) will be required in writing within the time mentioned, and which shall state whether a part of the cargo is destined to other foreign ports, or those of the republic. In cases where it is not intended to unload, the vessel will be required to depart within six working (*habiles*) days after her arrival, except in cases of arrival to repair damages, and under charge of inspectors, in which case the vessel can only be permitted to remain as long as may be strictly necessary. When the proprietor or consignee retains on board a part of the cargo, to be sent to other ports, the re-exportation must be made within ten days following the discharge of the residue of the cargo; and whilst remaining in port one or more inspectors will remain on board.

No unlading can take place without permission from the collector and comptroller.

The permit to discharge will be delivered to the commandant to have it carried into effect, under the following formalities: 1st. He will, in writing, order the inspectors on duty in the vessel to permit the unlading. 2d. The inspectors will take account of packages discharged, and in designating the marks and numbers, will class them by cases, bales, barrels, trunks, *guacabs*, &c. He will compare these notes with the packages discharged, and if they agree, will deliver them to the commandant, who will copy them into a register, and will transmit them to the custom-house, that they may serve for reception of the packages into store. 3d. The commandant will prepare, daily, a list (*nota*) of the packages discharged, according to the separate notes received from the inspectors, and will transmit them every day to the administrator of the customs, in order that, before closing the expedition, the said administrator or the comptroller may confront it with the packages deposited in the custom-house stores, and that he may sign it, if correct, or make therein such rectifications as may be necessary. 4th. Inflammable articles and all others which are not in packages, objects in use, may, after verification by the visiters, be expedited from the strand or wharf without being placed in store. 5th. Discharging will take place in custom-house hours, that is to say, from six o'clock in the morning to three o'clock in the afternoon, and at the places designated. 6th. The discharging finished, and information thereof given by the captain of the vessel to the administrator, the latter or the comptroller, accompanied by the commandant, will proceed to visit the vessel for the purpose of ascertaining whether any articles remain on board except such as were declared in the manifest to be destined to other ports. 7th. The visit completed, they will confront the manifest (*sobordo*) with the quotidien notes of discharging, and if they agree, the commandant will certify that the unlading is completed.

Invoices and declarations.—Within 24 hours after notice given of intention to discharge, the proprietor, consignee or agent, must present an invoice (*factura*) or declaration (*manifesto*) in the Spanish language, with the prices, measure, and value of merchandise coming from foreign ports.

Verification.—After the deposit in custom-house stores of all the articles composing the lading of a vessel other than inflammable articles, and all others which are not in packages, objects in use, the verification will be made by the administrator and the comptroller, who will be held personally responsible. For the port of Cumana, the depôt and the verification prescribed above will take place at the entrance of the river.

Damaged goods.—When, at the time of verification, goods shall appear to be damaged, the administrator and the comptroller, assisted by a merchant named by the interested, shall proceed to estimate the damage, and no duty shall be levied on the value of the damaged goods. Goods once removed from the public stores can receive no allowance for damage.

Duties and extra duties.—The duties of importation will be conformable to the tariffs established by law, or according to valuations, if the merchandise is imported by national vessels, or by vessels of countries having with the republic treaties based upon reciprocity.

When the importation shall be by any other vessels, and when the duty is specific, there will be added 10 per cent. on the amount of duty ; if the duty is ad valorem, there shall be an addition of five per cent. on the valuation.

To enjoy the equality of duties established by the preceding paragraph, between national vessels and those of countries having treaties of reciprocity, it must be shown by a certificate (*certification*) of the collector of the port, that all the articles comprising the cargo are the products of the soil or industry of the nation to which the vessel belongs.

Valuations.—The valuation of merchandise liable to ad valorem duty, will be made by two viewers, to be named by the administrator. The viewers thus named will be competent for all questions relative to the same declaration, (*manifesto.*)

The basis of the valuation referred to shall be the price current of the market in which such valuation is made. There shall, from this valuation, be a deduction of 20 per cent., and the duties shall be liquidated on the balance.

Contestations.—Doubts entertained by the administrator as to the denomination of merchandise designated in the manifesto (*declaration*) of the importer, shall be resolved by a majority, of the comptroller and two viewers, as is prescribed for valuations.

Viewers, named to exercise the functions mentioned, cannot refuse to serve, unless justified by an adequate excuse in the opinion of the administrator. When the excuse is not admitted, the viewers nominated shall be obliged to exercise the functions, under a penalty of $200.

Tares.—The tare on articles subject to duty by weight, shall be deducted as follows:

Grain, fruit, seed, flour of all sorts, in linen bags, two per cent.

Articles in cases, cajones, barrels, &c., will be allowed the tare marked on the packages, subject to reweighing when the administrator shall deem it necessary.

Gauging.—The executive powers shall fix for the customs the weight and measure for liquids, as well as the capacity of the vessels (*envasis*) containing them, until they shall have been regulated by law, and will supply the custom-houses with the acrometres and other necessary instruments.

Allowance.—On liquids, in wooden vessels, four per cent. shall be allowed for leakage; the same allowance shall be made for damage on liquids in bottles, cases and barrels; on queensware, china, glassware and crystals, when an estimation is not demanded.

On each invoice or declaration (*manifesto*) mention shall be made of the verifications, valuations and estimations of damage; and the invoice shall be signed by those who have concurred in said proceedings; after which the duties shall be liquidated.

Liquidation.—The liquidation shall be made by the administrator and comptroller, conformably to the tariff, and within eight days at farthest. There shall be delivered to the proprietor or consignee, a note (*planilla*) of the duties, regulated by the above two authorities, in order that, after having ascertained that it is conformably to law, or after having it rectified, he may return it signed, that it may be annexed to the document (*expediente*) of the vessel's entry.

The document of entry which ought to be open for every vessel, as a basis of the calculation of duties, ought to be formed within the ten days which follow the customs verification; in this interval, the merchant should present the note in question, and the other pieces which complete the document of entry. This *expediente* will consist, 1st. Of the *sobordo* and permit to discharge. 2d. Of the original *manifestos* and valuation. 3d. Of the daily notes (*notas*) of discharging, examined by the commandant. 4th. Of the process verbals of verifications and of weighing. 5th. Of the process verbaux of seizures, if there have been any. 6th. Of the liquidation (*liquidacion*) of the duties, and of a declaration from the proprietor or consignee, announcing when the duties have been paid or secured to be paid.

Submissions.—The proprietor or consignee will guaranty the payment of the duties, with one or two securities, to be approved by the administrator or comptroller. He will sign the obligations (*pagares*) upon stamped paper.

The payment of duties shall be:

Up to $100	cash.
300	30 days.
500	60 days.

Above $500, whatever may be the amount, in equal payments of three and six months.

If the proprietor, importer, or consignee of goods, consent to abandon a part in payment of duties, or if they desire to re-export, they shall be permitted to do so, provided that the abandonment or re-exportation be declared before the goods are withdrawn from the custom-house. In the first case, the articles will be sold at auction, for account of the treasury; in the second, they will pay only one per cent. a month, for the time they have remained in the custom-house.

Coasting trade.—This is confined to national vessels.

Foreign vessels are allowed to transport from one legal port to one or more other legal ports, such part of their cargo as has not been unloaded, and which has been declared for transit for another or other ports; and also to take on board commodities of the country on the coasts, rivers or lakes where they are produced, or in depôt, provided such vessels comply with the laws on the subject of importation and exportation.

When goods are to be transported from one port to another in the same vessel in which they have been imported, the administrator and comptroller shall give the master a literal and certified copy of the manifest delivered at his entry, on which shall be stated the merchandise remaining on board.

From the 1st April, 1836, all articles of importation to pay ten per cent. additional, to be calculated on amount of said duties.

From the 27th February, 1836, cotton will pay an export duty of 50 cents per quintal; cocoa, five cents per quintal additional; coffee, 30 cents per quintal additional; hides, two cents each additional; horned cattle, fifty cents each; mules, 100 cents each; sarsaparilla, 25 cents per quintal.

VENICE,

Once the first commercial city in the world, but, under Austrian control, sunk to comparative insignificance. Its principal commerce is now more particularly with the Levant, the produce of which is transmitted from hence to other countries, and the Levant supplied with groceries, Dutch and German linens, dried and salted fish, &c. The manufactories of Venice afford large quantities of wrought silk for foreign commerce, also velvets and embroideries. The Venitian turpentine and mirrors are celebrated all over Europe.

The bank of Venice is the oldest in the world, being instituted in 1587. All bills made payable in Venice, in banco, used to be paid through the bank; but since the French carried away the funds or capital of the bank, this has ceased.

In proportion as Venice has declined, a neighbouring city and port, Trieste, in one of the Austrian provinces on the Adriatic sea, advanced. It has a large and safe harbour, and a great trade, as most of the foreign produce for the consumption of the Austrian States is drawn from it, so that it necessarily becomes a great depôt for the produce of the Levant; in return, it supplies those countries with many foreign articles.

WEST INDIES.

These islands, lying at the mouth of the Gulf of Mexico, between lat. 10° and 28° N. are of great importance in the commercial world. Their products are abundant and valuable, viz.: sugar, coffee, rum, molasses, cotton, cocoa, ginger, spices, aloes, pimento, indigo, drugs and dyes.

Their imports are flour, grain, lumber, staves, fish, beef and pork, horses, cattle, vegetables, manufactures of the United States, furniture, staves, hoops and heads.

Different regulations are in force as to the terms of importation in the several islands. Hayti and Margarita are independent; the rest are in subjection to the European powers.

HISPANIOLA, OR HAYTI.

This island is situated between Jamaica and Cuba on the west, and Porto Rico on the east. It has naturally a fertile soil, and its productions, consisting of coffee, cotton, sugars and mahogany, are in great demand; but since the expulsion of the whites, its exports have greatly diminished. The independent parts are now united under the government of president Boyer, and great efforts are making by the public authorities to render the negroes civilized and industrious. The ports are Cape Henry, Port au Prince, the mole in the government of Boyer, and St. Domingo in the Spanish part of the island.

The following regulations were promulgated March 30th, 1817, by Christophe, before the independent parts were united.

The landing and embarking of cargoes cannot be effected but upon the established wharves appointed for that purpose, and upon the permits in writing of the weighmaster of the custom-house, signed by the consignee or by their clerks, in presence of the searchers. These permits are valid for the day only. Landing and loading can only be done from sunrise to sunset, Sundays and holidays excepted, on pain of forfeiture of the goods.

The unloading and loading of articles brought for the government, may be done any where as may be ordered by the collector of the customs.

All masters of vessels may load and unload with their own boats.

The offices of customs shall be open from six o'clock in the morning until noon, and from two o'clock in the afternoon until six o'clock in the evening in the long days, and until five o'clock in the short days. The searchers shall always attend at the wharves until sunset.

The translation of the invoices or manifests shall be deposited at the custom-house by the interpreter, within 48 hours at most. The whole of the cargo of the vessel must be reported in the invoice, and at the bottom a memorandum of the merchandise not to be unloaded.

The collector is obliged to furnish to the consignee a statement of the importation duties within six days after the vessel shall be unloaded, that he may not be delayed when he clears out the vessel.

Transporting merchandise to the custom-house, unpacking for inspection, and repacking, shall be at the expense of the owners, as also for the exportation of produce. The inspection and purification of goods can only be done in the presence of the consignees and their clerks.

All merchandise not unloaded, which shall be declared upon the manifest, translated by the interpreter and signed by the captain or consignee, to be re-exported, shall be free of import duties. If, however, he may find it necessary to land those goods, thus declared, in order to export them by another vessel, he may do it, and the goods shall be deposited in the store of the consignee, under his and the captain's responsibility, and under the custom-house seal, and shall pay duty on re-exporting the same at 2½ per cent. If at the expiration of three months from the day of the arrival of the vessel, the goods thus deposited shall not be re-exported, they will be subject to the full duties.

All captains of foreign vessels, entering any of the ports of the kingdom, are to declare on their arrival if they mean to sell or not.

If a vessel puts in on account of stress of weather, and should want any repair which requires the cargo to be unloaded, the same must be deposited in a merchant's store, under seal of the collector of customs, and shall not be subject to any duty, unless it may be found necessary to sell part of the cargo; in which case the goods sold will be subject to the importation duty as per tariff, the remainder may be shipped on board the same vessel or any other.

In the case of a wreck, the collector of the customs or a searcher, as soon as informed thereof, shall go to where the goods may have been carried, in order to have them deposited at the custom-house, where a descriptive declaration and recognizance shall be made in the presence of the proprietor, (if any there,) or of the captain or supercargo, and a copy shall be given to him; those goods shall afterwards be restored to the owners on payment of the duties as per tariff, and in conforming to the articles of the law upon wrecks. In case of the goods being damaged, and that the same is duly stated, the duties shall only be chargeable upon the estimated value of those goods.

Captains who may have paid all the duties and fees of the different offices in one port, and shall go to another port of the kingdom, with the whole or any part of their cargo, not being subject to any other duty excepting anchorage and flag staff money.

The collector of the customs of the port, where the duties shall have been paid, shall state in the clearance that the duties have been paid, and, if necessary, shall enumerate the goods.

The import and export duties shall be paid before the vessel obtains her clearance.

The period of six months allowed by decision of his majesty in favour of foreign trade, dated the 19th of February, 1813, for the re-examination of ardent spirits, which shall not be sold, is confirmed.

When the collector of the customs has strong presumption of fraud, he may, in concert with the comptrollers, make every necessary search and inspection on board of the suspected vessel, which they may judge necessary, to assure themselves that nothing more has been unloaded or loaded on board but the merchandise or produce declared and specified in the permits.

In case fraud should be discovered, the collector of the customs and the comptroller, are authorized to have the whole or part of the cargo unloaded: they shall make a fair statement of the cargo, and the captain or consignee shall be jointly condemned to a fine of double the value of the goods or produce confiscated.

Fraud exists when the weight of any kind of produce found on board shall exceed ten per cent., the weight specified in the custom-house books, or when a greater number of bales, cases, bags or tons, than what is in the permits of lading or landing.

All merchandise or produce seized, shall be deposited in the custom-stores, and a statement of the fraud shall be transmitted within 24 hours at the office of the minister of finances and of the interior, where penalty shall be ordered. The articles seized shall be sold at public sale, and the amount proceeding therefrom deposited in the treasury, to be disposed of as may be directed by the minister of finance and of the interior.

The collectors of the customs are bound to have in their offices the ordinances and tariff for their guide; to communicate them to all who may be desirous of information, but without allowing the same to be taken out of their office.

All spirituous liquors are prohibited in the island of St. Domingo, and if intended for exportation, must be so exported on arrival; otherwise it is subject to confiscation and a fine of five dollars for every gallon on board.

The exportation of the following articles is prohibited, viz.: arms of all kinds and all munitions of war, all gold and silver, and whether coined, manufactured, or not, jewelry, copper, old iron, castor oil, campeachy and yellow wood.

Duties on exportation.

Coffee, per cwt.	$1 21
Sugar, white or clayed	1 80
raw	60
Cotton	1 20
Indigo, per lb.	5
Cocoa, per cwt.	60
Molasses, per velt	5
Raw ox hides, each	50
sheep or kid	10
Dressed do. per side	50
Mahogany, per fast	50
Gum guyacum, per cwt.	1 00
Chocolate, per lb.	5
Confectionary, per lb.	5
Cassia medicinal.	1
Yellow wax	10
Shell	$0 50
Marine salt, per bl.	50
Liquors, per 12 bottles	40
Tobacco	80
Horses and mares	40 00
Oxen	24 00
Cows	20 00
Antelopes and calves	12 00
Mules	40 00
Asses	20 00
Sheep	2 00
Presses of mahogany	40 00
Sideboards	30 00
Tables	12 00
Bedsteads	25 00

The eastern or Spanish part of the island lately declared itself independent, and has solicited to be admitted into the republic of Colombia.

PORT AU PRINCE.

The duties upon imports at Port au Prince are 12 per cent., except British manufactures in British vessels, which pay 7 per cent.

Wharfage.—Fifty cents per 1000 pounds French, on all articles to be weighed, and from 4½ to 50 cents upon every package.

Tonnage duties.—Fifty cents per ton, and payable only in one port.

In January, 1822, an additional duty of 50 cents per ton was laid at Port au Prince, and the present tonnage duty on foreign shipping is therefore $1 per ton.

Port charges.—For all vessels under 200 tons, $72; above 200 tons, $108, and payable at every open port where they land or ship any part of their cargo.

Commissions on sales, five per cent.; on return, 2½ per cent.

Export duties, including wharfage, weighage and territorial:

On coffee, per 1000 lbs	$37
cotton	47
sugar	19
cocoa	24
logwood and lignumvitæ	7

Tariff for the fountain.—Vessels between 15 and 50 tons, pay $4, and $4 for every additional 50 tons to $20, which is the maximum.

Stamps for entering and clearing a vessel	$10 50
on any sum not exceeding $200	6 00
of $200 and not exceeding 500	12 00
of 500 and not exceeding 1000	25 00
of 1000 and not exceeding 3000	50 00
of 3000 and upwards	100 00

MARGARITA.

This island belongs to the republic of Colombia, and is of course subject to the commercial regulations of that government.

BRITISH ISLANDS.

These are Anguilla, Antigua, Bahama isles, Barbadoes, Barbuda, Dominica, Grenada, Jamaica, Montserat, Nevis, St. Christopher, St. Lucia, St. Vincent, partly independent, Torbago, Tortola, Trinidad and Virgin Gorda.

The regulations for Bermuda are included under this head, though not properly belonging to it.

A contest has existed for many years between the governments of the United States and Great Britain in relation to the commercial intercourse of these islands; the former contending for the principle of reciprocity, and the latter seeking to engross the trade in her own vessels.

An arrangement was made during the administration of general Jackson, by which this principle was in effect given up; and by means of high duties imposed upon certain articles, directly imported from the United States, a preference is secured for the circuitous route through the northern colonies, and the trade is now chiefly carried on in British vessels.

The trade is now carried on under the following regulations:

Certain free ports are opened in the West Indies, of which a list is below, in schedule A., for the importation of certain articles specified in schedule B.

American and British vessels are admitted in these ports from the United States upon equal terms, but enormous duties are imposed upon the chief articles of supply direct from the United States, while the same are admitted from the northern colonies free.

Schedule A.

List of free ports.—Kingston, Savannah Le Mar, Montego Bay, Santa Lucia, Antonio, Saint Ann, Falmouth, Maria, Morant Bay, Jamaica; Saint George, Grenada; Roseau, Dominica; Saint John's, Antigua; San Josef, Trinidad; Scarborough, Tobago; Road Harbour, Tortola; Nassau, New-Providence; Pitt's Town, Crooked Island; Kingston, St. Vincent; Port St. George and Port Hamilton, Bermuda; any port where there is a custom-house, Bahamas; Bridgetown, Barbadoes; St. John's, St. Andrew's, New-Brunswick; Halifax, Pictou, and Sidney, Nova Scotia; Quebec, Canada; St. John's, Newfoundland; Georgetown, Demarara; New-Amsterdam, Berbice; Castries, St. Lucia; Bassaterre, St. Kitts; the port in the island of Anguilla; Charlestown, Nevis; Plymouth, Montserat; Sidney, Cape Breton.

Schedule B.

Asses, barley, beans, biscuit, bread, beaver, and all sorts of fur, bowsprits, cocoa, cochineal, coin and bullion, cotton, wool, drugs of all sorts, diamonds and precious stones, flax, fruit, and vegetables, fustic, and all sorts of wood for dyers' use, flour, grain of any sort, hemp, heading boards, horses, hogs, hides, hard wood or mill timber, live stock of any sort, lumber, logwood, mahogany, and other wood for cabinet wares, masts, mules, neat cattle, oats, peas, potatoes, poultry, pitch, rice, staves, skins, shingles, sheep, tar, tallow, tobacco, turpentine, timber, tortoise shell, wool, wheat, yarns.

Import regulations.—The master of every ship arriving in any of the British possessions in America, or the island of Mauritius, shall directly and before breaking bulk, report, upon oath and in writing, to the proper officer of the customs, the arrival and voyage of such ship. He shall state in such report, "her name, country, and tonnage; the name and country of the master and owners; the number of the crew, and how many of them are of the country of such ship; whether she be laden or in ballast; the marks, numbers, and contents of every package on board, where the same was laden, and where and to whom consigned, and where any and what goods, if any, had been unladen during the voyage; and shall further answer upon oath, any question concerning the same, which the officer shall ask him. And for failure in any of the aforesaid requisitions, he shall forfeit £100, and the goods not reported shall be forfeited.

No goods shall be unladen in any of the above named places until duly entered, and warrant granted for unlading the same. Nor shall any goods be unladen, except at a duly appointed and authorized place, and in the presence, or with the permission in writing, of the proper officer. And all goods unladen contrary to these regulations shall be forfeited.

The person entering such goods, shall deliver to the proper officer a bill of the entry thereof, containing the names of the importer, of the ship, of the master, of the place from which bound, and of the place within the port where such goods are to be unladen; also, particulars of the quality and quantity of the goods, of the packages containing them, with their marks and numbers, and shall pay down all duties due upon the same, and the officer shall thereupon grant the warrant for unlading.

If the importer of any goods shall declare upon oath that he is unable to make a perfect entry thereof, the officer of the customs may receive an entry by "bill of sight," and grant a warrant for landing and securing the goods; and the importer shall have access to them, in the presence of the officer, and shall, within three days after landing such goods, make out a perfect entry thereof, and pay all the duties on the same; and in default of such entry, the goods shall be taken to the king's warehouse, and, if within one month after landing, such entry be not made, and duties and charges paid, the goods shall be sold for the payment of the same, and the overplus paid to the proprietor.

The importer of any goods subject to "ad valorem" duties, shall, on entry thereof, state their value, (either in person or by his authorized agent,) by declaration in writing, subscribed by himself or agent, in the presence of the officer. But if it shall appear to the officer that such goods are not truly valued, the importer or his agent shall declare upon oath the invoice price of the same, and that he believes such price to be the current value of the goods in the place whence imported, and such invoice price, with the addition of 10 per centum thereon, shall be the value upon which the duties shall be charged; and if it shall appear that such invoice price is not the current value of the goods in the place whence imported, or if the invoice price be unknown, the goods shall be examined by two persons duly appointed, who shall state upon oath their true value in the place where entered, and such value shall be deemed the true value, upon which the duties shall be charged.

If the importer refuse to pay the duties on such articles, the officer of the customs shall, at a proper time and place, cause the same to be sold publicly to the highest bidder, and the proceeds of the sale shall be applied to the payment of the duties and charges, and the overplus paid to the proprietor.

If the goods are not landed and entered within 20 days after the arrival of the importing ship, the officer of the customs may convey the same to the king's warehouse; and if the duties are not paid within three months after the seizure, the goods may be sold for the duties and charges.

In any entry, warrant for landing, or taking out of the warehouse, the description given of the goods must correspond with that given in the report of the ship or the document by virtue of which they have been imported, and a proper description must, in all cases, be given, so that the goods may be "correctly charged with duties, according to the meaning of this act;" otherwise, such goods shall be deemed forfeited.

Any goods which may be lawfully imported into any of the British possessions in America, from a foreign adjoining country, by sea, may be also brought from such country into such possessions, by land or inland navigation, as well in the vessels, boats and carriages of such country, as in British vessels, boats or carriages. Provided, that the goods thus imported be brought into some port or place of entry where there is a custom-house lawfully established, and be subject to the same duties, rules, regulations, restrictions, &c., as the like goods imported by sea.

No vessel or boat shall be admitted to be British, on the inland waters or lakes in America, unless it shall have been built at some place in the British dominions, and be wholly owned by British subjects, and shall not have been repaired at any foreign place, to a greater extent than in the proportion of 10 shillings in the ton at any one time.

No British ship or vessel shall sail from any place in the island of Jamaica, to any place in the island of St. Domingo, or from any place in the latter island to any place in the former. Nor shall any foreign ship or vessel, which shall have come from, or during her voyage shall have touched at, any place in the island of St. Domingo, be allowed to enter any port in the island of Jamaica; nor shall any person be landed in the island of Jamaica from such ship, except in case of urgent necessity, or by license from the governor of Jamaica; and this under penalty of forfeiture of ship and cargo.

All laws, by-laws, or customs, which shall be attempted to be enforced in any of the British possessions in America, repugnant in anywise to any act of parliament relating to such possessions, shall be null and void to all intents and purposes whatsoever.

If any person in the British possessions abroad, shall forge, or wilfully use when forged, any documents necessary for the importation or exportation of goods, or shall procure any such documents by a false statement, or shall falsely make any oath required by the laws regulating the trade, &c., of such possessions, or shall forge, or publish when forged, any such necessary oath, he shall forfeit for every such offence the sum of £200, to be prosecuted and recovered as the laws direct.

If any goods, ship, or vessel, be seized as forfeited, and detained in any of the British possessions in America, the judges of the court, with the consent of the customs officers, may order the delivery thereof, on security by bond with two sufficient and approved sureties, to answer double the value of the same, if condemned.

If any goods be seized for non-payment of duties, or any other cause of forfeiture, and dispute arise whether the laws and requisitions concerning the same have been complied with, the proof thereof shall lie on the owner or claimant of the goods seized, and not on the officer making the seizure.

No goods shall be imported from the United Kingdom to any British possession in Asia, Africa or America, except in British ships; nor shall any goods be carried from one of such possessions to another, nor from one part of any such possessions to another part of the same, except in British ships;* nor shall any goods be imported into any British possession in Asia, Africa or America, in any foreign ships, unless they be ships of the country of which the goods are the produce, and from which they are imported, on forfeiture of the goods and ships, and £100 by the master thereof.

No goods shall be imported into any British possession, as from the United Kingdom, or any other such possession, (if any advantage attach to the distinction,) unless they appear upon the cockets, &c., to have been duly cleared outwards from the United Kingdom, or such other possession, or unless the ground of advantage be stated in the cocket; nor shall any goods upon importation into any of the British possessions, be deemed to be of the growth, produce, or manufacture of the United Kingdom, or of any such possession, unless imported from the last named places respectively.

All masts, timber, staves, wood hoops, shingles, lathwood, and cord wood for fuel, imported from any British possession in North America, into any other British possession in America, or into the United Kingdom, shall be deemed to be the produce of the British possessions in North America, and ashes brought by land or inland navigation into Canada, and imported thence into the United Kingdom, shall be taken as the produce of some British possession.

If any of the goods shall be imported through the United Kingdom, (having been warehoused therein, and exported from the warehouse, or the duties thereon if then paid, having been drawn back,) one tenth part of the duties therein imposed shall be remitted, in respect of such goods. And if any of the goods mentioned as before, shall be imported through the United Kingdom, (not from the warehouse,) but after all duties shall have been paid thereon for home use, in the said United Kingdom, and not drawn back, such goods shall be free of all duties herein imposed. No greater proportion of the duties imposed by this act, shall be charged on any article which is subject also to duty, under any colonial law, than the amount, if any, by which the duty charged by this act shall exceed such other duty, except the duty of sixpence per gallon on rum, or other spirits, the produce of any British possession in South America, or the West Indies, and imported into Canada, from the United Kingdom, which shall be payable over and above any duty thereon, under any colonial law.

A foreign vessel may pass from one colonial free port to another, and discharge part of her cargo at one, and a part at the other. Portions of the return cargo may also be taken in at different ports, but cannot be landed either in any other colony or in the British European dominions.

A foreign vessel may clear for several colonial ports, and can on the voyage touch at an intermediate colonial or even foreign port.

---

* This refers to mere coasting trade.

Duties are paid only on so much of the cargo as is landed at any one port. The tonnage duty where there is any, is payable but once, and that at the first port of entry; that is, such tonnage dues as are imposed by acts of parliament. Local port charges, or dock fees, vary at the different ports, and are exacted indiscriminately from British, as well as from foreign vessels.

The collectors and comptrollers of the said ports respectively, may appoint warehouses, from time to time, for the free warehousing of goods therein, and also declare what sort of goods may be so warehoused; and the importers of any such goods may warehouse the same, in the warehouses so appointed, without payment of any duty, on the first entry thereof.

As there are many places situated on rivers and bays, at which it may be necessary to establish free warehousing ports, for limited purposes only, the king, when making such appointment, may, by his order in council, limit and confine the same to any and such purposes only, as shall be expressed in said order.

On the entry of goods to be warehoused, the importer shall give bond and security, in treble the amount of the duties on such goods, for the safe depositing of the same in the warehouse, and for the payment of all duties thereon, or for the exportation thereof, according to the account taken of the same, at the landing thereof, with further condition, that no part of the said goods shall be taken from the warehouse, until cleared from thence, by payment of duty, or entry for exportation; also, that the whole of said goods shall be cleared from such warehouse, and that the duty upon any deficiency in the same, according to the first account taken, shall be paid within two years after the first entry thereof. If the goods be sold in the warehouse, the purchaser may give a new bond, to the same effect, and the old bond may be cancelled.

Upon the entry and landing of goods to be warehoused, the officers shall take an account of them, to be entered in a book to be kept for that purpose, and no goods so warehoused shall be taken from the warehouse, except after due entry either for exportation or home use; and upon the delivery from the warehouse of the whole, or a part, of the said goods, an account shall be taken of the quantity removed and of the quantity remaining, also of the quantity upon which the duties have been paid, and in case of deficiency in the original quantity, the duties on such deficiency shall then be paid.

The officers may permit samples to be taken of any goods in the warehouse, without entry or payment of duty, except as the same may afterwards become payable, as on deficiency. The officers may also suffer goods in the warehouse to be sorted, separated, packed and repacked, or altered in any manner necessary for the preservation, sale, shipment, or legal disposal of the same; and they may permit the same to be destroyed, but without prejudice to the claims for the duties due thereon.*

* A whole package may be abandoned for the duties without any liability for the duty on the same.

If goods be not cleared for exportation or home use within two years after warehousing, they shall be liable to be sold for duties and charges; but the officers of the customs may permit the same to remain in the warehouse a longer time, if they shall think it proper to do so.

Upon the entry outwards of goods to be exported from the warehouse, the exporter shall enter into bond, with approved security, that the same shall be duly landed at the place for which they have been entered outwards, or otherwise accounted for to the satisfaction of the customs' officers.

Wheat flour which shall have been warehoused at any free warehousing port in the British possessions in North America, and imported direct from thence into any British possessions in the West Indies, or in South America, shall be liable to a duty of one shilling per barrel, instead of the duty of five shillings now payable on the same under this act.

Wood of all sorts, warehoused *in like manner*, and exported direct from the warehouse, shall, upon importation into any *other* British possession in America, be liable to one fourth part only of such duty as would be otherwise charged on it.

Goods may be entered with the proper officer on arrival at any frontier port in the Canadas, to be warehoused at any warehousing port in the same possessions, and will be delivered by such officer to be passed on to such warehousing port, bond being given for the due arrival and warehousing of the same. Goods warehoused in any British possessions in America, may, upon due entry thereof, be delivered without payment of duty (except for deficiency) for the purpose of removal to another warehousing port, in the *same possession*, under bond for their due arrival and re-warehousing in such other port.

Wheat being warehoused or entered to be warehoused in any British possession in America, may be delivered to the importer for the purpose of being ground into flour; the importer giving bond for the warehousing within three months thereafter, of one barrel of merchantable flour for every five bushels of wheat so delivered, and such flour shall be deemed to be flour duly imported and warehoused.

Export regulations.—The master of every ship bound from any British possession in America or the island of Mauritius, shall, before lading any goods therein, deliver to the proper officer an entry outwards, under his hand, of the destination of the ship, stating all the necessary particulars; and before such ship shall depart, the master shall deliver to the proper officer a content in writing, under his hand, of the cargo of such ship, and shall make oath to the truth of such content, as far as his knowledge goes; and the master shall also, before his departure, come before the officer and answer upon oath, all the questions concerning the ship and cargo, crew and voyage, which shall be demanded of him, and the officer shall thereupon make out and give to the master a certificate of the clearance of such ship for her intended voyage.

No goods shall be laden on board any ship, in any of the above named possessions, until they have been duly entered, and warrant granted, for lading the same; and none shall be so laden except at some place duly authorized or appointed, and except in the presence or with the permission in writing of the proper officer; and any person entering any goods for exportation shall deliver to the officer a bill of entry thereof in writing, containing all the necessary particulars with regard to the vessel, crew and cargo, and pay all duties upon the same, and thereupon the officer shall grant his warrant for lading.

Before any sugar, coffee, cocoa, nuts, spirits or mahogany, shall be shipped for exportation in any British possession in America or the island of Mauritius, as being the produce of such places, the exporter shall deliver to the customs' officer the affidavit of the grower of such goods, declaring that such goods are the produce of his estate; setting forth the name of the estate, and the name of the consignee at the port of shipment, and containing an accurate description of the goods; and the exporter shall make oath that the goods entered are the same mentioned in the affidavit, and the master of the ship shall make oath before clearance, that the goods shipped by virtue of such entry, are the same intended and mentioned in the affidavit, to the best of his knowledge; and thereupon the officers shall grant a certificate of production for such goods, and if any such goods shall be imported into any other British possession without such certificate, as being the produce of any British possession, the same shall be forfeited, except mahogany, which shall be deemed to be of foreign production.

Upon re-exportation of the same goods in any of the British possessions, as the produce of some other possession, a similar certificate of production will be required, founded upon the original certificate of production by which the goods were imported.

Upon the entry outwards of any goods in any of the British possessions in America, to be exported to any other British possession or to the United Kingdom, it shall be stated in such entry that such goods are the produce of some British possession in America, or of foreign produce, as the case may be; and no goods shall be stated in the certificate of clearance of any ship, to be the produce of such possessions, unless expressly so stated in the entry outwards; and unless stated in the certificate of clearance to be the produce of such possessions, they shall, upon arrival in any other possession, or in the United Kingdom, be deemed to be of foreign production.

Duties payable upon Goods, Wares, and Merchandise, not being of the growth, production, or manufacture of the United Kingdom, or of any of the British possessions in America, imported or brought into any of the British possessions in America, by sea, or by inland carriage or navigation.

Imported into the British possessions in the West Indies, or on the continent of South America, or into the Bahama or Bermuda islands, viz.:

Wheat flour, the barrel, 5s.; imported from any British possession in North America, or from the warehouse in the United Kingdom, free.

Shingles, not more than 12 inches in length, the 1000, 7s.; more than 12 inches in length, the 1000, 14s.; imported from any British possession in North America, or from the warehouse in the United Kingdom, free.

Red oak staves and headings, the 1000, 15s.; imported from any British possession in North America, or from the warehouse in the United Kingdom, free.

White oak staves and headings, the 1000, 12s.; imported from any British possession in North America, or from the warehouse in the United Kingdom, free.

Pitch pine lumber, 1 inch thick, the 1000, £1 1s.; imported from any British possession, &c., free.

White and yellow pine lumber, 1 inch thick, the 1000 ft., £1 1s.; imported from any British possession, &c., free.

Dyewood and cabinet-maker's wood, free.

Other kinds of wood and lumber, 1 inch thick, 1000 ft., £1 8s.

Wood hoops, the 1000, 5s. 3d.; imported from any British possession, &c., free.

Beef and pork, salted, of all sorts, per cwt., 12s.; imported from any British possession in North America, free.

Imported into New-Brunswick, Nova Scotia, or Prince Edward's Island, viz.:

Wheat flour, the barrel, 5s.

Beef and pork, salted, of all sorts, per cwt., 12s.; fresh, brought by land or inland navigation, free.

Imported into any of the British possessions in America, viz.:

Spirits, viz. brandy, Geneva, or cordials, and other spirits, except rum, the gallon, 1s.; and further, the amount of any duty payable for the time being, on spirits, the manufacture of the United Kingdom.

Rum, the gallon, 6d.; and further, the amount of any duty payable for the time being, on rum of the British possessions in South America, or the West Indies.

N. B.—Rum, although British, if imported from any British possession in which foreign rum is not prohibited, is treated as foreign, unless it had been warehoused, and exported from the warehouse.

Wine, in bottles, the tun, £7 7s.; and further, for every £100 of the value, £7 10s.; and on the bottles, the dozen, 1s.; bottled in, and imported from the United Kingdom, for every £100 of the value, £7 10s.; the bottles, free; not in bottles, for every £100 value, £7 10s.; imported into the British possessions in North America, from Gibraltar or Malta, subject to no higher duty than if imported from the United Kingdom, viz., one tenth of the duty remitted.

Coffee, cocoa, sugar, per cwt., 5s.; molasses, per cwt., 3s. And further, the amount of any duty payable for the time being, on coffee, cocoa, sugar, and molasses, respectively, being the produce of the British possessions in South America or the West Indies.

Clocks and watches, leather manufactures, linen, musical instruments, wires of all sorts, books and papers, silk manufactures, glass manufactures, for every £100 value, £30.

Soap, refined sugar, sugar candy, tobacco manufactured, and cotton manufactures, for every £100 value, £20.

Alabaster, anchovies, argol, aniseed, amber, almonds, brimstone, botargo, boxwood, currants, capers, cascasoo, cummin seed, coral, cork, cinnabar, dates, essence of bergamot, of lemon, of roses, of citron, of oranges, of lavender, of rosemary, emerystone fruit preserved in sugar or brandy, figs, honey, iron in bars, unwrought, and in pigs, juniper berries, incense of frankincense, lava and Malta stone for building, lentils, marble, rough and worked, mosaic work, medals, musk, maccaroni, nuts of all kinds, oil of olives, oil of almonds, orris root, ostrich feathers, ochres, orange buds and peel, olives, pitch, pickles in jars or bottles, paintings, pezzolano, pumice stone, punk, Parmasan cheese, pickles, prints, pearls, precious stones except diamonds, quicksilver, raisins, sausages, sponges, tar, turpentine, vermillion, vermicelli, whetstones, £100 value, £7 10s.

Goods, wares, and merchandise, not otherwise charged with duty, and not herein declared to be free of duty, for every £100 value, £15.

Coin, bullion, and diamonds, horses, mules, asses, neat cattle, and all other live stock, tallow and raw hides, rice, corn and grain unground, biscuit or bread, meal or flour, except wheat flour, fresh meat, fresh fish, carriages of travellers; wheat flour, beef and pork, hams and bacon, wood and lumber, imported into Canada; wood and lumber, imported into New-Brunswick, Nova Scotia, or Prince Edward's Island; hay and straw, fruit and vegetables, fresh, salt, cotton wool, free.

Goods, the produce of places within the limits of the East India Company's charter, imported from those places, or from the United Kingdom, or from some place in the British dominions, free.

Herrings, taken and cured by the inhabitants of the Isle of Man, and imported from thence, free.

Lumber, the produce of, and imported from any British possession on the West Coast of Africa, free.

Any sort of craft, food, and victuals, except spirits; and any sort of clothing, and implements, and materials, fit and necessary for the British fisheries in America, imported into the place at or from whence such fishery is carried on, free.

Drugs, gums or resins, dyewood and hard wood, cabinet-maker's wood, tortoise shell, hemp, flax, and tow, free.

Seeds, wheat flour, fruits, pickles, woods of all sorts, oakum, pitch, tar, turpentine, ochres, brimstone, sulphur, vegetable oils, burr stones, dog stones, hops, cork, sago, tapioca, sponge, sausages, cheese, cider, wax, spices, tallow, imported direct from the warehouses in the United Kingdom, free.

All goods imported from the United Kingdom, after having there paid the duties of consumption, and being exeported from thence without drawback, free.

BAHAMAS.

These islands, situated between lat. 26° and 21° N., and long. 79° and 71° W., belong to Great Britain. The most important of these are New-Providence, lat. 25° 05′, long. 77° 22′; Exuma, lat. 23° 36′, long. 75° 51′; Turk's Island, lat. 21° 30′, long. 71° 03′; and Crooked Island, lat. 22° 48′ N., long. 74° 18′ W., all being ports of entry for vessels of the United States to procure salt.

The articles of export are salt, cotton, pimento, dyewoods, fruit, &c.

BERMUDAS.

These islands are situated at 650 miles distance from our coast, in lat. 32° 22′ N., long. 64° 33′ W., containing about 20,000 acres of land. The soil is not fertile, and the productions neither abundant nor valuable; but on account of the difficulties in the direct trade between the United States and the British West India islands, they enjoy considerable commerce with the United States.

SPANISH POSSESSIONS.

CUBA.

This island is subject to Spain, and is the largest of the West India islands, being 235 leagues long, and from 45 to 14 broad. Its principal ports are Havana, lat. 23° 09′ N., long. 82° 19′ W.; St. Jago de Cuba, lat. 19° 57′ N., long. 76° 05′ W., and Matanzas, lat. 23° 02′ N., long. 81° 36′ W.

Havana is the entrepôt between Spain and Mexico, and has a good and spacious harbour.

Its exports are sugar, coffee, cocoa, copper, logwood, sarsaparilla, drugs, tallow, tortoise shell, hides, spirits, molasses, honey, segars, cotton, mahogany and ebony.

The commercial regulations which have been procured are as follows:

With the view of affording to the captain as well as to the consignee of a vessel, the opportunity of examining and comparing the manifests, by their advices or bills of lading, during the 12 hours allowed to make any additions or explanations to it, said manifest will remain with the administrator general during office hours, and if not office hours, he will send it to the custom-house to the office of the *resguarda*, in charge of the chief officer of the revenue at that place, or the person representing him, who is bound to produce it to those interested, during the 12 hours allowed; and every time, during that period, that request is made to see, or take copies of it, it shall be allowed; retaining carefully, in his custody, the originals, as sacred and inviolable documents. In case the administrator general's office is open, the said manifest shall there be free for inspection, under the rules referred to.

In extraordinary cases, in which it is for the interest of commerce to expedite the sailing of vessels, to save insurance, to be ready for a convoy, or for other similar motives, the administrator general will give particular permission, so that loading may go on at others, as well as at office hours, always seeing that it is not prejudicial to the royal interest. He will also give orders for the transporting of goods to the deposit warehouses, as well as from thence, for consumption or exportation, after the payment of the two per cent. duty. He will, also, when vessels, owing to their build, will not allow the discharge of the whole cargo, without taking weight in, allow a sufficient quantity of logwood and country produce to be taken in. He will see, also, that, without any impediment, or new demands of duties, the produce of the country, and other articles of exportation, regularly entered, and on which the duties have been paid, may pass from one vessel to another, which, for want of room, cannot be loaded in the vessel for which they were intended; and lastly, also to the arrangements of the warehousing operations, and the transfer of logwood, and other articles of the same nature, which, being only in transitu, may obtain these facilities.

When articles are manifested in transitu, their owners must deliver a detailed note of the contents of each package: those which are to be landed immediately and placed in security in one of the custom-house warehouses, from which will be excepted those which, from their bulk or kind, may, according to the judgment of the administrator general, remain on board, and those which will be landed in deposit until re-embarked, unless it seems proper to the owners to pass them to the mercantile deposit warehouses, or for the consumption of the place; in which case they will be inspected under the established regulations.

The permission to haul into the quay, the orders to leave it, permission to discharge, and all matters relative to these particulars, appertain to the powers of the administrator general.

All national or foreign vessels may load with molasses in any of the ports of entry in the island, or sailing in ballast from one of those ports, by permission of the administration of the revenue, thence to the port (not of entry) where they wish to load, requiring from the consignee, bonds compelling the vessel to return with its cargo of produce to the same port of entry from whence she sailed. In this port she will undergo a search visit, and will pay the established export duties, when she will be furnished with the necessary documents to prosecute her voyage from the island.

It is established as a general rule, that no damaged jerked beef shall be admitted, no matter from whence shipped; and if, of the quantity manifested, a part proves injured so as to require its being thrown into the sea, in this case the duties will be paid only on that portion which proves sound, without any deduction or release of the 6 or 14 per cent., according to whence it came, which must be settled, when the duties are calculated on the whole amount of the manifest.

Tonnage duty.—All vessels which shall enter any of the ports of entry of this island, shall pay 12 reals fuerte for each ton measurement, if foreign, and 5 if national vessels.

Those that arrive in ballast, and intend leaving in the same state, shall be exempted from the above duty; but should they have taken in any produce or goods, they shall pay the full tonnage duty.

Vessels arriving in want of water or provisions, will be exempt from the tonnage duty; but should they unload the whole or a part of their cargo, or take in the produce of the country, they shall pay the full tonnage duty.

National or foreign vessels, which have loaded goods for exportation at any of the ports of entry of the island, and secured the respective tonnage duty stated in this tariff, if obliged to put back to any of the ports to repair damages sustained at sea, or owing to other accidents, shall be exempt from having again to pay the tonnage duty.

National or foreign vessels, entering the port of Havana, shall pay one and a quarter reals for every ton measurement, for the maintenance of the dredging machine, over and above the foregoing tonnage duty.

Havana—Custom-house regulations.—Every master of a vessel is bound to have on his arrival, ready for delivery to the boarding-officers of the revenue, two manifests, containing a detailed statement of his cargo; and in the act of handing them over, has to write thereon the hour when he so delivered them, taking care that they be countersigned by the boarding-officers.

Within 12 hours from that time, he can make any alteration he pleases in these manifests, or deliver in new ones corrected.

After the expiration of the 12 hours, no alteration will be allowed; goods not placed on the manifests will be confiscated, without appeal; and if their value should not exceed $1000, masters of vessels will be liable to pay a penalty of double the amount of such goods; if they exceed that sum, and belong to the master, or are consigned to him, the vessel, freight, and other emoluments, will be forfeited to the revenue.

Goods on the manifest, but not on board, will pay duties as if they were on board.

Goods not on the manifest, but which are claimed in time by a consignee, will be delivered over to the latter; but the master will, in this case, be subjected to a fine, equal in amount to the value of the goods.

Gold and silver not on the manifest, or claimed in time by the master or a consignee, are liable to a duty of four per cent.

Goods falling short of the quantities set forth in the manifests, when landed, and not being included in the invoice of a consignee, will render the master liable to a penalty of $200 for each package so falling short.

Every consignee is obliged to present his invoice, or note of goods, within 48 hours after the arrival of the vessel; if he omit so to do, such goods are liable to a charge of 2 per cent. extra duty.

The same rule applies, if such invoice do not contain a statement of the number of pieces, contents, quantity, weight and measure.

All goods imported in vessels exceeding 80 tons burthen, except perishable provisions, bulky articles and liquors, may be placed in depôt, for an indefinite time, paying one per cent. inward, and one per cent. outward, on the preceding valuations each year.

When entered for home consumption, they are liable to the corresponding duty; if sold in depôt, the exporter pays the outward duty.

St. Jago de Cuba.—The superior authorities of Cuba have constituted St. Jago a port of entrepôt, with all the advantages attached thereto, now enjoyed by Havana.

Harbour regulations.—All masters of vessels entering the port of Havana, must observe the following regulations.

All vessels entering this port, must avoid anchoring in the channel, and in case the wind will not allow them to go up the harbour, they must anchor near the east side, and avail of the first opportunity to proceed to the anchorage destined for them, which is in the proximity of Casa Blanca, at the distance of 40 fathoms, moored head and stern, and to extend in tiers of two, from the guardship in a line to the king's warehouse, and thence in tiers of three to the wharf of D. Juan Perez; under no pretext, whatever, to approach a man-of-war nearer than a cable's length, otherwise a launch will be sent on board to remove said vessel, the expense of which, and a fine of $50, shall be paid by the master or consignee of any vessel disobeying this order.

The master, on coming ashore, must present himself at the harbour-master's office, with a list of passengers, if any. If he has powder on board, he must report the quantity, in order to make the necessary dispositions for its deposit; if notice is given of any being concealed on board, he (the master) shall pay a penalty of $80: as it has been observed that some delay its deposit, in order to profit time to haul to the wharf, and others keep their powder on board while in the stream, under pretext of there being but a small quantity. The firing of arms, of all kinds, in the harbour, is prohibited under a penalty of $50, without permission from the admiral, and giving notice at this office.

Every master of a vessel, at the time of anchoring, must take care that his cables do not get foul of others, as he will be liable to make good any damage that may arise from his carelessness.

No vessel shall be fastened to the buoys which are placed to indicate the sand banks in the channel, nor to those destined for the vessels of war. The master doing so, or moving a buoy from its place, shall pay a penalty of $100, and also the expense of all damage which may result from a violation of this order.

The master intending to haul his vessel to the wharf, must first have a place assigned him by the collector of customs. He shall by no means lay behind those fastened to the wharf, under a penalty of $50, and a liability for all damages that might follow; these are principally in case of hurricanes or fire, when it would be necessary to separate a vessel from the wharf. He must also place fore and aft the lower yards, take in the jib and flying jib, and main boom, and cockbill his anchors, in order to avoid damaging other vessels. They must be distant from each other at least one foot and a half by the beam, by which means they may haul from the wharf without difficulty. In hauling to the wharf, or leaving it, or moving from one place to another, permission must first be had from the harbour-master's office; and either one or the other can only be done from daylight until 9 o'clock in the morning, or from sunset till dark; but by no means can they remain in the channel, or disturb the free ingress and egress with lines or ropes, under penalty of $100, and payment of damages they may occasion.

At sunset, fires on board all vessels must be extinguished. The cabin light may be continued till the usual hour of retiring, provided it is kept in a lantern in good condition.

No vessel can take on board or discharge ballast without a written permission from the harbour-master's office, where the place will be pointed out from which it must be taken, or where it must be discharged. Care must be taken to place a tarpawlin to prevent its falling in the water. In neglect of this, the charges prescribed will be brought against the master. Equal care must be taken in discharging bricks; and, on no account, must any straw, sand, or sweepings, be thrown overboard, under a penalty of $50; for, if there be any on board, the master may call at the harbour-master's office, after putting it in the launch, in order to tell him where to discharge it.

In case a master should wish to caulk, repair, careen, heave down, or fumigate his vessel, he must first obtain permission at the harbour-master's office; but by no means will it be allowed at the wharf, or in the stream, as there are, for this purpose, several careening places, where it may be done without danger to the harbour. It is likewise prohibited to heat tar or pitch on board, as this can only be done on shore, and with the greatest precaution: it being understood that those who violate this article shall pay a penalty of $100, and, also, the damage resulting therefrom.

In case of any vessel getting unmoored, and being in danger of stranding, or being lost, by weather or other accident, it is the duty of all other vessels to render every possible assistance.

A master of a vessel, who may require a launch, is at liberty to make his selection; but he must give notice to the harbour-master's office, in order to have it examined, as prescribed by ordinance; and he who loads said launch without leaving the wales two inches out of water, shall be subject to a penalty of $20.

No vessel can pass the shoals and channels in the harbour without taking a pilot, to which purpose the master may call for one at the harbour-master's office, paying said pilot $5; which sum is allowed him, by tariff, after he has performed his duty: it being well understood that the master who does not call for a pilot, and notice being given of his having passed the shoals and channels without one, shall pay, in addition to the $5, the penalty incurred by violating this article.

In case of disturbances on board amongst the sailors at late hours in the evening, the master may call on board the flag-ship for assistance until the morning, when he may get an order from the harbour-master's office to lodge them in jail. No master of a vessel shall discharge his seamen without permission from his excellency the governor.

Every master of a merchantman must hoist his flag when he sees one displayed from the flag-ship. The day before he goes to sea he may call at the harbour-master's office for an order to take his powder on board, if he has any in deposit. No vessel will be allowed to leave port before sunrise or after sunset.

It is likewise prohibited to pass backward and forward in the harbour in boats after gun fire in the evening; on the contrary, they are exposed to being carried on board the flag-ship, where they will remain at the disposition of the admiral.

The wharf dues are, on Spanish vessels, 6 reals per day; on the vessels of other nations, 10 reals per day, for each 100 tons of their register measurement.

American vessels clearing out for Havana, or any port in Cuba, must procure certificates from the Spanish consul; and Americans intending to land, must procure a passport at the port of departure from the United States.

PORTO RICO.

Regulations.—Captains or supercargoes of Spanish vessels, from foreign ports, must hand in, on the first custom-house visit, to its officer, a manifest affirmed by him, comprehending his whole cargo, specifying the bales, casks, &c., and their contents; and if he intends proceeding to other ports of entry in the island, with the whole, or part of his cargo, will receive a permit for the ports he desires, he being required to return the permits; and in every port he must pay up the duties for such parts of the cargo as was there discharged.

Foreign vessels which do not unload, or which discharge only part of their cargo, and which take the balance to other places, will have to hand in a manifest, as mentioned for Spanish vessels, when they will be allowed to go where they please; and in lieu of the (guia) permit, he will be furnished with a certified copy of his original manifest, which, after being translated by the royal interpreter, will remain deposited in the archives of the custom-house of the port where he made his first entry.

The license, or permission to haul in at the mole, the orders for leaving it, permits for loading or unloading, and all those relative to these particulars, will proceed from the royal custom-house, where application must be made by those interested in those matters, as well as when, in extraordinary cases, in what interests commerce, for the prompt sailing of vessels, permission is required for extra business hours, or days for loading and unloading.

Decree, issued the 19*th July*, 1822.

The captains or supercargoes of foreign vessels, must deliver at the custom-house visit, which will be made whilst anchoring, a manifest of the cargo, signed and sworn to, and defining, in parcels, the casks, bales, &c., of which it is composed. This manifest shall be certified at the end, and signed on each of its leaves, by the boarding officer, in the presence of the captain or supercargo.

If any captain or supercargo deliver an incorrect or faulty manifest, or refuses making one, at the very instant of so doing, he will be fined the sum of one hundred dollars, without its affecting any additional fine, which, owing to the circumstances of the case, may be inflicted.

Within the first twenty-four hours, at furthest, the captain or supercargo must personally appear at the custom-house, with his consignee, and deliver a manifest containing a detailed statement of his cargo, with the original invoices, and he will also ratify the oath that he has not on board of his vessel any goods, &c., except those by him declared, and the interpreter will certify to this on the same manifest or invoices when translated.

For failing to deliver the detailed manifest within the twenty-four hours, as stated in the foregoing article, and ratifying and swearing to the same, a fine of one hundred dollars will be imposed on the captain or supercargo, and if any difference is found between the manifests which shall amount over three per cent., the excess shall be confiscated, but if not exceeding three per cent. the difference of duties will be received.

If the captain is not himself, or has no supercargo, and has not the invoices and individual manifests and entries, the consignee, or the persons concerned, are held bound to make the entries, and to present the original invoices within the twenty-four hours; which shall be translated by the royal interpreter within the forty-eight hours next succeeding their delivery.

Nothing must be taken on board, or landed from a vessel, before or after the delivery of the manifest or invoices, without the knowledge and permit of the custom-house. If attempted, or done, no matter of how little value, the article landed will be seized and condemned.

If goods are transported from one vessel to another in the bay, without the knowledge and consent of the custom-house, both the goods and the boat which conveyed them will be condemned.

Goods fraudulently landed, and seized by the custom-house officers, besides their own forfeiture, shall be immediately valued as per the rule laid down in the tariff, or if it does not contain the valuation, by the current wholesale prices of the port. If the value exceed six hundred dollars, and the vessel, from whence landed, is owned, or part owned by the captain or supercargo, the vessel and all its appurtenances shall be condemned.

The discharging of vessels shall always be done within office hours, as expressly ordered by his majesty, and at the wharf and place designated by the custom-house.

The goods and articles which have to be inspected, weighed or measured, must not be removed from one place to another without a permit from the custom-house. The infraction of these two articles will cause the seizure of the articles landed or removed.

It is expressly forbidden to sell any article whatever by retail on board of vessels: those seized as such will be condemned.

Goods and other articles manifested for transit or re-exportation, if landed, or are intended to be fraudulently introduced into the country, will be seized, wherever found, and condemned. In this case, if the goods seized, on being valued, amount to $500 or more, and the vessel is owned, in whole or in part, by the captain or supercargo, added to the condemnation of the goods seized, will be that of the vessel and all its appurtenances.

The stores and provisions of the voyage must also be entered on the manifest; and if there appears to be a considerable excess, taking into consideration the length of the voyage and the number of the regular consumers, duties will have to be paid on the excess.

The baggage of passengers comes under the same restrictions and inspection; and if any real fraud is discovered to be intended, the whole will be condemned.

Cargoes of produce, and other goods of the country, for exportation, will conform to the present established rules. Molasses, or any other article not subject to being weighed, must, indispensably, be measured, and inspected on the wharf, at which the boats lay which are to take it off. Without these formalities it cannot be embarked; and those who would evade them, or attempt it, will lose its value by condemnation, and be liable to further fines.

The officers of the customs who do not comply, as bound, in seeing the execution of this decree, either through neglect, evil intentions, or personal interest, will, without fail, be severely punished, according to, and with all the rigours of the law.

Hereby is permitted the transhipment of all kinds of goods for all the ports of Spanish America united to the mother country, and to those of foreign nations, friends or allies, as well in neutral as in Spanish vessels, by their paying a duty of 2 per cent. on the value of the exports.

If the transhipment and re-exportation is for any other port in the island, it will fully pay, at the first port of entry, not only the regular import duties on the goods, but also the 2 per cent. on the value of the exports.

All articles of commerce liable to duty, and manifested on arrival for the privilege of transit and re-exportation, if transhipped in the bay to another vessel, Spanish or foreign, bound to a Spanish port not on the island, or a foreign port, shall pay 2 per cent. on the value of the exports.

Nevertheless, if re-exported in the same vessel which imported them, without having been removed therefrom, no duty whatever shall be required.

Nor shall such part of the cargo, which, owing to damage or bad quality, is therefore re-exported without having been landed in any of the ports of this island, be required to pay any duty.

The articles of commerce mentioned in the three preceding articles, if landed and stored, will pay the full amount of duties; but a credit of 60 days (counting from the day of their landing and being inspected) will be allowed, on giving bonds for its payment to the custom-house, under the required security of the consignee, or another responsible person.

All articles of commerce landed and stored will be allowed to be re-exported in national or foreign vessels from this island, previous to having been fully four months stored, and the duties returned, deducting therefrom the two per cent. on the value of the exports.

After the four months allowed for the drawback of duties shall have expired, it will only depend on circumstances and weighty causes and reasons, such as being at a great distance from the owners, and the necessity of awaiting their orders or advice, which may cause its being granted; in which case one month more may be allowed for drawback.

Articles merely deposited on shore, will remain free of duty; duties being required only on those sold to pay those interested, or by their wish.

FRENCH POSSESSIONS.

The islands belonging to France, are Guadaloupe, Martinico, part of St. Martins, Marie Galante, and Deseada. The two last islands are not opened to any foreign vessels. In clearing out for these islands, it is necessary to procure the certificate of the French consul.

Business is done at these islands for cash; the commission merchant generally sells for a credit, but settles with the master for cash or good bills, or produce.

At the commencement of the French revolution in 1792, these islands were opened to the United States, and all nations at peace with France, without any restrictions, other than a small colonial duty on imports and exports. In this state of things the American trade rapidly increased, and became lucrative, as all the produce of the colonies was free from any restrictions. Sugar, coffee, cotton, &c., as well as molasses made up the return cargoes of American vessels; these again were exported to Europe, and found a ready market there; affording a large advance to the merchant thus employed.

The French merchant pays only one per cent. on all importations from France, and receives a bounty of 12 frs. on every cwt. of French fish imported from France into the colonies, and 15 francs on all codfish imported directly from Newfoundland or her dependencies in North America, in French vessels; while the American merchant pays three and a half francs duty on every cwt. of fish imported into the colonies. With this odds the American merchant cannot compete with the French, as the islands are abundantly supplied with French fish at all seasons,—though many of them of inferior quality, and in a decaying state when they arrive from France, owing to the long and circuitous route taken to convey them to the colonies. Many fish, however, are imported in as good a state of preservation as the American fish. Formerly the planters depended on the American fish entirely for their slaves; now they use the French fish only, as they come so much cheaper. All the American fish now consumed is for the retail market, say from 50 to 60 hhds. of 1000 lbs. each per month in both colonies, unless the French fish should be at any time short. This is not now to be expected, as the first new fish from Newfoundland is sent directly to the colonies, where the bounty secures a good profit. The American merchant may constantly use his liberty of carrying codfish to the islands and paying 3½ francs per 100 lb. duty. He must pay also nearly $2,75 on every barrel of beef, 7 per cent. on rice and tobacco on a high valuation, and an additional duty of one franc per hundred on tobacco. Taxes by the colony—same duty on all pickled fish as on dry; 2 francs on every barrel of 3½ bushels corn; and 4 per cent. on lumber of all kinds, all other articles being prohibited. It remains then that lumber, rice, tobacco and pickled fish, are the only articles wanted from the United States; even rice is imported in French vessels from Africa and Brazil—one ship arrived in April, 1835, at Point Petre from Africa, with 60 tons.

France not only supplies fish as before stated, but bread stuffs, flour, potatoes, peas, beans, and pulse of all kinds; pork, butter, lard, some beef, and all other productions from France, cheaper than they can be purchased by the United States, even if permitted on the same footing with French produce and manufactures. Live stock is furnished from Porto Rico and the Spanish Main much cheaper than they can be furnished by the United States.

Commissions on sales, are 5 per cent.

" on purchases, 2½ per cent.

St. Martins, 15 miles north-west of St. Bartholomews, 19 miles long and 14 broad, is held jointly by the French and Dutch governments. The French part being a dependance of Guadaloupe, and the Dutch being subject to the authority of St. Eustatius.

The plantations here are very handsomely laid out. The Dutch part of the island, though by far the handsomest portion, is not so fertile as the French; nor is agriculture so well attended to in the first as the last, if we except Cul de Sac, where the sugar estates vie with those of St. Croix, Barbadoes, and Antigua. In this quarter of the island the best planters reside; and the sugar manufactured here is, generally, superior to that made in any other part of the country.

The principal towns are Phillipsburg, the Dutch metropolis; and Mary-gut, the residence of the French commandant, and other public officers. Phillipsburg is located on a sand bank, on the south side of the island; contains a few neat buildings, and a great number of small houses; the population may possibly amount to 3000, including slaves and free people of colour. The police and custom-house regulations are pretty much like those of St. Eustatius, though the public officers are generally more addicted to extortion. Few Americans go here, as supplies can be procured very easily from St. Bartholomews and St. Eustatius, to which ports their produce is shipped.

The few vessels that trade here barter their cargoes for sugar, rum, &c., there being little or no money in circulation. The merchants here are generally correct dealing men.

The capital of the French part of St. Martins is Mary-gut, situated on the west side of the island. The French part is divided into four districts, viz.: Mary-gut, Columbia, Grand-Case, and Quartier d'Orleans; of these, Columbia is the handsomest and most fertile; and here, as in Dutch Cul De Sac, agriculture is well attended to, and the sugar is of a quality nearly equal to that of St. Kitts or St. Croix.

In St. Martins, the duties on imports in foreign vessels are 1½ per cent. ad valorem, except on beef, pork, and salt fish, which pay an additional duty of 3 francs per half metrical quintal. Sugars and cotton, exported in foreign vessels, pay 10 francs 80 centimes per 1000 weight. Molasses, rum, and tafias, pay 3 per cent. on exportation.

Port Charges in Martinique, Guadaloupe, and the French part of St. Martins.

	Clearance.		Pilot. & Anch.		Interpreter.		Health officer.	
Vessels of 50 tons and below,	21 fr.	60 cen.	27 fr.	0 cen.	16 fr.	20 cen.	5 fr.	40 cen.
From 50 to 100 tons,	25	20	32	40	21	60	8	10
100 to 150 tons,	32	40	43	20	27	00	8	10
150 to 200 tons,	43	20	54	00	34	43	10	80
Above 200 tons,	54	00	64	80	43	20	13	50

Strange vessels, standing off and on without coming to, are liable to pay 10 fr. 80 c.—though that is deducted from the port charges, if they afterwards come to.

In Guadaloupe and Martinique the importation of flour, soap, candles, butter, and lard, is prohibited.

DUTCH POSSESSIONS.

These are the remaining part of St. Martins, St. Eustatius, and Saba.

St. Eustatius, 25 miles S. W. by S. of St. Barts, is not more than 6 miles long, and about 3½ broad. The government is in the hands of a governor, appointed by the king, and a council chosen by the inhabitants. This body has the right of legislation and judicature. This island has almost the same political and commercial regulations as St. Barts; but St. Barts has considerable advantage in respect to its harbour, which is better calculated in every respect for landing, shipping, and transhipping of goods. St. Eustatius has but an open road, liable to heavy swells, and ground seas, which often very much impede the transacting of business; vessels being frequently obliged to quit their anchorage, and seek safety in putting to sea.

Foreign vessels are permitted to trade with St. Eustatius and Curacoa, on paying 5 per cent. more on the duties on imports and exports

than Dutch vessels. It is understood at the custom-house that not more than half of the cargo is cleared, but we do not know how this custom originated.

All exports from the colonies, except Surinam, to the Netherlands, pay the same duties upon their arrival as the same articles from other places. Exports from Surinam to Holland are free; the trade being confined to Dutch vessels.

Commissions on sales and purchases are $3\frac{1}{2}$ per cent. each.

No import duties are charged on American produce or manufactures in St. Eustatius.

Three per cent. ad valorem is paid on the exportation of sugar, which is never valued beyond 5 pieces of eight per cwt.

The import duties at St. Martins are $2\frac{1}{2}$ per cent. ad valorem.

The export duties on sugar are two dollars, good money, per 10 cwt.

The commerce with these places consists in the exchange of the produce or manufactures of the United States for the produce of the islands; scarcely any specie being in circulation.

In the Dutch part of St. Martins, an anchorage duty is paid of about 5 cents per ton. The port charges in all the islands are very light.

At St. Eustatius great facilities are afforded to American vessels to tranship their cargoes to the neighbouring islands.

DANISH POSSESSIONS.

The islands belonging to Denmark are St. Thomas, St. John, and Santa Cruz.

St. Thomas is a small but fertile island, about 12 leagues east of Porto Rico, and its exports include those of St. John. It has a safe and spacious harbour or road on the S. E. side of the island.

The port charges and duties are trifling, it being a free port. Commissions on sales and purchases are two and half per cent.

Santa Cruz lies north of St. Thomas, and has 346 plantations.

Its exports are chiefly sugar and cotton. Its imports, American manufactures.

American vessels are admitted to trade here, but not upon the same terms as Danish vessels.

At Christiansted, or Bass-end, the chief town, the pilotage is two pieces of eight, or 128 cents, per foot in, and the same out.

Custom-house fees, 8 per cent. on the duty.

Stamp for weigh bill, one st. per bill.

Brokerage here is two per cent.

At Fredricksted, the town on the west end of the island, you do not need a pilot.

Whilst the intercourse of foreigners with St. Croix was, in a manner, prohibited, that with St. Thomas was open. As a free port, a very general and extensive trade was carried on. The import and export duties are about one per cent. on the invoice, and the trader meets with few difficulties from the custom-house. The port charges, of every description, average about 20 cents per ton.

At St. John there is no port of entry. Sugar and molasses, which are the chief productions of the island, are shipped from St. Thomas.

Ordinance concerning the trade and navigation of the island of St. Croix, dated Copenhagen, 6th June, 1833.

Concerning the navigation.—All vessels, without exception, Danish or foreign, coming from Danish or foreign ports, will be admitted at St. Croix, and may discharge and reload in the harbour of Christiansted, or in the roads of Fredericksted.

The port charges hitherto exacted under the heads of anchorage fees, stamps, &c., are abolished, but the anchorage dues will be levied on the full burthen of the vessel.

The vessels not breaking bulk, are exempted from paying anchorage dues, as also the vessels belonging to the Danish islands, trading between St. Croix and the other Danish colonies. When the anchorage dues have been paid at one place in the island, no addition can be exacted, except when the goods landed or loaded on the same voyage, together with the goods previously landed or loaded, amount to a proportion subjecting the vessel to increased anchorage dues.

At Christiansted, an addition of 50 per cent. is exacted, for maintaining the quays, warping-anchors, and sea-marks.

Concerning the impcrtation of goods.—All goods, of Danish or foreign origin, coming from Danish or foreign ports, may be imported at Christiansted or Fredericksted.

When part of the cargo of a vessel is intended to be landed, it will be required, notwithstanding that a specification of the whole cargo be delivered on entering, and a similar specification of the remainder on clearing out.

On all foreign goods having paid duty at St. Thomas, when accompanied by a certificate from the custom office, showing the amount paid, will be deducted from the import duty at St. Croix, when the clearance is not older than 14 days. The trade and navigation to St. Croix, from free ports in Denmark and the Dutchies, will not enjoy the advantages granted to the ports where duties are paid.

Concerning the exportation of goods.—Goods of all descriptions may be exported from Christiansted or Fredericksted at St. Croix, in Danish or foreign vessels, on the following conditions, and subject to the following duties:

I. Sugars, produced at St. Croix, or there imported:

In vessels belonging to Denmark or to the Dutchies:

To a port in Denmark or Dutchies, where duties are levied, at 5 per cent.

To a Danish free port, or to foreign ports, at 12½ per cent.

In foreign vessels, in all cases, 12½ per cent.

When sugars, imported at St. Croix from St. Thomas or St. John, are re-exported, the duties there paid will be deducted.

II. Rum and molasses, produced at St. Croix, or there imported:

In vessels belonging to Denmark or to the Dutchies:

To a port in Denmark or the Dutchies, where duties are levied, at 2½ per cent.

To a Danish free port, or to a foreign port, 5 per cent.

In foreign vessels, in all cases, 5 per cent.

When rum or molasses, imported at St. Croix from St. Thomas or St. John, are re-exported, the duties there paid will be deducted.

III. Goods of other descriptions, in vessels of all nations:

On coffee and tobacco, exported to a Danish free port, or to a foreign port, $\frac{4}{5}$ths of the inward duty will be returned; and when exported to other ports in Denmark or the Dutchies, the full amount of inward duty will be returned against security to produce certificates from the port of discharge within six months.

On all other West India colonial produce imported free of duty, 1 per cent. will be paid when exported to a Danish free port, or to foreign ports, and no duty will be paid when exported to other ports in Denmark or the Dutchies, on security being given to produce certificates from the port of discharge within six months.

Goods of all other descriptions pay no export duty, whether they have been imported on or without paying duty.

General regulations at the importation or exportation of goods.—All goods sold by weight, whether free or subjected to duties, must be weighed on importation or exportation, and a certificate of the weight will immediately be granted. The weigh-money is two schillings per 100 pounds.

The duties *ad valorem*, are levied according to the taxation approved by the West Indian government.

In addition to the duties, one tenth part of their amount will be levied as fees to the custom officers.

The stamps hitherto required for certificates of all kinds, are abolished, and the duties on importation or exportation will accordingly not exceed what is stipulated by the 5th, 6th, 7th, and 9th sections.

Every owner or agent, whether a native or foreigner, may make his own declaration and clearance. Verbal declarations can be made out at the custom-house, and the within declarations be made out in the custom-house, for the signature of the parties, without expense to them.

The custom offices will be open from 7 o'clock till 3 o'clock, but goods may be landed and loaded from 6 o'clock in the morning until 6 o'clock in the evening. Special declarations must be made previously, and be attested by the inspectors.

When goods are landed or loaded without attestation from the inspector, or at other hours than stipulated, they are liable to confiscation.

SWEDISH POSSESSIONS.

St. Bartholomews, a small island, lying in lat. 17° 54′ N. long. 62° 40′ W., originally belonging to the French, but by them ceded to the Swedish crown many years ago, was formerly a place of considerable trade, chiefly carried on with the United States, from whence there are considerable importations of flour, rye, corn, and every article of American growth and manufacture. These are sold for cash or bartered for rum, molasses, sugar, coffee, and other West India productions. The island is about 12 miles long and 4 broad, and possesses little or no natural advantages, being very barren and rocky. It produces only a few liguminous and other vegetables, barely sufficient for the use of its inhabitants. The harbour, which opens to the northwest, is safe and commodious.

St. Bartholomews is the only island belonging to Sweden, and is a free port. No duties are charged on the importation of produce or manufactures of the United States, except on dry goods, on which 3 per cent. are paid.

The export duties on American and European articles are 1½ per cent. ad valorem.

Port charges, including achorage, harbour-master's fees, &c., do not exceed one dollar and fifty cents per 100 tons.

The commissions on sales and purchases are 2½ per cent. each.

Here are a few wealthy capitalists; but the generality of commercial men are merely commission agents—Americans, West Indians, and Frenchmen. Cargoes are sold for cash, or colonial produce, to be delivered at the option of the parties, never longer, however, than 30 days.

Upon giving one or two doubloons to some of the brokers, an American captain may retail his cargo on board, without any interference on the part of the governor; though the present governor is apt to take advantage of the necessities of foreigners, to extort from them as much as he can get.

WESTERN ISLANDS.

These islands belong to Portugal, and by a decree of 25th April, 1836, are directed to be governed as provinces of Portugal. They are nine in number, viz.: Corvo, Fayal, Flores, Gratiosa, Pico, St. George, St. Mary, St. Michael, and Terceira. They are situated in the Atlantic, between the parallels of 39° 30′ and 37° 00′ N. lat. and 25° 00′ and 31° 30′ W. long.

Their exports are wine, coffee, and fruits. Their imports are rice, fish, tar, staves, lumber, iron and East India goods.

Masters should be careful in clearing out for any of the Azores to comply with the following directions:

The manifest of the cargo, bills of lading, and custom-house clearance, should be accompanied by a certificate of their authenticity from the Portuguese consul of the district from whence the vessel shall have taken her departure. These papers must be attached together, numbered, and countersigned by the consul, so as to prevent the possibility of a substitution, and the whole must be addressed by him (under cover) to the judge of the custom-house of the port to which the vessel may be destined. It is provided, that in case of there being no Portuguese consul in the district from whence the vessel shall depart, the papers before mentioned must be duly authenticated by the highest officer in the custom-house department, and the fact of there being no Portuguese consul in that district, also certified by him. The non-observance of these regulations will prevent any vessel from being admitted to an entry in any of the custom-houses in the Azores.

A decree of the Cortes of Portugal prohibits the introduction of all spirituous liquors, (pure French brandy excepted,) and no vessel, having any on board will be admitted to an entry.

APPENDIX.

NEW-YORK PILOT LAWS.

A board of five commissioners, appointed by the governor and senate, is created for the licensing and regulating Sandy Hook pilots. The commissioners are chosen for two years.

The commissioners have an office in the city of New-York, where they meet the 1st and 3d Tueday in each month, and they are authorized to appoint a secretary and messengers, and make all needful rules and regulations, with penalties not exceeding $100 annexed, to enforce their own power, and the adequate discharge, by the pilots, of their duty; such regulations being calculated "to effect the objects of this act, *and to secure to each class of said pilots, as nearly as practicable, a chance for fair competition in proportion to their diligence, activity, industry and enterprise.*"

The commissioners keep regular minutes of all their proceedings, books containing their regulations, &c., a register of the pilots and their residences; which books are open to the inspection of any one.

The commissioners are required to license "all those persons now licensed to act as pilots by the way of Sandy Hook, and also every other person of full age, and good moral character, making application therefor, giving a preference to those who have served three years as an apprentice to a licensed pilot, by the way of Sandy Hook, and who, after an examination in the manner hereinafter prescribed, shall be found qualified to act as such pilots, and shall continue, from time to time, to increase the number of pilots in the manner just mentioned, as the public good may require."

Fee for a license, $2. The boats, and the names of the persons attached thereto, must be reported to the secretary of the board on the first Mondays of May and November in each year.

No person, except pilots licensed by New-York or New-Jersey, can pilot vessels to or from New-York, by the way of Sandy Hook, for hire, under the penalty of $50— This penalty is not incurred when the master is authorized to act as his own pilot, or when the vessel shall have been off Sandy Hook, with the usual signal for a pilot, two hours, without one having offered.

The commissioners have the power to suspend pilots, or to revoke their licenses for cause. When complaint is lodged with the commissioners against a pilot for misbehavior or neglect of duty, it must be reduced to writing, and sworn to. Notice thereof is then given to the pilot, and he is notified to appear in fifteen days to answer the complaint. If the answer be not satisfactory, he may be suspended, fined, not exceeding $100, or deprived of his license.

An appeal may be made by the pilot within fifteen days from the decision of the commissioners to the mayor, recorder, and first judge of the common pleas.

Applicants for licenses must be examined within one week, in the presence of one or more pilots, touching their qualifications, and in particular concerning their knowledge of the management of a square rigged vessel; of the tides, soundings, bearings and distances of the several shoals, rocks, bars, points of land, and night-lights of the harbour and bay.

Applications for pilots for outward bound vessels must be made one day previous— stating name of the vessel, where she lies, tonnage and draft of water; all which is to be entered in a book by the secretary, who then orders a pilot to the charge, giving preference to the pilot who brought the ship in. A pilot refusing or neglecting, is to be fined, not exceeding $100, or suspended, according to commissioners' discretion.

For false representation as to tonnage or draft of water, a penalty of $100 is incurred by the master; and if the vessel be run aground the pilot is not responsible.

Any pilot carried off is to receive $100 per month, in addition to pilotage, until his return. His charge, moreover, is to cease when blown off.

The pilots give bonds for $250 for the faithful discharge of their duties.

For casting away or losing a vessel the pilot loses his license, and is incapable of again being a pilot; for running a vessel aground, he loses his pilotage.

Neither commissioners, secretary nor messengers, can have any interest in pilot boats, or their earnings.

No licensed coasting sloop, or schooner, of or under 75 tons, is to be compelled to employ a pilot.

The master of any licensed coasting sloop or schooner, over 75 and not over 200 tons, may be his own pilot, on taking out a license from the commissioners, by a written application, specifying the name, tonnage, draft of water, and usual trade of his vessel, and on paying for such license four cents per ton as per register. The license is to continue in force one year, or until the termination of any voyage during which the license may expire.

If the master be changed before the end of the year, the new master can have a new license for the unexpired term without charge.

No pilot is to participate in the earnings of any pilot boat except that to which he belongs, under penalty of a forfeiture of his license, except authorized by the board.

Each boat must have three apprentices.

A journal must be kept on board each pilot boat; noting in detail all incidents of weather, station, &c. False entries therein subject pilots to loss of license. The journal is to be open to the inspection of the commissioners, to whom, moreover, every vessel, with all particulars, as names of master, owner, consignees, tonnage, draft of water, where boarded and where moored, is to be reported on arrival by the pilots.

For detention while tending a ship outward bound, $3 per diem is allowed to pilots; the same for detention by ice, on board inward bound ships, when over two days.

For detention at quarantine for having piloted a sickly vessel, $3 per day, and all necessary expenses of living.

Commissioners are to prepare printed instructions for pilots, which they are to exhibit under penalty of $10 for each offence, to the officer in charge of every vessel boarded—also to furnish each pilot with a copy of this act, and all rules and regulations.

The pilot on boarding is to present a printed request that the time and place of boarding be entered on the log-book; the failure to comply with this request bars all complaint to the commissioners against the pilot except in case of loss of life.

The pilot boat on the station where outward bound vessels discharge their pilots, must give every necessary aid for taking out and receiving the pilot, and also to send the pilot to the city or to quarantine.

Pilotage fees.—From a distance not exceeding 1 league from the southward and eastward of the white buoy on the eastern edge of the outer middle, to her moorings or wharf,

For 14 feet water	$2 00
Between 14 and 18 feet	2 50
Over 18 feet	3 00

Foreign vessels, not entitled to equality by treaty, pay one fourth more.

For American or foreign men-of-war, $5 per foot.

For taking charge at such distance south or east of Sandy Hook light, that from the deck of the vessel the light-house could not be seen in fair weather and in daylight, one fourth is to be added to the above rates, and half pilotage to be charged, if at that distance the pilot offer his services and they be refused, or intentionally avoided.

The same fees are to be paid on outward as on inward vessels.

No more than one half the pilotage allowed for a vessel boarded east or south of the white buoy, shall be allowed for piloting a vessel boarded between the white buoy and Flinn's Knoll.

No pilotage is chargeable on a vessel that has come in as far as Flinn's Knoll, unless a pilot then be asked for.

Half pilotage is allowed to the pilot offering to any inward vessel east or south of the buoy, and not received.

The law adds to the foregoing rates $4 for every vessel of 10 feet and upwards, and $2 for under 10 feet, between 1st November and 1st April.

The commissioners are entitled to receive 3 per cent. of the pilotage, to constitute a fund, out of which is paid $200 per annum to each of the commissioners, and $1500 to the secretary.

If a vessel bound to New-York be lost within 50 miles, after having been in sight of Sandy Hook without obtaining a pilot, inquiry must be made by the commissioners as to where the fault lies, and they must suspend or displace the parties implicated, publishing the result of their investigation.

Pilots are to be rewarded for extraordinary services to vessels in distress, according to agreement, or by the decision of the commissioners when the parties cannot agree.

A pilot becoming intoxicated while in the charge of a vessel, forfeits his pilotage, and is suspended six months; for a second offence he loses his license.

This act does not apply to Hell Gate pilots.

All pecuniary fines and penalties are to be sued for by commissioners, and paid either to the party aggrieved, or to the pilots' charitable fund.*

Pilots for the Hell Gate passage are appointed by the governor. They are subject to the regulations of the port-wardens, who act as commissioners for those pilots, and may suspend them for improper conduct.†

Fees of pilotage through Hell Gate.—Any Hell Gate pilot may demand from any person who employs him to pilot any vessel, or from the consignee or owner, from the eastward of Sands' Point or Execution rocks; or to take charge of any vessel at or to the eastward Sands' Point or Execution Rocks, and pilot her to the port of New-York; or to pilot her from the port of New-York to Execution rocks or Sand's Point, for every vessel $1 37 per foot; from the port of New-York to the eastward of Hell Gate or Riker's Island, or from the eastward of Hell Gate or Riker's Island to New-York, $1 per foot. The pilot who pilots any vessel into the port of New-York, by the way of Hell Gate, is entitled to a preference in piloting her out on the next outward voyage, if the said voyage be by the way of Hell Gate. From the 1st day of November to the 31st day of March inclusive, he is entitled to receive for every ship, barque, or brig, the sum of $2; and for every schooner or sloop, $1, in addition to the rates of pilotage.

The master, owner, or consignee of any vessel to whom any Hell Gate pilot shall have rendered, upon request of the master, any extra service for her preservation while in distress, must pay to said pilot in addition such amount for extra services as the board of wardens shall determine to be a reasonable reward. For every day's detention over and above 24 hours, he may demand from the master, owner or consignee, $2 a day.

Any pilot for Hell Gate, first tendering his services, may demand, in case his services are refused, 75 cents, from the eastward of Sand's Point or Execution rocks; and 50 cents from any other part of the channel of the East River, commonly called Hell Gate, for every foot said vessel may draw, except vessels sailing under a coasting license of less than 100 tons burthen; but such half pilotage shall not be more than once chargeable for the same passage.

$30 penalty is incurred for piloting a vessel through Hell Gate without a license.†

Coasting vessels making a signal for a pilot, and then refusing one, pay half pilotage.

Each and every pilot boat is to be numbered, and have the number on the foresail on each side, in black figures of 2 feet in length, and a proportionable width above the reefs.

The pilot taking charge of any vessel to pilot her through Hell Gate, must give orders to have one or more cables bent, and in readiness to anchor if required.

It is the duty of every pilot, on his arrival in the harbour of New-York, to have the vessel safely moored, or taken to such wharf as the master, or owner, or consignee may require.

If any commissioned pilot become intoxicated whilst having charge of any vessel as pilot, he shall for the first offence forfeit his pilotage, and pay a fine of $30; and for a second offence be suspended.

---

* Act of 12th April, 1837. † Act, 16th April, 1832.

TARIFF,

OR

RATES OF DUTIES,

Imposed by the Laws of Congress on all Goods, Wares and Merchandise imported into the United States of America, in American vessels.

When imported in a foreign vessel, not entitled to the privileges of American vessels, ten per cent. is added to the duty.

A.

ABSYNTH, extract of ... 60 cents per gal.
Absynth, oil of, or wormwood. 20 per cent.
Acacia, or gum arabic ... free.
Accordions ... 30 per cent.
Acetous acid ... 20 do.
Acetate of lead, or white lead. 4 cents per lb.
Acetate of potasse ... 20 per cent.
Acetic acid ... 20 do.
Acetate of quicksilver ... 20 do.
Acid, benzoic ... 20 do.
Acid, citric, white or yellow. 20 do.
Acid boracic ... 5 do.
Acid, muriatic ... 20 do.
Acid, nitric, or nitric fort ... 20 do.
Acid, oxalic ... 20 do.
Acid, pyroligneus ... 20 do.
Acid, tartaric, in crystals or powder ... 20 do.
Acid, sulphuric, or oil of vitriol ... 1 cent per lb.
Acorns ... 20 per cent.
Adhesive felt, for covering ships' bottoms ... free.
Adhesive plaster, salve ... 20 per cent.
Adianthum ... 20 do.
Adzes ... 30 do.
Agaric ... 20 do.
Agates ... 7 do.
Agates, bookbinders ... 7 do.
Alabata, or German silver in sheets ... 30 do.
Alabaster, or spar ornaments, 30 do.
Alba canella ... 20 do.
Alcornoque bark ... free.
Ale, in bottles ... 20 cents per gal.
Ale, otherwise than in bottles. 15 do.
Alkanet root ... 20 per cent.
Alkermes ... 20 do.
Allspice, oil of ... 20 do.
Almonds ... 3 cents per lb.
Almonds, oil of ... 9 do.
Almond paste ... 25 per cent.
Aloes ... free.
Alum ... $1\frac{1}{2}$ cents per lb.
Amber ... 20 per cent.
Amber beads ... 25 do.
Amber, oil of ... 20 do.
Ambergris ... 20 do.
Amethyst ... 7 do.
Ammonia, salts of ... 20 do.
Ammonia, volatile ... 20 do.
Ammoniac, gum ... 20 do.
Ammoniac, carbonate or nitrate of ... 20 do.
Ammoniac, bole ... 20 do.
Ammunition, viz:
canister shot ... 1 cent per lb.
cannon balls ... 1 do.
chain shot ... 1 do.
grape shot ... 1 do.
gunpowder ... 8 do.
langrel shot ... 1 do.
musket balls ... 4 do.
Anatomical preparations ... free.
Anchors, and all parts thereof, $2\frac{1}{2}$ cents per lb.
Anchovies, in pickle ... 100 cts. per brl.
Anchovies, in bottles or kegs .. 20 per cent.
Anchovies, in oil ... 20 do.
Angelica root ... 20 do.
Angora goat's wool or hair ... 1 cent per lb.
Angora gloves ... 20 per cent.
Angora mits ... 20 do.
Animals imported for breed .. free.
Animal oil, not otherwise enumerated ... 20 per cent.
Annatto ... 20 do.
Annealed iron wire to pay duty as other iron wire.
Aniseseed ... 20 do.
Aniseseed cordial ... 60 cents per gal.
Aniseseed, oil of ... 20 per cent.
Anthos, oil of ... 25 do.
Antimony, crude ... free.
Antique oil ... 25 per cent.

Antiquities specially imported, free.
Antiquities not specially imported, according to the materials of which they are composed.
Anvils, and parts thereof.....2¼ cents per lb.
Any goods, wares, or merchandise, of the growth, produce, or manufacture of the United States, or of its fisheries, upon which no drawback, bounty, or allowance has been paid................free.
Apothecaries' glass measures with engraved lines, according to weight. (See glass.)
Apothecaries' vials and bottles, 6 oz. and under.,.....$1 75 per gross.
Apothecaries' vials and bottles, *exceeding* the capacity of six, and *not* exceeding the capacity of *sixteen* oz. each.$2 25 do.
Apparatus, philosophical, specially imported by order and for the use of any society incorporated for philosophical or literary purposes, or for the encouragement of the fine arts, or by order and for the use of any seminary of learning, school or college within the United States, or the territories thereof......free.
Apparatus, philosophical, not specially imported, according to the materials of which they are composed.
Apparel, wearing and other personal baggage in actual use......................free.
Aqua ammonia, or hartshorn.20 per cent.
Aqua-fortis..................20 do.
Aqua-mellis..................25 do.
Arabic, gum..................free.
Arrack ....60 cents per gal.
Armenian, bole..............20 per cent.
Armenian, stone ....20 do.
Archelia, archil, or orchelia..20 do.
Argent, vivum ....20 do.
Argentine....................30 do.
Argol........................free.
Arms, fire (except muskets and rifles)..................30 per cent.
Arms, side..................30 do.
Arrow root..................20 do.
Arsenic, all................20 do.
Articles of the growth, produce, or manufacture of the United States, or its territories, and of its fisheries....free.
Articles, all, composed wholly or chiefly in *quantity* of gold, silver, pearl, and precious stones, not otherwise specified ....20 per cent.
Articles, all, not free, and not subject to any other rate of duty ....20 do.
Articles manufactured from copper, or of which copper is the material of chief value, not otherwise specified.....30 do.
Articles, all, imported for the use of the United States...free.
Artificial feathers...........25 per cent.
Artificial flowers............25 do.
Asphaltes...................15 do.
Assafœtida.................free.
Asses' skin.................25 per cent.
Asses' skin, imitation of......25 do.
Ava root....................free.
Aubuysson carpetings.......65 cts. p. sq. yd.
Augers......................30 per cent.
Auripigmentum, or orpiment..20 do.
Awl hafts...................30 do.
Awls........................30 do.
Axes........................30 do.
Ayr-stones..................20 do.

B.

Bacon....................... 3 cents per lb.
Baggage, personal, in actual use.......................free.
Bagging, called cotton bagging....................... 4 cts. p. sq. yd.
Bags, grass.................25 per cent.
Bags, gunny.................25 do.
Bags, woollen...............40 do.
Bags, worsted...............30 do.
Bags, flax..................25 do.
Bags, called carpet bags......40 do.
Baizes......................14 cts. p. sq. yd.
Balls, billiard...............20 per cent.
Balls, cannon............... 1 cent per lb.
Balls, musket............... 4 do.
Balls, wash ....30 per cent.
Balm of Gilead. ....25 do.
Balsam of Tolu ....25 do.
Balsam, medicinal ....25 do.
Balsam, all kinds of cosmetic.25 do.
Bamboos.....................free.
Band iron, rolled...........2½ cts. per. lb.
Bannanas .... free.
Bangups, a cotton stuff or cord. (See cotton.)
Bark of the cork tree unmanufactured....................free.
Barrége, worsted............30 per cent.
Barrége, cotton; if it cost less than 30 cents per square yard, it is to be deemed to have cost 30 cents per square yard. (See col'd cottons.) 40 do.
Barrége, if wool............40 do.
Barley,......................20 cts. pr. bush.
Barley, pearl................ 2 cents per lb.
Barytes..................... ½ do.
Band iron, slit or rolled...... 2¼ do.
Bar iron, when manufactured in whole or in part by rolling.........................$25 per ton.
Bar iron, not manufactured in whole or in part by rolling.$17 do.
Bar wood....................free.
Barilla......................free.
Bastard files.................30 per cent.
Bassoons....................30 do.
Baskets, wood or osier. .....25 do.
Baskets, palm leaf..........25 do.
Baskets, straw..............25 do.
Baskets, grass..............25 do.
Bast ropes................. 4½ cents per lb.
Battledoors..................30 per cent.
Bay water, or bay rum......25 do.
Bay wax, or myrtle wax.....20 do.
Bayonets....................30 do.
Bdellium....................20 do.
Beads of all descriptions....25 do.
Beads of precious stones.... 7 do.
Beans, tonkay...............20 do.
Beans, vanilla...............20 do.
Beans, all other. ....20 do.

Beaver, fur.................. 5 per cent.
Beam knives...............30 do.
Beams, scale...............30 do.
Bed feathers...............25 do.
Bed ticking, linen..........25 do.
Bed caps....................30 do.
Bed screws.................30 do.
Beef.........................2 cents per lb.
Beer in bottles..............20 cents pr. gal.
Beer, otherwise than in bottles.15 do.
Beeswax....................15 per cent.
Bellows' pipes.............30 do.
Bell cranks.................30 do.
Bell levers..................30 do.
Bell pulls....................30 do.
Bellows.......................35 do.
Belts, sword, leather........35 do.
Benzoates....................20 do.
Benzoic acid, or flor benzoin..20 do.
Benzoin.......................20 do.
Bed spreads, or covers, made of the scraps or waste ends of printed calicoes sewed together, not subject to the regulations on cotton cloths..30 do.
Bells, metal.................30 do.
Berries, used in dyeing......free.
Berries, juniper..............20 per cent.
Bezarr stones................20 do.
Bi, chromate of potash......20 do
Bick irons....................30 do.
Binding, carpet.............30 do.
Binding, cotton.............30 do.
Binding, woollen a component part.......................30 do.
Binding, worsted............30 do.
Binding, silk..................$2 50 per lb.
Binding, leather.............35 per cent.
Binding, linen...............25 do.
Binding, quality.............30 do.
Bird's eye stuff, linen........25 do.
Bird's eye worsted stuff......30 do.
Birds.........................20 do.
Bismuth, oxide of...........20 do.
Bismuth......................20 do.
Bits, carpenter's............30 do.
Bits, bridle. (See saddlery.)
Bitter apple..................20 do.
Bitumen......................15 do.
Black, ivory.................. ¾ cent per lb.
Black, lamp..................20 per cent.
Black lead, pots.............30 do.
Black glass bottles, not exceeding the capacity of one quart.......................$3 per gross.
Black glass bottles, exceeding one quart.................$4 do.
Black lead powder..........20 per cent.
Bleaching powder............ 1 cent per lb.
Blacking......................20 per cent.
Bladders......................20 do
Blacksmith's hammers.......2½ cents per lb.
Blacksmith's sledges.........2½ do.
Black lead pencils..........25 per cent.
Black frankfort..............20 do.
Blankets, the value not exceeding 75 cents each......15 do.
Blankets, the value exceeding 75 cents each..............25 do.
Blankets of Mohair or goat's hair........................20 do.
Blue, Prussian...............20 do.
Blue vitriol................. 4 cents per lb.
Blooms, iron in, subject to the same duty as iron in bolts or bars.
Boards, planed..............30 per cent.

Boards, rough..............20 per cent.
Bobinet lace................20 do.
Bobbin.......................30 do.
Bobbin wire.................. 8 cents per lb.
Bocking......................14 cts. p. sq. yd.
Bodkins, ivory..............20 per cent.
Bodkins, bone..............20 do.
Bodkins, silver.............30 do.
Bodkins, gold...............30 do.
Bodkins, plated.............30 do.
Bodkins, gilt................30 do.
Bodkins, iron................30 do.
Bodkins, steel..............30 do.
Bodkins, brass.............30 do.
Bodkins, copper............30 do.
Bohea tea from China, or places east of the Cape of Good Hope.......... free.
Bohea tea from any other place........................20 per cent.
Boiler plates.............. .. 4 cents per lb.
Bologna sausages.......... 25 per cent.
Bolting cloths of silk........20 do.
Bolts, iron, for fastenings....30 do.
Bolts, brass for do........30 do.
Bolts, copper................ 4 cents per lb.
Bolts, composition......... 30 per cent.
Bolt rope, as cordage, (tarred) 5 cents per lb.
Bolt rope, as cordage (untarred)..................... 4½ do.
Bolt, *iron, not* manufactured in whole or in part by *rolling*, $17 per ton.
Bolt, *iron*, when manufactured in whole or in part by *rolling*.$25 per ton.
Bole ammoniac, or Amenian bole.......................20 per cent.
Bombazine...................free.
Bonnets, Leghorn...........35 per cent.
Bonnets, chip...............35 do.
Bonnets, grass..............35 do.
Bonnets, straw..............35 do.
Bonnets, fur, leather.........35 do.
Bonnets, muslin............40 do.
Bonnets, silk or satin........$2 each.
Bonnet wire covered with silk,12 cents per lb.
Boncho leaves..............20 per cent.
Bone alphabets.............20 do.
Bone chessmen.............20 do.
Bone, whalebone............30 do.
Bone, tip..................... 5 do.
Bone, whale, not of the American fisheries............12½ per cent.
Bone, whale, manufactures of.20 do.
Bone, manufactures of ......20 do.
Boots.........................$1 25 per pair.
Boots, laced.................25 cts. do.
Bootees, silk.................75 do.
Boots and bootees, children's, of leather..................15 do.
Boots and bootees, men's, of leather........................$1 25 do.
Boots and bootees, women's, of leather....................50 cts. do.
Boot webb....................25 per cent.
Bookbinder's agates ferrulea. 7 do.
Books, blank.................20 cents per lb.
Books, printed 40 years...... 5 cents per vol.
Books, except English, Latin, and Greek................ 5 do.
Books, Latin (bound)........15 cents per lb.
Books, Latin (unbound)......13 do.
Books, Greek (unbound).....13 do.
Books, Greek (bound).......15 do.
Books, Hebrew (bound)......10 do.
Books, Hebrew (unbound)... 8 do.
Books of prints, drawings and engravings...................free.

Books, English, bound and half bound..............30 cents per lb.
Books, English, in sheets.....20 do.
Books, English, in boards.....20 do.
Books specially imported....free.
Books, the notes in any book, although in a different language from the work, do not change the duty; for instance, a Hebrew book with Latin notes, will still be subjected to a duty of only 5 cents per volume.
Books of engravings, or lithographic..................20 per cent.
Books in sheets, neither folded nor stitched, but printed in such a manner as to constitute a regular series of volumes, will pay the same duty as they would do if put up in volumes.
Boracic acid ....5 do.
Borax, or tincal.............25 do.
Botany, specimens in........free.
Bottles, apothecaries', exceeding the capacity of 6, and not exceeding the capacity of 16 ounces each.........$2 25 the gross.
Bottles, black glass, not exceeding one quart.........$3 00 do.
Bottles, black glass, exceeding one quart................$4 00 do.
Bottles, perfumery aad fancy, not exceeding the capacity of 4 oz. each..............$2 50 do.
When exceeding 4 oz. and not exceeding 16 oz...........$3 00 do.
Bougies......................30 per cent.
Boxes, gold or silver........30 do.
Boxes, musical..............30 do.
Boxes, japanned dressing....30 do.
Boxes, all wood.............30 do.
Boxes, sand or tin...........30 do.
Boxes, shell.................25 do.
Boxes, if paper only, not japanned.....................25 do.
Boxes, snuff, paper, japanned.25 do.
Boxes, snuff, paper, not japanned ....15 do.
Boxes, fancy, composed of pasteboard, gilt paper, cotton velvet, silk ribbon, &c..25 do.
Boxes, fancy, coloured paper, looking glass, silk velvet, gilt copper balls, ribbon, &c.25 do.
Boxes, fancy, paper, japanned, varnished, gilt, copper rim, &c.....................25 do.
Box boards, paper.......... 3 cents per lb.
Bracelets, gold or set.........20 per cent.
Bracelets, gilt...............25 do.
Bracelets, hair..............25 do.
Braces, carpenters', without bits.. ....30 do.
Braces and bits, carpenters'..30 do.
Brace bits...................30 do.
Braces or suspenders, silk, with buckles..............35 do.
Braces or suspenders, cotton.35 do.
Braces or suspenders, worsted or wool..................35 do.
Braces or suspenders, all leather ....35 do.
Brackets....................30 do.
Brads, not exceeding 16 oz. to the 1000.................. 5 cts. per 1000.
Brads, exceeding 16 oz. to the 1000..................... 5 cents per lb.
Braids, in ornaments for head dresses.....................25 per cent.
Braids, hair, not made up for head dresses...............25 do.
Braids, hair, made up for head dresses..................25 do.
Braids, of straw, for making bonnets or hats..........35 do.
Brandy....................$1 per gallon.
Brass, manufactures of, or of which it is a component material....................30 per cent.
Brass in bars...............free.
Brass in pigs...............free.
Brass, old, only fit to be remanufactured.............free.
Brass wire..................25 per cent.
Brass saddlery..............30 do.
Brass studs.................30 do.
Brass, in sheets, as brazier's copper...................free.
Brazier's rods, of 3-16 to 10-16 of an inch diameter......... $2\frac{1}{2}$ cents per lb.
Brazil paste, or pasta de Brazil.......................20 per cent.
Brazil pebbles................ 7 do.
Brazil wood................free.
Brazil pebbles prepared for spectacles................$2 per gross.
Bread baskets, japanned.....30 per cent.
Bread baskets, plated........30 do.
Bread baskets, silver........30 do.
Bricks.....................25 do.
Britannia ware............ 30 do.
Bridle bits, plated. (See saddlery.)...................30 do.
Bridles.....................35 do.
Brimstone, crude or sulphur..free.
Brimstone, rolled............25 per cent.
Bristol stones..............20 do.
Bristles.................... 1 cent per lb.
Brodequins, woollen.........40 per cent.
Brodequins, leather.........35 do.
Bronze casts...............30 do.
Bronze, all manufactures of..30 do.
Bronze powder.............20 do.
Bronze powder, pale, yellow, white and red............20 do.
Bronze liquid, gold or bronze colour.....................20 do.
Brown, Spanish, dry........ 1 cent per lb.
Brown, Spanish, in oil....... $1\frac{1}{2}$ do.
Brown smalts..............20 per cent.
Brooms, all kinds...........30 do.
Brucine....................20 do.
Brussels carpeting..........55 cts. p. sq. yd.
Brushes of all kinds.........30 per cent.
Buckles of copper, brass, iron, steel, pewter, tin, lead, or of which either of these articles is a component material....30 do.
Buckles, chiefly of gold or silver......................30 do
Buckram..................25 do.
Bugles and musical instruments.....................30 do.
Bugles, glass, if cut. (See glass.)
Bugles, glass, if not cut. do.
Building stones............20 per cent.
Bullets.................... 4 cents per lb.
Bullrushes.................20 per cent.
Bulbs or bulbous roots......free.
Bullion...................free.
Bunting...................30 per cent.
Burlaps...................25 do.

Burr stones, unwrought......free.
Burr stones, wrought........20 per cent.
Burgundy pitch............20 do.
Busts, lead................ 4 cents per lb.
Buttons, metal, all kinds of..30 per cent.
Buttons, all other...........25 do.
Butter .... 5 cents per lb.
Butchers' knives...........30 per cent.
Butt hinges, cast iron....... $2\frac{1}{2}$ cents per lb.
Button moulds............25 per cent.

C.

Cabinet wares..............30 per cent.
Cables, tarred.............. 5 cents per lb.
Cables, untarred........... $4\frac{1}{2}$ do.
Cables, made of grass........ $4\frac{1}{2}$ do.
Cables, iron or chain, or parts thereof .... $2\frac{1}{2}$ do.
Caddie balls................30 per cent.
Cadjeput, or cadjeputa, oil of,20 do.
Cakes, linseed..............20 do.
Calx ....20 do.
Calaminaris lapis ....20 do.
Calcined magnesia..........20 do.
Calf skins, raw .... 5 do.
Calf skins, salted, or in raw state..................... 5 do.
Calf skins, pickled, in casks...20 do.
Calf skins, tanned and dressed.$5 per doz.
Calomel, and all other mercurial preparations..........25 per cent.
Camblets of mohair or goats..20 do.
Cameos, real............... $7\frac{1}{2}$ do.
Cameo, imitation of.......... $7\frac{1}{2}$ do.
Camel's hair...............20 do.
Camel's hair pencils.........20 do.
Camomile flowers...........20 do.
Camphor, refined............20 cts. per lb.
Camphor, crude............ 5 do.
Camwood..................free.
Canary seed................20 per cent.
Cancrorum oculi or crab's eyes......................20 do.
Canella, alba...............20 do.
Candlesticks, alabaster......30 do.
Candlesticks, bone..........20 do.
Candlesticks, earthenware....30 do.
Candlesticks, brass ....30 do.
Candlesticks, bronze........30 do.
Candlesticks, gilt...........30 do.
Candlesticks. gold..........30 do.
Candlesticks glass, cut......45 cts. per lb.
Candlesticks, not cut. (See glass.
Candlesticks, iron..........30 per cent.
Candlesticks, japanned......30 do.
Candlesticks, marble........30 do.
Candlesticks, plated.........30 do.
Candlesticks, pewter.........30 do.
Candlesticks, porcelain......30 do.
Candlesticks, silver..........30 do.
Candlesticks, spa...........30 do.
Candlesticks, stoneware .....30 do.
Candlesticks, tin...... .. ..30 do.
Candlesticks, washed........30 do.
Candles, tallow............. 4 cents per lb.
Candles, wax.............. 8 do.
Candles, spermaceti......... 8 do.
Candy, sugar.............. 6 do.
Canes, walking.............30 per cent.
Cannetille, a wire ribbon, if covered with cotton thread.. 8 cents per lb.
Cannon, brass..............30 per cent.
Cannon, iron............... 1 cent per lb.
Cantharides...............free.
Canton crapes, coming from beyond the Cape of Good Hope....................$2 50 per lb.
Canvass, for floor cloths or wearing apparel...........25 per cent.
Canvass for sails, such as sail duck..................... 7 cts. p. sq. yd.
Caoutchouc gums..........free.
Capers ....30 per cent.
Cap wire, covered with silk, 12 cents per lb.
Cap wire, covered with cotton thread or other material.... 8 do.
Caps of chip..............35 per cent.
Caps of cotton.............40 do.
Caps of fur................35 do.
Caps, Kilmarnock..........30 do.
Caps of lace, made up.......40 do.
Caps of leather.............35 do.
Caps of linen..............25 do.
Caps of silk................30 do.
Caps of wool. ....30 do.
Caps, worsted.............30 do.
Cap pieces for stills.........30 do.
Caps or capes, lace, sewed...40 do.
Caps or capes, lace, not sewed40 do.
Carbines or carabines........30 do.
Carbonate of magnesia......20 do.
Carbonate (sal or brinal) of soda......................20 do.
Carbonate of ammonia.......20 do.
Carboys of half gallon......15 cents each.
Carboys above half gallon and not above 3 gallons.......30 do.
Carboys exceeding 3 gallons.50 do.
Carbuncles................ 7 per cent.
Cardamom seed...........20 do.
Cards, playing.............25 cts. per pack.
Cards, visiting..............12 cents per lb.
Cards, blank...............12 do.
Cards, wool................30 per cent.
Cards, cotton..............30 do.
Carmine...................20 do.
Caroline plaids, cotton and wool.....................40 do.
Caroline plaids, stripes, cotton.as cottons.
Carpeting, Aubusson........65 cts. p. sq. yd.
Capet binding ....30 per cent.
Carpets and carpeting, Brussels......................55 cts. p. sq. yd.
Carpets and carpeting, ingrained................. 30 do.
Carpets and carpeting, treble ingrained.............. 65 do.
Carpets and carpeting, Turkey 55 do.
Carpets and carpeting, Venitian........ ....30 do.
Carpets, Saxony............65 do.
Carpets and carpeting, Wilton.65 do.
Carpets and carpeting, oil cloth.....................35 do.
Carpets and carpeting, straw..25 per cent.
Carpeting matting ....25 do.
Carpets and carpeting, all other kinds of............30 do.
Carpet bags...............40 do.
Carriages of all descriptions, and parts thereof..........30 do.
Carriage springs...........30 do.
Carui, or caraway, oil of.....20 do.
Carvers....................30 do.
Cascarilla.................20 do.
Cashmere, borders of wool, in whole or in part..........40 do.
Cashmere, of Thibet........20 do.
Cashmere, of cloth..........40 do.
Cashmere gown patterns, wool being a component part....40 do.
Cashmere gowns, made......50 do.

Cashmere shawls, Thibet.....20 per cent.
Cashmere shawls, wool being a component part..........40 do.
Casement rods, iron for...... 2½ cents per lb.
Cases, fish skin..............20 per cent.
Cassimere, woollen...........40 do.
Cassimere, cotton, wool being a component part..........40 do.
Casks, empty..............30 do.
Cassada, or meal of..........20 do.
Cassia, Chinese, Calcutta and Sumatra.................. 5 cents per lb.
Cassia buds and fistula......20 per cent.
Castanas, or castinai......... 1 cent per lb.
Castings of plaster..........30 per cent.
Castings of iron, (except vessels,) all other, not specified, even if with wrought iron rings, hoops, handles, &c... 2½ cents per lb.
Castings, iron vessels........1½ do.
Castor beans..............20 per cent.
Castor oil..................40 cents per gal.
Castors, brass or iron........30 per cent.
Castors, wood..............30 do.
Castors or cruets, silver, with or without glasses........30 do.
Castors or cruets, plated, with or without glasses.........30 do.
Castors or cruets, wood, with or without glasses........30 do.
Castor glasses, not in frames or cruets, cut. (See glass.)
Castor glasses, not in frames or cruets, not cut. (See glass.)
Castorine lize, (woollen cloth)40 per cent.
Castorum..................20 do.
Cast shoe bills.............. 1 cent per lb.
Cast iron vessels, not otherwise specified............ 1½ do.
Catches, brass, copper or iron.30 per cent.
Catechu..................20 do.
Catgut....................15 do.
Catsup ....30 do.
Caulking mallets...........30 do.
Caustic....................20 do.
Cayenne pepper............10 cents per lb.
Cedar wood...............15 per cent.
Celtz water..............20 do.
Cement, Roman............20 do.
Cerise, eau de kerch wasser, or cherry water, a cordial...60 cents per gal.
Ceruse, dry or in oil......... 4 cents per lb.
Chafing dishes, copper. .....30 per cent.
Chafing dishes, iron or tin.....30 do.
Chain cables................ 2½ cents per lb.
Chain breeching, iron........ 4 do.
Chain curbs, gilt............30 per cent.
Chain curbs, iron...........30 do.
Chain curbs, plated..........30 do.
Chain curbs, silver..........30 do.
Chain curbs, steel...........30 do.
Chain curbs, tinned.........30 do.
Chain curbs, washed........30 do.
Chains, brass..............30 do.
Chains, copper.............30 do.
Chains, iron, suitable for cables.....................2½ cents per lb.
Chains, iron, for other purposes....................30 per cent.
Chains, gold or silver........20 do.
Chains, gilt................25 do.
Chains, plated.............30 do.
Chains, steel...............30 do.
Chains, tinned............. 4 cents per lb.
Chains, washed............ 4 do.
Chains, dog............... 4 do.
Chains, ox................. 4 cents per lb.
Chains, trace............... 4 do.
Chairs, sitting..............30 per cent.
Chalk, red..................20 do.
Chalk, French..............20 do.
Chalk, white...............free.
Chambray gauze, cotton .... as cottons.
Chambray, if wool is a component part..................40 per cent.
Chambray, of silk only......$2 50 per lb.
Chamomile flowers..........20 per cent.
Chandeliers, brass...........30 do.
Chandeliers, glass, cut...... 45 cents per lb.
Charbon, animal............20 per cent.
Charts....................20 do.
Charts, books of, not connected with any work of which they form a volume..20 do.
When so connected, will pay the same as the other volumes.
Checks, cotton. (See cotton.)
Checks, princess, wool......40 do.
Checks, princess, worsted.....30 do.
Checks, linen..............25 do.
Cheese.................... 9 cents per lb.
Chemical preparations, not otherwise enumerated......20 per cent.
Chemical salts, not otherwise enumerated..............20 do.
Chenille, cords or trimming of, cotton being a component part.................. 8 cents per lb.
Chenille, cords or trimmings of, entirely of silk.........free.
Cheroots.................40 cents per lb.
Cherry rum, a cordial.......60 cts. per gal.
Chessmen, bone, ivory or rice.20 per cent.
Chessmen, wood...........30 do.
Chest handles..............30 do.
Children's shoes............15 cts. per pair.
Children's slippers..........15 do.
China ware................30 do.
China root.................20 do.
Chinchilla skins, undressed.. 5 do.
Chinchilla skins, dressed.....25 do.
Chip hats, or bonnets. (See hats.)....................35 do.
Chissels, socket............30 do.
Chissels, all other...........30 do.
Chlorometers, glass. (See glass.)
Chloride of lime............ 1 cent per lb.
Chocolate.................. 4 do.
Choppa romals and bandanna handkerchiefs, (China goods)$2 50 per lb.
Chowdagary, a manufacture of cotton. (See cotton.)
Chromate of potash..........20 per cent.
Chromic yellow............. 1 cent per lb.
Chromic acid...............20 per cent.
Chronometers, ship or box...20 do.
Chrysolites.................20 do.
Chrystals of tin.............20 do.
Ciar, or coiar rope........... 4½ cents per lb.
Cicuta....................20 per cent.
Cigars.....................40 cents per lb
Chinchona.................20 per cent.
Chinchonine...............20 do.
Cinnabar..................20 do.
Cinnamon.................25 cents per lb.
Cinnamon, oil of............20 per cent.
Circingle, webb, woollen.....40 do.
Circassians, worsted.........30 do.
Citrate of lime..............20 do.
Citric acid.................20 do.
Citron, in its natural state....20 do.
Citron preserved............25 do

Citron, oil of................25 per cent.
Civit, oil of.................20 do.
Clasps, brass.................30 do.
Clasps, gold or silver........20 do.
Clasps, gilt or plated........25 do.
Clasps, steel.................30 do.
Clasps, set, gold or silver...20 do.
Clasps, iron..................30 do.
Clay, ground or prepared......20 do.
Clay, unwrought...............free.
Clayed sugar, white........ 4 cents per lb.
Cloaks........................50 per cent.
Cloak pins, gilt or plated....30 do.
Cloak pins, iron or steel.....30 do.
Clocks........................25 do.
Cloth, Indian rubber, wool being a component part......40 do.
Cloth, Indian rubber, linen being a component part......30 do.
Cloth, woollen................40 do.
Cloth, leopard spot, woollen..40 do.
Cloths, bolting, silk.........20 do.
Cloths, all oil, for floor, patent, stamped, printed, or painted.35 cts. p. sq. yd.
Cloths, oil, not denominated patent floor cloth..........10 do.
Cloths, hemp..................20 per cent.
Cloths, linen.................25 do.
Clothing, ready made..........50 do.
Clothing, all other, made wholly or in part by hand....40 do.
Cloves........................ 8 cents per lb.
Cloves, oil of................30 do.
Coaches, or parts thereof.....30 per cent.
Coach furniture, all..........30 do.
Coach lace, all kinds of......35 do.
Coal..........................$1 75 per ton.
Coal-hods, copper.............30 per cent.
Coal-hods, iron...............30 do.
Coating of mohair or goat's hair......................20 do.
Cobalt........................20 do.
Cochineal.....................free.
Coculus indicus...............20 per cent.
Cocks.........................30 do.
Cocoa......................... 1 cent per lb.
Codilla hemp..................$20 per ton.
Codfish, dry..................$1 per quintal.
Coffee, when imported in American vessels from the place of its growth..............free.
Coffee, other.................20 per cent.
Coffee mills..................30 do.
Coins, gold or silver.........free.
Coins, cabinets of, specially imported..................free.
Coins, cabinets of, not specially imported, and of copper...........................30 per cent.
Coins, copper.................30 do.
Coke.......................... 5 cts. pr. bush.
Colcother, dry................ 1 cent per lb.
Colcother, in oil............. 1½ do.
Cold cream....................25 per cent.
Colocynth.....................20 do.
Cologne water.................25 do.
Coloquintida..................20 do.
Colours, water................20 do.
Colombo root..................20 do.
Colt's foot...................20 do.
Cols, sanglier, cravat stiffners.40 do.
Combs, curry..................30 do.
Combs, all, for the hair, of whatever material.........25 do.
Commode handles...............30 do.
Commode knobs.................30 do.
Comforters, made of wool......30 per cent.
Comfits, preserved in sugar, brandy or molasses.........25 do.
Compasses, brass, iron or steel.........................30 do.
Compasses, mariners'..........30 do.
Compasses, wood...............30 do.
Concans, India................$2 50 per lb.
Coney wool....................25 per cent.
Confectionary, all............25 do.
Contrayema root...............20 do.
Copper, in plates or sheets, weighing over 34 oz., taken as braziers' copper.........30 do.
Copper plates, engraved.......30 do.
Copper plates or sheets to engrave upon, if polished....30 do.
Copper, manufactures of, not otherwise specified........30 do.
Copper wire...................25 do.
Copper vessels................30 do.
Copper, for the use of the mint.free.
Copper, suited to the sheathing of ships...............free.
But none is to be so considered except that which is 14 inches wide and 48 inches long, and weighing from 14 to 34 oz. per square foot.
Copper rods................... 4 cents per lb.
Copper bolts.................. 4 do.
Copper spikes................. 4 do.
Copper nails.................. 4 do.
Copper, in pigs...............free.
Copper, in bars...............free.
Copper, old, fit only to be remanufactured...............free.
Copper ore....................free.
Copperas...................... 2 cents per lb.
Copper bottoms, cut round.....30 per cent.
Copper bottoms, raised on the edge.........................30 do.
Copper still bottoms, and parts of............................30 do.
Copper chafing dishes.........30 do.
Copper, sulphate of........... 4 cents per lb.
Coral.........................20 per cent.
Cordage, tarred............... 5 cents per lb.
Cordage, untarred............. 4½ do.
Cordials......................60 cents per gal.
Coriander seed................20 per cent.
Corks.........................30 do.
Cork, manufactures of.........25 do.
Cork tree, bark of, unmanufactured.....................free.
Cornelian stone............... 7 per cent.
Corn fans.....................25 do.
Corn, Indian, or maize........10 cts. per bush.
Corrosive sublimate...........25 per cent.
Corsets.......................40 do.
Cosmetics.....................25 do.
Cotton bagging................ 4 cts. p. sq. yd.
Cotton, embroidery............30 do.
Cotton, unmanufactured........ 3 cents per lb.
Cotton cord...................30 per cent.
Cotton braces or suspenders...35 do.
Cotton, all manufactures of, or of which cotton shall be a component part, (not otherwise enumerated).........30 do.
Cotton, all manufactures of, not dyed, coloured, printed or stained, not exceeding in value 20 cents per square yard, shall be valued at 20 cents per square yard......30 do.

Cotton, all manufactures of, or cloths of which cotton shall be a component part, not otherwise described, if dyed, coloured, printed, or stained, in whole or in part, and *not* exceeding in value 30 cents the square yard, shall be taken and deemed to have cost 30 cents the square yard, and charged with duty accordingly.....30 per cent.
Cottons, all such velvets, cords, mole skins, fustians, buffalo cloths, or goods manufactured by napping or raising, cutting or shearing, not exceeding in value 35 cents per square yard, shall be valued at 35 cts. pr. sq. yd. and shall be charged accordingly ....30 do.
Cottons, kendal, the materials being cotton and wool.....40 do.
Cotton mits................30 do.
Cotton gloves..............30 do.
Cotton thread, twist and yarn, all unbleached and uncoloured, the original cost of which shall be less than 60 cents per lb., shall be deemed and taken to have cost 60 cents per lb., and shall be charged with duty accordingly.... ....25 do.
Cotton thread, twist and yarn, all bleached or coloured, the original cost of which shall be less than 75 cents per lb., shall be deemed and taken to have cost 75 cents per lb., and shall be charged with duty accordingly...........25 do.
Cotton twist, yarn and thread, all other on spools or otherwise....................30 do.
Cotton lace................20 do.
Cotton stockings...........30 do.
Counters, bone, ivory, pearl, or rice..................20 do.
Counters, gold or silver......30 do.
Counting-house boxes, entirely paper..................25 do.
Counting-house boxes, with brass rings...............30 do.
Court plaster..............30 do.
Cow hides, raw............ 5 do.
Cow hides, tanned.......... 6 cents per lb.
Cowage, or cowitch.........20 per cent.
Cowries, (shells)...........20 do.
Crab claws.................20 do.
Crapes, silk, from beyond the Cape of Good Hope....... $2 50 per lb.
Crash......................20 per cent.
Cranks, mill, of wrought iron, 4 cents per lb.
Cravats, in pieces or single, unmade, according to their material.
Cravats, ready made........50 per cent.
Cravat stiffeners............40 do.
Crayons....................25 do.
Crayon pencils, of lead......25 do.
Creas, cotton, as cotton.
Creas, linen...............25 per cent.
Cream of tartar............free.
Crocus powder..............20 per cent.
Crockery...................30 do.
Crowns, Leghorn hat........35 do.
Cross cut saws.............$1 00 each.
Crucibles, black lead ....30 per cent.
Crucibles, sand.............30 do.
Crystals, watch.............$2 00 per gross.
Crystals, glass, for seals. (See glass.)
Crystals, orange. (See glass.)
Cubebs.....................20 per cent.
Cudbear....................20 do.
Cummin seed...............20 do.
Cupboard turns.............30 do.
Curls, hair.................25 do.
Currier's knives............30 do.
Currants.................. 3 cents per lb.
Curtain rings...............30 per cent.
Custas, as manufactures of cotton. (See cotton.)
Cut iron nails.............. 3 cents per lb.
Cutting knives..............30 per cent.
Cut glassware, not otherwise specified. (See glass.)
Cutlasses..................30 do.
Cutlery....................30 do.
Cyanide of iodine...........20 do.
Cyanide of potassium........20 do.
Cyanide of zinc.............20 do.

D.

Daggers....................30 per cent.
Dates......................1 cent per lb.
Dacanters, cut glass. (See glass.)
Decanters, plain. (See glass.)
Delph......................30 per cent.
Delphine...................20 do.
Demijohns of half gal. or less, 15 cents each.
Demijohns above half gal. and not exceeding three gals..30 do.
Demijohns exceeding three gallons.................50 do.
Denmark stuff, or satteens, entirely stuff...............30 per cent.
Dentifrice.................20 do.
Devonshire kerseys.........40 do.
Diamonds.................. 7½ do.
Diamonds, set in steel, glaziers'...................25 do.
Diaper, linen...............25 do.
Diapers, cotton. (See cottons.)
Diapers, hemp..............20 do.
Dice, ivory or bone..........20 do.
Dimities and dimity muslin. (See cottons.)
Dimity furniture, dimity cambrics, and all other dimity. (See cottons.)
Directions for patent medicines....................20 do.
Dirks......................30 do.
Dishes, chafing, copper......30 do.
Dishes, chafing, iron or tin..30 do.
Distilled vinegar, medicinal..20 do.
Diuretic, sal................20 do.
Dividers, brass, iron or steel..30 do.
Dividers, silver.............30 do.
Dividers, wood.............30 do.
Dogs' chains............... 4 cents per lb. and 15 per cent. ad valorem.
Dolls, all..................30 per cent.
Domets, a flannel...........14 cts. p. sq. yd.
Dominos, bone or ivory......20 per cent.
Dowlas.....................25 do.
Doyley's cotton.............30 do.
Doyley's linen..............25 do.
Doyley's woollen...........40 do.
Down......................25 do.
Dragon's blood.............20 do.

Drawing pencils, (black lead)..25 per cent.
Drawing pencils, for drawing, (not black lead)..........25 do.
Drawings..................20 do.
Drawer knobs, of brass, iron, steel, washed, gilt or plated,30 do.
Drawer knobs, of brass and glass....................25 do.
Drawer knobs, entirely of cut glass. (See glass.)
Drawer knobs, entirely of plain glass. (See glass.)
Drawer knobs, ivory.........20 do.
Drawer knobs, bone,........20 do.
Drawing knives.............30 do.
Drawers, Guernsey, wool or worsted,.................30 do.
Drawers, knit, without needle work....................30 do.
Drawers, silk...............40 do.
Drawers, chest of,..........30 do.
Dressed furs, on the skin....25 do.
Dried pulp.................20 do.
Drillings, linen............25 do.
Drillings, if cotton be a component material, subject to the regulations respecting cotton cloths. (See cottons.)
Drugget, printed. (See baize.)
Drugs, dying, not otherwise enumerated..............20 do.
Drugs, medicinal, not otherwise enumerated...........20 do.
Duck, Holland, English, Russia, Ravens, half-duck, and all other sail-duck,........ 7 cts. p. sq. yd.
Dutch metal, in leaf........25 per cent.
Durants, worsted stuff......30 do.
Dust pans..................30 do.
Dutch pink.................20 do.
Dye woods.................free.
Dyeing drugs and materials for composing dyes, not otherwise enumerated.....20 per cent.
Dyeing, articles used principally for, not otherwise enumerated..................20 do.

E.

Earth, in oil................. 1½ cents per lb.
Earth, brown, red, blue, yellow, dry as ochre......... 1 do.
Earthenware...............30 per cent.
Ebony, unmanufactured.....free.
Ebony, manufactures of, or of which it is the material of chief value...............30 per cent.
Elastic garters, made of elastic wire, covered with leather, with metal clasps........35 do.
Elephant's teeth............free.
Elecampane...............20 per cent.
Embroidery, by hand, with a needle, and with thread of gold,.....................30 do.
Embroideries, all, in gold or silver, fine or half fine, other than clothing.............20 do.
Emeralds.................. 7 do.
Emery.....................free.
Emetic, tartar..............20 per cent.
Engraver's copper, prepared or polished...............30 do.
Engraver's scrapers.........30 do.
Engraver's burnishers.......30 do.
Engraved or lined apothecaries' glass measures. (See glass.)
Engravings, books of, with any letter press..........20 per cent.
Epaulets, of gold and silver..free.
Epauletts, of wool..........40 per cent.
Epauletts, of cotton.........30 do.
Epauletts, plated...........free.
Epauletts, gilt..............free.
Epauletts, mi. fin...........30 per cent.
Epsom salts...............20 do.
Equalizing files........... 30 do.
Escutcheons, silver.........30 do.
Escutcheons, brass, iron, steel, gilt or plated.............30 do.
Escutcheon pins............30 do.
Essence of aspic, or d'aspic..25 do.
Essence of bergamot........25 do.
Essence of cloves...........25 do.
Essence of juniper..........25 do.
Essence of lavender.........25 do.
Essence of lemons..........25 do.
Essence of muscade or nutmegs.....................25 do.
Essence of mustard..........25 do.
Essence of oranges..........25 do.
Essence of origanum or thyme,25 do.
Essence of rosemary........25 do.
Essence of rose.............25 do.
Essence of rue.............25 do.
Essence of sabine..........25 do.
Essence of spruce..........25 do.
Essence of Tyre............25 do.
Essence of ginger...........25 do.
Essence of peppermint......25 do.
Estoppillas, linen..........25 do.
Etchings or engravings......20 do.
Ether.....................20 do.
Etoile, or stars for ornaments, gold or silver, or mi. fin...30 do.
Ether, sulphuric............20 do.
Extract of Balladonna.......25 do.
Extract of Campeachy wood.25 do.
Extract of cicutæ...........25 do.
Extract of colocynth........25 do.
Extract of elaterium........25 do.
Extract of gentian..........25 do.
Extract of hyosciamus.......25 do.
Extract of logwood..........25 do.
Extract of nux vomica......25 do.
Extract of opium...........25 do.
Extract of rhatania..........25 do.
Extract of rhubarb..........25 do.
Extract of stramonium......25 do.
Eyes and rods for stairs......30 do.
Eyes, bull's, a bean.........20 do.
Eyes, bull's, a glass. (See glass, plain.)

F.

False collars...............40 per cent.
Fans......................25 do.
Fancy, or perfumed shaving soaps, including Windsor soap, and wash balls......30 do.
Fancy vials and bottles not exceeding the capacity of four ounces each, uncut.... $2 20 per gross.
Fancy vials and bottles exceeding 4 oz., and not exceeding 16 oz. each, uncut $3 00 do.
Fastenings, shutter or other, of copper, iron, steel, brass, gilt, plated or japanned....30 per cent.

Fearnought cloth...........40 per cent.
Feathers, ornamental.......25 do.
Feathers, for beds...........25 do.
Felt, patent adhesive, for ships' bottoms.................free.
Felts, or hat bodies, made in whole or in part of wool...18 cents each.
Felting, hatters'............40 per cent.
Fennel, essence of..........25 do.
Ferrets, cotton..............30 do.
Ferri, rubigo...............20 do.
Fiddles......................30 do.
Fids.........................30 do.
Fifes, bone..................30 do.
Fifes, ivory.................30 do.
Fifes, of wood...............30 do.
Figures, alabaster...........30 do.
Figures, brass...............30 do.
Figures, bronze..............30 do.
Figures, (such as are used in churches,) gold or silver...30 do.
Figures, gilt or plated.......30 do.
Figures, marble..............30 do.
Figures, plaster.............30 do.
Figs......... .... 2 cents per lb.
Fig blue.....................20 per cent.
Filberts..................... 1 cent per lb.
Files........................30 per cent.
File cuts....................30 do.
Filtering stones.............30 do.
Filtering stones, unmanufactured.....................20 do.
Fire arms, other than muskets and rifles ....30 do.
Fire crackers and fireworks..20 do.
Fire irons...................30 do.
Fish, pickled, other than in barrels or half barrels, not specified.................20 do.
Fish, foreign caught, dry... $1 00 per quintal.
Fish, mackerel and herring, pickled.................. 1 50 per barrel.
Fish, salmon, pickled or dry salted.................. 2 00 do.
Fish, salmon, smoked..... 1 00 p. qtl. 112 lb.
Fish, all other, pickled in barrels. .... 1 00 per barrel.
Fish for daily consumption...free.
Fish, other, in oil............20 per cent.
Fish glue, called isinglass....20 do.
Fish hooks...................30 do.
Fish sauce...................30 do.
Fish skins, raw..............20 do.
Fish skin cases..............20 do.
Fisheries of the United States and their territories, all products of the...............free.
Fishing nets, other than dip or scoop nets................ 7 cents per lb.
Flags, floor matting made of..25 per cent.
Flags, carpets and carpeting, mats and floor cloths made of.........................25 do.
Flageolets, wood.............30 do.
Flageolets, bone or ivory....30 do.
Flannels, all, except cotton..14 cts. pr. sq. yd.
Flap hinges, cast........... $2\frac{1}{2}$ cents per lb.
Flap hinges..................30 per cent.
Flasks or bottles that come in gin cases. (See bottles.)
Flasks, powder, brass, copper or japanned ....30 do.
Flasks, horn, entirely of......20 do.
Flat irons.................. $2\frac{1}{2}$ cents per lb.
Flats for making hats or bonnets....................35 per cent.
Flax, unmanufactured, or tow of......................$20 per ton.
Flax, all manufactures of, or which it is a component part, not otherwise specified........................25 per cent.
Flaxseed..................... 5 do.
Fleams.......................30 do.
Fleshers' (knives)...........30 do.
Flies, Spanish, or cantharides.free.
Flints.......................free.
Flint stone..................free.
Flint, ground................free.
Float files..................30 per cent.
Floor oil cloths, all stamped, printed or painted..........35 cts. p. sq. yd.
Floor, dish or table mats.....25 do.
Floor matting, all...........25 per cent.
Flor benzoin.................20 do.
Florentine buttons, covered with bombazet over a metal form.........................25 do.
Floss silk, and other similar silks purified from the gum..25 do.
Floss cotton. (See cotton thread.)
Flour, of wheat..............75 cts. per cwt.
Flour, of other grain........20 per cent.
Flour-sulphur................free.
Flower water, orange........25 per cent.
Flowers, chamomile..........20 do.
Flowers, artificial..........25 do.
Flutes, of wood..............30 do.
Flutes, of ivory or bone entirely.........................30 do.
Flushings....................40 do.
Foils, fencing...............30 do.
Foil, tin.................... $2\frac{1}{2}$ do.
Fol, digitalis...............20 do.
Forks, of gold or silver......30 do.
Forks, of brass, lead, pewter, iron, steel, tin, or of which either of these is a component part.................30 do.
Forks, wood, wholly of.....30 do.
Forks, with wood, ivory, turtle shell, mother of pearl, deer horn, or bone handles, and with iron or steel blades.30 do.
Forge hammers............ $2\frac{1}{2}$ cents per lb.
Forbidden fruit.............20 per cent.
Fossils......................20 do.
Fox glove....................20 do.
Frames, or sticks for umbrellas or parasols..............30 do.
Frames, plated cruet.........30 do.
Frames, quadrant.............30 do.
Frames, silver cruet.........30 do.
Frankfort black..............20 do.
Frankincense.................20 do.
French green.................20 do.
Fringes for coach makers or upholsterers, made of cotton.........................30 do.
Fringes, wool being a component material..............40 do.
Fringes, merino..............30 do.
Frize or ratteens, of wool....40 do.
Frizettes, hair..............25 do.
Frizettes, silk..............30 do.
Frocks, Guernsey.............30 do.
Frosts (glass)...............20 do.
Fruits, preserved in brandy or sugar.......................25 do.
Fruits, pickled..............30 do.
Fruits, green or ripe, from the West Indies, if in bulk....free.

Frying pans................30 per cent.
Fuller's Boards............12½ cents per lb.
Furniture, silver, coach and harness..........30 per cent.
Furniture, brass, copper, iron or steel, not coach or harness..................30 do.
Furnitures, calico or chintz. (See cotton.)
Furniture, household, not otherwise specified........30 do.
Furs, undressed, all on the skin...................... 5 do.
Fur, dressed, all on the skin..25 do,
Fur, hats or caps of.........35 do.
Fur, hat bodies or felts......25 do.
Furs, hatters, dressed or undressed, not on the skin...25 do.
Fustic....................free.
Fur muffs or tippets, or other manufactures not specified.35 per cent.

G.

Galanga...................20 per cent.
Gallengal, or gallengal root..20 do.
Galloons, gold or silver, fine or half fine............ 15 do.
Galls, nut.................free.
Gamboge..................20 per cent.
Game bags, leather.........35 do.
Game bags, twine..........25 do.
Garance, or madder..........free.
Garnets, glass............ 7½ per cent.
Garnets, a precious stone ... 7 do.
Garnets, imitation of, a composition .... 7½ do.
Garnets, hardware..........30 do.
Garden seeds, not otherwise specified................free.
Garters, elastic, made of wire covered with leather, with or without metal clasps...35 per cent.
Garters. Indian rubber, with clasps...................30 do.
Gauze cotton. (See cottons.)
Gelatine, a species of glue for clarifying..................30 do.
Gems, specially imported.... free.
Gems, not specially imported.. 7 do.
Gentian, or gentian root....20 do.
German silver, in sheets....30 do.
Gig hames..................30 do.
Gig springs.................30 do.
Gig handles................30 do.
Gilt bases..................30 do.
Gilt capitals................30 do.
Gilt chains.................25 do.
Gilt ear-rings...............25 do.
Gilt paper.................12½ cents per lb.
Gilt pins...................25 per cent.
Gilt rings..................25 do.
Gilt ware, silver............30 do
Gilt ware, of other metals..30 do.
Gilt wire...................30 do.
Gilt watch chains...........25 do.
Gilt watch seals............25 do.
Gilt watch keys............25 do.
Gilt wood..................30 do.
Gilt studs..................25 do.
Gimblets...................30 do.
Gimps, cotton..............30 do.
Gimps, silk...............$2 50 per lb.
Gimps, linen or thread .....25 per cent.
Gimps, wire being a a component part..................30 do.

Gin, 1st proof..............60 cents per gal.
Gin, 2d proof...............60 do.
Gin, 3d proof...............65 do.
Gin, 4th proof..............70 do.
Gin, 5th proof..............75 do.
Gin, above 5th proof........90 do.
Gin cases, with bottles in them, the cases pay............30 per cent. and the bottles. (See bottles.)
Ginger, essence of..........25 do.
Ginger, ground............. 4 cents per lb.
Ginger roots............... 2 do.
Ginghams, (as cottons.)
Ginseng...................20 per cent.
Girandoles, of metal........30 do.
Girandoles of glass and metal.25 do.
Glass, of antimony..........20 do.
Glass, manufactures of, all vessels or wares of cut glass, when the cutting does not exceed one third the height or length thereof..........25 cents per lb.
Glass, manufactures of, exceeding one third, but not half.....................35 do.
Glass, manufactures of, one half.....................45 do.
Glass, apothecaries' vials and bottles, not exceeding the capacity of six ounces.....$1 75 pr. gross.
Glass, apothecaries' vials, above six ounces, and not exceeding 16 ounces each..$2 25 do.
Glass bottles, black, not exceeding the capacity of one quart.....................$3 00 do.
Glass bottles, black, exceeding one quart................$4 00 do.
Glass, broken..............20 per cent.
Glass buttons, cut, entirely of..25 do.
Glass, coloured.............30 do.
Glass, green, pocket bottles..$3 00 pr. gross.
Glass, looking, plates, silvered.36 per cent.
Glasses, hour...............25 do.
Glasses, looking, with paper and wood frames.........30 do.
Glass, paintings on..........30 do.
Glass, shades for time pieces or mantel ornaments .....10 cents per lb.
Glass, all articles of, not specified, plain or moulded, weighing over 8 ounces...10 do.
Glass, plain or moulded, weighing under 8 ounces, except tumblers..........12 do.
Glass, cut, ornaments for chandeliers, &c..........45 do.
Glass tumblers, plain or moulded.................10 do.
Glass articles, plain or moulded, when stoppered or bottoms ground..............14 do.
Glass, watch, or watch crystals.....................$2 00 per gross.
Glass, window, cylinder or broad, not above 8 by 10 inches in size. .... 2 cts. per sq. ft.
Glass, window, not above 10 by 12 inches............. 2½ do.
Glass window, not above 10 by 14 inches............. 3½ do.
Glass, window, not above 11 by 16 inches............ 4 do.
Glass, window, not above 12 by 18 inches............. 5 do.
Glass, window, above 12 by 18 inches............. 6 do.

Glass, window, crown, not above 8 by 10 inches...... 3½ cts. p. sq. ft.
Glass, window, crown, not above 10 by 12........... 5 do.
Glass, window, crown, not above 14 by 10........... 6 do.
Glass, window, crown, not above 11 by 16........... 7 do.
Glass, window, crown, not above 12 by 18........... 8 do.
Glass, window, crown, above 12 by 18..............10 do.
Glass, polished plate, not exceeding 8 by 12........ 5 do.
Glass, polished plate, not above 10 by 14.......... 7 do.
Glass, polished plate, not above 11 by 16........... 8 do.
Glass, polished plate, not above 12 by 18...........10 do.
Glass, polished. plate, not above 14 by 22...........12 do.
Glass, polished plate, above 14 by 22...............30 per cent.
Glass, polished plate, silvered.36 do.
Glass, all articles not specified, connected with other materials, so as to prevent its being weighed........25 do.
Glauber salts...............20 do.
Glazier's diamonds, set in steel.....................25 do.
Globes.....................30 do.
Gloves, angora..............20 do.
Gloves, worsted............30 do.
Gloves, cotton..............30 do.
Gloves, linen...............25 do.
Gloves, silk................$2 50 per lb.
Gloves, woollen............30 per cent.
Gloves, mens', leatl ....$1 25 per doz.
Gloves, womens', leather, habit.......................$1 00 do.
Gloves, childrens,' leather, habit...................... 50 cts. do.
Gloves, womens,' leather, extra demi length.............$1 50 do.
Gloves, childrens,' extra demi length...................75 cts. do.
Gloves, hair,...............25 per cent.
Glue...................... 5 cents per lb.
Glue, a species for purifying liquors................... 5 do.
Goats' hair, or wool......... 1 do.
Goats' skins, raw.......... 5 per cent.
Goats' skins, tanned and dressed..................$2 50 per doz.
Gold epauletts and wings.....free.
Gold laces, galloons, tresses, tassels, knots, stars, fine or half fine.................15 per cent.
Gold embroideries, finished..20 do.
Gold embroideries, clothing..50 do.
Gold beaters' brime..........20 do.
Gold beaters' skins..........20 do.
Gold coin and bullion.......free.
Gold dust as bullion. ....free.
Gold or silver lace, even if mi. fin........................15 per cent.
Gold and silver leaf.........20 do.
Gold, muriate of ....20 do.
Gold ornaments, made by spreading gold leaf on very thin paper............... 30 do.
Gold, oxide of..............20 do.
Gold paper, in sheets, strips, or other forms............12½ cents per lb.
Gold size..................20 per cent.
Gold shell, for painting......20 per cent.
Gold studs.................20 do.
Gold watches and parts of.... 7½ do.
Golo shoes or clogs, wood...30 do.
Golo shoes, or clogs, leather.25 cts. per pair.
Gouges....................30 per cent.
Gowns ....50 do.
Gown patterns, wool being a component part..........40 do.
Grains, tawed or tanned. (See leather.)
Grains of Paradise..........20 do.
Grain tin................. 20 do.
Granella, or grana, is cochineal.....................free.
Granulated tin............ 20 do.
Granza or madder..........free.
Grapes, not dried in boxes, kegs or jars...............20 per cent.
Grass bags.................25 do.
Grass cables or cordage...... 4½ cents per lb.
Grass cloth................25 per cent.
Grass and cotton cloth, mixed; the same as manufactures of cotton.
Grass flats, braids, or plaits for making hats or bonnets.....35 do.
Grass hats or bonnets.......35 do.
Grass henguin..............$25 00 per ton.
Grass hopper springs........30 per cent.
Grass, manilla, or sisal..... $25 00 per ton.
Grass, mats of, flags, or other materials................25 per cent.
Grass rope,............... 4½ cents per lb.
Grease ....10 per cent.
Green glass pocket bottles....$3 00 per gross.
Green, French, mineral and olympian ....20 per cent.
Gridirons..................30 do.
Grindstones...............free.
Guava jelly, or paste........25 per cent.
Guernsey frocks............ 30 do.
Gunny bags................25 do.
Gunny cloth............... 5 cts. p. sq. yd.
Guana .... 20 per cent.
Guinea grains..............20 do.
Guitars....................30 do.
Guitar strings, gut..........15 do.
Guimauve or chamomile.....20 do.
Gum Arabic...............free.
Gum elastic bougies........30 per cent.
Gum elastic catheters ......30 do.
Gum elastic injection bags...30 do.
Gum elastic nipple shields...30 do.
Gum elastic pessaries...... 30 do.
Gum elastic setons..........30 do.
Gum elastic stomach tubes..30 do.
Gum Senegal..............free.
Gum tragacanth...........free.
Gum, all other resinous substances not specified, in a crude state. ....15 per cent.
Gum, all other not in a crude state.................. 25 do.
Guns, (except muskets and rifles)......................30 do.
Gun locks..................30 do.
Gunpowder............... 8 cents per lb.
Gypsum, or plaster of Paris..free.

H.

Hackles, flax...............30 per cent.
Hackles, hemp..............30 do.
Hackles, ropemakers'.......30 do.
Hair, angora, goats' or Thibet or mohair, unmanufactured, 1 cent per lb.

Hair, all manufactures of goats' or mohair.......20 per cent.
Hair, curled, for beds........10 do.
Hair prepared and cleaned for use.......................25 do.
Hair, made up for head dresses.25 do.
Hair, not made up for head dresses..................25 do.
Hair nets......................25 do.
Hair cloth.....................25 do.
Hair braids, for the head....25 do.
Hair belts.....................25 do.
Hair brooms..................30 do.
Hair bracelets,chains,ringlets and curls..................25 do.
Hair, unmanufactured.......10 do.
Hair powder, perfumed......30 do.
Hair powder, not perfumed..20 do.
Hair seating..................25 do.
Hair pencils..................30 do.
Halter chains.............. 4 cts pr. lb. and 15 pr. ct. ad val.
Halter rings..................30 per cent.
Hames. (See saddlery.)
Hammers, blacksmiths'......2½ cents per lb.
Hammers, hand............30 per cent.
Hammers, all other.........30 do.
Hams and bacon........... 3 cents per lb.
Handkerchiefs, linen........25 per cent.
Handkerchiefs, bandana, and choppa, and all of silk.....$2 50 per lb.
Handkerchiefs, cotton. (See cottons.)
Handkerchiefs, Madras. (See cottons.)
Handles for chests, japanned.30 per cent
Hangers......................30 do.
Hangings, paper.............35 do.
Hares' hair or fur, for hatters.25 do.
Hare skins, undressed....... 5 do.
Hare skins, dressed..........25 do.
Harlæm oil....................20 do.
Harness......................35 do.
Harness furniture, all........30 do.
Harp strings, gut. ....15 do.
Harp strings, wire..........30 do.
Harps and harpsicords......30 do.
Hartshorn....................20 do.
Hatchets .... 30 do.
Hat bodies, in whole or in part of wool ....18 do.
Hats, Leghorn...............35 do.
Hats, silk, for men...........15 do.
Hat linings, cotton, (as cotton.)
Hat linings, silk............free.
Hat or cap wire.............12 cents per lb.
Hats of chip, straw or grass.·35 per cent.
Hats, cotton cloth, complete, with the exception of the lining and band..........40 do.
Hats ....18 do.
Hats, fur.....................35 do.
Hat felts on bodies put in form or trimmed..........25 do.
Hatters' irons.............. 2½ cts. per lb.
Hats, leather ....35 per cent.
Hats, palm leaf ....35 do.
Hats, rattan................35 do.
Hats, silk, men's............$1 00 each.
Hats, japanned.............35 per cent.
Hautboys....................30 do.
Haversacks of leather......35 do.
Hay knives...... ....30 do.
Head dresses, ornaments for.25 do.
Head matter, if fishery of U.S.free.
Head pieces for stills......30 per cent.
Hearth rugs, wool, all.......40 do.
Hellebore root...............20 per cent.
Hemlock......................free.
Hempseed ....20 per cent.
Hempseed oil...............20 cents p. gal.
Hemp, all manufactures of, not otherwise specified, or of which hemp is a component part.................20 per cent.
Hemp, unmanufactured....$40 00 per ton.
Henbane......................20 per cent.
Herrings, pickled, in barrels $1 00 per barrel.
Herrings, pickled, in kegs..20 per cent.
Herrings, smoked or dry.....$1 00 p.qtl.112lb.
Hessians, German flax......25 per cent.
Hessians, hemp............20 do.
Hides, raw................. 5 do.
Hides, salted............... 5 do.
Hides, tanned.............. 6 cents per lb.
Hinges, brass, copper, iron or steel.........................30 per cent.
Hinges, silver or gold.......30 do.
Hobby horses, wood or paper.30 do.
Hods, coal, iron............30 do.
Hods, coal, copper..........30 do.
Hoes.........................30 do.
Hoisting chains, [4 cts. p. lb.].15 p. ct. ad val.
Hollands, brown............25 per cent.
Hones ....20 do.
Honey ....20 do.
Honey water.................25 do.
Hooks, fish..................30 do.
Hooks and eyes, gold or silver.........................30 do.
Hooks and eyes, other......30 do.
Hooks, reaping............ 30 do.
Hoop iron.................. 2½ cts. per lb.
Hoops, iron, fit for use......30 per cent.
Hops ....20 do.
Horn combs, even if with three small brass rivets........25 do.
Horn tips.................. 5 do.
Horn plates, for lanthorns..20 do.
Horns...................... 5 do.
Horse hair..................10 do.
Hose, cotton, wool or worsted.30 do.
Hose, leather...............35 do.
Hose, linen thread..........25 do.
Household furniture........30 do.
Hungary water.............25 do.
Hyacinth roots........... free.
Hydriodate of potash........20 per cent.
Hydrometers, of glass, according to weight. (See glass.)
It is understood that those which come from France have no metal connected with them.
And that those which come from England have brass or other metal as a component part; this being so, they will be subject to a duty of....30 do.

I.

Imitation of precious stones, other than glass.......... 7½ per cent.
Imitation of precious stones, glass..................... 7½ do.
Implements of trade of persons arriving in the United States.......................free.
Indian grass ....$25 00 per ton.
Indian rubber, in bottles or sheets, or otherwise, unmanufactured.............free.

Indian rubber oil cloth and shoes, or other manufactured articles, composed wholly or in part of Indian rubber....................30 per cent.

Indian rubber suspenders, but none to be taken at a less cost than $2 per dozen....30 do.

Indian rubber webbing .....30 do.

Indian meal................20 cts. p.112 lbs.

Indian corn................10 cts. p. bush.

Indigo..................... 5 cents per lb.

Indispensables, leather......35 per cent.

Indispensables, cotton.......30 do.

Indispensables, merino stuff..30 do.

Indispensables, silk.........30 do.

Indispensables, silk, with clasps.....................30 do.

Indispensables, bead........30 do.

Indispensables, bead, with clasps.....................30 do.

Ink and ink powder........25 do.

Inkstands, earthen..........30 do.

Inkstands, leather..........35 do.

Inkstands, wedgewood......30 do.

Inkstands, paper, with glass.25 do.

Inkstands, silver............30 do.

Inkstands, wood............30 do.

Inkstands, metal............30 do.

Inkstands, glass, plain, according to weight. (See glass.)

Inkstands, glass, cut, according to weight. (See glass.)

Instruments, philosophical, specially imported........free.

Instruments, philosophical, not specially imported; duty according to the materials they are composed of.

Instruments, musical........30 per cent.

Instruments, musical, brass..35 do.

Inventions, models of, all....free.

Iodine.....................20 per cent.

Iodine, salts of.............20 do.

Ipecac, or ipecacuanha......20 do.

Iris root, or orris...........20 do.

Iron anchors................ 2½ cents per lb.

Iron anchors, parts of........ 2½ do.

Iron anvils.................. 2½ do.

Iron, articles not enumerated, manufactured from iron, or of which iron is a component part................ 30 per cent.

Iron, in bars or bolts, made wholly or in part by rolling..$25 00 per ton.

Iron, in bars or bolts, not manufactured in whole *or* in part by rolling..........$17 00 per ton.

Iron boiler plates, with holes for rivets................... 4 cents per lb.

Iron boiler plates, *without* holes for rivets.......... 4 do.

Iron, band .... 2½ cents per lb.

Iron cables, or parts thereof.. 2½ do.

Iron castings, (except vessels). 1 do.

Iron in slabs, blooms, or other form less finished than iron in bars or bolts, and more advanced than pig iron, except castings, liable to the same duty as iron in bars or bolts.

Iron nail plates............2½ do

Iron, old, that has been in actual use, and fit only to be remanufactured...........$10 00 per ton.

Iron in pieces, except old, of more than six inches in length, or of sufficient length to be made into spikes and bolts, shall pay duty according to the articles of which it may consist, whether bolt, hoop, or other iron.

Iron casters.................30 per cent.

Iron combs.................30 do.

Iron cutting knives, for cutting hay or straw..........30 do.

Iron ferrules, piano..........30 do.

Iron filings.................30 do.

Iron hoop.................. 2½ cents p. lb.

Iron, cannon................25 per cent.

Iron, cast vessels........... 1½ cents p. lb.

Iron hoops, made fit for use..30 per cent.

Iron kentlege............... 1 cent per lb.

Iron liquor..................20 per cent.

Iron nails...................30 do.

Iron mill cranks, *of wrought iron*...................... 4 cents p. lb.

Iron mill irons, of *wrought iron*...................... 4 do.

Iron nails, cut............... 3 do.

Iron nails, wrought......... 4 do.

Iron nail or spike rods, whether slit, rolled, or hammered. 2½ do.

Iron in pigs.................$9 per ton.

Iron, round, or braziers' rods, of 3-16 to 10-16 of an inch diameter, *inclusive*........ 2½ cents p. lb.

Iron, sad or flat-irons........ 2½ do.

Iron screws for wood, called wood screws..............12 do.

Iron, screws, all other..... 30 per cent.

Iron, manufactures of, partly finished, pay the same rate of duty as if entirely finished.

Iron scythes................30 do.

Iron shot................... 1 cent per lb.

Iron, in sheet............... 2½ do.

Iron shovels.................30 per cent.

Iron sickles.................30 do.

Iron for band iron, round and hammered .... 2½ cents per lb.

Iron for scroll iron, round and hammered .... 2½ do.

Iron for casement rods, round and hammered............ 2½ do.

Iron spades.................30 per cent.

Iron squares................30 do.

Iron spikes................. 3 cents per lb.

Iron square wire, used for the manufacture of stretchers for umbrellas, and cut in pieces not exceeding the length used therefor .....12½ per cent.

Iron tacks, brads or sprigs, *not* exceeding 16 oz. per 1000.. 5 cents p. 1000.

Iron tacks, brads or sprigs, exceeding 16 oz. per 1000.... 5 cents per lb.

Iron tacks, shoemakers'....30 per cent.

Iron, vessels of, cast, even with wrought rings, hoops, handles, &c., &c., not otherwise specified........... 1½ cents per lb.

Iron weights, cast, even with wrought rings, hoops, handles, &c., &c., not otherwise specified............ 1 do.

Iron wire, not exceeding No. 14, 5 do.

Iron wire, exceeding No. 14, and not 25............... 8 do.

Iron wire, exceeding No. 25..11 do.

Iron chains for rail-roads, cast, 4 do.

Iron wheels for cars, cast.... 4 cents per lb.
Iron wire, tinned, as other iron wire.
Iron rods, ½ an inch thick and under.................... 3 do.
Iron, sulphate of...........20 per cent.
Iron wire, annealed, to pay duty the same as other iron wire.
Isinglass....................20 do.
Issue peas....................20 do.
Issue plaster..................20 do.
Ivory.........................free.
Ivory chessmen.............20 per cent.
Ivory combs..................25 do.
Ivory, manufactured ....20 do.
Ivory, unmanufactured......free.
Ivory black................ ¾ cents per lb.
Ivory parallel rules........30 per cent.
Ivory protractors............20 do.
Ivory scales...................20 do.
Ivory sectors..................30 do.

J.

Jacks, a part of piano fortes.30 per cent.
Jacks, clothiers'............30 do.
Jack chains, (4 cts. per lb.)..15 p. cent ad val.
Jack screws....................30 per cent.
Jalap...........................20 do.
Jallalpore Mamoody, cotton goods, (as cottons.)
Japanned saddlery, all......20 do.
Japanned wares of all other kinds.....................30 do.
Jassamin, or jasmine, oil of..25 do.
Jeanette, or jean, (as cottons.)
Jelly, and all similar preparations ....30 do.
Jerk beef.................. 2 cents per lb.
Jet, real.................... 7 per cent.
Jet, if composition.......... 7½ do.
Jet stones....................20 do.
Jet beads ....25 do.
Jewelry.......................20 do.
Jewelry, false, so called ...25 do.
Johntilly sawns, cotton goods, (as cottons.)
Joints, India..................free.
Jostic, or jos light..........free.
Juglandium, oil of..........20 per cent.
Juice of limes...............20 do.
Juice of lemons ....20 do.
Juice of oranges............20 do.
Juniper plants................free.
Juniper berries..............20 per cent.
Junk, old......................free.
Jute matting..................25 per cent.

K.

Kaleidescopes..............30 per cent.
Kalydor......................25 do.
Kelp..........................free.
Kentledge.................. 1 cent per lb.
Kermes ....free.
Kersey ratteen,woollen cloth.40 per cent.
Kerseys ....40 do.
Kerseymere ....40 do.
Kettles, brass, in nests......12 cents per lb.
Kettles, cast iron.......... 1½ do.
Kettles, copper..............30 per cent.
Keys, watch, of gold........20 do.
Keys, watch, of silver..... 20 do.
Keys, all other, of iron, brass or copper..................30 do.
Keys, all other, of gold or silver.........................30 per cent.
Kilmarnock caps............30 do.
King's yellow ....20 do.
Knitting needles............20 do.
Knives, cutting, (meaning those used for *hay* or *straw*)30 do.
Knives, curriers'............30 do.
Knives, drawing............30 do.
Knives, flesh.................30 do.
Knives, all other, of iron, steel, copper, brass, pewter, lead or tin..........................30 do.
Knives, silver or gold......30 do.
Knobs, brass, gilt, plated or washed iron; steel, copper or brass..................30 do.
Knobs, cut glass. (See glass.)
Knobs, glass, not cut. (See glass.)
Knobs, glass, with brass, iron, steel or composition shanks.25 per cent.
Knockers....................30 do.
Knots and stars of gold and silver, fine and half fine....15 do.

L.

Labels, printed.............20 per cent.
Labels, decanter or other, gilt or plated..................30 do.
Labels, decanter or other, gold or silver..................30 do.
Lac dye ....free.
Lace, all kinds of, made into wearing apparel..........40 per cent.
Lace, bobbinet..............20 do.
Lace, coach..................35 do.
Lace, gold....................15 do.
Lace, plated, or mi. fin......15 do.
Lace, silver..................15 do.
Lace, silk....................$2 50 per lb.
Lace shades..................20 per cent.
Lace shawls, cotton.........20 do.
Lace edgings................15 do.
Lace insertings, cotton......20 do.
Lace gimp, cotton...........20 do.
Lace quillings, cotton.......20 do.
Lace tatting, cotton.........20 do.
Lace purling, cotton.........20 do.
Lace bobbinet veils.........20 do.
Lace chemizettes, not trimmed..........................40 do.
Lace collars, not trimmed....40 do.
Lace pelerines, not trimmed..40 do.
Lace collarettes, not trimmed.40 do.
Lace cannezous, not trim'd..40 do.
Lace handkerchiefs..........20 do.
Lace caps, not trimmed....40 do.
Lace caps, made up and trimmed ....40 do.
Lace collars, trimmed ......40 do.
Lace collarettes, trimmed ...40 do.
Lace pelerines, trimmed....40 do.
Lace chemizettes, trimmed..40 do.
Lace cannezous, trimmed....40 do.
Lace handkerchiefs, trimmed, cotton ....40 do.
Lace collars and capes, ready to wear ....40 do.
Lace pelerines...............40 do.
Laces, gold and silver, invoiced fin, mi. fin, argent fin, and argent mi. fin ....15 do.
Laced boots or bootees......$1 25 per pair.
Lacets or lacings, silk ......$2 50 per lb.
Lacets or lacings, if cotton..30 per cent.

Article	Duty
Lacquered ware	30 per cent.
Ladles, gilt on copper	30 do.
Ladles, gilt on silver	30 do.
Ladles, gold or silver	30 do.
Ladles, iron, tin, Britannia, brass or copper	30 do.
Ladle heads	30 do.
Lake	20 do.
Lake drop	20 do.
Lake paints	20 do.
Lamp black	20 do.
Lamp hooks	30 do.
Lamp pullies, brass, copper or iron	30 do.
Lamp pullies, wood	30 do.
Lamps, brass, copper or tin	30 do.
Lamps, entirely of plain glass. (See glass.)	
Lamps, cut glass	45 cents per lb.
Lamps, with brass pillars and glass chimneys or domes imported in them	30 per cent.
Lancets	30 do.
Lancet cases, shagreen	30 do.
Lantern leaves, or horn plates	20 do.
Lanterns, japanned, tin, gilt, plated, brass, pewter or copper	30 do.
Lapis calaminaris	20 do.
Lapis infernalis	20 do.
Lapis tutia	20 do.
Lard	3 cents per lb.
Larding pins	30 per cent.
Latches, iron, steel, brass, gilt, plated, washed, or copper	30 do.
Latin books, bound	15 cents per lb.
Latin books, unbound	13 do.
Lattin, brass	30 per cent.
Laudanum	20 do.
Laurel, oil of	20 do.
Lavender, oil and essence of, double or single distilled	25 do.
Lavender, dry, flower of	20 do.
Lavender flowers	20 do.
Lawn, cotton. (See cottons.)	
Lawn, linen	25 per cent.
Lawn, or long lawn, linen	25 do.
Lavender water	25 do.
Lead, all manufactures of, not otherwise specified	4 cents per lb.
Lead in bars	3 do.
Lead, black	20 per cent.
Lead, powder of black	20 do.
Lead pencils, black	25 do.
Lead combs	25 do.
Lead, old	½ cent per lb.
Lead, in pigs	3 do.
Lead, scrap	1½ do.
Lead, sugar of	4 do.
Lead pots, black	30 per cent.
Lead, red, dry, or ground in oil	4 cents per lb.
Lead, nitrate of	20 per cent.
Lead, in sheets	4 cents per lb.
Lead shot	4 do
Lead, super acetate or sugar of lead	4 do.
Lead, white, dry or ground in oil	4 do.
Lead pipes	4 do.
Lead ore	3 do.
Lead, in any other form not specified	4 do.
Leaders, leather	35 per cent.
Leaders, worsted	30 do.
Leaf, gold and silver	20 do.
Leather bracelets, elastic	35 per cent.
Leather mits	35 do.
Leather garters, elastic	35 do.
Leather, and all manufactures thereof, or of which it is a material, not otherwise specified	35 do.
Leather, caps or hats of	35 do.
Leather bottles	35 do.
Leather, braces or suspenders, entirely of, or of which leather is a material	35 do.
Leaves of trees used for dyeing	20 do.
Leaves, not used in dyeing	20 do.
Leaves of bocoa	20 do.
Lees, wine, liquid	20 do.
Lees, wine, crystalized, or crude tartar	free.
Leghorn hats and bonnets, and all hats or bonnets of straw, chip or grass	35 per cent.
Leghorn flats, braids, crowns, brims or plaits	35 do.
Lemons, in bulk	free.
Lemons, in b'xs. bbls. or c'sks.	20 per cent.
Lemon juice	20 do.
Lemon, oil of	20 do.
Lemon peel	20 do.
Lemon, essence of	25 do.
Leno, linen	25 do.
Leno, muslin. (See cottons.)	
Leopard skins, raw	5 per cent.
Leopard skins, dressed	25 do.
Leopard spot cloth	40 do.
Limes, in bulk	free.
Lime juice	20 per cent.
Limets, oil of	20 do.
Lime, acetate of	20 do.
Lime	20 do.
Lime, citrat, or citrate of	20 do.
Lines, fishing, a twine	6 cents per lb.
Lines, fishing, complete	6 do.
Lines, worsted	30 per cent.
Linens, all manufactures of, not otherwise specified	25 do.
Linen bags	25 do.
Linen, bleached	25 do.
Linen mits	25 do.
Linen tape	25 do.
Linen, unbleached	25 do.
Linen canvas, black, in strips or patterns of the size exclusively for buttons, shoes, or bootees	5 do.
Linseed cakes	20 do.
Linseed	5 do.
Linseed oil	25 cents per gal.
Linsey woolsey	40 per cent.
Lint	25 do.
Liqueurs, or cordials	60 cents per gal.
Liquor, iron	20 per cent.
Liquor, purple	20 do.
Liquor, red	20 do.
Liquor, tin	20 do.
Liquor cases	30 do.
the bottles, if cut. (See glass.)	
if not cut. (See glass.)	
Liquorice paste	25 do.
Liquorice root	20 do.
Liquorice juice	20 do.
Litharge	4 cents per lb.
Lithontriptons	30 per cent.
Litmus	20 do.
Loadstones	20 do.

Loaf sugar................ 6 cents per lb.
Loaf sugar, in a pulverized liquid, or other forms...... 6 do.
Lotions, all cosmetic.........25 per cent.
Lotions, medicinal..........20 do.
Lozenges, all medicinal......25 do.
Locks, brass, iron, steel, wood and iron, wood and steel, or gun...................30 do.
Logwood..................free.
Logwood, extracts of........25 per cent.
Long cloths, (Madras and Calcutta,) liable to the regulations respecting manufactures of cotton.
Long cloths, linen..........25 do.
Looking glasses, framed......30 do.
Looking glasses, with paper and wood frames..........30 do.
Looking glass plates, if silvered....................36 do.
Looking glass plates, if not silvered...................30 do.
Looking glass frames, if gilt on metal..................30 do.
Looking glass frames, if wood, or gilt on wood. ....30 do.
Looking glass frames, if metal.....................30 do.
Lump sugar................ 6 cents per lb.
Lump sugar, in a pulverized, liquid or other form....... 6 do.
Lunar caustic................20 per cent.
Lupuline....................30 do.
Lustres, glass, cut ....45 cents per lb.
Lustres, brass and glass......25 per cent.
Lutes.......................30 do.
Lycopodium..................20 do.
Lye, soda...................20 do.

M.

Macaroni...................30 per cent.
Mace.......................50 cents per lb.
Macassar oil................25 per cent.
Machinery, models of........free.
Mackerel. (See fish.)
Madder...................free.
Madder root...............free.
Magnesia..................20 per cent.
Magnesia, sulphate of........20 do.
Mallets, caulkers, and other..30 do.
Malt.......................20 do.
Manganese.................20 do.
Manilla grass..............$25 00 per ton.
Manna......................20 per cent.
Manufactures of the United States and its territories exported and brought back...free.
Maps and charts specially imported.................free.
Maps and charts not specially imported.................20 per cent.
Marble, busts of, or statuary, specially imported........free.
Marble, unmanufactured....25 per cent.
Marble, all manufactures of...30 do.
Marmalade, a sweetmeat....25 do.
Mascade, essence of. ....25 do.
Marsh mallows.............20 do.
Mastic....................free.
Matches, for pocket lights, paper......................30 per cent.
Matches, for pocket lights, wood......................30 do.
Mathematical instruments, specially imported........free.
Mathematical instruments, of brass or iron..............30 per cent.
Mathematical instruments, of bone.....................20 do.
Mathematical instruments, of gold.....................30 do.
Mathematical instruments, of ivory....................20 do.
Mathematical instruments, of silver...................30 do.
Mathematical instruments, of wood or steel.............30 do.
Mats, table, straw, tow or flag.....................25 do.
Mats, table, wood...........25 do.
Mats, oil or floor cloth, dish or table ....25 do.
Mats, if wool be a component part.....................25 do.
Matting, all floor cloth.......25 do.
Mattresses, hair.............25 do.
Mattresses, moss............25 do.
Meal, cassada, linseed and oat.20 do.
Measures, glass, engraved. (See glass.)
Mecklin lace................15 do.
Medals, specially imported..free.
Medals, not specially imported....................20 per cent.
Medicinal drugs, all kinds of, not otherwise specified....20 do.
Mercury, cinabar, iodide and prussiate of..............25 do.
Metal, plated...............30 do.
Metallic slates, paper.......25 do.
Metallic slates, tin..........25 do.
Melting pots, if earthen......30 do.
Melting or glue pots........30 do.
Mercury or quicksilver...... 5 do.
Mercury, all preparations of..25 do.
Merino shawls..............40 do.
Merino cloth, wool..........40 do.
Merino fringe...............30 do.
Merino cloth, worsted.......30 do.
Manilla hemp...............$25 00 per ton.
Mica, or isinglass...........20 per cent.
Milk of roses...............25 do.
Millinery of all kinds........40 do.
Mill board paper............ 3 cents per lb.
Mill cranks, of wrought iron.. 4 do.
Mill irons, of wrought iron... 4 do.
Milpedes...................20 do.
Mill saws..................$1 00 each.
Mill stones.................20 per cent.
Mills, coffee................30 do.
Miniature cases or sheets, ivory.....................20 do.
Miniatures..................20 do.
Mineral, green..............20 do.
Mineral water...............20 do.
Mineral salts...............20 do.
Mirrors ....30 do.
Mirror glasses, silvered .....36 do.
Mirror glasses, *not* silvered. (See glass, window.)
Mittens of wool............30 do.
Mits, cotton................30 do.
Mits, silk..................$2 50 per lb.
Mits, leather...............35 per cent.
Mits, linen.................25 do.
Mits, Angora................20 do.
Mock jewelry...............25 do.
Mock pearls, being part glass, 7½ do.
Modellings, specially imported, free
Modellings *not* specially imported, according to the ma-

terials of which they are composed.
Models of invention or machinery..................free.
Mohair, for buttons.......... 5 per cent.
Mohair, unmanufactured..... 1 cent per lb.
Mohair blankets or coatings, camblets or camlets.......20 per cent.
Molasses..................... 4½ mills per lb.
Moon knives...............30 per cent.
Mops..........................30 do.
Mordant standards.........20 do.
Morebad-sawns, cotton. (See cottons.)
Morocco skins..............$2 50 per doz.
Morphine, acetate of ....20 per cent.
Morphine, sulphate or crystals of....................20 do.
Mortars, brass..............30 do.
Mortars, marble............30 do.
Mortars, composition.......30 do.
Moss, Iceland ....20 do.
Moss, for beds..............10 do.
Mother of pearl............free.
Mother of pearl shells......free.
Mother of pearl, articles made of, not otherwise enumerated.......................20 per cent.
Mother of pearl studs.......20 do.
Mother of pearl buttons, with metal eyes or shanks......25 do.
Moulds, button..............25 do.
Mouse traps, wire or wood...30 do.
Muffs, of fur.................35 do.
Munjeet, (a dyeing drug)....20 do.
Muriate of barytes, gold, tin, or strontian..............20 do.
Muriatic acid ....20 do.
Musical instruments.........30 do.
Musical instrument strings..15 do.
Mushrooms...................20 do.
Mushroom sauce............30 do.
Musk.........................20 do.
Muskets ....$1 50 per stand.
Musket bayonets and barrels.30 per cent.
Musket bullets .... 4 cents per lb.
Musket rods and stocks.....30 per cent.
Muslins......................40 do.
Muslin handkerchiefs, chemizettes, collars, bands, or canezous.....................40 do.
Mustard, including the bottles.25 do.
Myrrh, gum...................20 do.
Myrobalan...................20 do.
Mustard seed................ 5 do.

N.

Nails, brass.................30 per cent.
Nails, copper................ 4 cents per lb.
Nails, composition...........30 per cent.
Nails, iron, wrought........ 4 cents per lb.
Nails, iron, cut............. 3 do.
Nails, ornamental, with brass, gilt, or polished heads.....30 per cent.
Nail rods or plates.......... 2½ cents per lb.
Nails, zinc...................30 per cent.
Nankeens, imported directly from China, (as cottons.)
Nankeens, not imported direct from China, subject to the regulations on manufactures of cotton.
Nankeen shoes or slippers....25 cts. per pair.
Napkins, cotton..............30 per cent.
Napkins, linen...............25 do.
Napt or napped cottons, a manufacture of wool......40 do.
Naples soap..................30 per cent.
Narcotine.................... 20 do.
Natural history, specimens in.free.
Needles, all kinds ....20 per cent.
Nests, brass kettles in.......12 cents per lb.
Nests, birds'.................20 per cent.
Nets, fishing, other than dip or scoop nets.............. 7 cents per lb.
Nets, fishing, dip or scoop nets.30 per cent.
Nicaragua wood..............free.
Nippers......................30 per cent.
Nitrate of potash, or saltpetre unrefined................free.
Nitrate of potash, or saltpetre refined.................... 2 cents per lb.
Nitrate of iron...............20 per cent.
Nitrate of silver, or lunar caustic..........................20 do.
Nitrate of tin................20 do.
Nitrate of lead...............20 do.
Nitre mur. tin...............20 do.
Nitre, refined................ 2 cents per lb.
Nitre, unrefined.............free.
Nitric or nitrous acid.........20 per cent.
Nobs, or knobs, glass, with shanks or rivets...........25 per cent.
Nobs, or knobs, iron, steel, brass or copper...........30 do.
Norfolk latches.............30 do.
Noyeau.......................60 cents per gal.
Nutria skins.................. 5 per cent.
Nut-galls....................free.
Nutmegs.....................30 cents per lb.
Nutmegs, oil of..............15 per cent.
Nuts of all kinds............ 1 cent per lb.
Nuts used in dyeing........free.
Nux vomica..................free.
Nyansooks, (as cottons.)

O.

Oakum and junk............free.
Oats ....10 cts p. bush.
Oatmeal.....................20 per cent.
Ochre, dry................... 1 cent per lb.
Ochre........................ 1½ cents per lb.
Brown, blue, red and yellow earth, to be considered as ochre.
Odours or perfumes.........25 per cent.
Oil cakes....................20 do.
Oil cloth, table mats........25 do.
Oil cloth, table mats, lined with woollen...............25 do.
Oil, Harlem..................20 do.
Oil cloths, silk...............12½ cts. p. sq. yd.
Oil cloths, such as hat covers, over garments, &c., are usually made of...............12½ do.
Oil cloth aprons............50 per cent.
Oil cloth furniture..........16 cts. p. sq. yd.
Oil stones ....20 per cent.
Oil absynth, or wormwood...20 do.
Oil of almonds. .... 9 cents per lb.
Oil of amber, or ambre.......20 per cent.
Oil, animal, and animali......20 do.
Oil of aniseed................20 do.
Oil, bears'...................20 do.
Oil, cajaput, or cajaputa......20 do.
Oil, camomile...............20 do.
Oil of cassia, caryophil, cinnamon, cloves, cocoa-nuts, croton tiglium, fennell, hartshorn, juglandium, juniper, allspice, laurel, mace, minth or mint, mustard, nuts, poppies, pretoleum, caraway, rue, sage, savin, sassafras, spruce,

spike, spurge, and all essential oils not used principally as perfumes..............20 per cent.
Oil of palm bean and palm....free.
Oil of ambergris, anthos or rosemary, bergamot, cedrat, jasmine or jessamin, lavender, lemon, limets, limette...25 per cent
Oil, Macassar..............25 do.
Oil, neatsfoot...................20 do.
Oil of Nerol, or orange flower.25 do.
Oil of nutmegs, oranges, origanum or thyme, pimento, rhodium, roses, or otto of roses, rosemary or anthos........25 do.
Oil, succini, (drug)..........20 do.
Oil of sweet marjorum, thyme or origanum, tuberos, Vanilla beans, and all other essential oils used principally in perfumes...................25 do.
Oil, castor.......................40 cents per gal.
Oil, hemp seed and linseed..25 do.
Oil, olive, in casks...........20 do.
Oil, olive, in bottles or flasks..30 per cent.
Oil, rapeseed.................25 cents per gal.
Oil, salad...................30 per cent.
Oil, spermaceti, of foreign fishing......................25 cents per gal.
Oil of vitriol.............. 1 cent per lb.
Oil, whale, and other oil (not sperm) of foreign fishing.. 15 cents per gal.
Old iron, fit only to be remanufactured, and which has been in actual use........$10 00 per ton.
Old junk...................free.
Old brass, fit only to be remanufactured............free.
Old copper, fit only to be remanufactured............free.
Old lead and scrap.......... 1½ cents per lb.
Old pewter, fit only to be remanufactured............free.
Old silver, fit only to be remanufactured............free.
Olibanum...................20 per cent.
Olives.....................30 do.
Onions.....................20 do.
Opium......................75 cents per lb.
Opium, extract of...........25 per cent.
Orange crystal..............20 do.
Orange flowers..............20 do.
Oranges....................free.
Orange bitters..............20 per cent.
Orange peel.................20 do.
Orange issue peas...........20 do.
Orange flower water.........25 do.
Orange mineral..............20 do.
Orchilli, orchello, orchelia, or orchal.....................20 do.
Ore, specimens of...........20 do.
Organs.....................30 do.
Origanum, oil of............25 do.
Ornaments, gilt wood........30 do.
Ornaments, gold paper.......30 do.
Ornaments, for women's head dresses.....................30 do.
Ornaments, not for head dresses, of metal..............30 do.
Ornamental feathers.........25 do.
Orpiment...................20 do.
Ostrich feathers............25 do.
Orris root, or iris root.......20 do.
Ostrich plumes and feathers, manufactured............25 do.
Ostrich plumes and feathers, unmanufactured...........25 do.
Otto of roses...............25 per cent.
Oxalic acid.................20 do.
Oxide of bismuth............20 do.
Oxymuriate of lime..........20 do.
Oxymuriate or chlorate of potasse or potash..............20 do.
Oysters....................20 do.
Oznaburgs..................25 do.

P.

Pack thread................ 6 cents per lb.
Padding, woollen............40 per cent.
Pad screws..................30 do.
Paint brushes...............30 do.
Painted floor cloths, all......35 cts. p. sq. yd.
Painting brushes............25 per cent.
Paintings..................20 do.
Paintings, on glass or porcelain.......................30 do.
Paints, carmine, Dutch pink, desenna, Frankfort black, French green, lamp black, king's yellow, lakes, mineral green, olympian green, patent yellow, chalk; rose pink......................20 do.
Paint, terra umbra.......... 1 cent per lb.
Paint, ivory black.......... ¾ do.
Paint, red lead.............. 4 do.
Paint, Spanish brown, dry... 1 do.
in oil.. 1½ do.
Paint, white lead........... 4 do.
Painters' colours...........20 per cent.
Palm leaves................free.
Palm leaf hats..............35 per cent.
Palm leaf baskets...........25 do.
Palm oil...................free.
Palm leaf brooms............25 per cent.
Palmetto hats...............35 do.
Pamphlets, in English, Latin, or Greek, by the pound, as books.
Pannel saws.................30 do.
Pit saws...................$1 00 each.
Pans, warming, copper.......30 per cent.
Panilla grass...............$25 00 per ton.
Pantaloons, all.............50 per cent.
Paper, antiquarian..........15 cents per lb.
Paper, bank post............17 do.
Paper, binders' boards....... 3 do.
Paper, blotting..............15 do.
Paper, box boards.......... 3 do.
Paper, cartridge............ 3 do.
Paper, copying and coloured, for labels and needles.....15 do.
Paper, copperplate...........10 do.
Paper, demy, drawing, elephant and double elephant.15 do.
Paper, fancy coloured ..... 12½ do.
Paper, foolscap.............15 do.
Paper, like that in which blue nankeens are generally imported..................... 3 do.
Paper, folio................17 do.
Paper, fullers' boards....... 3 do.
Paper, glass................12½ do.
Paper, gold leaf.............12½ do.
Paper, gold, in sheets or strips12½ do.
Paper, silver, in sheets or strips.....................12½ do.
Paper, gilt or covered with metal......................25 per cent.
Paper, imperial.............15 cents per lb.
Paper, paper makers' boards.. 3 do.
Paper, medium..............15 do.
Paper, morocco.............12½ do.

Paper, mill board............ 3 cts. per lb.
Paper, pasteboard..........12½ do.
Paper, pott................15 do.
Paper, pressing boards......12½ do.
Paper, printing.............10 do.
Paper, pith.................15 do.
Paper, quarto post of all kinds.17 do.
Paper, rice.................17 do.
Paper, Bristol boards........15 do.
Paper, sand.................15 do.
Paper, sheathing............ 3 do.
Paper, letter...............20 do.
Paper, royal and segar......17 do.
Paper, super royal....... ..17 do.
Paper, stainers'............10 do.
Paper, tissue...............15 do.
Paper, wrapping............ 3 do.
Paper, writing............,.17 do.
Paper, counting house boxes.25 do.
Paper, counting house boxes, if mounted...............30 per cent.
Paper boxes.................25 do.
Paper hangings..............35 do.
Paper inkstands, with glass bottles...................25 do.
Paper inkstands, with earthen bottles...................30 do.
Paper pin cases.............25 do.
Paper pin cases mounted or ornamented with metal....30 do.
Paper segars................40 cents per lb.
Paper snuff boxes, not japanned...................25 per cent.
Paper snuff boxes, japanned, or with metal rim.........30 do.
Parasols....................30 do.
Parasol sticks or frames.....30 do.
Parallel rules, ivory, (not mounted)...................20 do.
Parallel rules, ivory, mounted.30 do.
Parchment...................25 do.
Paris white................ 1 cent per lb.
Parts of stills, viz.: sheets made by rolling, intended for the sides; globes and heads, made by hammering thick sheet copper; bottoms beat out of large pieces of copper, and shoulders made out of sheet copper by hammering...............30 per cent.
Pasteboard..................12½ cts. per lb.
Paste giggers...............30 per cent.
Paste, jujube...............25 do.
Paste, medicinal............25 do.
Paste, Brazil...............20 do.
Paste, almond...............25 do.
Paste, perfumed.............25 do.
Paste or pasta de Brazil, (ground Nicaragua wood, a dye)...................20 do.
Paste work that is set in gold or silver...................20 do.
Pastes, imitation of precious stones.................... 7½ do.
Pastel, or woad............ 1 cent per lb.
Patent floor cloth...........35 c. p. sq. yd.
Patent yellow...............20 per cent.
Paving stones...............20 do.
Paving tile.................25 do.
Pearl, mother of............free.
Pearl, mother of, buttons, without shanks or eyes........20 per cent.
Pearl, mother of, buttons, with shanks or eyes...........20 do.
Pearls, set or not set....... 7 do.
Pearls, all articles composed wholly or chiefly of.......20 per cent.
Pearls, composition......... 7½ do.
Pearls, mock pearls......... 7½ do.
Peas........................20 do.
Pelerines, lace.............40 do.
Pelham bits.................30 do.
Pellitory root..............20 do.
Pelts, salted............... 5 do.
Pencils, black lead..........25 do.
Pencils, camel's hair........20 do.
Pencils, red lead............20 do.
Pencils, slate...............20 do.
Pencil cases, gold...........30 do.
Pencil cases, silver.........30 do.
Pencil cases, gilt or plated...30 do.
Penknives...................30 do.
Pens of brass or copper......25 do.
Pens of gold................25 do.
Pens of iron................25 do.
Pens of quills..............25 do.
Pens of silver..............25 do.
Pens of steel or tin.........25 do.
Pepper, black or white....... 5 cents per lb.
Pepper, Cayenne.............10 do.
Peppers, red................10 do.
Perfumery vials and bottles, uncut, not exceeding the capacity of four ounces each....................$2 50 per gross.
Perfumery vials and bottles, uncut, exceeding four ounces, and not exceeding sixteen ounces each.......$3 00 do.
Percussian caps.............30 per cent.
Perfumes....................25 do.
Perfumed soap, for shaving..30 do.
Perry.......................60 cts. per gal.
Peruvian bark...............free.
Pestles and mortars, composition.....................30 per cent.
Pestles and mortars of marble30 do.
Pestles and mortars of stone..30 do.
Petershams, woollen cloth...40 do.
Petticoats, cotton patterns for, as manufactures of cotton. (See cottons.)
Petticoats, ready made......50 do.
Pewter, old, fit only to be remanufactured............free.
Pewter, articles of, not enumerated, manufactured from, or of which pewter is a component part..........30 per cent.
Philosophical apparatus, specially imported...........free.
Philosophical apparatus not specially imported........30 per cent.
Phosphate of lime...........20 do.
Phosphate of soda...........20 do.
Phosphorus lights, in glass bottles, with paper cases..25 do.
Phosphorus..................20 do.
Phosphuret of lime..........20 do.
Piano fortes................30 do.
Piano forte ferrules.........30 do.
Pickled fish, other than mackerel, herring and salmon.... $1 00 p. barrel.
Pickled herring.............$1 50 do.
Pickled herring, in kegs......20 per cent.
Pickled mackerel............ $1 50 p. barrel.
Pickled salmon..............$2 00 do.
Pickles.....................30 per cent
Picrotoxine.................20 do.
Picture glass. (See glass, window.)
Pictures....................20 do.
Pigs, brass in..............free.

Pigs, copper in..............free.
Pigs, iron in................$9 00 per ton.
Pigs, lead in............... 3 cents per lb.
Pigs, tin in................ 1 per cent.
Pimento.................... 5 cents per lb.
Pimento, oil of.............25 per cent.
Pin cases or needle cases of bone...................20 do.
Pin cases or needle cases of enamel...................30 do.
Pin cases or needle cases of gold....................30 do.
Pin or needle cases of ivory..20 do.
Pin or needle cases of leather.35 do.
Pin or needle cases of metal.30 do.
Pin or needle cases of mother of pearl.................20 do.
Pin or needle cases of paper.25 do.
Pin or needle cases set with pearl.................... 7 do.
Pin or needle cases, set with precious stones.......... 7 do.
Pin or needle cases of shell...25 do.
Pin or needle cases of silver..30 do.
Pin or needle cases of paper, mounted.................30 do.
Pin or needle cases of wood..30 do.
Pin cushions, silk...........30 do.
Pin cushions, cotton.........30 do.
Pin cushions, wool...........40 do.
Pincers......................30 do.
Pine apples..................free.
Pink, Dutch..................20 per cent.
Pink, rose...................20 do.
Pink, root...................20 do.
Pink saucers.................30 do.
Pins, solid-headed, and all other package pins not exceeding 5,000 to the pack of 12 papers.............40 cts. p. pack. And in the same proportion for a greater or less quantity.
Pins, rest (iron for inside of pianos)...................30 per cent.
Pins, silver.................30 do.
Pins, iron .... 30 do.
Piperine.....................20 do.
Pipes, clay, that is smoking...30 do.
Pipes, iron, not being castings.30 do.
Pipes, iron castings......... 1 cent per lb.
Pipes, lead................. 4 do.
Pipes, watch, carre, or canon. 7½ per cent.
Pipes, wood..................30 do.
Pistols......................30 do.
Pitch, Burgundy..............20 do.
Plaids, cotton. (See cottons.)
Plantain bark, or Manilla grass, or Manilla hemp....$25 00 per ton.
Plaits, for making hats or bonnets....................35 per cent.
Plaster, court, on silk........$2 50 per lb.
Plaster, court, on cambric....30 do.
Plaster, busts and casts of....30 do.
Plaster statues, castings, and ornaments..................30 do.
Plaitings of straw for hats or bonnets.....................35 do.
Planks, planed...............30 do.
Planks, rough................20 do.
Plants.......................free.
Plantain bark................20 per cent.
Plates or sheets, iron, ¾ to ½ inch thick............. 2½ cents per lb.
Plane irons and planes......30 per cent.
Plaster of Paris.............free.

Plata pina...................free.
Plate, silver................30 per cent.
Plated carriage and harness furniture....................30 do.
Plated epauletts.............30 do.
Plated metal, of copper and silver.....................30 do.
Plated moulding..............30 do.
Plated saddlery, all.........30 do.
Plated slides................30 do.
Plated wares of all kinds, not otherwise specified.........30 do.
Plated wire..................30 do.
Plats, for making hats or bonnets....................35 do.
Plates, boiler............... 4 cents per lb.
Plates, copper, suitable for sheathing ships, that is, 14 by 48 inches, and weighing from 14 to 34 ounces per square foot...............free.
Plates, nail................. 2½ cents per lb.
Plates, copper, engraved......30 per cent.
Plates, copper, prepared for engravers...................30 do.
Plates or rods, nails, iron in slits, rolled or hammered planes..................... 4 cents per lb.
Platillas, linen..............25 per cent.
Platina crucibles.............30 do.
Playing cards.................25 cts. per pack.
Pliers........................30 per cent
Ploughs.......................30 do.
Ploughs, (a plane)............30 do.
Plumes, ornamental, whether manufactured or not.......25 do.
Plush or shag, worsted, cut or not.........................30 do.
Plush, cotton, (as cottons.)
Plush, hair...................25 do
Plush, wool...................40 do.
Pocket books, leather, with iron or brass locks and mountings, of greater value than the leather..........25 do.
Pocket books, leather, or if leather is the article of chief value...............35 do.
Pocket books, paper...........35 do.
Pocket bottles, green glass. (See bottles.)
Pocket lights, phosphorus....30 do.
Poil de chevre, (wool and cotton)........................40 do.
Points, merino wool.......... 30 do.
Pole caps .... 30 do.
Pole, carriage hooks.........30 do.
Pole ferrules.................30 do.
Polishing stones.............free.
Polished steel, saddlery......30 per cent.
Polished or scraped brass....30 do.
Polypodium....................20 do.
Pomatum.......................25 do.
Pomegranates..................20 do.
Pomegranate peel..............20 do.
Pongees, if white.............$1 50 per lb.
Poplins.......................30 per cent.
Poppy heads...................20 do.
Poppy oil.....................20 do.
Poppies .... 20 do.
Porcelain.....................30 per cent.
Pork......................... 2 cents per lb.
Porphyry......................30 per cent.
Portable desks................30 do.
Porter in bottles, no duty on the bottles..................20 cents per gal.

Porter, imported otherwise than in bottles............15 cents per gal.
Potasse, or potash, prussiate of.......................20 per cent.
Potash, bichromate of........20 do.
Potash, chromate of.........20 do.
Potash, oxymuriate, or chlorate of...................20 do.
Potash, pure..................20 do.
Potash, iodate of.............20 do.
Potash, acetate of............20 do.
Potash, hydriodate of.......20 do.
Potatoes...................10 cts. per bush.
Pots, black lead............30 per cent.
Pots, blue..................30 do.
Pots, iron.................. 1½ cents per lb.
Pots, melting, earthen.......30 per cent.
Pounce.....................20 do.
Pound ribbon...............$2 50 per lb.
Powder, black lead.........20 per cent.
Powder, blue..............20 do.
Powder, of brass...........30 do.
Powder, of bronze..........20 do.
Powder, gun.............. 8 cents per lb.
Powder, hair, plain, or not perfumed.....................20 per cent.
Powder, hair, perfumed......25 do.
Powder, ink................25 do.
Powder puffs..............35 do.
Powder, subtil, for the skin..25 do.
Powder, tooth...............25 do.
Powders, paste, balls, balsams, ointments, oils, waters, washes, tinctures, essences, or other preparations, or compositions, commonly called sweet scents, odors, perfumes, or cosmetics, and all powders and preparations for the teeth or gums......................25 do.
Powdered sugar............ 6 cents per lb.
Precious stones, set or not set. 7 per cent.
Precious stones of all kinds, and articles composed wholly or chiefly of precious stones..................... 7 do.
Precious stones, glass, imitation of.................. 7½ do.
Precious stones, other imitations of................. 7½ do.
Prepared clay...............20 do.
Pressing boards............12½ cents per lb.
Preparations, anatomical....free.
Preparations, chemical, not otherwise enumerated.....20 per cent.
Preserves, that is, comfits or sweetmeats preserved in sugar or brandy............25 do.
Preserves, in molasses.......25 do.
Prince's stuff, woollen.......40 do.
Printed music, if in sheets or books.....................20 do.
Printing paper..............10 cents per lb.
Printing types, new or old..25 per cent.
Prints or engravings........20 do.
Prints, calico. (See cotton.)
Produce of, the growth, manufacture, or fisheries of the United States and its territories......................free.
Protractors, ivory...........30 per cent.
Prunelle..................30 do.
Prunes.................... 3 cents per lb.
Prussian blue.............20 per cent.
Prussiate of potash or potasse.20 do.
Pucheri....................20 do.
Pullies, iron, brass, copper or wood.....................30 per cent.
Pumice stone...............20 do.
Pumps, stomach............30 do.
Punches, shoe ....30 do.
Punjums, Madras, (as cottons.)
Purple brown..............20 do.
Purple tin liquor...........20 do.
Putty.................... 1½ cents per lb.
Pyroligneous acid..........20 per cent.
Pyrolignate of lead.........20 do.

Q.

Quadrants and sextants.....30 per cent.
Quadrant frames...........30 do.
Quality binding............30 do.
Quassia wood, in logs......free.
Queen's stones.............20 per cent.
Quicksilver, and all preparations of.................. 5 do.
Quill baskets...............25 do.
Quills, prepared or manufactured..................25 do.
Quills, unprepared.........15 do.
Quiltings or bed quilts, (as cotton.)
Quinine...................40 cents per oz.
Quinine, sulphate of........40 do.

R.

Radix or angelica root......20 per cent.
Rag stones.................20 do.
Raisins, muscatel or bloom, in boxes or jars.............. 3 cents per lb.
Raisins, all other.......... 2 do.
Rakes, iron, steel or wood.... 30 per cent.
Rape of grapes.............20 do.
Rape cakes................20 do.
Rape seed oil..............25 cents per gal.
Rappers, brass or iron.......30 per cent.
Rass, cornucervi...........20 do.
Rasps....................30 do.
Ratifia, (a liquor)..........60 cents per gal.
Rattans, unmanufactured....free.
Rattles, wood..............30 per cent.
Rattles, ivory, with bells....30 do.
Rattles, coral, with bells....30 do.
Rattles, with silver bells....30 do.
Ravens duck.............. 7 cts. p. sq. yd.
Raw skins, that is, undressed. 5 per cent.
Raw silk..................50 cents per lb.
Razors...................30 per cent.
Razors, in boxes or cases....30 do.
Razor cases, leather........35 do.
Razor cases, metal..........30 do.
Razor cases, paper..........25 do.
Razor cases, wood..........30 do.
Razor strops, leather........35 do.
Razor strops, wood.........35 do.
Reaping hooks, iron or steel..30 do.
Ready made clothing........50 do.
Red chalk.................20 do.
Red chromate of potash....20 do.
Red lead, dry............. 4 cents per lb.
Red lead, ground in oil...... 4 per cent.
Red lead pencils...........30 do.
Red mangrove bark.........free.
Red sanders...............free.
Red or crude tartar, or wine lees.....................free.
Red liquor.................20 per cent.
Red Venitian, dry.......... 1 cent per lb.
Red Venitian, ground in oil.. 1½ do.
Red wood, and red sanders wood....................free.

Red wool, for hatters........25 per cent.
Reeds, unmanufactured.....free.
Reeds, manufactured........30 per cent.
Reeds, weavers'............30 do.
Reeves' colours............20 do.
Regulus of antimony........20 do.
Reindeer skins, dressed......25 do.
Reindeer skins, undressed.... 5 do.
Reindeer skins, tanned....... 8 cents per lb.
Reindeer tongues...........20 per cent.
Reps, cotton...............$2 50 per lb.
Reps, silk.................$2 50 do.
Resin......................15 per cent.
Resin of jalap.............15 do.
Resin, nux vomica..........free.
Rest pins..................30 per cent.
Returned cargo of American growth or manufacture....free.
Returned cargo of foreign growth or manufacture, according to the material of which it is composed, and is liable to same duty as on its first importation.
Rhubarb....................free.
Ribbons, silk..............$2 50 per lb.
Rice.......................20 per cent.
Rifles.....................$2 50 each.
Rigotine, woollen cloth......40 per cent.
Rings, brass, iron, steel or copper......30 do.
Rivets, brass, iron, steel or copper.......... 30 do.
Ringlets of human hair ..... 25 do.
Rochelle salts.............20 do.
Roots, bulbous and others, not otherwise specified........free.
Roman cement...............20 per cent.
Rope, hemp, grass or bark. (See cordage.)
Rosewater..................25 per cent
Rosewood...................15 do.
Roses, otto of.............25 do.
Rosemary, essential oil of....20 do.
Rosin......................15 do.
Rotten stone...............free.
Rouge......................20 per cent.
Rubies..................... 7 do.
Rugs, hearth...............40 do.
Rugs, horse................40 do.
Rules, of bone or ivory......20 do.
Rules, of brass, wood, iron or steel.......................30 do.
Rum, 1st and 2d proof......60 cents per gal.
Rum, 3d proof..............65 do.
Rum, 4th proof.............70 do.
Rum, 5th proof.............75 do.
Rum, above 5th proof.......90 do.
Rum, cherry................60 do.
Rum, bay...................25 per cent.
Russia diaper..............25 do.
Russia sheetings, brown and white......................25 do.
Russia duck............... 7 cts. p. sq. yd.

S.

Sabres.....................30 per cent.
Saddlery, japanned and tinned.......................20 do.
Saddlery, plated, brass and polished steel............30 do.
Saddles....................30 do.
Sad irons.................. $2\frac{1}{2}$ cents per lb.
Saffron....................free.
Sago.......................20 per cent.
Sail duck.................. 7 cts. p. sq. yd.
Sal soda...................20 per cent.
Salmon, pickled............$2 00 per bbl
Salt....................... 8 cts. p. bushel of 56 lbs.
Salt, fossil or crude mineral..20 per cent.
Saltpetre, crude...........free.
Saltpetre, partially refined.. $\frac{1}{4}$ cent per lb.
Saltpetre, refined.......... 2 do.
Salts, Epsom...............20 per cent.
Salts, glauber.............20 do.
Salts, Rochelle............20 do.
Salts, all other, and all preparations of salts not enumerated.......................20 do.
Sandal wood................free.
Sardines, and other fish preserved in oil..............20 per cent.
Sarsaparilla...............free.
Sarsnets, silk.............$2 50 per lb.
Sassafras..................20 per cent.
Satin, silk................$2 50 per lb.
Satinwood..................15 per cent.
Sattinets..................40 do.
Saucepans, copper, wrought iron or tin................30 do.
Saucepans, cast iron, glazed or tinned................. $2\frac{1}{2}$ cents per lb.
Sausages, Bologna..........25 per cent.
Sausages, other............25 do.
Saws, mill, cross-cut and pit..$1 00 each.
Saws, all other............30 per cent.
Scagliola table tops.......30 do.
Scale beams................30 do.
Sculpture, specimens of, specially imported...........free.
Sculpture. (See marble.)
Scythes....................30 per cent.
Seating or haircloth.......25 do.
Sealingwax.................25 do.
Seed, anise, coriander, cardamum and canary..........20 do.
Seeds, garden..............free.
Segars.....................40 cents per lb.
Seines..................... 7 do.
Seneca root................20 per cent.
Senegal gum................free.
Senna......................20 per cent.
Seppia.....................20 do.
Serge, woollen.............40 do.
Services of gold and silver, or vessels and wares of which these metals are a component material.............30 do.
Sewing silk, or twist......$2 00 p. lb. av.
Sextants...................30 per cent.
Shawls, merino, of wool....40 do.
Shawls, of worsted.........40 do.
Shawls, of silk............30 do.
Shawls, of Cashmere of Thibet.......................40 do.
Shawls, of lace. (See laces.)
Shawls, of cotton. (See cotton.)......................40 do.
Shawls, of all kinds, made up ready for use.............40 do.
Sheathing copper, for ships... free.
Sheathing metal, composed in part of copper.......... 2 cents per lb.
Sheathing paper............ 3 do.
Sheep. (See animals.)
Sheet brass................30 per cent.
Sheet iron................. $2\frac{1}{2}$ cents per lb.
Sheeting, Russia and other hemp.......................25 per cent.
Sheeting, linen............25 do.
Sheeting, cotton. (See cotton).30 do.
Shellac....................free.
Shells, (except pearl.).......20 per cent.
Shells, cocoa..............20 do.

Shells, manufactures of......20 per cent.
Shell or fancy boxes, not otherwise specified........25 do.
Shoes, India rubber.........30 do.
Shoes and pumps, men's, of leather....................30 cts. per pair.
Shoes, double-soled pumps and welts, women's.......40 do.
Shoes or slippers, women's, (except silk.)..............25 do.
Shoes, children's boots and bootees..................15 do.
Shoes, women's or men's silk or satin, and slippers......30 do.
Shoes, children's silk or satin, and slippers..............15 do.
Shoes for horses, iron........30 per cent.
Shoe binding, wool..........30 do.
Shoe binding, leather.......35 do.
Shoe binding, silk...........30 do.
Shot lead.................... 4 cents per lb.
Shot, cast iron............... 1 do.
Shovels......................30 per cent.
Shovels and tongs...........30 do.
Shrub........................60 cents per gal.
Sickles.......................30 per cent.
Sieves, hair..................20 do.
Sieves, wire..................30 do.
Silk, raw, comprehending all silks in the gum...........50 cents per lb.
Silks, bolting cloths.........20 per cent.
Silk, sewing or twist.........$2 00 per lb.
Silk, floss, purified from the gum.........................25 per cent.
Silk, manufactures of, not otherwise specified........$2 50 per lb.
Silk, manufactures of, and cotton.........................30 per cent.
Silk, manufactures of, and wool.......................40 do.
Silk, manufactures of, and worsted....................30 do.
Silk, manufactures of, mixed with gold or silver........30 do.
Silk, pongee and plain white silk, for printing or coloring.$1 50 per lb.
Silk umbrellas, parasols and sun-shades...............30 per cent.
Silk or satin lace boots or bootees, for men or women.75 cents p. pair.
Silk or satin lace boots or bootees, for children.......25 do.
Silk shoes and slippers. (See shoes.)
Silk hats, for men...........$1 00 each.
Silk hats or bonnets, for women........................$2 00 do.
Silk shirts and drawers......40 per cent.
Silk, other articles of, made up by hand, in whole or in part, and not otherwise provided for..................30 do.
Silvered or plated wire.......30 do.
Silver jewelry................20 do.
Silver bullion................free.
Silver leaf....................20 per cent.
Silver epaulettes and wings. free.
Silver, manufactures of......30 per cent.
Silver watches and parts of watches.................... 7½ do.
Sisal grass..................$25 00 per ton.
Skins, calf and seal, tanned and dressed..............$5 00 per doz.
Skins, sheep or skivers, tanned and dressed..........$2 00 do.
Skins, goat or morocco, tanned and dressed..........$2 50 do.
Skins, kid or morocco, tanned and dressed..............$1 50 per doz.
Skins, tanned and not dressed, goat or sheep............$1 00 do.
Skins, kid and lamb, tanned and not dressed..........75 cts. per doz.
Skins, tanned and dressed, otherwise than in colour, viz: fawn, kid and lamb, usually known as chamois.$1 00 do.
Skins, raw or undressed, whether dried or salted, hides of all kinds............... 5 per cent.
Skins, pickled and in casks, not specified...............20 do.
Slates, of all kinds..........25 do.
Sledges and hammers, blacksmiths'.................... 2½ cents per lb.
Slit iron..................... 2½ do.
Smaltz.......................20 per cent.
Snuff........................12 cents per lb.
Snuff boxes, paper, japanned or not japanned...........25 per cent.
Soap, perfumed and Windsor, of all kinds...............30 do.
Soap, all others............ 4 cents per lb.
Soap, soft....................50 cents per bbl.
Soap stocks and soap stuffs..10 per cent.
Socket chisels...............30 do.
Soda ash..................... 5 do.
Soda, all carbonates of, except soda ash, carilla and kelp..20 do.
Soda powders................30 do.
Spades.......................30 do.
Spanish brown, dry.......... 1 cent per lb.
Spanish brown, ground in oil. 1½ do.
Spanish flies or cantharides. .free.
Spar and alabaster ornaments.30 per cent.
Spartere, or willow squares, for making bonnets or hats.35 do.
Specimens in botany, mineralogy and natural history.free.
Spectacles, gold, silver or shell, mounted..............20 per cent.
Spectacles, others...........30 do.
Spectacle glasses or pebbles, when not set..............$2 00 per gross.
Spectacle cases, (according to materials.)
Spelter.......................10 per cent.
Spermaceti candles, and wax and spermaceti combined.. 8 cents per lb
Spermaceti oil, of foreign fisheries......................25 cents pr. gal.
Spikes, iron.................. 3 cents per lb.
Spikes, copper............... 4 do.
Spirits, distilled from grain or other materials, 1st and 2d proof.......................60 cents pr. gal.
Third proof..................65 do.
Fourth proof.................70 do.
Fifth proof...................75 do.
Above fifth proof............90 do.
Sponges......................20 per cent.
Spoons, silver or gold.......30 do.
Spoons, plated iron, or other metal.......................30 do.
Sprigs. (See brads.)
Spunk........................20 per cent.
Spy glasses..................30 do.
Squares, of iron or steel.....30 do.
Squares, of brass or wood...30 do.
Starch........................ 2 cents per lb.
Statues and statuary, specially imported..............free.
Statuary, not specially imported........................30 per cent.

Statuary, by American artists abroad..................free.
Steel, cast, shear and German, in bars..................$1 50 per 112 lb.
Steel, all other, in bars......$2 50 do.
Steel, manufactures of, not otherwise specified, or of which steel is a component part....................30 per cent.
Steelyards....................30 do.
Stereotype plates..........25 do.
Sticks, walking, or canes....30 do.
Stockings, cotton, woollen, worsted....................30 do.
Stockings, Angora..........20 do.
Stockings, silk, if made by hand, in whole or in part..30 do.
Stockings, linen............25 do.
Stockinetts................30 do.
Stone ware................30 do.
Stone, rotten...............free.
Stones, burr, unwrought....free.
Stones, precious, set or not set....................... 7 per cent.
Stones, polishing ....free.
Straw baskets.................25 per cent.
Straw bonnets and hats......35 do.
Straw carpeting or Chinese matting..................25 do.
Straw manufactured for hats and bonnets..............35 do.
Strings for musical instruments, of cat-gut and whip-gut, and all other strings or thread of similar materials.15 do.
Stuff goods, (worsted.).......30 do.
Sublimate, corrosive........25 do.
Sugar, brown, in the raw state, syrup of sugar, or of sugar cane............ 2½ cents per lb.
Sugar, brown, clayed....... 2½ do.
Sugar, all other, advanced beyond the raw state, by claying, boiling, clarifying or otherwise, and not yet refined.................... 4 do.
Sugar, refined, whether loaf, lump, crushed, pulverized, or adulterated in any way, and on sugar candy....... 6 do.
Sugar, syrup of............ 2½ do.
Sugar of lead...............20 per cent.
Sulphate of quinine.........40 cts. p. oz. av.
Sulphate of copper, or blue vitriol.................. 4 cents per lb.
Sulphate of magnesia.......20 per cent.
Sulphate of barytes.........20 do.
Sulphur, flower of, and crude brimstone, (roll brimstone 25 per cent.).............free.
Sulphuric acid or oil of vitriol. 1 cent per lb.
Sumac.....................free.
Suspenders. (See braces.)
Sweetmeats of all kinds, preserved in molasses, sugar or brandy.....................25 per cent.
Swords and sword blades....30 do.
Sun shades, of silk.........30 do.
Syrup of sugar cane........ 2½ cents per lb.
Sun shades, frames and sticks for.......................30 per cent.

T.

Tacks. (See brads.)
Tacks, tinned..............30 per cent.
Taggers' iron............. 5 do.
Taggers' tin................ 2½ per cent.
Tailors' irons............... 2½ cents per lb.
Talc........................20 per cent.
Tallow..................... 1 cent per lb.
Tallow candles............ 4 do.
Tamarinds..................25 per cent.
Tapers, wax................30 do.
Tapes, linen................25 do.
Tapes, cotton...............30 do.
Tapioca.....................25 do.
Tar.........................15 do.
Tarred cordage and cables.. 5 cents per lb.
Tartaric acid...............20 per cent.
Tartar, crude...............free.
Tartar, cream of............free.
Tartar emetic...............20 per cent.
Teas of all kinds, imported from China, or other places where grown, in American vessels..................free.
Teas of all kinds from other places, or in foreign vessels.20 per cent.
Teasles....................20 do.
Teeth, elephants' and other animals, not manufactured, suitable for the manufacture of buttons exclusively 5 do.
Teeth or ivory, unmanufactured....................free.
Telescopes..................30 do.
Tentenague (or tenteneque)...free.
Thermometers..............30 do.
Thibet, cashmere of, real.....20 do.
Thibet shawls, &c., real, made up for use..........40 do.
Thibet shawls, of wool......40 do.
Thread, linen...............25 do.
Thread, cotton..............30 do.
Thread, pack............. 6 cts. per lb.
Ticking, hemp..............20 per cent.
Ticking, flax...............25 do.
Ticking, cotton. (See cottons.)30 do.
Ticklenburgs...............20 do.
Tiles (except marble) and bricks for paving..........25 do.
Tin, in pigs, bars or blocks... 1 do.
Tin foil, tin in sheets or plates, terne plates and taggers' tin........................2½ do.
Tin, all manufactures of, not otherwise specified.........30 do.
Tincal or borax............25 do.
Tinctures, not otherwise enumerated..................25 do.
Tips of bone or horn........ 5 do.
Tobacco, manufactured, other than snuff or cigars........10 cents per lb.
Tobacco, unmanufactured, in leaf......................20 per cent.
Tongues and sounds.........20 do.
Tools of trade of persons arriving in the United States.free.
Tooth brushes..............30 per cent.
Tortoise shell.............. 5 do.
Topaz..................... 7 do.
Tow, of hemp or flax, or codilla.....................$20 00 per ton.
Tow cloth of hemp..........20 per cent.
Tow cloth of flax...........25 do.
Toys and dolls, of every description, of whatever material composed...........30 do.
Trace chains, iron........... 4 cents per lb.
Trees and plants.............free.
Tumblers. (See glass.)
Turpentine, spirits of........10 cts. per gal.
Tumeric....................free.

Turtles....................20 per cent.
Twine, tarred.............. 5 cents per lb.
Twine, untarred or cleaned... 6 do.
Twist silk..................$2 00 per lb.
Twist, mohair, or silk and mohair...................$2 00 do.
Twist, cotton. (See cotton)..30 per cent.
Types, printing, old as well as new....................25 per cent.

U.

Umbrellas and parasols, of whatever materials made..30 per cent.
Umbrellas and parasols, frames and sticks for.......30 do.
Umbrellas and parasols, stretchers of iron or steel square wire...............12½ do.

V.

Valencias of wool..........40 per cent.
Valencias of worsted, or silk and worsted...............30 do.
Vanilla beans..............20 do.
Varnishes of all kinds.......20 do.
Vegetables, used principally in dyeing, of all kinds.....free.
Vegetables of all kinds, not used in dyeing and not enumerated..................20 per cent.
Veils, lace, made up.........50 do.
Veils, silk..................30 do.
Vellum and parchment......25 do.
Velvet silk.................$2 50 per lb.
Velvet cotton (minimum 35 cents per square yard).....30 per cent.
Venison hams.............. 3 cents per lb.
Verdigris..................20 per cent.
Vermicelli, and all similar preparations not specified.....30 do.
Vermilion...................20 do.
Vessels of copper...........30 do.
Vessels of cast iron, common. 1½ cts. per lb.
Vessels, glazed or tin........ 2½ do.
(See iron.)
Vessels of silver or gold......30 per cent.
Vials. (See glass.)
Vices.......................30 do.
Vinegar.................... 8 cts. per gal.
Violins.....................30 per cent.
Violin strings..............15 do.
Visiting cards..............12 cts. per lb.
Vitriol, blue, or sulphate of copper.................... 4 do.
Vitriol, white, or sulphate of zinc.....................20 per cent.
Vitriol, copperas and green... 2 cts. per lb.
Vitriol, oil of, or sulphuric acid...................... 1 do.
Vomica, nux................free.
Volatile and essential oils not otherwise specified.........20 per cent.

W.

Wafers.....................25 per cent.
Wagon boxes............... 1 cent per lb.
Walking canes and sticks....30 per cent.
Wares of all kinds, of gold or silver, not otherwise specified.....................30 do.
Watches, and parts of watches, and watch materials, not specified................. 7½ per cent.
Water colours.............. 20 do.
Waters, bay, Cologne, lavender, Hungary and honey...25 do.
Wax, bees, (bleached and unbleached)................15 do.
Wax, shoemakers'...........15 do.
Wax candles............... 8 cts. per lb.
Wax tapers................30 per cent.
Wax, amber, or composition beads....................25 do.
Wax, sealing...............25 do.
Wearing apparel, in actual use, of persons arriving in the United States.........free.
Webbing, silk, worsted or cotton....................30 per cent.
Webbing, hemp............20 do.
Webbing, flax..............25 do.
Webbing, india rubber.......30 do.
Weld......................free.
Whalebone, of foreign fisheries.....................12½ per cent.
Whale oil, of foreign fisheries.15 cts. per gal.
Wheat.....................25 c. per bush.
Wheat flour................70 c. p. 112 lbs.
Whips.....................35 per cent.
Whiskey. (See spirits.)
White lead, dry or ground in oil.......................4 cents per lb.
White, Paris, and whiting.... 1 do.
Wigs......................25 per cent.
Willow sheets, for hats......35 do.
Willow, for baskets.........free.
Willow baskets.............25 per cent.
Window glass. (See glass.)
Windsor soap..............30 do.
Wine, Madeira, in casks or bottles....................60 cts. per gal.
Wine, sherry...............60 do.
Wine, San Lucar or Canary, in casks or bottles........60 do.
Wine, Champaigne..........40 do.
Wine, Port, Burgundy and claret in bottles...........35 do.
Wine, Port, in casks........15 do.
Wine, Burgundy, in casks...15 do.
Wine, Teneriffe, in casks or bottles...................20 do.
Wine, claret, in casks........ 6 do.
Wine, white, not enumerated, of France, Austria, Prussia, Sardinia, Portugal and its possessions, in casks...... 7½ cts. per gal.
Do. do. in bottles.20 do.
Wine, red, not enumerated, of same countries, in casks.... 6 do.
Wine, red, in bottles.........20 do.
Wine, white and red, of Spain, Germany and the Mediterranean, in casks............12½ do.
Wine, do. in bottles.........20 do.
Wine, Sicily Madeira or Marsala, in casks or bottles.25 do.
Wine, other wines of Sicily, in casks or bottles........15 do.
Wine, all other, not enumerated, and other than those of France, Austria, Prussia, Sardinia and Portugal, and its possessions, when in bottles.................65 do.
Wine, do. when in casks.....25 do.

Wire, iron or steel, not exceeding No. 14............ 5 cents per lb.
Wire, do. over No. 14, and not exceeding No. 25......... 8 do.
Wire, do. over No. 25........11 do.
Wire, silver or plated........30 per cent.
Wire, brass or copper......25 do.
Wire, cap or bonnet, covered with silk.................12 cents per lb.
Wire, do. cotton thread...... 8 do.
Wire, square, for umbrellas..12½ per cent.
Woad or pastel.............. 1 cent per lb.
Wood, all manufactures of, not otherwise specified....30 per cent.
Wood used in dying, all kinds.free.
Wood, unmanufactured, of all kinds, not otherwise specified.....................do.
Wood, rose, satin, mahogany and cedar................15 per cent.
Wood, for fuel or fire wood, and timber for building wharves, and lumber in rough.....................20 do.
Wood, all dye, in sticks......free.
Wool, unmanufactured, the value whereof at the port of exportation shall not exceed 7 cents per lb...... 5 per cent.
Wool, all other descriptions of, a duty of three cents per pound, and...........30 per cent.
(See provisions respecting wool in the Act, sec. 1, article 1.)
Wool, all manufactures of, except carpetings, flannels, bockings, baizes, blankets, worsted stuff goods, ready made clothing, hosiery, mitts, caps, gloves and bindings, (which see)......40 do.
Woollen yarn..............30 do.
Worsted yarn...............30 do.
Worsted or stuff goods......30 do.

Y.

Yams.........................20 per cent.
Yarn, cotton. (See cotton)..25 do.
Yarn, woollen and worsted..30 do.
Yarn, flax.................. 6 cents per lb.

Z.

Zante currants............. 3 cents per lb.
Zinc, in sheets............10 per cent.
Zinc, manufactures of.......30 do.
Zinc, sulphate of...........20 do.